Shane Cavanagh

📖 SCHOLASTIC

Pocket Dictionary

📖 SCHOLASTIC

New York Toronto London Auckland
Sydney Mexico City New Delhi Hong Kong

Stone Cavone (handwritten, upside down)

Dictionary Staff

LEXICOGRAPHY TEAM
Chief Lexicographer: Orin Hargraves

Pronunciation Advisor: Constance Baboukis

Editor in Chief: Donnali Fifield

Editors: Johanna Baboukis, Daniel Barron,
Victoria Neufeldt, Marina Padakis,
Deborah M. Posner, Katherine C. Sietsema,
Sue Ellen Thompson

Assistant Editors: Carl Burnett,
Tyler Cassidy-Heacock, Rebecca Shapiro,
Jane Solomon

Copy Editor: Jane Sunderland

Designer/Art Director: Carol Farrar Norton

SPECIAL THANKS TO
Stephen Perkins, dataformat.com
Agnès Tabah, Esq.

PUBLISHED BY SCHOLASTIC INC.

Karyn Browne, Executive Managing Editor

Brenda Murray, Senior Editor,
Nonfiction & Reference

Elizabeth Krych, Production Editor

Produced by Potomac Global Media, LLC

Abridged from the *Scholastic Children's Dictionary*, 2011

ISBN 978-0-545-38371-4

10 9 8 7 6   14 15 16/0

Printed in the U.S.A.   40

First edition, August 2011

Cover photo credits: NASA: Astronaut/Andrew Fruchter and ERO Team; www.photolibrary.com: Globe/Indexstock and Dragonfly/Don Farrall; Shutterstock: ATV/PixArchi.

Contents

Part of speech labels usually appear on the first lines of entries. However, if a word's part of speech changes from one meaning to the next, the part of speech label starts each new meaning. When a meaning shows the word as part of a common phrase, which is known as an idiom, no part of speech is given.

Related words and word forms appear at the end of an entry or at the end of a meaning. This dictionary also lists irregular plural forms for noun entries, *–er* and *–est* forms for adjectives, and irregular, *–ed*, and *–ing* forms for verbs.

Usage labels tell you that a meaning of a word is informal or slang. Informal words are used in everyday speech but not usually in formal speech or in writing. Many slang terms or meanings are very popular only for a short period of time. Like informal words, they are not appropriate in formal writing such as term papers and essays.

Syllable breaks are indicated by small dots.

sat·el·lite (sat-uh-*lite*) *noun*
1. A spacecraft that is sent into orbit around the earth, the moon, or another heavenly body. **2.** A moon or other heavenly body that travels in an orbit around a larger heavenly body.

at·trib·ute
noun (**at**-ruh-*byoot*) A quality or characteristic that belongs to or describes a person or thing.
verb (uh-**trib**-yoot) When you attribute something to someone, you give him or her credit for it.
▶ *verb* attributing, attributed

rap (rap)
verb **1.** To hit something with a quick, sharp blow. **2.** (slang) To talk.
noun **1.** A type of popular music in which the words are spoken rhythmically to a musical background. **2.** A quick, sharp blow or knock.
Rap sounds like **wrap**.
▶ *verb* **rapping, rapped** ▶ *noun* **rapper**

tug (tuhg)
verb To pull something hard with a short, quick movement.
noun **1.** A brief, forceful pull. **2.** *See* tugboat.
▶ *verb* **tugging, tugged**

Pronunciations, given in parentheses, let you know how the entry words should sound. The pronunciation guide on page v explains which letters represent each sound. If the pronunciation of a word changes depending on its meaning, the appropriate pronunciation appears with the appropriate meaning.

Numbers appear at the beginning of each meaning when a word has more than one meaning. The most frequently used meanings generally appear first.

Definitions tell the meaning of words. When the main entry word is used within the definition, it is printed in **boldface**.

Homophones, words that sound alike but have different spellings, and meanings, are listed at or near the end of a definition.

Cross-references tell you where to turn in the dictionary for more information about the main entry word.

There are no strange symbols in this dictionary's pronunciation system. Instead, letters and letter combinations are used to stand for different sounds. To make our system as clear as possible, we have included more than one way to pronounce some sounds. These alternatives are indented, below. For example, the *ay-* sound is given the pronunciation symbol (ay), as in pay or rain. Sometimes, when the word ends with a consonant followed by a silent *e*, a *-consonant-e* spelling is used for the pronunciation, as in made or ate.

Many words contain two or more syllables. In most cases, those words have one syllable that receives a stronger stress than any other syllable. This accented syllable is marked in boldface letters, as in (**ak**-shuhn) for the word action. Some words also have a syllable with a lighter stress. This secondary, lighter-accented syllable is marked in italics, as in (**buht**-ur-*milk*) for buttermilk.

The symbol (uh) is used for both the accented vowel in the word cup (kuhp) and for many unaccented vowels in words, as in (uh-**bout**) for the word about. Here are the letters and letter combinations that stand for each sound in this dictionary.

Vowels

a	at, dash, hammer
ah	honor, father, drama, rock
ahr	art, dark, far
air	air, care
aw	autumn, caught, raw
ay	ail, rain, pay
	(a-*consonant*-e) made, ate
e	egg, men, insect
ee	each, beet, me
eer	ear, here, career
eye	item, iron
	(i-*consonant*-e) file, ripe
	(*consonant*-ye) rye, lie, my
i	it, still
oh	over, coat, foe, dough
	(o-*consonant*-e) code, stone
oi	oil, coin, toy
oo	pool, rude
oor	poor, tour, rural
or	orbit, corn, more
ou	ouch, house, cow
u	put, book
uh	sun, about, comma, camel, lesson, circus
ur	earn, dirt, worker, fur
yoo	music, few, beauty, cue

Consonants

b	bad, rabbit, sob
ch	chip, nature, ditch
d	dip, ladder, red
f	fun, offer, laugh
g	get, tiger, beg
h	ham, who
j	jam, giant, page, edge
k	keep, car, ache, sack
l	lap, salt, tell
m	man, common, lamb, condemn
n	now, annoy, ten, gnat, know
ng	hanger, wink, song
p	pan, upper, sip
r	rib, arrow, pour
s	set, castle, yes, pass
sh	ship, gracious, nation, rash
t	tub, battle, rat
th	thin, method, bath
TH	this, mother, bathe
v	van, over, hive
w	well, aware, whale, awhile
y	yell, canyon
z	zip, dazzle, has, those
zh	measure, occasion, azure

a (uh *or* ay) *indefinite article* **1.** Any. *Pick a card.* **2.** One. *I have a car.* **3.** Per. *They traveled more than 200 miles a day during the trip.*

aard·vark (**ahrd**-*vahrk*) *noun* An African mammal with a long, sticky tongue that it uses to catch insects.

ab·a·cus (**ab**-uh-kuhs) *noun* A frame with rows of sliding beads on wires, used for adding, subtracting, multiplying, and dividing. ▶ *noun, plural* **abacuses** *or* **abaci** (**ab**-uh-*sye or* **ab**-uh-*kye*)

ab·a·lo·ne (*ab*-uh-**loh**-nee) *noun* A large sea snail with a flat shell whose meat people eat and whose shell lining is shiny like a pearl.

a·ban·don (uh-**ban**-duhn) *verb* **1.** To leave somewhere or someone and not return. **2.** To give up. ▶ *verb* **abandoning, abandoned**

a·ban·doned (uh-**ban**-duhnd) *adjective* Deserted or no longer used.

a·bate (uh-**bate**) *verb* To become less intense. ▶ *verb* **abating, abated**

ab·bey (**ab**-ee) *noun* A group of buildings including a church where monks or nuns live and work.

ab·bre·vi·ate (uh-**bree**-vee-*ate*) *verb* To make something shorter, such as a word. ▶ *verb* **abbreviating, abbreviated** ▶ *adjective* **abbreviated**

ab·bre·vi·a·tion (uh-*bree*-vee-**ay**-shuhn) *noun* A shortened version of a word. For example, *St.* is an abbreviation of the word *street.*

ab·di·cate (**ab**-di-*kate*) *verb* To give up power. ▶ *verb* **abdicating, abdicated** ▶ *noun* **abdication**

ab·do·men (**ab**-duh-muhn) *noun* **1.** The front part of your body between your chest and hips. **2.** The rear section of an insect's body.

ab·duct (ab-**duhkt**) *verb* To take someone away by force. ▶ *verb* **abducting, abducted** ▶ *noun* **abduction**

ab·hor (ab-**hor**) *verb* To hate something. ▶ *verb* **abhorring, abhorred** ▶ *adjective* **abhorrent**

a·bide (uh-**bide**) *verb* **1.** If you **abide by** a rule, agreement, or law, you obey it or do what it requires. **2.** To stay or live somewhere. **3.** If you **cannot abide** something, you cannot tolerate it. ▶ *verb* **abiding, abided** *or* **abode** (uh-**bohd**)

a·bil·i·ty (uh-**bil**-i-tee) *noun* **1.** The mental or physical power to do something. **2.** Skill. ▶ *noun, plural* **abilities**

a·blaze (uh-**blaze**) *adjective* On fire.

a·ble (**ay**-buhl) *adjective* **1.** If you are **able** to do something, you can do it. **2.** Skillful or talented. ▶ *adjective* **abler, ablest** ▶ *adverb* **ably**

a·ble-bod·ied (**ay**-buhl-**bah**-deed) *adjective* Having a strong, healthy body.

ab·nor·mal (ab-**nor**-muhl) *adjective* Not normal, in a way that may cause problems. ▶ *noun* **abnormality** (*ab*-nor-**mal**-i-tee)

a·board (uh-**bord**) *adverb* On or onto a train, ship, or aircraft. ▶ *preposition* **aboard**

a·bode (uh-**bode**) *noun* **1.** Someone's home. **2.** The **right of abode** is the legal right to live in a particular place, especially a country that you were not born in.

a·bol·ish (uh-**bah**-lish) *verb* To put an end to something officially. ▶ *verb* **abolishes, abolishing, abolished** ▶ *noun* **abolition**

a·bo·li·tion·ist (*ab*-uh-**lish**-uh-nist) *noun* Someone who worked to abolish slavery before the Civil War.

a·bom·i·na·ble (uh-**bah**-muh-nuh-buhl) *adjective* Unpleasant or horrible. ▶ *adverb* **abominably**

ab·o·rig·i·ne (*ab*-uh-**rij**-uh-nee) *noun* **1.** One of the native peoples of Australia who have lived there since before the Europeans arrived. The name of this people is capitalized. **2.** **aborigine** The native people of a place, such as the Inuit and Native Americans in North America. ▶ *adjective* **aboriginal** (*ab*-uh-**rij**-uh-nuhl)

a·bort (uh-**bort**) *verb* To stop something from happening in the early stages. ▶ *verb* **aborting, aborted** ▶ *adjective* **abortive**

a·bor·tion (uh-**bor**-shuhn) *noun* A medical operation in which a fetus is removed from a pregnant woman before it is developed enough to live.

a·bound (uh-**bound**) *verb* To have or contain large amounts of something. ▶ *verb* **abounding, abounded**

a·bout (uh-**bout**)
preposition On a particular subject. *I'm reading a book about the Etruscans.*
adverb Almost; approximately.
adjective Moving around.

a·bove (uh-**buhv**)
adverb In a higher place.
preposition 1. Higher up than or over something. *The balloons were flying high above us.* 2. More than or better than. 3. At a higher volume or pitch than something. *When I sing, I can reach ten notes above middle C.*

a·bove·board (uh-**buhv**-bord) *adjective* If an action is **aboveboard,** it is completely honest and legal.

a·bra·sive (uh-**bray**-siv) *adjective* 1. Rough and coarse. 2. Rude and often offensive to others.

a·breast (uh-**brest**) *adverb* Side by side.

a·bridged (uh-**brijd**) *adjective* Shortened by leaving parts out. ▶ *verb* **abridge**

a·broad (uh-**brawd**) *adverb* In or to another country. In the United States, the word *abroad* usually means "overseas."

a·brupt (uh-**bruhpt**) *adjective* 1. Sudden and unexpected. 2. Quick, short, and rude. ▶ *adverb* **abruptly**

ab·scess (**ab**-ses) *noun* A painful infected area full of a yellow substance called pus. ▶ *noun, plural* **abscesses**

ab·scond (ab-**skahnd**) *verb* To go away suddenly and hide somewhere, often after stealing something. ▶ *verb* **absconding, absconded**

ab·sence (**ab**-suhns) *noun* The state of not being somewhere, or of not existing.

ab·sent (**ab**-suhnt) *adjective* Not present. ▶ *noun* **absentee** ▶ *noun* **absenteeism**

ab·sent-mind·ed (**ab**-suhnt-**mine**-did) *adjective* Not able to remember or notice things very well. ▶ *adverb* **absent-mindedly**

ab·so·lute (**ab**-suh-*loot*) *adjective* 1. Certain and without any doubt. 2. Complete, without any limit.

ab·so·lute·ly (*ab*-suh-**loot**-lee) *adverb* Fully and completely; without qualification or limit.

ab·solve (ab-**zahlv**) *verb* To officially remove the blame or responsibility for something bad from someone. ▶ *verb* **absolving, absolved** ▶ *noun* **absolution** (*ab*-suh-**loo**-shuhn)

ab·sorb (ab-**zorb**) *verb* 1. To soak up liquid. 2. To take in or learn information. 3. To get all of someone's attention. ▶ *verb* **absorbing, absorbed**

ab·sorbed (ab-**zorbd**) *adjective* If you are **absorbed,** you are giving all of your attention to an activity.

ab·sorb·ent (ab-**zor**-buhnt) *adjective* Something that soaks up liquid, such as a washcloth, towel, or sponge, is **absorbent.**

ab·sorp·tion (ab-**zorp**-shuhn) *noun* The process of soaking up something, as liquid, heat, or light.

ab·stain (ab-**stayn**) *verb* 1. To stop yourself from doing something that you might normally do. 2. To not participate in something such as a vote or a discussion. ▶ *verb* **abstaining, abstained** ▶ *noun* **abstention**

ab·sti·nence (**ab**-stuh-nuhns) *noun* The activity of completely avoiding an activity that some people find pleasurable, such as drinking alcohol or having sex. ▶ *adjective* **abstinent** (**ab**-stuh-nuhnt)

ab·stract (**ab**-strakt *or* ab-**strakt**) *adjective* 1. Based on ideas rather than things that you can touch and see. 2. Hard to understand.

ab·surd (ab-**surd** *or* ab-**zurd**) *adjective* Silly; ridiculous. ▶ *noun* **absurdity** ▶ *adverb* **absurdly**

A

a·bun·dance (uh-**buhn**-duhns) *noun* A large amount or supply of something.

a·bun·dant (uh-**buhn**-duhnt) *adjective* Widely available or present in great quantity. ▶ *adverb* **abundantly**

a·buse
noun (uh-**byoos**) **1.** Rude and offensive speech. **2.** Wrong or harmful use of something or treatment of someone. *verb* (uh-**byooz**) To treat a person or animal cruelly.
▶ *verb* **abusing, abused** ▶ *adjective* **abusive** (uh-**byoo**-siv) ▶ *noun* **abuser** (uh-**byoo**-zur)

a·bys·mal (uh-**biz**-muhl) *adjective* Extremely bad. ▶ *adverb* **abysmally**

a·byss (uh-**bis**) *noun* **1.** A very deep hole that seems to have no bottom. **2.** A situation that gets worse and worse.
▶ *noun, plural* **abysses**

a·ca·cia (uh-**kay**-shuh) *noun* A small tree or shrub that has feathery leaves and pleasant-smelling white or yellow flowers and grows in warm parts of the world.

ac·a·dem·ic (ak-uh-**dem**-ik)
adjective Of or having to do with study and learning.
noun Someone who teaches in a university or college or someone who does research.
▶ *adverb* **academically**

a·cad·e·my (uh-**kad**-uh-mee) *noun* **1.** A private junior high, middle school, or high school. **2.** A school that teaches special subjects.
▶ *noun, plural* **academies**

a·ca·i (ah-sah-**ee**) *noun* A kind of palm tree that grows in Central and South America. Its purple berries are thought to contain healthful substances.

ac·cel·er·ate (ak-**sel**-uh-rate) *verb* To get faster and faster. ▶ *verb* **accelerating, accelerated** ▶ *noun* **acceleration**

ac·cent (**ak**-sent)
noun **1.** The way that you pronounce sounds and put them together. **2.** A mark placed over or on a letter that changes its usual sound. **3.** A feature, decoration, or design that draws attention.

verb To emphasize or draw special attention to something.
▶ *verb* **accenting, accented**

ac·cen·tu·ate (ak-**sen**-choo-*ate*) *verb* To emphasize something, or make it stand out. ▶ *verb* **accentuating, accentuated**

ac·cept (ak-**sept**) *verb* **1.** To take or say yes to something that is offered. **2.** To agree that something is correct, satisfactory, or enough.
▶ *verb* **accepting, accepted**

ac·cept·a·ble (ak-**sep**-tuh-buhl) *adjective* **1.** Good enough; satisfactory. **2.** Within limits that are normal or that people can accept.

ac·cept·ance (ak-**sep**-tuhns) *noun* The act or fact of accepting something.

ac·cess (**ak**-ses)
noun **1.** A way to enter a place. **2.** Ability or permission to enter a place.
verb To get information from a computer.
▶ *noun, plural* **accesses** ▶ *verb* **accesses, accessing, accessed**

ac·ces·si·ble (ak-**ses**-uh-buhl) *adjective* **1.** Able to be accessed or reached, especially to people with disabilities. **2.** If someone is **accessible,** they are easy to talk to or get in contact with.

ac·ces·so·ry (ak-**ses**-ur-ee) *noun* **1.** An extra, optional part for something. **2.** A small item that you wear with your clothes, such as a belt, gloves, or scarf. **3.** An **accessory** to a crime is someone who helps another person commit it.
▶ *noun, plural* **accessories**

ac·ci·dent (**ak**-si-duhnt) *noun* **1.** An unfortunate and unplanned event. **2.** Lack of intention; chance.

ac·ci·den·tal (ak-si-**den**-tuhl) *adjective* Happening by accident; not planned or expected.

ac·ci·den·tal·ly (ak-si-**dent**-lee) *adverb* Not on purpose; without meaning to.

ac·claim (uh-**klaym**)
noun Praise.
verb To welcome and praise loudly.
▶ *verb* **acclaiming, acclaimed**

A

ac·cli·ma·tize (uh-**klye**-muh-tize) *verb*
To get used to a different climate
or to new surroundings. ▸ *verb*
acclimatizing, acclimatized ▸ *noun*
acclimatization

ac·com·mo·date (uh-**kah**-muh-date)
verb 1. To help out or reply to a request.
2. To provide with a place to stay.
▸ *verb* **accommodating,**
accommodated

ac·com·mo·da·tion (uh-kah-muh-
day-shuhn) *noun* 1. The act of
accommodating someone, or a thing
that you do to make things easier.
2. **Accommodations** is a somewhat
formal word for places to stay while
you are traveling.

ac·com·pa·ny (uh-**kuhm**-puh-nee) *verb*
1. To go somewhere with someone.
2. To play along with a singer on a
musical instrument.
▸ *verb* **accompanies, accompanying,**
accompanied ▸ *noun*
accompaniment ▸ *noun* **accompanist**

ac·com·plice (uh-**kahm**-plis) *noun*
Someone who helps another person
commit a crime.

ac·com·plish (uh-**kahm**-plish) *verb*
To do or complete something
successfully. ▸ *verb* **accomplishes,**
accomplishing, accomplished ▸ *noun*
accomplishment

ac·com·plished (uh-**kahm**-plisht)
adjective Skillful.

ac·cord (uh-**kord**) *noun* 1. A signed
agreement between countries about
the way they will deal with something
that concerns them. 2. If you do
something **of your own accord,** you do
it without being asked.

ac·cord·ing·ly (uh-**kor**-ding-lee) *adverb*
In a way that is suitable, appropriate,
or fitting.

ac·cord·ing to (uh-**kor**-ding) *preposition*
1. As someone has said or written.
According to the schedule, a bus stops
here every half hour. 2. In a way that
corresponds to something. *Babysitters*
are usually paid according to the number
of hours they work.

ac·cor·di·on (uh-**kor**-dee-uhn) *noun* A
keyboard wind instrument that you

hold to your chest and squeeze while
pressing keys and buttons.

ac·cost (uh-**kawst**) *verb* To start talking
to someone in a threatening or hostile
way. ▸ *verb* **accosting, accosted**

ac·count (uh-**kount**)
noun 1. A description of something that
has taken place. 2. An arrangement to
keep money in a bank.
noun, plural **accounts** A record of
money earned and spent.
verb If you **account for** something, you
explain it.
▸ *verb* **accounting, accounted**
▸ *adjective* **accountable**

ac·count·ant (uh-**koun**-tuhnt) *noun*
Someone whose job is keeping
accounts for a company or
business. ▸ *noun* **accounting**

ac·cu·mu·late (uh-**kyoo**-myuh-late)
verb To collect things or let them pile
up. ▸ *verb* **accumulating, accumulated**

ac·cum·u·la·tion (uh-kyoo-myuh-
lay-shuhn) *noun* 1. The process of
something getting bigger or thicker,
little by little. 2. An amount of
something that has slowly increased.

ac·cu·ra·cy (**ak**-yur-uh-see) *noun* The
quality of being correct and exact.

ac·cu·rate (**ak**-yur-it) *adjective* Correct in
details; exact.

ac·cu·rate·ly (**ak**-yur-it-lee) *adverb*
Correctly with respect to quantity, size,
or amount.

ac·cuse (uh-**kyooz**) *verb* To say that
someone has done something
wrong. ▸ *verb* **accusing,**
accused ▸ *noun* **accusation** (ak-yuh-
zay-shuhn) ▸ *noun* **accuser**

ac·cused (uh-**kyoozd**) *noun* **the accused**
A person or people who have been
charged with a crime.

ac·cus·tomed (uh-**kuhs**-tuhmd) *adjective*
1. Usual and familiar. 2. When you are
accustomed to something, you are
used to it.

ace (ase) *noun* 1. A playing card with
only one symbol on it. In most card
games, the ace has the highest value.
2. Someone who is an expert at
something. 3. A serve in tennis that is
not hit back by the other player.

ache (ake)
noun A dull pain that doesn't go away.
verb To hurt continuously.
▶ *verb* **aching, ached**

a·chieve (uh-**cheev**) *verb* To do
something successfully after
making an effort. ▶ *verb* **achieving,
achieved** ▶ *noun* **achiever**

a·chieve·ment (uh-**cheev**-muhnt) *noun*
1. The ability to reach goals and do
what you intend to do. 2. A thing that
has been achieved or accomplished.

ac·id (**as**-id)
noun A substance with a sour taste
that will react with a base to form a
salt. Acids turn blue litmus paper red.
Strong acids can burn your skin.
adjective Sour, or bitter.
▶ *adjective* **acidic** (uh-**sid**-ik)

ac·id rain (**as**-id **rayn**) *noun* Rain
that is polluted by chemicals in the
air, damaging lakes, forests, and
buildings.

ac·knowl·edge (ak-**nah**-lij) *verb* 1. To
accept the truth about something.
2. To show that you have noticed or
recognized something or someone.
3. To let the sender know that you have
received something.
▶ *verb* **acknowledging, acknowledged**
▶ *noun* **acknowledgment**

ac·ne (**ak**-nee) *noun* A skin condition
that causes inflammation and pimples
on the face, back, or chest.

a·corn (**ay**-korn) *noun* The seed of an
oak tree.

a·cou·stic (uh-**koo**-stik)
adjective Of or having to do with
sound or hearing.
noun, plural **acoustics** The qualities of
a place that affect how sound is heard
in it.

a·cous·tic gui·tar (uh-**koo**-stik gi-**tahr**)
noun A traditional guitar that is not
electrified.

ac·quain·tance (uh-**kwayn**-tuhns) *noun*
Someone you have met but do not
know very well.

ac·quire (uh-**kwire**) *verb* 1. To get
something so that you own it or
have it. 2. If something is an **acquired
taste,** you don't like it at first but

learn to like it.
▶ *verb* **acquiring, acquired**

ac·qui·si·tion (*ak*-wuh-**zish**-uhn) *noun*
1. The activity of acquiring something.
2. Something that has been acquired,
especially by paying a lot of money.

ac·quit (uh-**kwit**) *verb* To find someone
not guilty of a crime. ▶ *verb*
acquitting, acquitted ▶ *noun* **acquittal**

a·cre (**ay**-kur) *noun* A measurement of
area equal to 43,560 square feet. An
acre is almost the size of a standard
football field. ▶ *noun* **acreage**

ac·ro·bat (**ak**-ruh-*bat*) *noun* A person
who performs exciting gymnastic acts
that require great skill. Acrobats often
work with a circus.

ac·ro·bat·ics (*ak*-ruh-**bat**-iks) *noun,
plural* The difficult gymnastic acts
that acrobats perform. ▶ *adjective*
acrobatic

ac·ro·nym (**ak**-ruh-nim) *noun* A word
made from the first or first few letters
of the words in a phrase. Radar, for
example, is short for *radio detection
and ranging.*

a·cross (uh-**kraws**) *preposition* 1. From
one side of something to the other.
The cat ran across the room. 2. On the
other side of something. *Her house is
across from mine.*

a·cryl·ic (uh-**kril**-ik) *noun* A chemical
substance used to make fibers and
paints.

act (akt)
verb 1. To do something for a reason,
or in a particular way. 2. To perform
in a play, movie, or other form of
entertainment. 3. To have an effect.
noun 1. A short performance.
2. Anything that you do; a deed.
3. Behavior that is intended to fool
someone. 4. One of the parts of a
play. 5. A bill that has been passed by
Congress. If signed by the president,
it becomes law.
▶ *verb* **acting, acted**

ac·tion (**ak**-shuhn) *noun* 1. Something
that you do. 2. Things happening in
general. 3. When you **take action,** you
act to achieve some result.

A

A

ac·ti·vate (ak-tuh-*vate*) *verb* To turn on, or to cause to work. ▸ *verb* **activating, activated** ▸ *noun* **activator**

ac·tive (ak-tiv) *adjective* 1. Energetic and busy. 2. The subject of an **active** verb does an action, while the subject of a passive verb has something done to it. See **passive.**

ac·tiv·i·ty (ak-**tiv**-i-tee) *noun* 1. Things happening or people doing things. 2. Something that you do for pleasure. ▸ *noun, plural* **activities**

ac·tor (ak-tur) *noun* Someone whose job is to perform, as in the theater, movies, or television.

ac·tress (ak-tris) *noun* A girl or a woman whose job is to perform, as in the theater, movies, or television. ▸ *noun, plural* **actresses**

ac·tu·al (ak-choo-uhl) *adjective* Real, existing, or true.

ac·tu·al·ly (ak-choo-uh-lee) *adverb* In fact. People use **actually** to show that what they are saying is surprising, or that it contradicts something else.

ac·u·punc·ture (ak-yu-*pungk*-chur) *noun* A way of treating illness or pain by sticking needles in different parts of the body.

a·cute (uh-**kyoot**) *adjective* 1. Strong and severe. 2. Able to detect things easily and accurately. 3. An **acute** angle is an angle of less than 90 degrees. ▸ *noun* **acuteness** ▸ *adverb* **acutely**

A.D. (ay-dee) An abbreviation of the Latin phrase *Anno Domini*, which means "in the year of the Lord." A.D. shows that a date comes after the birth of Jesus.

ad (ad) *noun* An advertisement.

ad·age (ad-ij) *noun* An old saying that people generally believe is true.

a·dapt (uh-**dapt**) *verb* 1. To make something work in a different way or for a different purpose. 2. To change because you are in a different situation. ▸ *verb* **adapting, adapted** ▸ *adjective* **adaptable**

ad·ap·ta·tion (ad-uhp-**tay**-shuhn) *noun* 1. The act of adjusting, such as changing something from one form to another. 2. A change that a living thing goes through so it fits in better with its environment.

a·dapt·er *or* **a·dap·tor** (uh-**dap**-tur) *noun* A device that connects two parts that are of slightly different shapes or sizes.

a·dap·tive (uh-**dap**-tiv) *adjective* Done or used in order to adapt to something.

add (ad) *verb* 1. To find the sum of two or more numbers. 2. To put or mix one thing with another. ▸ *verb* **adding, added**

ADD (ay-dee-dee) *noun* A condition in which a person has trouble keeping still and concentrating. ADD is short for *attention deficit disorder.*

ad·dend (ad-end) *noun* Any number that is added to another to form a sum.

ad·der (ad-ur) *noun* 1. A North American snake that hisses and swells up its head when annoyed. 2. A small, poisonous European snake. Sometimes also called a **viper.**

ad·dict (ad-ikt) *noun* A person who cannot give up doing or using something. ▸ *noun* **addiction** ▸ *adjective* **addicted**

ad·dic·tive (uh-**dik**-tiv) *adjective* An **addictive** substance or activity makes you think you need it, even though it is harmful.

ad·di·tion (uh-**dish**-uhn) *noun* 1. The adding together of two or more numbers to come up with a sum. 2. A part of a building that is added on to the original. 3. Anything or anyone new.

ad·di·tion·al (uh-**dish**-uh-nuhl) *adjective* Extra, or more.

ad·di·tive (ad-i-tiv) *noun* Something added to a substance, especially food.

ad·dress
noun (uh-**dres** *or* ad-res) 1. Information such as the street, city, and state of a business or residence. 2. A speech on a particular subject. 3. **address book** A book in which you keep addresses, or a place on a computer where email addresses and other information are stored.
verb (uh-**dres**) 1. To write an address on a letter, card, or package. 2. To give

a speech to. **3.** To speak to someone or to a group in a formal way. **4.** When you **address** a problem, you tackle it or deal with it.
▶ *noun, plural* **addresses** ▶ *verb* **addresses, addressing, addressed**
▶ *noun* **addressee** (ad-res-**ee**)

ad·e·noid (**ad**-uh-*noid*) *noun* A spongy lump of flesh at the back of your nose that can become swollen, making it hard to breathe.

a·dept (uh-**dept**) *adjective* Able to do something well.

ad·e·quate (**ad**-i-kwit) *adjective* Just enough, or good enough. ▶ *adverb* **adequately**

ADHD (ay-*dee*-**aych**-*dee*) *noun* A set of behaviors including restlessness, too much activity, and poor concentration that may interfere with learning. ADHD is short for *attention deficit hyperactivity disorder.*

ad·here (ad-**heer**) *verb* **1.** To stick very tightly to something. **2.** To stick with an idea or plan.
▶ *verb* **adhering, adhered**

ad·he·sive (ad-**hee**-siv)
noun A substance, such as glue, that makes things stick together.
adjective Tending to stick when touched.

a·di·os (*ah*-dee-*ohs*) *interjection* The Spanish word for "good-bye."

ad·ja·cent (uh-**jay**-suhnt)
adjective Close or next to something. If two things are **adjacent,** they are next to each other.
preposition **adjacent to** Next to; beside. *My office is in a building adjacent to the new auditorium.*

ad·jec·tive (**aj**-ik-tiv) *noun* A word that describes a noun or pronoun. For example, in the phrase "the red house," the adjective *red* tells you how the house looks.

ad·journ (uh-**jurn**) *verb* To close or end something, especially a court session or government meeting. ▶ *verb* **adjourning, adjourned**

ad·just (uh-**juhst**) *verb* **1.** To move or change something slightly. **2.** To get used to something new and different.
▶ *verb* **adjusting, adjusted** ▶ *adjective* **adjustable**

ad·just·ment (uh-**juhst**-muhnt) *noun* **1.** The act or process of changing something slightly to make it work better. **2.** A small change to improve something.

ad-lib (**ad**-lib) *verb* To do something, especially speak in front of people, without preparing for it. ▶ *verb* **ad-libbing, ad-libbed** ▶ *adjective, adverb* **ad-lib**

ad·min·is·ter (ad-**min**-i-stur) *verb* **1.** To manage something so that it runs smoothly. **2.** To give something to someone in an official or controlled way.
▶ *verb* **administering, administered**

ad·min·is·tra·tion (ad-*min*-i-stray-shuhn) *noun* **1.** The activity of managing all the details of something, such as a business or project. **2.** The department or the people whose job it is to manage and supervise an organization. **3.** The government of a president, including the president's cabinet and advisors. The word *administration* also means the time that a particular president is in office.

ad·min·is·tra·tor (ad-**min**-i-stray-tur) *noun* Someone who works in administration.

ad·mi·ra·ble (**ad**-mur-uh-buhl) *adjective* Deserving praise or admiration.

ad·mi·ral (**ad**-mur-uhl) *noun* A high-ranking officer in a country's navy or coast guard.

ad·mire (ad-**mire**) *verb* **1.** To like and respect someone. **2.** To look at something with enjoyment.
▶ *verb* **admiring, admired** ▶ *noun* **admiration**

ad·mis·sion (ad-**mish**-uhn)
noun **1.** The act of allowing someone into a place. **2.** The price of getting into a place. **3.** An act of telling the truth about something you did or something that happened.
noun, plural **admissions** A department that decides and deals with who gets admitted to a place.

A

ad·mit (ad-**mit**) *verb* **1.** To say that you did something bad. **2.** To agree or accept that something is true. **3.** To allow someone or something to enter. ▶ *verb* **admitting, admitted** ▶ *noun* **admittance**

ad·mon·ish (ad-**mah**-nish) *verb* To scold someone sternly for his or her faults or mistakes. ▶ *verb* **admonishes, admonishing, admonished** ▶ *noun* **admonishment**

a·do·be (uh-**doh**-bee) *noun* Bricks made of clay mixed with straw and dried in the sun. *adjective* Made from adobe.

ad·o·les·cent (*ad*-uh-**les**-uhnt) *noun* A young person who is more grown-up than a child but is not yet an adult; a teenager. *adjective* Used to describe a young person who is more grown-up than a child but is not yet an adult. ▶ *noun* **adolescence**

a·dopt (uh-**dahpt**) *verb* **1.** To take a person or animal into your family. **2.** To accept a new way of doing things. ▶ *verb* **adopting, adopted** ▶ *noun* **adoption** ▶ *adjective* **adopted**

a·dor·a·ble (uh-**dor**-uh-buhl) *adjective* Sweet, cute, and lovable.

a·dore (uh-**dor**) *verb* **1.** To be very fond of someone or something. **2.** To be devoted to the point of worshiping someone or something. ▶ *verb* **adoring, adored** ▶ *noun* **adoration** (*ad*-uh-**ray**-shuhn)

a·dorn (uh-**dorn**) *verb* To decorate something.

ad·ren·a·line (uh-**dren**-uh-lin) *noun* A chemical that your body produces when you need more energy or when you sense danger.

A·dri·at·ic Sea (*ay*-dree-**at**-ik **see**) A part of the Mediterranean Sea separating Italy from Croatia and Bosnia and Herzegovina.

a·drift (uh-**drift**) *adverb, adjective* Drifting or floating freely through water or air.

a·dult (uh-**duhlt** *or* **ad**-uhlt) *noun* A fully grown person or animal.

adjective In the fully grown or fully developed form. ▶ *noun* **adulthood**

ad·vance (uhd-**vans**) *verb* **1.** To move forward. **2.** To make progress. **3.** To lend money. *adjective* Happening before something else. *noun* **1.** A movement forward in a military situation. **2.** The first part of a larger amount of money, paid early. **3.** A development that improves something. ▶ *verb* **advancing, advanced** ▶ *noun* **advancement**

ad·vanced (uhd-**vanst**) *adjective* **1.** At a higher or more developed level. **2.** More difficult or demanding.

ad·van·tage (uhd-**van**-tij) *noun* **1.** Something that helps you or puts you ahead. **2.** The first point in a tennis game after the score of deuce. *phrases* **1.** If you **take advantage of** someone, you use him or her for your own benefit. **2.** If you **take advantage of** something, you find a use for it that benefits you. ▶ *adjective* **advantageous** (*ad*-vuhn-**tay**-juhs)

ad·vent (**ad**-vent) *noun* **1.** The beginning of something new or important. **2. Advent** The period leading up to Christmas in the Christian calendar.

ad·ven·ture (uhd-**ven**-chur) *noun* An exciting or dangerous experience. ▶ *adjective* **adventurous**

ad·verb (**ad**-*vurb*) *noun* A word usually used to describe a verb, adjective, or other adverb. Adverbs indicate how, when, where, how often, or how much something happens. For example, in the sentence "He walks quickly," the adverb *quickly* tells you how he walks.

ad·ver·sar·y (**ad**-vur-*ser*-ee) *noun* An opponent or enemy. ▶ *noun, plural* **adversaries**

ad·verse (ad-**vurs**) *adjective* Unfavorable, negative, or causing a problem. ▶ *adverb* **adversely**

ad·ver·si·ty (ad-**vur**-si-tee) *noun* A difficult situation that lasts for a long time. ▶ *noun, plural* **adversities**

ad·ver·tise (**ad**-vur-*tize*) *verb* To give information about something that you want to promote or sell. ▸ *verb* **advertising, advertised** ▸ *noun* **advertiser**

ad·ver·tise·ment (ad-vur-**tize**-muhnt *or* ad-**vur**-tiz-muhnt) *noun* A broadcast or published notice that calls attention to something, such as a product or an event.

ad·ver·tis·ing (**ad**-vur-*tye*-zing) *noun* **1.** The activity or industry that brings products and services to people's attention. **2.** Advertisements of all kinds, considered together.

ad·vice (uhd-**vise**) *noun* A suggestion about what someone should do. ▸ *noun, plural* **advice**

ad·vis·a·ble (uhd-**vye**-zuh-buhl) *adjective* Sensible, wise, and worth doing. ▸ *adverb* **advisably**

ad·vise (uhd-**vize**) *verb* To give someone information or suggestions. ▸ *verb* **advising, advised** ▸ *adjective* **advisory**

ad·vis·er *or* **ad·vi·sor** (uhd-**vye**-zur) *noun* Someone who gives advice, especially someone who is qualified to do this or who does it as a job.

ad·vo·cate
verb (**ad**-vuh-*kate*) To support or call for an idea or a plan.
noun (**ad**-vuh-kit) A person who supports an idea or plan.
▸ *verb* **advocating, advocated**

Ae·ge·an Sea (i-**jee**-uhn **see**) An area of the Mediterranean Sea located between Greece and Turkey. The Aegean Sea is connected to the Black Sea at its northeast side and to the Ionian Sea at its western edge. Numerous island groups are located within the sea.

aer·i·al (**air**-ee-uhl)
noun An antenna that receives television or radio signals.
adjective Happening in the air.

aer·o·bics (air-**oh**-biks) *noun, plural* Energetic exercises that strengthen the heart and improve breathing. Aerobics are often done with music playing. ▸ *adjective* **aerobic**

aer·o·dy·nam·ic (*air*-oh-dye-**nam**-ik) *adjective* Designed to move through the air very easily and quickly.

aer·o·nau·tic (*air*-uh-**naw**-tik) *or* **aer·o·nau·ti·cal** (*air*-uh-**naw**-tik-uhl) *adjective* Of or having to do with the design and building of aircraft.

aer·o·sol (**air**-uh-*sawl*) *noun* **1.** A mass of tiny particles mixed in air or another gas. **2.** A product, such as a deodorant or insecticide, that is sold in a spray can.
▸ *adjective* **aerosol**

aer·o·space (**air**-oh-*spase*)
noun The earth's atmosphere and all the space beyond it.
adjective Of or having to do with the science and technology of jet flight or space travel.

af·fair (uh-**fair**)
noun A happening or event.
noun, plural **affairs** Matters connected with private or public life.

af·fect (uh-**fekt**)
verb **1.** To influence or change someone or something. **2.** To pretend to feel or think a certain way.
noun The display or expression of an emotion or mood.
▸ *verb* **affecting, affected**

af·fect·ed (uh-**fek**-tid) *adjective* Unnatural and not sincere.

af·fec·tion (uh-**fek**-shuhn) *noun* Love for someone or something familiar to you.

af·fec·tion·ate (uh-**fek**-shuh-nit) *adjective* Loving. ▸ *adverb* **affectionately**

af·fil·i·ate
verb (uh-**fil**-ee-*ate*) To join or connect closely with something.
noun (uh-**fil**-ee-it) **1.** Someone who is connected closely with something, usually as an employee or volunteer. **2.** A branch of a larger organization.
▸ *verb* **affiliating, affiliated**

af·fin·i·ty (uh-**fin**-i-tee) *noun* If you have an **affinity** for something, you like it and feel a natural attraction to it. ▸ *noun, plural* **affinities**

af·firm·a·tive (uh-**fur**-muh-tiv) *adjective* Giving the answer "yes," or stating that something is true.

A

af·firm·a·tive ac·tion (uh-**fur**-muh-tiv **ak**-shuhn) *noun* A program that promotes increased opportunities for minorities and women in order to make up for past discrimination.

af·flic·tion (uh-**flik**-shuhn) *noun* Something that causes suffering. ▶ *verb* **afflict**

af·flu·ent (**af**-loo-uhnt) *adjective* Having lots of money; wealthy. ▶ *noun* **affluence**

af·ford (uh-**ford**) *verb* **1.** To have enough money to buy something. **2.** To have enough time or ability to do something.
▶ *verb* **affording, afforded**

af·ghan (**af**-gan) *noun* A crocheted or knitted blanket.

Af·ghan·i·stan (af-**gan**-i-*stan*) A landlocked country in south-central Asia. It has been invaded many times over the centuries, most recently by the former Soviet Union (1979) and by the United States (2001). Alexander the Great conquered Afghanistan in 330 B.C. The expansion of his empire into Central Asia led to the establishment of the Silk Road trading routes, connecting Europe to India and China.

a·float (uh-**floht**) *adverb, adjective* **1.** Floating on water. **2.** If a business, plan, or program **stays afloat** or if someone **keeps it afloat,** it keeps going and does not fail.

a·fraid (uh-**frayd**) *adjective* **1.** Frightened; full of fear. **2.** If you begin or end a sentence with **I'm afraid,** you show that you are sorry that what you are saying is true.

Af·ri·ca (**af**-ri-kuh) The second-largest and second-most-populated continent in the world, after Asia. It is positioned over the equator, giving the continent a range of temperate zones, and is bordered by the Atlantic Ocean to the west, the Indian Ocean to the east, and the Mediterranean Sea to the north.

Af·ri·can A·mer·i·can (**af**-ri-kuhn uh-**mer**-i-kuhn) *noun* Someone who was born in the United States or who became a U.S. citizen and can trace his or her ancestors back to Africa. ▶ *adjective* **African-American**

Af·ro (**af**-roh) *noun* A hairstyle with tight curls in a full, rounded shape.

aft (aft) *adverb, adjective* Toward the back of a ship or an aircraft.

af·ter (**af**-tur) *preposition* **1.** Later than. **2.** Following behind. *The marching band passed by after the parade float.* **3.** Trying to catch someone or something. *The dog chased after the ball.*

af·ter·care (**af**-tur-kair) *noun* **1.** Care for children after school during the hours before their parents come home from work. **2.** Care for a person after a difficult event in his or her life, such as being in the hospital or being in prison.

af·ter·math (**af**-tur-*math*) *noun* The situation after a bad thing happens.

af·ter·noon (*af*-tur-**noon**) *noun* The time of day between noon and evening.

af·ter·shock (**af**-tur-shahk) *noun* A relatively small earthquake that comes soon after a stronger earthquake in the same general location.

af·ter·ward (**af**-tur-wurd) *or* **af·ter·wards** (**af**-tur-wurdz) *adverb* Later.

a·gain (uh-**gen**) *adverb* One more time.

a·gainst (uh-**genst**) *preposition* **1.** Next to and touching. *Lean against me if you get tired.* **2.** Competing with. *We've won every time we've gone up against them.* **3.** Directed at or toward. *What are the charges against him?* **4.** Opposed to. *The school board is against changing the dress code.*

age (ayj) *noun* **1.** The length of time someone has lived or that something has existed. **2.** A period of time in history. *verb* To become or seem older. *phrase* When you **come of age,** you become an adult in the eyes of the law.
▶ *verb* **aging** *or* **ageing, aged**

aged *adjective* **1.** (ayjd) Being a particular number of years old. **2.** (**ay**-jid) Very old.

A

noun, plural **the aged** (**ay**-jid) Old people in general.

a·gen·cy (**ay**-juhn-see) *noun* An office, business, or government department that provides a service to the public. ▶ *noun, plural* **agencies**

a·gen·da (uh-**jen**-duh) *noun* 1. A list of things that need to be done or discussed. 2. The real reasons that someone wants to do something, which may be secret or hidden.

a·gent (**ay**-juhnt) *noun* 1. Someone who arranges things for other people. 2. A spy.

ag·gra·vate (**ag**-ruh-*vate*) *verb* 1. To make something even worse. 2. To annoy or bother.
▶ *verb* **aggravating, aggravated**
▶ *noun* **aggravation** ▶ *adjective* **aggravating**

ag·gre·gate (**ag**-ri-git)
adjective Formed by adding together different things or amounts.
noun A total.

ag·gres·sion (uh-**gresh**-uhn) *noun* Violent or threatening behavior.

ag·gres·sive (uh-**gres**-iv) *adjective* Pushy and always ready to attack. ▶ *adverb* **aggressively**

ag·ile (**aj**-il *or* **aj**-ile) *adjective* 1. Able to move fast and easily. 2. Able to think quickly and accurately.

a·gil·i·ty (uh-**jil**-i-tee) *noun* Skill in doing something in a graceful, coordinated way.

ag·i·tate (**aj**-i-*tate*) *verb* 1. To make someone nervous and upset. 2. To stir or shake up.
▶ *verb* **agitating, agitated** ▶ *noun* **agitation** ▶ *adjective* **agitated**

ag·nos·tic (ag-**nah**-stik)
noun Someone who believes that it is impossible to know if God exists.
adjective Having or relating to the beliefs of an agnostic.

a·go (uh-**goh**) *adverb* Before now, or in the past.

ag·o·ny (**ag**-uh-nee) *noun* Severe pain or suffering. ▶ *noun, plural* **agonies** ▶ *adjective* **agonizing**

a·gree (uh-**gree**) *verb* 1. To say yes to something. 2. To share the same opinion. 3. To be suitable or acceptable to someone. 4. To be consistent with something else.
▶ *verb* **agreeing, agreed**

a·gree·a·ble (uh-**gree**-uh-buhl) *adjective* 1. Pleasing or likable. 2. Willing or ready to say yes.

a·gree·ment (uh-**gree**-muhnt) *noun* 1. If you are **in agreement** with someone, you think the same way about a particular topic. 2. A formal understanding between two sides.

ag·ri·cul·tur·al (ag-ri-**kuhl**-chur-uhl) *adjective* Of or having to do with farming.

ag·ri·cul·ture (**ag**-ri-*kuhl*-chur) *noun* The raising of crops and animals; farming.

a·ground (uh-**ground**) *adverb* Stuck on the bottom in shallow water.

a·head (uh-**hed**) *adverb* 1. In front. 2. Before. 3. Further on in time or space.

a·hoy (uh-**hoi**) *interjection* An exclamation used by sailors to call other ships or attract attention.

aid (ayd)
verb To help someone.
noun 1. An object or action that helps someone do something. 2. Money or equipment for people in need.
▶ *verb* **aiding, aided**

aide (ayd) *noun* A person who works along with others to help them do their jobs.

AIDS (aydz) *noun* An often fatal illness that attacks the immune system, which protects the body against disease. AIDS is short for *acquired immune deficiency syndrome.*

ai·ki·do (eye-**kee**-doh) *noun* A Japanese art of self-defense in which you use wrist, joint, and elbow grips to stop or throw your opponent.

ail (ayl) *verb* 1. To give pain or trouble to. 2. To have poor health.
▶ *verb* **ailing, ailed**

ai·le·ron (**ay**-luh-*rahn*) *noun* A movable piece on an aircraft wing that pilots control.

ail·ment (**ayl**-muhnt) *noun* An illness, especially one that isn't serious.

A

aim (aym)
verb **1.** To hit, throw, or shoot something in a particular direction. **2.** To plan or do something with a particular audience in mind. **3.** To intend or hope to achieve something. *noun* **1.** The act of aiming at something. **2.** Something that you want to achieve; the object of your action.
▶ *verb* **aiming, aimed**

aim·less (**aym**-lis) *adjective* Without direction or purpose. ▶ *adverb* **aimlessly**

ain't (aynt) *contraction* (slang) A short form of *am not, is not, are not, has not,* or *have not.*

air (air)
noun **1.** The mixture of gases around the earth that you need to breathe. **2.** An appearance, or a manner. *verb* **1.** To express publicly. **2.** To let air into a room.
Air sounds like **heir.** ▶ *verb* **airing, aired**

air·bag (**air**-bag) *noun* A bag in motor vehicles that automatically inflates during an accident to protect a driver or passenger.

air·con·di·tion·ing (**air**-kuhn-*dish*-uh-ning) *noun* A system for keeping the air inside cool, dry, and clean.

air·craft (**air**-*kraft*) *noun* A vehicle that can fly. ▶ *noun, plural* **aircraft**

air·craft car·ri·er (**air**-kraft *kar*-ee-ur) *noun* A warship with a large, flat deck where aircraft take off and land.

air·field (**air**-*feeld*) *noun* **1.** A large area that includes a runway for airplanes to take off and land. **2.** An airport.

air force (**air** *fors*) *noun* The part of a country's military that attacks and defends mainly with aircraft.

air·line (**air**-*line*) *noun* A company that carries passengers and freight by air in exchange for money.

air·mail (**air**-*mayl*) *noun* Letters and packages that are carried by aircraft, or the service that does this.

air mar·shal (**air** *mahr*-shuhl) *noun* A government security officer who wears ordinary clothes and flies on airplanes along with regular passengers.

air·plane (**air**-*plane*) *noun* A vehicle with wings and an engine that flies through the air.

air·port (**air**-*port*) *noun* A place where aircraft take off and land, with buildings for passengers, businesses, freight, and other services.

air pres·sure (**air** *presh*-ur) *noun* The density or weight of the air, which is greater near the earth than it is high up.

air·ship (**air**-*ship*) *noun* An inflated frame shaped like a sausage with engines and a passenger compartment hanging underneath it. Blimps and zeppelins are airships.

air·sick (**air**-*sik*) *adjective* Feeling sick to your stomach or dizzy from flying in a plane.

air·tight (**air**-*tite*) *adjective* Not allowing air in or out.

air·y (**air**-ee) *adjective* **1.** Full of fresh air. **2.** Lighthearted, or casual.
▶ *adjective* **airier, airiest** ▶ *adverb* **airily**

aisle (ile) *noun* **1.** The passage that runs between the rows of seats in a room or large area, as in a theater, house of worship, or aircraft. **2.** The passage between shelves in a store or supermarket, or the line of shelves.
Aisle sounds like **isle** or **I'll.**

a·jar (uh-**jahr**) *adjective, adverb* If a door is **ajar,** it is open or partly open.

a·kim·bo (uh-**kim**-boh) *adjective, adverb* If you have your arms **akimbo,** your hands or knuckles are on your hips and your elbows are turned outward.

a·kin (uh-**kin**) *adjective* **1.** Belonging to the same family. **2.** Similar.

Al·a·bam·a (*al*-uh-**bam**-uh) A state in the southeastern region of the United States. It was a focus of civil rights activity during the 1960s. The quarter for the state of Alabama depicts Helen Keller (1880–1968), who was born there. An author, lecturer, and political activist, she was the first deaf and blind person to receive a college degree.

a·la·bas·ter (**al**-uh-*bas*-tur) *noun* A smooth, white kind of stone,

often used for sculpture.
adjective Smooth, pale, and almost see-through.

a·larm (uh-**lahrm**)
noun 1. A mechanical, electric, or digital device with a bell, buzzer, or siren that wakes people or warns them of danger. 2. Fear that something bad will happen.
verb To make someone afraid that something bad might happen.
▶ *verb* **alarming, alarmed** ▶ *adjective* **alarming** ▶ *adverb* **alarmingly**

a·las (uh-**las**) *interjection* Unfortunately, or sadly.

A·las·ka (uh-**las**-kuh) The 49th and largest state in the United States. Alaska lies just across the Bering Strait from Russia, at the northwest extremity of the North American continent. Native Americans and native Alaskan tribes, such as the Inuit, also known as Eskimos, make up about 15 percent of the population.

Al·ba·ni·a (al-**bay**-nee-uh) A country in Southeastern Europe, across the Adriatic Sea from Italy. In the early 1990s, Albania ended 46 years of communist rule and established a democracy.

al·ba·tross (**al**-buh-*traws*) *noun* 1. A large seabird with webbed feet and long wings that can fly for a long time. 2. If something is an **albatross around your neck,** it is a burden.
▶ *noun, plural* **albatrosses**

Al·ber·ta (al-**bur**-tuh) A province in western Canada. It is the most populous and westernmost of Canada's three prairie provinces, which include Manitoba and Saskatchewan. Alberta and Saskatchewan are the only two Canadian provinces that are landlocked.

al·bi·no (al-**bye**-noh) *noun* A person or animal born with the absence of pigment. This condition makes hair and skin very pale or white, and sometimes makes eyes pink.

al·bum (**al**-buhm) *noun* 1. A book in which you keep things you collect. 2. A collection of music on a CD, tape, or vinyl record.

al·co·hol (**al**-kuh-*hawl*) *noun* 1. A colorless liquid found in drinks such as wine, whiskey, and beer that can make people drunk. 2. A drink that contains this liquid. 3. A liquid used in making medicines, chemicals, and fuels.

al·co·hol·ic (*al*-kuh-**haw**-lik) *adjective* Containing alcohol.
noun A person who is unable to stop the habit of drinking too much alcohol, even though it has very bad effects.
▶ *noun* **alcoholism**

al·cove (**al**-kove) *noun* A smaller part of a room that is separated from the main area.

al·der (**awl**-dur) *noun* A tree or bush with rough bark and jagged leaves that grows in cool, moist places.

ale (ayl) *noun* An alcoholic drink that is similar to beer but has a more bitter taste.

a·lert (uh-**lurt**)
adjective Paying attention to what is around you and ready to act.
verb To warn someone of possible danger.
noun A warning of possible danger.
▶ *verb* **alerting, alerted**

al·fal·fa (al-**fal**-fuh) *noun* A plant related to clover that is used mostly to feed farm animals.

al·gae (**al**-jee) *noun, plural* Small plants without roots or stems that grow mainly in water.

al·ge·bra (**al**-juh-bruh) *noun* A type of mathematics in which symbols and letters are used to represent numbers.

Al·ge·ri·a (al-**jeer**-ee-uh) A country in North Africa on the Mediterranean Sea. Algeria is the second-largest country in Africa, after Sudan, and it is the largest of the countries that border the Mediterranean. Ruled by France for more than a century, Algeria has been independent since 1962.

a·li·as (**ay**-lee-uhs) *noun* A false name, especially one used by a criminal. ▶ *noun, plural* **aliases**

A

al·i·bi (**al**-uh-*bye*) *noun* A claim that a person accused of a crime was somewhere else when the crime was committed.

a·li·en (**ay**-lee-uhn or **ayl**-yuhn) *noun* 1. A being from another planet. 2. A foreigner.
adjective Different and strange.

a·lign (uh-**line**) *verb* To put things in a straight line. ▸ *verb* **aligning, aligned**

a·lign·ment (uh-**line**-muhnt) *noun* 1. Arrangement in a straight line or an orderly way. 2. The way that text, columns, or data are arranged.

a·like (uh-**like**)
adjective Looking or acting the same.
adverb In a similar way.

al·i·men·ta·ry canal (*al*-uh-**ment**-ree) *noun* The path that food follows as it is digested by the body. It includes the esophagus, stomach, small intestine, and large intestine.

a·live (uh-**live**) *adjective* 1. Living; not dead. 2. Energetic or active.

al·ka·li (**al**-kuh-*lye*) *noun* A strong base, such as lye or ammonia, that dissolves in water and reacts with an acid to form a salt. Strong alkalis can burn your skin. ▸ *adjective* **alkaline** (**al**-kuh-*line*)

all (awl)
adjective **All** of a group or thing is the whole of it.
pronoun Everyone.
adverb 1. Completely. 2. For each side.
noun Everything.
All sounds like **awl**.

Al·lah (**ah**-luh or ah-**lah**) *noun* The Muslim name for God.

al·le·ga·tion (*al*-i-**gay**-shuhn) *noun* A claim without any proof that someone has done something wrong or that something illegal has happened.

al·lege (uh-**lej**) *verb* To say that something is true without offering proof. ▸ *verb* **alleging, alleged**

al·leged (uh-**lejd** or uh-**lej**-id) *adjective* Said to be true or to have happened, but without proof. ▸ *adverb* **allegedly**

al·le·giance (uh-**lee**-juhns) *noun* Loyal support for someone or something.

al·ler·gic (uh-**lur**-jik) *adjective* If you are **allergic** to a substance, it causes you to sneeze, develop a rash, or have another unpleasant reaction. ▸ *noun* **allergy** (**al**-ur-jee)

al·ley (**al**-ee) *noun* A narrow passageway between or behind buildings or backyards.

al·li·ance (uh-**lye**-uhns) *noun* An agreement to work together for some result.

al·lied (**al**-ide) *adjective* 1. Working together, or on the same side. 2. Similar or related.

al·li·ga·tor (**al**-i-*gay*-tur) *noun* A large reptile with strong jaws and very sharp teeth, related to the crocodile. Alligators live in parts of North America and China.

al·lit·er·a·tion (uh-*lit*-uh-**ray**-shuhn) *noun* Repetition of the same sound at the beginning of a group of words, for example, "Fred is the first to finish five files." ▸ *adjective* **alliterative**

al·lo·cate (**al**-uh-*kate*) *verb* To set something aside for a particular purpose. ▸ *verb* **allocating, allocated** ▸ *noun* **allocation**

al·lot (uh-**laht**) *verb* 1. To give out something in equal shares or parts. 2. To set aside for a particular purpose.
▸ *verb* **allotting, allotted** ▸ *noun* **allotment**

al·low (uh-**lou**) *verb* 1. To let someone have or do something. 2. To make something possible.
▸ *verb* **allowing, allowed**

al·low·ance (uh-**lou**-uhns) *noun* 1. Money given to someone regularly, especially from parents to a child. 2. A change that you make for a particular reason.

al·loy (**al**-oi) *noun* A metal made from mixing other metals, or mixing a metal with an element that is not a metal.

all right (awl rite)
adjective 1. Good enough or acceptable, but not very good. 2. Not hurt or sick.
interjection Yes; I agree or I will.

A

all-star (**awl**-*stahr*)
adjective Made up of the best people in a particular sport or skill.
noun A team member who has been selected for an all-star team.

al·lude (uh-**lood**) *verb* To hint at or mention briefly. ▶ *verb* **alluding, alluded**

al·ly (**al**-eye) *noun* A person or country that is on the same side during a war or disagreement. ▶ *noun, plural* **allies**

al·ma·nac (**awl**-muh-*nak*) *noun* A book published once a year with facts and statistics about a variety of subjects.

al·might·y (awl-**mye**-tee)
adjective 1. Thought to have total or great power. 2. (informal) Very large or great.
noun **the Almighty** God.

al·mond (**ah**-muhnd *or* **al**-muhnd) *noun* An oval-shaped nut that is used in cooking or baking or eaten alone.

al·most (**awl**-mohst) *adverb* Very nearly.

al·oe (**al**-oh) *noun* A plant whose thick gel can be used to help heal burns and cuts.

a·loft (uh-**lawft**) *adverb, adjective* High up in the air.

a·lo·ha (uh-**loh**-hah) *interjection* In Hawaiian, a term used to say hello or good-bye.

a·lone (uh-**lone**) *adjective, adverb* Without anyone or anything else.

a·long (uh-**lawng**)
preposition 1. Following the length or direction of. *I walked along the avenue.* 2. **all along** All the time. *I knew all along that Jonah would come back.*
adverb 1. Forward; in the same direction. 2. With someone else, as a companion.

a·long·side (uh-**lawng**-*side*)
adverb Near to the side.
preposition Parallel to. *The two boys ran alongside each other.*

a·loof (uh-**loof**)
adverb When you remain **aloof** from someone or something, you keep yourself apart and don't get involved.
adjective Not friendly or talkative.

a·loud (uh-**loud**) *adverb* So that other people can hear.

al·pac·a (al-**pak**-uh) *noun* A South American animal, related to the camel and the llama, that produces long, silky wool.

al·pha·bet (**al**-fuh-*bet*) *noun* All the letters of a language arranged in order. ▶ *adjective* **alphabetical**

al·pha·bet·ize (**al**-fuh-buh-*tize*) *verb* To arrange things so that they follow the order of the letters of the alphabet. ▶ *verb* **alphabetizing, alphabetized**

Alps (alps) A large mountain range of Europe, stretching across Austria, Slovenia, Italy, Switzerland, Liechtenstein, Germany, and France. The highest peak in the Alps is Mont Blanc, located at the border of France and Italy.

al·read·y (awl-**red**-ee) *adverb* Before now, or before a certain time in the past.

al·so (**awl**-soh) *adverb* As well; in addition.

al·tar (**awl**-tur) *noun* A large table in a house of worship, used for religious ceremonies. **Altar** sounds like **alter.**

al·ter (**awl**-tur) *verb* To change. **Alter** sounds like **altar.** ▶ *verb* **altering, altered**

al·ter·a·tion (*awl*-tuh-**ray**-shuhn) *noun* The act or process of changing something, or a change made.

al·ter·nate
adjective (**awl**-tur-nit) Every other one.
verb (**awl**-tur-*nate*) To take turns.
noun (**awl**-tur-nit) Someone or something available if the main person or thing is not.
▶ *verb* **alternating, alternated**

al·ter·na·tive (awl-**tur**-nuh-tiv)
noun A choice that is not the usual one.
adjective Different from the usual thing or kind.

al·ter·na·tive en·er·gy (awl-**tur**-nuh-tiv **en**-ur-jee) *noun* Energy from natural sources that are renewable and don't harm the environment, such as the sun, ocean waves, and wind.

al·ter·na·tive·ly (awl-**tur**-nuh-tiv-lee) *adverb* As an alternative.

A

al·though (*awl*-**THoh**) *conjunction* **1.** In spite of the fact that. **2.** But.

al·tim·e·ter (al-**tim**-i-tur) *noun* An instrument that measures how high something is above the ground.

al·ti·tude (**al**-ti-*tood*) *noun* The height of something above the ground or above sea level.

al·to (**al**-toh)
noun **1.** A singing voice that is higher than a tenor but lower than a soprano. **2.** A person with an alto voice.
adjective Of or having to do with an alto voice, as in *an alto soloist.*

al·to·geth·er (*awl*-tuh-**geTH**-ur) *adverb* **1.** With everything or everyone counted. **2.** Completely, or entirely. **3.** On the whole; in general.

a·lu·mi·num (uh-**loo**-mi-nuhm) *noun* A light, silver-colored metal.

al·ways (**awl**-*wayz*) *adverb* **1.** All the time or very many times. **2.** Since the beginning and up until now, or indefinitely into the future.

Alz·hei·mer's dis·ease (**awlts**-hye-murz di-*zeez*) *noun* A disease that damages brain cells, making it hard to remember even simple things, to speak, and eventually to move.

a.m. (**ay-em**) An abbreviation of the Latin phrase *ante meridiem,* which means "before noon."

am (am) *verb* The first person singular present tense of *be. Am* is used only with the pronoun *I.*

am·a·teur (**am**-uh-chur *or* **am**-uh-tur) *noun* Someone who does some activity for pleasure rather than for money.
adjective Not professional; done in a way that shows lack of skill.

a·maze (uh-**maze**) *verb* To make someone extremely surprised. ▶ *verb* **amazing, amazed** ▶ *noun* **amazement**

a·maz·ing (uh-**may**-zing) *adjective* Extremely impressive and perhaps difficult to believe. ▶ *adverb* **amazingly**

am·bas·sa·dor (am-**bas**-uh-dur) *noun* The top person sent by a government to represent it in another country.

am·ber (**am**-bur) *noun* **1.** A yellowish-brown substance formed from fossilized tree sap. **2.** A yellowish-brown color. ▶ *adjective* **amber**

AMBER a·lert (**am**-bur uh-*lurt*) *noun* A public notice or media broadcast that tells people about a missing child.

am·bi·dex·trous (*am*-bi-**dek**-struhs) *adjective* Able to use both hands equally well, especially for writing.

am·big·u·ous (am-**big**-yoo-uhs) *adjective* Having two possible meanings. ▶ *noun* **ambiguity** (*am*-bi-**gyoo**-i-tee) ▶ *adverb* **ambiguously**

am·bi·tion (am-**bish**-uhn) *noun* **1.** Something that you want to do in the future. **2.** A strong wish to be successful.

am·bi·tious (am-**bish**-uhs) *adjective* **1.** Having a strong desire and will to succeed. **2.** Requiring a lot of money, effort, or resources.

am·biv·a·lent (am-**biv**-uh-luhnt) *adjective* Having two different opinions about something at the same time. ▶ *noun* **ambivalence**

am·ble (**am**-buhl) *verb* To walk slowly because you are not in a hurry. ▶ *verb* **ambling, ambled**

am·bu·lance (**am**-byuh-luhns) *noun* A vehicle that takes ill or injured people to a hospital.

am·bush (**am**-*bush*)
verb To attack someone from a hiding place.
noun An attack from a hiding place.
▶ *verb* **ambushes, ambushing, ambushed** ▶ *noun, plural* **ambushes**

a·men (ay-**men** *or* ah-**men**) *interjection* **1.** People say **amen** after a prayer to mean "May it be so." **2. Amen** also shows agreement with a statement.

a·mend (uh-**mend**)
verb To change a legal document or a law.
idiom When you **make amends,** you do something to make up for a wrong or a mistake.
▶ *verb* **amending, amended**

a·mend·ment (uh-**mend**-muhnt) *noun* A change that is made to a law or a legal document.

A

A·mer·i·can (uh-**mer**-i-kuhn)
adjective **1.** Of or having to do with the United States. **2.** Of or having to do with North, Central, or South America.
noun **1.** Someone born or living in the United States. **2.** Someone born or living in North, Central, or South America.

A·mer·i·can In·di·an (uh-**mer**-i-kuhn **in**-dee-uhn)
noun A member of any of the original people of North, Central, or South America. American Indians are often called **Native Americans.**
adjective Of or having to do with American Indians.

A·mer·i·can Sa·mo·a (uh-**mer**-i-kuhn suh-**moh**-uh) An unincorporated U.S. territory in the South Pacific Ocean. Part of the Samoan Islands chain, American Samoa is the southernmost territory of the United States. It lies southeast of the country of Samoa and is located roughly halfway between Hawaii and New Zealand.

am·e·thyst (**am**-uh-thist) *noun* **1.** A type of quartz crystal that is usually purple and often is used in jewelry. **2.** A shade of purple.

a·mi·a·ble (**ay**-mee-uh-buhl) *adjective* Friendly and easygoing.

a·mid (uh-**mid**) *preposition* In the middle of or surrounded by. *The senator could be seen amid a large group of reporters.*

a·mi·go (uh-**mee**-goh) *noun* The Spanish word for "male friend." The Spanish word for "female friend" is *amiga* (uh-**mee**-guh).

A·mish (**ah**-mish)
noun, plural The members of a strict Christian group who live mostly in Pennsylvania and Ohio.
adjective Of or having to do with the Amish.

am·mo·nia (uh-**mohn**-yuh) *noun* A chemical with a strong smell. It dissolves in water and is used in some cleaning products.

am·mu·ni·tion (*am*-yuh-**nish**-uhn) *noun* **1.** Things such as bullets or shells that can be fired from weapons. **2.** Information that you can use to support or oppose something.

am·ne·sia (am-**nee**-zhuh) *noun* A partial or total loss of memory that can be temporary or permanent.

am·nes·ty (**am**-ni-stee) *noun* **1.** An official decision to release prisoners and pardon crimes or mistakes. **2.** A chance to correct a mistake you have made by keeping or owning something, without being punished.
▶ *noun, plural* **amnesties**

a·moe·ba *or* **a·me·ba** (uh-**mee**-buh) *noun* A microscopic creature made of only one cell that is able to move through fluid. ▶ *noun, plural* **amoebas** *or* **amoebae** (uh-**mee**-bee)

a·mong (uh-**muhng**) *preposition* **1.** In the middle of, or surrounded by. *Kerry felt safe because she was among friends.* **2.** Giving some to each person or thing. *Her mother baked a big chocolate cake and divided it among the five of us.* **3.** Included as part of a certain group. *These pieces are among the most popular for piano that Beethoven wrote.*

a·mount (uh-**mount**)
noun A quantity of something.
verb To add up to a certain figure or quantity.
▶ *verb* **amounting, amounted**

amp (amp) *noun* **1.** A unit used to measure the strength of an electrical current, short for **ampere** (**am**-peer). **2.** Short for **amplifier.**

am·per·sand (**am**-pur-*sand*) *noun* A symbol (&) that stands for the word *and.*

am·phi·bi·an (am-**fib**-ee-uhn) *noun* **1.** A cold-blooded animal with a backbone that lives in water and breathes with gills when young. As an adult, it develops lungs and lives on land. Frogs, toads, and salamanders are amphibians. **2.** A vehicle that can travel on land and in water.
▶ *adjective* **amphibious**

A

am·phi·the·a·ter (**am**-fi-*thee*-uh-tur) *noun* A large building or area with rows of seats in a high circle around a central place like a stage. In ancient Rome, amphitheaters were used for public entertainment.

am·ple (**am**-puhl) *adjective* 1. More than enough. 2. Large.
▶ *adjective* **ampler, amplest** ▶ *adverb* **amply** (**am**-plee)

am·pli·fi·er (**am**-pluh-*fye*-ur) *noun* A piece of equipment that makes sound louder. ▶ *noun* **amplification**

am·pli·fy (**am**-pli-*fye*) *verb* To make something louder or stronger. ▶ *verb* **amplifies, amplifying, amplified**

am·pu·tate (**am**-pyuh-*tate*) *verb* To cut off someone's limb, as an arm, leg, or finger, usually because it is damaged or diseased. ▶ *verb* **amputating, amputated** ▶ *noun* **amputation**

a·muse (uh-**myooz**) *verb* 1. To make someone laugh or smile. 2. To prevent someone from being bored in an enjoyable way.
▶ *verb* **amusing, amused** ▶ *noun* **amusement** ▶ *adjective* **amusing**

a·muse·ment park (uh-**myooz**-muhnt pahrk) *noun* A place where people pay to go on rides, play games of skill, and enjoy other forms of entertainment.

an (uhn *or* an) *indefinite article* A form of *a* used before a word that is pronounced with a vowel as its first sound.

an·a·con·da (*an*-uh-**kahn**-duh) *noun* A large, nonpoisonous South American snake that wraps itself tightly around its prey to kill it.

an·a·gram (**an**-uh-*gram*) *noun* A word or phrase made by rearranging the letters in another word or phrase.

an·a·log (**an**-uh-*lawg*) *adjective* 1. Using moving parts to show a continuous change in information. 2. Measuring or representing data by continuous changes in physical properties rather than by using numbers, as is the case for something that is digital.

a·nal·y·sis (uh-**nal**-i-sis) *noun* The process or result of analyzing something.

an·a·lyze (**an**-uh-*lize*) *verb* To examine something carefully in order to understand it. ▶ *verb* **analyzing, analyzed** ▶ *adjective* **analytical** (*an*-uh-**lit**-i-kuhl)

an·ar·chy (**an**-ur-kee) *noun* A situation with no order and no leaders. ▶ *noun* **anarchist**

a·nat·o·my (uh-**nat**-uh-mee) *noun* 1. The structure of a living thing, such as an animal or insect. 2. The scientific study of the structure of living things.
▶ *noun, plural* **anatomies** ▶ *adjective* **anatomical** (*an*-uh-**tah**-mi-kuhl)

an·ces·tor (**an**-ses-tur) *noun* A member of your family who lived long ago, usually before your grandparents. ▶ *adjective* **ancestral**

an·ces·try (**an**-ses-tree) *noun* Your ancestors, or some aspect of them.

an·chor (**ang**-kur)
noun 1. A heavy metal object that is lowered from a ship or boat when it stops, to keep it from drifting. 2. The main person on camera during a TV news show. 3. Something that makes another thing or person stable.
verb To keep a boat in place by dropping an anchor.

an·cho·vy (**an**-*choh*-vee) *noun* A small, edible fish that is often salted and canned. ▶ *noun, plural* **anchovies**

an·cient (**ayn**-shuhnt) *adjective* 1. Very old. 2. Belonging to a period long ago.

and (and *or* uhnd) *conjunction* 1. As well as. 2. Added to, or plus. 3. As a result.

An·des (**an**-deez) The longest continental mountain range in the world, stretching along the western coast of South America. The Andes are the highest range outside of Asia and occupy regions of the countries of Argentina, Bolivia, Chile, Colombia, Ecuador, Peru, and Venezuela.

An·dor·ra (an-**dor**-uh) A small country in the eastern Pyrenees Mountains between France and Spain. Tourism, especially for skiing, is one of the country's main industries. Andorra is also a banking center and is well known as a tax haven.

an·droid (**an**-droid) *noun* A robot that is designed to act and look like a human being.

an·ec·dote (**an**-ik-*dote*) *noun* A short, often funny story about an experience. ▶ *adjective* **anecdotal**

a·ne·mic (uh-**nee**-mik) *adjective* If you are **anemic,** you feel weak and become easily tired because your body isn't producing enough red blood cells. ▶ *noun* **anemia**

an·e·mom·et·er (*an*-i-**mah**-mi-tur) *noun* A scientific instrument used to measure the wind's speed.

a·nem·o·ne (uh-**nem**-uh-nee) *noun* **1.** A small plant with purple, red, white, or pink flowers. **2.** Short for *sea anemone.*

an·es·the·si·ol·o·gist (*an*-is-*thee*-zee-ah-luh-jist) *noun* A physician who specializes in giving people drugs or gas to prevent pain during operations.

an·es·thet·ic (*an*-is-**thet**-ik) *noun* A drug or a gas given to people to prevent or lessen pain.

a·new (uh-**noo**) *adverb* Again, or once more.

an·gel (**ayn**-juhl) *noun* **1.** In religion, a messenger of God. Most pictures of angels show them with wings. **2.** A very kind, gentle person.
▶ *adjective* **angelic** (an-**jel**-ik)

an·ger (**ang**-gur)
noun The strong feeling of being very annoyed or hostile toward someone.
verb To make someone angry or upset.
▶ *verb* **angering, angered**

an·gle (**ang**-guhl)
noun **1.** The area formed by two lines that start at the same point and go in different directions. Angles are measured in degrees. **2.** A way of looking at or dealing with something.
verb To move, turn, or bend at an angle.
phrase If something is **at an angle,** it is sloping.
▶ *verb* **angling, angled**

an·gling (**ang**-gling) *noun* The sport of fishing with a fishing rod rather than a net. ▶ *noun* **angler**

An·go·la (ang-**goh**-luh) A country on the Atlantic Ocean in south-central Africa. Angola was a Portuguese colony for centuries until its independence in 1975. After a fierce civil war that lasted until 2002, Angola is now one of Africa's major producers of oil and diamonds.

an·go·ra (ang-**gor**-uh) *noun* **1.** A long-haired variety of rabbit, goat, or cat. **2.** Fluffy fiber or yarn made from the hair of angora rabbits.

an·gry (**ang**-gree) *adjective* Feeling or showing annoyance or bad feelings toward someone or something. ▶ *adjective* **angrier, angriest** ▶ *adverb* **angrily**

an·guish (**ang**-gwish) *noun* A strong feeling of pain or distress. ▶ *adjective* **anguished**

an·gu·lar (**ang**-gyuh-lur) *adjective* Having straight lines and sharp turns or corners.

an·i·mal (**an**-uh-muhl)
noun Any living creature that can move around and that eats other organisms to survive. Humans are animals, too, but usually when people refer to animals they mean pigs, donkeys, elephants, or other such beings.
adjective Typical of the behavior or instincts of animals, as opposed to humans.

an·i·mal rights (**an**-uh-muhl *rites*) *noun* The idea that animals should be treated with kindness and respect, and that they should not suffer because of things that humans want.

an·i·mat·ed (**an**-uh-*may*-tid) *adjective* **1.** Lively. **2.** Made by projecting a series of slightly different images very quickly, one after the other, so that the characters in the images seem to move.
▶ *noun* **animator** ▶ *verb* **animate** ▶ *adverb* **animatedly**

an·i·ma·tion (*an*-uh-**may**-shuhn) *noun* The activity of making movies by using drawings, pictures, or computer graphics.

an·i·me (**an**-uh-*may*) *noun* Japanese animation for film, television, and video.

A

an·i·mos·i·ty (an-uh-**mah**-si-tee) *noun* A strong dislike for someone. ► *noun, plural* **animosities**

an·kle (**ang**-kuhl) *noun* The joint that connects your foot to your leg.

an·klet (**ang**-klit) *noun* 1. A band or chain worn around the ankle as a piece of jewelry. 2. A short sock that covers the ankle.

an·nex
verb (an-**eks** *or* **an**-eks) To take control of a country or territory by force.
noun (**an**-eks) A smaller building that is connected to or located near a main building.
► *verb* **annexes, annexing, annexed** ► *noun, plural* **annexes** ► *noun* **annexation** (an-ek-**say**-shuhn)

an·ni·hi·late (uh-**nye**-uh-*late*) *verb* To destroy something completely. ► *verb* **annihilating, annihilated** ► *noun* **annihilation**

an·ni·ver·sa·ry (an-uh-**vur**-sur-ee) *noun* A date that people remember each year because of an important event that happened on that date in an earlier year. ► *noun, plural* **anniversaries**

an·no·tate (**an**-uh-*tate*) *verb* To add notes to a text or picture in order to explain it better. ► *verb* **annotating, annotated** ► *noun* **annotation** ► *adjective* **annotated**

an·nounce (uh-**nouns**) *verb* To say something officially or publicly. ► *verb* **announcing, announced**

an·nounce·ment (uh-**nouns**-muhnt) *noun* 1. A public statement that gives new information about something. 2. The act of announcing something.

an·nounc·er (uh-**noun**-sur) *noun* 1. Someone who introduces programs on television or radio. 2. Someone who describes the action during a sports event.

an·noy (uh-**noi**) *verb* To make someone lose patience or feel angry. ► *verb* **annoying, annoyed** ► *noun* **annoyance** ► *adjective* **annoying** ► *adverb* **annoyingly**

an·nu·al (**an**-yoo-uhl)
adjective Happening once every year or over a period of one year.
noun 1. A book published once a year; a yearbook. 2. A plant that lives for only one year.
► *adverb* **annually**

a·noint (uh-**noint**) *verb* To honor someone during a religious ceremony by dabbing oil on his or her head. ► *verb* **anointing, anointed**

a·non·y·mous (uh-**nah**-nuh-muhs) *adjective* Written, done, or given by a person whose name is not known or made public. ► *noun* **anonymity** (an-uh-**nim**-i-tee) ► *adverb* **anonymously**

an·o·rex·i·a (an-uh-**rek**-see-uh) *noun* A mental illness that makes people think they are too fat when in fact they are dangerously thin because they won't eat enough. ► *adjective* **anorexic** (an-uh-**rek**-sik)

an·oth·er (uh-**nuhTH**-ur)
adjective One more of the same kind of thing.
pronoun A different one, or one more.

an·swer (**an**-sur)
verb 1. To say or write something as a reply. 2. To provide the solution to something. 3. **answer for** To be responsible for something.
noun 1. The response to a question. 2. The solution to a problem.
► *verb* **answering, answered**

an·swer·ing ma·chine (**an**-sur-ing muh-*sheen*) *noun* A machine connected to or built into a telephone that records messages from people who call while you are out.

ant (ant) *noun* A small but very strong insect that lives in a large group called a colony.

ant·ac·id (ant-**as**-id) *noun* A medicine that works by reducing the amount of acid in your stomach.

an·tag·o·nize (an-**tag**-uh-*nize*)
verb To make someone oppose you or be angry with you. ► *verb*

A

antagonizing, antagonized ▸ *noun*
antagonism ▸ *noun* **antagonist**

Ant·arc·tic (ant-**ahrk**-tik) *noun* The area
around the South Pole. ▸ *adjective*
Antarctic

Ant·arc·ti·ca (ant-**ahrk**-ti-kuh) *A*
continent that is located almost
entirely below the Antarctic Circle,
surrounding the South Pole.
Antarctica is surrounded by the
Southern Ocean and is the fifth-largest
continent. Because of its cold desert
climate, it is uninhabited, apart from
research teams who occupy the region
for short lengths of time.

ant·eat·er (**ant**-*ee*-tur) *noun* A mammal
with a long, sticky tongue that it uses
to search for ants and other small
insects. Anteaters are found in Central
and South America.

an·te·ced·ent (*an*-ti-**see**-duhnt) *noun*
The word or phrase that a pronoun
refers to. For example, in the sentence
"Ramón cooked the burger and then
ate it," the antecedent of the pronoun
it is "the burger."

an·te·lope (**an**-tuh-*lope*) *noun* An animal
that looks like a deer and runs very
fast. Antelopes have long horns
without branches and are found in
Africa and parts of Asia.

an·ten·na (an-**ten**-uh) *noun* **1.** A feeler on
the head of an insect. **2.** A device that
receives radio and television signals.
▸ *noun, plural* **antennas** or **antennae**
(an-**ten**-ee)

an·them (**an**-thuhm) *noun* A religious
or national song, or a song that
expresses the ideas of a particular
group.

an·ther (**an**-thur) *noun* The part of a
flower at the tip of the stamen that
contains its pollen.

an·thol·o·gy (an-**thah**-luh-jee) *noun* A
book that contains articles, poems, or
stories by different writers. ▸ *noun,
plural* **anthologies**

an·thra·cite (**an**-thruh-*site*) *noun* A type
of shiny, hard coal that burns very
cleanly.

an·thro·pol·o·gy (*an*-thruh-**pah**-luh-jee)
noun The study of the beliefs and

ways of life of different peoples and
cultures. ▸ *noun* **anthropologist**

an·ti·bi·ot·ic (*an*-ti-bye-**ah**-tik) *noun* A
drug that kills bacteria and is used to
treat infections and diseases.

an·ti·bod·y (**an**-ti-*bah*-dee) *noun* A
protein that your blood makes to stop
an infection that has entered your
body. ▸ *noun, plural* **antibodies**

an·tic·i·pate (an-**tis**-uh-*pate*) *verb* To
expect something to happen and be
prepared for it. ▸ *verb* **anticipating,
anticipated** ▸ *noun* **anticipation**

an·ti·cli·max (*an*-ti-**klye**-maks) *noun* An
event that you expect will be exciting,
interesting, or important but then
isn't. ▸ *noun, plural* **anticlimaxes**

an·ti·dote (**an**-ti-*dote*) *noun* Something
that stops a poison from working.

an·ti·freeze (**an**-tee-*freez*) *noun* A
chemical mixture that is added to
liquid to stop it from freezing.

An·ti·gua and Bar·bu·da (an-**teeg**-wuh
and bahr-**boo**-duh) *A* two-island nation
on the eastern edge of the Caribbean
Sea, near the Atlantic Ocean. Antigua
and Barbuda are surrounded by several
smaller islands and are part of the
Lesser Antilles.

an·ti·per·spi·rant (*an*-ti-**pur**-spur-uhnt)
noun A substance that you put on your
skin to stop you from sweating too
much.

an·tique (an-**teek**)
noun An object that is old and
considered valuable because it is rare
or beautiful.
adjective Very old.

an·ti·sep·tic (*an*-ti-**sep**-tik) *noun* A
substance that kills germs and
prevents infection by stopping the
growth of germs.

an·ti·so·cial (*an*-ti-**soh**-shuhl) *adjective*
1. An **antisocial** person does not
enjoy being with others. **2. Antisocial**
behavior upsets or harms other people.

an·ti·vi·rus (*an*-ti-**vye**-ruhs) *adjective*
Designed to protect computers from
viruses.

ant·ler (**ant**-lur) *noun* One of the two
large, branching, bony structures on
the head of a deer, moose, or elk.

A

an·to·nym (**an**-tuh-*nim*) *noun*
A word, often an adjective, that means the opposite of another word. *Hot* and *cold* are antonyms; so are *weak* and *strong, up* and *down*, and *over* and *under*.

anx·i·e·ty (ang-**zye**-i-tee) *noun* A feeling of worry or fear. ▸ *noun, plural* **anxieties**

anx·ious (**angk**-shuhs) *adjective*
1. Worried. 2. Very eager to do something.
▸ *adverb* **anxiously**

an·y (**en**-ee)
adjective 1. One or more. 2. Every. *pronoun* A way of suggesting people or things without naming them. *adverb* At all.

an·y·bod·y (**en**-ee-*buhd*-ee or **en**-ee-*bah*-dee) *pronoun* Any person.

an·y·how (**en**-ee-*hou*) *adverb* In any case.

an·y·more (*en*-ee-**mor**) *adverb* 1. Now, or from now on. 2. You use **anymore** to talk about differences between now and the past.

an·y·one (**en**-ee-*wuhn*) *pronoun* Any person.

an·y·place (**en**-ee-*plase*) *adverb* In any location; anywhere.

an·y·thing (**en**-ee-*thing*)
pronoun Any thing or item of any kind.
adverb At all.

an·y·time (**en**-ee-*time*) *adverb* At any hour or date, or whenever.

an·y·way (**en**-ee-*way*) *adverb* 1. In any case. 2. (informal) People sometimes use **anyway** at the beginning of a sentence to change the subject, or return to an earlier subject.

an·y·where (**en**-ee-*wair*) *adverb* In or to any place.

a·or·ta (ay-**or**-tuh) *noun* The main tube that carries blood away from the heart to the rest of the body, except the lungs.

A·pach·e (uh-**pach**-ee) *noun* A member of a group of Native Americans who live primarily in the southwestern United States. ▸ *noun, plural* **Apache** or **Apaches**

a·part (uh-**pahrt**) *adverb* 1. Separated in time or space. 2. **Apart** is used after verbs to say that something that was once a single thing is now divided or broken.

a·part·ment (uh-**pahrt**-muhnt) *noun* A set of rooms to live in, usually rented and on one floor of a building.

ap·a·thet·ic (*ap*-uh-**thet**-ik) *adjective* Not having or showing much interest in something.

ap·a·thy (**ap**-uh-thee) *noun* Lack of interest or concern.

a·pat·o·saur·us (uh-*pat*-uh-**sor**-uhs) *noun* A huge, plant-eating dinosaur with a small head, a long neck and tail, and four thick legs. Formerly called a **brontosaurus.** ▸ *noun, plural* **apatosauruses**

ape (ape)
noun A large animal related to monkeys and humans.
verb To copy the way someone behaves or speaks.
▸ *verb* **aping, aped**

Ap·en·nines (**ap**-uh-*ninez*) A mountain range stretching along the peninsula of Italy. The northeast end of the range joins a section of the Alps. The Apennines are sometimes called the Apennine Mountains.

ap·er·ture (**ap**-ur-chur) *noun* A hole behind a camera lens that can be opened or closed to control the amount of light that enters.

a·pex (**ay**-peks) *noun* The highest point of something. ▸ *noun, plural* **apexes**

a·phid (**ay**-fid) *noun* A tiny insect that feeds by sucking the juices from plants.

a·piece (uh-**pees**) *adverb* Each.

a·pol·o·gize (uh-**pah**-luh-*jize*) *verb* To say that you are sorry about something. ▸ *verb* **apologizing, apologized** ▸ *adjective* **apologetic** (uh-*pah*-luh-**jet**-ik)

apol·o·gy (uh-**pah**-luh-jee) *noun* Words that express that you are sorry for something you did. ▸ *noun, plural* **apologies**

a·pos·tle (uh-**pah**-suhl) *noun* 1. A close follower of another person or

A

cause. **2.** In Christianity, one of the 12 men chosen by Jesus to spread his teaching, plus Saint Paul.

a·pos·tro·phe (uh-**pah**-struh-fee) *noun*
1. A punctuation mark (') that is used with the letter *s* to show ownership. **2.** The punctuation mark used to show that letters have been left out, as in the word *didn't*.

app (ap) *noun* (informal) A computer application.

ap·pall·ing (uh-**paw**-ling) *adjective* Horrifying and shocking. ▸ *adverb* **appallingly**

ap·pa·rat·us (*ap*-uh-**rat**-uhs) *noun*
1. Equipment used for performing sports, especially gymnastics. **2.** Equipment or machines needed to do a job or experiment.
▸ *noun, plural* **apparatus** *or* **apparatuses**

ap·par·el (uh-**par**-uhl) *noun* Clothing.

ap·par·ent (uh-**par**-uhnt) *adjective*
1. Obvious or clear, so anyone can see or understand. **2.** Seeming to be real or true.

ap·par·ent·ly (uh-**par**-uhnt-lee) *adverb*
1. According to what seems true or obvious, or judging by what is known. **2.** You can begin a sentence with **apparently** as a way of showing that you have come to a conclusion about something from facts that imply it.

ap·peal (uh-**peel**)
verb **1.** To ask for something that is badly needed. **2.** To apply to a higher court for a change in a legal decision. **3.** To have an attractive quality.
noun **1.** A request for something needed, especially for donations. **2.** A request for a change in a legal decision. **3.** A quality that people find attractive.
▸ *verb* **appealing, appealed**

ap·pear (uh-**peer**) *verb* **1.** To come into view. **2.** To seem.
▸ *verb* **appearing, appeared**

ap·pear·ance (uh-**peer**-uhns) *noun*
1. An act of appearing. **2.** The way something or someone looks.

ap·pease (uh-**peez**) *verb* **1.** To make someone content or calm. **2.** To give

someone what is needed, or to satisfy someone.
▸ *verb* **appeasing, appeased**

ap·pen·di·ci·tis (uh-*pen*-di-**sye**-tis) *noun* An infection of the appendix; surgery to remove it is the most common treatment.

ap·pen·dix (uh-**pen**-diks) *noun* **1.** A small, closed tube attached to the large intestine. **2.** A section at the end of a book with extra information.
▸ *noun, plural* **appendixes** *or* **appendices** (uh-**pen**-di-seez)

ap·pe·tite (**ap**-uh-*tite*) *noun* **1.** Desire for food. **2.** Great ability to do something enthusiastically.

ap·pe·tiz·er (**ap**-uh-*tye*-zur) *noun* A small portion of food eaten before a meal or at the start of a meal.

ap·pe·tiz·ing (*ap*-uh-**tye**-zing) *adjective* **Appetizing** foods or smells make you want to eat.

ap·plaud (uh-**plawd**) *verb* To show that you like something, usually by clapping your hands. ▸ *verb* **applauding, applauded** ▸ *noun* **applause**

ap·ple (**ap**-uhl) *noun* A round, usually crisp fruit with a thin skin that is either red, green, or yellow when ripe.

ap·pli·ance (uh-**plye**-uhns) *noun* A machine that does a particular job, such as a dryer, toaster, or blender.

ap·pli·ca·ble (**ap**-li-kuh-buhl) *adjective* Relevant or appropriate; able to be applied.

ap·pli·cant (**ap**-li-kuhnt) *noun* Someone who applies for something, such as a job, a loan, or entrance to a school.

ap·pli·ca·tion (*ap*-li-**kay**-shuhn) *noun*
1. A written request for something. **2.** The act of applying something, or of applying for something. **3.** A form that you fill out to apply for something. **4.** A way of using something. **5.** A computer program that performs a certain task.

ap·ply (uh-**plye**) *verb* 1. To bring something into direct contact with something else. 2. To ask for something officially. 3. To be relevant. 4. To use something for a purpose. 5. If you **apply yourself** to something, you work hard at it.
▶ *verb* **applies, applying, applied**

ap·point (uh-**point**) *verb* 1. To choose someone for a job or position. 2. To arrange something officially.
▶ *verb* **appointing, appointed**

ap·point·ment (uh-**point**-muhnt) *noun* 1. The act of naming or choosing someone for a job. 2. An office, position, or job. 3. An arrangement to meet someone at a certain time.

ap·praise (uh-**praze**) *verb* To decide on the value of something by having an expert inspect it. ▶ *verb* **appraising, appraised**

ap·pre·cia·ble (uh-**pree**-shuh-buhl) *adjective* Enough to be noticed.

ap·pre·ci·ate (uh-**pree**-shee-*ate*) *verb* 1. To enjoy or value somebody or something. 2. To understand something. 3. To increase in worth.
▶ *verb* **appreciating, appreciated** ▶ *adjective* **appreciative** (uh-**pree**-shuh-tiv) ▶ *adverb* **appreciatively**

ap·pre·ci·a·tion (uh-**pree**-shee-**ay**-shuhn) *noun* A feeling or expression of being grateful for something.

ap·pre·hend (ap-ri-**hend**) *verb* 1. To capture and arrest someone. 2. To understand, or to capture the meaning of something.
▶ *verb* **apprehending, apprehended**

ap·pre·hen·sive (ap-ri-**hen**-siv) *adjective* Worried and slightly afraid that something bad will happen. ▶ *noun* **apprehension** ▶ *adverb* **apprehensively**

ap·pren·tice (uh-**pren**-tis) *noun* Someone who learns a skill by working with an expert. ▶ *noun* **apprenticeship**

ap·proach (uh-**prohch**) *verb* 1. To move nearer. 2. To go to a person with a question or request. 3. To begin to deal with something.

4. To come closer in time.
noun 1. The act of approaching or coming up to someone or something. 2. A particular way of doing something to get a result.
▶ *verb* **approaches, approaching, approached** ▶ *noun, plural* **approaches**

ap·proach·a·ble (uh-**proh**-chuh-buhl) *adjective* Friendly and easy to talk to.

ap·pro·pri·ate
adjective (uh-**proh**-pree-it) Suitable or right.
verb (uh-**proh**-pree-*ate*) To take something unfairly.
▶ *verb* **appropriating, appropriated** ▶ *adverb* **appropriately** (uh-**proh**-pree-it-lee)

ap·prov·al (uh-**proo**-vuhl) *noun* 1. A good and positive opinion about something. 2. Permission to do something.

ap·prove (uh-**proov**) *verb* 1. To have a good opinion about a person or thing. 2. To officially accept a plan or an idea.
▶ *verb* **approving, approved**

ap·prox·i·mate
adjective (uh-**prahk**-suh-mit) Close to or nearly accurate.
verb (uh-**prahk**-suh-mayt) 1. To form an estimate of something. 2. To be similar to something.
▶ *noun* **approximation** (uh-*prahk*-suh-**may**-shuhn)

ap·prox·i·mate·ly (uh-**prahk**-suh-mit-lee) *adverb* Not exactly; plus or minus a small amount.

a·pri·cot (**ay**-pri-*kaht* or **ap**-ri-*kaht*) *noun* A small, soft fruit similar to a peach.
adjective Having the color of this fruit.

A·pril (**ay**-pruhl) *noun* The fourth month on the calendar, after March and before May. April has 30 days.

Ap·ril Fools' Day (**ay**-pruhl **foolz** *day*) *noun* April 1, a day when it is customary to play practical jokes on people.

a·pron (**ay**-pruhn) *noun* 1. An article of clothing that you wear to protect your clothes when you are cooking or taking part in a messy activity. 2. The part of a stage in front of the curtain.

A

apt (apt) *adjective* **1.** Suitable for what is happening. **2.** Quick to learn things. **3.** If you are **apt** to do something, you are likely to do it.

ap·ti·tude (**ap**-ti-*tood*) *noun* A natural ability to learn quickly or do something well.

a·quar·i·um (uh-**kwair**-ee-uhm) *noun* **1.** A glass tank in which you can keep fish. **2.** A place set up for visitors to see different kinds of ocean creatures, such as dolphins, seals, and sharks. ▶ *noun, plural* **aquariums** or **aquaria** (uh-**kwair**-ee-uh)

a·quat·ic (uh-**kwat**-ik or uh-**kwah**-tik) *adjective* **1.** Living or growing in water. **2.** Performed in or on water.

aq·ue·duct (**ak**-wuh-*duhkt*) *noun* A man-made channel for carrying water over valleys and rivers. In Europe, many aqueducts were built in Roman times and are still standing.

A·ra·bi·an Pe·nin·su·la (uh-**ray**-bee-uhn puh-**nin**-suh-luh) A region of land between Africa and Asia, surrounded by water on three sides. The Arabian Peninsula is part of the area known as the Middle East. It is home to a diverse group of countries, languages, and peoples, mainly Arabs.

Ar·a·bic (**ar**-uh-bik)
noun A language spoken by many people in the Middle East and North Africa.
adjective Of or having to do with Arabs, their language, or their system of writing.

Ar·a·bic nu·mer·als (**ar**-uh-bik **noo**-mur-uhlz) *noun, plural* The figures 0, 1, 2, 3, 4, 5, 6, 7, 8, and 9 that we use today. These numerals were first taught to Europeans by Arab scholars.

ar·a·ble (**ar**-uh-buhl) *adjective* **Arable** land is suitable for farming.

ar·bi·trar·y (**ahr**-bi-*trer*-ee) *adjective* **1.** Based on personal feelings or opinions rather than on reason or logic. **2.** Not assigned or not having a particular or known value.

ar·bi·trate (**ahr**-bi-*trate*) *verb* To help two opposing sides reach an agreement about something they are arguing about. ▶ *verb* **arbitrating, arbitrated** ▶ *noun* **arbitration** ▶ *noun* **arbitrator**

ar·bor (**ahr**-bur) *noun* **1.** A small place that is surrounded by and shaded by trees, shrubs, and vines. **2. Arbor Day** is a day in spring that is set aside for planting trees. The actual date varies.

arc (ahrk) *noun* **1.** Part of a curve. **2.** In math, an **arc** is a curved line between two points, usually part of a circle. **Arc** sounds like **ark.**

ar·cade (ahr-**kade**) *noun* **1.** A row of arches supported by columns, in a building or standing freely as a separate structure. **2.** A business with machines for amusement, such as pinball games, which you pay to use.

arch (ahrch)
noun A curved shape over an opening. The structure of an arch often helps support the weight of a building, wall, or bridge.
verb To curve.
▶ *noun, plural* **arches** ▶ *verb* **arches, arching, arched** ▶ *adjective* **arched**

ar·chae·ol·o·gy or **ar·che·ol·o·gy** (*ahr*-kee-**ah**-luh-jee) *noun* The study of the distant past, which often involves digging up old buildings, objects, and bones and examining them carefully. ▶ *noun* **archaeologist** ▶ *adjective* **archaeological** (*ahr*-kee-uh-**lah**-ji-kuhl)

ar·cha·ic (ahr-**kay**-ik) *adjective* From the past and not used anymore.

arch·bish·op (ahrch-**bish**-uhp) *noun* A bishop of the highest rank in some Christian denominations.

arch·er·y (**ahr**-chur-ee) *noun* The sport of using a bow and arrow. ▶ *noun* **archer**

ar·chi·pel·a·go (*ahr*-kuh-**pel**-uh-goh) *noun* A group of islands.

ar·chi·tect (**ahr**-ki-*tekt*) *noun* Someone who designs buildings and supervises the way they are built.

ar·chi·tec·ture (**ahr**-ki-tek-chur) *noun* **1.** The activity of designing and drawing plans for buildings. **2.** A style of building.
▶ *adjective* **architectural**

A

ar·chive (**ahr**-kive)
noun A collection of related documents or other things that is stored in a library or other public place.
verb To put a document, object, or computer file into an archive.
▸ *adjective* **archival**

arc·tic (**ahrk**-tik)
adjective 1. Extremely cold and wintry. 2. About, at, or to the area around the North Pole.
noun **the Arctic** The area around the North Pole.

ar·dent (**ahr**-duhnt) *adjective* Feeling or showing very strong emotions. ▸ *adverb* **ardently**

ar·du·ous (**ahr**-joo-uhs) *adjective* Very difficult and requiring a lot of effort.

ar·e·a (**air**-ee-uh) *noun* 1. The amount of surface within a given boundary, measured in square units. 2. A part of a place. 3. A subject or activity.

ar·e·a code (**air**-ee-uh *kode*) *noun* A three-digit number that indicates a telephone service area, such as 202 for Washington, D.C.

a·re·na (uh-**ree**-nuh) *noun* A large area or building that is used for sports or entertainment.

aren't (ahrnt *or* **ahr**-uhnt) *contraction* A short form of *are not.*

Ar·gen·ti·na (**ahr**-juhn-**tee**-nuh) The second-largest country in South America, after Brazil. Argentina is the largest Spanish-speaking nation in the world in terms of land area.

ar·gue (**ahr**-gyoo) *verb* 1. To give your opinion about something. 2. To disagree in talking about or discussing something.
▸ *verb* **arguing, argued**

ar·gu·ment (**ahr**-gyuh-muhnt) *noun* 1. A set of reasons that supports an idea or opinion. 2. A verbal disagreement, especially a loud or angry one.
▸ *adjective* **argumentative** (ar-gyuh-**men**-tuh-tiv)

ar·id (**ar**-id) *adjective* Extremely dry because of a lack of rain.

a·rise (uh-**rize**) *verb* 1. To get up from bed or from lying down. 2. To come

into being; start existing.
▸ *verb* **arising, arose** (uh-**rohz**) **arisen** (uh-**riz**-uhn)

ar·is·toc·ra·cy (ar-i-**stah**-kruh-see) *noun* The group of people in a society who carry titles, or the most wealthy and prestigious group.

a·ris·to·crat (uh-**ris**-tuh-*krat*) *noun* A member of a group of people thought to be the best in some way, usually based on their social class. ▸ *adjective* **aristocratic**

a·rith·me·tic (uh-**rith**-muh-tik) *noun* The science of numbers and computation. Addition, subtraction, multiplication, and division are the four basic operations of arithmetic.

Ar·i·zo·na (ar-i-**zoh**-nuh) A state in the southwestern region of the United States. It has a desert landscape, with a dry climate and giant cacti, and is best known for being the site of the Grand Canyon.

ark (ahrk) *noun* 1. In the Bible, a boat built by Noah to carry his family and two of every kind of animal during the Great Flood. 2. In a synagogue, the cabinet in which the Torah scrolls are kept.
Ark sounds like **arc.**

Ar·kan·sas (**ahr**-kuhn-*saw*) A state in the southern region of the United States. The Mississippi River runs along its eastern border, and its mountains include the Ozarks and the Ouachita range. In addition to state and national parks, Arkansas has a dozen wilderness areas, covering about 150,000 acres.

arm (ahrm)
noun 1. The part of your body between your shoulder and your hand. 2. The part of an armchair or sofa where you rest your arms. 3. A branch or division of an organization.
verb To supply a person or group with weapons.
noun, plural **arms** Weapons, especially guns.
▸ *verb* **arming, armed**

ar·ma·da (ahr-**mah**-duh) *noun* A large group of warships.

A

ar·ma·dil·lo (*ahr*-muh-**dil**-oh) *noun* A mammal covered by hard, bony plates that is found in warm parts of North and South America.

ar·ma·ments (**ahr**-muh-muhnts) *noun, plural* Weapons and other equipment used for fighting wars.

arm·chair (**ahrm**-*chair*) *noun* A comfortable chair with flat rests on each side for the arms.

armed (ahrmd) *adjective* Carrying weapons.

armed forc·es (ahrmd **for**-siz) *noun, plural* All of the branches of a country's military. In the United States, the armed forces include the Army, Navy, Air Force, Marine Corps, and Coast Guard.

Ar·me·ni·a (ahr-**mee**-nee-uh) A mountainous, landlocked country located where western Asia meets eastern Europe. Once part of the Soviet Union, Armenia became independent in 1991 and is now a democratic state.

ar·mis·tice (**ahr**-mi-stis) *noun* A temporary agreement to stop a war.

ar·mor (**ahr**-mur) *noun* 1. Metal protection worn by soldiers in battle. 2. Strong metal protection for tanks and other military vehicles. 3. Protective scales, spines, or shells that cover some animals and plants.

ar·mored ve·hi·cle (**ahr**-murd **vee**-i-kuhl) *noun* A military or other vehicle with a strong metal covering.

ar·mor·y (**ahr**-mur-ee) *noun* A place where weapons are stored or soldiers are trained. ▸ *noun, plural* **armories**

arm·pit (**ahrm**-*pit*) *noun* The area under your arm where it joins your shoulder.

ar·my (**ahr**-mee) *noun* 1. A military group trained mainly to fight on land. 2. A large group of people doing the same thing. ▸ *noun, plural* **armies**

a·ro·ma (uh-**roh**-muh) *noun* A smell that is usually pleasant. ▸ *adjective* **aromatic** (ar-uh-**mat**-ik)

a·round (uh-**round**) *preposition* 1. Surrounding. *He put the belt around his waist.* 2. Close to some number, time, or quantity. *I'll pick you up around 4 p.m.* 3. On the other side of something. *They were waiting for me around the corner.* *adverb* 1. In many different places or parts of a place. 2. In a circle. 3. More or less.

a·rouse (uh-**rouz**) *verb* 1. To stir up a feeling. 2. To awaken from sleep. ▸ *verb* **arousing, aroused** ▸ *noun* **arousal**

ar·range (uh-**raynj**) *verb* 1. To make plans or prepare for something to happen. 2. To place things so that they are in order or look attractive. 3. To change a piece of music slightly, so that it can be played on different instruments. 4. In an **arranged marriage,** parents agree on a husband or wife for their son or daughter. ▸ *verb* **arranging, arranged**

ar·range·ment (uh-**raynj**-muhnt) *noun* 1. A plan for something to happen. 2. The way that something is arranged or set out. 3. A particular way for a piece of music to be sung or performed.

ar·ray (uh-**ray**) *noun* 1. A large number of things. 2. An orderly arrangement. *verb* To display or arrange something in a particular way. ▸ *verb* **arraying, arrayed**

ar·rest (uh-**rest**) *verb* 1. To stop and hold someone by the power of law. 2. To stop something from developing or happening anymore. *noun* The act of legally stopping and holding someone. ▸ *verb* **arresting, arrested**

ar·ri·val (uh-**rye**-vuhl) *noun* 1. The act of getting to a place. 2. Someone or something that has gotten to a place.

ar·rive (uh-**rive**) *verb* 1. To reach a place. 2. People say that an event or date **arrives** when they have been looking forward to it or dreading it. ▸ *verb* **arriving, arrived**

ar·ro·gant (**ar**-uh-guhnt) *adjective* Acting as if you are more important and smarter than other people. ▸ *noun* **arrogance** ▸ *adverb* **arrogantly**

A

ar·row (**ar**-oh) *noun* 1. A stick with a sharp point shot from a bow. 2. A sign (→) showing a direction, as on maps and road signs.

ar·row·head (**ar**-oh-*hed*) *noun* The sharp tip of an arrow, made of metal or (long ago) of stone.

ar·se·nal (**ahr**-suh-nuhl) *noun* A place where weapons and ammunition are made or stored.

ar·se·nic (**ahr**-suh-nik) *noun* An extremely poisonous chemical element that occurs naturally, usually as a gray-white crystal.

ar·son (**ahr**-suhn) *noun* The crime of setting fire to property with the intention of destroying it. ▶ *noun* **arsonist**

art (ahrt)
noun 1. The activity of creating something beautiful for others to enjoy, such as a painting, sculpture, piece of music, or poem. 2. Things that are created by this activity. 3. Something that requires practiced skill.
noun, plural **the arts** Making, showing, and performing works of art.

ar·ter·y (**ahr**-tur-ee) *noun* 1. One of the tubes that carries blood from your heart to all the rest of your body. 2. A main road.
▶ *noun, plural* **arteries** ▶ *adjective* **arterial** (ahr-**teer**-ee-uhl)

ar·thri·tis (ahr-**thrye**-tis) *noun* A disease in which joints become swollen and painful. ▶ *adjective* **arthritic** (ahr-**thrit**-ik)

ar·thro·pod (**ahr**-thruh-*pahd*) *noun* An animal without a backbone that has a hard outer skeleton and three or more pairs of legs that can bend. Insects, spiders, lobsters, and shrimp are all arthropods.

ar·ti·choke (**ahr**-ti-*chohk*) *noun* A tall plant in the thistle family, with large prickly flower heads that are cooked and eaten as a vegetable.

ar·ti·cle (**ahr**-ti-kuhl) *noun* 1. An object. 2. A piece of writing published in a newspaper, magazine, or online. 3. A word, such as *a, an,* or *the,* that goes in front of a noun.

ar·tic·u·late
adjective (ahr-**tik**-yuh-lit) Able to express yourself clearly in words.
verb (ahr-**tik**-yuh-*late*) To pronounce or say something in a particular way, especially in a clear way.
▶ *verb* **articulating, articulated** ▶ *adverb* **articulately** (ahr-**tik**-yuh-lit-lee)

ar·ti·fact (**ahr**-tuh-*fakt*) *noun* An object made or changed by human beings, especially a tool or weapon used in the past.

ar·ti·fi·cial (ahr-tuh-**fish**-uhl) *adjective* 1. Made by people rather than existing in nature. 2. Not sincere; pretended.
▶ *adverb* **artificially**

ar·ti·fi·cial in·tel·li·gence (ahr-tuh-**fish**-uhl in-**tel**-i-juhns) *noun* The science of making computers do things that previously needed human intelligence, such as understanding language. Abbreviated as *AI.*

ar·ti·fi·cial res·pi·ra·tion (ahr-tuh-**fish**-uhl *res*-puh-**ray**-shuhn) *noun* A method of helping someone start to breathe after the person's breathing has stopped. It is done by forcing air into and out of the lungs.

ar·til·ler·y (ahr-**til**-ur-ee) *noun* 1. Large, powerful guns that are mounted on wheels or tracks. 2. The part of an army that uses these weapons.

ar·ti·san (**ahr**-ti-zuhn) *noun* Someone who is skilled at working with his or her hands at a particular craft. Wood carvers and cheesemakers are artisans.

art·ist (**ahr**-tist) *noun* Someone very skilled at painting, making things, or performing in the arts.

ar·tis·tic (ahr-**tis**-tik) *adjective* 1. Showing or having creative skill. 2. Of, having to do with, or responsible for the creative aspects of something.
▶ *adverb* **artistically**

as (az *or* uhz)
conjunction 1. In comparison with. 2. In the same way that. 3. While or when. 4. Since or because.

adverb To the same degree.
preposition In the manner of, or in the role of. *As your mother, I know what's best for you.*

as·bes·tos (as-**bes**-tuhs) *noun* A grayish mineral whose fibers can be woven into a fireproof fabric. Asbestos is rarely used today, because breathing its fibers can cause serious illness.

as·cend (uh-**send**) *verb* To move or go up. ▶ *verb* **ascending, ascended** ▶ *noun* **ascent**

ash (ash) *noun* 1. The powder that remains after something has burned. 2. A kind of tree with long, thin leaves that fall off every year, or the wood of this tree.
▶ *noun, plural* **ashes**

a·shamed (uh-**shaymd**) *adjective* Feeling embarrassed and guilty.

a·shore (uh-**shor**) *adverb* On or to the shore or land.

A·sia (**ay**-zhuh) The world's largest continent, populated by about four billion people. Asia is part of the Eurasian landmass and is bordered by the Pacific Ocean to the east, the Arctic Ocean to the north, the Indian Ocean to the south, and the Ural Mountains to the west.

A·sian American (**ay**-zhuhn) *noun* Someone who was born in the United States or became a U.S. citizen and can trace his or her ancestors back to Asia. ▶ *adjective* **Asian-American**

a·side (uh-**side**)
adverb To one side, or out of the way.
noun A remark made quietly so only certain people can hear it.

ask (ask) *verb* 1. To make a request of someone. 2. To put a question to someone when you want information. 3. To invite someone to do something. 4. To want a certain amount in order to sell something.
▶ *verb* **asking, asked**

a·skew (uh-**skyoo**) *adverb, adjective* Crooked, or off-center.

a·sleep (uh-**sleep**) *adjective* Sleeping; not awake.

as·par·a·gus (uh-**spar**-uh-guhs) *noun* A green plant whose spear-shaped stalks can be cooked and eaten as a vegetable. ▶ *noun, plural* **asparagus**

as·pect (**as**-pekt) *noun* A feature or characteristic of something.

as·pen (**as**-puhn) *noun* A kind of poplar tree with white bark that grows typically in mountain areas.

as·phalt (**as**-fawlt) *noun* A black, tarlike substance that is mixed with sand and gravel and then rolled flat to make roads.

as·phyx·i·ate (as-**fik**-see-ate) *verb* To kill or attempt to kill people or animals by making them unable to breathe. ▶ *verb* **asphyxiating, asphyxiated** ▶ *noun* **asphyxiation**

as·pi·ra·tion (as-puh-**ray**-shuhn) *noun* A desire to achieve something in the future. ▶ *verb* **aspire** (uh-**spire**)

as·pi·rin (**as**-pur-in) *noun* A drug that relieves pain and reduces fever.

ass (as) *noun* 1. A donkey. 2. (informal) A silly or stupid person. Many people consider this word offensive.
▶ *noun, plural* **asses**

as·sas·si·nate (uh-**sas**-uh-*nate*) *verb* To murder someone who is well-known or important. ▶ *verb* **assassinating, assassinated** ▶ *noun* **assassin** ▶ *noun* **assassination**

as·sault (uh-**sawlt**) *verb* To attack someone or something violently. ▶ *verb* **assaulting, assaulted** ▶ *noun* **assault**

as·sem·ble (uh-**sem**-buhl) *verb* 1. To gather in one place. 2. To put together the parts of something.
▶ *verb* **assembling, assembled**

as·sem·bly (uh-**sem**-blee) *noun* 1. A meeting of lots of people. 2. In some states, the **assembly** is one of the two lawmaking bodies that voters in the state elect. 3. The process of putting something together from its parts. 4. **assembly line** An arrangement of machines and workers in a factory, where a product passes from one person or machine to the next, with each performing a small, separate task, until it is completely assembled.

A

as·sent (uh-**sent**)
verb To agree to something.
noun Agreement or consent.
▶ *verb* **assenting, assented**

as·sert (uh-**surt**) *verb* 1. To state something in a forceful or emphatic way. 2. If you **assert yourself,** you behave confidently and express yourself easily.
▶ *verb* **asserting, asserted**

as·ser·tive (uh-**sur**-tiv) *adjective* Able to behave confidently and express yourself positively. ▶ *noun* **assertiveness** ▶ *adverb* **assertively**

as·sess (uh-**ses**) *verb* To judge the value or qualities of something. ▶ *verb* **assesses, assessing, assessed** ▶ *noun* **assessor**

as·sess·ment (uh-**ses**-muhnt) *noun* The act or process of determining value or significance.

as·set (**as**-et) *noun* 1. A valuable thing that a person or business owns. 2. Someone who is helpful or useful.

as·sign (uh-**sine**) *verb* 1. To give someone a job to do. 2. To set apart for a specific purpose.

as·sign·ment (uh-**sine**-muhnt) *noun* A specific job that is given to somebody.

as·sist (uh-**sist**)
verb To help someone.
noun An **assist** in sports is an act of one player helping another, especially to score.
▶ *verb* **assisting, assisted**

as·sist·ance (uh-**sis**-tuhns) *noun* Help that makes things easier for someone.

as·sist·ant (uh-**sis**-tuhnt)
noun Someone who another to do something.
adjective Serving in a position under a head position.

as·sist·ed liv·ing (uh-**sis**-tid **liv**-ing) *noun* Housing for older people that provides the help they need to do things.

as·so·ci·ate
verb (uh-**soh**-see-ayt) 1. To form a connection between things in your mind. 2. To form a relationship or spend time with someone.
adjective (uh-**soh**-see-it) Having

responsibility at a lower level.
noun (uh-**soh**-see-it) Someone who works for a company.
▶ *verb* **associating, associated**

as·so·ci·a·tion (uh-**soh**-see-**ay**-shuhn) *noun* 1. A group of people who are organized to do something. 2. The condition of being connected with someone or something. 3. A connection that you make in your mind between thoughts and feelings and a person or thing.

as·so·nance (**as**-uh-nuhns) *noun* Repeated use of the same vowel sound in words that are close together, for example, the short *e* in "mellow wedding bells."

as·sort·ment (uh-**sort**-muhnt) *noun* A mixture of different things. ▶ *adjective* **assorted**

as·sume (uh-**soom**) *verb* 1. To suppose that something is true, without knowing for sure. 2. To begin to have responsibility or power to do something. 3. An **assumed name** is a false name.
▶ *verb* **assuming, assumed**

as·sump·tion (uh-**suhmp**-shuhn) *noun* 1. A thing that you assume. 2. The act of taking responsibility for something.

as·sur·ance (uh-**shoor**-uhns) *noun* A firm promise to do something.

as·sure (uh-**shoor**) *verb* 1. To say or promise something with confidence that it is true or that it will happen. 2. To make something certain.
▶ *verb* **assuring, assured**

as·ter (**as**-tur) *noun* A plant with flowers that have white, pink, yellow, or purple petals around a yellow center. Some asters look like daisies.

as·ter·isk (**as**-tuh-risk) *noun* The mark (*) used in printing and writing to tell readers to look elsewhere on the page for more information.

as·ter·oid (**as**-tuh-roid) *noun* A small rocky object that travels around the sun.

asth·ma (**az**-muh) *noun* A lung disease that causes coughing and difficulty in breathing. ▶ *noun* **asthmatic** (az-**mat**-ik) ▶ *adjective* **asthmatic**

A

as·ton·ish (uh-**stah**-nish) *verb*
To surprise someone very much. ▸ *verb* **astonishes, astonishing, astonished** ▸ *noun* **astonishment** ▸ *adjective* **astonishing** ▸ *adverb* **astonishingly**

as·tound (uh-**stound**) *verb* To amaze or astonish someone. ▸ *verb* **astounding, astounded**

a·stray (uh-**stray**) *adverb* 1. If something has gone **astray,** it has been lost. 2. If someone **leads** you **astray,** he or she encourages you to do something wrong or gives you incorrect information.

a·stride (uh-**stride**) *preposition* With a leg on either side of something. *In the story, the hero rides astride a majestic white horse.*

as·trol·o·gy (uh-**strah**-luh-jee) *noun* The study of how the positions of stars and planets supposedly affect people's lives. ▸ *noun* **astrologer** ▸ *adjective* **astrological** (as-truh-**lah**-ji-kuhl)

as·tro·naut (**as**-truh-*nawt*) *noun* Someone who travels in a spacecraft.

as·tro·nom·i·cal (as-truh-**nah**-mi-kuhl) *adjective* 1. Of or having to do with astronomy. 2. Very large or very high. ▸ *adverb* **astronomically**

as·tron·o·my (uh-**strah**-nuh-mee) *noun* The study of stars, planets, and space. ▸ *noun* **astronomer**

as·tute (uh-**stoot**) *adjective* Having or showing an ability to understand clearly and quickly.

a·sun·der (uh-**suhn**-dur) *adverb* If something is **torn asunder,** it is broken into pieces or separated.

a·sy·lum (uh-**sye**-luhm) *noun* 1. Protection given to someone who has left a dangerous place. 2. (old-fashioned) A hospital for people who are mentally ill and cannot live independently.

a·sym·met·ri·cal (ay-si-**met**-ri-kuhl) *adjective* Not the same on one half as on the other.

at (at) *preposition* 1. In a place or position. *We were at the movies.* 2. Describing a time. *We'll meet at* noon. 3. In the direction of. *Look at all those books!* 4. In a state or condition of. *The two countries were at war.* 5. For the amount or price of. *The store sells apples at $1 per pound.* 6. The **at sign** is a symbol (@) that means "at" and is used in email addresses.

ate (ayt) *verb* The past tense of **eat. Ate** sounds like **eight.**

a·the·ist (**ay**-thee-ist) *noun* Someone who does not believe that there is a God. ▸ *noun* **atheism**

ath·lete (**ath**-leet) *noun* Someone who is trained in or very good at sports and physical exercise. ▸ *adjective* **athletic** (*ath*-**let**-ik)

ath·lete's foot (**ath**-leets **fut**) *noun* An itchy rash caused by a fungus that can develop on your feet and between your toes.

ath·let·ics (ath-**let**-iks) *noun, plural* Sports and physical exercise. ▸ *adjective* **athletic**

At·lan·tic O·cean (at-**lan**-tik **oh**-shuhn) The world's second-largest ocean, covering about 20 percent of the earth's surface. The Atlantic Ocean stretches between the continents of North and South America and the continents of Europe and Africa.

at·las (**at**-luhs) *noun* A book of maps.

ATM (**ay**-*tee*-em) *noun* A machine linked to a bank that lets you put money into your account or take it out without actually going into the bank. ATM is short for *automatic teller machine* or *automated teller machine.*

at·mos·phere (**at**-muhs-*feer*) *noun* 1. The mixture of gases that surrounds a planet. 2. The air in a particular place. 3. The mood or feeling that you get in a place or situation.
▸ *adjective* **atmospheric**

at·oll (**at**-awl) *noun* One or more coral islands that form a ring around a lagoon.

at·om (**at**-uhm) *noun* The tiniest part of an element that has all the properties of that element. All the matter in the universe is made up of atoms.

a·tom·ic (uh-**tah**-mik) *adjective* **1**. Of or having to do with atoms. **2**. Using the power created when atoms are split.

a·tom·ic bomb (uh-**tah**-mik **bahm**) *noun* A very powerful bomb that explodes with great force, heat, and bright light. The explosion results from the energy that is released by splitting atoms.

a·tom·ic en·er·gy (uh-**tah**-mik **en**-ur-jee) *noun* The energy released when atoms are split apart or forced together. Also called **nuclear energy.**

a·tom·ic num·ber (uh-**tah**-mik **nuhm**-bur) *noun* The number of protons in the nucleus of an atom of a chemical element, which helps determine the element's properties and its place in the periodic table.

a·tone (uh-**tone**) *verb* To do something that makes up for a mistake you have made or a bad thing you have done. ▶ *verb* **atoning, atoned**

at-risk (**at**-**risk**) *adjective* Someone who is **at-risk** is in danger of getting into serious trouble.

a·tri·um (**ay**-tree-uhm) *noun* **1**. Either of two sections of the heart that receive blood from the veins; auricle. **2**. An open area inside a building.
▶ *noun, plural* **atriums** or **atria** (**ay**-tree-uh)

a·tro·cious (uh-**troh**-shuhs) *adjective* Very cruel or terrible.

a·troc·i·ty (uh-**trah**-si-tee) *noun* A very wicked or cruel act, often involving killing. ▶ *noun, plural* **atrocities**

at·tach (uh-**tach**) *verb* **1**. To join or fix one thing to another. **2**. If you **attach** a file to an email, you send that file along with the email. **3**. If you **attach** meaning or significance to something, you say that it has a particular meaning or significance. **4**. If you are **attached to** someone, you are very fond of that person.
▶ *verb* **attaches, attaching, attached** ▶ *noun* **attachment**

at·tack (uh-**tak**)
verb **1**. To use violence against someone or something. **2**. To criticize someone strongly.
noun **1**. The action of using violence against someone or something. **2**. A sudden onset of illness.
▶ *verb* **attacking, attacked** ▶ *noun* **attacker**

at·tain (uh-**tayn**) *verb* **1**. To achieve or get something. **2**. To reach a certain age, size, or amount.
▶ *verb* **attaining, attained** ▶ *adjective* **attainable**

at·tain·ment (uh-**tayn**-muhnt) *noun* Something you get as a result of effort.

at·tempt (uh-**tempt**) *verb* To try to do something. ▶ *verb* **attempting, attempted** ▶ *noun* **attempt**

at·tend (uh-**tend**) *verb* **1**. To be present in a place or at an event. **2**. To listen or pay attention. **3. attend to** To deal with something.
▶ *verb* **attending, attended**

at·tend·ance (uh-**ten**-duhns) *noun* **1**. The number of people who attend an event. **2**. The act or state of attending, especially regularly.

at·ten·dant (uh-**ten**-duhnt) *noun* Someone who takes care of a person or place.

at·ten·tion (uh-**ten**-shuhn) *noun* **1**. Concentration on one thing. **2**. If you **pay attention,** you concentrate on one thing. **3**. If something needs **attention,** it needs someone to do something to it. **4**. When soldiers **stand at attention,** they stand straight with their feet together and their arms by their sides.

at·ten·tive (uh-**ten**-tiv) *adjective* Alert and paying close attention to something or someone. ▶ *adverb* **attentively**

at·test (uh-**test**) *verb* **1**. To declare that something is true. **2**. To be proof of something.
▶ *verb* **attesting, attested**

at·tic (**at**-ik) *noun* A space in a building just under the roof.

at·tire (uh-**tire**) *noun* Clothing. ▶ *verb* **attire**

at·ti·tude (**at**-i-*tood*) *noun* **1**. Your opinions and feelings about someone or something that affect how you behave. **2**. The position in which you are standing or sitting.

A

at·tor·ney (uh-**tur**-nee) *noun* A lawyer.

at·tract (uh-**trakt**) *verb* **1.** To get your interest. **2.** If a person **attracts** you, you like him or her. **3.** To cause something to move closer or touch.
▶ *verb* **attracting, attracted**

at·trac·tion (uh-**trak**-shuhn) *noun* **1.** The power of attracting something. **2.** A person or thing that attracts people's attention, admiration, or interest.

at·trac·tive (uh-**trak**-tiv) *adjective* **1.** Enjoyable to look at or experience. **2.** Interesting or exciting.
▶ *noun* **attractiveness** ▶ *adverb* **attractively**

at·trib·ute
noun (**at**-ruh-byoot) A quality or characteristic that belongs to or describes a person or thing.
verb (uh-**trib**-yoot) When you **attribute** something to someone, you give him or her credit for it.
▶ *verb* **attributing, attributed**

ATV (**ay**-*tee*-vee) *noun* A vehicle with three or more large wheels, ridden like a motorcycle, that can travel over rough ground. ATV is short for *all-terrain vehicle.*

au·burn (**aw**-burn)
noun A reddish-brown color.
adjective Being reddish brown in color.

auc·tion (**awk**-shuhn) *noun* A sale where items are sold to those who offer the most money. ▶ *noun* **auctioneer** (*awk*-shuh-**neer**)

au·dac·i·ty (aw-**das**-i-tee) *noun* **1.** Extreme, reckless, or foolish boldness. **2.** Shameless behavior that offends someone.

au·di·ble (**aw**-duh-buhl) *adjective* Loud enough to be heard.

au·di·ence (**aw**-dee-uhns) *noun* **1.** The people who watch or listen to a performance, speech, or movie. **2.** A formal meeting with an important or powerful person.

au·di·o (**aw**-dee-*oh*)
adjective Of or having to do with how sound is heard, recorded, and played back.
noun Sound, especially the sound portion of a film or television program.

aud·i·o·book (**aw**-dee-oh-*buk*) *noun* A sound recording of a book being read aloud that can be listened to on a CD, audiotape, or computer.

au·di·o·tape (**aw**-dee-oh-*tape*) *noun* Magnetic tape that records sound.

au·di·o·vis·u·al (*aw*-dee-oh-**vizh**-oo-uhl) *adjective* Of or having to do with both sound and images.

au·di·tion (aw-**dish**-uhn)
noun A short performance by an actor, singer, musician, or dancer to see whether he or she is suitable for a part in a play, concert, or other performance.
verb To try out for a role in a play, concert, or other performance.
▶ *verb* **auditioning, auditioned**

au·di·to·ri·um (*aw*-di-**tor**-ee-uhm) *noun* A building or large room where people gather for meetings, plays, concerts, or other events.

aug·ment (awg-**ment**) *verb* You **augment** something when you add to it or make it larger. ▶ *verb* **augmenting, augmented**

Au·gust (**aw**-guhst) *noun* The eighth month on the calendar, after July and before September. August has 31 days.

aunt (ant *or* ahnt) *noun* The sister of your father or mother, or the wife of your uncle.

au pair (**oh** pair) *noun* A young person, usually from a foreign country, who lives with a family and helps with housework and child care in return for room and board.

au·ral (**or**-uhl) *adjective* Of or having to do with the ear or hearing. **Aural** sounds like **oral.**

au·ri·cle (**or**-i-kuhl) *noun* **1.** The outer part of the ear. **2.** Either of two sections of the heart that receive blood from the veins. Also called **atrium.**

au·ro·ra bo·re·al·is (uh-**ror**-uh bor-ee-**al**-is) *noun* Colorful bands of flashing lights that sometimes can be seen at night, especially near the Arctic Circle. Also called the **northern lights.**

aus·tere (aw-**steer**) *adjective* Severe or cold in manner or appearance.

A

aus·ter·i·ty (aw-**ster**-i-tee) *noun* A way of living without extras or comforts. ▶ *noun, plural* **austerities**

Aus·tral·ia (aw-**strayl**-yuh) A country in the Southern Hemisphere. Mainland Australia is the world's smallest continent. Until the late 18th century, it was inhabited only by indigenous people. Because of its long isolation and variety of habitats, it developed many distinctive animal species, such as koalas, kangaroos, platypuses, wombats, and emus.

Aus·tri·a (**aw**-stree-uh) A mountainous, landlocked country in central Europe. Its main city, Vienna, was the capital of European music during the 18th and 19th centuries, and was the home of Beethoven, Mozart, and many other classical composers.

au·then·tic (aw-**then**-tik) *adjective* Real, or genuine.

au·thor (**aw**-thur) *noun* The writer of a book, story, play, or article. ▶ *noun* **authorship**

au·thor·i·ta·tive (uh-**thor**-i-tay-tiv) *adjective* 1. Official, or coming from someone who has the power to give orders. 2. Expert.

au·thor·i·ty (uh-**thor**-i-tee) *noun* 1. The power to do something officially or to tell other people what to do. 2. An organization with power in a certain area. 3. Someone who knows a lot about a particular subject.
▶ *noun, plural* **authorities**

au·thor·ize (**aw**-thuh-rize) *verb* To give official permission for something to happen. ▶ *verb* **authorizing, authorized** ▶ *noun* **authorization**

au·tism (**aw**-tiz-uhm) *noun* A condition that causes someone to have trouble learning, communicating, and forming relationships with people. ▶ *adjective* **autistic** (aw-**tis**-tik)

au·to (**aw**-toh) *noun* Short for *automobile*.

au·to·bi·og·ra·phy (aw-toh-bye-**ah**-gruh-fee) *noun* A book in which the author tells the story of his or her life. ▶ *noun, plural* **autobiographies** ▶ *adjective*

autobiographical (aw-toh-bye-uh-**graf**-i-kuhl)

au·to·graph (**aw**-tuh-graf) *noun* A person's handwritten signature.

au·to·mat·ic (aw-tuh-**mat**-ik) *adjective* 1. Able to operate without direct control. 2. Done without your thinking about it.
▶ *adverb* **automatically**

au·to·ma·tion (aw-tuh-**may**-shuhn) *noun* The use of machines rather than people to do jobs, especially in factories. ▶ *verb* **automate**

au·to·mo·bile (**aw**-tuh-muh-beel) *noun* A car, SUV, or pickup.

au·ton·o·my (aw-**tah**-nuh-mee) *noun* 1. The right or condition of people being able to choose their government. 2. The state of being independent or self-governing.
▶ *adjective* **autonomous**

au·top·sy (**aw**-tahp-see) *noun* An examination performed on a dead person to find the cause of death. ▶ *noun, plural* **autopsies**

au·tumn (**aw**-tuhm) *noun* The season between summer and winter, from late September to late December in the Northern Hemisphere. Also called **fall**. ▶ *adjective* **autumnal** (aw-**tuhm**-nuhl)

aux·il·ia·ry (awg-**zil**-yur-ee) *adjective* Helping, or giving extra support.
noun A person or group that provides extra support.

a·vail·a·ble (uh-**vay**-luh-buhl) *adjective* 1. Ready to be used or bought. 2. Not busy, and therefore free to participate in something.
▶ *noun* **availability**

av·a·lanche (**av**-uh-lanch) *noun* A large mass of snow, ice, or earth that suddenly falls down the side of a mountain.

av·a·tar (**av**-uh-tahr) *noun* 1. A person who is an example of an idea. 2. In computer games, an **avatar** is a character that represents the person playing. 3. In online social networking, your **avatar** is the image or photo you use to identify yourself.

av·e·nue (**av**-uh-*noo*) *noun* A wide road in a town or city.

av·er·age (**av**-rij)
noun A number that you get by adding a group of numbers together and then dividing the sum by the number of figures you have added.
adjective Usual, or ordinary.
verb To add a group of numbers and divide the sum by the number of figures added.
▶ *verb* **averaging, averaged**

a·vert (uh-**vurt**) *verb* To turn away from something or avoid it. ▶ *verb* **averting, averted** ▶ *noun* **aversion** (uh-**vur**-zhuhn)

a·vi·ar·y (**ay**-vee-*er*-ee) *noun* An outdoor, enclosed area for birds. ▶ *noun, plural* **aviaries**

a·vi·a·tion (*ay*-vee-**ay**-shuhn) *noun* The practice and science of building and flying aircraft. ▶ *noun* **aviator**

av·id (**av**-id) *adjective* Very eager or committed. ▶ *adverb* **avidly**

av·o·ca·do (*av*-uh-**kah**-doh) *noun* A green or black pear-shaped fruit with a tough skin and a creamy, light green pulp.

av·o·ca·tion (*av*-uh-**kay**-shun) *noun* A hobby or pastime that is different from someone's regular job.

a·void (uh-**void**) *verb* **1.** To stay away from a person or place. **2.** To try to prevent something from happening.
▶ *verb* **avoiding, avoided** ▶ *noun* **avoidance** ▶ *adjective* **avoidable**

a·wait (uh-**wayt**) *verb* To wait for or expect someone or something. ▶ *verb* **awaiting, awaited**

a·wake (uh-**wake**)
adjective Not asleep.
verb To wake up.
▶ *verb* **awaking, awoke** (uh-**wohk**) **awoken** (uh-**woh**-kuhn) ▶ *noun* **awakening**

a·ward (uh-**word**)
verb **1.** To give someone something valuable as a reward or honor. **2.** To give someone something because of the decision of a court.
noun **1.** Something given to someone in recognition of achievement.

2. An amount of money provided to someone in order to study or carry out research.
▶ *verb* **awarding, awarded**

a·ware (uh-**wair**) *adjective* If you are **aware** of something, you notice it and are conscious of it.

a·ware·ness (uh-**wair**-nis) *noun* The condition or fact of being aware.

a·way (uh-**way**)
adverb **1.** Moving from a place, person, or thing. **2.** Distant from a place. **3.** Not at home, or not present. **4.** In a secure place.
adjective An **away** game in sports is one you play at your opponent's home field or court.

awe (aw) *noun* A feeling of admiration and respect, sometimes mixed with a little fear.

awe·some (**aw**-*suhm*) *adjective* **1.** Causing you to feel awe. **2.** (informal) Very good.

aw·ful (**aw**-fuhl)
adjective Terrible or horrible.
adverb, adjective (informal) **Awful** is sometimes used before nouns and adjectives with a negative meaning to make them more intense.
▶ *adverb* **awfully**

a·while (uh-**wile**) *adverb* For a short time.

awk·ward (**awk**-wurd) *adjective*
1. Difficult or embarrassing. **2.** Not able to relax and talk to people easily. **3.** Not graceful or smooth; clumsy.
▶ *noun* **awkwardness** ▶ *adverb* **awkwardly**

awl (awl) *noun* A sharp metal tool for making holes in leather or wood. **Awl** sounds like **all.**

aw·ning (**aw**-ning) *noun* A piece of cloth, metal, or wood that is fastened to the top of a window or to the front roof of a building to shade it from sun and help keep out rain.

ax *or* **axe** (aks)
noun A tool with a sharp blade on the end of a handle, used for chopping wood.
verb To bring something to an end.
▶ *noun, plural* **axes** ▶ *verb* **axes, axing, axed**

A

ax·is (**ak**-sis) *noun* **1.** An imaginary line through the middle of an object, around which that object spins. **2.** A line at the side or the bottom of a graph.
▶ *noun, plural* **axes** (**ak**-seez)

ax·le (**ak**-suhl) *noun* A rod in the center of a wheel, around which the wheel turns.

aye (eye)
noun A vote of "yes."
interjection A word used to say "yes."

a·za·lea (uh-**zayl**-yuh) *noun* A shrub with funnel-shaped pink, orange, or white flowers and dark green leaves.

Az·er·bai·jan (*az*-ur-bye-**jahn**) One of the six independent Turkic states at the crossroads of western Asia and eastern Europe. It was the first democratic and secular republic to be established in the Muslim world. It was also the first Muslim country to grant women the right to vote, providing this right in 1918, two years before women's suffrage became law in the United States.

Az·tec (**az**-tek)
noun A member of a Mexican Native American people who built a great civilization before the conquest of Mexico by Cortés in the 16th century.
adjective Of or having to do with the Aztecs, their language, or their culture.

az·ure (**azh**-ur)
noun A deep, clear blue, such as the color of the sky or deep, still water.
adjective Of or being the color azure.

B

bab·ble (**bab**-uhl) *verb* **1.** To talk quickly **bab·ble** (**bab**-uhl) *verb* **1.** To talk quickly and excitedly but without making any sense. **2.** To make a low, murmuring sound. **3.** When a baby **babbles,** he or she is making sounds that are similar to speech but have no meaning.
▶ *verb* **babbling, babbled**

babe (babe) *noun* A baby, as saying a *babe in arms* when you mean a very young infant.

ba·boon (ba-**boon**) *noun* A large African or Asian monkey with a long snout and large teeth.

ba·by (**bay**-bee)
noun **1.** An infant or very young child or animal. **2.** Someone who acts like a very young child.
verb To fuss over or treat someone like an infant.
▶ *noun, plural* **babies** ▶ *verb* **babying, babied** ▶ *adjective* **babyish**

ba·by boom (**bay**-bee *boom*) *noun* An increase in the number of babies born in a nation. The term is often used to refer to the generation of people born in the United States between 1946 and 1964. ▶ *noun* **baby boomer**

ba·by·sit (**bay**-bee-*sit*) *verb* To take care of someone else's child or children when the parents are unable to. ▶ *verb* **babysitting, babysat**

ba·by·sit·ter (**bay**-bee-*sit*-ur) *noun* Someone who takes care of children when their parents aren't home.

ba·by tooth (**bay**-bee *tooth*) *noun* A first tooth in infants and baby mammals. Baby teeth fall out and are replaced by permanent teeth. ▶ *noun, plural* **baby teeth**

bach·e·lor (**bach**-uh-lur) *noun* A man who has never been married.

back (bak)
noun **1.** The rear part of your body between your neck and the end of your spine. **2.** The part or area farthest from the front.
adverb **1.** In, to, or toward a place from which someone or something came. **2.** In the past. **3.** So as to return to an earlier or normal state.
adjective **1.** Located at or near the rear. **2.** Coming from an earlier time.
verb **1.** To give financial or other

support to someone or something.
2. To go backwards. **3. back down** To stop arguing for something. **4. back out** To withdraw from or change your mind about doing something you had promised to do. **5. back up** To make a copy of a computer file, or of all your computer files.
▶ *verb* **backing, backed** ▶ *noun* **backer**

back·board (**bak**-*bord*) *noun* The upright board behind a basketball hoop.

back·bone (**bak**-*bohn*) *noun* A set of connected bones that run down the middle of the back. The backbone is also called the **spine** and the **spinal column.**

back·fire (**bak**-*fire*) *verb* **1.** If an action **backfires,** it leads to the opposite of what you wanted or expected.
2. If a car **backfires,** there is a small explosion of unburned fuel that causes a loud bang in the exhaust pipe.
▶ *verb* **backfiring, backfired**

back·ground (**bak**-*ground*) *noun* **1.** The part of a picture or scene that lies behind the main figures. **2.** A person's past experience. **3.** Information that explains something.

back·hand (**bak**-*hand*) *noun* A stroke in tennis, badminton, and other racket sports that you play with your arm across your body and the back of your hand facing outward.

back·hoe (**bak**-*hoh*) *noun* A digging machine that has a bucket with teeth.

back·ing (**bak**-ing) *noun* Support that is meant to help someone or something succeed.

back·pack (**bak**-*pak*)
noun A bag that you carry on your back, which holds your supplies when you are hiking or camping.
verb To go on a long walk or hike carrying a backpack.
▶ *verb* **backpacking, backpacked**

back·slash (**bak**-*slash*) *noun* A character (\) that computers use to separate data and to perform some commands. ▶ *noun, plural* **backslashes**

back·sto·ry (**bak**-*stor*-ee) *noun* Information from the past about a person, thing, or character. ▶ *noun, plural* **backstories**

back·stroke (**bak**-*stroke*) *noun* A style of swimming in which you lie on your back and lift your arms, one at a time, in a backward circular movement while kicking your feet.

back·up (**bak**-*uhp*) *noun* **1.** Something or someone that can be used or called on if needed. **2.** An exact copy of a computer file that can be used if something happens to the original one. **3.** The job of making a copy of all the files on a computer or server.

back·ward (**bak**-wurd) *or* **back·wards** (**bak**-wurdz)
adverb **1.** In the reverse direction. **2.** In a way that is opposite to the normal or usual way.
adjective Lagging behind.

back·yard (**bak**-yahrd) *noun* An open area behind a house.

ba·con (**bay**-kuhn) *noun* Smoked or salted meat from the back or sides of a pig.

bac·te·ri·a (bak-**teer**-ee-uh) *noun, plural* Microscopic, single-celled living things that exist everywhere and that can either be useful or harmful. ▶ *noun, singular* **bacterium** (bak-**teer**-ee-uhm)

bad (bad) *adjective* **1.** Unwelcome or unpleasant. **2.** Serious or severe.
3. Rotten or spoiled. **4.** Not good; worse than others. **5.** Wicked or evil.
6. Sorry.
▶ *adjective* **worse, worst**

bade (bad *or* bayd) *verb* A past tense of **bid².**

badge (baj) *noun* A small, flat object that you pin to your clothes to show who you are or what you do.

badg·er (**baj**-ur)
noun A mammal with gray fur and a black and white head that lives in a burrow and feeds at night.
verb To pester someone.
▶ *verb* **badgering, badgered**

bad·ly (**bad**-lee) *adverb* **1.** Very much; intensely. **2.** Not well, or not skillfully.

B

bad·min·ton (**bad**-*min*-tuhn) *noun* A game in which players use light, long-handled rackets to hit a shuttlecock back and forth over a high, narrow net.

bad·mouth (**bad**-*mouth*) *verb* To say negative things about someone or something. ▶ *verb* **badmouthing, badmouthed**

baf·fle (**baf**-uhl) *verb* To make someone feel puzzled or confused. ▶ *verb* **baffling, baffled** ▶ *adjective* **baffling**

bag (bag)
noun A flexible container with an opening at the top, used for carrying things.
verb To put something in a bag or sack.
▶ *verb* **bagging, bagged**

ba·gel (**bay**-guhl) *noun* A chewy kind of bread that is shaped like a doughnut.

bag·gage (**bag**-ij) *noun* Travelers' suitcases, bags, and trunks.

bag·gy (**bag**-ee) *adjective* Hanging loosely. ▶ *adjective* **baggier, baggiest**

bag·pipes (**bag**-*pipes*) *noun, plural* A musical instrument popular in Scotland with a flexible bag that you blow into through a mouthpiece.

Ba·ha·mas (buh-**hah**-muhz) A country consisting of 29 islands in the Atlantic Ocean north of Cuba. One of these islands, San Salvador, is believed to be where Christopher Columbus first landed in 1492.

Bah·rain (bah-**rayn**) A country consisting of 33 islands in the Persian Gulf. It is connected to Saudi Arabia, which lies to the west, by a causeway.

bail (bayl) *noun* Money paid to a court for the release of someone accused of a crime, with the promise that he or she will show up for the trial.

bail·iff (**bay**-lif) *noun* An official in a court of law who maintains order in the court.

bail out (**bayl** out) *verb* 1. To jump out of an aircraft in an emergency, using a parachute. 2. To scoop water out of a boat. 3. If you **bail** someone **out**, you pay that person's bail or help him or her out of a difficult situation.
▶ *verb* **bailing out, bailed out**

bait (bayt)
noun A small amount of food put on a hook or in a trap to attract a fish or other animal.
verb To put bait on a hook or in a trap.
▶ *verb* **baiting, baited**

bake (bayk) *verb* 1. To cook food, especially bread or cake, with dry heat in an oven. 2. To heat something in order to make it hard. 3. To be or become very hot.
▶ *verb* **baking, baked** ▶ *noun* **baker** ▶ *noun* **bakery** (**bay**-kur-ee)

bak·ing pow·der (**bay**-king *pou*-dur) *noun* A white powder used in baking to make dough or batter rise.

bak·ing so·da (**bay**-king *soh*-duh) *noun* A white powder used to make dough rise, or to soothe an upset stomach. Also called **sodium bicarbonate.**

bal·ance (**bal**-uhns)
noun 1. Your **balance** is your ability to remain steady and upright. 2. A state or situation in which all elements are in the right proportion. 3. A device used for weighing things. 4. Remainder.
verb If you **balance** something, you keep it steady.
▶ *verb* **balancing, balanced**

bal·ance beam (**bal**-uhns *beem*) *noun* A narrow, horizontal beam, usually about four feet off the floor, used in gymnastics for doing various tumbling and dance movements.

bal·anced di·et (**bal**-uhnst **dye**-it) *noun* A diet that contains the proper kinds and amounts of food to keep you healthy.

bal·co·ny (**bal**-kuh-nee) *noun* 1. A platform surrounded by a railing or low wall on the outside of a building, usually above street level. 2. An upstairs seating area in a theater or auditorium that projects over the main floor.
▶ *noun, plural* **balconies**

bald (bawld) *adjective* 1. Having little or no hair on the head. 2. Without any natural covering.
▶ *adjective* **balder, baldest** ▶ *noun* **baldness** ▶ *adjective* **balding**

B

bald ea·gle (**bawld ee**-guhl) *noun*
An eagle with a brown body and a white head that appears bald from a distance. The bald eagle is the national symbol of the United States.

bale (bale)
noun A large bundle of things, such as straw or hay, that is tied tightly together.
verb To put hay or some other substance into a tightly packed bundle.
▶ *verb* **baling, baled**

balk (bawk) *verb* To stop and refuse to go on or be involved in something. ▶ *verb* **balking, balked**

Bal·kan Pe·nin·su·la (**bawl**-kuhn puh-**nin**-suh-luh) A region of Southeastern Europe, named after the mountain range that runs down its center. The Balkan Peninsula is surrounded by water on three sides, with the Mediterranean Sea to the south, the Adriatic Sea to the west, and the Black Sea to the east. The region encompasses the countries of Albania, Bosnia and Herzegovina, Bulgaria, Greece, Macedonia, and Montenegro, although other neighboring countries are sometimes included.

ball (bawl) *noun* **1.** A round object, especially one that is hit, thrown, or kicked in games. **2.** Something that has been squeezed or formed into a round shape. **3.** A formal gathering where people come to dance. **4.** In baseball, a pitch that a batter does not swing at and that does not cross home plate between the batter's shoulders and knees. **5.** (informal) If you are **on the ball,** you are quick at understanding things. **6.** If you **have a ball,** you have a very good time.
Ball sounds like **bawl.**

bal·lad (**bal**-uhd) *noun* A poem that tells a story and is meant to be sung.

bal·last (**bal**-uhst) *noun* **1.** Heavy material, such as water or sand, that is carried in the bottom of a ship or hot-air balloon to make it more stable.

2. ballast tank A large tank in a submarine that is filled with water to make the submarine sink or with air to make it come to the surface.

ball bear·ings (**bawl bair**-ingz) *noun, plural* Small metal balls, usually in a ring-shaped track, that keep machine parts moving smoothly against each other.

bal·le·ri·na (*bal*-uh-**ree**-nuh) *noun* A female ballet dancer.

bal·let (**bal**-ay *or* ba-**lay**) *noun* **1.** A style of dance that uses precise, graceful movements. **2.** A theatrical performance that uses dance, music, costumes, and scenery, often to tell a story.

bal·lis·tics (buh-**lis**-tiks) *noun, plural* The study of how things like bullets and missiles fly through the air.

bal·loon (buh-**loon**) *noun* **1.** A thin rubber bag filled with air and used as a toy or decoration. **2.** A **hot-air balloon** is an aircraft consisting of a very large bag filled with hot air or gas, with a basket for carrying passengers and equipment.

bal·lot (**bal**-uht) *noun* **1.** A way of voting secretly, using a machine or slips of paper. **2.** The list of candidates and questions tha people vote on in an election. **3. ballot box** A box with a long, narrow hole in the top for collecting completed ballots.

ball·park (**bawl**-pahrk) *noun* **1.** A place where people play a ball game, especially baseball. **2.** A **ballpark figure** is a number or amount that is partly a guess because there is not enough information available.

ball·point (**bawl**-*point*) *noun* A pen with a tiny ball for its point that transfers ink to a writing surface.

ball·room (**bawl**-*room*) *noun* A large room where parties and dances are held.

bal·sa (**bawl**-suh) *noun* A lightweight tropical wood used for making model airplanes.

bal·sam fir (**bawl**-suhm) *noun* A type of fragrant evergreen tree.

B

Bal·tic Sea (**bawl**-tik **see**) A small sea of northern Europe that separates the Scandinavian countries from Estonia, Latvia, and Lithuania.

bam·boo (bam-**boo**) *noun* A tropical plant with a hollow, woody stem, often used for making fishing poles and furniture.

ban (ban)
verb To officially forbid something or prevent someone from doing something.
noun A rule or law that forbids something.
▸ *verb* **banning, banned**

ba·nan·a (buh-**nan**-uh) *noun* A long, curved, tropical fruit with a thick yellow skin.

ba·nan·a split (buh-**nan**-uh **split**) *noun* A dessert of ice cream served on two halves of a banana with nuts, syrup, and other flavorings on top.

band (band)
noun 1. A thin strip of flexible material, such as rubber or plastic, that holds one or a number of things together. 2. A group of musicians who perform together. 3. A group of people with a common purpose. 4. A stripe of color or material.
verb When people **band** together, they form a group to achieve a common purpose.
▸ *verb* **banding, banded**

band·age (**ban**-dij)
noun A piece of cloth or material that protects an injured part of the body while it heals.
verb To apply a bandage to an injury.
▸ *verb* **bandaging, bandaged**

ban·dan·na (ban-**dan**-uh) *noun* A large, brightly colored square of fabric, usually worn around the head or neck.

ban·dit (**ban**-dit) *noun* An outlaw, usually a member of a gang, who robs people at gunpoint.

band·width (**band**-width) *noun* The amount of data that can move at one time on a computer network.

bang (bang)
noun A sharp, loud noise.

verb To hit forcefully and noisily.
▸ *verb* **banging, banged**

Bang·la·desh (*bahng*-gluh-**desh**) A country in South Asia. Formerly part of India, it is one of the most densely populated nations in the world, and is subject to flooding from the Ganges and two other large rivers.

ban·gle (**bang**-guhl) *noun* A rigid band of metal or plastic, worn as jewelry around the wrist or ankle.

bangs (bangz) *noun, plural* Hair that is cut short and often straight across a person's forehead.

ban·ish (**ban**-ish) *verb* To force someone to leave a place and never return. ▸ *verb* **banishing, banished** ▸ *noun* **banishment**

ban·is·ter (**ban**-is-tur) *noun* A handrail, usually supported by upright posts, that runs along the side of a stairway.

ban·jo (**ban**-joh) *noun* A musical instrument with a round body, a long neck, and four or five strings that are plucked or strummed. ▸ *noun, plural* **banjos** or **banjoes**

bank (bangk)
noun 1. A place where money is kept for saving and lending purposes. 2. The sloping land along the sides of a river or a canal. 3. A supply of something for future use.
verb 1. To put in a bank. 2. To maneuver an aircraft so that it is tilted. 3. If you **bank on** something, you are counting on it.
▸ *verb* **banking, banked**

bank·er (**bang**-kur) *noun* Someone who has an important job in a bank or owns a bank.

bank·roll (**bangk**-rohl) *verb* To supply with the money to do something. ▸ *verb* **bankrolling, bankrolled**

bank·rupt (**bangk**-ruhpt)
adjective If people or companies are **bankrupt**, they no longer have enough money to pay their debts.
verb To take or require all of a person's money.
▸ *verb* **bankrupting, bankrupted**
▸ *noun* **bankruptcy**

ban·ner (**ban**-ur) *noun* **1.** A long piece of material with writing, pictures, or designs on it, hung from a pole or displayed at sporting events or parades. **2. banner ad** An advertisement across the top, bottom, or side of a webpage.

ban·quet (**bang**-kwit) *noun* A formal meal for a large number of people, usually in honor of someone or something.

ban·ter (**ban**-tur) *verb* To tease someone in a friendly way. *noun* Playful and teasing comments. ▶ *verb* **bantering, bantered**

bap·tize (**bap**-tize) *verb* To pour water on someone's head or to immerse someone in water, as a sign that he or she has become a Christian. ▶ *verb* **baptizing, baptized** ▶ *noun* **baptism** (bap-*tiz*-uhm)

bar (bahr) *noun* **1.** A long, straight piece of something rigid. **2.** A block of something hard. **3.** A place where people can buy drinks, especially alcoholic drinks. **4.** In music, the same thing as a **measure.** *verb* To block someone, or to keep someone out. ▶ *verb* **barring, barred**

barb (bahrb) *noun* A sharp point that sticks out and backward, as on a hook or arrowhead. ▶ *adjective* **barbed**

Bar·ba·dos (bahr-**bay**-dohs) An island nation in the chain of islands known as the Lesser Antilles, situated in the western part of the North Atlantic Ocean, east of the Caribbean Sea. A British colony until it became independent in 1966, Barbados is known for its production of sugar, rum, and molasses as well as its tourist industry.

bar·bar·i·an (bahr-**bair**-ee-uhn) *noun* Someone who is considered wild and uncivilized.

bar·bar·ic (bahr-**bar**-ik) *adjective* Very cruel or primitive.

bar·be·cue (**bahr**-buh-kyoo) *noun* **1.** An outdoor grill for cooking meat and other food. **2.** An outdoor meal or party in which food is grilled over an open fire. *verb* To grill food on a barbecue. ▶ *verb* **barbecuing, barbecued**

barbed wire (barbd) *noun* Twisted strands of wire with small, sharp spikes, used for fences.

bar·ber (**bahr**-bur) *noun* Someone who cuts hair for men and boys, and trims or shaves beards.

bar code (**bahr** kode) *noun* A band of thick and thin lines printed on items sold in stores. When read electronically, the bar code gives the price and other information about the product.

bare (bair) *adjective* **1.** Wearing no clothes, or not covered. **2.** Empty or unfurnished. **3.** Basic. *verb* To expose or reveal something. **Bare** sounds like **bear.** ▶ *adjective* **barer, barest** ▶ *verb* **baring, bared**

bare·faced (**bair**-fayst) *adjective* Bold or shameless.

bare·foot (**bair**-fut) *adverb, adjective* Without shoes or socks.

bare·ly (**bair**-lee) *adverb* Hardly, or almost not.

bar·gain (**bahr**-guhn) *noun* **1.** Something offered or bought for a lower than usual price. **2.** A deal or agreement in which each side has to do certain things. *verb* When you **bargain** with someone, you discuss the price of something or the terms of an agreement. ▶ *verb* **bargaining, bargained**

barge (bahrj) *noun* A long, flat-bottomed boat that is often towed or pushed by another boat. *verb* If you **barge into** a place, you enter it rudely or abruptly. ▶ *verb* **barging, barged**

bar graph (**bahr** graf) *noun* A chart that compares information by showing it as rectangular bars of varying length.

B

bar·i·tone (**bar**-i-*tone*)
noun 1. The second-lowest male singing voice, higher than a bass voice but lower than a tenor voice. 2. A singer with such a voice.
adjective Of or for a baritone.

bar·i·um (**bair**-ee-uhm) *noun* A silver-colored chemical element used in paints, ceramics, and in medical imaging.

bark (bahrk)
noun 1. The tough outer covering on the stems of shrubs, trees, and other plants. 2. The usual sound that a dog makes.
verb 1. When a dog **barks,** it makes a sudden, harsh sound in its throat. 2. To speak sharply or abruptly.
▶ *verb* **barking, barked**

bar·ley (**bahr**-lee) *noun* A cereal plant whose grains are used for food, especially for farm animals. Barley is also used to make beer.

bar mitz·vah (*bahr* **mits**-vuh) *noun* A ceremony and celebration that takes place on or close to a Jewish boy's 13th birthday, after which he takes on the role of an adult in his religion.

barn (bahrn) *noun* A large farm building where crops, animals, and equipment are kept.

bar·na·cle (**bahr**-nuh-kuhl) *noun* A small shellfish that attaches itself firmly to underwater surfaces, such as rocks and the bottom of boats.

barn·yard (**bahrn**-*yahrd*) *noun* The area near a barn, usually surrounded by a fence.

ba·rom·e·ter (buh-**rah**-mi-tur) *noun* An instrument that measures changes in air pressure and is used to forecast the weather.

bar·on (**bar**-uhn) *noun* 1. A nobleman of the lowest rank. 2. Someone who has a lot of power and influence in a certain area.
▶ *adjective* **baronial** (buh-**roh**-nee-uhl)

bar·on·ess (**bar**-uh-nis) *noun* A noblewoman of the lowest rank. ▶ *noun, plural* **baronesses**

bar·racks (**bar**-uhks) *noun, plural* A large building or group of buildings where soldiers are housed.

bar·ra·cu·da (*bar*-uh-**koo**-duh) *noun* A fish with a long, narrow body and many sharp teeth.

bar·rage (buh-**rahzh**) *noun* 1. Concentrated firing from guns or other weapons. 2. A huge outpouring of something.

bar·rel (**bar**-uhl) *noun* 1. A large container that bulges out in the middle and has a flat top and bottom. It is used as a unit of measure for some products. 2. A tube-shaped part of something. 3. If someone has you **over a barrel,** he or she has put you in a difficult position.

bar·ren (**bar**-uhn) *adjective* 1. Unable to produce crops. 2. Bleak, lifeless, or without interest.

bar·rette (buh-**ret**) *noun* A plastic or metal clip used to hold the hair in place.

bar·ri·cade (**bar**-i-*kade*)
noun A barrier to stop people from getting past a certain point.
verb If people **barricade** themselves in a place, they put up obstacles to stop other people from getting to them.
▶ *verb* **barricading, barricaded**

bar·ri·er (**bar**-ee-ur) *noun* 1. A structure, such as a wall or a fence, that prevents people or things from going past it. 2. Anything that makes communication or progress difficult.

bar·ring (**bahr**-ing) *preposition* Except for; apart from. *Barring a major traffic tie-up, we should be there by noon.*

bar·ri·o (**bar**-ee-*oh*) *noun* A neighborhood where Spanish is the main language. Barrio means "neighborhood" in Spanish.

bar·row (**bar**-oh) *noun* A mound of earth or stones placed over a grave in ancient times.

bar·ten·der (**bahr**-ten-dur) *noun* Someone who mixes and serves drinks at a bar.

bar·ter (**bahr**-tur)
verb To do business by exchanging products or services, rather than paying for them.
noun An exchange or trade.
▶ *verb* **bartering, bartered**

base (base)
noun **1.** The lowest or supporting part of something. **2.** The headquarters or main place for something. **3.** An idea, quantity, or rule that is the starting point for everything that follows it. **4.** In baseball, a **base** is one of the four corners of the diamond to which you must run in order to score. **5.** In chemistry, a **base** is a substance that will react with an acid to form a salt. **6.** In mathematics, a **base** is the number on which a counting system is built.
verb **1.** To use something as the source for something else. **2.** If a company or operation is **based** somewhere, it has its headquarters there.
adjective Selfish or without moral standards.
▶ *verb* **basing, based** ▶ *adjective* **baser, basest**

base·ball (**base**-*bawl*) *noun* **1.** A game played on a large, grassy field with a bat and ball and two teams of nine players each. **2.** The ball used in this game.

base·ment (**base**-muhnt) *noun* The lowest room or area in a building, usually below ground level.

bash (bash)
verb To hit something hard or strike it with a heavy blow.
noun (informal) A very large party.
▶ *verb* **bashes, bashing, bashed** ▶ *noun, plural* **bashes**

bash·ful (**bash**-fuhl) *adjective* If you are **bashful,** you are shy and easily embarrassed. ▶ *adverb* **bashfully**

ba·sic (**bay**-sik)
adjective Essential and fundamental.
noun, plural **the basics** If you know **the basics,** you know the most important elements of something.

BASIC (**bay**-sik) *noun* A computer programming language that is easy to learn. BASIC is short for *beginner's all-purpose symbolic instruction code.*

ba·si·cal·ly (**bay**-sik-lee) *adverb* In most or all important ways.

ba·sin (**bay**-suhn) *noun* **1.** A round container that is wider than it is deep, usually used for holding liquids. **2.** An

area of land drained by a river system.

ba·sis (**bay**-sis) *noun* The underlying support for something.

bask (bask) *verb* **1.** To lie or sit in the sun for pleasure. **2.** If you **bask in** something, you take pleasure in it.
▶ *verb* **basking, basked**

bas·ket (**bas**-kit) *noun* **1.** A container, often with handles, made of woven material. **2.** The goal or the act of scoring in basketball.

bas·ket·ball (**bas**-kit-*bawl*) *noun* **1.** A game played by two teams of five players each that try to score points by throwing a ball through a hoop with a hanging net. The hoop is attached to a backboard at each end of the court. **2.** The large, round ball used in this game.

bass
noun **1.** (base) The lowest male singing voice. **2.** (base) A singer with such a voice. **3.** (base) A musical instrument, especially a double bass or bass guitar, that produces very low tones. **4.** (bas) Any of several freshwater or saltwater fish.
adjective (base) Low in pitch.
▶ *noun, plural* **bass** or **basses**

bass drum (base druhm) *noun* A very large drum that makes a deep, loud noise.

bas·soon (buh-**soon**) *noun* A wind instrument with keys, holes, and a small curved reed. The bassoon makes a very deep sound.

baste (bayst) *verb* **1.** To spoon juices from the pan over food while it is cooking in an oven. **2.** To sew something with loose stitches to hold it in place temporarily.
▶ *verb* **basting, basted**

bat (bat)
noun **1.** A small, flying mammal with leathery wings that feeds at night and finds its way around by listening for the echoes of its own squeaking cry. **2.** A piece of wood or aluminum used for hitting the ball in baseball and softball.
verb To take a turn at hitting the ball in baseball or softball.
▶ *verb* **batting, batted**

B

batch (bach) *noun* A group of things that are made at one time. ▶ *noun, plural* **batches**

bath (bath) *noun* **1.** The act of washing in a container of water. **2.** The water or the tub used in bathing. **3.** A bathroom.

bathe (bayTH) *verb* **1.** To take a bath. **2.** To give someone a bath. ▶ *verb* **bathing, bathed**

bath·ing suit (**bay**-THing soot) *noun* A piece of clothing that people wear to go swimming; a swimsuit.

bath·robe (**bath**-robe) *noun* A long, loose piece of clothing that people wear after a bath or shower or while relaxing.

bath·room (**bath**-room) *noun* A room that contains a sink and a toilet and often a bathtub or a shower.

bath·tub (**bath**-tuhb) *noun* A large, open container for water in which you sit and wash your whole body.

ba·tik (buh-**teek**) *noun* A method of printing colored designs on fabric by using wax to cover the parts that will not be dyed.

bat mitz·vah (baht **mits**-vuh) *noun* A ceremony and celebration that takes place on or close to a Jewish girl's 12th birthday, after which she can take part in her religion as an adult. Also known as a *bas mitzvah* (bahs **mits**-vuh).

ba·ton (buh-**tahn**) *noun* **1.** A thin stick used by a conductor to direct an orchestra or band. **2.** A stick that is twirled by a person in a parade. **3.** A short stick that one runner passes to the next in a relay race.

bat·tal·ion (buh-**tal**-yuhn) *noun* A large unit of soldiers.

bat·ter (**bat**-ur)
verb To injure someone by hitting him or her over and over.
noun **1.** A mixture consisting mainly of milk, eggs, and flour used to make pancakes or baked goods or to form a coating over food that is going to be fried. **2.** The player whose turn it is to bat in baseball or softball. ▶ *verb* **battering, battered** ▶ *noun* **battering** ▶ *adjective* **battered**

bat·ter·ing ram (**bat**-ur-ing ram) *noun* A heavy wooden beam used in the past as a weapon to break down walls or gates.

bat·ter·y (**bat**-ur-ee) *noun* **1.** A container filled with chemicals that produces electrical power. **2.** A large number or series of something. ▶ *noun, plural* **batteries**

bat·tle (**bat**-uhl)
noun **1.** A fight between two armies, ships, or aircraft. **2.** A long struggle or competition.
verb To take part in a battle; fight. ▶ *verb* **battling, battled**

bat·tle·ground (**bat**-uhl-ground) *noun* A field or an area where a battle is fought.

bat·tle·ment (**bat**-uhl-muhnt) *noun* A low wall at the top of a fort or castle with openings for soldiers to shoot through.

bat·tle·ship (**bat**-uhl-ship) *noun* A heavily armed warship.

bawl (bawl) *verb* **1.** To wail or cry loudly. **2.** To shout in an angry voice. **3.** When you **bawl** someone **out,** you scold him or her.
Bawl sounds like **ball.** ▶ *verb* **bawling, bawled**

bay (bay)
noun **1.** A portion of the ocean that is partly enclosed by land. **2.** If you keep someone or something **at bay,** you prevent someone or something from coming near or having an effect. **3. bay window** A window that is built out from the wall of a house or other building.
verb To make a howling sound, like wolves or hounds sometimes make.
adjective A **bay** horse is reddish brown. ▶ *verb* **baying, bayed**

Bay of Fundy (bay uhv **fuhn**-dee) A bay of the Atlantic Ocean, on the eastern coast of North America. The Bay of Fundy lies between the Canadian provinces of New Brunswick and Nova Scotia, and connects to the northeastern end of the Gulf of Maine. The bay experiences a

B

particularly high tidal range, with drastic changes in water level at roughly six-hour intervals.

bay·o·net (**bay**-uh-*net*) *noun* A long blade that can be fastened to the end of a rifle and used as a weapon.

bay·ou (**bye**-oo) *noun* A stream that runs slowly through a swamp and leads to or from a lake or river. Bayous are most common in Texas, Louisiana, and Mississippi.

ba·zaar (buh-**zahr**) *noun* 1. A fair or sale at which things are sold to raise money for charity. 2. A street market, especially one found in a Middle Eastern country.

B.C. (**bee**-**see**) An abbreviation for "before Christ," used after a date to show that it comes before the birth of Jesus.

be (bee) *verb* 1. To exist. *There is time left to play.* 2. To happen. *The start of our vacation was last week.* 3. To come or go. *I've been to the store many times today.* 4. To stay or continue. *They've been in class for over an hour.* 5. **Be** can connect the subject of a sentence to a noun, adjective, pronoun, or prepositional phrase. *Roses are beautiful. The cat is on the couch.* 6. **Be** can support the main verb in a sentence. *We are eating dinner together tonight.*

Be sounds like **bee.**

beach (beech) *noun* A strip of sand or gravel at the edge of a body of water. **Beach** sounds like **beech.** ▶ *noun, plural* **beaches**

bea·con (**bee**-kuhn) *noun* A light or fire used as a signal or for guidance.

bead (beed) *noun* 1. A small piece of glass, wood, or other material that can be threaded on a string to make a necklace or to decorate something. 2. A drop of liquid on the surface of something.

bea·gle (**bee**-guhl) *noun* A medium-sized dog with short legs, long ears, and a smooth coat. Beagles are often kept as pets or used as hunting dogs.

beak (beek) *noun* The horny, pointed jaw of a bird.

beak·er (**bee**-kur) *noun* A plastic or glass jar with a spout for pouring, used in a laboratory.

beam (beem)
noun 1. A ray or band of light from a flashlight, a car headlight, or the sun. 2. A long, thick piece of wood, concrete, or metal used as a support in a building.
verb 1. To shine. 2. To broadcast something, or to send information with electronic signals. 3. To smile broadly.
▶ *verb* **beaming, beamed**

bean (been)
noun The seed or pod of various climbing plants that can be eaten.
verb To hit someone on the head with something you throw, such as a baseball.
▶ *verb* **beaning, beaned**

bear (bair)
verb 1. To carry someone or something or to hold someone or something up. 2. To produce fruit, flowers, or leaves. 3. To accept or put up with someone or something. 4. If you **bear** a resemblance to someone, you look somewhat like the person.
noun A large, heavy mammal with thick, shaggy fur and a short tail that lives typically in forests.
Bear sounds like **bare.** ▶ *verb* **bearing, bore** (bor), **borne** (born) ▶ *adjective* **bearable**

beard (beerd) *noun* The hair on a man's chin and lower cheeks.

bear·ing (**bair**-ing)
noun 1. The way someone stands, moves, or behaves. 2. A connection to something else. 3. In machinery, a part that allows moving parts to work with as little friction as possible.
noun, plural Your **bearings** are your sense of direction in relation to where things are.

beast (beest) *noun* 1. An animal, especially one that is dangerous or that walks on four feet. 2. A cruel or wicked person.
▶ *noun* **beastliness** ▶ *adjective* **beastly**

B

beat (beet)
verb **1.** To hit someone or something over and over again. **2.** To defeat someone or something. **3.** In cooking, if you **beat** something, you stir it quickly with a machine, spoon, or fork.
noun **1.** The regular rhythm of something, such as your heart. **2.** A regular route.
Beat sounds like **beet.** ▸ *verb* **beating, beat, beaten** (bee-tuhn) ▸ *noun* **beating**

beau·ti·ful (byoo-ti-ful) *adjective* Very pleasing to the senses. ▸ *verb* **beautify** (byoo-ti-*fye*) ▸ *adverb* **beautifully**

beau·ty (byoo-tee) *noun* **1.** The quality of being very attractive and pleasing to people. **2.** A person, usually a woman, who is considered beautiful.
▸ *noun, plural* **beauties**

bea·ver (bee-vur) *noun* **1.** A rodent with a wide, flat tail and strong teeth that gnaws down trees and uses them to create dams and lodges in which to live and protect their young. **2.** Someone who is an **eager beaver** works very hard and is quick to volunteer.

be·cause (bi-kawz *or* bi-kuhz) *conjunction* Since; for the reason that.

beck·on (bek-uhn) *verb* To make a sign to someone, encouraging that person to come or to follow. ▸ *verb* **beckoning, beckoned**

be·come (bi-kuhm) *verb* **1.** To develop into or come to be. **2.** To suit, or to look good on.
▸ *verb* **becoming, became** (bi-kaym)

be·com·ing (bi-kuhm-ing) *adjective* Flattering or attractive.

bed (bed) *noun* **1.** A piece of furniture or a place for lying down and sleeping. **2.** A piece of land where flowers are planted. **3.** The bottom of a body of water.
▸ *verb* **bed**

bed·bug (bed-buhg) *noun* A kind of insect that lives in mattresses and bites people when they sleep, causing painful swelling and itching.

bed·ding (bed-ing) *noun* Sheets, blankets, comforters, quilts, and other such items for beds.

be·drag·gled (bi-drag-uhld) *adjective* Wet, limp, or soiled; messy.

bed·rid·den (bed-rid-uhn) *adjective* Unable to get out of bed, usually because of illness.

bed·rock (bed-rahk) *noun* The solid layer of rock under the soil.

bed·room (bed-room) *noun* A room that has a bed and is used for sleeping.

bed·side (bed-side)
noun The area next to a bed.
adjective Designed to be used next to a bed.

bed·spread (bed-spred) *noun* A decorative quilt or other cover for a bed.

bed·time (bed-time) *noun* The time when someone usually goes to bed.

bee (bee) *noun* **1.** An insect with four wings that collects pollen. Some types of bees make honey, and some bees sting. **2.** A group competition or work activity.
Bee sounds like **be.**

beech (beech) *noun* A tree with smooth, gray bark and small nuts that are eaten as food. **Beech** sounds like **beach.** ▸ *noun, plural* **beeches**

beef (beef) *noun* The meat from a steer, bull, ox, or cow.

bee·hive (bee-hive) *noun* A nest or house for a swarm of bees.

been (bin) *verb* The past participle of **be.**

beep (beep)
noun A short, high sound, as made by a horn or machine.
verb To make the sound of a beep.
▸ *verb* **beeping, beeps** ▸ *noun* **beeper** ▸ *adjective* **beeping**

beer (beer) *noun* An alcoholic drink made from malt and flavored with hops and other ingredients.

bees·wax (beez-waks) *noun* A waxy substance produced and used by bees to make their honeycombs.

beet (beet) *noun* A dark red root vegetable. **Beet** sounds like **beat.**

bee·tle (bee-tuhl) *noun* An insect with two pairs of wings. A pair of hard wings

B

in front protects a pair of soft flying wings, which are folded underneath.

be·fall (bi-**fawl**) *verb* To happen to someone. ▶ *verb* **befalling, befell, befallen**

be·fore (bi-**for**)
preposition **1.** Sooner, or earlier than. *Please get back before six.* **2.** In front of. *The criminal stood before the judge.*
adverb Earlier.
conjunction Rather than.

be·fore·hand (bi-**for**-hand) *adverb, adjective* Ahead of time.

be·friend (bi-**frend**) *verb* To make friends with someone. ▶ *verb* **befriending, befriended**

beg (beg) *verb* **1.** To ask someone in the street for food or money. **2.** To ask in a pleading way.
▶ *verb* **begging, begged**

beg·gar (**beg**-ur)
noun Someone who lives by asking others for food and money.
verb To cause someone to lose their money or possessions.
▶ *verb* **beggaring, beggared**

be·gin (bi-**gin**) *verb* To start or to take the first step in doing something. ▶ *verb* **beginning, began** (bi-**gan**), **begun** (bi-**guhn**) ▶ *noun* **beginner**

be·gin·ning (bi-**gin**-ing) *noun* The time or occasion when something starts; the first or earliest part of something.

be·go·ni·a (bi-**gohn**-yuh) *noun* A tropical plant with white, yellow, red, or pink flowers.

be·half (bi-**haf**) *noun* If you do something **on behalf** of someone else, you are acting in their interests or as their representative.

be·have (bi-**hayv**) *verb* **1.** To act in a polite or proper way. **2.** To act in a particular way.
▶ *verb* **behaving, behaved**

be·hav·ior (bi-**hayv**-yuhr) *noun* **1.** The way someone acts, either typically or in a particular situation. **2.** The way that a machine, software program, or piece of equipment operates.

be·head (bi-**hed**) *verb* To chop off someone's head. ▶ *verb* **beheading, beheaded**

be·held (bi-**held**) *verb* The past tense and past participle of **behold.**

be·hind (bi-**hinde**)
preposition **1.** At the back of something or on the opposite side. *Look behind that drawer if you want to find your missing sock.* **2.** In a lesser position, or farther back than. *He finished the race behind his younger brother.* **3.** Later than. *He had fallen behind schedule but wouldn't stop working.* **4.** In support of. *My friends were behind me all the way when I tried out for the team.*
adverb Slow or late in getting something done.

be·hold (bi-**hohld**) *verb* To look at something with great interest, or to see. ▶ *verb* **beholding, beheld**

beige (bayzh)
noun A pale grayish-brown color.
adjective Being beige in color.

be·ing (**bee**-ing) *noun* **1.** The state of existing. **2.** A person or creature that is alive.

Be·la·rus (**bel**-uh-**roos**) A country in eastern Europe bordered by Russia, Ukraine, Poland, Lithuania, and Latvia. Belarus was a republic of the Soviet Union until it won its independence in 1991.

be·lat·ed (bi-**lay**-tid) *adjective* Delayed, or late. ▶ *adverb* **belatedly**

belch (belch)
verb **1.** To burp or let gas from your stomach out through your mouth. **2.** To send out smoke or flames in an explosive way.
noun The act of belching.
▶ *verb* **belches, belching, belched** ▶ *noun, plural* **belches**

bel·fry (**bel**-free) *noun* The tower, or room in a tower, where a large bell is hung. ▶ *noun, plural* **belfries**

Bel·gium (**bel**-juhm) A country in northwest Europe just north of France. Occupied by Germany during World Wars I and II, it is now home to the headquarters of the European Union, NATO, and other major international organizations.

B

be·lief (bi-**leef**) *noun* **1.** Something that someone believes is true. **2.** One of a number of ideas that together form someone's religion. **3.** Confidence or trust in someone or in the truth of something.

be·lieve (bi-**leev**) *verb* **1.** To accept as true or real. **2.** To have faith in someone or something; to support. **3.** To be reasonably confident that something is true.
▶ *verb* **believing, believed** ▶ *noun* **believer** ▶ *adjective* **believable**

Be·lize (buh-**leez**) A country in Central America formerly known as British Honduras. It is the only country in Central America where English is the official language.

bell (bel) *noun* **1.** An instrument that is designed to make a ringing sound when it is struck. **2.** (informal) If something **rings a bell,** it sounds familiar. **3.** Something that is shaped like a bell, especially the part of a musical instrument where the sound comes out.

bel·lig·er·ent (buh-**lij**-ur-uhnt) *adjective* **1.** Eager to fight, or hostile. **2.** Warlike.
▶ *adverb* **belligerently**

bel·low (**bel**-oh)
verb To shout or make a deep roaring sound.
noun A shout or deep roar.
noun, plural **bellows** A device whose sides are squeezed to pump air into something, such as a fire.
▶ *verb* **bellowing, bellowed**

bel·ly (**bel**-ee) *noun* **1.** The stomach, or the part of the body below the ribs. **2. belly flop** A dive in which the front of your body lands flat against the water.
▶ *noun, plural* **bellies**

bel·ly but·ton (**bel**-ee *buht*-uhn) *noun* A hollow or raised dimple in the center of your stomach where your umbilical cord was attached to your mother before you were born; your navel.

be·long (bi-**lawng**) *verb* **1.** If something **belongs** to you, it is your property. **2.** To be a member of a group or club. **3.** To be in the proper place

or position.
▶ *verb* **belonging, belonged** ▶ *noun, plural* **belongings**

be·lov·ed (bi-**luhv**-id)
adjective Greatly loved or dear to someone's heart.
noun Someone who is greatly loved.

be·low (bi-**loh**)
preposition Beneath or in a lower position than. *The sun is below the horizon.*
adverb Toward or in a lower place.

belt (belt)
noun **1.** A long, narrow piece of leather or other material that you wear around your waist to support clothing, tools, or weapons. **2.** A continuous band of rubber used for moving things along or for transferring motion from one part of a machine to another. **3.** An area known for a particular thing.
verb **1.** (informal) To hit someone or something very hard. **2.** If you **belt something out,** you play or sing it very loudly. **3.** To put a belt on.
▶ *verb* **belting, belted**

bench (bench) *noun* **1.** A long, narrow seat for more than one person, usually made of wood or plastic. **2.** A table in a workshop or laboratory. **3.** The place where a judge sits in a court of law. Judges ask lawyers to "approach the bench" to discuss issues in private during a trial.
▶ *noun, plural* **benches**

bend (bend)
verb **1.** If you **bend** or **bend over,** you lean forward from the waist or curve your body downward. **2.** If something **bends,** it turns in a curved or angled direction. **3.** To give something that was straight a curved or angled shape.
noun A curve or angle.
▶ *verb* **bending, bent** (bent)

be·neath (bi-**neeth**)
preposition **1.** Of a lower status than, or not worthy of. *Don't apologize; it's beneath your dignity.* **2.** Underneath or hidden by. *We found the missing book beneath a pile of papers.*
adverb In or to a lower place; underneath.

B

ben·e·fi·cial (*ben*-uh-**fish**-uhl)
adjective Good for someone or
something. ▶ *adverb* **beneficially**
ben·e·fit (**ben**-uh-fit)
verb If you **benefit** from something,
you receive something that helps you
or gives you an advantage.
noun **1.** An event whose purpose is
to raise money for a cause, charity,
or cultural organization. **2.** An
advantage or valuable thing that
comes with a job in addition to the
pay. **3.** Something that gives you
an advantage or makes a situation
better.
noun, plural **benefits** Money that
people may receive in special
circumstances.
▶ *verb* **benefiting, benefited**
be·nev·o·lent (buh-**nev**-uh-luhnt)
adjective Known for doing
good; well-meaning. ▶ *noun*
benevolence ▶ *adverb* **benevolently**
be·nign (bi-**nine**) *adjective* Not
dangerous to your health; harmless.
Be·nin (buh-**neen**) A country on the
coast of West Africa. Formerly known
as Dahomey, it played a central role
in the slave trade during the 17th
century. Today, Benin attracts tourists
to its national parks to see animals
such as lions, leopards, elephants,
and monkeys.
bent (bent) *adjective* **1.** Crooked or
curved. **2.** If you're **bent on** doing
something, you are determined to
do it.
be·queath (bi-**kweeth**) *verb* To pass
something on to someone, or to
leave something to somebody
in your will. ▶ *verb* **bequeathing,
bequeathed** ▶ *noun* **bequest** (bi-
kwest)
be·reaved (bi-**reevd**) *adjective* A
bereaved person feels sad because
someone very close to him or her has
died. ▶ *noun* **bereavement**
be·ret (buh-**ray**) *noun* A round, flat cap
made of felt, wool, or some other soft
material.
Ber·ing Strait (**bair**-ing **strayt**) A
narrow waterway located far in the

north between Asia and North
America. In ancient times there was
a land bridge where the Bering Strait
is today, which allowed migration
into the Americas from Asia.
ber·ry (**ber**-ee) *noun* A small, fleshy
fruit that grows on bushes or trees.
Berry sounds like **bury.** ▶ *noun,
plural* **berries**
berth (burth)
noun **1.** A built-in bed or bunk on a
ship or train. **2.** A place in a harbor
where a ship is tied up or anchored.
verb To tie up to a dock or a pier.
Berth sounds like **birth.** ▶ *verb*
berthing, berthed
be·seech (bi-**seech**) *verb* To ask
someone in a very serious way; to
beg. ▶ *verb* **beseeching, besought**
(bi-**sawt**) **beseeched**
be·set (bi-**set**) *verb* To attack or
trouble someone. ▶ *verb* **besetting,
beset**
be·side (bi-**side**) *preposition* **1.** Next
to or at the side of someone or
something. *Walk beside me.* **2.** Apart
from. *Your excuse is beside the point.*
3. If you are **beside yourself,** you are
extremely worried, angry, or excited.
*My mother was beside herself until I
called to tell her where I was.*
be·sides (bi-**sidez**)
preposition In addition to, or other
than. *Who, besides Marian, will ever
know the truth?*
adverb Also, or furthermore.
be·siege (bi-**seej**) *verb* **1.** To surround
with armed forces. **2.** To crowd
around.
▶ *verb* **besieging, besieged**
best (best)
adjective Better than everyone or
everything else in some way.
verb To do better than someone else.
adverb More than any or all others.
noun A thing or person that is better
than all others.
phrase When you **do your best,**
you make a very great effort to do
something as well as you possibly
can.
▶ *verb* **besting, bested**

B

B

best man (**best man**) *noun* A brother or close male friend of a bridegroom, whose duties at the wedding include keeping the rings safe and making a toast.

be·stow (bi-**stoh**) *verb* To give someone a gift or a prize. ▶ *verb* bestowing, bestowed

bet (bet)
verb 1. To risk a sum of money on the outcome of something that is hard to predict, such as a race or a game. 2. If you **bet** someone that he or she can't do something, you challenge him or her to try it. 3. (informal) If you **bet** that someone will do something, you are confident that he or she will do it.
noun An act of betting money on something.
▶ *verb* betting, bet ▶ *noun* betting

be·tray (bi-**tray**) *verb* 1. To be disloyal to someone or something. 2. If you **betray** your feelings, you reveal them without meaning to do so.
▶ *verb* betraying, betrayed ▶ *noun* betrayal

bet·ter (**bet**-ur)
adjective 1. More suitable or satisfactory. 2. Recovering from illness or injury. 3. **better off** Having more money or being in a more favorable position.
adverb In a more complete, effective, or satisfactory way.
verb To improve something.
▶ *verb* bettering, bettered

be·tween (bi-**tween**) *preposition* 1. If something is **between** two things, it is in the place that separates them. *The car is parked between two trucks.* 2. From one to another. *The airfare between Chicago and Miami was a bargain.* 3. Somewhere in the period separating two points in time. *We should arrive between eight and nine o'clock.* 4. By comparing. *Please choose between the boots and the sneakers.*

bev·er·age (**bev**-rij) *noun* A drink, especially other than water.

be·ware (bi-**wair**) *verb* To be careful about or to guard against.

be·wil·der (bi-**wil**-dur) *verb* To confuse someone. ▶ *verb* bewildering, bewildered ▶ *noun* bewilderment ▶ *adjective* bewildered

be·witch (bi-**wich**) *verb* To cast a spell on someone. ▶ *verb* bewitching, bewitched

be·yond (bee-**ahnd**)
preposition 1. On the far side of or past something. *The dogs couldn't get beyond the chain-link fence.* 2. If something is **beyond** you, it is outside your experience or understanding. *How you can live in such a messy room is beyond me.*
adverb Farther on or farther away.

Bhu·tan (boo-**tahn**) A country in South Asia at the eastern end of the Himalaya Mountains between China and India. Formerly one of the most isolated countries in the world, modern-day Bhutan is known for its efforts to preserve its traditional culture and protect its natural environment.

bi·as (bye-uhs)
noun A tendency to favor or oppose a particular group or person; prejudice.
verb To influence someone in favor or against a group or individual.
▶ *verb* biasing, biased

bi·ased (bye-uhst) *adjective* Prejudiced, or favoring one person or point of view more than another.

bi·ath·lon (bye-**ath**-lahn) *noun* A sport in which the participants carry a rifle as they ski on a course and stop to shoot at targets along the way.

Bi·ble (bye-buhl) *noun* 1. The sacred book of the Christian religion that contains the Old and New Testaments. 2. The sacred book in the Jewish religion, consisting of the Old Testament.

bib·li·cal (**bib**-li-kuhl) *adjective* Of, from, or having to do with the Bible.

bib·li·og·ra·phy (*bib*-lee-**ah**-gruh-fee) *noun* A list of books and articles on a subject, especially one in the back of a book. ▶ *noun, plural* bibliographies ▶ *adjective* bibliographical (*bib*-lee-uh-**graf**-i-kuhl)

bi·ceps (**bye**-seps) *noun, plural* The large muscle on the front of your arm between your shoulder and inner elbow.

bick·er (**bik**-ur) *verb* To argue about small things. ▶ *verb* **bickering, bickered**

bi·coast·al (bye-**koh**-stuhl) *adjective* Living and working on both the East and West Coasts of the United States.

bi·cus·pid (bye-**kuhs**-pid) *noun* A tooth with two points located just beside the front sets of upper and lower teeth.

bi·cy·cle (**bye**-si-kuhl)
noun A light-framed vehicle with two wheels, handlebars for steering and braking, and pedals that you push with your feet.
verb To ride a bicycle.
▶ *verb* **bicycling, bicycled**

bid (bid)
verb To offer a certain amount of money for something, as at an auction.
noun An effort to win or achieve something.
▶ *verb* **bidding, bid** ▶ *noun* **bidder**

bid (bid) *verb* **1.** To order someone to do something. **2.** To express something.
▶ *verb* **bidding, bid** or **bade, bidden** or **bid**

bid·den (**bid**-uhn) *verb* A past participle of **bid²**.

bide (bide) *verb* To wait for the right moment. ▶ *verb* **biding, bided**

bi·en·ni·al (bye-**en**-ee-uhl)
adjective Happening or celebrated every two years.
noun A plant that lives for two growing seasons.

bi·fo·cals (bye-*foh*-kuhlz) *noun, plural* Glasses or lenses that have two sections, for seeing up close and farther away.

big (big) *adjective* **1.** Large in size. **2.** Of great importance.
▶ *adjective* **bigger, biggest**

Big Bang (**big** bang) *noun* An explosion of dense matter more than 13 billion years ago that most scientists believe was the beginning of the universe.

big·horn (**big**-*horn*) *noun* A type of wild sheep with large, curved horns, found in the Rocky Mountains and other mountain ranges in western North America.

big·ot (**big**-uht) *noun* Someone who has strong opinions and prejudices, especially against people of other races, nationalities, or religions. ▶ *noun* **bigotry** ▶ *adjective* **bigoted**

bike (bike)
noun A bicycle, motorcycle, or motorbike.
verb To ride a bicycle, motorcycle, or motorbike.
▶ *verb* **biking, biked** ▶ *noun* **biker**

bi·ki·ni (bi-**kee**-nee) *noun* A very small, close-fitting, two-piece bathing suit worn by women and girls.

bile (bile) *noun* A greenish-yellow fluid that is made by the liver. It is stored in the gallbladder and helps you digest your food.

bi·lin·gual (bye-**ling**-gwuhl) *adjective*
1. Able to speak two languages well.
2. Dealing with two languages.

bill (bil)
noun **1.** A document that tells you how much money you owe for certain goods or services. **2.** A written plan for a new law, to be debated and passed by a body of legislators. **3.** The beak or jaws of a bird. **4.** A piece of paper money.
verb To send someone a bill to be paid.
▶ *verb* **billing, billed**

bill·board (**bil**-bord) *noun* A large outdoor sign used to advertise products or services.

bill·fold (**bil**-*fohld*) *noun* A small folding wallet for paper money.

bil·liards (**bil**-yurdz) *noun, plural* A game in which you use a stick, called a cue, to hit balls around a rectangular, cloth-covered table.

bil·lion (**bil**-yuhn)
noun **1.** One thousand times one million, written numerically as 1,000,000,000. **2.** A very large amount.
adjective Equal to a very large amount.

B

Bill of Rights (bil uhv **rites**) *noun* The first ten amendments to the U.S. Constitution, which define the rights that protect every American.

bil·low (**bil**-oh)
verb 1. To bulge or swell out, especially when pushed by the wind. 2. If smoke or fog **billows**, it rolls or rises up like a huge wave.
noun A large wave or swell of water, or a large mass of smoke, fog, or clouds.
▸ *verb* **billowing, billowed**

bin (bin) *noun* A large covered container or box for storing things.

bi·na·ry (**bye**-nur-ee *or* **bye**-*ner*-ee) *adjective* 1. Having two parts or based on two things. 2. In mathematics, the **binary** number system uses only two digits, 1 and 0. 3. In computers, **binary** refers to files and codes that convert all numbers and letters into strings of 1s and 0s.

bind (binde) *verb* 1. To secure something by tying it up. 2. To enclose something by wrapping a piece of material around it. 3. If you **bind** a book, you fasten its pages together between covers. 4. To oblige.
▸ *verb* **binding, bound** (bound) ▸ *adjective* **binding** ▸ *noun* **binding**

bind·er (**bine**-dur) *noun* A detachable cover used for holding papers.

binge (binj)
verb To overdo an activity such as eating or drinking.
noun A period of overdoing something; a spree.
▸ *verb* **bingeing** *or* **binging, binged**

bin·go (**bing**-goh) *noun* A game of chance in which the players have cards with numbered squares on them, and they cross out the numbers that are drawn at random and announced by a caller.

bin·oc·u·lars (buh-**nah**-kyuh-lurz) *noun, plural* A device that you look through with both eyes to make things that are far away seem larger and nearer.

bi·o·de·grad·a·ble (*bye*-oh-di-**gray**-duh-buhl) *adjective* Able to be broken down by natural processes.

bi·o·di·ver·si·ty (*bye*-oh-duh-**vur**-si-tee) *noun* The condition of nature in which a wide variety of species live in a single area.

bi·o·fu·el (**bye**-oh-*fyoo*-uhl) *noun* A fuel that is made from renewable materials such as plants or animal waste.

bi·og·ra·phy (bye-**ah**-gruh-fee) *noun* A book that tells the life story of someone other than the author. ▸ *noun, plural* **biographies** ▸ *noun* **biographer** ▸ *adjective* **biographical** (bye-*uh*-**graf**-i-kuhl)

bi·ol·o·gy (bye-**ah**-luh-jee) *noun* The study of life and of all living things. ▸ *noun* **biologist** ▸ *adjective* **biological** (bye-uh-**lah**-ji-kuhl) ▸ *adverb* **biologically**

bi·o·mass (**bye**-oh-*mas*) *noun* The amount or weight of living matter in a certain area or volume of a habitat.

bi·o·rhythm (**bye**-oh-*riTH*-uhm) *noun* The natural rhythm of the human body.

bi·o·tech·nol·o·gy (*bye*-oh-tek-**nah**-luh-jee) *noun* The use of biological materials and processes in industry.

bi·plane (**bye**-*plane*) *noun* An airplane with a double set of wings, one above and one below the body of the plane.

birch (burch) *noun* A tree with hard wood and smooth bark that peels off easily in long strips. ▸ *noun, plural* **birches**

bird (burd) *noun* A warm-blooded animal with two legs, wings, feathers, and a beak.

bird flu (burd *floo*) *noun* A kind of flu that kills birds and that can also spread to people.

birth (burth) *noun* 1. The act or process of being born. 2. The starting point of something. 3. When a woman or female animal **gives birth,** she has a baby.
Birth sounds like **berth.**

birth·day (**burth**-*day*) *noun* The day that someone was born, or the anniversary of that date in the years that follow, often marked by a celebration.

birth·mark (**burth**-*mahrk*) *noun* A mark on the skin that was there from birth.

birth moth·er (**burth** *muhTH*-ur) *noun* The biological mother of a person. Used in reference to adoption, the term means the woman who actually gave birth to a child, as opposed to the woman who adopts and raises that child.

birth·place (**burth**-*plase*) *noun* The place where someone was born, or where something began.

birth·right (**burth**-*rite*) *noun* A right or privilege that someone has because of being born into a specific family or group.

bis·cuit (**bis**-kit) *noun* A small, round kind of bread, made from dough that is rolled out and cut into circles or dropped from a spoon.

bi·sect (**bye**-*sekt*) *verb* To cut or divide into two equal parts. ▸ *verb* **bisecting, bisected** ▸ *noun* **bisection**

bish·op (**bish**-uhp) *noun* **1.** A senior member of the Christian clergy, who is in charge of all the churches in an area. **2.** In chess, a piece that can move across the board in a diagonal direction.

bi·son (**bye**-suhn) *noun* A large animal with a big, shaggy head, a humped back, and short horns, found in western North America; a buffalo. ▸ *noun, plural* **bison**

bit (bit)
noun **1.** A small portion or amount of something. **2.** A unit of information that can be stored in a computer's memory. **3.** A metal mouthpiece that is attached to the reins and used to control a horse. **4.** The pointed part of a drill.
verb The past tense of **bite.**

bite (bite)
verb **1.** To cut into something with your teeth. **2.** If an insect or snake **bites** you, it makes a wound in your skin with its stinger or its teeth. **3.** If a fish **bites,** it takes the bait at the end of a fishing line into its mouth.
noun A small amount of food.

Bite sounds like **byte.** ▸ *verb* **biting, bit** (bit), **bitten** (bit-uhn)

bit·map (**bit**-*map*) *noun* A way of storing an image on a computer so that each pixel is represented by a code that tells its color and location.

bit·ten (**bit**-uhn) *verb* The past participle of **bite.**

bit·ter (**bit**-ur) *adjective* **1.** Tasting sharp, not sweet. **2.** If you feel **bitter,** you are angry or resentful because you don't think you've been treated fairly. **3.** Extremely cold.
▸ *noun* **bitterness**

bi·valve (**bye**-*valv*) *noun* A mollusk that lives inside two shells that close together. Bivalves include oysters, mussels, scallops, and clams.

bi·zarre (bi-**zahr**) *adjective* Very strange or odd.

black (blak)
noun A color that is completely dark, like that of coal or of the sky at night.
adjective Colored black.
▸ *adjective* **blacker, blackest**

black·ber·ry (**blak**-*ber*-ee) *noun* A small, juicy, black fruit that grows on a prickly, climbing shrub. ▸ *noun, plural* **blackberries**

black·bird (**blak**-*burd*) *noun* One of a large number of birds with black feathers. Crows and grackles are types of blackbirds.

black·board (**blak**-*bord*) *noun* A hard, smooth surface, often made of slate, that people write on with chalk.

black·en (**blak**-uhn) *verb* To make black or become black. ▸ *verb* **blackening, blackened**

black eye (**blak** eye) *noun* A bruise on the skin around the eye, caused by broken blood vessels.

Black·foot (**blak**-*fut*) *noun* A member of a group of Native Americans who live mainly in Montana and the Canadian province of Alberta. ▸ *noun, plural* **Blackfoot** or **Blackfeet**

black hole (**blak** hole) *noun* An area in space where a star has collapsed and where gravity is so strong that nothing can escape, not even light.

black·mail (**blak**-*mayl*)
noun The crime of demanding money from someone in exchange for not revealing information that might threaten or embarrass the person.
verb When you **blackmail** someone, you threaten or pressure the person to do something he or she doesn't want to do.
▶ *verb* **blackmailing, blackmailed**

black·out (**blak**-*out*) *noun* 1. A period of unconsciousness. 2. If a town or city has a **blackout,** the lights go off because the electricity has failed.
▶ *verb* **black out**

Black Sea (**blak** see) An inland sea located in Europe, north of the Mediterranean Sea. The Black Sea is surrounded by Turkey, Bulgaria, Romania, Ukraine, Georgia, and the southernmost tip of Russia.

black·smith (**blak**-*smith*) *noun* Someone who makes things by heating and bending iron.

black·top (**blak**-*tahp*) *noun* The hard black surface that covers roads and other paved areas; asphalt.

black wid·ow (**blak wid**-oh) *noun* A spider with a poisonous bite. The female black widow has a shiny black body and a red hourglass shape on the underside of its abdomen.

blad·der (**blad**-ur) *noun* The organ where urine is stored before your body gets rid of it.

blade (blade) *noun* 1. The flat, sharp-edged part of a tool or utensil, such as a knife, sword, or dagger. 2. The flat, wide part of an oar or propeller that pushes against the water. 3. A long, narrow leaf of a plant such as grass or wheat. 4. The metal runner on an ice skate.

blame (blame)
verb To feel or say that something is someone's fault.
noun Responsibility for a bad thing that has happened.
▶ *verb* **blaming, blamed**

bland (bland) *adjective* Without much flavor. ▶ *adjective* **blander, blandest**

blank (blangk)
adjective 1. Bare, empty, or with nothing written on it. 2. A **blank** expression or look doesn't tell you anything about what a person is thinking or feeling.
noun 1. An empty line or space. 2. A cartridge for a gun that contains gunpowder but no bullet, used for training.
idiom If you **go blank,** you suddenly cannot think of something.
▶ *adjective* **blanker, blankest**

blan·ket (**blang**-kit)
noun 1. A covering for a bed. 2. A thick layer of something.
adjective Applying to or covering all things or people equally.
verb To cover something evenly.

blare (blair) *verb* To make a very loud, harsh sound. ▶ *verb* **blaring, blared**

blas·phe·my (**blas**-fuh-mee) *noun* The act of speaking in a disrespectful way about God or holy things. ▶ *verb* **blaspheme** (blas-feem) ▶ *adjective* **blasphemous** (**blas**-fuh-muhs)

blast (blast)
noun 1. An explosion or sudden, loud noise. 2. A strong gust of air.
verb 1. To blow up with explosives. 2. When a rocket **blasts off,** it is launched.
▶ *verb* **blasting, blasted**

blast·off (**blast**-*awf*) *noun* The launching into space of a rocket, missile, or spaceship.

bla·tant (**blay**-tuhnt) *adjective* Open, obvious, and without shame. ▶ *adverb* **blatantly**

blaze (blayz)
verb 1. To burn fiercely or shine brightly. 2. If you **blaze a trail,** you mark out a path or set an example.
noun A large or fiercely burning fire.
▶ *verb* **blazing, blazed**

blaz·er (**blay**-zur) *noun* A solid color sports jacket, especially one with metal buttons.

bleach (bleech)
noun A chemical that takes color, dirt,

B

and stains out of materials.
verb To make something cleaner or lighter in color by using a bleach or the sun.
▸ *verb* **bleaches, bleaching, bleached**

bleach·ers (**blee**-churz) *noun, plural* Raised seats or benches arranged in rows. Bleachers are usually found in stadiums or along a parade route.

bleak (bleek) *adjective* **1.** Cold, miserable, and exposed to the weather. **2.** Unlikely to have a positive outcome.
▸ *adjective* **bleaker, bleakest**

bleat (bleet)
noun The cry of a sheep or a goat.
verb To make the sound of a sheep or goat.
▸ *verb* **bleating, bleated**

bleed (bleed) *verb* **1.** To lose blood as a result of illness or injury. **2.** If your heart **bleeds** for someone, you feel sorrow or pity for the person.
▸ *verb* **bleeding, bled**
(bled) ▸ *adjective* **bleeding**

bleep (bleep)
verb To make a short, high-pitched sound like that of an electronic device.
noun The sound made this way.
▸ *verb* **bleeping, bleeped**

blem·ish (**blem**-ish)
noun A mark or spot that makes something less than perfect; a flaw.
verb To make something less perfect than it was.
▸ *noun, plural* **blemishes** ▸ *verb* **blemishes, blemishing, blemished**

blend (blend) *verb* To mix two or more things together so that they combine. ▸ *verb* **blending, blended** ▸ *noun* **blend**

blend·ed fam·i·ly (**blen**-did **fam**-uh-lee) *noun* A family in which not all of the children have the same two parents.

blend·er (**blen**-dur) *noun* A small appliance that grinds and mixes food.

bless (bles) *verb* **1.** To make holy. **2.** To ask God to protect someone or something. **3.** "**Bless you!**" is what you say when a person has just sneezed, or if you want to thank someone.
▸ *verb* **blesses, blessing, blessed** ▸ *noun* **blessing**

blew (bloo) *verb* The past tense of **blow**. **Blew** sounds like **blue**.

blight (blite) *noun* **1.** A disease that destroys plants. **2.** Something that can hurt or destroy the health or beauty of something.

blimp (blimp) *noun* An airship, or dirigible, whose body does not have a rigid frame.

blind (blinde)
adjective **1.** Not able to see. **2.** A **blind** corner is so sharp that it is impossible to see around. **3.** If you are **blind to** something, you do not notice it or act on it.
noun **1.** A covering for a window that can be pulled down to keep out the light. **2.** A driver's **blind spot** is an area that cannot be seen in either the side or rearview mirrors.
verb To cause to lose judgment.
▸ *verb* **blinding, blinded** ▸ *noun* **blindness**

blind·fold (blinde-*fohld*)
verb To cover someone's eyes with a strip of material so that he or she cannot see.
noun A scarf or other material that is tied around the head to cover the eyes and keep the wearer from seeing.
▸ *verb* **blindfolding, blindfolded**

blink (blingk)
verb **1.** To close and open your eyes very quickly. **2.** To flash on and off.
noun The act of blinking.
▸ *verb* **blinking, blinked**

bliss (blis) *noun* A state of perfect happiness. ▸ *adjective* **blissful** ▸ *adverb* **blissfully**

blis·ter (**blis**-tur)
noun A small, fluid-filled bubble on the skin, caused by something burning or rubbing against it.
verb To form or cause to form blisters.
▸ *verb* **blistering, blistered**

bliz·zard (**bliz**-urd) *noun* A severe snowstorm with strong winds.

B

bloat·ed (**bloh**-tid) *adjective* Swollen with fluid or gas, often as a result of overeating.

blob (blahb) *noun* A small lump of something soft, wet, or thick.

block (blahk)
noun 1. A piece of something solid with flat sides. 2. The distance or area from one street to another. 3. The area or section in a city surrounded by four streets. 4. A large building.
verb 1. To come between one thing and another. 2. To prevent movement or progress.
▶ *verb* **blocking, blocked**

block·ade (blah-**kade**) *noun* The closing off of an area to keep people or supplies from going in or out.

block·house (**blahk**-*hous*) *noun* 1. A small fort or building designed as a defense against attack. 2. A strong concrete building used to protect the observers of a rocket launch or an explosion.

blog (blawg *or* blahg)
noun A webpage or website to which new messages are added easily. Blogs usually discuss a single subject or issue, and they may be written by a single person, like a diary, or as a discussion by many people.
verb To add new entries to a blog.
▶ *verb* **blogging, blogged** ▶ *noun* **blogger**

blond (blahnd)
adjective Having golden or pale yellow hair. When the word is spelled *blonde*, with an *e* at the end, it usually refers to a girl or woman with such hair.
noun **blond, blonde** A person who has hair like this.

blood (bluhd) *noun* The red fluid that your heart pumps through your veins and arteries. It carries oxygen to, and takes carbon dioxide from, all parts of the body.

blood bank (bluhd *bangk*) *noun* A place where blood is donated and stored. Hospitals use this stored blood to replace blood lost by someone during an operation or in an accident.

blood do·nor (bluhd *doh*-nur) *noun* A person who gives some of his or her own blood to someone who needs it.

blood·hound (**bluhd**-*hound*) *noun* A large dog with a wrinkled face, drooping ears, and a very good sense of smell.

blood·shed (**bluhd**-*shed*) *noun* The injury or killing of human beings, particularly as a result of a battle or war.

blood·shot (**bluhd**-*shaht*) *adjective* **Bloodshot** eyes are red and irritated.

blood·stream (**bluhd**-*streem*) *noun* The blood circulating through the body.

blood·thirst·y (**bluhd**-*thur*-stee) *adjective* Someone who is **bloodthirsty** is eager for or takes pleasure in violence or killing.

blood ves·sel (bluhd *ves*-uhl) *noun* Any of the tubes in your body through which your blood flows.

blood·y (**bluhd**-ee) *adjective* 1. Full of blood, or covered with blood. 2. Violent, or showing blood.
▶ *adjective* **bloodier, bloodiest**

bloom (bloom)
noun A flower.
verb 1. To produce flowers or to be in flower. 2. To flourish.
▶ *verb* **blooming, bloomed** ▶ *adjective* **blooming**

blos·som (**blah**-suhm)
noun A flower on a fruit tree or other plant.
verb To grow or to develop.
▶ *verb* **blossoming, blossomed**

blot (blaht)
noun 1. A mark or stain, such as one made by ink or paint. 2. A fault that spoils appearance, reputation, or enjoyment.
verb To dry by soaking up excess liquid.
▶ *verb* **blotting, blotted**

blotch (blahch) *noun* A stain or a large, irregular mark on the skin. ▶ *noun, plural* **blotches** ▶ *adjective* **blotchy**

blot·ter (**blah**-tur) *noun* A pad or piece of thick paper that absorbs extra ink.

blouse (blous) *noun* A loose-fitting shirt worn by women and girls that covers the area from the neck to the waist, or just below.

B

blow (bloh)
verb **1.** To force air out of your mouth through your lips. **2.** To force air into a device or instrument in order to produce a sound. **3.** To move in the wind or be carried as if by the wind. **4. blow up** To explode something or to destroy it with an explosion. **5. blow up** To lose your temper.
noun **1.** A sudden and forceful stroke with your hand or a weapon. **2.** A shock or a disappointment.
▶ *verb* **blowing, blew** (bloo), **blown** (blohn)

blow·torch (bloh-torch) *noun* A small torch with an intense flame that is used to melt metal or take off paint. ▶ *noun, plural* **blowtorches**

blub·ber (bluhb-ur)
noun The layer of fat under the skin of a whale, seal, or other large marine mammal.
verb To sob loudly.
▶ *verb* **blubbering, blubbered**

blue (bloo)
noun The color of the ocean or the sky on a sunny day.
adjective **1.** Of or being the color blue. **2.** Sad, gloomy, or depressed.
idiom If something comes to you **out of the blue**, it comes from a source or at a time when you didn't expect it. **Blue** sounds like **blew**. ▶ *adjective* **bluer, bluest**

blue·ber·ry (bloo-ber-ee) *noun* The sweet, dark blue fruit of a bush common in the northeastern United States. ▶ *noun, plural* **blueberries**

blue·bird (bloo-burd) *noun* A small songbird that has blue feathers on its back and wings.

blue·fish (bloo-fish) *noun* A silver-blue ocean fish. ▶ *noun, plural* **bluefish** or **bluefishes**

blue·grass (bloo-gras) *noun* **1.** A grass with a slightly blue tinge, used for lawns and for cattle and horse feed. **2.** A type of country music, typically played on banjos and guitars.

blue jay (bloo jay) *noun* A fairly large, blue and white bird, related to crows, with a crest of feathers on its head.

blue jeans (bloo jeenz) *noun, plural* Jeans made of blue denim.

blue·print (bloo-print) *noun* A model or detailed plan of action.

blues (blooz) *noun, plural* **1.** A type of music first sung by African Americans, with songs about difficulties in life and love. **2.** Low spirits.

blue whale (bloo wayl) *noun* A bluish-gray whale that is the largest living animal.

bluff (bluhf)
verb To try to mislead someone by appearing more confident than you really are.
noun **1.** A statement or action that is intended to mislead someone. **2.** A cliff or other mountain with a very steep face.
idiom If you **call** someone's **bluff,** you challenge the person to do something he or she has boasted about or threatened to do.
▶ *verb* **bluffing, bluffed**

blun·der (bluhn-dur)
noun A stupid or careless mistake.
verb **1.** To make a stupid mistake. **2.** To move in a confused or clumsy way.
▶ *verb* **blundering, blundered**

blunt (bluhnt)
adjective **1.** Having a dull edge or point. **2.** Abrupt and honest in what you say.
verb To make or become less sharp.
▶ *adjective* **blunter, bluntest** ▶ *verb* **blunting, blunted** ▶ *noun* **bluntness** ▶ *adverb* **bluntly**

blur (blur)
verb To make something less clear or unclear.
noun Something that can't be seen or remembered clearly.
▶ *verb* **blurring, blurred** ▶ *adjective* **blurred**

blurb (blurb) *noun* A short written piece that promotes a book, a movie, or a product.

blurt (blurt) *verb* If you **blurt** something out, you say it suddenly and without thinking about its effect. ▶ *verb* **blurting, blurted**

B

blush (bluhsh)
verb To become red in the face because you are shy, embarrassed, or ashamed.
noun The red color in your face when you blush.
▶ *verb* **blushes, blushing, blushed** ▶ *noun, plural* **blushes**

blus·ter (**bluhs**-tur)
verb **1.** To blow in violent gusts.
2. To act or speak in a bullying, overconfident way.
noun Bullying, overconfident talk.
▶ *verb* **blustering, blustered** ▶ *adjective* **blustery**

Blvd. (**bul**-uh-*vahrd*) Short for *boulevard*.

bo·a con·stric·tor (**boh**-uh kuhn-*strik*-tur) *noun* A large, nonpoisonous tropical snake that kills its prey by coiling around it and squeezing.

boar (bor) *noun* **1.** A male pig. **2.** A type of wild pig with tusks.
Boar sounds like **bore**.

board (bord)
noun **1.** A long, flat piece of wood, used for building or making things. **2.** The **board** of a company or organization is the group of people who control it. **3.** Meals provided to paying guests. **4.** A specially marked square or rectangle on which a game is played.
verb To get on or enter a ship, aircraft, or other vehicle.
▶ *verb* **boarding, boarded**

board·er (**bor**-dur) *noun* A person who pays to live in a house and receive meals there.

board·ing (**bor**-ding) *noun* The sport of riding a skateboard or snowboard.

board·ing school (**bor**-ding *skool*) *noun* A school that students may live in during the school year.

boast (bohst)
verb **1.** To brag about something in order to impress people. **2.** If a place **boasts** something, it has something that others would like to have.
noun Speech or writing in which you brag about something you have done, could do, or will do.
▶ *verb* **boasting, boasted** ▶ *adjective* **boastful** ▶ *adverb* **boastfully**

boat (boht)
noun A vessel that travels on water and is used to carry people and goods.
verb To travel in a boat.
▶ *verb* **boating, boated**

boat·house (**boht**-*hous*) *noun* A building where small boats are sheltered or stored.

boat peo·ple (**boht** *pee*-puhl) *noun, plural* People who are forced to leave their country in boats because of the poverty or difficult conditions there.

bob (bahb)
verb To keep moving up and down quickly.
noun A short hairstyle where all the hair is the same length.
▶ *verb* **bobbing, bobbed**

bob·bin (**bah**-bin) *noun* A spool inside a sewing machine or on a loom that holds the thread.

bob·by pin (**bah**-bee *pin*) *noun* A flat hairpin that keeps hair in place.

bob·cat (**bahb**-*kat*) *noun* A small wildcat with reddish-brown fur, black spots, and a short tail. A bobcat is a type of lynx.

bob·o·link (**bah**-buh-*link*) *noun* A North and South American songbird with black, white, and yellow feathers.

bob·sled (**bahb**-*sled*)
noun A long sled with a steering wheel and brakes, used for racing down a steep, icy run.
verb To race in a bobsled.
▶ *verb* **bobsledding, bobsledded**

bob·white (**bahb**-*wite*) *noun* A common North American quail with a reddish-brown body and white, black, and tan markings. A bobwhite's call sounds like its name. ▶ *noun, plural* **bobwhite** or **bobwhites**

bode (bode) *verb* To be a sign of something. ▶ *verb* **boding, boded**

bod·y (**bah**-dee) *noun* **1.** All the physical parts of a person or an animal. **2.** The physical part of something. **3.** Someone who has died; a corpse. **4.** A group of people working together. **5.** A mass of matter.
▶ *noun, plural* **bodies** ▶ *adjective* **bodily** (**bah**-duhl-ee)

B

bod·y·guard (**bah**-dee-*gahrd*) *noun*
A man or woman who protects
someone, especially a famous or
important person.

body mass in·dex (**bah**-dee *mas in*-
deks) *noun* A measure of whether
you are overweight, determined by
dividing your weight by the square of
your height.

bog (bahg)
noun An area of soft, wet land.
verb If you are **bogged down,** you are
stuck and can't make any progress.
▶ *verb* **bogging, bogged** ▶ *adjective*
boggy

bo·gey·man (bu-gee-*man*) *noun*
An imaginary, scary man that
is sometimes used to frighten
children. ▶ *noun, plural* **bogeymen**

bo·gus (**boh**-guhs) *adjective* Fake or not
true.

boil (boil)
verb 1. To heat a liquid to the point
where it bubbles and gives off steam.
2. To cook or clean something in
boiling water.
noun 1. A painful swelling on or under
the skin. 2. The condition of boiling.
▶ *verb* **boiling, boiled** ▶ *adjective*
boiling

boil·er (**boi**-lur) *noun* A device that
heats water for a house or for use in a
heating system.

boil·ing point (**boi**-ling *point*) *noun*
1. The temperature at which a liquid
turns to a gas. The boiling point of
water is 212 degrees Fahrenheit or 100
degrees Celsius. 2. When you reach
your **boiling point,** you are about to
lose your temper.

bois·ter·ous (**boi**-stur-uhs) *adjective*
Noisy and high-spirited. ▶ *noun*
boisterousness ▶ *adverb* **boisterously**

bold (bohld) *adjective* 1. Having or
showing confidence and courage.
2. **Bold** colors stand out because they
are bright and clear.
▶ *adjective* **bolder, boldest** ▶ *adverb*
boldly ▶ *noun* **boldness**

Bo·liv·i·a (buh-**liv**-ee-uh) A country in
central South America. Part of the

Inca Empire in the 15th and early 16th
centuries, it was a Spanish colony
until it became independent in 1825.
Bolivia has two capitals: La Paz, the
administrative capital, and Sucre, the
legislative capital. La Paz, located at
about 12,000 feet (3,660 meters), has
the highest elevation of all the world's
capital cities.

boll wee·vil (bohl wee-vuhl) *noun* A
beetle that lays eggs in cotton plants.

bol·ster (**bohl**-stur)
verb To support or give a boost to
someone or something.
noun A long, narrow pillow or cushion.
▶ *verb* **bolstering, bolstered**

bolt (bohlt)
noun 1. A metal pin or bar that slides
into place and fastens a door or
window. 2. A metal pin that screws
into a nut to fasten things together.
3. A flash of lightning or crack of
thunder. 4. A roll of something, such
as cloth.
verb 1. To run away or move suddenly.
2. If you **bolt your food,** you eat it very
quickly.
▶ *verb* **bolting, bolted**

bomb (bahm)
noun A container filled with
explosives, designed to destroy
someone or something.
verb To attack someone or something
with bombs.
▶ *verb* **bombing, bombed**

bom·bard (bahm-**bahrd**) *verb* 1. To
attack a place with bombs, missiles,
or gunfire. 2. To overwhelm someone
with questions, information, or
complaints.
▶ *verb* **bombarding,
bombarded** ▶ *noun* **bombardment**

bomb·er (**bah**-mur) *noun* 1. A large
airplane that drops bombs on targets.
2. Someone who sets off bombs.

bomb·shell (**bahm**-shel) *noun* 1. A
bomb. 2. An event that is very
surprising, usually not in a good way.

bo·na fide (**boh**-nuh *fide*) *adjective*
1. Genuine or sincere. 2. In good faith,
or without fraud.

B

bond (bahnd)

noun 1. A close connection with or strong feeling for someone. 2. A document that allows companies or governments to raise money. People buy the bonds and are later paid back, with interest added. 3. Something that holds two things together physically.

noun, plural **bonds** The ropes or chains that are used to tie up a prisoner.

verb When you **bond** two things, you make them stick together.

▶ *verb* **bonding, bonded**

bond·age (**bahn**-dij) *noun* The condition of being under the control of someone or something when it is against your will.

bone (bohn) *noun* The hard, whitish tissue that makes up the skeleton of a person or an animal.

bon·fire (**bahn**-*fire*) *noun* A large outdoor fire, typically used to celebrate something, to burn trash, or to send a signal.

bon·go drum (**bahng**-goh *druhm*) *noun* Either of a pair of small connected drums, held between the knees and struck with the fingers.

bon·net (**bah**-nit) *noun* A baby's or woman's hat, usually one with a brim and strings that tie under the chin.

bon·sai (**bahn**-sye) *noun* A miniature tree or shrub that is grown in a pot and shaped by pruning. ▶ *noun, plural* **bonsai**

bo·nus (**boh**-nuhs) *noun* 1. An extra reward or benefit. 2. Something that is unexpected but welcome.

▶ *noun, plural* **bonuses**

bon·y (**boh**-nee) *adjective* 1. Extremely thin or full of bones. 2. Made of bone.

▶ *adjective* **bonier, boniest**

boo (boo)

interjection A word used to surprise or startle someone, or to express dislike or disapproval.

verb To express dislike or disapproval by saying *boo*.

▶ *verb* **boos, booing, booed**

boo·by trap (**boo**-bee *trap*) *noun* 1. A harmless-looking object with a hidden device that explodes when someone or something touches it. 2. A situation that tricks you or catches you by surprise when you're not paying attention.

▶ *verb* **booby-trap**

book (buk)

noun A set of pages that are fastened along one side and put between two covers.

verb To arrange for something ahead of time.

▶ *verb* **booking, booked** ▶ *noun* **booking**

book·case (**buk**-*kase*) *noun* A cabinet or piece of furniture with shelves that hold books.

book·keep·er (**buk**-*kee*-pur) *noun* Someone who keeps financial records for a business or an organization. ▶ *noun* **bookkeeping**

book·let (**buk**-lit) *noun* A small, thin book with a soft cover.

book·mark (**buk**-*mahrk*)

noun 1. A piece of ribbon, paper, or other material used to mark a place in a book. 2. The address of a webpage that you have saved in your browser.

verb To save the address of a webpage by using the "Favorites" or "Bookmarks" feature in your browser.

▶ *verb* **bookmarking, bookmarked**

book·mo·bile (**buk**-muh-*beel*) *noun* A van or truck that is used as a small, mobile library.

book·worm (**buk**-*wurm*) *noun* Someone who loves books and spends a lot of time reading.

boom (boom)

noun 1. A very loud, deep sound. 2. A period of rapid growth or expansion.

verb To speak in a loud, deep voice.

idiom If you **lower the boom** on someone, you punish the person.

▶ *verb* **booming, boomed**

boo·mer·ang (**boo**-muh-*rang*) *noun* A curved stick made so that after it is thrown, it will return to the thrower. It was originally used as a weapon by the Aborigines of Australia.

B

boon (boon) *noun* Something that helps you or makes your life easier.

boor (boor) *noun* A person with bad manners and no consideration for others. ▶ *adjective* **boorish**

boost (boost)
verb 1. To lift someone or something by pushing from below. 2. To increase or encourage something.
noun If something gives you a **boost,** it cheers you up or makes you feel better.
▶ *verb* **boosting, boosted**

boost·er (boo-stur) *noun* 1. A rocket that helps a spacecraft get off the ground. 2. A person or thing that is encouraging or that makes something better. 3. A **booster shot** is an additional injection of a drug that makes the first dose more effective.

boot (boot)
noun A heavy, protective shoe that covers your foot and ankle and sometimes your lower leg.
verb 1. When you **boot up** a computer, you turn it on so that it can start working. 2. To kick something hard, especially the ball in football.
▶ *verb* **booting, booted**

boot·ee or **boot·ie** (**boo**-tee or boo-**tee**) *noun* A knitted sock for a baby.

booth (booth) *noun* 1. A temporary display area that is used to sell or show a product. 2. A restaurant dining area consisting of two benches with a table in between them. 3. A small enclosed place.

boo·ty (**boo**-tee) *noun* Valuable objects that are taken away by force, as by an army after a battle.

bor·der (**bor**-dur)
noun 1. The dividing line between two countries or regions. 2. A decorative band or design around the edge of something.
verb If two countries **border** each another, they share a common boundary.
▶ *verb* **bordering, bordered**

bore (bor)
verb 1. To make someone feel dull and weary. 2. To make a hole in something

with a drill or similar tool. 3. The past tense of **bear.**
noun The hollow part of a gun barrel.
Bore sounds like **boar.** ▶ *verb* **boring, bored**

bored (bord) *adjective* Not interested in what you are doing, or not having anything interesting to do.

bore·dom (**bor**-duhm) *noun* The state or experience of being bored.

bor·ing (**bor**-ing) *adjective* Not at all interesting or engaging.

born (born) *adjective* 1. Brought into life. 2. Naturally gifted at something.
Born sounds like **borne.**

borne (born) *verb* The past participle of **bear. Borne** sounds like **born.**

bor·ough (**bur**-oh) *noun* 1. In some states, a town or area that has its own local government. 2. One of the five political divisions of New York City.
Borough sounds like **burro** and **burrow.**

bor·row (**bor**-oh) *verb* To use something that belongs to someone else, with the understanding that you will return it as soon as you're done with it. ▶ *verb* **borrowing, borrowed**

Bos·ni·a and Her·ze·go·vi·na (**bahz**-nee-uh and *hert*-suh-goh-**vee**-nuh) A country on the Balkan Peninsula in Southeastern Europe. Bosnia and Herzegovina declared independence from the former Yugoslavia in 1992. Almost completely landlocked, it has a small coastline of only about 12 miles on the Adriatic Sea.

bos·om (**buz**-uhm or **boo**-zuhm)
noun The front part of a person's chest.
adjective Close and dear.

boss (baws)
noun Someone who is in charge of a company's employees or who has control or authority.
verb **boss around** To give orders to someone.
▶ *noun, plural* **bosses** ▶ *verb* **bosses, bossing, bossed**

bos·sy (**baw**-see) *adjective* A **bossy** person likes to give orders. ▶ *adjective* **bossier, bossiest** ▶ *noun* **bossiness**

B

bot (baht) *noun* 1. Short for **robot.**
2. A computer program that runs continuously on the Internet, doing a repetitive job such as crawling the web to get information for a search engine. While many bots are useful, some can be dangerous, such as those used by hackers to steal passwords and credit card numbers.

bot·a·ny (**bah**-tuh-nee) *noun* The scientific study of plant life. ▶ *noun* **botanist** ▶ *adjective* **botanical** (buh-**tan**-i-kuhl)

both (bohth)
pronoun Two things or people.
adjective Referring to the one and the other.
conjunction Equally, or as well.

both·er (**bah**-THur)
verb 1. If something **bothers** you, it disturbs or annoys you. 2. To take the trouble to do something.
noun Something that annoys you.
▶ *verb* **bothering, bothered**

Botox (**boh**-tahks) *noun* A trademark for an injected drug that relaxes muscles and makes wrinkles appear to be less deep.

Bot·swa·na (baht-**swah**-nuh) A country in southern Africa. One of Africa's poorest countries when it gained independence from Britain in 1966, Botswana now has one of the world's fastest-growing economies. It is the largest diamond producer in Africa.

bot·tle (**bah**-tuhl)
noun A glass or plastic container with a narrow neck and mouth and no handle.
verb 1. To put in a bottle. 2. If you **bottle up** something, you hold it in.
▶ *verb* **bottling, bottled**

bot·tle·neck (**bah**-tuhl-nek) *noun* A narrow section of road where traffic often backs up.

bot·tom (**bah**-tuhm)
noun 1. The lowest or deepest part of something. 2. A person's buttocks. 3. The most basic part of something.
adjective Lowest.

bough (bou) *noun* A tree branch, especially a large one.

bought (bawt) *verb* The past tense and past participle of **buy.**

boul·der (**bohl**-dur) *noun* A large, rounded rock.

bou·le·vard (**bul**-uh-*vahrd*) *noun* A wide city street that often has grass, trees, or flowers planted down the middle or along either side.

bounce (bouns)
verb 1. To move quickly in the opposite direction after hitting something. 2. If you **bounce a check,** you don't have enough money in your bank account to cover it.
noun If someone has lots of **bounce,** he or she is very energetic and cheerful.
▶ *verb* **bouncing, bounced** ▶ *adjective* **bouncy**

bound (bound)
verb 1. The past tense and past participle of **bind.** 2. To walk or run with leaps and jumps.
adjective If something is **bound** to happen, it will certainly or almost certainly take place.
noun, plural 1. A boundary or limit of an area, subject, or field. 2. Someone or something that is **out of bounds** is beyond the boundaries or limits that have been set. In sports, **out of bounds** means out of the field of play.
▶ *verb* **bounding, bounded**

bound·a·ry (**boun**-dur-ee) *noun* The line, fence, or other object that separates one area from another. ▶ *noun, plural* **boundaries**

boun·ti·ful (**boun**-ti-fuhl) *adjective* More than enough; generous; plentiful.

boun·ty (**boun**-tee) *noun* 1. Something that is given or that exists in generous amounts. 2. A reward offered for the capture of a criminal or a harmful animal.
▶ *noun, plural* **bounties**

bou·quet (boh-**kay** or boo-**kay**) *noun* 1. A bunch of picked or cut flowers. 2. The pleasant smell that something has.

bout (bout) *noun* 1. An attack or a spell. 2. An athletic match or contest.

bou·tique (boo-**teek**) *noun* A small shop that sells fashionable clothes or other specialty items.

B

bow
> *verb* (bou) To bend the head or upper body as a sign of respect, greeting, or shame, or to accept applause.
> *noun* **1.** (boh) A knot with two loops and two ends. **2.** (bou) The front section of a ship or boat. **3.** (boh) A long, flat piece of wood with horsehair stretched between the ends, used for playing instruments like the violin or the cello. **4.** (boh) A curved, flexible piece of wood with a string stretched between the two ends, used for shooting arrows.
> ▶ *verb* **bowing, bowed**

bow·els (**bou**-uhlz) *noun, plural* Intestines.

bowl (bohl)
> *noun* A round, open dish for food or liquid.
> *verb* When you **bowl**, you roll a heavy ball down an alley to knock over wooden pins.
> *idiom* When something **bowls you over,** it greatly surprises you.
> ▶ *verb* **bowling, bowled** ▶ *noun* **bowler**

bow·leg·ged (**boh**-leg-id) *adjective* If someone is **bowlegged,** he or she has legs that are curved outward so that the knees do not touch when the ankles are together.

bowl·ing (**boh**-ling) *noun* A game played by rolling a heavy ball down an alley at wooden pins.

bowl·ing al·ley (**boh**-ling al-ee) *noun* A building where people go to bowl.

bow tie (**boh** tye) *noun* A necktie in the shape of a bow, often worn on formal occasions.

box (bahks)
> *noun* A container with a flat bottom and sides.
> *verb* **1.** To fight someone with your fists. **2.** To put something in a box. **3.** If you **box** someone or something **in,** you create a situation where escape is impossible.
> ▶ *noun, plural* **boxes** ▶ *verb* **boxes, boxing, boxed** ▶ *noun* **boxer** ▶ *noun* **boxing**

box·car (**bahks**-kahr) *noun* An enclosed railroad car with sliding doors to load and unload freight.

box of·fice (**bahks** aw-fis) *noun* The ticket office at a theater. It is also a term used to describe how successful a play or movie is.

boy (boi) *noun* A male child or young person.

boy·cott (**boi**-kaht)
> *verb* To refuse to buy something or do business with someone as a punishment or protest.
> *noun* Refusal to do business as a punishment or protest.
> ▶ *verb* **boycotting, boycotted**

boy·friend (**boi**-frend) *noun* **1.** The man or boy with whom someone is having a romantic relationship. **2.** A male friend.

boy·hood (**boi**-hud) *noun* The time during which someone is a boy.

bra (brah) *noun* A women's undergarment that covers and supports the breasts. Bra is short for *brassiere.*

brace (brase)
> *noun* An object fastened to another object to support it.
> *noun, plural* **braces** A device worn inside your mouth, with wires attached to your teeth to straighten them.
> *verb* **1.** To fasten or strengthen with a brace. **2.** If you **brace yourself,** you prepare yourself for an attack or a shock.
> ▶ *verb* **bracing, braced**

brace·let (**brase**-lit) *noun* A band or chain worn around the arm or wrist.

brack·et (**brak**-it)
> *noun* **1.** A rigid support that is attached to a wall and used to hold up a shelf or cupboard. **2.** A grouping of similar people or things.
> *noun, plural* **Brackets** are the two symbols [ ] that are used to separate some material from the main written text.
> *verb* To put inside brackets.
> ▶ *verb* **bracketing, bracketed**

brag (brag) *verb* To talk in a boastful way. ▶ *verb* **bragging, bragged**

B

braid (brayd)
noun A length of hair or other material that has been divided into three or more parts and woven together.
verb To form a braid using three or four strands of hair or material.
▶ *verb* **braiding, braided**

Braille (brayl) *noun* A system of writing and printing for blind people that uses raised dots for letters and numbers.

brain (brayn) *noun* 1. The organ inside your skull that controls your body's activities as well as your thoughts, memories, and emotions. 2. Your mind or the power of your intelligence.

brain·storm (brayn-*storm*)
verb When people **brainstorm,** they get together to come up with ideas or a solution to a problem.
noun A great idea that comes to you all of a sudden.
▶ *verb* **brainstorming, brainstormed** ▶ *noun* **brainstorming**

brain·wash (brayn-*wahsh*) *verb* To force someone to accept or believe something by using various forms of mental pressure. ▶ *verb* **brainwashes, brainwashing, brainwashed** ▶ *noun* **brainwashing**

brain·y (bray-nee) *adjective* (informal) Very intelligent. ▶ *adjective* **brainier, brainiest**

brake (brake)
noun A device to slow down or stop a vehicle.
verb To slow down or stop a vehicle by using a brake.
Brake sounds like **break.** ▶ *verb* **braking, braked**

brake·man (brake-*muhn*) *noun* 1. A worker on a train who helps the conductor. Originally, the brakeman worked the brakes on the train. 2. The end person on a bobsled team, who operates the brakes.
▶ *noun, plural* **brakemen**

bram·ble (bram-buhl) *noun* A prickly bush or shrub, such as the blackberry or raspberry.

bran (bran) *noun* The outer covering of wheat or other grains that is sifted out when flour is made. Bran is used in baked goods and cereals.

branch (branch)
noun 1. A part of a tree that grows out of the main trunk or a bough. 2. A smaller extension of a river, railroad, or road that runs in a different direction. 3. A **branch** of a company or organization is one of its stores or offices in a particular area.
verb 1. To divide into two or more parts that go in different directions. 2. If you **branch out,** you start doing something new.
▶ *noun, plural* **branches** ▶ *verb* **branches, branching, branched**

brand (brand)
noun 1. A name that identifies a product or the company that makes it. 2. The mark put on a farm or ranch animal to identify its owner.
verb 1. To burn a mark on the skin of cattle and other animals to show who owns them. 2. To call by a shameful name.
▶ *verb* **branding, branded**

bran·dish (bran-dish) *verb* To hold up something, such as a weapon, and wave it around. ▶ *verb* **brandishes, brandishing, brandished**

brand-new (bran-noo) *adjective* Never used before; completely new, or recently purchased.

brand·y (bran-dee) *noun* A strong alcoholic drink made from wine or fruit juice.

brass (bras)
noun A shiny yellow metal made from copper and zinc.
noun, plural **the brasses** Musical instruments made of brass.
adjective The **brass** section of an orchestra is composed of musical instruments that are made of brass, such as the trumpet and the trombone.
▶ *noun, plural* **brasses** ▶ *adjective* **brassy**

brass rub·bing (bras *ruhb*-ing) *noun* A copy of a picture carved on a brass plate, made by rubbing crayon or chalk over a piece of paper laid on top of the plate.

B

brat (brat) *noun* An unpleasant or spoiled child who misbehaves.

bra·va·do (bruh-**vah**-doh) *noun* If you are full of **bravado,** you try to impress someone by pretending to be braver or more confident than you really are.

brave (brave)
adjective If you are **brave,** you have courage and are willing to face danger, difficulty, or pain.
verb If you **brave** something, you face it with courage and determination.
noun In history, a Native American warrior.
▶ *adjective* **braver, bravest** ▶ *verb* **braving, braved** ▶ *noun* **bravery** ▶ *adverb* **bravely**

bra·vo (**brah**-voh *or* brah-**voh**) *interjection* Well done!

brawl (brawl)
noun A rough or noisy fight.
verb To fight, especially in a rough and noisy way.
▶ *verb* **brawling, brawled**

bray (bray)
verb 1. When a donkey **brays,** it makes a loud, harsh cry. 2. When a person **brays,** he or she speaks or laughs in a way that sounds like a donkey.
noun The noise made by a donkey, or a noise that sounds like this.
▶ *verb* **braying, brayed**

braz·en (**bray**-zuhn) *adjective* 1. Bold, self-assured, and shameless.
2. Sounding harsh or loud.
▶ *adverb* **brazenly**

Bra·zil (bruh-**zil**) The largest and most populous country in South America. It is known for its diverse wildlife, vast natural resources, and fast-growing economy.

breach (breech)
verb To break through something; to make a hole in something.
noun 1. A failure to live up to a law or promise. 2. A break in a relationship.
▶ *verb* **breaches, breaching, breached** ▶ *noun, plural* **breaches**

bread (bred) *noun* 1. A food made from flour, water, and yeast, shaped into loaves and baked. 2. (slang) Money.

breadth (bredth) *noun* 1. The distance or measurement from one side of something to the other. 2. Wide range or scope.

bread·win·ner (**bred**-win-ur) *noun* Someone whose earnings are the main source of support for a family or household.

break (brayk)
verb 1. To cause something to crack, snap off, or separate into pieces. 2. To damage something so that it doesn't work. 3. To separate into pieces, usually by force. 4. To stop. 5. To do better than. 6. If someone **breaks** the rules, the person fails to obey them. 7. **break in** To force your way into a building. 8. **break out** To start suddenly.
noun 1. A short rest, pause, or vacation. 2. A gap or opening, especially one resulting from breaking. 3. An opportunity, often unexpected, that provides a chance for success.
Break sounds like **brake.** ▶ *verb* **breaking, broke** (brohk), **broken** (**brohk**-in) ▶ *noun* **breakage** ▶ *adjective* **broken**

break·a·ble (**bray**-kuh-buhl) *adjective* Subject to breaking; likely to break if dropped.

break danc·ing (**brayk** dan-sing) *noun* A very energetic form of street dancing that involves gymnastic skills and touching the ground with various parts of the body. ▶ *noun* **break-dancer** ▶ *verb* **break-dance**

break·down (**brayk**-doun) *noun* 1. If your car has a **breakdown,** it stops moving because something has gone wrong with it. 2. A sudden collapse in someone's health. 3. A case of something failing or falling apart.

break·er (**bray**-kur) *noun* A big sea wave that breaks into foam when it reaches the shore.

break·fast (**brek**-fuhst) *noun* The first meal of the day, or a meal eaten in the morning.

break-in (**brayk**-in) *noun* The act of forcibly entering a building or house in order to steal things.

B

break·through (**brayk**-throo) *noun* A successful, often sudden development that makes progress possible.

break·wa·ter (**brayk**-*waw*-tur) *noun* A barrier that protects a harbor or beach from the force of waves.

breast (brest) *noun* **1.** One of the glands in a female mammal that can produce milk to feed her young. **2.** The chest of a person or an animal.

breast·bone (**brest**-*bone*) *noun* The flat bone in your chest that is attached to your ribs.

breast·stroke (**brest**-*stroke*) *noun* A style of swimming face down in which you stretch your arms out in front of your head and then sweep them back to your sides while kicking your legs like a frog.

breath (breth) *noun* **1.** The air that you take into and send out of your lungs. **2.** If you are **out of breath,** you are having trouble breathing or are gasping for air. **3.** When you say something **under your breath,** you say it in a very quiet voice.

breathe (breeTH) *verb* **1.** To take air into and send it out of your lungs. **2.** To be alive, as shown by air entering and leaving your body. **3.** To whisper.
▶ *verb* **breathing, breathed**

breath·er (**bree**-THur) *noun* A short pause or rest.

breath·less (**breth**-lis) *adjective* **1.** Out of breath. **2.** If you are **breathless,** you are experiencing a strong feeling.
▶ *adverb* **breathlessly**

breath·tak·ing (**breth**-*tay*-king) *adjective* Very beautiful, impressive, or awe-inspiring. ▶ *adverb* **breathtakingly**

breech·es (**brich**-iz) *noun, plural* Old-fashioned knee-length pants that are tight at the bottom.

breed (breed)
verb **1.** To keep animals or plants under controlled conditions so they produce more and better quality offspring. **2.** When animals **breed,** they mate and give birth to their young.
noun A particular type of plant or animal.
▶ *verb* **breeding, bred** (bred)
▶ *noun* **breeder**

breed·ing (**bree**-ding) *noun* **1.** The mating or reproduction of animals, or the activity of controlling this. **2.** Good manners that come from being well brought up.

breeze (breez)
noun A light wind.
verb To move quickly and easily.
▶ *verb* **breezing, breezed** ▶ *adjective* **breezy**

brev·i·ty (**brev**-i-tee) *noun* The quality of being brief or short, especially with reference to language or to an event.

brew (broo)
verb **1.** To make tea or coffee by mixing it with hot water. **2.** To make beer. **3.** To start developing.
noun A brewed concoction of unusual ingredients.
▶ *verb* **brewing, brewed**

brew·er·y (**broo**-ur-ee) *noun* A place where beer is made. ▶ *noun, plural* **breweries**

bribe (bribe)
noun Money or a gift that you offer someone to persuade the person to do what you want him or her to do.
verb To persuade someone to do something by offering them money or a gift.
▶ *verb* **bribing, bribed** ▶ *noun* **bribery**

bric-a-brac (**brik**-uh-*brak*) *noun, plural* Small objects that are used as ornaments and that have only sentimental value.

brick (brik) *noun* A block of clay, baked in the sun or in a kiln and used for building.

bride (bride) *noun* A woman on her wedding day or one who has just gotten married. ▶ *adjective* **bridal**

bride·groom (**bride**-*groom*) *noun* A man on his wedding day or one who has just gotten married.

brides·maid (**bridez**-*mayd*) *noun* A female relative or close friend of a bride, who helps the bride get ready for the wedding and who assists at the ceremony.

B

bridge (brij)
noun 1. A structure built over a river, railroad, or road that allows people or vehicles to cross to the other side. 2. A card game in which a deck of cards is divided evenly among the four players. 3. The bony part of your nose between your eyes.
verb 1. To connect two places separated by water. 2. To connect two separated things.
idiom If something **bridges a gap**, it makes the difference between two groups or things seem less important.
▸ *verb* **bridging, bridged**

bri·dle (**brye**-duhl)
noun A harness that fits around a horse's head and is used to guide or control the horse.
verb To put a bridle on.
▸ *verb* **bridling, bridled**

bri·dle path (**brye**-duhl *path*) *noun* A track or path for riding or walking horses.

brief (breef)
adjective 1. Lasting only a little while. 2. Using as few words as possible.
verb To give information, instructions, or advice that will prepare someone.
noun An outline of the main information and arguments of a legal case.
▸ *verb* **briefing, briefed** ▸ *adjective* **briefer, briefest** ▸ *adverb* **briefly**

brief·case (**breef**-*kase*) *noun* A flat, rectangular bag with a handle, used for carrying books and papers.

bri·er (**brye**-ur) *noun* A prickly twig, or the shrub that it grows on.

brig (brig) *noun* 1. A military prison, usually on a ship. 2. A sailing ship with two masts and square sails.

bri·gade (bri-**gayd**) *noun* 1. A unit of an army, larger than a battalion but smaller than a division. 2. A group of workers organized for a special purpose.

brig·and (**brig**-uhnd) *noun* (old-fashioned) A member of a gang of robbers.

bright (brite) *adjective* 1. Giving out or reflecting a large amount of light. 2. A bright color is bold and vivid. 3. Smart.
▸ *adjective* **brighter, brightest** ▸ *noun* **brightness** ▸ *adverb* **brightly**

bright·en (**brye**-tuhn) *verb* To make something brighter or to become brighter. ▸ *verb* **brightening, brightened**

bril·liant (**bril**-yuhnt) *adjective* 1. Full of light or shining brightly. 2. Very smart. 3. Splendid, or terrific.
▸ *noun* **brilliance** ▸ *adverb* **brilliantly**

brim (brim) *noun* 1. The edge of a hat that sticks out over the face and neck of the person wearing it. 2. The edge of a cup or glass.

brine (brine) *noun* Seawater, or water that is very salty.

bring (bring) *verb* 1. To take someone or something with you. 2. To cause something to happen. 3. To sell for. 4. **bring out** To introduce a product and start selling it. 5. **bring up** To mention something. 6. **bring up** To raise a child.
▸ *verb* **bringing, brought** (brawt)

brink (bringk) *noun* 1. The edge of something, before it drops off steeply or meets the water. 2. **on the brink** The point at which something is about to begin.

brisk (brisk) *adjective* 1. Quick and lively. 2. If the wind or weather is **brisk**, it is chilly but refreshing.
▸ *adjective* **brisker, briskest** ▸ *adverb* **briskly**

bris·tle (**bris**-uhl)
noun A stiff animal or man-made hair, used to make a brush.
verb To show anger.
▸ *verb* **bristling, bristled** ▸ *adjective* **bristly**

Brit·ish Co·lum·bi·a (*brit*-ish kuh-**luhm**-bee-uh) The westernmost province of Canada. British Columbia has 17,000 miles of rugged coastline and about 6,000 islands, most of which are uninhabited.

brit·tle (**brit**-uhl) *adjective* Likely to snap off, crack, or break. ▸ *adjective* **brittler, brittlest**

broach (brohch) *verb* When you **broach** a subject, you bring it up for discussion. ▸ *verb* **broaches, broaching, broached**

B

B

broad (brawd) *adjective* **1.** Wider than usual from side to side. **2.** Including many things. **3.** Without a lot of detail.
▶ *adjective* **broader, broadest** ▶ *adverb* **broadly**

broad·band (**brawd**-band) *noun* A fast Internet connection over a cable modem or a telephone line. *adjective* Of or having to do with a broadband connection.

broad·cast (**brawd**-kast) *verb* To send out a radio or television program to its audience. *noun* A radio or television program.
▶ *verb* **broadcasting, broadcasted** ▶ *noun* **broadcaster** ▶ *noun* **broadcasting**

broad·en (**braw**-duhn) *verb* To make something broader or more tolerant. ▶ *verb* **broadening, broadened**

broad·mind·ed (**brawd**-mine-did) *adjective* If you are **broad-minded**, you are open to new ideas and other people's views.

bro·cade (broh-**kayd**) *noun* Fabric woven with a raised pattern.

broc·co·li (**brah**-kuh-lee) *noun* A vegetable with many clusters of green flower buds on thick stalks.

bro·chure (broh-**shoor**) *noun* A booklet with pictures that advertises or gives information about something.

broil (broil) *verb* **1.** To cook by exposing food directly to the source of heat from above. **2.** To be or make very hot.
▶ *verb* **broiling, broiled**

broil·er (**broi**-lur) *noun* The part of an oven that heats food from above.

broke (broke) *verb* The past tense of **break**. *adjective* (informal) Having no money.

bro·ken (**broh**-kuhn) *verb* The past participle of **break**. *adjective* **1.** In pieces; not whole. **2.** Not working. **3.** An animal that is **broken** can be controlled by humans.

bron·chi·al tubes (**brahng**-kee-uhl *toobz*) *noun, plural* Tubes in your lungs that air passes through when you breathe.

bron·chi·tis (brahng-**kye**-tis) *noun* A disease of the bronchial tubes inside your lungs.

bron·co (**brahng**-koh) *noun* A wild horse found in the western United States.

bronze (brahnz) *noun* **1.** A yellowish-brown metal that is a mixture of copper and tin. **2.** A yellowish-brown color. *adjective* Being yellowish brown in color. *verb* If you **bronze** yourself, you get a dark suntan.
▶ *verb* **bronzing, bronzed**

Bronze Age (brahnz *ayj*) *noun* A period of history, before the introduction of iron, when bronze was commonly used to make tools and weapons. This period occurred at different times in different parts of the world.

brooch (brohch *or* brooch) *noun* A large, decorative pin that you wear at or near your neck. ▶ *noun, plural* **brooches**

brood (brood) *verb* To worry or think deeply about something. *noun* **1.** A group of young birds who all hatched at the same time. **2.** (informal) All the children in one family.
▶ *verb* **brooding, brooded**

brook (bruk) *noun* A small stream; a creek.

broom (broom) *noun* A long-handled brush, used for sweeping floors.

broth (brawth) *noun* The liquid that remains after meat or vegetables have been cooked in water.

broth·er (**bruhTH**-ur) *noun* A boy or man who has the same parents as another person. ▶ *adjective* **brotherly**

broth·er·hood (**bruhTH**-ur-*hud*) *noun* **1.** Warm feelings and goodwill among people. **2.** A group that works or lives together in a brotherly way.

brother-in-law (**bruhTH**-ur-in-*law*) *noun* Someone's **brother-in-law** is the brother of his or her spouse or the husband of his or her sister. ▶ *noun, plural* **brothers-in-law**

brought (brawt) *verb* The past tense and past participle of **bring**.

brow (brou) *noun* 1. A person's forehead. 2. The upper part of a steep place.

brown (broun)
noun The color of chocolate, leather, or coffee.
verb To make something brown, especially by cooking it.
adjective Being brown in color.
▶ *verb* **browning, browned** ▶ *adjective* **browner, brownest**

brown·ie (**brou**-nee) *noun* A square piece of a heavy, rich chocolate cake.

brown·out (**broun**-out) *noun* A partial loss of electrical power that causes the lights to dim.

browse (brouz) *verb* 1. To look at something in a casual way. 2. To eat by nibbling on twigs, leaves, or shoots. 3. To spend time looking at different things that interest you on the Internet.
▶ *verb* **browsing, browsed**

brows·er (**brou**-zur) *noun* 1. A computer program that lets you find and look through webpages or other data. 2. An animal that eats by browsing.

bruise (brooz)
noun A discolored area that appears when blood vessels burst underneath your skin, usually because you have fallen or been hit by something.
verb To develop a bruise or to cause one.
▶ *verb* **bruising, bruised** ▶ *adjective* **bruised**

brunch (bruhnch) *noun* A late-morning meal that combines breakfast and lunch, typically eaten on a weekend. ▶ *noun, plural* **brunches**

Bru·nei (bru-**nye**) A Southeast Asian country on the north coast of the island of Borneo. The same family has ruled Brunei for more than six centuries.

bru·nette (broo-**net**)
adjective Having brown or black hair.
noun A person with brown or black hair.

brush (bruhsh)
noun 1. An object with bristles fastened to a handle, used for scrubbing, sweeping, painting, or smoothing hair. 2. An area of land where small trees and shrubs grow.
verb 1. To clean, groom, or apply with a brush. 2. To touch something lightly or gently.
▶ *noun, plural* **brushes** ▶ *verb* **brushes, brushing, brushed**

Brus·sels sprout (**bruhs**-uhlz *sprout*) *noun* A vegetable that looks like a small head of cabbage.

bru·tal (**broo**-tuhl) *adjective* Extremely cruel or violent. ▶ *noun* **brutality** (broo-**tal**-i-tee) ▶ *adverb* **brutally**

brute (broot)
noun A savage or violent person or animal.
adjective Involving physical strength rather than intelligence.

bub·ble (**buhb**-uhl)
noun 1. One of the tiny balls of gas that rise to the surface of boiling water, soda, or other fizzy drinks. 2. A thin film of liquid surrounding a ball of air or some other gas. 3. A **bubble** in a market is a situation where the price of something becomes higher than its actual worth.
verb To form or produce bubbles.
▶ *verb* **bubbling, bubbled**

bub·bly (**buhb**-lee) *adjective* 1. If a liquid is **bubbly**, it is full of bubbles. 2. If a person is **bubbly**, he or she is very cheerful and talkative.

buc·ca·neer (**buhk**-uh-**neer**) *noun* A pirate, especially one who attacked Spanish ships in the Caribbean in the 17th century.

buck (buhk)
noun 1. A male deer, antelope, or rabbit. 2. (slang) A dollar.
verb 1. If a horse **bucks**, it jumps in the air with its back arched. 2. To stubbornly resist something or go against it.
idiom If you **pass the buck,** you shift the responsibility for something to someone else.
▶ *verb* **bucking, bucked**

buck·et (**buhk**-it) *noun* A plastic, wooden, or metal container with a handle, used for carrying liquids or other things.

B

buck·le (**buhk**-uhl)
noun A flat frame with a pin, used to fasten shoes, belts, or straps.
verb 1. To collapse under pressure.
2. To connect a strap or belt using a buckle. 3. **buckle down** To work very hard.
▸ *verb* **buckling, buckled**

buck·skin (**buhk**-skin) *noun* A strong, soft material made from the skin of a deer or sheep.

buck·tooth (**buhk**-tooth) *noun* A longer front tooth that sticks out. ▸ *noun, plural* **buckteeth**

buck·wheat (**buhk**-weet) *noun* A plant with small seeds, used as cattle feed or made into flour.

bud (buhd)
noun A small knob on a plant that grows into a leaf, shoot, or flower.
verb To develop buds.
▸ *verb* **budding, budded**

Bud·dha (**boo**-duh) *noun* 1. The man whose teachings are the basis of Buddhism. He lived in India around 500 B.C. 2. A statue or picture of Buddha.

Bud·dhism (boo-*diz*-uhm) *noun* A way of life based on the teachings of Buddha. Buddhists believe that wanting things is the cause of most suffering, and that birth and death is a cycle that repeats again and again for everyone. ▸ *noun* **Buddhist** ▸ *adjective* **Buddhist**

bud·ding (**buhd**-ing) *adjective* In the early stages of maturity, or gaining skill.

bud·dy (**buhd**-ee) *noun* A close friend; a pal. ▸ *noun, plural* **buddies**

budge (buhj) *verb* 1. To make or cause a slight movement. 2. To give in or change your opinion.
▸ *verb* **budging, budged**

budg·et (**buhj**-it)
noun A plan for how much money you will earn and spend during a particular period of time.
verb If you **budget** your money, you plan how you will spend it.
adjective Not very expensive; suitable for somone on a budget.
▸ *verb* **budgeting, budgeted** ▸ *adjective* **budgetary**

buff (buhf)
noun 1. A yellowish-beige color.
2. (informal) Someone who is very interested in a subject and knows a lot about it.
adjective Being buff in color.
verb To polish something.
▸ *verb* **buffing, buffed**

buf·fa·lo (**buhf**-uh-loh) *noun* 1. A type of wild ox with horns that curve backward, found in Europe, Africa, and Asia. 2. An American bison.
▸ *noun, plural* **buffaloes** or **buffalos** or **buffalo**

buff·er (**buhf**-ur)
noun 1. Something that softens a blow or forms a protective barrier.
2. Someone who keeps opposing groups or individuals from harming each other or coming into direct contact.
verb To soften or cushion a blow or form a protective barrier.
▸ *verb* **buffering, buffered**

buf·fet
verb (**buhf**-it) To strike repeatedly.
noun (buh-**fay**) 1. A meal in which people serve themselves from a table on which many different foods are laid out. 2. A piece of furniture with a flat top for serving food and drawers for storing dishes and silverware.
▸ *verb* **buffeting, buffeted**

bug (buhg)
noun 1. A small insect. 2. An illness caused by a germ. 3. An error in a computer program or system.
verb 1. To hide microphones in a place in order to hear what people are saying. 2. (informal) If people or things **bug** you, they bother or annoy you.
▸ *verb* **bugging, bugged**

bug·gy (**buhg**-ee) *noun* 1. A light carriage with two wheels pulled by a horse. 2. A baby carriage.
▸ *noun, plural* **buggies**

B

bu·gle (byoo-guhl) *noun* A musical instrument shaped like a trumpet but without valves. Bugles are often used in the army to send signals to the troops. ▶ *noun* **bugler**

build (bild)
verb 1. To make something by putting parts or materials together. 2. **build up** To gradually increase or develop. *noun* The way a person's body is put together.
▶ *verb* **building, built**

build·ing (bil-ding) *noun* 1. A structure with walls and a roof, such as a house or a factory. 2. The process of making something that is intended to last a long time.

built-in (bilt-*in*) *adjective* Built as a permanent part of something.

bulb (buhlb) *noun* 1. The underground, onion-shaped part of some plants that stores food from which the plants grow. 2. The part of an electric light that glows when switched on.

Bul·gar·i·a (buhl-gair-ee-uh) A country in Southeastern Europe whose eastern boundary lies on the Black Sea. It became a communist state after World War II, but in 1990 Bulgaria began its transition to a democracy. It is now a member of the European Union.

bulge (buhlj)
verb To swell or stick out.
noun A small area that sticks out from a surface.
▶ *verb* **bulging, bulged**

bulk (buhlk) *noun* 1. Large size. 2. The **bulk** of something is the greater part of it. 3. When you buy something **in bulk,** you buy it in large quantities, usually for a lower price.

bulk·y (buhl-kee) *adjective* 1. Large and awkward to handle. 2. Taking up a lot of space.
▶ *adjective* **bulkier, bulkiest**

bull (bul) *noun* 1. An adult male of the cattle family. 2. An adult male of a large species of animals, such as elephants, seals, moose, or whales.

bull·dog (bul-*dawg*) *noun* A strong dog with a round head, powerful jaws, and short legs.

bull·doz·er (bul-*doh*-zur) *noun* A powerful tractor with a broad, curved blade in the front, used for clearing ground.

bul·let (bul-it) *noun* 1. A metal object fired from a gun, usually shaped like a pointed cylinder or ball. 2. A dot or symbol that is printed before items in a list so that they stand out.
▶ *adjective* **bulleted**

bul·le·tin (bul-i-tin) *noun* An official statement or brief news summary, broadcast on television or the radio.

bul·le·tin board (bul-i-tin *bord*) *noun* 1. A place on a wall where people can put signs and notices that they want others to see. 2. A place on the Internet where anyone, or members of an organization, can put notices for others to see.

bul·let·proof (bul-it-*proof*) *adjective* Something that is **bulletproof** is able to resist bullets.

bull·fight (bul-*fite*) *noun* A public entertainment in which people fight against bulls, popular in Spain, Portugal, and parts of Latin America. ▶ *noun* **bullfighter**

bull·frog (bul-*frawg*) *noun* A large frog with a deep croak.

bul·lion (bul-yuhn) *noun* Gold or silver shaped into bars.

bull's-eye (bulz-*eye*) *noun* The center of a target that is usually round and is used for archery or darts.

bul·ly (bul-ee)
verb 1. To frighten or pick on people who are smaller or weaker than you are. 2. If you **bully** someone **into** something, you make him or her do it by using force or threats.
noun Someone who uses force and threats to intimidate others.
▶ *verb* **bullies, bullying, bullied** ▶ *noun, plural* **bullies**

bum·ble·bee (buhm-buhl-*bee*) *noun* A large, hairy bee with yellow and black stripes that hums when it flies.

B

bump (buhmp)
verb 1. To knock or run into something. 2. If you **bump into** someone, you meet the person by chance. 3. To move or travel in a jolting way.
noun 1. A light blow or collision. 2. A round lump or swelling on the skin.
▶ *verb* **bumping, bumped**

bump·er (**buhm**-pur)
noun The horizontal bar or projecting piece on the front or back of a vehicle that helps protect it in an accident.
adjective Very large.

bump·y (**buhm**-pee) *adjective* Very uneven or full of bumps. ▶ *adjective* **bumpier, bumpiest**

bun (buhn) *noun* 1. A round bread roll. 2. A tight, round knot of hair worn at the back of the head.

bunch (buhnch)
noun A group of people or things of the same kind.
verb To bring or come together.
▶ *noun, plural* **bunches** ▶ *verb* **bunches, bunching, bunched**

bun·dle (**buhn**-duhl)
verb 1. To tie, wrap, or gather things together. 2. To push or carry someone in a forceful way. 3. To sell or deliver software programs together rather than separately.
noun A number of similar things grouped or tied together.
▶ *verb* **bundling, bundled**

bun·ga·low (**buhng**-guh-*loh*) *noun* A small house, usually with only one floor.

bun·gee (**buhn**-jee) *noun* An elastic cord with hooks at either end, used to hold things in place.

bun·gle (**buhng**-guhl) *verb* To do something badly or clumsily, resulting in failure or the wrong outcome. ▶ *verb* **bungling, bungled**

bunk (buhngk)
noun 1. A narrow bed built into or against a wall. 2. **bunk bed** A piece of furniture consisting of two beds, one stacked on top of another.
verb To sleep in a bed or spend the night.
▶ *verb* **bunking, bunked**

bun·ker (**buhng**-kur) *noun* 1. An underground shelter, especially during wartime. 2. A sand trap on a golf course.

bun·ny (**buhn**-ee) *noun* (informal) A rabbit. ▶ *noun, plural* **bunnies**

Bun·sen burn·er (**buhn**-suhn *bur*-nur) *noun* A device used in laboratories that burns gas to provide a small, hot flame.

bunt (buhnt) *verb* To tap a baseball lightly with a bat, so that the ball doesn't go very far. ▶ *verb* **bunting, bunted**

bun·ting (**buhn**-ting) *noun* 1. A light cloth used for making flags. 2. Decorations made of the same fabric and colors as the American flag.

bu·oy (**boo**-ee *or* boi) *noun* A floating marker, often with a bell or a light, that warns boats of underwater dangers or shows them where to go.

buoy·ant (**boi**-uhnt *or* **boo**-yuhnt) *adjective* 1. Able to float or stay afloat. 2. Cheerful and lighthearted.
▶ *adverb* **buoyantly** ▶ *noun* **buoyancy**

bur·den (**bur**-duhn)
noun 1. A heavy load that has to be carried. 2. A serious task or responsibility. 3. A source of great worry.
verb To load or overload someone.
▶ *verb* **burdening, burdened** ▶ *adjective* **burdensome**

bu·reau (**byoor**-oh) *noun* 1. A chest of drawers; a dresser. 2. An office or business that provides a specific service or kind of information.

burg·er (**bur**-gur) *noun* A sandwich consisting of a flat, round piece of beef or other food on a bun. Burger is short for *hamburger*.

bur·glar (**bur**-glur) *noun* Someone who breaks into a building and steals something. ▶ *noun* **burglary**

bur·i·al (**ber**-ee-uhl) *noun* The placing of a dead body in the earth or sea.

Bur·ki·na Fa·so (bur-**kee**-nuh **fah**-soh) A landlocked country in West Africa formerly known as Upper Volta. It

has the largest elephant population
in West Africa, and its wildlife
includes monkeys, hippos, lions, and
antelopes. Burkina Faso gained its
independence from France in 1960.

bur·lap (**bur**-*lap*) *noun* A tough, coarse
material used to make strong bags.

bur·ly (**bur**-lee) *adjective* Husky; strong
and with large muscles. ▸ *adjective*
burlier, burliest

burn (burn)
  verb **1.** To hurt or damage someone
or something by means of heat, a
chemical, or radiation. **2.** To feel very
hot or to cause or feel pain connected
with something hot. **3.** To feel strong
emotion. **4.** If you **burn** a CD or DVD
on your computer, you put data such
as music or video on it.
  noun An injury or mark caused by
burning.
  ▸ *verb* **burning, burned** *or* **burnt**
(burnt)

burn·er (**bur**-nur) *noun* **1.** The area on
top of a stove where a flame or heat
is used to cook things. **2.** A device on
a computer that can write data onto
CDs or DVDs.

burn·ing (**bur**-ning) *adjective* On fire.

burnt (burnt)
  verb A past tense and past participle
of **burn.**
  adjective Cooked too much, or
damaged by fire.

burp (burp)
  verb To make a noise as you release
gases that have been forced up from
your stomach out through your throat.
  noun The gases that are released from
your stomach; a belch.
  ▸ *verb* **burping, burped**

bur·qa (**bur**-kuh) *noun* A garment
worn by some Muslim women that
completely covers the head, body,
arms, and legs.

burr *or* **bur** (bur) *noun* **1.** A prickly pod
that sticks to the clothing of people
or the fur of animals. **2.** The bush that
produces these pods.

bur·ro (**bur**-oh) *noun* A small donkey.
  Burro sounds like **borough** and **burrow.**

bur·row (**bur**-oh)
  noun A tunnel or hole in the ground
made or used as a home by a rabbit or
other animal.
  verb To dig or live in such a tunnel or
hole.
  Burrow sounds like **borough** and
burro. ▸ *verb* **burrowing, burrowed**

burst (burst)
  verb **1.** To break apart suddenly and
violently. **2.** To suddenly begin doing
something. **3.** To be very full.
  noun A sudden, brief outbreak
of something, such as gunfire or
applause.
  ▸ *verb* **bursting, burst**

Bu·run·di (bu-**run**-dee) A country in
eastern Africa on Lake Tanganyika.
Burundi's first democratically elected
president was assassinated in 1993,
triggering widespread ethnic violence
between the Hutu and Tutsi people.
Peace talks between the two warring
factions brought the fighting to a
close, and Burundi is now rebuilding
its economy.

bur·y (**ber**-ee) *verb* **1.** To put a dead
body in a grave or tomb. **2.** To hide
something underground or at the
bottom of something.
  Bury sounds like **berry.** ▸ *verb* **buries,
burying, buried**

bus (buhs)
  noun A large vehicle for carrying
passengers, usually along a specific
route.
  verb To take people somewhere by
bus.
  ▸ *noun, plural* **buses** ▸ *verb* **busing** *or*
bussing, bused *or* **bussed**

bush (bush) *noun* **1.** A shrub with many
branches. **2.** Land or an area with
many plants but few people. **3.** If you
beat around the bush, you talk a lot
but don't come to the point.
  ▸ *noun, plural* **bushes**

bush·el (**bush**-uhl) *noun* A unit of
dry measure that tells how much
a container holds. A bushel equals
32 quarts.

B

bush·whack (**bush**-*wak*) *verb* 1. To make a path by cutting away at the underbrush with a machete or other sharp tool. 2. To ambush someone from a hiding place.
▶ *verb* **bushwhacking, bushwhacked** ▶ *noun* **bushwhacker**

bush·y (**bush**-ee) *adjective* Thick and spreading. ▶ *adjective* **bushier, bushiest**

busi·ness (**biz**-nis) *noun* 1. Commercial activity. 2. A person's job or profession. 3. A commercial organization. 4. A matter that concerns or interests you. If something is **none of your business,** it should not concern you.
▶ *noun, plural* **businesses**

busi·ness card (**biz**-nis *kahrd*) *noun* A small card printed with a person's name, job, and company.

busi·ness·like (**biz**-nis-*like*) *adjective* Practical and unemotional.

busi·ness·man (**biz**-nis-*man*) *noun* A man who has a high position in a company or who owns a business. ▶ *noun, plural* **businessmen**

bust (buhst)
noun A sculpture of a person's head, neck, and shoulders.
verb 1. (informal) To arrest someone. 2. (informal) To smash or break something.
▶ *verb* **busting, busted** *or* **bust** ▶ *adjective* **busted**

bus·tle (**buhs**-uhl)
verb To rush about or move energetically.
noun Energetic activity or commotion.
▶ *verb* **bustling, bustled**

bus·y (**biz**-ee)
adjective 1. Having a lot to do. 2. If a place is **busy,** it is full of people and activity. 3. In use.
verb If you **busy yourself,** you keep yourself occupied.
▶ *adjective* **busier, busiest** ▶ *verb* **busies, busying, busied** ▶ *adverb* **busily**

bus·y·bod·y (**biz**-ee-*bah*-dee) *noun* Someone who likes to know other people's business. ▶ *noun, plural* **busybodies**

but (buht)
conjunction On the other hand.
preposition 1. Other than. *There is no road to riches but through hard work.* 2. With the exception of. *We've chosen everyone but him.*
adverb Only, or just.
But sounds like **butt.**

butch·er (**buch**-ur) *noun* Someone who cuts up and sells meat.

but·ler (**buht**-lur) *noun* The chief male servant in a house.

butt (buht)
noun 1. Someone who is teased or made fun of by other people. 2. The thicker end.
verb To hit someone or something with the head or horns.
Butt sounds like **but.** ▶ *verb* **butting, butted**

butte (byoot) *noun* A hill or mountain with steep sides and a flat top that stands by itself, mostly found in the western United States.

but·ter (**buht**-ur) *noun* A yellowish fatty substance made by churning cream, used in cooking and to flavor food.

but·ter·cup (**buht**-ur-*kuhp*) *noun* A plant with bright yellow cup-shaped flowers.

but·ter·fly (**buht**-ur-*flye*) *noun* 1. An insect with a thin body and large, often colorful wings. 2. If you have **butterflies,** you are feeling very nervous.
▶ *noun, plural* **butterflies**

but·ter·milk (**buht**-ur-*milk*) *noun* The sour liquid left over after butter has been churned from cream.

but·ter·scotch (**buht**-ur-*skahch*) *noun* A flavor or candy made by mixing brown sugar, butter, and vanilla extract.

but·tocks (**buht**-uhks) *noun, plural* The fleshy part of your body that you sit on.

but·ton (**buht**-uhn)
noun 1. A disc-shaped fastener that is used to join two parts of a piece of clothing. 2. A small knob that you turn or press to control a machine, such

B

as a TV or radio.
verb To fasten a piece of clothing using buttons.
▶ *verb* **buttoning, buttoned**

but·ton·hole (**buht**-uhn-*hole*) *noun* The small hole that you push a button through in order to close a garment.

but·tress (**buht**-ris)
noun A structure built against a wall to help support it.
verb To give support or make stronger.
▶ *noun, plural* **buttresses** ▶ *verb* **buttresses, buttressing, buttressed**

buy (bye)
verb To get something in exchange for money.
noun A bargain.
Buy sounds like **by.** ▶ *verb* **buying, bought** (bawt)

buy·er (**bye**-ur) *noun* Someone who buys, or who is interested in buying something.

buzz (buhz)
verb To make a vibrating sound like that of a bee or a wasp.
noun The vibrating sound made by some flying insects or by an electric or electronic device.
▶ *verb* **buzzes, buzzing, buzzed** ▶ *noun, plural* **buzzes** ▶ *noun* **buzzer**

buz·zard (**buhz**-urd) *noun* A large bird of prey, similar to a vulture, with a hooked beak and long, sharp claws.

by (bye)
preposition 1. Next to, or beside.
2. Through the work of. *His portrait was painted by my father.* 3. Through

the means of. *We went home by bus.*
4. Beyond, or past. *They drove by the accident.*
adverb 1. Near, or close at hand. 2. Past.
idiom **by and by** After a while; soon.
By sounds like **buy.**

by·gone (**bye**-*gawn*) *adjective* Past or former.

by·pass (**bye**-*pas*)
noun A highway that goes around an urban area rather than through the middle of it.
verb To avoid something by using a different route.
adjective Enabling something to go around something else.
▶ *noun, plural* **bypasses** ▶ *verb* **bypasses, bypassing, bypassed**

by·prod·uct (**bye**-*prah*-duhkt) *noun* Something that is left over after you make or do something.

by·stand·er (**bye**-*stan*-dur) *noun* Someone who is at a place where something happens to someone else; a spectator.

byte (bite) *noun* A unit of information stored in a computer. **Byte** sounds like **bite.**

Byz·an·tine (**biz**-uhn-*teen*) *adjective* 1. Of or having to do with the ancient city of Byzantium (bi-**zan**-tee-uhm), where Istanbul, Turkey, is now located. 2. In the style of art or architecture popular in the Byzantine Empire. Byzantine buildings of the fifth and sixth centuries have large domes, rounded arches, and a lot of surface decoration, especially colored-glass mosaics.

C

cab (kab) *noun* 1. A car that takes people from one place to another in exchange for money; a taxi. 2. The driver's area of a large truck or machine, such as a bulldozer.

cab·bage (**kab**-ij) *noun* A large vegetable with green or purple leaves shaped into a round head.

cab·in (**kab**-in) *noun* 1. A small, simple

house, often built of wood. 2. A private room for passengers or members of the crew to sleep in on a ship.
3. A section of an airplane for the passengers, crew, or cargo.

cab·i·net (**kab**-uh-nit) *noun* 1. A piece of furniture with shelves or drawers. 2. A group of advisors for the head of a government.

ca·ble (kay-buhl)
noun **1.** A thick rope made of wire.
2. An insulated bundle of wires used for carrying electricity or communication signals, such as television. **3.** A message sent by cable. **4. cable car** A vehicle pulled by a moving cable, used for carrying people along city streets or up mountains. **5. cable modem** A modem that uses your cable television connection to provide high-speed access to the Internet. **6. cable television** A television service in which signals from the television stations are sent by cable to the homes of paying customers.
verb **1.** To send a message by cable. **2.** To provide with a cable.
▸ *verb* **cabling, cabled**

ca·boose (kuh-**boos**) *noun* The last car on a freight train, occupied by the crew.

ca·ca·o (kuh-**kou**) *noun* An evergreen tree found in warm climates that produces a seed from which cocoa and chocolate are made.

cack·le (**kak**-uhl)
verb **1.** To give a loud, clucking cry, like a hen or a goose. **2.** To laugh in a sharp, loud way.
noun This sound.
▸ *verb* **cackling, cackled**

ca·coph·o·ny (kuh-**kah**-fuh-nee) *noun* A harsh, unpleasant mixture of sounds. ▸ *noun, plural* **cacophonies** ▸ *adjective* **cacophonous**

cac·tus (**kak**-tuhs) *noun* A plant with a thick stem and sharp spikes in place of leaves, which grows in hot, dry areas. ▸ *noun, plural* **cacti** (**kak**-tye) or **cactuses**

CAD (kad) *noun* Short for **computer-aided design.**

ca·det (kuh-**det**) *noun* A young person who is training to become a member of the armed forces or a police force.

ca·fé (ka-**fay**) *noun* A small restaurant that serves light meals and drinks.

caf·e·te·ri·a (*kaf*-uh-**teer**-ee-uh) *noun* **1.** A self-service restaurant. **2.** A room in a

school or business where meals are served and eaten.

caf·feine (ka-**feen** or kaf-een) *noun* A chemical found in tea, coffee, and some soft drinks that acts as a stimulant.

caf·tan (**kaf**-tan) *noun* An ankle-length, loose piece of clothing with long sleeves, often worn in the Middle East.

cage (kayj)
noun A container in which something can be kept, made of wires or bars.
verb To put something, especially an animal, in a cage.
▸ *verb* **caging, caged**

ca·gey (**kay**-jee) *adjective* Cautious and reluctant to give away information. ▸ *adjective* **cagier, cagiest**

ca·jole (kuh-**johl**) *verb* To persuade someone to do something by flattering or coaxing the person. ▸ *verb* **cajoling, cajoled**

Ca·jun (**kay**-juhn)
noun A descendant of the French-speaking people who left eastern Canada for Louisiana in the 1700s.
adjective Of or having to do with a style of spicy cooking invented by the Cajuns.

cake (kake)
noun **1.** A sweet food made by combining flour, butter, eggs, sugar, and other ingredients, and then baking this mixture. **2.** A shaped mass of something.
verb To dry or harden into a solid mass.
▸ *verb* **caking, caked** ▸ *adjective* **caked**

ca·lam·i·ty (kuh-**lam**-i-tee) *noun* A terrible disaster. ▸ *noun, plural* **calamities** ▸ *adjective* **calamitous**

cal·ci·um (**kal**-see-uhm) *noun* A silver-white chemical element found in teeth and bones, which is necessary for many chemical processes in the human body.

cal·cu·late (**kal**-kyuh-*late*) *verb* To figure out by using mathematics. ▸ *verb* **calculating, calculated**

C

cal·cu·lat·ing (**kal**-kyuh-*lay*-ting) *adjective* Acting in a scheming way to get what you want.

cal·cu·la·tion (*kal*-kyuh-**lay**-shuhn) *noun* **1.** The process of finding a number or amount using math. **2.** An assessment of a course of action with respect to risks, cost, outcome, or other factors.

cal·cu·la·tor (**kal**-kyuh-*lay*-tur) *noun* An electronic machine used for figuring out math problems.

cal·en·dar (**kal**-uhn-dur) *noun* **1.** A chart showing all the days, weeks, and months in a year. **2.** A system of measuring time over a period of a year.

calf (kaf) *noun* **1.** The young of several large species of animals, such as cows, seals, elephants, giraffes, or whales. **2.** The fleshy part at the back of your leg, below your knee.
  ▶ *noun, plural* **calves**

cal·i·co (**kal**-i-koh)
  noun Cotton cloth printed with a colorful pattern.
  adjective Having spotted colors.
  ▶ *noun, plural* **calicoes** or **calicos**

Cal·i·for·nia (*kal*-uh-**forn**-yuh) A state on the West Coast of the United States. It is the most populous state in the country and the third-largest state, after Alaska and Texas. California is known for Hollywood, winemaking, and agriculture, and as the home of the Silicon Valley, the hub of the high-tech industry.

call (kawl)
  verb **1.** To give someone or something a name. **2.** To shout something out, especially someone's name. **3.** To telephone someone. **4. call for** To make necessary or to demand. **5. call on** To visit a person. **6. call off** To cancel.
  noun **1.** The sound of someone trying to get another's attention. **2.** If there is a **call**, or **no call**, for something, there is a reason, or no reason, for it to happen.
  phrase **call collect** To reverse telephone charges from the person who is making the call to the person who is receiving it.
  ▶ *verb* **calling, called** ▶ *noun* **caller**

call·er ID (**kaw**-lur *eye*-**dee**) *noun* A service that shows you the telephone number of the person who is calling, displayed in a window on the phone.

cal·lig·ra·phy (kuh-**lig**-ruh-fee) *noun* Decorative handwriting.

call·ing (**kawl**-ing) *noun* Your **calling** is the job, profession, or other important thing that you want to do in your life.

call num·ber (**kawl** *nuhm*-bur) *noun* A sequence of numbers and letters that identifies the location of an item in a collection, especially a library.

cal·lous (**kal**-uhs) *adjective* Having no tender feelings; cruel. ▶ *noun* **callousness** ▶ *adverb* **callously**

calm (kahm)
  adjective Peaceful and not troubled.
  verb To soothe or to quiet.
  noun **1.** Peacefulness; lack of trouble or violence. **2.** A lack of wind or motion.
  ▶ *adjective* **calmer, calmest** ▶ *verb* **calming, calmed** ▶ *noun* **calmness** ▶ *adverb* **calmly**

cal·o·rie (**kal**-ur-ee) *noun* A measurement of the amount of energy contained in food.

calves (kavz) *noun, plural* The plural of **calf.**

ca·lyp·so (kuh-**lip**-soh) *noun* A style of Caribbean music with a strong, lively rhythm.

Cam·bo·di·a (kam-**boh**-dee-uh) A country in Southeast Asia on the Gulf of Thailand. Angkor Wat, a Hindu temple complex in the northwestern part of the country, is a protected World Heritage Site. The ruins of Angkor Wat and of other nearby temples are Cambodia's main tourist attraction.

cam·cord·er (**kam**-*kor*-dur) *noun* A small video camera that also records sound.

cam·el (**kam**-uhl) *noun* A mammal with one or two humps on its back. It can survive for long periods of time without food or water, which makes it useful for carrying people and goods across the desert.

C

cam·e·o (**kam**-ee-*oh*) *noun* 1. A piece of jewelry with a raised portrait carved on it. 2. A small character part in a play or a movie, usually played by a famous actor or actress.

cam·er·a (**kam**-ur-uh) *noun* A device for capturing images through a lens and storing them digitally or on film.

Cam·e·roon (*kam*-uh-**roon**) A country in the western part of central Africa. Its diverse geography includes savannas, beaches, mountains, deserts, and rain forests. Cameroon's wildlife preserves are the habitats for such well-known African animals as elephants, hippos, and giraffes.

cam·ou·flage (**kam**-uh-*flahzh*)
noun A disguise or a natural coloring that allows animals, people, or objects to hide by making them look like their surroundings.
verb To disguise something so that it blends in with its surroundings.
▶ *verb* **camouflaging, camouflaged**

camp (kamp)
noun 1. A place where people stay in tents or cabins, usually as part of a vacation. 2. A place where people stay in an emergency because their homes are destroyed or not safe. 3. A place or a program devoted to a particular recreational activity.
verb To live or stay in a camp.
▶ *verb* **camping, camped** ▶ *noun* **camping**

cam·paign (kam-**payn**)
noun Organized action in order to achieve a particular goal.
verb To participate in a campaign.
▶ *verb* **campaigning, campaigned**

camp·er (**kam**-pur) *noun* 1. A person who stays or vacations at a camp. 2. A large motor vehicle in which you can sleep and cook meals when camping.

camp·fire (**kamp**-*fire*) *noun* A fire lit at the site of a camp for warmth and for cooking.

camp·ground (**kamp**-*ground*) *noun* A place where people camp.

camp·us (**kam**-puhs) *noun* The land and buildings of a school, college, or university. ▶ *noun, plural* **campuses**

can (kan) *verb* 1. To be able to.
2. (informal) To be allowed to do something.
▶ *verb* **could** (kud)

can (kan)
noun A metal container with the shape of a cylinder, used mainly for storing food.
verb To put into a jar or can; to preserve.
idiom **can of worms** An awkward or difficult situation.
▶ *verb* **canning, canned** ▶ *adjective* **canned**

Can·a·da (**kan**-uh-duh) The largest country in North America, bordered by the United States on the south. Canada is one of the world's wealthiest countries, with highly developed mining, manufacturing, and agricultural industries.

ca·nal (kuh-**nal**) *noun* 1. A channel that is dug across land so that boats or ships can travel between two bodies of water, or so that water can flow from one place to another. 2. A tube in a plant or animal, through which food, fluid, or air can travel.

ca·nar·y (kuh-**nair**-ee) *noun* 1. A bright yellow bird noted for its singing ability. 2. A bright yellow color.
▶ *noun, plural* **canaries**

can·cel (**kan**-suhl) *verb* 1. To decide or announce that a planned event is not going to happen. 2. To stop an action on a computer if you don't want to complete it. Usually you do this by clicking on a cancel button. 3. To mark a postage stamp with a postmark so that it cannot be used again. 4. **cancel out** To have one action stop the effect of another action.
▶ *verb* **canceling, canceled** ▶ *noun* **cancelation** or **cancellation**

can·cer (**kan**-sur) *noun* A serious disease in which some cells in the body grow faster than normal cells and destroy healthy organs and tissues. ▶ *adjective* **cancerous**

can·did (**kan**-did) *adjective* Speaking openly and honestly. ▶ *noun* **candor** ▶ *adverb* **candidly**

can·di·date (**kan**-di-*date*) *noun* A person who is applying for a job or running in an election. ▶ *noun* **candidacy** (**kan**-di-duh-see)

can·dle (**kan**-duhl) *noun* A stick of wax with a wick strung through it that you burn to produce light. ▶ *noun* **candlelight**

can·dle·stick (**kan**-duhl-*stik*) *noun* A holder for a candle or candles.

can·dy (**kan**-dee)
noun Food made with sugar or syrup and often chocolate, nuts, or other flavorings.
verb To coat with sugar.
▶ *noun, plural* **candies** ▶ *verb* **candies, candying, candied** ▶ *adjective* **candied**

cane (kane)
noun 1. The woody, sometimes hollow, stem of a plant such as bamboo or sugarcane. 2. A plant or grass with this kind of woody, jointed stem. 3. A stick, especially one used for assistance in walking or for beating someone.
verb To make or repair furniture with cane.
▶ *verb* **caning, caned**

ca·nine (**kay**-nine)
adjective Of or having to do with dogs.
noun One of the pointed teeth on each side of your upper and lower jaws. People have four canines.

can·ni·bal (**kan**-uh-buhl) *noun* A person who eats human flesh. ▶ *noun* **cannibalism**

can·non (**kan**-uhn) *noun* A heavy gun, usually mounted on wheels, that fires large metal balls.

can·not (**kan**-aht *or* ka-**naht**) *verb* To be unable to do something.

ca·noe (kuh-**noo**) *noun* A narrow boat with pointed ends that you move through the water with paddles.

can·o·py (**kan**-uh-pee) *noun* 1. A piece of cloth or other material suspended as a cover, shade, or decoration, especially over an entrance, a bed, or a throne. 2. A hanging shelter or cover. 3. A cover over an airplane or helicopter cockpit. 4. The upper level of a rain forest, consisting mostly of branches, vines, and leaves.
▶ *noun, plural* **canopies**

can't (kant) *contraction* A short form of *can not* or *cannot.*

can·ta·loupe (**kan**-tuh-*lope*) *noun* A melon with a rough skin and sweet, juicy, orange fruit.

can·teen (kan-**teen**) *noun* 1. A small portable metal container for holding water or other liquids. 2. The area in a factory, school, or office where people can take breaks and eat simple meals.

can·ter (**kan**-tur)
verb To run at a speed between a trot and a gallop on a horse.
noun The slow, relaxed gallop of a horse.
▶ *verb* **cantering, cantered**

can·tor (**kan**-tur) *noun* An official who sings and leads prayers in a synagogue.

can·vas (**kan**-vuhs) *noun* 1. A type of coarse, strong cloth used to make tents, sails, and clothing. 2. A piece of canvas stretched over a wooden frame for painting on, or the painting itself. **Canvas** sounds like **canvass.** ▶ *noun, plural* **canvases**

can·vass (**kan**-vuhs) *verb* To go around among a group of people, asking for their opinions or votes. **Canvass** sounds like **canvas.** ▶ *verb* **canvasses, canvassing, canvassed** ▶ *noun* **canvasser**

can·yon (**kan**-yuhn) *noun* A deep, narrow river valley with steep sides.

cap (kap)
noun 1. A soft, flat hat without a brim, sometimes with a visor in the front. 2. The cover of a bottle or a pen. 3. A small amount of explosive on a piece of paper that makes a bang when struck, often used in toy guns. 4. (informal) A capital letter.
verb To cover with a cap.
▶ *verb* **capping, capped**

ca·pa·bil·i·ty (*kay*-puh-**bil**-i-tee) *noun* The power or ability to do something. ▶ *noun, plural* **capabilities**

ca·pa·ble (**kay**-puh-buhl) *adjective* 1. Able to do something. 2. Adept and skillful. ▶ *adverb* **capably**

C

ca·pac·i·ty (kuh-**pas**-i-tee) *noun* **1.** The amount or number that something can hold. **2.** The ability to do a particular thing. **3.** A role or job.
▸ *noun, plural* **capacities**

cape (kape) *noun* **1.** A sleeveless coat that you wear over your shoulders and wrap around your body. **2.** A piece of land that sticks out into the sea.

ca·per (**kay**-pur)
noun **1.** A trick or prank. **2.** (slang) A criminal act.
verb To skip or dance around playfully.
▸ *verb* **capering, capered**

Cape Verde (**kape** vurd) An island country off the western coast of Africa. Once a trading center for African slaves, Cape Verde today is known for its peacefulness and stability. No war has ever been fought there.

cap·il·lar·y (**kap**-uh-*ler*-ee) *noun* One of many small tubes in your body that transfers blood between the arteries and the veins. ▸ *noun, plural* **capillaries**

cap·i·tal (**kap**-i-tuhl) *noun* **1.** A letter with the form A, B, C, D, E, rather than a, b, c, d, e, and so on. **2.** The city in a country or state where the government is based. **3.** An amount of money used to start a business. **Capital** sounds like **capitol.**

cap·i·tal·ism (**kap**-i-tuh-*liz*-uhm) *noun* A way of organizing a country's economy so that most of the land, houses, factories, and other property belong to individuals and private companies rather than to the government.

cap·i·tal·ist (**kap**-i-tuh-list)
noun Someone who supports capitalism and uses their wealth to invest.
adjective Of or having to do with capitalism.

cap·i·tal·ize (**kap**-i-tuh-*lize*) *verb* **1.** To put a capital letter at the beginning of a word or sentence. **2.** To write or print in capital letters. **3.** To benefit by taking advantage of something.
▸ *verb* **capitalizing, capitalized** ▸ *noun* **capitalization** (*kap*-i-tuhl-i-**zay**-shuhn)

cap·i·tal pun·ish·ment (**kap**-i-tuhl **puhn**-ish-muhnt) *noun* Punishment that causes death, carried out by a government.

cap·i·tol (**kap**-i-tuhl) *noun* **1.** The building where state lawmakers meet. **2. Capitol** The building in Washington, D.C., where the U.S. Congress meets. **Capitol** sounds like **capital.**

cap·puc·ci·no (*kap*-uh-**chee**-noh) *noun* Coffee made with steamed, foamy milk and often flavored with cinnamon.

ca·pri·cious (kuh-**prish**-uhs) *adjective* Unpredictable and tending to change without any obvious reason.

cap·size (**kap**-size) *verb* To turn over in the water. ▸ *verb* **capsizing, capsized**

cap·sule (**kap**-suhl) *noun* **1.** A small container made of gelatin that holds one dose of medicine for a person to swallow. **2.** The part of a spacecraft in which the crew travels.

cap·tain (**kap**-tuhn)
noun **1.** The person in charge of a ship or an aircraft. **2.** The leader of a team. **3.** A police or military officer at a certain level of authority.
verb If you **captain** a team, ship, or organization, you are the main person in charge.
▸ *verb* **captaining, captained**

cap·tion (**kap**-shuhn) *noun* A short title or description appearing with an illustration.

cap·ti·vate (**kap**-tuh-*vate*) *verb* To attract and hold someone's attention. ▸ *verb* **captivating, captivated**

cap·tive (**kap**-tiv)
noun A person who has been taken prisoner, or an animal that has been caught.
adjective Confined to a place and not able to escape.

cap·tiv·i·ty (kap-**tiv**-i-tee) *noun* **1.** The condition of being held or trapped by people. **2.** An animal raised **in captivity** is a normally wild animal that is raised and cared for by people.

cap·ture (**kap**-chur)
verb **1.** To take a person, an animal, or a place by force. **2.** To attract and hold.

C

noun The act of capturing.
▶ *verb* **capturing, captured**

car (kahr) *noun* **1.** A motor vehicle that has four wheels and two or four doors, designed to carry a driver and passengers; an automobile. **2.** A vehicle on wheels that carries passengers and freight, such as a unit of a train. **3.** The part of an elevator that carries people or freight.

car·a·mel (**kar**-uh-muhl *or* **kahr**-muhl) *noun* **1.** Sugar or syrup heated until it turns brown, used as a flavoring or coloring for food or drinks. **2.** Candy made from sugar and butter. **3.** A light brown color.
adjective Being the color of caramel.

car·at (**kar**-uht) *noun* A unit for measuring the weight of gemstones.
Carat sounds like **carrot.**

car·a·van (**kar**-uh-*van*) *noun* A group of people using animals or vehicles to travel together.

car·bo·hy·drate (*kahr*-buh-**hye**-drate) *noun* One of the substances in foods such as bread, rice, and potatoes that give you energy. Carbohydrates are made up of carbon, hydrogen, and oxygen and are produced by plants.

car·bon (**kahr**-buhn) *noun* **1.** A chemical element found in coal and diamonds and in all plants and animals. **2. carbon di·ox·ide** (dye-**ahk**-side) A gas that is a mixture of carbon and oxygen, with no color or odor. People and animals breathe this gas out, while plants absorb it during the day. **3. carbon mon·ox·ide** (muh-**nahk**-side) A poisonous gas produced by the engines of vehicles and other things that burn carbon-based fuels. **4. carbon footprint** A measure of the amount of carbon dioxide produced by a person, object, or organization and released into the atmosphere.
noun, plural **carbon emissions** Carbon dioxide that goes into the air from the burning of fossil fuels and forests, as well as other human activities.

carbs (kahrbz) *noun, plural* (informal) Carbohydrates or foods that contain them.

car·bu·re·tor (**kahr**-buh-*ray*-tur) *noun* The part of an engine where air and gasoline mix.

car·cass (**kar**-kuhs) *noun* The dead body of an animal. ▶ *noun, plural* **carcasses**

card (kahrd) *noun* **1.** A folded, decorated piece of stiff paper sent on special occasions. **2.** One of a set of rectangular pieces of stiff paper, used in games. **3.** A small, rectangular piece of plastic with electronic coding that allows you to do certain things, such as get cash from an ATM, make a telephone call, or open a locked door.

card·board (**kahrd**-*bord*) *noun* Thick, stiff paper used for making boxes and other things.

car·di·ac (**kahr**-dee-*ak*) *adjective* Of or having to do with the heart.

car·di·gan (**kahr**-di-guhn) *noun* A sweater that fastens down the front.

car·di·nal (**kahr**-duh-nuhl) *noun* **1.** A songbird with black coloring around the beak and a crest of feathers on its head. The male is bright red. **2.** One of the officials in the Roman Catholic Church, ranking just below the pope.
adjective Most important.

car·di·nal num·ber (**kahr**-duh-nuhl **nuhm**-bur) *noun* A number, such as one, two, three, or four, used to show the amount of something.

care (kair) *verb* **1.** To feel interest or concern about something. **2.** To want or to be willing.
noun **1.** Concern or attention. **2.** Supervision and protection. **3.** A worry or a fear about something.
idiom **1. take care of someone** To do what is needed to keep someone safe, well, happy, or comfortable. **2. take care of something** To solve a problem or deal with a situation.
▶ *verb* **caring, cared** ▶ *adjective* **caring**

ca·reer (kuh-**reer**) *noun* The work or the series of jobs that a person has.

care·free (**kair**-*free*) *adjective* Having no worries or responsibilities.

C

care·ful (**kair**-fuhl) *adjective* **1.** Cautious; paying close attention so as not to take risks. **2.** Thoughtful and attentive. ▶ *noun* **carefulness**

care·ful·ly (**kair**-fuh-lee) *adverb* **1.** In a way that shows close attention or concern. **2.** In a way that shows great care or caution.

care·giv·er (**kair**-*giv*-ur) *noun* Someone who takes care of children, old people, or sick people.

care·less (**kair**-lis) *adjective* Not paying attention, and making mistakes as a result. ▶ *noun* **carelessness** ▶ *adverb* **carelessly**

ca·ress (kuh-**res**) *verb* To stroke gently. *noun* A gentle touch. ▶ *verb* **caresses, caressing, caressed** ▶ *noun, plural* **caresses**

care·tak·er (**kair**-*tay*-kur) *noun* A person whose job is to take care of a building, property, animals, or other people.

car·go (**kahr**-goh) *noun* Freight that is carried by a ship or an aircraft. ▶ *noun, plural* **cargoes**

Ca·rib·be·an (kuh-**rib**-ee-uhn *or* kar-uh-**bee**-uhn) *noun* An area of sea and islands in the Atlantic Ocean, in the tropical area southeast of the Gulf of Mexico. *adjective* Of or having to do with the Caribbean, its islands, its people, or their culture.

car·i·bou (**kar**-uh-*boo*) *noun* A large North American mammal of the deer family. Caribou are related to reindeer. ▶ *noun, plural* **caribou** *or* **caribous**

car·i·ca·ture (**kar**-i-kuh-*choor*) *noun* An exaggerated drawing or verbal description of someone.

car·jack (**kahr**-*jak*) *verb* To steal a car by threatening to harm the driver. ▶ *verb* **carjacking, carjacked** ▶ *noun* **carjacking**

car·na·tion (kahr-**nay**-shuhn) *noun* **1.** A fragrant flower, usually pink, white, or red. **2.** A pink color.

car·ni·val (**kahr**-nuh-vuhl) *noun* A public celebration, often with rides, games, and parades.

car·ni·vore (**kahr**-nuh-*vor*) *noun* An animal that eats meat.

car·niv·o·rous (kahr-**niv**-ur-uhs) *adjective* Having meat as a regular part of the diet. Wolves, lions, dogs, and most people are carnivorous.

car·ob (**kar**-uhb) *noun* **1.** An evergreen tree whose beans are used to make a flavoring that tastes something like chocolate. **2.** Brown powder from carob beans, used as a food or flavoring.

car·ol (**kar**-uhl) *noun* A joyful song, especially one that people sing at Christmas. *verb* To celebrate by singing joyously. ▶ *verb* **caroling, caroled** ▶ *noun* **caroling**

carp (kahrp) *noun* A large fish that lives in fresh water and is used as food. *verb* To find fault with someone or something. ▶ *noun, plural* **carp** *or* **carps** ▶ *verb* **carping, carped**

car·pen·ter (**kahr**-puhn-tur) *noun* A person who works with wood or builds and repairs the wooden parts of buildings. ▶ *noun* **carpentry**

car·pet (**kahr**-pit) *noun* **1.** A thick floor covering made of a woven fabric. **2.** A thick layer of something. *verb* To cover with a carpet. ▶ *verb* **carpeting, carpeted**

car pool (**kahr** *pool*) *noun* **1.** A system in which a group of people travel together, often taking turns driving their own cars. **2.** A group of people involved in such a system. ▶ *verb* **car-pool**

car·riage (**kar**-ij) *noun* **1.** A vehicle with wheels, sometimes pulled by horses. **2.** Your posture; the way you stand, sit, and walk.

car·ri·er (**kar**-ee-ur) *noun* **1.** Someone or something that carries. **2.** A company whose business is to transport people or things. **3.** A company that provides telephone and other communications services.

C

car·rot (**kar**-uht) *noun* 1. An orange root eaten as a vegetable. 2. An offer of something nice in order to persuade someone to do something.
Carrot sounds like **carat.**

car·ry (**kar**-ee) *verb* 1. To move something from one place to another. 2. To support the weight of something. 3. To travel for some distance. 4. To offer something for sale. 5. To be infected with a disease that can be transmitted to others. 6. To continue or to extend. 7. **carry a tune** To be able to sing reasonably well. 8. **be carried away** *or* **get carried away** To become too enthusiastic about something. 9. **carry on** To continue to do something. 10. **carry on** To behave in an exaggerated or inappropriate way. 11. **carry out** To put a plan or an idea into practice.
▶ *verb* **carries, carrying, carried**

carry-on *noun* A bag or suitcase that you keep with you on an airplane instead of checking it.

car·sick (**kahr**-sik) *adjective* Having a dizzy, nauseated feeling from the motion of a moving vehicle such as a car, train, or bus.

cart (kahrt)
noun 1. A small wagon with two or four wheels, often pulled by an animal. 2. A light wagon that is pushed by someone and used to carry heavy items such as groceries.
verb To carry something with effort.
▶ *verb* **carting, carted**

car·ti·lage (**kahr**-tuh-lij) *noun* A strong, elastic tissue that forms the outer ear and nose of humans and mammals, and lines the bones at the joints.

car·tog·ra·phy (kahr-**tah**-gruh-fee) *noun* The science of making maps. ▶ *noun* **cartographer**

car·ton (**kahr**-tuhn) *noun* A cardboard or plastic box or container used for holding or shipping goods.

car·toon (kahr-**toon**) *noun* 1. A short film using animation rather than real people or objects. 2. A humorous or exaggerated drawing.
▶ *noun* **cartoonist**

car·tridge (**kahr**-trij) *noun* 1. A container that holds a bullet or shot and the explosive for firing it. 2. A small container that holds something and that is designed to be inserted into something else.

cart·wheel (**kahrt**-weel) *noun* A circular, sideways handspring with arms and legs extended.

carve (kahrv) *verb* 1. To cut meat into slices for eating. 2. To cut a piece of wood, stone, or other hard substance into a particular shape.
▶ *verb* **carving, carved** ▶ *noun* **carver** ▶ *noun* **carving**

cas·cade (kas-**kade**)
noun 1. A waterfall. 2. Anything arranged in a downward pattern, or falling in a downward pattern.
verb To fall like water over rocks.
▶ *verb* **cascading, cascaded**

Cas·cades (kas-**kaydz**) A North American mountain range extending along the western coastal area from Canada into the United States. The Cascades pass through the province of British Columbia and the states of Oregon, Washington, and California. The range includes both volcanic mountains and nonvolcanic mountains.

case (kase) *noun* 1. An instance or example of something. 2. A trial in a court of law. 3. A crime that the police are investigating. 4. An occurrence of an illness. 5. A set of circumstances. 6. A box or container that holds something. 7. **in any case** No matter what happens. 8. **just in case** In the event that something happens or that something is needed.

case sen·si·tive (**kase** sen-si-tiv) *adjective* Working only when you type it using the correct combination of capital and lowercase letters.

cash (kash)
noun Money in the form of bills and coins.
verb 1. To exchange something, like a check, for money. 2. **cash in** To take advantage of something.
▶ *verb* **cashes, cashing, cashed**

cash·ew (**kash**-oo) *noun* A nut that is shaped like a kidney bean. Cashews grow on evergreen trees in tropical countries.

cash·ier (ka-**sheer**) *noun* A person who takes in or pays out money in a store or bank.

cash ma·chine (kash muh-**sheen**) *noun* Another name for an **ATM.**

cash reg·is·ter (kash *rej*-i-stur) *noun* A machine used in stores that has a drawer for money and that keeps an account of each purchase.

cask (kask) *noun* A large, wooden barrel, usually used to make and store wine.

cas·ket (**kas**-kit) *noun* A wooden or metal container into which a dead person is placed for burial; a coffin.

cas·se·role (**kas**-uh-role) *noun* 1. A glass or ceramic dish with a lid that is used for cooking and serving. 2. Food that is cooked in such a dish.

cas·sette (kuh-**set**) *noun* A flat plastic box containing recording tape, used for recording and playing music, movies, and other sounds and images.

cast (kast)
noun 1. The actors in a play, movie, or television program. 2. A hard covering that holds a broken bone in place while it heals.
verb 1. To throw. 2. To register a vote. 3. To form something by pouring soft or molten material into a mold.
▶ *verb* **casting, cast**

cast·a·way (**kas**-tuh-*way*) *noun* A person who has been shipwrecked in an isolated place.

cast i·ron (**kast eye**-urn) *noun* A hard and brittle form of iron made by melting iron with other metals. The mixture is poured into a mold to make something.

cas·tle (**kas**-uhl) *noun* 1. A large building protected by thick walls and often a moat. Most castles were built in the Middle Ages. 2. A piece used in chess, also called a rook, that moves around the board in horizontal or vertical lines.

cas·u·al (**kazh**-oo-uhl) *adjective* 1. Informal. 2. Happening by chance. 3. Relaxed and unworried.
▶ *adverb* **casually**

cas·u·al·ty (**kazh**-oo-uhl-tee) *noun* A person who is injured or killed in an accident, a natural disaster, or a war. ▶ *noun, plural* **casualties**

cat (kat) *noun* 1. A small, furry animal with sharp claws and whiskers, often kept as a pet. 2. Any member of the cat family, including lions, tigers, and cheetahs. 3. **let the cat out of the bag** To tell a secret by mistake.

cat·a·log *or* **cat·a·logue** (**kat**-uh-*lawg*) *noun* 1. A book or magazine listing things you can buy from a company or the works of art in an exhibition, often including pictures and descriptions. 2. An alphabetical list of all the books in a library.
verb To make a list of.
▶ *verb* **cataloging** *or* **cataloguing, cataloged** *or* **catalogued**

cat·a·lyst (**kat**-uh-list) *noun* 1. A substance that causes or speeds up a chemical reaction. 2. A person or thing that causes something to happen.

cat·a·ma·ran (*kat*-uh-muh-**ran**) *noun* A boat with two hulls that are joined together.

cat·a·pult (**kat**-uh-*puhlt*)
noun 1. A device used to launch airplanes from the deck of a ship. 2. A weapon, similar to a large slingshot, used in the past for firing rocks or other objects over castle walls.
verb To cause someone to suddenly move ahead of many others.

cat·a·ract (**kat**-uh-rakt) *noun* 1. A cloudy film that sometimes grows on the lens of a person's eye, causing blindness or partial blindness. 2. A steep waterfall.

ca·tas·tro·phe (kuh-**tas**-truh-fee) *noun* A terrible and sudden disaster. ▶ *adjective* **catastrophic** (*kat*-uh-**strah**-fik)

cat·bird (**kat**-*burd*) *noun* A gray songbird with a call that sounds like a cat meowing.

C

catch (kach)
verb **1.** To seize something moving through the air. **2.** To get something or someone you are chasing. **3.** To arrive at a bus, train, or other kind of transportation in time to get on. **4.** To see someone doing something. **5.** To become sick with a particular disease. **6.** To become stuck or trapped. **7.** To attend or to watch. **8.** To hear and understand. **9. catch up with** To reach a person or thing after a chase. **10. catch up on** To complete work that should have been done earlier. **11. catch on** To become very popular. **12. catch on** To understand.
noun **1.** The act of catching something. **2.** A fastener on a door, box, piece of jewelry, or other object that needs to be held shut. **3.** A game in which two or more people throw a ball to one another. **4.** A hidden problem or disadvantage.
▶ *noun, plural* **catches** ▶ *verb* **catches, catching, caught** (kawt)

catch·er (**kach**-ur) *noun* A person who catches; the baseball player behind home plate who catches the balls thrown by the pitcher.

cat·e·gor·i·cal (*kat*-uh-**gor**-i-kuhl) *adjective* Completely clear. ▶ *adverb* **categorically**

cat·e·go·ry (**kat**-uh-*gor*-ee) *noun* A group of people or things that has certain characteristics in common. ▶ *noun, plural* **categories**

ca·ter (**kay**-tur) *verb* **1.** To provide food for a party or other social occasion. **2.** To provide people with the things they need or want, especially if it involves special requests.
▶ *verb* **catering, catered** ▶ *noun* **caterer** ▶ *noun* **catering**

cat·er·pil·lar (**kat**-ur-*pil*-ur) *noun* A larva that changes into a butterfly or moth. It looks like a worm and is sometimes hairy.

cat·fish (**kat**-*fish*) *noun* A freshwater fish with long feelers around its mouth that look like cat whiskers. ▶ *noun, plural* **catfish** *or* **catfishes**

ca·the·dral (kuh-**thee**-druhl) *noun* A large and important church, with a bishop or an archbishop as its main priest.

Cath·o·lic (**kath**-lik)
noun A member of the Roman Catholic Church.
adjective Of or belonging to the Roman Catholic Church.
▶ *noun* **Catholicism** (kuh-**thah**-luh-*siz*-uhm)

CAT scan (**kat** *skan*) *noun* An image made by computer from a series of X-rays, resulting in a single three-dimensional image. CAT is short for *computerized axial tomography.*

cat·tail (**kat**-*tayl*) *noun* A tall, thin plant with long, brown, furry pods at the top and narrow leaves. Cattails grow in large groups in marshes.

cat·tle (**kat**-uhl) *noun, plural* Cows, bulls, and steers that are raised for food or for their hides.

Cau·ca·sian (kaw-**kay**-zhuhn) *noun* A member of a race of peoples with light or tan skin. Caucasians may come from Europe, the Americas, northern Africa, India, and other regions.
adjective Of or having to do with Caucasians.

caul·dron (**kawl**-druhn) *noun* A large metal pot, used for cooking over an open fire.

cau·li·flow·er (**kaw**-li-*flou*-ur) *noun* A vegetable with a large, rounded, white head surrounded by leaves.

caulk (kawk)
noun A waterproof paste that is applied to a hole or a gap, such as the edges of a bathtub, to close it and make it watertight.
verb To apply a waterproof material to something in order to prevent water from leaking in or out.
▶ *verb* **caulking, caulked**

cause (kawz)
verb To make something happen.
noun **1.** The reason that something happens. **2.** A principle or a goal to which people commit themselves and for which they work.
▶ *verb* **causing, caused**

C

cause·way (**kawz**-way) noun A raised road built across water or low ground.

cau·tion (**kaw**-shuhn) noun Carefulness or watchfulness. verb To warn about something or someone. ▶ verb **cautioning, cautioned**

cau·tious (**kaw**-shuhs) adjective Acting carefully to avoid mistakes or danger. ▶ adverb **cautiously**

cav·al·ry (**kav**-uhl-ree) noun 1. In earlier times, the part of an army that fought on horseback. 2. In modern times, soldiers who fight in armored vehicles. ▶ noun, plural **cavalries**

cave (kave) noun A large opening underground, in a hillside, or in a cliff. verb **cave in** To fall down suddenly. ▶ verb **caving, caved**

cave-in (**kave**-in) noun The collapse of an underground structure such as a mine or tunnel.

cave·man (**kave**-man) noun A prehistoric man who lived in caves. ▶ noun, plural **cavemen**

cave paint·ing (**kave** payn-ting) noun A picture painted on a cave wall in prehistoric times.

cav·ern (**kav**-ern) noun A large cave, or a room in a cave. ▶ adjective **cavernous**

cave·wom·an (**kave**-wum-uhn) noun A prehistoric woman who lived in caves. ▶ noun, plural **cavewomen**

cav·i·ty (**kav**-i-tee) noun 1. An empty space in something solid. 2. A hole in a tooth, caused by decay. ▶ noun, plural **cavities**

CB (**see**-bee) noun A radio system that people, especially truck drivers, use to talk to each other over short distances. CB is short for *citizens band.*

CD (**see**-dee) noun Short for **compact disk.**

CD-ROM (**see**-dee-rahm) noun A compact disk that stores text, music, video clips, and other information that can be read by a computer. CD-ROM is short for *compact disk read-only memory.*

cease (sees) verb To stop. ▶ verb **ceasing, ceased**

cease-fire (**sees**-fire) noun A temporary pause during a war, usually to allow peace talks to take place.

ce·dar (**see**-dur) noun A type of evergreen tree with hard wood and leaves shaped like needles. The fragrant wood is used for furniture and moth-repellent linings.

ceil·ing (**see**-ling) noun 1. The overhead surface of a room. 2. The highest level that something can reach.

cel·e·brate (**sel**-uh-brate) verb To do something special to mark a happy occasion. ▶ verb **celebrating, celebrated** ▶ adjective **celebratory** (**sel**-uh-bruh-tor-ee)

cel·e·bra·tion (sel-uh-**bray**-shuhn) noun A joyous ceremony or gathering, usually to mark a major event.

ce·leb·ri·ty (suh-**leb**-ri-tee) noun A famous person. ▶ noun, plural **celebrities**

cel·er·y (**sel**-ur-ee) noun A vegetable with crisp white or green stalks, often eaten raw in salads or cooked in soups and stews.

ce·les·tial (suh-**les**-chuhl) adjective Of or having to do with the sky or the heavens. ▶ adverb **celestially**

cel·i·bate (**sel**-uh-bit) adjective Not engaging in any sexual activities with others. ▶ noun **celibacy** (**sel**-uh-buh-see)

cell (sel) noun 1. A small room in a place such as a prison or monastery, where people stay. 2. The smallest unit of an animal or a plant. 3. A box in a spreadsheet in which an item of data can be entered.

cel·lar (**sel**-ur) noun A room below ground level in a house, often used for storage.

cel·lo (**chel**-oh) noun A large stringed instrument that rests on the floor. It is played with a bow like a violin but is held between the knees.

cel·lo·phane (**sel**-uh-fane) noun Clear plastic material that is made from cellulose and is used as a wrapping.

C

cell phone (sel *fone*) *noun* A portable telephone that often has features like a camera and Internet access. A cell phone uses signals sent over radio channels.

cel·lu·lar (**sel**-yuh-lur) *adjective* 1. Made of or having to do with cells. 2. Of or having to do with cell phones and their technology.

cel·lu·loid (**sel**-yuh-*loid*) *noun* 1. A plastic material once used to make motion picture film. 2. Motion picture film.

cel·lu·lose (**sel**-yuh-*lohs*) *noun* The substance from which the cell walls of plants, and plant fibers, are made. Cellulose is used to make paper, cloth, and plastics.

Cel·si·us (**sel**-see-uhs) *adjective* A measurement of temperature using a scale on which water boils at 100 degrees and freezes at 0 degrees. It is also called *centigrade.*

ce·ment (suh-**ment**) *noun* 1. A gray powder made from crushed limestone that is used in building and that becomes hard when you mix it with water and let it dry. Cement is used to make concrete. 2. A substance that joins two things together. *verb* To attach one thing to another using glue, cement, or some other adhesive. ▶ *verb* **cementing, cemented**

cem·e·ter·y (**sem**-i-*ter*-ee) *noun* A place where dead people are buried. ▶ *noun, plural* **cemeteries**

cen·sor (**sen**-sur) *verb* To remove parts of a book, movie, or other work that are thought to be unacceptable or offensive. *noun* A person whose job is to examine books, movies, or other works for objectionable parts before they are published or released. ▶ *verb* **censoring, censored** ▶ *noun* **censorship**

cen·sus (**sen**-suhs) *noun* An official count of all the people living in a country or district. ▶ *noun, plural* **censuses**

cent (sent) *noun* A unit of money in the United States, Canada, Australia, many parts of Europe, and New Zealand. One hundred cents are equal to one dollar or one euro. **Cent** sounds like **scent** and **sent.**

cen·taur (**sen**-tor) *noun* A creature in Greek and Roman mythology that has the body and legs of a horse but the chest, arms, and head of a man.

cen·ten·ni·al (sen-**ten**-ee-uhl) *noun* The 100th-year celebration of an event. *adjective* Of or for a period of 100 years.

cen·ter (**sen**-tur) *noun* 1. The middle of something. 2. A place devoted to a particular activity. 3. **center of gravity** The point on an object at which half of its weight is on one side and half on the other. *verb* 1. To put something in the center. 2. To concentrate on something. 3. To put printed text in the middle of a line so that there is equal white space to the left and to the right of it. ▶ *verb* **centering, centered**

cen·ti·me·ter (**sen**-tuh-*mee*-tur) *noun* A unit of length in the metric system. A centimeter is equal to one-hundredth of a meter, or about four-tenths of an inch; 2.54 centimeters equals one inch.

cen·ti·pede (**sen**-ti-*peed*) *noun* A small creature with a very long, segmented body and one pair of legs per segment.

cen·tral (**sen**-truhl) *adjective* 1. In the middle. 2. Most important. ▶ *adverb* **centrally**

Cen·tral Af·ri·can Re·pub·lic (**sen**-truhl **af**-ri-kuhn ri-**puhb**-lik) A country in Central Africa. It is landlocked and mostly covered by savannas. A former colony of France, it has had an unstable government since gaining independence in 1960 and is one of the world's poorest countries.

Cen·tral A·mer·i·ca (**sen**-truhl uh-**mer**-i-kuh) The central region of the Americas, connecting North America to South America. Central America includes all the countries from Belize south to Panama.

C

cen·tral heat·ing (**sen**-truhl **hee**-ting)
noun A system for heating a building by heating water or air in one place and sending it through pipes or vents through the entire building.

cen·tri·fu·gal (sen-**trif**-yuh-guhl)
adjective Moving or tending to move away from the center.

cen·trip·e·tal (sen-**trip**-i-tuhl) *adjective* Moving or tending to move toward the center.

cen·tu·ri·on (sen-**toor**-ee-uhn) *noun* An officer in the ancient Roman army who was in command of 100 soldiers.

cen·tu·ry (**sen**-chur-ee) *noun* A period of 100 years. ▶ *noun, plural* **centuries**

ceph·a·lo·pod (**sef**-uh-luh-*pahd*) *noun* A sea creature that has tentacles attached to its head, such as an octopus or a squid.

ce·ram·ics (suh-**ram**-iks)
noun The art of making objects out of clay.
noun, plural Objects made of clay.
▶ *adjective* **ceramic**

ce·re·al (**seer**-ee-uhl) *noun* 1. A grain crop grown for food, such as wheat, corn, rice, oats, and barley. 2. A breakfast food made from grain, often eaten with milk.
Cereal sounds like **serial**.

cer·e·mo·ny (**ser**-uh-*moh*-nee) *noun* 1. A formal sequence of events to mark an important occasion. 2. The things that people do on special or formal occasions that make these occasions distinctive.
▶ *noun, plural* **ceremonies** ▶ *adjective* **ceremonial** ▶ *adverb* **ceremonially**

cer·tain (**sur**-tuhn) *adjective* 1. Sure, having no doubt. 2. Particular and usually known, but not specifically named.

cer·tain·ly (**sur**-tuhn-lee)
adverb You can use **certainly** with a verb when you want to emphasize your belief in the truth of what you are saying.
interjection You can say **certainly** or **certainly not** as an emphatic way of saying "yes" or "no," or to show that you strongly agree or disagree with

what someone has said. These two words are often used in sentences that end with an exclamation mark.

cer·tain·ty (**sur**-tuhn-tee) *noun* 1. The state or quality of being completely certain. 2. A statement or fact about which there is no doubt.
▶ *noun, plural* **certainties**

cer·tif·i·cate (sur-**tif**-uh-kit) *noun* A piece of paper that officially states that something is a fact.

cer·ti·fy (**sur**-tuh-fye) *verb* To state officially that something is true, correct, or genuine. ▶ *verb* **certifies, certifying, certified**

chad (chad) *noun* A small piece of paper made by punching a hole in a card, ballot, or paper.

Chad (chad) A country in Central Africa. It has a desert in the north, a fertile savanna in the south, and the second-largest wetland in Africa.

chafe (chafe) *verb* 1. To make something raw or sore by rubbing. 2. To be annoyed or irritated.
▶ *verb* **chafing, chafed**

chain (chayn)
noun 1. A flexible series of metal rings, called links, joined together. 2. A series of similar or connected items. 3. **chain store** A group of stores that is owned by the same company and sells similar products.
verb To attach with a chain.
▶ *verb* **chaining, chained**

chair (chair)
noun 1. A piece of furniture that you sit on, with a seat, legs, and a back. 2. A chairman or a chairwoman.
verb To be in charge of a meeting.
▶ *verb* **chairing, chaired**

chair·lift (**chair**-*lift*) *noun* A line of chairs attached to a moving cable that carries people up mountains, usually to ski.

chair·man (**chair**-muhn) *noun* A person who is in charge of a committee, a company, or a department in a school. The term usually applies to a man but can sometimes refer to a woman. ▶ *noun, plural* **chairmen**

chair·per·son (**chair**-*pur*-suhn) *noun* A chairman or a chairwoman.

C

chair·woman (**chair**-*wum*-uhn)
noun A woman who is in charge of a committee, a company, or a department in a school. ▶ *noun, plural* **chairwomen**

cha·let (sha-**lay**) *noun* A wooden house with a sloping roof and overhanging eaves, especially in mountainous areas of Europe.

chalk (chawk)
noun **1.** A soft, white rock, made from the remains of ancient sea creatures. **2.** A stick of this material, sometimes colored, used for writing or drawing.
verb To write using chalk.
 ▶ *verb* **chalking, chalked**

chalk·board (**chawk**-*bord*) *noun* Another name for a **blackboard.**

chal·lenge (**chal**-inj)
noun Something difficult that requires extra work or effort to do.
verb **1.** To invite someone to compete or to try to do something. **2.** To question whether something is right or not.
 ▶ *verb* **challenging, challenged** ▶ *adjective* **challenging**

cham·ber (**chaym**-bur) *noun* **1.** A room, especially a bedroom. **2.** A division of a legislative body. **3.** An enclosed space in a machine or an animal's body. **4. chamber music** Classical music for a small number of instruments.

cha·me·leon (kuh-**meel**-yuhn) *noun* A lizard that can change color, sometimes matching its surroundings.

cham·pagne (sham-**pane**) *noun* A white wine with small bubbles, often drunk at a celebration.

cham·pi·on (**cham**-pee-uhn)
noun **1.** The winner of a competition. **2.** A person who stands up for another person or an idea.
verb To support a cause.
 ▶ *verb* **championing, championed**

cham·pi·on·ship (**cham**-pee-uhn-*ship*)
noun A contest or final game of a series that determines which team or player will be the overall winner.

chance (chans)
noun **1.** The possibility of something happening. **2.** An opportunity to do something. **3. take a chance** To try something even though it is risky. **4. by chance** In an accidental or unplanned way.
adjective Happening accidentally and without planning or intention.
verb To do something by accident, without intending to.
 ▶ *verb* **chancing, chanced**

chan·cel·lor (**chan**-suh-lur) *noun* A title for a high-ranking government or university official.

chan·de·lier (*shan*-duh-**leer**) *noun* A light fixture that hangs from the ceiling and is usually lit by many small lights.

change (chaynj)
verb **1.** To become different or to make different. **2.** To put on different clothes. **3.** To exchange.
noun **1.** Something that is different, or the fact of being different. **2.** The money you receive back if you pay more than something costs. **3.** Coins rather than bills.
 ▶ *verb* **changing, changed**

chan·nel (**chan**-uhl) *noun* **1.** A narrow stretch of water between two areas of land. **2.** A television or radio station.

chan·nel-surf (**chan**-uhl-*surf*) *verb* To change television channels quickly in order to find something interesting. ▶ *verb* **channel-surfing, channel-surfed**

chant (chant)
verb **1.** To say or sing a phrase repeatedly. **2.** To sing, especially certain kinds of religious music.
noun A text, usually a religious one, that is chanted.
 ▶ *verb* **chanting, chanted**

cha·os (**kay**-ahs) *noun* Complete and usually noisy disorder. ▶ *adjective* **chaotic** (kay-**ah**-tik) ▶ *adverb* **chaotically**

chap (chap)
verb To make something, especially skin, so rough or dry that it cracks.
noun A man or boy; a fellow.
 ▶ *verb* **chapping, chapped** ▶ *adjective* **chapped**

C

chap·el (**chap**-uhl) *noun* 1. A small church. 2. A small, separate section of a large church or synagogue. 3. A place in a college, prison, or other institution where religious services are held.

chap·er·one or **chap·er·on** (**shap**-uh-*rohn*) *noun* An adult who protects the safety of young people at an event such as a dance or a class trip and who makes sure they behave well. *verb* To accompany in order to protect. ▶ *verb* **chaperoning, chaperoned**

chap·lain (**chap**-lin) *noun* A priest, minister, or rabbi who works in the military, or in a school or prison. A chaplain leads religious services and counsels people.

chaps (chaps) *noun, plural* Leather coverings that fit over jeans and protect the legs of people riding on horseback.

chap·ter (**chap**-tur) *noun* 1. A section of a book. 2. A branch of an organization.

char·ac·ter (**kar**-ik-tur) *noun* 1. The sort of person you are, or the qualities that make you that person. 2. One of the people in a story, book, play, movie, or television program. 3. A letter or symbol used in printing or on computers. All the letters of the alphabet are characters. 4. An unusual or amusing person.

char·ac·ter·is·tic (*kar*-ik-tuh-**ris**-tik) *noun* A typical feature or quality. *adjective* Typical. ▶ *adverb* **characteristically**

char·ac·ter·ize (**kar**-ik-tuh-*rize*) *verb* 1. To describe or identify the important qualities of someone or something. 2. To be a feature that identifies something. ▶ *verb* **characterizing, characterized**

char·coal (**char**-*kohl*) *noun* A substance made from incompletely burned wood. Charcoal is used in drawing pencils and as barbecue fuel.

charge (chahrj) *verb* 1. To demand a particular price for something. 2. To attack in a rush. 3. To put off paying for something by using a credit card or signing an agreement. 4. To accuse. 5. To pass an electric current through a battery so that it stores electricity. *noun* 1. The cost or price. 2. An attack. 3. An accusation or statement of blame. *idiom* **in charge** In a position of leadership or control. ▶ *verb* **charging, charged**

char·i·ot (**char**-ee-uht) *noun* A small vehicle pulled by a horse, used in ancient times in battles or for racing.

cha·ris·ma (kuh-**riz**-muh) *noun* A powerful personal appeal that attracts a great number of people. ▶ *adjective* **charismatic** (*kar*-iz-**mat**-ik)

char·i·ty (**char**-i-tee) *noun* 1. An organization that raises money to help people in need or some other worthy cause. 2. Money or other help that is given to people in need. 3. Kindness towards others. ▶ *noun, plural* **charities** ▶ *adjective* **charitable**

charm (chahrm) *noun* 1. Pleasing and attractive appearance and behavior. 2. A small object that is believed to bring good luck. *verb* To please someone and make the person like you. ▶ *verb* **charming, charmed** ▶ *noun* **charmer**

charm·ing (**chahr**-ming) *adjective* Attractive, full of charm, or delightful.

chart (chahrt) *noun* 1. A table, graph, or diagram that presents information. 2. A map of the stars or the oceans. *verb* To record or present information in the form of a chart. ▶ *verb* **charting, charted**

char·ter (**chahr**-tur) *noun* A formal document that states the rights or duties of a group of people, or that creates an institution such as a company or a university. *verb* To rent a form of transportation for private use. ▶ *verb* **chartering, chartered**

char·ter school (**chahr**-tur *skool*) *noun* A school that receives some money

C

from the government but that operates independently of other public schools.

chase (chase)
verb To run after someone or something in order to catch them or scare them away.
noun The act of chasing; pursuit.
▶ *verb* **chasing, chased**

chasm (**kaz**-uhm) *noun* A deep crack in the earth or in some other surface.

chas·sis (**chas**-ee *or* **shas**-ee) *noun* The frame of a vehicle, on which the body is assembled. ▶ *noun, plural* **chassis**

chat (chat)
verb 1. To talk in a friendly and informal way, usually about subjects that are not very serious. 2. To communicate with others in a chat room.
noun An informal conversation.
▶ *verb* **chatting, chatted**

châ·teau (sha-**toh**) *noun* A castle or large country house in France. ▶ *noun, plural* **châteaux** (sha-**toh** *or* sha-**tohz**)

chat room (**chat** room) *noun* An Internet site or website where people can type messages back and forth.

chat·ter (**chat**-ur)
verb 1. To talk continuously about unimportant things. 2. To knock together because you are cold; said of your teeth.
noun 1. The sharp, choppy sound of chattering. 2. Casual or foolish talk.
▶ *verb* **chattering, chattered**

chauf·feur (shoh-**fur**)
noun A person who is hired to drive a car for somebody else.
verb To act as a chauffeur.
▶ *verb* **chauffeuring, chauffeur**

chau·vin·ist (**shoh**-vuh-nist) *noun* A person who is overly proud of his or her nationality, gender, ethnic background, or other personal characteristic. ▶ *noun* **chauvinism** ▶ *adjective* **chauvinistic**

cheap (cheep) *adjective* 1. Not costing or worth very much. 2. Unkind and mean. 3. Not wanting to pay very much or spend very much.
▶ *adjective* **cheaper, cheapest** ▶ *noun* **cheapness** ▶ *adverb* **cheaply**

cheat (cheet)
verb To get something in a dishonest way.
noun A person who acts dishonestly.
▶ *verb* **cheating, cheated**

check (chek)
verb 1. To look at something in order to find out its condition. 2. To stop something from moving or growing. 3. To leave an item you own, such as a coat or a suitcase, in the care of someone else for a short time. 4. **check in** To register for a hotel room, a meeting, or some other facility or activity. 5. **check out** To pay your bill at a hotel or motel before leaving. 6. **check out** To remove items officially from their proper location. 7. **check out** To investigate something.
noun 1. A pattern of squares of different colors. 2. A printed piece of paper on which someone writes to tell the bank to pay a specific amount of money from his or her account to another person or to a company. 3. A mark (✓) used to show that a thing has been looked at or verified.
▶ *verb* **checking, checked** ▶ *adjective* **checked**

check·ers (**chek**-urz) *noun* A game for two people with 12 round pieces each, played on a board marked with squares of alternating colors.

check·out (**chek**-out) *noun* The place in a store where you pay for your purchases.

check·up (**chek**-uhp) *noun* A thorough medical or dental examination.

cheek (cheek) *noun* 1. Either side of your face below your eyes. 2. Rude and disrespectful behavior or speech.
▶ *adjective* **cheeky** ▶ *adverb* **cheekily**

cheer (cheer)
verb 1. To praise or encourage with shouts. 2. **cheer up** To begin to feel better after being sad or worried.
noun 1. A shout of encouragement. 2. Happiness; good spirits.
idiom **be of good cheer** To be happy.
▶ *verb* **cheering, cheered**

C

cheer·ful (**cheer**-fuhl) *adjective* Visibly happy. ▸ *noun* **cheerfulness** ▸ *adverb* **cheerfully**

cheese (cheez) *noun* A food made from the curds of milk.

cheese·bur·ger (**cheez**-*bur*-gur) *noun* A hamburger with cheese melted on top of the meat.

chee·tah (**chee**-tuh) *noun* A wild cat with a spotted coat that is found in Africa and southern Asia. Cheetahs are the fastest-running animals on land.

chef (shef) *noun* The chief cook in a restaurant.

chem·i·cal (**kem**-i-kuhl)
noun **1.** A substance used in or made by chemistry. **2. chemical symbol** A one- to three-letter abbreviation that is used to identify all of the elements.
adjective Of or having to do with chemistry or chemicals.
▸ *adverb* **chemically**

chem·ist (**kem**-ist) *noun* A person trained in chemistry.

chem·is·try (**kem**-i-stree) *noun* The scientific study of substances, what they are composed of, and how they react with each other.

che·mo·ther·a·py (*kee*-moh-**ther**-uh-pee) *noun* The use of chemicals to kill diseased cells in cancer patients. ▸ *noun* **chemotherapist**

cher·ish (**cher**-ish) *verb* **1.** To protect and care for someone or something lovingly. **2.** To value or hold dear.
▸ *verb* **cherishes, cherishing, cherished**

Cher·o·kee (**cher**-uh-*kee*) *noun* A member of a group of Native Americans who live primarily in Oklahoma and North Carolina. ▸ *noun, plural* **Cherokee** *or* **Cherokees**

cher·ry (**cher**-ee)
noun **1.** A small, sweet, red fruit with a pit inside. **2.** A tree that produces cherries. **3.** A medium to bright red color.
adjective Being a medium to bright red color.
▸ *noun, plural* **cherries**

Ches·a·peake Bay (**ches**-uh-*peek* **bay**) An estuary of the Atlantic Ocean, located on the eastern coast of the United States between Maryland and Virginia. The Chesapeake is fed by more than 150 rivers and streams and spans about 200 miles from the northern tip, where it meets the Susquehanna River, to the southern tip, where it meets the Atlantic Ocean.

chess (ches) *noun* A game for two people with 16 pieces each, played on a board marked with squares of alternating colors.

chest (chest) *noun* **1.** The front part of your body between your neck and belly. **2.** A large, strong box for storage or shipping.

chest·nut (**ches**-*nuht*)
noun **1.** A large, reddish-brown nut. **2.** A tree that produces chestnuts. **3.** A reddish-brown color.
adjective Being a reddish-brown color.

chest of draw·ers (**chest** uhv **drorz**) *noun* A piece of furniture with drawers, usually used for storing clothes. ▸ *noun, plural* **chests of drawers**

chew (choo) *verb* To grind food between your teeth. ▸ *verb* **chewing, chewed**

chew·ing gum (**choo**-ing *guhm*) *noun* A sweet, flavored substance that you chew for a long time but do not swallow.

Chey·enne (shye-**en**) *noun* A member of a group of American Indians who live primarily in Montana and Oklahoma. ▸ *noun, plural* **Cheyenne** *or* **Cheyennes**

Chi·ca·na (chi-**kah**-nuh) *noun* **1.** An American girl or woman born of Mexican parents; a Mexican American. **2.** A Mexican woman living and working in the United States.

Chi·ca·no (chi-**kah**-noh) *noun* **1.** An American boy or man born of Mexican parents; a Mexican American. **2.** A Mexican man living and working in the United States.

chick (chik) *noun* A very young bird, especially a very young chicken, or a small lobster.

chick·a·dee (**chik**-uh-*dee*) *noun* A kind of small bird with a black head and throat, gray wings, and a white belly. The call of the chickadee sounds like its name.

chick·en (**chik**-uhn) *noun* **1.** A common type of fowl that is raised on farms for its meat and eggs. **2.** The meat from this bird, used as food. **3.** (slang) A person who is too scared to do something.

chick·en pox (**chik**-uhn pahks) *noun* A common, contagious disease, especially among children, that causes red, itchy spots on the skin.

chick·pea (**chick**-*pee*) *noun* The edible seed of a plant originally grown in Asia. Another name for chickpea is *garbanzo*.

chide (chide) *verb* To scold or to find fault with someone. ▶ *verb* **chiding, chided**

chief (cheef)
noun The leader of a group.
adjective Main, or most important.

chief·ly (**cheef**-lee) *adverb* Mainly or mostly.

chief·tain (**cheef**-tuhn) *noun* The chief or leader of a tribe, clan, or community.

chig·ger (**chig**-ur) *noun* A tiny insect that feeds on skin cells, causing a rash and severe itching.

Chi·hua·hua (chi-**wah**-wuh) *noun* A breed of small, short-haired dog, originally from Mexico.

child (childe) *noun* **1.** A young boy or girl. **2.** A son or daughter. ▶ *noun, plural* **children** (**chil**-drin)

child·birth (**childe**-*burth*) *noun* The act or process of giving birth to a baby.

child·hood (**childe**-hud) *noun* The time when you are a child.

child·ish (**chile**-dish) *adjective* Immature and silly. ▶ *noun* **childishness** ▶ *adverb* **childishly**

Chil·e (**chil**-ee) A country in South America that runs in a long, narrow strip between the Pacific Ocean and the Andes Mountains. Stable and prosperous, it enjoys a better quality of life than most other South American nations.

chil·i (**chil**-ee) *noun* **1.** A kind of pepper with green or red skin that is used to make food spicy. **2.** A spicy food made with chilies, and often with beans and meat. ▶ *noun, plural* **chilies**

chill (chil)
verb **1.** To make someone or something cold. **2.** **chill** or **chill out** (slang) To relax or stop worrying.
noun **1.** A slight coldness. **2.** A shiver you feel in your body, often related to cold or fear.
adjective Cool or cold.
▶ *verb* **chilling, chilled** ▶ *adjective* **chilly** ▶ *adjective* **chilling**

chime (chime)
verb To make a ringing sound, like a bell or a clock.
noun A ringing sound.
▶ *verb* **chiming, chimed**

chim·ney (**chim**-nee) *noun* An upright pipe or channel that carries smoke away from a fire, usually out of a building.

chim·pan·zee (*chim*-pan-**zee** or chim-**pan**-zee) *noun* A small ape with dark fur that comes from Africa. Chimpanzees are the closest genetic relative of humans.

chin (chin) *noun* The part of your face below your mouth, formed by the point of the lower jaw.

chi·na (**chye**-nuh) *noun* **1.** A very thin, delicate ceramic material. **2.** Cups, plates, and dishes made of china.

Chi·na (**chye**-nuh) A country in East Asia. It is the most populous country in the world, with more than a billion people. A communist state since 1949, it is a rising power. China is now considered to have the world's second-largest economy, after the United States.

chin·chil·la (chin-**chil**-uh) *noun* A small South American rodent with very soft fur.

chink (chingk) *noun* A small crack or opening.

C

chip (chip)
noun 1. A small piece of something that is cut or broken off. 2. A very thin piece of food cooked in oil until it is crisp. 3. Short for **microchip**.
verb 1. To break a small piece off something. 2. **chip in** To add your money to other people's money to make a purchase together.
idiom **have a chip on your shoulder** To feel angry because you think you have been treated unfairly.
▶ *verb* **chipping, chipped**

chip·munk (**chip**-muhnk) *noun* A small animal related to the squirrel that has brown fur and dark stripes on its back and tail.

chi·ro·prac·tor (**kye**-ruh-*prak*-tur) *noun* A person who treats back pain and other illnesses by adjusting the spine.

chirp (churp)
noun A high-pitched sound made by some birds and insects.
verb To make such a sound.
▶ *verb* **chirping, chirped**

chis·el (**chiz**-uhl)
noun A tool with a broad, sharp end used to cut or shape wood, stone, or metal.
verb To cut something carefully and form it into a desired shape.
▶ *verb* **chiseling, chiseled**

chiv·al·ry (**shiv**-uhl-ree) *noun*
1. Courteous and helpful behavior, especially by a man toward a woman.
2. A code of noble and polite behavior that was expected of a medieval knight.
▶ *adjective* **chivalrous**

chlo·ri·nate (**klor**-i-nate) *verb* To add chlorine to water in order to kill germs. ▶ *verb* **chlorinating, chlorinated**

chlo·rine (**klor**-een) *noun* A chemical element that is a poisonous gas with a strong smell. It is added to water in very small amounts to keep it free from bacteria.

chlo·ro·phyll (**klor**-uh-fil) *noun* The green substance in plants that uses light to manufacture food from carbon dioxide and water.

choc·o·late (**chaw**-kuh-lit *or* **chawk**-lit)
noun A food made from roasting and grinding the beans that grow on the tropical cacao tree.
adjective Being made from or having the flavor of chocolate.
▶ *adjective* **chocolatey**

Choc·taw (**chahk**-taw) *noun* A member of a group of Native Americans who live primarily in Oklahoma, Mississippi, and Louisiana. ▶ *noun, plural* **Choctaw** *or* **Choctaws**

choice (chois)
noun 1. The thing or person that has been selected. 2. A group or range of things from which you can choose.
3. The chance to choose.
adjective Of very good quality.

choir (kwire) *noun* A group of people who sing together, especially in a church.

choke (choke) *verb* 1. To have great difficulty breathing because something is blocking your breathing passages or because of lack of air.
2. To cause someone to stop breathing by squeezing his or her neck. 3. To block something. 4. **choke back** To hide a feeling or refuse to express it.
▶ *verb* **choking, choked**

chol·e·ra (**kah**-lur-uh) *noun* A dangerous disease that causes severe vomiting and diarrhea, usually due to contaminated water.

cho·les·ter·ol (kuh-**les**-tuh-*rawl*) *noun* A fatty substance that humans and animals need to digest food and produce certain vitamins and hormones. Too much cholesterol in the blood can increase the possibility of heart disease.

choose (chooz) *verb* 1. To pick out one person or thing from several possibilities. 2. To decide to do something.
▶ *verb* **choosing, chose** (chohz), **chosen** (**choh**-zuhn)

choos·y (**choo**-zee) *adjective* Particular about what you want, especially in a situation where there is no great benefit in being particular. ▶ *adjective* **choosier, choosiest**

C

chop (chahp)
verb To cut by striking repeatedly with a knife or an ax.
noun A small piece of lamb, veal, or pork with a rib or other bone attached.
▶ *verb* **chopping, chopped**

chop·py (**chah**-pee) *adjective* Quite rough or uneven. ▶ *adjective* **choppier, choppiest**

chop·sticks (**chahp**-stiks) *noun, plural* A pair of thin, tapered sticks for handling food, used primarily by people in East Asian countries.

cho·ral (**kor**-uhl) *adjective* Sung by a choir, or having to do with a choir.
Choral sounds like **coral.**

chord (kord) *noun* **1.** Two or more musical notes played at the same time. **2.** A straight line that joins two points on a curve.
Chord sounds like **cord.**

chore (chor) *noun* A job that has to be done regularly, and that is usually considered unpleasant or tedious.

cho·re·og·ra·pher (kor-ee-ah-gruh-fur) *noun* A person who arranges steps and movements for a ballet or other forms of dance. ▶ *noun* **choreography** ▶ *verb* **choreograph** (**kor**-ee-uh-graf)

cho·rus (**kor**-uhs) *noun* **1.** The part of a song that is repeated after each verse. **2.** A large group of people who sing or recite together.
▶ *noun, plural* **choruses**

chose (choze) *verb* The past tense of **choose.**

chos·en (**choh**-zuhn) *verb* The past participle of **choose.**

chow·der (**chou**-dur) *noun* A thick soup made with clams or fish and vegetables.

Christ (kriste) *noun* Jesus, the person whom Christians worship as the son of God.

chris·ten·ing (**kris**-uh-ning) *noun* A ceremony in which a person is given a name and accepted into the Christian religion. ▶ *verb* **christen**

Chris·ti·an·i·ty (kris-chee-**an**-i-tee) *noun* The religion based on the life and teachings of Jesus. ▶ *noun* **Christian** ▶ *adjective* **Christian**

Christ·mas (**kris**-muhs) *noun* The Christian festival on December 25 that celebrates the birth of Jesus.
adjective Of, for, or because of Christmas.
▶ *noun, plural* **Christmases**

chro·ma·tog·ra·phy (kroh-muh-**tah**-gruh-fee) *noun* The process of separating parts of a chemical mixture by letting it travel through a material that absorbs each part at a different rate.

chrome (krohm) *noun* A shiny silver metal that is used as a protective covering or for decoration.

chro·mo·some (**kroh**-muh-*sohm*) *noun* The structure inside the nucleus of a cell that carries the genes that give living things their individual characteristics.

chron·ic (**krah**-nik) *adjective* Lasting for a long time or returning periodically. ▶ *adverb* **chronically**

chron·i·cle (**krah**-ni-kuhl)
verb To record historical events in a factual and detailed way.
noun A record of historical events.
▶ *verb* **chronicling, chronicled**

chron·o·log·i·cal (*krah*-nuh-**lah**-ji-kuhl) *adjective* Arranged in the order in which things occurred. ▶ *noun* **chronology** (kruh-**nah**-luh-jee) ▶ *adverb* **chronologically**

chrys·a·lis (**kris**-uh-lis) *noun* A butterfly or moth in a quiet stage of development between a caterpillar and an adult. It spends this stage inside a hard outer shell. ▶ *noun, plural* **chrysalises**

chry·san·the·mum (kruh-**san**-thuh-muhm) *noun* A flower of various shapes and colors that has many petals.

chub·by (**chuhb**-ee) *adjective* Slightly fat or plump. ▶ *adjective* **chubbier, chubbiest**

chuck·le (**chuhk**-uhl)
verb To laugh quietly or inwardly.
noun A quiet laugh.
▶ *verb* **chuckling, chuckled**

C

chuck·wag·on (**chuhk**-*wag*-uhn) *noun* A covered wagon or truck that serves as a portable kitchen.

chug (chuhg) *verb* **1.** To make a series of muffled explosive sounds while moving along. **2.** (informal) To drink a large quantity at once without stopping.
▶ *verb* **chugging, chugged**

chum (chuhm) *noun* A friend, buddy, or pal.

chunk (chuhngk) *noun* A thick, solid piece of something.

chunk·y (**chuhng**-kee) *adjective* **1.** Full of chunks or pieces. **2.** Short and solid in build; stocky.
▶ *adjective* **chunkier, chunkiest**

church (church) *noun* **1.** A building used by Christians for worship. **2.** A group of Christians who share similar beliefs. **3.** Christian religious services.
▶ *noun, plural* **churches**

churn (churn)
noun A machine or device in which cream is made into butter.
verb **1.** To form butter by stirring cream. **2.** To move a substance around roughly. **3.** If your stomach **churns,** you feel very upset or a little sick.
▶ *verb* **churning, churned**

chute (shoot) *noun* A narrow, tilted passage for sending things like garbage, laundry, grain, or coal to a lower level. **Chute** sounds like **shoot.**

chut·ney (**chuht**-nee) *noun* A relish of vegetables, fruit, and spices.

ci·der (**sye**-dur) *noun* A beverage made by pressing apples.

ci·gar (si-**gahr**) *noun* A cylinder of rolled-up tobacco leaves that people smoke.

cig·a·rette (*sig*-uh-**ret**) *noun* A thin roll of finely chopped tobacco covered with paper that people smoke.

cin·der (**sin**-dur) *noun* A small piece of wood or coal that has been partly burned.

cin·e·ma (**sin**-uh-muh) *noun* **1.** A movie theater. **2.** The movie industry.
▶ *adjective* **cinematic**

cin·na·mon (**sin**-uh-muhn) *noun*
1. A reddish-brown spice that comes from the inner bark of a tropical tree. **2.** A light reddish-brown color.

cir·ca (**sur**-kuh) *preposition* The Latin word for "around," indicating that something, especially a date, is not known exactly. Abbreviated as *c.* or *ca.* *My estimate is that he was born circa 1730.*

cir·cle (**sur**-kuhl)
noun **1.** A flat, perfectly round shape. **2.** A group of people who all know each other.
verb To run or form a circle around something.
idiom **go around in circles** To do something over and over again without accomplishing anything.
▶ *verb* **circling, circled** ▶ *adjective* **circular** (**sur**-kyuh-lur)

cir·cuit (**sur**-kit) *noun* **1.** A route or trip with several stops that ends in the place where it began. **2.** A complete path for an electrical current. **3.** An area that is under the authority of a particular court.

cir·cuit board (**sur**-kit *bord*) *noun* A piece of plastic that has electrical circuits printed onto it in the form of small metal strips.

cir·cuit break·er (**sur**-kit *bray*-kur) *noun* A safety device that switches the electricity off when there is too much current in the system.

cir·cu·late (**sur**-kyuh-*late*) *verb* **1.** To move in a circle or pattern. **2.** To follow a course from place to place or person to person.
▶ *verb* **circulating, circulated**

cir·cu·la·tion (*sur*-kyuh-**lay**-shuhn) *noun* **1.** The movement of blood in blood vessels through the body. **2.** The number of copies of a newspaper, magazine, or other publication that are bought in a day, week, month, or year.
▶ *adjective* **circulatory** (**sur**-kyuh-luh-*tor*-ee)

cir·cu·la·to·ry sys·tem (**sur**-kyuh-luh-*tor*-ee *sis*-tuhm) *noun* The group of organs that pump blood through the body.

cir·cum·fer·ence (sur-**kuhm**-fur-uhns) *noun* **1.** The outer edge of a circle or the length of this edge. **2.** The distance around something.

cir·cum·spect (**sur**-kuhm-spekt) *adjective* Cautious and unwilling to take risks. ▸ *noun* **circumspection** ▸ *adverb* **circumspectly**

cir·cum·stanc·es (**sur**-kuhm-*stan*-siz) *noun, plural* The facts or conditions that are connected to an event or period of time.

cir·cum·stan·tial (*sur*-kuhm-**stan**-shuhl) *adjective* Of or having to do with circumstances that suggest that someone is guilty but without any means of proving it.

cir·cus (**sur**-kuhs) *noun* **1.** A traveling show in which clowns, acrobats, trained animals, and other entertainers perform. **2.** A noisy and confused situation.
▸ *noun, plural* **circuses**

cis·tern (**sis**-turn) *noun* A reservoir or tank for storing water.

cite (site) *verb* **1.** To quote from a written work. **2.** To give someone a commendation or medal. **3.** To summon someone to appear in court. **4.** To use a thing or an event as proof of an argument.
Cite sounds like **site** and **sight**. ▸ *verb* **citing, cited**

cit·i·zen (**sit**-i-zuhn) *noun* **1.** A person who has full rights in a particular country, such as the right to live there, to work there, and to vote in the country's elections. **2.** A resident of a particular town or city.

cit·i·zen·ship (**sit**-i-zuhn-*ship*) *noun* The condition of being a citizen of a certain country.

cit·rus fruit (**sit**-ruhs *froot*) *noun* An acidic, juicy fruit such as an orange, a lemon, or a grapefruit.

cit·y (**sit**-ee) *noun* A very large or important town. ▸ *noun, plural* **cities**

civ·ic (**siv**-ik) *adjective* Of or having to do with a city or the people who live in it.

civ·ics (**siv**-iks) *noun* The study of the way government works, and of how to be a good citizen of a community or country.

civ·il (**siv**-uhl)
adjective **1.** Of or having to do with the government or people of a country, rather than its military forces or religion. **2.** Polite.
noun, plural **civil rights** The individual rights that all members of a democratic society have to freedom and equal treatment under the law.
noun **civil servant** A person who works for the government.
▸ *noun* **civility** (suh-**vil**-i-tee)

ci·vil·ian (suh-**vil**-yuhn) *noun* A person who is not a member of the armed forces or a police force.

civ·i·li·za·tion (*siv*-uh-li-**zay**-shuhn) *noun* **1.** An advanced stage of human organization, technology, and culture. **2.** A developed and organized society.

civ·i·lize (**siv**-uh-*lize*) *verb* **1.** To improve a person's manners and education. **2.** To bring a society to a level of development that is considered higher or better.
▸ *verb* **civilizing, civilized** ▸ *adjective* **civilized**

civ·il war (**siv**-uhl **wor**) *noun* **1.** A war between different groups within the same country. **2. Civil War** The war in the United States between the Confederacy, or Southern states, and the Union, or Northern states, that lasted from 1861 to 1865.

clad (klad) *adjective* Dressed in a particular way.

claim (klaym)
verb **1.** To demand something because you think that it belongs to you or that you have a right to it. **2.** To say that something is true.
noun **1.** A statement that something is true. **2.** A statement that you have a right to something, or the right itself.
▸ *verb* **claiming, claimed**

clam (klam)
noun A shellfish, often used as food, that has two tightly closed shells, which are hinged together.
verb **clam up** (informal) To refuse to speak.
▸ *verb* **clamming, clammed**

C

clam·bake (**klam**-*bake*) *noun* A party, often held at the beach, where clams and other foods are cooked on heated stones.

clam·ber (**klam**-bur) *verb* To climb or move quickly and awkwardly. ▶ *verb* **clambering, clambered**

clam·my (**klam**-ee) *adjective* Unpleasantly damp, sticky, and chilly. ▶ *adjective* **clammier, clammiest**

clam·or (**klam**-ur)
verb To demand something noisily.
noun A disturbance caused by a large group of people making noise or demanding something.
▶ *verb* **clamoring, clamored**

clamp (klamp)
noun A tool or instrument for holding things firmly in place.
verb **1.** To fasten something with a clamp. **2. clamp down** To try to stop something or control it more tightly.
▶ *verb* **clamping, clamped**

clan (klan) *noun* A large group of families descended from a common ancestor.

clap (klap)
verb To strike your hands together to show that you have enjoyed something, to keep time to music, or to get someone's attention.
noun A loud bang of thunder or other noise.
▶ *verb* **clapping, clapped**

clar·i·fy (**klar**-uh-*fye*) *verb* To explain something; to make something clear. ▶ *verb* **clarifies, clarifying, clarified** ▶ *noun* **clarification**

clar·i·net (*klar*-uh-**net**) *noun* A long, hollow woodwind instrument. A clarinet is played by blowing into a mouthpiece and pressing keys or covering holes with the fingers to change the pitch.

clar·i·ty (**klar**-i-tee) *noun* The quality of being clear, or easy to understand.

clash (klash)
verb **1.** To fight or argue vehemently. **2.** To not match or go together well. **3.** To make a loud ringing noise by striking two objects against each other.
noun **1.** A strong disagreement or fight.

2. A loud ringing noise.
▶ *verb* **clashes, clashing, clashed** ▶ *noun, plural* **clashes**

clasp (klasp)
verb To hold tightly.
noun A small fastener.
▶ *verb* **clasping, clasped**

class (klas) *noun* **1.** A group of students who are taught together. **2.** A group of people or things that are similar. **3.** A group of people in society with a similar way of life or range of income. **4.** In taxonomy, a **class** is a group of related plants and animals that is larger than an order but smaller than a phylum. **5.** (informal) Attractiveness and style in appearance or behavior.
▶ *noun, plural* **classes**

clas·sic (**klas**-ik)
adjective **1.** Very well liked or of very good quality, and therefore likely to remain popular for a long time. **2.** Typical.
noun An outstanding example of its kind.
noun, plural **classics** The languages and literature of ancient Greece and Rome.

clas·si·cal (**klas**-i-kuhl) *adjective* **1.** In the style of ancient Greece or Rome. **2.** Traditional or accepted. **3. Classical** music is serious music in the European tradition, such as opera, chamber music, and music for large orchestras.

clas·si·fied (**klas**-uh-fide) *adjective* **1.** Declared secret by the government or other authority. **2.** A **classified** ad in a newspaper is a small ad for a job, a service, an item for sale, or other similar transactions, organized in sections according to category.

clas·si·fy (**klas**-uh-fye) *verb* To put things into groups according to the characteristics they have in common. ▶ *verb* **classifies, classifying, classified** ▶ *noun* **classification**

class·mate (**klas**-mate) *noun* A person who is in the same class as another person.

class·room (**klas**-room) *noun* A room in a school in which classes take place.

clas·sy (**klas**-ee) *adjective* 1. (informal) Attractive and stylish. 2. (informal) Dignified and appropriate, especially under stress.
▶ *adjective* **classier, classiest**

clat·ter (**klat**-ur)
verb To fall or bang together noisily.
noun The noise of objects banging together or falling.
▶ *verb* **clattering, clattered**

clause (klawz) *noun* 1. A group of words that contains a subject and a predicate and forms a sentence or one part of a sentence. 2. One section of a formal legal document.

claus·tro·pho·bi·a (*klaws*-truh-**foh**-bee-uh) *noun* Extreme fear of being in small, enclosed places. ▶ *adjective* **claustrophobic**

claw (klaw)
noun A hard, sharp nail on the foot of an animal or a bird.
verb To scratch with nails or claws.
▶ *verb* **clawing, clawed**

clay (klay) *noun* A kind of earth that can be shaped when wet and baked to make bricks, pottery, or figures.

clean (kleen)
adjective 1. Not dirty, messy, or marked up. 2. Fair, or obeying the rules. 3. Not rude or offensive.
verb To remove the dirt from something.
idiom **keep your nose clean** To stay out of trouble.
▶ *verb* **cleaning, cleaned** ▶ *adjective* **cleaner, cleanest** ▶ *noun* **cleaner** ▶ *noun* **cleanness** ▶ *adverb* **cleanly**

clean·ing (**klee**-ning) *noun* An act or instance of removing the dirt, grime, or dust from something.

clean·li·ness (**klen**-lee-nis) *noun* Cleanness, especially of a person's body and surroundings.

cleanse (klenz) *verb* To make something thoroughly clean or pure. ▶ *verb* **cleansing, cleansed**

cleans·er (**klen**-zur) *noun* A powder or liquid used to clean or scrub things.

clear (kleer)
adjective 1. Easy to see through. 2. Colorless. 3. Bright; not dark or cloudy. 4. Easy to understand. 5. Free of obstructions. 6. Free of appointments or commitments. 7. Free from worry or guilt.
verb 1. To make or become bright. 2. To remove things that are covering or blocking a place. 3. To jump over something without touching it. 4. To declare that someone is not guilty of a crime.
adverb In a clear way; distinctly.
▶ *adjective* **clearer, clearest** ▶ *verb* **clearing, cleared** ▶ *noun* **clearness**

clear·ance (**kleer**-uhns) *noun* 1. The act of clearing. 2. The sale of merchandise at a low price to get rid of it quickly, usually in order to make room for newer items. 3. Permission to do something. 4. The space needed so that an object can move freely without touching something else.

clear·ing (**kleer**-ing) *noun* An open area in a forest.

clear·ly (**kleer**-lee) *adverb* 1. In a way that is clear. 2. Obviously and without a doubt.

clef (klef) *noun* A symbol written at the beginning of a line of music to show the pitch of the notes.

cleft (kleft) *noun* 1. A split or division. 2. An indentation similar to a dimple.

clench (klench) *verb* To close or hold something tightly. ▶ *verb* **clenches, clenching, clenched**

cler·gy (**klur**-jee) *noun* A group of people trained to lead religious groups, such as priests, ministers, and rabbis. ▶ *noun, plural* **clergies**

cler·i·cal (**kler**-i-kuhl) *adjective* 1. Of or having to do with the clergy. 2. Of or having to do with office work, especially routine work such as filing.

clerk (klurk) *noun* 1. A salesperson in a store. 2. A person who keeps records in an office, a bank, or a law court.

clev·er (**klev**-ur) *adjective* 1. Able to learn, understand, and do things quickly and easily. 2. Ingenious; well thought out.
▶ *adjective* **cleverer, cleverest** ▶ *noun* **cleverness** ▶ *adverb* **cleverly**

C

C

cli·ché (klee-**shay**) *noun* An idea or a phrase that is used often but that doesn't have very much meaning. *"If you know what I mean"* is a cliché.

click (klik)
verb 1. To make a short, sharp sound. 2. (informal) To become suddenly clear. 3. To instruct a computer to do something by pressing the mouse button when the cursor is over or pointing to the desired choice.
noun 1. A short sharp sound. 2. A single pressing down on a computer's mouse.
▶ *verb* **clicking, clicked**

cli·ent (**klye**-uhnt) *noun* 1. A customer of a professional person or company. 2. A computer that can exchange data with a server.

cliff (klif) *noun* A high, steep rock face.

cliff·hang·er (**klif**-hang-ur) *noun* 1. A story, movie, or television program presented in several parts that is exciting because each part ends at a moment of suspense. 2. A suspenseful situation.

cli·mate (**klye**-mit) *noun* 1. The weather typical of a place over a long period of time. 2. The general situation, mood, or public opinion at a particular time.
▶ *adjective* **climatic** (klye-**mat**-ik)

cli·mate change (**klye**-mit chaynj) *noun* Global warming and other changes in the weather and weather patterns that are happening because of human activity.

cli·max (**klye**-maks)
noun The most exciting or important part of a story or an event, usually happening near the end.
verb To reach the most important, exciting, or significant moment.
▶ *noun, plural* **climaxes** ▶ *verb* **climaxes, climaxing, climaxed**

climb (klime)
verb 1. To move upward, usually with effort. 2. To go in various directions using your hands to support and help you.
noun The process of moving upward, or an upward slope.
▶ *verb* **climbing, climbed** ▶ *noun* **climber**

clinch (klinch) *verb* To settle a matter definitely. ▶ *verb* **clinches, clinching, clinched**

cling (kling) *verb* To stick to or hold on to something or someone very tightly. ▶ *verb* **clinging, clung** (kluhng)

clin·ic (**klin**-ik) *noun* 1. A hospital department or other place where people receive medical treatment or advice. 2. A class or session for teaching some specific skill or information.

clip (klip)
verb 1. To fasten things together with a small, tight fastener. 2. To trim something.
noun 1. A small fastener. 2. A short piece of a movie or television program shown by itself. 3. A rapid pace.
▶ *verb* **clipping, clipped**

clip art (klip ahrt) *noun* Simple images or pictures that are stored on a computer or online for use in illustrating a document.

clip·board (**klip**-bord) *noun* 1. A thin board with a clip at the top for holding papers and writing on them. 2. A place on your computer where you can store text or pictures temporarily.

clip·per (**klip**-ur) *noun* 1. A tool that clips something, such as hedges or fingernails. 2. A fast-sailing ship with three masts, built in the United States in the 1800s and used to carry cargo.

clip·ping (**klip**-ing) *noun* Something clipped or cut from something else.

clique (kleek *or* klik) *noun* A small group of friends who do not easily allow others to join them. ▶ *adjective* **cliquish**

cloak (klohk) *noun* A loose, sleeveless coat that fastens at the neck and is wrapped around your body.

cloak·room (**klohk**-room) *noun* A room where you can hang coats and store umbrellas, hats, and bags.

clock (klahk)
noun An instrument that tells the time.
verb To measure the time or speed of something.
▶ *verb* **clocking, clocked**

clock·wise (**klahk**-*wize*) *adverb, adjective* In the direction in which the hands of a clock move.

clock·work (**klahk**-*wurk*) *noun* **1.** A mechanism with gears, springs, and wheels that makes things such as clocks and toys work. **2. like clockwork** Smoothly and without problems.

clod (klahd) *noun* **1.** A lump of earth or clay. **2.** A dull or awkward person.

clog (klahg)
verb To fill up or block something with foreign matter.
noun A sturdy, round-toed shoe. In the past, clogs usually had wooden soles.
▶ *verb* **clogging, clogged**

clois·ter (**kloi**-stur) *noun* **1.** A place where nuns or monks live; a convent or monastery. **2.** A covered walk with columns along the wall of a convent, monastery, or other building.

clone (klohn)
verb To grow an identical plant or animal from the cells of another plant or animal.
noun An identical plant or animal that has been grown from the cells of another.
▶ *verb* **cloning, cloned**

close
verb (kloze) **1.** To shut something that is open. **2.** To bring something to an end. **3.** To stop running a computer program.
noun (kloze) The end of something.
adverb (klose) Near.
adjective (klose) **1.** Only a short distance away. **2.** Careful. **3.** Almost even. **4.** Similar or alike.
▶ *verb* **closing, closed** ▶ *adjective* **closer, closest** ▶ *adverb, adjective* **closer, closest** ▶ *adverb* **closely**

close call (**klohs kawl**) *noun* A narrow escape from danger or trouble.

closed (klohzd) *adjective* **1.** Not open for business. **2.** Not welcoming to newcomers or strangers.

closed-cir·cuit tel·e·vi·sion (**klohzd**-*sur*-kit **tel**-uh-*vizh*-uhn) *noun* A television system that shows images on a limited number of television screens.

clos·et (**klah**-zit) *noun* A small room used for storing things.

close-up (**klohs**-*uhp*)
noun A very detailed look at something, especially a camera shot taken at close range.
adjective Of or like a close-up.

clot (klaht)
noun A mass of liquid that has become thicker and more solid.
verb To thicken.
▶ *verb* **clotting, clotted**

cloth (klawth) *noun* **1.** A material that is made from weaving or knitting threads, used to make clothing and many other things. **2.** A small piece of this material used for a particular purpose.

clothe (klohTH) *verb* To dress or provide with clothing. ▶ *verb* **clothing, clothed**

clothes (klohz) *noun, plural* Things that you wear, such as shirts, pants, and dresses. ▶ *noun, plural* **clothes**

clothes·pin (**klohz**-*pin*) *noun* A wooden or plastic clip used to hold clothes on a line while they dry.

cloth·ing (**kloh**-THing) *noun* Garments worn to cover the body; clothes.

cloud (kloud)
noun **1.** A visible white or gray mass of tiny water drops or ice particles suspended in the air. **2.** A mass of smoke or dust.
verb **cloud over** To become covered with clouds; to become less clear or less bright.
▶ *verb* **clouding, clouded**

cloud·burst (**kloud**-*burst*) *noun* A sudden, heavy rain shower.

cloud·y (**klou**-dee) *adjective* **1.** Covered with clouds. **2.** Not clear.
▶ *adjective* **cloudier, cloudiest**

clove (klove) *noun* **1.** The dried flower bud of a tropical tree, used whole or ground up as a spice in cooking. **2.** One of the sections of a bulb of garlic.

clo·ver (**kloh**-vur) *noun* A small plant with white or pink flowers and three-part leaves.

C

clown (kloun)
noun 1. A performer with a painted face and funny clothes, who tries to make people laugh. 2. A person who does silly things on purpose.
verb To do silly things in order to make people laugh or to cause disruption.
▶ *verb* **clowning, clowned**

club (kluhb)
noun 1. A group or organization devoted to a particular interest or activity. 2. The place where a group meets to share a common interest. 3. A stick with a metal or wooden head used for playing golf. 4. A thick, heavy stick, especially when used as a weapon.
noun, plural **clubs** One of the four suits in a deck of cards, with a black symbol having three leaves.
verb To hit with a club.
▶ *verb* **clubbing, clubbed**

clue (kloo) *noun* An object or a piece of information that helps you answer a question or solve a mystery.

clump (kluhmp)
noun A group of trees, plants, dirt, or other material.
verb To walk slowly, heavily, and noisily.
▶ *verb* **clumping, clumped**

clum·sy (kluhm-zee) *adjective* Careless and awkward. ▶ *adjective* **clumsier, clumsiest** ▶ *noun* **clumsiness** ▶ *adverb* **clumsily**

clung (kluhng) *verb* The past tense and past participle of **cling**.

clus·ter (kluhs-tur)
verb To form a group close together.
noun A group of things located or growing together.
▶ *verb* **clustering, clustered**

clutch (kluhch)
verb To grip something tightly.
noun 1. The pedal or lever of some motor vehicles that you press to change gears. 2. Someone's grip on something.
▶ *verb* **clutches, clutching, clutched** ▶ *noun, plural* **clutches**

clut·ter (kluht-ur)
verb To make a place messy by filling it up with a jumble of things.

noun A messy heap of things; a jumble.
▶ *verb* **cluttering, cluttered**

Co. (kuhm-puh-nee) Short for **company**.

coach (kohch)
noun 1. Someone whose job is to train a person or team and help them improve their skills. 2. A large carriage pulled by horses. 3. A section of passenger seats on a bus, a train, or an airplane that is less expensive than first class. 4. A bus or a railroad passenger car.
verb To train someone in a sport, a skill, or a subject.
▶ *verb* **coaches, coaching, coached** ▶ *noun, plural* **coaches**

coal (kohl) *noun* 1. A black mineral formed from the remains of ancient plants. Coal is mined underground and burned as a fuel. 2. A small piece of coal. 3. A piece of burned or slightly burning wood.

co·a·li·tion (koh-uh-lish-uhn) *noun* A group formed for a common purpose.

coarse (kors) *adjective* 1. Having a rough surface or texture. 2. Rude and offensive. 3. Having large particles.
Coarse sounds like **course**. ▶ *adjective* **coarser, coarsest** ▶ *noun* **coarseness** ▶ *adverb* **coarsely**

coast (kohst)
noun Land that lies along the sea.
verb 1. To move along in a car or other vehicle without using any power, or to move on a bicycle or skates without exerting any effort. 2. To complete a task without much effort.
idiom **the coast is clear** It is safe to act without being seen or caught.
▶ *verb* **coasting, coasted** ▶ *adjective* **coastal**

coast guard (kohst gahrd) *noun* The branch of a nation's armed forces that watches the sea for ships in danger and protects the coastline.

coast·line (kohst-line) *noun* The place where the land and the ocean meet; the outline of the coast.

coat (koht)
noun 1. A piece of clothing that you wear on your body over other clothes to keep you warm. 2. An animal's

C

covering of hair or fur. **3.** A thin layer.
verb To cover with a thin layer of
something.
► *verb* **coating, coated**

coat·ing (**koh**-ting) *noun* A layer that is
covering something.

coat of arms (**koht** uhv **ahrmz**) *noun*
A design on a shield that identifies a
noble family or person, a city, or an
organization. ► *noun, plural* **coats of
arms**

coax (kohks) *verb* To persuade someone
to do something, gradually or by
flattery. ► *verb* **coaxes, coaxing,
coaxed** ► *adjective* **coaxing** ► *adverb*
coaxingly

cob (kahb) *noun* The center part of an
ear of corn on which the kernels grow.

co·balt (**koh**-bawlt)
noun **1.** A silver-white metallic element
used to make alloys and paints. **2.** A
deep blue color.
adjective Being a deep blue color.

cob·bler (**kah**-blur) *noun* **1.** A person
who makes or repairs shoes. **2.** A
dessert made of fruit, with a top crust.

cob·ble·stone (**kah**-buhl-*stone*) *noun* A
flat, round rock used in construction
or formerly to pave roads. ► *adjective*
cobblestoned

co·bra (**koh**-bruh) *noun* A large,
poisonous snake that can raise its
head and spread its skin so that its
head and neck look like a hood.

cob·web (**kahb**-*web*) *noun* A spider's
web, especially one that is old and
covered with dust.

co·caine (koh-**kayn**) *noun* A powerful,
addictive drug that is sold illegally in
the form of a white powder or rock
crystals.

cock (kahk)
noun **1.** An adult male chicken. **2.** A
male bird of certain kinds.
verb To turn up to one side.
► *verb* **cocking, cocked**

cock·a·too (**kah**-kuh-*too*) *noun* A white
parrot with a crest of feathers, found
in Asia and Australia.

cock·er span·iel (**kah**-kur **span**-yuhl)
noun A popular breed of small dog,
with a long, silky coat and long ears.

cock·le (**kah**-kuhl) *noun* An edible
shellfish shaped like a heart.

cock·pit (**kahk**-*pit*) *noun* The control
area in the front of a plane, boat,
or spacecraft where the pilot and
sometimes the crew sits.

cock·roach (**kahk**-*rohch*) *noun* A brown
or black insect that lives in warm,
dark places and is a household
pest. ► *noun, plural* **cockroaches**

cock·tail (**kahk**-*tayl*) *noun* **1.** A drink,
usually alcoholic, made by mixing
several different kinds of liquids
together. **2.** Seafood or fruit served at
the start of a meal.

cock·y (**kah**-kee) *adjective* (informal)
Self-confident to the point of being
unpleasant. ► *adjective* **cockier,
cockiest**

co·coa (**koh**-koh) *noun* **1.** A chocolate
powder made from roasted and
ground cacao seeds. **2.** A hot drink
made with cocoa powder, sugar, and
milk or water.

co·co·nut (**koh**-kuh-nuht) *noun* A very
large nut with a hard, hairy shell
and white insides that can be eaten.
Coconuts grow on a kind of palm tree.

co·coon (kuh-**koon**) *noun* A covering
made from silky threads produced
by the larvae of some insects and by
certain other small animals to protect
themselves or their eggs.

C.O.D. (**see**-*oh*-**dee**) Short for *cash on
delivery*; a way to send packages so
that the receiver must pay for the
merchandise when it is delivered.

cod (kahd) *noun* A fish that is found in
the northern Atlantic Ocean, used for
food. ► *noun, plural* **cod**

code (kode)
noun **1.** A system of words, letters,
symbols, or numbers used instead of
ordinary words to send messages or
to store information, as in *a secret
code.* **2.** A set of rules or standards.
3. The instructions of a computer
program, written in a programming
language.
verb To put a message into code.
► *verb* **coding, coded** ► *adjective*
coded

C

co·ed·u·ca·tion·al (koh-ej-uh-**kay**-shuhn-uhl) *adjective* A **coeducational** school teaches both boys and girls. A **coeducational** dormitory has rooms for both males and females. Often shortened to *coed*.

co·erce (koh-**urs**) *verb* To persuade someone to do something by using threats or force. ▸ *verb* **coercing, coerced** ▸ *noun* **coercion** (koh-**ur**-shuhn)

cof·fee (**kaw**-fee) *noun* 1. A drink made from the roasted and ground beans of the coffee shrub. 2. Ground coffee beans.

cof·fin (**kaw**-fin) *noun* A box into which a dead person is placed for burial.

cog (kahg) *noun* 1. One of the teeth on the edge of a wheel or bar that makes machinery run. 2. **cogwheel** (**kahg**-weel) A wheel with teeth that makes machinery run.

co·her·ent (koh-**heer**-uhnt) *adjective* 1. Logical and consistent. 2. United; acting together to form a whole.

coil (koil)
verb 1. To wind something into a series of loops. 2. To wind or wrap around something.
noun A loop or series of loops.
▸ *verb* **coiling, coiled**

coin (koin)
noun A small piece of metal stamped with a design and used as money.
verb To invent a new word or a new meaning of a word.
▸ *verb* **coining, coined** ▸ *noun* **coinage**

co·in·cide (koh-in-**side**) *verb* To happen at the same time. ▸ *verb* **coinciding, coincided**

co·in·ci·dence (koh-**in**-si-duhns) *noun* A surprising or remarkable event that seems to happen by chance. ▸ *adjective* **coincidental** (koh-*in*-si-**den**-tuhl) ▸ *adverb* **coincidentally**

col·an·der (**kah**-luhn-dur) *noun* A bowl-shaped utensil with holes, used for draining liquid from foods.

cold (kohld)
adjective 1. At a low temperature. 2. Unfriendly.

noun 1. A common mild illness that causes sneezes, a sore throat, a stuffy nose, and sometimes a cough and a mild fever. 2. Wintry weather or low temperature.
▸ *adjective* **colder, coldest** ▸ *noun* **coldness** ▸ *adverb* **coldly**

cold-blood·ed (kohld-**bluhd**-id) *adjective* 1. Having a body temperature that changes according to the temperature of the surroundings, like reptiles or fish. 2. Done deliberately and cruelly.

cole·slaw (**kohl**-*slaw*) *noun* A salad made of shredded cabbage mixed with other ingredients.

col·i·se·um (*kah*-li-**see**-uhm) *noun* A large stadium or auditorium for sports or other events.

col·lab·o·rate (kuh-**lab**-uh-*rate*) *verb* To work together to do something. ▸ *verb* **collaborating, collaborated** ▸ *noun* **collaboration** ▸ *noun* **collaborator**

col·lage (kuh-**lahzh**) *noun* A piece of art made by gluing different things onto a surface, such as pieces of cloth or tissue onto cardboard.

col·lapse (kuh-**laps**)
verb 1. To fall down suddenly. 2. To fail suddenly and completely.
noun 1. A falling down or crumbling. 2. A complete failure.
▸ *verb* **collapsing, collapsed**

col·laps·i·ble (kuh-**lap**-suh-buhl) *adjective* Capable of being folded into a small space.

col·lar (**kah**-lur)
noun 1. The part of a piece of clothing, such as a shirt, blouse, or coat, that goes around your neck and is usually folded down. 2. A thin band of leather or other material worn around an animal's neck.
verb To catch someone, usually because the person is in trouble.
▸ *verb* **collaring, collared**

col·lards (**kah**-lurdz) *noun, plural* The green leaves of a vegetable related to cabbage, popular in the southern United States.

col·league (**kah**-leeg) *noun* A person who works with you.

col·lect (kuh-**lekt**) *verb* **1.** To gather things together. **2.** To assemble a group of similar objects in an organized way, often as a hobby. **3.** To receive money that someone owes you.
▶ *verb* **collecting, collected**

col·lec·tion (kuh-**lek**-shuhn) *noun* **1.** A group of similar things gathered on purpose. **2. take up a collection** To gather money for a specific purpose.

col·lec·tive (kuh-**lek**-tiv) *adjective* Shared by everyone in a group.

col·lege (**kah**-lij) *noun* A place of higher learning where students can continue to study after they have finished high school.

col·lide (kuh-**lide**) *verb* To crash together forcefully, often at high speed. ▶ *verb* **colliding, collided**

col·lie (**kah**-lee) *noun* A breed of large dog with a long nose, a narrow head, and a thick coat.

col·li·sion (kuh-**lizh**-uhn) *noun* A sudden and violent striking together of two objects.

col·lo·qui·al (kuh-**loh**-kwee-uhl) *adjective* Used in everyday informal conversation or writing.

Co·lom·bi·a (kuh-**luhm**-bee-uh) A country in northwestern South America. It has long been a center for the illegal drug trade, and parts of the country are still under the control of criminal groups. Colombia nevertheless continues to draw visitors, especially for its Spanish colonial architecture and ecological diversity, which includes coastlines on the Caribbean and the Pacific, tropical jungles, savannas, and deserts. It is also famed for the coffee it produces in its volcanic, mountainous interior.

co·lon (**koh**-luhn) *noun* **1.** The punctuation mark (:) used to introduce a list of things or a statement that will explain the preceding statement. **2.** The main part of your large intestine, where partially digested food is broken down by bacteria and water is removed from it.

colo·nel (**kur**-nuhl) *noun* An officer in the Army, Air Force, or Marine Corps ranking below a general. **Colonel** sounds like **kernel.**

col·o·nist (**kah**-luh-nist) *noun* A person who lives in a colony or who helps to establish a colony.

col·o·nize (**kah**-luh-nize) *verb* To establish a new colony in a place. ▶ *verb* **colonizing, colonized**

col·o·ny (**kah**-luh-nee) *noun* **1.** A group of people who leave their country to settle in a new area. **2.** A territory that has been settled by people from another country and is controlled by that country. **3.** A large group of animals that live together.
▶ *noun, plural* **colonies** ▶ *adjective* **colonial** (kuh-**loh**-nee-uhl)

col·or (**kuhl**-ur)
noun **1.** A property of an object that reflects light of a certain wavelength. The eye perceives such light as being red, blue, yellow, or some other color. **2.** The appearance of a person's skin.
verb To draw, paint, or turn something from one color to another.
▶ *verb* **coloring, colored** ▶ *adjective* **colorful** ▶ *adjective* **colorless**

Col·o·ra·do (*kah*-luh-**rah**-doh *or* *kah*-luh-**rad**-oh) A state in the western United States. It contains many of the highest peaks in the Rocky Mountains, including Pikes Peak, the most visited mountain in North America. Colorado also has several national parks and national monuments.

col·or·blind (**kuhl**-ur-*blinde*) *adjective* Unable to tell certain colors apart. ▶ *noun* **color-blindness**

col·or·ing (**kuhl**-ur-ing) *noun* **1.** The way in which something is colored. **2.** Something used to color something else.

col·or·ize (**kuhl**-u-rize) *verb* To add color to an image using a computer. ▶ *verb* **colorizing, colorized** ▶ *noun* **colorization**

co·los·sal (kuh-**lah**-suhl) *adjective* Extremely large.

colt (kohlt) *noun* A young horse, donkey, or zebra, especially the male of such animals.

col·um·bine (**kah**-luhm-*bine*) *noun* A tall flower with long, narrow petals, often in two colors.

Co·lum·bus Day (kuh-**luhm**-buhs *day*) *noun* A holiday celebrating Christopher Columbus's arrival in North America in 1492, observed on the second Monday in October.

col·umn (**kah**-luhm) *noun* 1. A pillar that helps support a building or statue. 2. A series of numbers or words arranged vertically. 3. A piece of writing by the same author, or on the same subject, that appears regularly in a printed periodical or on a website.
▶ *noun* **columnist** (**kah**-luhm-nist)

co·ma (**koh**-muh) *noun* A state of deep unconsciousness, usually caused by injury or illness.

comb (kohm)
noun 1. A flat piece of metal or plastic with a row of long, thin teeth, used for making your hair smooth and neat. 2. The brightly colored crest on the head of a rooster or a related bird.
verb 1. To use a comb to arrange your hair. 2. To search a place systematically.
▶ *verb* **combing, combed**

com·bat
noun (**kahm**-bat) Fighting between people or armies.
verb (kahm-**bat**) To fight against something in order to destroy it or prevent it.
▶ *verb* **combating, combated** *or* **combatting, combatted**

com·bi·na·tion (*kahm*-buh-**nay**-shuhn) *noun* 1. The act of combining two or more things, or the state of being so combined. 2. Two or more things put together to act or be used as one.

com·bine (kuhm-**bine**) *verb* To put two or more things together. ▶ *verb* **combining, combined**

comb·over (**kohm**-*oh*-vur) *noun* A men's hairstyle in which hair is combed over from the side of the head to cover a bald area.

com·bus·ti·ble (kuhm-**buhs**-tuh-buhl) *adjective* Capable of catching fire.

com·bus·tion (kuhm-**bus**-chuhn) *noun* The process of burning.

come (kuhm) *verb* 1. To move toward a place where the person who is speaking or writing is already located. 2. To arrive. 3. **come about** To happen. 4. **come across** To find by chance. 5. **come down with** To become sick with a particular illness. 6. **come from** To be born or grow up in a particular place. 7. **come into** To inherit something, such as money or property. 8. **come to** To become conscious again.
▶ *verb* **coming, came** (kame), **come**

co·me·di·an (kuh-**mee**-dee-uhn) *noun* An entertainer who tries to make people laugh by telling jokes and funny stories.

com·e·dy (**kah**-mi-dee) *noun* 1. A funny movie or play. 2. Actions or events that make people laugh.
▶ *noun, plural* **comedies**

com·et (**kah**-mit) *noun* A bright heavenly body with a long tail of light. A comet travels around the sun in a long, slow path.

com·fort (**kuhm**-furt)
verb To calm or reassure someone.
noun 1. The feeling of being at ease, without pain, unpleasantness, or worry. 2. Something that makes your life more pleasant and enjoyable.
▶ *verb* **comforting, comforted**
▶ *adjective* **comforting** ▶ *adverb* **comfortingly**

com·fort·a·ble (**kuhm**-fur-tuh-buhl) *adjective* 1. Relaxed in your body or your mind; free from pain or worry. 2. Allowing you to relax and feel pleasure; offering comfort.
▶ *adverb* **comfortably**

com·fort·er (**kuhm**-fur-tur) *noun* A thick, warm covering for a bed, filled with feathers or fibers.

com·ic (**kah**-mik)
noun A person who tells jokes and funny stories.
adjective Funny or amusing.
noun, plural **the comics** A group of comic strips.

C

com·i·cal (**kah**-mi-kuhl) *adjective* Causing amusement or laughter; funny. ▶ *adverb* **comically**

com·ic book (**kah**-mik *buk*) *noun* A booklet with stories told in cartoons.

com·ic strip (**kah**-mik *strip*) *noun* A story told in a sequence of panels or cartoons, found in a newspaper or comic book.

com·ing (**kuhm**-ing) *adjective* Getting closer in time; about to happen.

com·ma (**kah**-muh) *noun* The punctuation mark (,) used for separating parts of a sentence, words in a list, or groups of three digits in large numbers.

com·mand (kuh-**mand**) *verb* **1.** To order someone to do something. **2.** To have authority over a group of people, especially in the armed forces. *noun* **1.** A word or phrase that you type to tell a computer program what to do. You can also perform commands with computer features such as function keys, menu options, and on-screen buttons. **2.** An order. **3.** Your knowledge of a subject and your skill in using it. ▶ *verb* **commanding, commanded**

com·mand·er (kuh-**man**-dur) *noun* Someone who has official command over a uniformed force. Both police and military leaders can be called commanders.

com·mand·ment (kuh-**mand**-muhnt) *noun* A law or rule, especially one that is considered to come from a divine being.

com·mem·o·rate (kuh-**mem**-uh-*rate*) *verb* To honor and remember an important person or event. ▶ *verb* **commemorating, commemorated** ▶ *noun* **commemoration** ▶ *adjective* **commemorative**

com·mence (kuh-**mens**) *verb* To begin. ▶ *verb* **commencing, commenced**

com·mence·ment (kuh-**mens**-muhnt) *noun* **1.** The start or beginning of something. **2.** Graduation day, or a graduation ceremony.

com·mend (kuh-**mend**) *verb* To praise someone formally or officially. ▶ *verb* **commending, commended** ▶ *noun* **commendation** (*kah*-muhn-**day**-shuhn) ▶ *adjective* **commendable**

com·ment (**kah**-ment) *noun* A remark or note that expresses your opinion or gives an explanation. *verb* To give an explanation or an opinion about something. ▶ *verb* **commenting, commented**

com·men·tar·y (**kah**-muhn-*ter*-ee) *noun* **1.** A description of and comments about an event. **2.** Something that serves as an example or an illustration. ▶ *noun, plural* **commentaries** ▶ *noun* **commentator**

com·merce (**kah**-murs) *noun* The buying and selling of things, especially in large amounts.

com·mer·cial (kuh-**mur**-shuhl) *adjective* **1.** Of or having to do with buying and selling things. **2.** Of or having to do with making money. *noun* A television or radio advertisement.

com·mer·cial·ize (kuh-**mur**-shuh-*lize*) *verb* To organize, change, or use something in order to make money. ▶ *verb* **commercializing, commercialized** ▶ *noun* **commercialization**

com·mis·er·ate (kuh-**miz**-uh-*rate*) *verb* To sympathize with someone else's misfortune. ▶ *verb* **commiserating, commiserated** ▶ *noun* **commiseration**

com·mis·sion (kuh-**mish**-uhn) *noun* **1.** A group of people who meet to solve a particular problem or do certain tasks. **2.** An offer of money to do creative work, such as writing music or designing a building. **3.** A written order giving someone rank in the armed services. **4.** The act of doing some undesirable thing. **5.** Working order or condition. *verb* **1.** To give someone the authority to do something. **2.** To put a ship into service. ▶ *verb* **commissioning, commissioned**

C

com·mit (kuh-**mit**) *verb* **1.** To do something wrong or illegal. **2.** To promise to do a specific thing or to support a specific cause.
▶ *verb* **committing, committed**
▶ *adjective* **committed**

com·mit·ment (kuh-**mit**-muhnt) *noun* **1.** The state or fact of being committed or pledged to something. **2.** An engagement or appointment that prevents you from doing something else.

com·mit·tee (kuh-**mit**-ee) *noun* A group of people chosen to discuss a particular issue and make decisions or take action for a larger group.

com·mod·i·ty (kuh-**mah**-di-tee) *noun* **1.** A raw material or an agricultural product that is bought and sold. **2.** A useful or valuable thing.
▶ *noun, plural* **commodities**

com·mon (kah-muhn) *adjective* **1.** Existing in large numbers. **2.** Found or occurring often. **3.** Ordinary, usual, not special. **4.** Not refined or cultured; crude or vulgar. **5.** Shared by two or more people or things.
noun An area of public land that people use.
▶ *adjective* **commoner, commonest**

com·mon de·nom·i·na·tor (kah-muhn di-**nah**-muh-*nay*-tur) *noun* **1.** A denominator shared by several fractions. In the fractions ¼ and ¾, the common denominator is the number 4. **2.** A trait or belief held in common by many people.

com·mon noun (kah-muhn noun) *noun* A noun that refers to a class of people, places, or things and is generally not spelled with a capital letter. The words *boy* and *island* are common nouns in the sentence "The boy lives on an island." *See* **proper noun.**

com·mon·place (kah-muhn-*plase*) *adjective* Ordinary, easy to find, or not new.

com·mon sense (kah-muhn **sens**) *noun* The ability to think clearly and make good decisions.

com·mon·wealth (kah-muhn-*welth*) *noun* **1.** A nation or state that is governed by the people who live there. **2.** The people who live in and make up a nation.

com·mo·tion (kuh-**moh**-shuhn) *noun* A confused and noisy disturbance.

com·mu·nal (kuh-**myoo**-nuhl) *adjective* Shared by a number of people. ▶ *adverb* **communally**

com·mune (**kahm**-yoon) *noun* A group of people who live together and share possessions and responsibilities.

com·mu·ni·ca·ble (kuh-**myoo**-ni-kuh-buhl) *adjective* Easily passed from one person to another.

com·mu·ni·cate (kuh-**myoo**-ni-*kate*) *verb* To share information, ideas, or feelings with another person through language, eye contact, or gestures. ▶ *verb* **communicating, communicated** ▶ *adjective* **communicative** (kuh-**myoo**-ni-kuh-tiv)

com·mu·ni·ca·tion (kuh-*myoo*-ni-**kay**-shuhn) *noun* **1.** The activity of communicating. **2.** Something that is communicated; a message.

Com·mun·ion (kuh-**myoon**-yuhn) *noun* A Christian church service in which people eat bread and drink wine or grape juice to remember the last meal of Jesus.

com·mu·ni·qué (kuh-*myoo*-ni-**kay**) *noun* An official announcement or statement, especially one that is intended to be made public.

com·mun·ism (**kahm**-yuh-*niz*-uhm) *noun* A way of organizing the economy of a country so that all the land, property, businesses, and resources belong to the government or community, and the profits are shared by all. ▶ *noun* **communist** ▶ *adjective* **communist**

com·mu·ni·ty (kuh-**myoo**-ni-tee) *noun* **1.** A place and the people who live in it. **2.** A group of people who all have something in common.
▶ *noun, plural* **communities**

com·mu·ni·ty col·lege (kuh-**myoo**-ni-tee **kah**-lij) *noun* A college that has programs of study lasting two years or less, and that usually does not have dormitories where students live.

C

com·mut·er (kuh-**myoo**-tur)
noun A person who travels some distance to work or school each day, usually by car, bus, or train.
verb To travel some distance each day to work or school.
▶ *verb* **commuting, commuted**

Com·o·ros (**kah**-muh-*rohz*) An island nation in the Indian Ocean off the eastern coast of Africa. A former colony of France, it includes a number of small islands and three major islands. A fourth island, Mayotte, has elected to remain part of France and is a contested territory. Formed by volcanoes, the islands are hilly and mountainous.

com·pact
adjective (kuh-**pakt** *or* **kahm**-pakt)
1. Designed to take up very little space. **2.** Grouped closely together.
noun (**kahm**-pakt) **1.** A small, flat case containing face powder and a mirror. **2.** An agreement between people or groups.
verb (kuh-**pakt**) To press or crush something to make it take up less space.
▶ *verb* **compacting, compacted**
▶ *noun* **compactness**

com·pact disk (**kahm**-pakt disk) *noun* A disk with music, data, or other information stored on it that can be read by using a laser beam; a CD.

com·pan·ion (kuh-**pan**-yuhn)
noun A person who is with you, or whom you spend time with. ▶ *noun* **companionship**

com·pa·ny (**kuhm**-puh-nee) *noun*
1. An organization that produces or sells products or services. **2.** A visiting person or group of people. **3.** An army unit under the command of a captain. **4.** A group of performers. **5.** Companionship.
▶ *noun, plural* **companies**

com·pa·ra·ble (**kahm**-pur-uh-buhl) *adjective* Similar enough to be compared.

com·par·a·tive (kuh-**par**-uh-tiv) *adjective* **1.** Judged in relation to similar things. **2. Comparative**

forms of adjectives and adverbs are used when you compare two things or actions. For example, the comparative form of the adjective *young* is *younger,* and the comparative form of the adverb *slowly* is *more slowly.*
noun An adjective or adverb in the comparative form.
▶ *adverb* **comparatively**

com·pare (kuhm-**pair**) *verb* **1.** To judge one thing in relation to another in order to see the similarities and differences. **2.** To be like or as good as something or somebody else.
▶ *verb* **comparing, compared**

com·par·i·son (kuhm-**par**-i-suhn) *noun* The activity or result of comparing.

com·part·ment (kuhm-**pahrt**-muhnt) *noun* A separate part of a container, where certain things can be kept apart from others.

com·pass (**kuhm**-puhs) *noun* **1.** An instrument with a magnetic pointer that always points north, used for finding directions. **2.** An instrument with two legs connected by a movable joint, used for drawing circles and arcs.
▶ *noun, plural* **compasses**

com·pas·sion (kuhm-**pash**-uhn) *noun* A feeling of sympathy for and a desire to help someone who is suffering. ▶ *adjective* **compassionate** ▶ *adverb* **compassionately**

com·pat·i·ble (kuhm-**pat**-uh-buhl) *adjective* Able to get along well or to be used together. ▶ *noun* **compatibility**

com·pel (kuhm-**pel**) *verb* To force someone to do something. ▶ *verb* **compelling, compelled**

com·pen·sate (**kahm**-puhn-*sate*) *verb* **1.** To repay or make up for something. **2.** To pay.
▶ *verb* **compensating, compensated**

com·pen·sa·tion (*kahm*-puhn-**say**-shuhn) *noun* Money given to someone for work, for something they have given up, or for some loss or injury they have suffered.

com·pete (kuhm-**peet**) *verb* To try hard to outdo others at a task, race, or contest. ▶ *verb* **competing, competed**

com·pe·tence (**kahm**-pi-tuhns) *noun* The state or fact of being competent to do something.

com·pe·tent (**kahm**-puh-tuhnt) *adjective* Able to do something well. ▶ *adverb* **competently**

com·pe·ti·tion (*kahm*-puh-**tish**-uhn) *noun* 1. A situation in which two or more people are trying to obtain something of which there is only a limited amount. 2. A contest of some kind.

com·pet·i·tive (kuhm-**pet**-i-tiv) *adjective* 1. Having to do with a situation where the participants are trying to win a contest or obtain something. 2. Very eager to win, succeed, or excel. 3. Similar to, or better than, others of the same kind.

com·pet·i·tor (kuhm-**pet**-i-tur) *noun* Someone who competes, especially an athlete.

com·pile (kuhm-**pile**) *verb* To bring together many pieces of information into one larger unit. ▶ *verb* **compiling, compiled** ▶ *noun* **compilation** (*kahm*-puh-**lay**-shun)

com·pla·cent (kuhm-**play**-suhnt) *adjective* Overly satisfied or happy with your situation in life, so that you feel no need to change or improve it.

com·plain (kuhm-**playn**) *verb* 1. To express dissatisfaction about something. 2. To report, or to make an accusation. ▶ *verb* **complaining, complained**

com·plaint (kuhm-**playnt**) *noun* 1. A statement expressing dissatisfaction about something. 2. A cause for complaining, such as an illness. 3. A formal charge against someone.

com·ple·ment (**kahm**-pluh-muhnt) *noun* Something that completes something else or makes a thing whole or better. *verb* To complete or enhance something. ▶ *verb* **complementing, complemented**

com·plete (kuhm-**pleet**) *adjective* 1. Having all the parts that are needed or wanted. 2. Total. *verb* To finish something. ▶ *verb* **completing, completed**

com·plete·ly (kuhm-**pleet**-lee) *adverb* 1. Totally and fully; in every way. 2. People often use **completely** to emphasize the truth of what they are saying, or to emphasize their strong feeling about it.

com·ple·tion (kuhm-**plee**-shuhn) *noun* The act of completing something or the state of being complete.

com·plex *adjective* (kuhm-**pleks** or **kahm**-pleks) 1. Very complicated. 2. Having a large number of parts. *noun* (**kahm**-pleks) 1. A set of strong feelings that causes you anxiety. 2. A group of buildings that are near each other and are used for similar purposes. ▶ *noun, plural* **complexes** ▶ *noun* **complexity** (kuhm-**pleks**-i-tee)

com·plex·ion (kuhm-**plek**-shuhn) *noun* The color and look of the skin, especially the skin on your face.

compli·cate (**kahm**-pli-*kate*) *verb* To make something more difficult by introducing new elements. ▶ *verb* **complicating, complicated** ▶ *noun* **complicatation**

com·pli·cat·ed (**kahm**-pli-*kay*-tid) *adjective* Difficult to use or understand because of having many different parts or ideas.

com·pli·ment *noun* (**kahm**-pluh-muhnt) A remark or action that shows you appreciate something. *verb* (**kahm**-pluh-ment) To make a remark or do something to show appreciation. ▶ *verb* **complimenting, complimented**

com·pli·men·ta·ry (*kahm*-pluh-**ment**-ree) *adjective* 1. Full of praise or giving praise. 2. Costing nothing, especially when given as a gift.

com·ply (kuhm-**plye**) *verb* To act in agreement with rules or requests. ▶ *verb* **complies, complying, complied**

C

com·po·nent (kuhm-**poh**-nuhnt) *noun*
A part of a larger whole, especially a
machine or a system.

com·pose (kuhm-**poze**) *verb* To write
or create something, such as a piece
of music, a story, or a poem. ▸ *verb*
composing, composed

com·posed (kuhm-**pohzd**) *adjective*
Made of certain things.

com·pos·er (kuhm-**poh**-zur) *noun*
Someone who writes or composes
something, especially music.

com·pos·ite (kuhm-**pah**-zit) *adjective*
Made up of many parts from different
sources.

com·po·si·tion (*kahm*-puh-**zish**-uhn)
noun 1. The combining of parts to
form a whole. 2. What something is
made of. 3. Something that is created,
especially a written or musical work.

com·post (**kahm**-pohst) *noun* A mixture
of organic material, such as rotted
leaves, vegetables, or manure, that
is added to soil to make it more
productive.

com·po·sure (kuhm-**poh**-zhur) *noun* A
calm state; self-control.

com·pound
noun (**kahm**-*pound*) 1. An area of land,
usually fenced in and containing
one or more buildings. 2. Something
formed by combining two or more
parts. 3. A substance, such as salt
or water, made from two or more
chemical elements.
adjective (**kahm**-*pound*) Having two or
more parts.
verb (kahm-**pound**) To add to, or to
make more complicated.
▸ *verb* **compounding, compounded**

com·pre·hend (*kahm*-pri-**hend**)
verb To understand fully. ▸ *verb*
comprehending, comprehended

com·pre·hen·sion (*kahm*-pri-**hen**-
shuhn) *noun* Understanding, or the
power to understand.

com·pre·hen·sive (*kahm*-pri-
hen-siv) *adjective* Complete and
inclusive. ▸ *adverb* **comprehensively**

com·press
verb (kuhm-**pres**) 1. To press or flatten
something in order to fit it into a

smaller space. 2. To make a computer
file smaller so that it is easier to store
or send.
noun (**kahm**-*pres*) A small cloth pad
placed on a part of the body for
warmth, cold, or pressure.
▸ *verb* **compresses, compressing,
compressed** ▸ *noun, plural*
compresses ▸ *noun* **compression**
(kuhm-**presh**-uhn)

com·prise (kuhm-**prize**) *verb* To include
or to contain. ▸ *verb* **comprising,
comprised**

com·pro·mise (**kahm**-pruh-*mize*)
verb To agree to accept something that
is not entirely what you wanted, in
order to satisfy some of the requests
of other people.
noun An agreement that is reached
after people with opposing views each
give up some of their demands.
▸ *verb* **compromising, compromised**

com·pul·so·ry (kuhm-**puhl**-sur-ee)
adjective Required by a rule or a law.

com·pute (kuhm-**pyoot**) *verb* To find
an answer by using mathematics;
to calculate. ▸ *verb* **computing,
computed** ▸ *noun* **computation**

com·put·er (kuhm-**pyoo**-tur) *noun* An
electronic machine that can store and
retrieve large amounts of information,
do very quick and complicated
calculations, and perform many other
tasks. ▸ *noun* **computing**

com·pu·ter·aid·ed de·sign (kuhm-**pyoo**-
tur-*ay*-did di-**zine**) *noun* The process
of creating plans and drawings on a
computer to develop the design of
something, such as a vehicle, room,
or building. Abbreviated as *CAD*.

com·put·er graph·ics (kuhm-**pyoo**-tur
graf-iks) *noun, plural* The pictures
or images that can be made on a
computer.

com·put·er lan·guage (kuhm-**pyoo**-
tur *lang*-gwij) *noun* The words and
symbols used in computer programs
that give instructions to the computer.

com·put·er sci·ence (kuhm-**pyoo**-
tur *sye*-uhns) *noun* The study of
computers and how they work.

C

com·rade (**kahm**-rad) *noun* A good friend or a colleague. ▶ *noun* **comradeship**

con·cave (kahn-**kave** *or* kahng-**kave**) *adjective* Curved inward, like the inside of a bowl.

con·ceal (kuhn-**seel**) *verb* To hide something. ▶ *verb* **concealing, concealed** ▶ *noun* **concealment**

con·cede (kuhn-**seed**) *verb* **1.** To admit something is true after denying it first. **2.** To admit defeat in a competition or election. **3.** To give something up. ▶ *verb* **conceding, conceded**

con·ceit·ed (kuhn-**see**-tid) *adjective* Overly proud of yourself and what you can do. ▶ *noun* **conceit**

con·ceive (kuhn-**seev**) *verb* **1.** To come up with an idea. **2.** To become pregnant. ▶ *verb* **conceiving, conceived**

con·cen·trate (**kahn**-suhn-*trate*) *verb* **1.** To give all of your thought and attention to something. **2.** To come together in one place. **3.** To make a liquid thicker and stronger by removing water from it. *noun* A liquid that has been thickened by removing the water. ▶ *verb* **concentrating, concentrated** ▶ *adjective* **concentrated**

con·cen·tra·tion (*kahn*-suhn-**tray**-shuhn) *noun* **1.** The fact or state of being concentrated. **2.** A state of mind in which you are focused on one thing and not distracted.

con·cen·tric (kuhn-**sen**-trik) *adjective* Having their centers at the same point.

con·cept (**kahn**-sept) *noun* An abstract or general idea.

con·cep·tion (kuhn-**sep**-shuhn) *noun* **1.** A general idea, or the way in which something is understood. **2.** The process of becoming pregnant.

con·cern (kuhn-**surn**) *verb* **1.** To involve someone, or to be of interest or importance to someone. **2.** To be about a certain topic or idea. **3.** To worry. *noun* **1.** Something that makes you worry. **2.** A business or company. ▶ *verb* **concerning, concerned**

con·cerned (kuhn-**surnd**) *adjective* Worried or anxious about something.

con·cern·ing (kuhn-**sur**-ning) *preposition* Having to do with; about. *The call was concerning our lost dog.*

con·cert (**kahn**-surt) *noun* A performance by musicians.

con·cer·to (kuhn-**chair**-toh) *noun* A piece of music, usually fairly long, for one or more solo instruments playing with an orchestra. ▶ *noun, plural* **concertos** *or* **concerti** (kuhn-**chair**-tee)

con·cess·ion (kuhn-**sesh**-uhn) *noun* **1.** Something that is allowed or agreed, as a result of special conditions or a special request. **2.** Permission to sell something granted by a governing body to the seller. **3.** A **concession stand** is a small business in a building or stadium where food and drinks are sold.

conch (kahngk *or* kahnch) *noun* **1.** A marine animal that lives in a large spiral shell. **2.** The shell of this animal. ▶ *noun, plural* **conchs** (kahngks) *or* **conches** (**kahn**-chuhz)

con·cise (kuhn-**sise**) *adjective* Giving a lot of information clearly in a few words. ▶ *adverb* **concisely**

con·clude (kuhn-**klood**) *verb* **1.** To arrive at a decision or realization based on the facts that you have. **2.** To finish or end something. ▶ *verb* **concluding, concluded**

con·clu·sion (kuhn-**kloo**-zhuhn) *noun* **1.** The end or last part of an event or process. **2.** A judgment or decision that you make after thinking about it. **3.** The last part of a text, especially one that gives the main points.

con·clu·sive (kuhn-**kloo**-siv) *adjective* Proving something or contributing strongly to proof. ▶ *adverb* **conclusively**

con·coct (kahn-**kahkt** *or* kuhn-**kahkt**) *verb* **1.** To make something by combining several ingredients. **2.** To invent something, such as a story, a plan, or an excuse. ▶ *verb* **concocting, concocted** ▶ *noun* **concoction**

con·cord (**kahn**-kord) *noun* **1.** A state of harmony and peace, especially between

C

two people or groups. **2.** A treaty or an agreement.

con·crete (**kahn**-kreet *or* kahn-**kreet**)
noun A building material made from a mixture of sand, gravel, cement, and water, which becomes very hard when it dries.
adjective Physically real, not abstract.

con·cur (kuhn-**kur**) *verb* To agree. ▸ *verb*
concurring, concurred

con·cus·sion (kuhn-**kuhsh**-uhn) *noun*
An injury to the brain caused by a heavy blow to the head. ▸ *adjective*
concussed

con·demn (kuhn-**dem**) *verb* **1.** To disapprove strongly of something.
2. To sentence someone to a particular punishment. **3.** To state that something is unsafe.
▸ *verb* **condemning, condemned**
▸ *noun* **condemnation** (*kahn*-dem-**nay**-shuhn)

con·den·sa·tion (*kahn*-den-**say**-shuhn) *noun* **1.** The act or process of condensing something. **2.** Something that has been condensed. **3.** The changing of a gas or vapor into its liquid form.

con·dense (kuhn-**dens**) *verb* **1.** To turn from a gas into a liquid, usually as a result of cooling. **2.** To make a piece of writing shorter by removing parts of it. **3.** To make something thicker by boiling away liquid.
▸ *verb* **condensing, condensed**
▸ *adjective* **condensed**

con·de·scend (*kahn*-di-**send**) *verb* To behave in a way that shows you think you are better than others. ▸ *verb*
condescending, condescended ▸ *noun*
condescension

con·de·scend·ing (*kahn*-di-**sen**-ding) *adjective* Treating other people as though they were inferior to you.

con·di·tion (kuhn-**dish**-uhn)
noun **1.** The general state of a person, animal, or thing. **2.** General health or physical fitness. **3.** A medical problem that lasts for a long time. **4.** Something that must occur before another thing can occur.
verb **1.** To get into good health. **2.** To

train a person or animal to think or behave in a certain way, sometimes unintentionally.
▸ *verb* **conditioning, conditioned** ▸ *noun* **conditioning**

con·di·tion·al (kuhn-**dish**-uh-nuhl) *adjective* Requiring something else to happen first. ▸ *adverb* **conditionally**

con·di·tion·er (kuhn-**dish**-uh-nur) *noun* A liquid that you put on your hair after washing it to improve its appearance and condition.

con·do·lence (kuhn-**doh**-luhns) *noun* An expression of sympathy, especially when someone has just died.

con·do·min·i·um (*kahn*-duh-**min**-ee-uhm) *noun* An apartment house or other development in which each unit is owned by the person who lives in it.

con·dor (**kahn**-dor) *noun* A type of very large vulture that lives in North or South America.

con·duct
verb (kuhn-**duhkt**) **1.** To organize and carry out an activity or a process. **2.** To direct a group of musicians as they sing or play. **3.** To lead someone on a particular route. **4.** To allow heat, electricity, or sound to pass through.
noun (**kahn**-duhkt) Behavior.
▸ *verb* **conducting, conducted** ▸ *noun* **conduction**

con·duc·tor (kuhn-**duhk**-tur) *noun* **1.** A person who directs the playing or singing of a group of musicians. **2.** A person who collects fares or tickets on a train. **3.** A substance that allows heat, electricity, or sound to travel through it.

cone (kone) *noun* **1.** An object or a shape with a round base and a point at the other end. **2.** The hard, woody fruit of an evergreen tree.
▸ *adjective* **conical** (**kah**-ni-kuhl)

con·fed·er·a·cy (kuhn-**fed**-ur-uh-see) *noun* **1.** A union of states, provinces, tribes, towns, or people with a common goal. **2.** **the Confederacy** The group of 11 states that declared independence from the rest of the United States just before the Civil War.
▸ *noun, plural* **confederacies**

C

con·fed·er·ate (kuhn-**fed**-ur-it)
adjective 1. Belonging to a confederacy or union. 2. **Confederate** Of or having to do with the Confederacy before and during the Civil War.
noun A person who bands together with others for a common purpose.

con·fed·er·a·tion (kuhn-*fed*-uh-**ray**-shun) *noun* A union of several groups, such as labor unions, political parties, or countries.

con·fer (kuhn-**fur**) *verb* 1. To give someone something, such as a gift, an honor, or a reward. 2. To hold a meeting with someone; to seek someone's advice. ▶ *verb* **conferring, conferred**

con·fer·ence (**kahn**-fur-uhns) *noun* A formal meeting for discussion.

con·fess (kuhn-**fes**) *verb* To admit that you have done something wrong. ▶ *verb* **confesses, confessing, confessed** ▶ *noun* **confession**

con·fet·ti (kuhn-**fet**-ee) *noun* Small pieces of colored paper that are thrown at parades, carnivals, and other celebrations.

con·fide (kuhn-**fide**) *verb* To tell someone a secret. ▶ *verb* **confiding, confided**

con·fi·dence (**kahn**-fi-duhns) *noun*
1. The feeling that something or someone is good and can be trusted.
2. A belief that you have the necessary ability to succeed.

con·fi·dent (**kahn**-fi-duhnt) *adjective*
1. Self-assured; having a strong belief in your own abilities. 2. Certain that things will happen in the way you expect. ▶ *adverb* **confidently**

con·fi·den·tial (*kahn*-fi-**den**-shuhl) *adjective* Secret. ▶ *adverb* **confidentially**

con·fig·u·ra·tion (kuhn-*fig*-yuh-**ray**-shun) *noun* The way that parts or elements of something are arranged to work together.

con·fine (kuhn-**fine**) *verb* 1. To keep within certain bounds; to limit. 2. To shut or keep in or prevent from leaving a place.
▶ *verb* **confining, confined** ▶ *noun* **confinement**

con·firm (kuhn-**furm**) *verb* 1. To say that something is definitely true or will definitely happen, when it was previously just a rumor or a possibility. 2. To accept a person as a full member of a church or synagogue in a special ceremony.
▶ *verb* **confirming, confirmed** ▶ *noun* **confirmation**

con·fis·cate (**kahn**-fi-*skate*) *verb* To take something away as a punishment or because the item is not permitted. ▶ *verb* **confiscating, confiscated** ▶ *noun* **confiscation**

con·flict
noun (**kahn**-flikt) 1. A serious and usually lengthy disagreement. 2. A war or some other period of fighting.
verb (kuhn-**flikt**) To clash or to disagree.
▶ *verb* **conflicting, conflicted**

con·form (kuhn-**form**) *verb* 1. To think or behave in the same way as everyone else. 2. To follow a rule, a law, or an expectation.
▶ *verb* **conforming, conformed** ▶ *noun* **conformist** ▶ *noun* **conformity**

con·front (kuhn-**fruhnt**) *verb* 1. To meet or face someone in a hostile way. 2. To deal with something directly.
▶ *verb* **confronting, confronted**

con·fron·ta·tion (*kahn*-fruhn-**tay**-shuhn) *noun* A hostile meeting between enemies or opposing sides.

Con·fu·cius (kuhn-**fyoo**-shuhs) *noun* A Chinese philosopher who lived from 551 to 479 B.C. His teachings are called Confucianism, an important system of ethics. ▶ *adjective* **Confucian**

con·fuse (kuhn-**fyooz**) *verb* 1. To make someone uncertain or puzzled. 2. To mistake one thing for another. 3. To make something more complicated.
▶ *verb* **confusing, confused** ▶ *adjective* **confusing** ▶ *adjective* **confused**

con·fu·sion (kuhn-**fyoo**-zhuhn) *noun* 1. The mental state of being completely uncertain as to what is right or wrong, or what is true or false.

C

2. A condition in which there is no order or regularity.

con·geal (kuhn-**jeel**) *verb* To go from a liquid or semiliquid state to a thick or solid one. ▶ *verb* **congealing, congealed**

con·ges·ted (kuhn-**jes**-tid) *adjective* So blocked up or full that it is impossible to move. ▶ *noun* **congestion**

Con·go, Dem·o·crat·ic Re·pub·lic of the (*dem*-uh-**krat**-ik ri-**puhb**-lik uhv THuh **kahng**-goh) A country in Central Africa, formerly known as Zaire. Located near the equator, it has the second-largest rain forest in the world, after the Amazon. The country has been beset by ethnic warfare and government corruption since it became independent from Belgium in 1960.

Con·go, Re·pub·lic of (ri-**puhb**-lik uhv **kahng**-goh) A country in Central Africa, on the northwest border of the Democratic Republic of the Congo. It was a French colony until 1960. The Republic of Congo has large numbers of western lowland gorillas, the type of gorilla commonly found in zoos.

con·grat·u·late (kuhn-**grach**-uh-late) *verb* To offer good wishes to someone when something good has happened or when the person has done something special. ▶ *verb* **congratulating, congratulated** ▶ *noun, plural* **congratulations**

con·gre·gate (**kahng**-gri-*gate*) *verb* To gather together for a common activity. ▶ *verb* **congregating, congregated**

con·gre·ga·tion (*kahng*-gri-**gay**-shuhn) *noun* A group of people asembled for religious worship.

Con·gress (**kahng**-gris) *noun* The law-making body of the United States, made up of the Senate and the House of Representatives. ▶ *adjective* **congressional** (kuhn-**gresh**-uh-nuhl)

con·gru·ent (kuhn-**groo**-uhnt *or* **kahng**-groo-uhnt) *adjective* Equal in shape and size.

con·i·fer (**kah**-nuh-fur *or* **koh**-nuh-fur) *noun* An evergreen tree that produces its seeds in cones. ▶ *adjective* **coniferous** (kuh-**nif**-ur-uhs)

con·junc·tion (kuhn-**juhngk**-shuhn) *noun* A word that connects words or phrases within a sentence. The words *and, but,* and *if* are all conjunctions.

con·jur·er *or* **con·jur·or** (**kahn**-jur-ur) *noun* A person who performs magic tricks to entertain people. ▶ *noun* **conjuring** ▶ *verb* **conjure**

con·nect (kuh-**nekt**) *verb* To join together. ▶ *verb* **connecting, connected**

Con·nect·i·cut (kuh-**net**-i-kuht) A state in southern New England in the northeastern United States. Settled by the English in the 1630s, Connecticut was one of the 13 original colonies. It was the home of Mark Twain (1835–1910), who wrote *The Adventures of Tom Sawyer* and *The Adventures of Huckleberry Finn* while living in the Connecticut city of Hartford.

con·nec·tion (kuh-**nek**-shuhn) *noun* **1.** A link between things, such as objects, people, or ideas. **2.** A train, plane, or bus that you take in order to continue on a trip you have already begun on another train, plane, or bus.
noun, plural **connections** People you know, especially people who might be useful to you in your career.

con·nois·seur (*kah*-nuh-**sur**) *noun* A person who knows a lot about a subject, particularly how to recognize good quality in objects connected with that subject.

con·quer (**kahng**-kur) *verb* **1.** To defeat and take control of an enemy or a territory. **2.** To overcome a problem or a weakness.
▶ *verb* **conquering, conquered** ▶ *noun* **conqueror**

con·quest (**kahn**-kwest) *noun* **1.** Something that is won, such as land, treasure, or buildings. **2.** The act of conquering.

con·science (**kahn**-shuhns) *noun* Your moral sense that acts as a guide to help you tell right from wrong.

C

con·sci·en·tious (*kahn*-shee-**en**-shuhs)
adjective **1.** Doing things thoroughly
and well. **2.** A **conscientious objector**
is a person who refuses to serve
in the armed forces because he or
she believes that it is wrong to fight
and kill.
▶ *adverb* **conscientiously**

con·scious (**kahn**-shuhs) *adjective*
1. Awake and able to think and
perceive. **2.** Aware of something.
3. Deliberate.
▶ *adverb* **consciously**

con·scious·ness (**kahn**-shuhs-nis) *noun*
1. Awareness of something. **2.** The
faculty of mind that makes it possible
for you to be aware and process input
from your five senses.

con·sec·u·tive (kuhn-**sek**-yuh-
tiv) *adjective* One right after the
other. ▶ *adverb* **consecutively**

con·sen·sus (kuhn-**sen**-suhs) *noun* An
agreement among all the people in a
discussion or meeting.

con·sent (kuhn-**sent**)
verb To agree to something.
noun Official agreement that
something can happen.
▶ *verb* **consenting, consented**

con·se·quence (**kahn**-si-*kwens*) *noun*
The result of an action, a condition, or
a decision. ▶ *adjective* **consequent**

con·se·quent·ly (**kahn**-si-kwuhnt-lee)
adverb As a result; because of that.

con·ser·va·tion (*kahn*-sur-**vay**-
shuhn) *noun* The protection of
valuable things, especially forests,
wildlife, natural resources, or
artistic or historic objects. ▶ *noun*
conservationist

con·serv·a·tive (kuhn-**sur**-vuh-tiv)
adjective **1.** Moderate, cautious,
and traditional. **2.** Favoring smaller
government and businesses, and
being opposed to large social welfare
programs.
noun **1.** A candidate or office holder
who supports conservative political
ideas. **2.** A person who opposes big
changes and believes in traditional
ways of doing things.
▶ *adjective* **conservatively**

con·serv·a·to·ry (kuhn-**sur**-vuh-*tor*-ee)
noun **1.** A school for music or other
arts. **2.** A greenhouse, or a glass
room connected to a house and
used for growing plants.
▶ *noun, plural* **conservatories**

con·serve (kuhn-**surv**) *verb* To
save something from loss, decay,
or waste; to preserve. ▶ *verb*
conserving, conserved

con·sid·er (kuhn-**sid**-ur) *verb* **1.** To
think about something carefully,
usually before making a decision
or taking action. **2.** To believe
something. **3.** To take something into
account.
▶ *verb* **considering, considered**

con·sid·er·a·ble (kuhn-**sid**-ur-uh-buhl)
adjective Fairly large.

con·sid·er·a·bly (kuhn-**sid**-ur-uh-
blee) *adverb* More than a little; to a
noticeable degree or extent.

con·sid·er·ate (kuhn-**sid**-ur-it)
adjective Careful and concerned
for other people's needs and
feelings. ▶ *adverb* **considerately**

con·sid·er·a·tion (kuhn-*sid*-uh-**ray**-
shuhn) *noun* **1.** Care and concern for
other people's needs and feelings.
2. Careful thought before making a
decision. **3.** Something that needs to
be taken into account when making
a decision.

con·sign·ment (kuhn-**sine**-muhnt)
noun A group of things that are
shipped or delivered together.

con·sist (kuhn-**sist**) *verb* To be made
up of certain elements. ▶ *verb*
consisting, consisted

con·sis·tent (kuhn-**sis**-tuhnt) *adjective*
1. Always behaving in the same way
or according to the same principles.
2. In agreement with something.
▶ *noun* **consistency** ▶ *adverb*
consistently

con·sole
verb (kuhn-**sole**) To comfort
someone who is sad or
disappointed.
noun (**kahn**-sole) A cabinet for
something electronic, such as a
television or radio, designed to

stand on the floor.
▶ verb **consoling, consoled** ▶ noun **consolation** (kahn-suh-**lay**-shun)

con·sol·i·date (kuhn-**sah**-li-date) verb To bring several different parts together into one. ▶ verb **consolidating, consolidated** ▶ noun **consolidation**

con·so·nant (**kahn**-suh-nuhnt) noun A speech sound or letter that is not a vowel. Letters such as b, m, r, and k represent consonants.

con·spic·u·ous (kuhn-**spik**-yoo-uhs) adjective Easy to see or notice. ▶ adverb **conspicuously**

con·spir·a·cy (kuhn-**spir**-uh-see) noun A secret plan made by two or more people to do something illegal or harmful. ▶ noun, plural **conspiracies** ▶ noun **conspirator** ▶ verb **conspire** (kuhn-**spire**) ▶ adjective **conspiratorial** (kuhn-spir-uh-**tor**-ee-uhl)

con·sta·ble (**kahn**-stuh-buhl) noun A police officer, especially in a rural area of Great Britain.

con·stant (**kahn**-stuhnt) adjective 1. Never stopping. 2. Staying the same over a period of time.

con·stant·ly (**kahn**-stuhnt-lee) adverb All the time; without stopping.

con·stel·la·tion (kahn-stuh-**lay**-shuhn) noun A group of stars that forms a shape or figure and usually has a name.

con·sti·pat·ed (**kahn**-stuh-pay-tid) adjective Unable to move your bowels frequently or easily. ▶ noun **constipation**

con·stit·u·ent (kuhn-**stich**-oo-uhnt) noun A voter represented by an elected official.

con·sti·tute (**kahn**-sti-toot) verb 1. To form or to compose; to make up. 2. To set up or form legally.
▶ verb **constituting, constituted**

con·sti·tu·tion (kahn-sti-**too**-shuhn) noun 1. The basic laws of a country that state the rights of the people and the powers of the government. 2. **the Constitution** The written document containing the governmental

principles by which the United States is governed. It went into effect in 1789. 3. Your general physical condition.

con·sti·tu·tion·al (kahn-sti-**too**-shuh-nuhl) adjective 1. Of or having to do with a constitution. 2. Consistent with what is written in a constitution.

con·straint (kuhn-**straynt**) noun Something that limits your actions. ▶ verb **constrain**

con·strict (kuhn-**strikt**) verb To slow or stop a natural flow by making a passage narrower; to squeeze. ▶ verb **constricting, constricted**

con·struct (kuhn-**struhkt**) verb To make or build something. ▶ verb **constructing, constructed**

con·struc·tion (kuhn-**struhk**-shuhn) noun 1. The act or process of building or constructing something. 2. The industry or job of building.

con·struc·tive (kuhn-**struhk**-tiv) adjective Helpful, useful, and positive. ▶ adverb **constructively**

con·sul (**kahn**-suhl) noun A person appointed by the government of a country to live and work in another country. A consul's job is to protect fellow citizens who are working or traveling in the foreign country.

con·sult (kuhn-**suhlt**) verb 1. To check with someone for advice. 2. To use something as a source of information.
▶ verb **consulting, consulted**

con·sul·tant (kuhn-**suhl**-tuhnt) noun An expert in a particular field who is hired by others to give advice.

con·sul·ta·tion (kahn-suhl-**tay**-shuhn) noun The action of formally discussing something, or an instance of doing this.

con·sume (kuhn-**soom**) verb 1. To eat or drink something. 2. To use something up. 3. To destroy something.
▶ verb **consuming, consumed**

con·sum·er (kuhn-**soo**-mur) noun A person who buys and uses products and services.

con·sump·tion (kuhn-**suhmp**-shuhn) noun The act of consuming, using, or eating something.

C

con·tact (kahn-takt)
noun **1.** The state or action of physically touching someone or something. **2.** The state or action of communicating or meeting with someone. **3.** A person you know through working with them or being introduced to them professionally.
verb To communicate with someone.
▸ *verb* **contacting, contacted**

con·tact lens (kahn-takt *lenz***)** *noun* A small plastic lens that you wear on your eyeball to improve your vision. ▸ *noun, plural* **contact lenses**

con·ta·gious (kuhn-tay-juhs) *adjective* Spread by direct or indirect contact with an infected person or animal.

con·tain (kuhn-tayn) *verb* **1.** To hold or include something. **2.** To control an emotion.
▸ *verb* **containing, contained**

con·tain·er (kuhn-tay-ner) *noun* An object, such as a box, jar, or barrel, that is used to hold something.

con·tam·i·nat·ed (kuhn-tam-uh-nay-tid) *adjective* Containing harmful or undesirable substances. ▸ *noun* **contamination** ▸ *verb* **contaminate**

con·tem·plate (kahn-tuhm-plate) *verb* **1.** To think about something. **2.** To look thoughtfully at something.
▸ *verb* **contemplating, contemplated** ▸ *noun* **contemplation**

con·tem·po·rar·y (kuhn-tem-puh-rer-ee) *adjective* **1.** Belonging or occurring in the present; modern. **2.** Happening or existing at about the same time.
noun A person of about the same age as you.
▸ *noun, plural* **contemporaries**

con·tempt (kuhn-tempt) *noun* The belief that something is worthless and deserves no respect. ▸ *adjective* **contemptuous (kuhn-temp-choo-uhs)** ▸ *adverb* **contemptuously**

con·tend (kuhn-tend) *verb* **1.** To compete for a specific goal or prize. **2.** To claim. **3.** To deal with or put up with.
▸ *verb* **contending, contended** ▸ *noun* **contender**

con·tent
adjective **(kuhn-tent)** Peacefully happy.
noun **1.** (kuhn-**tent**) A feeling of ease and satisfaction with the way things are. **2.** (**kahn**-tent) The things that are held, contained, or included in something. **3.** (**kahn**-tent) The information on a website, in contrast to the commands that make the information look the way it does.
verb (kuhn-**tent**) **content oneself** To be satisfied with something.
▸ *verb* **contenting, contented** ▸ *noun* **contentment** ▸ *adjective* **contented** ▸ *adverb* **contentedly**

con·tents (kahn-tents) *noun, plural* The things that are inside something or that compose it.

con·test
noun (**kahn**-test) A competition.
verb (kuhn-**test**) **1.** To compete for something. **2.** To dispute a decision or a result.
▸ *verb* **contesting, contested**

con·test·ant (kuhn-tes-tuhnt) *noun* A participant in a competition.

con·text (kahn-tekst) *noun* **1.** The language around a word or phrase that affects or helps you understand its meaning. **2. in context** Taking into account all the things that affect something.

con·ti·nent (kahn-tuh-nuhnt) *noun* **1.** One of the seven large landmasses of the earth. They are Asia, Africa, Europe, North America, South America, Australia, and Antarctica. **2. the Continent** The mainland of Europe.
▸ *adjective* **continental**

con·ti·nen·tal shelf (kahn-tuh-nen-tuhl shelf) *noun* A comparatively shallow, gently sloping area of the sea floor near a coastline.

con·tin·u·al (kuhn-tin-yoo-uhl) *adjective* **1.** Happening repeatedly; frequent. **2.** Happening without a pause; continuous.

con·tin·u·al·ly (kuhn-tin-yoo-uh-lee) *adverb* Repeatedly; again and again.

con·tin·ue (kuhn-tin-yoo) *verb* **1.** To keep on doing something or keep on

C

happening. **2.** To restart an activity after a break.
▶ *verb* **continuing, continued** ▶ *noun* **continuation**

con·tin·u·ous (kuhn-**tin**-yoo-uhs) *adjective* Present or happening all the time and not stopping. ▶ *adverb* **continuously**

con·tort (kuhn-**tort**) *verb* To bend something out of its normal shape. ▶ *verb* **contorting, contorted** ▶ *noun* **contortion** ▶ *adjective* **contorted**

con·tour (**kahn**-toor) *noun* The outline of an object.

con·tra·band (**kahn**-truh-*band*) *noun* Things that are brought illegally from one place to another.
adjective Illegally transported across a border.

con·tract
noun (**kahn**-trakt) A legal agreement between people or companies stating what each of them has agreed to do and any amounts of money involved.
verb (kuhn-**trakt**) **1.** To become smaller. **2.** To catch a disease.
▶ *verb* **contracting, contracted**

con·trac·tion (kuhn-**trak**-shuhn) *noun* **1.** A shortening or shrinking of something. **2.** A shortening of a muscle in order to cause a part of the body to move. **3.** Two words combined with an apostrophe, such as *can't, wouldn't, I'd, won't.*

con·tra·dict (kahn-truh-**dikt**) *verb* To say the opposite of what has already been said. ▶ *verb* **contradicting, contradicted**

con·tra·dic·tion (*kahn*-truh-**dik**-shuhn) *noun* A combination of statements or conditions that are opposed to each other, or the act of making a statement that opposes another.

con·tra·dic·to·ry (*kahn*-truh-**dik**-tur-ee) *adjective* Opposite, contrary, or not consistent.

con·trap·tion (kuhn-**trap**-shuhn) *noun* A strange or complicated device or machine.

con·trar·y
adjective **1.** (**kahn**-trer-ee) Opposite.

2. (kuhn-**trair**-ee) Deliberately stubborn and difficult.
noun (**kahn**-trer-ee) **1.** An idea or position that is opposite to another.
2. When you say **on the contrary,** you are taking a position opposite to what someone has just said.

con·trast
verb (kuhn-**trast**) **1.** To differ greatly. **2.** To point out the differences between things.
noun (**kahn**-trast) The difference between two things.
▶ *verb* **contrasting, contrasted**

con·tri·bute (kuhn-**trib**-yoot) *verb* **1.** To give help or money in order to accomplish a specific goal. **2.** To help to bring about. **3.** To write for a publication.
▶ *verb* **contributing, contributed** ▶ *noun* **contributor**

con·tri·bu·tion (*kahn*-truh-**byoo**-shuhn) *noun* The act of giving or contributing something, or the thing given.

con·trive (kuhn-**trive**) *verb* **1.** To make something happen by using skill and cleverness. **2.** To make something up.
▶ *verb* **contriving, contrived**

con·trol (kuhn-**trohl**)
verb **1.** To make something or someone act in a particular way. **2.** To hold back.
noun Power or authority over people or a situation.
noun, plural **controls** The levers, switches, and other devices that make a machine work.
▶ *verb* **controlling, controlled**

con·trol pan·el (kuhn-**trohl** pan-uhl) *noun* **1.** The part of an aircraft or machine where all the controls are.
2. The place on a computer where you can change settings that affect the way the computer operates.

con·tro·ver·sial (*kahn*-truh-**vur**-shuhl) *adjective* Causing a great deal of disagreement.

con·tro·ver·sy (**kahn**-truh-*vur*-see) *noun* A situation that people hold and express strongly opposing views about. ▶ *noun, plural* **controversies**

C

con·va·les·cence (*kahn*-vuh-**les**-uhns)
noun The time during which a person
is recovering from an illness, an injury,
or an operation. ▶ *verb* **convalesce**

con·va·les·cent (*kahn*-vuh-**les**-uhnt)
noun A person who is recovering from
an illness, an injury, or an operation.
adjective Of or having to do with a
person recovering from an illness,
injury, or operation, or with a period of
convalescence.

con·vec·tion (kuhn-**vek**-shuhn) *noun*
The circulation of heat through liquids
and gases.

con·vene (kuhn-**veen**) *verb* To gather
together. ▶ *verb* **convening, convened**

con·ven·ience (kuhn-**veen**-yuhns) *noun*
1. Something that makes a job or a
situation easier and more pleasant.
2. **convenience food** Food that is quick
and easy to prepare, such as a frozen
dinner.

con·ven·ient (kuhn-**veen**-yuhnt)
adjective Useful, or easy to
use. ▶ *adverb* **conveniently**

con·vent (**kahn**-vent) *noun* A building
occupied by nuns.

con·ven·tion (kuhn-**ven**-shuhn) *noun*
1. A formal gathering of people who
have the same profession or interests.
2. A customary or accepted way to
behave.

con·ven·tion·al (kuhn-**ven**-shuh-
nuhl) *adjective* 1. Usual, accepted, or
traditional. 2. Preferring the traditional
way of doing things.
▶ *adverb* **conventionally**

con·verge (kuhn-**vurj**) *verb* To come
together from several directions and
meet. ▶ *verb* **converging, converged**

con·ver·sa·tion (*kahn*-vur-**say**-shuhn)
noun The act of talking with another
person for a while.

con·verse
verb (kuhn-**vurs**) To talk with
someone.
noun (**kahn**-vurs) Something that is
the reverse or opposite of something
else.
▶ *verb* **conversing, conversed**
▶ *adverb* **conversely** (**kahn**-vurs-lee)

con·vert
verb (kuhn-**vurt**) To turn something
into something else.
noun (**kahn**-vurt) A person who has
changed his or her religion or other
beliefs.
▶ *verb* **converting, converted** ▶ *noun*
conversion (kuhn-**vur**-zhuhn)

con·vert·i·ble (kuhn-**vur**-tuh-buhl)
adjective Able to be changed into
something else.
noun A car with a top that can be put
down.

con·vex (**kahn**-veks *or* kahn-**veks**)
adjective Curved outward, like the
outside of a bowl.

con·vey (kuhn-**vay**) *verb* 1. To carry or
take from one place to another. 2. To
tell or to communicate.
▶ *verb* **conveying, conveyed**

con·vey·or belt (kuhn-**vay**-ur belt) *noun*
A moving belt that carries objects
from one place to another.

con·vict
verb (kuhn-**vikt**) To declare that
someone is guilty of a crime.
noun (**kahn**-vikt) A person who is
in prison because he or she has
committed a crime.
▶ *verb* **convicting, convicted**

con·vic·tion (kuhn-**vik**-shuhn) *noun*
1. A strong belief or opinion. 2. A
formal declaration that a person has
committed a crime.

con·vince (kuhn-**vins**) *verb* To
persuade someone to do or believe
something. ▶ *verb* **convincing,
convinced**

con·vinc·ing (kuhn-**vin**-sing) *adjective*
Having qualities that make you
want to believe or change your
mind. ▶ *adverb* **convincingly**

con·voy (**kahn**-voi) *noun* A group of
vehicles or ships that travel together
for convenience or safety.

con·vul·sion (kuhn-**vuhl**-shuhn) *noun*
An involuntary jerking movement
of the muscles or the whole body,
sometimes causing the person to fall
or to lose consciousness.

cook (kuk)
verb To prepare and heat food

for eating.

noun A person whose job is to prepare food.

▶ *verb* **cooking, cooked** ▶ *noun* **cooking**

cook·book (kuk-*buk*) *noun* A book filled with recipes, cooking directions, and information about food.

cook·ie (kuk-ee) *noun* **1.** A small, sweet, usually flat cake. **2.** A small file that is stored on your computer by a website so that when you visit the site again, it will remember some things about you, such as the pages you visited.

cool (kool)
adjective **1.** Somewhat cold.
2. Unfriendly or unenthusiastic.
3. (informal) Attractive, impressive, or fashionable.
verb To reduce the temperature of something.

▶ *adjective* **cooler, coolest** ▶ *verb* **cooling, cooled** ▶ *noun* **coolness** ▶ *adverb* **coolly**

co-op (koh-ahp) *noun* A store, society, or building in which members own shares. Co-op is short for **cooperative.**

coop (koop)
noun A small building or pen used to house chickens or other small animals.
verb **coop up** To confine in a small space.

▶ *verb* **cooping, cooped**

co·op·er·ate (koh-ah-puh-*rate*) *verb* To work together toward the same goal. ▶ *verb* **cooperating, cooperated**

co·op·er·a·tion (koh-ah-puh-**ray**-shuhn) *noun* The activity of working together to achieve something.

co·op·er·a·tive (koh-**ah**-pur-uh-tiv)
adjective Willing to work with other people.
noun A business owned by all the people who work in it and who share the responsibilities and the profits.

▶ *adverb* **cooperatively** ▶ *noun* **cooperativeness**

co·or·di·nate
verb (koh-**or**-duh-*nate*) To organize activities or people so that they function smoothly together.

noun (koh-**or**-duh-nit) One of a set of numbers used to show the position of a point on a line, graph, or map.

▶ *verb* **coordinating, coordinated** ▶ *noun* **coordination** (koh-or-duh-**nay**-shuhn) ▶ *noun* **coordinator** (koh-**or**-duh-nay-tur)

co·or·di·nat·ed (koh-**or**-duh-nay-tid) *adjective* Able to make your arms and legs work well together; graceful.

cope (kope) *verb* To deal with something effectively. ▶ *verb* **coping, coped**

cop·i·er (kah-pee-ur) *noun* A machine that copies printed material.

co·pi·lot (koh-*pye*-luht) *noun* The assistant pilot of an airplane.

cop·per (kah-pur)
noun **1.** A reddish-brown metal that conducts heat and electricity well. **2.** A reddish-brown color.
adjective Made of copper, or of the color of copper.

▶ *adjective* **coppery**

cop·per·head (kah-pur-*hed*) *noun* A poisonous snake with a light brown body and dark brown markings. Copperheads are found in the eastern part of the United States.

cop·y (kah-pee)
verb **1.** To do or say the same as another person. **2.** To make a similar or identical version of something.
noun Something that looks, sounds, or acts exactly the same as the original.

▶ *verb* **copies, copying, copied** ▶ *noun, plural* **copies**

cop·y·right (kah-pee-*rite*) *noun* The legal right to control the use of something created, such as a song or book.

cor·al (kor-uhl) *noun* **1.** A substance found underwater, made up of the skeletons of tiny sea creatures. **2.** A pink-red color.
Coral sounds like **choral.**

cor·al reef (kor-uhl reef) *noun* A reef made of coral and other materials that have solidified into rock.

cor·al snake (kor-uhl *snake*) *noun* A poisonous snake with red, black, and yellow bands on its body.

C

cord (kord) *noun* **1.** A string or rope. **2.** A covered wire that connects an electrical appliance to an outlet. **3.** A pile of cut wood four feet wide, four feet high, and eight feet long.
Cord sounds like **chord.**

cor·dial (kor-juhl) *adjective* Friendly and cheerful. ▶ *adverb* **cordially**

cor·du·roy (kor-duh-*roi*) *noun* A heavy cotton material with a ribbed pattern.

core (kor)
noun **1.** The hard center part of a fruit, such as an apple or pear, which often contains seeds. **2.** The intensely hot, most inner part of the earth. **3.** The most important part of something. **4.** The place in a nuclear reactor where fission occurs.
verb To remove the core of a fruit.
Core sounds like **corps.** ▶ *verb* **coring, cored**

cork (kork)
noun Soft bark used to make mats, stoppers for bottles, wall covering, and other objects.
verb To seal by putting a cork stopper in.
▶ *verb* **corking, corked**

cork·screw (kork-*skroo*)
noun A tool for pulling corks out of bottles.
adjective Turning in circles or spirals.

cor·mor·ant (kor-mur-uhnt) *noun* A large diving bird with a long neck, a hooked bill, and mainly dark feathers.

corn (korn) *noun* **1.** A plant that produces its seeds in rows on the ears of the plant, grown for many consumer and industrial uses. **2.** The sweet yellow or white seeds of one variety of this plant, eaten as a vegetable. **3.** A small, painful patch of thick, hard skin on your foot.

Corn Belt (korn *belt*) A region of the midwestern United States where corn is the most important cultivated crop. The Corn Belt stretches across the states of Iowa, Illinois, Indiana, Nebraska, Kansas, Minnesota, and Missouri. A large percentage of the corn grown in the United States comes from this region, where the crop has been cultivated since the mid-19th century.

cor·ne·a (kor-nee-uh) *noun* The transparent outer layer of the eyeball. The cornea covers the iris and pupil.

cor·ner (kor-nur)
noun **1.** The place where two or more sides or edges of something meet. **2.** The place where two streets intersect.
verb To get a person or an animal into a situation or position that is a trap.
idioms and phrases **1. just around the corner** Very close by. **2. just around the corner** Expected to happen very soon. **3. corner the market** To control the supply or the price of a particular thing.
▶ *verb* **cornering, cornered**

cor·net (kor-net) *noun* A brass musical instrument that is similar to but shorter than a trumpet.

corn·meal (korn-*meel*) *noun* Ground dried corn.

corn·row (korn-*roh*)
noun A flat braid of hair arranged close to the scalp.
verb To braid hair into cornrows.
▶ *verb* **cornrowing, cornrowed**

corn·starch (korn-*stahrch*) *noun* Flour made from the starchy part of corn kernels, used to thicken sauces.

cor·o·nar·y (kor-uh-*ner*-ee)
adjective Of or having to do with the heart.
noun A heart attack.
▶ *noun, plural* **coronaries**

cor·o·na·tion (kor-uh-**nay**-shun) *noun* The ceremony in which a king, queen, or other ruler is crowned.

cor·o·ner (kor-uh-nur) *noun* An official who investigates sudden, violent, or unnatural deaths.

cor·po·ral (kor-pur-uhl) *noun* A soldier who ranks below a sergeant.

cor·por·al pun·ish·ment (kor-pur-uhl **puhn**-ish-muhnt) *noun* Physical punishment, such as spanking.

cor·po·ra·tion (kor-puh-**ray**-shuhn) *noun* A group of people who are allowed by law to run a company, college, or town as a single person. Like an individual, a corporation can enter into contracts and buy and sell property.

corps (kor) *noun* **1.** A group of people acting together or doing the same thing. **2.** A company of military officers and enlisted personnel.
Corps sounds like **core.** ▶ *noun, plural* **corps** (korz)

corpse (korps) *noun* A dead body, especially of a human.

cor·pus·cle (**kor**-*puhs*-uhl) *noun* A red or white blood cell.

cor·ral (kuh-**ral**)
noun A fenced area that holds horses, cattle, or other animals.
verb To gather people, animals, or things in an enclosed area.
▶ *verb* **corralling, corralled**

cor·rect (kuh-**rekt**)
adjective True, right, or having no errors.
verb To put an error right.
▶ *verb* **correcting, corrected**

cor·rec·tion (kuh-**rek**-shuhn) *noun* The act of making something correct, or a statement, number, or piece of information that does this.

cor·rect·ly (kuh-**rekt**-lee) *adverb* In the right way.

cor·res·pond (kor-uh-**spahnd**) *verb* **1.** To write letters or emails to someone. **2.** To match in some way.
▶ *verb* **corresponding, corresponded**

cor·re·spond·ence (kor-uh-**spahn**-duhns) *noun* **1.** Letters or other communications between people, or the activity of exchanging messages. **2.** Similarity in particular points.

cor·res·pond·ent (kor-uh-**spahn**-duhnt) *noun* **1.** A person who reports for television, radio, or a printed publication about a particular subject or place. **2.** A person who writes letters, especially to the same recipient on a regular basis.

cor·re·spond·ing (kor-uh-**spahn**-ding) *adjective* Similar with respect to form, position, scale, or change.

cor·ri·dor (**kor**-i-dur) *noun* A long hallway or passage in a building or train.

cor·rode (kuh-**rode**) *verb*
To destroy or eat away at

something little by little. ▶ *verb* **corroding, corroded** ▶ *noun* **corrosion** ▶ *adjective* **corrosive**

cor·ru·gat·ed (**kor**-uh-gay-tid) *adjective* Shaped into ridges or ripples.

cor·rupt (kuh-**ruhpt**)
verb To make someone dishonest or immoral.
adjective Containing errors that make a thing unreliable or useless.
▶ *verb* **corrupting, corrupted**

cor·rup·tion (kuh-**ruhp**-shuhn) *noun* **1.** Dishonesty and cheating in public officials. **2.** The condition of being corrupt or corrupted.

cor·sage (kor-**sahzh**) *noun* A small bouquet worn on clothing or fastened to the wrist.

cos·met·ic (kahz-**met**-ik)
noun, plural **cosmetics** Beauty products; makeup.
adjective Of or having to do with the way a person or thing looks.

cos·mic (**kahz**-mik) *adjective* Of or having to do with the universe apart from the earth. ▶ *adverb* **cosmically**

cos·mo·naut (**kahz**-muh-*nawt*) *noun* A Russian astronaut.

cos·mo·pol·i·tan (*kahz*-muh-**pah**-li-tuhn) *adjective* **1.** Able to understand and feel at home in more than one culture. **2.** Containing or influenced by many different cultures.

cos·mos (**kahz**-mohs) *noun* The universe.

cost (kawst)
verb **1.** To have a price; to be worth a certain amount. **2.** To cause the loss of something.
noun **cost of living** The amount of money you need to spend on necessary items, such as food, housing, and clothing.
▶ *verb* **costing, cost**

co-star (**koh**-*stahr*)
noun A famous performer who appears in a movie, play, or television show with another performer who is equally famous.
verb To appear in a performance as a co-star.
▶ *verb* **co-starring, co-starred**

C

Cos·ta Ri·ca (**kah**-stuh **ree**-kuh *or* **koh**-stuh **ree**-kuh) A country in Central America. Known as the "greenest" country in the world, Costa Rica hopes to become the first carbon-neutral nation by 2021.

cost·ly (**kawst**-lee) *adjective* 1. Expensive. 2. Causing a loss or disadvantage.
▸ *adjective* **costlier, costliest**

cos·tume (**kahs**-toom) *noun* 1. Clothes worn by actors or people dressing in disguise. 2. Clothes worn by people at a particular time or in a particular place.

cot (kaht) *noun* A small, narrow bed that can be folded up and put away.

Côte d'I·voire (**koht** deev-**wahr**) A country in West Africa. Elephants were once plentiful in the Côte d'Ivoire. European explorers traded for ivory there, and it later became a French colony. In English, it is often called the Ivory Coast, the English translation of its French name.

cot·tage (**kah**-tij) *noun* A small house, especially in a beach or country setting.

cot·tage cheese (**kah**-tij *cheez*) *noun* Soft, white cheese made from curdled milk.

cot·ton (**kah**-tuhn) *noun* 1. A plant that produces seed pods containing fluffy white fibers. 2. The cloth made from such fibers. *adjective* Made from cotton.

cot·ton·mouth (**kah**-tuhn-*mouth*) *noun* A poisonous snake that lives near water and in swamps in the southeastern part of the United States. It is also called a **water moccasin.**

cot·ton·tail (**kah**-tuhn-*tayl*) *noun* A rabbit with a short, fluffy, white tail.

cot·ton·wood (**kah**-tuhn-*wud*) *noun* A kind of poplar tree with seeds covered with whitish hairs that look like cotton.

couch (kouch) *noun* 1. A long, cushioned piece of furniture that two or more people can sit on at the same time. 2. **couch potato** (informal) A person who spends a lot of time watching television rather than being active.
▸ *noun, plural* **couches**

cou·gar (**koo**-gur) *noun* A member of the cat family with a small head, long legs, and a strong body. Cougars live in the mountains of North and South America; also called **mountain lion, panther,** or **puma.**

cough (kawf)
verb To force air out of your lungs with a sudden, sharp sound.
noun An illness or condition that makes you cough.
▸ *verb* **coughing, coughed**

could (kud) *verb* Past tense of **can.**

could·n't (**kud**-uhnt) *contraction* A short form of *could not.*

coun·cil (**koun**-suhl) *noun* A group of people chosen to run a town, a county, or an organization. **Council** sounds like **counsel.**

coun·sel (**koun**-suhl)
verb To give people advice about problems.
noun Advice.
Counsel sounds like **council.** ▸ *verb* **counseling, counseled** ▸ *noun* **counseling**

coun·sel·or (**koun**-suh-lur) *noun* 1. Someone trained to help with problems or give advice. 2. A lawyer.

count (kount)
verb 1. To say numbers in order. 2. To figure out how many there are of something. 3. To be worth something. 4. To consider. 5. **count on** To rely on something or someone.
noun A number of people or things that have been counted.
▸ *verb* **counting, counted** ▸ *noun* **counting**

count·down (**kount**-doun) *noun* A backward counting from a certain number down to zero, to mark the moment when something happens.

coun·ter (**koun**-tur)
noun 1. A long, flat surface, usually used for work or display. 2. A small piece of wood or plastic used in some games or to do math.
adjective Opposite.
adverb In opposition.

coun·ter·act (*koun*-tur-**akt**) *verb* To act against something in order to reduce its effect. ▶ *verb* **counteracting, counteracted**

coun·ter·clock·wise (*koun*-tur-**klahk**-*wize*) *adverb, adjective* In a direction opposite to the way the hands of a clock move.

coun·ter·feit (*koun*-tur-*fit*)
adjective Fake, but looking almost exactly like the real thing.
noun A fake.
verb To manufacture a fake.
▶ *verb* **counterfeiting, counterfeited**

coun·ter·part (*koun*-tur-*pahrt*) *noun*
1. A person or thing whose position or function is similar in some way to that of another. 2. One of two parts that complete each other.

count·less (*kount*-lis) *adjective* Too many to count.

coun·try (*kuhn*-tree)
noun 1. A part of the world with its own territory and government. 2. Land away from towns or cities, containing farmland, forests, or other land that has not been built on and where few people live. 3. The people of a nation.
adjective Of, in, or about the countryside.
▶ *noun, plural* **countries**

coun·try·man (*kuhn*-tree-muhn)
noun Someone from your own country. ▶ *noun, plural* **countrymen**

coun·try·side (*kuhn*-tree-*side*) *noun* Land outside of towns or cities, with few inhabitants or buildings.

coun·ty (*koun*-tee)
noun A division of a state with its own local government.
adjective Of or in a county.
▶ *noun, plural* **counties**

coup (koo) *noun* 1. An achievement that comes suddenly and unexpectedly. 2. The sudden overthrow of a government.

cou·ple (*kuhp*-uhl) *noun* 1. Two of the same kind of thing. 2. Two people paired together.

cou·pon (*koo*-pahn) *noun* 1. A small piece of paper, sometimes cut out of a newspaper or magazine, that gives you a discount on something. 2. A small form that you fill out and mail to get information about something or to order merchandise.

cour·age (*kur*-ij) *noun* Bravery; the ability to do something that scares you. ▶ *adjective* **courageous** (kuh-*ray*-juhs) ▶ *adverb* **courageously**

cour·i·er (*kur*-ee-ur *or* *koor*-ee-ur) *noun* A person or a service that carries messages or packages for somebody else.

course (kors) *noun* 1. A part of a meal served by itself. 2. A series of lessons or classes. 3. An area where certain sports are played. 4. A route.
Course sounds like **coarse.**

court (kort)
noun 1. A place where legal cases are heard and decided. 2. An area where certain sports are played. 3. An open space closed in by walls or buildings.
verb 1. To try to win the love of someone, especially so as to marry. 2. To try to attract. 3. To risk misfortune by behaving carelessly.
▶ *verb* **courting, courted**

cour·te·ous (*kur*-tee-uhs)
adjective Polite, respectful, and considerate. ▶ *noun* **courteousness** ▶ *adverb* **courteously**

cour·te·sy (*kur*-ti-see) *noun* 1. Well-mannered behavior. 2. A thoughtful act; a favor.
▶ *noun, plural* **courtesies**

court·house (*kort*-*hous*) *noun* A building where trials and government business are conducted.

court·mar·tial (*kort*-*mahr*-shuhl)
noun A court in which military trials are held, using military law.
verb To try someone in a military court.
▶ *noun, plural* **courts-martial** ▶ *verb* **court-martialing, court-martialed**

court·ship (*kort*-ship) *noun* Attempts by one person to win the love and affection of another, usually with the intention of marrying.

court·yard (*kort*-*yahrd*) *noun* An open area surrounded by walls or buildings; a court.

C

cous·cous (**koos**-koos) *noun* A dish made from tiny grains of pasta.

cous·in (**kuhz**-in) *noun* A child of your uncle or aunt.

cove (kove) *noun* A small, sheltered inlet along a coast.

cov·e·nant (**kuhv**-uh-nuhnt) *noun* A formal and often legal agreement to do or to avoid a certain thing.

cov·er (**kuhv**-ur)
verb 1. To put something on top of or in front of something else. 2. To hide something by putting another thing over it. 3. To teach or study a particular topic. 4. To travel a certain distance. 5. To extend or apply over a certain area. 6. To provide compensation for a loss.
noun 1. A thing that covers or holds another thing; a top, lid, or container. 2. A blanket or bedspread. 3. Protection for someone doing something dangerous.
▶ *verb* **covering, covered** ▶ *noun* **coverage**

covered wag·on (**kuhv**-urd **wag**-uhn) *noun* A large wooden wagon with a canvas cover spread over metal hoops, used by American pioneers crossing the country during the nation's westward expansion.

cov·er·up (**kuhv**-ur-*uhp*) *noun* An attempt to prevent people from finding out about something bad, especially a crime.

cov·et (**kuhv**-it) *verb* To want something very much even though it may belong to someone else. ▶ *verb* **coveting, coveted**

cow (kou) *noun* 1. An adult female farm animal, raised especially for her milk. 2. An adult female of some other large mammals, including elk, seals, and whales. 3. **have a cow** (informal) To become angry or agitated about something. 4. **till the cows come home** (informal) For a very long time.

cow·ard (**kou**-urd) *noun* A person who lacks the courage to face dangerous or unpleasant situations.

cow·ard·ice (**kou**-ur-dis) *noun* Lack of bravery.

cow·ard·ly (**kow**-urd-lee) *adjective* Having or showing a lack of courage that also suggests weakness.

cow·boy (**kou**-*boi*) *noun* A man or boy who herds and takes care of cattle.

cow·girl (**kou**-*gurl*) *noun* A woman or girl who herds and takes care of cattle.

cow·hand (**kou**-*hand*) *noun* A person who works on a ranch.

cow·hide (**kou**-*hide*) *noun* The skin of a cow, used to make leather goods.

coy·o·te (kye-**oh**-tee *or* **kye**-oht) *noun* An animal that looks like a small wolf and is native to the western United States. ▶ *noun, plural* **coyote** *or* **coyotes**

co·zy (**koh**-zee) *adjective* Comfortable, snug, and warm. ▶ *adjective* **cozier, coziest** ▶ *noun* **coziness** ▶ *adverb* **cozily**

CPR (see-*pee*-**ahr**) *noun* A method of reviving victims of a heart attack or suffocation using mouth-to-mouth breathing and rhythmic compressing of the chest. CPR is short for *cardiopulmonary resuscitation*.

CPU (see-*pee*-**yoo**) *noun* The part of a computer that processes commands and manages the programs that are running. CPU is short for *central processing unit*.

crab (krab) *noun* A creature that lives in water and has a hard shell, eight legs, and two claws. Some kinds of crabs can be eaten.

crab ap·ple (**krab** *ap*-uhl) *noun* A small, sour apple used to make jelly.

crab·by (**krab**-ee) *adjective* Grouchy or irritable. ▶ *adjective* **crabbier, crabbiest** ▶ *noun* **crabbiness** ▶ *adverb* **crabbily**

crack (krak)
verb 1. To break or split without completely separating, often with a loud, sharp noise. 2. To solve a puzzle. *noun* 1. A break or a narrow opening. 2. (informal) A nasty or sarcastic remark. 3. (slang) A form of the drug cocaine.
idiom **take a crack at something** (informal) To try to do something.
▶ *verb* **cracking, cracked**

C

crack·er (**krak**-ur) *noun* A thin, crisp biscuit or wafer.

crack·le (**krak**-uhl)
verb To make a lot of quick, sharp sounds.
noun Quick, sharp sounds.
▶ *verb* **crackling, crackled**

cra·dle (**kray**-duhl)
noun 1. A small bed for a young baby, usually on rockers. 2. The place where something starts.
verb To hold something or someone in or as if in a cradle.
▶ *verb* **cradling, cradled**

craft (kraft)
noun 1. Skillful work involving making things with your hands. 2. A boat, ship, spaceship, or plane.
verb To make something by hand.
▶ *verb* **crafting, crafted**

crafts·man·ship (**krafts**-muhn-*ship*)
noun Skill in making or doing something, especially with your hands.

crafts·per·son (**krafts**-*pur*-suhn) *noun* A person who is skilled in a particular craft. People sometimes use the word *craftsman* to refer to a male craftsperson and *craftswoman* to refer to a female craftsperson. ▶ *noun, plural* **craftspeople**

craft·y (**kraf**-tee) *adjective* Good at tricking people. ▶ *adjective* **craftier, craftiest** ▶ *adverb* **craftily**

crag (krag) *noun* A steep, rough cliff or rock face. ▶ *adjective* **craggy**

cram (kram) *verb* 1. To force things into a small or crowded space. 2. To study very hard over a short period of time.
▶ *verb* **cramming, crammed**

cramp (kramp)
noun A painful muscle contraction, often caused by strain or fatigue.
verb **cramp your style** (informal) To keep you from expressing yourself freely.
noun, plural **cramps** Sharp pains in your abdomen.
▶ *verb* **cramping, cramped**

cramped (krampt) *adjective* Too small or crowded to hold the people or things that need to fit.

cran·ber·ry (**kran**-*ber*-ee) *noun* A small, red, sour berry that grows on low bushes in bogs and in swamps. ▶ *noun, plural* **cranberries**

crane (krane)
noun 1. A large wading bird with long legs and a long neck and bill. 2. A machine with a long arm used to lift and move heavy objects.
verb To stretch your neck so that you can see over or around something better.
▶ *verb* **craning, craned**

crank (krangk)
noun 1. A handle that is attached at a right angle to a shaft and is turned to make a machine work. 2. (informal) Someone with strange ideas.
verb To start something, or make something happen, by turning a crank.
adjective Produced by someone mentally unstable or malicious.
▶ *verb* **cranking, cranked**

crank·y (**krang**-kee) *adjective* Acting in an annoyed way; grouchy. ▶ *adjective* **crankier, crankiest**

crash (krash)
verb 1. To make a loud, smashing noise. 2. To collide violently with another object. 3. To fail completely.
noun A violent collision, especially an accident involving a vehicle.
▶ *verb* **crashes, crashing, crashed** ▶ *noun, plural* **crashes**

crate (krate)
noun A large wooden or plastic box used for transporting and storing things.
verb To put or pack in a crate.
▶ *verb* **crating, crated**

cra·ter (**kray**-tur) *noun* 1. The mouth of a volcano or geyser. 2. A large hole in the ground caused by something falling or exploding, such as a meteorite or a bomb.

crave (krave) *verb* To want something very much. ▶ *verb* **craving, craved** ▶ *noun* **craving**

craw·dad (**kraw**-dad) *or* **craw·fish** (**kraw**-fish) *noun* (informal) Other names for **crayfish**. ▶ *noun, plural* **crawdads, crawfish** *or* **crawfishes**

C

crawl (krawl)
verb 1. To move on your hands and knees. 2. To move slowly.
noun 1. A style of swimming face down in which you alternate your arm strokes while kicking your legs rapidly. 2. A very slow rate of movement. 3. A crawling movement.
▶ *verb* **crawling, crawled**

cray·fish (**kray**-*fish*) *noun* A small animal related to the lobster that lives in freshwater and is used for food. ▶ *noun, plural* **crayfish** or **crayfishes**

cray·on (**kray**-uhn or **kray**-ahn) *noun* A stick of colored wax used for drawing and coloring.
verb To draw or color with a crayon.
▶ *verb* **crayoning, crayoned**

craze (kraze) *noun* A very popular fashion or pastime that usually does not stay popular very long.

cra·zy (**kray**-zee) *adjective* 1. Insane or foolish. 2. (informal) Extremely enthusiastic.
▶ *adjective* **crazier, craziest** ▶ *noun* **craziness** ▶ *adverb* **crazily**

creak (kreek)
verb To make a high-pitched squeaking noise when something is moved or weight is put on it.
noun A high-pitched squeaking noise.
Creak sounds like **creek.** ▶ *verb* **creaking, creaked** ▶ *adjective* **creaky** ▶ *adverb* **creakily**

cream (kreem)
noun 1. A thick, fatty liquid found in whole milk. 2. A thick, smooth liquid that you put on your skin to soften and protect it. 3. A yellow-white color, or the color of cream. 4. The best part.
adjective Being the color of cream.
▶ *noun* **creaminess** ▶ *adjective* **creamy**

cream cheese (**kreem** *cheez*) *noun* A soft white cheese that is spread on bread or used to make dip or cheesecake.

crease (krees)
verb To make folds or lines in something, especially fabric or paper.
noun A wrinkle or fold.
▶ *verb* **creasing, creased**

cre·ate (kree-**ate**) *verb* 1. To make something new. 2. To make something happen as a result of an action or a situation.
▶ *verb* **creating, created**

cre·a·tion (kree-**ay**-shuhn) *noun* 1. Something that has been made or invented, especially something that shows artistic talent. 2. The act of making something.

cre·a·tive (kree-**ay**-tiv) *adjective* Skillful at using your imagination and thinking of new ideas. ▶ *noun* **creativity** ▶ *adverb* **creatively**

cre·a·tor (kree-**ay**-tur) *noun* A person who creates something.

crea·ture (**kree**-chur) *noun* A living being, human or animal.

crèche (kresh) *noun* A model of the baby Jesus with his parents, visitors, and animals, in the stable where he was born.

cre·den·tials (kri-**den**-shuhlz) *noun, plural* Written proof of someone's background, experience, or certification, such as a diploma or certificate.

cred·i·ble (**kred**-uh-buhl) *adjective* Believable. ▶ *noun* **credibility**

cred·it (**kred**-it)
noun 1. The balance in your favor in an account. 2. Public acknowledgment or praise. 3. **on credit** To be paid for later.
noun, plural **credits** A list of names at the end of a movie or television program that tells you who made it.
verb To give public acknowledgment to.
▶ *verb* **crediting, credited**

cred·it card (**kred**-it *kahrd*) *noun* A small, plastic card used in stores and restaurants to purchase products and services on credit.

cred·i·tor (**kred**-i-tur) *noun* A person or company to whom another person or company owes money.

creed (kreed) *noun* A system of beliefs; a guiding belief.

creek (kreek) *noun* A stream, usually one that is smaller than a river. **Creek** sounds like **creak.**

C

creep (kreep)
  verb **1.** To move very slowly and carefully so as not to make noise. **2.** To move slowly because of an obstruction.
  noun (slang) An unpleasant person.
  idiom **give someone the creeps** (informal) To be unpleasant and frightening.
  ▶ *verb* **creeping, crept** (krept) ▶ *adjective* **creepy**

cre·mate (**kree**-mate) *verb* To burn a dead body to ashes. ▶ *verb* **cremating, cremated** ▶ *noun* **cremation**

Cre·ole (**kree**-ohl)
  noun **1.** Someone of mixed European and African descent born in the West Indies or South America. **2.** Someone of French or Spanish descent living in Louisiana or Texas. **3.** The languages based on French that are spoken in Louisiana and Haiti.
  adjective **creole** or **Creole** Prepared with a spicy sauce of tomatoes, peppers, and okra. The word usually comes after a noun rather than before it.

crepe (krape) *noun* A very thin pancake that is sometimes rolled up around a filling.

crepe pa·per (krape *pay*-pur) *noun* A thin paper with a wrinkled texture, often used in party decorations.

cres·cent (**kres**-uhnt)
  noun A curved shape similar to that of the moon when it is just a sliver in the sky.
  adjective Being in the shape of a crescent.

crest (krest)
  noun **1.** The top of something, especially a mountain, a hill, or a wave. **2.** A tuft of feathers on the top of a bird's head. **3.** Part of a coat of arms.
  verb To reach the highest point.
  ▶ *verb* **cresting, crested** ▶ *adjective* **crested**

crev·ice (**krev**-is) *noun* A narrow opening in something, such as a rock.

crew (kroo) *noun* A team of people who work together on a ship, an aircraft, or a specific job.

crib (krib) *noun* **1.** A small bed for a baby, usually with bars on the sides. **2.** A small farm building in which grain is stored.

crick·et (**krik**-it) *noun* **1.** A jumping insect that makes a high-pitched chirping sound. **2.** An outdoor game played by two teams of 11 players with smooth, flat bats and a small, hard ball.

crime (krime) *noun* An act that is against the law.

crim·i·nal (**krim**-uh-nuhl)
  noun A person who commits a crime.
  adjective Of or having to do with crime.
  ▶ *adverb* **criminally**

crim·son (**krim**-zuhn)
  noun A dark red color.
  adjective Being a dark red in color.

crin·kle (**kring**-kuhl)
  verb **1.** To wrinkle or to crumple. **2.** To make a soft, slight, rustling sound.
  noun A soft rustling sound.
  ▶ *verb* **crinkling, crinkled** ▶ *adjective* **crinkled**

crip·ple (**krip**-uhl)
  noun A person who has a physical limitation that makes it hard for him or her to walk or move easily. This word is now considered offensive by many people. The preferred term is *person with a disability.*
  verb **1.** To injure someone in a way that causes a serious handicap. **2.** To stop someone or something from moving or working properly, or to cause severe damage.
  ▶ *verb* **crippling, crippled** ▶ *adjective* **crippled**

cri·sis (**krye**-sis) *noun* A time of severe difficulty or danger. ▶ *noun, plural* **crises** (**krye**-seez)

crisp (krisp) *adjective* **1.** Firm, dry, and easily broken. **2.** Pleasantly cool and fresh.
  ▶ *adjective* **crisper, crispest** ▶ *adverb* **crisply** ▶ *adjective* **crispy**

C

criss·cross (**kris**-kraws)
verb To form or move in a pattern of intersecting lines.
noun A pattern of intersecting lines.
adjective Marked with intersecting lines.
▶ *verb* **crisscrosses, crisscrossing, crisscrossed** ▶ *noun, plural* **crisscrosses**

cri·te·ri·a (**krye**-teer-ee-uh) *noun, plural* Facts or qualities that you use as a standard when you judge something. Note that the word *criteria* is a plural noun; the singular, which is not used often, is *criterion*.

crit·ic (**krit**-ik) *noun* **1.** A person who finds something wrong with people or things. **2.** A person whose job is to judge and write about books, movies, plays, or restaurants.

crit·i·cal (**krit**-i-kuhl) *adjective* **1.** Expressing a negative opinion or finding fault. **2.** Dangerous or serious.
▶ *adverb* **critically**

crit·i·cism (**krit**-i-siz-uhm) *noun* **1.** A critical comment or complaint about something. **2.** The activity of evaluating books, movies, performances, or works of art.

crit·i·cize (**krit**-i-size) *verb* **1.** To tell someone what he or she has done wrong, often in a hostile or impatient way. **2.** To evaluate something, such as a book, movie, play, or television program.
▶ *verb* **criticizing, criticized**

croak (krohk)
verb **1.** To make a deep, hoarse sound like a frog. **2.** To speak with a deep, hoarse voice. **3.** (slang) To die.
noun A deep, hoarse sound, like that of a frog.
▶ *verb* **croaking, croaked** ▶ *adjective* **croaky**

Cro·a·tia (kroh-**ay**-shuh) A country on the Adriatic Sea in Central Europe. Croatia declared its independence from the former Yugoslavia in 1991, but it took four years of fighting before the occupying Serb army was finally forced out.

cro·chet (kroh-**shay**) *verb* To make patterned cloth from thread or yarn using a hooked needle. ▶ *verb* **crocheting, crocheted** ▶ *noun* **crocheting**

crock·er·y (**krah**-kur-ee) *noun* Pottery that you use for food, such as plates, cups, and saucers.

croc·o·dile (**krah**-kuh-dile) *noun* A large reptile with a long body, short legs, and strong jaws. Crocodiles live in water and are related to alligators.

cro·cus (**kroh**-kuhs) *noun* A small plant with purple, yellow, or white flowers and thin leaves like blades of grass. Most crocuses bloom early in the spring. ▶ *noun, plural* **crocuses**

crois·sant (kruh-**sahnt**) *noun* A flaky roll that is shaped like a crescent moon.

crook (kruk)
noun **1.** A bent or curved part of something. **2.** A criminal or a dishonest person. **3.** A long, hooked staff used by shepherds.
verb To bend something, especially your finger.
▶ *verb* **crooking, crooked**

crook·ed (**kruk**-id) *adjective* **1.** Not straight. **2.** Dishonest or illegal.

crop (krahp)
noun **1.** A plant grown for food for people or animals. **2.** The amount of food produced in a single harvest. **3.** The pouch in a bird's throat where food is stored or prepared for digestion.
verb **1.** To eat the top part of grass while grazing. **2.** To cut off or remove the edges from something.
▶ *verb* **cropping, cropped**

cro·quet (kroh-**kay**) *noun* An outdoor game played by hitting wooden balls with mallets through wire hoops that are stuck into the ground.

cross (kraws)
verb **1.** To travel from one side of something to the other. **2.** To draw a line through. **3.** To intersect. **4.** To oppose someone, or to obstruct someone's plans. **5.** To reach from one side to the other.
adjective Annoyed or irritable.

noun **1.** A shape made up of two intersecting lines, such as the x or the plus sign (+). **2.** An upright post with a horizontal bar that crosses it, or a pendant shaped this way. The cross is the symbol of Christianity.

idiom If you **cross your heart,** you move your hand in an X shape on your chest to show that you are telling the truth or that you will keep a promise.

▶ *verb* **crosses, crossing, crossed** ▶ *noun, plural* **crosses**

cross·bow (**kraws**-boh) *noun* A weapon with a bow mounted across a piece of wood. Crossbows were used in the Middle Ages.

cross·coun·try (**kraws**-kuhn-tree) *adjective* Run through the countryside instead of on a track.

cross·ex·am·ine (**kraws**-ig-**zam**-in) *verb* To question a witness in a court case who has already been questioned by the lawyers on the other side. ▶ *verb* **cross-examining, cross-examined** ▶ *noun* **cross-examination**

cross-eyed (**kraws**-ide) *adjective* Having eyes that turn inward, toward each other, so that they are difficult to focus and the person cannot see clearly.

cross·ref·er·ence (**kraws**-**ref**-ur-uhns) *noun* A mention in one part of a book that tells you where to find more information on the same subject in another part. A cross-reference can be in the index or in the text of the book.

cross·roads (**kraws**-rohdz) *noun, plural* **1.** A place where two or more roads meet. **2.** A point where an important decision must be made.

cross sec·tion (**kraws** sek-shuhn) *noun* **1.** A diagram that shows the inside of something, as if it had been cut through. **2.** A selection of different types of people or things.

▶ *adjective* **cross-sectional**

cross·walk (**kraws**-wawk) *noun* A place where pedestrians can safely cross a street, often marked with painted lines.

cross·word puz·zle (**kraws**-wurd **puhz**-uhl) *noun* A puzzle in which you answer clues in order to fill blank squares with words, writing one letter in each square.

crotch (krahtch) *noun* The area of the body where your legs meet. ▶ *noun, plural* **crotches**

crouch (krouch)
verb To bend your legs and lower your body.
noun A crouching position.
▶ *verb* **crouches, crouching, crouched**
▶ *noun, plural* **crouches**

croup (kroop) *noun* A children's disease that causes frequent coughing and difficulty in breathing.

crow (kroh)
noun **1.** A large black bird with a loud, rough voice. **2.** A noise like that of a rooster.
verb **1.** To make a loud, crying noise like a rooster. **2.** To brag in a satisfied way about something.
▶ *verb* **crowing, crowed**

crow·bar (**kroh**-bahr) *noun* A heavy steel or iron bar with a flat end that can be used to lift heavy things or to pry something open.

crowd (kroud)
noun A large number of people gathered together.
verb To not give someone else enough room.
▶ *verb* **crowding, crowded** ▶ *adjective* **crowded**

crown (kroun)
noun **1.** A headdress worn by a king, a queen, or another ruler, made from gold or silver and jewels. **2.** The top part of something. **3.** A wreath or headdress given to the winner of a competition.
verb **1.** To put someone into a position of authority or honor by placing a crown on his or her head. **2.** To declare someone to be the winner.
▶ *verb* **crowning, crowned** ▶ *noun* **crowning**

crow's nest (krohz nest) *noun* A small platform used for a lookout, found on top of the mast of a sailing ship.

cru·cial (**kroo**-shuhl) *adjective* Decisive; extremely important for the success of something. ▶ *adverb* **crucially**

C

crude (krood) *adjective* 1. Rough, not refined or finished. 2. Rude and in poor taste.
▶ *adjective* **cruder, crudest** ▶ *noun* **crudity** ▶ *adverb* **crudely**

cru·el (kroo-uhl) *adjective* 1. Deliberately causing pain to others, or happy to see them suffer. 2. Hurtful or humiliating.
▶ *adjective* **crueler, cruelest** ▶ *noun* **cruelty** ▶ *adverb* **cruelly**

cruise (krooz)
noun A vacation on a ship that docks at several places.
verb To travel smoothly and easily.
▶ *verb* **cruising, cruised**

cruis·er (**kroo**-zur) *noun* 1. A boat with a cabin that is used for short cruises. 2. A warship that is faster than a battleship and has fewer guns.

crumb (kruhm) *noun* A tiny piece of bread or other baked food.

crum·ble (**kruhm**-buhl) *verb* To break into tiny pieces. ▶ *verb* **crumbling, crumbled** ▶ *adjective* **crumbly**

crum·ple (**kruhm**-puhl) *verb* 1. To crush something, usually paper or fabric, into wrinkles and folds. 2. To collapse into bent pieces.
▶ *verb* **crumpling, crumpled**
▶ *adjective* **crumpled**

crunch (kruhnch)
verb To crush or chew something noisily.
noun The act or sound of crunching.
▶ *verb* **crunches, crunching, crunched** ▶ *noun, plural* **crunches** ▶ *adjective* **crunchy**

cru·sade (kroo-**sade**) *noun* 1. A battle or fight for which someone feels a great deal of emotion. 2. **Crusade** One of the battles fought in the 11th, 12th, and 13th centuries by European Christians attempting to capture biblical lands from the Muslims.

cru·sad·er (kroo-**say**-dur) *noun* 1. A person who works very hard to bring change to a social or political situation. 2. **Crusader** One of the soldiers or knights who took part in the Crusades of the 11th, 12th, and 13th centuries.

crush (kruhsh)
verb 1. To damage or destroy something by pressing it under a heavy weight. 2. To bring a sudden end to something.
noun Strong romantic feelings toward someone, usually lasting only for a short time.
▶ *verb* **crushes, crushing, crushed**
▶ *noun, plural* **crushes**

crust (kruhst) *noun* 1. The crisp, outer layer of bread or pastry. 2. The hard outer layer of the earth.

crus·ta·cean (kruh-**stay**-shuhn) *noun* A sea creature that has an outer skeleton, such as a crab, lobster, or shrimp.

crutch (kruhch) *noun* A long stick with a padded top, used to help support someone with a leg or foot injury. ▶ *noun, plural* **crutches**

cry (krye)
verb 1. To produce tears because of strong feelings. 2. To shout.
noun The sound of someone crying, shouting, or yelling.
▶ *verb* **cries, crying, cried** ▶ *noun, plural* **cries**

cryp·tic (**krip**-tik) *adjective* Not clear or easy to understand, mysterious.

crys·tal (**kris**-tuhl)
noun 1. A clear or nearly clear mineral or rock with many flat faces, such as quartz. 2. A substance that forms a pattern of many flat surfaces when it becomes a solid. Salt and snowflakes are crystals. 3. Glass of superior quality, used to make fine things, such as drinking glasses or vases.
adjective Made of crystal, as *a crystal chandelier.*
▶ *adjective* **crystalline** (**kris**-tuh-lin)

crys·tal·lize (**kris**-tuh-*lize*) *verb* 1. To form crystals. 2. To take form.
▶ *verb* **crystallizing, crystallized**

CT scan (**see-tee** *skan*) *noun* Another term for **CAT scan.**

cub (kuhb) *noun* A young animal, such as a lion, tiger, or bear.

Cu·ba (**kyoo**-buh) The largest and most populous island nation in the Caribbean. Cubans began fleeing

C

the country after its communist revolution in 1959. Their illegal immigration to the United States, often on homemade rafts, has been a continuing problem along the Florida coast.

cube (kyoob)
noun A three-dimensional shape with six square faces. Dice are cubes.
verb To multiply a number by itself twice. *The number 4 cubed is 4 x 4 x 4. It is written 4³*
▸ *verb* **cubing, cubed** ▸ *adjective* **cubic**

cu·bi·cle (**kyoo**-bi-kuhl) *noun* A small office or area surrounded by partitions.

cu·bit (**kyoo**-bit) *noun* An ancient form of measurement based on the length of the forearm, measured from the elbow to the tip of the middle finger.

cuck·oo (**koo**-koo)
noun A bird with a distinct call and a long tail. Some cuckoos lay their eggs in other birds' nests.
adjective (informal) Silly, or acting in a scatterbrained manner.

cu·cum·ber (**kyoo**-*kuhm*-bur) *noun* A long, crisp, green vegetable with a soft center filled with seeds.

cud (kuhd) *noun* Food that some animals, such as cows and sheep, bring up from the first part of their stomachs to chew again.

cud·dle (**kuhd**-uhl)
verb To hold someone or something closely and lovingly in your arms.
noun An act of cuddling.
▸ *verb* **cuddling, cuddled**

cue (kyoo)
noun **1.** The signal to say lines or perform an action in a play. **2.** Any signal to do something. **3.** A long stick used to hit the ball in billiards and pool.
verb To give a signal.
Cue sounds like **queue**. ▸ *verb* **cueing, cued**

cuff (kuhf) *noun* **1.** The band or folded part of the sleeve of a shirt or blouse that goes around your wrist. **2.** The folded part at the bottom of a pant leg. **3. off the cuff** Without preparation.

cui·sine (kwi-**zeen**) *noun* A style or manner of cooking or presenting food.

cul-de-sac (**kuhl**-duh-sak) *noun* A road that is closed at one end.

cul·mi·nate (**kuhl**-muh-nate) *verb* To reach the highest or final point. ▸ *verb* **culminating, culminated** ▸ *noun* **culmination**

cul·prit (**kuhl**-prit) *noun* A person who is guilty of doing something wrong or of committing a crime.

cult (kuhlt) *noun* **1.** A particular form of religious worship, especially one that people who don't share its beliefs think is strange or allows no freedom. **2.** A strong, almost religious devotion to a person, thing, idea, or way of life. **3. cult hero** A person who is very popular with a small group of followers.

cul·ti·vate (**kuhl**-tuh-vate) *verb* **1.** To grow crops on land. **2.** To develop by studying.
▸ *verb* **cultivating, cultivated** ▸ *noun* **cultivation**

cul·ture (**kuhl**-chur) *noun* **1.** An appreciation for the arts, such as music, literature, and painting. **2.** An artificial growth of cells or tissue in a laboratory. **3.** The ideas, customs, traditions, and way of life of a group of people.
▸ *adjective* **cultural**

cul·tured (**kuhl**-churd) *adjective* Well-educated or refined.

cum·ber·some (**kum**-bur-suhm) *adjective* Heavy or bulky and difficult to move around.

cun·ning (**kuhn**-ing)
adjective Having or showing the ability to trick people.
noun The ability to trick people.
▸ *adverb* **cunningly**

cup (kuhp) *noun* **1.** A small container for holding liquids, often with a handle. **2.** A unit of measurement equal to eight fluid ounces. **3.** Any ornament shaped like a cup.

cup·board (**kuhb**-urd) *noun* A cabinet or closet for storing things, such as dishes or food.

C

cup·cake (**kuhp**-*kake*) *noun* A small, round cake with frosting, for one person to eat.

cup·ful (**kuhp**-*ful*) *noun* 1. The amount a cup can hold. 2. An amount equal to eight fluid ounces; half a pint.

cur·a·ble (**kyoor**-uh-buhl) *adjective* Able to be cured with proper medical treatment.

cu·ra·tor (**kyoor**-ay-tur *or* kyoo-**ray**-tur) *noun* A person who is in charge of a collection of art or an exhibit in a museum.

curb (kurb)
noun A raised border along the edge of a paved street.
verb To control or hold back something.
▸ *verb* **curbing, curbed**

curd (kurd) *noun* The solid part of milk that is sour or separated, often used to make cheese.

cur·dle (**kur**-duhl) *verb* To separate into curds or lumps, either because a food has gone sour or because something has been added to it. ▸ *verb* **curdling, curdled** ▸ *adjective* **curdled**

cure (kyoor)
verb To make someone better when he or she has been sick.
noun 1. A drug or some other kind of treatment that ends an illness. 2. A return to good health.
▸ *verb* **curing, cured**

cur·few (**kur**-fyoo) *noun* A rule or an order that prevents people from traveling around freely, especially after dark.

cu·ri·ous (**kyoor**-ee-uhs) *adjective* 1. Eager to know or learn about something. 2. Unusual or remarkable.
▸ *noun* **curiosity** (**kyoor**-ee-**ah**-si-tee) ▸ *adverb* **curiously**

curl (kurl)
noun A coiled lock of hair.
verb To move, or to make something move, in a spiral or curved direction.
▸ *verb* **curling, curled**

cur·ly (**kur**-lee) *adjective* Having curls; twisted. ▸ *adjective* **curlier, curliest**

cur·rant (**kur**-uhnt) *noun* 1. A small dried berry used in cooking and baking. 2. A small sour berry used in making jelly.
Currant sounds like **current**.

cur·ren·cy (**kur**-uhn-see) *noun* The form of money used in a country. ▸ *noun, plural* **currencies**

cur·rent (**kur**-uhnt)
noun The movement of water in a definite direction in a river or an ocean, or the movement of electricity through a cable or wire.
adjective Happening now.
Current sounds like **currant**. ▸ *adverb* **currently**

cur·rent af·fairs (**kur**-uhnt uh-**fairz**) *noun, plural* Important events, usually political, that are happening now and that are often reported on television or in newspapers and magazines.

cur·ric·u·lum (kuh-**rik**-yuh-luhm) *noun* An organized program of study in a school or college. ▸ *noun, plural* **curricula** (kuh-**rik**-yuh-luh)

cur·ry (**kur**-ee) *noun* 1. A powder with a hot, spicy taste, made from various spices. 2. A dish made with curry and meat, fish, or vegetables.
▸ *noun, plural* **curries** ▸ *adjective* **curried**

curse (kurs)
noun A spell intended to harm someone by calling on evil spirits or other such powers.
verb To use offensive language.
▸ *verb* **cursing, cursed**

cur·sor (**kur**-sur) *noun* A small indicator on a computer screen that shows where the computer's next action will take place.

curt (kurt) *adjective* Short and abrupt; delivered in a rude manner. ▸ *adjective* **curter, curtest**

cur·tain (**kur**-tuhn) *noun* A piece of fabric that can be pulled across a window, a stage, or a similar opening to cover it.

curt·sy (**kurt**-see)
verb To bend slightly at the knees, with one foot in front of the other. Women and girls sometimes curtsy to show respect or to acknowledge applause.

C

noun A bow made by women by bending at the knee, with one foot in front of the other.
▶ *verb* **curtsies, curtsying, curtsied** ▶ *noun, plural* **curtsies**

curve (kurv)
verb To bend or turn continuously.
noun 1. A continuous bend in something. 2. **curve ball** A baseball or softball pitch that spins away from a straight path as it approaches the batter.
▶ *verb* **curving, curved** ▶ *adjective* **curved** ▶ *adjective* **curvy**

cush·ion (**kush**-uhn)
noun 1. A pillow used to make furniture more comfortable to sit or lie on. 2. Something that forms an area or layer of protection.
verb To soften the effect of something.
▶ *verb* **cushioning, cushioned**

cus·tard (**kuhs**-turd) *noun* A sweet, thick dessert made from milk, eggs, sugar, and sometimes other flavorings.

cus·to·di·an (kuhs-**toh**-dee-uhn) *noun* 1. A person who has responsibility for something valuable, such as a museum collection or a set of standards and ideals. 2. A person whose job is to clean and maintain a building or institution.

cus·to·dy (**kuhs**-tuh-dee) *noun* 1. The legal right to supervise and take care of a child. 2. Police supervision.
▶ *adjective* **custodial** (kuhs-**toh**-dee-uhl)

cus·tom (**kuhs**-tuhm)
noun 1. A tradition in a culture or society. 2. Something that you do regularly.
noun, plural **customs** A place at a country's borders, ports, or airports where officials may ask questions and check your luggage to make sure that you are not bringing in anything illegal.

cus·tom·ar·y (**kus**-tuh-**mer**-ee) *adjective* Happening regularly by habit or custom; usual.

cus·tom·er (**kuhs**-tuh-mur) *noun* A person who buys things from a particular store or business.

cus·tom·ize (**kuhs**-tuh-**mize**)
verb To change something to suit an individual's needs or preferences. ▶ *verb* **customizing, customized**

cut (kuht)
verb 1. To use a sharp instrument, such as scissors or a knife, to separate something into smaller pieces, to remove part of it, or to change its shape. 2. To reduce something. 3. To shorten or trim. 4. To stop or interrupt. 5. **cut back** To reduce the amount of money you spend, or the amount of something that you use. 6. **cut down** To have or use something less often. 7. **cut off** To isolate a person or thing from others.
noun A skin wound caused by a sharp object.
phrase **cut and paste** To move words or images from one place to another on a computer.
▶ *verb* **cutting, cut**

cute (kyoot) *adjective* Charming, pretty, or attractive. ▶ *adjective* **cuter, cutest**

cu·ti·cle (**kyoo**-ti-kuhl) *noun* The tough layer of skin around the edges of a fingernail or a toenail.

cut·ler·y (**kuht**-lur-ee) *noun* Knives, forks, and spoons used for eating or serving food.

cut·ting (**kuht**-ing)
noun A small part of a plant taken off to put in the ground and grow a new plant.
adjective Mean and hurtful.

cy·ber·space (**sye**-bur-*spase*) *noun* The world of communication and interaction represented by the Internet.

cy·cle (**sye**-kuhl)
verb To ride a bicycle.
noun 1. A bicycle. 2. A series of events that are repeated in the same order.
▶ *verb* **cycling, cycled** ▶ *noun* **cyclist**

cy·clone (**sye**-klone) *noun* A storm with very strong, destructive winds that rotate.

cyg·net (**sig**-nit) *noun* A young swan.

C

cyl·in·der (**sil**-uhn-dur) *noun* **1.** A shape with flat, circular ends and sides shaped like the outside of a tube. **2.** A chamber in an engine that is shaped like a tube.
> ▶ *adjective* **cylindrical** (suh-**lin**-dri-kuhl)

cym·bal (**sim**-buhl) *noun* A musical instrument made of brass and shaped like a plate. It is played by striking it with a stick or another cymbal.
Cymbal sounds like **symbol.**

cyn·i·cal (**sin**-i-kuhl) *adjective* Believing that the worst will always happen and that people are basically selfish and dishonest. ▶ *noun* **cynic** ▶ *noun* **cynicism** (**sin**-i-*siz*-uhm) ▶ *adverb* **cynically**

cy·press (**sye**-pruhs) *noun* An evergreen tree with small, dark green leaves that resemble scales. ▶ *noun, plural* **cypresses**

Cy·prus (**sye**-pruhs) An island country in the eastern Mediterranean, off the southern coast of Turkey. It is the third-largest island in the Mediterranean and a popular tourist destination.

cyst (sist) *noun* A small sac of tissue inside the body that fills with some substance, such as air, fluid, or pus.

cy·to·plasm (**sye**-tuh-*plaz*-uhm) *noun* The contents of a living cell, except for the nucleus.

czar *or* **tsar** (zahr) *noun* An emperor of Russia before the revolution of 1917.

cza·ri·na *or* **tsa·ri·na** (zah-**ree**-nuh) *noun* A former empress of Russia or wife of a czar.

Czech Re·pub·lic (**chek** ri-**puhb**-lik) A country in Central Europe. It is the western part of the former Czechoslovakia, a country that existed from 1918 through 1992. Czechoslovakia resisted communist rule and eventually regained its freedom and reverted to two separate countries, the Czech Republic and Slovakia.

D

DA (**dee**-ay) *noun* Short for *district attorney.*

dab (dab)
verb **1.** To touch something lightly and quickly. **2.** To apply.
noun A little bit.
> ▶ *verb* **dabbing, dabbed**

dab·ble (**dab**-uhl) *verb* **1.** If you **dabble** in something, you do not do it very seriously or very thoroughly. **2.** To dip something playfully in and out of water.
> ▶ *verb* **dabbling, dabbled** ▶ *noun* **dabbler**

dachs·hund (**dahks**-*hunt*) *noun* A breed of dog with a long body, brownish fur, very short legs, and drooping ears.

dad (dad) *or* **daddy** (**dad**-ee) *noun* (informal) Father. ▶ *noun, plural* **dads** *or* **daddies**

dad·dy-long-legs (**dad**-ee-**lawng**-*legz*) *noun* An animal that looks like a spider but has a small, rounded body and very long, spindly legs. ▶ *noun, plural* **daddy-longlegs**

daf·fo·dil (**daf**-uh-dil) *noun* A plant that has yellow, bell-like flowers and long, narrow leaves.

daft (daft) *adjective* (informal) Silly or foolish. ▶ *adjective* **dafter, daftest**

dag·ger (**dag**-ur) *noun* A short, pointed weapon that is used for stabbing.

dai·ly (**day**-lee)
adjective Produced or happening every day, or every working day.
adverb Every day.
noun A newspaper that is printed every day.
> ▶ *noun, plural* **dailies**

dain·ty (**dayn**-tee) *adjective* Attractively delicate. ▶ *adjective* **daintier, daintiest** ▶ *noun* **daintiness** ▶ *adverb* **daintily**

dair·y (**dair**-ee)
noun A business that buys milk from farmers and sells milk and other

products made from it.
adjective Of or having to do with milk and milk cows.
▶ *noun, plural* **dairies**

da·is (**day**-is) *noun* A raised platform in a large room used to seat special guests or to speak from. ▶ *noun, plural* **daises**

dai·sy (**day**-zee) *noun* A flower with white, pink, or yellow petals and a yellow center. ▶ *noun, plural* **daisies**

dale (dayl) *noun* A valley.

dal·ma·tian (dal-**may**-shuhn) *noun* A breed of large dog with a white coat and black or brown spots.

dam (dam) *noun* A barrier across a stream or river that holds back water.

dam·age (**dam**-ij)
verb To harm or spoil something.
noun The harm caused by something.
noun, plural **damages** Money awarded to individuals by a court to try to make up for an injury or a loss that they have suffered.
▶ *verb* **damaging, damaged** ▶ *adjective* **damaging**

damp (damp) *adjective* Slightly wet, or moist. ▶ *adjective* **damper, dampest** ▶ *noun* **dampness**

damp·en (**dam**-puhn) *verb* 1. To make something moist or slightly wet.
2. To make dull or depressed.
▶ *verb* **dampening, dampened**

dam·sel (**dam**-zuhl) *noun* A young woman. This word is now used mainly in stories, or in a joking way.

dance (dans)
verb To move in time to music.
noun 1. An event where people dance. 2. A particular set of steps, such as a waltz or a square dance.
▶ *verb* **dancing, danced** ▶ *noun* **dancing**

danc·er (**dan**-sur) *noun* Someone who knows how to dance, or who dances as a job.

dan·de·li·on (**dan**-duh-**lye**-uhn) *noun* A plant with bright yellow flowers, often found growing in lawns.

dan·druff (**dan**-druhf) *noun* Small flakes of dead skin from the scalp, sometimes found in hair or seen on people's clothes.

dan·dy (**dan**-dee)
noun A man who pays too much attention to his appearance or clothing.
adjective Great, or fine.
▶ *noun, plural* **dandies** ▶ *adjective* **dandier, dandiest**

dan·ger (**dayn**-jur) *noun* 1. A strong possibility that something bad or harmful may happen. 2. Something that may cause harm or injury.

dan·ger·ous (**dayn**-jur-uhs) *adjective* Likely to cause harm or injury; not safe; risky. ▶ *adverb* **dangerously**

dan·gle (**dang**-guhl) *verb* To swing or hang down loosely. ▶ *verb* **dangling, dangled**

dank (dangk) *adjective* Unpleasantly damp and smelly. ▶ *adjective* **danker, dankest**

dap·pled (**dap**-uhld) *adjective* Marked with areas of light and dark.

dare (dair)
verb 1. To challenge someone to do something that involves a risk. 2. To be brave enough to do something.
noun A challenge to someone to do something risky.
▶ *verb* **daring, dared**

dare·dev·il (**dair**-*dev*-uhl) *noun* Someone who enjoys doing risky things.

dar·ing (**dair**-ing) *adjective* Involving some risk and requiring courage. ▶ *adverb* **daringly**

dark (dahrk)
adjective 1. Without any or very much light. 2. Containing more black than white. 3. Having skin or hair that is brown or black. 4. Bad, or evil. 5. Gloomy, or dismal.
noun 1. The time of day when sunlight ends. 2. Lack or absence of light.
▶ *adjective* **darker, darkest**

dark·en (**dahr**-kuhn) *verb* To make or become darker. ▶ *verb* **darkening, darkened** ▶ *adjective* **darkened**

D

dark en·er·gy (dahrk en-ur-jee)
noun A form of energy that does
not give off light, and so can't be
seen directly. Even though it is not
visible, scientists believe it is present
throughout space, and think it exists
because it helps explain why the
universe is expanding ever faster.

dark mat·ter (dahrk *mat*-ur) *noun*
A form of matter that does not
generate light, and so can't be
seen directly. Even though it is not
visible, scientists believe it is present
throughout space, and think it
exists because it helps explain the
gravitational influences on such
objects as stars and galaxies.

dark·ness (dahrk-nis) *noun* Lack of
light; the state of being dark.

dark·room (dahrk-room) *noun* A room
with all the light blocked out and with
special equipment for developing
photographs.

dar·ling (dahr-ling)
noun Someone who is dearly loved.
adjective **1.** Loved very much.
2. Charming, or adorable.

darn (dahrn) *verb* To mend a hole
in a piece of cloth by sewing back
and forth across it. ▸ *verb* **darning,
darned** ▸ *noun* **darning**

dart (dahrt)
noun **1.** A pointed object like a small
arrow that you throw in the game
of darts. **2. darts** A game in which
players score by throwing darts at
a target that usually has concentric
circles and a bull's-eye in the center.
3. A kind of pleat in a piece of clothing
that makes it fit better.
verb To move suddenly and quickly.
▸ *verb* **darting, darted**

dash (dash)
noun **1.** A very small amount of
something. **2.** A horizontal line (—)
used as a punctuation mark to show a
pause in a sentence. **3.** A short race.
verb **1.** To move quickly, usually over a
short distance. **2.** To destroy or bring
an end to.
▸ *noun, plural* **dashes** ▸ *verb* **dashes,
dashing, dashed**

dash·board (dash-bord) *noun* **1.** The
instrument panel of a car or truck,
where the gauges and warning
lights are located. **2.** A window on
a computer screen that provides
information about a program that is
currently running.

da·ta (day-tuh *or* **dat**-uh) *noun*
Information collected in a place so
that something can be done with it.

da·ta·base (day-tuh-*base or* **dat**-uh-*base*)
noun A set of related information that
is organized and stored in a computer.

date (date)
noun **1.** A particular day. **2.** An
appointment to meet someone,
especially for romance. **3.** A small
brown fruit from a palm tree with a
long, thin pit.
verb **1.** To go out with someone on
a date. **2.** If something **dates** from a
certain time, it was made then. **3.** To
accurately determine the time that
something was made or first existed.
idioms **1.** If something is **up to date,** it
is modern or has the latest features or
information. **2.** If something is **out of
date,** it is old-fashioned and dated, or
lacks modern features or information.
▸ *verb* **dating, dated**

dat·ed (day-tid) *adjective* Old-fashioned
or lacking modern features or
information.

daub (dawb) *verb* To smear or coat with
a substance such as plaster, paint, or
mud. ▸ *verb* **daubing, daubed**

daugh·ter (daw-tur) *noun* Someone's
female child.

daugh·ter-in-law (daw-tur-in-*law*) *noun*
The wife of someone's son. ▸ *noun,
plural* **daughters-in-law**

daunt (dawnt) *verb* To make someone
feel frightened or discouraged. ▸ *verb*
daunting, daunted

daw·dle (daw-duhl) *verb* To do
something slowly, or to waste
time. ▸ *verb* **dawdling, dawdled**
▸ *noun* **dawdler**

dawn (dawn)
noun **1.** The beginning of the day when
light first appears in the sky. **2.** The
start of a new period of time.

D

verb If something **dawns** on you, you start to understand it.
▶ *verb* **dawning, dawned**

day (day) *noun* **1.** A 24-hour period, especially as measured from midnight to midnight. **2.** The period of light between sunrise and sunset. **3.** The part of the day spent at work. **4.** A certain period of time.

day·break (**day**-brayk) *noun* Dawn, or the time when the first rays of sunlight appear.

day care (**day** kair) *noun* Care given by adults to young children away from their homes during the day. ▶ *adjective* **day-care**

day·dream (**day**-dreem)
noun A pleasant dream you have while you are awake.
verb To let your mind wander and imagine things.
▶ *verb* **daydreaming, daydreamed** ▶ *noun* **daydreamer**

day·light (**day**-lite) *noun* **1.** The light of the sun during daytime hours. **2.** If something happens **in broad daylight,** it is not secret or hidden.

day·time (**day**-time) *noun* The hours of daylight, from dawn till dusk.

daze (dayz)
noun A condition in which you are not able to think clearly.
verb To confuse or bewilder someone.
▶ *verb* **dazing, dazed**

daz·zle (**daz**-uhl) *verb* **1.** To blind someone for a moment with a bright light. **2.** To amaze and impress someone.
▶ *verb* **dazzling, dazzled** ▶ *adjective* **dazzling**

dea·con (**dee**-kuhn) *noun* In the Christian church, a person who helps a minister or preacher.

dead (ded)
adjective **1.** Not alive. **2.** Without activity or excitement. **3.** Extremely tired.
adverb Completely.
noun, plural **the dead** All those who are no longer alive.

dead·en (**ded**-uhn) *verb* To weaken or make less sharp. ▶ *verb* **deadening, deadened**

dead end (ded end)
noun A street that ends without a place to enter another street.
adjective **dead-end** Leading to nothing better.

dead·line (**ded**-line) *noun* A time when something must be finished.

dead·lock (**ded**-lahk) *noun* A situation where two sides cannot agree.

dead·ly (**ded**-lee)
adjective **1.** Capable of killing. **2.** Aiming to kill or destroy someone. **3.** Extremely dull and boring.
adverb In a way that could end in death.
▶ *adjective* **deadlier, deadliest**

deaf (def) *adjective* **1.** Unable to hear. **2.** If you are **deaf to** something, you are not willing to consider or accept it.
▶ *adjective* **deafer, deafest** ▶ *noun* **deafness**

deaf·en·ing (**def**-uh-ning) *adjective* Very loud. ▶ *adverb* **deafeningly**

deal (deel)
verb **1.** To do business. **2.** To give or to deliver. **3.** When a text **deals with** a subject, it is about that subject. **4.** When you **deal with** something, you take some sort of action about it.
noun An agreement.
▶ *verb* **dealing, dealt** (delt)

deal·er (**dee**-lur) *noun* **1.** Someone who buys and sells things. **2.** Someone who gives out cards during a card game.

dealt (delt) *verb* The past tense and past participle of **deal.**

dear (deer)
adjective **1.** Much loved. **2.** You use **dear** at the beginning of a letter.
noun A kind or sweet person.
Dear sounds like **deer.** ▶ *adjective* **dearer, dearest**

dear·ly (**deer**-lee) *adverb* Very much.

death (deth) *noun* **1.** The end of life. **2.** The destruction or end of something.

death·ly (**deth**-lee) *adjective* Reminding you of death or of something dead.

death trap (deth trap) *noun* A situation, place, or vehicle that is very dangerous.

D

de·bate (di-**bate**)
noun A discussion in which people express different opinions.
verb To discuss or think about something from different points of view.
▶ *verb* **debating, debated** ▶ *adjective* **debatable**

deb·it (**deb**-it)
noun A record of money that is taken out of an account.
verb To remove money from an account.
▶ *verb* **debiting, debited**

deb·it card (**deb**-it *kahrd*) *noun* A plastic card that is connected to a bank account and that can be used to pay for things, just like a check or cash.

de·bris (duh-**bree**) *noun* The pieces of something that has been broken or destroyed.

debt (det) *noun* **1.** Money or something else that someone owes. **2.** The condition of owing money or something else to someone.

debt·or (**det**-ur) *noun* Someone who owes money.

de·bug (dee-**buhg**) *verb* To remove the defects or errors in a computer program. ▶ *verb* **debugging, debugged**

de·but (day-**byoo** or **day**-byoo)
noun A first public appearance or performance.
verb To perform something for the first time.
▶ *verb* **debuting, debuted**

dec·ade (**dek**-ayd) *noun* A period of ten years.

de·caf (**dee**-*kaf*)
adjective Having the caffeine removed from a drink such as coffee or tea.
noun Coffee with the caffeine removed.

de·caf·fein·at·ed (dee-**kaf**-uh-*nay*-tid) *adjective* Having the caffeine removed. ▶ *verb* **decaffeinate**

de·cal (**dee**-*kal*) *noun* A picture or label on specially treated paper that can be transferred to glass, metal, or other hard surfaces.

de·cant·er (di-**kan**-tur) *noun* A fancy glass bottle with a stopper, used to hold and serve liquids, especially wine.

de·cap·i·tate (di-**kap**-i-*tate*) *verb* To cut off the head of a person, animal, or thing. ▶ *verb* **decapitating, decapitated** ▶ *noun* **decapitation**

de·cath·lon (di-**kath**-lahn) *noun* A track-and-field contest made up of ten athletic events.

de·cay (di-**kay**)
verb **1.** To rot or break down. **2.** To decline in quality.
noun **1.** The breaking down of plant or animal matter by natural causes. **2.** A decline in quality.
▶ *verb* **decaying, decayed**

de·ceased (di-**seest**) *adjective* Dead.

de·ceit (di-**seet**) *noun* The act of lying to or deceiving someone.

de·ceit·ful (di-**seet**-fuhl) *adjective* Intentionally deceiving or misleading. ▶ *adverb* **deceitfully**

de·ceive (di-**seev**) *verb* To trick someone into believing something that is not true. ▶ *verb* **deceiving, deceived**

De·cem·ber (di-**sem**-bur) *noun* The 12th month on the calendar. December follows November and has 31 days.

de·cent (**dee**-suhnt) *adjective*
1. Acceptable or satisfactory.
2. Respectful and proper.
3. Thoughtful or kind.
▶ *noun* **decency** ▶ *adverb* **decently**

de·cep·tion (di-**sep**-shuhn) *noun* Something that makes people believe what is not true; a lie.

de·cep·tive (di-**sep**-tiv) *adjective* Misleading, or not telling the true situation. ▶ *adverb* **deceptively**

dec·i·bel (**des**-uh-buhl) *noun* A unit for measuring the loudness of sounds.

de·cide (di-**side**) *verb* **1.** To make up your mind. **2.** To settle something that has more than one possible result.
▶ *verb* **deciding, decided**

de·cid·u·ous (di-**sij**-oo-uhs) *adjective* Shedding all leaves every year in the fall.

D

dec·i·mal (**des**-uh-muhl)
adjective Using the number 10 as a base.
noun A number that is written with a decimal point, for example, 0.75, 5.56, and 92.50.

dec·i·mal point (**des**-uh-muhl *point*)
noun A period used in a number to show that all the numbers to its right are less than 1. The number 3.14 combines the whole number 3 and the fraction .14, or 14/100.

de·ci·pher (di-**sye**-fur) *verb* To figure out something that is written in code or is hard to understand. ▶ *verb* **deciphering, deciphered** ▶ *adjective* **decipherable**

de·ci·sion (di-**sizh**-uhn) *noun* 1. The act of making up your mind about something. 2. The result of making up your mind; a conclusion. 3. A judgment by a court or other authority.

de·ci·sive (di-**sye**-siv) *adjective* 1. Able to make choices quickly and easily. 2. Causing a certain result. 3. Not leaving any doubt about the result. ▶ *adverb* **decisively**

deck (dek) *noun* 1. The floor of a boat or ship. 2. A platform with railings on the outside of a building. 3. A full set of playing cards.

dec·la·ra·tion (*dek*-luh-**ray**-shuhn) *noun* The act of announcing something, or the announcement made.

Dec·la·ra·tion of In·de·pen·dence (*dek*-luh-**ray**-shuhn uhv *in*-duh-**pen**-duhns) *noun* A document declaring the freedom of the 13 American colonies from British rule. It was adopted on July 4, 1776.

de·clare (di-**klair**) *verb* 1. To say something firmly. 2. To announce something formally or officially. ▶ *verb* **declaring, declared**

de·cline (di-**kline**)
verb 1. To refuse something, especially in a way that is polite. 2. To get worse, smaller, or lower. 3. To bend or slope downward.
noun 1. The act or process of getting worse; deterioration. 2. A lowering or lessening in value or amount, as *a decline in population* or *a decline in property values*.
▶ *verb* **declining, declined**

de·code (dee-**kode**) *verb* To change information into a form that is easier to understand. ▶ *verb* **decoding, decoded** ▶ *noun* **decoder**

de·com·pose (*dee*-kuhm-**poze**) *verb* To rot or decay. ▶ *verb* **decomposing, decomposed** ▶ *noun* **decomposition**

de·con·ges·tant (*dee*-kuhn-**jes**-tuhnt) *noun* A drug or treatment that makes it easier for you to breathe when you have a cold or infection. ▶ *noun* **decongestion** ▶ *verb* **decongest**

de·con·tam·i·nate (*dee*-kuhn-**tam**-uh-*nate*) *verb* To remove harmful substances from a thing or place. ▶ *verb* **decontaminating, decontaminated** ▶ *noun* **decontamination**

dec·o·rate (**dek**-uh-*rate*) *verb* 1. To add color, design, or other features that improve the appearance of something. 2. To give a medal or badge to someone.
▶ *verb* **decorating, decorated** ▶ *noun* **decorating** ▶ *adjective* **decorative** (**dek**-ur-uh-tiv)

dec·o·ra·tion (*dek*-uh-**ray**-shuhn) *noun* 1. Something that makes an object or a place more attractive. 2. The act of decorating something. 3. A badge or pin given to someone for achievement, especially in the military.

dec·o·ra·tor (**dek**-uh-*ray*-tur) *noun* Someone whose job is to decorate the inside of buildings.

de·cou·page (*day*-koo-**pahzh**) *noun* The art of decorating a surface by pasting on pieces of paper and then covering the whole object with layers of varnish.

de·coy (**dee**-koi) *noun* 1. A carved model of a bird used by hunters to attract real birds. 2. Someone who lures a person into a trap or draws attention away from something.

D

de·crease

verb (di-**krees**) To become less, smaller, or fewer.

noun (**dee**-krees) A loss, or the amount by which something gets less or smaller.

▸ *verb* **decreasing, decreased**
▸ *adjective* **decreasing** ▸ *adverb* **decreasingly**

de·cree (di-**kree**)

verb To give an order officially.

noun An official decision or order.

▸ *verb* **decreeing, decreed**

de·crep·it (di-**krep**-it) *adjective* Weakened by old age or too much use.

ded·i·cate (**ded**-i-*kate*) *verb* 1. If you are **dedicated** to something or if you **dedicate** yourself to something, you give a lot of time and energy to it. 2. To put someone's name in or on something, usually to say thanks or show appreciation. 3. To set aside an amount of money for a particular purpose.

▸ *verb* **dedicating, dedicated**

ded·i·ca·tion (*ded*-i-**kay**-shun) *noun* 1. Devotion or concentration of effort. 2. The inscription written in a book. 3. The opening of a place such as a new bridge or hospital, with a special ceremony.

de·duce (di-**doos**) *verb* To figure something out from the amount of information that you have. ▸ *verb* **deducing, deduced**

de·duct (di-**duhkt**) *verb* To take away or subtract. ▸ *verb* **deducting, deducted** ▸ *adjective* **deductible**

de·duc·tion (di-**duhk**-shuhn) *noun* 1. An amount that is taken away or subtracted. 2. Something that is figured out from a little information.

deed (deed) *noun* 1. Something that is done. 2. A legal document that shows who owns property.

deem (deem) *verb* To have an opinion or to think about something in a particular way. ▸ *verb* **deeming, deemed**

deep (deep)

adjective 1. Going down a long way.

2. Very intense and strong. 3. Low in pitch. 4. Not easy to understand.

noun **the deep** The deep part of the ocean.

▸ *adjective* **deeper, deepest** ▸ *adverb* **deeply**

deep·en (**dee**-puhn) *verb* 1. To become deeper. 2. To become larger, more important, or more intense.

deep-sea (**deep**-*see*) *adjective* Living or happening far under the ocean.

deer (deer) *noun* An animal with hoofs that runs very fast and eats plants. Male deer grow bony, branching antlers. **Deer** sounds like **dear.** ▸ *noun, plural* **deer**

de·face (di-**fase**) *verb* To spoil the way something looks by writing on it or scratching it. ▸ *verb* **defacing, defaced**

de·fault (di-**fawlt**)

noun A setting or option that will be effective if you don't specifically choose one in a computer program.

adjective Standard; in effect unless you choose something else.

verb 1. To use a standard setting that has already been chosen. 2. To fail to pay back a loan.

▸ *verb* **defaulting, defaulted**

de·feat (di-**feet**)

verb To beat someone in a war or a competition.

noun An instance of losing something such as a competition, an election, or a war.

▸ *verb* **defeating, defeated**

de·fect

noun (**dee**-fekt *or* di-**fekt**) A fault or weakness that makes something less valuable or useful.

verb (di-**fekt**) To leave your country or political party and go to another.

▸ *verb* **defecting, defected** ▸ *adjective* **defective** (di-**fek**-tiv) ▸ *noun* **defector** (di-**fek**-tur) ▸ *noun* **defection** (di-**fek**-shuhn)

de·fend (di-**fend**) *verb* 1. To protect from harm. 2. To give the reasons for something or for your support of someone. 3. To try to stop points being scored in a game with opposing sides or teams.

D

▸ *verb* **defending, defended** ▸ *noun* **defender**

de·fend·ant (di-**fen**-duhnt) *noun* The person in a court case who has been accused or who is being sued.

de·fense *noun* **1.** (di-**fens**) The ability to protect from harm or attack, or something that does this. **2.** (di-**fens**) The accused person or party in a trial, or the lawyer who represents the accused person or party. **3.** (di-**fens**) An explanation that supports someone or some action. **4.** (di-**fens** or **dee**-fens) In sports, the **defense** is the side that doesn't have the ball, and tries to prevent the other team from scoring.

de·fen·sive (di-**fen**-siv) *adjective* **1.** Serving to defend yourself or others. **2.** If you are **defensive** or **on the defensive,** you act as if you are being attacked or criticized. ▸ *noun* **defensiveness** ▸ *adverb* **defensively**

de·fer (di-**fur**) *verb* **1.** To postpone until later. **2.** To give in to another's wishes or opinions. ▸ *verb* **deferring, deferred** ▸ *noun* **deferment**

de·fi·ant (di-**fye**-uhnt) *adjective* Refusing to obey, or showing an attitude of opposition. ▸ *noun* **defiance** ▸ *adverb* **defiantly**

de·fi·cient (di-**fish**-uhnt) *adjective* Lacking something necessary. ▸ *noun* **deficiency**

def·i·cit (**def**-i-sit) *noun* **1.** A situation where more money has been spent than has come in. **2.** A situation where there is less of something than normal.

de·fine (di-**fine**) *verb* **1.** To explain the meaning of something. **2.** To describe something exactly and in detail. ▸ *verb* **defining, defined** ▸ *noun* **definer**

def·i·nite (**def**-uh-nit) *adjective* **1.** Certain. **2.** Easy to see or understand.

def·i·nite ar·ti·cle (**def**-uh-nit **ahr**-ti-kuhl) *noun* The term for the word *the*. A definite article is used before a noun when the noun refers to something specific.

def·i·nite·ly (**def**-uh-nit-lee) *adverb* Without any doubt; with certainty.

def·i·ni·tion (*def*-uh-**nish**-uhn) *noun* An explanation of the meaning of a word or phrase.

de·flate (di-**flate**) *verb* **1.** To let the air out of something. **2.** To reduce in size or importance. ▸ *verb* **deflating, deflated** ▸ *noun* **deflation**

de·flect (di-**flekt**) *verb* To make something go in a different direction. ▸ *verb* **deflecting, deflected** ▸ *noun* **deflection**

de·for·est (dee-**for**-ist) *verb* To remove or cut down forests. ▸ *verb* **deforesting, deforested** ▸ *noun* **deforestation**

de·formed (di-**formd**) *adjective* Twisted, bent, or disfigured. ▸ *noun* **deformity** ▸ *verb* **deform**

de·fraud (di-**frawd**) *verb* To cheat someone out of something that belongs to him or her, such as money or property. ▸ *verb* **defrauding, defrauded**

de·frost (di-**frawst**) *verb* **1.** To completely thaw out an item that is frozen. **2.** To remove ice from something, such as a refrigerator or freezer. ▸ *verb* **defrosting, defrosted**

deft (deft) *adjective* Skillful, quick, and effective. ▸ *adjective* **defter, deftest** ▸ *noun* **deftness** ▸ *adverb* **deftly**

de·fuse (dee-**fyooz**) *verb* **1.** To make a bomb safe so that it cannot explode. **2.** To make a situation calmer. ▸ *verb* **defusing, defused**

de·fy (di-**fye**) *verb* **1.** To refuse to obey a person, order, rule, or law. **2.** To challenge or dare someone to do something. ▸ *verb* **defies, defying, defied**

de·gen·er·ate (di-**gen**-uh-*rate*) *verb* To become worse or inferior in quality. ▸ *verb* **degenerating, degenerated**

de·grad·ing (di-**gray**-ding) *adjective* Making you lose your self-respect or dignity. ▸ *noun* **degradation** (*deg*-ruh-**day**-shuhn) ▸ *verb* **degrade**

D

de·gree (di-**gree**) *noun* **1.** A step in a series. **2.** A unit for measuring temperature. The symbol for a degree is °. **3.** A unit for measuring arcs and angles. **4.** A title given by a college or university.

de·hy·drat·ed (dee-**hye**-dray-tid) *adjective* **1.** With all the water removed. **2.** Lacking enough water in your body for normal functioning.
▸ *noun* **dehydration** ▸ *verb* **dehydrate**

de·ice (dee-**ise**) *verb* To remove or keep free of ice. ▸ *verb* **deicing, deiced** ▸ *noun* **deicer**

de·i·ty (**dee**-i-tee) *noun* **1.** A god or a goddess. **2. the Deity** God.
▸ *noun, plural* **deities**

de·ject·ed (di-**jek**-tid) *adjective* Sad and depressed. ▸ *noun* **dejection** ▸ *adverb* **dejectedly**

Del·a·ware (**del**-uh-*wair*) A state on the East Coast of the United States. Delaware was one of the 13 original colonies. On December 7, 1787, it was the first colony to ratify the Constitution of the United States, thereby becoming the first state. The date is on the state's flag and is commemorated in the state each year on the seventh of December as "Delaware Day."

de·lay (di-**lay**)
verb **1.** To make someone or something late. **2.** To postpone until later.
noun A period of time during which something planned, intended, or expected does not happen.
▸ *verb* **delaying, delayed**

del·e·gate
verb (**del**-i-*gate*) To give someone responsibility to do something.
noun (**del**-i-git) Someone who represents other people at a meeting or in a legislature.
▸ *verb* **delegating, delegated**

del·e·ga·tion (*del*-i-**gay**-shuhn) *noun* A group of people who represent an organization or a government at meetings.

de·lete (di-**leet**) *verb* To remove something from a text or from a computer storage area. ▸ *verb* **deleting, deleted** ▸ *noun* **deletion**

del·i (**del**-ee) *noun* Short for **delicatessen.**

de·lib·er·ate
adjective (duh-**lib**-ur-it) **1.** Done on purpose; intentional. **2.** Careful and slow.
verb (duh-**lib**-uh-*rate*) To consider something carefully.
▸ *verb* **deliberating, deliberated**
▸ *noun* **deliberation** (duh-*lib*-uh-**ray**-shuhn)

de·lib·er·ate·ly (duh-*lib*-ur-it-lee) *adverb* On purpose; with a specific intention.

del·i·cate (**del**-i-kit) *adjective* **1.** Very pleasant to the senses. **2.** Finely made or sensitive. **3.** Not very strong and likely to become ill. **4.** Likely to hurt feelings or cause an unpleasant reaction in someone.
▸ *adverb* **delicately**

del·i·ca·tes·sen (*del*-i-kuh-**tes**-uhn) *noun* A store that sells prepared foods, such as salads and sliced meats.

de·li·cious (di-**lish**-uhs) *adjective* Tasting or smelling very good. ▸ *adverb* **deliciously**

de·light (di-**lite**)
noun Great pleasure.
verb To please someone very much.
▸ *verb* **delighting, delighted** ▸ *adjective* **delightful** ▸ *adverb* **delightfully**

de·light·ed (di-**lye**-tid) *adjective* Feeling very happy because of something that has happened.

de·lin·quent (di-**ling**-kwuhnt)
noun A person who is often in trouble with the law.
adjective **1.** Overdue for payment. **2.** Relating to juvenile delinquents.
▸ *noun* **delinquency**

de·lir·i·ous (di-**leer**-ee-uhs) *adjective* Unable to think straight either because of a high fever or extreme happiness. ▸ *adverb* **deliriously**

de·liv·er (di-**liv**-ur) *verb* **1.** To take something to someone. **2.** To say or state, usually in a formal way. **3.** To help a baby to be born. **4.** To free someone from something bad.
▸ *verb* **delivering, delivered** ▸ *noun* **deliverance**

D

de·liv·er·y (di-**liv**-ur-ee) *noun* **1.** The act of handing over something that is expected or has been ordered. **2.** The gestures, tone, and behavior of someone speaking before people. **3.** The act of bringing a baby out of his or her mother's womb.
▶ *noun, plural* **deliveries**

del·ta (**del**-tuh) *noun* **1.** An area of land shaped like a triangle where a river enters the sea. **2.** The fourth letter of the Greek alphabet.

del·uge (**del**-yooj)
noun Heavy rain, often causing flooding.
verb **1.** To cover a place in water. **2.** To send or give large amounts of something.
▶ *verb* **deluging, deluged**

de·lu·sion (di-**loo**-zhuhn) *noun* A false idea or a hallucination. ▶ *verb* **delude**

de·luxe (di-**luhks**) *adjective* Of the best quality, or having extra, expensive features.

delve (delv) *verb* If you **delve** into something, you find out everything about it that you can by studying or asking questions. ▶ *verb* **delved, delving**

de·mand (di-**mand**)
verb **1.** To ask for something firmly because you think it is right. **2.** To require.
noun **1.** Desire to buy or use something. **2.** An official or urgent request.
▶ *verb* **demanding, demanded**

de·mand·ing (di-**man**-ding) *adjective* Requiring a lot of time, attention, or effort.

dem·o (**dem**-oh) *noun* **1.** (informal) A recording made to introduce a new performer or piece of music. **2.** (informal) Something that shows you how another thing will work.

de·moc·ra·cy (di-**mah**-kruh-see) *noun* **1.** A form of government in which the people choose their leaders in elections. **2.** A country that has this kind of government.
▶ *noun, plural* **democracies**

dem·o·crat (**dem**-uh-**krat**) *noun* **1.** Someone who agrees with the system of democracy. **2. Democrat** A member of the Democratic Party.

dem·o·crat·ic (*dem*-uh-**krat**-ik) *adjective* **1.** Having to do with or in favor of democracy. **2. Democratic** Belonging to or connected with the Democratic Party.
▶ *adverb* **democratically**

Dem·o·crat·ic Par·ty (*dem*-uh-**krat**-ik **pahr**-tee) *noun* One of the two main political parties in the United States. The other is the Republican Party.

de·mo·graph·ics (*dem*-uh-**graf**-iks) *noun, plural* Population statistics, including data on age and income. Companies often use demographics to decide how and where to sell their products. ▶ *adjective* **demographic**

de·mol·ish (di-**mah**-lish) *verb* To knock down or destroy something. ▶ *verb* **demolishes, demolishing, demolished** ▶ *noun* **demolition** (*dem*-uh-**lish**-uhn)

de·mon (**dee**-muhn) *noun* A devil or an evil spirit. This word is sometimes used in a positive way to describe someone who seems to have magical ability because he or she works very hard. ▶ *adjective* **demonic** (di-**mah**-nik)

dem·on·strate (**dem**-uhn-*strate*) *verb* **1.** To show how to do something or use something. **2.** To show something clearly. **3.** To join together with other people to protest something.
▶ *verb* **demonstrating, demonstrated**

dem·on·stra·tion (*dem*-uhn-**stray**-shuhn) *noun* **1.** The act or process of showing how something works. **2.** A public protest.

dem·on·stra·tive (duh-**mahn**-struh-tiv) *adjective* Showing and expressing feelings freely.
noun A word that tells you which one or ones. The pronouns *this*, *that*, *these*, and *those* are the main demonstratives in English.

de·mo·nym (**dem**-uh-nim) *noun* A name for a person who comes from a particular place.

D

de·mor·al·ized (di-**mor**-uh-*lized*)
adjective Depressed and hopeless.

den (den) *noun* 1. The home of a wild animal, such as a lion. 2. A comfortable room where you can work or play.

de·ni·al (di-**nye**-uhl) *noun* 1. The act of saying that something is not true or valid. 2. If someone is **in denial,** he or she refuses to believe something that is true.

den·im (**den**-uhm)
noun Strong cotton material used to make jeans and other articles of clothing.
adjective Made of denim.

Den·mark (**den**-mahrk) A Scandinavian country with an extensive coastline on the North Sea. It is a constitutional monarchy. Denmark was the home of Hans Christian Andersen (1805–1875), the author of "The Little Mermaid," "The Ugly Duckling," and many other well-known fairy tales.

de·nom·i·na·tion (di-*nah*-muh-**nay**-shuhn) *noun* 1. An organized branch of a religion. 2. A value or unit in a system of measurement.

de·nom·i·na·tor (di-**nah**-muh-*nay*-tur) *noun* The number in a fraction that is under the line and that shows how many equal parts the whole number can be divided into.

de·note (di-**note**) *verb* 1. To show or be a sign of something. 2. To mean.
▶ *verb* **denoting, denoted** ▶ *noun* **denotation**

de·nounce (di-**nouns**) *verb* To say in public that something is wrong or that someone has done something wrong. ▶ *verb* **denouncing, denounced**

dense (dens) *adjective* 1. Crowded or thick. 2. (informal) Slow to understand; stupid.
▶ *adjective* **denser, densest** ▶ *noun* **denseness** ▶ *adverb* **densely**

den·si·ty (**den**-si-tee) *noun* 1. A measure of how heavy or light an object is for its size. Density is measured by dividing an object's mass by its volume. 2. The amount of something per unit.

▶ *noun, plural* **densities**

dent (dent)
verb To damage something by bashing it in.
noun The damage produced when something is dented.
▶ *verb* **denting, dented**

den·tal (**den**-tuhl) *adjective* Of or having to do with your teeth.

den·tist (**den**-tist) *noun* A doctor who is qualified to examine, clean, and treat teeth. ▶ *noun* **dentistry**

den·tures (**den**-churz) *noun, plural* A set of false teeth.

de·ny (di-**nye**) *verb* 1. To say that something is not true. 2. To refuse to allow something.
▶ *verb* **denies, denying, denied**

de·o·dor·ant (dee-**oh**-dur-uhnt) *noun* A substance used to cover up or get rid of unpleasant smells.

de·part (di-**pahrt**) *verb* 1. To leave, especially to go on a trip. 2. To change a course of action. 3. You can say that someone has **departed** or has **departed this life** as an indirect way of saying that they have died.
▶ *verb* **departing, departed**

de·part·ment (di-**pahrt**-muhnt) *noun* A part of a place like a store, hospital, or university that has a particular function or purpose. ▶ *adjective* **departmental**

de·part·ment store (di-**pahrt**-muhnt *stor*) *noun* A large store with sections for the different kinds of goods sold.

de·par·ture (di-**pahr**-chur) *noun* 1. The act of leaving a place. 2. A change in the way that something is usually done.

de·pend (di-**pend**) *verb* 1. To rely on someone or something. 2. If a thing **depends on** something else, it is determined or influenced by it.
▶ *verb* **depending, depended** ▶ *noun* **dependence** ▶ *adjective* **dependable**

de·pend·ent (di-**pen**-duhnt)
noun 1. A person who is taken care of and supported by someone else. 2. A **dependent clause** is a part of a sentence that cannot stand on its own. *See* **independent clause.**
adjective Depending on or controlled by something or someone else.

D

de·pict (di-**pikt**) *verb* To show something using pictures or language. ▶ *verb* **depicting, depicted**

de·plete (di-**pleet**) *verb* To empty, or to use up. ▶ *verb* **depleting, depleted** ▶ *noun* **depletion** (di-**plee**-shuhn)

de·plor·a·ble (di-**plor**-uh-buhl) *adjective* Very bad. ▶ *verb* **deplore** ▶ *adverb* **deplorably**

de·ploy (di-**ploi**) *verb* 1. To be ready for use and come into action. 2. To send troops or weapons.
▶ *verb* **deploying, deployed**

de·port (di-**port**) *verb* To send someone back to his or her own country. ▶ *verb* **deporting, deported** ▶ *noun* **deportation** (*dee*-por-**tay**-shuhn)

de·port·ment (di-**port**-muhnt) *noun* The way that you behave.

de·pose (di-**poze**) *verb* 1. To remove a ruler from office, usually by force. 2. To testify or to examine someone under oath in a legal case.
▶ *verb* **deposing, deposed** ▶ *noun* **deposition** (*dep*-uh-**zish**-uhn)

de·pos·it (di-**pah**-zit)
noun 1. Money given as a first payment or as a promise to buy or take part in something. 2. A natural layer of rock, sand, or minerals.
verb 1. To place, or to lay down. 2. To put money into a bank account.
▶ *verb* **depositing, deposited**

de·pot (**dee**-poh) *noun* A bus or railroad station.

de·pre·ci·ate (di-**pree**-shee-ate) *verb* To lose value. ▶ *verb* **depreciating, depreciated** ▶ *noun* **depreciation**

de·pressed (di-**prest**) *adjective* Sad and unhappy with life. ▶ *adjective* **depressing** ▶ *verb* **depress**

de·pres·sion (di-**presh**-uhn) *noun* 1. Unhappiness that doesn't go away. 2. A medical condition in which you feel unhappy or hopeless and can't concentrate or sleep well. 3. A time when the economy of a country is shrinking severely and many people lose their jobs. 4. A hollow or concave place.

de·prive (di-**prive**) *verb* To take a thing away from someone, or prevent him or her from having it. ▶ *verb* **depriving, deprived** ▶ *noun* **deprivation** (*dep*-ruh-**vay**-shuhn) ▶ *adjective* **deprived**

depth (depth) *noun* 1. Deepness, or a measurement of how deep something is. 2. Something done **in depth** is very thorough. 3. If you are **out of your depth,** something is too complex for you to understand it fully.

dep·u·ty (**dep**-yuh-tee) *noun* Someone who helps or acts for somebody else. ▶ *noun, plural* **deputies** ▶ *verb* **deputize**

de·ranged (di-**raynjd**) *adjective* Insane.

der·by (**dur**-bee) *noun* 1. A stiff hat with a narrow brim and a round top. 2. A race or contest, especially one involving horses.
▶ *noun, plural* **derbies**

der·e·lict (**der**-uh-likt)
adjective 1. Neglected and falling apart. 2. Someone who has been derelict in their duties or responsibilities has not undertaken them.
noun A wandering, homeless person.

de·rive (di-**rive**) *verb* 1. To take or receive something from another thing. 2. If a word is **derived** from another word, it has developed from it.
▶ *verb* **deriving, derived** ▶ *noun* **derivation** (*der*-i-**vay**-shuhn)

der·rick (**der**-ik) *noun* 1. A tall crane with a long, movable arm that can raise or lower heavy objects. 2. A tall framework that holds the machines used to drill oil wells.

de·scend (di-**send**) *verb* 1. To go down to a lower level. 2. If you are **descended** from someone, that person is one of your ancestors.
▶ *verb* **descending, descended** ▶ *noun* **descent**

de·scend·ant (di-**sen**-duhnt) *noun* Your **descendants** are your children, their children, and so on into the future.

de·scribe (di-**skribe**) *verb* To tell about something so that your listener gets an understanding of it. ▶ *verb* **describing, described** ▶ *adjective* **descriptive** (di-**skrip**-tiv)

D

de·scrip·tion (di-**skrip**-shuhn) *noun*
A written or spoken statement that tells about someone or something. ▶ *noun, plural* **descriptions**

de·seg·re·gate (dee-**seg**-ruh-*gate*)
verb To do away with the practice of separating people of different races in schools, restaurants, and other public places. ▶ *verb* **desegregating, desegregated** ▶ *noun* **desegregation**

de·sert
verb (di-**zurt**) To go away from a person, place, or thing for good, or to run away from the army.
noun (**dez**-urt) A dry area where hardly any plants grow because there is so little rain.
adjective (**dez**-urt) Without features or interest; bare.
Desert (the verb) sounds like **dessert.** ▶ *verb* **deserting, deserted** ▶ *noun* **deserter** (di-**zur**-tur) ▶ *noun* **desertion** (di-**zur**-shuhn)

de·sert·ed (di-**zur**-tid) *adjective* Empty of people; without anyone around.

de·serve (di-**zurv**) *verb* To earn something because of something you have done. ▶ *verb* **deserving, deserved** ▶ *adjective* **deserving**

de·sign (di-**zine**)
verb To draw a plan for something that can be made.
noun The shape or style of something. ▶ *verb* **designing, designed**

des·ig·nate (**dez**-ig-nate) *verb* **1.** To name or mark something. **2.** To call or name something. **3.** To choose someone for an office or duty. ▶ *verb* **designating, designated** ▶ *noun* **designation**

des·ig·nat·ed driv·er (**dez**-ig-*nay*-tid **drye**-vur) *noun* A person who has agreed not to drink alcohol so that he or she can drive for others who are drinking.

des·ig·nat·ed hit·ter (**dez**-ig-*nay*-tid **hit**-ur) *noun* In baseball, a player who is named at the start of the game to bat in the pitcher's place without causing the pitcher to be taken out of the game.

de·sign·er (di-**zye**-nur) *noun* Someone who designs something, especially as a job.

de·sir·a·ble (di-**zire**-uh-buhl) *adjective* Having qualities that make people want it.

de·sire (di-**zire**)
noun A strong feeling of needing to do or have something.
verb To want something. ▶ *verb* **desiring, desired**

desk (desk) *noun* A piece of furniture with a flat top where you sit and do work.

desk·top (**desk**-*tahp*)
noun **1.** The surface on the top of a desk where you do work. **2.** An image on a computer screen showing icons of files and programs in the computer.
adjective Designed to be used on a desk.

desk·top pub·lish·ing (**desk**-*tahp* **puhb**-li-shing) *noun* The process of writing, editing, and designing pages on a computer to publish in print or electronic form.

des·o·late (**des**-uh-lit) *adjective* **1.** Empty of people. **2.** Extremely sad and lonely. ▶ *noun* **desolation** ▶ *adverb* **desolately**

de·spair (di-**spair**)
verb To lose hope that something will happen.
noun Extreme sadness after something terrible has happened. ▶ *verb* **despairing, despaired** ▶ *adjective* **despairing** ▶ *adverb* **despairingly**

des·per·a·do (*des*-puh-**rah**-doh) *noun* A bold, reckless criminal; a bandit. ▶ *noun, plural* **desperadoes** or **desperados**

des·per·ate (**des**-pur-it) *adjective* **1.** Willing to do anything to change a situation. **2.** Dangerous but done only because there is no other choice. ▶ *adverb* **desperately** ▶ *noun* **desperation** (*des*-puh-**ray**-shuhn)

de·spise (di-**spize**) *verb* To dislike and disrespect someone or something very strongly. ▶ *verb* **despising, despised** ▶ *adjective* **despicable** (di-**spik**-uh-buhl)

D

de·spite (di-**spite**) *preposition* In spite of. *We enjoyed the hike, despite the chilly wind.*

de·spond·ent (di-**spahn**-duhnt) *adjective* Miserable and depressed. ▶ *adverb* **despondently**

des·sert (des-**zurt**) *noun* A sweet food, such as ice cream, fruit, or cake, usually served at the end of a meal.

des·ti·na·tion (des-tuh-**nay**-shuhn) *noun* The place that a person or vehicle is traveling to.

des·tined (**des**-tuhnd) *adjective* **1.** Having a certain fate. **2.** Bound for a certain place.

des·ti·ny (**des**-tuh-nee) *noun* **1.** The future events in your life, as determined by something that happened earlier. **2.** A force that is believed to control the future and the course of people's lives; fate. ▶ *noun, plural* **destinies**

des·ti·tute (**des**-ti-toot) *adjective* Lacking food, shelter, and clothing. ▶ *noun* **destitution**

de·stroy (di-**stroi**) *verb* To ruin something completely so that nothing usable is left. ▶ *verb* **destroying, destroyed**

de·stroy·er (di-**stroi**-ur) *noun* A very fast warship that uses guns, missiles, and torpedoes to protect other ships from submarines.

de·struc·tion (di-**struhk**-shuhn) *noun* The act of destroying something.

de·struc·tive (di-**struhk**-tiv) *adjective* Causing damage and harm. ▶ *adverb* **destructively**

de·tach (di-**tach**) *verb* To separate one thing from another. ▶ *verb* **detaches, detaching, detached** ▶ *adjective* **detachable**

de·tached (di-**tacht**) *adjective* **1.** Able to stand back from a situation and not get too involved in it. **2.** Separate and not connected to something else. ▶ *noun* **detachment**

de·tail (di-**tayl** *or* dee-tayl) *noun* **1.** A small part of a whole item. **2.** The treatment of something item by item.

noun, plural **details** Items of specific information.

verb To name or describe the details of something. ▶ *verb* **detailing, detailed** ▶ *adjective* **detailed**

de·tain (di-**tayn**) *verb* To hold somebody back when he or she wants to go. ▶ *verb* **detaining, detained** ▶ *noun* **detainee**

de·tect (di-**tekt**) *verb* To notice or discover something. ▶ *verb* **detecting, detected** ▶ *noun* **detection** ▶ *adjective* **detectable**

de·tec·tive (di-**tek**-tiv) *noun* Someone who investigates crimes, usually for or with the police.

de·tec·tor (di-**tek**-tur) *noun* A machine used to reveal the presence of something, such as smoke, metal, or radioactivity.

de·ten·tion (di-**ten**-shuhn) *noun* **1.** A punishment in which a student has to stay after school or has to report early to school. **2.** The state of being forced to stay in a place, usually by authorities.

de·ter (di-**tur**) *verb* To prevent or discourage something. ▶ *verb* **deterring, deterred**

de·ter·gent (di-**tur**-juhnt) *noun* A substance similar to soap for cleaning things.

de·te·ri·o·rate (di-**teer**-ee-uh-rate) *verb* To get worse. ▶ *verb* **deteriorating, deteriorated** ▶ *noun* **deterioration**

de·ter·mi·na·tion (di-tur-muh-**nay**-shuhn) *noun* **1.** A strong will to do something. **2.** The act of deciding or determining something.

de·ter·mine (di-**tur**-min) *verb* **1.** To have an effect on. **2.** To make a discovery or to find out. **3.** If you **determine** the solution to a problem, you are able to settle or resolve it. **4.** If you **determine** a date or time, you decide it after considering everything necessary. ▶ *verb* **determining, determined**

de·ter·mined (di-**tur**-mind) *adjective* Having or showing a strong intention to do something. ▶ *adverb* **determinedly**

D

de·ter·rent (di-**tur**-uhnt) *noun* A thing that stops something else from happening.

de·test (di-**test**) *verb* To dislike very much. ▶ *verb* **detesting, detested** ▶ *adjective* **detestable**

det·o·nate (**det**-uh-nate) *verb* To set off an explosion. ▶ *verb* **detonating, detonated** ▶ *noun* **detonator**

de·tour (**dee**-toor)
noun A different, usually longer way to go somewhere when the direct route is closed or blocked.
verb To take a route other than the planned or usual one, or to send traffic elsewhere.
▶ *verb* **detouring, detoured**

de·tract (di-**trakt**) *verb* To reduce the enjoyment or value of something. ▶ *verb* **detracting, detracted**

det·ri·men·tal (*det*-ri-**men**-tuhl) *adjective* Harmful. ▶ *noun* **detriment**

deuce (doos) *noun* **1.** A two, especially in cards or dice. **2.** The tennis score of 40 to 40, in which one player must score two points in a row in order to win.

de·val·ue (dee-**val**-yoo) *verb* To reduce the value of something, especially a currency. ▶ *verb* **devaluing, devalued** ▶ *noun* **devaluation**

dev·as·tate (**dev**-uh-*stayt*) *noun* **1.** To damage severely or destroy. **2.** To upset extremely.
▶ *adjective* **devastating** ▶ *noun* **devastation**

de·vel·op (di-**vel**-uhp) *verb* **1.** To grow in a natural way to a more mature or advanced state. **2.** To make something grow in this way. **3.** To bring something into existence. **4.** To treat film with chemicals in order to bring out the photos that have been taken on the film, or to make prints of photos taken with a digital camera.
▶ *verb* **developing, developed** ▶ *noun* **developer**

de·vel·op·ing coun·try (di-**vel**-uh-ping **kuhn**-tree) *noun* A country in which most people are poor and there is not yet much industry.

de·vel·op·ment (di-**vel**-uhp-muhnt) *noun* **1.** The natural and expected growth or change in something. **2.** The appearance of something that wasn't there before. **3.** Something that happens in a process and that is seen as a change in that process. **4.** An area of land that has been modified for a particular use.

de·vi·ate (**dee**-vee-ate) *verb* To do something differently from the usual way. ▶ *verb* **deviating, deviated** ▶ *noun* **deviation**

de·vice (di-**vise**) *noun* **1.** A piece of equipment that does a particular job. **2.** If you are **left to your own devices,** you can do what you want.

dev·il (**dev**-uhl) *noun* **1. the devil** In many religions, the primary spirit of evil. The word is often capitalized. **2.** A person who is full of mischief or is wicked.
▶ *adjective* **devilish**

de·vi·ous (**dee**-vee-uhs) *adjective* Misleading or not direct in communicating the real reasons for something. ▶ *noun* **deviousness** ▶ *adverb* **deviously**

de·vise (di-**vize**) *verb* To think of a way to do or create something. ▶ *verb* **devising, devised**

de·void (di-**void**) *adjective* Lacking something that you would expect to be present.

de·vote (di-**voht**) *verb* To give your time, effort, or attention to some purpose. ▶ *verb* **devoting, devoted**

de·vot·ed (di-**voh**-tid) *adjective* Having or showing strong feelings of loyalty and love. ▶ *noun* **devotion** ▶ *adverb* **devotedly**

de·vour (di-**vour**) *verb* To eat something quickly and hungrily. ▶ *verb* **devouring, devoured**

de·vout (di-**vout**) *adjective* Deeply religious. ▶ *noun* **devoutness** ▶ *adverb* **devoutly**

dew (doo) *noun* Moisture in the form of small drops that collects overnight on cool surfaces outside. ▶ *adjective* **dewy**

dew·lap (**doo**-lap) *noun* The loose skin that hangs under an animal's chin or neck.

D

dex·ter·i·ty (dek-**ster**-i-tee) *noun* Skill in using your hands or in thinking or speaking. ▶ *adjective* **dexterous** (**dek**-struhs)

di·a·be·tes (dye-uh-**bee**-tis *or* dye-uh-**bee**-teez) *noun* A disease in which there is too much sugar in the blood. ▶ *adjective* **diabetic** (dye-uh-**bet**-ik)

di·a·bol·i·cal (dye-uh-**bah**-li-kuhl) *or* **di·a·bol·ic** (dye-uh-**bah**-lik) *adjective* 1. Wicked and evil. 2. Of or having to do with the devil.
▶ *adverb* **diabolically**

di·ag·nose (dye-uhg-**nohs**) *verb* To determine what disease a patient has or what the cause of a problem is. ▶ *verb* **diagnosing, diagnosed** ▶ *noun* **diagnosis**

di·ag·o·nal (dye-**ag**-uh-nuhl) *adjective* Joining opposite corners of a square or rectangle.
noun A line that joins opposite corners of a square or rectangle.
▶ *adverb* **diagonally**

di·a·gram (**dye**-uh-gram) *noun* A drawing or plan that explains something with the use of arrows, colors, shapes, and other things. ▶ *adjective* **diagrammatic**

di·al (**dye**-uhl)
noun 1. The face on a clock, gauge, or other measuring instrument. 2. A disk on certain devices, such as a radio, that is moved to operate the device. 3. **dial tone** The sound that you hear when you first pick up the receiver of a phone. This sound tells you that the phone is working.
verb To enter a phone number by pushing buttons or, on older phones, by turning a dial.
▶ *verb* **dialing, dialed**

di·a·lect (**dye**-uh-lekt) *noun* A way a language is spoken in a particular place or among a particular group of people.

di·a·log box (**dye**-uh-lawg bahks) *noun* A window on a computer screen that requires you to input text or make a choice. ▶ *noun, plural* **dialog boxes**

di·a·logue *or* **di·a·log** (**dye**-uh-*lawg*) *noun* Conversation, especially in a play, movie, television program, or book.

di·al-up (**dye**-uhl-*uhp*) *noun* The slowest form of Internet connection. It sends signals over a standard telephone line.

di·am·e·ter (dye-**am**-i-tur) *noun* 1. A straight line through the center of a circle, connecting opposite sides. 2. The length of this line.

dia·mond (**dye**-muhnd *or* **dye**-uh-muhnd)
noun 1. A clear, precious stone that is a form of carbon and is the hardest known mineral. 2. A shape with four equal sides, resting on one of its points. 3. The area of a baseball field enclosed by first, second, and third base and home plate.
noun, plural **diamonds** One of the four suits in a deck of cards.

di·a·per (**dye**-pur *or* **dye**-uh-pur) *noun* A piece of soft, absorbent clothing worn as underwear by babies and young children.

di·a·phragm (**dye**-uh-*fram*) *noun* The wall of muscle in your lower chest that draws air into and pushes air out of your lungs.

di·ar·rhe·a (dye-uh-**ree**-uh) *noun* A condition in which normally solid waste from your body becomes liquid.

di·a·ry (**dye**-ur-ee) *noun* A book in which people write down things that happen every day, or at regular intervals. ▶ *noun, plural* **diaries**

dice (dise)
noun, plural Cubes with a different number of dots on each face, used in games. The singular of *dice* is *die*, although some people use *dice* as the singular.
verb To cut something into small cubes.
▶ *verb* **dicing, diced** ▶ *adjective* **diced**

dic·tate (**dik**-tate) *verb* 1. To say something so that someone can write down what you say. 2. To order something with authority.
▶ *verb* **dictating, dictated** ▶ *noun* **dictation** (dik-**tay**-shuhn)

D

dic·ta·tor (**dik**-tay-tur) *noun* A ruler who has complete control of a country, often by force. ▶ *noun* **dictatorship**

dic·ta·to·rial (dik-tuh-**tor**-ee-uhl) *adjective* 1. Of or having to do with a dictator. 2. Extremely bossy.

dic·tion·ar·y (**dik**-shuh-*ner*-ee) *noun* A book such as this one that lists words in a language in alphabetical order and explains what they mean. ▶ *noun, plural* **dictionaries**

did·n't (**did**-uhnt) *contraction* A short form of *did not.*

die (dye)
verb 1. To come to the end of life. 2. To come to an end because nothing supports continuing. 3. If you are **dying** to do something, you really want to do it.
noun The singular form of the word **dice.**
Die sounds like **dye.** ▶ *verb* **dying, died**

die·sel (**dee**-zuhl) *noun* A fuel used in diesel engines that is heavier than gasoline.

die·sel en·gine (**dee**-zuhl *en*-jin) *noun* A type of engine that works using heat produced by compressing air. By contrast, a gasoline engine uses an electric spark to start the burning process.

di·et (**dye**-it)
noun 1. The food you usually or typically eat. 2. A planned way of eating, usually for losing weight.
verb To eat less according to a plan in order to lose weight.
▶ *verb* **dieting, dieted** ▶ *adjective* **dietary** (**dye**-i-*ter*-ee) ▶ *noun* **dieter**

dif·fer (**dif**-ur) *verb* 1. To be unlike something or someone else. 2. To disagree about something.
▶ *verb* **differing, differed**

dif·fer·ence (**dif**-ur-uhns *or* **dif**-ruhns) *noun* 1. A way in which one thing is not like another. 2. The amount left after you subtract one number from another.

dif·fer·ent (**dif**-ur-uhnt *or* **dif**-ruhnt) *adjective* 1. Not the same. 2. Various or several. 3. Not usual, typical, or expected.

dif·fer·ent·ly (**dif**-ur-uhnt-lee *or* **dif**-ruhnt-lee) *adverb* Not in the same way.

dif·fi·cult (**dif**-i-*kuhlt*) *adjective* 1. Not easy. 2. Not easy to get along with.

dif·fi·cul·ty (**dif**-i-*kuhl*-tee) *noun* A problem that prevents or slows down progress. ▶ *noun, plural* **difficulties**

dig (dig)
verb 1. To break up or move earth. 2. To look very hard for information.
noun 1. A push or a poke. 2. A critical and thoughtless remark. 3. An archaeological excavation.
▶ *verb* **digging, dug** (duhg)

di·gest
verb (dye-**jest** *or* di-**jest**) To break down food in the organs of digestion so that it can be absorbed into the blood and used by the body.
noun (**dye**-jest) A shortened form of a book or other written work, or a collection of such shortened forms.
▶ *verb* **digesting, digested**

di·ges·tion (dye-**jes**-chuhn *or* di-**jes**-chuhn) *noun* The process of breaking down food and separating from it the things that the body needs. ▶ *adjective* **digestive**

dig·it (**dij**-it) *noun* 1. Any one of the numerals from 1 to 9, and sometimes 0. 2. A finger or toe.

dig·it·al (**dij**-i-tuhl) *adjective* 1. Represented in or by numerals. 2. Using the binary number system for recording text, images, or sound in a form that can be used on a computer.

dig·i·tal rights (**dij**-i-tuhl **rites**) *noun, plural* The rights of artists, musicians, writers, and others to protect the things that they create and put on the Internet or on other electronic media.

dig·i·tize (**dij**-i-*tize*) *verb* To convert or change data or graphic images to digital form, usable by a computer. ▶ *verb* **digitizing, digitized**

dig·ni·fied (**dig**-nuh-*fide*) *adjective* Calm and serious in a way that deserves respect.

dig·ni·ty (**dig**-ni-tee) *noun* The quality or manner that makes a person worthy of honor or respect.

D

dike (dike) *noun* A high wall or dam that is built to hold back water and prevent flooding.

di·lap·i·dat·ed (duh-**lap**-i-*day*-tid) *adjective* Shabby and falling apart. ▸ *noun* **dilapidation**

di·lem·ma (duh-**lem**-uh) *noun* A situation in which any possible choice has some disadvantages.

dil·i·gence (**dil**-i-juhns) *noun* A constant and sincere effort to do what is necessary to accomplish something, usually with careful attention to details.

dil·i·gent (**dil**-i-juhnt) *adjective* Working hard and carefully. ▸ *adverb* **diligently**

di·lute (duh-**loot** *or* dye-**loot**) *verb* To make something weaker by adding water or some other liquid to it.
▸ *verb* **diluting, diluted** ▸ *noun* **dilution**

dim (dim)
adjective 1. Somewhat dark.
2. Formless, or hard to see.
verb To make less bright.
▸ *verb* **dimming, dimmed**

dime (dime) *noun* A small coin of the United States and Canada that is worth ten cents.

di·men·sion (duh-**men**-shuhn) *noun* Any of the three measures of an object: length, width, or height. ▸ *adjective* **dimensional**

di·min·ish (duh-**min**-ish) *verb* To make or become smaller or weaker. ▸ *verb* **diminishes, diminishing, diminished**

di·min·u·tive (duh-**min**-yuh-tiv) *adjective* Tiny, or very small.
noun A word that indicates a smaller version of something.

dim·ple (**dim**-puhl) *noun* A small hollow in a person's cheek or chin. ▸ *adjective* **dimpled**

din (din) *noun* A great deal of noise.

dine (dine) *verb* To have a meal, especially dinner, in a formal way. ▸ *verb* **dining, dined**

din·er (**dye**-nur) *noun* 1. A person eating in a public place like a restaurant or hotel. 2. A restaurant where people sit at a long counter or in booths.

di·nette (dye-**net**) *noun* 1. A small space, usually next to a kitchen, for eating meals. 2. A **dinette set** is a table and chairs used for eating in such an area.

din·ghy (**ding**-ee) *noun* A small rowboat. ▸ *noun, plural* **dinghies**

din·gy (**din**-jee) *adjective* Dull and dirty. ▸ *adjective* **dingier, dingiest**

din·ing room (**dye**-ning *room*) *noun* A room where meals are served at a table.

din·ner (**din**-ur) *noun* 1. The main meal of the day. 2. A formal banquet.

di·no·saur (**dye**-nuh-*sor*) *noun* A kind of large reptile that lived in prehistoric times.

di·o·cese (**dye**-uh-sis *or* **dye**-uh-*seez*) *noun* A church district under the authority of a bishop.

dip (dip)
verb 1. To put something briefly into a liquid. 2. To slope downward.
noun 1. If you **take a dip**, you go for a short swim. 2. A thick sauce into which you dip foods such as raw vegetables and chips. 3. A downward slope.
▸ *verb* **dipping, dipped**

di·plo·ma (duh-**ploh**-muh) *noun* A certificate from a school showing that you have finished a course of study.

dip·lo·mat (**dip**-luh-*mat*) *noun* Someone who officially represents his or her country's government in a foreign country as a job.

dip·lo·mat·ic (*dip*-luh-**mat**-ik) *adjective* 1. Of or having to do with being a diplomat. 2. Tactful and good at dealing with people.
▸ *noun* **diplomacy** (duh-**ploh**-muh-see)

dip·per (**dip**-ur) *noun* A cup with a long handle used to scoop liquid out of a large container.

dire (dire) *adjective* Dreadful or urgent. ▸ *adjective* **direr, direst**

di·rect (duh-**rekt**)
adjective 1. Moving or laid out in a straight line. 2. Communicating straight to the point; frank.
verb 1. To supervise people, especially in a play, movie, or television program. 2. To tell someone the way to reach a place.
▸ *verb* **directing, directed**

D

di·rec·tion (duh-**rek**-shuhn)
noun **1.** The line that someone or something is moving on or pointing toward. **2.** Guidance or supervision.
noun, plural **directions** Instructions, especially for getting to a place.

di·rec·tive (duh-**rek**-tiv) *noun* An order from an authority.

di·rect·ly (duh-**rekt**-lee) *adverb* Immediately and straight through, without changing direction or stopping.

di·rec·tor (duh-**rek**-tur) *noun* **1.** Someone who directs a play, a movie, or a radio or television program. **2.** One of a group of people responsible for the important decisions of a company.

di·rec·to·ry (duh-**rek**-tur-ee) *noun* **1.** A book that gives addresses, phone numbers, or other information in alphabetical order. **2.** A named area of disk memory that can hold a number of computer files; a folder.
▶ *noun, plural* **directories**

dirge (durj) *noun* A poem or song that is very sad, especially one that is part of a funeral.

di·ri·gi·ble (**dir**-i-juh-buhl) *noun* An aircraft that is shaped like a fat cigar, filled with a gas that makes it rise, and powered by a motor.

dirt (durt) *noun* **1.** Earth or soil. **2.** Mud, dust, and other unclean substances.

dir·ty (**dur**-tee)
adjective **1.** Not clean. **2.** Unfair or dishonest. **3.** Concerned with sex in an impolite or offensive way. **4.** Showing hostile feelings toward someone.
verb To make something dirty.
▶ *adjective* **dirtier, dirtiest** ▶ *verb* **dirties, dirtying, dirtied**

dis (dis) *verb* (slang) To show disrespect for someone. ▶ *verb* **disses, dissing, dissed**

dis·a·bil·i·ty (*dis*-uh-**bil**-i-tee) *noun* **1.** Something that prevents someone from being able to move easily, or from being able to act or think in ways typically expected of a person. **2.** The lack of an ability to do something.
▶ *noun, plural* **disabilities**

dis·a·ble (dis-**ay**-buhl) *verb* To take away the ability to do something. ▶ *verb* **disabling, disabled**

dis·a·bled (dis-**ay**-buhld) *adjective* Not able to do the things that most people can do, usually because of an illness or injury or from a condition present from birth.

dis·ad·van·tage (*dis*-uhd-**van**-tij) *noun* **1.** Something that makes success more difficult. **2. at a disadvantage** Less likely to succeed.

dis·ad·van·taged (*dis*-uhd-**van**-tijd) *adjective* Poor and lacking many opportunities.

dis·a·gree (*dis*-uh-**gree**) *verb* **1.** To have a different opinion. **2.** To cause discomfort after being eaten.
▶ *verb* **disagreeing, disagreed**

dis·a·gree·ment (*dis*-uh-**gree**-muhnt) *noun* **1.** A difference of opinion with someone, especially when it causes unpleasant feelings. **2.** The fact of not being in agreement.

dis·ap·pear (*dis*-uh-**peer**) *verb* To go out of sight. ▶ *verb* **disappearing, disappeared** ▶ *noun* **disappearance**

dis·ap·point (*dis*-uh-**point**)
verb To let someone down by not doing what he or she expected. ▶ *verb* **disappointing, disappointed** ▶ *adjective* **disappointed** ▶ *adjective* **disappointing**

dis·ap·point·ment (*dis*-uh-**point**-muhnt) *noun* **1.** A person or thing that disappoints you. **2.** Unhappiness or discouragement that you feel when you get a bad result or when something turns out worse than you expected.

dis·ap·prove (*dis*-uh-**proov**) *verb* To think that a particular action or behavior is bad. ▶ *verb* **disapproving, disapproved** ▶ *noun* **disapproval**

dis·arm (dis-**ahrm**) *verb* **1.** To take weapons away from somebody. **2.** To give up weapons. **3.** To win over.
▶ *verb* **disarming, disarmed** ▶ *adjective* **disarming** ▶ *noun* **disarmament** (dis-**ahr**-muh-muhnt)

D

dis·as·ter (di-**zas**-tur) *noun* **1.** An event that causes great damage, loss, or suffering, such as a flood or a plane crash. **2.** A result or outcome in which everything goes wrong.
▶ *adjective* **disastrous** ▶ *adverb* **disastrously**

dis·be·lief (*dis*-bi-**leef**) *noun* Refusal to believe something.

dis·be·lieve (*dis*-bi-**leev**) *verb* To think that something is not true. ▶ *verb* **disbelieving, disbelieved**

disc (disk) *noun* Another spelling of **disk.**

dis·card (dis-**kahrd**) *verb* To throw something away. ▶ *verb* **discarding, discarded**

dis·charge
verb (dis-**chahrj**) **1.** To tell someone officially that he or she can go or leave. **2.** To release a substance into the open.
noun (**dis**-chahrj) **1.** An official release. **2.** A gas or liquid that comes out of something.
▶ *verb* **discharging, discharged**

dis·ci·ple (di-**sye**-puhl) *noun* Someone who follows the teachings of a leader.

dis·ci·pline (**dis**-uh-plin)
noun **1.** Control over your own or someone else's behavior.
2. Punishment for misbehavior or breaking rules. **3.** The activities required to learn and master a skill. **4.** An area of study.
verb To punish someone for breaking a rule or causing disruption.
▶ *verb* **disciplining, disciplined** ▶ *adjective* **disciplinary**

disc jock·ey (**disk** *jah*-kee) *noun* Someone who plays music on the radio or at a party or club. Abbreviated as *DJ.*

dis·close (dis-**klohz**) *verb* To reveal something. ▶ *verb* **disclosing, disclosed** ▶ *noun* **disclosure** (dis-**kloh**-zhur)

dis·co (**dis**-koh)
noun A club where music is played for dancing.
adjective Of or having to do with the type of music played at discos.

dis·com·fort (dis-**kuhm**-furt) *noun* A feeling of pain or uneasiness that keeps you from relaxing.

dis·con·nect (*dis*-kuh-**nekt**) *verb* To separate things that are joined or break a connection. ▶ *verb* **disconnecting, disconnected** ▶ *noun* **disconnection**

dis·con·tent·ed (*dis*-kuhn-**ten**-tid) *adjective* Not satisfied. ▶ *noun* **discontent** ▶ *adverb* **discontentedly**

dis·con·tin·ue (*dis*-kuhn-**tin**-yoo) *verb* To stop doing or providing something. ▶ *verb* **discontinuing, discontinued**

dis·cord (**dis**-kord) *noun* Disagreement or conflict, especially in a group. ▶ *adjective* **discordant** (dis-**kord**-uhnt)

dis·count (**dis**-kount)
noun **1.** A reduction in price. **2.** A **discount store** sells things at reduced prices.
verb To reduce the price of something.
▶ *verb* **discounting, discounted**

dis·cour·age (dis-**kur**-ij) *verb* **1.** To try to persuade someone not to do something. **2.** To cause someone to lose their enthusiasm for doing something.
▶ *verb* **discouraging, discouraged** ▶ *noun* **discouragement**

dis·cour·aged (dis-**kur**-ijd) *adjective* Feeling less confident or enthusiastic because of some setback.

dis·course (**dis**-kors) *noun* Communication in words between people or groups.

dis·cov·er (dis-**kuhv**-ur) *verb* **1.** To find something. **2.** To become aware of or learn something.
▶ *verb* **discovering, discovered** ▶ *noun* **discoverer**

dis·cov·er·y (dis-**kuhv**-ur-ee) *noun* **1.** The act of discovering something. **2.** A thing that has been discovered.
▶ *noun, plural* **discoveries**

dis·creet (dis-**kreet**) *adjective* Careful to avoid hurting or upsetting others, especially by revealing a secret. **Discreet** sounds like **discrete.** ▶ *adverb* **discreetly**

D

discrete (dis-**kreet**) *adjective* Separate
and distinct. **Discrete** sounds like
discreet.

dis·cre·tion (dis-**kresh**-uhn) *noun*
1. Sensitivity and good judgment
about matters that might upset,
offend, injure, or embarrass someone.
2. Freedom to decide what to do.

dis·crim·i·nate (dis-**krim**-uh-*nate*) *verb*
1. To treat someone unfairly while
you treat someone else better. 2. To
recognize differences between types
of things.
▶ *verb* **discriminating, discriminated**
▶ *adjective* **discriminating**
▶ *adjective* **discriminatory**
(dis-**krim**-uh-nuh-*tor*-ee)

dis·crim·i·na·tion (dis-*krim*-i-**nay**-
shuhn) *noun* 1. Prejudice or unfair
behavior to others based on
differences in such things as age,
race, or gender. 2. The ability to
recognize small differences, especially
in the quality of things.

dis·cus (**dis**-kuhs) *noun* A large, heavy
disk that is thrown in a track-and-field
event. ▶ *noun, plural* **discuses**

dis·cuss (dis-**kuhs**) *verb* To talk about
something in order to understand it
better or to reach a decision about
it. ▶ *verb* **discusses, discussing,
discussed**

dis·cus·sion (dis-**kuhsh**-uhn) *noun* A
conversation with a purpose, in which
different opinions are expressed.

dis·ease (di-**zeez**) *noun* 1. A specific
illness. 2. Sickness in general.
▶ *adjective* **diseased**

dis·fig·ure (dis-**fig**-yur) *verb* To spoil
the way something looks. ▶ *verb*
disfiguring, disfigured ▶ *noun*
disfigurement ▶ *adjective* **disfigured**

dis·grace (dis-**grase**)
noun Something that causes shame or
disapproval.
verb To cause shame or dishonor to
yourself or your family.
▶ *verb* **disgracing,
disgraced** ▶ *adjective* **disgraceful**

dis·grun·tled (dis-**gruhn**-tuhld) *adjective*
Unhappy or dissatisfied.

dis·guise (dis-**gize**)
verb To hide something, especially by
changing the way it appears.
noun A way of dressing or behaving
that hides your identity or your
intentions.
▶ *verb* **disguising, disguised**

dis·gust (dis-**guhst**)
verb To make someone feel very
strong dislike and disapproval.
noun A strong feeling of dislike or
disapproval, sometimes combined
with anger.
▶ *verb* **disgusting, disgusted**

dis·gust·ing (dis-**guhs**-ting)
adjective Very unpleasant and
offensive. ▶ *adverb* **disgustingly**

dish (dish)
noun 1. A container, such as a plate or
bowl, used for serving food. 2. Food
made in a certain way.
verb If you **dish up** food, you put or
serve it in a dish.
▶ *noun, plural* **dishes** ▶ *verb* **dishes,
dishing, dished**

di·shev·eled (di-**shev**-uhld) *adjective*
Very messy.

dis·hon·est (dis-**ah**-nist) *adjective*
Not honest or truthful. ▶ *adverb*
dishonestly

dis·hon·est·y (dis-**ah**-nis-tee) *noun* A
failure to be truthful and honest.

dis·hon·or (dis-**ah**-nur)
verb To bring shame or disgrace upon
yourself or others.
noun Shame or disgrace.
▶ *verb* **dishonoring,
dishonored** ▶ *adjective* **dishonorable**

dish·wash·er (**dish**-*wah*-shur) *noun*
1. A machine for washing dishes.
2. Someone whose job is to wash
dishes.

dis·il·lu·sion (*dis*-i-**loo**-zhuhn) *verb*
To take away someone's mistaken
ideas or unrealistic hopes. ▶ *verb*
disillusioning, disillusioned ▶ *noun*
disillusionment

dis·in·fect·ant (*dis*-in-**fek**-tuhnt) *noun* A
chemical used to kill germs, as on a
cut or on a household surface. ▶ *verb*
disinfect

D

dis·in·te·grate (dis-**in**-tuh-*grate*) *verb*
1. To break into small pieces. 2. To fall apart.
▶ *verb* **disintegrating, disintegrated** ▶ *noun* **disintegration**

dis·in·ter·est·ed (dis-**in**-tuh-*res*-tid *or* dis-**in**-tri-stid) *adjective* Having no personal feelings for either side of a contest or an argument.

dis·joint·ed (dis-**join**-tid) *adjective* Not connected, or not flowing smoothly.

disk *or* **disc** (disk) *noun* 1. A flat, circular object. 2. A circular object that can store information usable by a computer.

disk drive (**disk** *drive*) *noun* The part of a computer that reads information from, or saves information onto, a disk.

dis·like (dis-**like**)
verb To have a feeling of displeasure about someone or something.
noun The feeling of displeasure about something or someone.
▶ *verb* **disliking, disliked**

dis·lo·cate (dis-**loh**-kate *or* **dis**-loh-kate) *verb* To move something out of its usual place. ▶ *verb* **dislocating, dislocated** ▶ *noun* **dislocation** ▶ *adjective* **dislocated**

dis·lodge (dis-**lahj**) *verb* To force something out of position. ▶ *verb* **dislodging, dislodged**

dis·loy·al (dis-**loi**-uhl) *adjective* Hurting someone whom you should support; not loyal.

dis·mal (**diz**-muhl) *adjective* 1. Gloomy, sad, or dreary. 2. Extremely bad; failed.

dis·man·tle (dis-**man**-tuhl) *verb* To take something apart. ▶ *verb* **dismantling, dismantled**

dis·mayed (dis-**mayd**) *adjective* Concerned or worried about something. ▶ *noun* **dismay**

dis·miss (dis-**mis**) *verb* 1. To allow someone to leave. 2. To fire someone from a job. 3. To put something out of your mind.
▶ *verb* **dismisses, dismissing, dismissed**

dis·mis·sal (dis-**mis**-uhl) *noun* 1. The act of letting someone leave, or officially making them leave. 2. A **dismissal** by

a judge or court is a decision not to consider a case anymore. 3. **Dismissal** of an idea or suggestion is rejecting it without any serious thought or consideration.

dis·mount (dis-**mount**)
verb To get off of a horse, vehicle, or apparatus.
noun A move in gymnastics, in which the gymnast leaves the piece of equipment and lands on his or her feet.
▶ *verb* **dismounting, dismounted**

dis·o·be·di·ence (*dis*-oh-**bee**-dee-uhns) *noun* Failure to obey.

dis·o·be·di·ent (*dis*-uh-**bee**-dee-uhnt) *adjective* Failing or refusing to obey. ▶ *adverb* **disobediently**

dis·o·bey (*dis*-uh-**bay**) *verb* To go against the rules or someone's wishes. ▶ *verb* **disobeying, disobeyed**

dis·or·der (dis-**or**-dur) *noun* 1. Lack of order. 2. A physical or mental illness.

dis·or·der·ly (dis-**or**-dur-lee) *adjective*
1. Messy and disorganized.
2. Uncontrolled and possibly violent.
▶ *noun* **disorderliness**

dis·or·gan·i·zed (dis-**or**-guh-*nized*) *adjective* Not properly planned, controlled, or in order. ▶ *noun* **disorganization**

dis·own (dis-**ohn**) *verb* 1. To refuse to accept someone as your relative any longer. 2. If you **disown** a statement or a responsibility, you say that you have nothing to do with it.
▶ *verb* **disowning, disowned**

dis·patch (dis-**pach**)
noun A message or a report.
verb To send something or somebody off.
▶ *noun, plural* **dispatches** ▶ *verb* **dispatches, dispatching, dispatched**

dis·pel (dis-**pel**) *verb* To put an end to something. ▶ *verb* **dispelling, dispelled**

dis·pense (dis-**pens**) *verb* To give something out. ▶ *verb* **dispensing, dispensed**

dis·pens·er (dis-**pen**-sur) *noun* A device or machine that gives out one thing or a small amount at a time.

D

dis·perse (dis-**purs**) *verb* To scatter or move in different directions. ▶ *verb* **dispersing, dispersed** ▶ *noun* **dispersal**

dis·place (dis-**plase**) *verb* 1. To move someone or something from its usual place. 2. To take the place of something or somebody else.
▶ *verb* **displacing, displaced** ▶ *noun* **displacement**

dis·play (dis-**play**)
verb To show something.
noun 1. A public show or exhibition. 2. A screen or panel on electronic equipment that shows information. 3. Special behavior by an animal to attract a mate.
▶ *verb* **displaying, displayed**

dis·please (dis-**pleez**) *verb* If you **displease** someone, you annoy the person or cause him or her to be dissatisfied. ▶ *verb* **displeasing, displeased** ▶ *noun* **displeasure** (dis-**plezh**-ur) ▶ *adjective* **displeased**

dis·pos·a·ble (dis-**poh**-zuh-buhl) *adjective* Made to be thrown away after use.

dis·pos·al (dis-**poh**-zuhl) *noun* 1. The act of throwing away or recycling something. 2. A **garbage disposal** is a small machine under a sink that grinds up leftover food and sends it into the sewer system.

dis·pose (dis-**poze**) *verb* 1. If you **dispose of** something, you get rid of it or throw it away. 2. If you are **disposed to** do something, or **disposed toward** something, you are willing to do it.
▶ *verb* **disposing, disposed**

dis·po·si·tion (dis-puh-**zish**-uhn) *noun* 1. A person's general attitude or mood. 2. The act of disposing of something. 3. The way that something is arranged or ordered.

dis·prove (dis-**proov**) *verb* To show that something cannot be true. ▶ *verb* **disproving, disproved**

dis·pute (dis-**pyoot**)
noun A disagreement about an issue.
verb To say that you think something said or written is not true or accurate.
▶ *verb* **disputing, disputed**

dis·qual·i·fy (dis-**kwah**-luh-*fye*) *verb* To say that someone cannot take part in an activity, often because the person has broken a rule. ▶ *verb* **disqualifies, disqualifying, disqualified** ▶ *noun* **disqualification**

dis·re·gard (*dis*-ri-**gahrd**)
verb To ignore someone or something.
noun Neglect or lack of attention to.
▶ *verb* **disregarding, disregarded**

dis·rep·u·ta·ble (dis-**rep**-yuh-tuh-buhl) *adjective* Having or deserving a bad reputation. ▶ *noun* **disrepute** (*dis*-ri-**pyoot**)

dis·res·pect (*dis*-ri-**spekt**) *noun* A lack of respect, or rudeness. ▶ *adjective* **disrespectful** ▶ *adverb* **disrespectfully**

dis·rupt (dis-**ruhpt**) *verb* To disturb or interrupt something that is happening. ▶ *verb* **disrupting, disrupted** ▶ *noun* **disruption** ▶ *adjective* **disruptive**

dis·sat·is·fied (dis-**sat**-is-*fide*) *adjective* Unhappy or discontented. ▶ *noun* **dissatisfaction** (dis-*sat*-is-**fak**-shuhn) ▶ *verb* **dissatisfy**

dis·sect (di-**sekt**) *verb* 1. To cut apart an animal or a human body so as to examine it. 2. To examine and analyze something very carefully.
▶ *verb* **dissecting, dissected** ▶ *noun* **dissection**

dis·sent (di-**sent**)
verb To disagree with an idea or opinion.
noun Disagreement with an opinion or idea.
▶ *verb* **dissenting, dissented** ▶ *noun* **dissension** (di-**sen**-shuhn)

dis·si·dent (**dis**-i-duhnt) *noun* Someone who opposes the laws of a country. ▶ *noun* **dissidence**

dis·solve (di-**zahlv**) *verb* 1. To seem to disappear when mixed with liquid. 2. To end something officially.
▶ *verb* **dissolving, dissolved** ▶ *noun* **dissolution** (*dis*-uh-loo-shuhn)

dis·tance (**dis**-tuhns) *noun* 1. The space between two places. 2. A distant place or area. 3. If you **keep your distance** from somebody, you keep away from the person.

D

dis·tant (**dis**-tuhnt) *adjective* **1.** Not close in space or time. **2.** Not closely related. **3.** Not warm or friendly.

dis·taste (dis-**tayst**) *noun* A feeling of not liking.

dis·taste·ful (dis-**tayst**-fuhl) *adjective* Unpleasant or not to a person's taste; offensive.

dis·tem·per (dis-**tem**-pur) *noun* An often deadly disease of dogs and some other animals. It is caused by a virus, and its symptoms include fever and loss of appetite.

dis·till (di-**stil**) *verb* To purify a liquid by boiling it, collecting the steam, and then letting it cool until it takes a liquid form again. ▶ *verb* **distilling, distilled** ▶ *noun* **distillation** (dis-tuh-**lay**-shuhn) ▶ *noun* **distiller** ▶ *adjective* **distilled**

dis·tinct (di-**stingkt**) *adjective* **1.** Very clear and easy to notice. **2.** Different in an obvious way. ▶ *adverb* **distinctly**

dis·tinc·tion (di-**stingk**-shuhn) *noun* **1.** A difference. **2.** Excellence. **3.** Something that makes an object or a person unusual or different.

dis·tinc·tive (di-**stingk**-tiv) *adjective* Making a person or thing different from all others.

dis·tin·guish (di-**sting**-gwish) *verb* **1.** To recognize the difference between things. **2.** To see or hear clearly. ▶ *verb* **distinguishes, distinguishing, distinguished** ▶ *adjective* **distinguishable**

dis·tin·guished (di-**sting**-gwisht) *adjective* Well-known or honored for important achievements.

dis·tort (di-**stort**) *verb* **1.** To twist out of the normal shape. **2.** To lie about something in order to mislead someone. ▶ *verb* **distorting, distorted** ▶ *noun* **distortion** (di-**stor**-shuhn) ▶ *adjective* **distorted**

dis·tract (di-**strakt**) *verb* To weaken your concentration on what you are doing. ▶ *verb* **distracting, distracted** ▶ *noun* **distraction**

dis·tress (di-**stres**) *noun* **1.** A feeling of emotional pain or sadness. **2. in distress** In need of help. *verb* To cause emotional pain or sadness. ▶ *verb* **distresses, distressing, distressed** ▶ *adjective* **distressed** ▶ *adjective* **distressing**

dis·trib·ute (di-**strib**-yoot) *verb* To give things out to a number of people, or at different places. ▶ *verb* **distributing, distributed**

dis·tri·bu·tion (dis-truh-**byoo**-shuhn) *noun* **1.** The activity of delivering things to people or places. **2.** The way that something is found or arranged within an area.

dis·trib·u·tor (di-**strib**-yuh-tur) *noun* **1.** A company that buys products from one company and arranges for other companies to sell them. **2.** The part of a car engine that sends electricity from the ignition system to the spark plugs.

dis·trict (**dis**-trikt) *noun* **1.** An area or a region. **2. district attorney** An elected official who represents a state government in court and who has the power to bring government cases to court. Abbreviated as *DA*.

dis·trust (dis-**truhst**) *verb* To think that someone or something is false and cannot be relied on. *noun* The feeling that someone or something cannot be relied on. ▶ *verb* **distrusting, distrusted** ▶ *adjective* **distrustful** ▶ *adverb* **distrustfully**

dis·turb (di-**sturb**) *verb* **1.** To cause someone to stop doing something. **2.** To bother someone who is busy or doing something quiet. **3.** To worry or upset someone. **4.** To change the way that something is arranged. ▶ *verb* **disturbing, disturbed** ▶ *adjective* **disturbing**

dis·turb·ance (dis-**tur**-buhns) *noun* An action or event that upsets a calm and orderly situation.

dis·use (dis-**yoos**) *noun* If something **falls into disuse,** people stop using it. ▶ *adjective* **disused** (dis-**yoozd**)

D

ditch (dich)
noun A long, narrow trench that drains water away or that carries water to fields.
verb 1. To land an aircraft on water in an emergency. 2. (slang) To suddenly leave or stop seeing someone.
▶ *noun, plural* **ditches** ▶ *verb* **ditches, ditching, ditched**

dit·to (**dit**-oh)
adverb As indicated before; similarly.
noun **Ditto** marks (") are used in lists to show that what is written above is repeated on the line with the marks.

dive (dive)
verb 1. To go headfirst into water with your arms out in front of you. 2. To drop down suddenly.
noun An act of diving.
▶ *verb* **diving, dived** *or* **dove** (dove)

div·er (**dye**-vur) *noun* 1. Someone who dives underwater, especially in a competition. 2. Someone who uses special equipment to swim or explore underwater.

di·verse (di-**vurs** *or* dye-**vurs**) *adjective* Having many different types or kinds; varied.

di·ver·sion (di-**vur**-zhuhn) *noun* Something that is amusing and takes your mind away from work.

di·ver·si·ty (di-**vur**-si-tee) *noun* Variety.

di·vert (di-**vurt** *or* dye-**vurt**) *verb* 1. To change the course or direction that something is moving in. 2. To take someone's attention away from something.
▶ *verb* **diverting, diverted** ▶ *adjective* **diverting**

di·vide (di-**vide**) *verb* 1. To separate into parts. 2. If you **divide** one number by another, you figure out how many times the second number will go into the first. 3. To share something by giving everyone a portion. 4. To split into opposing groups.
▶ *verb* **dividing, divided**

div·i·dend (**div**-i-dend) *noun* 1. In a division problem, the number that is divided. 2. A share of the money earned by an investment or a business.

di·vid·er (di-**vye**-dur) *noun* A thing that makes a boundary or separation between two things.

di·vine (di-**vine**)
adjective 1. Having to do with God or from God. 2. Wonderful.
verb To discover something by intuition or guessing.
▶ *verb* **divining, divined**

div·ing board (**dye**-ving bord) *noun* A plank that sticks out over a swimming pool, allowing people to jump or dive into the water.

di·vis·i·ble (di-**viz**-uh-buhl) *adjective* Able to be divided.

di·vi·sion (di-**vizh**-uhn) *noun* 1. The operation of dividing one number by another. 2. One of the parts into which something has been divided. 3. A part of an organization that does some things independently. 4. Part of an army made up of several regiments. 5. The action of dividing.

di·vi·sor (di-**vye**-zur) *noun* In a division problem, the number that you divide by.

di·vorce (di-**vors**)
noun The official ending of a marriage by a court.
verb 1. To end a marriage legally. 2. To separate completely.
▶ *verb* **divorcing, divorced** ▶ *adjective* **divorced**

di·vulge (di-**vuhlj**) *verb* To reveal information that was secret or unknown. ▶ *verb* **divulging, divulged**

diz·zy (**diz**-ee) *adjective* 1. If you are **dizzy,** you feel very unsteady on your feet, and your head seems to be turning. 2. Bewildered and confused.
▶ *adjective* **dizzier, dizziest** ▶ *adjective* **dizzying** ▶ *noun* **dizziness**

DJ (**dee**-jay) *noun* Short for **disc jockey.**

Dji·bou·ti (juh-**boo**-tee) A country in the Horn of Africa, where the Red Sea meets the Gulf of Aden. A former French colony, it still maintains close ties with France

D

today. Djibouti has the only American military base in sub-Saharan Africa.

DNA (**dee**-en-ay) *noun* The molecule that carries our genes, found inside the nucleus of cells. DNA is short for *deoxyribonucleic acid.*

do (doo) *verb* **1.** To perform an action. **2.** To complete or deal with. **3.** To be acceptable. **4.** To get along. **5.** To behave or act in a certain way. **6.** To create or perform. **7.** To bring about a result.
▸ *verb* **does** (duhz), **doing, did** (did), **done** (duhn)

Do·ber·man pin·scher (**doh**-bur-muhn **pin**-chur) *noun* A breed of dog with a long head; a large, muscular body; and a short, black or brown coat.

doc·ile (**dah**-suhl) *adjective* Calm and easy to manage or train.

dock (dahk)
noun **1.** A platform that sticks out over the water so boats and ships can stop beside it. **2.** A part of a building with large doors where trucks load and unload.
verb To stop at a dock.
▸ *verb* **docked, docking**

doc·tor (**dahk**-tur)
noun **1.** Someone who is trained and licensed to treat illnesses. Abbreviated as *Dr.* **2.** Someone who has the highest academic degree given by a college or university.
verb To treat someone or something as a doctor would, with the intention to heal.

doc·trine (**dahk**-trin) *noun* A belief or teaching of a religion, political party, or other group.

doc·u·dra·ma (**dahk**-yuh-*drah*-muh) *noun* A television program that tells a story based on true and dramatic events, using actors.

doc·u·ment
noun (**dahk**-yuh-muhnt) **1.** A piece of paper containing official information. **2.** A computer file containing information that can be viewed on the screen or printed.
verb (**dahk**-yuh-*ment*) To write down all the important details.
▸ *verb* **documenting, documented**

doc·u·men·ta·ry (*dahk*-yuh-**ment**-ree) *noun* A movie or television program about real people and events. ▸ *noun, plural* **documentaries**

do·dec·a·he·dron (doh-*dek*-uh-**hee**-druhn) *noun* A solid shape with 12 faces.

dodge (dahj)
verb **1.** To avoid something or somebody by moving quickly. **2.** To avoid something in a clever or dishonest way.
noun A quick move to avoid something.
▸ *verb* **dodging, dodged**

dodge·ball (**dahj**-*bawl*) *noun* A team game in which players on the defending team are out if they get hit by a ball thrown by the other team.

do·do (**doh**-doh) *noun* **1.** An extinct bird that had a large body and wings so small it was unable to fly. Dodos lived on an island in the Indian Ocean. **2.** (slang) A stupid person.
▸ *noun, plural* **dodos** or **dodoes**

doe (doh) *noun* A female deer or the female of various other mammals where the male is called a buck, for example, kangaroos and rabbits. **Doe** sounds like **dough.**

does (duhz) *verb* The third-person singular present tense form of **do.**

does·n't (**duhz**-uhnt) *contraction* A short form of *does not.*

doff (dahf) *verb* **1.** To remove an article of clothing. **2.** If you **doff your hat** or **cap,** you tip it as a sign of greeting.
▸ *verb* **doffing, doffed**

dog (dawg *or* dahg)
noun A domestic mammal with four legs that is often kept as a pet or as a work animal. Dogs are related to wolves, coyotes, and foxes.
verb To follow someone closely.
▸ *verb* **dogging, dogged**

dog·ma (**dawg**-muh) *noun* Ideas that a religion or group expects you to believe without questioning.

dog·mat·ic (dawg-**mat**-ik) *adjective* If you are **dogmatic,** you insist very strongly that you are right about things.

dog pad·dle (**dawg** *pad*-uhl) *noun*
A swimming stroke in which your
arms and legs move the same way
that a dog's limbs move when it is
swimming. ▶ *verb* **dog-paddle**

dog·wood (**dawg**-*wud*) *noun* A tree or
shrub that has small, green flowers
surrounded by pink or white leaves
that look like petals.

doi·ly (**doi**-lee) *noun* A small piece of
lace or cut paper placed under a plate
or other item as a decoration or on
furniture to protect it. ▶ *noun, plural*
doilies

do-it-your·self (**doo**-it-yur-**self**) *adjective*
Of or having to do with home
improvements, repairs, or projects that
you do yourself. Abbreviated as *DIY*.

dole (dohl) *verb* If you **dole** out
something, such as food or
money, you give it out in small
quantities. ▶ *verb* **doling, doled**

doll (dahl) *noun* A small model of a
human used as a child's toy.

dol·lar (**dah**-lur) *noun* The main unit of
money in the United States, Canada,
Australia, and New Zealand.

doll·house (**dahl**-*hous*) *noun* A small
toy house.

dol·phin (**dahl**-fin) *noun* An intelligent
water mammal with a long snout.
Dolphins are related to whales but are
smaller.

do·main (doh-**mayn**) *noun* 1. A region or
place controlled by a government or
person. 2. A part of the Internet where
all the sites have the same letters after
the period in their address. 3. **domain
name** A general address on the World
Wide Web, such as scholastic.com.

dome (dohm) *noun* A roof shaped like
half of a sphere.

do·mes·tic (duh-**mes**-tik) *adjective* 1. Of
or having to do with the home. 2. Of,
having to do with, or within your
own country. 3. **Domestic animals** are
animals that have been tamed. People
use them as a source of food or as
work animals, or keep them as pets.

do·mes·ti·cate (duh-**mes**-ti-
kate) *verb* To tame an animal
so it can live with or be used by

people. ▶ *verb* **domesticating,
domesticated** ▶ *adjective*
domesticated

dom·i·nant (**dah**-muh-nuhnt) *adjective*
Most influential or powerful.

dom·i·nate (**dah**-muh-*nate*) *verb* 1. To
control, or to rule. 2. To be the main
feature of a something.
▶ *verb* **dominating, dominated** ▶ *noun*
domination

Dom·i·ni·ca (*dah*-muh-**nee**-kuh *or*
duh-**min**-i-kuh) An island nation in
the Caribbean Sea. It is known for
its rare wildlife and lush rain forests.
Dominica's Boiling Lake is the world's
second-largest hot spring, smaller
only than Frying Pan Lake in New
Zealand.

Do·min·i·can Re·pub·lic (duh-**min**-
i-kuhn ri-**puhb**-lik) A country on
the eastern side of the island of
Hispaniola in the Caribbean Sea.
Haiti occupies the western side of the
island. Hispaniola is the second-
largest island in the Caribbean, after
Cuba.

do·min·ion (duh-**min**-yuhn) *noun* 1. A
large area of land controlled by a
single ruler or government. 2. Power
to rule over something.

dom·i·no (**dah**-muh-*noh*)
noun A small rectangular tile that is
divided into two halves that are blank
or contain dots.
noun, plural **dominoes** A game played
with a number of these tiles.

don (dahn) *verb* If you **don** clothing, you
put it on. ▶ *verb* **donning, donned**

do·nate (**doh**-nate) *verb* To give
something to a charity or
cause. ▶ *verb* **donating, donated**

do·na·tion (doh-**nay**-shuhn) *noun* A gift,
usually of money, to an organization,
such as a charity.

done (duhn) *verb* The past participle
of **do.**

don·key (**dahng**-kee) *noun* A mammal
with long ears that is sometimes used
as a work animal. Donkeys are related
to horses but are smaller.

do·nor (**doh**-nur) *noun* 1. Someone
who gives something, usually to an

D

organization or a charity. **2.** Someone who agrees to give his or her body, or a part of it, to medical science to help sick people.

don't (dohnt) *contraction* A short form of *do not*.

doo·dle (**doo**-duhl)
verb To draw absent-mindedly while you are listening or thinking.
noun A drawing or scribble made without thought.
▸ *verb* **doodling, doodled**

doom (doom)
noun A terrible situation that cannot be escaped, especially one that involves death or destruction.
verb To be the cause of a bad thing that happens.
▸ *verb* **dooming, doomed** ▸ *adjective* **doomed**

door (dor) *noun* **1.** A tall, flat panel that opens and closes at the entrance or exit of a building or room. **2.** A house or a building, as in *Muriel lives two doors away from me.*

door·bell (**dor**-bel) *noun* A bell or buzzer outside a door that is rung by someone who wants the door to be opened.

door·knob (**dor**-nahb) *noun* A handle that you turn to open a door.

door·man (**dor**-man) *noun* A man who works at the door of a large building to provide security and to help visitors. ▸ *noun, plural* **doormen**

door·step (**dor**-step) *noun* A step or steps on the outside doorway of a building.

door·way (**dor**-way) *noun* The space between two rooms, or between the inside and outside of a building, that can be closed by a door.

dope (dohp) *noun* **1.** (informal) A stupid person. **2.** (informal) An illegal or addictive drug.

dor·mant (**dor**-muhnt) *adjective* **1.** A **dormant** animal is one that is hibernating. **2.** A **dormant** volcano is not doing anything now but could erupt again. **3.** A **dormant** plant or seed is alive but not growing.

dor·mi·to·ry (**dor**-mi-tor-ee) *noun* A building with many separate sleeping rooms. ▸ *noun, plural* **dormitories**

dor·mouse (**dor**-mous) *noun* A European, African, or Asian rodent that looks like a small squirrel, with black or gray fur and a furry tail. ▸ *noun, plural* **dormice** (**dor**-mise)

dose (dohs) *noun* **1.** An amount of a medicine or chemical that is used or taken at one time. **2.** A small amount, especially of something unpleasant.

dot (daht)
noun A small, round point.
verb **1.** To write a dot over a letter that requires one. **2.** To be here and there around an area.
▸ *verb* **dotting, dotted**

dot-com (**daht**-kahm) *noun* A company that does business mainly online, especially one whose website has ".com" at the end of the address.

dote (doht) *verb* To pay a lot of attention to, or to show a lot of fondness for, someone. ▸ *verb* **doting, doted**

dou·ble (**duhb**-uhl)
adjective Twice the amount, the number, or the strength.
adverb Twice as much.
verb **1.** To make something twice as big. **2.** To bend or fold in two. **3.** To serve more than one purpose.
noun **1.** A person who looks just like you. **2.** A hit in baseball that allows the player to get to second base.
noun, plural **doubles** Team play with two players on each side.
▸ *verb* **doubling, doubled**

dou·ble bass (**duhb**-uhl base) *noun* The largest string instrument in the violin family. You play it by standing next to it and plucking the strings or using a bow.

dou·ble-click (**duhb**-uhl-**klik**) *verb* To quickly click twice on a mouse button in order to make something happen on a computer.

dou·ble-cross (**duhb**-uhl-**craws**) *verb* To tell someone you will do one thing, knowing that you are really going to do something else. ▸ *verb* **double-crosses, double-crossing, double-crossed** ▸ *noun* **double cross**

D

dou·ble·head·er (**duhb**-uhl-**hed**-ur)
noun Two baseball games played one
right after the other.

doubt (dout)
noun The state or quality of being
uncertain.
verb To be uncertain about something.
▶ *verb* **doubting, doubted**

doubt·ful (**dout**-ful) *adjective* 1. Full of
doubts. 2. Uncertain and unlikely.
▶ *adverb* **doubtfully**

dough (doh) *noun* 1. A thick mixture
of mainly flour and water, used to
make bread, cookies, and other foods.
2. (slang) Money.
Dough sounds like **doe.**

dough·nut or **do·nut** (**doh**-nuht) *noun* A
cake fried in oil. A doughnut is round
and usually has a hole in the middle.

dove (duhv) *noun* A plump bird that
makes a cooing sound. Doves are
often used as a symbol of peace.

down (doun)
preposition 1. In a direction lower
or farther away. 2. From a higher to
a lower place. *We raced down the
mountain.*
adverb To a lower place or condition.
noun 1. In football, one of a series of
four attempts to advance the ball ten
yards. 2. The soft feathers of a bird.
3. One of a group of series of gentle
hills.
adjective 1. (informal) Sad or
depressed. 2. If a computer, system,
or communications link is **down,** it is
not working and you can't use it.
verb 1. To defeat or wreck someone or
something, especially by knocking it
down or bringing it down. 2. To drink
something quickly.
▶ *adjective* **downward** (**doun**-
wurd) ▶ *adverb* **downward** or
downwards ▶ *adjective* **downy**

down·cast (**doun**-kast) *adjective* Very
sad.

down·fall (**doun**-fawl) *noun* 1. A sudden
negative change in position or
reputation. 2. Something that causes
a downfall.

down·hill
adverb (**doun**-hil) 1. From the higher

to the lower part of a slope or hill.
2. From a better to a worse position or
situation.
adjective (**doun**-hil) Going downwards
or getting worse.

down·load (**doun**-lohd) *verb* To transfer
information from a larger to a smaller
computer, or from an Internet location
to your own computer. ▶ *verb*
downloading, downloaded

down·pour (**doun**-por) *noun* A very
heavy rain.

down·right (**doun**-rite)
adjective (informal) Total, or complete.
adverb Absolutely, or completely.

downs (dounz) *noun, plural* An area of
rolling hills, especially in England.

down·size (**doun**-size) *verb* To reduce
the size of something, such as the
scale of an automobile or the number
of employees in a company. ▶ *verb*
downsizing, downsized

down·stairs
adverb (**doun**-stairz) Down the stairs
or to a lower floor.
adjective (**doun**-stairz) On a lower level
of a house.
noun (**doun**-stairz) The bottom or
lower level of a house.

down·stream (**doun**-streem) *adverb,
adjective* In the direction of the flowing
current in a river or stream.

Down syn·drome (**doun** sin-drohm)
noun A genetic condition in which
a person is born with learning
disabilities and with eyes that appear
to slant, a broad skull, and shorter
fingers than normal. Also called
Down's syndrome.

down·town (**doun**-toun)
adverb To or in a city's main business
district.
adjective Being in the city's main
business district.
noun The main business disctrict of
a city.

dow·ry (**dou**-ree) *noun* Money or
property that a woman's family
supplies to a man or his family in
some cultures when the woman
marries him. ▶ *noun, plural* **dowries**

doze (dohz)
verb To sleep lightly or take a brief, unintentional nap.
noun A light sleep or unintentional nap.
▶ *verb* **dozing, dozed**

doz·en (**duhz**-uhn) *noun* A group of 12.

dpi (**dee**-*pee*-**eye**) *noun* A measure of the sharpness of an image on a scanner or printer based on the number of dots per inch. The higher the dpi, the sharper the image. Dpi is short for *dots per inch.*

Dr. (**dahk**-tur) Short for **Doctor.**

drab (drab) *adjective* Plain and uninteresting to look at. ▶ *noun* **drabness**

draft (draft)
noun 1. A flow of air, especially a cold one. 2. A first version of a document, or one that is not final. 3. The **draft** was the system that required young men in the United States to serve in the armed forces. It ended in 1973.
verb 1. To write a first rough copy of a document. 2. To make someone join the armed forces.
adjective Drawn out of a barrel or keg.
▶ *verb* **drafting, drafted** ▶ *adjective* **drafty**

drag (drag)
verb 1. To pull something along the ground. 2. To move something from one place to another on a computer, using the mouse. 3. If an activity or event **drags,** it seems to go slowly.
noun (informal) A boring activity or event.
▶ *verb* **dragging, dragged**

drag and drop (**drag** uhn **drahp**) *noun* A method of moving text or an image on a computer by selecting it and holding down the mouse button while you move the cursor to a new position. When you release the button, the moved material will be inserted in the new place. ▶ *verb* **drag-and-drop**

drag·on (**drag**-uhn) *noun* An imaginary monster that breathes fire.

drag·on·fly (**drag**-uhn-*flye*) *noun* A large insect with two sets of wings and a long, slender body. ▶ *noun, plural* **dragonflies**

drain (drayn)
verb 1. To remove the liquid from something. 2. To tire, or to use up.
noun An opening leading to a pipe or channel that takes away liquid.
▶ *verb* **draining, drained**

drain·age (**dray**-nij) *noun* The act or process of removing liquid from an area.

drained (draynd) *adjective* If you feel **drained,** you have no energy left.

dra·ma (**drah**-muh) *noun* 1. A play that is serious rather than funny. 2. The subject or practice of acting. 3. Something that causes people to experience strong, usually unpleasant feelings.

dra·mat·ic (druh-**mat**-ik) *adjective* 1. Of or having to do with acting and the theater. 2. Exciting in the way that a movie or a play can be. 3. Very noticeable. 4. Expressing or showing more feeling than is really necessary.
▶ *adverb* **dramatically**

dram·a·tist (**dram**-uh-tist) *noun* Someone who writes plays.

dram·a·tize (**dram**-uh-*tize*) *verb* 1. To adapt a story into a play. 2. To make an event seem more exciting than it really was.
▶ *verb* **dramatizing, dramatized**

drank (drank) *verb* The past tense of **drink.**

drape (drape)
noun A piece of material placed across a window or stage to cover it.
verb To cover with a loosely hanging cloth.
▶ *noun* **drapery**

dras·tic (**dras**-tik) *adjective* Serious and likely to have important or long-lasting effects. ▶ *adverb* **drastically**

draw (draw)
verb 1. To make a picture with something you write with, such as a pencil, pen, or crayon. 2. To pull something. 3. To attract. 4. To figure out by using your power of reason. 5. To inhale.
noun An equal score for both teams at the end of a competition.
▶ *verb* **drawing, drew** (droo), **drawn** (drawn)

D

draw·back (**draw**-bak) noun A problem or disadvantage.

draw·bridge (**draw**-brij) noun A bridge that can be raised or moved to let boats pass underneath.

draw·er (dror) noun A storage compartment that slides out of a piece of furniture.

draw·ing (**draw**-ing) noun A picture made by hand, such as with pen, pencil, crayons, or chalk.

drawl (drawl)
verb To speak in a slow manner, stretching out the vowel sounds.
noun A slow manner of speaking.
▶ verb **drawling, drawled**

draw·string (**draw**-string) noun A string or cord that closes or tightens a bag or piece of clothing when you pull the ends.

dread (dred)
verb To be afraid of something you expect in the near future. People often use the word **dread** for things they do not actually fear, but do not look forward to.
noun Fear of something that you expect to happen.
▶ verb **dreading, dreaded** ▶ adjective **dreaded**

dread·ful (**dred**-fuhl) adjective 1. Very frightening; awful. 2. Very bad.
▶ adverb **dreadfully**

dread·locks (**dred**-lahks) noun, plural A hairstyle in which the hair is grown long and worn in thick, ropelike strands.

dream (dreem)
verb 1. To imagine events while you are asleep. 2. To have a strong wish for something in the future.
noun 1. An experience while you are asleep that feels like it is happening in real life. 2. Something you hope for in the future.
▶ verb **dreaming, dreamed** or **dreamt** (dremt) ▶ noun **dreamer**

dream·y (**dree**-mee) adjective Vague or soft. ▶ adjective **dreamier, dreamiest** ▶ adverb **dreamily**

drear·y (**dreer**-ee) adjective Dull, unattractive, or sad. ▶ adjective **drearier, dreariest** ▶ adverb **drearily**

dredge (drej) verb To scrape the bottom of a body of water to make it deeper or to find or catch something. ▶ verb **dredging, dredged**

dregs (dregz) noun, plural The solid bits that drop to the bottom of some liquids, such as coffee.

drench (drench) verb To make someone or something completely wet. ▶ verb **drenches, drenching, drenched**

dress (dres)
verb 1. To put clothes on. 2. If you **dress** a salad, you mix a sauce into it in order to add flavor. 3. If you **dress** a wound or injury, you put an ointment on it and bandage it.
noun 1. A piece of women's clothing that covers the body from the shoulders to the legs. 2. Clothes in general.
▶ verb **dresses, dressing, dressed**
▶ noun, plural **dresses**

dress·er (**dres**-ur) noun A piece of furniture with drawers, used for storing clothes.

dress·ing (**dres**-ing) noun 1. A type of sauce for salads. 2. A mixture used to stuff a chicken or turkey before it is roasted. 3. A covering for a wound.

dress·ing table (**dres**-ing tay-buhl) noun A piece of bedroom furniture with a mirror and drawers.

dress re·hears·al (dres ri-hur-suhl) noun The last rehearsal of a play or concert, performed as if an audience were present.

drib·ble (**drib**-uhl) verb 1. To let liquid trickle from your mouth. 2. To drop liquid in small amounts. 3. To bounce a basketball while walking or running, keeping it under your control.
▶ verb **dribbling, dribbled**

dri·er (**drye**-ur) adjective The comparative of **dry.**

dri·est (**drye**-ist) adjective The superlative of **dry.**

drift (drift)
verb 1. To move in the same direction as water or wind. 2. To move or act without any sense of purpose.
noun A pile of sand or snow created by the wind.

D

idiom (informal) If you **get someone's drift,** you understand what the person is saying.

▸ *verb* **drifting, drifted** ▸ *noun* **drifter**

drift·wood (**drift**-*wud*) *noun* Wood that floats ashore or is floating on water.

drill (dril)

noun **1.** A rotating tool used for making holes. **2.** An exercise in which you learn something by doing it repeatedly.

verb **1.** To use a drill. **2.** To teach someone how to do something by having the person do it over and over again.

▸ *verb* **drilling, drilled**

drink (dringk)

noun **1.** A liquid that you swallow. **2.** An amount of a drink that you can hold in your mouth. **3.** An alcoholic liquid.

verb **1.** To swallow liquid. **2.** To drink alcoholic beverages, or to have the habit of doing this.

▸ *verb* **drinking, drank, drunk** ▸ *noun* **drinker**

drip (drip)

verb To fall in drops, or to make liquid fall in drops.

noun **1.** A slow leak that falls in drops. **2.** (informal) A boring person.

▸ *verb* **dripping, dripped**

drip·pings (**drip**-ingz) *noun, plural* Fat and juice that comes from meat while it is cooking.

drive (drive)

verb **1.** To operate and control a vehicle. **2.** To take someone somewhere in a vehicle. **3.** To hit something hard and far. **4.** To force someone into a desperate state.

noun **1.** A computer device that can read and sometimes write to some form of storage media. **2.** A trip that you make by driving, or a distance that you can drive. **3.** A road, especially one that is scenic and often winding. **4.** Energy and determination. **5.** An organized campaign to do something.

▸ *verb* **driving, drove, driven** (driv-uhn) ▸ *noun* **driving**

drive-in (**drive**-*in*) *adjective* Designed so that customers may be served or entertained in their cars. ▸ *noun* **drive-in**

driv·el (**driv**-uhl) *noun* Nonsense, in speech or writing.

driv·er (**drye**-vur) *noun* **1.** Someone who drives a vehicle. **2.** A computer program that controls the way a connected device works.

drive-through *or* **drive-thru** (**drive**-*throo*)

adjective Offering services to people while they are still in their cars.

noun A window, as at a restaurant or bank, that can be used by the driver of a car.

drive·way (**drive**-*way*) *noun* A private road that leads from the street to a house or garage.

driz·zle (**driz**-uhl)

noun Light rain.

verb To rain lightly.

▸ *verb* **drizzling, drizzled**

drom·e·dar·y (**drah**-mi-*der*-ee) *noun* A camel with one hump, found in the Middle East and northern Africa. It is also known as an *Arabian camel.* ▸ *noun, plural* **dromedaries**

drone (drone)

verb **1.** To make a low, dull, steady humming or buzzing sound, like the noise an engine makes. **2.** To talk in a dull, monotonous way.

noun **1.** A military aircraft without a pilot that is controlled remotely. **2.** A male insect, such as a bee, whose function is to mate with the queen.

▸ *verb* **droning, droned**

drool (drool) *verb* **1.** To let saliva trickle from your mouth. **2. drool over** To think that someone or something is very attractive and desirable.

▸ *verb* **drooling, drooled**

droop (droop) *verb* **1.** To hang downward; sag. **2.** To run out of energy and feel very tired.

▸ *verb* **drooping, drooped** ▸ *adjective* **drooping**

D

drop (drahp)
verb **1.** To let something fall. **2.** To fall down or move to a lower place. **3.** To leave out. **4.** To stop using someone or something, or to stop doing something. **5. drop by** To pay a short visit. **6. drop off** To deliver. **7. drop out** To stop taking part in something.
noun **1.** The distance from a higher to a lower place. **2.** A small quantity of liquid. **3.** Any small amount. **4.** A small piece of candy or medication for the throat.
idioms **1.** A **drop in the bucket** is a very small amount. **2.** If you **drop the ball,** you fail to do what is expected of you.
▶ *verb* **dropping, dropped**

drop·out (**drahp**-out) *noun* Someone who has left a school or course before finishing, especially high school.

drought (drout) *noun* A long period without rain.

drove (drove)
noun **1.** A large herd of animals being moved as a group. **2.** A large crowd of people.
verb The past tense of **drive.**

drown (droun) *verb* **1.** To die from a lack of air when under water or another liquid. **2. drown out** To make a louder noise than something else.
▶ *verb* **drowning, drowned**

drow·sy (**drou**-zee) *adjective* Not fully awake; sleepy. ▶ *adjective* **drowsier, drowsiest** ▶ *noun* **drowsiness** ▶ *verb* **drowse** ▶ *adverb* **drowsily**

drudg·er·y (**druhj**-ur-ee) *noun* Difficult, boring, or unpleasant work.

drug (druhg)
noun **1.** A substance, either natural or synthetic, used to treat an illness. **2.** A chemical substance that people take because they like its effect on them. Drugs are dangerous and usually cause addiction. **3. drug addict** Someone who cannot give up using drugs.
verb To make someone unconscious by giving him or her a drug.
▶ *verb* **drugging, drugged** ▶ *adjective* **drugged**

drug·store (**druhg**-stor) *noun* A store that contains a pharmacy and also sells other medicines, cosmetics, and personal items.

drum (druhm)
noun **1.** A percussion instrument shaped like a cylinder with one closed end that makes a noise when you hit it with your hands or drumsticks. **2.** A container shaped like a drum.
verb To play a drum or other surface with drumsticks or with your fingers.
▶ *verb* **drumming, drummed** ▶ *noun* **drummer**

drum·stick (**druhm**-stik) *noun* **1.** A stick used to hit a drum. **2.** The leg portion of a chicken or turkey.

drunk (druhngk)
adjective If people are **drunk,** they have had too much alcohol to drink and cannot control their actions or emotions.
noun **drunk** or **drunkard** (**druhng**-kurd) A person who often gets drunk.
verb The past participle of **drink.**
▶ *adjective* **drunken** (**druhng**-kuhn)

drunk·ard (**druhng**-kurd) *noun* Someone who drinks too much alcohol or who is often drunk.

dry (drye)
verb **1.** To remove the moisture from something. **2.** To lose moisture.
adjective **1.** Not wet. **2.** Lacking rain. **3.** Lacking features that are interesting; dull. **4.** Without butter or margarine.
▶ *adjective* **drier, driest** ▶ *verb* **dries, drying, dried** ▶ *adverb* **drily**

dry cell (drye sel) *noun* A small electric battery that contains no liquid. Most common sizes of batteries for toys and appliances are dry cells.

dry clean·ing (drye **klee**-ning) *noun* A method of cleaning clothes with liquid chemicals that remove stains. Dry cleaning is used for fabrics and materials that would be damaged by soap and water. ▶ *noun* **dry cleaner** ▶ *verb* **dry-clean**

dry·er (**drye**-ur) *noun* A machine that dries something.

dry goods (drye gudz) *noun, plural* Fabrics, clothing, and related

D

materials, such as threads and ribbons.

DSL (*dee-es-el*) *noun* A fast form of Internet connection that uses a special telephone line. DSL is short for *digital subscriber line*.

du·al (**doo**-uhl) *adjective* 1. Combining two things or aspects in one. 2. Made up of two parts or pieces.
Dual sounds like **duel**.

du·bi·ous (**doo**-bee-uhs) *adjective* Having or showing doubts. ▶ *adverb* **dubiously**

du·chess (**duhch**-is) *noun* The wife or widow of a duke, or a woman with the rank that is equal to that of a duke. ▶ *noun, plural* **duchesses**

duck (duhk)
noun A bird with webbed feet that swims and feeds in water.
verb 1. To bend low to avoid something. 2. To avoid or to evade.
▶ *verb* **ducking, ducked**

duck·ling (**duhk**-ling) *noun* A young duck.

duct (duhkt) *noun* A tube that carries air or liquid from one place to another.

dud (duhd)
noun 1. A bomb or firework that does not explode as expected. 2. A dull and unsuccessful entertainment or event.
adjective Being something that does not work out as expected.

dude (dood) *noun* 1. A person from a town or city who has little or no experience on a Western ranch.
2. (informal) A man or boy.

due (doo)
adjective 1. Expected to arrive or happen. 2. Owed. 3. Suitable or appropriate.
preposition **due to** Because of. *We're hurrying to finishing the school paper due to the deadline.*
adverb **Due** south (or north, east, or west) means exactly in that compass direction.
▶ *adverb* **duly** (**doo**-lee)

du·el (**doo**-uhl) *noun* A fight between two people using swords or guns, fought according to strict rules. **Duel** sounds like **dual**.

du·et (doo-**et**) *noun* A piece of music for two singers or performers, or the performers themselves.

duf·fel bag (**duhf**-uhl *bag*) *noun* A bag made from strong cloth in the shape of a cylinder, often used by soldiers or campers.

dug (duhg) *verb* The past tense and past participle of **dig.**

dug·out (**duhg**-out) *noun* 1. A long, low shelter where baseball players sit when they are not at bat or in the field. 2. A rough shelter dug out of the ground or in the side of a hill. 3. A canoe made from the outer portion of a large log.

duke (dook) *noun* A nobleman. In Britain, a duke holds the rank just below that of a prince.

dull (duhl)
adjective 1. Not bright; dim. 2. Not perceptive or intelligent. 3. Boring. 4. Not shiny. 5. Not sharp. 6. Slow or sluggish.
verb To make or become dull.
▶ *adjective* **duller, dullest** ▶ *adverb* **dully**

dumb (duhm) *adjective* (informal) Stupid. ▶ *adjective* **dumber, dumbest**

dumb·bell (**duhm**-bel) *noun* 1. A short bar with heavy weights at each end, used to exercise and strengthen the muscles. 2. (slang) A stupid person.

dumb·found·ed (**duhm**-foun-did) *adjective* So amazed that you cannot speak.

dum·my (**duhm**-ee) *noun* 1. A model of a person or object made for some practical purpose. 2. (informal) A stupid person.
▶ *noun, plural* **dummies**

dump (duhmp)
verb 1. To put something somewhere by tipping its container or turning it upside down. 2. To put something down thoughtlessly or roughly. 3. (informal) To end a relationship with someone.
noun (informal) A place where garbage and other unwanted things are left; a landfill.
▶ *verb* **dumping, dumped**

dump·ling (**duhmp**-ling) *noun* Dough that has been boiled, fried, or steamed, sometimes with meat, vegetables, or fruit wrapped inside.

dune (doon) *noun* A sand hill formed by wind or tides.

dun·geon (**duhn**-juhn) *noun* An underground prison.

dunk (duhngk) *verb* 1. To dip something into liquid. 2. To push someone under water in a playful way. 3. To jump and force a basketball down through the basket.
▶ *verb* **dunking, dunked**

du·pli·cate
verb (**doo**-pli-*kate*) To make an exact copy of something.
noun (**doo**-pli-kit) An exact copy of something, especially one that is not needed.
▶ *verb* **duplicating, duplicated**
▶ *noun* **duplication** (*doo*-pli-**kay**-shuhn) ▶ *noun* **duplicator** (**doo**-pli-*kay*-tur)

du·ra·ble (**door**-uh-buhl) *adjective* Tough and lasting for a long time. ▶ *noun* **durability** (door-uh-**bil**-i-tee)

du·ra·tion (du-**ray**-shuhn) *noun* The period of time that something lasts.

dur·ing (**door**-ing) *preposition* Within a particular time. *The gym is open during the day.*

dusk (duhsk) *noun* The time of day after sunset when it starts getting dark.

dust (duhst)
noun Tiny particles of something like dirt or fluff that gather on surfaces or in the air.
verb To remove these particles from surfaces.
▶ *verb* **dusting, dusted** ▶ *noun* **duster**

dust·pan (**duhst**-*pan*) *noun* A small tray with a handle that you use with a broom to pick up dust and dirt from the floor.

dust·y (**duhs**-tee) *adjective* Full of or covered with dust. ▶ *adjective* **dustier, dustiest**

du·ti·ful (**doo**-ti-fuhl) *adjective* Obedient and careful to do what you are supposed to do. ▶ *adverb* **dutifully**

du·ty (**doo**-tee) *noun* 1. A thing a person must do or ought to do. 2. A tax charged on imported products. 3. If you are **on duty,** you are at work or responsible for something.
▶ *noun, plural* **duties**

DVD (**dee**-*vee*-**dee**) *noun* A disk the size of a compact disk but that can hold much more information. A DVD can contain computer data or recordings of movies or music. DVD is short for *digital versatile disk* or *digital video disk.*

DVR (**dee**-*vee*-**ahr**) *noun* A device that receives a video broadcast signal and stores it digitally on a hard drive so that the broadcast can be watched later. DVR is short for *digital video recorder.*

dwarf (dworf)
noun A person, animal, or plant that is smaller than normal.
verb To make something else seem small.
adjective Being smaller than normal in size.
▶ *noun, plural* **dwarfs** or **dwarves** (dworvz) ▶ *verb* **dwarfing, dwarfed**

dwarf plan·et (**dworf** *plan*-it) *noun* A round heavenly body that orbits the sun or another star. A dwarf planet is smaller than a planet.

dwell (dwel) *verb* To live in a place. ▶ *verb* **dwelling, dwelt** (dwelt) or **dwelled**

dwell·ing (**dwel**-ing) *noun* The place where someone lives, such as a house or an apartment.

dwin·dle (**dwin**-duhl) *verb* To become smaller or less till very few or little is left. ▶ *verb* **dwindling, dwindled**

dye (dye)
noun A substance used to change the color of something.
verb To change the color of something, especially fabric, by soaking it in dye.
Dye sounds like **die.** ▶ *verb* **dying, dyed** ▶ *adjective* **dyed**

dy·nam·ic (dye-**nam**-ik) *adjective* 1. If someone is **dynamic,** he or she is very energetic and good at getting things done. 2. If a situation is **dynamic,** it is

D

constantly changing because there are many things that influence it.
▶ *noun* **dynamism** (**dye**-nuh-*miz*-uhm)

dy·na·mite (**dye**-nuh-*mite*) *noun* A very powerful explosive.

dy·na·mo (**dye**-nuh-*moh*) *noun* 1. A machine for converting the power of a turning wheel into electricity; a generator. 2. A forceful person who works very hard.

dy·nas·ty (**dye**-nuh-stee) *noun* 1. A series of rulers belonging to the same family. 2. A group, family, or team that succeeds for a long time.
▶ *noun, plural* **dynasties**

dys·lex·i·a (dis-**lek**-see-uh) *noun* A condition that makes it difficult to read, write, and distinguish letters properly or in the correct order. ▶ *adjective* **dyslexic** (dis-**lek**-sik)

E

each (eech)
adjective Every one of two or more people or things.
pronoun Every person or thing.
adverb Apiece; for each one.

ea·ger (**ee**-gur) *adjective* Having or showing a lot of interest and excitement. ▶ *noun* **eagerness** ▶ *adverb* **eagerly**

ea·gle (**ee**-guhl) *noun* A large bird of prey that can see very well and eats small birds and animals.

ear (eer) *noun* 1. The organ on either side of the head that we use to hear with. 2. The part of some plants on which grain or seeds grow.

ear·ache (**eer**-*ake*) *noun* A pain inside the ear.

ear·drum (**eer**-*druhm*) *noun* A thin piece of skin inside the ear that vibrates when sound hits it, which makes us able to hear.

ear·ly (**ur**-lee)
adverb At or near the beginning.
adjective 1. Before the usual time.
2. Near the beginning of a period of time.
▶ *adjective* **earlier, earliest**

ear·mark (**eer**-*mahrk*)
verb To decide that money will be used for a particular purpose.
noun 1. A quality that is typical of something and that helps you to identify it. 2. An amount of money that has been set aside for a purpose.
▶ *verb* **earmarking, earmarked**

ear·muffs (**eer**-*muhfs*) *noun, plural* Thick pads attached to a band, which cover the ears to keep them warm in cold weather.

earn (urn) *verb* 1. To get money by doing work. 2. To get something that you deserve.
Earn sounds like **urn**. ▶ *verb* **earning, earned** ▶ *noun* **earner**

ear·nest (**ur**-nist) *adjective* Honest and serious. ▶ *adverb* **earnestly**

earn·ings (**ur**-ningz) *noun, plural* Money that is paid for work.

ear·phone (**eer**-*fohn*) *noun* Either of a pair of small speakers that are worn on or in the ears.

ear·ring (**eer**-ing) *noun* A piece of jewelry worn on or through the ear.

earth (urth) *noun* 1. The planet that we live on. The earth is the third planet from the sun, between Venus and Mars. The name of the planet is sometimes capitalized. 2. Soil.
3. The ground. 4. **down to earth** Realistic, practical, and easy to deal with.
▶ *adjective* **earthly**

earth·en (**ur**-thuhn) *adjective* Made of earth.

earth·quake (**urth**-kwayk) *noun* A sudden, violent shaking of the earth that may damage buildings and cause injuries.

earth·worm (**urth**-*wurm*) *noun* A worm that lives in the ground and eats the nutrients in soil.

ease (eez)
noun **1.** Freedom from hard work, pain, or discomfort. **2.** A state of feeling relaxed.
verb **1.** To make something less difficult. **2.** To lessen. **3.** To move something slowly and carefully into a tight space.
▶ *verb* **easing, eased**

ea·sel (**ee**-zuhl) *noun* A folding stand with a small shelf that can hold something up, such as a painting or sign.

eas·i·ly (**ee**-zuh-lee) *adverb* If something is easy to do, you can do it **easily.**

east (eest)
noun **1.** One of the four main points of the compass. **2. East** Any area or region lying in this direction. **3. the East** In the United States, the states lying along the Atlantic coast. **4. the East** A name sometimes used to mean the countries of Asia, such as Japan, China, and Korea.
adjective Having to do with or existing in the east.
adverb To or toward the east.
▶ *adjective* **eastern** ▶ *adjective* **Eastern**

Eas·ter (**ee**-stur) *noun* The holiday on which Christians celebrate that Jesus rose from the dead, according to Christian belief.

Eas·ter egg (**ee**-stur *eg*) *noun* A hard-boiled egg that is colored or decorated, or a candy egg that looks like this.

East·ern Hem·i·sphere (**ee**-sturn **hem**-i-*sfeer*) *noun* The half of the world east of the Atlantic Ocean. It includes Europe, Africa, Asia, and Australia, and surrounding waters.

East·ern Or·tho·dox (**ee**-sturn or-thuh-*dahks*) *adjective* Belonging to or having to do with a group of churches that goes back to the beginning of Christianity.

east·ward (**eest**-wurd) *adverb* To or toward the east. ▶ *adjective* **eastward**

eas·y (**ee**-zee) *adjective* **1.** Not requiring much effort, ability, or training. **2.** Not stressful or difficult. **3.** Not strict or

hard to please.
▶ *adjective* **easier, easiest** ▶ *noun* **easiness**

eat (eet) *verb* **1.** To put food in your mouth, then chew and swallow it. **2.** To have a meal. **3. eat away** To destroy slowly. **4. eat up** To use all of something.
▶ *verb* **eating, ate** (ayt), **eaten** (**ee**-tin)

eaves (eevz) *noun, plural* The edges of a roof that hang over the side of a building.

eaves·drop (**eevz**-*drahp*) *verb* To listen to a conversation secretly. ▶ *verb* **eavesdropping, eavesdropped** ▶ *noun* **eavesdropper**

ebb (eb)
verb **1.** When the tide **ebbs,** it goes down and back out to sea. **2.** To fade or to get weaker.
noun **1.** The flowing out of the tide. **2.** A low point.
▶ *verb* **ebbing, ebbed**

eb·on·y (**eb**-uh-nee)
noun **1.** A very hard, black wood, or the African tree that it comes from. **2.** A deep black color.
adjective Being deep black in color.

e-book (**ee**-*buk*) *noun* An electronic book that can be read on a computer or on a special device.

ec·cen·tric (ek-**sen**-trik)
adjective Unusual or strange, but in a harmless or amusing way.
noun Someone with strange or unusual habits.
▶ *adverb* **eccentrically**

e·chi·no·derm (i-**kye**-nuh-*durm*) *noun* A sea creature that has five similar body parts and rough or pointy skin, such as a starfish or sea urchin.

ech·o (**ek**-oh)
verb **1.** When a sound **echoes,** it repeats because sound waves bounce back from a hard surface. **2.** When you **echo** what another person says, you repeat what he or she said, sometimes to show that you agree.
noun A reflected sound.
▶ *verb* **echoes, echoing, echoed** ▶ *noun, plural* **echoes**

e·clec·tic (i-**klek**-tik) *adjective* Having or showing a wide variety.

e·clipse (i-**klips**)
noun **1. eclipse of the moon** A time when the earth comes between the sun and the moon so that all or part of the moon's light is blocked. **2. eclipse of the sun** A time when the moon comes between the sun and the earth so that all or part of the sun's light is blocked.
verb **1.** To make something invisible by coming between it and a viewer. **2.** To become better, more well-known, or more important than someone else.
▶ *verb* **eclipsing, eclipsed**

e·co-friend·ly (**ee**-kou-*frend*-lee or **ek**-oh-*frend*-lee) *adjective* Not harmful to the environment; nonpolluting.

e·col·o·gy (i-**kah**-luh-jee) *noun* **1.** The scientific study of the relationships between living things and their environment. **2.** The study of how human activity affects the earth. This is also known as *human ecology.*
▶ *noun* **ecologist** ▶ *adjective* **ecological** (ee-kuh-**lah**-ji-kuhl) ▶ *adverb* **ecologically**

e·com·merce (**ee**-*kah*-murs) *noun* The activity of buying and selling on the Internet.

e·co·nom·ic (ee-kuh-**nah**-mik or ek-uh-**nah**-mik) *adjective* Of or having to do with economics or the economy.

e·co·nom·i·cal (ee-kuh-**nah**-mi-kuhl or ek-uh-**nah**-mi-kuhl) *adjective* Not wasteful or expensive. ▶ *adverb* **economically**

e·co·nom·ics (ee-kuh-**nah**-miks or ek-uh-**nah**-miks) *noun* The study of the way that money, resources, and services are used in a society.

e·con·o·mist (i-**kah**-nuh-mist) *noun* A person who is trained in economics.

e·con·o·mize (i-**kah**-nuh-*mize*) *verb* To cut down on spending in order to save money. ▶ *verb* **economizing, economized**

e·con·o·my (i-**kah**-nuh-mee) *noun* **1.** The system of buying, selling, making things, and managing money in a place. **2.** The careful use of money and other things to cut down on waste.
▶ *noun, plural* **economies**

e·co·sys·tem (ee-koh-*sis*-tuhm or ek-oh-*sis*-tuhm) *noun* All the living things in a place and their relation to their environment.

ec·sta·sy (**ek**-stuh-see) *noun* A feeling of great joy. ▶ *noun, plural* **ecstasies**

ec·stat·ic (ek-**stat**-ik) *adjective* Feeling or expressing extreme joy. ▶ *adverb* **ecstatically**

Ec·ua·dor (**ek**-wuh-*dor*) A country in the northwestern part of South America on the Pacific Ocean. Ecuador is named after the equator, which runs right through it, and it includes the Galápagos Islands. Located about 600 miles west of the mainland, the Galápagos have giant tortoises and hundreds of other species unique to the islands.

ec·ze·ma (**ek**-suh-muh or eg-**zee**-muh) *noun* A medical condition that makes the skin dry, rough, and itchy.

ed·dy (**ed**-ee)
noun A current in water or air that makes it move in a circle.
verb To swirl around.
▶ *noun, plural* **eddies** ▶ *verb* **eddies, eddying, eddied** ▶ *adjective* **eddying**

edge (ej)
noun **1.** The part of an object or area that is farthest from the center. **2.** The sharp side of a cutting tool. **3.** An advantage.
verb To move very carefully and slowly.
idiom If you are **on edge,** you feel anxious.
▶ *verb* **edging, edged** ▶ *adjective* **edgy**

edge·wise (**ej**-*wize*) *adverb* **1.** With the edge first. **2.** If you cannot **get a word in edgewise** in a discussion, you do not get a chance to speak because others are talking a lot.

ed·i·ble (**ed**-uh-buhl) *adjective* Able to be eaten.

ed·it (**ed**-it) *verb* **1.** To correct a piece of writing and shorten it if it is too long. **2.** To prepare video or film for viewing.
▶ *verb* **editing, edited**

E

e·di·tion (i-**dish**-uhn) *noun* **1.** The form or version of a book or newspaper that is printed at a particular time. **2.** The number of copies of a newspaper, book, or magazine that are printed at the same time.

ed·i·tor (**ed**-i-tur) *noun* **1.** Someone whose job is to edit writing before it is published, and sometimes to choose which books will be published. **2.** The person who is in charge of a newspaper or a magazine. **3.** A computer program for editing documents. *See* **text editor.**

ed·i·to·ri·al (ed-i-**tor**-ee-uhl) *adjective* Of or having to do with putting together a publication.
noun An article that gives the opinion of the writer or of a newspaper, rather than just reporting facts in the news.

ed·u·cate (**ej**-uh-kate) *verb* **1.** To give someone knowledge or a skill through teaching. **2.** To arrange for someone's education.
▶ *verb* **educating, educated** ▶ *noun* **educator**

ed·u·cat·ed (**ej**-uh-kay-tid) *adjective* Having finished a course of education, especially high school or college education.

ed·u·ca·tion (ej-uh-**kay**-shuhn) *noun* **1.** The process of teaching and learning. **2.** The knowledge, skills, and abilities that you learn from school, college, or some other experience.

ed·u·ca·tion·al (ej-uh-**kay**-shuh-nuhl) *adjective* **1.** Of or having to do with education. **2.** Providing an education.

eel (eel) *noun* A long, slippery, snakelike fish.

ee·rie (**eer**-ee) *adjective* Strange and spooky. ▶ *adjective* **eerier, eeriest**
▶ *adverb* **eerily**

ef·fect (i-**fekt**)
noun **1.** Something that happens because of something else; a result. **2.** Influence or power to make something happen. **3.** When something **goes into effect,** it starts to happen.
verb To cause or bring about.
▶ *verb* **effecting, effected**

ef·fec·tive (i-**fek**-tiv) *adjective* **1.** Having the intended effect. **2.** Skillful and able to get things done. **3.** In force.

ef·fec·tive·ly (i-**fek**-tiv-lee) *adverb* **1.** In a way that produces a good result. **2.** For all practical purposes; in effect.

ef·fec·tive·ness (i-**fek**-tiv-nis) *noun* The quality or state of being effective.

ef·fer·ves·cent (ef-ur-**ves**-uhnt) *adjective* **1.** Full of bubbles. **2.** Very lively and cheerful.
▶ *noun* **effervescence**

ef·fi·cien·cy (i-**fish**-uhn-see) *noun* **1.** The quality of working or operating well, quickly, and without waste. **2.** An **efficiency** or **efficiency apartment** is an apartment of only one room where the occupant lives, eats, and sleeps.
▶ *noun, plural* **efficiencies**

ef·fi·cient (i-**fish**-uhnt) *adjective* Working very well and not wasting time or energy. ▶ *adverb* **efficiently**

ef·flu·ent (**ef**-loo-uhnt) *noun* Waste that flows out from factories or sewers.

ef·fort (**ef**-urt) *noun* The activity of trying hard to achieve something.

ef·fort·less (**ef**-urt-lis) *adjective* Something that is **effortless** is easy to do. ▶ *adverb* **effortlessly**

e.g. (ee-**jee**) The initials of the Latin phrase *exempli gratia,* which means "for example."

egg (eg)
noun **1.** An oval or round object that contains a baby bird, reptile, fish, or insect. It is produced by the females of these species to protect their young as they develop. **2.** A chicken's egg, used as food. **3.** A cell created inside the female body that grows into a new individual if it is fertilized.
verb To urge or challenge someone to do something.
▶ *verb* **egging, egged**

egg·nog (**eg**-nahg) *noun* A sweet, thick drink made with eggs and milk, usually flavored with nutmeg.

egg·plant (**eg**-plant) *noun* A purple vegetable with white flesh and tiny seeds inside.

e·go·cen·tric (ee-goh-**sen**-trik) *adjective* Being a lot more interested in yourself

E

than you are in others. ▶ *noun*
egocentricity (ee-goh-sen-**tris**-i-tee)

e·gret (**ee**-grit) *noun* A tall white bird
with long legs that lives near water.

E·gypt (**ee**-jipt) A country that connects
North Africa to Southwest Asia via the
Sinai Peninsula. Its civilization is very
ancient, and it is home to such world-
famous monuments as the Giza
pyramids and the Great Sphinx.

ei·der (**eye**-dur) *noun* A large, northern
sea duck. The males are mainly black
and white, and the females are brown.

ei·der·down (**eye**-dur-*doun*) *noun* **1.** The
soft feathers of an eider duck. **2.** A
warm comforter filled with eiderdown.

eight (ayt)
noun The number that comes after
seven and before nine, written
numerically as 8.
adjective Referring to the number that
comes after seven and before nine.
Eight sounds like **ate.**

eight·een (**ay**-teen) *noun* The number
that comes after 17 and before 19,
written numerically as 18.

eighth (ayth)
adjective Next after seventh and before
ninth, written numerically as 8th.
noun One part of something that has
been divided into eight parts, written
numerically as 1/8.

eight·y (**ay**-tee) *noun* The number
that is equal to 8 times 10, written
numerically as 80.

ei·ther (**ee**-THur *or* **eye**-THur)
conjunction **Either** can be used to
indicate a choice.
pronoun One of two.
adjective **1.** One or the other of two.
2. Each of two.
adverb Also, or similarly.

e·ject (ee-**jekt**) *verb* **1.** To push or force
something out. **2.** To force someone
to leave. **3.** To leave the cockpit of a
fighter plane quickly, using a special
mechanism.
▶ *verb* **ejecting, ejected**

eke (eek) *verb* To barely manage to do
something. ▶ *verb* **eking, eked**

e·lab·o·rate
adjective (i-**lab**-ur-it) Complex and

detailed.
verb (i-**lab**-uh-*rate*) To give more
details about something.
▶ *verb* **elaborating,**
elaborated ▶ *adverb* **elaborately** (i-**lab**-
ur-it-lee)

e·lapse (i-**laps**) *verb* To pass, usually
used in reference to time. ▶ *verb*
elapsing, elapsed

e·las·tic (i-**las**-tik)
noun A type of rubber that returns to
its original shape after you stretch it.
adjective Able to stretch and then
return to its original shape.
▶ *noun* **elasticity** (i-las-**tis**-i-tee)

e·lat·ed (i-**lay**-tid) *adjective* Very excited
and happy. ▶ *noun* **elation**

el·bow (**el**-boh) *noun* The joint that
connects the upper arm to the lower
arm.

eld·er (**el**-dur)
adjective Older.
noun **1.** An old person, especially one
who is respected or is an authority.
2. When a father and son share the
same name and both of them are well
known, the father is often called **the**
Elder.

eld·er·ly (**el**-dur-lee) *adjective* Old. The
word *elderly* is usually considered a
polite way of saying "old."

eld·est (**el**-dist) *adjective* The oldest in
a group.

e·lect (i-**lekt**) *verb* To choose someone
by voting for him or her. ▶ *verb*
electing, elected

e·lec·tion (i-**lek**-shuhn) *noun* The act
or process of choosing someone or
deciding something by voting.

e·lec·tive (i-**lek**-tiv)
adjective **1.** If something is **elective,**
you are free to choose whether or not
to do it. For example, an elective class
is a class that you are not required to
take in order to complete your grade.
2. Decided by an election.
noun A class that you can choose to
take or not take.

e·lec·tric (i-**lek**-trik) *adjective* **1.** Supplied
by or having to do with electricity.
2. Extremely exciting and stimulating.
▶ *adjective* **electrical**

E

E

e·lec·tric eel (i-**lek**-trik **eel**) *noun* A long, snakelike fish that can give off electric shocks to protect itself and stun its prey.

e·lec·tri·cian (i-lek-**trish**-uhn) *noun* Someone who installs electrical systems and fixes electrical equipment.

e·lec·tric·i·ty (i-lek-**tris**-i-tee) *noun* 1. A form of energy caused by the motion of electrons and protons. 2. Electrical power that is generated in special large plants and distributed to all parts of a country through wires.

e·lec·tro·cute (i-**lek**-truh-*kyoot*) *verb* To injure or kill with a severe electric shock. ▶ *verb* **electrocuting, electrocuted** ▶ *noun* **electrocution**

e·lec·trode (i-**lek**-trode) *noun* A point through which an electric current can flow into or out of a device or substance.

e·lec·tro·lyte (i-**lek**-truh-*lite*) *noun* A substance that electricity can travel through.

e·lec·tro·mag·net (i-*lek*-troh-**mag**-nit) *noun* A magnet that is formed when electricity flows through a coil of wire. ▶ *adjective* **electromagnetic**

e·lec·tron (i-**lek**-trahn) *noun* A tiny particle that moves around the nucleus of an atom. Electrons carry a negative electrical charge.

e·lec·tron·ic (i-lek-**trah**-nik) *adjective* Powered or achieved by very small amounts of electricity. ▶ *adverb* **electronically**

e·lec·tron·ics (i-lek-**trah**-niks) *noun* 1. The scientific study of the behavior of electrons. 2. Electronic equipment.

el·e·gance (**el**-uh-guhns) *noun* The quality of being graceful or stylish in appearance or manner.

el·e·gant (**el**-uh-guhnt) *adjective* Graceful and pleasing to look at. ▶ *adverb* **elegantly**

el·e·gy (**el**-uh-jee) *noun* A poem or speech in memory of someone who has died. An elegy is often reflective and sad. ▶ *noun, plural* **elegies**

el·e·ment (**el**-uh-muhnt) *noun* 1. One of the simple, basic parts of something. 2. A substance that cannot be divided up into simpler substances. 3. The part of an electric heater or toaster that heats up when electricity passes through it. *noun, plural* **the elements** The weather.

el·e·men·ta·ry (*el*-uh-**ment**-ree) *adjective* Simple or basic, but still important.

el·e·men·ta·ry school (*el*-uh-**ment**-ree *skool*) *noun* A school that children attend, usually from kindergarten through fifth or sixth grade.

el·e·phant (**el**-uh-fuhnt) *noun* A large, gray animal with a long trunk and ivory tusks. Elephants are mammals and are native to Africa or Asia.

el·e·vate (**el**-uh-*vate*) *verb* 1. To raise something up. 2. To give someone a more important position. ▶ *verb* **elevating, elevated** ▶ *adjective* **elevated**

el·e·va·tion (*el*-uh-**vay**-shuhn) *noun* 1. A place that is higher than the surrounding land. 2. A move to a more important position. 3. The height above sea level.

el·e·va·tor (**el**-uh-*vay*-tur) *noun* 1. A large box that carries people or things up and down between different floors of a building. 2. A very large, hollow building used for storing crops after they are harvested.

el·ev·en (i-**lev**-uhn) *noun* The number that comes after 10 and before 12, written numerically as 11. *adjective* Referring to the number that comes after 10 and before 12.

elf (elf) *noun* A small, imaginary person with pointed ears and magical powers. Elves are usually mischievous characters in fairy tales. ▶ *noun, plural* **elves** (elvz) ▶ *adjective* **elfin** (**el**-fin)

el·i·gi·ble (**el**-i-juh-buhl) *adjective* 1. Having the right abilities or qualifications for something. 2. Suitable for someone to marry. ▶ *noun* **eligibility**

e·lim·i·nate (i-**lim**-uh-*nate*) *verb* 1. To leave out, or to get rid of. 2. To remove from a competition by a defeat.

▶ *verb* **eliminating, eliminated** ▶ *noun*
elimination

e·lite (i-**leet** *or* ay-**leet**)
noun A group of people who have more advantages and privileges than other people.
adjective Designed for very rich or important people, or made up of them.
▶ *noun* **elitism**

elk (elk) *noun* A type of large deer that lives in the Rocky Mountains and in parts of Asia. ▶ *noun, plural* **elk** *or* **elks**

el·lipse (i-**lips**) *noun* A flat oval shape. ▶ *adjective* **elliptical** (i-**lip**-ti-kuhl)

elm (elm) *noun* A tall shade tree with spreading branches, or the wood that comes from it.

El Ni·ño (el **neen**-yoh) *noun* Warm water temperatures, currents, and wind conditions in the Pacific Ocean that affect weather conditions over much of the earth.

e·lon·gate (i-**lawng**-gate) *verb* To make something longer or more stretched out. ▶ *verb* **elongating, elongated**

e·lope (i-**lope**) *verb* To run away and get married secretly. ▶ *verb* **eloping, eloped** ▶ *noun* **elopement**

el·o·quent (**el**-uh-kwuhnt) *adjective* Using language in a graceful way that persuades people. ▶ *noun* **eloquence** ▶ *adverb* **eloquently**

El Sal·va·dor (el **sal**-vuh-dor) The smallest, most densely populated country in Central America. It has more than 20 volcanoes, some of which are still active. The Santa Ana Volcano, the highest volcano in the country, last erupted in 2005, spewing rocks as large as cars.

else (els) *adverb* **1.** Another, or a different place, person, or thing. **2.** More.

else·where (**els**-wair) *adverb* Somewhere different.

e·lude (i-**lood**) *verb* To escape or get away from someone. ▶ *verb* **eluding, eluded**

e·lu·sive (i-**loo**-siv) *adjective* **1.** Very hard to find or capture. **2.** Difficult to understand.
▶ *noun* **elusiveness** ▶ *adverb* **elusively**

elves (elvz) *noun, plural* The plural of **elf.**

e·mail *or* e-mail (ee-*mayl*)
noun **1.** Electronic messages that are sent through a computer network or over the Internet. Short for *electronic mail*. **2.** A single message sent in this way.
verb To send a message by email.
adjective Sent by email.
▶ *verb* **emailing, emailed** *or* **e-mailing, e-mailed** ▶ *noun, plural* **emails** *or* **e-mails**

e·man·ci·pate (i-**man**-suh-*pate*) *verb* To free a person or group from slavery or control. ▶ *verb* **emancipating, emancipated** ▶ *noun* **emancipation**

em·balm (em-**bahm**) *verb* To treat a dead body with substances that will keep it from decaying for a long time. ▶ *verb* **embalming, embalmed**

em·bank·ment (em-**bangk**-muhnt) *noun* **1.** A high wall at the sides of a river that keeps it from flooding. **2.** A long piece of raised earth built to support railroad tracks or a road.

em·bar·go (em-**bahr**-goh) *noun* An official order that forbids something from happening.
verb To forbid that a particular thing be imported or exported.
▶ *noun, plural* **embargoes** ▶ *verb* **embargoes, embargoing, embargoed**

em·bark (em-**bahrk**) *verb* **1.** To get on a ship or an airplane that is ready to travel. **2.** To start something that is new or difficult.
▶ *verb* **embarking, embarked**

em·bar·rass (em-**bar**-uhs) *verb* To make someone feel ashamed and uncomfortable. ▶ *verb* **embarrasses, embarrassing, embarrassed** ▶ *adjective* **embarrassing** ▶ *adjective* **embarrassed**

em·bar·rass·ment (em-**bar**-uhs-muhnt) *noun* **1.** The feeling of being ashamed. **2.** Someone or something that causes people to feel ashamed.

E

em·bas·sy (**em**-buh-see) *noun* The official place in a foreign country where an ambassador works. ▶ *noun, plural* **embassies**

em·bed (em-**bed**) *verb* To **embed** something is to put it inside something else so that it cannot be easily removed. ▶ *verb* **embedding, embedded**

em·bers (**em**-burz) *noun, plural* The hot, glowing pieces of a fire after the flames are gone.

em·bez·zle (em-**bez**-uhl) *verb* To secretly steal money from the place you work for. ▶ *verb* **embezzling, embezzled** ▶ *noun* **embezzler** ▶ *noun* **embezzlement**

em·blem (**em**-bluhm) *noun* A symbol or a sign that represents something.

em·bod·y (em-**bah**-dee) *verb* To give a solid form to an idea or feeling. ▶ *verb* **embodies, embodying, embodied**

em·boss (em-**baws**) *verb* To create raised lettering or designs on a flat surface. ▶ *verb* **embosses, embossing, embossed**

em·brace (em-**brase**)
verb **1.** To hug. **2.** To start doing something eagerly, or to think of something in a very positive way. **3.** To include.
noun The act of taking someone in your arms; a hug.
▶ *verb* **embracing, embraced**

em·broi·der (em-**broi**-dur) *verb* To sew a picture or a design onto cloth, using different colors of thread or yarn. ▶ *verb* **embroidering, embroidered** ▶ *noun* **embroiderer** ▶ *noun* **embroidery**

em·bry·o (**em**-bree-oh) *noun* **1.** A baby, animal, or plant in the very early stages of development before birth. **2.** A plant in its first stage of development, contained inside a seed.

em·bry·on·ic (*em*-bree-**ah**-nik) *adjective* **1.** Made from or using embryos. **2.** Capable of developing or being developed further.

em·er·ald (**em**-ur-uhld)
noun **1.** A bright green gem. **2.** A bright green color.

adjective Being bright green in color.

e·merge (i-**murj**) *verb* **1.** To come out from a place where you are hidden. **2.** To become apparent or publicly known.
▶ *verb* **emerging, emerged** ▶ *noun* **emergence** ▶ *adjective* **emergent**

e·mer·gen·cy (i-**mur**-juhn-see) *noun* A sudden and dangerous situation that requires immediate action. ▶ *noun, plural* **emergencies**

em·i·grate (**em**-i-grate) *verb* To leave your home country to live in another country. ▶ *verb* **emigrating, emigrated** ▶ *noun* **emigrant** (**em**-i-gruhnt) ▶ *noun* **emigration**

em·i·nent (**em**-uh-nuhnt) *adjective* Well-known and highly respected. ▶ *noun* **eminence** ▶ *adverb* **eminently**

em·is·sar·y (**em**-i-ser-ee) *noun* An **emissary** is a person who is sent to do a special job as a representative for someone. ▶ *noun, plural* **emissaries**

e·mis·sion (i-**mish**-uhn)
noun The release of something, especially chemicals, into the atmosphere.
noun, plural **emissions** Substances released into the atmosphere.

e·mit (i-**mit**) *verb* To produce or send out something such as heat, light, signals, or sound. ▶ *verb* **emitting, emitted**

e·mo·ti·con (i-**moh**-ti-*kahn*) *noun* A small image of a face expressing some emotion, used in email and instant messaging to communicate a feeling or attitude.

e·mo·tion (i-**moh**-shuhn) *noun* A feeling, such as happiness, love, or anger.

e·mo·tion·al (i-**moh**-shuh-nuhl) *adjective* **1.** Of or having to do with your feelings. **2.** Showing or expressing strong feelings.
▶ *adverb* **emotionally**

em·per·or (**em**-pur-ur) *noun* The male ruler of an empire.

em·pha·sis (**em**-fuh-sis)
noun Importance given to something. ▶ *noun, plural* **emphases** (**em**-fuh-*seez*)

em·pha·size (**em**-fuh-*size*) *verb* To make something stand out or draw attention

E

to it because you think it is important or true. ▸ *verb* **emphasizing, emphasized**

em·phat·ic (em-**fat**-ik) *adjective* Forceful and strong so that people pay attention. ▸ *adverb* **emphatically**

em·pire (**em**-pire) *noun* 1. A group of countries or states that have the same ruler. 2. A country that is ruled over by an emperor or empress. 3. A large group of companies that is controlled by one person or organization.

em·ploy (em-**ploi**) *verb* 1. To pay someone to do work. 2. To use something.
▸ *verb* **employing, employed**

em·ployed (em-**ploid**) *adjective* Having a job.

em·ploy·ee (em-**ploi**-ee) *noun* A person who is paid to work for another person or business.

em·ploy·er (em-**ploy**-ur) *noun* A person or company that employs people.

em·ploy·ment (em-**ploy**-munt) *noun* 1. Work for salary or wages. 2. The number of people working in a particular area or time.

em·press (**em**-pris) *noun* The female ruler of an empire, or the wife of an emperor.

emp·ty (**emp**-tee)
adjective 1. With nothing inside. 2. Not being used or enjoyed by people. 3. Without meaning or value.
verb To take everything out of a container.
noun An empty bottle or can.
▸ *adjective* **emptier, emptiest** ▸ *verb* **empties, emptying, emptied** ▸ *noun, plural* **empties** ▸ *noun* **emptiness**

e·mu (**ee**-myoo) *noun* A large bird from Australia that does not fly but can run very fast.

e·mul·sion (i-**muhl**-shuhn) *noun* A mixture of two liquids in which the particles of one liquid mix with the other liquid but do not dissolve. This occurs, for example, when mixing oil and vinegar.

en·a·ble (en-**ay**-buhl) *verb* To allow or make it possible for someone

to do something. ▸ *verb* **enabling, enabled** ▸ *noun* **enabler**

e·nam·el (i-**nam**-uhl)
noun 1. A shiny substance made from melted glass that is used to coat and protect different materials. 2. The hard, white surface of your teeth. 3. Paint that dries to a hard, shiny surface.
verb To apply enamel to a surface.
▸ *verb* **enameling, enameled**
▸ *adjective* **enameled**

en·chant (en-**chant**) *verb* To delight or charm someone. ▸ *verb* **enchanting, enchanted**

en·chant·ed (en-**chan**-tid) *adjective* Magical, or under a magic spell.

en·chant·ing (en-**chan**-ting) *adjective* Delightful and charming. ▸ *adverb* **enchantingly**

en·chant·ment (en-**chant**-muhnt) *noun* 1. Something that causes you to feel charmed and delighted. 2. The state of being enchanted.

en·close (en-**kloze**) *verb* 1. To put a fence or a wall around something. 2. To put something in with a letter or a package that you are sending.
▸ *verb* **enclosing, enclosed** ▸ *adjective* **enclosed**

en·clo·sure (en-**kloh**-zhur) *noun* 1. An area surrounded by a barrier such as a fence or walls. 2. Something that is put in with a letter or a package.

en·com·pass (en-**kuhm**-puhs) *verb* 1. To include something. 2. To form a circle around something.
▸ *verb* **encompasses, encompassing, encompassed**

en·core (**ahng**-kor *or* **ahn**-kor)
noun A small, extra performance after an event because the audience is still clapping enthusiastically.
interjection Again, please!

en·coun·ter (en-**koun**-tur)
noun An unexpected or difficult situation or meeting.
verb To meet someone or experience something without expecting to, especially someone or something difficult.
▸ *verb* **encountering, encountered**

E

en·cour·age (en-**kur**-ij) *verb* To give someone confidence, usually by using praise and support. ▶ *verb* **encouraging, encouraged** ▶ *adjective* **encouraging** ▶ *adverb* **encouragingly**

en·cour·age·ment (en-**kur**-ij-muhnt) *noun* The act of encouraging someone, or the state of being encouraged.

en·cy·clo·pe·di·a (en-*sye*-kloh-**pee**-dee-uh) *noun* A book or set of books with very detailed information, usually arranged in alphabetical order. ▶ *adjective* **encyclopedic**

end (end)
noun **1.** The last part or final point of something. **2.** A point that is farthest from the middle of an object or place.
verb **1.** To finish. **2.** To bring about the end of something.
▶ *verb* **ending, ended**

en·dan·ger (en-**dayn**-jur) *verb* To put someone or something in a dangerous situation. ▶ *verb* **endangering, endangered** ▶ *adjective* **endangered**

en·dan·gered spe·cies (en-**dayn**-jurd **spee**-sheez) *noun* A plant or animal that is in danger of becoming extinct, usually because of human activity.

en·deav·or (en-**dev**-ur)
verb To try very hard to do something.
noun A serious attempt or effort.
▶ *verb* **endeavoring, endeavored**

end·ing (en-ding) *noun* The final part of something, especially a story, movie, or book.

end·less (**end**-lis) *adjective* Having no end or seeming to have no end. ▶ *adverb* **endlessly**

en·dor·phin (en-**dor**-fin) *noun* A substance created by the brain that reduces pain and causes pleasant feelings.

en·dorse (en-**dors**) *verb* **1.** To support or approve of someone or something. **2.** To sign your name on the reverse side of a document, especially a check.
▶ *verb* **endorsing, endorsed** ▶ *noun* **endorsement**

en·dow (en-**dou**) *verb* **1.** If you are **endowed** with a gift or a talent, you have it naturally. **2.** To give money or property.
▶ *verb* **endowing, endowed**

en·dow·ment (en-**dou**-muhnt) *noun* The money and investments that a big institution like a university owns and earns money on.
noun, plural **endowments** Attractive qualities that someone has naturally.

en·dur·ance (en-**door**-uhns) *noun* **1.** The ability to do something difficult for a long time. **2.** The quality of being able to last for a long time.

en·dure (en-**door**) *verb* **1.** To put up with something difficult or painful. **2.** To last for a long time.
▶ *verb* **enduring, endured** ▶ *adjective* **enduring**

end zone (end *zohn*) *noun* The part of a football field at each end, in front of the goal post. The end zone is ten yards deep.

en·e·my (**en**-uh-mee) *noun* **1.** Someone who hates another person and wants to hurt him or her. **2.** The country or army that your country is fighting against in a war.
▶ *noun, plural* **enemies**

en·er·get·ic (*en*-ur-**jet**-ik) *adjective* Strong, active, and full of energy. ▶ *adverb* **energetically**

en·er·gy (**en**-ur-jee) *noun* **1.** The ability or strength to do things without getting tired. **2.** Power from coal, electricity, or other sources that makes machines work and produces heat. **3.** The ability of something to do work. Energy is a concept in physics and is measured in **joules.**

en·force (en-**fors**) *verb* To make sure that a law or rule is obeyed. ▶ *verb* **enforcing, enforced** ▶ *noun* **enforcement**

en·gage (en-**gayj**) *verb* **1.** To hire someone to do a job. **2.** To attract something.
▶ *verb* **engaging, engaged**

en·gaged (en-**gayjd**) *adjective* **1.** If two people are **engaged,** they are going to get married. **2.** Busy doing something.

en·gage·ment (en-**gayj**-muhnt) *noun*
1. The period between a proposal of marriage and the wedding ceremony. 2. The act of engaging a person or group in something. 3. An appointment or date that carries responsibilities.

en·gine (**en**-jin) *noun* 1. A machine that makes something move by using gasoline, steam, or another energy source. 2. The front part of a train that pulls the cars; a locomotive.

en·gi·neer (en-juh-**neer**) *noun* Someone who is specially trained to design and build machines or large structures such as bridges and roads.
verb To plan or do something in a clever way.
▶ *verb* engineering, engineered ▶ *noun* engineering

Eng·lish (**ing**-glish) *noun* The main language spoken in the United States, Canada, Great Britain, Australia, New Zealand, and many other countries.
adjective 1. Of or having to do with the English language. 2. From England, or having to do with England.

Eng·lish Chan·nel (**ing**-glish **chan**-uhl) A small arm of the Atlantic Ocean that connects it to the North Sea. The English Channel separates the south coast of England from the north coast of France.

en·grave (en-**grave**) *verb* To cut a design or writing into a metal or other hard surface. ▶ *verb* engraving, engraved ▶ *noun* engraver ▶ *noun* engraving ▶ *adjective* engraved

en·grossed (en-**grohst**) *adjective* Giving all of your attention to something. ▶ *adjective* engrossing

en·gulf (en-**guhlf**) *verb* To cover up or completely surround someone or something. ▶ *verb* engulfing, engulfed

en·hance (en-**hans**) *verb* To make something bigger, better, or more attractive. ▶ *verb* enhancing, enhanced ▶ *noun* enhancement

e·nig·ma (i-**nig**-muh) *noun* A mystery or something that is hard to understand. ▶ *adjective* enigmatic (en-ig-**mat**-ik)

en·joy (en-**joi**) *verb* 1. To get pleasure or satisfaction from doing something. 2. To get a benefit from something. ▶ *verb* enjoying, enjoyed ▶ *noun* enjoyment ▶ *adjective* enjoyable ▶ *adverb* enjoyably

en·large (en-**lahrj**) *verb* To make bigger. ▶ *verb* enlarging, enlarged ▶ *noun* enlarger

en·large·ment (en-**lahrj**-muhnt) *noun* 1. The act of making something bigger. 2. A bigger version of something.

en·light·en (en-**lye**-tuhn) *verb* To teach or explain something to someone. ▶ *verb* enlightening, enlightened ▶ *noun* enlightenment

en·list (en-**list**) *verb* 1. To join or get someone to join the army, navy, or one of the other armed forces. 2. To get someone's help. ▶ *verb* enlisting, enlisted

e·nor·mous (i-**nor**-muhs) *adjective* Extremely big. ▶ *noun* enormousness ▶ *adverb* enormously

e·nough (i-**nuhf**) *adjective* As much as you need or is necessary.
pronoun An amount equal to as much as needed or necessary.
adverb In an amount that is as much as is necessary.

en·rage (en-**rayj**) *verb* To make someone very angry. ▶ *verb* enraging, enraged

en·rich (en-**rich**) *verb* 1. To improve something by adding good things to it. 2. To make richer. 3. To fertilize. ▶ *verb* enriches, enriching, enriched ▶ *noun* enrichment ▶ *adjective* enriching ▶ *adjective* enriched

en·roll (en-**rohl**) *verb* To register as a student or a member of something. ▶ *verb* enrolling, enrolled ▶ *noun* enrollment

en route (ahn **root**) *adverb, adjective* On the way.

en·sem·ble (ahn-**sahm**-buhl) *noun* A group of musicians, actors, or dancers who usually perform together.

E

en·sue (en-**soo**) *verb* To happen next, usually as a result of something. ▶ *verb* **ensuing, ensued** ▶ *adjective* **ensuing**

en·sure (en-**shoor**) *verb* To make sure that something happens. ▶ *verb* **ensuring, ensured**

en·tail (en-**tayl**) *verb* To involve or require something, especially something difficult or complicated. ▶ *verb* **entailing, entailed**

en·tan·gle (en-**tang**-guhl) *verb* 1. To catch or trap something, especially accidentally. 2. To involve someone in a difficult situation.
▶ *verb* **entangling, entangled** ▶ *noun* **entanglement**

en·ter (en-tur)
verb 1. To go or come into a place. 2. To sign up for a competition or a race. 3. To type information into a computer or write it in a book.
noun The large key at the far right-hand side of the middle row of a keyboard that you hit to end a line or to move to another place on your screen.
▶ *verb* **entering, entered**

en·ter·prise (en-tur-*prize*) *noun* 1. A plan that has several steps leading to a result, especially the making of money. 2. A business. 3. The activity of starting businesses and developing an economy.

en·ter·pris·ing (en-tur-*prize*-ing) *adjective* Having or showing a lot of good ideas for solving problems or making money.

en·ter·tain (en-tur-**tayn**) *verb* 1. To amuse someone in an enjoyable way. 2. To invite people to your home for a party, a visit, or a meal.
▶ *verb* **entertaining, entertained** ▶ *noun* **entertainer** ▶ *adjective* **entertaining**

en·ter·tain·ment (en-tur-**tayn**-muynt) *noun* 1. The activity or industry of making people laugh and enjoy themselves. 2. A thing that provides entertainment.

en·thrall (en-**thrawl**) *verb* To excite or charm someone. ▶ *verb* **enthralling, enthralled**

en·thu·si·asm (en-**thoo**-zee-*az*-uhm) *noun* Great eagerness or interest.

en·thu·si·as·tic (en-**thoo**-zee-**as**-tik) *adjective* Having or showing feelings of excitement and interest about something. ▶ *noun* **enthusiast** ▶ *adverb* **enthusiastically**

en·tice (en-**tise**) *verb* To persuade someone to do something. ▶ *verb* **enticing, enticed** ▶ *noun* **enticement** ▶ *adjective* **enticing**

en·tire (en-**tire**) *adjective* Whole.

en·tire·ly (en-**tire**-lee) *adverb* Completely, wholly, or fully.

en·ti·tle (en-**tye**-tuhl) *verb* 1. To give a right or a privilege to someone. 2. To give a name to a book or other work.
▶ *verb* **entitling, entitled** ▶ *noun* **entitlement**

en·trance
noun (**en**-truhns) The way into a place.
verb (en-**trans**) To fill someone with feelings of pleasure.
▶ *verb* **entrancing, entranced** ▶ *adjective* **entrancing**

en·trant (**en**-truhnt) *noun* Someone who enters a contest, competition, or race.

en·trap (en-**trap**) *verb* To trick someone, especially into doing something wrong or admitting they did something wrong. ▶ *verb* **entrapping, entrapped**

en·tre·pre·neur (ahn-truh-pruh-**noor**) *noun* Someone who starts businesses and finds new ways to make money. ▶ *adjective* **entrepreneurial** (ahn-truh-pruh-**noor**-ee-uhl)

en·trust (en-**truhst**) *verb* 1. To give someone responsibility for doing something. 2. To give something valuable or important to someone who will take care of it for you.
▶ *verb* **entrusting, entrusted**

en·try (en-tree) *noun* 1. A way into a place. 2. Something such as a picture or story that you enter in a

E

competition. **3.** A piece of information in a dictionary, diary, computer program, or other work.
▶ *noun, plural* **entries**

e·nun·ci·ate (i-**nuhn**-see-*ate*) *verb* To speak or pronounce words. ▶ *verb* **enunciating, enunciated** ▶ *noun* **enunciation**

en·vel·op (en-**vel**-uhp) *verb* To completely cover or surround something. ▶ *verb* **enveloping, enveloped**

en·ve·lope (**en**-vuh-*lope* or **ahn**-vuh-*lope*) *noun* A paper or plastic container for anything flat, like a card or folded papers.

en·vi·a·ble (**en**-vee-uh-buhl) *adjective* Making you wish that you had something; desirable.

en·vi·ous (**en**-vee-uhs) *adjective* Wishing you could have something that someone else has. ▶ *adverb* **enviously**

en·vi·ron·ment (en-**vye**-ruhn-muhnt) *noun* **1.** All the things that are part of your life and have an effect on it, such as your family and your school, the place where you live, and the events that happen to you. **2.** The natural surroundings of living things, such as the air, land, or sea. **3.** The situation or set of circumstances that affects how something happens.
▶ *noun* **environmentalist** ▶ *adjective* **environmental** ▶ *adverb* **environmentally**

en·vi·ron·men·tal·ly friend·ly (en-vye-ruhn-**men**-tuh-lee **frend**-lee) *adjective* **1.** Made of substances that do not damage or pollute the natural environment. **2.** Done in a way that does not damage or pollute the natural environment.

en·vi·sion (en-**vizh**-uhn) *verb* To imagine something for the future, especially something pleasant. ▶ *verb* **envisioning, envisioned**

en·vy (**en**-vee)
verb To wish that you could have something that someone else has, or could do something that someone else has done.

noun A strong feeling of wanting something that someone else has.
▶ *verb* **envies, envying, envied**

en·zyme (**en**-zime) *noun* A protein produced by a plant or animal that causes chemical reactions to occur inside.

e·on (**ee**-ahn) *noun* A very long period of time.

ep·ic (**ep**-ik)
noun A long story, poem, or movie about heroic adventures and great battles that happened in the past, or in some imaginary place.
adjective **1.** Ambitious or impressive. **2.** Very large.

ep·i·cen·ter (**ep**-i-sen-tur) *noun* The area directly above where an earthquake occurs. Often, the people who live at or near the epicenter are in the greatest danger during an earthquake.

ep·i·dem·ic (ep-i-**dem**-ik)
noun An infectious disease present in a large number of people at the same time.
adjective Spreading or likely to spread very quickly and dangerously.

ep·i·gram (**ep**-i-*gram*) *noun* A short, witty saying. ▶ *adjective* **epigrammatic**

ep·i·lep·sy (**ep**-uh-*lep*-see) *noun* A disease of the brain that may cause a person to have sudden blackouts or to lose control of his or her movements. ▶ *noun* **epileptic** (*ep*-uh-**lep**-tik) ▶ *adjective* **epileptic**

ep·i·logue (**ep**-i-*lawg*) *noun* A short speech or piece of writing at the end of a play, story, or poem.

ep·i·sode (**ep**-i-*sode*) *noun* **1.** One of the programs in a television series. **2.** An event in your life that is unusual or remarkable.

ep·i·taph (**ep**-i-*taf*) *noun* Something written on a person's gravestone about him or her.

e·poch (**ep**-uhk) *noun* A period of important events in history.

ep·o·nym (**ep**-uh-nim) *noun* A name for something that is based on a person's name.

E

e·qual (**ee**-kwuhl)
adjective **1.** The same as something else in size, value, or amount. **2.** The same for each member of a group.
noun A person of equal ability or position, or a thing of equal quality.
verb To do or be the same as something else in amount, score, or quantity.
▶ *verb* **equaling, equaled** ▶ *adverb* **equally**

e·qual·i·ty (i-**kwah**-li-tee) *noun* The right of everyone to be treated the same, with no one getting special advantages.

e·qua·tion (i-**kway**-zhuhn) *noun* A mathematical statement in which one set of numbers or values is equal to another. For example, 5 x 4 = 20 is an equation.

e·qua·tor (i-**kway**-tur) *noun* An imaginary line around the middle of the earth that is an equal distance from the North and South poles. ▶ *adjective* **equatorial** (ee-kwuh-**tor**-ee-uhl)

E·qua·to·ri·al Guin·ea (ee-kwuh-**tor**-ee-uhl **gin**-ee) A country in Central Africa, just south of the equator. It is the third-largest exporter of oil in sub-Saharan Africa. A former colony of Spain, it is the only country in Africa where Spanish is spoken as an official language.

e·ques·tri·an (i-**kwes**-tree-uhn)
adjective Of or having to do with horseback riding.
noun Someone who rides a horse as a hobby or to compete in events.

e·qui·lat·er·al (ee-kwuh-**lat**-ur-uhl)
adjective Having sides of equal length.

e·qui·lib·ri·um (ee-kwuh-**lib**-ree-uhm) *noun* **1.** The ability to keep from falling over. **2.** A state in which everything is balanced, in a place or in your mind.

e·qui·nox (**ee**-kwuh-*nahks*) *noun* One of the two days each year, in March and in September, when day and night last exactly the same length of time all over the world. ▶ *noun, plural* **equinoxes**

e·quip (i-**kwip**) *verb* To provide with the things that are needed. ▶ *verb* **equipping, equipped**

e·quip·ment (i-**kwip**-muhnt) *noun* The tools, machines, or products needed for a particular purpose.

eq·ui·ties (**ek**-wi-teez) *noun, plural* Shares of stock issued by publicly traded companies.

eq·ui·ty (**ek**-wi-tee) *noun* Equal treatment for everyone in a situation.

e·quiv·a·lent (i-**kwiv**-uh-luhnt)
adjective The same in amount, value, or importance.
noun A thing that is equal to or can be used in place of another thing.
▶ *noun* **equivalence**

e·ra (**er**-uh *or* **eer**-uh) *noun* A long period of time in history that has some consistent feature.

e·rad·i·cate (i-**rad**-i-kate) *verb* To get rid of something completely, especially something bad such as disease, crime, or poverty. ▶ *verb* **eradicating, eradicated** ▶ *noun* **eradication** ▶ *noun* **eradicator**

e·rase (i-**rase**) *verb* **1.** To remove writing with an eraser. **2.** To delete something stored in a computer or recorded on a tape. **3.** To get rid of completely.
▶ *verb* **erasing, erased** ▶ *noun* **erasure** (i-**ray**-shur)

e·ras·er (i-**ray**-sur) *noun* Something used for removing pencil marks from paper, or chalk marks from a surface such as a blackboard.

e·read·er (**ee**-ree-dur) *noun* An electronic device that stores and enables you to read e-books.

e·rect (i-**rekt**)
adjective Standing up straight.
verb To put up a building or other structure.
▶ *verb* **erecting, erected** ▶ *adverb* **erectly** ▶ *noun* **erection**

Er·i·tre·a (er-i-**tree**-uh) A country in the Horn of Africa on the Red Sea. It is involved in border disputes with Ethiopia, which lies to its south. Eritrea is the first country in the world to announce that it plans to make its entire coastline an environmentally protected zone.

er·mine (**ur**-min) *noun* A kind of weasel. Its brown fur turns white in

E

winter. ▶ *noun, plural* **ermines** or **ermine**

e·rode (i-**rode**) *verb* **1.** To wear away gradually by water or wind. **2.** To become weaker or less powerful. ▶ *verb* **eroding, eroded**

e·ro·sion (i-**roh**-zhuhn) *noun* The wearing away of something by water or wind.

er·rand (**er**-uhnd) *noun* A small job that involves going somewhere to take or get something.

er·rat·ic (i-**rat**-ik) *adjective* Not following a regular or normal pattern. ▶ *adverb* **erratically**

er·ror (**er**-ur) *noun* A mistake.

e·rupt (i-**ruhpt**) *verb* **1.** When a volcano **erupts,** it suddenly and violently throws out lava, hot ashes, and steam. **2.** To happen suddenly. **3.** To suddenly get very angry. ▶ *verb* **erupting, erupted** ▶ *noun* **eruption**

es·ca·la·tor (**es**-kuh-*lay*-tur) *noun* A staircase that moves up or down.

es·cape (e-**skape**)
verb **1.** To get out of a place where you have been kept against your will. **2.** To avoid something. **3.** To leak out.
noun **1.** The act of getting out of a place, especially suddenly or when there is danger. **2.** A way of escaping.
▶ *verb* **escaping, escaped**

es·cort
verb (es-**kort**) To go with or follow someone, especially for protection.
noun (**es**-kort) A group or individual who goes with someone officially.
▶ *verb* **escorting, escorted**

Es·ki·mo (**es**-kuh-*moh*) *noun* A native person of the Arctic. Eskimos live today mainly in Alaska, Canada, and Greenland. They are also called the **Inuit.** ▶ *noun, plural* **Eskimo** or **Eskimos**

e·soph·a·gus (uh-**sah**-fuh-guhs) *noun* The tube that carries food from the throat to the stomach. ▶ *noun, plural* **esophaguses** or **esophagi** (uh-**sah**-fuh-gye)

es·pe·cial·ly (e-**spesh**-uh-lee) *adverb* **1.** More so; particularly. **2.** To a great degree; very or very much.

es·pi·o·nage (**es**-pee-uh-*nahzh*) *noun* The act of spying, or the work of a spy for a government or organization.

es·say (**es**-ay) *noun* A short piece of writing on a particular subject.

es·sence (**es**-uhns) *noun* **1.** The most important quality of something that makes it what it is. **2.** A substance, usually from a plant, used to make perfume.

es·sen·tial (uh-**sen**-shuhl)
adjective Necessary or very important.
noun Something that you consider necessary and that you cannot do without.

es·sen·tial·ly (uh-**sen**-shuh-lee) *adverb* In all important respects; in every way that matters.

es·tab·lish (e-**stab**-lish) *verb* **1.** To start up something that will last for some time. **2.** To determine that something is true or correct. ▶ *verb* **establishes, establishing, established**

es·tab·lish·ment (e-**stab**-lish-muhnt) *noun* **1.** The process or act of establishing something. **2.** A business or store.

es·tate (e-**state**) *noun* **1.** A large area of land, usually with a house on it. **2.** All the money, property, and other things that someone leaves behind when he or she dies.

es·teem (e-**steem**)
noun A feeling of respect and admiration for someone.
verb To have a feeling of respect and admiration for.
▶ *verb* **esteeming, esteemed** ▶ *adjective* **esteemed**

es·ti·mate
noun (**es**-tuh-mit) A rough guess or calculation about an amount, distance, cost, or other quantity.
verb (**es**-tuh-*mate*) To calculate something such as a value, amount, or distance in a way that is not exact.
▶ *verb* **estimating, estimated** ▶ *noun* **estimator** (**es**-tuh-*may*-tur) ▶ *noun* **estimation** (*es*-tuh-**may**-shuhn)

E

es·ti·mat·ed (**es**-tuh-*may*-tid) *adjective*
Guessed at, usually because exact
measurement or calculation is not
possible.

Es·to·ni·a (e-**stoh**-nee-uh) A country
in northern Europe on the Baltic
Sea. Estonia has the world's highest
number of craters caused by
meteorite hits, per unit of land area.
Occupied by the Soviet Union in 1940,
it regained its freedom in 1991 when
the Soviet Union collapsed.

es·tu·ar·y (**es**-choo-er-ee) *noun* The
wide part of a river, where it joins the
ocean. ▶ *noun, plural* **estuaries**

etc. (*et* **set**-ur-uh) An abbreviation of the
Latin phrase *et cetera*, which means
"and the rest." *Etc.* is used at the end
of a list to mean that other, similar
items could be added.

etch (ech) *verb* To cut a design on
metal or glass, using a sharp object
or acid. ▶ *verb* **etches, etching,
etched** ▶ *adjective* **etched**

etching (**ech**-ing) *noun* A picture or
print that is made from an etched
plate.

e·ter·nal (i-**tur**-nuhl) *adjective* Lasting
or staying the same forever. ▶ *adverb*
eternally

e·ter·ni·ty (i-**tur**-ni-tee) *noun* **1.** All of
time, without beginning or end. **2.** A
seemingly endless amount of time.
▶ *noun, plural* **eternities**

e·ther (**ee**-thur) *noun* A clear liquid with
a strong smell. Ether was once used
to put a person to sleep before an
operation.

eth·i·cal (**eth**-i-kuhl) *adjective* Something
that is **ethical** is good and honest.

E·thi·o·pi·a (*ee*-thee-**oh**-pee-uh)
A country in the Horn of Africa.
Ethiopia has more than 2,000 years
of recorded history, making it Africa's
oldest state. It is also one of the
oldest Christian nations in the world.
For most of its history, it has been an
independent monarchy.

eth·nic (**eth**-nik) *adjective* Of or having
to do with a group of people sharing
the same national origins, language,
or culture. ▶ *adverb* **ethnically**

eth·nic cleans·ing (**eth**-nik **klen**-
zing) *noun* The killing or removal
of a particular ethnic group by a
government or by another ethnic
group.

et·i·quette (**et**-i-kit) *noun* Rules of
polite behavior that most people in a
society are aware of.

E·trus·can (i-**truhs**-kuhn) *adjective*
Of or having to do with an ancient
civilization in an area that later
became part of Italy.

et·y·mol·o·gy (*et*-uh-**mah**-luh-jee) *noun*
The history of a word, including its
earlier forms and meanings. ▶ *noun,
plural* **etymologies**

EU (**ee yoo**) *noun* Short for the
European Union.

eu·ca·lyp·tus (*yoo*-kuh-**lip**-tuhs) *noun*
An evergreen tree originally from
Australia that is now grown in many
places. ▶ *noun, plural* **eucalyptuses**
or **eucalypti** (*yoo*-kuh-**lip**-tye)

Eu·phra·tes (yoo-**fray**-teez) The
longest river of Southwest Asia.
The Euphrates originates in the
mountains of Turkey and flows
through Syria and Iraq, meeting with
the Tigris and then emptying into the
Persian Gulf.

Eur·a·sia (yoor-**ay**-zhuh) A landmass
consisting of the continents of
Europe and Asia, covering about 10
percent of the earth's total surface.
Eurasia is located in the Eastern
and Northern Hemispheres and is
inhabited by over 70 percent of the
total population of the earth.

eu·ro (**yoor**-oh) *noun* The main unit of
money in many of the countries in
the European Union.

Eu·rope (**yoor**-uhp) The continent
located on the far western edge of
the Eurasian landmass. Europe is
surrounded by the Arctic Ocean to
the north, the Mediterranean Sea to
the south, and the Atlantic Ocean to
the west. It is separated from Asia
on its western boundary by water,
including the Ural River and Caspian
Sea, and mountains, especially the
Ural Mountains.

E

Eu·ro·pe·an (yoor-uh-**pee**-uhn) *adjective* From Europe or having to do with Europe.
noun Someone who was born in Europe or whose parents come from there.

Eu·ro·pe·an Un·ion (**yoor**-uh-*pee*-uhn **yoon**-yuhn) *noun* A group of 27 European countries that have joined together to encourage economic and political cooperation. The European Union is continuing to expand. Abbreviated as *EU*.

eu·tha·na·sia (yoo-thuh-**nay**-zhuh) *noun* The ending of a life to save an animal or a person from horrible suffering. Opinions vary widely on whether euthanasia should be legal for people.

e·vac·u·ate (i-**vak**-yoo-*ate*) *verb* To move away from an area or building because it is dangerous there. ▶ *verb* **evacuating, evacuated** ▶ *noun* **evacuation**

e·vade (i-**vade**) *verb* 1. To avoid someone or something unpleasant. 2. To avoid answering or giving information.
▶ *verb* **evading, evaded**

e·val·u·ate (i-**val**-yoo-*ate*) *verb* To decide the value of something by thinking carefully about it. ▶ *verb* **evaluating, evaluated** ▶ *noun* **evaluator**

e·val·u·a·tion (i-*val*-yoo-**ay**-shuhn) *noun* The process of forming an idea of the value or qualities of something.

e·van·gel·i·cal (ee-van-**jel**-i-kuhl) *adjective* An **evangelical** Christian is very enthusiastic about his or her religious beliefs and wants others to be as well. ▶ *noun* **evangelism** (ee-**van**-juh-*liz*-uhm) ▶ *noun* **evangelist** (ee-**van**-juh-list)

e·vap·o·rate (i-**vap**-uh-*rate*) *verb* 1. To change into a vapor or gas. 2. To become less and then disappear completely.
▶ *verb* **evaporating, evaporated** ▶ *noun* **evaporation**

e·va·sion (i-**vay**-zhuhn) *noun* 1. The activity of avoiding something unpleasant. 2. Something that you do or say as a way of avoiding what you should do or say.

e·va·sive (i-**vay**-siv) *adjective* Intending or intended to avoid something unpleasant.

eve (eev) *noun* The evening or day before an important or special day.

e·ven (**ee**-vuhn) *adjective* 1. Staying about the same. 2. An **even** number can be divided evenly by two. 3. Equal in amount, size, score, or other quantity. 4. Flat and level.
verb To make something smooth, level, or equal.
adverb 1. Surprisingly or unexpectedly. 2. **even if** Whether or not.
▶ *verb* **evening** (**ee**-vuh-ning) **evened** ▶ *adverb* **evenly**

eve·ning (**eev**-ning) *noun* The time of day between late afternoon and night.

e·vent (i-**vent**) *noun* 1. Something that happens, especially something that is planned, interesting, or important. 2. A contest in a sports competition.
▶ *adjective* **eventful**

e·ven·tu·al (i-**ven**-choo-uhl) *adjective* Final, or happening at the end.

e·ven·tu·al·ly (i-**ven**-choo-uh-lee) *adverb* 1. Finally or after a long time. 2. At some indefinite time in the future.

ev·er (**ev**-ur) *adverb* 1. At any time. 2. All the time or continually. 3. **Ever** is sometimes used to give emphasis.

ev·er·glade (**ev**-ur-*glade*) *noun* An area of swampy land with tall grasses and many swamps.

ev·er·green (**ev**-ur-*green*)
noun A bush or tree that has green leaves throughout the year.
adjective Being a bush or tree that has green leaves all year long.

ev·er·last·ing (*ev*-ur-**las**-ting) *adjective* Lasting forever or for a very long time.

eve·ry (**ev**-ree) *adjective* Each of the people or things in a group or all the parts of something.

eve·ry·bod·y (**ev**-ree-*buhd*-ee *or* ev-ree-*bah*-dee) *pronoun* Each and every person.

eve·ry·day (**ev**-ree-*day*) *adjective* 1. Happening every day. 2. All right for ordinary, daily use.

E

eve·ry·one (**ev**-ree-*wuhn*) *pronoun* Every person; everybody.

eve·ry·place (**ev**-ree-*plase*) *adverb* (informal) Another word for **everywhere**.

eve·ry·thing (**ev**-ree-*thing*) *pronoun* **1.** Each and every thing. **2.** (informal) Other things that are related or similar to something you have mentioned. **3.** A very important thing.

eve·ry·where (**ev**-ree-*wair*) *adverb* In all places.

e·vict (i-**vikt**) *verb* To force someone to move out of a place. ▶ *verb* **evicting, evicted** ▶ *noun* **eviction**

ev·i·dence (**ev**-i-duhns) *noun* Information and facts that help prove something is true or not true.

ev·i·dent (**ev**-i-duhnt) *adjective* Easy to see or understand; obvious.

ev·i·dent·ly (**ev**-i-duhnt-lee) *adverb* In a way that is clear and obvious, especially if it was not clear before.

e·vil (**ee**-vuhl)
adjective Cruel and immoral.
noun Bad or wicked qualities or events.

ev·o·lu·tion (ev-uh-**loo**-shuhn) *noun* **1.** The gradual change of living things that takes place very slowly from generation to generation. **2.** Gradual change or development into another form.
▶ *adjective* **evolutionary**

e·volve (i-**vahlv**) *verb* **1.** To change slowly and naturally over time. **2.** To develop and change as a result of many small steps.
▶ *verb* **evolving, evolved**

ewe (yoo) *noun* A female sheep. **Ewe** sounds like **you** and **yew**.

ex (eks) *noun* A person who used to have a particular position, especially a former husband or wife. ▶ *noun, plural* **exes**

ex·act (ig-**zakt**) *adjective* **1.** Correct, complete, and accurate. **2.** **Exact** is sometimes used for emphasis.
▶ *noun* **exactness**

ex·act·ly (ig-**zakt**-lee) *adverb* Accurately in every detail; precisely.

ex·ag·ger·ate (ig-**zaj**-uh-*rate*) *verb* To make something seem bigger, better, more important, or more extreme than it really is. ▶ *verb* **exaggerating, exaggerated** ▶ *adjective* **exaggerated**

ex·ag·ger·a·tion (ig-*zaj*-uh-**ray**-shuhn) *noun* The act of exaggerating something, or a statement that does this.

ex·am (ig-**zam**) *noun* An official test of your knowledge of a subject. Exam is short for **examination.**

ex·am·i·na·tion (ig-*zam*-uh-**nay**-shuhn) *noun* **1.** An official test of your knowledge of a subject. Often shortened to **exam. 2.** A careful check or study of something in order to learn more about it or to determine something.

ex·am·ine (ig-**zam**-in) *verb* **1.** To look carefully at something in order to learn about it. **2.** To check a person's body to discover if anything is not normal.
▶ *verb* **examining, examined** ▶ *noun* **examiner**

ex·am·ple (ig-**zam**-puhl) *noun* **1.** Someone or something that shows what a whole group is like. **2.** A way of behaving that others should copy. **3.** A question or a problem, given with its answer. **4.** You use **for example** to help explain what you are saying or to show that it is true. **5.** If you **make an example** of someone, you punish him or her as a way to warn others not to do the same thing.

ex·as·per·ate (ig-**zas**-puh-*rate*) *verb* To make someone very annoyed. ▶ *verb* **exasperating, exasperated** ▶ *noun* **exasperation** ▶ *adjective* **exasperating** ▶ *adjective* **exasperated**

ex·ca·vate (**ek**-skuh-*vate*) *verb* To dig a large hole in the earth to search for something buried, as in archaeological research, or to prepare the ground for the construction of a building. ▶ *verb* **excavating, excavated** ▶ *noun* **excavation** ▶ *noun* **excavator**

E

ex·ceed (ik-**seed**) *verb* 1. To be bigger or better than something else. 2. To do or be more than is allowed or expected.
▶ *verb* **exceeding, exceeded**

ex·cel (ik-**sel**) *verb* To do something extremely well. ▶ *verb* **excelling, excelled**

ex·cel·lence (**ek**-suh-luhns) *noun* The quality or state of being extremely good or superior.

ex·cel·lent (**ek**-suh-luhnt) *adjective* Very good. ▶ *adverb* **excellently**

ex·cept (ik-**sept**)
preposition Apart from; not including. *Everyone except Jamie stayed at the hotel.*
conjunction However, but for the fact that.

ex·cep·tion (ik-**sep**-shuhn) *noun*
1. Something that is different or not included. 2. If you **make an exception,** you do not include something or you do something in a different way than usual.

ex·cep·tion·al (ik-**sep**-shuh-nuhl) *adjective* 1. Unusual or rare. 2. Very good.

ex·cerpt
noun (**ek**-surpt) A short piece taken from a longer piece of writing, music, or film.
verb (ik-**surpt**) To take a short section of a longer piece of writing, music, or film.
▶ *verb* **excerpting, excerpted**

ex·cess (**ek**-ses *or* ik-**ses**)
noun 1. A larger amount than is needed or wanted. 2. **in excess of** More than an amount. 3. If you do something **to excess,** you do it too much.
adjective Extra; more than is needed or wanted.
▶ *noun, plural* **excesses**

ex·ces·sive (ik-**ses**-iv) *adjective* More than necessary. ▶ *adverb* **excessively**

ex·change (eks-**chaynj**)
verb To give one thing and receive a similar thing back.
noun 1. The act or process of giving and taking. 2. A place where people meet to buy and sell such things as stocks or merchandise. 3. **exchange rate** A comparison of the worth of money in different countries. You use the exchange rate to calculate how much money you will get when you exchange one country's money for another.
▶ *verb* **exchanging, exchanged**

ex·cite (ik-**site**) *verb* To make someone feel eager and interested. ▶ *verb* **exciting, excited**

ex·cit·ed (ik-**sye**-tid) *adjective* Eagerly interested and stimulated.

ex·cite·ment (ik-**site**-muhnt) *noun* A state or condition of being excited.

ex·cit·ing (ik-**sye**-ting) *adjective* Causing eager enthusiasm and interest about something.

ex·claim (ik-**sklaym**) *verb* To say something suddenly or with force, especially because you are surprised or excited. ▶ *verb* **exclaiming, exclaimed** ▶ *noun* **exclamation** (ek-skluh-**may**-shuhn)

ex·cla·ma·tion point (eks-kluh-**may**-shuhn *point*) *noun* The punctuation mark (!) used after a sentence or word to show surprise, excitement, or another strong feeling. It is also known as an *exclamation mark.*

ex·clude (ik-**sklood**) *verb* 1. To keep someone from joining or taking part in something. 2. To leave out or not consider something.
▶ *verb* **excluding, excluded** ▶ *noun* **exclusion** ▶ *preposition* **excluding**

ex·clu·sive (ik-**skloo**-siv)
adjective 1. Available or offered only to one person, or to a special group. 2. Complete or whole.
noun A story that appears in one place only.

ex·clu·sive·ly (ik-**skloo**-siv-lee) *adverb* Only; in a way that excludes all others.

ex·crete (ik-**skreet**) *verb* To get rid of waste matter or other substances from the body. ▶ *verb* **excreting, excreted** ▶ *noun* **excretion** ▶ *adjective* **excretory** (ek-**skruh**-tor-ee)

ex·cru·ci·a·ting (ik-**skroo**-shee-ay-ting) *adjective* Very painful. ▶ *adverb* **excruciatingly**

ex·cur·sion (ik-**skur**-zhuhn) *noun* **1.** A short trip for pleasure, often to an interesting place. **2.** An **excursion fare**, on a plane, train, or other form of passenger transportation, is cheaper than the standard fare.

ex·cuse
noun (ik-**skyoos**) **1.** A reason you give to explain a mistake or why you have done something wrong. **2.** A false reason someone gives for not doing something.
verb (ik-**skyooz**) **1.** To allow someone not to do something. **2.** To forgive someone who has done something wrong or offensive.
▶ *verb* **excusing, excused** ▶ *adjective* **excusable** (ik-**skyoo**-zuh-buhl)

ex·e·cute (**ek**-suh-*kyoot*) *verb* **1.** To do something that you have planned. **2.** To kill someone to punish him or her for a crime.
▶ *verb* **executing, executed**

ex·e·cu·tion (*ek*-suh-**kyoo**-shuhn) *noun* **1.** The way that something is carried out, done, or performed. **2.** The killing of a person who has been condemned to death, usually for a crime.

ex·ec·u·tive (ig-**zek**-yuh-tiv)
noun Someone who has one of the highest jobs in a company or organization.
adjective **1.** Of or having to do with the branch of government that carries out the laws of the United States or any state. **2.** Performed by or at the level of an executive.

ex·empt (ig-**zempt**)
adjective Excused from having to do something that others have to do.
verb To officially excuse someone, or leave something out of a rule or law.
▶ *verb* **exempting, exempted** ▶ *noun* **exemption**

ex·er·cise (**ek**-sur-*size*)
noun **1.** Physical activity that you do to stay strong and healthy. **2.** Something that you do in order to practice a skill.
verb **1.** To do physical activities, such as sports, in order to stay strong and healthy. **2.** To put something, such as

a skill or right, into practice.
▶ *verb* **exercising, exercised**

ex·ert (ig-**zurt**) *verb* **1.** To make an effort to do something. **2.** To use power or control to make something happen.
▶ *verb* **exerting, exerted** ▶ *noun* **exertion**

ex·hale (eks-**hale**) *verb* To breathe out of your mouth or nose. ▶ *verb* **exhaling, exhaled** ▶ *noun* **exhalation**

ex·haust (ig-**zawst**)
verb **1.** To make someone feel very tired. **2.** To use up all of something.
noun **1.** The gases or steam produced by the engine of a motor vehicle. **2.** The pipe on a motor vehicle that releases waste gases.
▶ *verb* **exhausting, exhausted** ▶ *adjective* **exhausting** ▶ *adjective* **exhausted**

ex·haus·tion (ig-**zaws**-chuhn) *noun* The state of being extremely tired and unable to continue.

ex·hib·it (ig-**zib**-it)
verb To show a thing or a group of things to the public.
noun A public showing or display; exhibition.
▶ *verb* **exhibiting, exhibited** ▶ *noun* **exhibitor**

ex·hi·bi·tion (*ek*-suh-**bish**-uhn) *noun* A public display of things that interest people.

ex·hil·a·rat·ing (ig-**zil**-uh-*ray*-ting) *adjective* Very exciting and enjoyable. ▶ *noun* **exhilaration** ▶ *verb* **exhilarate**

ex·ile (**eg**-zile or **ek**-sile)
verb To send someone away from his or her own country, usually for political reasons.
noun **1.** A person who has been sent away from his or her country. **2.** A situation in which you are forbidden to live in your own country.
▶ *verb* **exiling, exiled**

ex·ist (ig-**zist**) *verb* **1.** To be real or alive. **2.** To have barely enough food to stay alive.
▶ *verb* **existing, existed**

ex·ist·ence (ig-**zis**-tuhns) *noun* **1.** The fact or state of being real or alive. **2.** Continuation of life.

ex·it (**eg**-zit *or* **ek**-sit)
verb To leave or go out of a place.
noun **1.** The way out of a place, such
as a door. **2.** The act of going away or
leaving.
▶ *verb* **exiting, exited**

ex·o·dus (**ek**-suh-duhs) *noun* A
departure of a large number of people
at one time. ▶ *noun, plural* **exoduses**

ex·o·skel·e·ton (*ek*-soh-**skel**-i-tuhn)
noun A bony structure on the outside
of an animal, such as the shell of a
lobster or a crab.

ex·ot·ic (ig-**zah**-tik) *adjective* **1.** Unusual
and fascinating. **2.** From a faraway
country.

ex·pand (ik-**spand**) *verb* To become
larger. ▶ *verb* **expanding,**
expanded ▶ *adjective* **expandable**

ex·panse (ik-**spans**) *noun* A large, open
area.

ex·pan·sion (ik-**span**-shuhn) *noun* The
act or process of expanding or being
expanded.

ex·pect (ik-**spekt**) *verb* **1.** To wait for
someone or something to arrive. **2.** To
think that something should happen.
3. If a woman is **expecting,** she is
going to have a baby.
▶ *verb* **expecting, expected**

ex·pec·ta·tion (ek-spek-**tay**-shuhn) *noun*
A strong belief that something will
happen or be true.

ex·pe·di·tion (ek-spuh-**dish**-uhn) *noun*
1. A long trip made for a specific
purpose, such as for exploration. **2.** A
short trip to do something you enjoy.

ex·pel (ik-**spel**) *verb* **1.** To make
someone leave a school or
organization, usually because of
poor behavior. **2.** To send or push
something out.
▶ *verb* **expelling, expelled** ▶ *noun*
expulsion (ik-**spuhl**-shuhn)

ex·pen·di·ture (ik-**spen**-di-chur) *noun*
1. The spending or using up of time
or money for a purpose. **2.** The total
amount of money that a person,
company, or government spends.

ex·pense (ik-**spens**) *noun* Money for a
particular job or task.

ex·pen·sive (ik-**spen**-siv) *adjective*
Costing a lot of money. ▶ *adverb*
expensively

ex·pe·ri·ence (ik-**speer**-ee-uhns)
noun **1.** Something that happens to
you. **2.** The knowledge and skills that
you gain by doing a job or activity.
verb If you **experience** something, it
happens to you.
▶ *verb* **experiencing,**
experienced ▶ *adjective* **experienced**

ex·per·i·ment (ik-**sper**-uh-ment)
noun A test to try out a theory or
to see the effect of something.
verb **1.** To scientifically test or
try something in order to learn
something particular. **2.** To try
something new to find out what
it is like.
▶ *verb* **experimenting, experimented**

ex·per·i·men·tal (ik-*sper*-uh-**men**-tuhl)
adjective Not yet tested thoroughly
or proven.

ex·pert
noun (**ek**-spurt) Someone who has
a special skill or knows a lot about a
particular subject.
adjective (**ek**-spurt *or* ek-**spurt**) Of,
coming from, or having do with with
an expert.

ex·per·tise (eks-pur-**teez**) *noun* Expert
skill or knowledge about something.

ex·pire (ik-**spire**) *verb* **1.** When
something **expires,** it reaches the end
of the time when it can be legally or
properly used. **2.** To die.
▶ *verb* **expiring, expired** ▶ *noun*
expiration (ek-spuh-**ray**-shuhn)

ex·plain (ik-**splayn**) *verb* **1.** To make
something easier to understand. **2.** To
give or be a reason for something.
▶ *verb* **explaining,**
explained ▶ *adjective* **explanatory** (ik-
splan-uh-tor-ee)

ex·pla·na·tion (ek-spluh-**nay**-shuhn)
noun A statement or fact that explains
or provides the reason for something.

ex·plic·it (ik-**splis**-it) *adjective* **1.** Very
clearly stated. **2.** Containing sex,
violence, bad language, or other
material that many people do not like
to see.

E

ex·plode (ik-**splode**) verb 1. To burst into pieces with a loud noise and great force. 2. To get very loud and angry suddenly. 3. To prove an idea or opinion false.
▶ verb **exploding, exploded**

ex·ploit
noun (**ek**-sploit) A brave or exciting action.
verb (ek-**sploit**) 1. To treat someone unfairly for your own advantage. 2. To use something for your own advantage.
▶ verb **exploiting, exploited** ▶ noun **exploitation** (ek-sploi-**tay**-shuhn)

ex·plo·ra·tion (ek-spluh-**ray**-shuhn) noun The act of studying an unknown thing or place.

ex·plore (ik-**splor**) verb 1. To travel and look around in order to discover things. 2. To think carefully about something.
▶ verb **exploring, explored** ▶ adjective **exploratory** ▶ noun **explorer**

ex·plo·sion (ik-**sploh**-zhuhn) noun 1. A sudden and loud burst of energy. 2. A sudden increase in the number or amount of something.

ex·plo·sive (ik-**sploh**-siv)
noun Something that can blow up.
adjective 1. Able to cause an explosion. 2. If a situation is **explosive,** it is likely to make people angry or violent.
▶ adverb **explosively**

ex·po·nent (ik-**spoh**-nuhnt) noun A number placed next to and above another to show how many times that number is to be multiplied by itself.

ex·port
verb (ek-**sport** or **ek**-sport) 1. To send products to another country to sell them there. 2. To create a copy of a computer file in a different format so you can use it with another program.
noun (**ek**-sport) The act of selling something to another country, or a product sold this way.
▶ verb **exporting, exported** ▶ noun **exporter**

ex·pose (ik-**spoze**) verb 1. To uncover something so it can be seen. 2. To reveal a secret about someone or something. 3. To let light fall on photographic film. 4. To leave in the open, without protection. 5. To put someone in danger. 6. To let someone experience something.
▶ verb **exposing, exposed**

ex·po·sé (ek-spuh-**zay**) noun An article that investigates and exposes a serious problem.

ex·po·sure (ik-**spoh**-zhur) noun 1. The act of coming into contact with something harmful. 2. The act of coming into contact with something. 3. The harmful effect of severe weather on someone's body. 4. A piece of film that produces a photo when it is exposed to light. 5. The length of time that the shutter is open when you take a picture. 6. The orientation of a place to sunlight.

ex·press (ik-**spres**)
verb To show what you feel or think with words, writing, or actions.
noun A fast train or bus that does not stop in many places.
adjective 1. Faster than usual. 2. Specific; particular.
▶ verb **expresses, expressing, expressed** ▶ noun, plural **expresses**

ex·pres·sion (ik-**spresh**-uhn) noun 1. A phrase that has a particular meaning. 2. The look on someone's face that shows what he or she is feeling or thinking. 3. A way of showing your feelings.

ex·pres·sive (ik-**spres**-iv) adjective Full of meaning or feeling. ▶ adverb **expressively**

ex·press·way (ik-**spres**-way) noun A wide highway without traffic lights or stop signs that you can only get onto and get off of at certain places.

ex·quis·ite (ek-**skwiz**-it or **ek**-skwi-zit) adjective Very beautiful and finely done. ▶ adverb **exquisitely**

ex·tend (ik-**stend**) verb 1. To make something longer or larger. 2. To stretch out, or go as far as. 3. To offer.
▶ verb **extending, extended**

ex·ten·sion (ik-**sten**-shuhn) noun 1. The increasing of something in time or space. 2. A new part added to an existing building.

E

ex·ten·sive (ik-**sten**-siv) *adjective*
1. Covering a wide area. 2. Containing or including a lot of things.

ex·tent (ik-**stent**) *noun* How large, serious, or important something is.

ex·te·ri·or (ek-**steer**-ee-ur)
noun The outer part of something, especially a building.
adjective 1. Being on the outer part of something, as *the exterior surface* or *exterior lights.* 2. Meant for the outer part of something.

ex·ter·mi·nate (ek-**stur**-muh-*nate*) *verb* To kill large numbers of something, especially insects or animals. ▸ *verb* **exterminating, exterminated** ▸ *noun* **extermination** ▸ *noun* **exterminator**

ex·ter·nal (ek-**stur**-nuhl) *adjective* On the outside of something. ▸ *adverb* **externally**

ex·tinct (ik-**stingkt**) *adjective* 1. No longer found alive; known about only through fossils or history. 2. If a volcano is **extinct,** it does not erupt anymore. ▸ *noun* **extinction**

ex·tin·guish (ik-**sting**-gwish) *verb* 1. To make a fire stop burning. 2. To cause the end or death of something.
▸ *verb* **extinguishes, extinguishing, extinguished** ▸ *noun* **extinguisher**

ex·tra (**ek**-struh)
adjective More than the usual or normal amount.
adverb Extremely, or more than usual.
noun Something that is added to the usual or the normal.

ex·tract
verb (ek-**strakt**) To remove or pull something out.
noun (**ek**-strakt) A short piece taken from a book, speech, song, or other work.
▸ *verb* **extracting, extracted** ▸ *noun* **extraction** (ek-**strak**-shuhn)

ex·traor·di·nar·y (ek-**stror**-duh-ner-ee) *adjective* Very unusual or impressive. ▸ *adverb* **extraordinarily**

ex·tra·ter·res·tri·al (ek-struh-tuh-**res**-tree-uhl)
adjective Coming from a place beyond the earth, or beyond our solar system.
noun A being from outer space.

ex·trav·a·gant (ik-**strav**-uh-guhnt)
adjective Very wasteful of money or resources. ▸ *adverb* **extravagantly**

ex·treme (ik-**streem**)
adjective 1. Very great. 2. Farthest from the center. 3. Exciting and very dangerous.
noun Either of two opposites.

ex·treme·ly (ik-**streem**-lee) *adverb* To a high or extreme degree; very.

ex·trem·ist (ik-**stree**-mist)
noun A person who has extreme views, usually about religion or politics.
adjective Of or having to do with extremists.

ex·trem·i·ty (ik-**strem**-i-tee) *noun* 1. The extreme point or end of something.
2. **extremities** Your hands and feet.
▸ *noun, plural* **extremities**

ex·tro·vert (**ek**-struh-*vurt*)
noun Someone who enjoys being with other people and is confident and talkative.
adjective Characteristic of an extrovert.
▸ *adjective* **extroverted**

ex·u·ber·ant (ig-**zoo**-bur-uhnt) *adjective* Very cheerful and bubbly. ▸ *noun* **exuberance** ▸ *adverb* **exuberantly**

eye (eye)
noun 1. Either of the pair of organs that you use to see with. 2. The small hole on one end of a needle. 3. The calm, clear area at the center of a hurricane.
verb To look at someone or something in a close or careful way.
idiom If you **have an eye for something,** you are able to assess its value accurately.
▸ *verb* **eyeing, eyed**

eye·ball (**eye**-*bawl*)
noun The round part of the eye that is found in nearly all animals with backbones.
verb To estimate something by looking.
▸ *verb* **eyeballing, eyeballed**

eye·brow (**eye**-*brou*) *noun* The line of hair that grows at the base of your forehead, above each of your eyes.

eye·glass·es (**eye**-glas-iz) noun, plural
A pair of lenses in a frame that helps
a person see better.

eye·lash (**eye**-lash) noun One of the
short, curved hairs that grows on
the edge of an eyelid. ▶ noun, plural
eyelashes

eye·lid (**eye**-lid) noun One of the folds
of skin that covers the eye when it is
closed.

eye·sight (**eye**-site) noun The ability
to see.

eye·sore (**eye**-sor) noun Something that
is ugly and out of place.

eye·wit·ness (**eye**-wit-nis) noun
Someone who has seen something
happen and can describe it. ▶ noun,
plural **eyewitnesses**

F

fa·ble (**fay**-buhl) noun 1. A story that
teaches a lesson. Fables often have
animal characters that talk and act like
people. 2. A lie or an untrue story.

fab·ric (**fab**-rik) noun Cloth or material.

fab·u·lous (**fab**-yuh-luhs) adjective
1. Wonderful or marvelous. 2. Amazing
or hard to believe.
▶ adverb **fabulously**

fa·cade (fuh-**sahd**) noun 1. The front
of a building. 2. A person's **facade** is
the way he or she wants to be seen or
thought of.

face (fase)
noun 1. The front part of your head,
from your forehead to your chin.
2. An expression or look on the face.
3. The front, outer, or upper surface of
something.
verb 1. To look toward something. 2. To
deal with something boldly or bravely.
▶ verb **facing, faced** ▶ adjective **facial**
(**fay**-shuhl) ▶ adjective **facing**

face·book (**fase**-buk) verb To bring
attention to something by writing
about it on the social networking
site Facebook. ▶ verb **facebooking,
facebooked**

fac·et (**fas**-it) noun 1. A flat, polished
surface of a cut gem. 2. A part or side
of something.

fa·cial (**fay**-shuhl)
adjective Of or having to do with
the face.
noun A relaxing treatment that
cleanses and tones the skin of
your face.

fa·cil·i·tate (fuh-**sil**-i-tate) verb To make
something easier. ▶ verb **facilitating,
facilitated** ▶ noun **facilitator**

fa·cil·i·ty (fuh-**sil**-i-tee) noun 1. The
ability to do something easily or
skillfully. 2. A place or building for
a particular activity.
▶ noun, plural **facilities**

fac·sim·i·le (fak-**sim**-uh-lee) noun
1. A reproduction or exact copy of
something written or of a work of
art. 2. See **fax.**

fact (fakt) noun 1. A piece of
information that is known to be true.
2. **in fact** Actually or really.

fac·tion (**fak**-shuhn) noun A small
group that opposes the ideas or
aims of the larger group it belongs
to.

fac·tor (**fak**-tur) noun 1. Something
that helps produce a result. 2. A
whole number that can be divided
into a larger number without a
remainder.

fac·to·ry (**fak**-tur-ee) noun A building
where products, such as cars
or chemicals, are made in large
numbers, often using machines.
Also called a **plant.** ▶ noun, plural
factories

fac·tu·al (**fak**-choo-uhl) adjective If
something is **factual,** it is real, or
true; it contains a fact. ▶ adverb
factually

fac·ul·ty (**fak**-uhl-tee) noun 1. The
teachers and professors at a school,
college, or university, or a group of

them. **2.** One of the powers of the body or mind, such as memory, reason, sight, or speech. **3.** A unique talent or ability.
▶ *noun, plural* **faculties**

fad (fad) *noun* Something that is very popular for a short time.

fade (fade) *verb* **1.** To lose color and become paler. **2.** To lose freshness and strength. **3.** To disappear slowly or become weaker.
▶ *verb* **fading, faded**

Fahr·en·heit (**far**-uhn-*hite*) *adjective* Based on the measurement of temperature using a scale in which water boils at 212 degrees and freezes at 32 degrees.

fail (fayl)
verb **1.** If you **fail** to do something, you do not do it. **2.** If you **fail** a test, you do not pass it. **3.** If you **fail** someone, you do not do what is expected of you. **4.** To break down or stop working. **5.** To lose power or strength. **6.** To go bankrupt.
phrase **without fail** Surely, certainly, or every single time.
▶ *verb* **failing, failed**

fail·ure (**fayl**-yur) *noun* **1.** Someone or something that is not successful. **2.** Lack of favorable results. **3.** A weakening or loss of ability. **4.** The fact that you did not do something you were supposed to do.

faint (faynt)
adjective **1.** Not clear or strong. **2.** Dizzy and weak. **3.** Weak or feeble; small.
verb To suddenly lose consciousness for a short time.
adjective Weak or feeble; small.
noun The state of losing consciousness.
Faint sounds like **feint.** ▶ *adjective* **fainter, faintest** ▶ *verb* **fainting, fainted** ▶ *noun* **faintness** ▶ *adverb* **faintly**

faint·heart·ed (**faint**-*hahr*-tid) *adjective* Timid or scared; not confident.

fair (fair)
adjective **1.** Reasonable and just.

2. Fair hair or skin is light-colored. **3.** Neither good nor bad. **4. Fair** weather is clear and sunny. **5.** Having a pleasing appearance.
noun An outdoor show of farm products and animals, often with entertainment, food, and rides.
adverb By the rules.
Fair sounds like **fare.** ▶ *adjective* **fairer, fairest** ▶ *adjective, adverb* **fairer, fairest** ▶ *noun* **fairness** ▶ *adverb* **fairly**

fair·ground (**fair**-ground) *noun* A large outdoor area where fairs are held.

fair·ly (**fair**-lee) *adverb* Quite; somewhat. **2.** In a way that is reasonable and just.

fair·y (**fair**-ee) *noun* An imaginary creature with magical abilities that looks like a tiny person with wings, found in fairy tales. ▶ *noun, plural* **fairies**

fairy tale *noun* **1.** A children's story about magical beings such as fairies, giants, and witches. Some fairy tales, such as "Cinderella," are many hundreds of years old. **2.** A made-up story, usually meant to deceive.

faith (fayth) *noun* **1.** Confidence in someone or something. **2.** Belief in God, or in a system or religion. **3.** A religion.

faith·ful (**fayth**-fuhl) *adjective* **1.** Loyal and worthy of trust. **2.** True with reference to an original text, work of art, or other creation.
▶ *noun* **faithfulness** ▶ *adverb* **faithfully**

fake (fake)
verb **1.** To pretend that something is genuine. **2.** To make a copy of something and pretend that it is the real thing.
noun Someone or something that is not what it seems to be.
adjective Not genuine or real.
▶ *verb* **faking, faked** ▶ *noun* **faker**

fa·la·fel (fuh-**lah**-fuhl) *noun* A spicy mixture of ground beans or chickpeas that is shaped into a ball or a patty and fried.

F

fal·con (**fawl**-kuhn *or* **fal**-kuhn) *noun*
A bird that hunts small birds and animals, and has long wings and hooked claws.

fall (fawl)
verb **1.** To drop from a higher place to a lower place. **2.** To lessen or become lower. **3.** To become. **4.** To happen or take place. **5.** To be defeated, captured, or overthrown. **6.** If two people **fall out,** they argue and stop getting along well. **7.** If something **falls through,** it doesn't happen.
noun **1.** The season between summer and winter, when it gets colder, the sun sets earlier, and the leaves turn color and then fall from the trees. Also called **autumn. 2.** The act of falling.
▶ *verb* **falling, fell, fallen**

fall·en (**faw**-luhn) *verb* The past participle of **fall.**

fall·out (**fawl**-*out*) *noun* **1.** Radioactive dust from a nuclear explosion. **2.** The result of an action.

fal·low (**fal**-oh) *adjective* Land that is **fallow** has not been planted with crops and is being allowed to rest, so that its nutrients can be restored.

false (fawls) *adjective* **1.** Not true or correct. **2.** Not loyal. **3.** Not real.
▶ *adverb* **falsely**

false·hood (**fawls**-hud) *noun* A lie.

fal·ter (**fawl**-tur) *verb* **1.** To act or move in an unsteady way. **2.** To pause while speaking because you are unsure or confused.
▶ *verb* **faltering, faltered**

fame (fame) *noun* The condition of being well-known. ▶ *adjective* **famed**

fa·mil·iar (fuh-**mil**-yur) *adjective* **1.** Well-known, common, or easily recognized. **2.** Knowing something well. **3.** Friendly.

fam·i·ly (**fam**-uh-lee)
noun **1.** A group of people related to one another, especially parents or guardians and their children. **2.** A group of living things that are related to each other. **3. family room** A room in a house that is used for relaxing, playing, and watching television.
adjective **1.** Suitable for children and adults. **2.** Connected with a family.
▶ *noun, plural* **families**

fam·i·ly name (**fam**-uh-lee *name*) *noun* The part of your name that you share with any brothers and sisters and that is the same as one of your parents, usually your father.

fam·i·ly tree (**fam**-uh-lee **tree**) *noun* A diagram that shows how all the members of a family are related, going back many generations.

fam·ine (**fam**-in) *noun* A serious lack of food in a geographic area.

fam·ished (**fam**-isht) *adjective* Very hungry.

fa·mous (**fay**-muhs) *adjective* Very well known to many people.

fan (fan)
noun **1.** A person who is very interested in or enthusiastic about something. **2.** A wooden or cardboard object that you use to wave air onto you in order to keep cool. **3.** A machine that blows air around a room in order to cool it.
verb **1.** To move air around or toward someone or something with a fan. **2.** To make a person or group of people feel an emotion more strongly and therefore be more likely to be angry or violent.
▶ *verb* **fanning, fanned**

fa·nat·ic (fuh-**nat**-ik) *noun* Someone who is very and sometimes overly enthusiastic about a belief, a cause, or an interest. ▶ *adjective* **fanatical** ▶ *adverb* **fanatically**

fan·cy (**fan**-see)
adjective Decorated; not plain or ordinary.
noun **1.** Imagination. **2.** A great liking.
verb To imagine.
▶ *adjective* **fancier, fanciest** ▶ *verb* **fancies, fancying, fancied** ▶ *noun, plural* **fancies**

fang (fang) *noun* An animal's long, pointed tooth.

fan·ny pack (**fan**-ee *pak*) *noun* A small bag on a belt. It is worn around the waist and used to carry personal items.

F

fan·ta·size (fan-tuh-*size*) *verb* To imagine that something that is not real is happening. ▶ *verb* **fantasizing, fantasized**

fan·tas·tic (fan-tas-tik) *adjective* 1. Very strange and unbelievable. 2. Terrific or wonderful.
▶ *adverb* **fantastically**

fan·ta·sy (fan-tuh-see *or* **fan**-tuh-zee) *noun* 1. Something you imagine happening that is not realistic or likely to occur. 2. A story with magical or strange characters, places, or events.
▶ *noun, plural* **fantasies**

FAQ (fak) *noun* A file, document, or webpage that contains answers to questions people commonly ask. FAQ is short for *frequently asked questions.*

far (fahr)
adverb 1. A great distance. 2. Very much.
adjective Distant or not near.
▶ *adverb, adjective* **farther, farthest** *or* **further, furthest**

far·a·way (fahr-uh-*way*) *adjective* 1. Distant or remote. 2. Dreamy or lost in thought.

farce (fahrs) *noun* 1. A funny play in which there are many silly misunderstandings. 2. A ridiculous situation.
▶ *adjective* **farcical**

fare (fair)
noun 1. The cost of a ticket to travel on a plane, bus, or other vehicle. 2. A particular kind of available foods.
verb To get along.
Fare sounds like **fair.** ▶ *verb* **faring, fared**

Far East (fahr eest) *noun* The countries in eastern Asia, such as China, Japan, and Korea.

fare·well (fair-wel)
interjection Good-bye and good luck.
noun A statement of good wishes for a journey.
adjective Last or final.

far-fetched (fahr-fecht) *adjective* Difficult to believe; not likely.

farm (fahrm)
verb To grow crops and raise animals.
noun An area of land used for growing crops or raising animals, usually with a house and other buildings.
adjective Related to a farm or farming.
▶ *verb* **farming, farmed**

farm·er (fahr-mur) *noun* Someone who works on or owns a farm.

farm·ing (fahr-ming)
noun The activity or business of running a farm.
adjective Of or having to do with farms.

Far·si (fahr-see) *noun* Another name for **Persian.**

far·sight·ed (fahr-sye-tid) *adjective* 1. Able to see things in the distance more clearly than things that are close. 2. Able to imagine and plan for the future.

far·ther (fahr-THur)
adjective or adverb A comparative of **far.** *Further* is a more common comparative of *far* than the word *farther,* but you can use *farther* when you are talking about physical distances.
adverb At greater distance than something else.
adjective More distant or remote.

far·thest (fahr-THist) *adjective, adverb* Most distant or remote.

fas·ci·nate (fas-uh-*nate*) *verb* To attract and hold the attention of. ▶ *verb* **fascinating, fascinated** ▶ *noun* **fascination**

fas·ci·nat·ing (fas-uh-*nay*-ting) *adjective* Attractive and interesting in a way that holds all your attention.

fas·cism (fash-iz-uhm) *noun* A form of government in which a dictator and the dictator's political party have complete power over a country. ▶ *noun* **fascist**

fash·ion (fash-uhn)
noun 1. A style or a piece of clothing that is popular at a certain time. 2. A way of doing things.
verb To make or shape something.
▶ *verb* **fashioning, fashioned**

fash·ion·a·ble (fash-uh-nuh-buhl) *adjective* Liked and admired by many people at a particular time; in fashion. ▶ *adverb* **fashionably**

F

fast (fast)
adjective 1. Moving quickly; rapid.
2. If a dye or color is **fast,** it will not fade when you wash the material.
3. Ahead of the real time.
verb To stop eating all food or particular foods for a time.
adverb In a quick way.
noun A period of time when a person does not eat any food.
▶ *adjective* **faster, fastest** ▶ *adverb* **faster, fastest** ▶ *verb* **fasting, fasted**

fas·ten (**fas**-uhn) *verb* To tie, attach, or close firmly. ▶ *verb* **fastening, fastened** ▶ *noun* **fastening**

fas·ten·er (**fas**-uh-nur) *noun* An object such as a button, buckle, or clip that is used to hold something together.

fast food (**fast food**) *noun* Food such as hamburgers, fried chicken, and pizza that is prepared and served quickly by restaurants.

fast track (**fast** *trak*) *noun* A way of doing something that gets results or success faster than the usual way.

fat (fat)
adjective 1. Heavy or plump; weighing much more than normal.
2. Thick and heavy.
noun An oily substance found in the body tissues of animals and some plants. Fats are found in foods such as meat, milk, cheese, nuts, and avocados.
▶ *adjective* **fatter, fattest** ▶ *noun* **fatness** ▶ *verb* **fatten** ▶ *adjective* **fatty**

fa·tal (**fay**-tuhl) *adjective* 1. Causing or leading to death. 2. Likely to have very bad or harmful results.
▶ *adverb* **fatally**

fa·tal·i·ty (fay-**tal**-i-tee) *noun* A death that results from an accident, disaster, war, or other violent cause. ▶ *noun, plural* **fatalities**

fate (fate) *noun* 1. A force that some believe controls events and people's lives in unpredictable ways.
2. Destiny.

fate·ful (**fate**-fuhl) *adjective* Having a strong and usually bad effect on future events. ▶ *adverb* **fatefully**

fa·ther (**fah**-THur) *noun* 1. A male parent.
2. A priest.
▶ *noun* **fatherhood**

fa·ther-in-law (**fah**-THur-in-*law*) *noun* Your **father-in-law** is the father of your wife or husband. ▶ *noun, plural* **fathers-in-law**

fa·ther·ly (**fah**-THur-lee) *adjective* Of, like, or typical of a father.

Fa·ther's Day (**fah**-THurz *day*) *noun* A holiday that honors fathers, celebrated on the third Sunday in June.

fath·om (**faTH**-uhm)
noun A unit for measuring how deep the water is. One fathom equals six feet.
verb If you **can't fathom** something, you are not able to understand it.
▶ *verb* **fathoming, fathomed**

fa·tigue (fuh-**teeg**)
noun The feeling of being very tired or weary.
verb To make someone feel very tired.
▶ *verb* **fatiguing, fatigued**

fau·cet (**faw**-sit) *noun* A device with a valve used to turn the flow of a liquid on or off.

fault (fawlt)
noun 1. If something is your **fault,** you caused it to happen. 2. Something wrong that keeps another thing from working well. 3. A weakness in a person's character. 4. A large break in the earth's surface that can cause an earthquake.
verb To criticize or find problems with something or someone.
▶ *verb* **faulting, faulted**

fau·na (**faw**-nuh) *noun* The animals of a particular area or region.

fa·vor (**fay**-vur)
noun 1. Something helpful or nice that you do for someone else. 2. A small gift.
verb 1. To prefer someone or something more than others; have as a favorite.
2. To look like or be like someone from an earlier generation in your family.
idiom If you are **in favor of** something, you approve of it and think it is good.
▶ *verb* **favoring, favored**

fa·vor·a·ble (**fay**-vur-uh-buhl) *adjective*
1. Helpful. 2. Approving. 3. Pleasing.

F

fa·vor·ite (**fay**-vur-it)
noun 1. The person or thing that you like more than all the others. 2. The person, team, or animal that most people think will win a race.
adjective Referring to the person or thing that you like more than all the others.

fa·vor·it·ism (**fay**-vur-i-*tiz*-uhm) *noun* Unfair advantage shown to one person more than others.

fawn (fawn)
noun 1. A deer less than a year old. 2. A light brown color.
adjective Light brown in color.

fax (faks)
noun A copy of a document printed on a special machine, generated by an electrical signal sent on a telephone line. Fax is short for **facsimile.**
verb To send a fax.
▶ *noun, plural* **faxes** ▶ *verb* **faxes, faxing, faxed**

fear (feer)
noun The feeling you have when you are afraid that something dangerous or bad will happen.
verb 1. To be afraid of someone or something. 2. To be worried about something.
▶ *verb* **fearing, feared** ▶ *adjective* **fearful**

fear·less (**feer**-lis) *adjective* Not afraid, even when there is danger; very brave. ▶ *adverb* **fearlessly**

fear·some (**feer**-suhm) *adjective* Very scary.

fea·si·ble (**fee**-zuh-buhl) *adjective* Able to be achieved successfully. ▶ *noun* **feasibility** ▶ *adverb* **feasibly**

feast (feest)
noun A large, special meal, usually for a lot of people on a holiday or other occasion.
verb To eat a large meal and enjoy it, especially with a lot of people.
▶ *verb* **feasting, feasted**

feat (feet) *noun* An achievement that shows great courage, strength, or skill.

feath·er (**feTH**-ur) *noun* One of the light, soft parts that cover a bird's body. ▶ *adjective* **feathered** ▶ *adjective* **feathery**

fea·ture (**fee**-chur)
noun 1. A particular part or quality of something. 2. The different parts of a person's face. 3. A full-length movie. 4. A newspaper or magazine article, or a part of a TV show, that presents a particular subject.
verb To include a particular part or quality.
▶ *verb* **featuring, featured**

Feb·ru·ar·y (**feb**-roo-er-ee *or* **feb**-yoo-er-ee) *noun* The second month on the calendar, after January and before March. February has 28 days except in a leap year, when it has 29.

fed (fed) *verb* The past tense and the past participle of **feed.**

fed·er·al (**fed**-ur-uhl) *adjective* In a country with a **federal** government, such as the United States, several states are united under and controlled by one central power or authority. However, each state also has its own government and can make its own laws.

fed·er·a·tion (*fed*-uh-**ray**-shuhn) *noun* A union of states, nations, or other groups joined together by an agreement.

fed up (**fed uhp**) *adjective* (informal) If you are **fed up,** you are annoyed, bored, or disgusted about something.

fee (fee) *noun* The amount of money that is charged for a service.

fee·ble (**fee**-buhl) *adjective* Weak; not strong enough. ▶ *adjective* **feebler, feeblest**

feed (feed)
verb 1. To give food to a person or an animal. 2. When animals **feed,** they eat. 3. To supply, or to put in.
noun 1. Food for animals. 2. An electronic signal or program that is sent to a receiving station or computer, such as information sent by a news organization to its subscribers.
▶ *verb* **feeding, fed**

feed·back (**feed**-*bak*) *noun* 1. Written or spoken reactions to something that you are doing. 2. The sharp, loud noise made when a sound produced by an amplifier goes through it again.

F

feel (feel)
  verb **1.** To touch something or to experience something touching you. **2.** To have a certain emotion or sensation. **3.** To think or to have an idea about something. **4.** To have some quality that you can notice by touching.
  noun The act of touching something.
  ▶ *verb* **feeling, felt**

feel·ing (**fee**-ling) *noun* **1.** The ability to note touch and physical sensations. **2.** A thought, belief, or emotion. **3. feelings** Your inner self; your emotions.

feet (feet) *noun, plural* The plural of **foot.**

feign (fayn) *verb* To pretend in order to fool someone. ▶ *verb* **feigning, feigned**

feint (faynt)
  noun A blow or movement meant to take attention away from the real point of attack.
  verb To make a small move in one direction or pretend to attack in order to fool an opponent.
  Feint sounds like **faint.** ▶ *verb* **feinting, feinted**

feist·y (**fye**-stee) *adjective* **1.** Easily angered or likely to quarrel. **2.** Very lively or frisky.

fe·line (**fee**-line)
  adjective **1.** Of or having to do with cats. **2.** Like a cat.
  noun Any animal of the cat family.

fell (fel) *verb* **1.** To cut something down on purpose. **2.** To cause someone or something to fall. **3.** The past tense of **fall.**
  ▶ *verb* **felling, felled**

fel·low (**fel**-oh)
  noun A man or a boy.
  adjective Being in the same group, category, or situation.

fel·low·ship (**fel**-oh-*ship*) *noun* **1.** A group of people sharing an interest. **2.** A friendly feeling among people who share an interest or do something together.

fel·on (**fel**-uhn) *noun* A person who has committed a serious crime, such as murder or burglary. ▶ *noun* **felony** (**fel**-uh-nee)

felt (felt)
  noun A thick cloth made of wool or other fibers that are pressed and shrunk together in layers.
  verb The past tense and past participle of **feel.**

fe·male (**fee**-male)
  noun A person or an animal of the sex that can give birth to young or lay eggs.
  adjective Of, having to do with, or typical of the sex that can give birth to young or lay eggs.

fem·i·nine (**fem**-uh-nin) *adjective* **1.** Of or having to do with women. **2.** Having qualities that are supposed to be typical of women.
  ▶ *noun* **femininity**

fem·i·nist (**fem**-uh-nist)
  noun Someone who believes strongly that women are equal to men and should have the same rights and opportunities.
  adjective Having to do with the belief that women are equal to men and should have the same rights and opportunities.
  ▶ *noun* **feminism**

fence (fens)
  noun **1.** A structure, often made of wood or wire, used to surround, protect, or mark off an area. **2.** A person who knowingly sells or receives stolen goods.
  verb **1.** To fight with special swords called foils, which are long and very thin, as a sport. **2.** To build a fence around something.
  idiom If you are **on the fence,** you are undecided about which side you are on.
  ▶ *verb* **fencing, fenced** ▶ *noun* **fencer**

fenc·ing (**fen**-sing) *noun* **1.** The sport of fighting with long, thin swords called foils. **2.** Fences, or the material used to make them.

fend (fend) *verb* **1.** If you **fend** for yourself, you take care of yourself. **2.** When you **fend off** someone who is attacking you, you defend yourself and hold off the attack.
  ▶ *verb* **fending, fended**

F

fend·er (**fen**-dur) *noun* A cover over the wheel of a car or bicycle that protects the wheel against damage and reduces splashing.

fer·ment (fur-**ment**) *verb* When a liquid **ferments**, the sugars in the liquid turn into alcohol. ▶ *verb* **fermenting, fermented** ▶ *noun* **fermentation**

fern (furn) *noun* A plant that has feathery leaves, or fronds, and no flowers. Ferns usually grow in damp places and reproduce by spores instead of seeds.

fe·ro·cious (fuh-**roh**-shuhs) *adjective* Very dangerous, violent, and savage. ▶ *noun* **ferocity** (fuh-**rah**-si-tee) ▶ *adverb* **ferociously**

fer·ret (**fer**-it)
noun A long, thin animal that is related to the weasel and is sometimes kept as a pet.
verb To search.
▶ *verb* **ferreting, ferreted**

Fer·ris wheel (**fer**-is *weel*) *noun* A large, spinning wheel with seats hung on its side, used as a ride in a carnival or amusement park.

fer·ry (**fer**-ee)
noun A boat that regularly carries people across a body of water such as a river, lake, or bay.
verb To carry people or things from one place to another.
▶ *noun, plural* **ferries** ▶ *verb* **ferries, ferrying, ferried**

fer·tile (**fur**-tuhl) *adjective* **1.** Land that is **fertile** is good for growing crops and plants. **2.** Able to have babies. **3.** Having a lot of ideas.
▶ *noun* **fertility**

fer·ti·lize (**fur**-tuh-*lize*) *verb* **1.** To put an organic or synthetic substance into the soil to make it richer so that plants grow better. **2.** To begin reproduction in an animal or a plant by causing a sperm cell to join with an egg cell or pollen to come into contact with the reproductive part of the animal or plant.
▶ *verb* **fertilizing, fertilized** ▶ *noun* **fertilization** ▶ *noun* **fertilizer**

fer·vent (**fur**-vuhnt) *adjective* Showing strong or intense feeling. ▶ *adverb* **fervently**

fes·ti·val (**fes**-tuh-vuhl) *noun* **1.** A celebration or holiday. **2.** An organized program of cultural, artistic, or musical events, often held every year around the same time.

fes·tive (**fes**-tiv) *adjective* Cheerful and lively.

fes·tiv·i·ty (fes-**tiv**-i-tee) *noun* A celebration or an activity that is part of a celebration. ▶ *noun, plural* **festivities**

fes·toon (fes-**toon**) *verb* To cover something with flowers, ribbons, or other decorations. ▶ *verb* **festooning, festooned**

fetch (fech) *verb* **1.** To go after and bring back something or somebody. **2.** To sell for a particular price.
▶ *verb* **fetches, fetching, fetched**

fetch·ing (**fech**-ing) *adjective* Charming or attractive.

fet·tuc·ci·ne *or* **fet·tuc·ci·ni** (*fet*-uh-**chee**-nee) *noun* Pasta in narrow strips shaped like a ribbon.

fe·tus (**fee**-tuhs) *noun* A baby or an animal before birth, at a later stage of development in the mother's body than an embryo.

feud (fyood)
noun An angry argument between two people or families that lasts for a long time, sometimes for many generations.
verb To have an angry argument that lasts for a long time.
▶ *verb* **fencing, fenced**

feu·dal·ism (**fyoo**-duh-*liz*-uhm) *noun* The medieval system in which a lord gave people land and protection. In return, they had to work and fight for him. ▶ *adjective* **feudal**

fe·ver (**fee**-vur) *noun* **1.** A body temperature that is higher than normal. Most people have a fever if their temperature is more than 98.6 degrees Fahrenheit. **2.** Great excitement or activity.
▶ *adjective* **feverish** ▶ *adverb* **feverishly**

F

few (fyoo)
adjective Not many.
noun Not many things or people.
▶ *adjective* **fewer, fewest**

fez (fez) *noun* A cylindrical cap with no brim. Often made of red felt and decorated with a tassel, fezzes are worn by men, mainly in Turkey and other eastern Mediterranean countries. ▶ *noun, plural* **fezzes**

fi·an·cé (*fee*-ahn-**say** or fee-**ahn**-say) *noun* A man who is engaged to be married.

fi·an·cée (*fee*-ahn-**say** or fee-**ahn**-say) *noun* A woman who is engaged to be married.

fi·as·co (fee-**as**-koh) *noun* A total failure. ▶ *noun, plural* **fiascoes**

fib (fib)
verb To tell a small lie.
noun A small lie.
▶ *verb* **fibbing, fibbed** ▶ *noun* **fibber**

fi·ber (**fye**-bur) *noun* **1.** A thin strand of material such as cotton, wool, hemp, or nylon. **2.** A part of fruits, vegetables, and grains that passes through the body but is not digested. Fiber helps food move through the intestines.
▶ *adjective* **fibrous** (**fye**-bruhs)

fi·ber·glass (**fye**-bur-*glas*) *noun* A strong insulating material made from very fine glass fibers, used in buildings, cars, boats, and many other things.

fi·ber op·tics (**fye**-bur **ahp**-tiks) *noun, plural* Bundles of extremely thin glass or plastic fibers through which light passes. Fiber optics are used in medical operations and for sending data signals.

fick·le (**fik**-uhl) *adjective* Changing very often, or inconsistent. ▶ *noun* **fickleness**

fic·tion (**fik**-shuhn) *noun* **1.** Stories about characters and events that are not real. **2.** Something that is made up.
▶ *adjective* **fictional** ▶ *adjective* **fictitious** (fik-**tish**-uhs)

fid·dle (**fid**-uhl)
noun (informal) A violin.
verb **1.** To touch or play nervously with something. **2.** To waste.
▶ *verb* **fiddling, fiddled** ▶ *noun* **fiddler**

fidg·et (**fij**-it) *verb* To keep moving because you are restless, bored, or nervous. ▶ *verb* **fidgeting, fidgeted** ▶ *adjective* **fidgety**

field (feeld)
noun **1.** A piece of open land, sometimes used for growing crops or grazing animals **2.** An outdoor area where certain sports are played. **3.** A space in a spreadsheet or database where you can enter a particular kind of data. **4.** An area of interest, study, or occupation.
verb In baseball, to catch or stop a ball that has been hit.
▶ *verb* **fielding, fielded**

field·er (**feel**-dur) *noun* A baseball player who is not batting and has a position on the field.

field goal (feeld *gohl*) *noun* **1.** In football, a play in which the ball is kicked from the field, scoring three points. **2.** In basketball, a basket made when the ball is in play, scoring two or three points.

field hock·ey (feeld *hah*-kee) *noun* A team game played on a rectangular field using curved sticks and a small ball. Players attempt to hit the ball along the ground and into the other team's goal.

field trip (feeld *trip*) *noun* A group trip to a place where you can see things and learn.

fiend (feend) *noun* **1.** An evil spirit. **2.** An evil or cruel person.
▶ *adjective* **fiendish** ▶ *adverb* **fiendishly**

fierce (feers) *adjective* **1.** Violent or dangerous. **2.** Very strong or extreme.
▶ *adjective* **fiercer, fiercest** ▶ *noun* **fierceness** ▶ *adverb* **fiercely**

fier·y (**fire**-ee or **fye**-ur-ee) *adjective* **1.** Like fire; very hot or glowing. **2.** Very emotional and spirited.
▶ *adjective* **fierier, fieriest**

fi·es·ta (fee-**es**-tuh) *noun* A religious festival or other public holiday, especially in Latin America and Spain.

fife (fife) *noun* A small instrument, similar to a flute, that has a high pitch.

F

fifth (fifth)
adjective Next after fourth and before sixth, written numerically as 5th.
noun One part of something that has been divided into five equal parts, written numerically as 1/5.

fif·ti·eth (fif-tee-ith) *adjective* Next after 49th and before 51st, written numerically as 50th.

fif·ty (fif-tee) *noun* The number that is equal to 5 times 10, written numerically as 50.

fig (fig) *noun* A small, sweet fruit with tiny seeds, eaten fresh or dried.

fight (fite)
noun 1. A battle in which each side tries to hurt the other. 2. A violent disagreement between two or more people. 3. A hard struggle to gain a goal.
verb To have an argument or a quarrel.
▶ *verb* **fighting, fought**

fight·er (fye-tur) *noun* 1. A soldier. 2. A boxer. 3. A strong-willed person who does not give up in a difficult situation.

fig·ure (fig-yur)
noun 1. A symbol that represents a number, such as 1, 2, 3, and so on. 2. An amount given in numbers. 3. A shape or an outline. 4. A person's shape. 5. A well-known person.
noun, plural **figures** Arithmetic.
verb **figure out** To come to understand something.
▶ *verb* **figuring, figured**

fig·ure·head (fig-yur-hed) *noun* 1. Someone who holds an important position or office but has no real power. 2. A carved statue found on the bow of a ship.

fig·ure of speech (fig-yur uhv speech) *noun* An expression, such as a simile, in which words are used in a poetic way. Authors often use figures of speech to make their writing more colorful. For example, the phrase "as strong as an ox" is a figure of speech that means someone is very strong. ▶ *noun, plural* **figures of speech**

Fi·ji (fee-jee) An island nation in the South Pacific Ocean northeast of New Zealand. It is an archipelago of more than 330 islands and 500 islets. Only about a third of the islands are inhabited.

fil·a·ment (fil-uh-muhnt) *noun* A very fine wire or thread. In a lightbulb, the filament is a fine thread of tungsten that glows and produces light.

file (file)
noun 1. A folder or binder for papers or documents. 2. A tool used to make something smoother. 3. A collection of information stored on a computer and given a name that identifies it.
verb 1. To sharpen something using a file. 2. To put papers or documents in a file, in some particular order.
idiom **in single file** In a line with one person behind another.
▶ *verb* **filing, filed**

file ex·ten·sion (file ik-sten-shuhn) *noun* The letters that come after the period in the name of a computer file that indicate what kind of file it is, or which program can open it.

file·name (file-naym) *noun* The name of a computer file.

fill (fil) *verb* 1. To make or become full. 2. To take up the whole space of. 3. To stop or plug up. 4. If you **fill in** or **fill out** a form, you put information wherever it is required. 5. If you **fill in** for someone, you do that person's job while he or she is away.
▶ *verb* **filling, filled**

fil·let (fi-lay *or* fil-ay)
noun A piece of meat or fish with the bones removed.
verb To remove the bones from a piece of fish or meat.
▶ *verb* **filleting** (fi-lay-ing), **filleted** (fi-layd)

fill·ing (fil-ing) *noun* 1. Material that a dentist puts into holes in your teeth to prevent more decay. 2. The substance that is used to repair the holes or cracks in something, as a piece of wood or other material. 3. The food inside a sandwich, pie, or cake.

fil·ly (fil-ee) *noun* A young female horse. ▶ *noun, plural* **fillies**

F

film (film)
noun **1.** A thin layer of something.
2. A roll of thin plastic that you put in older kinds of cameras so you can take photographs or motion pictures. The film reacts to the light and allows the images on the film to appear when the film is developed. **3.** A movie.
verb To record something with a film or video camera.
▶ *verb* **filming, filmed**

fil·ter (**fil**-tur)
noun A device that cleans liquids or gases as they pass through it.
verb **1.** To put something through a filter. **2.** To go through very slowly or sparsely.
▶ *verb* **filtering, filtered**

filth (filth) *noun* **1.** Dirt. **2.** Foul or obscene language or images.
▶ *noun* **filthiness** ▶ *adjective* **filthy**

fin (fin) *noun* **1.** A part on the body of a fish shaped like a flap that is used for moving and steering through the water.
2. A small, flat structure on an airplane or boat, used to help with steering.
3. One of two long, flat attachments worn on the feet to help you swim underwater. Also called a **flipper.**

fi·nal (**fye**-nuhl)
adjective **1.** Last. **2.** Not to be changed or discussed.
noun **1.** The last and usually most important examination in a school subject. **2.** The last and final round, game, or match in a series to determine who is the absolute winner.

fi·na·le (fuh-**nal**-ee *or* fuh-**nah**-lee) *noun* The last part of a show or piece of music.

fi·nal·ist (**fye**-nuh-list) *noun* Someone who has reached the last part of a competition.

fi·nal·ize (**fye**-nuh-*lize*) *verb* To make something final; to complete all the details. ▶ *verb* **finalizing, finalized**

fi·nal·ly (**fye**-nuh-lee) *adverb* **1.** After many attempts. **2.** Eventually; at last.

fi·nance (fuh-**nans** *or* **fye**-nans)
noun The management and use of money by businesses, banks, and governments.
verb To provide money for something.
noun, plural **finances** The total amount of money that an individual, a company, or a government has.
▶ *verb* **financing, financed**

fi·nan·cial (fuh-**nan**-shuhl *or* fye-**nan**-shuhl) *adjective* Of or having to do with money, income, and spending. ▶ *adverb* **financially**

finch (finch) *noun* A small songbird with a strong, thick bill used for cracking seeds. ▶ *noun, plural* **finches**

find (finde)
verb **1.** To come across something by chance. **2.** To come to and state a decision. **3.** **find out** To learn about something or someone.
noun An important or valuable discovery.
▶ *verb* **finding, found**

find·ing (**fine**-ding) *noun* One of the results of an investigation or a study.

fine (fine)
adjective **1.** Very well or healthy. **2.** Very good or excellent. **3.** Not cloudy or rainy. **4.** Thin or delicate.
noun A sum of money to be paid as a punishment for doing something wrong.
verb To make someone pay a sum of money as punishment for doing something wrong.
▶ *adjective* **finer, finest** ▶ *verb* **fining, fined** ▶ *noun* **fineness**

fin·ger (**fing**-gur)
noun One of the long parts of your hands that you can move. Our hands have five fingers each, enabling us to pick up and hold things.
verb **1.** To touch something lightly with your fingers. **2.** To blame or accuse someone of something.
▶ *verb* **fingering, fingered**

fin·ger·nail (**fing**-gur-*nayl*) *noun* The hard protective layer at the upper tip of each finger that grows and requires regular trimming.

fin·ger·print (**fing**-gur-*print*) *noun* The print made by the pattern of curved ridges on the tips of your fingers.

fin·ick·y (**fin**-i-kee) *adjective* Fussy, especially about food.

F

fin·ish (**fin**-ish)
verb 1. To end or complete something.
2. To use the last of something. 3. To
give an attractive or protective surface
to something after it is built.
noun 1. The end of something, such as
a race. 2. A coating on a surface such
as metal or wood.
▶ *verb* **finishes, finishing, finished**
▶ *noun, plural* **finishes**

fi·nite (**fye**-nite) *adjective* Having an
end.

Fin·land (**fin**-luhnd) A country in
northern Europe between Sweden
and Norway on the west and north
and Russia on the east. It is the most
sparsely populated country in the
European Union. Forests cover more
than three-quarters of the country.

fir (fur) *noun* An evergreen tree with
needle-like leaves and upright cones.

fire (fire)
noun 1. Flames, heat, and light
produced by burning. 2. The use of
guns or other weapons that use high-
speed ammunition. 3. Strong emotion.
verb 1. To shoot a gun or other
weapon. 2. To dismiss someone from
his or her job.
▶ *verb* **firing, fired**

fire·arm (**fire**-ahrm) *noun* A weapon
that shoots bullets. Rifles, pistols, and
shotguns are firearms.

fire·crack·er (**fire**-krak-ur) *noun* A
paper tube containing gunpowder
and a fuse. Firecrackers make a loud
popping noise when they explode.

fire en·gine (**fire** en-jin) *noun* A large
truck that carries powerful pumps,
hoses, ladders, and firefighters to a
fire.

fire es·cape (**fire** e-skape) *noun* A set
of metal stairs on the outside of a
building, designed to allow people to
escape in case of fire.

fire ex·tin·guish·er (**fire** ik-sting-gwi-
shur) *noun* A portable metal container
that holds chemicals and sometimes
water, used to put out a fire.

fire·fight·er (**fire**-fye-tur) *noun* Someone
who is trained to put out fires.

fire·fly (**fire**-flye) *noun* A small beetle
that flies at night and gives off flashes
of green light from its abdomen. Also
called a **lightning bug.** ▶ *noun, plural*
fireflies

fire·house (**fire**-hous) *noun* A building
where fire engines are kept and where
firefighters wait until they are called to
put out a fire. Also called a **fire station.**

fire·man (**fire**-muhn) *noun* A male
firefighter. ▶ *noun, plural* **firemen**

fire·place (**fire**-plase) *noun* A structure,
usually made of brick or stone, in
which a fire can burn safely.

fire·proof (**fire**-proof) *adjective* Made
from a material that has been
chemically treated so that it will
not burn.

fire·side (**fire**-side) *noun* The area around
a fireplace.

fire sta·tion (**fire** stay-shuhn) *noun*
Another term for **firehouse.**

fire·trap (**fire**-trap) *noun* A building that
would be hard to escape from if it
caught on fire.

fire·wall (**fire**-wawl) *noun* 1. A wall in a
building that is designed to keep a fire
from spreading. 2. Software designed
to control access to a computer
in order to protect it from outside
attacks.

fire·wood (**fire**-wud) *noun* Logs or other
pieces of wood that are burned as fuel.

fire·works (**fire**-wurks) *noun, plural*
Devices that make very loud noises
and colorful lights when they are
burned or exploded.

firm (furm)
adjective 1. Strong and solid. 2. Definite
and not easily changed. 3. Steady.
noun A business or a company.
▶ *adjective* **firmer, firmest** ▶ *adverb*
firmly

first (furst)
adjective 1. Before the second of
something, written numerically as 1st.
2. Before every other. 3. Earliest in time.
4. Best, or most important.
noun Someone or something that acts
or happens before any other.
adverb Before something else; earliest
of all.

F

first aid (furst ayd) *noun* Emergency care given to an injured or sick person before he or she is examined by a doctor.

first class (furst klas)
noun 1. The most expensive level of service offered to travelers on trains, ships, and airplanes. 2. The standard level of mail service used for letters, postcards, and bills.
adjective **first-class** Being of the highest quality.
adverb **first-class** Traveling by means of the most expensive level of service.

first·hand (furst-hand)
adjective Direct from the original source.
adverb In a way that comes directly from the original source.

first-rate (first-rate) *adjective* Excellent.

first re·spond·er (furst ri-spahn-dur)
noun Someone whose job is to respond first in an emergency, such as a police officer, firefighter, or paramedic.

fis·cal (fis-kuhl) *adjective* Of or having to do with government income and spending. ▶ *adverb* **fiscally**

fish (fish)
noun A cold-blooded animal that lives in water and has scales, fins, and gills.
verb 1. To try to catch fish. 2. When a person **fishes** for information, he or she is trying to find something out in a sly or indirect way.
▶ *noun, plural* **fish** *or* **fishes** ▶ *verb* **fishes, fishing, fished** ▶ *noun* **fishing**

fish·er·man (fish-ur-muhn) *noun* A person who catches fish to earn a living or for sport. ▶ *noun, plural* **fishermen**

fish·er·y (fish-ur-ee) *noun* 1. A place where fish are bred commercially. 2. A place where fish are caught.
▶ *noun, plural* **fisheries**

fish·hook (fish-huk) *noun* A small hook with a barb, used for catching fish.

fish·ing rod (fish-ing rahd) *noun* A long, flexible pole used with a hook, line, and reel to catch fish.

fish·y (fish-ee) *adjective* 1. Having a strong smell or taste of fish.

2. (informal) Unlikely, doubtful, or suspicious.
▶ *adjective* **fishier, fishiest**

fis·sion (fish-uhn) *noun* 1. The act of splitting into parts. 2. **nuclear fission** The splitting of the nucleus of an atom, which creates energy.

fist (fist) *noun* A tightly closed hand.

fit (fit)
verb 1. To be the right shape or size to cover something. 2. To be the right shape or size to contain something. 3. To be right for.
adjective 1. Strong and healthy. 2. Good enough.
noun 1. A sudden attack of something that cannot be controlled. 2. An angry outburst.
▶ *verb* **fitting, fitted** *or* **fit** ▶ *adjective* **fitter, fittest**

fit·ness (fit-nis) *noun* Your **fitness** is how healthy and strong you are. You can improve your fitness by exercising and eating healthy foods.

fit·ting (fit-ing)
adjective Suitable or proper.
noun A small metal or plastic part that connects things.

five (five)
noun The number that comes after four and before six, written numerically as 5.
adjective Referring to the number that comes after four and before six.

fix (fiks)
verb 1. To repair something. 2. To arrange or tidy something. 3. To get something ready to eat. 4. To place or fasten firmly.
noun A repair, change, or solution to something.
idiom **in a fix** In a difficult situation or in trouble.
▶ *verb* **fixes, fixing, fixed** ▶ *noun, plural* **fixes**

fix·a·tion (fik-say-shuhn) *noun* An overly strong attachment to a person, idea, or thing. ▶ *verb* **fixate**

fixed (fikst) *adjective* 1. Not changing. 2. Scheduled. 3. Held in place; firmly attached.

F

fix·ture (**fiks**-chur) *noun* Something that is fixed firmly and permanently in place, especially in a house or building.

fizz (fiz)
verb To make bubbles and a hissing noise.
noun A lot of tiny, hissing bubbles.
▶ *verb* **fizzes, fizzing, fizzed** ▶ *adjective* **fizzy**

fiz·zle (**fiz**-uhl) *verb* **1.** To make a hissing or sputtering sound. **2.** (informal) To fail or die out, especially after a good start.
▶ *verb* **fizzling, fizzled**

fjord (fyord) *noun* A long, narrow inlet of the ocean between high cliffs.

flab (flab) *noun* Extra fat on your body. ▶ *noun* **flabbiness** ▶ *adjective* **flabby**

flab·ber·gast·ed (**flab**-ur-*gas*-tid) *adjective* (informal) Stunned and surprised.

flac·cid (**flas**-id *or* **flak**-sid) *adjective* Limp or soft.

flag (flag)
noun A square or rectangular piece of cloth with a pattern on it that is a symbol of a country or an organization.
verb To stop, or to signal.
▶ *verb* **flagging, flagged**

Flag Day (**flag** day) *noun* A holiday that celebrates the day in 1777 when the Stars and Stripes became the official flag of the United States. It is observed on June 14.

flag·pole (**flag**-pole) *noun* A tall pole made of wood or metal for raising and flying a flag.

flair (flair) *noun* A natural ability or skill. **Flair** sounds like **flare**.

flak (flak) *noun* **1.** Shots fired against an aircraft. **2.** (informal) Criticism and negative reactions.

flake (flake)
noun A small, flat piece of something.
verb To peel off in small, flat pieces.
▶ *verb* **flaking, flaked** ▶ *adjective* **flaky**

flam·boy·ant (flam-**boi**-uhnt) *adjective* Brightly colored or showy.

flame (flame) *noun* The light given off by a fire.

fla·min·go (fluh-**ming**-goh) *noun* A pink bird with a long neck, long legs, and webbed feet. ▶ *noun, plural* **flamingos** *or* **flamingoes**

flam·ma·ble (**flam**-uh-buhl) *adjective* Quick to catch fire and burn.

flank (flangk)
noun **1.** The side of an animal, between its ribs and hips. **2.** The far left or right side of something such as a group of soldiers, a fort, or a naval fleet.
verb To guard or be at the side of something or someone.
▶ *verb* **flanking, flanked**

flan·nel (**flan**-uhl) *noun* A soft, woven cloth, usually made of cotton or wool.

flap (flap)
verb **1.** To move up and down. **2.** To swing loosely and make a noise.
noun **1.** A part of something that hangs on the side or edge. **2.** A movable part on an airplane wing, used to control the plane's rise and fall.
▶ *verb* **flapping, flapped**

flap·jack (**flap**-jak) *noun* A pancake.

flare (flair)
verb **1.** To burn with a sudden, very bright light. **2.** To break out in sudden or violent feeling. **3. flare out** To spread out in a bell shape at the bottom. **4. flare up** To suddenly become stronger and more intense or violent.
noun A stick that produces a flame or bright light to warn people of something.
Flare sounds like **flair.** ▶ *verb* **flaring, flared**

flash (flash)
noun **1.** A short burst of light. **2.** A very brief period of time. **3.** A sudden outburst. **4. news flash** A brief report of very recent or important news.
verb To move rapidly.
▶ *noun, plural* **flashes** ▶ *verb* **flashes, flashing, flashed**

flash·back (**flash**-bak) *noun* **1.** A scene in a movie or a story that tells you something that happened in the past. **2.** A sudden memory of something that happened and was forgotten.

F

flash drive (**flash** *drive*) *noun* A form of computer memory that has no moving parts and is small enough to carry in your pocket.

flash·light (**flash**-*lite*) *noun* A portable light that is powered by a battery.

flash·y (**flash**-ee) *adjective* Very bright and attracting attention. ▶ *adjective* **flashier, flashiest**

flask (flask) *noun* **1.** A small, flat bottle made to be carried in the pocket. **2.** A bottle with a narrow neck used in science laboratories.

flat (flat)
adjective **1.** Smooth and even. **2.** Not very deep or thick; shallow. **3.** Absolute. **4.** Containing no air. **5.** Dull or lifeless. **6.** Lower than the correct or usual pitch.
adverb Fully stretched out or spread out against a surface.
noun **1.** In music, a **flat** is a note that is one half step lower in pitch than the usual note. **2.** A written sign in sheet music that shows that the next note is a flat.
▶ *adjective* **flatter, flattest**

flat·bed (**flat**-*bed*) *noun* A truck with a large, flat cargo area in the back, designed to carry a heavy load, like a car.

flat·car (**flat**-*kahr*) *noun* A railroad car that has no roof or sides and is used to carry freight.

flat·fish (**flat**-*fish*) *noun* A fish with a flat body and both eyes on its upper side, such as halibut, sole, or flounder. ▶ *noun, plural* **flatfish** or **flatfishes**

flat·ten (**flat**-uhn) *verb* To make something flat or almost flat by pressing on it. ▶ *verb* **flattening, flattened**

flat·ter (**flat**-ur)
verb To praise too much or insincerely, especially when you want a favor.
adjective Something is **flattering** if it makes you look good.
▶ *verb* **flattering, flattered** ▶ *noun* **flatterer** ▶ *noun* **flattery**

flaunt (flawnt) *verb* To show off in order to impress others. ▶ *verb* **flaunting, flaunted**

fla·vor (**flay**-vur)
noun Taste.
verb To add taste to food during its preparation.
▶ *verb* **flavoring, flavored** ▶ *adjective* **flavored** ▶ *adjective* **flavorless** ▶ *noun* **flavoring**

flaw (flaw) *noun* A weakness.

flax (flaks) *noun* **1.** A plant with blue flowers that produces oil and fiber. **2.** The fiber of the flax plant, which can be woven into thread that is used to make linen.

flea (flee) *noun* **1.** A small, wingless insect that lives on the blood of people and other animals. **2. flea market** An indoor or outdoor market selling mainly secondhand items and used clothing. **Flea** sounds like **flee.**

fleck (flek) *noun* A tiny piece of something. ▶ *adjective* **flecked**

fled (fled) *verb* The past tense and the past participle of **flee.**

fledg·ling (**flej**-ling) *noun* A young bird that has just grown the feathers it will need to fly.

flee (flee) *verb* To run away, especially from danger. **Flee** sounds like **flea.** ▶ *verb* **fleeing, fled** (fled)

fleece (flees)
noun The woolly coat of a sheep.
verb To swindle someone out of his or her money or possessions, especially by doing it in a tricky way.
▶ *verb* **fleecing, fleeced** ▶ *adjective* **fleecy**

fleet (fleet)
noun **1.** A group of warships under one command. **2.** A number of ships, planes, or cars that form a group.
adjective Swift or fast.

fleet·ing (**flee**-ting) *adjective* Not lasting long. ▶ *adverb* **fleetingly**

flesh (flesh) *noun* **1.** The soft part of your body that covers your bones. Flesh is made up of fat and muscle. **2.** The meat of an animal. **3.** The parts of a fruit or vegetable that people eat.
▶ *adjective* **fleshy**

F

flew (floo) *verb* The past tense of **fly.**

flex (fleks) *verb* **1.** To tighten a muscle.
2. To bend or stretch something.
▶ *verb* **flexes, flexing, flexed**

flex·i·ble (flek-suh-buhl) *adjective* **1.** Able to bend. **2.** Able to change.
▶ *noun* **flexibility** ▶ *adverb* **flexibly**

flex·time (fleks-*time*) *noun* A system of adjusting the hours of work so that employees may select their own starting and finishing times.

flick (flik)
noun A light, quick movement.
verb To touch or move something with a quick, snapping movement.
▶ *verb* **flicking, flicked**

flick·er (flik-ur)
verb To burn or shine unsteadily.
noun A movement of light that burns or shines unsteadily.
▶ *verb* **flickering, flickered**

fli·er *or* **fly·er** (flye-ur) *noun* **1.** Someone who flies, such as an airplane pilot.
2. A paper advertisement sent or given to people.

flight (flite) *noun* **1.** The act or manner of flying, or the ability to fly. **2.** An airplane journey. **3.** A set of stairs or steps between floors or landings of a building. **4.** When a person **takes flight,** he or she runs away. **5.** When a bird **takes flight,** it flies up from the ground or a tree.

flight at·ten·dant (flite uh-*ten*-duhnt) *noun* Someone who helps passengers and serves food and drinks on an airplane.

flim·sy (flim-zee) *adjective* Easy to tear or break. ▶ *adjective* **flimsier, flimsiest** ▶ *noun* **flimsiness** ▶ *adverb* **flimsily**

flinch (flinch)
verb To draw back with a quick, sudden movement from a source of pain or fear.
noun A quick, sudden movement away from a source of pain or fear.
▶ *verb* **flinches, flinching, flinched** ▶ *noun, plural* **flinches**

fling (fling)
verb To throw something with force or violence.

noun A short period of time during which you do things you enjoy and do not worry about other things.
▶ *verb* **flinging, flung** (fluhng)

flint (flint) *noun* A very hard kind of rock that makes sparks when steel is struck against it. In prehistoric times, flint was used to make tools and weapons.

flip (flip)
verb **1.** To toss or fling something.
2. To turn something over.
3. (informal) If someone **flips** or **flips out,** he or she suddenly becomes extremely angry.
noun A somersault.
▶ *verb* **flipping, flipped**

flip·pant (flip-uhnt) *adjective* Lacking respect or seriousness. ▶ *noun* **flippancy** (flip-uhn-see) ▶ *adverb* **flippantly**

flip·per (flip-ur) *noun* **1.** One of the broad, flat limbs that sea mammals such as seals, whales, and dolphins use when they swim. **2.** One of the two long, flat rubber attachments that you wear on your feet to help you swim.

flirt (flurt)
verb **1.** If you **flirt** with someone, you show romantic interest in that person, but in a casual way. **2.** To consider an idea, but not seriously.
noun A person who likes to flirt with other people.
▶ *verb* **flirting, flirted**

float (floht)
verb **1.** To rest or move on a liquid or in the air. **2.** To move without effort.
noun **1.** A small floating object attached to the end of a fishing line that holds the line up. **2.** A decorated truck or platform that forms part of a parade.
▶ *verb* **floating, floated**

flock (flahk)
noun **1.** A group of animals of one kind that live, travel, or feed together. **2.** A large group of people.
verb To come together in a large group.
▶ *verb* **flocking, flocked**

F

floe (floh) *noun* A large sheet or block of floating ice in a sea, lake, or river.

flog (flahg) *verb* To beat with a whip or a stick. ▶ *verb* **flogging, flogged** ▶ *noun* **flogging**

flood (fluhd)
verb 1. To overflow with water beyond its normal limits. 2. To come in large amounts.
noun 1. A large amount of water that overflows into an area of land that is usually dry. 2. A large number or amount that arrives or happens at the same time.
▶ *verb* **flooding, flooded**

flood·light (fluhd-*lite*) *noun* An outside lamp that produces a broad and very bright beam of light.

flood plain (fluhd *playn*) *noun* An area of low land near a stream or river that becomes flooded during heavy rains.

floor (flor)
noun 1. The flat surface that you walk or stand on inside a building. 2. A story in a building.
verb (informal) To surprise.
▶ *verb* **flooring, floored** ▶ *noun* **flooring**

flop (flahp)
verb 1. To fall or drop heavily. 2. To flap or move about. 3. (informal) To fail.
noun (informal) A failure.
▶ *verb* **flopping, flopped**

flop·py (flah-pee) *adjective* Soft and flexible; hanging down loosely. ▶ *adjective* **floppier, floppiest**

flo·ra (flor-uh) *noun* All the plants of a particular area as a group.

flo·ral (flor-uhl) *adjective* Of, having to do with, or showing flowers.

Flor·i·da (flor-i-duh) A state in the southeastern United States consisting of a large peninsula surrounded by the Gulf of Mexico, the Atlantic Ocean, and the Caribbean Sea. It is known as "the Sunshine State" because of its warm climate and is a popular place for older Americans to retire.

flo·rist (flor-ist) *noun* Someone who sells flowers and plants.

floss (flaws *or* flahs)
noun A thin strand of thread used to clean between the teeth. Also called **dental floss.**
verb To clean your teeth using dental floss.
▶ *verb* **flossing, flossed**

flot·sam (flaht-suhm) *noun* Objects from a shipwreck that float in the sea or are washed up on the shore.

floun·der (floun-dur)
verb 1. To have difficulty moving through snow, mud, or water. 2. To have trouble doing something.
noun A flat ocean fish used for food.
▶ *verb* **floundering, floundered**

flour (flour) *noun* Ground wheat or other grain that you use for baking or frying.

flour·ish (flur-ish)
verb 1. To grow well. 2. To develop and succeed. 3. To wave something around, especially to show it off.
noun A dramatic way of doing something that makes people notice you.
▶ *verb* **flourishes, flourishing, flourished** ▶ *noun, plural* **flourishes**

flout (flout) *verb* To break rules on purpose. ▶ *verb* **flouting, flouted**

flow (floh)
verb To move smoothly, like water.
noun 1. The movement of the ocean toward the land. 2. The steady, smooth movement of something in one direction, such as liquid or electricity.
▶ *verb* **flowing, flowed**

flow·chart (floh-*chahrt*) *noun* A diagram that shows how something develops and progresses, step by step.

flow·er (flou-ur)
noun 1. The colorful blossoms of a plant that produces seeds or fruit. 2. A plant that is grown for its flowers.
verb To produce flowers.
▶ *verb* **flowering, flowered**

flown (flohn) *verb* The past participle of **fly.**

flu (floo) *noun* An illness, caused by a virus, that is like a bad cold, with fever and muscle pains. Flu is short for **influenza.**

fluc·tu·ate (fluhk-choo-*ate*) *verb* To change back and forth or up

F

and down. ▸ *verb* **fluctuating, fluctuated** ▸ *noun* **fluctuation**

flue (floo) *noun* A hollow part or passage, such as the pipe inside a chimney that carries smoke away from a fire.

flu·ent (**floo**-uhnt) *adjective* Able to speak easily and well, especially in another language. ▸ *noun* **fluency** (**floo**-uhn-see) ▸ *adverb* **fluently**

fluff (fluhf)
noun A light, soft, tiny mass of material, as from wool or cotton.
verb **1.** To shake something out, as a bird does its feathers, or to plump something up, as a pillow. **2.** To make a mistake in speaking or reading something.
▸ *verb* **fluffing, fluffed**

fluff·y (**fluhf**-ee) *adjective* **1.** Light and airy. **2.** Covered with soft, fine hair or feathers.
▸ *adjective* **fluffier, fluffiest**

flu·id (**floo**-id)
noun A substance that can flow, such as a liquid or a gas.
adjective Flowing.
▸ *noun* **fluidity** (floo-**id**-i-tee)

fluke (flook) *noun* **1.** An accident, especially a lucky accident. **2.** Part of the tail of a sea creature such as a whale or dolphin.

flung (fluhng) *verb* The past tense and the past participle of **fling**.

flunk (fluhngk) *verb* **1.** Another word for fail, used especially for not passing a test or not moving on to the next year in school. **2.** **flunk out** To leave school with failing grades.
▸ *verb* **flunking, flunked**

fluo·res·cent (flu-**res**-uhnt) *adjective* **1.** Giving out a bright light by using a certain type of energy, such as ultraviolet light or X-rays. **2.** A **fluorescent** color seems to glow when you shine a light on it.
▸ *noun* **fluorescence**

fluor·i·date (**flor**-i-date) *verb* To add fluoride in order to fight tooth decay. ▸ *verb* **fluoridating, fluoridated**

fluor·ide (**flor**-ide) *noun* A chemical compound put in toothpaste and

added to the public water supply to prevent tooth decay.

flur·ry (**flur**-ee) *noun* **1.** A confusion or a commotion. **2.** A brief snow shower.
▸ *noun, plural* **flurries**

flush (fluhsh)
verb **1.** To turn red or to blush. **2.** To flood something with water in order to clean or empty it.
adjective Exactly even.
noun **1.** A flow of blood to the cheeks that makes your face red, as with embarrassment or anger. **2.** The act of flooding something, such as a toilet, with water in order to clean or empty it.
▸ *verb* **flushes, flushing, flushed** ▸ *noun, plural* **flushes**

flushed (fluhsht) *adjective* A **flushed** face has turned red, as with embarrassment or anger.

flus·ter (**fluhs**-tur) *verb* To confuse or disturb someone. ▸ *verb* **flustering, flustered**

flute (floot) *noun* A long, cylindrical wind instrument played by blowing air across a hole at one end and fingering keys to change notes.

flut·ter (**fluht**-ur)
verb To wave back and forth rapidly.
noun **1.** When you are in a **flutter,** you are excited and nervous. **2.** A quick, beating sensation or movement.
▸ *verb* **fluttering, fluttered**

fly (flye)
verb **1.** To travel through the air. **2.** To travel through the air in an aircraft. **3.** To move or pass quickly.
noun **1.** An insect with two wings. **2.** The opening at the top of a pair of pants where they fasten. **3.** A fishhook used for fishing. **4.** A baseball hit high in the air.
▸ *verb* **flies, flying, flew, flown** ▸ *noun, plural* **flies**

fly·catch·er (**flye**-kach-ur) *noun* A kind of songbird that feeds on insects caught in the air.

fly·er (**flye**-ur) *noun* Another spelling of **flier**.

F

fly·fish·ing (**flye**-*fish*-ing) *noun* A type of fishing using fake flies attached to a fishhook and made from such materials as feathers, bits of fur, thread, and plastic.

fly·ing fish (**flye**-ing **fish**) *noun* A type of fish with large fins that spread open like wings, allowing it to jump out of the water and glide in the air for a short time. ▶ *noun, plural* **flying fish** or **flying fishes**

fly·ing sau·cer (**flye**-ing **saw**-sur) *noun* A spacecraft that some people believe has come from another planet, shaped like a saucer.

foal (fohl) *noun* A young horse, mule, donkey, or zebra. *verb* To give birth to a young horse, mule, donkey, or zebra. ▶ *verb* **foaling, foaled**

foam (fohm) *noun* A mass of small bubbles. *verb* To make bubbles. ▶ *verb* **foaming, foamed**

foam rub·ber (**fohm ruhb**-ur) *noun* A light spongy material, used for mattresses and pillows and to make certain toys.

fo·cus (**foh**-kuhs) *noun* **1.** The point where rays of light meet after being bent by a lens. **2.** The center of activity, interest, or attention. *verb* **1.** To adjust your eyes or the lens of a camera to see something clearly. **2.** To concentrate on something or somebody. ▶ *noun, plural* **focuses** or **foci** (**foh**-*sye*) ▶ *verb* **focuses, focusing, focused** ▶ *adjective* **focal**

fod·der (**fah**-dur) *noun* Food for cattle and horses.

foe (foh) *noun* An opponent or enemy.

fog (fahg *or* fawg) *noun* **1.** A cloud of mist near the ground. **2.** A state of confusion or unclear thinking. *verb* To become or make something become covered with a cloud of mist and therefore difficult to see through. ▶ *verb* **fogging, fogged** ▶ *adjective* **foggy**

fog·horn (**fahg**-*horn*) *noun* A very loud, deep horn used to warn ships in foggy weather that the coast is near.

foil (foil) *noun* **1.** Very thin, silvery sheets of metal. **2.** A long, thin sword used in fencing. *verb* To prevent someone from doing something. ▶ *verb* **foiling, foiled**

fold (fohld) *verb* **1.** To bend something over on itself. **2.** To bring together, or to bend close to the body. **3.** If a company **folds,** it goes out of business. *noun* **1.** A line or crease made by folding. **2.** A small, enclosed area for sheep. ▶ *verb* **folding, folded**

fold·er (**fohl**-dur) *noun* **1.** A cardboard holder to keep papers in. **2.** A named area of disk memory that can hold a number of computer files; a directory.

fo·li·age (**foh**-lee-ij) *noun* Leaves of a plant or tree.

folk (fohk) *noun* People. *noun, plural* **folks** Family members, especially parents. *adjective* Traditional and belonging to the common people in a region. ▶ *noun, plural* **folk** or **folks**

folk dance (**fohk** *dans*) *noun* A kind of dance that is native to a particular area or group.

folk·lore (**fohk**-*lor*) *noun* The stories, customs, and beliefs of the common people that are handed down from one generation to the next.

folk mu·sic (**fohk** *myoo*-zik) *noun* Traditional music of an area that is often handed down from one generation to the next.

folk sing·er (**fohk** *sing*-ur) *noun* Someone who sings folk music.

folk song (**fohk**-*sawng*) *noun* A traditional song with music and words, usually with a simple melody.

folk·tale (**fohk**-*tale*) *noun* A story that is passed down orally from one generation to the next.

F

fol·low (**fah**-loh) *verb* **1.** To go after someone or something. **2.** To come after something. **3.** To go behind someone. **4.** To obey. **5.** To imitate or copy. **6.** If you **follow up** on something, you return to something that you started.
▶ *verb* **following, followed** ▶ *noun* **follower**

fol·low·er (**fah**-loh-ur) *noun* A **follower** follows someone or something.

fol·low·ing (**fah**-loh-ing)
preposition Next, after, or coming after. *Following the ceremony, dessert will be served.*
adjective Next in time or order of occurrence.
noun A group of supporters or admirers.

fol·ly (**fah**-lee) *noun* Foolishness. ▶ *noun, plural* **follies**

fond (fahnd) *adjective* **1.** Liking someone or something very much. **2.** A **fond memory** or a **fond hope** is a memory or hope that you care for very much.
▶ *adjective* **fonder, fondest** ▶ *noun* **fondness** ▶ *adverb* **fondly**

font (fahnt) *noun* **1.** A bowl or other large container used in a church to hold the water for baptisms. **2.** A style of type.

food (food) *noun* Substances that living things eat to stay alive and grow.

food chain (**food** chayn) *noun* An ordered arrangement of animals and plants in which each feeds on the one below it in the chain.

food court (**food** kort) *noun* The area in a shopping mall or other place where there are food sellers and tables.

food proc·es·sor (**food** prah-ses-ur) *noun* A machine that cuts up, purees, or liquefies food.

food web (**food** web) *noun* The complex network of related food chains within an ecosystem.

fool (fool)
noun A person who lacks good sense.
verb To trick or cheat someone.
▶ *verb* **fooling, fooled**

fool·ish (**foo**-lish) *adjective* Not showing good sense; not wise. ▶ *noun* **foolishness**

fool·proof (**fool**-proof) *adjective* Something so simple to use or so well planned that anyone can use it or do it without failing.

foot (fut) *noun* **1.** The end part of many animals' bodies at the end of the leg. **2.** The bottom or lowest part of something. **3.** A unit of length that equals 12 inches. **4.** If you **put your foot down,** you insist on something and act firmly. **5.** If you **put your foot in your mouth,** you say something that hurts or upsets someone and you get embarrassed.
▶ *noun, plural* **feet** (feet)

foot·ball (**fut**-bawl) *noun* **1.** A game played by two teams of 11 players each on a long field with goals at each end. Each team tries to score points by getting the ball across the opponent's goal line. **2.** The ball used in this game.

foot·hill (**fut**-hil) *noun* A low hill at the base of a mountain or mountain range.

foot·ing (**fut**-ing) *noun* **1.** A secure place on which to stand. **2.** In architecture, the **footing** of a building is the bottom of its foundation, next to the earth. **3.** If you **lose your footing,** you are no longer standing firmly.

foot·lights (**fut**-lites) *noun, plural* Lights arranged along the front floor of a stage that allow the audience to see the actors.

foot·note (**fut**-note) *noun* A note at the bottom of a page that explains something in the text.

foot·print (**fut**-print) *noun* **1.** A mark made by a foot or shoe. **2.** The shape and the amount of space that something takes up on the floor, ground, or some other surface. **3.** Something that is left behind by an activity, especially an amount of pollution or damage to the environment.

foot·step (**fut**-step) *noun* **1.** The act of placing the foot on the ground or floor. **2.** The sound that the foot makes when it hits the ground or floor.

F

for (for)
preposition **1.** Intended to be used on or with. *These markers are for posters.* **2.** Meeting the needs of; in order to benefit. *I take vitamins for my health.* **3.** Over the time or distance of. *We marched for miles.* **4.** Due to; because of. *She has to travel for her job.* **5.** In honor of, or on behalf of. *He picked the flowers for me.* **6.** Worth the amount of. *I bought a pack of gum for 50 cents.* **7.** Intended to be given or sent to. *This is for you.* **8.** In place of. *In the recipe, we substituted honey for sugar.*
conjunction Because.

for·age (**for**-ij)
noun Hay, grain, and other food for horses, cattle, and similar animals.
verb To go in search of food.
▶ *verb* **foraging, foraged**

for·bade (fur-**bad**) *verb* The past tense of **forbid.**

for·bid (fur-**bid**) *verb* To order someone not to do something. ▶ *verb* **forbidding, forbade, forbidden** ▶ *adjective* **forbidden**

for·bid·den (fur-**bid**-uhn)
verb The past participle of **forbid.**
adjective Not allowed to be done or used.

for·bid·ding (fur-**bid**-ing)
adjective Looking unfriendly or dangerous. ▶ *adverb* **forbiddingly**

force (fors)
noun **1.** Strength or power. **2.** In physics, a **force** is any action that produces, stops, or changes the shape or the movement of an object. **3.** A group of people who work together.
verb To make someone do something.
▶ *verb* **forcing, forced** ▶ *adjective* **forceful** ▶ *adverb* **forcefully**

for·ceps (**for**-seps) *noun, plural* Tongs used for grasping, holding, or pulling, especially by dentists or surgeons.

ford (ford)
noun A shallow part of a stream or river where you can cross.
verb To cross at a ford.
▶ *verb* **fording, forded**

fore·arm (**for**-ahrm) *noun* The part of your arm from your wrist to your elbow.

fore·cast (**for**-kast)
verb To tell what you believe will happen in the future.
noun A prediction of what you believe will happen in the future.
▶ *verb* **forecasting, forecast** or **forecasted** ▶ *noun* **forecaster**

fore·fa·ther (**for**-fah-THur) *noun* An ancestor.

fore·fin·ger (**for**-fing-gur) *noun* The finger used for pointing; the index finger.

fore·gone (**for**-gawn) *adjective* Decided in advance.

fore·ground (**for**-ground) *noun* The part of a picture that is or seems to be nearest to the person looking at it.

fore·head (**for**-id or **for**-hed) *noun* The top part of your face above your eyes.

for·eign (**for**-uhn) *adjective* **1.** Of, having to do with, or coming from another country. **2.** Unfamiliar and strange.
▶ *noun* **foreigner**

for·eign·er (**for**-uh-nur) *noun* A person who is staying or living in a country that is not his or her own country; an alien.

fore·leg (**for**-leg) *noun* One of the front legs of an animal with four legs.

fore·man (**for**-muhn) *noun* **1.** Someone, usually in a factory, who is in charge of a group of workers. **2.** The lead man or woman on a jury.
▶ *noun, plural* **foremen**

fore·most (**for**-mohst) *adjective* First in rank, position, or importance.

fo·ren·sic (fuh-**ren**-sik) *adjective* Using science and technology to investigate evidence and establish facts for use in a court of law. A forensic laboratory looks at clues such as fingerprints, DNA, and blood spatters.

fore·per·son (**for**-pur-suhn) *noun* A foreman or a forewoman.

fore·run·ner (**for**-ruhn-ur) *noun*
1. Someone who has come before, such as an ancestor or a predecessor. **2.** Something that has come before and led to something else. **3.** A sign of something to come.

F

fore·see (for-**see**) *verb* To expect or know beforehand. ▸ *verb* **foreseeing, foresaw, foreseen** ▸ *adjective* **foreseeable**

fore·sight (**for**-*site*) *noun* The ability to see into or plan for the future.

for·est (**for**-ist) *noun* A large area thickly covered with full-grown trees and plants. ▸ *adjective* **forested**

for·est rang·er (**for**-ist *rayn*-jur) *noun* Someone whose job is to manage and protect a forest.

fore·tell (for-**tel**) *verb* To forecast or predict something. ▸ *verb* **foretelling, foretold**

for·ev·er (fur-**ev**-ur) *adverb* **1.** For all time. **2.** Always or continually.

fore·wom·an (**for**-*wum*-an) *noun* **1.** A woman who leads a group of people who work together. **2.** The lead woman on a jury.
▸ *noun, plural* **forewomen**

for·feit (**for**-fit)
noun A penalty for something not done or badly done.
verb To give up the right to something.
▸ *verb* **forfeiting, forfeited** ▸ *noun* **forfeiture** (**for**-fi-chur)

for·gave (fur-**gave**) *verb* The past tense of **forgive.**

forge (forj)
verb **1.** To make a copy of something, such as money or a person's signature; to counterfeit. **2.** If you **forge ahead,** you move forward steadily or continue to make progress. **3.** To make or form something slowly and steadily, such as a friendship or an agreement.
noun A blacksmith's shop or the furnace in a blacksmith's shop.
▸ *verb* **forging, forged** ▸ *noun* **forger**

for·ger·y (**for**-jur-ee) *noun* Something that has been forged; an illegal copy.

for·get (fur-**get**) *verb* If you **forget** something, you fail to remember it. ▸ *verb* **forgetting, forgot, forgotten**

for·get·ful (fur-**get**-fuhl) *adjective* Having a habit of forgetting things. ▸ *noun* **forgetfulness**

for·get-me-not (fur-**get**-mee-*naht*) *noun* A plant with clusters of small, blue flowers, often used as a symbol of friendship.

for·give (fur-**giv**) *verb* To stop being angry with someone, or to stop blaming the person for something. ▸ *verb* **forgiving, forgave** (fur-**gayv**), **forgiven** (fur-**giv**-uhn) ▸ *adjective* **forgiving**

for·give·ness (fur-**giv**-nis) *noun* The act of forgiving someone.

fork (fork)
noun **1.** A kitchen tool with prongs used for eating. **2.** A farm tool with prongs used for lifting hay. **3.** A place where something, such as a road, river, or tree, branches into two or more directions.
verb **1.** To branch into two or more directions. **2.** If you **fork out** or **fork over** money, you give it even though you don't want to.
▸ *verb* **forking, forked** ▸ *adjective* **forked**

fork·lift (**fork**-*lift*) *noun* A vehicle with two long horizontal bars at the front, used for lifting and carrying large loads.

for·lorn (for-**lorn**) *adjective* **1.** Sad and lonely. **2.** A **forlorn** attempt or hope is one that has little chance of success, or of coming true.
▸ *adverb* **forlornly**

form (form)
noun **1.** Type or kind. **2.** Shape. **3.** A printed document with a list of questions and spaces for answers to be filled in. **4.** In grammar, one of the ways a word appears, depending on how it is used. For example, the word *children* is the plural form of the word *child*.
verb **1.** To make up or create something. **2.** To gradually appear, develop, or come into being. **3.** To make or to organize.
▸ *verb* **forming, formed** ▸ *adjective* **formless**

for·mal (**for**-muhl)
adjective **1.** Dressy and not casual. **2.** Official.
noun A social event, such as a dance, at which you are required to wear formal clothes.
▸ *adverb* **formally**

F

for·mat (for-mat)
noun The appearance, shape, or style of something.
verb To prepare a computer disk for use by erasing anything that may be on it.
▸ verb **formatting, formatted**

for·ma·tion (for-may-shuhn) noun
1. The process of something coming into existence. 2. A pattern or a shape. 3. The way in which the members of a group are arranged.

for·mer (for-mur)
noun The first of two things that have been mentioned.
adjective Previous or earlier.

for·mer·ly (for-mur-lee) adverb In the past, or at an earlier time.

for·mi·da·ble (for-mi-duh-buhl) adjective Frightening and awesome. ▸ adverb **formidably**

for·mu·la (for-myuh-luh) noun 1. A scientific or mathematical rule or principle that is written with numbers and symbols. 2. A suggested series of actions. 3. A mixture with several ingredients, or the recipe that you use to make one. 4. A liquid substitute for mother's milk.
▸ noun, plural **formulas** or **formulae (for-**myuh-lee)

for·mu·late (for-myuh-late) verb To work out an idea and then state it clearly. ▸ verb **formulating, formulated**

for·sake (for-sake) verb To give up, leave, or abandon. ▸ verb **forsaking, forsook (for-suk), forsaken**

for·sak·en (for-say-kuhn) adjective Abandoned or left.

for·syth·i·a (for-sith-ee-uh) noun A bush with bright yellow flowers that blooms in spring.

fort (fort) noun 1. A structure that is built to survive enemy attacks. 2. If you **hold the fort,** you take care of things for someone who is away.

forte
noun (fort or **for-**tay) Your **forte** is your strong point.
adverb (**for-**tay) **Forte** is the Italian word for loud. It is used in music.

forth (forth) adverb 1. Forward, or onward. 2. Out from hiding.

3. Away, or abroad.
Forth sounds like **fourth.**

forth·com·ing (forth-kuhm-ing) adjective 1. Coming soon. 2. If someone is not very **forthcoming,** he or she talks very little, or does not tell the entire truth.

for·ti·eth (for-tee-ith) adjective Next after 39th and before 41st, written numerically as 40th.

for·ti·fy (for-tuh-fye) verb 1. To build walls for protection from attack. 2. If you **fortify** yourself, you make yourself feel better and stronger. 3. To improve or to enrich.
▸ verb **fortifies, fortifying, fortified** ▸ noun **fortification**

fort·night (fort-nite) noun A period of two weeks. ▸ adjective **fortnightly** ▸ adverb **fortnightly**

for·tress (for-tris) noun A place such as a castle that is fortified against attack. ▸ noun, plural **fortresses**

for·tu·nate (for-chuh-nit) adjective Lucky. ▸ adverb **fortunately**

for·tune (for-chuhn) noun 1. Fate or destiny. 2. Chance or good luck. 3. A large amount of money.

for·ty (for-tee) noun The number that is equal to 4 times 10, written numerically as 40.

fo·rum (for-uhm) noun 1. The town square of an ancient Roman city. 2. A public discussion of an issue.

for·ward (for-wurd)
adverb 1. To or toward the front, or ahead. 2. If you **look forward** to something, you are eager to do it or experience it.
adjective 1. Bold or rude. 2. In front of, or ahead of, or to the front.
noun A player in basketball, hockey, or soccer who plays in an attacking position and tries to score goals.
verb To send something to a different person or address after it has been received.
▸ adverb **forwards**

fos·sil (fah-suhl) noun A bone, shell, or other trace of an animal or plant from millions of years ago, preserved as rock. ▸ verb **fossilize** ▸ adjective **fossilized**

F

fos·sil fu·el (**fah**-suhl *fyoo*-uhl) *noun*
Coal, oil, or natural gas, formed from
the remains of prehistoric plants and
animals.

fos·ter (**faws**-tur)
verb **1.** To bring up a child who is not
your own, without officially adopting
that child. **2.** To help the growth and
development of something.
adjective Having to do with a person or
family that brings up a child who is not
their own, without adopting that child.
▶ *verb* **fostering, fostered**

fought (fawt) *verb* The past tense and
the past participle of **fight.**

foul (foul)
adjective **1.** Filthy and disgusting.
2. Foul weather is rainy, stormy, and
unpleasant.
verb **1.** To break an important rule in a
sport. **2.** To pollute.
noun Something done in a sport that
is against the rules.
Foul sounds like **fowl.** ▶ *adjective*
fouler, foulest ▶ *verb* **fouling,
fouled** ▶ *noun* **foulness** ▶ *adverb*
foully

foul line (**foul** line) *noun* **1.** In baseball,
either of the two lines drawn from
home plate to first and third bases. A
ball hit outside of the foul lines is a
foul ball. 2. In basketball, the line on
either side of the court from which a
player shoots a penalty shot.

found (found) *verb* **1.** The past tense
and past participle of **find. 2.** To
establish something, such as a school,
a business, or an organization.
▶ *verb* **founding, founded**

foun·da·tion (foun-**day**-shuhn) *noun*
1. A solid structure on which a
building is constructed. **2.** The basis
of something. **3.** An organization that
gives money to worthwhile causes.

found·er (**foun**-dur) *noun* Someone
who establishes something that lasts
a long time.

found·ry (**foun**-dree) *noun* A factory for
melting and shaping metal. ▶ *noun,
plural* **foundries**

foun·tain (**foun**-tuhn) *noun* **1.** A
controlled stream or jet of water used
for drinking or for decoration.
2. A rich or abundant source.

foun·tain pen (**foun**-tuhn *pen*) *noun*
A pen with a point that is supplied
with liquid ink from a container
inside the pen.

four (for)
noun The number that comes
after three and before five, written
numerically as 4.
adjective Referring to the number that
comes after three and before five.

Four-H Club (**for**-aych *kluhb*) *noun* A
club for young people that teaches
community values through farming
and other useful skills. The four Hs
stand for head, heart, hands, and
health.

fourth (forth)
adjective Next after third and before
fifth, written numerically as 4th.
noun One part of something that has
been divided into four equal parts,
written numerically as 1/4.
Fourth sounds like **forth.**

Fourth of Ju·ly (**forth** uhv juh-**lye**) *noun*
A holiday that celebrates the signing
of the Declaration of Independence
on July 4, 1776.

fowl (foul) *noun* A bird, such as a
chicken, turkey, or duck, often raised
for its eggs or its meat. **Fowl** sounds
like **foul.** ▶ *noun, plural* **fowl** or **fowls**

fox (fahks) *noun* A wild animal
related to the dog, with thick fur, a
pointed nose and ears, and a bushy
tail. ▶ *noun, plural* **foxes**

fox·hound (**fahks**-hound) *noun* A breed
of dog of medium size that is trained
to hunt foxes.

foy·er (**foi**-ur *or* foi-**ay**) *noun* An entrance
hall, especially of a theater, an
apartment building, or a hotel.

frac·tal (**frak**-tuhl) *noun* A shape, often
drawn on a computer, that repeats
itself in a pattern over and over again.

frac·tion (**frak**-shuhn) *noun* **1.** A part of a
whole number. For example, 1/4, 1/2,
and 3/4 are all fractions. **2.** A part of a
whole. **3.** A small amount.
▶ *adjective* **fractional** ▶ *adverb*
fractionally

F

frac·ture (frak-chur)
verb To crack or break something, such as a bone or a tooth.
noun A crack or break in something, such as a bone or a tooth.
▶ *verb* **fracturing, fractured**

frag·ile (fraj-uhl) *adjective* Easily broken.

frag·ment
noun (frag-muhnt) A small piece or a part that is broken off.
verb (frag-ment) To break or cause something to break into small pieces or parts.
▶ *verb* **fragmenting, fragmented**

fra·grant (fray-gruhnt) *adjective* Having a sweet smell. ▶ *noun* **fragrance**

frail (frayl) *adjective* Weak. ▶ *adjective* **frailer, frailest** ▶ *noun* **frailty**

frame (frame)
noun 1. A basic structure that provides the support for a building. 2. A border that surrounds and holds something. 3. A **frame** on a webpage is a separate, self-contained area that works independently of the rest of the page. 4. The way in which a person's body is built.
verb 1. (informal) To make an innocent person seem guilty by providing false information or evidence. 2. To create or act as a border that surrounds something and makes it look attractive.
▶ *verb* **framing, framed**

frame·work (frame-wurk) *noun* 1. A structure that gives shape or support to something. 2. The rules, guidelines, or structure that controls how something works or happens.

franc (frangk) *noun* The main unit of money in Switzerland, many African countries, and formerly in France and Belgium. **Franc** sounds like **frank.**

France (frans) A country in western Europe. More foreign tourists visit France than any other country in the world. It is known for its cultural traditions, its wine and food, and its capital city, Paris.

fran·chise (fran-chize)
noun 1. The right to vote. 2. Permission given by a company to sell its services or distribute its products in a certain area. 3. A single location of a chain store or restaurant.
verb To give the right to someone to sell a product or service in a certain area.
▶ *verb* **franchising, franchised** ▶ *noun* **franchiser** ▶ *noun* **franchisee** (fran-chye-zee)

frank (frangk) *adjective* Honest in saying what you think or feel. **Frank** sounds like **franc.** ▶ *adjective* **franker, frankest** ▶ *noun* **frankness** ▶ *adverb* **frankly**

Fran·ken·food (frang-kuhn-food) *noun* (informal) Food made from genetically modified crops.

frank·fur·ter (frangk-fur-tur) *noun* A hot dog or small smoked sausage made of beef, pork, chicken, or other meat.

fran·tic (fran-tik) *adjective* Having or showing extreme worry or fear. ▶ *adverb* **frantically**

fraud (frawd) *noun* 1. Dishonest behavior and tricks that are intended to deceive people or get money from them. 2. If someone is a **fraud,** the person pretends to be something he or she is not.
▶ *adjective* **fraudulent** (fraw-juh-luhnt) ▶ *adverb* **fraudulently**

fray (fray)
verb To unravel.
noun A noisy argument or fight.
▶ *verb* **fraying, frayed**

freak (freek)
noun 1. A person, an animal, or a plant that has not developed normally. 2. (informal) A person who is very enthusiastic about or devoted to something.
adjective Very odd or unusual.

freck·le (frek-uhl) *noun* A small, light brown spot on the skin. ▶ *adjective* **freckled** *adjective* **freckly**

free (free)
adjective 1. If something is **free,** you can use it or enjoy it without having to pay for it. 2. If people or animals are **free,** they can do what they like without being stopped or controlled. 3. Not held

F

back. **4.** Not busy. **5.** Not affected by something.
verb To let a person or animal go from a prison or cage.
▶ *adjective* **freer, freest** ▶ *verb* **freeing, freed**

free·bie (**free**-bee) *noun* Something that is given for free.

free·dom (**free**-duhm) *noun* The right or power to do and say what you like.

free·lance (**free**-*lans*) *adjective* If you are a **freelance** worker, you get paid for each individual job you do, instead of earning a salary like an employee. ▶ *noun* **freelancer**

free·ly (**free**-lee) *adverb* **1.** Not under another's control; independently. **2.** Without limits or restrictions.

free-range (**free**-*raynj*) *adjective* **Free-range** animals are not kept indoors in cages, pens, or stalls. They are free to feed and move around outside.

free·ware (**free**-*wair*) *noun* Software that doesn't cost anything and that you usually download from the Internet.

free·way (**free**-*way*) *noun* A wide highway that you can travel on without paying tolls.

freeze (freez) *verb* **1.** To become solid or turn into ice at a very low temperature. **2.** To make or become very cold. **3.** To suddenly stop moving because you are very afraid. **4.** If your computer **freezes** or **freezes up,** it stops responding, usually because a program has caused it to stop. **5.** To be damaged or killed from the cold. **6.** To keep from rising. **Freeze** sounds like **frieze.** ▶ *verb* **freezing, froze** (frohz), **frozen** ▶ *adjective* **freezing**

freez·er (**free**-zur) *noun* An appliance or part of a refrigerator that freezes food quickly and keeps it from spoiling.

freez·ing point (**free**-zing *point*) *noun* The temperature at which a liquid turns solid or freezes. The freezing point of water is 32 degrees Fahrenheit, or 0 degrees Celsius.

freight (frayt) *noun* Goods that are carried by trains, ships, planes, or trucks.

freight·er (**fray**-tur) *noun* A ship or plane that carries cargo.

French fries (**french** frize) *noun, plural* Strips of potato that are fried in deep fat or oil.

French horn (**french** horn) *noun* A brass instrument made of a coiled tube that opens outward into a bell shape at the end. The French horn plays in a musical range below the trumpet and above the tuba.

fren·zy (**fren**-zee) *noun* If you are in a **frenzy,** you are wildly excited or frantic about something. ▶ *noun, plural* **frenzies** ▶ *adjective* **frenzied**

fre·quen·cy (**free**-kwuhn-see) *noun* **1.** If something happens with **frequency,** it happens often. **2.** The number of times that something happens. **3.** The number of cycles per second of a radio wave. **4.** The numbers that identify where on the dial a radio station can be found. **5.** The number of vibrations per second in a light wave.
▶ *noun, plural* **frequencies**

fre·quent
adjective (**free**-kwuhnt) Happening often.
verb (free-**kwent** *or* **free**-kwent) To visit somewhere often or regularly.
▶ *verb* **frequenting, frequented**

fre·quent·ly (**free**-kwuhnt-lee) *adverb* Often; at frequent intervals.

fres·co (**fres**-koh) *noun* A painting made on the damp plaster of a wall or ceiling. ▶ *noun, plural* **frescoes** *or* **frescos**

fresh (fresh) *adjective* **1.** Clean or new. **2.** Recently harvested. **3.** Cool or refreshing. **4.** Not salty. **5.** Rude.
▶ *adjective* **fresher, freshest** ▶ *adverb* **freshly**

fresh·en (**fresh**-uhn) *verb* To make something fresh, or fresher than it was before. ▶ *verb* **freshening, freshened**

fresh·man (**fresh**-muhn) *noun* Someone in the first year of high school or college.

F

fresh·wa·ter (**fresh**-*waw*-tur)
adjective Of or having to do with or living in water that does not contain salt.
noun Water that does not contain salt.

fret (fret)
verb To worry, get upset, or complain.
noun One of the bars or ridges on the neck of a stringed musical instrument, such as a guitar.
▶ *verb* **fretting, fretted** ▶ *noun* **fretfulness** ▶ *adjective* **fretful** ▶ *adverb* **fretfully**

fric·tion (**frik**-shuhn) *noun* 1. The rubbing of one object against another. 2. The force that slows down objects when they rub against each other. 3. Disagreement or anger.

Fri·day (**frye**-day *or* **frye**-dee) *noun* The sixth day of the week, after Thursday and before Saturday.

fridge (frij) *noun* Short for *refrigerator.*

friend (frend)
noun 1. Someone you like and know well. 2. Someone who supports a group or cause. 3. A contact on a social networking site.
verb To add someone to your list of friends on a social networking site.
▶ *verb* **friending, friended**

friend·ly (**frend**-lee) *adjective* 1. Warm, kind, or helpful; acting like a friend. 2. Not angry or hostile.
▶ *adjective* **friendlier, friendliest** ▶ *noun* **friendliness**

friend·ship (**frend**-ship) *noun* The state of being a friend or having friends.

fries (frize) *noun, plural* A short form of **French fries.**

frieze (freez) *noun* A horizontal band of decoration, usually along the top of a wall. **Frieze** sounds like **freeze.**

fright (frite) *noun* A sudden, intense feeling of fear or alarm.

fright·en (**frye**-tuhn) *verb* 1. To make someone afraid. 2. If you **frighten** someone **off,** you make that person too afraid to get involved or to stay nearby.
▶ *verb* **frightening, frightened**
▶ *adjective* **frightening**

fright·ful (**frite**-fuhl) *adjective* Terrifying, horrifying, or shocking. ▶ *adverb* **frightfully**

frig·id (**frij**-id) *adjective* 1. Extremely cold. 2. Stiff and formal; unfriendly.

frill (fril) *noun* A ruffled, gathered, or pleated edge or border. ▶ *adjective* **frilly**

fringe (frinj)
noun 1. A border of cords or threads attached to something. 2. Something that resembles a border or edging.
verb To form an edge or a border.
▶ *verb* **fringing, fringed**

Fris·bee (**friz**-bee) *noun* A trademark for a plastic disk tossed from person to person in various outdoor games.

frisk (frisk) *verb* 1. To search someone for something hidden, especially weapons or drugs. 2. To move in a lively and playful way.
▶ *verb* **frisking, frisked**

frisk·y (**fris**-kee) *adjective* Playful and full of energy. ▶ *adjective* **friskier, friskiest** ▶ *adverb* **friskily**

frit·ta·ta (free-**tah**-tuh) *noun* A flat omelet stuffed with a filling such as chopped vegetables, cheese, or meat.

frit·ter (**frit**-ur)
verb To use up in a careless, wasteful way.
noun A small fried cake containing corn, clams, fruit, or other ingredients.
▶ *verb* **frittering, frittered**

friv·o·lous (**friv**-uh-luhs) *adjective* 1. Silly or without any real purpose. 2. Not important; trivial.
▶ *adverb* **frivolously**

frog (frawg *or* frahg) *noun* A small amphibian with webbed feet and long hind legs that allow it to jump far. Frogs live in or near water.

frol·ic (**frah**-lik)
verb To behave playfully and happily.
noun Playful and happy activity.
▶ *verb* **frolicking, frolicked**

from (fruhm *or* frahm) *preposition* 1. Starting at or in. *The hurricane came from the south.* 2. In relative distance to. *The garage is not far from the house.* 3. In contrast to. *I can't tell him apart from his twin brother.* 4. Out of. *The first*

F

little pig's house was made from straw.
5. Because of. *I became sick from eating fried clams.* **6.** At. *I got this sundae from the ice-cream shop.*

frond (frahnd) *noun* A large leaf with many divisions, such as a fern or palm leaf.

front (fruhnt)
noun **1.** The part of something that comes first. **2.** The forward-facing part of someone or something. **3.** The area where two armies meet and fight. **4.** The forward edge of a mass of air. **5.** If you **put up a front,** you try to fool people by behaving in a certain way.
adjective Located at or on the front of something.

fron·tier (fruhn-**teer**) *noun* **1.** The far edge of a country, where few people live. **2.** The border separating two countries. **3.** A subject or an area of study that is just beginning to be understood.

frost (frawst)
noun **1.** A fine layer of powdery ice that forms on things when the temperature goes below freezing. **2.** A period of cold weather when the temperature falls below the freezing point.
verb **1. frost up** To get covered with frost. **2.** To put frosting on. ▶ *verb* **frosting, frosted**

frost·bite (frawst-*bite*) *noun* A condition that occurs when extremely cold temperatures damage parts of a person's body, such as fingers, toes, ears, or nose. ▶ *adjective* **frostbitten**

frost·ing (**fraw**-sting) *noun* Icing used to decorate cakes and pastries.

frost·y (**fraw**-stee) *adjective* **1.** Covered with powdery ice. **2.** Cold enough to form frost. **3.** Not at all friendly. ▶ *adjective* **frostier, frostiest** ▶ *noun* **frostiness** ▶ *adverb* **frostily**

froth (frawth)
noun A mass of small bubbles that forms in or on a liquid.
verb To produce a mass of small bubbles in or on a liquid. ▶ *verb* **frothing, frothed** ▶ *adjective* **frothy**

frown (froun)
verb **1.** To have an angry or annoyed look on your face. **2.** If you **frown on** something, you disapprove of it.
noun An expression on your face that shows you are angry, sad, or upset. ▶ *verb* **frowning, frowned**

fro·zen (**froh**-zuhn) *adjective* **1.** Forming into ice or turned into ice because of extremely low temperatures. **2.** Extremely cold. **3.** Chilled until hard, then stored in a freezer. **4.** Plugged up with ice. **5.** Too frightened to move.

fru·gal (**froo**-guhl) *adjective* Not wasteful; using money wisely. ▶ *noun* **frugality** (froo-**gal**-i-tee) ▶ *adverb* **frugally**

fruit (froot) *noun* **1.** The fleshy, juicy product of a plant that contains one or more seeds and is usually edible. **2.** The part of a flowering plant that contains seeds. **3.** The result or outcome.
▶ *noun, plural* **fruit** *or* **fruits** ▶ *adjective* **fruity**

fruit·ful (**froot**-fuhl) *adjective* Producing results. ▶ *noun* **fruitfulness** ▶ *adverb* **fruitfully**

fruit·less (**froot**-lis)
adjective Unproductive or unsuccessful. ▶ *adverb* **fruitlessly**

frus·trate (**fruhs**-trate) *verb* **1.** To prevent something from happening or from being successful. **2.** To make someone feel helpless or discouraged.
▶ *verb* **frustrating, frustrated** ▶ *adjective* **frustrated** ▶ *adjective* **frustrating**

frus·tra·tion (fruh-**stray**-shuhn) *noun* Annoyance caused by a failure, difficulty, or delay.

fry (frye) *verb* To cook food in hot fat or oil. ▶ *verb* **fries, frying, fried** ▶ *adjective* **fried**

fudge (fuhj)
noun A sweet, rich candy made with butter, sugar, milk, and usually chocolate.
verb To cheat or be dishonest about something.
▶ *verb* **fudging, fudged**

F

fu·el (**fyoo**-uhl)
noun Something that is used as a source of heat or energy, such as coal, wood, gasoline, or natural gas.
verb **1.** To supply the power for something. **2.** To cause something to become bigger or more widely known or believed.
▶ *verb* **fueling, fueled**

fu·gi·tive (**fyoo**-ji-tiv)
noun Someone who is running away, especially from the police.
adjective Running away and trying to avoid being captured.

ful·crum (**ful**-kruhm) *noun* The point on which a lever rests or turns. For example, the support on which a seesaw balances acts as a fulcrum. ▶ *noun, plural* **fulcrums** or **fulcra** (**ful**-kruh)

ful·fill (ful-**fil**) *verb* **1.** To perform or to do what is needed. **2.** To satisfy or measure up to something.
▶ *verb* **fulfilling, fulfilled** ▶ *noun* **fulfillment**

full (ful) *adjective* **1.** With no empty space left inside. **2.** Not leaving anything out. **3.** Having a large number. **4.** Not hungry anymore; having eaten enough.
▶ *adjective* **fuller, fullest**

full moon (ful moon) *noun* The phase of the moon when it is a full circle in the sky.

full-time (**ful**-time) *adjective* If you have a **full-time** job, the job takes up most of your day. You usually work five days a week for seven or eight hours a day.

full·y (**ful**-ee) *adverb* Completely; to the greatest or fullest extent.

fum·ble (**fuhm**-buhl)
verb **1.** To look for something in a clumsy way. **2.** To drop something or to handle it clumsily. **3.** To lose control of a football or a baseball after you have touched it.
noun A clumsy, awkward, or unsuccessful action.
▶ *verb* **fumbling, fumbled**

fume (fyoom)
noun, plural **fumes** Unpleasant or harmful gas, smoke, or vapor.

verb To feel anger, frustration, or resentment.
▶ *verb* **fuming, fumed**

fun (fuhn) *noun* A good time, or something that provides enjoyment.

func·tion (**fuhngk**-shuhn)
verb If something **functions,** it works properly.
noun **1.** A role, job, or activity that is someone's or something's purpose. **2.** A formal social gathering, such as a wedding. **3.** One of the things that a computer program can do.
▶ *verb* **functioning, functioned**

func·tion·al (**fuhngk**-shuh-nuhl) *adjective* If something is **functional,** it works well or is designed to be practical and useful.

func·tion key (**fuhngk**-shuhn *kee*) *noun* Any of the keys on the top row of a computer keyboard, numbered F1 to F12, that have different jobs in different programs.

fund (fuhnd)
noun **1.** Money kept for a special purpose. **2.** A supply.
noun, plural **funds** Money that is ready to use.
verb To provide the money for something to happen.
▶ *verb* **funding, funded**

fun·da·men·tal (**fuhn**-duh-**men**-tuhl)
adjective **1.** Basic and indispensable. **2.** Very important; major.
noun, plural **fundamentals** The most basic and indispensable parts of something.
▶ *adverb* **fundamentally**

fu·ner·al (**fyoo**-nur-uhl) *noun* The memorial ceremony that is held shortly after someone has died and that includes the person's burial or cremation.

fun·gus (**fuhng**-guhs) *noun* A plant-like organism that has no leaves, flowers, roots, or chlorophyll and grows on other plants or decaying matter. Some fungi can be poisonous. ▶ *noun, plural* **fungi** (**fuhn**-jye or **fuhng**-gye)

fun·nel (**fuhn**-uhl)
noun **1.** An open cone that narrows to a tube, used for pouring something

F

into a container that has a narrow neck. **2.** A smokestack on a ship or locomotive.
verb To pour something through or as if through a funnel.
▶ *verb* **funneling, funneled**

fun·ny (**fuhn**-ee)
adjective **1.** Amusing or humorous. **2.** Peculiar.
noun, plural **The funnies** are the comic strips or the comic section of a newspaper.
▶ *adjective* **funnier, funniest** ▶ *adverb* **funnily**

fur (fur) *noun* The coat of thick, soft hair on the skin of an animal.

fu·ri·ous (**fyoor**-ee-uhs) *adjective* **1.** Full of anger. **2.** Fierce or violent.
▶ *adverb* **furiously**

fur·long (**fur**-lawng) *noun* A distance of 220 yards.

fur·lough (**fur**-loh) *noun* **1.** Time off from duty for military people. **2.** Time off from work for a government employee when there is a budget problem.

fur·nace (**fur**-nis) *noun* A large, enclosed metal chamber in which fuel is burned to produce heat. Furnaces are used to heat buildings and to melt metals, glass, and other materials.

fur·nish (**fur**-nish) *verb* **1.** To equip a room or a house with furniture. **2.** To supply, provide, or equip someone with something.
▶ *verb* **furnishes, furnishing, furnished** ▶ *noun, plural* **furnishings**

fur·ni·ture (**fur**-ni-chur) *noun* The large, movable things in a room or office that make it a place to live or work, such as chairs, tables, desks, and beds.

fur·row (**fur**-oh)
noun The long, narrow groove that a plow cuts in the ground.
verb If you **furrow** your brow, you wrinkle up your forehead because you are puzzled or worried.
▶ *verb* **furrowing, furrowed**

fur·ry (**fur**-ee)
adjective Something that is **furry** has a lot of fur.
noun **furry friend** Pets such as dogs,

cats, rabbits, and other animals are sometimes called our **furry friends.**
▶ *adjective* **furrier, furriest**

fur·ther (fur-**THur**)
adjective or adverb A comparative of **far.**
adverb **1.** To a greater degree or extent. **2.** At a greater distance; farther.
adjective **1.** Additional. **2.** More distant or remote.
verb To help advance or go forward.
▶ *verb* **furthering, furthered**

fur·ther·more (fur-**THur**-mor) *adverb* In addition; besides.

fur·thest (fur-**THist**) *adjective, adverb* Another form of **farthest.**

fur·tive (**fur**-tiv) *adjective* Sly or sneaky. ▶ *noun* **furtiveness** ▶ *adverb* **furtively**

fu·ry (**fyoor**-ee) *noun* **1.** Extreme anger, rage, or violence. **2.** A dangerous or violent force.
▶ *noun, plural* **furies**

fuse (fyooz)
noun **1.** A safety device in electrical equipment that cuts off the power if something goes wrong. **2.** A cord that burns slowly and then causes a bomb or firework to explode.
verb To melt two pieces of something, such as metal or plastic, together by heating them.
▶ *verb* **fusing, fused**

fu·se·lage (**fyoo**-suh-*lahzh*) *noun* The main body of an aircraft where the passengers, crew, and cargo are carried.

fu·sion (**fyoo**-zhuhn) *noun* The joining together of two different things by blending or melting.

fuss (fuhs)
verb To be in a state of nervous, worried, or useless activity.
noun A flurry of needless activity or excitement.
▶ *verb* **fusses, fussing, fussed** ▶ *noun, plural* **fusses**

fuss·y (**fuhs**-ee) *adjective* **1.** Overly concerned with small details. **2.** If you are a **fussy** eater, there are many foods that you don't like or won't eat.
▶ *adjective* **fussier, fussiest**

F

fu·tile (**fyoo**-tuhl) *adjective* If an action is **futile,** it has no useful outcome. ▶ *noun* **futility** (fyoo-**til**-i-tee)

fu·ton (**foo**-tahn) *noun* A hard mattress that is filled with cotton or similar material and does not contain springs.

fu·ture (**fyoo**-chur)
noun 1. The time yet to come.
2. Another name for the **future tense.**
adjective Coming or happening after the present time.

future tense (**fyoo**-chur **tens**) *noun* A form of a verb using the words *will, be going to,* or *shall* to indicate future time. The sentences "I will mow the lawn tomorrow," "She is going to travel to the East Coast," and "We shall obey the rules" are examples of the future tense.

fuzz (fuhz) *noun* A coating of short, soft hair or fibers.

fuzz·y (**fuhz**-ee) *adjective* 1. Like fuzz, or covered with fuzz. 2. Not clear or distinct.
▶ *adjective* **fuzzier, fuzziest**

G

gab (gab) *verb* (slang) To chat or to gossip. ▶ *verb* **gabbing, gabbed**

ga·ble (**gay**-buhl) *noun* The triangular part of the outside wall of a building between the eaves and the ridge of the roof.

Ga·bon (gah-**bawn**) A country in western Central Africa on the Gulf of Guinea. Much of the country is covered by a dense rain forest, the habitat for what is believed to be the largest population of forest-dwelling elephants in Central Africa. A French colony until 1960, Gabon is now a democracy.

gad·get (**gaj**-it) *noun* A small tool that does a particular job.

gag (gag)
verb 1. To tie a piece of cloth around someone's mouth to stop the person from talking or crying out. 2. If you **gag,** you feel as though you are about to choke or throw up.
noun 1. Something put over the mouth to stop someone from making a noise.
2. (informal) A joke.
▶ *verb* **gagging, gagged**

gain (gayn)
verb 1. To get or win something. 2. To increase the amount of something.
3. If you **gain on** someone, you start to catch up with the person.
noun A profit, or an increase.
▶ *verb* **gaining, gained**

gait (gayt) *noun* A way of walking. **Gait** sounds like **gate.**

ga·la (**gay**-luh *or* **gal**-uh)
noun A special event that usually includes food, entertainment, and important guests.
adjective Including a party, decorations, celebration, and similar activities.

gal·ax·y (**gal**-uhk-see) *noun* A very large group of stars and planets. ▶ *noun, plural* **galaxies** ▶ *adjective* **galactic** (guh-**lak**-tik)

gale (gale) *noun* 1. A very strong wind.
2. A noisy outburst.

gal·lant (**gal**-uhnt) *adjective* 1. Brave and selfless. 2. Courteous and attentive, especially to women.
▶ *adverb* **gallantly**

gall·blad·der (**gawl**-blad-ur) *noun* The organ in your body that stores a liquid called bile, or gall, that helps you digest food.

gal·le·on (**gal**-ee-uhn) *noun* A sailing ship with three masts used in the 15th to early 18th centuries for trading and warfare.

gal·ler·y (**gal**-ur-ee) *noun* 1. A place where paintings, sculpture, and other works of art are exhibited and sometimes sold. 2. An upstairs seating area or balcony, especially in large halls and theaters.
▶ *noun, plural* **galleries**

gal·ley (**gal**-ee) *noun* 1. The kitchen on a boat or an airplane. 2. A long, flat boat with many oars, used in ancient times.

gal·lon (**gal**-uhn) *noun* A liquid measure equal to four quarts.

gal·lop (**gal**-uhp)
verb When a horse **gallops,** it runs as fast as it can with all four feet off the ground at once.
noun 1. The movement of a horse at its fastest speed. 2. A very fast speed.
▶ *verb* **galloping, galloped**

gal·lows (**gal**-ohz) *noun* A wooden frame with two standing posts and a beam from which a noose is suspended, once used for hanging criminals.

ga·loot (guh-**loot**) *noun* (slang) A clumsy person.

ga·lore (guh-**lor**) *adjective* In large numbers.

ga·losh·es (guh-**lah**-shiz) *noun, plural* Waterproof shoes that fit over ordinary shoes and protect them from rain and snow.

gal·va·nize (**gal**-vuh-*nize*) *verb* 1. To coat steel or iron with zinc to keep it from rusting. 2. To strongly encourage and bring about action, support, or change.
▶ *verb* **galvanizing, galvanized**

Gam·bi·a (**gam**-bee-uh) A country in western Africa on the Atlantic Ocean. The smallest nation in Africa, it occupies a long, narrow strip of land on both sides of the Gambia River.

Gam·bi·a Riv·er (**gam**-bee-uh **riv**-ur) A major river of western Africa, which flows into the Atlantic Ocean. The Gambia River originates in northern Guinea, and passes through part of Senegal and then Gambia before reaching the Atlantic.

gam·ble (**gam**-buhl) *verb* 1. To bet money on the outcome of a race, game, or contest. 2. To take a risk or behave recklessly.
▶ *verb* **gambling, gambled** ▶ *noun* **gambler**

gam·bling (**gam**-bling) *noun* The activity of betting money on cards, horses, or the outcome of future events.

game (game)
noun 1. An activity with rules that can be played by one or more people. 2. Wild animals that are hunted for sport or for food.
adjective Eager and willing to do something.

game con·sole (game *kahn*-sole) *noun* A computer that is used in combination with other equipment, including a TV or monitor, to play video games.

gam·er (**gay**-mur) *noun* Someone who plays video games or who plays games online.

gam·ing (**gay**-ming) *noun* 1. The activity of playing video games or playing games online. 2. The activity or business of gambling.

gan·der (**gan**-dur) *noun* 1. A male goose. 2. (informal) If you **take a gander** at something, you look or glance at it.

gang (gang)
noun 1. A group of people who spend a lot of time together. 2. An organized group of criminals or young people involved in crime. 3. A group of people organized to do physical work.
verb If several people **gang up** on you, they all turn against you.
▶ *verb* **ganging, ganged**

gang·plank (**gang**-*plangk*) *noun* A movable bridge or wooden ramp used for walking onto and off a ship or boat.

gan·grene (**gang**-green) *noun* A dangerous condition in which your skin or organs decay, usually because the blood supply has been cut off to a part of the body.

gang·ster (**gang**-stur) *noun* A member of an organized group of criminals.

gang·way
noun (**gang**-*way*) 1. A passageway on a ship or walkway between buildings. 2. A gangplank.
interjection (**gang**-way) A word used to tell people that they need to get out of the way.

G

gap (gap) *noun* **1.** A space between things. **2.** Something that is missing. **3.** A difference between people or things.

gape (gape)
verb **1.** To open your mouth wide and stare in surprise. **2.** To open widely.
noun **1.** A large opening. **2.** The part of a beak that opens.
▶ *verb* **gaping, gaped**

ga·rage (guh-**rahzh** *or* guh-**rahj**) *noun* **1.** A building used for storing vehicles. **2.** A place where cars and other vehicles are repaired.

gar·bage (**gahr**-bij) *noun* **1.** Food or things thrown away. **2.** Something considered worthless or meaningless.

gar·bled (**gahr**-buhld) *adjective* Garbled language or speech is mixed up and does not make sense.

gar·den (**gahr**-duhn)
noun A piece of land, often near a house, where flowers, vegetables, herbs, and shrubs are planted.
verb To grow or take care of plants in a garden.
▶ *verb* **gardening, gardened** ▶ *noun* **gardener** ▶ *noun* **gardening**

gar·de·nia (gahr-**deen**-yuh) *noun* A tropical evergreen tree or bush with fragrant, usually white flowers.

gar·gle (**gahr**-guhl) *verb* To breathe out with liquid in your mouth while your head is held back, usually to clean or treat your throat. ▶ *verb* **gargling, gargled**

gar·goyle (**gahr**-goil) *noun* A grotesque animal head or figure carved out of stone and used to carry rainwater away from the wall of a building.

gar·ish (**gair**-ish) *adjective* Too brightly colored and overly decorated; flashy. ▶ *adverb* **garishly**

gar·land (**gahr**-luhnd) *noun* A wreath of flowers and leaves, often worn on the head as a mark of honor.

gar·lic (**gahr**-lik) *noun* **1.** A strong-smelling plant related to an onion. **2.** The strong-tasting bulb of the garlic plant, used in cooking to add flavor and in home remedies.

gar·ment (**gahr**-muhnt) *noun* A piece of clothing.

gar·net (**gahr**-nit) *noun* A dark red stone worn as jewelry or used in industry.

gar·nish (**gahr**-nish)
verb To decorate food that is going to be served.
noun Something that is used to decorate food that is going to be served.
▶ *verb* **garnishes, garnishing, garnished** ▶ *noun, plural* **garnishes**

gar·ri·son (**gar**-i-suhn)
noun **1.** A group of soldiers assigned to defend a town. **2.** The building occupied by these soldiers.
verb To send a group of soldiers to a town or building in order to defend it.
▶ *verb* **garrisoning, garrisoned**

gar·ter (**gahr**-tur) *noun* An elastic band that people wear to keep a piece of clothing, such as a stocking or sock, from sliding down.

gar·ter snake (**gahr**-tur *snake*) *noun* A small, harmless snake with yellow stripes on its back.

gas (gas) *noun* **1.** A substance, such as air, that will spread to fill any space that contains it. **2.** A source of energy made from coal; natural gas. **3.** A liquid fuel used in many vehicles. Gas is short for **gasoline**. **4.** The accelerator pedal on a motor vehicle. **5.** (informal) If someone or something is **a gas**, it is entertaining or amusing.
▶ *noun, plural* **gases** ▶ *adjective* **gaseous** (**gas**-ee-uhs *or* **gash**-uhs)

gash (gash)
noun A long, deep cut.
verb To make a deep cut in something.
▶ *noun, plural* **gashes** ▶ *verb* **gashes, gashing, gashed**

gas·o·line (**gas**-uh-*leen*) *noun* A liquid fuel made from oil, which is used in many vehicles. Also called **gas.**

gasp (gasp)
verb **1.** To breathe in suddenly because you are surprised, in pain, or have exercised heavily. **2.** To speak while out of breath.
noun A loud and sudden breath.
▶ *verb* **gasping, gasped**

G

gas sta·tion (**gas** *stay*-shuhn) *noun* A place that sells gasoline, oil, and other things needed to keep motor vehicles running.

gas·tric (**gas**-trik) *adjective* Of or having to do with the stomach.

gas·tro·pod (**gas**-truh-*pahd*) *noun* An animal that slides on a long foot that also contains its mouth parts, such as a slug or a snail.

gate (gayt) *noun* 1. A frame on hinges in an outdoor wall or fence, that opens like a door. 2. The number of people paying to see a game, a sporting event, or a performance, such as a concert. **Gate** sounds like **gait.**

gate·way (**gate**-*way*) *noun* 1. An opening through which you can enter by a gate. 2. A way to get something you want. 3. A place where people enter a country.

gath·er (**gaTH**-ur) *verb* 1. To collect things into one place. 2. To come together in a group. 3. To learn something by listening or watching. 4. To gain little by little. 5. To attract or accumulate. 6. To draw toward yourself. ▶ *verb* **gathering, gathered**

gaud·y (**gaw**-dee) *adjective* If someone's clothing is **gaudy,** it is too brightly colored and fancy. If someone's jewelry is **gaudy,** it is too large and showy. ▶ *adjective* **gaudier, gaudiest**

gauge (gayj) *verb* 1. To judge something or make a guess about it. 2. To measure the amount or level of something. *noun* 1. An instrument for measuring something. 2. A set measurement, such as the distance between two rails of a railroad track. ▶ *verb* **gauging, gauged**

gaunt (gawnt) *adjective* Very thin and bony.

gaunt·let (**gawnt**-lit) *noun* 1. A long, protective glove, worn in the past by soldiers to prevent injury from weapons. 2. If you **throw down the gauntlet,** you challenge someone to do something. If you **take up the gauntlet,** you accept a challenge that someone has made.

gauze (gawz) *noun* A thin woven cloth used as a bandage.

gave (gayv) *verb* The past tense of **give.**

gav·el (**gav**-uhl) *noun* A small wooden hammer that is used to signal the beginning of a meeting or to call for quiet. A gavel is used by an auctioneer or a judge.

gay (gay) *adjective* 1. A **gay** person is attracted to people of the same sex. 2. Lighthearted and lively. 3. Decorated with bright colors. ▶ *adjective* **gayer, gayest** ▶ *adverb* **gaily**

gaze (gayz) *verb* To look at something steadily. *noun* A long steady look at someone or something. ▶ *verb* **gazing, gazed**

ga·zelle (guh-**zel**) *noun* A graceful, fast-running antelope found in Africa and Asia.

gear (geer) *noun, plural* **gears** A set of wheels with teeth that fit together to control the flow of energy and movement in a machine. *noun* Equipment or clothing. *verb* 1. To make suitable. 2. If you **gear up** for something, you get ready for it. ▶ *verb* **gearing, geared**

geck·o (**gek**-oh) *noun* A kind of small, harmless lizard often found in houses in warm countries. ▶ *noun, plural* **geckos** or **geckoes**

geese (gees) *noun, plural* The plural of **goose.**

Gei·ger count·er (**gye**-gur *koun*-tur) *noun* An instrument that finds and measures radioactivity.

gel (jel) *noun* A substance between a liquid and a solid, as in *hair gel.* **Gel** sounds like **jell.**

gel·a·tin (**jel**-uh-tin) *noun* A clear substance with thickening properties used in making glue and such desserts as Jell-O and marshmallows. Gelatin is made from animal bones and other tissues.

gem (jem) *noun* A precious stone often used in jewelry, such as a diamond, a ruby, or an emerald.

G

gen·der (jen-dur) *noun* 1. The male or female sex. 2. A category of nouns. In English we show the gender of a noun mainly by the kind of pronoun that can refer to it. Feminine nouns such as *girl* use *she*, masculine nouns such as *boy* use *he*, neuter nouns such as *table* use *it*, and plural nouns such as *children* use *they*.

gene (jeen) *noun* One of the parts that make up chromosomes. Genes are passed from parents to children and determine how you look and the way you grow.

ge·ne·al·o·gy (jee-nee-**al**-uh-jee) *noun* 1. The study of family history over many generations. 2. The history of a family.
▶ *noun, plural* **genealogies** ▶ *noun* **genealogist**

gen·er·a (jen-ur-uh) *noun, plural* A plural of **genus**.

gen·er·al (jen-ur-uhl)
adjective 1. Of or having to do with everybody or everything. 2. Not detailed or specialized. 3. Not very specific or definite.
noun A very high-ranking officer in the army, air force, or marines.

gen·er·al·ize (jen-ur-uh-*lize*) *verb* 1. To make a statement that applies to everyone or everything. 2. To discuss something in a vague or general way.
▶ *verb* **generalizing, generalized**
▶ *noun* **generalization**

gen·er·al·ly (jen-ur-uh-lee) *adverb* Usually; under most circumstances or in most cases.

gen·er·ate (jen-uh-*rate*) *verb* To create or produce something. ▶ *verb* **generating, generated**

gen·er·a·tion (jen-uh-**ray**-shuhn) *noun* 1. All the people born around the same time. 2. The average amount of time between the birth of parents and that of their children. A generation is 25 to 30 years. 3. The descendants from a shared ancestor. 4. The process of bringing something into being.

gen·er·a·tor (jen-uh-*ray*-tur) *noun* A machine that produces electricity by turning a magnet inside a coil of wire.

ge·ner·ic (juh-**ner**-ik) *adjective* 1. Of or having to do with a whole group or class of something. 2. Not sold under a trademark and available from different companies.

gen·er·os·i·ty (jen-uh-**rah**-si-tee) *noun* The quality of or an act of being generous and giving.

gen·er·ous (jen-ur-uhs) *adjective* 1. Willing and happy to give to and share with others. 2. Larger than expected or larger than usual.
▶ *adverb* **generously**

ge·net·ic (juh-**net**-ik) *adjective* Controlled by or having to do with genes and heredity. ▶ *adverb* **genetically**

ge·net·i·cal·ly mod·i·fied (juh-**net**-ik-lee **mah**-duh-*fide*) *adjective* Containing genes that have been changed in order to produce a desirable quality.

ge·net·ics (juh-**net**-iks) *noun* The study of how personal characteristics are passed from one generation to the next through genes.

ge·nial (jeen-yuhl) *adjective* Friendly and welcoming. ▶ *noun* **geniality** (jee-nee-**al**-i-tee) ▶ *adverb* **genially**

ge·nie (jee-nee) *noun* A magical spirit who grants the wishes of the person who summons it.

gen·ius (jeen-yuhs) *noun* 1. A highly intelligent or talented person. 2. An exceptional or natural ability.
▶ *noun, plural* **geniuses**

ge·nome (jee-nohm) *noun* A full set of chromosomes in an organism.

gen·re (**zhahn**-ruh) *noun* A particular kind of creative work. For example, science fiction and fantasy are two genres of story writing.

gen·teel (jen-teel) *adjective* Extremely polite and careful in your behavior. ▶ *noun* **gentility** (jen-**til**-i-tee)

gen·tile *or* **Gen·tile** (jen-tile) *noun* A person who is not Jewish.

gen·tle (jen-tuhl) *adjective* 1. Not rough. 2. Kind and sensitive to people. 3. Not steep or extreme.
▶ *adjective* **gentler, gentlest** ▶ *noun* **gentleness** ▶ *adverb* **gently**

G

gen·tle·man (jen-tuhl-muhn) *noun*
1. A polite term for a man. **2.** A man with good manners who treats other people well. **3.** A man who belongs to a high social class.
▸ *noun, plural* **gentlemen** ▸ *adjective* **gentlemanly**

gen·tle·wom·an (jen-tuhl-*wum*-uhn) *noun* **1.** A polite term for a woman. It is frequently used in Congress to refer to a female senator or representative. **2.** A woman with good manners who treats other people well. **3.** A woman who belongs to a high social class.
▸ *noun, plural* **gentlewomen**

gen·tri·fi·ca·tion (jen-truh-fi-**kay**-shuhn) *noun* The rebuilding of old city neighborhoods to attract people with more money. ▸ *verb* **gentrify**

gen·u·ine (jen-yoo-in) *adjective* **1.** Real and not fake. **2.** Honest and sincere.

gen·u·ine·ly (jen-yoo-in-lee) *adverb* **1.** Truly; really. **2.** Sincerely.

ge·nus (jee-nuhs) *noun* In taxonomy, a **genus** is a group of related plants or animals that is larger than a species but smaller than a family. Dogs and wolves, for example, belong to the genus *Canis*. ▸ *noun, plural* **genera** (**jen**-ur-uh) *or* **genuses**

ge·o·des·ic (jee-uh-**des**-ik) *adjective* Of or having to do with the geometry of curved surfaces.

ge·og·ra·phy (jee-**ah**-gruh-fee) *noun* **1.** The study of the earth, its people, climate, natural resources, and physical features, such as its mountains, rivers, oceans, and continents. **2.** The physical features of a place or an area.
▸ *noun, plural* **geographies** ▸ *noun* **geographer** ▸ *adjective* **geographical** (jee-uh-**graf**-i-kuhl)

ge·ol·o·gy (jee-**ah**-luh-jee) *noun* The study of the earth's physical structure, especially its layers of soil and rock. ▸ *noun* **geologist** ▸ *adjective* **geological** (jee-uh-**lah**-ji-kuhl)

ge·o·met·ric (jee-uh-**met**-rik) *adjective* **1.** Of or having to do with geometry. **2.** Having a regular shape on the outside. **3.** A **geometric** design is one that uses simple lines, circles, or squares to form a pattern.

ge·om·e·try (jee-**ah**-muh-tree) *noun* The branch of mathematics that deals with points, lines, angles, shapes, and solids.

Geor·gia (jor-juh) A country in the Caucasus region of Europe where eastern Europe meets western Asia. Formerly part of the Soviet Union, Georgia takes its name from its patron saint, St. George. According to tradition, the Catholic saint slew a dragon. The large red cross in the middle of the country's flag is known as a St. George's Cross.

Geor·gia (jor-juh) A state in the southeastern United States. One of the original 13 colonies, it was the only one to be named after a king, George II of England. Atlanta is the state's capital and largest city. Many major U.S. corporations have their headquarters in the Atlanta metropolitan area, one of the fastest-growing regions in the country.

ge·o·ther·mal (jee-oh-**thur**-muhl) *adjective* Of or having to do with the heat inside the earth and its commercial use.

ge·ra·ni·um (juh-**ray**-nee-uhm) *noun* A common house or garden plant with thick stems and clusters of red, pink, or white flowers.

ger·bil (**jur**-buhl) *noun* A mouselike rodent with long hind legs and a tufted tail, often kept as a pet.

ger·i·at·rics (jer-ee-**at**-riks) *noun, plural* The study of the health and care of very old people. ▸ *adjective* **geriatric**

germ (jurm) *noun* **1.** A tiny living organism that can cause disease. **2.** The very beginning of something.

Ger·man·ic (juhr-**man**-ik) *noun* A language that scholars believe was the parent of modern English, German, Dutch, and other related languages.
adjective Of or having to do with Germans, Germany, or languages related to German.

G

Ger·man mea·sles (jur-muhn **mee**-zuhlz) noun A contagious illness that gives you a rash and a slight fever.

Ger·man shep·herd (jur-muhn **shep**-urd) noun A breed of large dog with pointed ears, a narrow nose, and black, brown, or gray fur. German shepherds are often used for police work and as guide dogs for blind people.

Ger·ma·ny (jur-muh-nee) A country in Central Europe. It was divided after World War II into East Germany and West Germany, but it was reunified in 1990 after the fall of the Berlin Wall.

ger·mi·nate (jur-muh-nate) verb 1. When seeds or beans **germinate,** they start to put out shoots. 2. To come into being and develop.
▶ verb **germinating, germinated**
▶ noun **germination**

ges·ture (jes-chur)
verb To move a part of the body in order to communicate a feeling or an intention.
noun 1. An action that shows a feeling or that communicates something. 2. Something that is done for show, even though it is unlikely to have any effect.
▶ verb **gesturing, gestured**

get (get) verb 1. To obtain something or begin to have it in your possession. 2. To capture. 3. To become. 4. To arrive somewhere. 5. To be present and affected by something that happens. 6. To become sick with something. 7. (informal) To fully understand something. 8. **get away with** To escape blame or punishment. 9. **get by** To manage with very little money. 10. **get over** To recover from something. 11. **get to** To annoy or upset.
▶ verb **getting, got** (gaht), **got** or **gotten (gah**-tuhn)

get·a·way (get-uh-way) noun 1. A fast escape. 2. A short vacation.

gey·ser (gye-zur) noun An underground hot spring that shoots boiling water and steam into the air.

Gha·na (gah-nuh) A country in West Africa on the Gulf of Guinea. Its Lake Volta reservoir, which covers more than 3,000 square miles (7,770 square kilometers), is one of the largest man-made lakes in the world. Ghana is the world's second-largest producer of cocoa, after Côte d'Ivoire.

ghast·ly (gast-lee) adjective 1. Horrible. 2. (informal) Very bad or unpleasant. 3. If you feel or look **ghastly,** you feel or look very ill.
▶ adjective **ghastlier, ghastliest**

ghet·to (get-oh) noun A usually poor neighborhood in a city where people of the same race, religion, or ethnic background live. ▶ noun, plural **ghettos** or **ghettoes**

ghost (gohst) noun 1. The spirit of a dead person that haunts a place or is visible to the living. 2. A faint trace.

ghost·ly (gohst-lee) adjective Like a ghost.

ghost town (gohst toun) noun A deserted town with few or no people living there.

GI (jee-eye) noun 1. An American soldier. 2. **GI Bill** A set of laws that give benefits to people who have served in the military.

gi·ant (jye-uhnt)
noun In folktales and fairy tales, a **giant** is a mythical being of superhuman size.
adjective Very large.

gib·bon (gib-uhn) noun A kind of small ape that lives in trees in Southeast Asia.

gid·dy (gid-ee) adjective 1. Feeling dizzy and unsteady from being unwell. 2. Feeling excited.
▶ adjective **giddier, giddiest** ▶ noun **giddiness** ▶ adverb **giddily**

GIF (jif or gif) noun A common format for image files. GIF is short for graphics interchange format.

gift (gift) noun 1. A present. 2. A natural ability or special talent.

gift·ed (gif-tid) adjective Having a special, natural ability to do something.

G

gig (gig) *noun* **1.** (informal) A job for a musician or band playing jazz or popular music. **2.** (informal) A temporary job. **3.** (informal) Short for **gigabyte.**

gig·a·byte (**gig**-uh-*bite*) *noun* A unit for measuring the amount of data in a computer memory or file. A gigabyte is about 1 billion bytes.

gi·ga·hertz (**gig**-uh-*hurts*) *noun* A measure of frequency equal to one billion cycles per second. Gigahertz is used to measure the speed of some computers, and also the frequency of some radio broadcasts.

gi·gan·tic (jye-**gan**-tik) *adjective* Huge in size or extent.

gig·gle (**gig**-uhl)
verb To laugh in a nervous or silly way.
noun A quick, nervous and silly laugh.
▶ *verb* **giggling, giggled** ▶ *adjective* **giggly**

gild (gild)
verb To coat something with a thin layer of gold.
adjective **gilded** Very wealthy or privileged.
▶ *verb* **gilding, gilded**

gill (gil) *noun* Either of the pair of organs near a fish's mouth through which it breathes by extracting oxygen from water.

gilt (gilt) *adjective* Decorated with a thin coating of gold or gold paint. **Gilt** sounds like **guilt.**

gim·mick (**gim**-ik) *noun* A clever gadget, trick, or idea that gets people's attention.

gin·ger (**jin**-jur)
noun **1.** A fragrant plant root that gives a spicy flavor to food and drink. **2.** A light reddish-yellow or reddish-brown color.
adjective Having a light reddish-yellow or reddish-brown color.
▶ *adjective* **gingery**

gin·ger·bread (**jin**-jur-*bred*) *noun* A brown cake or cookie flavored with ginger and other spices.

gin·ger·ly (**jin**-jur-lee) *adverb* In a cautious or careful way.

ging·ham (**ging**-uhm) *noun* Lightweight cotton cloth with a checked pattern.

gink·go (**ging**-koh) *noun* A tree with leaves shaped like a fan, originally from China but now grown in many places.

gi·raffe (juh-**raf**) *noun* A large African mammal with a very long neck and legs and dark brown patches on its coat. The giraffe is the tallest animal in the world.

gird·er (**gur**-dur) *noun* A large, heavy beam made of steel or concrete, used in construction.

girl (gurl) *noun* A female child or young woman.

girl·friend (**gurl**-frend) *noun* **1.** The girl or woman with whom someone is having a romantic relationship. **2.** A female friend.

girl·hood (**gurl**-hud) *noun* The time during which someone is a girl.

girl·ish (**gur**-lish) *adjective* Like a girl or like what girls usually do.

girth (gurth) *noun* A measure around something.

gist (jist) *noun* The main point or general meaning of something.

give (giv) *verb* **1.** To hand something to another person. **2.** To pay. **3.** To supply. **4.** To offer. **5.** To cause to happen. **6. give in** To stop fighting or arguing with someone. **7. give rise to** To be the cause or source of. **8. give up** To stop trying. **9. give up on** To lose faith in.
▶ *verb* **giving, gave** (gayv), **given** (**giv**-uhn)

gla·cier (**glay**-shur) *noun* A slow-moving mass of ice found in mountain valleys or polar regions. A glacier is formed when snow falls and does not melt because the temperature remains below freezing.

glad (glad) *adjective* Pleased or happy. ▶ *adjective* **gladder, gladdest** ▶ *noun* **gladness** ▶ *verb* **gladden** ▶ *adverb* **gladly**

glade (glade) *noun* An open, grassy space in the middle of a forest or wooded area.

G

glad·i·a·tor (**glad**-ee-ay-tur) *noun* A man in ancient Rome who fought other men or wild animals, often to the death, in order to provide entertainment. Some gladiators were professional fighters, but others were slaves, criminals, or captives from other countries.

glad·i·o·lus (glad-ee-**oh**-luhs) *noun* A popular plant for bouquets, with long, sword-shaped leaves and brightly colored flowers arranged in a row on a long stem. ▸ *noun, plural* **gladioli** (glad-ee-**oh**-lye)

glam·or·ous (**glam**-ur-uhs) *adjective* Attractive and exciting.

glam·our *or* **glam·or** (**glam**-ur) *noun* An exciting or fascinating quality that makes people or things attractive.

glance (glans)
verb 1. To look at something or someone quickly. 2. To hit something and bounce off at an angle.
noun A quick look at something or someone.
▸ *verb* **glancing, glanced** ▸ *adjective* **glancing**

gland (gland) *noun* An organ in the body that produces or releases natural chemicals. ▸ *adjective* **glandular** (**glan**-juh-lur)

glare (glair)
noun 1. Very bright light that makes it hard for you to see. 2. An angry look.
verb 1. To look at someone in an angry way. 2. To shine with a very bright light that makes it hard for you to see.
▸ *verb* **glaring, glared**

glar·ing (**glair**-ing) *adjective* 1. Very bright and gaudy. 2. Very obvious.
▸ *adverb* **glaringly**

glass (glas) *noun* 1. A transparent material made from melted sand, used in windows, bottles, and lenses. 2. A container for drinking, made from glass or plastic.
▸ *noun, plural* **glasses**

glass·es (**glas**-iz) *noun, plural* Lenses set in frames that rest on a person's nose and ears, worn to correct eyesight.

glaze (glayz)
noun 1. A thin coat of liquid that is applied to pottery before it is fired to give it a shiny, colorful finish. 2. A liquid used to form a coating on food. 3. A thin coating of something.
verb 1. To put glass into a window. 2. If you are bored or tired, your eyes may **glaze over,** taking on a fixed and vacant appearance.
▸ *verb* **glazing, glazed** ▸ *adjective* **glazed**

gleam (gleem)
verb To shine.
noun A brief or faint light or sign of emotion.
▸ *verb* **gleaming, gleamed**

glee (glee) *noun* Great enjoyment or excitement. ▸ *adjective* **gleeful** ▸ *adverb* **gleefully**

glen (glen) *noun* A narrow or small valley.

glide (glide)
verb 1. To move smoothly and without effort. 2. To fly without power, as in a glider.
noun A smooth and effortless movement.
▸ *verb* **gliding, glided**

glid·er (**glye**-dur) *noun* A very light aircraft designed to fly without engine power.

glim·mer (**glim**-ur)
verb To shine faintly or for brief periods.
noun 1. A trace. 2. A faint light that shines for brief periods.
▸ *verb* **glimmering, glimmered**

glimpse (glimps)
verb To see something or someone very briefly.
noun A brief look at something or someone.
▸ *verb* **glimpsing, glimpsed**

glint (glint)
verb To reflect light in small flashes.
noun A hint of emotion, especially in a person's eyes.
▸ *verb* **glinting, glinted**

glis·ten (**glis**-uhn)
verb To shine and sparkle.
noun A sparkling light reflected off a moist surface.
▸ *verb* **glistening, glistened**

glitch (glich) *noun* (informal) Any sudden thing that goes wrong or

G

causes a problem, usually with machinery. ▶ *noun, plural* **glitches**

glit·ter (**glit**-ur) *verb* To shine with many small flashes of reflected light. ▶ *verb* **glittering, glittered**

gloat (gloht) *verb* To take satisfaction or delight in your own success or someone else's misfortune. ▶ *verb* **gloating, gloated**

glob·al (**gloh**-buhl) *adjective* Of or having to do with the whole world, or globe. ▶ *adverb* **globally**

glob·al warm·ing (**gloh**-buhl **wor**-ming) *noun* A gradual rise in the temperature of the earth's atmosphere, caused by human activities that pollute.

globe (glohb) *noun* 1. The world. 2. A round model of the world used for study or decoration. 3. A ball-shaped object.

glock·en·spiel (**glah**-kuhn-*speel*) *noun* A musical instrument consisting of a frame with tuned metal bars. The bars are struck with small hammers to sound different notes.

gloom (gloom) *noun* 1. A sense of hopelessness and depression. 2. Shade or darkness.

gloom·y (**gloo**-mee) *adjective* 1. Overcast or dimly lit. 2. Feeling or expressing sadness and pessimism. ▶ *adjective* **gloomier, gloomiest**

glo·ri·fy (**glor**-uh-*fye*) *verb* 1. To praise or treat as very important or splendid. 2. To honor or promote the glory of. ▶ *verb* **glorifies, glorifying, glorified**

glo·ry (**glor**-ee) *noun* 1. Great fame or honor. 2. Splendor or magnificence. ▶ *noun, plural* **glories** ▶ *adjective* **glorious**

gloss (glaws *or* glahs) *noun* A shine on a surface. ▶ *noun, plural* **glosses** ▶ *adjective* **glossy**

glos·sa·ry (**glah**-sur-ee) *noun* A list of technical or specialized words and phrases along with their definitions. ▶ *noun, plural* **glossaries**

glove (gluhv) *noun* 1. A warm or protective hand covering that has separate parts for the thumb and each finger. 2. A padded leather covering for the hand, worn by players of

sports such as boxing and baseball. 3. If something **fits like a glove,** it fits exactly.

glow (gloh)
verb 1. To give off a steady, low light, because of heat or chemical activity. 2. To show a color suggesting warmth or good health. 3. To show a warm feeling.
noun 1. A steady light. 2. A bright, warm, or healthy color.
▶ *verb* **glowing, glowed** ▶ *adjective* **glowing**

glow·er (**glou**-ur)
verb To stare angrily.
noun An angry stare.
▶ *verb* **glowering, glowered**

glow·worm (**gloh**-*wurm*) *noun* The larva of a firefly, or a wingless female firefly that glows to attract males.

glu·cose (**gloo**-kose) *noun* 1. A naturally produced sugar in plants and in the blood of animals. It is a source of energy for living things. 2. A syrup made from cornstarch and widely used in the food industry.

glue (gloo)
noun A substance used to make materials or objects stick together tightly.
verb 1. To stick things together with or as if with glue. 2. (informal) If you are **glued to** something, you are not leaving or letting your attention stray from it.
▶ *verb* **gluing, glued**

glum (gluhm) *adjective* Looking or feeling unhappy. ▶ *adjective* **glummer, glummest** ▶ *adverb* **glumly**

glut (gluht) *noun* An overabundant supply.

glut·ton (**gluht**-uhn) *noun* 1. A person who is greedy, especially for food. 2. A person who is always eager for something difficult or unpleasant. ▶ *noun* **gluttony** ▶ *adjective* **gluttonous**

gnarled (nahrld) *adjective* Twisted and knobby, especially with age.

gnash (nash) *verb* To grind together in anger or grief. ▶ *verb* **gnashes, gnashing, gnashed**

G

gnat (nat) *noun* A small, winged, biting insect similar to a mosquito.

gnaw (naw) *verb* 1. To bite or nibble persistently. 2. If something **gnaws at** you, it is a source of distress or anxiety. ▸ *verb* **gnawing, gnawed**

gnome (nome) *noun* 1. In folktales and fairy tales, **gnomes** are dwarflike old men believed to live underground and guard the earth's treasure. 2. A garden statue that looks like an old man with a beard and a pointy hat.

gnu (noo) *noun* A kind of antelope found in Africa that has a head like an ox, a short mane, curved horns, and a long tail. **Gnu** sounds like **knew** and **new**. ▸ *noun, plural* **gnus** or **gnu**

go (goh)
verb 1. To move away from or closer to a place. 2. To function properly. 3. To pass. 4. To have a certain place. 5. If you are **going to** do something, you intend to do it in the future. 6. To be suitable. 7. To turn out.
adjective Ready to happen.
noun An attempt to do something.
▸ *verb* **goes, going, went** (went), **gone** (gawn)

goad (gohd) *verb* To tease or urge someone into doing something. ▸ *verb* **goading, goaded**

goal (gohl) *noun* 1. An area or a frame with a net that is the target of scoring in a game. 2. The act of sending a ball or puck into or past a goal and scoring because of this. 3. Something that you aim to do.

goal·ie (**goh**-lee) *noun* Someone who guards the goal in soccer or hockey to prevent the other team from scoring.

goal·keep·er (**gohl**-*kee*-pur) *noun* A goalie.

goat (goht) *noun* 1. An animal with a beard and horns that curve backward, often raised on farms for its milk. 2. If someone **gets your goat,** he or she has succeeded in annoying you.

goa·tee (goh-**tee**) *noun* A small beard around the mouth and chin, pointed like that of a goat.

gob·ble (**gah**-buhl) *verb* 1. To eat food in a hurry. 2. To make the sound a turkey makes.
▸ *verb* **gobbling, gobbled**

gob·let (**gah**-blit) *noun* A tall drinking glass with a stem and a base.

gob·lin (**gah**-blin) *noun* In fairy tales, **goblins** are small, ugly creatures who like to cause trouble.

God (gahd) *noun* 1. The creator and ruler of the universe in Christianity and other religions. 2. **god** A superhuman being who is worshiped. 3. **god** A much-loved, admired, or influential person.

god·dess (**gah**-dis) *noun* 1. A female god. 2. A woman who is much-loved or greatly admired, especially for her beauty.

god·par·ent (**gahd**-*pair*-uhnt) *noun* In the Christian religion, someone who promises to oversee a child's religious education when the child is baptized.

goes (gohz) *verb* The third person singular present form of **go.**

gog·gles (**gah**-guhlz) *noun, plural* Protective glasses that fit tightly around your eyes.

go-kart *or* **go-cart** (**goh**-*kahrt*) *noun* A small racing vehicle that is low on the ground and built without doors or a roof.

gold (gohld)
noun 1. A chemical element that is a precious metal used in jewelry and to guarantee the value of a country's currency. 2. A deep yellow or yellow-brown color.
adjective 1. Made of gold. 2. Having a deep yellow or yellow-brown color.
▸ *adjective* **golden**

gold·en·rod (**gohl**-duhn-*rahd*) *noun* A tall, wild plant with short spikes of small, yellow flowers. Goldenrods bloom in the late summer and fall.

gold·finch (**gohld**-*finch*) *noun* A small bird that looks very much like a canary. The male goldfinch is yellow with black markings. ▸ *noun, plural* **goldfinches**

gold·fish (**gohld**-*fish*) *noun* A reddish-golden fish often seen in ponds and

G

kept in aquariums. ▶ *noun, plural*
goldfish *or* **goldfishes**

golf (gahlf)
noun A game in which players use clubs to hit a small white ball around a special grassy course and into a series of holes. A golf course has either 9 or 18 holes.
verb To play golf.
▶ *verb* **golfing, golfed** ▶ *noun* **golfer** ▶ *noun* **golfing**

gon·do·la (**gahn**-duh-luh) *noun* **1.** A light, flat-bottomed rowboat with high, pointed ends. Gondolas are used to transport people and goods through the canals of Venice, Italy. **2.** A railroad freight car with low sides and no roof. **3.** A cabin or enclosure for passengers on a ski lift or under a hot-air balloon or blimp.

gone (gawn) *verb* The past participle of **go.**

gong (gahng *or* gawng) *noun* A metal disk that, when hit with a hammer, makes a resonant sound.

good (gud)
adjective **1.** Well-behaved. **2.** Pleasant or agreeable. **3.** Suitable for or beneficial to. **4.** Of high quality. **5.** Full. **6.** Clever or skillful. **7.** Kind or helpful. **8.** If you **make good** at something, you are doing well at it.
noun Something that is useful or helps someone or something.
▶ *adjective* **better, best**

good·bye *or* **good·by** (gud-**bye**)
interjection A word of farewell said when leaving or ending a conversation.

Good Fri·day (gud **frye**-day) *noun* A date commemorated by Christian religions as the day Jesus died on the cross; the Friday before Easter.

good·na·tured (gud-**nay**-churd)
adjective Pleasant and generally warm and kind.

good·ness (**gud**-nis) *noun* Generosity or kindness.

goods (gudz) *noun, plural* Things that are sold or things that someone owns.

good·will (gud-**wil**) *noun* **1.** A kindly feeling of support and cooperation.

2. The value a business has because of a good relationship with its customers.

goo·ey (**goo**-ee) *adjective* (informal) Soft and sticky. ▶ *adjective* **gooier, gooiest** ▶ *noun* **gooeyness**

goo·gle (**goo**-guhl) *verb* To search for information about someone or something on the Internet, using the Google search engine or some other online search service. ▶ *verb* **googling, googled**

goose (goos) *noun* A large waterbird with a long neck, short legs, and webbed feet. ▶ *noun, plural* **geese** (gees)

goose bumps (**goos** buhmps)
noun, plural When you are cold or frightened, you can sometimes get **goose bumps.** Tiny bumps appear on your skin, and the hairs on your skin stand up.

go·pher (**goh**-fur) *noun* A small, furry animal related to the squirrel. Gophers live underground.

gore (gor)
noun Clotted blood or blood that has been shed as a result of violence.
verb If you are **gored** by an animal, you are pierced by its horns or tusks.
▶ *verb* **goring, gored** ▶ *adjective* **gory**

gorge (gorj)
noun A deep valley or ravine.
verb To eat greedily or stuff yourself with food.
▶ *verb* **gorging, gorged**

gor·geous (**gor**-juhs) *adjective* Very attractive or beautiful.

go·ril·la (guh-**ril**-uh) *noun* A dark, broad-shouldered ape with a large head and a short neck, found in Africa. **Gorilla** sounds like **guerrilla.**

gos·ling (**gahz**-ling) *noun* A young goose.

gos·pel (**gahs**-puhl) *noun* **1.** The teachings of Jesus. **2. Gospel** One of the first four books in the New Testament of the Bible, which tell the story of Jesus' life and teachings. **3.** Something that is absolutely true or accepted as truth.

gos·sa·mer (**gah**-suh-mur)
noun A very delicate film spun by a spider; a cobweb.
adjective Fine, delicate, or insubstantial.

gos·sip (**gah**-sip)
noun **1.** Idle talk about other people's personal business. **2.** A person who likes to talk about other people's personal business.
verb To talk about other people's personal business.
▶ *verb* **gossiping** or **gossipping, gossiped** or **gossipped**

got (gaht) *verb* The past tense of **get.** The word *got* is also used as the past participle of the verb *get* in some meanings.

Goth (gahth)
noun **1.** A member of the Germanic tribes that invaded the Roman Empire between the third and fifth centuries A.D. **2. goth** A young person who dresses in black, has piercings, and wears a lot of shiny jewelry.
adjective **goth** Belonging to a style of music or fashion that goths like.

Goth·ic (**gah**-thik) *adjective* **1.** Of or having to do with the style of art or architecture used in Europe between the 12th and 16th centuries. **2. Gothic** stories and fiction are often set in the past and are full of scary things.

got·ten (**gah**-tuhn) *verb* A past participle of **get.** The word *gotten* is used as the past participle in sentences where the verb *get* means "become" or "obtain."

gouge (gouj)
noun **1.** A tool used to make deep impressions in wood or other hard materials. **2.** A deep cut caused by such a tool or other object.
verb **1.** To cut something deeply with or as if with a sharp tool. **2.** To cheat or steal from someone.
▶ *verb* **gouging, gouged**

gourd (gord) *noun* A hard-skinned fruit that grows on a vine, similar to a squash or pumpkin.

gour·met (goor-**may**)
noun An expert on food and wine, or someone who appreciates them.

adjective Of or having to do with good food.

gov·ern (**guhv**-urn) *verb* **1.** To control or exercise authority over a country, organization, or group. **2.** To control, influence, or regulate.
▶ *verb* **governing, governed**

gov·ern·ment (**guhv**-urn-muhnt or **guhv**-ur-muhnt) *noun* **1.** The system by which a country, state, or organization is governed. **2.** The group of people who govern a country or state.
▶ *adjective* **governmental**

gov·er·nor (**guhv**-ur-nur) *noun* **1.** The highest elected official of a U.S. state. **2.** A person in charge of certain types of organizations.

gown (goun) *noun* **1.** A long dress worn on special or formal occasions. **2.** A loose robe worn by judges, surgeons and patients, and by students at their graduation ceremonies.

GP (jee-**pee**) *noun* A family doctor who is not a specialist and who performs physicals and treats common illnesses. GP is short for *general practitioner*.

GPS (jee-pee-**es**) *noun* A system of satellites and devices that people use to find out where they are, or to get directions to a place. GPS is short for *Global Positioning System*.

grab (grab) *verb* **1.** To take hold of something suddenly. **2.** To obtain something hastily or when the opportunity arises.
▶ *verb* **grabbing, grabbed**

grace (grase) *noun* **1.** Movement that shows smoothness and elegance. **2.** Pleasant and polite behavior. **3.** A short prayer or blessing before a meal.
▶ *adjective* **graceful** ▶ *adverb* **gracefully** ▶ *adjective* **gracious** (**gray**-shuhs) ▶ *adverb* **graciously**

grack·le (**grak**-uhl) *noun* A type of blackbird that has shiny black feathers and a long tail.

grade (grade)
noun **1.** A letter or number rating the quality of work done in school. **2.** Quality. **3.** A class or year in a

G

school, or the students in it. **4.** The amount that a road slants up or down. *verb* **1.** To even out or make level. **2.** To assign a grade to a student or a student's work.
▶ *verb* **grading, graded**

grad·u·al (**graj**-oo-uhl) *adjective* Happening slowly and steadily. ▶ *adverb* **gradually**

grad·u·ate
noun (**graj**-oo-it) Someone who has finished the course requirements of a school and has received a diploma. *verb* (**graj**-oo-*ate*) **1.** To finish the course requirements of a school and receive a diploma. **2.** To move up to a higher level.
▶ *verb* **graduating, graduated**

grad·u·a·tion (*graj*-oo-**ay**-shuhn) *noun* **1.** The successful completion of the highest grade in a school, or of a degree program in a college. **2.** A ceremony in which graduating students receive their diplomas or degrees.

graf·fi·ti (gruh-**fee**-tee) *noun, plural* Drawings or words people put on walls, buses, subway cars, or other surfaces that are not supposed to be there.

graft (graft)
noun **1.** The taking of money dishonestly, especially in politics or government. **2.** Bribery or money that is taken dishonestly. **3.** An operation that involves attaching a patch of skin to repair an injury to another part of a body, or a shoot from one plant to repair damage in another. *verb* **1.** To perform an operation that removes a patch of skin to help repair an injury to another part of the body. **2.** To insert a shoot from one plant into the trunk or stem of another so that they grow together.
▶ *verb* **grafting, grafted**

gra·ham crack·er (**gram** *krak*-ur) *noun* A sweet cracker made with whole wheat flour.

grain (grayn) *noun* **1.** A very small piece of something. **2.** Cereal plants in general. Grains include such cereals

as barley, oats, wheat, and rye. **3.** The seed or fruit of a cereal plant.

gram (gram) *noun* A metric unit of measurement or weight that is equal to one thousandth of a kilogram.

gram·mar (**gram**-ur) *noun* The rules that tell you how to speak and write correctly.

gram·mar school (**gram**-ur *skool*) *noun* Another name for an **elementary school.**

gram·mat·i·cal (gruh-**mat**-i-kuhl) *adjective* Correct according to the rules of a language.

gra·na·ry (**gray**-nur-ee or **gran**-ur-ee) *noun* A building where grain is stored. ▶ *noun, plural* **granaries**

grand (grand) *adjective* **1.** Large and admirable. **2.** Important or dignified. **dignified 3.** Wonderful or very enjoyable. **4.** Complete or added up.
▶ *adjective* **grander, grandest** ▶ *adverb* **grandly**

grand·child (**grand**-childe) *noun* The child of someone's son or daughter. ▶ *noun, plural* **grandchildren** (**grand**-*chil*-druhn)

grand·daugh·ter (**gran**-*daw*-tur) *noun* Someone's **granddaughter** is the daughter of that person's child.

grand·fa·ther (**grand**-*fah*-THur) *noun* The father of your mother or father.

grand·fa·ther clock (**grand**-*fah*-THur *klahk*) *noun* A clock built into the top of a tall, narrow, usually wooden cabinet.

grand ju·ry (**grand joor**-ee) *noun* A group of people that meet to decide if there is enough evidence to try someone for a crime. ▶ *noun, plural* **grand juries**

grand·moth·er (**grand**-*muhTH*-ur) *noun* The mother of your mother or father.

grand·pa·rent (**grand**-*pair*-uhnt) *noun* The parent of your mother or father.

grand·son (**grand**-*suhn*) *noun* Someone's **grandson** is the son of that person's child.

grand·stand (**grand**-*stand*) *noun* The main area at an arena or stadium with seats for spectators.

G

gran·ite (**gran**-it) *noun* A hard, gray rock used in construction.

gra·no·la (gruh-**noh**-luh) *noun* A food made with grains, nuts, and dried fruit and often eaten as a breakfast cereal.

grant (grant)
verb 1. To agree to give or allow something. 2. To admit or agree that something is true.
noun An amount of money given by an organization or government for a particular purpose.
idiom If you **take** someone or something **for granted,** you fail to appreciate it because it is too familiar.
▶ *verb* **granting, granted**

grape (grape) *noun* A juicy, smooth-skinned berry that grows on a vine and can be eaten fresh, dried to make raisins, or crushed to make wine.

grape·fruit (**grape**-*froot*) *noun* A large, round citrus fruit with a yellow or pink rind and pulp, and a rather bitter taste. ▶ *noun, plural* **grapefruits** or **grapefruit**

grape·vine (**grape**-*vine*) *noun* 1. A vine on which grapes grow. 2. If you receive information **through the grapevine,** you hear it unofficially or as a rumor.

graph (graf)
noun A diagram that shows the relationship between numbers or amounts. Common graphs use bars, lines, or parts of a circle to display data.
verb To trace or represent on a graph.
▶ *verb* **graphing, graphed**

graph·ic (**graf**-ik) *adjective* 1. Giving a very realistic picture with explicit detail. 2. Of or having to do with the visual arts, especially involving drawing, lettering, or engraving. 3. Of or having to do with handwriting.

graph·ics (**graf**-iks) *noun, plural* Images such as drawings, maps, or graphs.

graph·ite (**graf**-ite) *noun* A common black or gray mineral used as lead in pencils.

grap·ple (**grap**-uhl) *verb* 1. To engage in a close physical struggle that doesn't involve weapons. 2. To try to figure out or deal with something.
▶ *verb* **grappling, grappled**

grasp (grasp)
verb 1. To seize something or someone and hold it firmly. 2. To fully understand something.
noun 1. A strong hold of something. 2. The ability to achieve or find something.
▶ *verb* **grasping, grasped**

grass (gras) *noun* 1. Any of several plants whose leaves are long, thin blades, such as grains, bamboo, and sugarcane. 2. An area of these plants growing wild, planted as a crop, or used for a lawn.
▶ *noun, plural* **grasses** ▶ *adjective* **grassy**

grass·hop·per (**gras**-*hah*-pur) *noun* An insect that eats plants and has long rear legs adapted for leaping.

grass·land (**gras**-*land*) *noun* A large, open area of grass, often used as pasture for animals.

grate (grayt)
verb 1. To shred food by rubbing it back and forth on a device covered with sharp-edged holes. 2. If something **grates on** you, it has an annoying or irritating effect.
noun A framework of bars or wires that covers or protects something.
Grate sounds like **great.** ▶ *verb* **grating, grated**

grate·ful (**grate**-fuhl) *adjective* If you are **grateful** for someone or something, you are thankful and appreciative. ▶ *adverb* **gratefully**

grat·er (**gray**-tur) *noun* A tool that has a flat surface with holes with sharp, raised edges for grating food such as cheese and vegetables.

grat·i·fy (**grat**-uh-*fye*) *verb* To give pleasure to someone by fulfilling his or her needs or desires. ▶ *verb* **gratifies, gratifying, gratified** ▶ *noun* **gratification**

grat·i·tude (**grat**-i-tood) *noun* A feeling of being grateful or thankful.

grave (grave)
noun A hole in the ground in which someone is buried or going

G

to be buried.
adjective Very serious or alarming.
▶ *adjective* **graver, gravest** ▶ *adverb*
gravely

grav·el (**grav**-uhl) *noun* A loose mixture of small stones used on paths and roads.

grave·stone (**grave**-*stone*) *noun* A piece of carved stone that marks someone's grave.

grave·yard (**grave**-*yahrd*) *noun* A cemetery, especially a small one next to a church.

grav·i·ty (**grav**-i-tee) *noun* **1.** The force that pulls things toward the center of the earth and keeps them from floating away. **2.** Extreme importance or seriousness.

gra·vy (**gray**-vee) *noun* **1.** A flavored sauce served with meat and usually made by adding flour and seasoning to the fat and juices of cooked meat. **2.** Something unearned or unexpected.
▶ *noun, plural* **gravies**

gray (gray)
noun A color between black and white, such as the color of ashes or of an overcast sky.
adjective Having a color between black and white.
▶ *adjective* **grayer, grayest**

graze (graze)
verb **1.** To feed on grass that is growing in a field. **2.** To scrape or break the skin. **3.** To touch just barely.
noun An injury caused by something scraping or breaking the skin.
▶ *verb* **grazing, grazed**

grease (grees)
noun **1.** A thick, oily substance, used to keep the parts of something moving smoothly against each other. **2.** An oily substance found in animal fat, used in cooking.
verb To apply grease to something in order to keep the parts moving smoothly against each other.
▶ *verb* **greasing, greased** ▶ *adjective*
greasy

great (grayt)
adjective **1.** Very large. **2.** Of very good or excellent ability or quality.
3. Extremely enjoyable.
interjection Used to express happiness or excitement.
Great sounds like **grate.** ▶ *adjective*
greater, greatest ▶ *adverb*
greatly ▶ *noun* **greatness**

Great Bear Lake (**grayt bair lake**) A lake in the Northwest Territories of Canada, on the Arctic Circle. It is the largest lake that is entirely within Canada, and is the third-largest lake in North America, after Lake Superior and the combined Great Lakes of Huron and Michigan.

Great Dane (**grayt dane**) *noun* A very large, powerful dog with a short coat and long legs.

great·grand·child (**grayt**-*grand*-
childe) *noun* The son or daughter of someone's grandchild.

great·grand·par·ent (**grayt**-*grand*-*pair*-
uhnt) *noun* The father or mother of one of your grandparents.

Great Lakes (**grayt laykz**) A group of five freshwater lakes located in North America. The Great Lakes make up the largest group of freshwater lakes in the world, and contain about 20 percent of the freshwater on the earth's surface. The group includes Lake Superior, Lake Huron, Lake Ontario, Lake Michigan, and Lake Erie, and are all located in the border area between the United States and Canada.

great·ly (**grayt**-lee) *adverb* Very much.

Greece (grees) A country in Southeastern Europe, surrounded by the Aegean Sea, the Ionian Sea, and the Mediterranean Sea. It is often referred to as the birthplace of Western civilization and is where the first Olympic Games were held.

greed (greed) *noun* Extreme selfishness; wanting everything for yourself.

greed·y (**gree**-dee) *adjective* Having a strong or selfish desire for something. ▶ *adjective* **greedier, greediest** ▶ *adverb* **greedily**

G

Greek (greek) *adjective* **1.** Of, from, or having to do with modern Greece. **2.** Of, from, or having to do with the ancient civilization or the language from the area where modern Greece is today.

green (green)
noun **1.** A color like that of grass. **2.** An area of grass for public use, especially in the center of a town. **3.** An area of very short grass surrounding the hole on a golf course.
adjective **1.** Not ripe. **2.** Being or having the color green. **3.** Having little experience. **4.** Supporting or concerned with the protection of the environment. The word is sometimes capitalized.
noun, plural **greens** Green leaves or stems used as food.
▶ *adjective* **greener, greenest**

green bean (green *been*) *noun* A kind of bean that is grown for its long green pods, which are eaten with the seeds inside, while they are still small and soft.

green card (green *kahrd*) *noun* A permit or identification card that allows someone who is not a citizen to live and work in the United States.

green·house (green-*hous*) *noun* An enclosed structure for plants that has controlled lighting and heat so that the plants can grow even when it's cold.

green·house ef·fect (green-*hous* i-*fekt*) *noun* The warming of the lower layers of the earth's atmosphere, caused by carbon dioxide and other gases that prevent the sun's heat from escaping.

green·house gas·es (green-*hous* gas-iz) *noun, plural* Gases such as carbon dioxide and methane that contribute to the greenhouse effect.

Green Mountains (green *moun*-tuhnz) A mountain range in Vermont that stretches from north to south along the state's western border. The Green Mountains are part of the larger Appalachian Mountain range.

green thumb (green *thuhm*) *noun* A talent for making plants grow.

greet (greet) *verb* **1.** To give a sign of recognition or welcome when you meet someone. **2.** To acknowledge or respond to something in a particular way.
▶ *verb* **greeting, greeted** ▶ *noun* **greeting** ▶ *noun* **greeter**

Gre·na·da (gruh-*nay*-duh) An island nation in the southeastern Caribbean Sea consisting of the island of Grenada and six smaller islands. Called the Spice Isle, it is one of the world's largest exporters of nutmeg, mace, and other spices. Nutmeg is so important to Grenada's economy that it is shown on the country's flag.

gre·nade (gruh-*nade*) *noun* A small bomb that is thrown by hand or launched mechanically.

grew (groo) *verb* The past tense of **grow.**

grey·hound (*gray*-hound) *noun* A thin dog with a smooth coat that can run very fast. Greyhounds are often used for racing.

grid (grid) *noun* **1.** A network of uniformly spaced vertical and horizontal lines that forms a regular pattern of squares. **2.** A network of cables and wires for supplying electricity.

grid·dle (*grid*-uhl) *noun* **1.** A large, flat, heated surface used for cooking. **2.** A flat pan with a handle, used for frying food.

grid·i·ron (*grid*-eye-urn) *noun* A playing field marked with evenly spaced parallel lines for football.

grid·lock (*grid*-lahk) *noun* A severe traffic jam that results in blocking many intersections in a grid of streets so that vehicles cannot move in any direction.

grief (greef) *noun* A feeling of great sadness or deep distress.

griev·ance (*gree*-vuhns) *noun* If you have a **grievance,** you feel angry or annoyed enough about something that you complain about it or want to complain about it.

grieve (greev) *verb* To feel intense sorrow, usually because someone you love has died or gone away. ▶ *verb* **grieving, grieved**

G

grill (gril)
noun An outdoor cooking device consisting of a metal framework on which food is suspended over a source of intense heat.
verb 1. To cook food on a grill. 2. (informal) To question someone aggressively.
▶ *verb* **grilling, grilled**

grim (grim) *adjective* Very serious or forbidding. ▶ *adjective* **grimmer, grimmest** ▶ *adverb* **grimly**

gri·mace (**grim**-is *or* gri-**mase**)
noun A facial expression that usually expresses a negative reaction.
verb To make a facial expression that shows pain or disgust.
▶ *verb* **grimacing, grimaced**

grime (grime) *noun* Dirt or soot that accumulates on a surface. ▶ *adjective* **grimy**

grin (grin)
verb To smile broadly in amusement or pleasure.
noun A broad smile.
▶ *verb* **grinning, grinned**

grind (grinde)
verb 1. To crush something into small pieces or into a powder. 2. To sharpen a blade or change the shape of something by rubbing it on a rough, hard surface.
noun A period of very hard work or study.
phrase If you **grind your teeth,** you rub them together, sometimes making a noise.
▶ *verb* **grinding, ground** (ground)

grind·stone (**grinde**-*stone*) *noun* 1. A rotating stone used to sharpen or shape something. 2. If you **keep your nose to the grindstone,** you do not let anything distract you from your work.

grip (grip)
verb 1. To keep a tight hold on something. 2. If something **grips** you, it holds your attention or interest.
noun 1. A hold on something. 2. (informal) An understanding.
▶ *verb* **gripping, gripped** ▶ *adjective* **gripping**

gris·tle (**gris**-uhl) *noun* A tough, inedible substance found in meat. Gristle is cartilage tissue.

grit (grit)
noun 1. Fine particles of sand or stone. 2. The ability to keep on doing something even though it is very difficult.
verb To grind your teeth together.
▶ *verb* **gritting, gritted** ▶ *adjective* **gritty**

grits (grits) *noun, plural* Coarsely ground grain, especially white corn, boiled and eaten as a cereal or side dish.

griz·zly bear (**griz**-lee *bair*) *noun* A large brown or gray bear found in the Northwest and in Alaska. Grizzly bears are often very aggressive.

groan (grohn)
verb To make a long, low sound because you are suffering or unhappy.
noun A long, low sound.
▶ *verb* **groaning, groaned**

gro·cer·y (**groh**-sur-ee)
noun A store that sells food and household goods. Also called a *grocery store.*
noun, plural **groceries** Food and household goods that you buy in a grocery store.
▶ *noun, plural* **groceries**

grog·gy (**grah**-gee) *adjective* Sleepy or dazed and unsteady. ▶ *adjective* **groggier, groggiest**

groin (groin) *noun* The front of your body where your legs meet.

groom (groom)
noun 1. A man who is about to get married or has just gotten married. 2. Someone who takes care of horses.
verb 1. To take care of your appearance and your clothing. 2. To brush and clean an animal. 3. To teach or prepare someone to take over a job.
▶ *verb* **grooming, groomed** ▶ *noun* **grooming**

groove (groov) *noun* 1. A long, narrow cut in the surface of something hard. 2. A habitual or routine way of doing something.

G

grope (grope) *verb* 1. To search for something with your hands that you cannot see. 2. To look for or think about in an uncertain way.
▶ *verb* **groping, groped**

gross (grohs)
adjective 1. Very large. 2. Very rude and improper. 3. Unpleasantly big and ugly or capable of making you feel that way. 4. The **gross** amount is the total amount earned, before subtracting taxes or anything else.
noun A group of 12 dozen (or 144) things.
▶ *adjective* **grosser, grossest** ▶ *adverb* **grossly**

gro·tesque (groh-**tesk**) *adjective* Very strange or ugly. ▶ *adverb* **grotesquely**

grot·to (**grah**-toh) *noun* A small cave, or a structure built to look like one.

grouch (grouch) *noun* Someone who is in a bad mood. ▶ *noun, plural* **grouches**

grouch·y (**grou**-chee) *adjective* Mean, nasty, or grumpy. ▶ *adjective* **grouchier, grouchiest**

ground (ground)
noun 1. The earth's surface. 2. Land used for a certain activity. *See also* **grounds.** 3. A wire that will carry an electric current into the ground or to a place where it won't be dangerous. 4. **ground ball** In baseball, a ball hit along the ground by a batter.
verb 1. In baseball, to hit a ball that bounces along the ground. 2. To restrict the activity of someone or something.
▶ *verb* **grounding, grounded**

ground·ed (**groun**-did) *adjective* 1. If an aircraft is **grounded,** it cannot fly. 2. If an electrical appliance is **grounded,** it is connected directly to the earth and is safe to use.

ground·hog (**ground**-hawg) *noun* A small, furry, burrowing animal with large front teeth. Also called a **woodchuck.**

Ground·hog Day (**ground**-hawg *day*) *noun* According to legend, people can predict when spring will arrive by watching the behavior of a groundhog

on **Groundhog Day,** February 2. If it comes out of its burrow and sees its shadow, there will be six more weeks of winter. If it does not see its shadow, spring will come early.

grounds (groundz) *noun, plural* 1. The land surrounding a large building or a group of buildings. 2. A reason for doing or thinking something. 3. The particles of coffee that remain after the coffee is brewed.

ground·wa·ter (**ground**-*waw*-tur) *noun* Water far below the ground that can be used for drinking and other purposes when wells are dug into it.

group (groop)
noun 1. A number of people or things that go together or have something in common. 2. A number of people who gather together or share a common purpose.
verb To put people or things together or to place in a group.
▶ *verb* **grouping, grouped**

grouse (grous)
noun A small, plump game bird.
verb To complain about something.
▶ *verb* **grousing, groused**

grove (grove) *noun* A group of trees growing or planted near one another.

grov·el (**gruhv**-uhl *or* **grah**-vuhl) *verb* To behave in a very humble way toward a person of much greater rank, such as a king, or because you want someone to forgive you or give you something. ▶ *verb* **groveling, groveled**

grow (groh) *verb* 1. To increase in size, develop, or change physically. 2. To plant and care for something so that it gets bigger. 3. To gradually become. 4. If something **grows on** you, it gradually becomes more acceptable or appealing.
▶ *verb* **growing, grew, grown**

growl (groul)
verb To show anger by making a low, deep sound.
noun A low, deep sound that shows anger.
▶ *verb* **growling, growled**

grown (grohn) *verb* The past participle of **grow.**

G

grown-up (**grohn**-*uhp*)
noun An adult.
adjective Suitable for an adult.

growth (grohth) *noun* **1.** The process of increasing in size, value, or maturity. **2.** A tumor or abnormal lump of body tissue.

grub (gruhb) *noun* **1.** The wormlike larva of some insects. **2.** (slang) Food.

grudge (gruhj) *noun* A long-lasting feeling of resentment toward someone who has hurt or insulted you.

gru·el·ing (**groo**-uh-ling) *adjective* Very tiring or demanding.

grue·some (**groo**-suhm) *adjective* Very unpleasant, disgusting, or horrible.

gruff (gruhf) *adjective* Abrupt, rough, or unfriendly. ▶ *adjective* **gruffer, gruffest** ▶ *adverb* **gruffly**

grum·ble (**gruhm**-buhl) *verb* To complain about something in a grouchy but not very loud or angry way. ▶ *verb* **grumbling, grumbled**

grump·y (**gruhm**-pee) *adjective* Easily irritated; grouchy. ▶ *adjective* **grumpier, grumpiest** ▶ *adverb* **grumpily**

grunt (gruhnt)
verb To make a low, gruff sound like a pig, especially to express effort or agreement.
noun A low, gruff sound like that made by a pig.
▶ *verb* **grunting, grunted**

gua·ca·mo·le (*gwah*-kuh-**moh**-lee) *noun* A dip made of avocado, onions, lime juice, and seasonings.

Guam (gwahm) An island territory of the United States in the western Pacific Ocean. Guam is the largest of the Mariana Islands, and has one of the most important U.S. military bases in the Pacific.

guar·an·tee (*gar*-uhn-**tee**)
noun **1.** A promise made by manufacturers that if their product breaks within a certain time or is defective, they will repair or replace it. **2.** A promise that something will be done or will happen.
verb To promise that something will be done or happen.
▶ *verb* **guaranteeing, guaranteed**

guard (gahrd)
verb **1.** To protect someone from harm. **2.** To watch over someone so that he or she can't escape. **3.** If you **guard against** something, you take steps to keep it from happening.
noun **1.** Someone whose job it is to protect a person or control access to a place. **2.** A football player whose job is often to protect the quarterback or tackle the opposition's quarterback. **3.** A basketball player whose job is often to initiate plays. **4.** A device worn by a person or placed on something to prevent injury or damage.
▶ *verb* **guarding, guarded**

guard·i·an (**gahr**-dee-uhn)
noun **1.** Someone who is not a child's parent but who is legally responsible for him or her. **2.** Someone who defends or protects something.
adjective Having to do with someone who defends or protects someone.

Gua·te·ma·la (*gwah*-tuh-**mah**-luh) A country in Central America just south of Mexico. The ancient Mayan civilization flourished there during the first millennium A.D.

gua·va (**gwah**-vuh) *noun* A tropical fruit with pink flesh and a very sweet taste.

guer·ril·la (guh-**ril**-uh)
noun A member of a small group of fighters or soldiers that often launches surprise attacks against an official army.
adjective Of or having to do with guerrilla fighting techniques.
Guerrilla sounds like **gorilla.**

guess (ges)
verb **1.** To give an answer without being sure that you're right. **2.** To suppose or believe something.
noun An answer that you are not sure is right.
▶ *verb* **guesses, guessing, guessed** ▶ *noun, plural* **guesses**

guest (gest) *noun* **1.** Someone who has been invited to visit or to stay in another person's home. **2.** Someone who pays to stay in a hotel, a motel, or an inn.

G

guid·ance (**gye**-duhns) *noun* 1. Advice or counsel, especially about a student's future plans. 2. Direction or supervision.

guide (gide)
verb To help someone, usually by showing the way or by providing advice or instruction.
noun Someone who helps people by showing them around a place or by providing advice or instruction.
▶ *verb* **guiding, guided**

guide·book (**gide**-*buk*) *noun* A book containing information about a place, for use by tourists and visitors.

guide dog (**gide** *dawg*) *noun* A dog trained to lead a visually impaired person.

guide·line (**gide**-*line*) *noun* A rule or suggestion that tells how something should be or will be done.

guide word (**gide** *wurd*) *noun* One of the words at the top of a page in a dictionary or encyclopedia that show the part of the alphabet included on that page.

guild (gild) *noun* A group or organization of people who do the same kind of work or have the same interests.

guile (gile) *noun* Clever but dishonest or misleading behavior.

guil·lo·tine (**gil**-uh-*teen* or **gee**-uh-*teen*) *noun* A large machine with a sharp blade that slides down a frame, formerly used to cut off the heads of criminals.

guilt (gilt) *noun* 1. The state of being responsible for having committed a crime or for having done something wrong. 2. A feeling of shame or remorse for having done something wrong or for having failed to do something.
Guilt sounds like **gilt.**

guilt·y (**gil**-tee) *adjective* 1. If you are **guilty,** you are responsible for committing a crime or doing something wrong. 2. If you feel **guilty,** you are ashamed or filled with regret because you know that you've done something wrong.
▶ *adjective* **guiltier, guiltiest** ▶ *adverb* **guiltily**

Guin·ea (**gin**-ee) A country in West Africa on the Atlantic Ocean. Formerly known as French Guinea, it was a French colony until it declared its independence in 1958. To prevent confusion with its neighbor, Guinea-Bissau, it is sometimes referred to as Guinea-Conakry. Conakry is the name of its capital.

Guin·ea-Bis·sau (**gin**-ee-bi-**sou**) A country in West Africa on the Atlantic Ocean. Formerly known as Portuguese Guinea, it became independent from Portugal in 1974. To distinguish itself from Guinea, its southern neighbor, it added the name of its capital, Bissau, to its name and became known as Guinea-Bissau.

guin·ea pig (**gin**-ee *pig*) *noun* 1. A small, stout rodent with short ears and legs, a smooth coat, and no visible tail. Guinea pigs are often kept as pets or used in laboratory research. 2. A person who is used in an experiment.

gui·tar (gi-**tahr**) *noun* A musical instrument with six or twelve strings on a long neck.

gulch (guhlch) *noun* A valley that often fills with water when it rains. ▶ *noun, plural* **gulches**

gulf (guhlf) *noun* 1. An area of the sea that is partly surrounded by land. 2. A difference between two people or situations.

Gulf of A·den (**guhlf** uhv **ay**-duhn) A waterway of the Arabian Sea. The Gulf of Aden runs between Yemen to the north and Somalia to the south, and is connected by a narrow strait to the Red Sea.

Gulf of Guin·ea (**guhlf** uhv **gin**-ee) A gulf of the eastern Atlantic Ocean, off the coast of Africa and near Ghana, Nigeria, Cameroon, and Gabon. The equator passes through the Gulf of Guinea. Major rivers drain into it, including the Niger and the Volta.

Gulf of Hon·du·ras (**guhlf** uhv hahn-**door**-uhs) An inlet of the Caribbean Sea, off the eastern coast of Central

G

America. The Gulf of Honduras lies next to the eastern coasts of Belize, Guatemala, and Honduras.

Gulf of Mex·i·co (**guhlf** uhv **mek**-si-*koh*) A large gulf of the Atlantic Ocean, also connected to the Caribbean Sea on its southeast side. The Gulf of Mexico is the world's ninth-largest body of water, and adjoins the Gulf Coast of the United States to the north and the eastern coast of Mexico to the south.

Gulf of Thai·land (**guhlf** uhv **tye**-*land*) A region of the South China Sea, located along the southern coast of the continent of Asia. The Gulf of Thailand is surrounded on three sides by Cambodia, Thailand, and Vietnam, and flows into the South China Sea at its southern end.

gull (guhl) *noun* Short for **seagull.**

gul·li·ble (**guhl**-uh-buhl) *adjective* If you are **gullible,** it's easy to fool you because you believe anything you are told. ▶ *noun* **gullibility**

gul·ly (**guhl**-ee) *noun* A long, narrow ditch created by running water. ▶ *noun, plural* **gullies**

gulp (guhlp)
verb To swallow food or drink quickly in large mouthfuls.
noun A mouthful of something that is swallowed.
▶ *verb* **gulping, gulped**

gum (guhm) *noun* **1.** Your **gums** are the areas of firm, pink flesh around the roots of your teeth in your upper and lower jaws. **2.** A thick, sticky substance produced by various plants. **3.** Glue made from such a substance and used to stick paper and other materials together. **4.** A sweet substance used for chewing. Also called **chewing gum.**

gum·drop (**guhm**-*drahp*) *noun* A small, chewy candy covered with sugar.

gun (guhn)
noun A weapon that uses explosive force to fire bullets through a long metal tube.
verb **1. gun down** To shoot someone deliberately with a gun. **2.** To speed up something quickly.
▶ *verb* **gunning, gunned**

gun·fire (**guhn**-*fire*) *noun* The repeated firing of guns.

gun·pow·der (**guhn**-*pou*-dur) *noun* A powder that explodes easily. Gunpowder is used in bullets, in fireworks, and in blasting.

gup·py (**guhp**-ee) *noun* A tiny freshwater fish popular in home aquariums. ▶ *noun, plural* **guppies**

gur·gle (**gur**-guhl)
verb **1.** When water **gurgles,** it makes a hollow, bubbling sound, like water being poured out of a bottle. **2.** To make a sound like gurgling water.
noun A hollow, bubbling sound, like water being poured out of a bottle.
▶ *verb* **gurgling, gurgled**

gu·ru (**goo**-roo) *noun* **1.** A spiritual leader or guide in the Hindu religion. **2.** A person who has special knowledge and who is looked up to by many people.

gush (guhsh)
verb **1.** When liquid **gushes,** it flows quickly in a sudden stream. **2.** A person who **gushes** speaks or writes with exaggerated enthusiasm.
noun A quick flow of something, especially a liquid, in a sudden stream.
▶ *verb* **gushes, gushing, gushed**
▶ *noun, plural* **gushes** ▶ *adjective* **gushing**

gust (guhst) *noun* A brief, strong rush of wind or sudden burst of something.

gus·to (**guhs**-toh) *noun* If you do something with **gusto,** you do it with energy and enthusiasm.

gut (guht)
noun Your stomach or intestines.
noun, plural **1. guts** Internal organs that have been exposed or removed from the body. **2. guts** (informal) Personal courage and determination.
verb To destroy the inside of a building.
▶ *verb* **gutting, gutted**

gut·ter (**guht**-ur) *noun* A shallow trough or channel through which rain is carried away from a road or the roof of a building.

G

guy (gye)
noun (informal) A man or a boy.
noun, plural **guys** (informal) Two or more people, male or female.

Guy·a·na (gye-**ah**-nuh) A country on the northern coast of South America. It is the only country in South America where English is the official language.

guz·zle (**guhz**-uhl) verb To drink something in a noisy or greedy manner. ▶ verb **guzzling, guzzled**

gym (jim) noun 1. A large room or building with special equipment for exercising and playing games. Gym is short for gymnasium. 2. A class or course in physical education.

gym·na·si·um (jim-**nay**-zee-uhm) noun A gym.

gym·nast (**jim**-nuhst) noun Someone who practices gymnastics.

gym·nas·tics (jim-**nas**-tiks) noun Physical exercises, often performed on special equipment such as ropes or parallel bars, that involve flexibility, strength, balance, and coordination. ▶ adjective **gymnastic**

Gypsy (**jip**-see) noun 1. A term sometimes used, especially formerly, for one of the Romany people, who often travel around instead of living in one place. Another name for a Gypsy is a **Rom**. 2. **gypsy** Someone who moves around a lot or has an unconventional lifestyle. ▶ noun, plural **Gypsies**

gy·rate (**jye**-rate) verb 1. To move in a circle or spiral. 2. To dance by rotating the hips. ▶ verb **gyrating, gyrated**

gy·ro·scope (**jye**-ruh-skope) noun A device consisting of a wheel or disk that spins rapidly around an axis that can be tilted in any direction. Gyroscopes are used to provide stability on ships and airplanes.

H

ha (hah) interjection 1. A word used to express joy, surprise, or triumph. 2. A word used to express laughter.

hab·it (**hab**-it) noun 1. An activity or behavior that you do regularly, often without thinking about it. 2. A strong need to smoke or take a drug regularly. 3. Special clothing for a particular activity, or for members of a religious order.

hab·it·a·ble (**hab**-i-tuh-buhl) adjective Safe and good enough for people to live in.

hab·i·tat (**hab**-i-tat) noun The place where an animal or a plant is usually found is its **habitat.**

ha·bit·u·al (huh-**bich**-oo-uhl) adjective 1. Behaving from habit. 2. Done over and over again. 3. Regular or usual.

ha·bit·u·al·ly (huh-**bich**-oo-uh-lee) adverb Usually or regularly.

ha·ci·en·da (hah-see-**en**-duh) noun A large ranch or estate found in the southwestern part of the United States or in Spanish-speaking countries.

hack (hak)
verb 1. To cut something roughly or violently. 2. If you **hack** into a computer system, you secretly change it or get information from it without permission. 3. To cough loudly.
noun A loud, dry cough.
▶ verb **hacking, hacked**

hack·er (**hak**-ur) noun Someone who has a special skill for getting into a computer system without permission.

had·n't (**had**-uhnt) contraction A short form of had not.

hag·gard (**hag**-urd) adjective Someone who is **haggard** looks sick and thin, usually because the person is tired, worried, or in pain.

hag·gle (**hag**-uhl) verb To argue with someone, usually in order to agree on the price of something. ▶ verb **haggling, haggled**

hai·ku (**hye**-koo) noun A short Japanese poem in three lines containing a total of 17 syllables.

hail (hayl)
verb **1.** When it **hails,** small balls of ice fall from the sky. **2.** To get someone's attention, especially by calling out or making a signal.
noun Small balls of ice that fall from the sky.
▶ *verb* **hailing, hailed**

hair (hair) *noun* The mass of thin, soft strands that grow from your head or body or from the body of an animal.

hair·cut (**hair**-*kuht*) *noun* The act of someone cutting and styling your hair.

hair·do (**hair**-*doo*) *noun* The way a person's hair is styled or arranged. Also called a *hairstyle.*

hair·dress·er (**hair**-*dres*-ur) *noun* Someone whose job is to cut and style people's hair.

hair·pin (**hair**-*pin*)
noun A piece of bent wire with sides that press together to hold hair in place.
adjective Shaped like a hairpin.

hair·rais·ing (**hair**-*ray*-zing) *adjective* Extremely exciting or frightening.

hair·y (**hair**-ee) *adjective* **1.** Having a lot of hair. **2.** (slang) Frightening and dangerous.
▶ *adjective* **hairier, hairiest**

Hai·ti (**hay**-tee) A country that occupies the western end of the island of Hispaniola. It is the birthplace of voodoo, a religion developed by slaves brought from Africa to Haiti in the 16th century. One of the poorest countries in the Americas, Haiti was devastated by an earthquake in 2010 that killed more than 200,000 people.

half (haf)
noun **1.** One of the two equal parts that something can be divided into. **2.** One of two equal lengths of time played in a game.
adverb Not completely.
adjective Being one of two equal or nearly equal parts that something can be divided into.
▶ *noun, plural* **halves**

half broth·er (haf *bruhTH*-ur) *noun* A brother who shares only one parent with someone else.

half·heart·ed (haf-**hahr**-tid) *adjective* Without much enthusiasm or interest. ▶ *adverb* **halfheartedly**

half·mast (haf-**mast**) *noun* The position halfway between the top and bottom of a flagpole or mast. Flags are flown at this position as a sign of respect for a person who has just died.

half sis·ter (haf *sis*-tur) *noun* A sister who shares only one parent with someone else.

half·time (haf-*time*) *noun* A short break in the middle of a game such as football, basketball, hockey, or soccer.

half·way (haf-**way**)
adjective **1.** Half the distance from one point to another. **2.** Not thorough or complete.
adverb To or at half the distance.

hal·i·but (**hal**-uh-buht) *noun* A type of fish found in both the Atlantic and Pacific oceans and used as food. ▶ *noun, plural* **halibut** or **halibuts**

hall (hawl) *noun* **1.** A long, narrow passage that goes to other rooms. **2.** An area of a house just inside the entrance. **3.** A large room or building used for public events such as meetings.
Hall sounds like **haul.**

hal·le·lu·jah (*hal*-uh-**loo**-yuh) *interjection* A word used to express joy, praise, or thanks, especially to God.

hal·lowed (**hal**-ohd) *adjective* Sacred or holy. ▶ *verb* **hallow**

Hal·low·een (*hal*-uh-**ween**) *noun* The evening of October 31, once thought to be the night witches and ghosts came out and haunted people. On Halloween, children dress up in costumes and go out to trick-or-treat.

hal·lu·ci·nate (huh-**loo**-suh-*nate*) *verb* To see or hear something or someone that is not really there. ▶ *verb* **hallucinating, hallucinated** ▶ *noun* **hallucination**

ha·lo (**hay**-loh) *noun* **1.** A ring of light around an object. **2.** A circle of light shown in pictures around the heads of angels and sacred people.
▶ *noun* **haloes** or **halos**

H

halt (hawlt)
noun A temporary or sudden stop.
verb To stop or cause someone or something to stop.
▸ *verb* **halting, halted**

hal·ter (**hawl**-tur) *noun* 1. A rope or strap used to lead or tie an animal such as a horse. A halter fits over the animal's nose and behind its ears.
2. A woman's top with a band that ties behind the neck, leaving the back and shoulders bare.

halve (hav) *verb* 1. To divide or cut something into two equal parts. 2. To reduce something by half.
Halve sounds like **have.** ▸ *verb* **halving, halved**

ham (ham) *noun* 1. The meat from the top part of a pig's hind leg that has been salted and sometimes smoked.
2. A bad actor who exaggerates emotions when performing.

ham·burg·er (**ham**-bur-gur) *noun* 1. A round, flat piece of chopped beef that is cooked and usually served on a bun. 2. Ground beef.

ham·let (**ham**-lit) *noun* A very small village.

ham·mer (**ham**-ur)
noun A tool with a handle and a heavy metal head, used especially for hitting nails.
verb To hit something very hard repeatedly.
▸ *verb* **hammering, hammered**

ham·mock (**ham**-uhk) *noun* A piece of strong net or cloth that is hung up by each end and used as a bed or as a place to relax.

ham·per (**ham**-pur)
noun A large box or basket used for carrying food or for storing dirty clothing.
verb To make it difficult for something to succeed, or for someone to do something.
▸ *verb* **hampering, hampered**

ham·ster (**ham**-stur) *noun* A small furry animal that is kept as a pet.

hand (hand)
noun 1. The part of your body on the end of your arm. The hand includes your wrist, palm, fingers, and thumb.
2. A set of cards that you hold during a card game. 3. One of the parts of a clock that points to the numbers. 4. A worker or a work crew. 5. A round of applause.
verb 1. To give or pass something to someone. 2. If you **hand** something **in,** you give it to someone.
idioms and phrases 1. If something is **at hand,** it is available to use, or will happen soon. 2. If something is made **by hand,** a person has done it with his or her hands rather than with a machine. 3. If you **give** or **lend a hand** to someone, you help the person. 4. If people or things work **hand in hand,** they are cooperating to achieve something. 5. If you **have your hands full** with something, you are very busy with it. 6. If you are in **good hands,** you are well taken care of. 7. If something is **on hand,** it is nearby and handy to use. 8. If something is **out of hand,** it is not under control. 9. If you **wash your hands of** something, you refuse to have anything more to do with it.
▸ *verb* **handing, handed**

hand·bag (**hand**-bag) *noun* A bag or purse in which a woman carries her wallet and other small things.

hand·ball (**hand**-bawl) *noun* 1. A game played in a large room or outdoors in which two or four players take turns hitting a small, hard rubber ball against a wall with their hands. 2. The rubber ball used for playing handball.

hand·book (**hand**-buk) *noun* A book containing useful information or instructions.

hand·cuffs (**hand**-kuhfs) *noun, plural* Metal rings joined by a chain that are put around a prisoner's wrists to keep him or her from escaping. ▸ *verb* **handcuff**

hand·ful (**hand**-ful) *noun* 1. The amount of something that can be held in a hand. 2. A small number of things or people. 3. (informal) If someone is a **handful,** he or she is difficult to control.

H

hand·i·cap (**han**-dee-*kap*) *noun* **1.** A physical or mental limitation. The word *disability* is now the preferred term to describe the inability to do some things, such as walk or see. **2.** A situation or condition that makes it difficult for you to do something. **3.** A disadvantage given in a sport, such as golf, to the stronger players in order to make the competition more equal. *verb* To make more difficult.
▶ *verb* **handicapping, handicapped** ▶ *adjective* **handicapped**

hand·i·craft (**han**-dee-*kraft*) *noun* A skill, such as sewing or pottery, that involves using your hands to make things.

hand·ker·chief (**hang**-kur-chif) *noun* A small square of cloth that you use for wiping your face, hands, or nose.

han·dle (**han**-duhl) *noun* The part of an object that you use to hold, carry, move, or open that object. *verb* **1.** To pick up, touch, or feel something with your hands. **2.** To deal with someone or something, such as a situation, in a successful way.
▶ *verb* **handling, handled**

han·dle·bars (**han**-duhl-*bahrz*) *noun, plural* The bar at the front of a bicycle or motorcycle that you use for steering.

hand·made (**hand**-made) *adjective* Made by hand, not by a machine.

hand·me·down (**hand**-mee-*doun*) *noun* An article of clothing or another item that belongs to someone and is passed along for use by another person.
▶ *noun, plural* **hand-me-downs**

hand·out (**hand**-out) *noun* **1.** Money, food, or clothing that is given to a needy person. **2.** An informative pamphlet or leaflet that is given out for free at an event such as a meeting or lecture, or during a class.

hand·rail (**hand**-*rayl*) *noun* A narrow rail that can be held for support, usually used on stairways.

hand·shake (**hand**-*shake*) *noun* A way of greeting or saying good-bye to someone by shaking the person's hand.

hand·some (**han**-suhm) *adjective* **1.** Attractive in appearance, used especially to describe a man. **2.** Generous.

hand·spring (**hand**-*spring*) *noun* A gymnastic movement in which you spring forward or backward onto both hands, then flip all the way over to land back on your feet.

hand·stand (**hand**-*stand*) *noun* When you do a **handstand,** you balance on your hands and put your feet in the air.

hand·writ·ing (**hand**-*rye*-ting) *noun* **1.** The way the letters and words look when you write. **2.** Writing done by a person, not a machine.
▶ *adjective* **handwritten**

hand·y (**han**-dee) *adjective* **1.** Useful, convenient, and easy to use. **2.** Skillful, especially with your hands. **3.** Near to someone or something.
▶ *adjective* **handier, handiest**

hang (hang) *verb* **1.** To put an object on a thing, such as a hook or rod, that holds it up. **2.** To kill someone by putting a rope around the person's neck and then letting the person's body drop. **3. hang up** To end a phone conversation by putting down the receiver or by turning off the phone. **4. hang out** (informal) To spend a lot of time in a place. **5.** If you **get the hang of** something, you learn how to do it and become comfortable doing it.
▶ *verb* **hanging, hung** (huhng) *or* **hanged** ▶ *noun* **hangout**

han·gar (**hang**-ur) *noun* A large building in which planes are kept and repaired. **Hangar** sounds like **hanger.**

hang·er (**hang**-ur) *noun* A frame used for hanging clothes that is made of wood, metal, or plastic and has a hook. **Hanger** sounds like **hangar.**

hang gli·der (**hang** *glye*-dur) *noun* A small aircraft like a giant kite, which you control through the motions of your body and that you hang from in order to fly. ▶ *noun* **hang gliding**

H

hang·over (**hang**-oh-vur) *noun* A headache, nausea, and other unpleasant feelings caused by drinking too much alcohol.

hang-up (**hang**-uhp) *noun* (informal) If you have a **hang-up** about something, it bothers you.

han·ker (**hang**-kur) *verb* To want something very much. ▶ *verb* **hankering, hankered** ▶ *noun* **hankering**

Ha·nuk·kah (**hah**-nuh-kuh) *noun* An eight-day Jewish holiday, also called the Feast or Festival of Lights, that usually falls in December. During this celebration, Jews light a menorah, a special candleholder with eight branches.

hap·haz·ard (*hap*-**haz**-urd) *adjective* Without any plan or organization. ▶ *adverb* **haphazardly**

hap·less (**hap**-lis) *adjective* Unlucky or unfortunate. ▶ *adverb* **haplessly** ▶ *noun* **haplessness**

hap·pen (**hap**-uhn) *verb* 1. To occur or to take place. 2. If you **happen** to do something, you do it by chance. ▶ *verb* **happening, happened**

hap·pi·ness (**hap**-ee-nis) *noun* The state or feeling of being happy, especially over a period of time.

hap·py (**hap**-ee) *adjective* 1. Feeling or showing pleasure or enjoyment. 2. Fortunate or lucky. ▶ *adjective* **happier, happiest** ▶ *adverb* **happily**

hap·py-go-luck·y (**hap**-ee-goh-**luhk**-ee) *adjective* A person who is **happy-go-lucky** is carefree and does not have many worries or troubles.

har·ass (huh-**ras** or **har**-uhs) *verb* To bother or annoy someone again and again. ▶ *verb* **harasses, harassing, harassed** ▶ *noun* **harassment**

har·bor (**hahr**-bur) *noun* An area of calm water near land where ships can safely dock or put down their anchors, often to unload cargo. *verb* 1. To keep bad thoughts in your mind for a long time. 2. To hide someone. ▶ *verb* **harboring, harbored**

hard (hahrd) *adjective* 1. Firm and stiff. 2. Difficult to do or understand. 3. Strong and forceful. 4. Strong and powerful enough to cause addiction. 5. Energetic. 6. Difficult and severe. *adverb* Energetically. ▶ *adjective* **harder, hardest** ▶ *noun* **hardness**

hard-boiled (**hahrd**-boild) *adjective* 1. Cooked by boiling until solid. 2. Tough and not sympathetic.

hard cop·y (**hahrd kah**-pee) *noun* A printed copy of a document created by a computer.

hard drive (**hahrd drive**) or **hard disk** (**hahrd disk**) *noun* A device fixed inside a computer containing a disk that can store large amounts of data. A hard drive connected to the outside of a computer is known as an *external hard drive*.

hard·en (**hahr**-duhn) *verb* 1. To become firm or stiff, or to make something firm or stiff. 2. To make or become tough and less sensitive to others. ▶ *verb* **hardening, hardened** ▶ *adjective* **hardened**

hard·ly (**hahrd**-lee) *adverb* 1. Barely or only just. 2. Surely not.

hard·ship (**hahrd**-ship) *noun* Something that makes life difficult, such as not having enough money or food.

hard·ware (**hahrd**-wair) *noun* 1. Tools and other equipment that are used especially in the house or yard. 2. Computer equipment, such as a printer, a monitor, or a keyboard.

hard·wired (**hahrd**-wired) *adjective* 1. Doing something in a particular way or by instinct, without having to learn it. 2. Operating with or involving connections using wires or hardware.

hard·wood (**hahrd**-wud) *noun* Very strong, heavy wood from trees such as oak, maple, beech, and mahogany.

har·dy (**hahr**-dee) *adjective* Strong and healthy and able to survive in very difficult conditions. ▶ *adjective* **hardier, hardiest**

H

hare (hair) *noun* A mammal that runs very fast and is like a large rabbit but with longer ears and strong hind legs.

harm (hahrm)
verb To hurt, injure, or damage someone or something.
noun Damage or injury.
▶ *verb* **harming, harmed** ▶ *adjective* **harmful**

harm·less (**hahrm**-lis) *adjective* Not able or likely to cause injury or damage. ▶ *noun* **harmlessness** ▶ *adverb* **harmlessly**

har·mon·i·ca (hahr-**mah**-ni-kuh) *noun* A small musical instrument that you play by blowing out and breathing in through the mouthpiece.

har·mo·nize (**hahr**-muh-*nize*) *verb* 1. To sing or play musical notes that sound pleasing together. 2. To go together in a pleasing or agreeable way.
▶ *verb* **harmonizing, harmonized**

har·mo·ny (**hahr**-muh-nee) *noun* 1. A situation in which people work or live together in a peaceful way. 2. A pleasing combination or arrangement. 3. A set of musical notes played or sung at the same time that are part of a chord and that sound pleasing together.
▶ *noun, plural* **harmonies** ▶ *adjective* **harmonious** (hahr-**moh**-nee-uhs)

har·ness (**hahr**-nis)
noun 1. A set of leather straps and metal pieces that connect a horse or another animal to a plow, cart, or wagon. 2. A set of straps used to connect you to something and keep you safe.
verb To control something and use it for a particular purpose.
▶ *verb* **harnesses, harnessing, harnessed** ▶ *noun, plural* **harnesses**

harp (hahrp)
noun A large, triangular musical instrument with strings. It is played by plucking the strings with your fingers.
verb If you **harp on** something, you keep talking about it in a way that is annoying.
▶ *verb* **harping, harped** ▶ *noun* **harpist**

har·poon (hahr-**poon**)
noun A long spear with an attached rope that can be thrown or shot out of a special gun. It is usually used for hunting large fish or whales.
verb To hit or kill with a harpoon.
▶ *verb* **harpooning, harpooned**

harp·si·chord (**hahrp**-si-*kord*) *noun* A keyboard instrument that looks like a small piano. A harpsichord has wire strings that are plucked rather than being struck like the strings in a piano.

harsh (hahrsh) *adjective* 1. Cruel or rough. 2. Unpleasant or hard on the body or senses.
▶ *adjective* **harsher, harshest** ▶ *adverb* **harshly**

har·vest (**hahr**-vist)
noun 1. The gathering of crops that are ripe, or the crops that have been gathered. 2. The season in which crops become ripe and are gathered.
verb To gather crops from a field.
▶ *verb* **harvesting, harvested**

har·vest·er (**hahr**-vi-stur) *noun* A machine used to harvest crops.

hash (hash) *noun* 1. A hot dish of small pieces of meat and potatoes cooked together. 2. (*informal*) If you **make a hash of** something, you do it badly.
▶ *noun, plural* **hashes**

has·n't (**haz**-uhnt) *contraction* A short form of *has not.*

has·sle (**has**-uhl)
verb (*informal*) If someone **hassles** you, the person keeps bothering you about something.
noun (*informal*) Something that is annoying and causes problems.
▶ *verb* **hassling, hassled**

haste (hayst) *noun* Speed in doing something, especially because you do not have enough time.

has·ten (**hay**-suhn) *verb* 1. To move quickly. 2. To make someone or something move or happen faster. 3. To be quick to do or say something.
▶ *verb* **hastening, hastened**

has·ty (**hay**-stee) *adjective* Done too quickly, especially with bad results. ▶ *adjective* **hastier, hastiest** ▶ *adverb* **hastily**

hat (hat) *noun* A piece of clothing that you wear on your head.

H

hatch (hach)
verb 1. When an egg **hatches,** it breaks open and a baby bird or reptile comes out of it. 2. To think of a plan, usually in secret.
noun An opening in a floor, deck, wall, or ceiling, or the door that covers it.
▶ *verb* **hatches, hatching, hatched** ▶ *noun, plural* **hatches**

hatch·back (**hach**-bak) *noun* A car with a large back door that opens upward.

hatch·et (**hach**-it) *noun* A small ax with a short handle.

hate (hate)
verb To strongly dislike someone or something.
noun A very strong feeling of dislike for someone or something.
▶ *verb* **hating, hated**

hate·ful (**hate**-fuhl) *adjective* Full of hatred and ill will. ▶ *adverb* **hatefully**

hat·red (**hay**-trid) *noun* Intense dislike; the feeling of someone who hates.

haugh·ty (**haw**-tee) *adjective* If you are **haughty,** you are very proud and think you are better or smarter than other people. ▶ *adjective* **haughtier, haughtiest** ▶ *noun* **haughtiness** ▶ *adverb* **haughtily**

haul (hawl)
verb 1. To pull or drag something with a lot of effort or difficulty. 2. To transport with a vehicle.
noun 1. A large amount of something that has been caught or captured. 2. The distance someone travels or over which something is transported.
Haul sounds like **hall.** ▶ *verb* **hauling, hauled**

haunch (hawnch) *noun* The hip, buttock, and upper thigh of an animal or a person. ▶ *noun, plural* **haunches**

haunt (hawnt)
verb 1. If a ghost **haunts** a place, it appears there often. 2. If something **haunts** you, it upsets you and you are unable to forget it.
noun A place someone often visits.
▶ *verb* **haunting, haunted** ▶ *adjective* **haunting**

haunt·ed (**hawn**-tid) *adjective* 1. A house or other place that is **haunted** is thought to be lived in or visited by ghosts. 2. If a person is **haunted,** he or she has terrible memories of a past experience or action.

have (hav) *verb* 1. To own, possess, or hold something. 2. To experience something. 3. To receive or get something. 4. To need or be obliged to do. 5. To contain or consist of. 6. To be the parent or parents of. 7. To be sick with something. 8. To arrange for. **Have** sounds like **halve.** ▶ *verb* **has** (haz), **having, had** (had)

ha·ven (**hay**-vuhn) *noun* A safe place for animals or people.

have·n't (**hav**-uhnt) *contraction* A short form of *have not.*

hav·oc (**hav**-uhk) *noun* Great destruction or confusion.

Ha·wa·ii (huh-**wye**-ee) A state west of the continental United States in the Pacific Ocean that consists of eight main islands and many smaller ones. The newest of the 50 states, Hawaii is popular with tourists who come to enjoy its tropical climate, pristine beaches, and active volcanoes.

hawk (hawk)
noun A large bird with a hooked beak and sharp claws that eats small animals and other birds.
verb To sell something, especially by offering goods in the street or some other public place and shouting to draw attention to them.
▶ *verb* **hawking, hawked**

hay (hay) *noun* Long grass that is dried and used as food for farm animals. **Hay** sounds like **hey.**

hay fe·ver (**hay** *fee*-vur) *noun* A sickness like a cold that affects your eyes, nose, and throat. It is an allergy caused by breathing in pollen from plants.

hay·loft (**hay**-*lawft*) *noun* A platform high above the floor of a barn where hay is stored.

hay·stack (**hay**-*stak*) *noun* A big, firm pile of hay.

hay·wire (**hay**-*wire*) *adjective* 1. Out of order or not working properly. 2. Wild or out of control.

H

haz·ard (**haz**-urd)
noun Something that is dangerous or likely to cause problems.
verb To make a guess or suggestion, even though you know it might be wrong.
▶ *verb* **hazarding, hazarded**

haz·ard·ous (**haz**-ur-duhs) *adjective* Dangerous or risky.

haz·ard·ous waste (**haz**-ur-duhs **wayst**)
noun Dangerous materials that should not be thrown away without some sort of protective covering.

haze (haze) *noun* Smoke, dust, or moisture in the air that prevents you from seeing very far.

ha·zel (**hay**-zuhl)
noun **1.** A small tree or shrub that produces light brown nuts; a hazelnut tree. **2.** A green-brown color.
adjective Having a green-brown color.

haz·y (**hay**-zee) *adjective* **1.** Unclear because of smoke, dust, or moisture. **2.** If you have a **hazy** memory of something, the details are unclear in your mind.
▶ *adjective* **hazier, haziest** ▶ *adverb* **hazily**

he (hee) *pronoun* **1.** The male person or animal mentioned before. **2.** Any person.

head (hed)
noun **1.** The top part of your body where your brain, eyes, ears, nose, and mouth are. **2.** The person who leads an organization or group of people. **3.** The top or front of something. **4.** A single person or animal. **5.** A cluster of leaves or flowers.
noun, plural **heads** The main side of a coin, which usually shows a head or a face.
verb **1.** To lead. **2.** To move in the direction of something.
adjective Leading a group or organization.
idioms **1.** If something **goes to your head,** it makes you dizzy. **2.** If a compliment **goes to your head,** it makes you think you are better than other people. **3.** If you **keep a cool head** in an emergency, you remain calm and relaxed.
▶ *verb* **heading, headed**

head·ache (**hed**-ake) *noun* **1.** An ache or pain in your head. **2.** Something or someone that is a nuisance and causes problems.

head·band (**hed**-band) *noun* A strip of cloth or plastic worn around the head to soak up sweat or keep hair out of the face.

head·dress (**hed**-dres) *noun* A covering for the head, usually worn as a decoration on special occasions. ▶ *noun, plural* **headdresses**

head·first (**hed**-furst) *adverb* With the head first, or leading with the head.

head·hunt·er (**hed**-huhn-tuhr) *noun* Someone whose job is to find the best people for important jobs and introduce them to employers.

head·ing (**hed**-ing) *noun* Words written as a title at the top of a page or over a section of writing in a magazine, newspaper, or book.

head·light (**hed**-lite) *noun* A bright light on the front of a vehicle that allows the driver to see ahead in the dark.

head·line (**hed**-line)
noun The title of a newspaper, magazine, or web article, appearing in large, usually bold type.
verb To give an article a particular headline.
▶ *verb* **headlining, headlined**

head·long (**hed**-lawng) *adverb* **1.** With the head first. **2.** Without thinking about what you are doing.

head·mas·ter (**hed**-mas-tur) *noun* A man who is in charge of a private school.

head·mis·tress (**hed**-mis-tris) *noun* A woman who is in charge of a private school. ▶ *noun, plural* **headmistresses**

head·on (**hed**-awn) *adjective, adverb* With the head or front end first.

head·phones (**hed**-fohnz) *noun, plural* Small speakers that you wear in or over your ears to listen to music or other audio.

H

head·quar·ters (hed-*kwor*-turz) *noun*
The main building or office of a
company or organization. Abbreviated
as *HQ*.

head start (hed stahrt) *noun* An
advantage, usually in a race when one
runner is allowed to start first.

head·strong (hed-*strawng*) *adjective*
Determined to do what you want and
not listen to advice.

head·way (hed-*way*) *noun* Progress or
forward movement.

heal (heel) *verb* 1. To get better. 2. To
cure someone or make the person
healthy.
Heal sounds like **heel.** ▸ *verb* **healing,
healed** ▸ *noun* **healer** ▸ *noun* **healing**

health (helth) *noun* 1. The state of being
free from disease. 2. The condition of
your body or mind. 3. The condition
of something such as a business or
organization.

health food (helth *food*) *noun* Food that
is considered to be healthy because
it is grown in a natural way and does
not contain anything artificial.

health·y (hel-thee) *adjective* 1. If you are
healthy, you are strong and not likely
to become sick. 2. Something that
is **healthy** is good for the health of
your body. 3. Successful and working
effectively.
▸ *adjective* **healthier,
healthiest** ▸ *adverb* **healthily**

heap (heep)
noun 1. A large, messy pile of things.
2. (informal) A lot of something.
verb To pile things on top of each
other.
▸ *verb* **heaping, heaped**

hear (heer) *verb* 1. To take in sounds
through your ears. 2. To get news.
3. To listen to.
Hear sounds like **here.** ▸ *verb*
hearing, heard (hurd)

hear·ing (heer-ing) *noun* 1. The ability
to hear. 2. An opportunity for an
accused person in a court case to tell
their version of what happened. 3. An
opportunity to state an idea and have
it be heard and respected.

hear·ing aid (heer-ing *ayd*) *noun* A small
device worn behind one or both ears
that helps a person hear better.

hear·say (heer-*say*) *noun* Something you
have heard from someone else but
have not seen or experienced yourself;
a rumor.

hearse (hurs) *noun* A car that carries a
coffin to a funeral and burial.

heart (hahrt)
noun 1. The organ in your chest that
pumps blood all through your body.
2. The part of you that feels emotion.
3. Love and caring. 4. Courage or hope.
5. The center or most important part
of something. 6. A shape like this (♥)
that people use as a symbol for love,
or in place of the verb *love.* 7. If you
learn something **by heart,** you have
memorized it and know it very well.
8. If you **take something to heart,** you
think about it seriously.
noun, plural **hearts** One of the four
suits in a deck of cards. Hearts have a
red symbol shaped like a heart.

heart at·tack (hahrt uh-*tak*) *noun* If
someone has a **heart attack,** the
person's heart suddenly stops
pumping blood properly to the rest of
the body. This can cause death in the
most serious cases.

heart·beat (hahrt-*beet*) *noun* One
complete pumping movement of the
heart.

heart·bro·ken (hahrt-*broh*-kuhn)
adjective Extremely sad.

hearth (hahrth) *noun* The floor in front
of or inside a fireplace.

heart·less (hahrt-lis) *adjective*
Cruel and feeling no sympathy
for other people. ▸ *noun*
heartlessness ▸ *adverb* **heartlessly**

heart·y (hahr-tee) *adjective* 1. Friendly
and enthusiastic. 2. Large and filling.
3. If you have a **hearty** appetite, you are
able to eat a lot of food.
▸ *adjective* **heartier, heartiest** ▸ *noun*
heartiness ▸ *adverb* **heartily**

heat (heet)
noun 1. The quality of being very
warm. 2. Hot weather. 3. The level of

H

temperature, such as on a stove or in a building. **4.** An early round in a race. **5.** Strong emotions, such as anger or excitement. **6.** In physics, energy that comes from the motion of molecules passing from one substance to another, which increases temperature. **7. heat wave** A long period of unusually hot weather.
verb To cause something to become hot or warm.
▶ *verb* **heating, heated** ▶ *adjective* **heated** ▶ *adverb* **heatedly**

heat·er (**hee**-tur) *noun* A device that produces heat, such as a radiator or a furnace.

heath (heeth) *noun* An area of open land that is covered with grass and small, wild plants.

hea·then (**hee**-THuhn) *noun* **1.** Someone who does not believe in one of the major religions. **2.** (informal) Someone who is not civilized or educated.

heath·er (**heTH**-ur) *noun* A small bush with pink, purple, or white flowers.

heave (heev)
verb **1.** To lift, pull, push, or throw something heavy using a lot of effort. **2.** To go up and down with regular movements.
noun A strong push, pull, throw, or lift.
▶ *verb* **heaving, heaved**

heav·en (**hev**-uhn)
noun **1.** The home of God, according to Christianity and some other religions. It is thought to be a glorious place where good people go after they die. **2.** A wonderful situation or place.
noun, plural **the heavens** The sky.

heav·en·ly (**hev**-uhn-lee) *adjective* **1.** Of or having to do with heaven. **2.** Of or having to do with the sky or outer space. **3.** Delightful or wonderful.

heav·y (**hev**-ee) *adjective* **1.** Weighing a lot; hard to move or lift. **2.** Larger, stronger, or more than usual. **3.** Needing a lot of effort or physical strength. **4.** Making you feel very full. **5.** Serious, difficult, or hard to understand.
▶ *adjective* **heavier, heaviest** ▶ *noun* **heaviness** ▶ *adverb* **heavily**

heav·y met·al (**hev**-ee **met**-uhl) *noun* A type of rock 'n' roll music with a strong beat and very loud electric guitars.

He·brew (**hee**-broo)
noun **1.** The language of the ancient Hebrews, used today as a language of prayer. Hebrew is also the language spoken by the people who live in Israel. **2.** A member of or descendant from one of the Jewish tribes of ancient times.
adjective Of or having to do with the Hebrews or their language.

heck·le (**hek**-uhl) *verb* To interrupt a speaker or a performer in a rude way by making loud comments. ▶ *verb* **heckling, heckled** ▶ *noun* **heckler**

hect·are (**hek**-tair) *noun* A unit of area in the metric system. One hectare is equal to 10,000 square meters, or about 2.5 acres.

hec·tic (**hek**-tik) *adjective* Very busy and filled with activity and excitement. ▶ *adverb* **hectically**

hedge (hej)
noun A row of bushes or small trees that are planted very close to each other, usually used as a border around yards or fields.
verb To avoid giving a direct answer.
▶ *verb* **hedging, hedged**

hedge·hog (**hej**-hawg or **hej**-hahg) *noun* A small, insect-eating mammal with a pointed nose and spines on its back. It rolls into a ball to protect itself when it is frightened.

heed (heed)
verb To pay close attention to someone or something.
noun Attention.
▶ *verb* **heeding, heeded**

heel (heel) *noun* **1.** The back part of your foot. **2.** The part of a shoe or sock that covers the back of your foot. **3.** The part on the bottom of a shoe or boot that raises the back. **4.** If you **kick up your heels,** you are having a very good time.
Heel sounds like **heal.**

H

hef·ty (**hef**-tee) *adjective* **1.** (informal) Large, heavy, or strong. **2.** (informal) A **hefty** amount of something, such as money, is very large.
▶ *adjective* **heftier, heftiest** ▶ *noun* **heftiness** ▶ *adverb* **heftily**

heif·er (**hef**-ur) *noun* A young cow that has not yet had a baby.

height (hite) *noun* **1.** A measurement of how tall someone or something is. **2.** A measurement of how high above the ground something is. **3.** The most important or peak point of something.

height·en (**hye**-tuhn) *verb* To increase something or make it stronger. ▶ *verb* **heightening, heightened**

Heim·lich ma·neu·ver (**hime**-lik muh-*noo*-vur) *noun* A way of helping someone who is choking by putting your arms around the person from behind, below the ribs, and squeezing in order to force food out of the person's throat.

heir (air) *noun* Someone who receives someone else's money, property, or title when that person dies. **Heir** sounds like **air.**

heir·ess (**air**-uhs) *noun* A girl or woman who receives someone else's money, property, or title when that person dies. ▶ *noun, plural* **heiresses**

heir·loom (**air**-*loom*) *noun* Something valuable, such as an antique, that is passed from one generation of a family to the next.

hel·i·cop·ter (**hel**-i-*kahp*-tur) *noun* An aircraft with large, rotating blades on top and no wings. A helicopter can fly straight up and down and does so for takeoff and landing, requiring little space.

he·li·um (**hee**-lee-uhm) *noun* A light, colorless gas that does not burn. It is used to fill airships and balloons.

hell (hel) *noun* A very hot, miserable place where evil people go when they die in order to be punished, according to some Christian and other religious groups. ▶ *adjective* **hellish**

hel·lo (he-**loh** *or* huh-**loh**) *interjection* A word you say to greet a person you meet or speak to on the telephone.

helm (helm) *noun* **1.** The wheel or handle used to steer a boat or ship. **2.** Someone who is **at the helm** is in charge of something.

hel·met (**hel**-mit) *noun* A hard hat that covers and protects your head.

help (help)
verb **1.** To make it possible or easier for another person to do something. **2.** To make a situation better. **3.** If you **help yourself,** you take something you want, such as food or drink, often without asking for permission. **4.** If you can't **help** something, you can't avoid it or stop doing it.
noun Something you do that makes it possible or easier for another person to do something.
▶ *verb* **helping, helped**

help·er (**hel**-pur) *noun* A person or thing that helps someone.

help·ful (**help**-fuhl) *adjective* **1.** Willing to help. **2.** Able to make a situation better or easier.
▶ *noun* **helpfulness** ▶ *adverb* **helpfully**

help·ing (**hel**-ping) *noun* An amount of food that is put on a person's plate.

help·ing verb (**hel**-ping *vurb*) *noun* A verb, such as *may* or a form of *be, do,* or *have,* that is used together with another verb to complete the meaning of that verb.

help·less (**help**-lis) *adjective* If you are **helpless,** you cannot take care of yourself. ▶ *noun* **helplessness** ▶ *adverb* **helplessly**

hem (hem)
noun An edge of material that has been folded over and sewn down.
verb **1.** To sew down an edge of material after you have folded it over. **2.** If you are **hemmed in,** you are surrounded and cannot move or get out.
▶ *verb* **hemming, hemmed**

hem·i·sphere (**hem**-i-*sfeer*) *noun* One half of a round object, especially of the earth.

hem·lock (**hem**-lahk) *noun* **1.** A very poisonous plant of the carrot family, or the poison made from this plant. **2.** A tree similar to the pine that has green leaves throughout the year.

H

he·mo·glo·bin (**hee**-muh-*gloh*-bin) *noun* A substance in your red blood cells that carries oxygen to all parts of your body.

he·mo·phil·i·a (*hee*-muh-**fil**-ee-uh) *noun* A serious disease in which a person bleeds too much from cuts or bruises.

hem·or·rhage (**hem**-ur-ij) *noun* A serious medical condition in which a person bleeds a lot and cannot stop it.

hemp (hemp) *noun* A plant that is used to make rope and cloth.

hen (hen) *noun* **1.** An adult female bird. **2.** A female bird raised for its eggs and meat.

hence (hens) *adverb* As a result; for this reason.

hep·tath·lon (hep-**tath**-luhn) *noun* An athletic competition, usually for women, made up of seven events.

her (hur)
pronoun The form of the word *she* used as a grammatical object.
adjective Belonging to or related to a girl or woman.

her·ald (**her**-uhld)
noun A person in the past who carried messages and made announcements on behalf of a ruler.
verb To signal the approach of something.
▶ *verb* **heralding, heralded**

her·ald·ry (**her**-uhl-dree) *noun* The study of the history of families and their symbols, such as their coats of arms.

herb (urb) *noun* A plant or part of a plant that is used in cooking or medicine. ▶ *noun* **herbalist** ▶ *adjective* **herbal**

her·bi·vore (**hur**-buh-*vor*) *noun* An animal that only eats plants. ▶ *adjective* **herbivorous** (hur-**biv**-ur-uhs)

herd (hurd)
noun A large number of animals that stay together or move together.
verb To move people or animals together in a group.
▶ *verb* **herding, herded** ▶ *noun* **herder**

here (heer)
adverb **1.** At or in this place. **2.** At this point or time.
interjection A word used to answer a roll call.
noun This place.
Here sounds like **hear.**

here·af·ter (*heer*-af-tur) *adverb* From now on.

here·by (**heer**-bye *or* heer-**bye**) *adverb* By means of or as a result of these words or this statement.

he·red·i·tar·y (huh-**red**-i-ter-ee) *adjective* Passed from parent to child before the child is born.

he·red·i·ty (huh-**red**-i-tee) *noun* **1.** The process of passing physical and mental qualities from a parent to a child before the child is born. **2.** All of the qualities that are passed on in this way.

her·e·tic (**her**-uh-tik) *noun* Someone whose views are thought to be wrong or evil by a particular religion or by people in authority. ▶ *noun* **heresy** (**her**-i-see) ▶ *adjective* **heretical** (huh-**ret**-i-kuhl)

her·i·tage (**her**-i-tij) *noun* Traditions and beliefs that a country or society considers an important part of its history.

her·mit (**hur**-mit) *noun* Someone who prefers to live alone and stay away from other people.

he·ro (**heer**-oh) *noun* **1.** A person who is admired for doing something brave or good. **2.** The main character in a book, play, movie, or any kind of story.
▶ *noun, plural* **heroes** ▶ *noun* **heroism**

he·ro·ic (hi-**roh**-ik) *adjective* **1.** Very brave and admired by many people. **2.** Involving the actions of heroes.
▶ *adverb* **heroically**

her·o·in (**her**-oh-in) *noun* A powerful and illegal drug that can cause addiction. **Heroin** sounds like **heroine.**

her·o·ine (**her**-oh-in) *noun* **1.** A girl or woman who is admired for doing something brave or good. **2.** The main female character in a book, play, movie, or any kind of story.
Heroine sounds like **heroin.**

H

her·on (**her**-uhn) *noun* A bird with a long, thin beak and long legs that lives near water.

her·pes (**hur**-peez) *noun* A disease caused by a virus, resulting in painful blisters.

her·ring (**her**-ing) *noun* A fish that swims in the northern Atlantic and Pacific oceans and is used for food. ▶ *noun, plural* **herring** or **herrings**

hers (hurz) *pronoun* The thing or things belonging to or related to a girl or woman.

her·self (hur-**self**) *pronoun* Her and no one else.

hertz (hurts) *noun* A unit for measuring the frequency of vibrations and waves, equal to one cycle per second. Abbreviated as *Hz*. ▶ *noun, plural* **hertz**

hes·i·tate (**hez**-i-*tate*) *verb* To pause before saying or doing something, especially because you feel nervous or unsure. ▶ *verb* **hesitating, hesitated** ▶ *noun* **hesitation** ▶ *adjective* **hesitant**

hex·a·gon (**hek**-suh-*gahn*) *noun* A shape with six straight sides. ▶ *adjective* **hexagonal** (hek-**sag**-uh-nuhl)

hey (hay) *interjection* A word used to get someone's attention or to show surprise or joy. **Hey** sounds like **hay**.

hey·day (**hay**-*day*) *noun* The time when someone or something was most successful or popular.

hi (hye) *interjection* A word used as a greeting; hello. **Hi** sounds like **high**.

hi·ber·nate (**hye**-bur-*nate*) *verb* When animals **hibernate,** they sleep for the entire winter. This protects them and helps them survive when the temperatures are cold and food is hard to find. ▶ *verb* **hibernating, hibernated** ▶ *noun* **hibernation**

hic·cup (**hik**-uhp) *noun* A sound in your throat caused by a sudden movement in your chest that you cannot control. Hiccups are usually caused by drinking or eating too quickly.

noun, plural **hiccups** The condition of having a series of these for a period of time. Sometimes also known as *the hiccups.*

hick·o·ry (**hik**-ur-ee) *noun* A tall tree with hard wood and a nut that you can eat. *adjective* Made of the wood of a hickory tree. ▶ *noun, plural* **hickories**

hid·den (**hid**-uhn) *verb* The past participle of **hide.** *adjective* Not in view; not obvious or known about.

hide (hide) *verb* **1.** To put something in a place where it cannot be seen. **2.** To go to a place where you cannot be seen. **3.** To keep something secret, such as a feeling. *noun* The skin of an animal that is used to make leather. *phrase* If someone is **in hiding,** they are in a secret place that most people don't know about. ▶ *verb* **hiding, hid** (hid), **hidden** (**hid**-uhn)

hide-and-seek (**hide**-uhn-**seek**) *noun* A game in which people hide while one person looks for them.

hid·e·ous (**hid**-ee-uhs) *adjective* Very ugly or horrible. ▶ *noun* **hideousness** ▶ *adverb* **hideously**

hide·out (**hide**-out) *noun* A place where someone can hide, especially a criminal trying to escape from the police.

hi·er·ar·chy (**hye**-ur-*ahr*-kee) *noun* An arrangement in which people or things have different ranks or levels of importance. ▶ *adjective* **hierarchical** (hye-ur-**ahr**-ki-kuhl)

hier·o·glyph·ics (*hye*-ruh-**glif**-iks) *noun, plural* A system of writing used by ancient Egyptians, made up of pictures and symbols that stand for words.

high (hye) *adjective* **1.** Something that is **high** is a long way above the ground. **2.** Measuring a particular distance

H

from top to bottom. **3.** A **high** voice, sound, or note is near the top of the range of sounds that people can hear. **4.** More or better than the normal level, amount, or quality.

adverb At or to a high level, amount, or quality.

noun The highest level or degree.

High sounds like **hi.** ▶ *adjective* **higher, highest** ▶ *adverb* **higher, highest**

high-def (hye-def) *adjective* Short for **high-definition.**

high-def·i·ni·tion (hye-def-uh-**nish**-uhn) *adjective* Using new technology that creates very clear and detailed images. Often shortened to *high-def.*

high·er ed·u·ca·tion (hye-ur ej-uh-**kay**-shuhn) *noun* Education at a college or university.

high jump (hye juhmp) *noun* A track-and-field event in which athletes must jump over a bar without knocking it down. The bar is raised higher each time they successfully jump over it. ▶ *noun* **high jumper**

high·land (hye-luhnd)
noun An area of land with mountains or hills.
adjective Relating to an area of land with mountains or hills.

high·light (hye-lite)
verb **1.** To make something easy to notice. **2.** To mark text using a pen with brightly colored ink that you can see through. **3.** To select text or an image on a computer monitor in order to do something with it.
noun The most interesting or important part of something.
noun, plural **highlights** Areas of a light color in hair.
▶ *verb* **highlighting, highlighted**

high·light·er (hye-lye-tur) *noun* A special pen with brightly colored ink that you can see through, used to mark important text.

high·ly (hye-lee) *adverb* At or to a high degree or level.

high-rise (hye-rize)
noun A tall building. High-rises are

found mostly in cities.
adjective Very tall, with many floors.

high school (hye skool)
noun A school that usually includes grades nine through twelve or ten through twelve.
adjective **high-school** Of or having to do with a high school.

high seas (hye seez) *noun, plural* The parts of an ocean or a sea that are not controlled by any country.

high-strung (hye-struhng) *adjective* Very nervous or easily excited.

high-tech (hye-tek)
adjective Using the most modern technology.
noun The most modern technology.

high tide (hye tide) *noun* The time at which the water level in an ocean, a gulf, or a bay is at its highest point.

high·way (hye-way) *noun* A large public road that connects cities or towns.

hi·jack (hye-jak) *verb* If someone **hijacks** a vehicle, such as a plane, the person takes illegal control of it and forces its pilot or driver to go somewhere. ▶ *verb* **hijacking, hijacked** ▶ *noun* **hijacker** ▶ *noun* **hijacking**

hike (hike)
noun A long walk, especially in the country or the mountains.
verb To walk in the outdoors as exercise or for pleasure.
▶ *verb* **hiking, hiked** ▶ *noun* **hiker** ▶ *noun* **hiking**

hi·lar·i·ous (hi-lair-ee-uhs) *adjective* Very funny. ▶ *noun* **hilarity**

hill (hil) *noun* A raised area of land that is not as high as a mountain.

hill·side (hil-side) *noun* The sloping side of a hill.

hill·top (hil-tahp) *noun* The highest part of a hill.

hilt (hilt) *noun* **1.** The handle of a sword or knife. **2. to the hilt** As much as possible; completely.

him (him) *pronoun* The form of the word *he* used as a grammatical object. **Him** sounds like **hymn.**

H

Him·a·lay·as (*him*-uh-**lay**-uhz) The world's highest mountain range, stretching across south-central Asia. The Himalayas run from west to east, through the countries of Bhutan, China, Myanmar, India, Nepal, Pakistan, and Afghanistan. Mount Everest is the highest peak in the range.

him·self (him-**self**) *pronoun* Him and no one else.

hind (hinde) *adjective* At the back or rear.

hin·der (**hin**-dur) *verb* To make it more difficult for something to happen or succeed. ▶ *verb* **hindering, hindered**

Hin·du·ism (**hin**-doo-*iz*-uhm) *noun* A religion and philosophy practiced mainly in India. Hindus worship many gods and believe in reincarnation. ▶ *noun* **Hindu** ▶ *adjective* **Hindu**

hinge (hinj) *noun* A metal joint on a door, gate, or lid that allows it to open and close easily. *verb* To depend on something completely. ▶ *verb* **hinging, hinged** ▶ *adjective* **hinged**

hint (hint) *noun* 1. A helpful piece of information that makes it easier for you to do something or guess an answer. 2. A very small amount of something. *verb* To suggest something without saying it directly. ▶ *verb* **hinting, hinted**

hip (hip) *noun* The part of your body below your waist that sticks out on either side, right above the top of your leg.

hip-hop (**hip**-*hahp*) *noun* A style of dancing, art, music, and dress that began in cities. Hip-hop includes rap music, break dancing, and graffiti art.

hip·pie (**hip**-ee) *noun* A young person, especially one in the 1960s, who rejected traditional values. Hippies often had long hair, wore bright

clothes, and were against war and violence.

hip·po·pot·a·mus (*hip*-uh-**pah**-tuh-muhs) *noun* A large African mammal with thick gray skin, a big head and mouth, and short legs. Hippopotamuses eat plants and live in or near water. The animal is also known as a *hippo*. ▶ *noun, plural* **hippopotamuses** *or* **hippopotami** (*hip*-uh-**pah**-tuh-*mye*)

hire (hire) *verb* 1. To give someone a job. 2. To get the use of something temporarily in exchange for money. ▶ *verb* **hiring, hired**

his (hiz) *adjective* Belonging to or related to a boy or man. *pronoun* The thing or things belonging to or related to him.

His·pan·ic (hi-**span**-ik) *adjective* Coming from or related to countries where Spanish is spoken. *noun* Someone who comes from a country where Spanish is spoken.

hiss (his) *verb* To make a sound like a long "s," especially to show that you do not like something or someone. *noun* A sound like a long "s." ▶ *verb* **hisses, hissing, hissed** ▶ *noun, plural* **hisses**

his·to·ri·an (his-**tor**-ee-uhn) *noun* Someone who writes about or knows about history.

his·tor·ic (hi-**stor**-ik) *adjective* If an event is **historic,** it was important in the past and will be remembered in the future, as in *the historic signing of the Declaration of Independence.*

his·tor·i·cal (hi-**stor**-i-kuhl) *adjective* Of or having to do with people or events of the past. ▶ *adverb* **historically**

his·to·ry (**his**-tur-ee) *noun* 1. The study of things that happened in the past. 2. A description of things that happened in the past. ▶ *noun, plural* **histories**

hit (hit) *verb* 1. To strike something with your hand or with an object such as a

H

bat or a hammer. **2.** To fall or crash into something with force. **3.** To have a strong, often harmful effect on someone or something.
noun **1.** The impact that results from striking or hitting something. **2.** Something, such as a song or play, that is popular or successful. **3.** A result from a search that you do on the Internet. **4.** A play in baseball, in which a batter hits the ball and is able to reach a base safely.
idiom (informal) If you **hit it off** with someone, you get along well with the person.
▶ *verb* **hitting, hit** ▶ *noun* **hitter**

hitch (hich)
verb **1.** To connect one thing to another using something such as a rope. **2.** (informal) To hitchhike.
noun A problem or difficulty.
idiom (slang) If you **get hitched,** you get married.
▶ *noun, plural* **hitches** ▶ *verb* **hitches, hitching, hitched**

hitch·hike (**hich**-hike) *verb* To travel by getting rides in other people's vehicles, often by standing on the side of the road and holding out your thumb to get someone to stop. ▶ *verb* **hitchhiking, hitchhiked** ▶ *noun* **hitchhiker**

hith·er (**hiTH**-ur) *adverb* Here.

HIV (aych-*eye*-vee) *noun* **1.** A virus that can develop into AIDS. HIV is short for *human immunodeficiency virus.* **2.** If someone is **HIV positive,** the person has the HIV virus and his or her immune system is weakened. People who are HIV positive can develop AIDS.

hive (hive)
noun Short for **beehive.**
noun, plural **hives** An allergic reaction of the skin, producing a rash that itches or burns.

HMO (aych-*em*-oh) *noun* An organization that provides all the health care for its members who make a regular payment to it. HMO is short for *health maintenance organization.*

hoard (hord)
verb **1.** To collect and store things, sometimes secretly. **2.** To buy up a lot of supplies because you think they will be gone soon.
noun A large supply of something that has been collected.
Hoard sounds like **horde.** ▶ *verb* **hoarding, hoarded** ▶ *noun* **hoarder**

hoarse (hors) *adjective* A **hoarse** voice is rough and sounds croaky, often because of a sore throat. **Hoarse** sounds like **horse.**

hoax (hohks) *noun* A trick that makes people believe something that is not true. ▶ *noun, plural* **hoaxes**

hob·ble (**hah**-buhl) *verb* To walk with difficulty because you are injured or weak. ▶ *verb* **hobbling, hobbled**

hob·by (**hah**-bee) *noun* Something that you enjoy doing when you have free time. ▶ *noun, plural* **hobbies**

Hodg·kin's lym·pho·ma (**hahj**-kinz lim-**foh**-muh) *noun* A disease in which the lymph glands, spleen, and liver gradually become larger.

hoe (hoh)
noun A gardening tool with a long handle and flat blade, used to turn over soil and remove weeds.
verb To turn over soil and remove weeds with a hoe.
▶ *verb* **hoeing, hoed**

hog (hawg *or* hahg)
noun **1.** A fully grown pig. **2.** (informal) A selfish person who takes or uses more than his or her fair share of something.
verb (informal) To take or use more than one's fair share of something.
▶ *verb* **hogging, hogged**

ho·gan (**hoh**-gahn) *noun* A Navajo house made with logs and branches and covered with soil.

hoist (hoist)
verb To lift something heavy, usually with rope or a piece of equipment.
noun A piece of equipment used for lifting heavy things.
▶ *verb* **hoisting, hoisted**

H

hold (hohld)
verb **1.** To have something in your hand, hands, or arms. **2.** To contain or have enough room for something. **3.** To support the weight of something or someone. **4.** To cause something to happen. **5.** To have a particular position or job. **6.** To have an opinion or belief. **7.** To keep control of something or someone, for example by defending something that is being attacked. **8.** If you **hold something against** someone, you have a bad opinion of that person because of something he or she did in the past. **9. hold off** To delay doing something, especially because you are waiting for something else to happen or finish. **10. hold on** To succeed in doing something, even though it is difficult to do. **11.** If you ask someone to **hold on,** you ask the person to wait briefly. **12.** If you **hold out** in a difficult situation, you continue with what you are doing. **13. hold up** To rob a person or business with a weapon. **14.** If you **hold up** someone or something, you delay the person or thing.
noun The part of a ship where goods are stored.
▶ *verb* **holding, held** (held)

hold·er (**hohl**-dur) *noun* **1.** An object that holds something. **2.** A person who holds or owns something.

hold·ing (**hohl**-ding) *noun* **1.** A penalty in various sports in which one player illegally obstructs another. **2. holdings** *noun, plural* Things that a company or a person owns, especially investments or real estate.

hold·up (**hohld**-*uhp*) *noun* **1.** A robbery by someone who has a weapon. **2.** A delay in activity.

hole (hole) *noun* **1.** A hollow place or an opening in something solid. **2.** A weakness or flaw. **3.** A small animal's home. **4.** (informal) A small, dark, unpleasant place.
Hole sounds like **whole.**

hol·i·day (**hah**-li-*day*) *noun* **1.** A day when most people do not work or go to school, and many businesses are closed, especially because of a religious or national celebration. **2.** A vacation.

ho·lis·tic (hoh-**lis**-tik) *adjective* Considering the whole of something rather than its individual parts. Holistic medicine deals with the whole patient, meaning both the patient's mind and body, not just the place where the patient feels the injury or pain.

hol·low (**hah**-loh)
adjective If something is **hollow,** it is empty inside.
verb **hollow out** If you **hollow** something **out,** you take its inside parts out.
noun An empty hole inside something.
▶ *adjective* **hollower, hollowest** ▶ *verb* **hollowing, hollowed**

hol·ly (**hah**-lee) *noun* A tree or bush with red berries and leaves with sharp points. Holly is often used as a decoration at Christmas. ▶ *noun, plural* **hollies**

hol·ly·hock (**hah**-lee-*hahk*) *noun* A tall garden plant grown for its large, brightly colored flowers.

ho·lo·caust (**hah**-luh-*kawst*) *noun* **1.** Total destruction and great loss of life, especially by fire. **2. the Holocaust** The killing of millions of European Jews and others by the Nazis during World War II.

ho·lo·gram (**hah**-luh-*gram*) *noun* An image made by laser beams that looks as if it has depth and is three-dimensional. ▶ *noun* **holography** (huh-**lah**-gruh-fee)

hol·ster (**hohl**-stur) *noun* A holder for a gun worn on a belt.

ho·ly (**hoh**-lee) *adjective* Related to or belonging to God or a higher being. **Holy** sounds like **wholly.** ▶ *adjective* **holier, holiest**

Ho·ly Com·mu·nion (**hoh**-lee kuh-**myoon**-yuhn) *noun* A Christian ceremony in which people eat bread and sip wine or grape juice, which represent the body and blood of Jesus.

home (home)
noun **1.** Your **home** is where you live,

H

belong, or come from. **2.** A house or apartment. **3.** A place where you are likely to find something. **4.** A place where sick, old, or homeless people can receive proper care. **5.** A place in some sports or games, such as baseball, where players must go in order to score a point. **6.** If you feel **at home,** you feel comfortable and relaxed with a particular person or in a particular place.
adverb To or at the place where you live.

home·land (home-*land*) *noun* The country or region that you or your family comes from.

Home·land Se·cu·ri·ty (home-*land* si-**kyoor**-i-tee) *noun* The federal government department that is responsible for protecting the United States from attacks and danger.

home·less (home-*lis*)
adjective Without a permanent home or place to sleep.
noun, plural **the homeless** People who have no place to live are called **the homeless.**

home·ly (home-*lee*) *adjective* **1.** Not attractive; plain. **2.** Simple and not fancy.
▶ *adjective* **homelier, homeliest**

home·made (home-*made*) *adjective* Made at home or by hand.

home·mak·er (home-*may*-kur)
noun Someone who takes care of a house and family. ▶ *noun* **homemaking** ▶ *adjective* **homemaking**

ho·me·op·a·thy (hoh-*mee*-ah-puh-thee) *noun* A system of treating diseases with a very small amount of the substance that causes the condition that a person is suffering from. ▶ *adjective* **homeopathic (hoh-**mee-uh-**path**-ik)

home·page (home-*payj*) *noun* **1.** The main page of a website. It usually has links to other webpages or websites. **2.** The first page that appears when you open a web browser to go online. It is typically of a website that you use often.

home plate (home plate) *noun* In baseball, the base next to which a batter stands to hit the ball. The batter must run to all the bases and touch home plate to score a run.

home·room (home-*room*) *noun* A classroom in which students meet with a teacher before classes begin.

home run (home ruhn) *noun* In baseball, a hit that allows the batter to run all the way around the bases and score a run.

home·school (home-*skool*) *verb* To educate someone at home rather than at a school. ▶ *verb* **homeschooling, homeschooled** ▶ *noun* **homeschooler**

home·sick (home-*sik*) *adjective* If you are **homesick,** you miss your home, family, and friends when you are away.

home·spun (home-*spuhn*) *adjective* **1.** Plain and simple. **2.** Made at home, especially fabric.

home·stead (home-*sted*) *noun* **1.** A house, especially a farmhouse, with its buildings and land. **2.** In the American West, a piece of land measuring 160 acres (65 hectares) given to a settler by the U.S. government. The settler was required to build a house and farm the land.
verb To move to government land, build a house on it, and farm it.
▶ *verb* **homesteading, homesteaded**
▶ *noun* **homesteader**

home·ward (hohm-*wurd*)
adverb In the direction of home.
adjective Going in the direction of home.

home·work (home-*wurk*) *noun* Schoolwork that is to be done at home.

ho·mi·cide (hah-*mi-*side*) *noun* The crime of killing someone; murder. ▶ *adjective* **homicidal**

ho·mog·e·nize (huh-*mah*-juh-nize) *verb* To mix milk so that the cream in it is spread evenly and does not rise to the top. ▶ *verb* **homogenizing, homogenized** ▶ *noun* **homogenization**

H

hom·o·graph (**hah**-muh-*graf*) *noun*
One of two or more words that
have the same spelling but different
meanings and sometimes different
pronunciations. For example, the
noun *wind*, meaning "a current of air,"
and the verb *wind*, meaning "to wrap
around," are homographs that aren't
pronounced the same.

hom·o·nym (**hah**-muh-nim) *noun* One
of two or more words that have the
same pronunciation and often the
same spelling but different meanings.
For example, the verb *sew*, meaning
"to fix or make something with a
needle and thread," and the verb *sow*,
meaning "to put seeds in the soil,"
are homonyms that aren't spelled
the same.

hom·o·phone (**hah**-muh-*fone*) *noun*
One of two or more words that have
the same pronunciation but different
spellings and different meanings,
such as the words *to, too,* and *two.*

hon·cho (**hahn**-choh) *noun* (informal)
A leader, boss, or other important
person.

Hon·du·ras (hahn-**door**-uhs) A
country in Central America, between
the Pacific Ocean and the Gulf of
Honduras. Discovered in 1502 by
Christopher Columbus on his last
voyage to the Americas, it became
a Spanish colony. It was known as
Spanish Honduras so that it wouldn't
be confused with its neighbor, British
Honduras, a colony of England.
British Honduras is now called Belize.

hon·est (**ah**-nist) *adjective* 1. Truthful
and never stealing or cheating.
2. Done without lying or cheating.

hon·est·ly (**ah**-nist-lee) *adverb* 1. In an
honest and truthful way. 2. People use
honestly to emphasize that they are
telling the truth.

hon·est·y (**ah**-nis-tee) *noun* The quality
or trait of being honest and truthful.

hon·ey (**huhn**-ee) *noun* A sweet, sticky
substance that is made by bees and
eaten as food.

hon·ey·comb (**huhn**-ee-*kohm*) *noun* A
wax structure made by bees to store

honey and pollen, and to raise young
bees. A honeycomb is made up of
many rows of cells with six sides.

hon·ey·moon (**huhn**-ee-*moon*) *noun*
A trip that a bride and groom take
together after their wedding.

hon·ey·suck·le (**huhn**-ee-*suhk*-uhl) *noun*
A climbing plant with white, red, or
yellow flowers that have a pleasant
smell.

honk (hahngk *or* hawngk)
noun 1. The sound a car horn makes.
2. The sound a goose makes.
verb To make the sound of a car horn
or of a goose.
▶ *verb* **honking, honked**

hon·or (**ah**-nur)
noun 1. A person's good reputation
and the respect that a person gets
from other people. 2. A special
privilege.
verb 1. To praise someone or give him
or her an award. 2. To do what you
have promised to do.
▶ *verb* **honoring, honored**

hon·or·a·ble (**ah**-nur-uh-buhl) *adjective*
1. Deserving respect and praise. 2. An
honorable person is honest and has
good moral character.

hon·or·ar·y (**ah**-nuh-*rer*-ee) *adjective*
Given as an honor without the usual
requirements or duties.

hood (hud) *noun* 1. A part attached to
the top of a coat or jacket that goes
over your head. 2. The cover for a car's
engine, usually found in the front of
a car.

hood·lum (**hood**-luhm) *noun* 1. A
violent criminal. 2. A young adult who
is rough, mean, or violent.

hoof (huf *or* hoof) *noun* 1. The hard part
that covers the foot of an animal such
as a horse or deer. 2. The entire foot
of an animal such as a horse or deer.
▶ *noun, plural* **hoofs** *or* **hooves** (huvz
or hoovz) ▶ *adjective* **hoofed**

hook (huk)
noun 1. A curved piece of metal or
plastic used for hanging things. 2. A
fishhook. 3. A punch in boxing made
when the elbow is bent.
verb To bend a part of your body, such

as your arm or leg, around something in order to move or hold it.
▶ *verb* **hooking, hooked**

hooked (hukt) *adjective* **1.** Curved or shaped like a hook. **2.** If you are **hooked** on something, you are very interested in it and want to do it as much as possible.

hoo·li·gan (**hoo**-luh-guhn) *noun* A noisy, violent person, especially a young man who causes trouble. ▶ *noun* **hooliganism**

hoop (hoop *or* hup) *noun* **1.** A large ring made of a material such as metal or plastic. **2.** A ring with a net attached, used as a goal in basketball.
noun, plural **hoops** (informal) Basketball.

hoot (hoot) *verb* **1.** To make a sound like an owl. **2.** To show dislike or disapproval by shouting loudly.
noun A short, loud sound or laugh.
▶ *verb* **hooting, hooted**

hop (hahp) *verb* **1.** To jump on one foot. **2.** To move with short jumps or leaps. **3.** To jump over something.
noun, plural **hops** The seed cases of hop plants, which are dried and used to make beer.
noun A short jump.
▶ *verb* **hopping, hopped**

hope (hope) *verb* To wish for something to happen and believe that it is possible.
noun **1.** A feeling of wishing for something to happen and confidence that it will happen. **2.** Something that you wish for.
▶ *verb* **hoping, hoped**

hope·ful (**hope**-ful) *adjective* **1.** Believing that what you wish for will happen. **2.** Making you feel that what you wish for will happen.
▶ *noun* **hopefulness**

hope·ful·ly (**hope**-fuh-lee) *adverb* **1.** Used to say what you hope will happen. **2.** In a hopeful way.

hope·less (**hope**-lis) *adjective* **1.** Not likely to happen or be successful.

2. Bad at doing something.
▶ *noun* **hopelessness** ▶ *adverb* **hopelessly**

Ho·pi (**hoh**-pee) *noun* A member of a group of Native Americans who live primarily in northeastern Arizona. ▶ *noun, plural* **Hopi** *or* **Hopis**

hop·scotch (**hahp**-skahch) *noun* A game in which players throw a stone or other object into a pattern of numbered shapes drawn on the ground. The players hop into the shapes in a certain order and try to pick up the stone.

horde (hord) *noun* A large, noisy crowd of people, animals, or insects. **Horde** sounds like **hoard.**

ho·ri·zon (huh-**rye**-zuhn) *noun* **1.** The line where the earth or ocean seem to meet the sky. **2.** The limit of your experience, knowledge, or interests.

hor·i·zon·tal (hor-i-**zahn**-tuhl) *adjective* Straight and level; parallel to the ground. ▶ *adverb* **horizontally**

hor·mone (**hor**-mone) *noun* Your **hormones** are chemical substances made by your body that affect the way your body grows, develops, and functions. ▶ *adjective* **hormonal**

horn (horn) *noun* **1.** A hard, pointed growth on the heads of some animals, such as goats and sheep. **2.** A device that gives a signal by making a loud sound. **3.** A brass musical instrument that you blow into.

hor·net (**hor**-nit) *noun* A large wasp with a painful sting that lives in a large group and builds a large nest.

Horn of Africa (**horn** uhv **af**-ri-kuh) An area of northeastern Africa that extends outward from the mainland into the Arabian Sea. The region includes Somalia, Eritrea, Djibouti, and Ethiopia.

hor·o·scope (**hor**-uh-skope) *noun* A diagram of the stars and planets on the day when you were born, used by astrologers to talk about your personality and predict events in your future.

H

hor·ri·ble (**hor**-uh-buhl) *adjective*
1. Shocking or frightening. **2.** Very bad or unpleasant.
▶ *adverb* **horribly**

hor·rid (**hor**-id) *adjective* Nasty or shocking.

hor·rif·ic (hor-**if**-ik) *adjective* Shocking or frightening.

hor·ri·fy (**hor**-uh-*fye*) *verb* If something **horrifies** you, it shocks, frightens, or disgusts you. ▶ *verb* **horrifies, horrifying, horrified** ▶ *adjective* **horrifying**

hor·ror (**hor**-ur)
noun **1.** A feeling of fear, terror, or shock. **2.** Something that brings on such a feeling.
adjective Frightening or terrifying.

horse (hors)
noun **1.** A large, strong animal with four legs that people ride or use to pull things, such as carts or plows. **2.** A piece of gymnastics equipment that you jump over.
verb If you **horse around,** you play in a rough and noisy way.
Horse sounds like **hoarse.** ▶ *verb* **horsing, horsed**

horse·back (**hors**-*bak*)
noun The back of a horse.
adverb On the back of a horse.

horse·fly (**hors**-*flye*) *noun* A large fly. The female bites and sucks the blood of humans, horses, cattle, and other animals. ▶ *noun, plural* **horseflies**

horse·play (**hors**-*play*) *noun* Rough, noisy, and playful behavior, especially by children.

horse·pow·er (**hors**-*pou*-ur) *noun* A unit for measuring the power of an engine.

horse·rad·ish (**hors**-*rad*-ish) *noun* A plant with a hard white root that is used to make a sauce with a very strong taste, usually eaten with meat. ▶ *noun, plural* **horseradishes**

horse·shoe (**hors**-*shoo*)
noun A piece of metal shaped like a U and nailed to the bottom of a horse's hoof to protect it.
noun, plural **horseshoes** A game in which horseshoes are thrown around a metal stake.

hor·ti·cul·ture (**hor**-ti-*kuhl*-chur) *noun* The science of growing flowers, fruits, and vegetables. ▶ *adjective* **horticultural**

hose (hohz)
noun **1.** A long rubber or plastic tube that liquids or gases can flow through. **2.** Stockings or socks.
verb To wash or water something with a hose.
▶ *verb* **hosing, hosed**

ho·sier·y (**hoh**-zhur-ee) *noun* Stockings and socks.

hos·pice (**hahs**-pis) *noun* A place that provides care for people who are dying and comfort for their families.

hos·pi·ta·ble (**hah**-spi-tuh-buhl) *adjective* Friendly, welcoming, and generous to visitors or strangers.

hos·pi·tal (**hah**-spi-tuhl) *noun* A place where sick or injured people receive medical treatment and are taken care of.

hos·pi·tal·i·ty (hah-spi-**tal**-i-tee) *noun* A generous and friendly way of treating guests, so that they feel comfortable and at home. ▶ *noun, plural* **hospitalities**

hos·pi·tal·ize (**hah**-spi-tuh-*lize*) *verb* To keep a person in a hospital for medical treatment. ▶ *verb* **hospitalizing, hospitalized** ▶ *noun* **hospitalization**

host (hohst)
noun **1.** A person who entertains guests. **2.** A large number of people or things. **3.** A person who is in charge of a TV show, especially one that includes music or conversation with celebrities. **4.** An animal or plant from which a parasite gets nutrition.
verb To entertain guests.

hos·tage (**hah**-stij) *noun* Someone who is kept prisoner by a person who demands something, such as money, before the captured person is released.

hos·tel (**hah**-stuhl) *noun* A building with cheap, basic rooms where people can stay overnight. Hostels are used especially by young people who are traveling. **Hostel** sounds like **hostile.**

H

host·ess (**hoh**-stis) *noun* 1. A woman who entertains guests. 2. A woman who greets people in a restaurant.
▶ *noun, plural* **hostesses**

hos·tile (**hah**-stuhl) *adjective* Angry and aggressive. **Hostile** sounds like **hostel.**

hos·til·i·ty (hah-**stil**-i-tee) *noun* Strong feelings against someone or something. ▶ *noun, plural* **hostilities**

hot (haht) *adjective* 1. Having a high temperature. 2. Very spicy and strong in taste. 3. Showing anger very easily. 4. (informal) Eager. 5. (informal) New, exciting, and popular.
▶ *adjective* **hotter, hottest**

hot dog (**haht** dawg) *noun* A long sausage usually eaten in a bun.

ho·tel (hoh-**tel**) *noun* A place where you pay to stay overnight when you are traveling. Many hotels serve meals.

hot spot (**haht** spaht) *noun* 1. A place, such as a restaurant, club, or resort, that is popular and attracts a lot of people. 2. A place where there is a lot of trouble happening. 3. A place where there is a wireless signal available so you can use the Internet.

hot spring (**haht** spring) *noun* A source of hot water that flows naturally from the ground.

hound (hound)
noun A kind of dog with a very good sense of smell that has been bred to hunt.
verb To keep chasing or bothering somebody.
▶ *verb* **hounding, hounded**

hour (our) *noun* 1. A unit of time equal to 60 minutes. There are 24 hours in a day. 2. A fixed period of time when a particular activity happens.

hour·glass (**our**-glas) *noun* An instrument for measuring time. It is made of two glass bulbs joined in the middle by a narrow glass tube. A quantity of sand falls from the upper bulb into the lower one in exactly one hour.

house
noun (hous) 1. A building made for people to live in. 2. All the people who

live in a house. 3. A large building used for a particular purpose. 4. A group of people who meet to make the laws of a country. In the United States, the houses are the Senate and the House of Representatives. 5. If something in a restaurant is **on the house,** you do not have to pay for it.
verb (houz) If you **house** someone, you provide the person with a place to stay or live.
▶ *verb* **housing, housed**

house·boat (**hous**-boht) *noun* A boat that you can live on, with places for cooking and sleeping.

house·fly (**hous**-flye) *noun* A common fly found in most parts of the world, which lives in or around people's houses.

house·hold (**hous**-hohld)
noun All the people who live in a house.
adjective Of or having to do with a house or a family.

House of Rep·re·sen·ta·tives (hous uhv *rep*-ri-**zen**-tuh-tivz) *noun* One of the two houses of the U.S. Congress that makes laws. In this body, members are elected for two-year terms, and the number of members from each state is based on population.

house·sit (**hous**-sit) *verb* To live in or take care of a home while the owners or regular residents are away. ▶ *verb* **house-sitting, house-sat** ▶ *noun* **house sitter**

house·wife (**hous**-wife) *noun* A married woman who spends her time managing her household, for example, by cooking, cleaning, and taking care of her children.

house·work (**hous**-wurk) *noun* Work done to keep a house neat and clean.

hous·ing (**hou**-zing) *noun* 1. Buildings or other shelters where people live. 2. A frame or cover that protects a machine's moving parts.

hov·el (**huhv**-uhl *or* **hah**-vuhl) *noun* A small house, hut, or room that is dirty and in bad condition, especially one that a very poor person lives in.

H

hov·er (**huhv**-ur) *verb* **1.** To remain in one place in the air. **2.** To stay attentively nearby. **3.** To wait nearby, especially because you do not know what to do. ▶ *verb* **hovering, hovered**

how (hou) *adverb* **1.** In what way, or by what means. **2.** In what condition. **3.** To what extent, amount, or degree. **4.** For what reason, or why.

how·ev·er (hou-**ev**-ur) *conjunction* In spite of that. *adverb* In whatever way.

howl (houl) *verb* **1.** To make a loud noise that sounds like a dog or a wolf. **2.** To yell out with laughter, anger, or excitement. **3.** If the wind **howls**, it makes a loud, sad noise. *noun* A loud noise made by a dog or wolf, or a sound like that. ▶ *verb* **howling, howled**

HTML (**aych**-tee-em-el) *noun* The set of computer codes that is used to make basic webpages. HTML is short for *hypertext markup language*.

HTTP (**aych**-tee-tee-pee) *noun* The set of rules that controls how data travels over the Internet. HTTP is short for *hypertext transfer protocol*.

HTTPS (**aych**-tee-tee-pee-es) *noun* A secure form of HTTP that is used, for example, when you buy something online, so that no one can steal information about you. HTTPS is short for *hypertext transfer protocol secure*.

hub (huhb) *noun* **1.** The center part of a wheel. **2.** The center or most important part of an activity or organization.

huck·le·ber·ry (**huhk**-uhl-ber-ee) *noun* A shiny, dark blue or black berry that is similar to a blueberry and grows on a shrub. The name *huckleberry* can mean both the berry and the shrub. ▶ *noun, plural* **huckleberries**

hud·dle (**huhd**-uhl) *verb* To come together closely in a group. *noun* **1.** A grouping of players in football who gather to prepare for the next play. **2.** A group of people or objects that are close together. ▶ *verb* **huddling, huddled**

hue (hyoo) *noun* A color, or a type of a color.

huff (huhf) *noun* If you are **in a huff,** you are in a bad mood because someone upset or annoyed you.

hug (huhg) *verb* To put your arms around someone or something in a caring or loving way. *noun* If you give someone a **hug,** you put your arms around them to make them feel good. ▶ *verb* **hugging, hugged**

huge (hyooj) *adjective* Extremely large. ▶ *adjective* **huger, hugest**

hulk (huhlk) *noun* **1.** The remains of a wrecked ship or vehicle. **2.** A large, heavy person. ▶ *adjective* **hulking**

hull (huhl) *noun* **1.** The frame or body of a boat or ship. **2.** The outer covering of certain fruits, seeds, or nuts. *verb* To remove the outer skin of a seed or nut. ▶ *verb* **hulling, hulled**

hum (huhm) *verb* **1.** To sing a tune with your mouth closed. **2.** To make a steady, buzzing sound. *noun* A steady, buzzing sound. ▶ *verb* **humming, hummed**

hu·man (**hyoo**-muhn) *noun* **human** or **human being** A person. *adjective* **1.** Of, from, or having to do with people. **2.** Typical and understandable. *noun, plural* **human rights** Everyone's right to justice, fair treatment, and free speech.

hu·man be·ing (**hyoo**-muhn **bee**-ing) *noun* A person.

hu·mane (hyoo-**mane**) *adjective* Someone or something that is **humane** is kind and not cruel to people or animals. ▶ *adverb* **humanely**

hu·man·i·tar·i·an (hyoo-**man**-i-tair-ee-uhn) *adjective* Of or having to do with helping people and improving their lives.

H

hu·man·i·ty (hyoo-**man**-i-tee)
noun 1. All people. 2. Kindness and sympathy toward other people.
noun, plural **the humanities** Subjects outside the sciences, such as literature, history, and art.

hum·ble (**huhm**-buhl)
adjective 1. Not thinking you are better or more important than other people.
2. Having a low social position.
verb To make someone feel not as good, important, or proud as before.
▶ *adjective* **humbler, humblest** ▶ *verb* **humbling, humbled** ▶ *adverb* **humbly**

hum·drum (**huhm**-*druhm*) *adjective* Dull and ordinary.

hu·mid (**hyoo**-mid) *adjective* **Humid** weather is moist and usually very warm, in a way that is uncomfortable.

hu·mid·i·ty (hyoo-**mid**-i-tee) *noun* The amount of moisture in the air.

hu·mil·i·ate (hyoo-**mil**-ee-*ate*) *verb* To make someone look or feel foolish or embarrassed. ▶ *verb* **humiliating, humiliated** ▶ *noun* **humiliation**

hu·mil·i·ty (hyoo-**mil**-i-tee) *noun* If you show **humility,** you do not think you are better or more important than others, and you recognize your own faults.

hum·ming·bird (**huhm**-ing-*burd*) *noun* A very small, brightly colored bird that moves its wings very quickly and makes a humming sound.

hum·mus (**huhm**-uhs) *noun* A dip or sandwich spread made of chickpeas and sesame paste.

hu·mor (**hyoo**-mur)
noun 1. The quality of something that makes it funny or amusing. 2. If you have a **sense of humor,** you are quick to laugh or to make others laugh.
3. Mood or state of mind.
verb To agree with someone or do what the person wants so the person does not become upset.
▶ *verb* **humoring, humored**

hu·mor·ous (**hyoo**-mur-uhs) *adjective* Amusing or funny.

hump (huhmp) *noun* A large lump that sticks out or up from something.

hu·mus (**hyoo**-muhs) *noun* Rich, dark soil made from decaying plant and animal matter.

hunch (huhnch)
verb To sit or stand with your head lowered into your shoulders and your body leaning forward so that your back is curved.
noun An idea that is based on a feeling you have and not backed by facts or information.
▶ *verb* **hunches, hunching, hunched** ▶ *noun, plural* **hunches**

hun·dred (**huhn**-drid)
noun The number that is equal to 10 times 10, written numerically as 100.
adjective Of or having to do with the number 100.

hun·dredth (**huhn**-dridth)
adjective Next after 99th and before 101st, written numerically as 100th.
noun 1. One part of something that has been divided into 100 equal parts, written numerically as 1/100. 2. In decimal notation, the **hundredths place** is the position of the second number to the right of the decimal point. In the number 4.0129, the digit 1 is in the hundredths place.

hung (huhng) *verb* The past tense and past participle of the word *hang* when it means "put an object on a hook."

Hun·ga·ry (**huhng**-gur-ee) A country in Central Europe. Hungary was a very powerful nation until World War I, after which it lost much of its land and a third of its population under the terms of a peace treaty. The Danube runs through the country. It is the second-longest river in Europe, after the Volga.

hun·ger (**hung**-ger) *noun* 1. The state of not having enough food to eat for a long time, especially when it causes sickness or death. 2. The feeling of wanting to eat. 3. The feeling of wanting something very much.

hun·gry (**huhng**-gree) *adjective*
1. Wanting to eat food. 2. Wanting something very much.
▶ *adjective* **hungrier, hungriest**
▶ *adverb* **hungrily**

H

hunk (huhngk) *noun* A large piece of something, such as bread, cheese, or meat.

hunt (huhnt)
verb 1. To chase and kill wild animals for food or sport. 2. To try to find something.
noun An attempt to try to find someone or something.
▶ *verb* **hunting, hunted** ▶ *noun* **hunting**

hunt·er (**huhn**-tur) *noun* 1. Someone who hunts. 2. A horse or a dog that you use to help during hunting.

hur·dle (**hur**-duhl)
noun 1. A small barrier, like a fence, that you jump over in a race. 2. A problem that you need to deal with to achieve something.
verb To jump over something while you are running.
▶ *verb* **hurdling, hurdled** ▶ *noun* **hurdler**

hurl (hurl) *verb* To throw something with great effort. ▶ *verb* **hurling, hurled**

hur·ray (huh-**ray**) *interjection* A word used when people cheer. Also spelled as "hooray" (huh-**ray**) and "hurrah" (huh-**rah**).

hur·ri·cane (**hur**-i-*kane*) *noun* A violent storm with heavy rain and high winds.

hur·ry (**hur**-ee)
verb To move or do things quickly, especially because you do not have much time.
phrase When you are **in a hurry,** you do things very quickly because you do not have much time.
▶ *verb* **hurries, hurrying, hurried** ▶ *adjective* **hurried**

hurt (hurt) *verb* 1. To cause physical or emotional pain. 2. To feel pain. 3. To cause problems or difficulty.
▶ *verb* **hurting, hurt** ▶ *adjective* **hurtful**

hur·tle (**hur**-tuhl) *verb* To move with force at great speed. ▶ *verb* **hurtling, hurtled**

hus·band (**huhz**-buhnd) *noun* The man that a woman is married to.

hush (huhsh)
noun A sudden period of silence, especially after a period of noise.
interjection Used to tell someone to be quiet.
verb 1. To be quiet or make someone be quiet. 2. **hush up** To keep something secret, especially something that is embarrassing.
adjective **hush-hush** (informal) Very secret.
▶ *noun, plural* **hushes** ▶ *verb* **hushes, hushing, hushed**

husk (huhsk) *noun* The outer covering of seeds and some types of grains and fruits.

husk·y (**huhs**-kee)
adjective 1. A **husky** voice sounds low and rough. 2. Large and powerful, used especially to describe men or boys.
noun A strong dog with a thick coat, bred to pull sleds in the snow.
▶ *noun, plural* **huskies** ▶ *adjective* **huskier, huskiest** ▶ *noun* **huskiness**

hus·tle (**huhs**-uhl) *verb* 1. To push or move someone roughly in order to make the person move quickly. 2. To work quickly and energetically.
▶ *verb* **hustling, hustled** ▶ *noun* **hustler**

hut (huht) *noun* A small, very simple house.

hutch (huhch) *noun* 1. A cage used to hold rabbits or other small pets. 2. A piece of furniture with shelves on top to hold dishes.
▶ *noun, plural* **hutches**

hy·a·cinth (**hye**-uh-*sinth*) *noun* A plant with small, pleasant-smelling blue, white, or pink flowers that grow closely together.

hy·brid (**hye**-brid)
noun 1. A plant or an animal, such as a mule, that has parents of two different types or species. 2. Something that is made by combining two or more things.
adjective Combining or produced by two or more things.

H

hy·drant (**hye**-druhnt) *noun* A large pipe in the street that supplies water to use against fires and in other emergencies.

hy·drau·lic (hye-**draw**-lik) *adjective* **Hydraulic** machines work on power created by liquid moving through pipes under pressure. ▶ *noun* **hydraulics**

hy·dro·e·lec·tric (hye-droh-i-**lek**-trik) *adjective* Using the power of water to produce electricity. Hydroelectric power plants are often built at dams.

hy·dro·e·lec·tric·i·ty (hye-droh-i-lek-**tris**-i-tee) *noun* Electricity made from the power of running water.

hy·dro·gen (**hye**-druh-juhn) *noun* A gas with no smell or color that is lighter than air and catches fire easily. Hydrogen mixed with oxygen makes water.

hy·dro·gen bomb (**hye**-druh-juhn bahm) *noun* An extremely powerful nuclear bomb. Its tremendous force comes from the energy that is released when hydrogen atoms combine to form helium atoms. Also called an *H-bomb*.

hy·e·na (hye-**ee**-nuh) *noun* A wild animal that looks somewhat like a dog. It eats meat and makes a sound similar to a laugh.

hy·giene (**hye**-jeen) *noun* Keeping yourself and the things around you clean, in order to stay healthy. ▶ *adjective* **hygienic** (hye-**jen**-ik) ▶ *adverb* **hygienically**

hy·gien·ist (hye-**jeen**-ist or hye-**jen**-ist) *noun* Someone trained to help people stay healthy and clean.

hymn (him) *noun* A song that praises God. **Hymn** sounds like **him.**

hym·nal (**him**-nuhl) *noun* A book of religious songs used in religious services.

hype (hipe)
noun Claims that make something seem very important or exciting in order to get people interested.
verb To try to make something seem important or exciting in order to get people interested.
▶ *verb* **hyping, hyped**

hy·per·ac·tive (hye-pur-**ak**-tiv) *adjective* If someone, especially a child, is **hyperactive,** the person has difficulty sitting quietly or keeping still. ▶ *noun* **hyperactivity**

hy·per·link (**hye**-pur-*lingk*) *noun* A piece of text on a webpage that is linked to another webpage, so that when you click on it you go to the second webpage.
verb To link one webpage to another by using a hyperlink.
▶ *verb* **hyperlinking, hyperlinked**

hy·phen (**hye**-fuhn) *noun* The punctuation mark (-) used in a word made of two or more parts or words. Words such as *half-mast, middle-aged,* and *part-time* use hyphens. ▶ *noun* **hyphenation** ▶ *verb* **hyphenate**

hyp·no·sis (hip-**noh**-sis) *noun* A state in which a person appears to be sleeping but can still see and hear and respond to suggestions and questions.

hyp·no·tize (**hip**-nuh-*tize*) *verb* To put someone into a state in which the person appears to be asleep but is still able to respond to suggestions and questions. ▶ *verb* **hypnotizing, hypnotized** ▶ *noun* **hypnotism** (**hip**-nuh-tiz-uhm) ▶ *noun* **hypnotist**

hy·po·chon·dri·ac (hye-puh-**kahn**-dree-ak) *noun* Someone who continually thinks that he or she is sick even when healthy. ▶ *noun* **hypochondria**

hyp·o·crite (**hip**-uh-krit) *noun* Someone who pretends or claims to have certain beliefs or feelings that he or she does not really have. ▶ *noun* **hypocrisy** (hi-**pah**-kri-see)

hyp·o·crit·i·cal (*hip*-uh-**krit**-i-kuhl) *adjective* Pretending or claiming to have certain beliefs or values when this is not true. ▶ *adverb* **hypocritically**

hy·pot·e·nuse (hye-**pah**-tuh-*noos*) *noun* The side opposite the right angle in a right triangle.

H

hy·poth·e·sis (hye-**pah**-thi-sis) *noun*
An idea that could explain how something works but that has to be tested through experiments to be proven right. ▶ *noun, plural* **hypotheses** (hye-**pah**-thi-seez)

hys·ter·i·a (hi-**ster**-ee-uh) *noun* Wild, uncontrolled feeling and expression in a person or group.

hys·ter·i·cal (hi-**ster**-i-kuhl) *adjective*
Someone who is **hysterical** laughs or cries in an uncontrolled way because he or she is very excited, frightened, or angry. ▶ *adverb* **hysterically**

I (eye) *pronoun* The person who is speaking or writing.

ice (ise)
noun 1. Frozen water. 2. A frozen dessert made from fruit juice and sweetened water.
verb 1. To turn into ice. 2. To cool with ice. 3. To cover a cake or cupcake with icing.
idiom **break the ice** To say or do something to relieve tension or help people get acquainted.
▶ *verb* **icing, iced**

Ice Age *or* **ice age** (ise ayj) *noun* A period of time in history, many centuries ago, when a large part of the earth was covered with ice.

ice·berg (**ise**-burg) *noun* A large mass of ice that has broken off from a glacier and is floating in the sea.

ice·box (**ise**-bahks) *noun* 1. A box or chest kept cool with blocks of ice.
2. A refrigerator.
▶ *noun, plural* **iceboxes**

ice·break·er (**ise**-bray-kur) *noun* 1. A ship designed to break through the ice in frozen waters so that other ships can pass through. 2. An event or comment that relieves the tension at a social gathering.

ice·cap (**ise**-kap) *noun* A very thick layer of ice that covers an area of land and may get bigger or smaller as the climate cools or warms.

ice cream (**ise** kreem) *noun* A frozen dessert made from milk or cream, various flavors, and sweeteners.

ice hock·ey (**ise** hah-kee) *noun* A team game played on ice with sticks and a flat disk called a puck that skaters try to hit into their opponents' net to make a goal.

Ice·land (**ise**-luhnd) A European island nation in the North Atlantic Ocean. It is just south of the Arctic Circle and is the second-largest island in Europe, after Great Britain. A wealthy and highly developed country, Iceland is known for its glaciers, high number of active volcanoes, and geothermal landscape, which includes geysers and hot springs.

ice skate (**ise** skate) *noun* A shoe or boot with a metal blade attached to the sole, used for gliding on ice.

i·ci·cle (**eye**-si-kuhl) *noun* A vertical ice formation caused by water that freezes as it drips.

ic·ing (**eye**-sing) *noun* A sweet layer of creamy mixture used to decorate cakes or cookies.

i·con (**eye**-kahn) *noun* 1. A graphic symbol on the desktop of a computer screen representing a program, function, or file. 2. A picture of a holy figure that is present in Christian churches and homes for veneration, especially those of the Eastern Orthodox faith.

i·cy (**eye**-see) *adjective* 1. Extremely cold, or covered with ice. 2. Very unfriendly.
▶ *adjective* **icier, iciest**

I.D. (**eye**-dee) *noun* Short for **identification.**

I'd (ide) *contraction* A short form of *I had* or *I would.*

I·da·ho (**eye**-duh-hoh) A state in the Pacific Northwest region of the United

States. Idaho is the largest producer of potatoes in the United States. It is primarily mountainous and is known as the Gem State because of the wide variety of gems that have been found there.

i·de·a (eye-**dee**-uh) *noun* 1. A thought, a plan, or an opinion. 2. An aim or purpose.

i·de·al (eye-**dee**-uhl) *adjective* The best or most suitable. *noun* 1. Someone or something considered perfect. 2. A standard of excellence.

i·de·al·ist (eye-**dee**-uh-list) *noun* A person who believes in the highest ideals, even if they seem unrealistic. ▶ *noun* **idealism** (eye-**dee**-uh-*liz*-uhm)

i·de·al·is·tic (eye-*dee*-uh-**lis**-tik) *adjective* Believing that ideals are more important than practical matters.

i·den·ti·cal (eye-**den**-ti-kuhl) *adjective* Exactly the same. ▶ *adverb* **identically**

i·den·ti·fi·ca·tion (eye-*den*-tuh-fi-**kay**-shuhn) *noun* A document or other item that proves who you are.

i·den·ti·fy (eye-**den**-tuh-*fye*) *verb* To recognize or tell what something is or who someone is. ▶ *verb* **identifies, identifying, identified**

i·den·ti·ty (eye-**den**-ti-tee) *noun* Who or what you are. ▶ *noun, plural* **identities**

i·den·ti·ty theft (eye-**den**-ti-tee *theft*) *noun* The crime of pretending that you are another person so that you can spend that person's money or use his or her credit.

i·de·ol·o·gy (eye-dee-**ah**-luh-jee) *noun* A system of ideas that something is based on, such as a political party, economy, or society. ▶ *noun, plural* **ideologies**

id·i·om (**id**-ee-uhm) *noun* A commonly used expression whose meaning is not obvious, or not what you would expect. For example, if a homework assignment is "a piece of cake," it means that it is easy. ▶ *adjective* **idiomatic** (id-ee-uh-**mat**-ik)

id·i·ot (**id**-ee-uht) *noun* A stupid or foolish person. ▶ *adjective* **idiotic** (id-ee-**ah**-tik) ▶ *adverb* **idiotically**

i·dle (**eye**-duhl) *adjective* 1. Not busy, or not working; lazy. 2. Not active, or not in use. *verb* 1. To run slowly without being connected to the transmission. 2. To spend time doing nothing useful. **Idle** sounds like **idol.** ▶ *adjective* **idler, idlest** ▶ *verb* **idling, idled** ▶ *noun* **idleness** ▶ *noun* **idler** ▶ *adverb* **idly**

i·dol (**eye**-duhl) *noun* 1. An image or object that is worshiped. 2. A popular person admired and loved for his or her accomplishments. **Idol** sounds like **idle.**

i.e. (**eye-ee**) An abbreviation of the Latin phrase *id est,* which means "that is." It is used to show that what follows is a fuller explanation of something.

if (if) *conjunction* You use **if** in a sentence to show that there is a condition that may or may not happen, or that may or may not be true.

ig·loo (**ig**-loo) *noun* The traditional house of the Eskimo, or Inuit, people, made in the shape of a dome out of sod, stone, blocks of ice, or hard snow.

ig·ne·ous (**ig**-nee-uhs) *adjective* Produced by great heat or by a volcano.

ig·nite (ig-**nite**) *verb* To set fire to something, or to catch fire. ▶ *verb* **igniting, ignited**

ig·ni·tion (ig-**nish**-uhn) *noun* 1. The activation of a machine by means of an electrical spark. 2. The firing or blasting off of a rocket.

ig·no·rance (**ig**-nur-uhns) *noun* The state or condition of not knowing something.

ig·no·rant (**ig**-nur-uhnt) *adjective* 1. Not aware of something. 2. Uneducated, or lacking knowledge in general. ▶ *adverb* **ignorantly**

ig·nore (ig-**nor**) *verb* To pay no attention to something. ▶ *verb* **ignoring, ignored**

i·gua·na (i-**gwah**-nuh) *noun* A large tropical American lizard that can grow to more than five feet in length.

I

I'll (ile) *contraction* A short form of
I will or *I shall*. **I'll** sounds like **aisle**
and **isle**.

ill (il)
adjective 1. Sick; not enjoying good
health. 2. Bad, or negative.
adverb In a bad or negative way. When
used in this way, the word *ill* is often
attached to a participle with a hyphen.

il·le·gal (i-**lee**-guhl) *adjective* Against the
law. ▶ *adverb* **illegally**

il·leg·i·ble (i-**lej**-uh-buhl) *adjective*
Difficult or impossible to read.

Il·li·nois (*il*-uh-**noy**) A state in the
Midwest region of the United States.
Its largest city is Chicago. The state
is sometimes called the Land of
Lincoln. Illinois has many museums
devoted to him, especially in the state
capital, Springfield, where he lived and
worked as a lawyer before becoming
president.

il·lit·er·ate (i-**lit**-ur-it) *adjective* Unable to
read or write. ▶ *noun* **illiteracy**

ill·ness (**il**-nis) *noun* The condition
of not being in good health;
sickness. ▶ *noun, plural* **illnesses**

il·log·i·cal (i-**lah**-ji-kuhl) *adjective*
Making no sense. ▶ *adverb* **illogically**

il·lu·mi·nate (i-**loo**-muh-nate) *verb*
1. To bring light to or on something;
to light up something, such as a
building. 2. To make something
easier to understand. 3. To decorate
a text with pictures and other
artwork. This was often done in
the Middle Ages.
▶ *verb* **illuminating, illuminated**
▶ *noun* **illumination** ▶ *adjective*
illuminated ▶ *adjective* **illuminating**

il·lu·sion (i-**loo**-zhuhn) *noun*
1. Something you see that does not
really exist. 2. A false idea.
▶ *adjective* **illusory** (i-**loo**-sur-ee)

il·lus·trate (**il**-uh-strate) *verb* 1. To add
visual images to text. 2. To make
clear or explain by using examples or
comparisons.
▶ *verb* **illustrating, illustrated** ▶ *noun*
illustrator ▶ *adjective* **illustrated**

il·lus·tra·tion (*il*-uh-**stray**-shuhn) *noun*
1. A picture in a book, magazine, or
other publication or document. 2. An
example.
▶ *adjective* **illustrative** (i-**luhs**-truh-tiv)

illustrious (i-**luhs**-tree-uhs) *adjective*
Famous because of doing something
very well or making something
important.

ill will (**il** wil) *noun* Unfriendly feeling
or hatred.

I'm (ime) *contraction* A short form of
I am.

IM (*eye*-**em**) *verb* To send messages
back and forth over the Internet using
an instant messaging computer
program. IM is short for *instant
message.* ▶ *verb* **IMing, IMed** or
IM'd ▶ *noun* **IMing**

im·age (**im**-ij) *noun* 1. An idea of how
something looks. 2. A representation
of something. 3. The way a person
appears to other people. 4. A person
or thing that closely resembles
another. 5. A picture formed in a lens
or mirror.

im·age·ry (**im**-ij-ree) *noun* Language
that describes how something looks.

i·mag·i·nar·y (i-**maj**-uh-**ner**-ee) *adjective*
Existing in the imagination and not
the real world.

i·mag·i·na·tion (i-*maj*-uh-**nay**-shuhn)
noun 1. The ability to form pictures
in your mind of things that are not
present or real, or to create new
images or ideas. 2. The part of your
mind that imagines things.

i·mag·i·na·tive (i-**maj**-uh-nuh-tiv)
adjective 1. Creative or having great
imagination. 2. Showing imagination.
▶ *adverb* **imaginatively**

im·ag·ine (i-**maj**-in) *verb* 1. To form an
image of something in your mind.
2. To believe that something exists
when it does not. 3. To believe that
something is true without having
proof.
▶ *verb* **imagining, imagined**

im·be·cile (**im**-buh-suhl) *noun* A stupid
person.

im·i·tate (**im**-i-*tate*) *verb* To copy or mimic someone or something. ▶ *verb* **imitating, imitated**

im·i·ta·tion (*im*-i-**tay**-shuhn) *noun* 1. The act of imitating somebody or something. 2. A copy; something that is not real.
adjective Made to be like something else.

im·mac·u·late (i-**mak**-yuh-lit) *adjective* Very clean or neat. ▶ *adverb* **immaculately**

im·ma·ture (*im*-uh-**choor** or *im*-uh-**toor**) *adjective* 1. Not fully developed. 2. Behaving in a silly, childish way. ▶ *noun* **immaturity** ▶ *adverb* **immaturely**

im·mea·sur·a·ble (i-**mezh**-ur-uh-buhl) *adjective* Too great or vast to be measured. ▶ *adverb* **immeasurably**

im·me·di·ate (i-**mee**-dee-it) *adjective* 1. Happening or done at once. 2. Close or near.

im·me·di·ate·ly (i-**mee**-dee-it-lee) *adverb* 1. Right away. 2. Closely, or next.

im·mense (i-**mens**) *adjective* Extremely large. ▶ *noun* **immensity** ▶ *adverb* **immensely**

im·merse (i-**murs**) *verb* 1. To cover someone or something with a liquid. 2. In some religions, to baptize someone by placing the person completely under water for a moment. 3. To be totally absorbed in something. ▶ *verb* **immersing, immersed** ▶ *noun* **immersion** (i-**mur**-zhuhn)

im·mi·grant (**im**-i-gruhnt) *noun* Someone who moves from one country to another and settles there. ▶ *noun* **immigration** (*im*-i-**gray**-shuhn) ▶ *verb* **immigrate**

im·mi·nent (**im**-uh-nuhnt) *adjective* About to happen. ▶ *adverb* **imminently**

im·mo·bi·lize (i-**moh**-buh-lize) *verb* To prevent something or someone from moving. ▶ *verb* **immobilizing, immobilized**

im·mor·al (i-**mor**-uhl) *adjective* Bad, or without a sense of right and wrong. ▶ *adverb* **immorally**

im·mor·al·i·ty (*im*-uh-**ral**-i-tee) *noun* Immoral actions, or the condition of being without morals.

im·mor·tal (i-**mor**-tuhl) *adjective* 1. Living or lasting forever. 2. Famous or remembered forever. *noun* Someone or something that lives or is famous forever. ▶ *noun* **immortality** (*im*-or-**tal**-i-tee)

im·mune (i-**myoon**) *adjective* 1. If you are **immune** to a disease, you don't get sick from it. 2. Protected from physical or emotional harm. ▶ *noun* **immunity**

im·mune sys·tem (i-**myoon** *sis*-tuhm) *noun* The system that protects your body against disease and infection. It includes white blood cells and antibodies.

im·mu·nize (**im**-yuh-*nize*) *verb* To make someone immune to a disease. ▶ *verb* **immunizing, immunized** ▶ *noun* **immunization**

imp (imp) *noun* 1. A small demon who is full of mischief. 2. A cute child who is full of mischief.

im·pact (**im**-pakt) *noun* 1. When two things collide. 2. A strong impression someone or something has made on a person.

im·pair (im-**pair**) *verb* To damage something or make it less effective. ▶ *verb* **impairing, impaired** ▶ *noun* **impairment**

im·pal·a (im-**pal**-uh) *noun* A small African antelope with curved horns and a reddish-brown coat, which can leap great distances. ▶ *noun, plural* **impala** or **impalas**

im·par·tial (im-**pahr**-shuhl) *adjective* Treating all persons or points of view equally. ▶ *adverb* **impartially**

im·pass·a·ble (im-**pas**-uh-buhl) *adjective* Not providing any way through.

im·pa·tient (im-**pay**-shuhnt) *adjective* 1. In a hurry and unwilling to wait. 2. Easily annoyed. ▶ *noun* **impatience** ▶ *adverb* **impatiently**

I

im·peach (im-**peech**) *verb* To bring formal charges against a public official for misconduct. An official can be impeached for committing a crime and be removed from office. ▶ *verb* **impeaches, impeaching, impeached** ▶ *noun* **impeachment**

im·pede (im-**peed**) *verb* To slow something down or stop it from making progress. ▶ *verb* **impedes, impeding, impeded**

im·per·a·tive (im-**per**-uh-tiv) *adjective* 1. Extremely important. 2. Expressing a command, an order, or a request.
noun Something that is extremely important.

im·per·fect (im-**pur**-fikt) *adjective* Faulty or not perfect. ▶ *noun* **imperfection** ▶ *adverb* **imperfectly**

im·pe·ri·al (im-**peer**-ee-uhl) *adjective* 1. Of or having to do with an empire. 2. Of or having to do with an emperor or empress.

im·per·son·al (im-**pur**-suh-nuhl) *adjective* 1. Lacking in feeling. 2. Having a style that is not emotional or meant to have personality. ▶ *adverb* **impersonally**

im·per·son·ate (im-**pur**-suh-*nate*) *verb* To pretend to be someone else. ▶ *verb* **impersonating, impersonated** ▶ *noun* **impersonation** ▶ *noun* **impersonator**

im·per·ti·nent (im-**pur**-tuh-nuhnt) *adjective* Disrespectful and not courteous. ▶ *noun* **impertinence** ▶ *adverb* **impertinently**

im·pet·u·ous (im-**pech**-oo-uhs) *adjective* Done quickly and without thinking first. ▶ *adverb* **impetuously**

im·plant
verb (im-**plant**) 1. To establish or instill firmly and deeply. 2. To put an organ or a device into the body by surgery.
noun (**im**-plant) Something placed into the body by surgery. ▶ *verb* **implanting, implanted**

im·ple·ment
noun (**im**-pluh-muhnt) A tool or a utensil.
verb (**im**-pluh-*ment*) To put a plan or an idea into action. ▶ *verb* **implementing, implemented** ▶ *noun* **implementation** (*im*-pluh-men-**tay**-shuhn)

im·pli·ca·tion (*im*-pli-**kay**-shuhn) *noun* 1. The meaning or significance of something. 2. Something suggested but not said directly.

im·plic·it (im-**plis**-it) *adjective* Known or understood without being talked about. ▶ *adverb* **implicitly**

im·ply (im-**plye**) *verb* To suggest or mean something without stating it directly. ▶ *verb* **implies, implying, implied**

im·po·lite (*im*-puh-**lite**) *adjective* Not courteous; inconsiderate. ▶ *adverb* **impolitely**

im·port
verb (im-**port**) 1. To bring into a place or country from somewhere else. 2. To transfer data into a file or document.
noun (**im**-port) A good that is brought into a place or country from somewhere else. ▶ *verb* **importing, imported** ▶ *noun* **importer**

im·por·tance (im-**por**-tuhns) *noun* The quality of being important.

im·por·tant (im-**por**-tuhnt) *adjective* 1. Having great significance or impact. 2. Powerful, or necessary in a particular situation.

im·por·tant·ly (im-**por**-tuhnt-lee) *adverb* People use **importantly,** usually with the word *more* or *most,* to give emphasis to part of what they are saying.

im·pose (im-**poze**) *verb* 1. To force to accept by legal means. 2. To take advantage of someone or make unfair demands. ▶ *verb* **imposing, imposed** ▶ *noun* **imposition** (*im*-puh-**zish**-uhn)

im·pos·si·ble (im-**pah**-suh-buhl) *adjective* 1. Not able to happen or exist. 2. Very difficult to deal with. ▶ *noun* **impossibility** (im-*pah*-suh-**bil**-i-tee) ▶ *adverb* **impossibly**

im·pos·tor (im-**pah**-stur) *noun* Someone who pretends to be someone that he or she is not.

I

im·prac·ti·cal (im-**prak**-ti-kuhl) *adjective*
Not useful or sensible.

im·press (im-**pres**) *verb* 1. To make someone feel admiration or respect. 2. To make something very clear to someone. 3. To have an effect on someone's mind. 4. To make a mark on something, using pressure.
▶ *verb* **impresses, impressing, impressed**

im·pres·sion (im-**presh**-uhn) *noun* 1. An idea or a feeling based on something you saw, read, or heard. 2. An imitation of someone or something. 3. A strong effect. 4. A mark made by pressing or stamping something into a surface or substance.

im·pres·sion·a·ble (im-**presh**-uh-nuh-buhl) *adjective* Easily influenced.

im·press·ive (im-**pres**-iv) *adjective* Creating a strong and good impression.

im·print
noun (**im**-print) 1. A mark made by pressing or stamping something on a surface. 2. A strong influence or effect.
verb (im-**print**) 1. To fix firmly in the mind or memory. 2. To leave a mark by pressing or stamping something on a surface.
▶ *verb* **imprinting, imprinted**

im·pris·on (im-**priz**-uhn) *verb* 1. To put someone into prison. 2. To confine to a particular place.
▶ *verb* **imprisoning, imprisoned**
▶ *noun* **imprisonment**

im·prop·er (im-**prah**-pur) *adjective* 1. Wrong. 2. Showing bad manners or bad taste. 3. An **improper fraction** is a fraction whose numerator is greater than its denominator, as in $4/3$ or $15/13$.
▶ *adverb* **improperly**

im·prove (im-**proov**) *verb* To get better or to make better. ▶ *verb* **improving, improved** ▶ *adjective* **improved**

im·prove·ment (im-**proov**-muhnt) *noun* 1. Something that makes a person or thing better. 2. The process of getting better.

im·pro·vise (**im**-pruh-*vize*) *verb* 1. To create or achieve something with whatever is available. 2. To make something up on short notice.
▶ *verb* **improvising, improvised**
▶ *noun* **improvisation** (im-**prah**-vuh-zay-shuhn) ▶ *noun* **improviser**

im·pru·dent (im-**proo**-duhnt) *adjective* Lacking in good judgment; unwise.

im·pu·dent (**im**-pyuh-duhnt) *adjective* Bold and disrespectful. ▶ *noun* **impudence** ▶ *adverb* **impudently**

im·pulse (**im**-puhls) *noun* 1. A sudden urge to do something. 2. A pulse of force or energy.

im·pul·sive (im-**puhl**-siv) *adjective* Acting on impulse, or done on impulse. ▶ *adverb* **impulsively**

im·pure (im-**pyoor**) *adjective* 1. Unclean or contaminated. 2. Mixed with foreign substances.
▶ *adverb* **impurely**

in (in)
preposition 1. Inside an enclosed space. *Your socks are in the top drawer.* 2. Into. *Let's put it in the house.* 3. During, as in *in the autumn.*
adverb 1. In or into some condition, relation, or place. 2. Inside a certain place.
In sounds like **inn.**

in·a·bil·i·ty (*in*-uh-**bil**-i-tee) *noun* Lack of power or ability.

in·ac·ces·si·ble (*in*-uhk-**ses**-uh-buhl) *adjective* Not reachable; not able to be accessed, reached, or contacted.

in·ac·cu·rate (in-**ak**-yur-it) *adjective* 1. Not precise or correct. 2. Off the mark; not on target.
▶ *noun* **inaccuracy** (in-**ak**-yur-uh-see) ▶ *adverb* **inaccurately**

in·ad·e·quate (in-**ad**-i-kwit) *adjective* Not enough or not good enough. ▶ *adverb* **inadequately**

in·an·i·mate (in-**an**-uh-mit) *adjective* Something that has no life is **inanimate.** Rocks and buildings are inanimate objects.

in·ap·pro·pri·ate (*in*-uh-**proh**-pree-it) *adjective* Unsuitable for the situation. ▶ *adverb* **inappropriately**

in·ar·tic·u·late (*in*-ahr-**tik**-yuh-lit) *adjective* Unable to express yourself clearly in speech or writing.

I

in·au·di·ble (in-**aw**-duh-buhl) *adjective*
Impossible to hear. ▶ *noun*
inaudibility ▶ *adverb* **inaudibly**

in·au·gu·rate (in-**aw**-gyuh-*rate*) *verb*
1. To swear a public official into office
with a formal ceremony. **2.** To open
formally, or to begin to use publicly.
▶ *verb* **inaugurating, inaugurated**

in·au·gu·ra·tion (in-*aw*-gyuh-**ray**-shuhn)
noun The ceremony of swearing in a
public official.

in·born (**in**-born) *adjective* Existing from
birth and natural to a person.

in·box (**in**-*bahks*) *noun* **1.** A tray on
a desk or table for mail and other
paperwork that needs to be done. **2.** In
a computer mail system, the folder
that contains all the emails that have
come in.
▶ *noun, plural* **inboxes**

in·can·des·cent (*in*-kuhn-**des**-uhnt)
adjective **1.** Glowing with light as a
result of being heated. **2.** Radiant or
brightly shining.

in·ca·pa·ble (in-**kay**-puh-buhl) *adjective*
Unable to do something.

in·cense
noun (**in**-sens) A substance that is
burned to produce a pleasant smell.
verb (in-**sens**) To make very angry.
▶ *verb* **incensing, incensed**

in·cen·tive (in-**sen**-tiv) *noun* Inspiration
to do something.

in·ces·sant (in-**ses**-uhnt) *adjective*
Without stopping. ▶ *adverb*
incessantly

inch (inch)
noun **1.** A unit of length equal to 1/12
of a foot. The diameter of a quarter
measures about an inch. **2.** A very
small distance.
verb To move very slowly.
▶ *noun, plural* **inches** ▶ *verb* **inches,
inching, inched**

inch·worm (**inch**-*wurm*) *noun* A
caterpillar that moves by arching and
stretching its body.

in·ci·dent (**in**-si-duhnt) *noun* Something
that happens; an event.

in·ci·den·tal·ly (in-si-**dent**-lee) *adverb* A
word used to add a remark unrelated
to the original subject.

in·cin·er·a·tor (in-**sin**-uh-*ray*-tur) *noun* A
furnace for burning garbage and other
waste materials.

in·ci·sion (in-**sizh**-uhn) *noun* A precise
cut made by a knife or blade.

in·ci·sor (in-**sye**-zur) *noun* A kind of
tooth in the front of the mouth that is
used for cutting. Humans have four
upper incisors and four lower incisors.

in·cite (in-**site**) *verb* To stir up feelings
that make someone do something
violent or foolish. ▶ *verb* **inciting,
incited**

in·cline (in-**kline**)
verb To lean or slant.
noun (**in**-kline) A slope.
▶ *verb* **inclining, inclined**

in·clined (in-**klinde**) *adjective* **1.** Leaning
or slanting. **2.** Liking or tending to do
something.
▶ *noun* **inclination** (*in*-kluh-**nay**-shuhn)

in·clude (in-**klood**) *verb* To contain
something or someone as part of a
whole. ▶ *verb* **including, included**

in·clu·sion (in-**kloo**-zhuhn) *noun* The act
of including somebody or something.

in·clu·sive (in-**kloo**-siv) *adjective*
1. Covering everything. **2.** Welcoming
to everyone.
▶ *noun* **inclusiveness**

in·co·her·ent (*in*-koh-**heer**-uhnt)
adjective Not clear or logical; difficult
to understand. ▶ *adverb* **incoherently**

in·come (**in**-kuhm) *noun* The money that
a person earns or receives, especially
from working.

in·come tax (**in**-kuhm *taks*) *noun* A
payment made to the government
based on the amount of money a
person earns. ▶ *noun, plural* **income
taxes**

in·com·pat·i·ble (*in*-kuhm-**pat**-uh-
buhl) *adjective* **1.** Unable to get along.
2. Unable to work together or to be
used together.
▶ *noun* **incompatibility**

in·com·pe·tent (in-**kahm**-pi-tuhnt)
adjective Unable to do something
successfully. ▶ *noun* **incompetence**
▶ *adverb* **incompetently**

in·com·plete (*in*-kuhm-**pleet**) *adjective*
Not having all the necessary parts;

I

not finished or complete. ▶ *adverb* **incompletely**

in·com·pre·hen·si·ble (*in*-kahm-pri-**hen**-suh-buhl) *adjective* Impossible to understand.

in·con·ceiv·a·ble (*in*-kuhn-**see**-vuh-buhl) *adjective* Not believable. ▶ *adverb* **inconceivably**

in·con·clu·sive (*in*-kuhn-**kloo**-siv) *adjective* Unclear or uncertain. ▶ *adverb* **inconclusively**

in·con·sid·er·ate (*in*-kuhn-**sid**-ur-it) *adjective* Not caring about other people's needs or feelings. ▶ *adverb* **inconsiderately**

in·con·spic·u·ous (*in*-kuhn-**spik**-yoo-uhs) *adjective* Not easy to see; not attracting attention. ▶ *adverb* **inconspicuously**

in·con·ven·ience (*in*-kuhn-**veen**-yuhns) *noun* 1. Trouble or difficulty. 2. Something that causes trouble or difficulty.
verb To cause trouble or difficulty. ▶ *verb* **inconveniencing, inconvenienced**

in·con·ven·ient (*in*-kuhn-**veen**-yuhnt) *adjective* Causing difficulty or discomfort. ▶ *adverb* **inconveniently**

in·cor·po·rate (in-**kor**-puh-*rate*) *verb* 1. To include something as part of another thing. 2. To make or become a corporation. ▶ *verb* **incorporating, incorporated** ▶ *noun* **incorporation** ▶ *adjective* **incorporated**

in·cor·rect (*in*-kuh-**rekt**) *adjective* Wrong. ▶ *adverb* **incorrectly**

in·crease
verb (in-**krees**) To become larger.
noun (**in**-krees) A rise in number, amount, size, or degree. ▶ *verb* **increasing, increased** ▶ *adverb* **increasingly**

in·cred·i·ble (in-**kred**-uh-buhl) *adjective* Unbelievable or amazing. ▶ *adverb* **incredibly**

in·cred·u·lous (in-**krej**-uh-luhs) *adjective* Unable to believe something or accept that something is true. ▶ *adverb* **incredulously**

in·crim·i·nate (in-**krim**-uh-*nate*) *verb* To provide evidence that someone is guilty of something. ▶ *verb* **incriminating, incriminated** ▶ *noun* **incrimination**

in·cu·bate (**ing**-kyuh-*bate*) *verb* 1. To keep eggs warm before they hatch. 2. To keep a premature or sick baby safe and warm in a specially heated apparatus. 3. To nurture, or to allow to develop. ▶ *verb* **incubating, incubated** ▶ *noun* **incubation**

in·cu·ba·tor (**ing**-kyuh-*bay*-tur) *noun* 1. A heated container in which premature or sick babies are kept safe and warm. 2. A container that keeps eggs warm until they hatch.

in·cur (in-**kur**) *verb* To make something happen, especially something that is not good. ▶ *verb* **incurring, incurred**

in·cur·a·ble (in-**kyoor**-uh-buhl) *adjective* Unable to be made well or healthy.

in·debt·ed (in-**det**-id) *adjective* 1. You can be **indebted** to someone for a favor that person did for you. 2. A person who owes money to a bank is **indebted** to the bank. ▶ *noun* **indebtedness**

in·de·cent (in-**dee**-suhnt) *adjective* Inappropriate or obscene. ▶ *noun* **indecency** ▶ *adverb* **indecently**

in·deed (in-**deed**) *adverb* Truly.

in·def·i·nite (in-**def**-uh-nit) *adjective* Unclear or uncertain.
noun **indefinite article** The grammatical term for *a* or *an*, used before a noun when it refers to something general or not specific. ▶ *adverb* **indefinitely**

in·dent
verb (in-**dent**) To start a line of writing or typing farther from the margin.
noun (**in**-dent) An empty space at the beginning of a line of writing. ▶ *verb* **indenting, indented** ▶ *noun* **indentation** (*in*-den-**tay**-shuhn)

in·de·pen·dence (*in*-di-**pen**-duhns) *noun* Freedom; the condition of being independent.

In·de·pen·dence Day (*in*-di-**pen**-duhns day) *noun* A U.S. holiday, celebrated on July 4th, to commemorate the signing of the Declaration of Independence in 1776. Also known as the **Fourth of July.**

in·de·pend·ent (*in*-di-**pen**-duhnt)
adjective 1. Not controlled or affected
by other people or things. 2. Not
wanting or needing much help from
other people.
noun **independent clause** A sentence
that can stand alone and be
grammatical. *See* **dependent clause.**

in·de·pen·dent·ly (*in*-di-**pen**-duhnt-lee)
adverb 1. With no outside control or
interference. 2. If one thing works,
acts, or operates **independently of**
another, neither one influences the
other.

in·de·struc·ti·ble (*in*-di-**struhk**-
tuh-buhl) *adjective* Unable to be
destroyed. ▸ *adverb* **indestructibly**

in·dex (**in**-deks)
noun An alphabetical list showing
where to find things in a book.
verb 1. To supply with an index. 2. To
arrange in the form of an index.
▸ *noun, plural* **indexes** *or* **indices**
(**in**-di-*seez*) ▸ *verb* **indexes, indexing,**
indexed ▸ *noun* **indexer**

in·dex fin·ger (**in**-deks *fing*-gur) *noun*
The finger next to the thumb, used for
pointing.

In·di·a (**in**-dee-uh) A country in South
Asia. It is the second-most-populated
country in the world and has one of
the fastest-growing economies.

In·di·an (**in**-dee-uhn)
noun 1. A person from India. 2. A
Native American. *See* **American**
Indian, Native American.
adjective 1. Of or having to do with
India, its people, or its culture. 2. Of or
having to do with Native Americans,
also known as American Indians.

In·di·an·a (*in*-dee-**an**-uh) A state in the
Midwest region of the United States.
Its inhabitants are known as Hoosiers,
but the origin of the term is unknown.
Some people say that it comes from
"Who's there?" or "Whose ear?"

In·di·an O·cean (*in*-dee-uhn **oh**-shuhn)
The third-largest ocean in the world.
It is bounded by Africa to the west,
India to the north, and Indochina and
Australia to the east.

in·di·cate (**in**-di-*kate*) *verb* 1. To show
something. 2. To point out something.
▸ *verb* **indicating, indicated** ▸ *adjective*
indicative (in-**dik**-uh-tiv)

in·di·ca·tion (*in*-di-**kay**-shuhn) *noun*
Something that indicates or points out.

in·di·ca·tor (**in**-di-*kay*-tur) *noun*
Something that shows or points out
something else.

in·dict (in-**dite**) *verb* To officially charge
someone with a crime. ▸ *verb*
indicting, indicted ▸ *noun* **indictment**

in·dif·fer·ent (in-**dif**-ur-uhnt)
adjective Not to care much
about something. ▸ *noun*
indifference ▸ *adverb* **indifferently**

in·di·ges·tion (*in*-di-**jes**-chuhn) *noun*
Discomfort in the stomach because of
difficulty digesting food.

in·dig·nant (in-**dig**-nuhnt) *adjective*
Annoyed about something that seems
unfair. ▸ *noun* **indignation** ▸ *adverb*
indignantly

in·di·go (**in**-di-*goh*) *noun* 1. A plant with
dark purple berries from which a dark
blue dye can be made. 2. A dark violet-
blue color or dye.
▸ *noun, plural* **indigos** *or* **indigoes**

in·di·rect (*in*-duh-**rekt**) *adjective*
1. Not in a straight line. 2. Not
directly connected. 3. Not to the
point. 4. **indirect object** Someone or
something that is affected by the action
of a verb in a sentence, but is not
the direct object. For example, in the
sentence "Josh threw me the ball," the
word *ball* is the direct object and *me* is
the indirect object.
▸ *adverb* **indirectly**

in·dis·crim·i·nate (*in*-dis-**krim**-uh-nit)
adjective Not carefully chosen or
thought out.

in·dis·pen·sa·ble (*in*-di-**spen**-
suh-buhl) *adjective* Absolutely
necessary. ▸ *adverb* **indispensably**

in·dis·tin·guish·a·ble (*in*-dis-**ting**-gwi-
shuh-buhl) *adjective* Impossible to tell
apart. ▸ *adverb* **indistinguishably**

in·di·vid·u·al (*in*-di-**vij**-oo-uhl)
noun A person.
adjective 1. Single and separate.
2. Unusual or different.

in·di·vid·u·al·i·ty (in-di-*vij*-oo-**al**-i-tee) *noun* The qualities that set a person apart from all others.

in·di·vid·u·al·ly (in-di-**vij**-oo-uh-lee) *adverb* Separately or one at a time.

in·di·vis·i·ble (in-di-**viz**-uh-buhl) *adjective* Unable to be divided or broken into pieces. ▶ *adverb* **indivisibly**

In·do·ne·sia (in-duh-**nee**-zhuh) A country in Southeast Asia that consists of more than 17,000 islands. A Dutch colony for more than 300 years, Indonesia became independent after World War II and currently has the world's largest Muslim population.

in·door (**in**-dor) *adjective* Used, done, or built inside.

in·doors (**in**-dorz) *adverb* Inside a building.

in·duce (in-**doos**) *verb* 1. To persuade someone to do something. 2. To cause something to happen. ▶ *verb* **inducing, induced**

in·dulge (in-**duhlj**) *verb* 1. To give in to a person's wishes. 2. If you **indulge in** something, you take pleasure in it. ▶ *verb* **indulging, indulged** ▶ *noun* **indulgence** ▶ *adjective* **indulgent**

in·dus·tri·al (in-**duhs**-tree-uhl) *adjective* 1. Of or having to do with factories and making things in large quantities. 2. Having an economy that is based on factories and making things. ▶ *adverb* **industrially**

in·dus·tri·al·ize (in-**duhs**-tree-uh-lize) *verb* To set up businesses and factories in an area. ▶ *verb* **industrializing, industrialized** ▶ *noun* **industrialization** (in-*duhs*-tree-uh-li-**zay**-shuhn)

in·dus·try (**in**-duh-stree) *noun* 1. Manufacturing companies and other businesses, taken together. 2. A single branch of business or trade. 3. Hard work or effort. ▶ *noun, plural* **industries**

in·ef·fi·cient (in-uh-**fish**-uhnt) *adjective* Ineffective and wasteful. ▶ *noun* **inefficiency** ▶ *adverb* **inefficiently**

in·e·qual·i·ty (in-i-**kwah**-li-tee) *noun* Differences that seem unfair between people or things. ▶ *noun, plural* **inequalities**

in·ert (i-**nurt**) *adjective* 1. Not moving. 2. Not reacting easily with other chemicals or substances.

in·er·tia (i-**nur**-shuh) *noun* 1. Unwillingness to move or act because of laziness or tiredness. 2. A physical property of objects that means they stay at rest or keep moving in the same way unless an outside force acts on them.

in·ev·i·ta·ble (i-**nev**-i-tuh-buhl) *adjective* Certain to happen. ▶ *noun* **inevitability** ▶ *adverb* **inevitably**

in·ex·cus·a·ble (in-ik-**skyoo**-zuh-buhl) *adjective* So bad that it cannot be excused.

in·ex·pen·sive (in-ik-**spen**-siv) *adjective* Not costing a lot of money. ▶ *adverb* **inexpensively**

in·ex·pe·ri·enced (in-ik-**speer**-ee-uhnst) *adjective* Having little practice in doing something.

in·ex·pli·ca·ble (in-ik-**splik**-uh-buhl or in-**ek**-spli-kuh-buhl) *adjective* Impossible to explain. ▶ *adverb* **inexplicably**

in·fal·li·ble (in-**fal**-uh-buhl) *adjective* Not capable of making mistakes or of being wrong. ▶ *noun* **infallibility** (in-*fal*-uh-**bil**-i-tee)

in·fa·mous (**in**-fuh-muhs) *adjective* Having a very bad reputation.

in·fant (**in**-fuhnt) *noun* A newborn child. Babies are considered infants until the time they can walk. ▶ *noun* **infancy** (**in**-fuhn-see)

in·fan·try (**in**-fuhn-tree) *noun* The foot soldiers of an army.

in·fat·u·at·ed (in-**fach**-oo-*ay*-tid) *adjective* So strongly attracted to someone that you can no longer think sensibly about that person. ▶ *noun* **infatuation**

in·fect (in-**fekt**) *verb* To cause disease or contaminate by introducing germs or viruses. ▶ *verb* **infecting, infected** ▶ *adjective* **infected**

in·fec·tion (in-**fek**-shuhn) *noun* An illness caused by bacteria or viruses.

in·fec·tious (in-**fek**-shuhs) *adjective*
1. Spread from one person to another by bacteria or viruses in the air or on objects. 2. Easily passed from one person to another.

in·fer (in-**fur**) *verb* To draw a conclusion after considering all the facts. ▶ *verb* **inferring, inferred** ▶ *noun* **inference** (**in**-fur-uhns)

in·fe·ri·or (in-**feer**-ee-ur) *adjective* Not as good; lower in quality. ▶ *noun* **inferiority** (in-*feer*-ee-**or**-i-tee)

in·fer·tile (in-**fur**-tuhl) *adjective*
1. Unsuitable for growing crops and plants. 2. Unable to have offspring. ▶ *noun* **infertility** (*in*-fur-**til**-i-tee)

in·fest (in-**fest**) *verb* To be present in a way that causes harm or disease. ▶ *verb* **infesting, infested** ▶ *noun* **infestation** (in-fes-**tay**-shuhn)

in·fes·ted (in-**fes**-tid) *adjective* Full of harmful animals or insects.

in·field (**in**-feeld) *noun* In baseball, the area enclosed by home plate and the bases, or the group of players at first base, second base, shortstop, and third base. ▶ *noun* **infielder**

in·fil·trate (**in**-fil-*trate*) *verb* To enter an enemy's side secretly in order to spy or cause some sort of damage. ▶ *verb* **infiltrating, infiltrated** ▶ *noun* **infiltration**

in·fi·nite (**in**-fuh-nit) *adjective* 1. Without end. 2. Too large to be measured or counted.
▶ *noun* **infinity** (in-**fin**-i-tee) ▶ *adverb* **infinitely**

in·fin·i·tive (in-**fin**-i-tiv) *noun* The basic form of a verb, often preceded by *to*, for example, *to run, to be, to write.*

in·firm (in-**furm**) *adjective* Weak or ill. ▶ *noun* **infirmity** (in-**fur**-mi-tee)

in·fir·ma·ry (in-**fur**-mur-ee) *noun* A place where sick people are cared for.

in·flame (in-**flame**) *verb* 1. To make hot, red, or swollen, usually as the result of an infection or injury. 2. To stir up or excite the emotions of a person or group.
▶ *verb* **inflaming, inflamed**

in·flam·ma·ble (in-**flam**-uh-buhl) *adjective* Able to catch fire easily.

in·flam·ma·tion (*in*-fluh-**may**-shuhn) *noun* Redness, swelling, heat, and pain, usually caused by an infection or injury.

in·flat·a·ble (in-**flay**-tuh-buhl) *adjective* Able to be expanded by filling with air.
noun An object, such as a boat, that must be filled with air in order to be used.

in·flate (in-**flate**) *verb* 1. To make something expand by blowing or pumping air into it. 2. To increase or improve, sometimes deceptively.
▶ *verb* **inflating, inflated**

in·fla·tion (in-**flay**-shuhn) *noun* 1. A general increase in prices. 2. The process of making something expand by blowing air into it.
▶ *adjective* **inflationary** (in-**flay**-shuh-ner-ee)

in·flect (in-**flekt**) *verb* To change the form of a word according to the job it is doing in a sentence. ▶ *verb* **inflecting, inflected**

in·flec·tion (in-**flek**-shuhn) *noun* A slightly changed form of a word that affects some aspect of its meaning. For example, *striking, struck,* and *stricken* are inflections of the verb *strike.*

in·flex·i·ble (in-**flek**-suh-buhl) *adjective*
1. Unable to bend. 2. Unable to change; rigid.
▶ *noun* **inflexibility** (in-*flek*-suh-**bil**-i-tee) ▶ *adverb* **inflexibly**

in·flict (in-**flikt**) *verb* To harm someone or something. ▶ *verb* **inflicting, inflicted** ▶ *noun* **infliction**

in·flu·ence (**in**-floo-uhns)
verb To have an effect on someone or something.
noun Someone or something that has an effect on someone or something else.
▶ *verb* **influencing, influenced**

in·flu·en·tial (*in*-floo-**en**-shuhl) *adjective* Having the power to change or affect someone or something.

I

in·flu·en·za (in-floo-**en**-zuh) *noun* An illness caused by a virus. *See* **flu.**

in·fo·mer·cial (**in**-foh-*mur*-shuhl) *noun* A program-length TV commercial with detailed information about a service or product.

in·form (in-**form**) *verb* 1. To tell someone something. 2. To give information to the police about a criminal.
▶ *verb* **informing, informed** ▶ *noun* **informer** ▶ *noun* **informant**

in·for·mal (in-**for**-muhl) *adjective* 1. Relaxed and casual. 2. Unofficial. 3. **Informal** language is used in everyday speech but not usually in formal speaking or in writing. For example, saying that Ivy is "gonna have a cow" is an informal way of saying that she is "going to be very upset."
▶ *adverb* **informally** ▶ *noun* **informality** (in-for-**mal**-i-tee)

in·for·ma·tion (in-fur-**may**-shuhn) *noun* Facts and knowledge you get from exploring something, or that you learn by listening.

in·for·ma·tion su·per·high·way (in-fur-**may**-shuhn **soo**-pur-*hye*-way) *noun* A vast network of information available to a computer user with a modem.

in·for·ma·tion tech·nol·o·gy (in-fur-**may**-shuhn tek-*nah*-luh-jee) *noun* The use of computers and other electronic equipment to find, create, store, or communicate information. Abbreviated as *IT.*

in·for·ma·tive (in-**for**-muh-tiv) *adjective* Providing useful information.

in·fre·quent (in-**free**-kwuhnt) *adjective* Not happening very often. ▶ *adverb* **infrequently**

in·fu·ri·ate (in-**fyoor**-ee-*ate*) *verb* To make someone extremely angry. ▶ *verb* **infuriating, infuriated** ▶ *adjective* **infuriating** ▶ *adverb* **infuriatingly**

in·gen·ious (in-**jeen**-yuhs) *adjective* Inventive and original. ▶ *adverb* **ingeniously**

in·ge·nu·i·ty (in-juh-**noo**-i-tee) *noun* The ability to be inventive and original, especially in order to solve a problem.

in·got (**ing**-guht) *noun* A mass of metal that has been shaped into a block or bar.

in·gre·di·ent (in-**gree**-dee-uhnt) *noun* An item used to make something.

in·hab·it (in-**hab**-it) *verb* To live in a place. ▶ *verb* **inhabiting, inhabited**

in·hab·i·tant (in-**hab**-i-tuhnt) *noun* Someone who lives in a particular place.

in·hale (in-**hayl**) *verb* To breathe in. ▶ *verb* **inhaling, inhaled** ▶ *noun* **inhalation** (in-huh-**lay**-shuhn)

in·hal·er (in-**hay**-lur) *noun* A small device for inhaling medicine through your mouth.

in·her·ent (in-**heer**-uhnt *or* in-**her**-uhnt) *adjective* Existing naturally as an inseparable part of something. ▶ *adverb* **inherently**

in·her·it (in-**her**-it) *verb* 1. To receive money, property, or a title from someone who has died. 2. To receive a particular characteristic from one of your parents.
▶ *verb* **inheriting, inherited**

in·her·it·ance (in-**her**-i-tuhns) *noun* 1. The money and property that someone inherits, usually from parents or grandparents. 2. The action of inheriting.

in·hu·man (in-**hyoo**-muhn) *adjective* Lacking human qualities like sympathy or mercy; cruel. ▶ *noun* **inhumanity** (in-hyoo-**man**-i-tee) ▶ *adverb* **inhumanly**

in·i·tial (i-**nish**-uhl) *noun* The first letter of a name or word. *adjective* First. *verb* To write your initials on.
▶ *verb* **initialing, initialed** ▶ *adverb* **initially**

i·ni·ti·ate (i-**nish**-ee-*ate*) *verb* 1. To introduce or start something new. 2. To bring someone into a club or group, often with a ceremony.
▶ *verb* **initiating, initiated** ▶ *noun* **initiation**

in·i·tia·tive (i-**nish**-uh-tiv) *noun* The ability to take action without being told what to do.

in·ject (in-**jekt**) *verb* 1. To put medicine or nourishment into someone's body through a needle. 2. To add something needed.
▶ *verb* **injecting, injected**

in·jec·tion (in-**jek**-shuhn) *noun* 1. The introduction of medicine into the body through a thin needle; a shot. 2. The act of adding something needed.

in·jure (**in**-jur) *verb* To hurt or harm yourself or someone else. ▶ *verb* **injuring, injured**

in·ju·ry (**in**-jur-ee) *noun* Damage or harm. ▶ *noun, plural* **injuries**
▶ *adjective* **injurious** (in-**joor**-ee-uhs)

in·jus·tice (in-**juhs**-tis) *noun* 1. Unfairness or lack of justice. 2. An unfair situation or action.

ink (ingk) *noun* A colored liquid used for writing and printing.

ink·jet (**ingk**-jet) *adjective* Of or having to do with a kind of printer that forms words and images by shooting tiny drops of ink onto paper.

in·land (**in**-luhnd)
adjective Located away from the sea.
adverb In a direction away from the sea.

in·law (**in**-law) *noun* A person who is related to someone because of a marriage, not because they both share the same ancestor. Usually when people refer to their in-laws, they mean their husband's or wife's parents.

in·let (**in**-let) *noun* A narrow body of water that leads inland from a larger body of water, such as an ocean.

in·line skate (**in**-line skate) *noun* A skate whose wheels are in a straight line.

in·mate (**in**-mate) *noun* A person in prison or a hospital.

inn (in) *noun* A small hotel that often includes a restaurant.

in·ner (**in**-ur) *adjective* 1. Inside, or near the center. 2. Inside a person's own mind or self.

in·ning (**in**-ing) *noun* A part of a baseball game in which each team gets a turn at bat.

in·no·cent (**in**-uh-suhnt) *adjective* 1. Not guilty. 2. Not knowing about something or not being involved in something.
▶ *noun* **innocence** ▶ *adverb* **innocently**

in·no·va·tion (*in*-uh-**vay**-shuhn) *noun* A new idea or invention. ▶ *verb* **innovate** ▶ *adjective* **innovative**

in·oc·u·late (i-**nah**-kyuh-*late*) *verb* To inject a weakened form of a disease into someone's body so that the person becomes protected against it. *See also* **vaccine.** ▶ *verb* **inoculating, inoculated** ▶ *noun* **inoculation**

in·pa·tient (**in**-pay-shuhnt) *noun* A person who stays in the hospital while being treated for an illness or injury.

in·put (**in**-put)
noun 1. Advice or information offered by a person. 2. Information fed into a computer. 3. Something that is put in, such as energy to be used by a machine.
verb To put information into a computer.
▶ *verb* **inputting, inputted** *or* **input**

in·quire (in-**kwire**) *verb* To ask about someone or something. ▶ *verb* **inquiring, inquired** ▶ *adjective* **inquiring** ▶ *adverb* **inquiringly**

in·quir·y (in-**kwye**-ree *or* **in**-kwur-ee) *noun* 1. An official attempt to discover the facts about something. 2. A request for information.
▶ *noun, plural* **inquiries**

in·quis·i·tive (in-**kwiz**-i-tiv) *adjective* Curious or asking a lot of questions.
▶ *noun* **inquisitiveness** ▶ *adverb* **inquisitively**

in·sane (in-**sane**) *adjective* 1. Mentally ill. 2. Very foolish.
▶ *noun* **insanity** (in-**san**-i-tee) ▶ *adverb* **insanely**

in·san·i·tar·y (in-**san**-i-*ter*-ee) *adjective* Dirty and unhealthy.

in·scribe (in-**skribe**) *verb* 1. To write, carve, or engrave letters on a surface. 2. To write a special message in a book.
▶ *verb* **inscribing, inscribed** ▶ *adjective* **inscribed**

in·scrip·tion (in-**skrip**-shuhn) *noun* A specially written message, usually to identify an object or a person.

in·sect (**in**-sekt) *noun* A small animal with three pairs of legs; three main parts to its body: the head, thorax, and abdomen; and usually wings, with either one or two pairs of wings. Insects have a hard outer skeleton and do not have a backbone.

in·sec·ti·cide (in-**sek**-tuh-side) *noun* A chemical used to kill insects.

in·se·cure (in-si-**kyoor**) *adjective* 1. Unsafe, or not providing any security. 2. Anxious and uncertain. ▶ *noun* **insecurity** ▶ *adverb* **insecurely**

in·sen·si·tive (in-**sen**-si-tiv) *adjective* Thoughtless and unconcerned about other people's feelings. ▶ *noun* **insensitivity** ▶ *adverb* **insensitively**

in·sep·a·ra·ble (in-**sep**-ur-uh-buhl) *adjective* Not able to be separated; always found together.

in·sert
verb (in-**surt**) To put something inside something else.
noun (**in**-surt) Something extra that is put inside something else.
▶ *verb* **inserting, inserted** ▶ *noun* **insertion** (in-**sur**-shuhn)

in·side
noun (**in**-side) The interior of something.
preposition (in-**side**) 1. In less than. *You should be able to finish your homework inside an hour.* 2. Within. *Put the letter inside the envelope.*
adverb (in-**side**) Into an enclosed space, such as a house.
adjective (in-**side** or **in**-side) Located on or near the interior of something.

in·sid·i·ous (in-**sid**-ee-uhs) *adjective* 1. Quietly harmful or deceitful. 2. Working in a hidden but harmful way.

in·sight (**in**-site) *noun* The ability to understand something that is not obvious.

in·sig·ni·a (in-**sig**-nee-uh) *noun* A badge, emblem, or design that shows someone's rank or membership in an organization. ▶ *noun, plural* **insignias** or **insignia**

in·sig·nif·i·cant (in-sig-**nif**-i-kuhnt) *adjective* Small and unimportant.

▶ *noun* **insignificance** ▶ *adverb* **insignificantly**

in·sin·cere (in-sin-**seer**) *adjective* Not genuine or honest. ▶ *noun* **insincerity** (in-sin-**ser**-i-tee) ▶ *adverb* **insincerely**

in·sip·id (in-**sip**-id) *adjective* 1. Having little or no taste. 2. Uninteresting.

in·sist (in-**sist**) *verb* To demand something and refuse to accept a negative reply. ▶ *verb* **insisting, insisted** ▶ *noun* **insistence** ▶ *adjective* **insistent**

in·so·lent (**in**-suh-luhnt) *adjective* Disrespectful and outspoken. ▶ *noun* **insolence** ▶ *adverb* **insolently**

in·sol·u·ble (in-**sahl**-yuh-buhl) *adjective* 1. Unable to be dissolved in water or other liquid. 2. Impossible to solve.

in·som·ni·a (in-**sahm**-nee-uh) *noun* Difficulty falling asleep or staying asleep. ▶ *noun* **insomniac** (in-**sahm**-nee-ak)

in·spect (in-**spekt**) *verb* To examine something carefully. ▶ *verb* **inspecting, inspected**

in·spec·tion (in-**spek**-shuhn) *noun* A careful look at something or someone; an examination.

in·spec·tor (in-**spek**-tur) *noun* 1. A person who checks or examines things. 2. A high-ranking detective.

in·spi·ra·tion (in-spuh-**ray**-shuhn) *noun* 1. The act of inspiring someone, or the feeling of being inspired. 2. Something that inspires someone, such as a person, an event, or an idea.

in·spire (in-**spire**) *verb* 1. To fill someone with an emotion, an idea, or an attitude. 2. To influence and encourage someone to achieve or do something.
▶ *verb* **inspiring, inspired** ▶ *adjective* **inspiring** ▶ *adjective* **inspirational** (in-spuh-**ray**-shuh-nuhl)

in·stall (in-**stawl**) *verb* 1. To put something into a place where it can be used. 2. To put a program or part of a program on a computer's hard drive.
▶ *verb* **installing, installed**

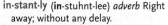

in·stal·la·tion (*in*-stuh-**lay**-shuhn)
noun The act or process of installing something.

in·stall·ment (in-**stawl**-muhnt)
noun **1.** One of a series of regular payments over a period of time for a purchased object. **2.** One part of a story that is printed or shown in separate parts.

in·stance (**in**-stuhns) *noun* **1.** An example. **2. for instance** As an example.

in·stant (**in**-stuhnt)
adjective **1.** Happening right away. **2.** Already mixed and prepared, needing only quick preparation.
noun A moment.
▶ *adjective* **instantaneous** (in-stuhn-**tay**-nee-uhs) ▶ *adverb* **instantaneously**

in·stant·ly (**in**-stuhnt-lee) *adverb* Right away; without any delay.

in·stant mes·sag·ing (**in**-stuhnt **mes**-i-jing) *noun* The use of a computer program that allows people to email messages back and forth very quickly over the Internet. ▶ *noun* **instant message** ▶ *verb* **instant message**

in·stead (in-**sted**) *adverb* In place of another person or thing.

in·step (**in**-*step*) *noun* The top part of the foot between the toes and the ankle.

in·sti·gate (**in**-sti-*gate*) *verb* To start something, especially something that leads to trouble.

in·still (in-**stil**) *verb* To put into a person's mind slowly, over a period of time. ▶ *verb* **instilling, instilled**

in·stinct (**in**-stingkt) *noun* **1.** Behavior that is natural rather than learned. **2.** Knowledge that comes without thinking or studying.
▶ *adjective* **instinctive** ▶ *adverb* **instinctively** ▶ *adjective* **instinctual** (in-**stingk**-choo-uhl)

in·sti·tute (**in**-sti-*toot*)
noun A society or organization with a particular goal.
verb To begin or establish something.
▶ *verb* **instituting, instituted**

in·sti·tu·tion (*in*-sti-**too**-shuhn) *noun* **1.** A large organization where people live or work together. **2.** A custom or tradition.
▶ *adjective* **institutional**

in·struct (in-**struhkt**) *verb* **1.** To teach a subject or a skill. **2.** To give instructions.
▶ *verb* **instructing, instructed** ▶ *noun* **instructor**

in·struc·tion (in-**struhk**-shuhn)
noun The act of teaching or giving lessons.
noun, plural **instructions** Directions on how to do something, or orders on what to do.

in·stru·ment (**in**-struh-muhnt) *noun* **1.** An object that is used to make music. **2.** A tool designed to do a specific thing, especially something difficult or delicate.
▶ *adjective* **instrumental** (in-struh-**men**-tuhl) ▶ *noun* **instrumentalist**

in·suf·fi·cient (*in*-suh-**fish**-uhnt) *adjective* Not enough or inadequate. ▶ *adverb* **insufficiently**

in·su·late (**in**-suh-*late*) *verb* To cover something with material in order to stop heat, electricity, or sound from escaping. ▶ *verb* **insulating, insulated** ▶ *noun* **insulation** ▶ *noun* **insulator** ▶ *adjective* **insulating**

in·su·lin (**in**-suh-lin) *noun* A hormone produced in the pancreas that regulates the level of sugar in the blood. People who have diabetes do not produce enough of this hormone and may need to receive it through injections.

in·sult
verb (in-**suhlt**) To say or do something disrespectful and upsetting to somebody.
noun (**in**-suhlt) A comment or action that is offensive and upsetting to somebody.
▶ *verb* **insulting, insulted** ▶ *adjective* **insulting**

in·sur·ance (in-**shoor**-uhns) *noun* An arrangement in which someone pays money to a company that agrees to pay the person a certain amount in the event of sickness, fire, accident, or other loss.

in·sure (in-**shoor**) *verb* To buy insurance on something. ▶ *verb* **insuring, insured** ▶ *adjective* **insured**

in·tact (in-**takt**) *adjective* Not broken or damaged; complete.

in·take (**in**-take) *noun* **1.** The amount of something taken in. **2.** The act of taking something in.

in·te·ger (**in**-ti-jur) *noun* A whole number, either positive or negative. Examples of integers include −3, −2, −1, 0, 1, 2, and 3.

in·te·grate (**in**-tuh-grate) *verb* **1.** To combine several things or people into one. **2.** To include people of all races. ▶ *verb* **integrating, integrated**

in·te·grat·ed (**in**-tuh-gray-tid) *adjective* **1.** Not separated by race; open to or used by all sorts of people. **2.** Combining different elements to work together effectively.

in·te·gra·tion (**in**-tuh-gray-shuhn) *noun* The act or practice of making facilities or an organization open to people of all races and ethnic groups.

in·teg·ri·ty (in-**teg**-ri-tee) *noun* The quality of being honest and having high moral principles.

in·tel·lect (**in**-tuh-lekt) *noun* The power of the mind to think, reason, understand, and learn.

in·tel·lec·tu·al (**in**-tuh-lek-choo-uhl) *adjective* Involving thought and reason.
noun A person with a highly developed intellect. ▶ *adverb* **intellectually**

in·tel·li·gence (in-**tel**-i-juhns) *noun* **1.** The fact or state of being intelligent. **2.** Information about what is happening or is going to happen, especially when obtained by spying.

in·tel·li·gent (in-**tel**-i-juhnt) *adjective* Quick to understand, think, and learn. ▶ *adverb* **intelligently**

in·tel·li·gi·ble (in-**tel**-i-juh-buhl) *adjective* Able to be understood. ▶ *adverb* **intelligibly**

in·tend (in-**tend**) *verb* **1.** To mean to do something. **2.** Designed for a particular purpose. ▶ *verb* **intending, intended**

in·tense (in-**tens**) *adjective* **1.** Very strong. **2.** Showing strong feelings about something. ▶ *adverb* **intensely**

in·ten·si·fy (in-**ten**-suh-*fye*) *verb* To make something stronger or more powerful. ▶ *verb* **intensifies, intensifying, intensified**

in·ten·si·ty (in-**ten**-si-tee) *noun* The quality of being intense.

in·tent (in-**tent**) *adjective* Determined to do something.
noun A plan or a purpose. ▶ *adverb* **intently**

in·ten·tion (in-**ten**-shuhn) *noun* Something that you mean to do.

in·ten·tion·al (in-**ten**-shuh-nuhl) *adjective* Done on purpose; deliberate. ▶ *adverb* **intentionally**

in·ter·act (*in*-tur-**akt**) *verb* When you play a game or talk with people, you are **interacting** with them. ▶ *verb* **interacting, interacted** ▶ *noun* **interaction**

in·ter·ac·tive (*in*-tur-**ak**-tiv) *adjective* **1.** Working together or influencing each other. **2.** Allowing the users of a computer program to make choices in order to control or change features of the program.

in·ter·cept (*in*-tur-**sept**) *verb* To prevent someone or something from moving from one place to another. ▶ *verb* **intercepting, intercepted** ▶ *noun* **interception**

in·ter·change·a·ble (*in*-tur-**chayn**-juh-buhl) *adjective* Easily switched with someone or something else. ▶ *adverb* **interchangeably**

in·ter·com (**in**-tur-kahm) *noun* A system that uses a microphone and speaker through which a person can listen and talk to someone in another location. Intercom is short for *intercommunication system.*

in·ter·est (**in**-trist)
verb To attract a person's curiosity or attention.
noun 1. A feeling of curiosity or concern. 2. The power to cause curiosity or concern. 3. Something that you do because you enjoy the way it occupies you. 4. A legal share, as in a business. 5. A fee paid for borrowing money, usually a percentage of the amount borrowed. 6. Money paid to you by a bank for keeping your savings there.
phrase If it is **in your interest** to do something, it will benefit you in some way.
▶ *verb* **interesting, interested**
▶ *adjective* **interested**

in·ter·est·ing (**in**-tri-sting *or* in-tuh-*res*-ting) *adjective* Able to get and hold your attention.

in·ter·face (**in**-tur-*fase*)
noun The point at which two different things meet.
verb To connect and communicate.
▶ *verb* **interfacing, interfaced**

in·ter·fere (in-tur-**feer**) *verb* 1. To become involved in a situation or activity without being asked to do so. 2. To hinder.
▶ *verb* **interfering, interfered** ▶ *adjective* **interfering**

in·ter·fer·ence (in-tur-**feer**-uhns) *noun* 1. An unwelcome involvement in the affairs of others. 2. Interruption in a broadcast or an electronic signal so that you cannot see or hear the program or the message properly. 3. In sports, the illegal obstruction of an opponent.

in·ter·ga·lac·tic (in-tur-guh-**lak**-tik) *adjective* Happening or situated between galaxies.

in·te·ri·or (in-**teer**-ee-ur)
noun The inside of something.
adjective On the inside of something.

in·ter·jec·tion (in-tur-**jek**-shuhn) *noun* A word spoken suddenly and used to express surprise, pain, delight, or some other emotion. An interjection is often used with an exclamation point.

in·ter·me·di·ate (in-tur-**mee**-dee-*it*)
adjective Between two things, or in the middle of a series of things.

in·ter·mis·sion (in-tur-**mish**-uhn) *noun* A short break in a performance.

in·ter·mit·tent (in-tur-**mit**-uhnt)
adjective Stopping and starting, not continuous. ▶ *adverb* **intermittently**

in·tern (**in**-turn)
noun 1. Someone who is learning a skill or job by working with an expert in that field. 2. A newly graduated doctor of medicine who is working at a hospital to get practical experience.
verb To work as an intern.
▶ *verb* **interning, interned** ▶ *noun* **internship**

in·ter·nal (in-**tur**-nuhl) *adjective* 1. On the inside of someone or something. 2. Of or having to do with matters inside a country or an organization.
▶ *adverb* **internally**

in·ter·na·tion·al (in-tur-**nash**-uh-nuhl) *adjective* Involving more than one country. ▶ *adverb* **internationally**

In·ter·net (**in**-tur-*net*) *noun* The electronic network that allows millions of computers around the world to connect together.

in·ter·pret (in-**tur**-prit) *verb* 1. To translate a conversation between people who speak different languages. 2. To figure out what something means.
▶ *verb* **interpreting, interpreted** ▶ *noun* **interpreter**

in·ter·pre·ta·tion (in-tur-pri-**tay**-shuhn) *noun* An explanation of the meaning of something.

in·ter·ro·gate (in-**ter**-uh-*gate*) *verb* To question someone in detail, usually in connection with a crime. ▶ *verb* **interrogating, interrogated** ▶ *noun* **interrogation**

in·ter·rupt (in-tuh-**ruhpt**) *verb* 1. To stop or hinder for a short time. 2. To start talking while someone else is talking.
▶ *verb* **interrupting, interrupted** ▶ *noun* **interruption** ▶ *adjective* **interruptive**

in·ter·sect (in-tur-**sekt**) *verb* To meet or cross something. ▶ *verb* **intersecting, intersected**

in·ter·sec·tion (*in*-tur-**sek**-shuhn *or* in-tur-*sek*-shuhn) *noun* The point at which two things meet and cross each other.

in·ter·state (*in*-tur-**state**) *adjective* Connecting, between, or having to do with two or more states.

in·ter·val (**in**-tur-vuhl) *noun* A time between two events, or a space between two objects.

in·ter·vene (*in*-tur-**veen**) *verb* 1. To get involved in a situation in order to change it. 2. To occur between two other events.
▸ *verb* **intervening, intervened**

in·ter·ven·tion (*in*-tur-**ven**-shuhn) *noun* The act of becoming involved in something that is happening in a way that stops it or changes its course.

in·ter·view (**in**-tur-*vyoo*)
noun A meeting at which someone is asked questions.
verb To ask a person a series of questions in order to get information.
▸ *verb* **interviewing, interviewed**

in·tes·tine (in-**tes**-tin) *noun* A long tube in the body extending below the stomach that digests food and absorbs liquids and salts. It consists of the **small intestine** and the **large intestine.**

in·ti·mate (**in**-tuh-mit) *adjective* Very closely acquainted or connected. ▸ *noun* **intimacy** (**in**-tuh-muh-see) ▸ *adverb* **intimately**

in·tim·i·date (in-**tim**-i-*date*)
verb To frighten someone, especially in order to make him or her do something. ▸ *verb* **intimidating, intimidated** ▸ *noun* **intimidation** ▸ *adjective* **intimidating**

in·to (**in**-too *or* **in**-tuh) *preposition*
1. To the inside of. *She went into the tent.* 2. To the occupation of. *She went into biology.* 3. To the condition or form of. *The cat got into trouble.*
4. To the subject or situation of. *The police are looking into the burglary.*
5. Against. *Her car bumped into ours.*
6. Toward. *The kite flew into the wind.*
7. (informal) Extremely interested in. *Ben is into surfing.*

in·tol·er·a·ble (in-**tah**-lur-uh-buhl) *adjective* Impossible to endure.
▸ *adverb* **intolerably**

in·tol·er·ant (in-**tah**-lur-uhnt) *adjective* Unable or unwilling to accept another kind of person, idea, or behavior. ▸ *noun* **intolerance** ▸ *adverb* **intolerantly**

in·tox·i·cate (in-**tahk**-si-*kate*) *verb* 1. To make drunk, especially with alcohol. 2. To excite or to make enthusiastic.
▸ *verb* **intoxicating, intoxicated** ▸ *noun* **intoxication**

in·tran·si·tive (in-**tran**-suh-tiv) *adjective* If a verb is **intransitive,** it does not need an object in order to complete its meaning. For example, in the sentences "Where are we going to sleep?" and "It's raining," the verbs *sleep* and *rain* are intransitive. *See also* **transitive.**

in·trep·id (in-**trep**-id) *adjective* Very brave, especially when exploring something unknown.

in·tri·cate (**in**-tri-kit) *adjective* Complicated or containing many small parts or details. ▸ *noun* **intricacy** ▸ *adverb* **intricately**

in·trigue
verb 1. (in-**treeg**) To be very interesting or fascinating to someone. 2. To plot or scheme.
noun (**in**-treeg *or* in-**treeg**) A secret plot or scheme.
▸ *verb* **intriguing, intrigued** ▸ *adjective* **intriguing**

in·tro·duce (*in*-truh-**doos**) *verb* 1. To bring in something new. 2. To tell someone your name upon first meeting. 3. To start.
▸ *verb* **introducing, introduced**

in·tro·duc·tion (*in*-truh-**duhk**-shuhn) *noun* 1. A person's first experience of something. 2. The presentation of one person to another. 3. The opening section of a book, speech, or other presentation.
▸ *adjective* **introductory** (*in*-truh-**duhk**-tur-ee)

in·tro·vert (**in**-truh-*vurt*) *noun* A shy person who does not share his or her thoughts or feelings easily. ▸ *adjective* **introverted**

I

in·trude (in-**trood**) *verb* To go into a place or get involved in a situation where you are not wanted. ▶ *verb* **intruding, intruded** ▶ *noun* **intruder** ▶ *noun* **intrusion** (in-**troo**-zhuhn) ▶ *adjective* **intrusive** (in-**troo**-siv)

in·tu·i·tion (*in*-too-**ish**-uhn) *noun* An understanding of something that is based on feelings rather than reason or logic. ▶ *verb* **intuit** (in-**too**-it) ▶ *adjective* **intuitive** (in-**too**-i-tiv)

In·u·it (in-**oo**-it *or* in-**yoo**-it) *noun* A native person of the Arctic. The Inuit live today mainly in Alaska, Canada, and Greenland. The Inuit are also known as **Eskimos.**
adjective Of or having to do with the Inuit people or Inuit culture.
▶ *noun, plural* **Inuit** *or* **Inuits**

in·un·date (in-uhn-*date*) *verb* 1. To flood. 2. To bring so much of something that it is hard or impossible to deal with.
▶ *verb* **inundating, inundated** ▶ *noun* **inundation**

in·vade (in-**vade**) *verb* 1. To enter a place or situation in large numbers, usually with a negative effect. 2. To send armed forces into a place in order to occupy or control it.
▶ *verb* **invading, invaded** ▶ *noun* **invader**

in·va·lid
noun (**in**-vuh-lid) A person whose movements and activitives are limited because he or she is seriously ill.
adjective (in-**val**-id) Unable to be used because it is no longer legal or in effect.

in·val·u·a·ble (in-**val**-yuh-buhl) *adjective* Indispensible, necessary, or precious. ▶ *adverb* **invaluably**

in·va·sion (in-**vay**-zhuhn) *noun* 1. The act of intruding. 2. The act of invading by a military force.

in·vent (in-**vent**) *verb* 1. To think up and create something new. 2. To make something up, especially with the idea of deceiving someone.
▶ *verb* **inventing, invented** ▶ *noun* **inventor**

in·ven·tion (in-**ven**-chuhn) *noun* 1. Some useful thing that is newly designed or created. 2. The activity of inventing things. 3. A statement that is made up and not true; a lie.

in·ven·tive (in-**ven**-tiv) *adjective* Good at thinking up new ideas or ways of doing things; creative.

in·ven·to·ry (in-**vuhn**-*tor*-ee) *noun* 1. A complete list of items someone owns. 2. All the items on hand for sale in a store.
verb To count and list the items someone owns, or the items available for sale in a store.
▶ *noun, plural* **inventories** ▶ *verb* **inventories, inventorying, inventoried**

in·vert (in-**vurt**) *verb* 1. To turn something upside down. 2. To reverse the order of something.
▶ *verb* **inverting, inverted**

in·ver·te·brate (in-**vur**-tuh-brit) *noun* An animal without a backbone. *adjective* Not having a backbone.

in·vest (in-**vest**) *verb* 1. To give or lend money to something, such as a company, with the intention of getting more money back later. 2. To devote time or effort to something.
▶ *verb* **investing, invested** ▶ *noun* **investment** ▶ *noun* **investor**

in·ves·ti·gate (in-**ves**-ti-*gate*) *verb* To gather information about something. ▶ *verb* **investigating, investigated** ▶ *noun* **investigator** ▶ *adjective* **investigative**

in·ves·ti·ga·tion (in-*ves*-ti-**gay**-shuhn) *noun* The act or process of looking into how something works or why something happened.

in·vest·ment (in-**vest**-mint) *noun* 1. An activity that involves giving money, time, or effort in the hope of getting something back. 2. Something in which someone has invested money, time, or effort. 3. Something in which someone may invest, or has invested.

in·vin·ci·ble (in-**vin**-suh-buhl) *adjective* Impossible to defeat. ▶ *adverb* **invincibly**

in·vis·i·ble (in-**viz**-uh-buhl) *adjective*
Impossible to see. ▶ *noun* **invisibility**
(in-*viz*-uh-**bil**-i-tee) ▶ *adverb* **invisibly**

in·vi·ta·tion (*in*-vuh-**tay**-shuhn) *noun* A
spoken or written notice to someone
inviting them to attend an event.

in·vite (in-**vite**) *verb* To ask someone to
do something or to go somewhere,
usually enjoyable. ▶ *verb* **inviting,
invited**

in·voice (**in**-vois)
noun An itemized bill for goods
shipped to a customer or for work
done or to be done for a customer.
verb To send a customer an itemized
bill for goods shipped or for work
done or to be done.
▶ *verb* **invoiced, invoicing**

in·vol·un·tar·y (in-**vah**-luhn-*ter*-ee)
adjective **1.** Not done willingly or by
choice. **2.** Done without a person's
control.

in·volve (in-**vahlv**) *verb* To include
something. ▶ *verb* **involving,
involved** ▶ *noun* **involvement**

in·volved (in-**vahlvd**) *adjective* **1.** Taking
part in something. **2.** Complicated.

in·ward (**in**-wurd) *or* **in·wards**
(**in**-wurdz)
adverb Toward the inside.
adjective **1.** Opening toward the inside.
2. Of or having to do with the mind
or soul.

i·o·dine (**eye**-uh-*dine*) *noun* **1.** A
chemical element found in seaweed
and saltwater that is used in medicine
and photography. **2.** A brown medicine
containing iodine and alcohol that is
used to kill germs on wounds.

i·on (**eye**-uhn *or* **eye**-ahn) *noun* An
electrically charged atomic particle.
Ions are either positive or negative.

I·o·ni·an Sea (eye-**oh**-nee-uhn **see**)
A region of the Mediterranean Sea,
located along its northern side
between Italy and Greece. It is heavily
populated with small islands, most of
which are Greek territories.

I·o·wa (**eye**-uh-wuh) A state in the
Midwest region of the United States.
Located in the heart of the Corn Belt,
Iowa is often referred to as the "Food

Capital of the World." It received
its nickname, the Hawkeye State,
after a newspaper publisher in Iowa
changed the name of his paper from
The Iowa Patriot to *The Hawk-Eye
and Iowa Patriot* as a tribute to Black
Hawk, a famous Native American
chief who was a friend of his.

IQ (**eye**-kyoo) *noun* A number that
represents a measure of someone's
intelligence. IQ is short for
intelligence quotient.

I·ran (i-**ran** *or* i-**rahn**) A country in
western Asia. Iran was known as
Persia for thousands of years. Persia
controlled a huge empire until
Alexander the Great conquered it
in the fourth century B.C. Today,
Iran is an Islamic state. It has large
amounts of natural gas and some
of the world's biggest known oil
reserves.

I·raq (i-**rak** *or* i-**rahk**) A country in
western Asia. The area between
the Tigris and Euphrates rivers
was the site of some of the world's
oldest civilizations, including
the Babylonian and Assyrian
empires. It was formerly known as
Mesopotamia.

i·rate (eye-**rate**) *adjective* Extremely
angry or annoyed. ▶ *adverb* **irately**

Ire·land (**ire**-luhnd) An island nation
that lies to the west of Great Britain.
Ireland was ruled by England for
several centuries, until it won its
independence in 1922. Its abundant
rainfall makes the whole island green
with vegetation, earning the country
the name of the Emerald Isle.

i·ris (**eye**-ris) *noun* **1.** The round,
colored part of the eye around the
pupil. **2.** A plant with long, thin
leaves and large flowers in a variety
of colors, which blooms in the
spring.

I·rish Sea (**eye**-rish **see**) A small sea
that separates Ireland from Great
Britain. The Irish Sea runs along
the eastern coast of Ireland, and
is connected at its northern and
southern ends to the Atlantic Ocean.

I

I·rish set·ter (**eye**-rish **set**-ur) *noun* A large hunting dog with a silky red coat. These dogs originally were bred in Ireland.

i·ron (**eye**-urn)
noun 1. A strong, hard metal that is magnetic and that is used to make a great variety of things. It is also found in some foods as well as in the body's red blood cells. 2. An electrical appliance with a handle and a heated surface, used to smooth wrinkles out of clothing.
verb 1. **iron out** To solve a problem or arrange details. 2. To use an iron to smooth wrinkles out of clothing.
adjective Made of iron.
▶ *verb* **ironing, ironed**

I·ron Age (**eye**-urn *ayj*) *noun* A period of history when iron was commonly used to make tools and weapons. This period occurred at different times in different parts of the world.

i·ron·ic (eye-**rah**-nik) *adjective*
1. Happening in the opposite way to what is expected. 2. Slightly sarcastic.
▶ *adverb* **ironically**

i·ro·ny (**eye**-ruh-nee) *noun* A way of speaking or writing that means the opposite of what the words say, especially when it is meant humorously, such as saying "Beautiful weather, isn't it?" when it is raining.

I·ro·quois (**eer**-uh-*kwoi*) *noun* A member of a confederation of Native American tribes originally of New York. ▶ *noun, plural* **Iroquois**

ir·ra·tio·nal (i-**rash**-uh-nuhl) *adjective* Not logical or reasonable. ▶ *adverb* **irrationally**

ir·reg·u·lar (i-**reg**-yuh-lur) *adjective*
1. Not standard in shape, timing, size, or arrangement. 2. Contrary to the normal rules or pattern. 3. An **irregular** verb is one whose main parts are not formed according to a regular pattern. For example, the verb *sink* is irregular because its past tense is *sank* rather than *sinked*.
▶ *adverb* **irregularly** ▶ *noun* **irregularity** (i-*reg*-yuh-**lar**-i-tee)

ir·rel·e·vant (i-**rel**-uh-vuhnt) *adjective* Having nothing to do with a particular subject. ▶ *noun* **irrelevance** ▶ *adverb* **irrelevantly**

ir·re·sist·i·ble (*ir*-i-**zis**-tuh-buhl) *adjective* Impossible to resist. ▶ *adverb* **irresistibly**

ir·re·spon·si·ble (*ir*-i-**spahn**-suh-buhl) *adjective* Careless and lacking a sense of responsibility. ▶ *noun* **irresponsibility** ▶ *adverb* **irresponsibly**

ir·re·vers·i·ble (*ir*-uh-**ver**-suh-buhl) *adjective* Unable to be changed or undone.

ir·ri·gate (**ir**-uh-*gate*) *verb* To supply water to crops by artificial means, such as channels and pipes. ▶ *verb* **irrigating, irrigated** ▶ *noun* **irrigation**

ir·ri·ta·ble (**ir**-i-tuh-buhl) *adjective* Grumpy and quick to be annoyed. ▶ *adverb* **irritably**

ir·ri·tate (**ir**-i-*tate*) *verb* 1. To annoy or make angry. 2. To make sore or sensitive.
▶ *verb* **irritating, irritated** ▶ *noun* **irritation** ▶ *adjective* **irritating**
▶ *adverb* **irritatingly**

is (iz) *verb* The third person present singular form of **be.**

Is·lam (is-**lahm** or iz-**lahm**) *noun* The religion based on the teachings of Muhammad. Muslims believe that Allah is the only God and that Muhammad is Allah's prophet. The religion is based on prayer, fasting, charity, and pilgrimage, as taught through the Koran. ▶ *adjective* **Islamic**

is·land (**eye**-luhnd) *noun* A piece of land completely surrounded by water.

is·land·er (**eye**-luhn-dur) *noun* A person who comes from or lives on an island.

isle (ile) *noun* An island, especially a small one. **Isle** sounds like **aisle** and **I'll.**

is·n't (**iz**-uhnt) *contraction* A short form of *is not.*

i·so·late (**eye**-suh-*late*) *verb* 1. To keep something or someone alone or separate. 2. To identify something so as to deal with it separately.
▶ *verb* **isolating, isolated**

i·so·lated (**eye**-suh-*lay*-tid) *adjective*
1. Far separated from other people or things. 2. If someone feels **isolated,** they feel lonely and not connected with other people.

i·so·la·tion (*eye*-suh-*lay*-shuhn) *noun*
1. The state of being completely apart from other things or people. 2. The act or process of isolating something.

i·sos·ce·les (eye-**sah**-suh-*leez*) *adjective* An **isosceles** triangle has two equal sides.

ISP (**eye**-*es*-**pee**) *noun* A company that provides people with access to the Internet in exchange for a monthly fee. ISP is short for *Internet service provider.*

Is·ra·el (**iz**-ree-uhl) A country in western Asia on the eastern shore of the Mediterranean Sea. Established in 1948 on land that had been part of Palestine, Israel is the world's only predominantly Jewish state.

is·sue (**ish**-oo)
noun 1. The main topic for debate or decision. 2. An edition of a newspaper, magazine, or other periodical. 3. A problem or difficulty.
verb 1. To provide or distribute. 2. To come out of. ▶ *verb* **issuing, issued**

isth·mus (**is**-muhs) *noun* A narrow strip of land that lies between two bodies of water and connects two larger land masses.

IT (**eye**-**tee**) *noun* Short for **information technology.**

it (it)
pronoun 1. An object or situation mentioned earlier or later. 2. The subject of some verbs that shows an action or condition.
noun The player in a game who performs the main action, such as trying to find others in hide-and-seek.

i·tal·ics (i-**tal**-iks) *noun, plural* A slanting form of print used to emphasize certain words or to show that they are special in some way. ▶ *verb* **italicize** (i-**tal**-i-*size*) ▶ *adjective* **italic**

It·a·ly (**it**-uh-lee) A country in southern Europe consisting of a peninsula and the two largest islands in the Mediterranean Sea, Sicily and Sardinia. Its capital, Rome, was the center of the Roman Empire. A popular tourist destination, Italy is known for its food, wine, and Roman ruins.

itch (ich)
verb To experience an uncomfortable tickling sensation on the skin that makes the person want to scratch it.
noun An uncomfortable tickling sensation on the skin that makes the person want to scratch it. ▶ *verb* **itches, itching, itched** ▶ *noun, plural* **itches** ▶ *adjective* **itchy**

it'd (**it**-uhd) *contraction* A short form of *it had* or *it would.*

i·tem (**eye**-tuhm) *noun* One of a list or collection of things.

i·tem·ize (**eye**-tuh-*mize*) *verb* To list the individual units or parts of something. ▶ *verb* **itemizing, itemized** ▶ *adjective* **itemized**

i·tin·er·ant (eye-**tin**-ur-uhnt) *adjective* Traveling from place to place, usually to find or do work.

i·tin·er·ar·y (eye-**tin**-uh-*rer*-ee) *noun* A plan for a trip. ▶ *noun, plural* **itineraries**

it'll (**it**-uhl) *contraction* A short form of *it will.*

it's (its) *contraction* A short form of *it is* or *it has.*

its (its) *adjective* Belonging to or related to something.

it·self (it-**self**) *pronoun* 1. It and nothing else. 2. Used when the subject of a verb is also the object.

I've (ive) *contraction* A short form of *I have.*

i·vo·ry (**eye**-vur-ee)
noun 1. A hard, whitish substance that forms the tusks of mammals, especially elephants. 2. A creamy white color.
adjective 1. Made of ivory. 2. Being a creamy white color.

i·vy (**eye**-vee) *noun* An evergreen climbing or trailing plant with pointed leaves.

I

jab (jab)
verb To poke someone or something quickly with a pointed object.
noun A short, quick punch.
▶ *verb* **jabbing, jabbed**

jab·ber (jab-ur)
verb To talk quickly in an unclear or confused way that is hard to understand.
noun Talk that is unclear, confused, and hard to understand.
▶ *verb* **jabbering, jabbered**

jack (jak)
noun 1. A device for raising a heavy vehicle off the ground. 2. A playing card with a picture of a soldier or servant, with a value of ten. 3. A small metal piece with six points used in the game of jacks. 4. A hole or set of holes arranged in a particular way that a plug fits into; a socket. 5. A game played with jacks and a rubber ball.
verb To use a jack to raise a heavy vehicle off the ground.
▶ *verb* **jacking, jacked**

jack·al (jak-uhl) *noun* A long-legged wild dog, found in Africa and southern Asia, that feeds off dead animals.

jack·et (jak-it) *noun* 1. A short coat. 2. An outer covering, as for a book.

jack·ham·mer (jak-ham-ur) *noun* A machine that uses compressed air to drill through rock, concrete, and similar hard materials.

jack-in-the-box (jak-in-THuh-bahks) *noun* A toy box with a clown's head that pops out when the lid is opened. ▶ *noun, plural* **jack-in-the-boxes**

jack·knife (jak-nife)
noun 1. A knife with a blade that folds into a handle. 2. A type of dive that involves bending at the waist in the air, then straightening out before entering the water headfirst.
verb To bend or fold in like a jackknife.

▶ *verb* **jackknifing, jackknifed** ▶ *noun, plural* **jackknives**

jack-o'-lan·tern (jak-uh-lan-turn) *noun* A hollowed-out pumpkin with a face carved into it and a candle inside, used at Halloween.

jack·pot (jak-paht) *noun* The top prize in a game or contest.

jack·rab·bit (jak-rab-it) *noun* A large hare, common in the western part of the United States. The jackrabbit has very long ears and strong back legs for leaping.

Ja·cuz·zi (juh-koo-zee) *noun* A trademark for a large hot tub with a system of underwater jets that massage the body.

jade (jade)
noun 1. A hard stone, usually green and occasionally white, used for making ornaments and jewelry. 2. A light bluish-green color.
adjective 1. Made of jade. 2. Being a light bluish-green color.

jag·ged (jag-id) *adjective* With sharp, uneven points sticking out.

jag·uar (jag-wahr) *noun* A large wildcat with a yellowish-brown coat and black spots, found in the southwestern United States, Mexico, and South and Central America.

jail (jayl)
noun A building for keeping people who are awaiting trial or who have been found guilty of minor crimes.
verb To put someone in jail.
▶ *verb* **jailing, jailed** ▶ *noun* **jailer**

jam (jam)
noun 1. A sweet, thick food made from boiled fruit and sugar. 2. A situation in which things or people are stuck. 3. (informal) An awkward, difficult position to be in. 4. **jam session** A time when musicians play together without using written music.
verb 1. To pack or press something tightly into a space. 2. To become

stuck and not work. **3.** To bruise or crush by squeezing. **4.** To practice or play with other musicians, not using printed music.
▶ *verb* **jamming, jammed**

Ja·mai·ca (juh-**may**-kuh) An island nation in the Caribbean Sea south of Cuba. Jamaica was discovered by Christopher Columbus, settled by the Spanish, and ruled by the British for 300 years before it became independent in 1962.

jan·gle (**jang**-guhl) *verb* To make a ringing, metallic sound. ▶ *verb* **jangling, jangled**

jan·i·tor (**jan**-i-tur) *noun* Someone who maintains a building.

Jan·u·ar·y (**jan**-yoo-*er*-ee) *noun* The first month on the calendar. January is followed by February and has 31 days.

Ja·pan (juh-**pan**) An island nation in East Asia consisting of four large islands and thousands of smaller ones. Home to the world's largest metropolitan area, Tokyo.

Jap·a·nese bee·tle (jap-uh-*neez* **bee**-tuhl) *noun* An insect that eats leaves and can destroy plants, brought to the United States from Japan.

jar (jahr)
noun A container with a wide mouth.
verb **1.** To send a painful shock through a part of the body. **2.** If something **jars** you, it has a surprising, unpleasant effect. **3.** If something **jars** with the facts, it conflicts with them.
▶ *verb* **jarring, jarred**

jar·gon (**jahr**-guhn) *noun* Words or expressions used only by a particular group of people.

jaun·dice (**jawn**-dis) *noun* A medical condition that turns the skin or the whites of the eyes a yellowish color.

jaunt (jawnt) *noun* A short trip for pleasure.

jaun·ty (**jawn**-tee) *adjective* Having or expressing a lively and self-confident manner. ▶ *adjective* **jauntier, jauntiest** ▶ *adverb* **jauntily**

jave·lin (**jav**-uh-lin) *noun* A long metal spear that is thrown for distance in a track-and-field event.

jaw (jaw)
noun **1.** Either of the two bones that frame your mouth and hold your teeth in place. **2.** The lower part of your face, just above your neck.
noun, plural **jaws** The parts of a tool that close to grip an object.

jay (jay) *noun* A bold, noisy bird that is related to crows. North America has several kinds of jays, including the common blue jay.

jay·walk (**jay**-*wawk*) *verb* To cross a street illegally, against the traffic light or not at a crosswalk. ▶ *verb* **jaywalking, jaywalked** ▶ *noun* **jaywalker**

jazz (jaz) *noun* A type of music that was started by African Americans at the turn of the 20th century. It has a strong rhythm and does not follow written notes. ▶ *adjective* **jazzy**

jeal·ous (**jel**-uhs) *adjective* **1.** Feeling envious of what someone else possesses or has achieved. **2.** Afraid that a person you love cares more for someone else than for you.
▶ *noun* **jealousy** ▶ *adverb* **jealously**

jeans (jeenz) *noun, plural* Pants for casual wear made of denim or similar strong cloth. ▶ *noun, plural* **jeans**

Jeep (jeep) *noun* A trademark for a small, powerful vehicle with four-wheel drive.

jeer (jeer)
verb To make loud, mocking remarks about someone.
noun A loud, mocking remark.
▶ *verb* **jeering, jeered** ▶ *adverb* **jeeringly**

Je·ho·vah (juh-**hoh**-vuh) *noun* A Hebrew name for God, used in the Old Testament.

jell (jel) *verb* **1.** To change from a liquid to a somewhat solid form like jelly. **2.** To become more certain.
Jell sounds like **gel.** ▶ *verb* **jelling, jelled**

Jell-O (**jel**-oh) *noun* A trademark for a dessert made with gelatin and a flavoring, which is boiled and then allowed to set.

J

jel·ly (**jel**-ee) *noun* A sweet, clear food that is soft, somewhat solid, and made from boiled fruit and sugar. ▶ *noun, plural* **jellies**

jel·ly·fish (**jel**-ee-*fish*) *noun* A sea creature with a soft, almost transparent body, and long, trailing tentacles that sometimes can sting. ▶ *noun, plural* **jellyfish** or **jellyfishes**

jeop·ard·ize (**jep**-ur-*dize*) *verb* To put someone or something into a situation in which danger, harm, or failure is likely. ▶ *verb* **jeopardizing, jeopardized**

jeop·ard·y (**jep**-ur-dee) *noun* Danger of loss, harm, or failure.

jerk (jurk)
verb **1.** To move or pull someone or something very suddenly and sharply. **2.** If someone **jerks** you **around,** he or she treats you in an unfair or dishonest way.
noun **1.** A sudden, sharp movement. **2.** An annoyingly stupid or foolish person.
▶ *verb* **jerking, jerked** ▶ *adjective* **jerky** ▶ *adverb* **jerkily**

jer·sey (**jur**-zee) *noun* **1.** A knitted material used for clothing. **2.** A knitted pullover top worn by athletes, such as football or hockey players, as part of their uniform.

jest (jest)
noun Something said or done in a mocking or amusing tone.
verb To say something in a mocking or amusing tone.
▶ *verb* **jesting, jested**

jest·er (**jes**-tur) *noun* A professional joker or entertainer in medieval courts.

Je·sus (**jee**-zuhs) *noun* A Jewish religious teacher who lived in Palestine around 2,000 years ago. His teachings became the basis of Christianity. Also called *Jesus Christ.* See **Christ.**

jet (jet)
noun **1.** A stream of liquid or gas forced through a small opening with great pressure. **2.** An aircraft powered by one or more jet engines.
verb To travel by jet.
▶ *verb* **jetting, jetted**

jet en·gine (jet **en**-jin) *noun* An engine that is powered by a stream of gases made by burning a mixture of fuel and air inside the engine itself.

jet lag (jet *lag*) *noun* Extreme tiredness felt by someone who has taken a long flight across several time zones.

jet pro·pul·sion (jet pruh-**puhl**-shuhn) *noun* A way of moving an aircraft in one direction by using a stream of hot gas propelled in the opposite direction.

jet·sam (**jet**-suhm) *noun* Cargo that has been thrown overboard to lighten a ship's load.

jet stream (jet *streem*) *noun* A very strong current of wind, usually found between four and nine miles above the earth's surface. Jet streams usually move west to east at speeds reaching more than 200 miles per hour.

jet·ti·son (**jet**-i-suhn) *verb* To abandon or get rid of something you no longer need. ▶ *verb* **jettisoning, jettisoned**

jet·ty (**jet**-ee) *noun* A structure projecting out into the sea to protect a waterfront area from the waves. ▶ *noun, plural* **jetties**

Jew (joo) *noun* **1.** Someone who is descended from the ancient Hebrew tribes of Israel. **2.** Someone whose religion is Judaism.

jew·el (**joo**-uhl) *noun* **1.** A precious stone, usually cut into a shape with many flat sides or facets, worn as an ornament. **2.** A person or thing that is greatly admired or valued.

jew·el·er (**joo**-uh-lur) *noun* A person who designs, makes, repairs, or sells jewelry.

jew·el·ry (**joo**-uhl-ree) *noun* Personal ornaments, such as rings, bracelets, and necklaces, often made of gold and gems. ▶ *noun, plural* **jewelry**

Jew·ish (**joo**-ish) *adjective* Of or having to do with Jews, their religion, or their culture.

J

jib (jib) *noun* **1.** The arm of a mechanical crane that can move up, down, and sideways. **2.** A triangular sail that is set in front of the mast and attached to the bow of a boat or ship.

jif·fy (**jif**-ee) *noun* A very short time; a moment. ▶ *noun, plural* **jiffies**

jig (jig) *noun* **1.** A fast, lively dance, or the music played during this dance. **2.** (informal) If **the jig is up,** the trick you are playing or the secret you are keeping is over because someone has caught on to you. ▶ *verb* **jig**

jig·saw (**jig**-saw) *noun* An electric saw with a very narrow blade for cutting curves and patterns in wood.

jig·saw puz·zle (**jig**-saw *puhz*-uhl) *noun* A wooden or cardboard puzzle made up of many small, interlocking pieces of a picture that have to be fitted together.

jin·gle (**jing**-guhl) *noun* **1.** A light ringing sound made from small bells or from metal objects hitting each other. **2.** A simple, upbeat tune or song used to advertise a product. *verb* To make a light ringing sound. ▶ *verb* **jingling, jingled**

jinx (jingks) *noun* A person or thing believed to bring bad luck. *verb* To seem to bring bad luck. ▶ *noun, plural* **jinxes** ▶ *verb* **jinxes, jinxing, jinxed**

job (jahb) *noun* **1.** Work to be done. **2.** A paid position of employment.

jock (jahk) *noun* (informal) A male athlete, especially one who is not very interested in other things.

jock·ey (**jah**-kee) *noun* A professional rider in a horse race. *verb* **1.** If you **jockey for** something, you try every possible way to gain or achieve it. **2.** To act or work as a jockey. ▶ *verb* **jockeying, jockeyed**

joc·u·lar (**jah**-kyuh-lur) *adjective* Joking, or fond of making jokes.

jodh·purs (**jahd**-purz) *noun, plural* Pants worn for horseback riding. Jodhpurs are loose around the thigh and fit tightly below the knee.

jog (jahg) *verb* **1.** To run at a slow, steady pace, especially for exercise. **2.** To shake or to push. **3.** If something **jogs your memory,** it causes you to suddenly remember something. ▶ *verb* **jogging, jogged** ▶ *noun* **jogging** ▶ *noun* **jogger**

join (join) *verb* **1.** To secure or link two things together. **2.** To come into the company of something or someone. **3.** To become a member of a group or an employee of an organization. **4.** If you **join up,** you become a member of the armed forces. *noun* The place where two things are secured or linked together. ▶ *verb* **joining, joined**

joint (joint) *noun* **1.** A connection between two bones of a skeleton. **2.** A place where two or more things meet or come together. **3.** (informal) A cheap, often unattractive place to eat, drink, or spend the night. *adjective* Done or shared by two or more people.

jo·jo·ba (hoh-**hoh**-buh) *noun* A large evergreen shrub or small tree that grows in the southwestern part of the United States and Mexico. Jojoba oil is used in products such as shampoos and lotions.

joke (joke) *verb* To amuse people with funny stories or remarks; to play tricks on people. *noun* **1.** A short, funny story. **2.** A funny trick you play on someone. ▶ *verb* **joking, joked**

jol·ly (**jah**-lee) *adjective* Cheerful and in good humor; high-spirited. ▶ *adjective* **jollier, jolliest**

jolt (johlt) *verb* To move with sudden, rough jerks. *noun* **1.** A sudden surprise or shock. **2.** A sudden, rough movement. ▶ *verb* **jolting, jolted**

J

jon·quil (**jahn**-kwil) *noun* A plant that grows from a bulb and has long, narrow leaves and fragrant white or yellow flowers. The jonquil is a kind of daffodil.

Jor·dan (**jor**-duhn) A country in the Middle East. Home to a number of ancient civilizations, Jordan today plays a crucial role in Middle East politics and maintains close ties with the United States and the United Kingdom.

jos·tle (**jah**-suhl) *verb* To bump or push roughly. ▶ *verb* **jostling, jostled**

jot (jaht) *verb* To write something quickly. ▶ *verb* **jotting, jotted**

joule (jool) *noun* A unit for measuring work or energy.

jour·nal (**jur**-nuhl) *noun* **1.** A diary in which you regularly write down your thoughts and experiences. **2.** A magazine or newspaper that deals with a particular subject.

jour·na·lism (**jur**-nuh-*liz*-uhm) *noun* The work of gathering and reporting news for newspapers, magazines, and other media.

jour·nal·ist (**jur**-nuh-list) *noun* Someone who writes for newspapers, magazines, television, or radio. ▶ *adjective* **journalistic**

jour·ney (**jur**-nee)
noun A long trip.
verb To take a long trip.
▶ *verb* **journeying, journeyed**

joust (joust)
noun A competition between two knights on horseback with lances.
verb To compete closely.

jo·vi·al (**joh**-vee-uhl) *adjective* Someone who is **jovial** is cheerful and friendly.
▶ *noun* **joviality** (*joh*-vee-**al**-i-tee)
▶ *adverb* **jovially**

jowl (joul) *noun* A layer of loose flesh that hangs down around the throat or lower jaw.

joy (joi) *noun* **1.** A feeling of great delight or happiness. **2.** A person or thing that brings great happiness to someone.

joy·ful (**joi**-fuhl) *adjective* Feeling or causing great happiness. ▶ *noun* **joyfulness** ▶ *adverb* **joyfully**

joy·stick (**joi**-*stik*) *noun* A lever that can be moved in several directions, used to control an aircraft or the movement of an image in a computer game.

JPEG (**jay**-*peg*) *noun* A common format for image files. JPEG is short for *Joint Photographic Experts Group*.

Jr. (**joon**-yur) *noun* The abbreviation for *Junior*. See **Junior**.

ju·bi·lant (**joo**-buh-luhnt) *adjective* Filled with or expressing great happiness or triumph. ▶ *noun* **jubilation** (*joo*-buh-**lay**-shuhn) ▶ *adverb* **jubilantly**

ju·bi·lee (**joo**-buh-*lee*) *noun* The celebration of an important event, such as a 25th or 50th anniversary.

Ju·da·ism (**joo**-dee-*iz*-uhm) *noun* The religion of the Jewish people, based on a belief in one God and the teachings of the Torah, the first five books of the Old Testament.

judge (juhj)
noun **1.** The person in charge in a court of law who decides the matters brought to the court. **2.** A person who decides the result or rules in a competition.
verb **1.** To decide the results of a competition. **2.** To form an opinion or come to a conclusion about something or someone.
▶ *verb* **judging, judged**

judg·ment *or* **judge·ment** (**juhj**-muhnt) *noun* **1.** An opinion or conclusion about someone or something. **2.** A decision made by a judge or a court of law. **3.** The ability to decide or form opinions wisely.

ju·di·cial (joo-**dish**-uhl) *adjective* Of or having to do with a court of law or a judge. ▶ *adverb* **judicially**

ju·di·cious (joo-**dish**-uhs)
adjective Showing good sense or judgment. ▶ *adverb* **judiciously**

ju·do (**joo**-doh) *noun* An Asian martial art in which two people try to throw each other off balance by using quick, controlled movements.

jug (juhg) *noun* A container with a narrow neck and a small handle.

jug·ger·naut (**juhg**-ur-*nawt*) *noun* A very powerful force that can destroy anything in its path.

jug·gle (**juhg**-uhl) *verb* To keep objects such as balls or clubs up in the air by catching them and then quickly tossing them up again, over and over. Jugglers usually juggle three or more objects at a time. ▶ *verb* **juggling, juggled** ▶ *noun* **juggler**

juice (joos) *noun* A liquid derived from fruit, vegetables, or meat, that is often made into a drink or sauce.

juke·box (**jook**-*bahks*) *noun* A machine that, when you put coins in it, automatically plays a piece of music you have selected. ▶ *noun, plural* **jukeboxes**

Ju·ly (ju-**lye**) *noun* The seventh month on the calendar, after June and before August. July has 31 days.

jum·ble (**juhm**-buhl)
verb To mix things up so that they are messy or confused.
noun A group of things mixed together in a messy or confused way.
▶ *verb* **jumbling, jumbled**

jum·bo (**juhm**-boh)
adjective Very large.
noun **jumbo jet** A very large jet airplane, such as the wide-body Boeing 747.

jump (juhmp)
verb **1.** To push off with your legs and feet and move through or into the air. **2.** To move or get up suddenly. **3.** If you **jump at** an offer or an opportunity, you accept it eagerly. **4.** If you **jump on** someone, you attack or criticize the person.
noun **1.** The act of jumping or the distance covered by a jump. **2.** A sudden rise or increase.
▶ *verb* **jumping, jumped**

jump·er (**juhm**-pur) *noun* A dress without sleeves or a collar, usually worn over a blouse or sweater.

jump·er ca·bles (**juhm**-pur *kay*-buhlz) *noun, plural* **Jumper cables** are used to start the engine of a car with a dead battery, by connecting the battery to one in another car.

jump rope (**juhmp** rohp) *noun* **1.** A rope that you swing over your head and under your feet as a game or exercise. **2.** A game in which this rope is used.

junc·tion (**juhngk**-shuhn) *noun* A place where two or more roads or railroad lines meet.

June (joon) *noun* The sixth month on the calendar, after May and before July. June has 30 days.

jun·gle (**juhng**-guhl) *noun* A forest in tropical geographic areas that is thickly covered with trees, vines, and bushes.

jun·ior (**joon**-yur)
adjective **1.** **Junior** is used after the name of a son who has the same name as his father. It is often abbreviated as *Jr.* and means "the younger of two." **2.** Lower in rank or position. **3.** For younger people.
noun A third-year high school or college student.

ju·nior high school (**joon**-yur **hye** *skool*) *noun* A school between elementary school and high school. It usually includes the seventh and eighth grades and sometimes includes the ninth grade.

ju·ni·per (**joo**-nuh-pur) *noun* An evergreen bush or tree similar to a pine. It bears purple fruit that look like berries.

junk (juhngk) *noun* **1.** Old metal, wood, rags, or other items that are thrown away. **2.** Something that has no value or use. **3.** A flat-bottomed boat with square sails, used in China and the East Indies.

junk food (**juhngk** *food*) *noun* Food with very little nutritional value that is prepared and packaged ahead of time, such as potato chips, candy, and cookies.

junk mail (**juhngk** *mayl*) *noun* Advertisements and catalogs that are sent to you without your asking for them.

junk·yard (**juhnk**-*yahrd*) *noun* An area used to collect, store, and sometimes sell discarded materials, such as old or wrecked cars.

J

Ju·pi·ter (**joo**-pi-tur) *noun* The fifth planet from the sun. Jupiter is the largest planet in our solar system.

ju·ris·dic·tion (*joor*-is-**dik**-shuhn) *noun* 1. The authority to make legal judgments and decisions. 2. An area over which a court, official, or authority has control.

ju·ror (**joor**-ur) *noun* A member of a jury.

ju·ry (**joor**-ee) *noun* A group of people, usually 12 in number, who listen to the facts at a trial and decide whether the accused person is innocent or guilty. ▶ *noun, plural* **juries**

just (juhst) *adjective* Based on or acting according to what is fair. *adverb* 1. Exactly. 2. A short while ago. 3. Barely or by a small amount. 4. Nothing more than. ▶ *adverb* **justly**

jus·tice (**juhs**-tis) *noun* 1. Fair and impartial behavior or treatment. 2. A country's system for carrying out laws and punishing those who break them. 3. A judge. 4. **justice of the peace** Someone who hears cases in a local court of law and performs marriages.

jus·ti·fi·ca·tion (*juhs*-tuh-fi-**kay**-shuhn) *noun* A reason for something that exists or for an action taken.

jus·ti·fy (**juhs**-tuh-*fye*) *verb* 1. To explain your actions to try to prove that they are right. 2. To arrange text so that the left and right margins are in a straight line. ▶ *verb* **justifies, justifying, justified**

jut (juht) *verb* To stick out. ▶ *verb* **jutting, jutted**

jute (joot) *noun* A strong fiber that is used to make rope and a coarse material called burlap. Jute comes from a plant that grows in tropical Asia.

ju·ve·nile (**joo**-vuh-nuhl) *noun* 1. A person who is legally below the age at which he or she can be treated as an adult for a crime. 2. **juvenile delinquent** A young person who repeatedly breaks the law but can't be sent to prison because of his or her age. *adjective* 1. Of or for young people. 2. Childish or immature. ▶ *noun* **juvenile delinquency**

jux·ta·pose (*juhk*-stuh-**poze**) *verb* To place things next to each other, sometimes to compare or contrast them. ▶ *verb* **juxtaposing, juxtaposed** ▶ *noun* **juxtaposition** (*juhk*-stuh-puh-**zish**-uhn)

K

ka·bob *or* **ke·bab** (kuh-**bahb**) *noun* Small pieces of meat or vegetables that have been roasted or grilled on a skewer.

Ka·bu·ki (kuh-**boo**-kee) *noun* A type of Japanese drama traditionally performed by men in elaborate costumes.

ka·lei·do·scope (kuh-**lye**-duh-*skope*) *noun* 1. A tube containing mirrors and pieces of colored glass that you twist or turn as you look into it to see an endless variety of patterns. 2. A changing pattern or sequence. ▶ *adjective* **kaleidoscopic** (kuh-*lye*-duh-**skah-pik**)

kan·ga·roo (*kang*-guh-**roo**) *noun* An Australian marsupial with short front legs and long, powerful hind legs that are used for leaping—its principal means of moving. The female carries her young in a pouch. The kangaroo is a national symbol of Australia.

Kan·sas (**kan**-zuhs) A state in the Midwest region of the United States. Located in almost the exact center of the country, Kansas consists primarily of farmland. It grows the most wheat in the country and is known for its fields of sunflowers. The state is the third-largest producer of sunflowers, after North Dakota and South Dakota.

Ka·ra·kum Des·ert (*kar*-uh-**koom** **dez**-urt) A large Central Asian desert, located within Turkmenistan. The Karakum Desert covers nearly 70 percent of the landmass of Turkmenistan, stretching east from the Caspian Sea, with the Aral Sea forming a northern border.

kar·a·o·ke (*kar*-ee-oh-**kee**) *noun* A form of entertainment that originated in Japan in which people sing the words of popular songs to recorded background music.

ka·ra·te (kuh-**rah**-tee) *noun* An Asian martial art of self-defense in which people fight each other using controlled kicks and punches.

ka·ty·did (**kay**-tee-*did*) *noun* A large, green insect that is related to the grasshopper. The noise that the male makes when it rubs its front wings together sounds like its name.

kay·ak (**kye**-ak) *noun* A covered, narrow boat with a small opening in the top in which you sit and paddle. Kayaks were first used by the Inuit.

Ka·zakh·stan (kuh-**zahk**-stan) A country in Central Asia. Kazakhstan is the world's largest landlocked country, covering more territory than all of western Europe. It was the last former Soviet republic to declare independence, doing so in 1991.

KB (**kil**-uh-*bite*) *noun* Short for **kilobyte.**

keel (keel)
noun The structure along the bottom of a boat or ship that keeps it stable and upright.
verb **keel over** (informal) To fall over or collapse.
▶ *verb* **keeling, keeled**

keen (keen) *adjective* 1. Very sharp.
2. Highly developed. 3. Quick or alert.
4. Interested in or enthusiastic about.
▶ *adjective* **keener, keenest**

keep (keep)
verb 1. To have something and not give it up. 2. To remain in the same condition. 3. To continue an activity.
4. To store. 5. To hold back or to stop.
6. To carry out or to fulfill.
noun 1. The amount of money needed for basic items such as food, clothing, and a place to live. 2. A large tower that is the strongest part inside a castle or fort.
▶ *verb* **keeping, kept** (kept)

keep·er (**kee**-pur) *noun* 1. Someone who manages or takes care of someone or something. 2. (informal) Something or someone that is worth keeping.

keg (keg) *noun* A small barrel, especially one that holds less than 16 gallons.

kelp (kelp) *noun* A large, edible, brown seaweed, also used to produce iodine, fertilizer, and other products. ▶ *noun, plural* **kelp**

ken·nel (**ken**-uhl) *noun* 1. A shelter where dogs and cats are kept. 2. A place where dogs and cats are raised and trained or cared for when their owners are away.

Ken·tuck·y (ken-**tuhk**-kee) A state in the east central United States. Known for its fertile soil, bluegrass pastures, and thoroughbred racehorses, it is the home of the Kentucky Derby, one of the oldest thoroughbred horse races in the country.

Ken·ya (**ken**-yuh or **keen**-yuh) A country in East Africa on the Indian Ocean. It is named after Mount Kenya, Africa's second-highest mountain peak, and is known for its many wildlife reserves.

kept (kept) *verb* The past tense and past participle of **keep.**

ker·chief (**kur**-chif) *noun* A piece of cloth, usually square, worn around the head or neck.

ker·nel (**kur**-nuhl) *noun* 1. A grain or seed of corn, wheat, or other cereal plant. 2. The soft part inside the shell of a nut that is good to eat. 3. The central or most important part of something.
Kernel sounds like **colonel.**

ker·o·sene (**ker**-uh-*seen*) *noun* A colorless liquid fuel that is made from petroleum.

ketch·up (**kech**-uhp) *noun* A thick, red sauce made with tomatoes, onions, salt, sugar, and spices.

ket·tle (**ket**-uhl) *noun* A metal pot mainly used for boiling liquids.

K

ket·tle·drum (**ket**-uhl-*druhm*) *noun*
A large drum with a metal body
shaped like a bowl that makes a deep,
booming sound.

key (kee)
noun 1. A piece of metal shaped to fit
into a lock to open it or to start an
engine. 2. Something that provides a
solution or an explanation. 3. One of
many buttons on a panel that is used
to operate a computer or typewriter.
4. One of the black or white bars that
you press when you play an organ or
a piano. 5. A list or chart that explains
the symbols on a map. 6. A group
of musical notes based around one
particular note.
adjective Very important.
Key sounds like **quay.**

key·board (**kee**-*bord*) *noun* 1. The set
of keys on a computer, typewriter, or
musical instrument. 2. An **electronic
keyboard** is an electric musical
instrument that has keys like a piano
and buttons that you control to
change the sound in some way.

key·board short·cut (**kee**-bord *short-
kuht*) *noun* A combination of two or
three keys that you can press on a
computer keyboard to do something
that would take longer if you used the
mouse.

key·hole (**kee**-*hole*) *noun* The hole in a
lock where a key fits.

key·pad (**kee**-*pad*) *noun* A small panel
of keys or buttons used for operating
an electronic machine such as a
calculator.

key·stone (**kee**-*stone*) *noun* 1. A wedge-
shaped piece at the top of an arch
that keeps the other pieces in place.
2. Something necessary or very
important that other things depend on.

key·stroke (**kee**-*strohk*) *noun* The action
of hitting a key on a computer or
typewriter keyboard.

key·word (**kee**-*wurd*) *noun* A word that
can be used to find a particular book,
website, or computer file.

kha·ki (**kak**-ee *or* **kah**-kee)
noun 1. A dull, brownish-yellow color.
2. A strong cotton cloth of this color,

often used for soldiers' uniforms.
adjective 1. Made of khaki. 2. Being a
dull, brownish yellow in color.

kib·butz (ki-**buts**) *noun* A farming
settlement in Israel where people live
and work together. ▶ *noun, plural*
kibbutzim (ki-*but*-**seem**)

kick (kik)
verb To strike something with your
foot.
noun 1. (informal) A feeling of
excitement or pleasure. 2. The act of
kicking.
▶ *verb* **kicking, kicked**

kick·off (**kik**-*awf*) *noun* 1. A kick of
the ball that starts the action in a
football or soccer game. 2. The start of
something.

kid (kid)
noun 1. (informal) A child. 2. A young
goat.
verb To make fun of or tease someone.
▶ *verb* **kidding, kidded**

kid·nap (**kid**-*nap*) *verb* The illegal activity
of capturing someone and keeping
the person as a prisoner. ▶ *verb*
kidnapping *or* **kidnaping, kidnapped**
or **kidnaped** ▶ *noun* **kidnapper** *or*
kidnaper

kid·ney (**kid**-nee) *noun* One of a pair of
organs in your body that clean your
blood by filtering out waste matter
and turning it into urine.

kid·ney bean (**kid**-nee *been*) *noun* A
bean plant with kidney-shaped seeds.
Many of the beans we eat are different
kinds of kidney beans.

kill (kil) *verb* 1. To cause the death of a
person, animal, or other living thing.
2. To end or to destroy. 3. To hurt very
much.
▶ *verb* **killing, killed**

kill·deer (**kil**-*deer*) *noun* A bird that is a
kind of plover, with a high, piercing
call and a white breast with two black
bands. ▶ *noun, plural* **killdeers** *or*
killdeer

kill·er (**kil**-ur) *noun* Someone who kills
another person or an animal.

kiln (kil *or* kiln) *noun* A very hot oven
used to bake or dry bricks, pottery, or
other objects made of clay.

ki·lo (**kee**-loh *or* **kil**-oh) *noun* Short for **kilogram.**

kil·o·byte (**kil**-uh-*bite*) *noun* A unit for measuring the amount of data in a computer memory or file. A kilobyte is equal to 1,024 bytes.

kil·o·gram (**kil**-uh-*gram*) *noun* A unit of mass or weight in the metric system equal to 1,000 grams, or 2.2 pounds.

kil·o·hertz (**kil**-uh-*hurts*) *noun* A unit for measuring the frequency of radio waves. One kilohertz is equal to 1,000 vibrations per second. ▶ *noun, plural* **kilohertz**

kil·o·joule (**kil**-uh-*jool*) *noun* A unit for measuring energy or work. One kilojoule is equal to 1,000 joules.

ki·lo·me·ter (ki-**lah**-mi-tur *or* **kil**-uh-*mee*-tur) *noun* A unit of length in the metric system equal to 1,000 meters, or about 0.6 miles. Abbreviated as *km.*

kil·o·watt (**kil**-uh-*waht*) *noun* A unit for measuring electrical power. One kilowatt equals 1,000 watts.

kilt (kilt) *noun* A pleated, knee-length plaid skirt, often worn by Scottish men as part of their traditional costume.

kil·ter (**kil**-tur) *noun* The usual or proper state of something; now usually used only in the phrases **out of kilter** or **off kilter.**

ki·mo·no (ki-**moh**-nuh) *noun* A long, loose robe with wide sleeves and a sash, traditionally worn by women in Japan.

kin (kin) *noun* Your family and relatives.

kind (kinde)
adjective Having or showing a caring and generous nature.
noun A group of things that share a number of qualities; a type or sort.
idiom If something is **one of a kind,** there is no other like it.
▶ *adjective* **kinder, kindest** ▶ *noun* **kindness** ▶ *adverb* **kindly**

kin·der·gar·ten (**kin**-dur-*gahr*-tuhn) *noun* A class for children ages four to six that is usually attended before entering first grade.

kind·heart·ed (**kinde**-*hahr*-tid) *adjective* Having or showing a friendly, helpful, and generous nature. ▶ *adverb* **kindheartedly**

kin·dle (**kin**-duhl) *verb* 1. To set on fire. 2. To stir up or to excite. ▶ *verb* **kindling, kindled**

kin·dling (**kind**-ling) *noun* Small pieces of wood or twigs used to start a fire.

kind·ly (**kinde**-lee)
adjective Kind.
adverb 1. In a kind way. 2. If you **take kindly** to something, you accept it willingly.

kind·ness (**kinde**-nis) *noun* The quality of being friendly, helpful, and generous. ▶ *noun, plural* **kindnesses**

ki·net·ic (ki-**net**-ik) *adjective* Of or having to do with motion. ▶ *adverb* **kinetically**

king (king) *noun* 1. A male ruler of a country, especially one who comes from a royal family. 2. A playing card with a picture of a king on it. 3. The most important piece in a game of chess.

king·dom (**king**-duhm) *noun* 1. A country that is ruled by a king or queen. 2. An area that is associated with or under the control of a person or thing. 3. One of the main groups into which all living things are divided, such as the animal kingdom and the plant kingdom.

king·fish·er (**king**-*fish*-ur) *noun* A colorful bird with a long, sharp beak that lives near water and dives for fish.

kink (kingk) *noun* 1. A tight curl or twist in a rope, wire, hose, chain, or hair. 2. A painful or stiff feeling. 3. An imperfection or obstacle that is likely to cause problems.

kin·ship (**kin**-ship) *noun* 1. A family relationship. 2. Any close connection.

ki·osk (**kee**-ahsk) *noun* A small structure with one or more open sides, often used as a stand for selling newspapers.

Ki·ri·ba·ti (*keer*-uh-**bah**-tee *or* **keer**-uh-*bahs*) An island nation in the Pacific Ocean. Straddling the equator, Kiribati has a tropical climate. It was known as the Gilbert Islands until it became independent from the United Kingdom in 1979.

K

kiss (kis)
verb To touch someone with your lips as a greeting or sign of love or affection.
noun The act of touching your lips to another person, especially on the face.
▶ *verb* **kisses, kissing, kissed** ▶ *noun, plural* **kisses**

kit (kit) *noun* **1.** A set of parts needed to put something together. **2.** A set of tools and materials for a certain purpose.

kitch·en (**kich**-uhn) *noun* A room or area where food is prepared and cooked.

kite (kite) *noun* A light frame covered with paper or other material that is attached to a long piece of string and flown in the wind.

kit·ten (**kit**-uhn) *noun* A young cat.

kit·ty (**kit**-ee) *noun* **1.** (informal) A kitten. **2.** A fund of money, to which everyone in a group contributes, that is used to buy something.
▶ *noun, plural* **kitties**

ki·wi (**kee**-wee) *noun* **1.** A bird from New Zealand that cannot fly, with a downcurved bill and hairlike feathers. **2.** A small, round fruit with fuzzy brown skin and green flesh. Kiwis are grown in New Zealand. Also called *kiwifruit*.

Klee·nex (**klee**-neks) *noun* A trademark for a soft tissue paper that can be used as a handkerchief.

klutz (kluhts) *noun* (slang) A clumsy person.

km (ki-**lah**-mi-tur) *noun* Short for **kilometer** or the plural form **kilometers.**

knack (nak) *noun* A skill or natural ability.

knap·sack (**nap**-sak) *noun* A canvas or leather bag used to carry books or supplies on your back.

knave (nave) *noun* **1.** A tricky and dishonest man. **2.** A playing card with a picture of a soldier or servant and with a value of ten. Also called a **jack.**

knead (need) *verb* To press, fold, and stretch dough with your hands to make it smooth. **Knead** sounds like **need.** ▶ *verb* **kneading, kneaded**

knee (nee) *noun* The joint between your thigh and lower leg, which bends when you walk.

knee·cap (**nee**-kap) *noun* The round bone at the front of the knee.

kneel (neel) *verb* To support your weight on one or both knees. ▶ *verb* **kneeling, knelt** (nelt)

knew (noo) *verb* The past tense of **know. Knew** sounds like **new** and **gnu.**

knick·knack (**nik**-nak) *noun* A small object used as a decoration.

knife (nife)
noun A tool with a handle and a sharp blade for cutting things.
verb To stab or wound someone with a knife.
▶ *noun, plural* **knives** ▶ *verb* **knifing, knifed**

knight (nite)
noun **1.** In the Middle Ages, a **knight** was a soldier who wore armor and fought on horseback. **2.** In Great Britain, a man who is rewarded for service to his country and can use the title "Sir." **3.** In the game of chess, a piece with a horse's head that can make an L-shaped move.
verb To make a man a knight.
Knight sounds like **night.** ▶ *verb* **knighting, knighted** ▶ *noun* **knighthood**

knit (nit) *verb* **1.** To make fabric out of yarn using a pair of pointed needles to create rows of interconnected loops. **2.** When a broken bone **knits,** it grows together again during healing.
▶ *verb* **knitting, knitted** or **knit** ▶ *noun* **knitting**

knives (nivez) *noun, plural* The plural of **knife.**

knob (nahb) *noun* **1.** A ball-shaped handle on a drawer or door. **2.** A round button used to control a radio, television, or other device. **3.** A roundish lump.
▶ *adjective* **knobby**

K

knock (nahk)
verb **1.** To strike something or someone forcefully. **2.** To hit and cause to fall. **3.** To criticize harshly. **4. knock out** To cause someone to lose consciousness.
noun The action of knocking on something, or the sound produced by it.
▶ *verb* **knocking, knocked**

knock·er (**nah**-kur) *noun* A hinged, metal object fastened to a door that can be used to knock on the door loudly.

knoll (nohl) *noun* A small hill.

knot (naht)
noun **1.** A fastening made by tying one or more pieces of string or rope. **2.** A round, hard spot in a piece of wood where a branch grew out of the trunk. **3.** A unit for measuring the speed of a ship or an aircraft, equal to 6,076 feet per hour.
verb To make a knot in.
Knot sounds like **not**. ▶ *verb* **knotting, knotted**

knot·ty (**nah**-tee) *adjective* **1.** Having many knots. **2.** Difficult to understand or solve.
▶ *adjective* **knottier, knottiest**

know (noh) *verb* To be aware of or familiar with someone or something.
Know sounds like **no**. ▶ *verb* **knowing, knew** (noo), **known** (nohn)

know-how (**noh**-*hou*) *noun* The knowledge and skill needed to complete a task or job correctly.

knowl·edge (**nah**-lij) *noun*
1. Understanding and information that someone gets by study and experience. **2.** Awareness of a fact or situation.

knowl·edge·a·ble (**nah**-li-juh-buhl) *adjective* Well-informed.

known (nohn) *verb* The past participle of **know.**

knuck·le (**nuhk**-uhl) *noun* One of the joints in a finger.

ko·a·la (koh-**ah**-luh) *noun* An Australian animal with thick gray fur that looks like a teddy bear and eats eucalyptus leaves.

kook (kook) *noun* (slang) Someone who acts in a silly or strange way or who has crazy ideas. ▶ *adjective* **kooky**

kook·a·bur·ra (**kuk**-uh-*bur*-uh) *noun* An Australian bird, in the kingfisher family, whose loud, cackling call sounds like someone laughing.

Ko·ran *or* **Qu·r'an** (kuh-**rahn** *or* kuh-**ran**) *noun* The holy book of the Muslim religion.

Ko·re·a, North (north kuh-**ree**-uh) A country in East Asia on the northern half of the Korean Peninsula. Korea was split in half after World War II, with South Korea backed by the United States and North Korea backed by the Soviet Union. Today, North Korea is a dictatorship and keeps itself isolated from the rest of the world.

Ko·re·a, South (south kuh-**ree**-uh) A country in East Asia on the southern half of the Korean Peninsula. Unlike communist North Korea, with whom it shares the most heavily fortified boundary in the world, South Korea is a democracy with a very high standard of living.

ko·sher (**koh**-shur) *adjective* Prepared according to the laws of the Jewish religion.

Ko·so·vo (**koh**-suh-*voh*) A territory on the Balkan Peninsula in Southeastern Europe. Part of the former Yugoslavia, and then a part of Serbia, Kosovo was the site of armed conflict in the late 1990s between the Serbians and the Albanians. The majority of people in Kosovo are ethnic Albanians. In 2008, it declared its independence from Serbia. Although a number of nations have recognized it as a country, Serbia is contesting its independence.

Ku·wait (kuh-**wayt**) A country in western Asia on the Persian Gulf. Kuwait, which has one of the largest oil reserves in the world, was invaded by Iraq in 1990, resulting in the Persian Gulf War. Its supply of oil has made it one of the wealthiest countries in the world.

K

Kwan·zaa (**kwahn**-zuh) *noun* An African-American holiday started in the mid-1960s, based on a traditional African harvest festival. Kwanzaa, meaning "first fruits" in Swahili, is celebrated for seven days beginning on December 26 and ending on New Year's Day, January 1. Each day is devoted to a different principle, such as faith, creativity, unity, and purpose.

Kyr·gyz·stan (**keer**-gi-*stan*) A landlocked, mountainous country in Central Asia. Kyrgyzstan has some of the largest walnut forests in the world. A former Soviet republic, it achieved independence when the Soviet Union dissolved in 1991.

lab (lab) *noun* Short for **laboratory**.

la·bel (**lay**-buhl)
noun **1.** A small piece of paper or other material that is attached to something and identifies its owner, use, or contents. **2.** A descriptive word or phrase.
verb **1.** To attach a label to something. **2.** To say what someone or something is like using nouns or adjectives.
▸ *verb* **labeling, labeled**

la·bor (**lay**-bur)
verb To work hard, either physically or mentally.
noun **1.** The process of giving birth to a child. **2.** Workers as a group, especially those who do physical work. **3.** Work.
▸ *verb* **laboring, labored** ▸ *noun* **laborer**

lab·o·ra·tor·y (**lab**-ruh-*tor*-ee) *noun* A room or building that has special equipment for people to use in scientific experiments. ▸ *noun, plural* **laboratories**

La·bor Day (**lay**-bur *day*) *noun* A legal holiday in the United States to honor people who work. It is celebrated on the first Monday in September.

la·bor un·ion (**lay**-bur *yoon*-yuhn) *noun* An organized group of workers set up to help improve working conditions and pay.

lace (lase)
noun **1.** A fine, patterned cloth with large spaces between the threads, used mainly for decoration. **2.** A long piece of thin string, cord, or leather used to tie shoes.
verb To fasten a shoe or piece of clothing with a lace.
▸ *verb* **lacing, laced** ▸ *adjective* **lacy**

lack (lak)
verb To be without or not to have enough of something.
noun **1.** The complete absence or a shortage of something. **2.** Something that is needed or is missing.
▸ *verb* **lacking, lacked**

lack·ing (**lak**-ing) *adjective* Not having something that is considered important or essential.

lac·quer (**lak**-ur)
noun A liquid coating that is put on wood or metal to give it a shiny finish and protect it.
verb To coat with this liquid.
▸ *verb* **lacquering, lacquered**

la·crosse (luh-**kraws**) *noun* A ball game for two teams in which each player uses a long-handled stick with a net on the end to run with the ball, pass it, and try to throw it in the other team's goal.

lac·tose (**lak**-tohs) *noun* A substance naturally found in milk. Lactose is a kind of sugar.

lad (lad) *noun* A boy or a young man.

lad·der (**lad**-ur) *noun* A structure made of metal, rope, or wood that is used to climb up and down.

lad·en (**lay**-duhn) *adjective* Loaded down.

la·dle (**lay**-duhl)
noun A large, long-handled spoon with

a deep bowl, used for serving soups and other liquids.

verb To use a ladle to serve soup, or another liquid.

▸ *verb* **ladling, ladled**

la·dy (**lay**-dee) *noun* **1.** A woman. **2.** A girl or woman who has good manners. **3. Lady** In Great Britain, a title used by a woman who has been rewarded for serving her country or who is married to a man who has the title "Sir."

▸ *noun, plural* **ladies**

la·dy·bug (**lay**-dee-*buhg*) *noun* A small, round beetle with a red or orange back and black spots.

lag (lag)

verb **1.** To move so slowly that you fall behind the others. **2.** To drop, or to lessen.

noun A delay.

▸ *verb* **lagging, lagged**

la·goon (luh-**goon**) *noun* A shallow body of water separated from the sea by a reef.

laid (layd) *verb* The past tense and past participle of **lay.**

laid-back (**layd-bak**) *adjective* (informal) Very relaxed and easygoing.

lain (layn) *verb* The past participle of **lie.**

lair (lair) *noun* A wild animal's resting place or den.

lake (lake) *noun* A large body of water surrounded by land. Most lakes contain freshwater rather than saltwater.

Lake Tan·gan·yi·ka (lake *tan*-guhn-**yee**-kuh) A large lake in Africa that flows into the Congo River system, which empties into the Atlantic Ocean. Lake Tanganyika is one of the world's largest freshwater lakes. It stretches through parts of Burundi and Tanzania along its eastern shore and parts of the Democratic Republic of the Congo and Zambia on the west.

Lake Vic·to·ri·a (lake vik-**tor**-ee-uh) Africa's largest lake and the second-largest freshwater lake in the world. Lake Victoria is located in the southeast and is territorially divided between the countries of Tanzania to

the south, Kenya to the northeast, and Uganda to the northwest.

Lake Vol·ta (lake vohl-tuh) A large man-made lake in Ghana. The largest reservoir in the world by surface area, it lies inland from Ghana's coast and stretches north along the country's eastern border. Lake Volta is formed by a dam at its southernmost end and is fed by the White Volta River and the Black Volta River, which converge and exit the reservoir as the Volta River.

lamb (lam) *noun* **1.** A young sheep. **2.** The flesh of a young sheep, eaten for food.

lame (laym) *adjective* **1.** Someone who is **lame** is having trouble walking due to illness or injury to the foot or leg. **2.** (informal) Unsatisfactory or unconvincing.

▸ *adverb* **lamely** ▸ *noun* **lameness**

la·ment (luh-**ment**)

verb To express great sadness or regret about something.

noun **1.** A song or poem expressing deep sadness, especially about someone's death. **2.** An expression of grief.

▸ *verb* **lamenting, lamented**

lamp (lamp) *noun* A gas, oil, or electric device that gives off light.

LAN (lan) *noun* A system of computers in a small area that are linked by cables or wirelessly so that users can share information and equipment. LAN is short for *local area network*.

lance (lans)

noun A long spear with a pointed metal tip, used in the past by soldiers fighting on horseback.

verb To cut open with a sharp knife.

▸ *verb* **lancing, lanced**

land (land)

noun **1.** The part of the earth's surface that is solid ground. **2.** Earth or soil. **3.** An area of ground that is owned by someone. **4.** A country.

verb **1.** To arrive on the ground after being in the air or on the water. **2.** To get or achieve something you want. **3.** To cause you to end up somewhere.

▸ *verb* **landing, landed**

L

land·fall (**land**-fawl) *noun* **1.** The act of arriving on land after being on a boat. **2.** The time when a hurricane over the ocean hits land.
▶ *adjective* **landfalling**

land·fill (**land**-fil) *noun* **1.** A place where garbage is stacked and covered with earth. **2.** A low-lying area or shallow water that is filled with land to make it usable. **3. landfill site** A large area where garbage is buried.

land·ing (**lan**-ding) *noun* **1.** The act of coming to land or coming ashore after a flight or voyage. **2.** The place on a dock or pier where boats load and unload. **3.** A level area of floor at the top of or partway up a staircase. **4. landing strip** A level area of ground used by aircraft for taking off and landing.

land·la·dy (**land**-lay-dee) *noun* A woman who owns and rents out an apartment, a room, a house, or other property. ▶ *noun, plural* **landladies**

land·locked (**land**-lahkt) *adjective* A country that does not have any border on the sea is called **landlocked.**

land·lord (**land**-lord) *noun* A man who owns and rents out an apartment, a room, a house, or other property.

land·mark (**land**-mahrk) *noun* **1.** An object in a landscape that stands out. **2.** An important event. **3.** A building or place selected and pointed out as important.

land·scape (**land**-skape) *noun* **1.** A large area of land that can be seen in a single view. **2.** A painting, drawing, or photograph that shows such a stretch of land. **3. landscape gardening** Laying out trees, shrubs, and gardens in an attractive way.

land·slide (**land**-slide) *noun* **1.** A mass of earth and rocks that suddenly slides down a mountain or a hill. **2.** An overwhelming majority of votes in an election.

lane (lane) *noun* **1.** A narrow road or a passageway between walls, fences, or hedges. **2.** A strip of road that has been marked out as wide enough for a single line of vehicles. **3.** One of a series of parallel courses into which a running track or swimming pool is divided. **4.** A narrow wooden path on which bowling balls are rolled.

lan·guage (**lang**-gwij) *noun* **1.** A system of words used together according to rules to communicate thoughts and feelings. **2.** Speech used by one country or group of people. **3.** The communication of thoughts and ideas by using signs, symbols, or movements.

lan·guage arts (**lang**-gwij **ahrts**) *noun, plural* Reading, composition, grammar, and spelling, taught as a single subject in school.

lank·y (**lang**-kee) *adjective* Someone who is **lanky** is tall and thin in an awkward way. ▶ *adjective* **lankier, lankiest**

lan·tern (**lan**-turn) *noun* A kind of lamp with a metal frame and glass sides. Lanterns can also be made out of paper.

lan·yard (**lan**-yurd) *noun* A cord looped around the neck to which a whistle, key, or other small object can be attached.

La·os (**lah**-ohs) A country in Southeast Asia. A landlocked country, it is surrounded by China, Myanmar, Vietnam, Cambodia, and Thailand. Laos has had a communist government since 1975. Tourists come to Laos to see its wild elephants and its mysterious Plain of Jars, which holds thousands of large stone jars more than 2,000 years old.

lap (lap) *noun* **1.** The flat area between your waist and knees when you are sitting down. **2.** One complete trip around something, such as a racetrack. *verb* **1.** To lie partly upon or over something else; to overlap. **2.** When water **laps** against something, it washes up against it with a gentle rippling sound. **3.** When an animal **laps up** a drink, it takes the liquid into its mouth with rapid motions of its tongue.
▶ *verb* **lapping, lapped**

L

la·pel (luh-**pel**) *noun* The part of a coat or jacket collar that folds back over against the front opening.

lapse (laps)
noun **1.** A brief failure. **2.** The time that passes between two events.
verb **1.** To drop or fall off little by little. **2.** To come to an end.
▶ *verb* **lapsing, lapsed**

lap·top (**lap**-tahp) *noun* A portable computer that is small and light enough to use while traveling.

lar·ce·ny (**lahr**-suh-nee) *noun* The crime of taking something that belongs to someone else and intending to keep it. ▶ *noun, plural* **larcenies** ▶ *adjective* **larcenous**

larch (lahrch) *noun* A type of pine tree with small cones and needles that drop off in the fall. ▶ *noun, plural* **larches**

lard (lahrd) *noun* A solid, white grease made from the melted-down fat of pigs and hogs, used in cooking.

lar·der (**lahr**-dur) *noun* A small room or pantry for storing food.

large (lahrj)
adjective Great in size or amount.
idiom **at large** Escaped and not yet captured; free.
▶ *adjective* **larger, largest** ▶ *noun* **largeness**

large in·tes·tine (lahrj in-**tes**-tin) *noun* The thick, lower end of the digestive system, containing the appendix, colon, and rectum.

large·ly (**lahrj**-lee) *adverb* To a great degree, or in general.

lar·i·at (**lar**-ee-uht) *noun* A lasso.

lark (lahrk) *noun* **1.** A small, brown bird that sings as it flies. **2.** A harmless prank or playful adventure.

lark·spur (**lahrk**-spur) *noun* A tall plant that has long stalks of blue, purple, or white flowers.

lar·va (**lahr**-vuh) *noun* An insect at the stage of development between an egg and a pupa, when it looks like a worm. A caterpillar is the larva of a moth or a butterfly. ▶ *noun, plural* **larvae** (**lahr**-vee)

lar·yn·gi·tis (*lar*-in-**jye**-tis) *noun* An infection of the larynx that makes it difficult to talk.

lar·ynx (**lar**-ingks) *noun* An organ in your throat that holds your vocal cords and makes it possible for you to speak.

la·sa·gna (luh-**zahn**-yuh) *noun* An Italian dish made with layers of wide noodles, chopped meat or vegetables, tomato sauce, and cheese.

la·ser (**lay**-zur) *noun* **1.** A device that produces a very narrow, intense beam of light that can be used for surgery, for cutting things, and for reading CDs. Laser is short for *light amplification by stimulated emission of radiation*. **2. laser beam** The concentrated beam of light that a laser produces.

la·ser print·er (**lay**-zur *prin*-tur) *noun* A computer printer that reproduces high-quality images using a laser.

lash (lash)
noun **1.** An eyelash. **2.** A blow with a whip or stick.
verb **1.** To fasten something securely using rope or cord. **2.** To whip back and forth. **3. lash out** To hit or to speak out against someone suddenly and angrily.
▶ *noun, plural* **lashes** ▶ *verb* **lashes, lashing, lashed**

lass (las) *noun* A girl or a young woman. ▶ *noun, plural* **lasses**

las·so (**las**-oh *or* la-**soo**)
noun A length of rope with a large loop at one end that can be used to catch wild horses or cattle. Also called a **lariat**.
verb To catch or stop something by throwing a lasso around it.
▶ *noun, plural* **lassos** or **lassoes** ▶ *verb* **lassoing, lassoed**

last (last)
adjective **1.** Being or coming after all others. **2.** Being the only one left. **3.** Just passed; most recent.
noun The last person or thing.
verb **1.** To exist or to go on or for a certain length of time. **2.** To stay in good condition.
▶ *verb* **lasting, lasted** ▶ *adverb* **lastly**

last·ing (**las**-ting) *adjective* Continuing or remaining for a long time.

L

last name (**last name**) *noun* Your family name or surname. In English-speaking countries, it usually comes after your given names, which means your first name and any middle names you may have.

latch (lach)
noun A bar that fits into a notch, used to close a door or gate.
verb **1.** To fasten or close something with a latch. **2. latch on** To become very attached to someone or something.
▶ *noun, plural* **latches** ▶ *verb* **latches, latching, latched**

latch·key (**lach**-*kee*) *noun* **1.** The key that opens an outside door. **2. Latchkey children** are alone at home after school because their parents are working.

late (late)
adjective **1.** Arriving, acting, or happening after the correct or usual time. **2.** Toward the end of a period of time. **3.** No longer living.
adverb After the correct or usual time.
▶ *adjective* **later, latest** ▶ *noun* **lateness**

late·com·er (**late**-*kuhm*-ur) *noun* Someone who arrives late or has just recently become a part of something.

late·ly (**late**-lee) *adverb* Not long ago; recently.

la·tent (**lay**-tuhnt) *adjective* Present but not active or visible yet.

lat·er (**lay**-tur) *adjective* Following in time or space.

lat·er·al (**lat**-ur-uhl) *adjective* On, at, from, or to the side.

la·tex (**lay**-teks) *noun* **1.** A milky liquid that comes from certain plants. This natural liquid is used to make rubber. **2.** A similar liquid that is produced artificially and is used to make rubber, paints, and chewing gum.

lathe (layTH) *noun* A machine that holds a piece of wood or metal while turning it against a cutting tool that shapes it.

lath·er (**laTH**-ur)
noun A thick, creamy foam formed when soap is mixed with water.
verb To produce a foam or froth by rubbing.
▶ *verb* **lathering, lathered**

Lat·in (**lat**-in) *noun* The language of ancient Rome.

La·ti·na (lah-**tee**-nuh *or* luh-**tee**-nuh) *noun* **1.** A woman or girl who was born in or lives in Latin America. **2.** A woman or girl born in Latin America who lives in the United States.
▶ *adjective* **Latina**

Lat·in A·mer·i·ca (**lat**-in uh-**mer**-i-kuh) *noun* All of the Americas found south of the United States, including Mexico as well as the countries of Central America and South America.

Lat·in·A·mer·i·can (**lat**-in-uh-**mer**-i-kuhn) *adjective* Of or having to do with the people, cultures, and countries of Mexico, Central America, and South America. ▶ *noun* **Latin American**

La·ti·no (lah-**tee**-noh *or* luh-**tee**-noh) *noun* **1.** A person who was born in or lives in Latin America. **2.** A person born in Latin America who lives in the United States.
▶ *adjective* **Latino**

lat·i·tude (**lat**-i-*tood*) *noun* The distance north or south of the equator, measured in degrees. ▶ *adjective* **latitudinal** (*lat*-i-**too**-duh-nuhl)

lat·ter (**lat**-ur)
noun The second of two persons or things just mentioned.
adjective Nearer the end than the beginning.

lat·tice (**lat**-is) *noun* A structure made from crossed strips of something to form a pattern of diamond shapes. ▶ *adjective* **latticed**

Lat·vi·a (**lat**-vee-uh) A country in northern Europe on the Baltic Sea. A former Soviet republic, it became independent in 1991 when the Soviet Union dissolved. More than 80 percent of the world's amber is found in the Baltic region. The area that is now Latvia was part of the ancient Amber Road, a major trade route for Baltic amber that extended from Scandinavia to the Mediterranean Sea.

L

laugh (laf)

verb When you **laugh,** you make sounds and move your face and body in a way that shows you think something is funny.

noun The act of laughing or the sound you make when laughing.

▶ *verb* **laughing, laughed** ▶ *noun* **laughter**

laugh·a·ble (**laf**-uh-buhl) *adjective* If something is **laughable,** it is ridiculous and people don't take it seriously.

laugh·ter (**laf**-tur) *noun* The action or sound of people laughing.

laugh track (**laf** trak) *noun* Previously recorded laughter of a studio audience that is added to the sound track of a television program.

launch (lawnch)

verb 1. To set a boat or ship afloat, especially if it has just been built. 2. To send a rocket or missile into space. 3. To get something started or to introduce something new.

noun 1. A type of boat that is often used for sightseeing. 2. An act of launching something, especially a rocket or missile. 3. **launching pad** or **launch pad** The platform from which a rocket or missile is sent into space.

▶ *noun, plural* **launches** ▶ *verb* **launches, launching, launched**

laun·der (**lawn**-dur) *verb* To wash and iron clothes. ▶ *verb* **laundering, laundered**

Laun·dro·mat (**lawn**-druh-*mat*) *noun* Trademark for a place where you pay to use washing machines and clothes dryers.

laun·dry (**lawn**-dree) *noun* 1. Clothes, towels, sheets, and other such items that need to be washed or are being washed. 2. A room or an area for doing the wash.

▶ *noun, plural* **laundries**

lau·rel (**lor**-uhl) *noun* 1. An evergreen shrub or tree with dark green, shiny leaves and black berries. 2. **laurels** The leaves of this tree, especially when woven into a wreath and given to the winner of a race or contest to wear as a crown. 3. If you **rest on your laurels,** you are satisfied with what you have already achieved and you no longer strive to do better.

la·va (**lah**-vuh or **lav**-uh) *noun* 1. The hot, liquid rock that pours out of a volcano when it erupts. 2. The rock formed when this liquid has cooled and hardened.

lav·a·to·ry (**lav**-uh-*tor*-ee) *noun* A bathroom. ▶ *noun, plural* **lavatories**

lav·en·der (**lav**-uhn-dur)

noun 1. A plant with fragrant bluish-purple flowers and narrow leaves. 2. A pale bluish-purple color.

adjective Bluish purple.

lav·ish (**lav**-ish)

adjective Extravagant, generous, or luxurious.

verb To give large amounts of something to someone.

▶ *verb* **lavishes, lavishing, lavished** ▶ *adverb* **lavishly**

law (law) *noun* 1. A rule established and enforced by a government. 2. A statement in science or math about what always happens whenever certain events take place. 3. The profession and work of a lawyer.

law·a·bid·ing (**law**-uh-*bye*-ding) *adjective* If you are **law-abiding,** you respect and obey the laws of society.

law·ful (**law**-fuhl) *adjective* Following or allowed by the law. ▶ *noun* **lawfulness** ▶ *adverb* **lawfully**

lawn (lawn) *noun* An area of mown grass around a house.

lawn mow·er (**lawn** moh-ur) *noun* A machine with a rotating blade that cuts grass.

law·suit (**law**-soot) *noun* A legal action or case brought against a person or a group in a court of law.

law·yer (**law**-yur or **loi**-ur) *noun* A person who has studied the law and is trained to advise people and represent them in court. ▶ *noun, plural* **lawyers**

lax (laks) *adjective* Not strict or careful enough. ▶ *noun* **laxity** ▶ *noun* **laxness** ▶ *adverb* **laxly**

L

lay (lay) *verb* **1.** The past tense of **lie.**
2. To put something down or to place it somewhere. **3.** To produce an egg or eggs. **4.** If a person has been **laid off,** he or she has been dismissed from a job. **5.** If you are **laid up,** you are in bed with an injury or illness.
Lay sounds like **lei.** ▶ *verb* **laying, laid** (layd)

lay·er (**lay**-ur)
noun A thickness or coating of something.
verb To cut or arrange something in layers.
▶ *verb* **layering, layered** ▶ *adjective* **layered**

lay·off (**lay**-*awf*) *noun* A period in which employees are dismissed from their jobs because there is not enough work for them to do or enough money to pay them.

lay·out (**lay**-*out*) *noun* The arrangement or plan of something, such as a book or a newspaper.

la·zi·ness (**lay**-zee-nis) *noun* Lazy behavior, or the trait of being lazy.

la·zy (**lay**-zee) *adjective* If you are **lazy,** you are unwilling to work or be active. ▶ *adjective* **lazier, laziest** ▶ *verb* **laze** ▶ *adverb* **lazily**

lb. (pound) An abbreviation for a pound. *See* **pound.**

LCD (**el**-*see*-**dee**) *noun* Short for **liquid crystal display.**

lead
verb (leed) **1.** To show the way by going first. **2.** To guide or direct.
noun **1.** (leed) A person's position at the front. **2.** (leed) A piece of helpful advice or information. **3.** (leed) The main actor or role in a play or movie. **4.** (led) A heavy, soft, bluish-gray metal. **5.** (led) The black or gray material used in pencils; graphite. **6.** (leed) A leash.
▶ *verb* **leading, led**

lead·er (**lee**-dur) *noun* Someone who leads, governs, or has authority over others.

lea·der·ship (**lee**-dur-*ship*) *noun* The ability to lead people and the skills associated with this.

lead·ing (**lee**-ding) *adjective* Most important, successful, or best.

leaf (leef)
noun **1.** A flat and usually green structure attached to a stem and growing from a branch of a tree or plant. **2.** A single sheet of paper, especially as part of a book. **3.** A flat, removable part of a table that can expand its surface.
verb To turn pages and glance at them quickly.
▶ *noun, plural* **leaves** (leevz) ▶ *verb* **leafing, leafed** ▶ *adjective* **leafy**

leaf·let (**leef**-lit) *noun* **1.** A single sheet of paper giving information or advertising something. **2.** A small or young leaf.

league (leeg) *noun* **1.** A group of people with a common interest or activity, such as sports or politics. **2.** A measure of distance equal to about three miles.

leak (leek)
verb **1.** If a container **leaks,** it allows whatever it was holding to escape from it. **2.** If a liquid or gas **leaks,** it escapes or enters accidentally through a hole or crack. **3.** To allow a secret to become known.
noun A hole or other place where a liquid or gas escapes.
Leak sounds like **leek.** ▶ *verb* **leaking, leaked** ▶ *adjective* **leaky**

lean (leen)
verb **1.** To stand at a slant or bend from an upright position. **2.** To rest part of your weight on something. **3.** To rely on for help.
adjective **1.** Someone who is **lean** is slender and muscular, with no excess fat. **2.** If meat is **lean,** it contains very little fat.
noun Meat that has little or no fat.
▶ *verb* **leaning, leaned** ▶ *adjective* **leaner, leanest**

leaning (**lee**-ning) *noun* If you have a **leaning** toward something, you think about it in a favorable or positive way.

leap (leep)
verb **1.** To jump up or across something. **2.** If you **leap at** something, you accept it eagerly.

L

noun A jump up or across something.
▶ *verb* **leaping, leaped** *or* **leapt** (lept)
leap·frog (leep-*frawg***)**
noun A game in which one player
bends over and another jumps over
his or her back, using the hands for
support.
verb **1.** To jump over someone's back.
2. To get ahead by overtaking others.
▶ *verb* **leapfrogging, leapfrogged**
leap year (leep *yeer***)** *noun* A year that
has 366 days. An extra day is added at
the end of February every four years
to make up for the difference between
the calendar year and the solar year.
learn (lurn) *verb* **1.** To gain knowledge,
understanding, or a skill. **2.** To
memorize. **3.** To become aware of
something.
▶ *verb* **learning, learned**
learn·ed (lur-nid**)** *adjective* Having
or showing a lot of knowledge or
education.
learn·er (lur-nur**)** *noun* Someone who is
learning something.
learn·ing dis·a·bled (lur-ning dis-*ay*-
buhld**)** *adjective* Having difficulty in
learning a basic skill, such as reading,
because of a physical condition,
such as dyslexia. Abbreviated as
LD. ▶ *noun* **learning disability**
lease (lees)
noun An agreement that a landlord
and tenant sign when renting an
apartment, a house, or other property.
verb To rent something.
▶ *verb* **leasing, leased**
leash (leesh)
noun A strap, cord, or chain that you
use to hold and control an animal.
verb To restrain with or as if with a
leash.
▶ *noun, plural* **leashes** ▶ *verb* **leashes,
leashing, leashed**
least (leest)
noun The smallest in size, amount, or
importance.
adverb In the smallest degree; less
than anything else.
adjective Smallest in size, degree, or
amount.
phrase **at least** Not less or fewer than.

leath·er (leTH-ur**)** *noun* Animal skin
that has been treated with chemicals
so it can be used to make things like
shoes and handbags. ▶ *adjective*
leathery
leave (leev)
verb **1.** To go away from someone
or something. **2.** To allow someone
or something to remain. **3.** To give
property to someone through a will,
after death. **4.** To quit. **5.** To have
remaining. **6.** If you **leave** something
behind, you don't bring it with you.
7. If you **leave** something **out,** you do
not include it.
noun Time away from work.
▶ *verb* **leaving, left** (left)
leav·en (lev-uhn**)**
noun A substance, such as yeast,
added to dough or batter to produce
gas bubbles. These bubbles cause
the dough or batter to rise, so that it
becomes bigger and lighter.
verb To cause dough or batter to
become bigger and lighter.
▶ *verb* **leavening, leavened**
leaves (leevz) *noun, plural* The plural
of **leaf.**
Leb·a·non (leb-uh-nuhn *or* **leb-**uh-*nahn***)**
A country on the eastern shore of the
Mediterranean Sea. In ancient times,
it was the site of the Phoenician
civilization. Lebanon suffered
considerable damage and civilian
deaths during the war between Israel
and Hezbollah in 2006.
lec·ture (lek-chur**)**
noun **1.** A talk prepared ahead of time
and given to a class or an audience.
2. A scolding that lasts a long time.
verb **1.** To teach or give information
by talking to a group. **2.** To scold
someone.
▶ *verb* **lecturing, lectured** ▶ *noun*
lecturer
led (led) *verb* The past tense and past
participle of **lead.**
ledge (lej) *noun* **1.** A narrow surface that
sticks out like a shelf. **2.** Something
that looks like a shelf on the side of a
mountain or a cliff.

L

lee (lee) *noun* The side of something, such as a ship or mountain, that is away from the wind; shelter. ▶ *adjective* **lee**

leech (leech) *noun* **1.** A worm that lives in water or wet earth and survives by sucking blood from animals. In the past, doctors often used leeches to take blood from patients. **2.** A person who clings to others, hoping to get something from them.
▶ *noun, plural* **leeches**

leek (leek) *noun* A vegetable with a slender white bulb and green, overlapping leaves. Leeks taste like mild onions.

leer (leer)
noun A sly or evil grin.
verb To look at someone or something in a sly or unpleasant way.
▶ *verb* **leering, leered**

left (left)
noun **1.** The side you begin to read from in a line of English writing; the side on which the heart is located in the human body. **2.** In politics, people **on the left** have liberal, progressive views about society and government.
adjective Located on or having to do with the side of someone or something that faces west when the person or thing is facing north.
adverb On or toward the left side.

left·hand·ed (left-**han**-did) *adjective* **1.** If you are **left-handed,** you write with your left hand and use it more easily than your right hand. **2.** If you receive a **left-handed compliment,** you are not sure if it really is a compliment because it seems to you that it could be insincere. The sentence "You're smarter than you look!" is an example of a left-handed compliment.
▶ *noun* **left-hander**

left·o·vers (left-*oh*-vurz) *noun, plural* Food that was not eaten at one meal and can be used for another meal.

leg (leg) *noun* **1.** One of the lower limbs of your body, between your hip and your foot. **2.** The part of a pair of stockings or pants that covers your leg. **3.** The supporting part of a chair,

table, or other piece of furniture. **4.** A stage in a journey or race. **5.** Either of two sides of a triangle besides the base. **6.** (informal) If you **pull** someone's **leg,** you tease the person by telling him or her something untrue. **7.** If something is **on its last legs,** it is about to collapse or die.

leg·a·cy (**leg**-uh-see) *noun* **1.** Money or property that someone has left you in his or her will. **2.** Something handed down from one generation to another.
▶ *noun, plural* **legacies**

le·gal (**lee**-guhl) *adjective* **1.** Of or having to do with the law or required by law. **2.** Allowed by law.
▶ *verb* **legalize** ▶ *adverb* **legally**

leg·end (**lej**-uhnd) *noun* **1.** A story handed down from earlier times. Legends are often based on fact, but they are not entirely true. **2.** Someone who is famous and well-known for something. **3.** The words written beneath or beside a map or chart to explain it.

leg·end·ar·y (**lej**-uhn-*der*-ee) *adjective* **1.** Very well known, usually because of some remarkable event or action. **2.** Based on or known about through legends.

leg·gings (**leg**-ingz) *noun, plural* Leg coverings that fit like tights.

leg·i·ble (**lej**-uh-buhl) *adjective* If handwriting or print is **legible,** it is clear enough to be read easily. ▶ *noun* **legibility** ▶ *adverb* **legibly**

le·gion (**lee**-juhn)
noun **1.** A unit in the Roman army consisting of 3,000 to 6,000 soldiers. **2.** A large group of soldiers or former soldiers.
adjective Great in number.

leg·is·la·tion (**lej**-is-*lay*-shuhn) *noun* Laws that have been proposed or made. ▶ *noun* **legislator** ▶ *verb* **legislate**

leg·is·la·ture (**lej**-is-*lay*-chur) *noun* A group of people who have the power to make or change laws for a country or state.

le·git·i·mate (luh-**jit**-uh-mit) *adjective* **1.** In keeping with the law or rules.

L

2. Reasonable or justified.
▸ *adverb* **legitimately**

le·gume (**leg**-yoom) *noun* A plant with seeds that grow in pods. Peas, beans, lentils, and peanuts are legumes.

leg warm·ers (**leg** wor-murz) *noun, plural* Knitted leg coverings usually worn from the ankle to the thigh.

lei (lay) *noun* A necklace of leaves or flowers, often given as a gift of welcome in Hawaii. **Lei** sounds like **lay.**

leis·ure (**lee**-zhur *or* **lezh**-ur) *noun* Free time in which you can relax and enjoy yourself. *adjective* Relaxed and enjoyable.

lei·sure·ly (**lee**-zhur-lee *or* **lezh**-ur-lee) *adjective* Not hurried or not rushed.

lem·on (**lem**-uhn) *noun* **1.** A yellow citrus fruit with a thick skin and a sour taste. **2.** Something that is defective.

lem·on·ade (*lem*-uh-**nade**) *noun* A drink made from lemon juice, water, and sugar.

lend (lend) *verb* To let someone have something that you expect to get back. ▸ *verb* **lending, lent** (lent)

length (lengkth) *noun* **1.** The measurement of something from end to end. **2.** The amount or extent of something from beginning to end. **3.** A piece of something.

length·en (**lengk**-thuhn) *verb* To make or become longer. ▸ *verb* **lengthening, lengthened**

length·wise (**lengkth**-wize) *adverb* In the direction of the length. *adjective* Lying or moving in the direction of the length.

le·ni·ent (**lee**-nee-uhnt) *adjective* Not harsh or strict. ▸ *adverb* **leniently**

lens (lenz) *noun* **1.** A piece of glass or plastic with one or both sides curved that brings together or spreads rays of light as they pass through, making things look larger or clearer. **2.** The clear part of your eye that focuses light on the retina.
▸ *noun, plural* **lenses**

Lent (lent) *noun* The 40 days before Easter, not including Sundays. During this period, some Christian denominations expect their members to pray and cut back on luxuries.

len·til (**len**-tuhl) *noun* The flat, round seed of a plant related to beans and peas. Lentils are often cooked in soups and stews.

leop·ard (**lep**-urd) *noun* A large wildcat with a light brown, spotted coat, found in Africa, India, and eastern Asia.

le·o·tard (**lee**-uh-*tahrd*) *noun* A tight-fitting one-piece garment worn for dancing, gymnastics, and exercise.

lep·re·chaun (**lep**-ri-*kahn*) *noun* A playful and annoying elf in Irish folklore who promises gold or other treasure if you can catch him.

Le·so·tho (luh-**soo**-too *or* luh-**soh**-toh) A country entirely surrounded by South Africa. Formerly known as Basutoland, it is the southernmost landlocked country in the world.

less (les)
adjective **1.** Smaller in quantity; not as much of something. **2.** Made up of a smaller number than wanted, needed, or expected.
adverb To a smaller extent; not so much.
preposition Minus. *My bike was cheap because I bought it at the sale price less a $15 discount from a gift coupon.*

les·sen (**les**-uhn) *verb* To decrease or diminish. **Lessen** sounds like **lesson.** ▸ *verb* **lessening, lessened**

less·er (**les**-ur) *adjective* Smaller or less important.

Less·er An·til·les (**les**-ur an-**til**-eez) A group of islands in the Caribbean Sea, which form part of the West Indies. To the west of the Lesser Antilles lies the Caribbean Sea and to the east, the Atlantic Ocean. To the south, they adjoin Venezuela and to the north, Puerto Rico, Haiti, and the Dominican Republic.

les·son (**les**-uhn) *noun* **1.** An assignment or exercise. **2.** What students are taught during one class or period of instruction. **3.** An experience from which you learn something important. **Lesson** sounds like **lessen.**

L

let (let) *verb* 1. To allow or give permission for something. 2. To allow to pass or go. 3. To rent out a house or an apartment. 4. If you are **let down** by someone, you are disappointed because the person did not help or support you as promised.
▶ *verb* **letting, let**

le·thal (lee-thuhl) *adjective* Very harmful or deadly. ▶ *adverb* **lethally**

let's (lets) *contraction* A short form of *let us.*

let·ter (let-ur)
noun 1. A mark that is part of an alphabet. A letter stands for a sound or sounds and is used in writing. 2. A written or printed message, especially one sent by mail.
verb To write letters on.
▶ *verb* **lettering, lettered**

let·ter·ing (let-ur-ing) *noun* Letters that have been drawn, painted, or printed on something, such as a sign or a greeting card.

let·tuce (let-is) *noun* A green plant with leaves that can be eaten, used in salads.

leu·ke·mi·a (loo-kee-mee-uh) *noun* A serious disease in which the bone marrow produces too many abnormal white blood cells.

lev·ee (lev-ee) *noun* 1. A bank built up near a river to prevent flooding. 2. A place for boats or ships to land. **Levee** sounds like **levy.**

lev·el (lev-uhl)
adjective 1. Flat and even. 2. At the same height.
noun 1. A floor or story of a structure. 2. A height or depth. 3. A flat, horizontal surface. 4. A position or rank in a series. 5. A carpentry tool used to show if a surface is flat and even.
verb 1. To make or become even or level. 2. To destroy. 3. If something **levels off**, it becomes more stable or consistent.
▶ *verb* **leveling, leveled**

lev·er (lev-ur *or* lee-vur)
noun 1. A bar resting on a pivot, used to move or lift an object placed on one end by pushing down on the other end. 2. A bar or a handle that you use to work or control a machine.
verb To lift or move with a lever or with great effort.
▶ *verb* **levering, levered**

lev·i·tate (lev-i-tate) *verb* 1. To rise in the air and float, seeming to defy gravity. 2. To cause to rise in the air and float.
▶ *noun* **levitation**

lev·y (lev-ee)
verb To impose or collect by lawful actions or by force.
noun A tax.
Levy sounds like **levee.** ▶ *verb* **levies, levying, levied** ▶ *noun, plural* **levies**

lex·i·cog·ra·pher (lek-si-kah-gruh-fur) *noun* Someone whose job is to research and write the entries for a dictionary.

lex·i·cog·ra·phy (lek-si-kah-gruh-fee) *noun* The work of researching and writing the entries for dictionaries.

li·a·bil·i·ty (lye-uh-bil-i-tee) *noun* 1. Responsibility. 2. Somebody or something that causes problems or holds a person back.
▶ *noun, plural* **liabilities**

li·a·ble (lye-uh-buhl) *adjective* 1. Likely to do something. 2. Legally required or responsible.
▶ *noun* **liability**

li·ar (lye-ur) *noun* A person who tells lies.

lib·er·al (lib-ur-uhl)
adjective 1. Given or used in generous amounts. 2. Plentiful or large. 3. Broad-minded and tolerant of opinions and ideas that are different from your own. 4. In favor of political change and reform. *See also* **left.**
noun A person with liberal views.
▶ *noun* **liberalism**

lib·er·ate (lib-uh-rate) *verb* To set free or release from captivity. ▶ *verb* **liberating, liberated** ▶ *noun* **liberator**

lib·er·at·ed (lib-uh-ray-tid) *adjective* Someone who is **liberated** has been set free or feels free, especially from rules about acceptable behavior.

L

lib·er·a·tion (*lib*-uh-**ray**-shuhn) *noun* The act of freeing someone or something from imprisonment, slavery, or oppression.

Li·be·ri·a (lye-**beer**-ee-uh) A country in West Africa on the Atlantic Ocean. It was founded in the 1820s by freed American slaves, who named their new capital Monrovia after the U.S. president at the time, James Monroe.

lib·er·ty (**lib**-ur-tee) *noun* Freedom.

li·brar·i·an (lye-**brair**-ee-uhn) *noun* A person who works in a library, especially one who is trained in managing a library.

li·brar·y (**lye**-brer-ee) *noun* A place where books, magazines, newspapers, records, and videos are kept for reading or borrowing. ▶ *noun, plural* **libraries** ▶ *noun* **librarian** (lye-**brair**-ee-uhn)

Lib·y·a (**lib**-ee-uh) A country in North Africa on the Mediterranean Sea. The Sahara Desert covers most of the country. Libya is rich in oil, making it one of the wealthiest countries in Africa.

lice (lise) *noun, plural* Small, wingless insects that attach themselves to animals or people, often in their hair. Lice is the plural form of **louse.**

li·cense (**lye**-suhns)
noun **1.** A document that officially grants permission for you to own, use, or do something. **2.** Permission to do something.
verb If someone is **licensed** to do something, such as practice medicine, he or she is authorized to do it.
▶ *verb* **licensing, licensed**

li·chen (**lye**-kuhn) *noun* A flat, spongelike growth on rocks, walls, and trees that consists of algae and fungi growing close together.

lick (lik)
verb **1.** To pass your tongue over or along something. **2.** To pass over something lightly, like a tongue. **3.** (informal) To defeat.
noun **1.** An act of licking. **2.** (informal)

A strike or blow. **3.** A small amount.
▶ *verb* **licking, licked** ▶ *noun* **licking**

lic·o·rice (**lik**-ur-ish *or* **lik**-ur-is) *noun*
1. A plant with a sweet, edible root that is used to flavor medicine and candy.
2. A candy flavored with licorice.

lid (lid) *noun* **1.** A removable top or a hinged cover. **2.** An eyelid.

lie (lye) *verb* **1.** To get into or be in a flat, horizontal position. **2.** To be situated somewhere. **3.** To stay in a certain place or condition.
Lie sounds like **lye.** ▶ *verb* **lying, lay** (lay), **lain** (layn)

lie (lye)
verb To deliberately say something that is not true.
noun A statement that is deliberately false.
Lie sounds like **lye.** ▶ *verb* **lying, lied**

Liech·ten·stein (**lik**-tuhn-stine) A mountainous country in western Europe between Switzerland and Austria. Liechtenstein is the smallest German-speaking country in the world. It is the only alpine country whose borders are entirely within the Alps, and it is one of only two nations in the world that are doubly landlocked: Both Liechtenstein and Uzbekistan, in Central Asia, are landlocked by other countries that are themselves landlocked.

lie de·tec·tor (lye di-**tek**-tur) *noun* A machine that is meant to find out if a person is lying. It measures small physical changes that often happen when a person lies in response to questions.

lieu·ten·ant (loo-**ten**-uhnt) *noun* An officer of low rank in the armed forces.

life (life) *noun* **1.** The quality that makes it possible for people and things to grow, breathe, and reproduce, and that separates people, animals, and plants from things that are not alive. **2.** The period of time from your birth until your death. **3.** A living person. **4.** Living things. **5.** An energetic feeling.
▶ *noun, plural* **lives** (livez)

L

life·boat (**life**-*boht*) *noun* A strong boat, usually carried on a larger ship, that is used in case of emergencies.

life cy·cle (**life** *sye*-kuhl) *noun* The series of changes each living thing goes through from birth to death.

life·guard (**life**-*gahrd*) *noun* An expert swimmer who is trained to rescue other swimmers when they are in danger at a beach or swimming pool.

life jack·et (**life** *jak*-it) *noun* A life preserver that looks like a sleeveless jacket or vest and that keeps you afloat in the water.

life·less (**life**-lis) *adjective* 1. Dead or without life. 2. Boring or dull.
▶ *noun* **lifelessness** ▶ *adverb* **lifelessly**

life·like (**life**-*like*) *adjective* Looking alive or real.

life·long (**life**-*lawng*) *adjective* Lasting for a lifetime.

life pre·serv·er (**life** pri-*zur*-ver) *noun* A belt, vest, or ring designed to keep a person afloat in water. Also called a **life jacket.**

life·sav·ing (**life**-*say*-ving) *adjective* Saving a person from serious harm or death.

life span (**life** *span*) *noun* The period of time a person, an animal, a plant, or an object is expected to live or last.

life·style (**life**-*stile*) *noun* The way someone lives.

life·time (**life**-*time*) *noun* The period of time that a person lives or an object lasts.

lift (lift)
verb 1. To raise something or someone to a higher position or level. 2. To rise into the air. 3. To rise and disappear.
noun 1. A ride in a vehicle given to someone going in the same direction. 2. A happy feeling.
▶ *verb* **lifting, lifted**

lift·off (**lift**-*awf*) *noun* The movement of a rocket or spacecraft as it rises from its launching pad.

lig·a·ment (**lig**-uh-muhnt) *noun* A tough band of tissue that connects bones and holds some organs in place.

light (lite)
verb 1. To set on fire. 2. To fill with light or cause something to give off light.
noun 1. Brightness or illumination. 2. Something that gives off light, such as a flashlight or lamp. 3. An instance of supplying a flame for something.
adjective 1. Pale in color. 2. Gentle or having little impact. 3. Not having much weight; not strongly made. 4. Moving easily or gracefully. 5. Not serious. 6. Low in calories or fat.
phrases If you **shed light** or **throw light on** something, you make it clear.
▶ *adjective* **lighter, lightest** ▶ *verb* **lighting, lighted** or **lit** (lit) ▶ *noun* **lightness**

light·en (**lye**-tuhn) *verb* 1. To make brighter or lighter. 2. To make or become lighter in color. 3. To make or become lighter in weight or quantity. 4. To make or become more cheerful.
▶ *verb* **lightening, lightened**

light·heart·ed (**lite**-*hahr*-tid) *adjective* Funny and not very serious; cheerful.

light·house (**lite**-*hous*) *noun* A tower set in or near the sea with a flashing light at the top that helps ships avoid danger. ▶ *noun, plural* **lighthouses**

light·ning (**lite**-ning) *noun* A flash of light in the sky when electricity moves between clouds or between a cloud and the ground.

light pen (**lite** *pen*) *noun* A penlike device used to draw or to change or move information or images on a computer screen.

light·weight (**lite**-*wayt*)
adjective 1. Not weighing very much. 2. Not serious; not having much influence.
noun Someone who is not that important, influential, or smart.

light-year (**lite**-*yeer*) *noun* 1. The distance that light travels in one year. 2. A very long way.

lik·a·ble (**lye**-kuh-buhl) *adjective* Easy to like.

like (like)
verb 1. To find someone or something pleasant or enjoyable. 2. To wish for or want something.
preposition 1. Similar to or resembling

closely. *My computer is like the one Simon has.* **2.** Typical or characteristic of. *It isn't like Alina to be late for a party.* **3.** Such as; as for example. *I do well in subjects like reading and language arts.*
adjective Similar or equal.
conjunction (informal) As if.
▶ *verb* **liking, liked** ▶ *noun* **liking**

like·ly (**like**-lee) *adjective* Probable or to be expected. ▶ *adjective* **likelier, likeliest** ▶ *noun* **likelihood**

lik·en (**lye**-kuhn) *verb* To compare one thing or person to another. ▶ *verb* **likening, likened**

like·ness (**like**-nis) *noun* **1.** A strong similarity or resemblance. **2.** A picture or portrait.

like·wise (**like**-*wize*) *adverb* Also, or in a similar way.

lik·ing (**lye**-king) *noun* **1.** Enjoyment of something or someone. **2.** If you **take a liking** to someone, that means you begin to like him or her.

li·lac (**lye**-lak *or* **lye**-lahk) *noun* **1.** A shrub or tree with large clusters of fragrant purple, pink, or white flowers. **2.** A pale purple color.

lil·y (**lil**-ee) *noun* Any of several plants that grow from bulbs and have flowers that are shaped like trumpets. ▶ *noun, plural* **lilies**

lil·y of the val·ley (**lil**-ee uhv THuh **val**-ee) *noun* A plant of the lily family with broad leaves and a stem covered with small, white flowers shaped like bells. ▶ *noun, plural* **lilies of the valley**

li·ma bean (**lye**-muh been) *noun* A flat, light green, edible bean, or the plant it grows on.

limb (lim) *noun* **1.** A part of a body used in moving or grasping. Arms, legs, wings, and flippers are limbs. **2.** A large tree branch.

lim·ber (**lim**-bur)
adjective Bending or moving easily.
verb When you **limber up,** you warm up your muscles before exercising or beginning an activity.
▶ *verb* **limbering, limbered**

lime (lime) *noun* **1.** A small, round citrus fruit with a green rind and sour taste. **2.** A white substance obtained by burning limestone, shells, and similar materials, used to make cement and as a fertilizer.

lime·light (**lime**-*lite*) *noun* If you are **in the limelight,** you are the focus of everyone's attention.

lim·er·ick (**lim**-ur-ik) *noun* A funny poem made up of five lines that rhyme in a set pattern.

lime·stone (**lime**-*stohn*) *noun* A hard rock used in building and in making lime and cement. Limestone is formed from the remains of shells or coral.

lim·it (**lim**-it)
noun A point beyond which someone or something cannot or should not go.
verb To set a limit on someone or something.
noun, plural **limits** Boundaries.
▶ *verb* **limiting, limited** ▶ *adjective* **limitless** ▶ *adverb* **limitlessly**

lim·i·ta·tion (lim-i-**tay**-shuhn) *noun* **1.** A fact, rule, or situation that limits something. **2.** The act of limiting something.

lim·it·ed (**lim**-i-tid) *adjective* Small or restricted in size, amount, or ability.

lim·ou·sine (**lim**-uh-zeen) *noun* **1.** An automobile that is bigger and more luxurious than a regular car. Limousines are often driven by a chauffeur. The word is sometimes shortened as *limo* (**lim**-oh). **2.** A van or small bus that takes people to and from an airport or other destination for a set fee.

limp (limp)
verb To walk with difficulty, placing more weight on one leg than the other, usually because of an injury.
adjective Lacking strength, spirit, or firmness.
noun A slow way of walking in which more weight is placed on one leg than the other, usually because of an injury.
▶ *verb* **limping, limped** ▶ *adjective* **limper, limpest** ▶ *adverb* **limply**

L

Lin·coln's Birth·day (**ling**-kuhnz **birth**-*day*) *noun* A holiday on February 12 when some states celebrate the birth of Abraham Lincoln (1809–1865), 16th president of the United States. The holiday is observed in some states on Presidents' Day, the third Monday in February.

line (line)
noun **1.** A long, thin mark made by a pen, pencil, or other tool. **2.** A row or series of people or things. **3.** A long, thin rope, string, or cord. **4.** A boundary. **5.** A short letter. **6.** A wire or set of wires that carries electricity or connects points in a telephone system. **7.** A transportation system that runs on a specific route. **8.** In mathematics, a set of points extending in a straight path without end in either direction. **9.** An attitude toward something.
noun, plural **lines** Words that you speak in a play.
verb **1.** To cover the inside surface of something. **2.** To form a straight line. ▶ *verb* **lining, lined**

lin·e·ar (**lin**-ee-ur) *adjective* **1.** Using or having to do with lines. **2.** Of or having to do with length. Feet, miles, centimeters, and kilometers are linear measures.

line·man (**line**-muhn) *noun* **1.** A person whose work is installing or repairing electric power lines or telephone lines. **2.** A football player who is part of the forward line of a team. A lineman blocks or tackles players of the other team in a game. ▶ *noun, plural* **linemen**

lin·en (**lin**-uhn) *noun* **1.** Cloth woven from fibers of the flax plant. **2.** Household items, such as tablecloths and sheets, that were once made of linen.

line spac·ing (**line** *spay*-sing) *noun* The amount of space between lines in a typed or printed document.

lines·per·son (**linez**-*pur*-suhn) *noun* An official who decides whether the ball has gone out of bounds in games such as football, soccer, hockey, and tennis.

lin·ger (**ling**-gur) *verb* To be slow in leaving or to continue to stay. ▶ *verb* **lingering, lingered** ▶ *adjective* **lingering**

lin·gui·ne (ling-**gwee**-nee) *noun* Pasta cut into long, thin strips.

lin·guist (**ling**-gwist) *noun* Someone who studies the structure and nature of languages or speaks them well. ▶ *noun* **linguistics** (ling-**gwis**-tiks)

lin·ing (**lye**-ning) *noun* The layer or coating that covers the inside of something.

link (lingk)
noun **1.** One of the rings or loops that make up a chain. **2.** A connection or relationship between people or things. **3.** A connection between one webpage or website and another; a hyperlink.
verb To connect or become connected. ▶ *verb* **linking, linked**

link·ing verb (**ling**-king *vurb*) *noun* A verb that does not show action. Its function is to link the subject of a sentence to what is said about the subject. For example, the verb *be* is a linking verb, as in the sentence "Paul is happy."

li·no·le·um (luh-**noh**-lee-uhm) *noun* A material with a strong, shiny surface and a canvas or cloth back. Linoleum is used as a floor covering, most commonly in kitchens.

lin·seed oil (**lin**-seed *oil*) *noun* Oil from the seed of certain flax plants used to make paints, varnishes, printing inks, patent leather, and linoleum.

lint (lint) *noun* Very small bits of thread or fluff from cloth.

li·on (**lye**-uhn) *noun* A large, light brown wildcat found in sub-Saharan Africa and India. Male lions have manes.

li·on·ess (**lye**-uh-nis) *noun* A female lion. ▶ *noun, plural* **lionesses**

lip (lip) *noun* **1.** Your **lips** are the two fleshy parts that form the edges of your mouth and that help to form speech sounds. **2.** The edge or rim

L

of something, especially of a pitcher, a cup, a bowl, or other container. **3.** (slang) Disrespectful talk.

lip-read (**lip**-reed) *verb* To understand what someone is saying by watching his or her lip movements. ▶ *verb* **lip-reading, lip-read** (red) ▶ *noun* **lipreading**

lip·stick (**lip**-stik) *noun* A small, crayonlike stick used to color the lips.

liq·ue·fy (**lik**-wuh-*fye*) *verb* To make something solid into a liquid. ▶ *verb* **liquefies, liquefying, liquefied**

liq·uid (**lik**-wid)
noun A substance that flows and can be easily poured.
adjective Able to flow freely like water; not a solid or a gas.

liq·uid crys·tal dis·play (**lik**-wid **kris**-tuhl dis-*play*) *noun* A way of showing numbers and letters on clocks, calculators, and digital watches by putting a liquid between layers of plastic or glass and then passing an electric current through it. Abbreviated as *LCD.*

liq·uor (**lik**-ur) *noun* A strong alcoholic drink, such as vodka, whiskey, or rum.

li·ra (**leer**-uh) *noun* The currency in Turkey and formerly in Italy, which now uses the euro. ▶ *noun, plural* **lire** (**leer**-uh)

lisp (lisp)
noun A speech defect in which "s" is pronounced like "th."
verb To speak with a lisp.
▶ *verb* **lisping, lisped**

list (list)
noun A series of names or items, often written in a particular order.
verb **1.** To put into a list. **2.** To lean to one side.
▶ *verb* **listing, listed**

lis·ten (**lis**-uhn) *verb* To make a conscious effort to hear something. ▶ *verb* **listening, listened** ▶ *noun* **listener**

list·less (**list**-lis) *adjective* Showing no interest in or enthusiasm about anything.

lit (lit) *verb* The past tense and past participle of **light.**

li·ter (**lee**-tur) *noun* A unit of measurement in the metric system. A liter is equal to about 1.1 quarts.

lit·er·a·cy (**lit**-ur-uh-see) *noun* The ability to read and write.

lit·er·al (**lit**-ur-uhl) *adjective* **1.** Following the original text exactly. **2.** True to the facts and not exaggerated; actual.

lit·er·al·ly (**lit**-ur-uh-lee) *adverb* **1.** Word for word. **2.** Actually. **3.** If you **take** something **literally,** you believe it without questioning it at all.

lit·er·ate (**lit**-ur-it) *adjective* **1.** Able to read and write. **2.** Highly educated.

lit·er·a·ture (**lit**-ur-uh-chur) *noun* Written works that have lasting value or interest. Literature includes novels, plays, short stories, essays, and poems. ▶ *adjective* **literary** (**lit**-uh-rer-ee)

Lith·u·a·ni·a (*lith*-oo-**ay**-nee-uh) A country in northern Europe on the Baltic Sea. It is one of the three Baltic states, which include Latvia and Estonia. Lithuania was occupied by the Soviet Union during World War II. In 1990, it became the first Soviet republic to declare independence.

lit·mus pa·per (**lit**-muhs *pay*-pur) *noun* Paper soaked in a dye that changes from red to blue in a base solution and from blue to red in an acid solution.

lit·ter (**lit**-ur)
noun **1.** Bits or scraps of paper or other garbage scattered around carelessly. **2.** A number of baby animals that are born at the same time to the same mother. **3.** A stretcher for carrying a sick or wounded person.
verb To make an area untidy by scattering trash around.
▶ *verb* **littering, littered**

lit·tle (**lit**-uhl)
adjective **1.** Small in size or amount. **2.** Not much.
noun A small quantity or amount of something.
▶ *adjective* **littler, littlest** ▶ *adjective* **less** (les), **least** (leest)

L

live

verb (liv) **1.** To be alive. **2.** To remain alive. **3.** To make your home in a particular place. **4.** To support yourself. **5.** If you can **live with** a difficult situation, you can put up with it or bear it.

adjective (līve) **1.** Living. **2.** Broadcast while actually being performed; not recorded. **3.** Burning. **4.** If an electrical wire or device is **live,** it is connected to a source of electricity and can give you a shock. **5.** Not yet exploded.

idiom If you **live and let live,** you are tolerant and able to accept or respect the behavior, customs, beliefs, or opinions of others.

▶ *verb* **living, lived**

live·li·hood (līve-lee-*hud*) *noun* The way that you earn money in order to live.

live·ly (līve-lee) *adjective* **1.** Full of life and energy. **2.** Bright. **3.** Exciting. **4.** Creative.

▶ *adjective* **livelier, liveliest** ▶ *noun* **liveliness**

liv·er (**liv**-ur) *noun* **1.** The organ in a human or animal body that cleans the blood and produces bile, which helps digest food. **2.** A food prepared from the liver of a calf, pig, or other animal.

liv·er·y (**liv**-ur-ee) *noun* **1.** A uniform worn by servants or members of a profession. **2.** A stable where horses are taken care of or rented for a fee.

lives

noun, plural (līvez) The plural of **life.**

verb (livz) The third person singular present form of **live.**

lives·tock (līve-*stahk*) *noun* Sheep, horses, cows, pigs, or other animals that are kept or raised on a farm or ranch. They are used to do work, to provide a profit from the sale of their fur or meat, or to provide pleasure, such as horseback riding.

liv·id (**liv**-id) *adjective* **1.** Having a pale, usually white or somewhat blue color. **2.** Very angry. **3.** Purple or dark in color because of a bruise.

liv·ing (**liv**-ing)

adjective **1.** Alive now; not dead.

2. Still active or in use.

noun A way of earning an income.

liv·ing room (**liv**-ing *room*) *noun* A room in a house intended for social and leisure activities.

liz·ard (**liz**-urd) *noun* A reptile with a scaly body, four legs, and a long tail.

lla·ma (**lah**-muh) *noun* A large South American mammal raised for its wool and used to carry loads. The llama is related to the camel.

load (lohd)

noun **1.** Something heavy or bulky that is being carried or is about to be carried. **2.** The amount carried at one time.

verb **1.** To put things on or into a carrier. **2.** To insert something into a device, such as a gun or a camera, so that it works.

noun, plural (informal) If you have **loads** of something, you have a great number or amount of it.

▶ *verb* **loading, loaded**

loaf (lohf)

noun **1.** Bread baked in one piece. **2.** Food in the shape of a rectangular loaf of bread.

verb To spend time doing little or nothing.

▶ *noun, plural* **loaves** (lohvz) ▶ *verb* **loafing, loafed**

loaf·er (**loh**-fur) *noun* **1.** Someone who lounges around and doesn't do much. **2. Loafer** A trademark for a flat, casual shoe.

loam (lohm) *noun* Loose, rich soil made of sand, clay, and decayed leaves and plants. ▶ *adjective* **loamy**

loan (lohn)

noun **1.** The act of lending something to someone. **2.** Something borrowed, especially money.

verb To lend something to someone. **Loan** sounds like **lone.** ▶ *verb* **loaning, loaned**

loathe (lohTH) *verb* To feel great dislike or disgust for someone or something. ▶ *verb* **loathing, loathed** ▶ *noun* **loathing**

loath·some (**lohTH**-suhm) *adjective* Causing hatred or disgust.

L

lob (lahb)
verb To throw or hit something, especially a ball, in a high arc.
noun A ball hit or thrown in a high arc.
▶ *verb* **lobbing, lobbed**

lob·by (lah-bee)
noun **1.** A hall or room at the entrance to a building. **2.** A group of people who try to influence politicians on a specific issue.
verb To work to influence someone about something, especially about a specific political issue.
▶ *noun, plural* **lobbies** ▶ *verb* **lobbying, lobbied**

lob·by·ist (lah-bee-ist) *noun* A person who works on behalf of a particular group to persuade members of the government to act or vote in support of that group's interests.

lob·ster (lahb-stur) *noun* A sea creature used for food, with a hard shell and five pairs of legs. The front pair of legs are large, heavy claws.

lo·cal (loh-kuhl)
adjective **1.** Of or having to do with the area in which you live. **2.** Affecting only a part of the body.
noun A train, subway, or bus that makes all the stops on a route.
▶ *adverb* **locally**

lo·cal·i·ty (loh-kal-i-tee) *noun* A district, an area, or a neighborhood. ▶ *noun, plural* **localities**

lo·cate (loh-kate) *verb* **1.** To find out the exact place or position of something. **2.** To put or place somewhere. **3.** To settle in a particular place.
▶ *verb* **locating, located**

lo·ca·tion (loh-kay-shuhn) *noun* **1.** A place or position. **2.** If a movie is made **on location**, it is filmed in the type of place where the story is set, not in the studio.

lo·ca·vore (loh-kuh-vor) *noun* Someone who tries to eat foods that are grown or made in the area where he or she lives.

lock (lahk)
verb **1.** To fasten or secure something with or as if with a lock. **2.** To join or link together.
noun **1.** A device for keeping a door or container fastened that you can open and shut with a key. **2.** A section of a canal with gates at each end, used for raising and lowering boats by changing the water level. **3.** A tuft of hair.
▶ *verb* **locking, locked**

lock·er (lah-kur) *noun* A small chest or closet, especially at a school or gym, that can be locked and where you can store your belongings.

lock·et (lah-kit) *noun* A piece of jewelry that women wear on a chain around their necks and that often contains a photograph, lock of hair, or other memento.

lock·smith (lahk-smith) *noun* Someone who makes and repairs locks and also makes keys.

lo·co·mo·tion (loh-kuh-moh-shuhn) *noun* The act of moving from one place to another, or the ability to do so.

lo·co·mo·tive (loh-kuh-moh-tiv) *noun* An engine used to push or pull railroad cars.

lo·cust (loh-kuhst) *noun* A type of grasshopper that moves in huge swarms and destroys crops and vegetation.

lode·stone (lohd-stone) *noun* A stone with iron in it that acts as a magnet.

lodge (lahj)
noun **1.** A small house, cottage, or cabin, often used for a short stay. **2.** The den of a beaver.
verb **1.** If you **lodge** with someone, you live in the person's house and usually pay rent. **2.** If something **lodges** somewhere, it comes to rest there and becomes firmly fixed. **3.** To bring to the attention of someone in charge.
▶ *verb* **lodging, lodged**

lodg·er (lah-jur) *noun* Somebody who rents a room in someone else's house. ▶ *noun* **lodgings**

loft (lawft) *noun* **1.** A room or space under the roof of a building. **2.** An upper story in a business building used as a place to live in or as an artist's studio.

L

loft·y (**lawf**-tee) *adjective* 1. Very tall and impressive. 2. Aloof and proud.
▶ *adjective* **loftier, loftiest**

log (lawg *or* lahg)
noun 1. A part of a tree that has fallen or been cut off. 2. A written record of a ship's speed, progress, and what happens on its voyage, kept by the captain. 3. A written record of the progress of something, such as a trip or an experiment.
verb 1. To cut down trees. 2. To keep a record of something. 3. When you **log on** or **log in** to a computer, you take whatever steps are required to begin using it, such as entering a username or a password. 4. When you **log off** or **log out,** you go through the steps required to finish using a computer.
▶ *verb* **logging, logged** ▶ *noun* **logger**

lo·gan·ber·ry (**loh**-guhn-*ber*-ee) *noun* A large, dark red berry that grows on a prickly shrub. The loganberry is a cross between the blackberry and the raspberry. ▶ *noun, plural* **loganberries**

log·ic (**lah**-jik) *noun* 1. Good or valid thinking or reasoning. 2. The study of the rules for correct reasoning. 3. A particular way of thinking.

log·i·cal (**lah**-ji-kuhl) *adjective* Consistent with logic; easily explainable. ▶ *adverb* **logically**

log·in (**lawg**-in) *or* **log·on** (**lawg**-awn) *noun* 1. An act of logging in to a network, website, computer, or online account. 2. A username.

lo·go (**loh**-goh) *noun* A distinctive symbol or trademark that identifies a particular company or organization.

loin (loin)
noun, plural **loins** In people or animals, the part of the sides and back of the body between the ribs and the hip.
noun A cut of meat from this part of an animal.

loi·ter (**loi**-ter) *verb* To stand around aimlessly or move slowly with many stops. ▶ *verb* **loitering, loitered** ▶ *noun* **loiterer**

loll (lahl) *verb* 1. To sit or stand in a lazy or relaxed way. 2. To hang loosely or to let something droop.
▶ *verb* **lolling, lolled**

lol·li·pop (**lah**-lee-*pahp*) *noun* A piece of hard candy on a stick.

lone (lohn) *adjective* 1. Alone or solitary. 2. Only or single.
Lone sounds like **loan.**

lone·ly (**lone**-lee) *adjective* 1. If you are **lonely,** you miss the company of other people. 2. Remote and standing apart from others like it.
▶ *adjective* **lonelier, loneliest** ▶ *noun* **loneliness**

lone·some (**lone**-suhm) *adjective* 1. If you are **lonesome,** you are sad because you feel alone. 2. Not often visited or used by people.

long (lawng)
adjective 1. Of greater than usual length, height, distance, or time. 2. Measured from end to end. 3. Lasting a long time.
adverb 1. For a long time. 2. Throughout the length or duration of.
noun A long time.
verb To wish for something or to want someone or something very much.
▶ *adjective* **longer, longest** ▶ *verb* **longing, longed** ▶ *noun* **longing**

long-dis·tance (**lawng**-dis-tuhns) *adjective, adverb* 1. Covering or able to cover a long distance. 2. Connecting distant places.

long·hand (**lawng**-hand) *noun* Ordinary writing in which you use a pencil or pen to write the words out in full.

lon·gi·tude (**lahn**-ji-*tood*) *noun* The distance east or west, measured in degrees, of an imaginary line that runs through Greenwich, England. On a map or globe, lines of longitude are drawn from the North Pole to the South Pole. ▶ *adjective* **longitudinal** (*lahn*-ji-**too**-duh-nuhl)

long-range (**lawng**-raynj) *adjective* 1. Of or having to do with the future. 2. Able to be used over a long distance.

L

long·ship (**lawng**-*ship*) *noun* A long, narrow, double-ended ship with many oars and a sail, used by the Vikings during the 8th to the 11th centuries for trading and exploring, and to transport warriors.

long shot (**lawng** *shaht*) *noun* 1. If something is not likely to happen, it can be called a **long shot.** 2. If someone asks you if your school will win the trophy, and you think it won't happen, you might answer, **"Not by a long shot!"**

long-term (**lawng**-*turm*) *adjective* Having to do with or extending over a long period of time.

long-wind·ed (**lawng**-**win**-did) *adjective* Speaking or writing at great length, often in a boring way.

loo·fah (**loo**-fuh) *noun* A rough sponge made from the dried inner parts of a tropical fruit.

look (luk)
verb 1. To use your eyes to see someone or something. 2. To turn your eyes or attention. 3. To seem or appear to be. 4. To face in a certain direction. 5. If you **look after** someone or something, you take care of or watch over him, her, or it. 6. If you **look down on** someone, you think you are superior to the person. 7. If you **look for** someone or something, you try to find them. 8. If you **look forward to** something, you can't wait for it to happen. 9. If you **look** something **up,** you search for information about it in a book or other reference. 10. If you **look up to** a person, you respect him or her.
noun 1. The act of looking at something. 2. A glance or facial expression that reveals how you are feeling or what you are thinking. 3. Appearance, style, or fashion.
▶ *verb* **looking, looked**

look·ing glass (**luk**-ing *glas*) *noun* A mirror.

look·out (**luk**-out) *noun* Someone who keeps watch for danger or trouble.

loom (loom)
verb 1. To take shape or come into view in a threatening way. 2. To be about to happen.
noun A machine or device used for weaving cloth.
▶ *verb* **looming, loomed**

loon (loon) *noun* A large diving bird with webbed feet, short legs, and a speckled back. The cry of the loon sounds like wild laughter.

loop (loop)
noun The shape formed when a piece of string, rope, or some other flexible material bends around and crosses itself.
verb To form into a loop.
▶ *verb* **looping, looped**

loose (loos) *adjective* 1. Not fastened or attached firmly. 2. Free. 3. Not fitting tightly or closely. 4. Not held together or attached in one place. 5. Not placed or packed tightly together.
▶ *adjective* **looser, loosest** ▶ *adverb* **loosely**

loose-leaf (**loos**-*leef*) *adjective* Holding or made to hold pages that have holes and are easily removed.

loos·en (**loo**-suhn) *verb* 1. To make something loose. 2. To set free. 3. If you **loosen up,** you relax, talk more freely, or warm up for an activity.
▶ *verb* **loosening, loosened**

loot (loot)
verb To steal from shops or homes during a riot, war, natural disaster, or other crisis.
noun Items that have been stolen or taken by force.
Loot sounds like **lute.** ▶ *verb* **looting, looted** ▶ *noun* **looter**

lop·sid·ed (**lahp-sye**-did) *adjective* Unbalanced, with one side heavier, larger, or higher than the other.

lord (lord) *noun* 1. A person who has great power or authority over others. In the Middle Ages, a lord lived in a castle and had many people under his rule. 2. **Lord** A name for God. 3. **Lord** In Great Britain, a title for a man of noble birth. Some British men earn this title as a reward for service to their country.

L

lose (looz) *verb* **1.** If you **lose** something, you no longer have it or know where it is. **2.** To fail to keep or hold on to something. **3.** To fail to win something, such as a contest, election, or argument. **4.** To waste or fail to take advantage of something. ▶ *verb* **losing, lost** (lawst) ▶ *noun* **loser**

loss (laws) *noun* **1.** The act or an instance of losing something. **2.** The person, thing, or amount that is lost. ▶ *noun, plural* **losses**

lost (lawst)
adjective **1.** If an object or pet is **lost,** its owner doesn't know where it is. **2.** Not knowing how to get back to a place that is familiar to you. **3.** Extremely confused, sometimes so much so that you cannot behave or live normally.
verb The past tense and past participle of **lose.**

lot (laht)
noun **1.** A great number or amount of something. **2.** A piece of land. **3.** A group of objects or people.
adverb **a lot** *or* **lots** Much.

lo·tion (loh-shuhn) *noun* A thin cream that is used to clean, soften, or heal the skin.

lot·ter·y (lah-tur-ee) *noun* A way of raising money in which people buy numbered tickets in the hope of winning a prize if their number is drawn. ▶ *noun, plural* **lotteries**

lo·tus (loh-tuhs) *noun* A water plant with large flowers that float on the surface. The flowers are usually pink, yellow, or white. ▶ *noun, plural* **lotuses**

loud (loud)
adjective **1.** Producing a very big sound. **2.** Bright and colorful but in poor taste.
adverb In a loud manner.
▶ *adjective* **louder, loudest** ▶ *adverb* **loudly**

loud·speak·er (loud-spee-kur) *noun* A machine that turns electrical signals into sounds that are loud enough to be heard in a large room or area.

Lou·i·si·an·a (loo-ee-zee-an-uh) A state in the southern United States on the Gulf of Mexico. Originally a colony of France, it was sold to the United States in 1803 in what became known as the Louisiana Purchase. Some of its residents still speak Cajun, a local French dialect. Louisiana has been struck by many hurricanes, most notably Hurricane Katrina in 2005, which flooded 80 percent of the city of New Orleans.

lounge (lounj)
verb To stand, sit, or lie in a lazy or relaxed way.
noun A room in a hotel or airport where people can sit and relax.
▶ *verb* **lounging, lounged**

louse (lous) *noun* A small, wingless insect that lives on people or animals and sucks their blood. ▶ *noun, plural* **lice** (lise)

lous·y (lou-zee) *adjective* **1.** (informal) Really bad; terrible. **2.** (informal) Unpleasant, immoral, or dishonest. **3.** Infested with lice.
▶ *adjective* **lousier, lousiest** ▶ *adverb* **lousily** ▶ *noun* **lousiness**

lov·a·ble (luhv-uh-buhl) *adjective* Easy to love. ▶ *adverb* **lovably**

love (luhv)
verb To feel a deep affection for or strong attachment to someone or something.
noun **1.** A strong and emotional liking for something or someone. **2.** A person that you love. **3.** In tennis, a score of zero; the score you have at the start of a game.
idiom If you are **in love** with someone, you are fond of him or her in a tender, passionate way.
▶ *verb* **loving, loved**

love·ly (luhv-lee) *adjective* **1.** If someone is **lovely,** the person has pleasing looks or has inner qualities that inspire love, affection, or admiration. The word is more often used for girls and women than for boys and men. **2.** Enjoyable or delightful.
▶ *adjective* **lovelier, loveliest** ▶ *noun* **loveliness**

L

lov·er (**luhv**-ur) *noun* 1. Someone who loves something. 2. Someone involved in a romantic relationship.

lov·ing (**luhv**-ing) *adjective* Having or showing a lot of love and affection.

low (loh) *adjective* 1. Not high or tall. 2. Below the usual level. 3. Near the bottom of a range of sounds in pitch. 4. Below average. 5. A **low** sound is not very loud or intense. 6. Not having enough. 7. If someone feels **low,** the person is depressed and has no energy.
▶ *adjective* **lower, lowest**

lower (**loh**-ur)
verb 1. To move or bring something down. 2. To make or become less. 3. To make less loud.
adjective Not as high in position, authority, or importance.
▶ *verb* **lowering, lowered**

low·er·case (**loh**-ur-**kase**)
adjective Using letters that are not capitals.
noun Small letters, not capitals.
verb To put in lowercase letters.
▶ *verb* **lowercasing, lowercased**

low tide (**loh tide**) *noun* The time at which the water level in an ocean, a gulf, or a bay is at its lowest point.

loy·al (**loi**-uhl) *adjective* Firm in supporting or faithful to one's country, family, friends, or beliefs. ▶ *adverb* **loyally**

loy·al·ty (**loi**-uhl-tee) *noun* The quality of being loyal and faithful. ▶ *noun, plural* **loyalties**

lu·bri·cate (**loo**-bri-*kate*) *verb* To add a substance such as oil or grease to make something move or operate more smoothly. ▶ *verb* **lubricating, lubricated** ▶ *noun* **lubricant** (**loo**-bri-kuhnt) ▶ *noun* **lubrication**

luck (luhk) *noun* 1. The chance occurrence of good or bad events. 2. Good fortune or success.

luck·y (**luhk**-ee) *adjective* 1. Having good luck or happening as a result of good luck. 2. Something that is **lucky** happens by chance and is fortunate. 3. A **lucky** number or charm is one that you think will bring you good luck.
▶ *adjective* **luckier, luckiest** ▶ *adverb* **luckily**

lu·di·crous (**loo**-di-kruhs) *adjective* Someone or something that is **ludicrous** is laughable because it is so ridiculous or absurd. ▶ *adverb* **ludicrously**

lug (luhg) *verb* To carry something with great difficulty or effort. ▶ *verb* **lugging, lugged**

luge (loozh)
noun A small sled on which the rider lies face up with feet forward and races down an icy course.
verb To ride in a luge.
▶ *verb* **luging, luged** ▶ *noun* **luger**

lug·gage (**luhg**-ij) *noun* Suitcases and bags that travelers fill with their belongings.

luke·warm (**look**-*worm*) *adjective* 1. Barely or only slightly warm. 2. Not very enthusiastic.

lull (luhl)
verb To soothe someone or send him or her to sleep.
noun A short pause or period of calm.
▶ *verb* **lulling, lulled**

lul·la·by (**luhl**-uh-*bye*) *noun* A soothing song sung to help a baby fall asleep. ▶ *noun, plural* **lullabies**

lum·ber (**luhm**-bur)
noun Wood or timber that has been sawed into planks or boards.
verb To move in a slow, heavy, clumsy way.
▶ *verb* **lumbering, lumbered**

lum·ber·jack (**luhm**-bur-*jak*) *noun* Someone whose job is to cut down trees and get the logs to a sawmill.

lu·mi·nous (**loo**-muh-nuhs) *adjective* Shining or giving off light, especially in the dark. ▶ *adverb* **luminously**

lump (luhmp)
noun 1. A shapeless piece of something. 2. A swelling or a bump.
verb 1. To pull or bring together. 2. To form lumps.
adjective Whole.
▶ *verb* **lumping, lumped**

L

lu·nar (**loo**-nur) *adjective* Of or having to do with the moon or resembling the moon.

lu·na·tic (**loo**-nuh-tik)
noun Someone who is insane or who behaves wildly and foolishly.
adjective Wildly foolish or insane.

lunch (luhnch)
noun A meal eaten in the middle of the day, after breakfast and before dinner.
verb To eat lunch.
▶ *verb* **lunches, lunching, lunched** ▶ *noun, plural* **lunches**

lunch·eon (**luhn**-chuhn) *noun* A lunch, especially a large, formal one.

lung (luhng) *noun* One of a pair of baglike organs inside your chest that fill with air when you breathe. The lungs supply the blood with oxygen and rid the blood of carbon dioxide.

lunge (luhnj)
verb To leap or plunge forward suddenly.
noun A sudden forward movement.
▶ *verb* **lunging, lunged**

lu·pus (**loo**-puhs) *noun* A disease that causes severe skin sores, body aches, shortness of breath, and heart or kidney problems.

lurch (lurch)
verb To stagger or move forward in a sudden, unsteady way.
noun A sudden, unsteady movement.
idiom If you **leave** someone **in the lurch,** you leave the person in a difficult situation, needing help.
▶ *verb* **lurches, lurching, lurched** ▶ *noun, plural* **lurches**

lure (loor)
verb To attract or tempt someone or something.
noun Something that has a strong power to attract.
▶ *verb* **luring, lured**

lurk (lurk) *verb* **1.** To lie hidden, especially for an evil purpose. **2.** To view but not participate in online social networks.
▶ *verb* **lurking, lurked**

lus·cious (**luhsh**-uhs) *adjective* Having a rich, sweet taste. ▶ *adverb* **lusciously**

lush (luhsh) *adjective* Growing thickly or in abundance. ▶ *adjective* **lusher, lushest**

lust (luhst)
verb If you **lust after** something, you feel a strong desire for it.
noun A strong desire.
▶ *verb* **lusting, lusted** ▶ *adjective* **lustful**

lus·ter (**luhs**-tur) *noun* A bright shine or glow of soft, reflected light.

lute (loot) *noun* A stringed instrument with a body shaped like a pear, played by plucking the strings. **Lute** sounds like **loot.**

Lux·em·bourg (**luhk**-suhm-*burg*) A small, landlocked country in western Europe. It was one of the six countries that founded the European Economic Community, now known as the European Union, in 1957.

lux·u·ry (**luhk**-shur-ee *or* **luhg**-zhur-ee) *noun* **1.** Something expensive that is nice to have but that you do not really need. **2.** Something that you enjoy or welcome that you are not always able to have or do. **3.** If you live **in luxury,** you live a very comfortable life, surrounded by expensive and beautiful things.
adjective Expensive and beautiful but not necessary.
▶ *adjective* **luxurious** (luhg-**zhoor**-ee-uhs)

lye (lye) *noun* A very strong substance that is used in making soap and detergents. Lye is made through a chemical process or by soaking wood ashes in water. **Lye** sounds like **lie.**

Lyme disease (**lime** di-*zeez*) *noun* A bacterial disease transmitted by the bite of a tick. If it is not treated early, it can lead to joint pain, arthritis, and heart and nerve problems.

lymph (limf) *noun* A clear liquid that carries nutrients and white blood cells throughout the body while cleansing waste.

lynx (lingks) *noun* A wildcat with long legs, a short tail, light brown or orange fur, and tufts of hair on its ears. ▶ *noun, plural* **lynx** *or* **lynxes**

L

lyre (lire) *noun* A small, stringed, harplike instrument played mostly in ancient Egypt, Israel, and Greece.

lyr·ic (**lir**-ik)
noun, plural **lyrics** The words of a song.
noun A short poem expressing the writer's feelings or mood.

lyr·i·cal (**lir**-i-kuhl) *adjective* **1.** Expressing a strong, personal emotion, especially in a way that suggests a song. **2.** Like a song, or fit for singing.

M

---

ma'am (mam) *noun* A polite or respectful way of addressing a woman. Ma'am is short for **madam.**

ma·ca·bre (muh-**kahb** *or* muh-**kah**-bruh) *adjective* Terrifying and gruesome.

mac·a·ro·ni (*mak*-uh-**roh**-nee) *noun* Pasta in the shape of curved, hollow tubes.

Mac·e·do·ni·a (*mas*-uh-**doh**-nee-uh) A country on the Balkan Peninsula in Southeastern Europe. Alexander the Great (356–323 B.C.), a Greek king of Macedonia, conquered the Persian Empire and extended Greek culture throughout many parts of the world. In modern times, Macedonia was part of Yugoslavia, becoming independent in 1991.

Mach (mahk) *noun* A unit for measuring speed, often used for aircraft. Mach 1 is the speed of sound, 761 miles per hour at sea level.

ma·chet·e (muh-**shet**-ee) *noun* A long, heavy knife with a broad blade, used as a tool and weapon.

ma·chine (muh-**sheen**) *noun* **1.** A piece of equipment whose different pieces work together to do a job, often using electricity or an engine. **2.** A simple device that makes it easier to move something. Levers, screws, and pulleys are simple machines. **3. machine gun** An automatic gun that can fire bullets very quickly one after another.

ma·chin·er·y (muh-**shee**-nur-ee) *noun* The parts of a machine, or a group of machines that do the same work or related kinds of work.

ma·chin·ist (muh-**shee**-nist) *noun* A person who runs machines that make tools and parts.

mack·er·el (**mak**-ur-uhl) *noun* A shiny saltwater fish that can be used as food. ▸ *noun, plural* **mackerel** *or* **mackerels**

mac·ro (**mak**-roh) *noun* A short computer program that performs a number of instructions with a single command.

mad (mad) *adjective* **1.** Very angry. **2.** Insane; mentally ill. **3.** Extremely foolish or crazy. **4.** Having the disease rabies. **5. be mad about** (informal) To like someone or something very much.
▸ *adjective* **madder, maddest** ▸ *adverb* **madly** ▸ *noun* **madness**

Mad·a·gas·car (*mad*-uh-**gas**-kur) A large island nation in the Indian Ocean. It lies off the southeastern coast of Africa, opposite Mozambique. A former French colony, Madagascar is famous for its thousands of unique species of plants and animals, in particular its 99 species of tree-dwelling primates called lemurs. Only Australia, which is 13 times larger than Madagascar, has more unique species.

mad·am (**mad**-uhm) *noun* A polite or respectful way of addressing a woman, used in formal speech and writing.

made (made) *verb* The past tense and past participle of **make.** Made sounds like **maid.**

mag·a·zine (**mag**-uh-*zeen*) *noun* **1.** A monthly or weekly publication that can contain stories, articles, photographs, advertisements, and other material. **2.** A room or building for storing ammunition or weapons. **3.** The part of a gun that holds the bullets.

mag·got (**mag**-uht) *noun* The larva of certain flies that looks like a small worm. It often feeds on rotting animal flesh.

Ma·gi (**may**-*jye*) *noun, plural* In the New Testament, the three kings who visited the baby Jesus, bringing gifts.

mag·ic (**maj**-ik)
noun **1.** The power or forces that some people believe can make impossible things happen. **2.** Tricks done to entertain people, such as pulling a rabbit out of a hat or making something disappear.
adjective Having the power to make impossible things happen or appear to happen.
▶ *adjective* **magical** ▶ *adverb* **magically**

ma·gi·cian (muh-**jish**-uhn) *noun* **1.** Someone who is thought to have the ability to perform magic and make impossible things happen. **2.** An entertainer who performs tricks before an audience.

mag·is·trate (**maj**-i-*strate*) *noun* A government official who can act as a judge in a court.

mag·lev (**mag**-*lev*) *noun* Short for *magnetic levitation*, a system of high-speed train transportation in which the train uses powerful magnets to float above its track.

mag·ma (**mag**-muh) *noun* Melted rock found beneath the earth's surface that becomes lava when it flows out of volcanoes.

mag·ne·si·um (mag-**nee**-zee-uhm) *noun* An element that is a light, silver-white metal that burns with a bright white light.

mag·net (**mag**-nit) *noun* A piece of metal that attracts iron or steel. Magnets have two ends, or poles, called north and south. ▶ *noun* **magnetism** (**mag**-ni-*tiz*-uhm)

mag·net·ic (**mag**-*net*-ik) *adjective* **1.** Acting like or including a magnet. **2.** Very attractive or exciting.

mag·net·ic field (mag-**net**-ik **feeld**) *noun* The area around a magnet or electric current that has the power to attract other metals, usually iron or steel.

mag·net·ic pole (mag-**net**-ik **pole**) *noun* **1.** Either of the two points of a magnet where its magnetic force seems to be strongest. **2.** Either of the two points of the earth's surface where the earth's magnetic pull is strongest. One of these points is near the North Pole; the other is near the South Pole.

mag·net·ic tape (mag-**net**-ik **tape**) *noun* A thin ribbon of plastic coated with a magnetic material on which sound, images, and other information can be recorded or stored.

mag·net·ize (mag-nuh-*tize*) *verb* To make something magnetic, either by exposing it to an electric current or by attaching a magnet to it. ▶ *verb* **magnetizing, magnetized** ▶ *noun* **magnetization**

mag·nif·i·cent (mag-**nif**-i-suhnt) *adjective* Extremely beautiful, good, or big. ▶ *noun* **magnificence** ▶ *adverb* **magnificently**

mag·ni·fy (**mag**-nuh-fye) *verb* **1.** To make something appear larger so that it is easier to see, usually using a lens or mirror. **2.** To make something seem bigger, more important, or more effective.
▶ *verb* **magnifies, magnifying, magnified** ▶ *noun* **magnification** ▶ *adjective* **magnified**

mag·ni·fy·ing glass (**mag**-nuh-*fye*-ing glas) *noun* A lens that is thicker in the middle than at the edges, causing small things to appear large. ▶ *noun, plural* **magnifying glasses**

mag·ni·tude (**mag**-ni-tood) *noun* The size or importance of something.

mag·no·li·a (mag-**nohl**-yuh) *noun* A tree or tall shrub that has large, fragrant, white, pink, purple, or yellow flowers.

M

mag·pie (**mag**-pye) *noun* A noisy, long-tailed, black and white bird that is related to crows.

ma·hog·a·ny (muh-**hah**-guh-nee) *noun* 1. A tropical tree with hard, dark, reddish-brown wood, or the wood from this tree. 2. A dark, reddish-brown color. ▶ *noun, plural* **mahoganies**

maid (mayd) *noun* 1. A woman who is paid to clean a house or hotel rooms. 2. **maid of honor** An unmarried woman who is the bride's chief attendant at a wedding.

maid·en (**may**-duhn) *noun* 1. A young, unmarried woman. 2. **maiden voyage** *or* **maiden flight** The first trip made by a particular ship or plane.

maid·en name (**may**-duhn **name**) *noun* The last name that a married woman used before she was married. Some women continue to use their maiden names after they marry.

mail (mayl) *noun* 1. Letters and packages sent through a public postal system. 2. **mail order** A way to buy things in which you order and pay for the item and it is mailed to you. *verb* To send a letter or package through the mail. **Mail** sounds like **male.** ▶ *verb* **mailing, mailed**

mail·box (**mayl**-bahks) *noun* 1. A large, public box that you put letters and packages in so they can be picked up by a mail carrier. 2. A box for letters and packages that are delivered to a home or business. ▶ *noun, plural* **mailboxes**

mail car·ri·er (**mayl** kar-ee-ur) *noun* A person who delivers mail to a house or business or picks it up from mailboxes. Also called a *letter carrier*.

mail·man (**mayl**-man) *noun* A male mail carrier. ▶ *noun, plural* **mailmen**

maim (maym) *verb* To injure a part of the body so it is permanently damaged. ▶ *verb* **maiming, maimed**

main (mayn) *adjective* Largest, or most important. *noun* A large pipe that supplies water or gas to a building or that removes waste.

Main sounds like **mane.**

Maine (mayn) A state in the northeastern United States. It is the northernmost state in New England and the easternmost state in the country, known for its lobsters and scenic, rocky coastline.

main·frame (**mayn**-frame) *noun* A large and very powerful computer that can help to run smaller computers.

main·land (**mayn**-luhnd) *noun* The largest part of a country, territory, or continent, rather than its islands or peninsulas.

main·ly (**mayn**-lee) *adverb* For the most part.

main·stay (**mayn**-stay) *noun* 1. A heavy rope or cable that supports or steadies the mast of a sailing ship. 2. A person or thing that is the most basic or important part of something.

main·stream (**mayn**-streem) *noun* People, ideas, or activities that are thought to be normal or typical. *verb* To place a child with disabilities in a regular classroom. ▶ *verb* **mainstreaming, mainstreamed**

main·tain (mayn-**tayn**) *verb* 1. To keep something in good condition. 2. To state an opinion strongly. 3. To make an effort to keep something at the same level or rate. 4. To provide support for somebody. ▶ *verb* **maintaining, maintained**

main·te·nance (**mayn**-tuh-nuhns) *noun* 1. The process of keeping something in good condition by checking and repairing it. 2. Money that helps to take care of someone.

maize (maze) *noun* Corn. **Maize** sounds like **maze.**

ma·jes·tic (muh-**jes**-tik) *adjective* 1. Having the appearance or qualities of a powerful ruler. 2. Having a lot of power or beauty. ▶ *adverb* **majestically**

maj·es·ty (**maj**-i-stee) *noun* 1. Impressiveness or dignity. 2. **His Majesty** *or* **Her Majesty** A formal title for a king or queen.

M

ma·jor (**may**-jur)
adjective 1. Larger, more serious, or more important. 2. A **major** scale in music has a half step between the third and fourth and the seventh and eighth notes.
noun 1. The main subject studied by a student at a college or university. 2. An officer in the army and other branches of the armed forces who ranks above a captain.

ma·jor·ette (*may*-juh-**ret**) *noun* A girl or woman who twirls a baton in a marching band.

ma·jor·i·ty (muh-**jor**-i-tee) *noun*
1. More than half the people or things in a group. 2. The number of votes by which someone wins an election. 3. The status of being legally an adult, usually by reaching the age of 18 or 21.
▶ *noun, plural* **majorities**

make (make)
verb 1. To build, create, produce, or say something. 2. To do a specific action. 3. To cause something to happen. 4. To add up to. 5. To earn. 6. To turn out to be. 7. To cause to become. 8. To get on a team. 9. **make believe** To pretend or imagine. 10. **make out** To be able to see something. 11. **make up** To become friends again after a fight. 12. **make up** To do something later because you could not do it at the original time.
noun A particular brand or type of product.
▶ *verb* **making, made**

make-be·lieve (**make**-bi-*leev*)
noun Playful pretending or imagination.
adjective Imaginary, or not real.

make·shift (**make**-*shift*) *adjective* Made from things that are available to use for a short time.

make·up (**make**-*uhp*) *noun* 1. A substance applied to the face to change or improve its appearance, used mainly by women. 2. The way something is put together. 3. Personality.

ma·lar·i·a (muh-**lair**-ee-uh) *noun* A serious disease that people get from a particular kind of mosquito. Symptoms include chills, fever, and sweating.

Ma·la·wi (muh-**lah**-wee) A country in southeast Africa. Malawi has the largest concentration of rock drawings in Central Africa: Its Chongoni Rock Art Area is a World Heritage Site and includes some rock drawings that go back to the Stone Age. One of the most densely populated countries in the world, Malawi is among the least developed and has a largely agricultural economy.

Ma·lay Pe·nin·su·la (muh-**lay** puh-**nin**-suh-luh) A peninsula extending off the mainland of Southeast Asia, forming the southernmost part of Asia. The Malay Peninsula stretches south and includes the countries of Thailand, Myanmar, Singapore, and Malaysia.

Ma·lay·sia (muh-**lay**-zhuh) A country in Southeast Asia that is separated into two regions by the South China Sea. Part of the country lies just south of Thailand on the Malay Peninsula, and the rest of Malaysia occupies the northern one-third of the island of Borneo. Orangutans are found only in the rain forests of Borneo and of the neighboring Indonesian island of Sumatra.

Mal·dives (**mawl**-deevz *or* **mal**-divez) An island nation in the Indian Ocean consisting of 26 atolls. Because of their low elevation, the Maldives are at particular risk of being lost to rising sea levels from global warming.

male (mayl)
noun A person or animal of the sex that cannot lay eggs or have babies.
adjective Of, having to do with, or typical of men.
Male sounds like **mail.**

Ma·li (**mah**-lee) A country in West Africa. Much of northern Mali lies in the Sahara Desert. A French colony until 1960, Mali is now a stable democracy. For centuries, Timbuktu, Mali's most famous city, has been a trading site for salt, with caravans of camels arriving from the salt mines hundreds of miles away. The camels cross the Sahara carrying the large slabs of salt.

mal·ice (**mal**-is) *noun* A desire to hurt or embarrass someone.

ma·li·cious (muh-**lish**-uhs) *adjective* Intended to hurt or embarrass someone. ▸ *adverb* **maliciously**

ma·lign (muh-**line**)
verb To say hurtful or untrue things about someone.
adjective Evil or intended to cause harm.
▸ *verb* **maligning, maligned**

ma·lig·nan·cy (muh-**lig**-nuhn-see) *noun* A cancerous tumor. ▸ *noun, plural* **malignancies**

ma·lig·nant (muh-**lig**-nuhnt) *adjective*
1. Dangerous because it cannot be controlled and usually causes death.
2. Evil and threatening.
▸ *adverb* **malignantly**

mall (mawl) *noun* A large, enclosed shopping center. **Mall** sounds like **maul.**

mal·lard (**mal**-urd) *noun* A common wild duck. The male has a green head, a white band around the neck, and a dark body.

mal·le·a·ble (**mal**-ee-uh-buhl) *adjective*
1. Soft and easily formed into different shapes. 2. Easily controlled or influenced by other people.

mal·let (**mal**-it) *noun* 1. A wooden hammer with a heavy round head. 2. A wooden club with a long handle, used to hit the ball in croquet or polo.

mal·nu·tri·tion (*mal*-noo-**trish**-uhn) *noun* Sickness or weakness caused by not eating enough food, or by eating food that is not good for you.

malt (mawlt) *noun* Grain, usually barley, that has been soaked and dried. It is often used to make alcoholic drinks. ▸ *adjective* **malted**

Mal·ta (**mawl**-tuh) A southern European country consisting of a group of islands off the south coast of Sicily. Many different nations have invaded and ruled Malta over the centuries because of its strategic location in the Mediterranean Sea.

malt·ed milk (**mawl**-tid **milk**) *noun* A milkshake flavored with malt.

mal·treat (mal-**treet**) *verb* To be cruel to a person or an animal. ▸ *verb* **maltreating, maltreated** ▸ *noun* **maltreatment**

mal·ware (**mal**-wair) *noun* Software that is intended to harm or create problems. Malware gets onto computers through an Internet connection or email attachment.

mam·mal (**mam**-uhl) *noun* A warm-blooded animal that has hair or fur and usually gives birth to live babies. Female mammals produce milk to feed their young.

mam·moth (**mam**-uhth)
noun An animal that looked like a large elephant, with long, curved tusks and shaggy hair. Mammoths lived during the Ice Age and are now extinct.
adjective Huge or taking a lot of effort.

man (man)
noun 1. An adult male human being.
2. Humans in general. 3. A piece used in games such as chess and checkers.
verb To work with a piece of equipment.
▸ *noun, plural* **men** ▸ *verb* **manning, manned** ▸ *noun* **manhood** ▸ *noun* **manliness** ▸ *adjective* **manly**

man·age (**man**-ij) *verb* 1. To be in charge of a store, business, or process. 2. To succeed in doing something that is difficult.
▸ *verb* **managing, managed**

man·age·ment (**man**-ij-muhnt) *noun*
1. The act of controlling or dealing with people, animals, or things. 2. The people who run a business or an organization.

man·a·ger (**man**-i-jur) *noun* Someone in charge of a store, a business, or a process, or in charge of a group of people at work. ▸ *adjective* **managerial** (man-i-**jeer**-ee-uhl)

man·a·tee (**man**-uh-tee) *noun* A large, plant-eating ocean mammal with flippers and a flat tail that lives in warm coastal waters and rivers.

M

man·da·rin (**man**-dur-in) *noun* **1.** A high official in ancient China. **2. Mandarin** The official language of the People's Republic of China. **3.** A small, sweet orange with a thin rind that is easy to peel. It is also called a **mandarin orange.**

man·date (**man**-date)
noun **1.** A task or policy that an elected official has to carry out. **2.** An order given by someone in charge.
verb To authorize or require.
▶ *verb* **mandating, mandated**

man·da·to·ry (**man**-duh-*tor*-ee) *adjective* Necessary or required, usually because of a rule or law.

man·do·lin (**man**-duh-lin) *noun* A small, pear-shaped instrument like a guitar.

mane (mayn) *noun* The long, thick hair on the head and neck of lions, horses, and some other animals. **Mane** sounds like **main.**

ma·neu·ver (muh-**noo**-vur)
noun A difficult movement that requires planning and skill.
noun, plural **maneuvers** Training exercises for battle that involve a large number of soldiers, tanks, and other equipment.
verb To move something carefully.
▶ *verb* **maneuvering, maneuvered**

man·ga (**mahng**-guh) *noun* A kind of Japanese comic that often has stories with a science fiction theme.

man·ger (**mayn**-jur) *noun* A large, open box that holds food for cattle and horses.

man·gle (**mang**-guhl) *verb* To spoil or destroy something by cutting, tearing, or crushing it. ▶ *verb* **mangling, mangled** ▶ *adjective* **mangled**

man·go (**mang**-goh) *noun* A tropical fruit with a large flat seed and sweet orange flesh. ▶ *noun, plural* **mangoes** *or* **mangos**

man·hole (**man**-*hole*) *noun* A covered hole in the street that leads to sewers or underground pipes or wires.

man·hood (**man**-hud) *noun* **1.** The time or state of being a man instead of a boy. **2.** Men as a group.

ma·ni·ac (**may**-nee-*ak*) *noun* **1.** A person who is crazy or acts in a dangerous or violent way. **2.** A person who is very enthusiastic about something.
▶ *adjective* **maniacal** (muh-**nye**-uh-kuhl)

man·i·cure (**man**-i-kyoor)
noun The cleaning, shaping, and polishing of the fingernails.
verb To clean, shape, and polish, especially the fingernails.
▶ *verb* **manicuring, manicured**

ma·nip·u·late (muh-**nip**-yuh-*late*)
verb **1.** To use or control a person or an event for your own benefit. **2.** To handle or control something skillfully.
▶ *verb* **manipulating, manipulated**
▶ *noun* **manipulation** ▶ *adjective* **manipulative**

Man·i·to·ba (*man*-i-**toh**-buh) A province in the middle of Canada. It has more than 110,000 lakes and is home to large Ukrainian and Icelandic communities. The northern Manitoba town of Churchill, in the Canadian Arctic, is known as the polar bear capital of the world and attracts visitors who take expeditions across the tundra to see the polar bears.

man·kind (**man**-*kinde*) *noun* The human race, or human beings as a group.

man·made (**man**-made) *adjective* Made by people, not produced naturally.

man·ne·quin (**man**-i-kin) *noun* A life-sized model of a human being, used especially to display clothing for sale in a store.

man·ner (**man**-ur)
noun **1.** The way in which something is done. **2.** The way in which a person behaves around other people. **3.** Kind.
noun, plural **manners** Polite behavior. **Manner** sounds like **manor.**

man·ner·ism (**man**-uh-*riz*-uhm) *noun* A small gesture or other movement that a person has a habit of making, usually without thinking.

man·or (**man**-ur) *noun* **1.** A lord's estate in the Middle Ages. **2.** A mansion. **Manor** sounds like **manner**.

man·sion (**man**-shuhn) *noun* A very large and impressive house.

man·slaugh·ter (**man**-*slaw*-tur) *noun* The crime of killing someone without intending to do it.

man·tel (**man**-tuhl) *noun* A wooden or stone shelf above a fireplace. **Mantel** sounds like **mantle**.

man·tle (**man**-tuhl) *noun* **1.** A loose cloak without sleeves. **2.** Something that covers or hides like a mantle. **3.** The part of the earth between the crust and the core. **Mantle** sounds like **mantel**.

man·u·al (**man**-yoo-uhl) *adjective* **1.** Operated or done with your hands rather than with electricity or machines. **2. manual labor** Hard work that uses your hands or your strength. *noun* A book of instructions that tells you how to do something or operate a machine.
▶ *adverb* **manually**

man·u·fac·ture (*man*-yuh-**fak**-chur) *verb* **1.** To make something, often with machines. **2.** To make something up, usually a story or an explanation.
▶ *verb* **manufacturing, manufactured** ▶ *noun* **manufacturer**

man·u·fac·tured (*man*-yuh-**fak**-churd) *adjective* Made by people or in a factory, rather than occurring naturally.

man·u·fac·tur·ing (*man*-yuh-**fak**-chur-ing) *noun* The activity or industry of making something on a large scale using special equipment or machinery. *adjective* Of or having to do with the large-scale production of something.

ma·nure (muh-**noor**) *noun* Animal waste that is used as fertilizer.

man·u·script (**man**-yuh-*skript*) *noun* An original handwritten or typed document, especially the content of a book before it is printed.

man·y (**men**-ee) *adjective* **1.** A lot of. **2.** Questions or sentences with **how many** are about the number of people or things involved.
pronoun A large number of people or things.
noun A large but indefinite number.
▶ *adjective* **more, most**

map (map) *noun* A drawing of an area, showing natural features, roads, towns, and other important objects.
verb **1.** To make a map of a place. **2. map out** To plan something carefully.
▶ *verb* **mapping, mapped**

ma·ple (**may**-puhl) *noun* A tree that has large, pointed leaves and hard wood. Some maples produce sap that is used to make maple syrup.

mar (mahr) *verb* To damage or spoil something. ▶ *verb* **marring, marred**

mar·a·thon (**mar**-uh-*thahn*) *noun* **1.** A running race that is 26 miles and 385 yards long. **2.** Any task or competition that is tiring and takes a long time.

mar·ble (**mahr**-buhl) *noun* **1.** A type of hard stone used to make buildings, sculptures, and fixtures for kitchens and bathrooms. Marble is usually white but can have different colors or streaks of color. **2.** A small, hard glass ball used in children's games. **3. marbles** A game in which these balls are rolled on the ground.

march (mahrch) *verb* **1.** To walk with even steps, often in a group. **2.** To walk somewhere quickly and in a determined way. *noun* **1.** A piece of music with a strong beat, intended to accompany marching. **2.** A large, organized group of people walking together to protest or show support for something.
▶ *noun, plural* **marches** ▶ *verb* **marches, marching, marched**

March (mahrch) *noun* The third month on the calendar, after February and before April. March has 31 days.

mare (mair) *noun* The female of certain animals, such as the horse, donkey, and zebra.

M

mar·ga·rine (**mahr**-jur-in) *noun* A yellow spread, similar to butter, that is usually made from vegetable oil.

mar·gin (**mahr**-jin) *noun* 1. The blank space that runs around the outer edges of a page. 2. An amount, especially of time, in addition to what is needed. 3. An amount by which something wins or falls short, especially in a contest or vote.

mar·gin·al (**mahr**-juh-nuhl) *adjective* 1. Written in the margin of a page. 2. Small or not very important. 3. Barely good enough.

mar·i·gold (**mar**-ri-gohld) *noun* A garden plant that has orange, yellow, or red flowers.

mar·i·juan·a (*mar*-uh-**wah**-nuh) *noun* A drug made from the dried leaves and buds of the hemp plant.

ma·rim·ba (muh-**rim**-buh) *noun* A kind of xylophone, originally from Africa, with wooden bars on top of gourds or tubes to make the sound louder.

ma·ri·na (muh-**ree**-nuh) *noun* A special harbor for small private boats.

mar·i·na·ra (*mar*-uh-**nar**-uh) *adjective* Made with tomatoes.

ma·rine (muh-**reen**)
adjective 1. Of or having to do with the ocean. 2. Of or having to do with ships or navigation.
noun **Marine** A member of the U.S. Marine Corps.

Ma·rine Corps (muh-**reen** kor) *noun* One of the armed forces of the United States. Marines are trained to fight on both land and water.

mar·i·o·nette (*mar*-ee-uh-**net**) *noun* A puppet, usually made of wood, that you move by pulling strings or wires attached to parts of its body.

mar·i·time (**mar**-i-*time*) *adjective* 1. Of or having to do with the sea, ships, or navigation. 2. Of, relating to, or near the sea.

mark (mahrk)
noun 1. A small, visible area usually caused by damage. 2. A written sign or symbol. 3. A line or an object that shows the position of something. 4. A grade on a piece of schoolwork.

5. Something that shows clearly.
verb To show clearly where something is or was.
idiom **make your mark** To have an impressive and lasting effect in a particular field.
▶ *verb* **marking, marked**

marked (mahrkt) *adjective* 1. Having one or more visible marks. 2. Very noticeable.

mark·er (**mahr**-kur) *noun* 1. A pen that has a wide tip, usually made of felt. 2. An object or event that gives information about something. 3. An object such as a stone or sign that tells people something important about a place. 4. A small object used in a game to show a player's position.

mar·ket (**mahr**-kit)
noun 1. A place or a business where people buy and sell food or other goods. 2. The amount of demand for something.
verb 1. To offer for sale. 2. To advertise or promote something so people will want to buy it.
idiom **on the market** Available for people to buy.

mar·ket·ing (**mahr**-ki-ting) *noun* The act of promoting and selling products or services.

market·place (**mahr**-kit-*plase*) *noun* 1. A place, such as a town square, where many individual sellers offer their goods for sale. 2. Business and trade in general or as a whole.

mar·ket re·search (**mahr**-kit *ree*-surch) *noun* The process of collecting information about the products that customers buy and new products that they might want.

marks·man (**mahrks**-muhn) *noun* A person who is an expert at shooting a gun. ▶ *noun, plural* **marksmen**

mar·ma·lade (**mahr**-muh-*lade*) *noun* A jam made from the peel and juice of oranges or other citrus fruit.

ma·roon (muh-**roon**)
noun A dark reddish-brown color.
adjective Dark reddish brown.
verb To leave someone in a place that is difficult to escape from.
▶ *verb* **marooning, marooned**

mar·quee (mahr-**kee**) *noun* A large sign above a theater entrance that displays the name of the current play or movie.

mar·riage (**mar**-ij) *noun* **1.** The state of being married, or the relationship between husband and wife. **2.** The act of marrying someone, or the wedding ceremony.

mar·ried (**mar**-eed) *adjective* Having a husband or wife.

mar·row (**mar**-oh) *noun* The soft substance inside bones that produces blood cells.

mar·ry (**mar**-ee) *verb* **1.** To legally become someone's husband or wife in a formal ceremony. **2.** To perform a marriage ceremony.
▶ *verb* **marries, marrying, married**

Mars (mahrz) *noun* The fourth planet in distance from the sun, between the earth and Jupiter. Mars is the second-smallest planet in our solar system.

marsh (mahrsh) *noun* An area of wet, muddy land. ▶ *noun, plural* **marshes** ▶ *adjective* **marshy**

marshal (**mahr**-shuhl)
noun **1.** A police officer who is responsible for a particular area.
2. An officer in the fire department.
3. A person who helps organize a public event such as a parade.
verb To bring together a group of people or things and arrange them for a purpose.
Marshal sounds like **martial**. ▶ *verb* **marshaling, marshaled**

Mar·shall Is·lands (**mahr**-shuhl **eye**-luhnds) A nation of atolls and islands in the middle of the Pacific Ocean, just north of the equator. Independent since 1986, the Marshall Islands were the site of U.S. nuclear tests between 1947 and 1962, when they were a U.S. territory.

marsh·mal·low (mahrsh-**mel**-oh) *noun* A soft, white, spongy candy.

mar·su·pi·al (mahr-**soo**-pee-uhl) *noun* Any of a large group of animals that includes the kangaroo, the koala, and the opossum. Female marsupials carry their babies in pouches on their abdomens.

mar·tial (**mahr**-shuhl)
adjective Of or having to do with war or soldiers.
noun **1. martial art** A style of fighting or self-defense that comes mostly from Asia. Judo and karate are martial arts.
2. martial law Rule by the army in time of war or disaster.
Martial sounds like **marshal**.

mar·tin (**mahr**-tin) *noun* A bird related to swallows that eats insects while flying.

Mar·tin Lu·ther King, Jr., Day (**mahr**-tin **loo**-thur **king joon**-yur *day*) *noun* A national holiday that honors the birth of Dr. Martin Luther King, Jr., the African-American civil rights leader who was assassinated in 1968. It is celebrated on the third Monday of January.

mar·tyr (**mahr**-tur) *noun* A person who is killed or made to suffer because of his or her beliefs. ▶ *noun* **martyrdom** (**mahr**-tur-duhm)

mar·vel (**mahr**-vuhl)
verb To be filled with surprise, admiration, or wonder.
noun Someone or something that causes a feeling of wonder.
▶ *verb* **marveling, marveled**

mar·vel·ous (**mahr**-vuh-luhs) *adjective* **1.** Causing surprise, wonder, or admiration. **2.** Very good or outstanding.
▶ *adverb* **marvelously**

Mar·y·land (**mer**-uh-luhnd) A state in the Mid-Atlantic region of the United States. It lies on both sides of the Chesapeake Bay, which is the largest estuary in the U.S. Maryland is known for seafood, especially crabs, and for the wild horses that live on Assateague, an island off the eastern coast of Maryland and Virginia.

mas·car·a (mas-**kar**-uh) *noun* Makeup put on eyelashes to darken them and make them look thicker and longer.

mas·cot (**mas**-kaht) *noun* An animal or symbol that is supposed to bring good luck, especially an animal that represents a sports team.

M

M

mas·cu·line (**mas**-kyuh-lin) *adjective*
1. Of or having to do with men.
2. Having qualities that are supposed to be typical of men.
▶ *noun* **masculinity** (*mas*-kyuh-**lin**-i-tee)

mash (mash)
verb To crush something into a soft mass.
noun A soft, pulpy mixture.
▶ *verb* **mashes, mashing, mashed**

mask (mask)
noun A covering for the face to hide, protect, or disguise it.
verb To hide or disguise something.
▶ *verb* **masking, masked** ▶ *adjective* **masked**

ma·son (**may**-suhn) *noun* A person who makes or builds with stone, cement, or bricks.

ma·son·ry (**may**-suhn-ree) *noun* Part of a building or wall that is made of stone, cement, or bricks.

mas·quer·ade (*mas*-kuh-**rade**)
noun A party or other event at which all the people dress up in costumes.
verb 1. To dress up in order to disguise yourself at a party or other event. 2. To pretend to be something you are not.
▶ *verb* **masquerading, masqueraded**

mass (mas)
noun 1. A large amount of something. 2. A large number of people or things grouped together in a messy way. 3. In science, the amount of physical matter that an object contains.
noun, plural **the masses** The ordinary people in a society.
verb To gather together or collect in a mass or single body.
adjective Done or carried out by a large number of people or things.
▶ *noun, plural* **masses** ▶ *verb* **massing, massed**

Mass (mas) *noun* The main religious service in the Roman Catholic Church and some other churches.

Mas·sa·chu·setts (*mas*-uh-**choo**-sits) A state in the New England region of the northeastern United States. It is where the Pilgrims landed in 1620

and established the second permanent English settlement in North America. The state has numerous universities and colleges, including Harvard, Wellesley, and the Massachusetts Institute of Technology, or MIT.

mas·sa·cre (**mas**-uh-kur)
noun The violent killing of a large number of people at the same time, often in battle.
verb To kill a large number of people in a brutal way.
▶ *verb* **massacring, massacred**

mas·sage (muh-**sahzh**)
verb To rub someone's body with the hands in order to loosen the muscles, relieve pain, or help the person relax.
noun The act of rubbing parts of the body with the hands to relieve tension or pain.
▶ *verb* **massaging, massaged**

mas·sive (**mas**-iv) *adjective* Large in size or amount. ▶ *adverb* **massively**

mass me·di·a (mas **mee**-dee-uh) *noun, plural* Forms of communication, such as television, radio, newspapers, and the Internet, that reach a large number of people.

mass pro·duc·tion (mas pruh-**duk**-shuhn) *noun* The method of making large amounts of identical things with machines in a factory. ▶ *verb* **mass-produce**

mass tran·sit (mas **tran**-sit) *noun* A system of subways, buses, and trains that transport large numbers of people into and around major cities.

mast (mast) *noun* A tall, upright pole on a boat or ship that holds up one or more sails.

mas·ter (**mas**-tur)
noun 1. A person with power, rule, or authority over another. 2. An expert.
verb 1. To become very good at something. 2. To have control over something.
adjective Most important or largest.
▶ *verb* **mastering, mastered**

mas·ter·mind (**mas**-tur-*minde*)
verb To plan and control a complicated or difficult activity.
noun The main person who plans and

controls an activity, often a harmful or illegal one.

▶ *verb* **masterminding, masterminded**

mas·ter·piece (**mas**-tur-*pees*) *noun*
1. An extremely good piece of work, especially in the areas of art, literature, or music. 2. A person's greatest achievement.

mas·ter·y (**mas**-tur-ee) *noun* When you have become very good at something, you have **mastery** of it. ▶ *noun, plural* **masteries**

mat (mat)
noun 1. A thick pad of material used to cover and protect a floor, a table, or some other surface. 2. A large, thick floor pad used to protect wrestlers, gymnasts, and other athletes. 3. A thick, tangled mass, especially of hair.
verb To form into a thick mass or become entangled.
Mat sounds like **matte**. ▶ *verb* **matting, matted**

mat·a·dor (**mat**-uh-*dor*) *noun* A person who fights bulls.

match (mach)
noun 1. A small, thin piece of wood or cardboard with a chemical tip that produces a flame when you strike it. 2. Someone or something that is similar to or goes well with another. 3. Someone or something that is equal to another. 4. A game or a sporting competition.
verb 1. To go well with. 2. To equal. 3. To put into competition.
▶ *noun, plural* **matches** ▶ *verb* **matches, matching, matched**

mate (mate)
noun 1. One of a pair. 2. A husband or a wife. 3. The male or female partner of a pair of animals. 4. An officer on a merchant ship. 5. A friend.
verb To join together to produce babies.
▶ *verb* **mating, mated** ▶ *noun* **mating**

ma·te·ri·al (muh-**teer**-ee-uhl)
noun 1. Cloth or fabric. 2. Things you need for a particular project or activity.
adjective 1. Of or having to do with possessions or money rather than ideas or values. 2. Of or having to do with the body.

ma·te·ri·al·is·tic (muh-*teer*-ee-uh-**lis**-tik) *adjective* Too concerned or impressed with money and possessions. ▶ *noun* **materialism**

ma·te·ri·al·ize (muh-**teer**-ee-uh-*lize*) *verb* To appear or to happen. ▶ *verb* **materializing, materialized**

ma·ter·nal (muh-**tur**-nuhl) *adjective* Of or typical of a mother.

ma·ter·ni·ty (muh-**tur**-ni-tee) *noun*
1. Motherhood. 2. **maternity leave** Time off from a job for a woman to give birth and take care of her baby.

math (math) *noun* Short for **mathematics.**

math·e·ma·ti·cian (*math*-uh-muh-**tish**-uhn) *noun* An expert in mathematics.

math·e·mat·ics (*math*-uh-**mat**-iks) *noun* The study of numbers, quantities, shapes, and measurements and how they relate to each other. ▶ *adjective* **mathematical**

mat·i·nee (*mat*-uh-**nay**) *noun* An afternoon performance of a play or showing of a movie.

mat·ri·mo·ny (**mat**-ruh-*moh*-nee) *noun* Marriage. ▶ *adjective* **matrimonial** (*mat*-ruh-**moh**-nee-uhl)

ma·trix (**may**-triks) *noun* An arrangement of numbers or other items in columns and rows. A chart showing the standings of major league baseball teams is a type of matrix. ▶ *noun, plural* **matrices** (**may**-tri-*seez*)

ma·tron (**may**-truhn) *noun* 1. An older woman who is married or widowed.
2. **matron of honor** A married woman who is a bride's most important attendant in her wedding.

matte (mat) *adjective* Dull rather than shiny. **Matte** sounds like **mat.**

mat·ter (**mat**-ur)
noun 1. Something that has weight and takes up space, such as a solid, liquid, or gas. 2. Content or material. 3. Something that you talk about or are interested in. 4. A situation, event, or task that you have to deal with.
verb To be important.
▶ *verb* **mattering, mattered**

M

mat·tress (**mat**-ris) *noun* A large, soft, thick pad that you put on a bed to make it comfortable to sleep on. ▶ *noun, plural* **mattresses**

ma·ture (muh-**choor** *or* muh-**toor**) *adjective* **1.** Adult or fully grown. **2.** Ripe or completely developed. **3.** Behaving in a sensible, responsible way.
verb To develop and become fully mature.
▶ *verb* **maturing, matured** ▶ *adverb* **maturely**

ma·tur·i·ty (muh-**choor**-i-tee) *noun* The state of being fully mature, ripe, or developed.

maul (mawl) *verb* To attack and damage or injure someone or something. **Maul** sounds like **mall**. ▶ *verb* **mauling, mauled**

Mau·ri·ta·ni·a (mor-i-**tay**-nee-uh) A country in North Africa on the Atlantic Ocean. It is on the western edge of the Sahara. About three-fourths of the country is desert or partially desert. Mauritania was a French colony until 1960, and today is an Islamic republic.

Mau·ri·tius (maw-**rish**-uhs) An island nation off the southeast coast of Africa in the Indian Ocean. Uninhabited until it was settled by the Dutch in the 17th century, Mauritius was the home of the dodo, a bird that has been extinct since the late 1600s.

mau·so·le·um (*maw*-suh-**lee**-uhm *or maw*-zuh-**lee**-uhm) *noun* A building that contains a tomb or tombs.

mauve (mohv)
noun A light purple color.
adjective Light purple.

mav·er·ick (**mav**-ur-ik) *noun* A person who does not follow rules and does not think or behave in the same way as other people.

max. (maks) Short for **maximum.**

max·i·mize (**mak**-suh-*mize*) *verb* **1.** To make something as large or as important as possible. **2.** To make a window on a computer desktop fill the entire screen.
▶ *verb* **maximizing, maximized**

max·i·mum (**mak**-suh-muhm) *noun* The largest amount possible.
adjective The greatest in quantity, size, or degree.

may (may) *verb* A helping verb that is used in the following ways: **1.** To say that something is possible or true. **2.** To ask for or give permission. **3.** To say you hope or wish for something.

May (may) *noun* The fifth month on the calendar, after April and before June. May has 31 days.

Ma·ya (**mye**-uh) *noun* A member of a group of Native American tribes who live in southern Mexico and Central America. The Maya flourished until about A.D. 1000. They were conquered by the Spanish during the 16th century. ▶ *noun, plural* **Maya** *or* **Mayas** ▶ *adjective* **Mayan** (**mye**-uhn)

may·be (**may**-bee) *adverb* Used to say that you are uncertain or you do not know if something is true.

May·day (**may**-*day*) *noun* **Mayday** is a word used all over the world to ask for help or rescue.

may·hem (**may**-hem) *noun* Confused or violent disorder.

may·on·naise (**may**-uh-*naze*) *noun* A thick white sauce made from egg yolks, oil, and vinegar or lemon juice.

may·or (**may**-ur) *noun* A person who is elected to be the leader of a town or city government.

maze (maze) *noun* A complicated system of paths or passages, used as a puzzle or as a way of keeping people away from something. **Maze** sounds like **maize.**

MB (**meg**-uh-*bite*) *noun* Short for **megabyte.**

MD (**em**-dee) *noun* Short for the Latin words *medicinae doctor*, which mean "teacher of medicine." This abbreviation is used after a doctor's name.

me (mee) *pronoun* The form of the pronoun *I* used as the object of a verb or a preposition.

mead·ow (**med**-oh) *noun* A grassy field, especially one used for grazing or for harvesting hay.

mead·ow·lark (**med**-oh-*lahrk*) *noun*
A songbird with a pointed bill and
a yellow chest with a black crescent
across it.

mea·ger (**mee**-gur) *adjective* Very small,
or not enough.

meal (meel) *noun* 1. Food that you eat
at a regular time each day. Breakfast,
lunch, and dinner are meals. 2. Grain
that has been crushed into tiny pieces.

mean (meen)
verb 1. To express or refer to
something. 2. To do something
deliberately. 3. To be defined as. 4. To
matter or be important.
adjective 1. Unkind or cruel. 2. Selfish,
greedy, and inconsiderate of others.
3. (slang) Very skillful or excellent.
noun In mathematics, another word
for **average.**
▶ *verb* **meaning, meant** ▶ *adjective*
meaner, meanest ▶ *noun* **meanness**

me·an·der (mee-**an**-dur) *verb* To follow
a route that has a lot of bends. ▶ *verb*
meandering, meandered

mean·ing (**mee**-ning) *noun* 1. The idea
that someone or something expresses
or refers to. 2. The importance or
significance of something.

mean·ing·ful (**mee**-ning-fuhl) *adjective*
Having meaning, significance, or
value; not trivial.

means (meenz) *noun, plural* 1. A way of
getting something done or arriving at
a goal. 2. The money or resources you
need to do something.

meant (ment) *verb* The past tense and
past participle of **mean.**

mean·time (**meen**-*time*) *noun* The time
between two events.

mean·while (**meen**-*wile*) *adverb* 1. In
or during the time between. 2. At the
same time.

mea·sles (**mee**-zuhlz) *noun, plural* An
infectious disease, caused by a virus
that produces fever and a red rash.

mea·sly (**meez**-lee) *adjective*
(informal) Small in size or number;
not enough. ▶ *adjective* **measlier,
measliest**

mea·sure (**mezh**-ur)
verb 1. To find out the size or weight

of something. 2. To have a particular
size, length, or amount.
noun 1. A unit of measurement.
2. An action that has a particular
purpose. 3. The strength or amount
of something. 4. One of the short
sections into which written music is
divided, having a certain number of
beats.
▶ *verb* **measuring, measured**

meas·ure·ment (**mezh**-ur-muhnt) *noun*
1. The act or process of measuring.
2. The size, weight, or amount of
something that has been measured.
3. **measurements** All the measured
dimensions of an object, taken
together. 4. Measures of various parts
of your body, used as a guide to what
size clothing to buy.

meat (meet) *noun* 1. The flesh of an
animal that is eaten as food. 2. The
edible part of a fruit or nut. 3. The
most important part of something.
Meat sounds like **meet.**

me·chan·ic (muh-**kan**-ik) *noun* A person
who repairs machinery, especially
engines.

me·chan·i·cal (muh-**kan**-i-kuhl) *adjective*
1. Of or having to do with machines
or engines. 2. Operated by a machine.
3. Done without thinking.
▶ *adverb* **mechanically**

me·chan·ics (muh-**kan**-iks) *noun* 1. The
science that deals with motion and
forces. 2. The operating parts of
something.

mech·a·nism (**mek**-uh-*niz*-uhm) *noun*
A system of parts working together
inside a machine.

med·al (**med**-uhl) *noun* A piece of metal
with a special shape or design that is
given to someone as an award or for
a special event. **Medal** sounds like
meddle.

med·dle (**med**-uhl) *verb* To get involved
in someone else's personal business.
Meddle sounds like **medal.** ▶ *verb*
meddling, meddled ▶ *noun* **meddler**

med·dle·some (**med**-uhl-suhm)
adjective Inclined to interfere in other
people's business.

M

me·di·a (**mee**-dee-uh) *noun, plural*
1. A plural of **medium**. 2. Ways of communicating with large numbers of people, considered as a group.
3. Substances used to create a work of art.

me·di·an (**mee**-dee-uhn)
noun 1. The middle number, or the average of the two middle numbers, in a series of numbers listed from smallest to largest. 2. A narrow strip of land that separates the opposite sides of a large road.
adjective Located or having a value in the middle.

med·ic (**med**-ik) *noun* A person who is trained to give medical treatment in an emergency or in the military.

Med·i·caid (**med**-i-*kayd*) *noun* A government system that provides medical care for people who cannot afford it.

med·i·cal (**med**-i-kuhl) *adjective* Of or having to do with doctors or medicine. ▶ *adverb* **medically**

Med·i·care (**med**-i-*kair*) *noun* A government system that provides medical care to people over the age of 65.

med·i·ca·tion (*med*-i-**kay**-shuhn) *noun* A substance used for treating an injury or illness.

me·dic·i·nal (muh-**dis**-uh-nuhl) *adjective* Of or having the curing properties of a medicine.

med·i·cine (**med**-i-sin) *noun* 1. A substance, such as a drug, that is used to treat an illness. 2. The study and treatment of diseases and injuries.

me·di·e·val (mee-**dee**-vuhl *or med*-ee-**ee**-vuhl) *adjective* Of or having to do with the Middle Ages, the period of history between approximately A.D. 1000 and 1450.

me·di·o·cre (*me*-dee-**oh**-kur) *adjective* Of only average quality; not very good.

me·di·oc·ri·ty (*mee*-dee-**ah**-kri-tee) *noun* A condition or quality that is only average and not very good.

med·i·tate (**med**-i-*tate*) *verb* 1. To make your mind very quiet by focusing it on a single thing, such as your breath, for a period of time. 2. To think about something in a very focused way.
▶ *verb* **meditating, meditated**

med·i·ta·tion (*med*-i-**tay**-shuhn) *noun* 1. The activity of making your mind quiet by focusing on a single thing. 2. Serious thoughts on a subject that are put into a speech or essay.

Med·i·ter·ra·ne·an Sea (**med**-i-tuh-**ray**-nee-uhn **see**) A sea connected to the Atlantic Ocean on its western edge. It is bordered by Africa to the south and Europe to the north.

me·di·um (**mee**-dee-uhm)
adjective Average or middle in size.
noun 1. The substance that something lives or grows in. 2. A way of communicating information to large numbers of people. 3. Something that is used for a particular purpose. 4. A substance used to create a work of art.
▶ *noun, plural* **media** (**mee**-dee-uh) *or* **mediums**

me·di·um (**mee**-dee-uhm) *noun* A person who claims to communicate with spirits of dead people. ▶ *noun, plural* **mediums**

med·ley (**med**-lee) *noun* 1. A musical piece that consists of parts of different songs. 2. A mixture or assortment of things.

meek (meek) *adjective* Quiet, gentle, and eager to please. ▶ *adjective* **meeker, meekest** ▶ *adverb* **meekly**

meet (meet)
verb 1. To come together with someone or something. 2. To join. 3. To see or be introduced to for the first time. 4. To go to a place and wait for someone to arrive. 5. To fulfill or to be equal to; satisfy.
noun A sports competition.
Meet sounds like **meat**. ▶ *verb* **meeting, met** (met)

meet·ing (**mee**-ting) *noun* A scheduled event in which people meet to discuss or decide something.

meg (meg) *noun* Short for **megabyte**.

meg·a·byte (**meg**-uh-*bite*) *noun* A unit measuring computer memory or file

M

size. A megabyte is about one million bytes. Abbreviated as *MB*.

meg·a·hertz (**meg**-uh-*hurts*) *noun* A unit used to measure the frequency of radio waves and the speed of computer processors. It is equal to one million hertz. Abbreviated as *MHz*.

meg·a·phone (**meg**-uh-*fone*) *noun* A device used to make the voice louder, sometimes shaped like a cone.

meg·a·pix·el (**meg**-uh-*pik*-suhl) *noun* A unit used to tell how precise an image is, or how much space a digital camera can use to store a photograph. It is equal to one million pixels.

mel·an·cho·ly (**mel**-uhn-*kah*-lee) *adjective* Sad or depressed. *noun* Sadness or gloom.
▶ *adjective* **melancholic**

mel·low (**mel**-oh) *adjective* **1.** Soft, rich, and soothing. **2.** Soft, smooth, and fully ripe. *verb* To become gentler and more relaxed.
▶ *verb* **mellowing, mellowed**
▶ *adjective* **mellower, mellowest**

me·lo·di·ous (muh-**loh**-dee-uhs) *adjective* Pleasant to hear, like a melody. ▶ *noun* **melodiousness** ▶ *adverb* **melodiously**

mel·o·dra·mat·ic (*mel*-uh-druh-**mat**-ik) *adjective* Too dramatic or emotional. ▶ *noun* **melodrama** (**mel**-uh-*drah*-muh)

mel·o·dy (**mel**-uh-dee) *noun* An arrangement of musical notes that makes a tune. ▶ *noun, plural* **melodies** ▶ *adjective* **melodic** (muh-**lah**-dik)

mel·on (**mel**-uhn) *noun* A large, round, juicy fruit with a hard skin. Melons grow on vines.

melt (melt) *verb* **1.** To change something from a solid to a liquid by heating it. **2.** To dissolve in liquid. **3.** To fade away or disappear. **4.** If something **melts your heart,** or if your heart melts, you become more gentle and understanding.
▶ *verb* **melting, melted**

melt·down (**melt**-*doun*) *noun* **1.** The melting of the core of a nuclear reactor, which allows dangerous radiation to escape into the atmosphere. **2.** Loss of emotional control because you are tired or stressed.

mem·ber (**mem**-bur) *noun* **1.** A person, animal, or thing that belongs to a group. **2.** A part of the body, especially an arm or a leg.

mem·ber·ship (**mem**-bur-*ship*) *noun* **1.** The state of being a member of something. **2.** All the members of a club or other group.

mem·brane (**mem**-brane) *noun* **1.** A very thin layer of tissue that lines or covers certain organs or cells. **2.** A thin layer of plastic or other material that protects something.

me·men·to (muh-**men**-toh) *noun* A small item you keep to remind you of a person or place.

mem·o (**mem**-oh) *noun* Short for **memorandum.**

mem·o·ra·ble (**mem**-ur-uh-buhl) *adjective* Worth remembering, or easy to remember because of some special feature. ▶ *adverb* **memorably**

mem·o·ran·dum (*mem*-uh-**ran**-duhm) *noun* **1.** A short, written reminder. **2.** A short letter written to people who work in the same organization.
▶ *noun, plural* **memorandums** or **memoranda** (*mem*-uh-**ran**-duh)

me·mo·ri·al (muh-**mor**-ee-uhl) *noun* Something that is built, such as a statue or monument, or done to help people remember a person or an event.
adjective Done to help people remember a person or event.

Me·mo·ri·al Day (muh-**mor**-ee-uhl *day*) *noun* A holiday celebrated on the last Monday of May to honor Americans who have died in wars.

mem·o·rize (**mem**-uh-*rize*) *verb* To learn something so that you remember it exactly later. ▶ *verb* **memorizing, memorized**

M

mem·o·ry (**mem**-ur-ee) *noun* 1. The ability to remember things. 2. A thought of something that you remember from the past. 3. Honor and respect for people or events from the past. 4. The part of a computer in which instructions and information are stored.
▶ *noun, plural* **memories**

mem·o·ry foam (**mem**-ur-ee *fohm*) *noun* A kind of foam that takes the shape of something that touches it but returns to its original shape when the touching stops.

men (men) *noun, plural* The plural of **man.**

men·ace (**men**-is)
noun Something that is dangerous or can cause harm.
verb To endanger or be a threat to someone or something.
▶ *verb* **menacing, menaced** ▶ *adjective* **menacing**

mend (mend)
verb To fix or repair something, especially clothing.
noun If someone or something is **on the mend,** they are getting better after an injury or illness.
▶ *verb* **mending, mended**

me·no·rah (muh-**nor**-uh) *noun* A special holder for seven or nine candles. Menorahs for nine candles are used during Hanukkah, the Jewish "Festival of Lights."

men·tal (**men**-tuhl) *adjective* Having to do with or done in the mind. ▶ *adverb* **mentally**

men·tion (**men**-shuhn)
verb To bring up or speak about briefly.
noun A short statement that refers to someone or something.
▶ *verb* **mentioning, mentioned**

men·u (**men**-yoo) *noun* 1. A list of foods available in a restaurant. 2. A list of choices you can click on in a computer program.

men·u bar (**men**-yoo *bahr*) *noun* A bar across the top of a computer display that contains the titles of menus.

me·ow (mee-**ou**)
verb To make the crying sound a cat makes.
noun The cry of a cat.
▶ *verb* **meowing, meowed**

mer·ce·nar·y (**mur**-suh-*ner*-ee)
noun A professional soldier who works for money, rather than serving in his own country's forces.
adjective Interested only in getting or making money.
▶ *noun, plural* **mercenaries**

mer·chan·dise (**mur**-chuhn-*dize* or **mur**-chuhn-*dise*) *noun* Goods that are bought or sold; things for sale.

mer·chant (**mur**-chuhnt) *noun* 1. A person who sells goods to make money, especially in a store. 2. A country's **merchant marine** is made up of crews and ships that carry goods for trade.

mer·cu·ry (**mur**-kyur-ee) *noun* A silvery metal element that is poisonous and liquid at room temperature. Mercury was once commonly used in thermometers and barometers.

Mer·cu·ry (**mur**-kyur-ee) *noun* The smallest planet in our solar system and the closest planet to the sun.

mer·cy (**mur**-see) *noun* 1. Compassion or forgiveness for someone who should be punished. 2. Something to be thankful for because it stops something unpleasant.
▶ *noun, plural* **mercies** ▶ *adjective* **merciful** ▶ *adverb* **mercifully**

mere (meer) *adjective* Nothing more than; unimportant. ▶ *adjective* **merest**

mere·ly (**meer**-lee) *adverb* Only or just.

merge (murj) *verb* To join together into one. ▶ *verb* **merging, merged**

merg·er (**mur**-jur) *noun* The act of joining two businesses, teams, or other units into one.

me·rid·i·an (muh-**rid**-ee-uhn) *noun* An imaginary circle on the earth's surface that passes through the North and South poles. Meridians are used to show locations of places on earth.

mer·it (**mer**-it)
noun 1. If something has **merit,** it is valuable or praiseworthy. 2. A good point or feature.

M

verb To deserve praise or attention.
noun, plural merits The actual facts of a matter.

▶ **verb meriting, merited**

mer·maid (mur-mayd) **noun** An imaginary sea creature with a woman's head and upper body and a fish's tail instead of legs.

mer·ry (mer-ee) **adjective** Lively and cheerful. ▶ **adjective merrier, merriest**

mer·ry-go-round (mer-ee-goh-round) **noun** A revolving ride at amusement parks and fairs with seats that look like horses or other animals.

me·sa (may-suh) **noun** A large hill with steep sides and a flat top.

mesh (mesh)
noun A woven material made of threads or wires with open spaces between them.
verb To fit together or closely match.
▶ **noun, plural meshes** ▶ **verb meshes, meshing, meshed**

mess (mes)
noun 1. Something that is dirty or untidy. 2. A situation that is full of problems. 3. A meal served to a group of soldiers, sailors, or campers.
4. mess hall A room or building in a military unit or a camp where meals are served and eaten.
verb 1. **mess up** To make something dirty or untidy, or to make something go wrong. 2. If you **mess with** something, you alter it in a way that is not helpful.
▶ **noun, plural messes** ▶ **verb messes, messing, messed**

mes·sage (mes-ij) **noun** 1. A piece of information sent to or left for someone. 2. The meaning or lesson of something.

mes·sage board (mes-ij bord) **noun** A website where people can exchange messages with others.

mes·sen·ger (mes-uhn-jur) **noun** A person who delivers messages and documents.

mess·y (mes-ee) **adjective** Not neat or tidy; not arranged or orderly. ▶ **adjective messier, messiest** ▶ **adverb messily**

met (met) **verb** The past tense and past participle of **meet.**

me·tab·o·lism (muh-tab-uh-liz-uhm) **noun** The process in our bodies that changes the food we eat into the energy we need to breathe, digest, and grow.

met·al (met-uhl) **noun** A solid material such as iron or silver that is usually hard and shiny. Many metals are good conductors of heat and electricity.

me·tal·lic (muh-tal-ik) **adjective** 1. Made of metal or partly of metal. 2. Seeming like metal.

met·a·mor·phic (met-uh-mor-fik) **adjective** Of or having to do with rock that has been formed by pressure and heat.

met·a·mor·pho·sis (met-uh-mor-fuh-sis) **noun** 1. A series of changes some animals, such as caterpillars, go through as they develop into adults. 2. A complete or great change in appearance or form; a transformation.
▶ **noun, plural metamorphoses** (met-uh-mor-fuh-seez)

met·a·phor (met-uh-for) **noun** A word or phrase you use to compare something to something different that has a similar feature, for example, "That performer is a shining star" or "That cat is a lightning bolt when she's scared." ▶ **adjective metaphorical**

me·te·or (mee-tee-ur) **noun** A piece of rock or metal from space that speeds into the earth's atmosphere and forms a streak of light as it burns and falls to the earth.

me·te·or·ite (mee-tee-uh-rite) **noun** A piece of rock from space that falls to the earth.

me·te·o·rol·o·gist (mee-tee-uh-rah-luh-jist) **noun** An expert in the study of the earth's atmosphere and weather.

me·te·or·ol·o·gy (mee-tee-uh-rah-luh-jee) **noun** The study of the earth's atmosphere, especially in relation to climate and weather. ▶ **adjective meteorological** (mee-tee-ur-uh-lah-ji-kuhl)

M

me·ter (mee-tur)
noun **1.** The basic unit of length in the metric system, equal to 39.37 inches or a little more than 3 feet. **2.** A device that measures the amount or speed of something, especially the amount of something that has been used. **3.** The pattern of rhythm in a line of poetry formed by stressing some syllables and not others.
verb To measure with a meter.
▸ *verb* **metering, metered**

meth·ane (meth-ane) *noun* A colorless, odorless gas that burns easily and is used for fuel.

meth·od (meth-uhd) *noun* A particular way of doing something.

me·thod·i·cal (muh-**thah**-di-kuhl) *adjective* Done in a careful or logical way. ▸ *adverb* **methodically**

me·tic·u·lous (muh-**tik**-yuh-luhs) *adjective* Very careful and thorough; paying great attention to detail. ▸ *adverb* **meticulously**

met·ric (met-rik) *adjective* Of or having to do with a measuring system based on the meter and related units.

met·ric sys·tem (met-rik *sis*-tuhm) *noun* A system of measurement based on the meter. In the metric system, the meter is the basic unit of length, the gram is the basic unit of mass or weight, and the liter is the basic unit of liquid volume.

met·ro·nome (met-ruh-*nome*) *noun* A device that makes a regular beat to help musicians play at the correct speed.

met·ro·pol·i·tan (*met*-ruh-**pah**-li-tuhn) *adjective* Of or having to do with a large city, and sometimes its surrounding area.

Mex·i·co (mek-si-*koh*) A country that lies just south of the southwestern United States. Ruled by the Spanish for three centuries, Mexico is a popular tourist destination. Its attractions include enormous pyramids built by the ancient Mayans and Aztecs.

mg (mil-i-*gram*) *noun* Short for **milligram** or the plural form **milligrams.**

MHz (meg-uh-*hurts*) *noun* Short for **megahertz.**

mice (mise) *noun, plural* The plural of **mouse.

Mich·i·gan (mish-i-guhn) A state located in the Great Lakes region of the United States. It consists of two peninsulas and has more freshwater shoreline than any other state, in addition to almost 65,000 inland lakes and ponds. Michigan takes its name from a Native American Ojibwa word that means "large water" or "large lake."

mi·crobe (mye-krobe) *noun* An extremely small living thing, especially one that causes disease.

mi·cro·chip (mye-kroh-*chip*) *noun* A very thin piece of silicon that contains electronic circuits, used in computers and other electronic equipment. Often shortened as **chip.**

Mi·cro·ne·sia (*mye*-kruh-**nee**-zhuh) **1.** A group of thousands of small islands in the western Pacific Ocean, northeast of Australia and New Guinea. Guam, Kiribati, the Marshall Islands, Nauru, the Northern Mariana Islands, and the Federated States of Micronesia are all included in Micronesia. **2. Federated States of Micronesia** An island nation in Micronesia made up of a group of about 607 small islands, spread over almost 1,700 miles in the western Pacific Ocean.

mi·cro·or·gan·ism (*mye*-kroh-**or**-guh-niz-uhm) *noun* A living thing that is so small it can be seen only with a microscope, such as a bacterium or virus.

mi·cro·phone (mye-kruh-*fone*) *noun* An instrument that is used to record sound or make sound louder.

mi·cro·pro·ces·sor (mye-kroh-*prah*-ses-ur) *noun* A computer chip that controls the functions of an electronic device. Microprocessors are often used to program small devices like appliances.

mi·cro·scope (mye-kruh-*skope*) *noun* An instrument that makes very small things look larger so that they can be seen and studied.

mi·cro·scop·ic (mye-kruh-**skah**-pik) *adjective* Extremely small. ▶ *adverb* **microscopically**

mi·cro·wave (**mye**-kroh-*wave*) *noun* **1.** An electromagnetic wave that can pass through solid objects. Microwaves are primarily used in radar, to send messages over long distances, and to cook food in microwave ovens. **2. microwave oven** An oven that cooks food very quickly by sending microwaves into it. Microwaves cook the food from the inside by making the moisture in the food vibrate and heat up.

mid (mid)
adjective In the middle of something. Mid is often used in combination with another word. Mid-January means in the middle of January.
preposition In the middle. This use of mid is found mainly in old songs and poems. *Mid the snows of winter, the house stood snug and warm.*

mid·day (**mid**-*day*)
noun Noon, or the middle part of the day.
adjective Of or having to do with the middle of the day.

mid·dle (**mid**-uhl)
adjective Halfway between two things, sides, or points.
noun The center; the place between the two ends or sides.
idiom **in the middle** Involved in doing something.

mid·dle-aged (**mid**-uhl-**ayjd**) *adjective* A person who is **middle-aged** is between about 45 and 65 years old.

Mid·dle Ag·es (**mid**-uhl **ay**-jiz) *noun* The period of European history from approximately A.D. 1000 to 1450.

mid·dle class (**mid**-uhl **klas**) *noun* The social class that is neither rich nor poor. It falls between the upper class and lower class. ▶ *adjective* **middle-class**

Mid·dle East (**mid**-uhl **eest**) *noun* A region in North Africa and West Asia. It includes Egypt, Iran, Iraq, Israel,

Saudi Arabia, Syria, Lebanon, Turkey, and smaller nearby countries. The countries in the Middle East border on the Mediterranean Sea, the Red Sea, the Arabian Sea, the Caspian Sea, and the Persian Gulf. ▶ *adjective* **Middle Eastern**

Mid·dle Eng·lish (**mid**-uhl **ing**-glish) *noun* The English language that was spoken from around A.D. 1100 to 1500.

mid·dle school (**mid**-uhl *skool*) *noun* A school between elementary school and high school. It usually includes the seventh and eighth grades and sometimes the fifth and sixth grades.

mid·get (**mij**-it) *noun* A very small thing or person. Many people consider this word offensive.

mid·night (**mid**-*nite*)
noun Twelve o'clock at night.
adjective Of or having to do with twelve o'clock at night.

midst (midst) *noun* The middle part.

mid·way
adverb and adjective (**mid**-way) Halfway.
noun (**mid**-way) An area of a carnival or fair in which games, rides, and other amusements are located.

Mid·west (**mid**-west) *noun* The north-central region of the United States, roughly between the Ohio River in the East and the Rocky Mountains in the West.

mid·wife (**mid**-*wife*) *noun* A person who is trained to help women give birth. ▶ *noun, plural* **midwives** ▶ *noun* **midwifery** (mid-**wif**-ur-ee)

might (mite)
noun Strength or power.
verb The past tense of **may**.
Might sounds like **mite.**

might·y (**mye**-tee) *adjective* Powerful. ▶ *adjective* **mightier, mightiest** ▶ *adverb* **mightily** (**mye**-tuh-lee)

mi·graine (**mye**-grane) *noun* A very severe kind of headache that can make you sick.

M

mi·grant (**mye**-gruhnt)
noun A person or thing that moves from one area or country to another, especially to work.
adjective Of or having to do with someone who moves around to do work in different seasons.

mi·grate (**mye**-grate) *verb* **1.** To move from one country or area to another. **2.** To move to another area or climate at a particular time of year.
▶ *verb* **migrating, migrated** ▶ *adjective* **migratory**

mi·gra·tion (mye-**gray**-shuhn) *noun* Movement of people or animals from one region or habitat to another.

mild (milde) *adjective* **1.** Moderate, not harsh. **2.** Gentle and not easily provoked.
▶ *adjective* **milder, mildest** ▶ *noun* **mildness** ▶ *adverb* **mildly**

mil·dew (**mil**-doo)
noun A white, powdery fungus that can grow on damp cloth, paper, food, and other substances.
verb To grow mildew.
▶ *verb* **mildewing, mildewed**
▶ *adjective* **mildewed** ▶ *adjective* **mildewy**

mile (mile) *noun* A unit of length equal to 5,280 feet. It takes about 20 minutes to walk one mile.

mile·age (**mye**-lij) *noun* **1.** The total distance traveled or measured in miles. **2.** The average number of miles a vehicle travels on a gallon of fuel.

mile·stone (**mile**-stone) *noun* **1.** A marker on the side of a road that shows the distance to other points. **2.** An important event or development.

mil·i·tant (**mil**-i-tuhnt) *adjective* Very aggressive or willing to use force to support a cause you believe in. ▶ *noun* **militancy** (**mil**-i-tuhn-see) ▶ *adverb* **militantly**

mil·i·tar·y (**mil**-i-*ter*-ee)
adjective Of or having to do with soldiers, the armed forces, or war.
noun The armed forces of a country, such as the army or navy.

mi·li·tia (muh-**lish**-uh) *noun* A group of people who are trained to fight but are not professional soldiers.

milk (milk)
noun **1.** The white fluid produced by female mammals to feed their young. **2.** A white liquid that is made in plants. **3.** This fluid from cows, which many people drink.
verb To take milk from a cow or other animal.
▶ *verb* **milking, milked** ▶ *adjective* **milky** (**mil**-kee)

Milk·y Way (**mil**-kee **way**) *noun* The galaxy that includes the earth and our solar system. The Milky Way is made up of more than 100 billion stars and can be seen as a white streak in the night sky.

mill (mil)
noun **1.** A building that contains machinery for grinding grain into flour. **2.** A factory that produces fabrics, paper, steel, or other processed materials. **3.** A small machine used for grinding something into powder.
verb **mill around** To wander around within an area with a group.

mil·len·ni·um (muh-**len**-ee-uhm)
noun A time period of a thousand years. ▶ *noun, plural* **millenniums** or **millennia** (muh-**len**-ee-uh) ▶ *adjective* **millennial**

mil·let (**mil**-it) *noun* Small, edible seeds from a grass similar to wheat.

mil·li·gram (**mil**-i-gram) *noun* A metric measure equal to 1/1000 gram.

mil·li·li·ter (**mil**-uh-*lee*-tur) *noun* A liquid metric measure equal to 1/1000 of a liter.

mil·li·me·ter (**mil**-uh-*mee*-tur) *noun* A metric measure equal to 1/1000 meter.

mil·lion (**mil**-yuhn)
noun **1.** A thousand thousands, written numerically as 1,000,000. **2.** A very large amount.
adjective Equal to a very large amount.

mil·lion·aire (*mil*-yuh-**nair**) *noun* A person whose money and property are worth a million dollars or more; a rich person.

M

mime (mime)
noun **1.** Acting that uses movements and facial expressions instead of words. **2.** A performer who acts without words.
verb To act out with gestures or body movements.
▶ *verb* **miming, mimed**

mim·ic (**mim**-ik)
verb To imitate someone else, especially to make fun of the person.
noun A person who is good at imitating others.
▶ *verb* **mimicking, mimicked**

min. (min) Short for **minimum.** Also short for **minute** or the plural form **minutes.**

min·a·ret (*min*-uh-**ret**) *noun* The tall, slim tower of a mosque, from which Muslims are called to prayer.

mince (mins) *verb* To cut into tiny pieces. ▶ *verb* **mincing, minced**

mince·meat (**mins**-*meet*) *noun* A sweet mixture of finely chopped dried fruit, spices, and other ingredients, used in pies.

mind (minde)
noun **1.** The part of you that thinks, feels, and remembers. **2.** An opinion or thoughts about something. **3.** Thoughts or attention. **4.** Memory.
verb **1.** To take care of something or someone. **2.** To care about or to be annoyed by something. **3.** To watch out for something. **4.** To respect an authority and do what you are told. **5.** To be reluctant or unwilling to do something.
▶ *verb* **minding, minded**

mine (mine)
pronoun The one or ones belonging to me.
verb To dig up minerals that are in the ground.
noun **1.** A place where valuable minerals are taken out of the earth. **2.** A bomb placed underground or underwater. **3.** A good source of something.
▶ *verb* **mining, mined** ▶ *noun* **miner**

min·er·al (**min**-ur-uhl)
noun A solid substance found in the earth that does not come from an animal or plant.

adjective Of or having to do with minerals.

min·gle (**ming**-guhl) *verb* To combine things or people. ▶ *verb* **mingling, mingled**

min·i·a·ture (**min**-ee-uh-chur)
adjective Much smaller than usual.
noun Something that is much smaller than normal, especially a copy, model, or picture.

min·i·mal (**min**-uh-muhl) *adjective* As little as possible in amount or degree.

min·i·mize (**min**-uh-*mize*) *verb* **1.** To reduce something as much as possible. **2.** To shrink a window on the display of a computer screen. **3.** To make something seem less important or significant than it really is.
▶ *verb* **minimizing, minimized**

min·i·mum (**min**-uh-muhm)
noun The least amount or the smallest number possible.
adjective Of or having to do with the least or smallest amount, extent, or degree.

min·i·ser·ies (**min**-ee-*seer*-eez) *noun* A television production of a drama presented in separate parts, usually three to six.

min·i·skirt (**min**-ee-*skurt*) *noun* A very short skirt.

min·is·ter (**min**-i-stur)
noun **1.** A person who leads religious ceremonies in a church, especially a Protestant church. **2.** In certain countries, the head of a government department.
verb To take care of or serve someone.
▶ *verb* **ministering, ministered**

min·is·try (**min**-i-stree) *noun* **1.** The work and duties of a member of the clergy; religious service. **2.** In some countries, a government department.
▶ *adjective* **ministerial** (*min*-i-**steer**-ee-uhl)

mink (mingk)
noun **1.** A small animal related to the otter with soft, dark brown fur, often raised for its fur. **2.** A coat made from this animal's fur.
adjective Made from the fur of a mink.
▶ *noun, plural* **mink** or **minks**

M

Min·ne·so·ta (*min*-uh-**soh**-tuh) A state in the Midwest region of the United States. Minnesota is one of the border states with Canada and is the northernmost state in the U.S., except for Alaska. Known as the "Land of 10,000 Lakes," it also has more than 6,000 rivers and streams, as well as sizable wetlands, and is a popular place for outdoor recreation.

min·now (**min**-oh) *noun* A small freshwater fish, often used as bait.

mi·nor (**mye**-nur)
adjective 1. Not very serious or important. 2. A **minor** scale in music has a half step between the second and third and the fifth and sixth notes.
noun A person who is under the legal adult age.

mi·nor·i·ty (muh-**nor**-i-tee) *noun* 1. Less than half of a group. 2. A group of people of a particular race, ethnic group, or religion living among a larger group of a different race, ethnic group, or religion.
▶ *noun, plural* **minorities**

min·strel (**min**-struhl) *noun* A performer in medieval times who played or sang music or recited poems.

mint (mint)
noun 1. The leaves of a plant that have a strong scent and are used for flavoring. 2. A candy flavored with mint. 3. A place where coins are made. 4. (informal) A very large amount of money.
verb To make a coin out of metal.
▶ *verb* **minting, minted**

min·u·end (**min**-yoo-*end*) *noun* The number from which another number is subtracted. In the problem 60 – 40, 60 is the minuend.

mi·nus (**mye**-nuhs)
adjective 1. A **minus** sign (–) is used in a subtraction problem. *5 minus 3 equals 2, or 5 – 3 = 2.* 2. Less than zero. 3. On the lower end of a scale.
preposition Without. *Scott will be minus a bike while it gets fixed.*
noun 1. A disadvantage. 2. The sign (–) used in a subtraction problem.

min·ute
noun (**min**-it) 1. A unit of time equal to 60 seconds. 2. A very short time.
adjective (mye-**noot**) Extremely small.
noun, plural **minutes** (**min**-its) A written record of what happened in a meeting.
▶ *adjective* **minuter, minutest** ▶ *adverb* **minutely** (mye-**noot**-lee)

min·ute·man (**min**-it-*man*) *noun* A volunteer soldier in the American Revolutionary War who was ready to fight at a minute's notice. ▶ *noun, plural* **minutemen**

mir·a·cle (**mir**-uh-kuhl) *noun* 1. An amazing act or event that has no obvious explanation. 2. An extraordinary and lucky event.

mi·rac·u·lous (mi-**rak**-yuh-luhs) *adjective* By a miracle or like a miracle. ▶ *adverb* **miraculously**

mi·rage (muh-**rahzh**) *noun* Something that you think you see that is not really there, especially water. Mirages are caused by the bending of light rays by hot air.

Mi·ran·da (muh-**ran**-duh) *noun, plural* 1. **Miranda rights** The legal rights that protect a person when he or she is arrested by the police. These rights were established following a 1966 Supreme Court case, *Miranda v. Arizona.* 2. **Miranda warnings** The things that a police officer must tell a person who is being arrested, so that the person will know what his or her rights are.

mir·ror (**mir**-ur)
noun 1. A metal or glass surface that reflects a clear image of the things in front of it. 2. Something that clearly shows what another thing is like.
verb To clearly show what another thing is like.
▶ *verb* **mirroring, mirrored**

mirth (murth) *noun* A feeling of great amusement and joy, usually with laughter.

mis·be·have (*mis*-bi-**hayv**) *verb* To behave badly. ▶ *verb* **misbehaving, misbehaved** ▶ *noun* **misbehavior**

mis·cal·cu·late (mis-**kal**-kyuh-late) *verb* To estimate something

M

incorrectly or to misjudge a situation. ▸ *verb* **miscalculating, miscalculated** ▸ *noun* **miscalculation**

mis·car·riage (mis-**kar**-ij *or* mis-**kar**-ij) *noun* **1.** A pregnant woman's natural loss of a fetus that cannot survive. **2. miscarriage of justice** Failure of the legal system to make a good decision, especially when an innocent person is convicted of a crime.
▸ *verb* **miscarry**

mis·cel·la·ne·ous (*mis*-uh-**lay**-nee-uhs) *adjective* Of varied kinds, or from different sources. ▸ *noun* **miscellany** (**mis**-uh-*lay*-nee)

mis·chief (**mis**-chif) *noun* Playful behavior that may cause annoyance or harm to others.

mis·chie·vous (**mis**-chuh-vuhs) *adjective* **1.** Tending to get in trouble and create mischief. **2.** Expressing a sense of mischief.
▸ *adverb* **mischievously**

mis·con·duct (mis-**kahn**-duhkt) *noun* Unacceptable or dishonest behavior, especially by a professional person.

mis·count
verb (mis-**kount**) To count something wrongly.
noun (**mis**-*kount*) An inaccurate count of something.
▸ *verb* **miscounting, miscounted**

mi·ser (**mye**-zur) *noun* A very stingy person who spends as little money as possible. ▸ *noun* **miserliness** ▸ *adjective* **miserly**

mis·er·a·ble (**miz**-ur-uh-buhl) *adjective* **1.** Very unhappy. **2.** Depressing or uncomfortable.
▸ *adverb* **miserably**

mis·er·y (**miz**-ur-ee) *noun* Great suffering, because of poverty, pain, or sorrow. ▸ *noun, plural* **miseries**

mis·for·tune (mis-**for**-chuhn) *noun* **1.** An unlucky event or accident that causes trouble or disappointment. **2.** Bad luck.

mis·giv·ings (mis-**giv**-ingz) *noun, plural* Worries or doubts.

mis·guid·ed (mis-**gye**-did) *adjective* Wrong because you have not understood or judged something correctly. ▸ *adverb* **misguidedly**

mis·hap (**mis**-*hap*) *noun* A small or unlucky accident.

mis·lay (mis-**lay**) *verb* To lose something because you cannot remember where you put it. ▸ *verb* **mislaying, mislaid**

mis·lead (mis-**leed**) *verb* To give someone the wrong idea or inaccurate information about something, usually on purpose. ▸ *verb* **misleading, misled** ▸ *adjective* **misleading** ▸ *adverb* **misleadingly**

mis·place (mis-**plays**) *verb* To forget where you have put something. ▸ *verb* **misplacing, misplaced** ▸ *noun* **misplacement**

mis·print
noun (**mis**-*print*) A mistake in printed text, such as in a book or newspaper.
verb (mis-**print**) To print something incorrectly.
▸ *verb* **misprinting, misprinted**

mis·pro·nounce (*mis*-pruh-**nouns**) *verb* To say a word the wrong way. ▸ *verb* **mispronouncing, mispronounced** ▸ *noun* **mispronunciation** (*mis*-pruh-*nuhn*-see-**ay**-shuhn)

miss (mis)
verb **1.** To fail to hit or reach something. **2.** To fail to catch, see, meet, or do something. **3.** To fail to attend or be present for. **4.** To feel sad because you cannot see someone or do something you like. **5.** To notice the absence of something. **6.** To avoid or to escape.
noun **1.** A situation in which something fails to hit or happen.
2. Miss A title given to a girl or an unmarried woman. It is written before a name.
▸ *noun, plural* **misses** *or* **Misses**
▸ *verb* **misses, missing, missed**

mis·shap·en (mis-**shay**-puhn) *adjective* Twisted or bent; not having the usual shape.

mis·sile (**mis**-uhl) *noun* A weapon that is aimed at a target.

M

missing (**mis**-ing) *adjective* **1.** Not found or included. **2.** Not at home or in the usual place.

mis·sion (**mish**-uhn) *noun* **1.** An important job or task. **2.** A group of people who travel to do an important job. **3.** A church or other place where missionaries live and work.

mis·sion·ar·y (**mish**-uh-*ner*-ee) *noun* Someone who is sent to a foreign country to teach about religion and do good works. ▶ *noun, plural* **missionaries**

Mis·sis·sip·pi (*mis*-i-**sip**-ee) A state in the southern United States. It is named for the Mississippi River, which forms its western boundary. The name Mississippi, in the Native American language of the Ojibwa, means "Great River." The Mississippi Delta had an influential role in the development of the blues. This history is commemorated by the Mississippi Blues Trail, with markers to sites connected with the blues musicians of the region.

Mis·sis·sip·pi Riv·er (*mis*-i-**sip**-ee **riv**-ur) The longest river system in the United States. It originates in Minnesota and flows mainly southward until it empties into the Gulf of Mexico, near New Orleans, Louisiana.

Mis·sour·i (mi-**zoor**-ee *or* mi-**zoor**-uh) A state in the Midwest region of the United States. It was originally part of the Louisiana Purchase and was known as the Missouri Territory until it became a state in 1821. The state was called the gateway to the West. In the 19th century, many settlers and explorers headed west from Missouri, including the Lewis and Clark expedition, which reached the Pacific.

mis·spell (mis-**spel**) *verb* To spell something incorrectly. ▶ *verb* **misspelling, misspelled** ▶ *noun* **misspelling**

mist (mist) *noun* A cloud of tiny water droplets that hangs low in the air, like fog. *verb* To cover or become covered with tiny water droplets. ▶ *verb* **misting, misted** ▶ *adjective* **misty**

mis·take (mi-**stake**) *noun* An error, a misunderstanding, or a misjudgment. *verb* To believe that a person or thing is a different person or thing. ▶ *verb* **mistaking, mistook, mistaken**

mis·tak·en (mi-**stay**-kuhn) *verb* The past participle of **mistake**. *adjective* **1.** Based on an error or misunderstanding. **2.** Wrong in opinion or judgment. ▶ *adverb* **mistakenly**

mis·ter (**mis**-tur) *noun* A title for a man. It is written **Mister** or **Mr.** before a name.

mis·tle·toe (**mis**-uhl-*toh*) *noun* A plant with thick leaves and white berries that grows on trees. Mistletoe is often used as a Christmas decoration.

mis·took (mi-**stuk**) *verb* The past tense of **mistake.**

mis·treat (mis-**treet**) *verb* To treat cruelly, unfairly, or unkindly. ▶ *verb* **mistreating, mistreated** ▶ *noun* **mistreatment**

mis·tress (**mis**-tris) *noun* A woman with power or responsibility over something. ▶ *noun, plural* **mistresses**

mis·trust (mis-**truhst**) *verb* To be suspicious of someone; to have no confidence in someone. *noun* Lack of trust. ▶ *verb* **mistrusting, mistrusted**

mis·un·der·stand (*mis*-uhn-dur-**stand**) *verb* To not understand something, or understand it incorrectly. ▶ *verb* **misunderstanding, misunderstood**

mis·un·der·stand·ing (*mis*-uhn-dur-**stan**-ding) *noun* **1.** A situation in which something is not understood correctly. **2.** A disagreement between people.

mis·use
verb (mis-**yooz**) To use something

M

the wrong way or for the wrong purpose.

noun (mis-**yoos**) Improper or incorrect use of something.

▶ *verb* **misusing, misused**

mite (mite) *noun* 1. A tiny animal with eight legs that is like a spider. Mites mostly live on plants and animals.
2. A small person or animal. 3. A small amount of anything.

Mite sounds like **might.**

mitt (mit) *noun* 1. A padded leather glove worn to catch a baseball.
2. (informal) Someone's hand.

mit·ten (**mit**-uhn) *noun* A warm covering for the hand with one part for the thumb and another for the rest of the fingers.

mix (miks)

verb 1. To combine different things into one mass or substance. 2. To associate with other people. 3. **mix up** To confuse someone.

noun 1. A combination of people, things, or qualities. 2. A prepared combination of ingredients for making a certain kind of food. 3. A version of a recording that is different in some ways from the original one.

▶ *verb* **mixes, mixing, mixed**

▶ *adjective* **mixed-up**

mixed num·ber (**mikst nuhm**-bur) *noun* A number made up of a whole number and a fraction, such as 6 1/2.

mix·ture (**miks**-chur) *noun* A combination of different things mixed together.

mix-up (**miks**-*uhp*) *noun* A situation that is confused because a mistake has been made.

ml (**mil**-uh-*lee*-tur) *noun* Short for **milliliter** or the plural form **milliliters.**

mm (**mil**-uh-*mee*-tur) *noun* Short for **millimeter** or the plural form **millimeters.**

moan (mohn)

verb 1. To make a long, low sound because of sadness or pain. 2. To complain in a sad way.

noun A low, long sound of pain or grief.

▶ *verb* **moaning, moaned**

moat (moht) *noun* A deep, wide ditch dug around a castle, fort, or town and filled with water to prevent enemy attacks.

mob (mahb)

noun 1. A crowd of people, especially one that is violent and may cause trouble. 2. Any large crowd.

verb To gather around in a crowd.

▶ *verb* **mobbing, mobbed**

mo·bile

adjective (**moh**-buhl) Able to move or be moved easily.

noun (**moh**-beel) A decoration made of several items hanging from wires or threads that are balanced at different heights.

mo·bile home (**moh**-buhl **home**) *noun* A long, narrow house on wheels.

mo·bile phone (**moh**-buhl **fone**) *noun* A cell phone.

mo·bil·i·ty (moh-**bil**-i-tee) *noun* 1. The ability to move freely and easily. 2. The ability to move from one social or economic class to another.

mo·bil·ize (**moh**-buh-*lize*) *verb* 1. To assemble armed forces to be ready to fight, or to be assembled in this way.
2. To organize something so that it can be used effectively to accomplish something.

▶ *verb* **mobilizing, mobilized**

moc·ca·sin (**mah**-kuh-sin) *noun* A flat, soft leather shoe or slipper.

mock (mahk)

verb To tease or laugh at someone in a mean way, especially by imitating him or her.

adjective Imitation; not real.

▶ *verb* **mocking, mocked**

mock·er·y (**mah**-kur-ee) *noun* 1. The act of imitating or making fun of someone or something. 2. An action or decision that is ridiculous or unfair.

mock·ing·bird (**mah**-king-*burd*) *noun* A gray and white songbird that imitates the calls of other birds.

mode (mohd) *noun* 1. A particular way of doing something. 2. In mathematics, the number that appears most often in a set.

M

mod·el (**mah**-duhl)
adjective **1.** Identical but smaller.
2. Perfect or ideal.
noun **1.** A thing someone builds as an example of something larger, to see how it will work or look.
2. A person who poses for an artist or a photographer or who wears clothing to show it to people who might want to buy it. **3.** A thing or person who is a good example of something. **4.** A particular type or design of a product.
verb **1.** To create something so that it is deliberately very similar to something else. **2.** To wear clothes in order to show them to someone, especially someone who might want to buy them. **3.** To work as an artist's or photographer's model.
▸ *verb* **modeling, modeled** ▸ *noun* **modeling**

mo·dem (**moh**-duhm) *noun* An electronic device that allows computers to exchange data, especially over a telephone line.

mod·er·ate
adjective (**mah**-dur-it) Not excessive or extreme.
verb (**mah**-duh-*rate*) **1.** To make or become less severe or extreme. **2.** To lead or be in charge of a meeting, a debate, or a discussion.
noun (**mah**-dur-it) A person with opinions that are not extreme.
▸ *verb* **moderating, moderated** ▸ *adverb* **moderately** (**mah**-dur-it-lee) ▸ *noun* **moderation** (*mah*-duh-**ray**-shuhn) ▸ *noun* **moderator** (**mah**-duh-*ray*-tur)

mod·ern (**mah**-durn) *adjective* **1.** Of or having to do with the present or recent times. **2.** New, or having the latest technology.

mod·ern·ize (**mah**-dur-*nize*) *verb* To make something more up-to-date. ▸ *verb* **modernizing, modernized** ▸ *noun* **modernization**

mod·est (**mah**-dist) *adjective*
1. Not talking very much about your abilities, possessions, or achievements. **2.** Not large, showy, or expensive. **3.** Shy about showing your body.
▸ *adverb* **modestly** ▸ *noun* **modesty**

mod·i·fi·ca·tion (*mah*-duh-fi-**kay**-shuhn) *noun* A change or adjustment.

mod·i·fi·er (**mah**-duh-*fye*-ur) *noun* A word that limits the meaning of another word or phrase. In the sentence "I tripped over the sleeping dog," the word *sleeping* is a modifier of the word *dog*.

mod·i·fy (**mah**-duh-*fye*) *verb* **1.** To change something slightly in order to meet a specific need. **2.** To restrict the meaning of a word or phrase.
▸ *verb* **modifies, modifying, modified**

mod·ule (**mah**-jool) *noun* A separate unit that can be joined to others to make things such as machines and buildings.

Mo·hawk (**moh**-hawk) *noun* **1.** A member of a group of Native Americans who live primarily near the Mohawk River in New York. The Mohawk are part of the Iroquois Confederation. **2.** A haircut in which a strip of longer hair runs down the middle of the head front to back, with shorter hair on the sides.
▸ *noun, plural* **Mohawk, Mohawks**

Mo·he·gan (moh-**hee**-guhn) or **Mo·hi·can** (moh-**hee**-kuhn) *noun* A member of a group of Native Americans who originally lived in southeastern Connecticut. ▸ *noun, plural* **Mohegan, Mohegans** or **Mohican, Mohicans**

moist (moist) *adjective* Slightly wet. ▸ *adjective* **moister, moistest** ▸ *noun* **moisture** (**mois**-chur) ▸ *verb* **moisten** (**moi**-suhn)

mo·lar (**moh**-lur) *noun* One of the wide, flat teeth at the back of the mouth used for crushing and chewing food.

mo·las·ses (muh-**las**-iz) *noun* A thick, dark, sweet syrup made when sugarcane is processed into sugar.

mold (mohld)
noun **1.** A kind of fungus that grows

on old food or on things that are warm and moist. **2.** A container in a particular shape that you can pour liquid into so that it sets in that shape.
verb To shape a substance into a particular form.
▸ *verb* **molding, molded** ▸ *noun* **moldiness** ▸ *adjective* **moldy**

mold·ing (**mohl**-ding) *noun* A strip of wood or other material around the edges of windows or doorways.

Mol·do·va (mawl-**doh**-vuh) A country in eastern Europe. At one time part of Romania, Moldova was incorporated into the Soviet Union after World War II and didn't become independent until 1991. The country is landlocked and hilly, and is near the Black Sea.

mole (mohl) *noun* **1.** A small, furry mammal that burrows and lives underground. **2.** A small, slightly raised spot on the skin. Moles are usually brown or black.

mol·e·cule (**mah**-luh-*kyool*) *noun* The smallest unit that a chemical compound can be divided into that still displays all of its chemical properties. A molecule is made up of more than one atom. ▸ *adjective* **molecular** (muh-**lek**-yuh-lur)

mol·lusk (**mah**-luhsk) *noun* An animal with a soft body, no spine, and usually a hard shell that lives in water or a damp habitat.

molt (mohlt) *verb* To lose old fur, feathers, shell, or skin so that new ones can grow. ▸ *verb* **molting, molted**

mol·ten (**mohl**-tuhn) *adjective* Melted at a high temperature, usually describing metal or rock.

mom (mahm) *or* **mommy** (**mah**-mee) *noun* (informal) Mother. ▸ *noun, plural* **moms** *or* **mommies**

mo·ment (**moh**-muhnt) *noun* **1.** A short time. **2. at this moment** Right now.

mo·men·tar·y (**moh**-muhn-*ter*-ee) *adjective* Lasting only a moment. ▸ *adverb* **momentarily** (*moh*-muhn-**ter**-uh-lee)

mo·men·tum (moh-**men**-tuhm) *noun* Force or speed that something gains when it is moving.

Mon·a·co (**mah**-nuh-*koh*) A small city-state surrounded by France on the northern central coast of the Mediterranean Sea. Ruled by the Grimaldi family since the 13th century, Monaco is a world-famous tourist and recreation center.

mon·arch (**mah**-nurk) *noun* **1.** A person who rules a country, such as a king or queen. **2.** A large, orange and black butterfly.

mon·arch·y (**mah**-nur-kee) *noun* **1.** A government in which the head of state is a king or queen. **2.** A country with this type of government.
▸ *noun, plural* **monarchies**

mon·as·ter·y (**mah**-nuh-*ster*-ee) *noun* A building or group of buildings where monks or nuns live and work. ▸ *noun, plural* **monasteries** ▸ *adjective* **monastic** (muh-**nas**-tik)

Mon·day (**muhn**-day *or* **muhn**-dee) *noun* The second day of the week, after Sunday and before Tuesday.

mon·e·tar·y (**mah**-ni-*ter*-ee) *adjective* Of or having to do with money.

mon·ey (**muhn**-ee) *noun* The coins and bills that people use to buy things; what you earn when you work. ▸ *noun, plural* **moneys** *or* **monies**

Mon·go·li·a (mahng-**goh**-lee-uh) A country in the eastern part of Central Asia, between Russia and China. It is the most sparsely populated country in the world, and about a third of its population is nomadic. Mongolia was the center of the Mongol Empire, founded by Genghis Khan in the 13th century.

mon·goose (**mahng**-goos) *noun* An animal with a slender body, a long tail, and brown or black fur. Mongooses are known for killing poisonous snakes and rats. ▸ *noun, plural* **mongooses**

mon·grel (**mahng**-gruhl) *noun* A dog or other animal that is a mixture of different breeds.

M

mon·i·tor (**mah**-ni-tur)
noun 1. A student who is given a special job to do at school. 2. A person or a device that keeps track of or checks on people, machines, or a situation. 3. The visual display screen of a computer. 4. A television screen in a studio that shows or selects what is being recorded or transmitted.
verb To regularly check something over a period of time.
▶ *verb* **monitoring, monitored**

monk (muhngk) *noun* A man who lives apart from society in a religious community according to strict rules.

mon·key (**muhng**-kee)
noun An animal related to an ape, usually with a long tail.
verb To play in a silly or naughty way.
▶ *verb* **monkeying, monkeyed**

mon·key wrench (**muhng**-kee *rench*)
noun A tool that adjusts to fit different sizes of nuts and bolts. ▶ *noun, plural* **monkey wrenches**

mon·o·cle (**mah**-nuh-kuhl) *noun* A glass lens worn on one eye to improve eyesight, held in place by the muscles around the eye.

mon·o·gram (**mah**-nuh-gram)
noun A design made from two or more letters, usually someone's initials, often embroidered onto clothing or stamped onto paper.
verb To decorate with a monogram.
▶ *verb* **monogramming, mongrammed** ▶ *adjective* **monogrammed**

mon·o·lin·gual (*mah*-nuh-**ling**-gwuhl) *adjective* Speaking or using only one language.

mon·o·logue (**mah**-nuh-*lawg*) *noun* A long speech made by one person, usually in a play or movie.

mon·o·nu·cle·o·sis (*mah*-nuh-*noo*-klee-**oh**-sis) *noun* An infectious illness that gives you a sore throat, swollen glands, and a high temperature and that can last for many weeks. Often abbreviated as *mono*.

mo·nop·o·lize (muh-**nah**-puh-*lize*)
verb To control or keep the largest part of something for yourself so it isn't shared. ▶ *verb* **monopolizing, monopolized**

mo·nop·o·ly (muh-**nah**-puh-lee)
noun 1. The complete possession or control of the supply of a product or service. 2. A group or company that has such control.
▶ *noun, plural* **monopolies** ▶ *adjective* **monopolistic** (muh-*nah*-puh-**lis**-tik)

mon·o·rail (**mah**-nuh-*rayl*) *noun* 1. A railroad that runs on one rail, usually high above the ground, with the train hanging from it or balanced on it. 2. A railroad track that has only one rail.

mo·not·o·nous (muh-**nah**-tuh-nuhs) *adjective* Repetitive and boring. ▶ *noun* **monotony** ▶ *adverb* **monotonously**

mon·soon (mahn-**soon**) *noun* 1. Very strong winds that occur in different parts of the world. In summer the winds blow from the ocean, causing heavy rains; in winter they blow toward the ocean, creating hot, dry weather. 2. The rainy summer season brought on by the monsoon.

mon·ster (**mahn**-stur)
noun 1. A large, ugly, frightening creature, usually imaginary. 2. A very evil or cruel person.
adjective Huge.

mon·stros·i·ty (mahn-**strah**-si-tee) *noun* Something huge, frightening, ugly, or very badly wrong.

mon·strous (**mahn**-struhs) *adjective* 1. Ugly or frightening. 2. Very large. 3. Evil and shocking.
▶ *adverb* **monstrously**

Mon·tan·a (mahn-**tan**-uh) A state in the western United States. Named after the Spanish word for mountain, it has numerous mountain ranges, including the Rockies. Montana is the home of Glacier National Park and is also the site of the Battle of the Little Bighorn, where the chiefs Sitting Bull, Crazy Horse, and Gall led a combined force of Native American tribes that defeated General George Custer in 1876.

Mon·te·ne·gro (*mahn*-tuh-**neg**-roh) A mountainous country

M

in Southeastern Europe, with a coastline on the Adriatic Sea. In 2006, Montenegro declared its independence from Serbia. Both Serbia and Montenegro were previously part of the former Yugoslavia.

month (muhnth) *noun* One of the 12 parts that make up a year.

mon·u·ment (**mahn**-yuh-muhnt) *noun* 1. A statue, building, or other structure that reminds people of an event or a person. 2. An example of important work or a great achievement.

mon·u·men·tal (*mahn*-yuh-**men**-tuhl) *adjective* Extremely important or having a lot of influence. ▶ *adverb* **monumentally**

mood (mood) *noun* The way that you are feeling at a particular time; your emotional state.

mood·y (**moo**-dee) *adjective* 1. Upset or unhappy. 2. Having moods or feelings that change often.
▶ *adjective* **moodier, moodiest** ▶ *noun* **moodiness** ▶ *adverb* **moodily**

moon (moon) *noun* 1. The natural satellite that moves around the earth once each month and is visible because it reflects light from the sun. 2. A natural satellite of another planet.

moon·light (**moon**-*lite*) *noun* The light of the moon. *verb* (informal) To hold a second job that is usually done secretly.
▶ *verb* **moonlighting, moonlighted** ▶ *adjective* **moonlit**

moor (moor) *verb* To tie up a boat to land, to a pier, or to an anchor. *noun* In the British Isles, a high, grassy open area that is not used for farming. It is often covered with heather and marshes.
▶ *verb* **mooring, moored** ▶ *noun, plural* **moorings**

moose (moos) *noun* A large animal in the deer family that lives in the cold forests of North America, Europe, and Asia. **Moose** sounds like **mousse**. ▶ *noun, plural* **moose**

mop (mahp) *noun* 1. A long stick with a sponge or cloth strips at one end, used to clean floors. 2. A thick, tangled mass. *verb* To clean a floor or soak up liquid with a mop, towel, or sponge.
▶ *verb* **mopping, mopped**

mope (mope) *verb* To feel depressed and sorry for yourself. ▶ *verb* **moping, moped**

mo·ped (**moh**-*ped*) *noun* A heavy bicycle with a motor.

mor·al (**mor**-uhl) *adjective* 1. Concerned with right and wrong behavior. 2. Fair and honest. *noun, plural* **morals** Beliefs about what is right and acceptable. *noun* The lesson taught by a story or an experience.
▶ *adverb* **morally**

mo·rale (muh-**ral**) *noun* The mood or spirit of a person or group.

mo·ral·i·ty (muh-**ral**-i-tee) *noun* Principles about what is right and wrong that guide your actions.

mor·bid (**mor**-bid) *adjective* Unusually interested in death and unpleasant things. ▶ *adverb* **morbidly**

more (mor) *adjective* 1. Greater in number, size, amount, or degree. 2. Additional. *adverb* 1. To a larger extent or degree. 2. In addition or again. *pronoun* A greater number. *phrase* **more or less** Nearly or approximately.

more·o·ver (mor-**oh**-vur) *adverb* In addition to or supporting what has already been said.

Mor·mon (**mor**-muhn) *noun* A member of the Church of Jesus Christ of Latter-day Saints, a religion founded in 1830 by Joseph Smith in Fayette, New York.

morn·ing (**mor**-ning) *noun* The early part of a day between midnight and noon or sunrise and noon. **Morning** sounds like **mourning.**

morn·ing glo·ry (**mor**-ning *glor*-ee) *noun* A climbing vine with trumpet-shaped flowers that open early in the morning and close in the afternoon. ▶ *noun, plural* **morning glories**

M

Mo·roc·co (muh-**rah**-koh) A Muslim country in North Africa on the Atlantic Ocean. It is ruled by a king with an elected parliament. Morocco has a varied landscape, with a Mediterranean coastline in the north, snow-capped mountains in the center, and the Sahara Desert in the south.

mo·rose (muh-**rohs**) *adjective* Depressed and not talking very much. ▸ *adverb* **morosely**

morph (morf) *verb* To change smoothly from one shape to another or into something different, especially as done by computer animation. ▸ *verb* **morphing, morphed**

Morse code (**mors** kode) *noun* A communication system that uses light or sound in patterns of dots and dashes to represent letters and numbers.

mor·sel (**mor**-suhl) *noun* A small piece of something, especially food.

mor·tal (**mor**-tuhl)
adjective **1.** Not able to live forever. **2.** Causing death or likely to cause death. **3.** Lasting until death. **4.** Very intense or extreme.
noun A human being.
▸ *adverb* **mortally**

mor·tal·i·ty (mor-**tal**-i-tee) *noun* **1.** The state of being human and not living forever. **2.** The rate at which people die of a particular cause.

mor·tar (**mor**-tur) *noun* **1.** A mixture of lime, sand, water, and cement that is used to hold bricks and stones together. **2.** A heavy, hard bowl, used with a pestle for crushing things into powder or paste, especially in cooking and pharmacy. **3.** A heavy gun that fires shells or rockets high in the air.

mort·gage (**mor**-gij)
noun A loan from a bank used to buy a house or other property.
verb To give a bank the right to hold a house or other property as security for a loan it has granted.
▸ *verb* **mortgaging, mortgaged**

mor·tu·ar·y (**mor**-choo-er-ee) *noun* A room or building where dead

bodies are kept until they are buried or cremated. ▸ *noun, plural* **mortuaries**

mo·sa·ic (moh-**zay**-ik) *noun* A pattern or picture made up of small pieces of colored stone, tile, or glass.

Mo·ses (**moh**-zis *or* **moh**-ziz) *noun* A prophet in the Old Testament who led the ancient Jews out of Egypt.

mo·sey (**moh**-zee) *verb* (informal) To walk slowly or aimlessly. ▸ *verb* **moseying, moseyed**

mosh·ing (**mah**-shing) *noun* The activity of swaying, dancing, and flinging yourself around to loud music while banging into other people at a concert. ▸ *verb* **mosh** (mahsh)

mosh pit (**mahsh** pit) *noun* The place in front of the stage at a concert where people mosh.

mosque (mahsk) *noun* A building where Muslims worship.

mos·qui·to (muh-**skee**-toh) *noun* A small insect that bites animals and humans and sucks their blood. Female mosquitoes can spread diseases such as malaria and yellow fever. ▸ *noun, plural* **mosquitoes** *or* **mosquitos**

moss (maws) *noun* A small, fuzzy, green plant that grows on damp soil, rocks, and tree trunks. Mosses do not have roots, flowers, or fruit, and reproduce from spores. ▸ *noun, plural* **mosses** ▸ *adjective* **mossy**

most (mohst)
adjective **1.** Largest in number, amount, or degree. **2.** The majority of.
noun The largest number, amount, or degree.
adverb **1.** Very; completely. **2.** To the largest degree or extent.

most·ly (**mohst**-lee) *adverb* Usually or mainly.

mo·tel (moh-**tel**) *noun* A small hotel on a main road that provides parking next to the rooms.

moth (mawth) *noun* An insect similar to a butterfly with a thicker body, a dull color, and feathery antennae.

moth·er (**muhTH**-ur)
noun A female parent of a child or animal.
adjective Native, as in *mother country*.

M

verb To look after someone in protective way.
▶ *verb* **mothering, mothered** ▶ *noun* **motherhood**

moth·er·board (**muhTH**-ur-*bord*) *noun* The main circuit board in a computer, which usually holds the computer's main processor and memory.

moth·er-in-law (**muhTH**-ur-in-*law*) *noun* Your **mother-in-law** is the mother of your wife or husband. ▶ *noun, plural* **mothers-in-law**

moth·er·ly (**muhTH**-ur-lee) *adjective* Of, like, or typical of a mother.

Moth·er's Day (**muhTH**-urz *day*) *noun* A special day for honoring mothers, celebrated on the second Sunday in May.

mo·tion (**moh**-shuhn)
noun 1. The act or process of moving or the way something moves. 2. A formal suggestion or proposal made at a meeting or in a court of law.
verb To use a movement to communicate something.
▶ *verb* **motioning, motioned**

mo·tion·less (**moh**-shun-lis) *adjective* Not moving; still. ▶ *adverb* **motionlessly**

mo·tion pic·ture (**moh**-shuhn **pik**-chur) *noun* A formal term for **movie.**

mo·ti·vate (**moh**-tuh-*vate*) *verb* To encourage someone to do something or want to do something. ▶ *verb* **motivating, motivated** ▶ *adjective* **motivated**

mo·ti·va·tion (*moh*-tuh-**vay**-shuhn) *noun* 1. Desire to accomplish something. 2. A reason for doing something.

mo·tive (**moh**-tiv) *noun* A reason for doing something.

mo·to·cross (**moh**-tuh-*kraws*) *noun* A motorcycle race over rough ground.

mo·tor (**moh**-tur)
noun A machine that provides the power to make something run or move.
adjective Of or having to do with a motor or something run by a motor.
verb To drive.

▶ *verb* **motoring, motored** ▶ *noun* **motoring**

mo·tor·bike (**moh**-tur-*bike*) *noun*
1. A bicycle that has a small motor.
2. A small or light motorcycle.

mo·tor·cade (**moh**-tur-*kade*) *noun* A group of cars traveling together, often to transport an important person.

mo·tor·cy·cle (**moh**-tur-*sye*-kuhl) *noun* A road vehicle with two wheels and an engine.

mo·tor·ist (**moh**-tur-ist) *noun* A person who drives a car or travels by car.

mot·tled (**mah**-tuhld) *adjective* Covered with shapes of different colors in an irregular pattern.

mot·to (**mah**-toh) *noun* A short sentence that states someone's beliefs, or is used as a rule for behavior. ▶ *noun, plural* **mottoes** or **mottos**

mound (mound)
noun 1. A hill or a pile of something.
2. A small hill for the pitcher in the middle of a baseball diamond.
verb To make a pile of something.
▶ *verb* **mounding, mounded**

mount (mount)
verb 1. To get on or to climb up.
2. To increase gradually. 3. To put in place for display or to be examined.
4. To place on a raised support.
noun 1. A horse or other animal you ride on. 2. Mountain. This word is used in place names.
▶ *verb* **mounting, mounted**

moun·tain (**moun**-tuhn) *noun* 1. A very large and high hill. 2. A large amount or number of something.

moun·tain bike (**moun**-tuhn *bike*) *noun* A strong bicycle with many gears, wide tires, and heavy treads designed for riding on rough ground.

moun·tain·eer (*moun*-tuh-**neer**) *noun* A person who climbs mountains for fun. ▶ *noun* **mountaineering**

moun·tain li·on (**moun**-tuhn *lye*-uhn) *noun* A large, powerful wildcat that lives in the mountains of North, Central, and South America. The mountain lion is also known as a **cougar, puma,** or **panther.**

M

Mount Ev·er·est (mount ev-ur-ist) The highest mountain in the world, measuring 29,029 feet (8,848 meters) in height. Located on the border between Tibet and Nepal, Mount Everest is part of the Himalayas.

Mount Kil·i·man·ja·ro (mount *kil-*uh-muhn-**jahr-**oh) A mountain in northeastern Tanzania. It is the highest mountain in Africa, measuring 19,340 feet (5,895 meters) in height. It is an inactive volcano, and not part of a range of mountains.

Mount Mc·Kin·ley (mount muh-kin-lee) A mountain in Alaska that is the highest mountain in North America. It has two summits, the higher of which is 20,320 feet (6,194 meters) above sea level. Mount McKinley is sometimes called **Denali**, which is the Inuit name for it.

Mount Rush·more (mount ruhsh-*mor***)** A granite mountain in the Black Hills of South Dakota. Mount Rushmore is renowned for its 60-foot sculptures of the American presidents George Washington, Thomas Jefferson, Theodore Roosevelt, and Abraham Lincoln, which were carved between 1927 and 1941.

Mount St. Hel·ens (mount *saynt* **hel-**uhnz) An active volcano located in the Pacific Northwest. Mount St. Helens measures 8,365 feet (2,550 meters) in height and is in the state of Washington, about 95 miles south of the city of Seattle. The mountain's most recent large eruption occurred in 1980 and caused more destruction than any other U.S. volcanic eruption on record.

mourn (morn) *verb* To feel and show you are sad for a death or for some other kind of loss. ▶ *verb* **mourning, mourned** ▶ *noun* **mourner** ▶ *noun* **mourning**

mourn·ful (morn-fuhl) *adjective* Feeling, showing, or filled with grief. ▶ *adverb* **mournfully**

mourn·ing (mor-ning) *noun* 1. Sadness because someone has died. 2. A symbol of sadness because of death, such as black clothes or a black armband. In the past, it was usual for people to wear mourning for a time when a family member died.

Mourning sounds like **morning.**

mouse (mous) *noun* 1. A small, furry mammal with a pointed nose, small ears, and a long tail. 2. A small handheld device that you use to move the cursor on your computer screen.

▶ *noun, plural* **mice (mise)**

mousse (moos) *noun* 1. A cold dessert containing beaten egg whites and cream. Mousse is like a light and fluffy pudding. 2. A foamy substance that you use to style your hair.

Mousse sounds like **moose.**

mous·y (mou-see) *adjective* 1. Dull light brown, usually used to describe hair. 2. Timid and shy; not having a strong personality.

▶ *noun* **mousiness** ▶ *adverb* **mousily**

mouth
noun (mouth) 1. The opening in the face and the area inside the head through which people and animals eat, speak, and breathe. 2. An opening or entrance to something. 3. The part of a river where it joins the ocean or other large body of water. *verb* (mouTH) To move your lips as if you are talking without making any sound.

▶ *verb* **mouthing, mouthed**

mouth or·gan (mouth *or*-guhn) *See* **harmonica.**

mouth·piece (mouth-*pees***)** *noun* 1. The part of a telephone that you speak into. 2. The part of a musical instrument that you put in or near your mouth. 3. A person who speaks for an individual or a group.

move (moov)
verb 1. To change place or position, or to change the place or position of someone or something. 2. To change the place you live or work. 3. To cause someone to have strong feelings. 4. To put or keep in motion.

M

5. To cause to do something.
6. To formally make a proposal at a meeting.
noun **1.** A step or a movement. **2.** The act or process of changing your home or job. **3.** An action planned to achieve something. **4.** A person's turn to change the position of a playing piece in games such as chess or checkers.
▶ *verb* **moving, moved** ▶ *adjective* **movable** *or* **moveable**

move·ment (**moov**-muhnt) *noun*
1. The act of moving, or moving something, from one place to another. **2.** The act of moving a part of the body. **3.** A group of people working together to promote a cause. **4.** One of the main sections of a long piece of classical music.

mov·ie (**moo**-vee)
noun Moving pictures, usually with sound, that tell a story, shown on a screen.
noun, plural **movies** The industry or profession of making or starring in motion pictures.

mov·ing (**moo**-ving) *adjective* **1.** In motion or capable of changing position. **2.** Of or having to do with changing where you live. **3.** Triggering deep emotion or sympathy.

mow (moh) *verb* To cut grass or other long plants, such as grain or hay. ▶ *verb* **mowing, mowed, mown** (mohn) ▶ *noun* **mower**

Mo·zam·bique (*moh*-zam-**beek**) A country in southeastern Africa on the Indian Ocean. It was a Portuguese colony for 500 years, gaining independence in 1975. Today, Mozambique has one of the fastest-growing economies in the world.

MP3 (**em**-*pee*-**three**) *noun* A type of computer file that records sound. MP3 files can be played by a computer program or a device known as an *MP3 player.*

MPEG (**em**-*peg*) *noun* The standard electronic format for storing video in a compact space. MPEG is short for *Moving Picture Experts Group.*

mph *or* **m.p.h.** (**em**-*pee*-**aych**) *noun* Short for *miles per hour.*

Mr. (**mis**-ter) *noun* A title put in front of a man's name.

Mrs. (**mis**-iz) *noun* A title put in front of a married woman's name.

Ms. (miz) *noun* A title put in front of a woman's name whether she is married or unmarried.

much (muhch)
adjective Large in amount or degree.
adverb Very.
noun A large amount or degree of something.

mu·ci·lage (**myoo**-suh-lij) *noun* A liquid glue.

muck (muhk) *noun* Anything that is thick and dirty, wet, sticky, or slimy, especially mud or manure.

mu·cus (**myoo**-kuhs) *noun* A thick slimy liquid that coats and protects the inside of your mouth, nose, throat, and other breathing passages. ▶ *adjective* **mucous** (**myoo**-kuhs)

mud (muhd) *noun* **1.** Wet earth that is sticky and soft. **2. your name is mud** You are in trouble or disgrace with someone.

mud·dle (**muhd**-uhl)
verb **1.** To mix things up or put them in the wrong order. **2. muddle through** To accomplish something even though you are unsure of how to go about it or do not have the right equipment.
noun A mess or a state of confusion.
▶ *verb* **muddling, muddled** ▶ *adjective* **muddled**

mud·dy (**muhd**-ee)
adjective Covered with wet, soft dirt.
verb To make something unclear by adding something.
▶ *adjective* **muddier, muddiest** ▶ *verb* **muddies, muddying, muddied**

muf·fin (**muhf**-in) *noun* A small cake or bread baked in a cup.

muf·fle (**muhf**-uhl) *verb* To make a sound quieter or less clear. ▶ *verb* **muffling, muffled**

muf·fler (**muhf**-lur) *noun* **1.** A device on a vehicle that reduces engine noise. **2.** A warm scarf.

M

mug (muhg)
noun A tall cup with a handle.
verb (informal) To attack someone violently in public and try to steal the person's money.
▶ *verb* **mugging, mugged** ▶ *noun* **mugger**

mug·gy (**muhg**-ee) *adjective* Warm and damp. ▶ *adjective* **muggier, muggiest** ▶ *noun* **mugginess**

Mu·ham·mad (mu-**ham**-uhd *or* mu-**hah**-muhd) *or* **Mo·ham·mad** (moh-**ham**-uhd *or* moh-**hah**-muhd) *noun* The founder of the Islamic religion. Muslims believe that Muhammad is God's last and most important prophet. Also spelled **Mohammed.**

mul·ber·ry (**muhl**-*ber*-ee) *noun* 1. A tree that produces dark purple berries. Mulberry leaves are sometimes used as food for silkworms. 2. The edible berry produced by this tree. 3. A dark red or purple color.

mule (myool) *noun* An animal that comes from a female horse and a male donkey.

mul·ti·cul·tur·al (muhl-ti-**kuhl**-chur-uhl) *adjective* Involving or made up of people from different countries or cultures. ▶ *adverb* **multiculturally**

mul·ti·lin·gual (muhl-ti-**ling**-gwuhl) *adjective* Using or able to speak several different languages.

mul·ti·me·di·a (muhl-ti-**mee**-dee-uh) *adjective* Using several different media at the same time, such as text, sound, and video.
noun The combined use of several different media.

mul·ti·na·tion·al (muhl-ti-**nash**-uh-nuhl) *adjective* Involving or operating in more than one country.
noun A company operating in more than two countries.

mul·ti·ple (**muhl**-tuh-puhl) *adjective* 1. Involving many people or things. 2. A **multiple-choice** test gives you several answers to choose from for each question.
noun A number that can be exactly divided by a smaller number.

mul·ti·ple scle·ro·sis (**muhl**-tuh-puhl skluh-**roh**-sis) *noun* A serious disease that damages small areas of the brain and spinal cord. It causes numbness, paralysis, and other problems in the nervous system.

mul·ti·pli·cand (muhl-tuh-pli-**kand**) *noun* A number that is to be multiplied by another number. In the problem 2 × 8, 8 is the multiplicand.

mul·ti·pli·ca·tion (muhl-tuh-pli-**kay**-shuhn) *noun* 1. In math, the multiplying of numbers. 2. A **multiplication table** is a list of all the multiples of the numbers from one to twelve. 3. Growth in the number or amount of something.

mul·ti·pli·er (**mul**-tuh-*plye*-ur) *noun* The number by which you multiply another. In the problem 2 × 8, 2 is the multiplier.

mul·ti·ply (**muhl**-tuh-*plye*) *verb* 1. To add a number to itself a particular number of times. 2. To increase or make something increase.
▶ *verb* **multiplies, multiplying, multiplied**

mul·ti·ra·cial (muhl-ti-**ray**-shuhl) *adjective* Made up of people of different races. ▶ *adverb* **multiracially**

mul·ti·task (muhl-tee-*task*) *verb* To do two or more things at the same time.

mul·ti·tude (**muhl**-ti-*tood*) *noun* 1. A large number of people; a crowd. 2. A large or varied number of things.

mul·ti·vi·ta·min (muhl-ti-**vye**-tuh-min) *noun* A pill that contains several different vitamins.

mum·ble (**muhm**-buhl) *verb* To speak quietly in an unclear way. ▶ *verb* **mumbling, mumbled**

mum·my (**muhm**-ee) *noun* A dead body that has been preserved with special chemicals and wrapped in cloth. Sometimes bodies that have been preserved accidentally, by ice or natural chemicals, are also called mummies. ▶ *noun, plural* **mummies** ▶ *verb* **mummify** (**muhm**-uh-*fye*) ▶ *adjective* **mummified**

mumps (muhmps) *noun, plural* An infectious illness caused by a virus

M

that causes painful swelling of the glands around your face.

munch (muhnch) *verb* To eat in a noisy way, especially something crunchy. ▶ *verb* **munches, munching, munched**

mun·dane (muhn-**dane**) *adjective* Ordinary and everyday.

mu·nic·i·pal (myoo-**nis**-uh-puhl) *adjective* Of or having to do with a city or town and its services.

mu·ral (**myoor**-uhl) *noun* A large painting done on a wall.

mur·der (**mur**-dur) *verb* To kill someone deliberately. *noun* The crime of killing someone deliberately. ▶ *verb* **murdering, murdered** ▶ *noun* **murderer**

murk·y (**mur**-kee) *adjective* Dark, cloudy, or dirty. ▶ *adjective* **murkier, murkiest**

mur·mur (**mur**-mur) *verb* 1. To say something very quietly. 2. To make a low, continuous sound. *noun* 1. Quiet, unclear speech or other sound. 2. An abnormal sound made by your heart that is sometimes a sign of disease or damage. ▶ *verb* **murmuring, murmured**

mus·cle (**muhs**-uhl) *noun* 1. A type of tissue in the body that can contract to produce movement. Your muscles are attached to your skeleton and pull on your bones to make them move. 2. Strength or power. *verb* To accomplish something with strength. **Muscle** sounds like **mussel.** ▶ *verb* **muscling, muscled**

mus·cu·lar (**muhs**-kyuh-lur) *adjective* 1. Having strong muscles. 2. Involving a muscle or muscles.

muse (myooz) *verb* To think carefully or to reflect on something. *noun* A person or thing, either real or imaginary, that serves as an inspiration to an artist. ▶ *verb* **musing, mused** ▶ *noun* **musing**

mu·se·um (myoo-**zee**-uhm) *noun* A place where interesting and valuable objects of art, history, or science are preserved and displayed.

mush (muhsh) *noun* 1. A thick cereal made of cornmeal boiled in water or milk. 2. A thick, soft mixture or mass.

mush·room (**muhsh**-room) *noun* A small fungus that has a short stem and a top shaped like an umbrella. Many mushrooms can be eaten, but some are poisonous. *verb* To grow or spread rapidly. ▶ *verb* **mushrooming, mushroomed**

mu·sic (**myoo**-zik) *noun* 1. Sounds that are arranged in a way that is pleasant to hear, produced by voices or instruments. 2. Symbols that represent such sounds.

mu·si·cal (**myoo**-zi-kuhl) *adjective* 1. Fond of or skilled in music. 2. Of or having to do with music. 3. Resembling music. *noun* A play or movie that includes a lot of singing and dancing. ▶ *adverb* **musically**

mu·si·cal in·stru·ment (**myoo**-zi-kuhl **in**-struh-muhnt) *noun* An instrument for playing music.

mu·si·cian (myoo-**zish**-uhn) *noun* A person who plays, sings, or writes music.

musk (muhsk) *noun* A substance with a strong smell that is used in perfume, medicine, and soap. Musk is produced by some male deer.

mus·ket (**muhs**-kit) *noun* A type of long gun that was used by soldiers before the rifle was invented.

mus·ket·eer (**muhs**-ki-**teer**) *noun* A soldier who carried a musket.

musk·rat (**muhsk**-rat) *noun* A small rodent with webbed hind feet, a flat tail, and thick, brown fur. Muskrats live in and around water. ▶ *noun, plural* **muskrat** or **muskrats**

Mus·lim (**muhz**-lim or **muz**-lim) or **Mos·lem** (**mahz**-lim) *noun* A person whose religion is Islam. ▶ *adjective* **Muslim** or **Moslem**

M

mus·lin (**muhz**-lin) *noun* A thin cotton cloth used to make sheets, curtains, and clothing.

mus·sel (**muhs**-uhl) *noun* A type of shellfish that has a black shell and can be eaten. **Mussel** sounds like **muscle.**

must (muhst)
verb **1.** You use **must** to show that you have to do something, or that something has to happen. **2.** You also use **must** when you think something is true but don't have proof. **3.** You can use **must** to make a strong suggestion.
noun Something that you need or should have.

mus·tache *or* **mous·tache** (muh-**stash** *or* **muhs**-*tash*) *noun* Hair that grows on a man's upper lip.

mus·tang (**muhs**-tang) *noun* A small wild horse found mostly on the western plains of the United States.

mus·tard (**muhs**-turd) *noun* **1.** A leafy plant related to cabbage that is eaten as a vegetable in many parts of the world. **2.** A yellowish, spicy paste made from the seeds of the mustard plant.

mus·ter (**muhs**-tur) *verb* **1.** To gather in a group, especially to prepare for a battle. **2.** To collect or call up. **3. pass muster** To be adequate or acceptable. ▶ *verb* **mustering, mustered**

must·n't (**muhs**-uhnt) *contraction* A short form of *must not.*

mus·ty (**muhs**-tee) *adjective* Smelling of dampness or decay because there is no fresh air. ▶ *adjective* **mustier, mustiest** ▶ *noun* **mustiness**

mu·tant (**myoo**-tuhnt) *noun* A living thing that is different from others of its kind because of a change in its genes. ▶ *noun* **mutation** (myoo-**tay**-shuhn) ▶ *verb* **mutate** (**myoo**-tate)

mute (myoot)
adjective Not speaking; silent.
noun **1.** A person who cannot speak. **2.** A device that can be put on a musical instrument to soften its sounds.
verb To make a sound softer.

▶ *adjective* **muter, mutest** ▶ *verb* **muting, muted** ▶ *adverb* **mutely**

mut·ed (**myoo**-tid) *adjective* **1.** Muffled or softened. **2.** Quieter or less brilliant.

mu·ti·late (**myoo**-tuh-*late*) *verb* To injure or damage something or someone by disfiguring it. ▶ *verb* **mutilating, mutilated** ▶ *noun* **mutilation**

mu·ti·ny (**myoo**-tuh-nee)
noun A revolt against or refusal to obey authority, especially in the military.
verb To rebel against someone in authority.

▶ *noun, plural* **mutinies** ▶ *verb* **mutinying, mutinied** ▶ *noun* **mutineer** (*myoo*-tuh-**neer**) ▶ *adjective* **mutinous** (**myoo**-tuh-nuhs)

mutt (muht) *noun* A dog that comes from several breeds; a mongrel.

mut·ter (**muht**-ur)
verb To speak in a quiet voice with the mouth almost closed, especially because you are annoyed.
noun Something that is said very quietly and not very clearly.

▶ *verb* **muttering, muttered**

mut·ton (**muht**-uhn) *noun* The flesh of a sheep, eaten for food.

mu·tu·al (**myoo**-choo-uhl) *adjective* Shared or experienced by all the people involved. ▶ *adverb* **mutually**

muz·zle (**muhz**-uhl)
noun **1.** An animal's nose and mouth. **2.** A cover you put over an animal's mouth to keep it from biting. **3.** The open end of a gun barrel where bullets come out.
verb To restrain.

▶ *verb* **muzzling, muzzled**

my (mye) *adjective* Belonging to or having to do with me.

My·an·mar (mye-ahn-**mahr**) The largest country in mainland Southeast Asia. Formerly known as Burma, Myanmar is ruled by a military junta. The nation accounts for 90 percent of the world's rubies.

my·nah *or* **my·na** (**mye**-nuh) *noun* A dark brown Asian bird that can imitate the human voice.

M

my·ri·ad (**mir**-ee-uhd)
noun An extremely large or uncountable number.
adjective Unable to be counted.

my·self (mye-**self**) *pronoun* Me and no one else.

mys·te·ri·ous (mi-**steer**-ee-uhs)
adjective Very hard to explain or understand. ▶ *adverb* **mysteriously**

mys·ter·y (**mis**-tur-ee) *noun*
1. Something that is hard to explain or understand. **2.** A story containing strange events or crimes that have to be solved.
▶ *noun, plural* **mysteries**

mys·ti·fy (**mis**-tuh-*fye*) *verb* To confuse someone completely. ▶ *verb*
mystifies, mystifying, mystified ▶ *noun* **mystification** (*mis*-tuh-fi-**kay**-shuhn)

myth (mith) *noun* **1.** An old story that expresses the beliefs or history of a group of people or explains some natural event. **2.** A belief held by many people that is false or does not exist.

myth·i·cal (**mith**-i-kuhl) *adjective*
1. Found in or having to do with myths. **2.** Imaginary or untrue.

my·thol·o·gy (mi-**thah**-luh-jee)
noun A group of myths, especially ones that belong to a particular culture or religion. ▶ *noun, plural* **mythologies** ▶ *adjective* **mythological** (*mith*-uh-**lah**-ji-kuhl)

N

nag (nag)
verb To keep asking someone to do something or complaining to someone in a way that is annoying.
noun A horse, especially one that is old or worn-out.
▶ *verb* **nagging, nagged**

nail (nayl)
noun **1.** A small, thin, pointed piece of metal that you force into wood with a hammer. **2.** The thin, hard layer that grows on the tips of your fingers and toes.
verb To attach something to something else with a nail or nails.

na·ive *or* **na·ïve** (nah-**eev**) *adjective* Not having much experience of life or very much knowledge, and believing or trusting people too much. ▶ *noun* **naiveté** *or* **naïveté** (nah-*eev*-**tay**)
▶ *adverb* **naively**

na·ked (**nay**-kid) *adjective* **1.** Not wearing any clothes. **2.** Bare, or without what usually covers it. **3.** Expressed in a strong way. **4.** Without the help of an instrument like a telescope or microscope.
▶ *noun* **nakedness** ▶ *adverb* **nakedly**

name (name)
noun **1.** A word that you call a person,
an animal, a place, or a thing. **2.** A bad or mean word or phrase that you call a person. **3.** The reputation or opinion that others have of someone or something.
verb **1.** To say the name of someone or something. **2.** To give someone or something a name. **3.** To choose someone for a position or job.
▶ *verb* **naming, named**

name·ly (**name**-lee) *adverb* You use **namely** to let a listener or reader know that you are going to explain more or give details about something.

Na·mib·i·a (nuh-**mib**-ee-uh) A country in southern Africa on the Atlantic Ocean. Much of its territory is covered by two deserts, the Namib and the Kalihari. Namibia is sparsely populated. Only the country of Mongolia has fewer people per square mile.

nan·ny (**nan**-ee) *noun* **1.** A woman who takes care of young children as a job, especially in the children's home.
2. nanny goat A female goat.
▶ *noun, plural* **nannies**

nan·o·tech·nol·o·gy (*nan*-oh-tek-**nah**-luh-jee) *noun* Technology that attempts to harness extremely small things such as atoms and molecules.

nap (nap)
verb To sleep for a short time, especially during the day.
noun 1. A short period of sleep during the day. 2. The short, fuzzy threads on some kinds of cloth.
▶ *verb* **napping, napped**

nape (nape) *noun* The back part of your neck.

nap·kin (**nap**-kin) *noun* A small piece of paper or cloth used to clean your hands and mouth while eating.

nar·cis·sist (**nahr**-si-sist) *noun*
Narcissists are people who admire themselves too much, especially their looks. ▶ *noun* **narcissism** ▶ *adjective* **narcissistic**

nar·cis·sus (nahr-**sis**-uhs) *noun* A spring plant that has yellow or white flowers and long, thin leaves. The daffodil is a kind of **narcissus.** ▶ *noun, plural* **narcissuses** *or* **narcissus**

nar·cot·ic (nahr-**kah**-tik)
noun A strong drug that relieves pain or helps you relax or sleep better.
adjective Causing drowsiness or mental lethargy.

nar·rate (**nar**-ate) *verb* To tell a story or speak the words in a program or documentary. ▶ *verb* **narrating, narrated** ▶ *noun* **narration**

nar·ra·tive (**nar**-uh-tiv)
noun A story or a description of events.
adjective Telling a story or describing a sequence of events.

nar·ra·tor (**nar**-ay-tur) *noun* A person who tells a story. A narrator can be someone telling a story to another person, or it can be the character in a book who tells the story as he or she experienced it or heard about it.

nar·row (**nar**-oh)
adjective 1. Measuring a short distance from one side to the other. 2. Limited, or small in amount.
3. If you have a **narrow** escape, you almost do not avoid something. 4. If you are **narrow-minded,** you do not want to listen to or understand new or different ideas or opinions.
verb To become or make something narrower.
▶ *adjective* **narrower, narrowest** ▶ *verb* **narrowing, narrowed** ▶ *noun* **narrowness** ▶ *adverb* **narrowly**

na·sal (**nay**-zuhl) *adjective* 1. Of or having to do with the nose.
2. Sounding as if produced through the nose instead of the mouth. *M, n,* and *ng* are nasal sounds.

nas·tur·tium (nuh-**stur**-shuhm) *noun* A plant with yellow, red, or orange flowers that can be eaten.

nas·ty (**nas**-tee) *adjective* 1. Unkind or mean. 2. Bad or unpleasant.
3. Dangerous or severe.
▶ *adjective* **nastier, nastiest** ▶ *noun* **nastiness** ▶ *adverb* **nastily**

na·tion (**nay**-shuhn) *noun* 1. A country whose people share a language, culture, and history and have the same government. 2. All the people in a certain country. 3. A group of people who share a culture, language, or ancestry.

na·tion·al (**nash**-uh-nuhl)
adjective Of, having to do with, or shared by a whole nation.
noun A citizen of a particular country.
▶ *adverb* **nationally**

Na·tion·al Guard (**nash**-uh-nuhl **gahrd**) *noun* A volunteer military organization with units in each state that are commanded by the governor.

na·tion·al·ist (**nash**-uh-nuh-list)
noun Someone who is very proud of his or her country, or who wants it to be independent. ▶ *noun* **nationalism** ▶ *adjective* **nationalistic**

na·tion·al·i·ty (nash-uh-**nal**-i-tee) *noun*
1. The legal right to be a citizen of a certain country. 2. A group of people with the same language, culture, and history.
▶ *noun, plural* **nationalities**

na·tion·al·ize (**nash**-uh-nuh-*lize*)
verb If a company or industry is **nationalized,** the government owns and controls it. ▶ *verb* **nationalizing, nationalized** ▶ *noun* **nationalization**

N

na·tion·al park (**nash**-uh-nuhl **pahrk**)
noun A large section of land that is protected by the government for people to visit, such as Yellowstone National Park or Grand Canyon National Park.

na·tive (**nay**-tiv)
noun 1. A person who was born in or lives in a particular country or place. 2. An animal or a plant that lives or grows naturally in a certain place.
adjective Connected to the place where you were born or lived during the early part of your life.

Na·tive A·mer·i·can (**nay**-tiv uh-**mer**-i-kuhn)
noun One of the peoples who originally lived in North, Central, or South America or a descendant of these peoples. Native Americans are sometimes called **American Indians.**
adjective Of or having to do with Native Americans.

Na·tiv·i·ty (nuh-**tiv**-i-tee) *noun* 1. The birth of Jesus. 2. A display or scene that shows the story and place of the birth of Jesus.

NATO (**nay**-toh) *noun* An organization of countries that have agreed to give each other military help. This group includes the United States, Canada, and some countries in Europe. NATO stands for *North Atlantic Treaty Organization.*

nat·u·ral (**nach**-ur-uhl)
adjective 1. Found in or made by nature instead of people. 2. Normal or as you would expect. 3. Present or developing in a person from birth. 4. Lifelike or closely following nature. 5. Relaxed; not pretending to be different. 6. In music, a **natural** note is one that is not flat or sharp. 7. In a musical score, a **natural** sign shows that the next note is natural.
noun A person who has a special talent or ability.
▶ *adverb* **naturally**

nat·u·ral gas (**nach**-ur-uhl **gas**) *noun* A gas that is found under the ground or the ocean. It mostly consists of methane and is used for fuel.

nat·u·ral his·to·ry (**nach**-ur-uhl **his**-tur-ee) *noun* The study of plants and animals and the places they come from.

nat·u·ral·ist (**nach**-ur-uh-list) *noun* Someone who studies plants, animals, and other living things.

nat·u·ral·ize (**nach**-ur-uh-*lize*) *verb* To make someone a citizen of a country where they were not born. ▶ *verb* **naturalizing, naturalized** ▶ *noun* **naturalization**

nat·u·ral·ly (**nach**-ur-uh-lee) *adverb* 1. In a natural way. 2. Of course.

nat·u·ral re·source (**nach**-ur-uhl **ree**-sors) *noun* A material produced by the earth that is necessary or useful to people. Forests, water, oil, and minerals are some natural resources.

na·ture (**nay**-chur) *noun* 1. Things in the world, such as animals, plants, and the weather, that are not made by people. 2. The qualities or character of a person or thing.

naught (nawt) *noun* Nothing.

naught·y (**naw**-tee) *adjective* Badly behaved and disobedient. ▶ *adjective* **naughtier, naughtiest** ▶ *noun* **naughtiness** ▶ *adverb* **naughtily**

Na·u·ru (nah-**oo**-roo) An island nation in Micronesia in the South Pacific Ocean. The island is shaped like an oval and is surrounded by coral reefs. Nauru is the smallest island country in the world. It was a major exporter of phosphates, but its reserves have now been exhausted by mining, which damaged the island's environment.

nau·se·a (**naw**-zee-uh *or* **naw**-zhuh) *noun* A feeling of wanting to throw up. ▶ *adjective* **nauseous** (**naw**-shuhs) ▶ *adjective* **nauseated** (**naw**-zee-*ay*-tid)

nau·ti·cal (**naw**-ti-kuhl)
adjective Of or having to do with ships or sailing.
noun **nautical mile** A unit that measures distance in the sea or in the air. One nautical mile equals 6,076 feet.

N

Nav·a·jo *or* **Nav·a·ho** (**nav**-uh-*hoh*)
noun A member of the second-largest group of Native Americans. The Navajo live primarily in New Mexico, Arizona, and Utah. ▶ *noun, plural* **Navajo, Navajos** *or* **Navaho, Navahos**

na·val (**nay**-vuhl) *adjective* Of or having to do with the navy of a country.
Naval sounds like **navel**.

na·vel (**nay**-vuhl) *noun* The small, round hollow or raised part in the middle of your stomach where your umbilical cord used to be attached.
Navel sounds like **naval**.

nav·i·gate (**nav**-i-*gate*) *verb* **1.** To find where you are and where you need to go when you travel in a ship, an aircraft, or other vehicle. **2.** To travel along or across a place.
▶ *verb* **navigating, navigated** ▶ *noun* **navigation** ▶ *noun* **navigator**

na·vy (**nay**-vee)
noun **1.** The part of a country's military that fights at sea, using ships, aircraft, weapons, land bases, and people. **2.** A dark blue.
adjective Having a dark blue color.
▶ *noun, plural* **navies**

na·vy blue (**nay**-vee **bloo**)
noun A dark blue color.
adjective Being or having the color navy blue.

nay (nay)
noun A word used to say "no" when you are voting.
adverb **Nay** is used to show that you have thought of a word that is better or stronger than the one you just said.
Nay sounds like **neigh**.

Na·zi (**naht**-see)
noun **1.** A member of the National Socialist German Workers' Party, a political group that ruled Germany from 1933 to 1945. Led by Adolf Hitler, the Nazis killed millions of Jews, Gypsies, and others before and during World War II. **2. nazi** *or* **Nazi** A person who uses his or her power in a cruel way or is violently racist.
adjective Of, having to do with, or typical of a member of the National Socialist German Workers' Party.
▶ *noun* **Nazism** (**naht**-siz-uhm)

near (neer)
preposition A short distance to. *Brian lives near me.*
adverb Close, or a short distance away.
verb To get closer to something.
adjective **1.** Close to being something. **2.** Not far; close by. **3.** Closely related or similar.
▶ *adverb* **nearer, nearest** ▶ *adjective* **nearer, nearest** ▶ *verb* **nearing, neared** ▶ *noun* **nearness**

near·by (**neer**-bye) *adjective* A short distance away. ▶ *adverb* **nearby**

near·ly (**neer**-lee) *adverb* Almost or not completely.

near·sight·ed (**neer**-sye-tid) *adjective* Able to see objects clearly only if they are close to you.

neat (neet) *adjective* **1.** Not messy; in good order. **2.** Good or excellent.
▶ *adjective* **neater, neatest** ▶ *adverb* **neatly** ▶ *noun* **neatness**

Ne·bras·ka (nuh-**bras**-kuh) A state in the Midwest region of the United States. It is largely prairie land, and its economy is based on farming and ranching. Nebraska is the only state whose legislature is composed of a single body. It is called the Legislature or the Unicameral, which means "one chamber." Nebraska also has the only state legislature that is meant to be free of party influence. Its members, known as senators, are elected without having their party affiliation listed on the ballot.

neb·u·la (**neb**-yuh-luh) *noun* A bright area made of stars or gas and dust that can be seen in the night sky. ▶ *noun, plural* **nebulae** (**neb**-yuh-lee) *or* **nebulas**

nec·es·sar·i·ly (nes-uh-**ser**-uh-lee) *adverb* As a necessary result; unavoidably.
phrase **not necessarily** Possibly but not always true.

nec·es·sar·y (**nes**-uh-ser-ee) *adjective* If something is **necessary**, you need to do it or it needs to happen. ▶ *adverb* **necessarily**

ne·ces·si·ty (nuh-**ses**-i-tee) *noun* 1. The fact that something needs to happen or be done. 2. **Necessities** are the things you must have and cannot live without, such as food and shelter.

neck (nek) *noun* 1. The part of your body between your head and your shoulders. 2. The part of a piece of clothing that goes around your neck. 3. A long, narrow part of something.

neck·er·chief (**nek**-ur-chif) *noun* A square of cloth that you tie around your neck.

neck·lace (**nek**-lis) *noun* A piece of jewelry you wear on your neck.

neck·tie (**nek**-tye) *noun* A long, narrow piece of cloth that wraps around the neck and hangs down in front.

nec·tar (**nek**-tur) *noun* A sweet liquid from flowers that bees gather and make into honey.

nec·tar·ine (*nek*-tuh-**reen**) *noun* A fruit like a peach but without fuzz on its skin.

need (need)
verb 1. To require something because it is important or necessary. 2. Used to show that you should or have to do something.
noun 1. Something that you must have to survive. 2. Something that is necessary or required. 3. A situation of not having enough money or food.
Need sounds like **knead.** ▶ *verb* **needing, needed**

nee·dle (**nee**-duhl)
noun 1. A small, thin piece of metal with a sharp point and a hole for thread, used for sewing. 2. A long, thin piece of metal or plastic with a pointed end, used for knitting. 3. A very thin, hollow piece of metal with a sharp point that is used for putting a drug into your body or taking blood. 4. A pointer on a scientific instrument that shows a measurement or direction. 5. A thin, pointy leaf on a pine tree.
verb (informal) To annoy someone on purpose.
▶ *verb* **needling, needled**

need·less (**need**-lis) *adjective* Not necessary, because it could have been avoided. ▶ *adverb* **needlessly**

nee·dle·work (**need**-uhl-*wurk*) *noun* Something that is sewn or made with a needle, such as embroidery or needlepoint.

need·n't (**need**-uhnt) *contraction* A short form of *need not.*

need·y (**nee**-dee) *adjective* Not having enough money, food, or clothes. ▶ *adjective* **needier, neediest**

neg·a·tive (**neg**-uh-tiv)
adjective 1. Showing only the bad side of someone or something. 2. Damaging or bad. 3. Giving "no" as an answer. 4. Less than zero in number. 5. Producing one of two opposite kinds of electricity. 6. Not showing that something, such as a disease, is present.
noun Photographic film that has been developed. A negative shows light areas dark and dark areas light.
▶ *adverb* **negatively**

neg·lect (ni-**glekt**)
verb 1. To not take care of or not pay attention to someone or something. 2. To fail or forget to do something.
noun The failure to take care of or pay attention to something or someone.
▶ *verb* **neglecting, neglected**
▶ *adjective* **neglectful**

neg·li·gent (**neg**-li-juhnt) *adjective* Not caring or paying attention to someone or something, especially when this causes serious problems. ▶ *noun* **negligence**

ne·go·ti·ate (ni-**goh**-shee-*ate*) *verb* To try to reach an agreement by discussing something or making a bargain. ▶ *verb* **negotiating, negotiated** ▶ *noun* **negotiation** ▶ *noun* **negotiator**

neigh (nay)
noun The sound made by a horse.
verb To make a sound like that of a horse.
Neigh sounds like **nay.** ▶ *verb* **neighing, neighed**

neigh·bor (**nay**-bur) *noun* 1. Someone who lives next to you or nearby. 2. A person, place, or thing that is located near another. 3. Any other person.

neigh·bor·hood (**nay**-bur-*hud*) *noun*
1. The people who live in a particular area, especially near your house.
2. In a city or town, a small area or section where people live.

neigh·bor·ly (**nay**-bur-lee) *adjective* Friendly, welcoming, and helpful.

nei·ther (**nee**-THur *or* **nye**-THur) *adjective* Not either.
pronoun Not one or the other of two things.
conjunction 1. Nor. 2. Used with the conjunction *nor* to show something negative about two things or people.

ne·on (**nee**-ahn) *noun* A gas that glows brightly when electricity is passed through it, used in lights and signs.

Ne·pal (nuh-**pahl**) A country in the Himalayan Mountains of South Asia. Eight of the world's ten highest mountains, including Mount Everest, are in Nepal.

neph·ew (**nef**-yoo) *noun* The son of your brother or sister.

Nep·tune (**nep**-toon) *noun* The eighth planet in distance from the sun. Neptune is the fourth-largest planet in our solar system.

nerd (nurd) *noun* (slang) A person who is very smart, but considered unfashionable or awkward. ▶ *adjective* **nerdy**

nerve (nurv)
noun 1. A **nerve** is one of the threads that sends messages between your brain and other parts of your body so you can move and feel. 2. Courage to do something difficult or dangerous. 3. (informal) Being bold or rude.
noun, plural **nerves** (informal) Feelings of being frightened or worried.

nerv·ous (**nur**-vuhs) *adjective*
1. Anxious or worried about something. 2. Easily upset or tense and often worried. 3. Of or having to do with the nerves.
▶ *noun* **nervousness** ▶ *adverb* **nervously**

nerv·ous sys·tem (**nur**-vuhs *sis*-tuhm) *noun* A system in the body that includes the brain, spinal cord, and nerves. In humans and animals, the nervous system controls all the feelings and actions of the body.

nest (nest)
noun 1. A place built by birds and other small creatures to live in and take care of their young. 2. A comfortable place or shelter.
verb To make or settle in a nest or home.
▶ *verb* **nesting, nested**

nes·tle (**nes**-uhl) *verb* To sit or lie down in a safe and comfortable place. ▶ *verb* **nestling, nestled**

net (net)
noun 1. Material made from a grid of threads or ropes with small spaces in between. 2. A bag made of this material used to catch something, such as fish or butterflies. 3. A **net amount** of money is the amount that remains after taking out taxes and expenses. 4. The **net weight** of something is its weight without its container or wrapping. 5. the **Net** Short for the **Internet.**
verb 1. To catch something in a net. 2. To gain an amount of money as profit.
▶ *verb* **netting, netted**

net·book (**net**-buk) *noun* A small laptop computer that can access the Internet and does most other tasks that an ordinary laptop can do, but that usually does not have as much memory as an ordinary laptop.

Neth·er·lands (**neTH**-ur-luhndz) A country in northwestern Europe on the North Sea. Often referred to as Holland, the Netherlands is very flat, with about one-fifth of its land below sea level. The windmills that dot the Dutch landscape are used to pump water out of these areas.

net·tle (**net**-uhl) *noun* A plant with hairs on its stems and leaves that sting you if you touch them.

net·work (**net**-wurk)
noun 1. A large number of lines that cross over each other or are connected to each other. 2. A group of televison or radio stations in

N

different places that broadcast the same programs at the same time. **3.** A group of connected computers or communications equipment. **4.** A group of people who share professional or social information with each other.
verb **1.** To connect computers and other equipment to each other so that they can work together and share information. **2.** To meet and talk with people in order to get and give helpful information.
▶ *verb* **networking, networked** ▶ *noun* **networking**

neu·ron (**noor**-ahn) *noun* A cell that carries information between the brain and other parts of the body; a nerve cell.

neu·ro·sci·ence (*noor*-oh-**sye**-uhns) *noun* The science that deals with the brain, the nervous system, and how they work. ▶ *noun* **neuroscientist**

neu·rot·ic (nu-**rah**-tik) *adjective* Unable to behave or think normally because of deep conflicts in your mind. ▶ *adverb* **neurotically**

neu·ter (**noo**-tur)
adjective In some languages, nouns, pronouns, verbs, and adjectives that are neither masculine nor feminine in gender are **neuter.** In English, the pronoun *it* refers to neuter nouns, such as *table.*
verb To make an animal unable to produce young.

neu·tral (**noo**-truhl)
adjective **1.** Not supporting or agreeing with either side of a disagreement or competition, such as a war or a sports event. **2. Neutral** colors are pale and not colorful, such as beige and gray. **3.** In chemistry, a **neutral** substance is neither an acid nor a base.
noun When a car is in **neutral,** the gears cannot give power to the wheels.
▶ *noun* **neutrality** (noo-**tral**-i-tee)
▶ *adverb* **neutrally**

neu·tral·ize (**noo**-truh-*lize*) *verb* To stop something from working or

having an effect. ▶ *verb* **neutralizing, neutralized**

neu·tron (**noo**-trahn) *noun* One of the extremely small parts that form the nucleus of an atom. The neutron has no electrical charge.

Ne·vad·a (nuh-**vad**-uh or nuh-**vah**-duh) A state in the western United States. A part of the Mojave Desert is in Nevada, the most arid state in the country. Its largest city, Las Vegas, is known for its gambling casinos. Nevada is the second-largest producer of silver, after Alaska. The Comstock Lode, the first major silver mining area in the U.S., was discovered in the mountains of Nevada in the 1850s and set off a silver rush to the state.

nev·er (**nev**-ur) *adverb* Not at any time or not ever.

nev·er·the·less (*nev*-ur-THuh-**les**) *adverb* In spite of something you have just mentioned.

new (noo) *adjective* **1.** Just begun, made, or thought of. **2.** Already existing but seen or known for the first time. **3.** Unfamiliar or strange. **4.** Not yet used to or experienced at. **5.** Recently arrived or established in a place, position, relationship, or role. **6.** Not worn or used. **7.** Repeating or beginning again. **8.** Taking the place of a previous one.
New sounds like **gnu** and **knew.**
▶ *adjective* **newer, newest**

new·bie (**noo** -bee) *noun* A beginner at an activity, especially in using computers or the Internet.

new·born (**noo**-*born*)
adjective Recently born.
noun A child who has just been born.

New Bruns·wick (noo **bruhnz**-wik) One of Canada's three maritime provinces. The other two are Nova Scotia and Prince Edward Island. New Brunswick's southern border lies on the Bay of Fundy, which has the highest tides in the world.

new·com·er (**noo**-*kuhm*-ur) *noun* Someone who has just arrived in a place or started a new activity.

N

New Eng·land (noo ing-gluhnd)
noun A region of the northeastern
United States made up of six states:
Maine, New Hampshire, Vermont,
Massachusetts, Rhode Island, and
Connecticut. The New England states
include some of the earliest regions
to be settled by European colonists in
the United States in the 17th and 18th
centuries.

New·found·land and Lab·ra·dor (noo-
fuhnd-luhnd and **lab**-ruh-*dor*) The
easternmost province of Canada, on
the Atlantic Ocean. It consists of two
parts: Labrador, on the mainland; and
the island of Newfoundland, which is
where most of the population lives.

New Hamp·shire (noo **hamp**-shur) A
New England state in the northeastern
United States. Every four years, it
holds the first presidential primary
in the U.S. Its White Mountains
range includes Mount Washington,
the highest peak in the northeastern
U.S. The hurricane-like winds at its
summit have given the top of Mount
Washington the reputation of having
the worst weather in the world, with
record wind speeds.

New Jer·sey (noo **jur**-zee) A state
in the Mid-Atlantic region of the
United States. It is the most densely
populated state in the U.S. and is
known for its Atlantic Ocean beaches.
Edison, New Jersey, is named after
Thomas Edison (1847–1931), who
lived in the area and whose many
inventions include the lightbulb.

new·ly (noo-lee) *adverb* Recently.

New Mex·i·co (noo **mek**-si-*koh*) A
state in the southwestern United
States. Various Native American
tribes have lived there for centuries,
and it is still home to large Navajo
and Pueblo populations, as well as
to a large Hispanic population. Its
buildings and mesa landscapes have
become well known through the work
of the photographer Ansel Adams
(1902–1984) and the painter Georgia
O'Keeffe (1887–1986).

new moon (noo moon) *noun* The phase
of the moon when it is completely
dark or just after this, when it is a very
thin crescent.

news (nooz) *noun* 1. New information
or facts about something that has
happened recently. 2. A broadcast
or story of new information about
subjects that interest people.

news·cast (nooz-kast) *noun* A television
or radio broadcast that presents the
news. ▶ *noun* **newscaster**

news·pa·per (nooz-*pay*-pur) *noun*
Large, printed sheets of paper, folded
together, that contain news reports,
articles, letters, and photographs.
Newspapers are usually published
daily.

news·stand (nooz-*stand*) *noun* A kiosk,
booth, or stall where newspapers,
magazines, and sometimes snacks
and tobacco are sold.

newt (noot) *noun* A small salamander
with short legs and a long tail that
lives on land and in water.

New Tes·ta·ment (noo tes-tuh-muhnt)
noun The second section of the
Christian Bible that deals with the life
and teachings of Jesus Christ and his
followers.

new·ton (noo-tuhn) *noun* A unit used in
physics to measure force.

New World (noo wurld) *noun* North and
South America. European explorers
used this term to compare them to
Europe and places east of Europe.

New Year's Day (noo *yeerz* **day)** *noun*
January 1, a holiday celebrating the
first day of the new year.

New York (noo york) A state in the
northeastern United States. New York
City, the largest and most populous
city in the U.S., is located at the
state's southern tip. Its skyscrapers
include the Empire State Building and
the Chrysler Building. The Statue of
Liberty and Ellis Island, once the entry
point for millions of immigrants to the
U.S., are nearby landmarks. The rest of
New York State is more rural and has
forests, mountains, rivers, and lakes.

N

New Zea·land (noo **zee**-luhnd) An island country in the southwestern Pacific Ocean. It is geographically isolated, lying 1,200 miles southeast of Australia, but frequently visited for its unspoiled environment, dramatic scenery, and livable cities.

next (nekst)
adjective 1. Coming right after this one or the previous one. 2. Nearest or closest.
adverb After something else.

next door (**nekst dor**) *adverb* In or at the nearest house, building, or room. ▸ *adjective* **next-door**

Nez Percé (**nez purs**) *noun* A member of a group of Native Americans who live primarily in Idaho, and also in Washington and Oregon. French explorers called them Nez Percé, or "pierced nose," in error. ▸ *noun, plural* **Nez Percé** or **Nez Percés**

nib·ble (**nib**-uhl)
verb To eat something by taking small bites.
noun A small bite.
▸ *verb* **nibbling, nibbled**

Nic·a·ra·gua (nik-uh-**rah**-gwuh) The largest country in Central America, bordered on the west by the Pacific Ocean and on the east by the Caribbean Sea. Nicaragua has numerous volcanoes, rain forests, and lakes.

nice (nise) *adjective* 1. Pleasant or enjoyable. 2. Kind or friendly. 3. Polite. 4. Of good quality.
▸ *adjective* **nicer, nicest** ▸ *adverb* **nicely**

niche (nich or neesh) *noun* 1. A place, job, or situation that suits someone very well. 2. A hollow place in a wall that is often used to display a statue.

nick (nik)
noun A small cut or chip on the surface or edge of something.
idiom If something happens **in the nick of time,** it happens at the last moment or just in time before something bad could happen.
verb To make a small cut or notch in something.
▸ *verb* **nicking, nicked**

nick·el (**nik**-uhl) *noun* 1. A hard, silver-gray metal that is added to alloys to make them strong. 2. A coin of the United States and Canada equal to five cents.

nick·name (**nik**-*name*)
noun 1. A name for a person that friends use instead of the person's real name. 2. A familiar or shortened form of a name.
verb To give someone or something a nickname.
▸ *verb* **nicknaming, nicknamed**

nic·o·tine (**nik**-uh-*teen*) *noun* A poisonous substance in tobacco that causes people to become addicted to it.

niece (nees) *noun* The daughter of your brother or sister.

Ni·ger (**nye**-jur) A country in West Africa. More than 80 percent of the land in Niger is covered by the Sahara Desert. It was once a French colony, and its most profitable export is uranium.

Ni·ge·ri·a (nye-**jeer**-ee-uh) A country in West Africa. A former British colony, it is the most populous country in Africa and has one of the fastest-growing economies in the world.

night (nite) *noun* The dark time between days; the time between sunset and sunrise.

night·fall (**nite**-*fawl*) *noun* The time of day when it begins to get dark.

night·gown (**nite**-*goun*) *noun* A long, loose dress that is worn in bed.

night·in·gale (**nye**-tin-*gale*) *noun* A small brown and white bird. The male is known for its beautiful song.

night·ly (**nite**-lee)
adverb Every night.
adjective Done or happening every night or during the night.

night·mare (**nite**-*mair*) *noun* 1. A frightening or unpleasant dream. 2. A difficult or frightening experience.

night·time (**nite**-*time*) *noun* The time between days when it is dark, from sunset until sunrise.

N

nim·ble (**nim**-buhl) *adjective* Able to move quickly and easily. ▶ *adjective* **nimbler, nimblest** ▶ *adverb* **nimbly** (**nim**-blee)

NIMBY (**nim**-bee) *adjective* Opposed to a project or development that might happen or be built close to your house. NIMBY is short for *not in my backyard*.

nine (nine) *noun* The number that comes after eight and before ten, written numerically as 9.

nin·ja (**nin**-juh) *noun* A person who is very skilled in Japanese martial arts, especially one hired as a spy or to kill someone.

nip (nip)
verb 1. To bite or pinch quickly but not hard. 2. To cut off by pinching. 3. To sting or damage with cold.
noun 1. A feeling of coldness. 2. A bite or pinch.
▶ *verb* **nipping, nipped** ▶ *adjective* **nippy**

nip·ple (**nip**-uhl) *noun* 1. The raised part of a breast that in females contains ducts for milk. 2. A small rubber cap with a hole, attached to the top of a baby bottle.

ni·tro·gen (**nye**-truh-juhn) *noun* A colorless, odorless gas that makes up about four-fifths of the earth's atmosphere.

nits (nits) *noun, plural* Eggs laid by lice.

no (noh)
adverb 1. Used as a negative response to a question. 2. Not.
interjection A word used to show surprise or disbelief.
adjective 1. Not any; not one. 2. Not a.
noun 1. A word used to show that you do not agree. 2. A vote of "no" or a voter who votes "no."
No sounds like **know**. ▶ *noun, plural* **noes**

no·ble (**noh**-buhl)
adjective 1. Having or showing admirable qualities, such as courage, honesty, and generosity. 2. Belonging to a family that is of a very high social class. 3. Impressive or magnificent in size or quality.

noun A person who belongs to a family that is of a very high social class.
▶ *adjective* **nobler, noblest** ▶ *noun* **nobility** (noh-**bil**-i-tee) ▶ *adverb* **nobly** ▶ *noun* **nobleman** ▶ *noun* **noblewoman**

no·bod·y (**noh**-*bah*-dee or **noh**-buh-dee)
pronoun No one.
noun Someone who is not thought to be important.
▶ *noun, plural* **nobodies**

noc·tur·nal (nahk-**tur**-nuhl) *adjective* 1. Happening at night. 2. A **nocturnal** animal is active at night.
▶ *adverb* **nocturnally**

nod (nahd)
verb 1. To move your head up and down, to show that you agree or understand. 2. To let your head fall forward when you are falling asleep sitting up. 3. To indicate or say something by nodding. 4. To bend or to sway.
noun An up-and-down movement of the head.
▶ *verb* **nodding, nodded**

noise (noiz) *noun* A sound or sounds, especially loud or disturbing ones.

nois·y (**noi**-zee) *adjective* Loud. ▶ *adjective* **noisier, noisiest** ▶ *adverb* **noisily** ▶ *noun* **noisiness**

no·mad (**noh**-mad) *noun* 1. A member of a community that travels from place to place instead of living in the same place all the time. 2. A person who wanders from place to place.
▶ *adjective* **nomadic** (noh-**mad**-ik)

nom·i·nate (**nah**-muh-*nate*) *verb* To suggest that someone would be a good person to do an important job or to receive an honor. ▶ *verb* **nominating, nominated** ▶ *noun* **nomination**

nom·i·nee (*nah*-muh-**nee**) *noun* Someone who is suggested to run in an election, to fill a job, or to receive an honor.

none (nuhn)
pronoun 1. Not one of a group of

N

people or things. **2.** Not any or no part.

adverb Not at all; not very.

None sounds like **nun.**

none·the·less (*nuhn*-THuh-**les**) *adverb* Despite that.

non·fic·tion (*nahn*-**fik**-shuhn) *noun* Writing about real things, people, and events.

non·sense (**nahn**-*sens*) *noun* **1.** Ideas or statements that are silly, untrue, or make no sense. **2.** Behavior that is silly or annoying.

▶ *adjective* **nonsensical**

non·stop (**nahn**-stahp)
adjective Without any pauses or stops.
adverb Without stopping.

noo·dle (**noo**-duhl) *noun* A flat strip of dried dough, usually made from flour, water, and eggs.

nook (nuk) *noun* **1.** A corner or section of a room. **2.** A small, private area or place.

noon (noon) *noun* Twelve o'clock in the middle of the day.

no one (**noh** wuhn) *pronoun* Not anyone; not a single person.

noose (noos) *noun* A large loop tied in a piece of rope that closes up tightly when the rope is pulled.

nor (nor) *conjunction* And not. Often used together with *neither* to show something negative about two things or people.

norm (norm) *noun* An accepted standard or the usual thing.

nor·mal (**nor**-muhl)
adjective **1.** Usual or typical.
2. Healthy.
noun What you would expect.
▶ *noun* **normality** (nor-**mal**-i-tee)
▶ *noun* **normalcy** (**nor**-muhl-see)

nor·mal·ly (**nor**-muh-lee) *adverb* Under typical conditions.

north (north)
noun **1.** One of the four main points of the compass. North is the direction to your left when you face the sunrise. **2. North** Any area or region lying in this direction. **3. the North** In the United States, the

region that is north of Maryland, the Ohio River, and Missouri, especially the states that fought against the Confederacy in the Civil War.

adjective In or having to do with the north.

adverb In, from, or toward the north.

▶ *adjective* **northern** (nor-**THuhrn**)

North A·mer·i·ca (**north** uh-**mer**-i-kuh) *noun* The continent in the Western Hemisphere that includes the United States, Canada, Mexico, and Central America. North America is bordered by the Atlantic Ocean to the east and the Pacific Ocean to the west. ▶ *noun* **North American** ▶ *adjective* **North American**

North Car·o·li·na (**north** *kar*-uh-**lye**-nuh) A state on the Atlantic coast of the southern United States. North Carolina has beaches on its eastern shore, and has mountains in the western section of the state. The mountains are part of the Appalachian range and include the Blue Ridge Mountains and the Great Smoky Mountains.

North Da·ko·ta (**north** duh-**koh**-tuh) A state in the Midwest region of the United States, along the Canadian border. It is the third least populated state in the U.S., after Wyoming and Vermont, and most of it is covered in grassland. North Dakota has one of the largest Native American populations in the country and is the site of a major annual tribal gathering, known as a powwow.

North·east (*north*-**eest**) *noun* **the Northeast** The northeast area of the United States that includes New England, New York, New Jersey, and sometimes Pennsylvania.

North·ern Hem·i·sphere (**nor**-THurn **hem**-i-sfeer) *noun* The half of the earth that is north of the equator.

north·ern lights (**nor**-THurn **lites**) *noun, plural* Bright, colorful streaks of light that appear in the night sky in the far north. The northern lights are also called the **aurora borealis.**

North·ern Mar·i·an·a Is·lands
(**nor**-THurn *mair*-ee-**an**-uh **eye**-luhdz) A group of 15 islands in the western Pacific Ocean, about three-quarters of the way from Hawaii to the Philippines. The islands are considered a commonwealth in political union with the United States.

North Pole (**north pole**) *noun* The most northern point on earth, located at the top of the earth's axis.

North Sea (**north see**) A sea of the Atlantic Ocean between Great Britain and Scandinavia. It is bordered by Norway to the northeast, Great Britain to the west, Denmark and Germany to the east, and the Netherlands, Belgium, and France to the southeast.

North Star (**north stahr**) *noun* A bright star that is located directly over the North Pole.

north·ward (**north**-wurd)
adverb To or toward the north.
adjective Toward the north.

North·west (*north*-**west**) *noun* **the Northwest** The area of the United States that includes Washington, Oregon, and Idaho.

North·west Ter·ri·to·ries (**north**-west *ter*-i-*tor*-eez) A territory in northern Canada, between Yukon to the west and Nunavut to the east. It includes several islands to the north as well as Great Bear Lake, the largest lake entirely within Canada.

Nor·way (**nor**-way) A country in northern Europe on the western side of the Scandinavian Peninsula. Norway is known for the deep fjords, or inlets, in its extensive and mountainous North Atlantic coastline.

nose (nohz)
noun **1.** The part of your face above your mouth that you use to smell and breathe. **2.** The pointed front part of planes and some other aircraft.
verb To move forward slowly and carefully.
▸ *verb* **nosing, nosed**

nose·bleed (**nohz**-*bleed*) *noun* Bleeding in or from the nose.

nose cone (**nohz** *kone*) *noun* The front part of a missile, rocket, or jet engine. It is shaped like a cone to reduce friction with the air.

nosh (nahsh)
noun A snack or a small meal.
verb To eat a snack.
▸ *noun, plural* **noshes** ▸ *verb* **noshes, noshing, noshed** ▸ *noun* **nosher**

nos·tal·gia (nah-**stal**-juh) *noun* A feeling of longing for good times in the past and wishing things hadn't changed.

nos·tal·gic (nah-**stal**-jik) *adjective* Remembering good times in the past and wishing things had remained the same. ▸ *noun* **nostalgia** (nah-**stal**-juh) ▸ *adverb* **nostalgically**

nos·tril (**nah**-struhl) *noun* One of the two openings in your nose that you breathe and smell through.

nos·y (**noh**-zee) *adjective* Someone who is **nosy** is too interested in other people's business, especially things that do not concern them. ▸ *adjective* **nosier, nosiest** ▸ *adverb* **nosily** (**noh**-zuh-lee)

not (naht) *adverb* At no time or in no way. The word *not* is used to make a statement negative. **Not** sounds like **knot.**

no·ta·ble (**noh**-tuh-buhl)
adjective Important, remarkable, or deserving to be noticed.
noun An important or famous person.

no·ta·bly (**noh**-tuh-blee) *adverb* In a noticeable way.

no·ta·tion (noh-**tay**-shuhn) *noun* **1.** A system of signs or symbols used to represent information, especially in music, math, or science. **2.** A short note.

notch (nahch)
noun **1.** A V-shaped cut or nick. **2.** A level or degree on a scale.
verb To make a V-shaped cut in something.
▸ *noun, plural* **notches** ▸ *verb* **notches, notching, notched**

note (note)
noun **1.** A short message or letter. **2.** A word, phrase, or short sentence you write down to help you remember

something. **3.** A short comment in a book or article that gives more information. **4.** A quality in someone's voice or in music that suggests a feeling or mood. **5.** A piece of paper money. **6.** A musical sound, or the symbol that represents it.
verb **1.** To notice or pay attention to something. **2.** To write something down so you do not forget it. **3.** To mention something important.
▶ *verb* **noting, noted**

note·book (**note**-*buk*) *noun* **1.** A small book of blank or lined pages used for writing. **2.** A small computer that is easy to carry.

not·ed (**noh**-tid) *adjective* Famous or distinguished.

note·pad (**note**-*pad*) *noun* A pad of small paper for writing notes on.

noth·ing (**nuhth**-ing)
pronoun **1.** Not anything. **2.** Not anything important or interesting.
noun Zero.

no·tice (**noh**-tis)
verb To see or become aware of something.
noun **1.** Attention or knowledge. **2.** A printed paper giving information, especially one that is in a public place. **3.** A warning or an announcement.
phrase If someone **gives notice,** the person tells his or her employer that he or she will be leaving that job soon.
▶ *verb* **noticing, noticed** ▶ *adjective* **noticeable** ▶ *adverb* **noticeably**

no·ti·fy (**noh**-tuh-*fye*) *verb* To tell someone about something officially or formally. ▶ *verb* **notifies, notifying, notified** ▶ *noun* **notification**

no·tion (**noh**-shun)
noun **1.** An idea or something you believe. **2.** A sudden desire to do something.
noun, plural **notions** Small items for sewing, such as needles, pins, buttons, thread, and ribbons.

no·to·ri·ous (noh-**tor**-ee-uhs) *adjective* Well known for being bad or doing something bad.

noun (noun) *noun* A word that names a person, place, or thing. The words *cat, Miami,* and *goodness* are all nouns.

nour·ish (**nur**-ish) *verb* To keep a person or an animal strong and healthy by feeding them. ▶ *verb* **nourishes, nourishing, nourished** ▶ *noun* **nourishment** ▶ *adjective* **nourishing**

No·va Sco·tia (**noh**-vuh **skoh**-shuh) A province of southeastern Canada on the North Atlantic Ocean. It was named after Scotland, and people of Scottish descent constitute the largest ethnic group living there today.

nov·el (**nah**-vuhl)
noun A book that tells a made-up story about people and events.
adjective New and different.
▶ *noun* **novelist**

nov·el·ty (**nah**-vuhl-tee)
noun **1.** Something new, different, and interesting. **2.** The quality of being new and different.
adjective Intended to be amusing because it is new or unusual.
▶ *noun, plural* **novelties**

No·vem·ber (noh-**vem**-bur) *noun* The 11th month on the calendar, after October and before December. November has 30 days.

nov·ice (**nah**-vis) *noun* **1.** A beginner or someone who is not very experienced in a job or activity. **2.** Someone who joins a religious group in order to become a monk or a nun.

now (nou)
adverb **1.** At the present time. **2.** Right away; from this moment on. **3.** In the recent past.
noun The present time.
conjunction Since.

now·a·days (**nou**-uh-*days*) *adverb* At the present time, as compared to the past.

no·where (**noh**-*wair*)
adverb Not in or to any place.
noun An unknown or unimportant place or state of being.

N

noz·zle (**nah**-zuhl) *noun* A short tube or opening on a hose or pipe that controls the flow of liquid, gas, or air.

nu·cle·ar (**noo**-klee-ur)
adjective 1. Of or having to do with the nucleus of an atom or cell. 2. Of or having to do with the energy created by splitting atoms.
noun 1. **nuclear energy** Energy created by splitting atoms. 2. **nuclear power** Power created by splitting atoms. 3. **nuclear reactor** A large device in a power station that produces nuclear power. 4. **nuclear weapon** A weapon that uses the power created by splitting atoms.

nu·cle·us (**noo**-klee-uhs) *noun* 1. A central part around which other things are grouped or located. 2. The central part of an atom that is made up of neutrons and protons. 3. The central part of a cell that contains the chromosomes.
▸ *noun, plural* **nuclei** (**noo**-klee-*eye*)

nude (nood)
adjective Not wearing any clothes.
noun A naked human figure in a work of art, such as a sculpture or painting.
▸ *noun* **nudist** ▸ *noun* **nudity** (**noo**-di-tee)

nudge (nuhj)
verb To push someone or something gently, especially with the elbow.
noun A gentle push.
▸ *verb* **nudging, nudged**

nug·get (**nuhg**-it) *noun* 1. A small lump of something, especially precious metal. 2. A small bit of something.

nui·sance (**noo**-suhns) *noun* Someone or something that is annoying and causes problems.

numb (nuhm)
adjective 1. Not able to feel anything. 2. Stunned; not able to react.
verb To make someone or something incapable of feeling anything.
▸ *verb* **numbing, numbed** ▸ *noun* **numbness**

num·ber (**nuhm**-bur)
noun 1. A word or symbol used for counting and for adding and subtracting; a numeral. 2. A number that is used to identify someone or something. 3. An amount or group.
verb 1. To give a number to something in a set or list. 2. To make up a particular number.
▸ *verb* **numbering, numbered**

nu·mer·al (**noo**-mur-uhl) *noun* A sign or symbol that represents a number, such as "8" or "VIII."

nu·mer·a·tor (**noo**-muh-ray-tur) *noun* In fractions, the **numerator** is the number above the line. The numerator shows how many parts of the denominator are taken.

nu·mer·i·cal (noo-**mer**-i-kuhl) *adjective* Relating to or expressed with numbers. ▸ *adverb* **numerically**

nu·mer·ic key·pad (noo-**mer**-ik **kee**-*pad*) *noun* The small keypad on the right side of most computer keyboards that consists mainly of number keys.

nu·mer·ous (**noo**-mur-uhs) *adjective* Many, or made up of a large number.

nun (nuhn) *noun* A woman who lives in a religious community of women and has devoted her life to God. **Nun** sounds like **none.**

Nu·na·vut (**noo**-nuh-*voot*) A territory in northern Canada, east of the Northwest Territories. It is Canada's largest and most northern territory. It is also the newest, formed in 1999 after separating from the Northwest Territories. Its name means "our land" in Inuktitut, an Inuit language. Most of the people in Nunavut are Inuit, and their small population is spread out over an area three times the size of Texas.

nurse (nurs)
noun Someone whose job is taking care of people who are sick or injured, usually in a hospital.
verb 1. To take care of someone who is sick or injured. 2. To feed a baby milk from a breast. 3. To treat with care or attention.
▸ *verb* **nursing, nursed**

nurs·er·y (**nur**-sur-ee) *noun* 1. A baby's bedroom. 2. A place that sells trees,

N

plants, and seeds. **3. nursery rhyme** A short poem, especially for very young children. **4. nursery school** A school for children aged three to five years old, before they go to kindergarten.
▶ *noun, plural* **nurseries**

nurs·ing home (**nur**-sing *home*) *noun* A place where old or disabled people live and are cared for, because they cannot take care of themselves.

nur·ture (**nur**-chur) *verb* To protect and take care of something or someone while they are growing, especially like a child. ▶ *verb* **nurturing, nurtured**

nut (nuht) *noun* **1.** A small fruit or seed from a tree with a hard shell and softer parts inside. **2.** The inside part of a nut that can be eaten. **3.** A small piece of metal with a hole in the middle that screws on to a bolt and holds it in place. **4.** A strange or silly person. **5.** Someone who is very enthusiastic about something.

nut·crack·er (**nuht**-krak-ur) *noun* A tool for cracking nuts open.

nut·hatch (**nuht**-hach) *noun* A small bird that eats insects and can climb down trees headfirst. ▶ *noun, plural* **nuthatches**

nut·meg (**nuht**-meg) *noun* A spice used in cooking that is made from the ground-up seeds of a tropical tree.

nu·tri·ent (**noo**-tree-uhnt) *noun* A substance such as a protein, a mineral, or a vitamin that is needed by people, animals, and plants to stay strong and healthy.

nu·tri·tion (noo-**trish**-uhn) *noun* **1.** Something that nourishes. **2.** The process by which the body changes food into living tissues.
▶ *adjective* **nutritional**

nu·tri·tious (noo-**trish**-uhs) *adjective* Containing substances that help you stay healthy and strong. ▶ *adverb* **nutritiously**

nuz·zle (**nuhz**-uhl) *verb* **1.** To rub or touch with the nose or mouth as an animal does. **2.** To lie very close to someone or something.
▶ *verb* **nuzzling, nuzzled**

ny·lon (**nye**-lahn)
noun A strong artificial fiber used to make things such as clothing, carpets, and rope.
noun, plural **nylons** Women's stockings made from nylon.

nymph (nimf) *noun* **1.** In ancient Greek and Roman stories, a beautiful female spirit or goddess who lived in a forest, a meadow, a mountain, or a stream. **2.** A young form of an insect, such as a grasshopper, that changes into an adult by shedding its skin many times.

O

oak (ohk) *noun* A tree that produces acorns and a very hard wood used in building houses and making furniture.

oar (or) *noun* A long, usually wooden pole with a flat blade at one end, used for rowing or steering a boat. **Oar** sounds like **or** and **ore.**

oar·lock (**or**-lahk) *noun* A curved piece of metal attached to the side of a rowboat, used to hold the oar in place while you row.

o·a·sis (oh-**ay**-sis) *noun* A place in a desert where water can be found above the ground and where plants and trees can grow. ▶ *noun, plural* **oases** (oh-**ay**-seez)

oat (oht) *noun* The grain from a kind of grass plant used as food for humans and animals.

oath (ohth) *noun* **1.** A solemn, formal promise or declaration. **2.** A curse or swear word.

oat·meal (**oht**-meel) *noun* **1.** Meal made from oats that have been ground or rolled flat. **2.** A hot cereal made from oats.

o·be·di·ent (oh-**bee**-dee-uhnt) *adjective* If you are **obedient,** you do what you are told or are willing to follow orders. ▶ *noun* **obedience** ▶ *adverb* **obediently**

o·bese (oh-**bees**) *adjective* Extremely fat, in a way that is not healthy. ▶ *noun* **obesity** (oh-**bee**-si-tee)

o·bey (oh-**bay**) *verb* 1. To do what you are told to do. 2. To carry out or to follow orders or instructions.
▶ *verb* **obeying, obeyed**

o·bi (**oh**-bee) *noun* A wide sash worn with a Japanese kimono.

ob·ject
noun (**ahb**-jikt) 1. A thing that takes up space and can be seen or touched. 2. A person or thing that someone pays attention to, discusses, or thinks about. 3. Something that you are trying to achieve. 4. The **object** or **direct object** of a verb is the noun or pronoun that is affected by the action of the verb. In the sentence "Billy hit the ball," the noun *ball* is the object of the verb *hit*. The **indirect object** of a verb is the noun or pronoun that the action is done for or to. In "Mona gave her an apple," *her* is the indirect object.
verb (uhb-**jekt**) If you **object** to something, you don't like it or don't agree with it.
▶ *verb* **objecting, objected** ▶ *noun* **objector** (uhb-**jek**-tur)

ob·jec·tion (uhb-**jek**-shuhn) *noun* An expression or a feeling of not liking or not approving of something.

ob·jec·tion·a·ble (uhb-**jek**-shuh-nuh-buhl) *adjective* Unpleasant or offensive to others.

ob·jec·tive (uhb-**jek**-tiv)
noun A goal or something you are trying to achieve.
adjective Based on or influenced by facts, instead of opinions or feelings; fair.
▶ *noun* **objectivity** (ahb-juhk-**tiv**-i-tee) ▶ *adverb* **objectively**

ob·li·gate (**ahb**-li-gate) *verb* To force someone to do something because of a law, contract, or promise. ▶ *verb* **obligating, obligated**

ob·li·ga·tion (ahb-li-**gay**-shuhn) *noun* Something you have to do because it is your duty or you have promised. ▶ *adjective* **obligatory** (uh-**blig**-uh-tor-ee)

o·blige (uh-**blije**) *verb* 1. If you are **obliged** to do something, you must do it because it is a law or responsibility. 2. To do something to help or please someone by doing a favor.
▶ *verb* **obliging, obliged** ▶ *adjective* **obliging** ▶ *adverb* **obligingly**

o·blit·er·ate (uh-**blit**-uh-rate) *verb* To destroy or cover something completely, so that nothing remains or can be seen. ▶ *verb* **obliterating, obliterated**

ob·long (**ahb**-lawng)
adjective Having a shape that is longer than it is wide.
noun A shape like a rectangle, longer than it is wide.

ob·nox·ious (uhb-**nahk**-shuhs) *adjective* Very unpleasant or annoying in a way that offends people. ▶ *adverb* **obnoxiously**

o·boe (**oh**-boh) *noun* A long, thin woodwind instrument with a double-reed mouthpiece. An oboe makes a high, sweet sound. ▶ *noun* **oboist** (**oh**-boh-ist)

ob·scene (ahb-**seen**) *adjective* Offensive or vulgar. ▶ *noun* **obscenity** (ahb-**sen**-i-tee) ▶ *adverb* **obscenely**

ob·scure (ahb-**skyoor**)
adjective 1. Not well known, or not yet discovered. 2. Difficult to understand.
verb To hide from view.
▶ *verb* **obscuring, obscured** ▶ *noun* **obscurity**

ob·serv·ant (uhb-**zur**-vuhnt) *adjective* 1. Able to pay close attention and notice things quickly. 2. Adhering strictly to the rules of a religion.
▶ *adverb* **observantly**

ob·ser·va·tion (ahb-zur-**vay**-shuhn) *noun* 1. The act of watching someone or something carefully, especially to learn something. 2. Something that you have noticed by watching carefully. 3. A remark.

ob·serv·a·to·ry (uhb-**zur**-vuh-tor-ee) *noun* A special building that has telescopes or other instruments for studying the stars and the weather. ▶ *noun, plural* **observatories**

O

ob·serve (uhb-**zurv**) *verb* 1. To watch someone or something closely, especially to learn something. 2. To notice someone or something. 3. To make a comment. 4. To follow or to obey. 5. To celebrate.
▶ *verb* **observing, observed**

ob·serv·er (uhb-**zur**-vur) *noun* A person who sees or observes something, especially someone who does this in an official capacity.

ob·sess (uhb-**ses**) *verb* If something **obsesses** you, you are constantly talking or thinking about it. ▶ *verb* **obsesses, obsessing, obsessed** ▶ *adjective* **obsessive**

ob·ses·sion (uhb-**sesh**-uhn) *noun* Something that you can't stop doing or thinking about, even though you should.

ob·so·lete (*ahb*-suh-**leet**) *adjective* Out-of-date; no longer made or used because something new has been invented.

ob·sta·cle (**ahb**-stuh-kuhl) *noun* Something that makes it difficult to do or achieve something.

ob·sti·nate (**ahb**-stuh-nit) *adjective* If someone is **obstinate,** the person is stubborn and refuses to change his or her mind or behavior. ▶ *noun* **obstinacy** ▶ *adverb* **obstinately**

ob·struct (uhb-**struhkt**) *verb* 1. To block a road or passage. 2. To get in the way of. 3. To slow down the progress of something or prevent it from happening.
▶ *verb* **obstructing, obstructed** ▶ *noun* **obstruction** ▶ *adjective* **obstructive**

obtain (uhb-**tayn**) *verb* To get something, especially after making an effort. ▶ *verb* **obtaining, obtained**

ob·tuse (uhb-**toos**) *adjective* 1. If someone is **obtuse,** he or she is slow or not willing to understand something. 2. An **obtuse** angle is more than 90 degrees and less than 180 degrees.

ob·vi·ous (**ahb**-vee-uhs) *adjective* If something is **obvious,** you can see or understand it easily.

ob·vi·ous·ly (**ahb**-vee-uhs-lee) *adverb* In a way that is clearly seen or understood.

oc·ca·sion (uh-**kay**-zhuhn) *noun* 1. A time when something takes place. 2. A special event or celebration.

oc·ca·sion·al (uh-**kay**-zhuh-nuhl) *adjective* Happening sometimes but not often.

oc·ca·sion·al·ly (uh-**kay**-zhuh-nuh-lee) *adverb* Not very often or not on a regular basis.

oc·cu·pant (**ahk**-yuh-puhnt) *noun* A person who occupies a place.

oc·cu·pa·tion (*ahk*-yuh-**pay**-shuhn) *noun* 1. A job or profession. 2. The invasion and control of a country or an area by a foreign army.
▶ *adjective* **occupational**

oc·cu·py (**ahk**-yuh-*pye*) *verb* 1. To live or work in a place. 2. To fill or use a space or an amount of time. 3. If an army **occupies** a country or an area, it enters and takes control of it by force. 4. To fill up time or keep yourself busy.
▶ *verb* **occupies, occupying, occupied** ▶ *noun* **occupier**

oc·cur (uh-**kur**) *verb* 1. To take place; to happen. 2. If something **occurs to you,** it comes into your mind suddenly.
▶ *verb* **occurring, occurred**

oc·cur·rence (uh-**kur**-uhns) *noun* Something that happens.

o·cean (**oh**-shuhn) *noun* 1. The mass of saltwater that covers about 71 percent of the earth's surface. 2. One of the five main parts of this mass of water.

o·cean·og·ra·phy (*oh*-shuh-**nah**-gruh-fee) *noun* The scientific study of the ocean and the plants and animals that live in it. ▶ *noun* **oceanographer**

oce·lot (**ah**-suh-*laht*) *noun* A wildcat with spotted fur. The ocelot lives in the southwestern United States, Central America, and parts of South America.

o'clock (uh-**klahk**) *adverb* Used to say what hour it is.

oc·ta·gon (**ahk**-tuh-*gahn*) *noun* A flat shape with eight sides and eight angles. ▶ *adjective* **octagonal** (ahk-**tag**-uh-nuhl)

O

oc·ta·he·dron (ahk-tuh-**hee**-druhn) *noun* A solid shape with eight surfaces that are usually triangles.

oc·tave (**ahk**-tiv) *noun* The eight-note difference on a musical scale between two notes with the same name.

Oc·to·ber (ahk-**toh**-bur) *noun* The 10th month on the calendar, after September and before November. October has 31 days.

oc·to·pus (**ahk**-tuh-pus) *noun* A sea creature with a soft body and eight long arms, or tentacles, with suckers that it uses to move along the ocean bottom and catch its prey. ▶ *noun, plural* **octopuses** *or* **octopi** (**ahk**-tuh-pye)

odd (ahd) *adjective* 1. Strange, unusual, or hard to explain. 2. An **odd** number cannot be divided evenly by two; it will always have a remainder of one. 3. Not with the pair or set that something matches or belongs to. 4. Not frequent or regular.
▶ *adjective* **odder, oddest** ▶ *adverb* **oddly**

odd·i·ty (**ah**-di-tee) *noun* A person or thing that seems unusual or strange.

odds (ahdz) *noun, plural* The chances that something is likely to happen.

odds and ends (**ahdz** uhn **endz**) *noun, plural* 1. Small items that are not part of a set. 2. Small jobs to be done.

ode (ohd) *noun* A long poem that praises a person or thing or celebrates an event.

o·di·ous (**oh**-dee-uhs) *adjective* Unpleasant or disgusting.

o·dor (**oh**-dur) *noun* 1. A smell, especially a bad one. 2. An overall feeling or impression of something.

of (uhv *or* ahv) *preposition* 1. Belonging to. *She is a friend of mine.* 2. Made with, as in *a ring of silver.* 3. Named or called, as in *the city of Atlanta.* 4. Containing or holding, as in *a glass of milk.* 5. Before or until. *It is ten minutes of six.* 6. About or concerning. *I thought of you yesterday.*

off (awf)
preposition Away from. *Please get your feet off the couch.*

adverb 1. Away from a place. 2. Not turned on or not operating. 3. In the future.
adjective 1. Not at work. 2. Not as good as usual. 3. Not correct.

of·fend (uh-**fend**) *verb* To make someone feel upset or angry. ▶ *verb* **offending, offended**

of·fend·er (uh-**fen**-dur) *noun* A criminal or someone who commits an offense.

of·fense
noun 1. (uh-**fens**) Something that breaks a law or rule; a crime. 2. (**aw**-fens) In sports, the team or part of a team that is attacking or trying to score.
phrases 1. (uh-**fens**) If you **cause offense,** you hurt or insult someone. 2. (uh-**fens**) If you **take offense,** you feel hurt or insulted by something that someone has done or said.

of·fen·sive (uh-**fen**-siv)
adjective 1. Causing upset or hurt feelings. 2. Unpleasant or disgusting. 3. Aggressive or attacking.
noun An attack, especially by armed forces.

of·fer (**aw**-fur)
verb 1. To present something to someone that he or she might want, or to make something available. 2. To express that you are willing to do something. 3. To suggest something.
noun 1. The act of presenting something to someone, or expressing that you are willing to do something, and allowing that person the opportunity to accept it. 2. An amount of money that someone is willing to pay for something.
▶ *verb* **offering, offered**

of·fer·ing (**aw**-fur-ing)
noun Something that is given or made for others to use or enjoy.
plural noun **offerings** The food or other merchandise that a business sells.

off·hand (**awf**-hand)
adjective Showing little thought, interest, or preparation.
adverb Without thinking about it ahead of time.

O

of·fice (**aw**-fis) *noun* **1.** A room or building in which people work at desks or business is conducted. **2.** An important position of authority or power. **3.** The people who work in an office.

of·fi·cer (**aw**-fi-sur) *noun* **1.** Someone who is in charge or holds a position of authority, especially in the armed forces or the police. **2.** Someone who has a responsible position in a club or similar group.

of·fi·cial (uh-**fish**-uhl)
adjective Of or having to do with someone in a position of authority.
noun **1.** Someone who is in an important position or public office.
2. In sports, the person who enforces the rules of the game, such as the referee or umpire.
▶ *adverb* **officially**

off·line (**awf**-line)
adjective Not controlled by or directly connected to a computer or to the Internet.
adverb While not connected to a computer or the Internet.

off·peak (**awf**-peek) *adjective* When activity, use, or demand is less.

off·put·ting (**awf**-put-ing) *adjective* Annoying or disturbing, in a way that makes you dislike something.

off·road (**awf**-rohd) *adjective* Made for or involving traveling away from public roads.

off·set (*awf*-set) *verb* To cancel out, or to make up for. ▶ *verb* **offsetting, offset**

off·shoot (**awf**-shoot) *noun* **1.** A new stem that grows from the main stem of a plant. **2.** Something that develops or grows from something else.

off·side (**awf**-side) *adjective* In football, soccer, or hockey, in an illegal position ahead of the ball or puck.

off·spring (**awf**-spring) *noun* The young of an animal or a human being. ▶ *noun, plural* **offspring**

of·ten (**aw**-fuhn) *adverb* Frequently.

o·gre (**oh**-gur) *noun* **1.** A cruel giant or monster, usually in stories, that eats human beings. **2.** A person who is cruel or scary.

oh (oh) *interjection* A word used to express emotion such as surprise, disappointment, fear, or pain. **Oh** sounds like **owe.**

O·hi·o (oh-**hye**-oh) A state in the Midwest region of the United States. Ohio was originally part of the Northwest Territory. The state's name comes from the Iroquois word *ohi-yo*, meaning "great river." Ohio is known as the birthplace of aviation. Orville and Wilbur Wright, the inventors of the first successful airplane, lived in the city of Dayton. The brothers launched the first manned, powered flight at Kitty Hawk, North Carolina, in 1903.

ohm (ohm) *noun* A unit for measuring resistance to the flow of electricity through a substance.

oil (oil)
noun **1.** A thick, greasy liquid that burns easily and does not mix with water. **2.** A nontechnical term for **petroleum. 3.** A paint that is used by an artist and contains oil.
verb To smear, polish, or put oil on something.
▶ *verb* **oiling, oiled** ▶ *adjective* **oily**

oil rig (oil rig) *noun* A large platform that is built above the sea as a base for drilling for oil under the ocean floor.

oil well (oil wel) *noun* A deep hole made in the ground to get oil.

oint·ment (**oint**-muhnt) *noun* A thick, oily substance used to heal or protect the skin.

O·jib·wa (oh-**jib**-way) *noun* A member of a group of Native Americans who settled near the western Great Lakes in the United States and Canada. The Ojibwa are also called the **Chippewa.** ▶ *noun, plural* **Ojibwa** or **Ojibwas**

OK *or* **o·kay** (**oh**-kay)
adjective All right; acceptable but not very good.
verb If you **OK** something, you agree to it or allow it to happen.
noun Permission or approval.
▶ *verb* **OKing, OKed**

O

O·kla·ho·ma (*oh*-kluh-**hoh**-muh) A state in the South Central region of the United States. It is known for its production of natural gas and crude oil. The state has one of the largest Native American populations in the U.S., with 25 different languages. More Native American languages are spoken in Oklahoma than in any other state.

ok·ra (**oh**-kruh) *noun* A tall plant whose long seed pods are eaten as a vegetable.

old (ohld) *adjective* **1.** Having lived for a long time. **2.** Existing or used for a long time. **3.** Of a particular age. **4.** Worn out by a lot of use. **5.** Former, or from a time past.
▸ *adjective* **older, oldest**

old age (ohld ayj) *noun* The later years of a person's life, when he or she has less strength and energy.

old·en days (**ohl**-duhn *dayz*) *noun, plural* A time long ago.

Old Eng·lish (ohld **ing**-glish) *noun* The English language that was spoken before the 12th century.

old·er (**ohl**-dur) *adjective* Existing or starting earlier in time.

old-fash·ioned (ohld-**fash**-uhnd) *adjective* **1.** Outdated or no longer fashionable. **2.** Attached to or keeping the ways, ideas, or customs of an earlier time.

Old Tes·ta·ment (ohld **tes**-tuh-muhnt) *noun* A collection of writings that makes up the Jewish Bible and the first part of the Christian Bible.

Old World (ohld **wurld**) *noun* Europe, Asia, and Africa. They are called by this name usually in comparison with North and South America, known as the New World.

ol·ive (**ah**-liv) *noun* **1.** The small, black or green fruit of a Mediterranean evergreen tree. Olives are eaten whole or crushed for their oil. **2.** A grayish-green color.

ol·ive oil (**ah**-liv *oil*) *noun* A yellow or green oil that is made by crushing olives. It is used for cooking and as a salad dressing.

O·lym·pic Games (uh-**lim**-pik **gaymz**) *noun, plural* A competition for athletes from all over the world. The Olympic Games are held every two years, alternating summer and winter sports. Also called the *Olympics*.

O·man (oh-**mahn**) An Arab country on the southeast coast of the Arabian Peninsula, between Yemen and the United Arab Emirates. Its economy is heavily dependent on dwindling oil reserves.

om·e·let *or* **om·e·lette** (**ahm**-lit *or* **ah**-muh-lit) *noun* Beaten eggs that have been cooked in a pan, filled with cheese, vegetables, or meat, and folded over.

o·men (**oh**-muhn) *noun* A sign or warning about your luck in the future.

om·i·nous (**ah**-muh-nuhs) *adjective* Threatening or making you feel that something bad is going to happen. ▸ *adverb* **ominously**

omit (oh-**mit**) *verb* To leave something out or fail to do something. ▸ *verb* **omitting, omitted** ▸ *noun* **omission** (oh-**mish**-uhn)

om·ni·vore (**ahm**-nuh-*vor*) *noun* An animal or person that eats both plants and meat. Pigs and chickens are omnivores. ▸ *adjective* **omnivorous** (ahm-**niv**-ur-uhs)

on (awn *or* ahn) *preposition* **1.** Over and supported by. *The book is on the shelf.* **2.** Next to and touching. *Pin the poster on the wall.* **3.** During a day or date. *There is no practice on Saturday.* **4.** In the direction of. *The sugar is in the cabinet on your left.* **5.** In a state of. *The store is on fire!* **6.** Using. *I go to school on the bus.* **7.** About. *I'm looking for a book on bears.* *adverb* **1.** In contact with or covering something. **2.** Into use. **3.** Forward in time or space. *adjective* In operation.

once (wuhns) *adverb* **1.** For one time only. **2.** In the past; formerly. **3. at once** Immediately or at the same time. *conjunction* As soon as something has happened.

on·com·ing (**awn**-*kuhm*-ing) *adjective*
Coming nearer or towards you.

one (wuhn)
noun **1.** The number that comes after zero and before two, written numerically as **1. 2.** A single thing.
adjective **1.** Single or alone. **2.** Some.
pronoun **1.** A certain person or thing.
2. Any person.

one-sid·ed (**wuhn-sye**-did) *adjective*
1. Showing only one side of a situation, or favoring one side. **2.** Not equal or balanced.

one-way (**wuhn** *way*) *adjective*
1. Allowing travel in only one direction. **2.** A **one-way** ticket allows you to travel to a place but not back again.

on·go·ing (**awn**-*goh*-ing) *adjective* If something is **ongoing,** it is still in progress or developing.

on·ion (**uhn**-yuhn) *noun* A round vegetable with many layers that is known for its strong smell and taste.

on·line (**awn**-line)
adjective Connected to or controlled by a central computer or a system of computers and modems.
adverb Connected to a computer network.

on·ly (**ohn**-lee)
adverb No one or nothing except; just.
adjective Alone of its or their kind.
conjunction Except that.
noun An **only child** is one who has no brothers or sisters.

on·o·mat·o·poe·ia (*ah-nuh-mat-uh-***pee**-uh) *noun* The use of a word that sounds like the thing or action it describes. *Buzz* and *sizzle* are examples of onomatopoeia.
▶ *adjective* **onomatopoeic** (*ah-nuh-mat-uh-***pee**-ik)*or* **onomatopoetic** (*ah-nuh-mat-uh-poh-***et**-ik)

on·set (**awn**-*set*) *noun* The beginning or start of something.

On·tar·i·o (ahn-**tair**-ee-oh) A province in the east-central part of Canada. It is the second-largest province in Canada, after Quebec, and is the most populated. Ottawa, the capital of Canada, is in Ontario, as is Toronto, the capital of the province and Canada's biggest city.

on·to (**awn**-*too* or **awn**-tuh) *preposition* To a place or position on or upon. *She stepped up onto the bus.*

on·ward (**awn**-wurd) *or* **on·wards** (**awn**-wurdz)
adverb Ahead or in a forward direction.
adjective Forward-moving.

ooze (ooz)
verb To flow or seep out slowly.
noun Very soft mud, usually found underwater in a pond or stream.
▶ *verb* **oozing, oozed**

o·pal (**oh**-puhl) *noun* A precious stone that shows different colors when you move it in the light.

o·paque (oh-**pake**) *adjective* Not clear enough to let light through; not transparent.

o·pen (**oh**-puhn)
adjective **1.** Not shut, closed, or fastened. **2.** Exposed; not covered or protected. **3.** If a company or store is **open,** people are working there and you can do business.
4. If you are **open** about something, you are willing to talk about it honestly. **5.** Not limited or restricted to only a few. **6.** If a computer file is **open,** this usually means that it can be worked on, read from, or written to.
verb **1.** To move something so that you can go in, see in, or get in. **2.** To start or begin something. **3.** To begin working hours.
noun If you have an **open mind,** you are willing to listen to new ideas and arguments.
▶ *verb* **opening, opened** ▶ *noun*
openness ▶ *adverb* **openly**

o·pen·ing (**oh**-puh-ning)
noun **1.** A hole, gap, or space in something. **2.** A job that is available. **3.** The first time a play is performed.
adjective Coming at the beginning; initial.

o·pen-mind·ed (**oh**-puhn-**mine**-did) *adjective* Willing to listen to new or different ideas about something. ▶ *noun* **open-mindedness**

op·er·a (**ah**-pur-uh) *noun* A play in which all or most of the words are sung, accompanied by an orchestra. ▶ *adjective* **operatic** (*ah*-puh-**rat**-ik)

op·er·ate (**ah**-puh-*rate*) *verb* **1.** To work in a particular way. **2.** To make something work or to put something in action. **3.** To repair or remove something from someone's body; to perform surgery.
▶ *verb* **operating, operated**

op·er·at·ing sys·tem (**ah**-puh-*ray*-ting *sis*-tuhm) *noun* The software in a computer that supports all the programs that run on it. Abbreviated as *OS*.

op·er·a·tion (*ah*-puh-**ray**-shuhn) *noun* **1.** The act of cutting open someone's body to remove or repair a damaged or diseased part. **2.** A well-organized plan, project, or event that involves a lot of people. **3. in operation** Working or functioning.
▶ *adjective* **operational**

op·er·a·tor (**ah**-puh-ray-tur) *noun* **1.** Someone whose job is to help people make telephone calls. **2.** Someone who works a machine or device.

op·er·et·ta (*ah*-puh-**ret**-uh) *noun* A short, usually humorous opera with spoken lines.

oph·thal·mol·o·gist (*ahf*-thuhl-**mah**-luh-jist) *noun* A medical doctor who studies and treats diseases of the eye. ▶ *noun* **ophthalmology**

o·pin·ion (uh-**pin**-yuhn) *noun* **1.** Your personal feelings about someone or something. **2.** The beliefs or views of people in general. **3.** The judgment of an expert. **4. opinion poll** A survey of what people think about something, made by asking questions to a selected group of people.

o·pos·sum (uh-**pah**-suhm) *noun* A gray, furry animal with a hairless tail that lives mostly in trees and carries its young in a pouch. If it is threatened, the opossum lies still and pretends to be dead. It is also called a **possum.**

op·po·nent (uh-**poh**-nuhnt) *noun* The person or team you play or compete against in a fight, contest, debate, or election.

op·por·tu·ni·ty (*ah*-pur-**too**-ni-tee) *noun* A chance or a good time to do something. ▶ *noun, plural* **opportunities**

op·pose (uh-**poze**) *verb* To disagree with someone or something; to try to prevent or to resist. ▶ *verb* **opposing, opposed**

op·po·site (**ah**-puh-sit *or* **ah**-puh-zit) *preposition* Across from or facing. *My friend and I sat opposite each other on the bus.*
adjective **1.** Located or facing directly across. **2.** Facing or moving in the other direction. **3.** Different in every way.
noun A person, thing, or idea that is completely different from another.

op·po·si·tion (*ah*-puh-**zish**-uhn) *noun* **1.** Resistance to or disagreement with someone or something. **2.** The person or team that you play against in a game or competition.

op·press (uh-**pres**) *verb* **1.** To use power or authority in a cruel and unfair way. **2.** If something **oppresses** you, it makes you feel worried or anxious because you cannot stop thinking about it.
▶ *verb* **oppresses, oppressing, oppressed** ▶ *adjective* **oppressive**
▶ *noun* **oppression** ▶ *noun* **oppressor**

opt (ahpt) *verb* **1.** To choose or decide something. **2.** If you **opt out** of something, you choose not to participate in it.
▶ *verb* **opting, opted**

op·ti·cal (**ahp**-ti-kuhl)
adjective **1.** Of or having to do with eyes or eyesight. **2.** Designed to help eyesight.
noun **optical illusion** Something that tricks your eye by seeming to be what it is not.

op·ti·cian (ahp-**tish**-uhn) *noun* Someone who examines your eyes and makes or sells glasses and contact lenses.

O

op·ti·mis·tic (ahp-tuh-**mis**-tik)
adjective People who are **optimistic** believe that things will usually turn out well or for the best. ▶ *noun* **optimism** ▶ *noun* **optimist**

op·tion (**ahp**-shuhn) *noun* A choice.

op·tion·al (**ahp**-shuh-nuhl) *adjective* If something is **optional,** you can choose whether or not you want to do it. ▶ *adverb* **optionally**

op·tom·e·trist (ahp-**tah**-muh-trist) *noun* A person who is licensed to test your vision and prescribe glasses or contact lenses.

or (or) *conjunction* **1.** A word used to show choices or alternatives. **2.** A word used to introduce words or phrases that have the same meaning. **3.** A word used with *either* or *whether* to show choices.
Or sounds like **oar** and **ore.**

o·ral (**or**-uhl) *adjective* **1.** Spoken instead of written. **2.** Of or having to do with your mouth.
Oral sounds like **aural.** ▶ *adverb* **orally**

or·ange (**or**-inj)
noun **1.** A color between red and yellow, or the color of a pumpkin. **2.** A round citrus fruit with a thick, reddish-yellow skin and a juicy inside that is divided in sections.
adjective Having the color of a pumpkin.

o·rang·u·tan (uh-**rang**-uh-*tan*) *noun* A large ape of Southeast Asia with long, reddish-brown hair and long, strong arms.

or·bit (**or**-bit)
noun The curved path followed by a moon, planet, or satellite as it circles another planet or the sun.
verb To travel in a circular path around something, especially a planet or the sun.
▶ *verb* **orbiting, orbited** ▶ *adjective* **orbital**

or·chard (**or**-churd) *noun* An area of land where fruit or nut trees are grown.

or·ches·tra (**or**-kuh-struh) *noun* An often large group of musicians who play a variety of musical instruments together. ▶ *adjective* **orchestral** (or-**kes**-truhl)

or·chid (**or**-kid) *noun* A plant known for its colorful flowers with unusual shapes. There are many varieties of orchids, especially in tropical areas.

or·dain (or-**dane**) *verb* **1.** To formally make someone a member of the clergy in an official ceremony. **2.** To order by law.
▶ *verb* **ordaining, ordained** ▶ *noun* **ordination** (or-duh-**nay**-shuhn)

or·deal (or-**deel**) *noun* A long and very difficult or unpleasant experience.

or·der (**or**-dur)
verb **1.** To instruct or command someone to do something. **2.** To ask for something to be served or supplied. **3.** To arrange something so that all the parts are in the right place.
noun **1.** An arrangement. **2.** A state in which everything is neatly arranged. **3.** A state in which everyone or everything is calm and obeys the rules. **4.** A command from someone in authority. **5.** Written instructions to pay money to someone. **6.** A religious community or the people in it. **7.** A group of related plants or animals that is bigger than a family but smaller than a class.
phrases **1.** If you put things **in order,** you arrange them so that everything is in the right sequence or position. **2.** If something is **out of order,** it is not working properly or not working at all. **3.** If a person is **out of order,** he or she is not behaving properly.
▶ *verb* **ordering, ordered**

or·der·ly (**or**-dur-lee)
adjective **1.** Arranged in a neat and careful way. **2.** Behaving well.
noun A person who cleans and does other jobs in a hospital.
▶ *noun* **orderliness**

or·di·nal num·ber (**or**-duh-nuhl **nuhm**-bur) *noun* A number that shows the position of something in a series, such as first, second, or third.

or·di·nance (**or**-duh-nuhns) *noun* A law or regulation, especially one for a town or city.

or·di·nar·y (**or**-duh-*ner*-ee) *adjective* 1. Not different or unusual in any way. 2. Not having features that are interesting or unusual.
▶ *adverb* **ordinarily** (or-duh-**nair**-uh-lee)

ore (or) *noun* A rock or earth that contains a metal or valuable mineral. **Ore** sounds like **oar** and **or.**

Or·e·gon (**or**-i-guhn *or* **or**-i-*gahn*) A state in the Pacific Northwest region of the United States. It is known for its coastline and for the volcanic peaks of its Cascade Mountains. The Cascades include Mount Hood, the highest mountain in Oregon.

or·gan (**or**-guhn) *noun* 1. A musical instrument that looks like a piano, with one or more keyboards. Some organs have rows of pipes that make sounds when air passes through them. 2. A part of the body, such as the heart or the kidneys, that has a certain purpose.
▶ *noun* **organist**

or·gan·ic (or-**gan**-ik) *adjective* 1. Grown without artificial chemicals or fertilizers. 2. From or produced by living things.
▶ *adverb* **organically**

or·gan·ism (**or**-guh-*niz*-uhm) *noun* A living thing, such as a plant or animal.

or·gan·i·za·tion (or-guh-ni-**zay**-shuhn) *noun* 1. A number of people joined together for a particular purpose. 2. The act or process of planning and running something. 3. The way in which the parts of something are planned or arranged.

or·gan·ize (**or**-guh-*nize*) *verb* 1. To prepare for and run an event or activity. 2. To arrange the parts of something in a particular order or structure.
▶ *verb* **organizing, organized** ▶ *noun* **organizer**

O·ri·ent (**or**-ee-uhnt) *noun* The countries of the Far East, especially Japan and China. ▶ *adjective* **Oriental** (or-ee-**en**-tuhl)

o·ri·en·ta·tion (or-ee-uhn-**tay**-shuhn) *noun* 1. The position of something or the direction something faces, especially in relation to the compass. 2. Someone's feelings or beliefs about a particular issue. 3. The way a page is turned in relation to the information on it. The usual kinds of page orientation are portrait and landscape. 4. A set of activities that get you ready to take part in something new.

o·ri·en·teer·ing (or-ee-uhn-**teer**-ing) *noun* A race in which players use a map and a compass to find their way across rough country.

o·ri·ga·mi (or-i-**gah**-mee) *noun* The Japanese art of folding paper into decorative shapes.

or·i·gin (**or**-i-jin) *noun* 1. The point where something starts, or the cause of something. 2. A person's family background.

o·rig·i·nal (uh-**rij**-uh-nuhl) *adjective* 1. First, earliest, or existing from the beginning. 2. New or interesting.
noun A work of art or a piece of writing that is not a copy.
▶ *noun* **originality** (uh-*rij*-uh-**nal**-i-tee)

o·rig·i·nal·ly (uh-**rij**-uh-nuh-lee) *adverb* At the beginning; at first.

o·rig·i·nate (uh-**rij**-uh-*nate*) *verb* To happen or to begin in a particular place or situation. ▶ *verb* **originating, originated** ▶ *noun* **origination**

o·ri·ole (**or**-ee-*ohl*) *noun* Any of a group of songbirds in which the male has bright orange or yellow markings.

or·na·ment (**or**-nuh-muhnt) *noun* A small object that is used for decoration. ▶ *adjective* **ornamental**

or·nate (or-**nayt**) *adjective* Covered with a lot of decorations. ▶ *adverb* **ornately**

or·ner·y (**or**-nur-ee) *adjective* Stubborn and difficult.

or·ni·thol·o·gy (or-nuh-**thah**-luh-jee) *noun* The scientific study of birds.
▶ *noun* **ornithologist**

or·phan (**or**-fuhn) *noun* A child whose parents are not alive. ▶ *adjective* **orphaned**

or·phan·age (**or**-fuh-nij) *noun* A place where orphans live and are cared for.

or·tho·don·tist (or-thuh-**dahn**-tist) *noun* A dentist who straightens crooked teeth and corrects jaw and bite problems.

or·tho·dox (**or**-thuh-dahks) *adjective* **1.** A religion is described as **orthodox** if it has very traditional and established teachings. **2. Orthodox** views and beliefs are ones that are generally accepted or approved. *See also* **Eastern Orthodox.**
▶ *noun* **orthodoxy**

or·tho·pe·dic (or-thuh-**pee**-dik) *adjective* Of or having to do with the branch of medicine that deals with bones and joints. ▶ *noun* **orthopedics**

os·mo·sis (ahz-**moh**-sis *or* ahs-**moh**-sis) *noun* **1.** The process in which a more concentrated solution passes through a membrane into a less concentrated one, until the concentrations on both sides are equal. **2.** The process of absorbing ideas, attitudes, or information gradually.

os·trich (**aws**-trich) *noun* A large African bird with a long neck that can run very fast but cannot fly. The ostrich is the largest living bird and can weigh up to 300 pounds (140 kilograms). ▶ *noun, plural* **ostriches**

oth·er (uhTH-ur)
adjective **1.** Different; not the same. **2.** Remaining. **3.** More or extra. **4.** In the recent past.
pronoun The rest, or in addition to those already mentioned.

oth·er·wise (uhTH-ur-wize)
conjunction Or else.
adverb In a different way.

ot·ter (**ah**-tur) *noun* A fish-eating mammal with webbed feet and a long tail that lives partly in water and partly on land. Some otters live in the sea most of the time. Otters are related to weasels and minks.

ot·to·man (**ah**-tuh-muhn) *noun* A low padded seat without arms or a back. In addition to being used as a seat, an ottoman may also serve as a footrest or have a lid and serve as a storage box.

ouch (ouch) *interjection* A cry of sudden pain.

ought (awt) *verb* A helping verb used in the following ways: **1.** To show something you must do. **2.** To show what you expect or think will happen. **3.** To give advice.

ounce (ouns) *noun* **1.** A unit of weight equal to 1/16 of a pound. A mouse weighs about one ounce. *See also* **measurement. 2.** A **fluid ounce** is a unit used in liquid measurement. There are 16 fluid ounces in a pint and 32 fluid ounces in a quart. **3.** A small amount.

our (our *or* ahr) *adjective* Belonging to or connected with us.

ours (ourz *or* ahrz) *pronoun* The one or ones belonging to or connected with us.

our·selves (our-**selvz**) *pronoun* Us and no one else.

oust (oust) *verb* To force someone out of a place, a job, or a position of power. ▶ *verb* **ousting, ousted**

out (out)
adverb **1.** Away from the inside or middle of a place or thing. **2.** Away from home or work. **3.** Into the open, or into the public. **4.** No longer on fire or lit. **5.** Aloud or forcefully.
adjective **1.** In baseball, no longer a batter or base runner. **2.** Removed from a game or contest.
noun In baseball, a play in which a batter or runner is retired.

out·board mo·tor (**out**-bord **moh**-tur) *noun* A small motor with a propeller that can be attached to a small boat.

out·box (**out**-bahks) *noun* **1.** A box where you place letters that are ready to mail or go to another office. **2.** A place on a computer where email can wait until you send it.
▶ *noun, plural* **outboxes**

out·break (**out**-brake) *noun* The sudden start of something unpleasant.

out·burst (**out**-burst) *noun* A sudden release of emotion or violence.

out·cast (**out**-kast) *noun* Someone who has been rejected by other people.

O

out·come (**out**-kuhm) *noun* The result of an action or an event.

out·cry (**out**-krye) *noun* Protests or complaints from many people. ▶ *noun, plural* **outcries**

out·dat·ed (out-**day**-tid) *adjective* Old-fashioned.

out·do (out-**doo**) *verb* To go beyond or do better than someone else can. ▶ *verb* **outdoes, outdoing, outdid, outdone**

out·doors (out-**dorz**)
adverb In or into the open air; outside.
noun The open air.
adjective **outdoor** Done, located, or used outdoors.

out·er (**ou**-tur) *adjective* Farthest from the center or middle; on the outside.

out·er space (**ou**-tur **spase**) *noun* The universe beyond the earth's atmosphere.

out·field (**out**-feeld) *noun* 1. The part of a baseball field beyond the infield and inside the foul lines. 2. The group of baseball players assigned to this area when not at bat.

out·fit (**out**-fit)
noun 1. Pieces of clothing that are worn together. 2. A group of people who work together or form a team.
verb To obtain all the equipment you need to do something.
▶ *verb* **outfitting, outfitted**

out·go·ing (**out**-goh-ing) *adjective* Someone who is **outgoing** is very warm, friendly, and confident.

out·grow (out-**groh**) *verb* 1. To grow too big for something. 2. To lose interest in someone or something as you grow older.
▶ *verb* **outgrowing, outgrew, outgrown**

out·ing (**ou**-ting) *noun* A short trip for pleasure or education.

out·law (**out**-law)
noun A criminal, especially one who is hiding from the police.
verb To make something illegal.
▶ *verb* **outlawing, outlawed**

out·let (**out**-let) *noun* 1. A place where electronics and appliances can be plugged in and connected to electricity. 2. A pipe or hole that can release liquid or gas. 3. A store where a company's goods can be bought for lower prices. 4. A way of expressing your talents, energy, or feelings.

out·line (**out**-line)
noun 1. A line that shows the outer edges of something. 2. A brief description of the main points; a summary.
verb To give a summary of something.
▶ *verb* **outlining, outlined**

out·look (**out**-luk) *noun* 1. Your general attitude toward life and the world around you. 2. The way that something is likely to happen.

out·num·ber (out-**nuhm**-bur) *verb* To be greater in number than. ▶ *verb* **outnumbering, outnumbered**

out-of-date *adjective* Old-fashioned or no longer used.

out·pa·tient (**out**-pay-shuhnt) *noun* Someone who is treated in a hospital or clinic but does not stay the night.

out·post (**out**-pohst) *noun* 1. A military camp set up away from the main camp, used to keep watch on the enemy. 2. A town or buildings in a remote area.

out·put (**out**-put)
noun 1. The amount of something that a person, machine, or company makes or produces. 2. The information a computer produces.
verb To produce as output.
▶ *verb* **outputting, outputted** *or* **output**

out·rage (**out**-rayj)
noun 1. A strong feeling of anger or shock. 2. An act that is very violent, cruel, or extremely offensive.
verb To make someone feel very shocked or angry.
▶ *verb* **outraging, outraged**

out·ra·geous (out-**ray**-juhs)
adjective Very shocking or unacceptable. ▶ *adverb* **outrageously**

out·right (**out**-rite)
adjective Complete and total.
adverb Immediately.

out·run (out-**ruhn**) *verb* To run faster or farther than someone or something. ▶ *verb* **outrunning, outran, outrun**

out·set (**out**-set) *noun* The start or the beginning.

out·side
adverb (out-**side**) In or into the open air; outdoors.
noun (**out**-side) The outer surface or side.
preposition (out-**side**) Away from, or not in a certain place. *My aunt lives just outside Chicago.*
adjective (**out**-side) Located on the outer surface or side.

out·sid·er (out-**sye**-dur) *noun* Someone who is not part of a particular group.

out·skirts (**out**-skurts) *noun, plural* The outer edges of a city or town.

out·smart (out-**smahrt**) *verb* To get an advantage over someone else by being more clever. ▶ *verb* **outsmarting, outsmarted**

out·source (**out**-sors) *verb* 1. To get products or services from an outside company or source. 2. To move a job to a place where workers are cheaper.

out·spo·ken (out-**spoh**-kuhn) *adjective* Very honest and direct, especially when criticizing someone or something.

out·stand·ing (out-**stan**-ding) *adjective* 1. Extremely good or better than others of its kind. 2. Not yet paid or collected.

out·ward (**out**-wurd) *or* **out·wards** (**out**-wurdz)
adjective 1. Showing the way things seem rather than how they really are; on the surface. 2. Of, on, or toward the outside; external.
adverb Away from a place, especially one that will be returned to.
▶ *adverb* **outwardly**

out·weigh (out-**way**) *verb* 1. To be more important or more valuable than something else. 2. To weigh more than something or somebody else.
▶ *verb* **outweighing, outweighed**

out·wit (out-**wit**) *verb* To fool or get an advantage over someone by being more clever. ▶ *verb* **outwitting, outwitted**

o·val (**oh**-vuhl)
noun An egg-shaped form or object.
adjective Having the shape of an egg.

o·va·ry (**oh**-vur-ee) *noun* 1. The part of a flowering plant that produces seeds. 2. One of a pair of female organs that produce eggs.
▶ *noun, plural* **ovaries**

o·va·tion (oh-**vay**-shuhn) *noun* A loud and enthusiastic outburst of clapping.

ov·en (**uhv**-uhn) *noun* The part of a stove in which you can bake or roast food.

o·ver (**oh**-vur)
preposition 1. In a position higher than but not touching something. *We hung the chandelier over the table.* 2. On top of and touching something. *Spread the frosting over the cake.* 3. More than. *My shoes cost over $50.* 4. Across or to the other side of something. *Take the bridge that goes over the stream.*
adjective Finished or done with.
adverb 1. Remaining or left. 2. Again. 3. Leaning, falling, or hanging downward.
idiom If you **get over** something, it doesn't bother you anymore.

o·ver·all
adverb (oh-vur-**awl**) Taken as a whole, or considering everything.
adjective (**oh**-vur-awl) Total.

o·ver·alls (**oh**-vur-awlz) *noun, plural* Loose pants with a front flap over the chest held up by shoulder straps.

o·ver·bear·ing (oh-vur-**bair**-ing) *adjective* Acting in a forceful or bossy way.

o·ver·board (**oh**-vur-bord) *adverb* 1. Over the side of a boat and into the water. 2. If you **go overboard** with something, you are too enthusiastic or excited about it.

o·ver·cast (**oh**-vur-kast) *adjective* Covered with clouds or mist.

o·ver·coat (**oh**-vur-kote) *noun* A long, heavy coat worn in cold weather.

o·ver·come (oh-vur-**kuhm**) *verb* 1. To defeat or get control of a problem. 2. To strongly affect someone.
▶ *verb* **overcoming, overcame, overcome**

o·ver·do (oh-vur-**doo**) *verb* To do too much of something. ▶ *verb* **overdoes, overdoing, overdid, overdone** ▶ *adjective* **overdone**

O

o·ver·dose
noun (**oh**-vur-*dohs*) A large dose of a drug that can make you sick or kill you.
verb (oh-vur-**dohs**) To give or take too large a dose of something.
▶ *verb* **overdosing, overdosed**

o·ver·draft (**oh**-vur-*draft*) *noun* An amount of money you owe to the bank because you have withdrawn more than what you have in your account.

o·ver·dress (oh-vur-**dres**) *verb* To wear clothes that are too dressy or too warm for an event. ▶ *verb* **overdresses, overdressing, overdressed**

o·ver·due (oh-vur-**doo**) *adjective* Past the time payment or arrival is due; late.

o·ver·eat (oh-vur-**eet**) *verb* To eat more than you need. ▶ *verb* **overeating, overate**

o·ver·flow (oh-vur-**floh**) *verb* 1. To flow over the brim or edges of something. 2. To flood.
▶ *verb* **overflowing, overflowed**

o·ver·grown (oh-vur-**grohn**) *adjective* Covered with weeds or plants that have been allowed to grow wild.

o·ver·hand (**oh**-vur-*hand*) *adjective* Done with your arm raised above your shoulder.

o·ver·haul
verb (oh-vur-**hawl**) To thoroughly examine equipment or machinery and make necessary repairs.
noun (**oh**-vur-*hawl*) A thorough examination of equipment or machinery, including repairs if necessary.
▶ *verb* **overhauling, overhauled**

o·ver·head
adverb (oh-vur-**hed**) Above your head; in the sky.
adjective (**oh**-vur-*hed*) Located, operating, or coming from above your head.
noun (**oh**-vur-*hed*) The regular expenses involved in running a business, such as salaries, rent, and utilities.

o·ver·hear (oh-vur-**heer**) *verb* To hear something without meaning to or without the speaker's knowledge. ▶ *verb* **overhearing, overheard**

o·ver·joyed (oh-vur-**joid**) *adjective* If you are **overjoyed,** you are filled with happiness.

o·ver·lap
verb (oh-vur-**lap**) 1. To extend over or partly cover something. 2. To cover the same period of time or the same area of interest or responsibility.
noun (**oh**-vur-*lap*) The amount by which something overlaps something else.
▶ *verb* **overlapping, overlapped**

o·ver·load
verb (oh-vur-**lohd**) 1. To give something or someone too much to carry or too much work or responsibility. 2. To put too much demand on an electrical system or device so that it burns out.
noun (**oh**-vur-*lohd*) An excessive load or demand.
▶ *verb* **overloading, overloaded**

o·ver·look (oh-vur-**luk**) *verb* 1. To be able to look down on something from above. 2. To fail to notice or consider something. 3. To excuse or choose to ignore something.
▶ *verb* **overlooking, overlooked**

o·ver·ly (**oh**-vur-lee) *adverb* Too or excessively.

o·ver·night
adverb (oh-vur-**nite**) 1. During or for the night. 2. Suddenly or very quickly.
adjective (**oh**-vur-*nite*) 1. For one night. 2. To be used for one night or for short trips.

o·ver·pass (**oh**-vur-*pas*) *noun* A road or bridge that goes over another road or a railroad. ▶ *noun, plural* **overpasses**

o·ver·pop·u·la·tion (oh-vur-*pahp*-yuh-**lay**-shuhn) *noun* The situation in which the number of humans or animals in an area is too large to be sustained by the natural resources available.

o·ver·pow·er (oh-vur-**pou**-ur) *verb* 1. To defeat someone because you have more strength. 2. If something

O

overpowers you, it overwhelms you or makes you helpless.
▶ *verb* **overpowering, overpowered**

o·ver·rat·ed (*oh-vur-***ray**-tid) *adjective* If you think something is **overrated,** other people think it is better or more valuable than you do.

o·ver·rule (*oh-vur-***rool**) *verb* If someone in authority **overrules** a decision, the person reverses that decision or does not allow it to stand. ▶ *verb* **overruling, overruled**

o·ver·run (*oh-vur-***ruhn**) *verb* **1.** To fill a place or spread out over it in large numbers. **2.** To flood over, or go beyond a boundary or limit.
▶ *verb* **overrunning, overran, overrun**

o·ver·seas
adverb (**oh**-vur-**seez**) To or in a foreign country, or across an ocean.
adjective (**oh**-vur-**seez**) Of or having to do with foreign countries or countries across an ocean.

o·ver·sight (**oh**-vur-**site**) *noun* **1.** A mistake you make because you forget or do not notice something. **2.** The responsibility for seeing that something is done correctly.

o·ver·sleep (*oh-vur-***sleep**) *verb* To sleep later than you meant to. ▶ *verb* **oversleeping, overslept**

o·ver·take (*oh-vur-***take**) *verb* **1.** To catch up to and pass someone. **2.** To happen suddenly or by surprise and strongly affect everything.
▶ *verb* **overtaking, overtook, overtaken**

o·ver·throw (*oh-vur-***throh**)
verb **1.** To put an end to something or to force someone from power. **2.** To throw a ball past where it should go.
noun An instance of defeating, and usually replacing, someone in power.
▶ *verb* **overthrowing, overthrew, overthrown**

o·ver·time (**oh**-vur-*time*)
noun **1.** Time you spend working after you have worked your normal number of hours. **2.** Extra time in a game or competition because the score was tied at the end of normal play.
adjective Of or having to do with time spent working beyond the normal

number of hours.
adverb Beyond the established time limit or working hours.

o·ver·ture (**oh**-vur-*chur*) *noun* A piece of music played at the beginning of an opera, a ballet, or a musical.

o·ver·turn (*oh-vur-***turn**) *verb* **1.** To turn something upside down or on its side. **2.** To reverse something, especially a decision.
▶ *verb* **overturning, overturned**

o·ver·weight (**oh**-vur-**wate**) *adjective* Above a normal or desirable weight.

o·ver·whelm (*oh-vur-***welm**) *verb* **1.** To defeat someone or something completely. **2.** To have a very strong emotional effect.
▶ *verb* **overwhelming, overwhelmed**
▶ *adjective* **overwhelming**

o·ver·work (*oh-vur-***wurk**) *verb* To work or to make someone or something work too hard. ▶ *verb* **overworking, overworked**

owe (oh) *verb* **1.** To be responsible for giving money or goods to someone, especially if you have borrowed something from that person. **2.** To feel you should do or give something to someone, especially in return for something they have done. **3.** To exist or be successful because of someone or something.
Owe sounds like **oh.** ▶ *verb* **owing, owed**

owl (oul) *noun* A bird that has a round head, large eyes, and a hooked beak. Owls hunt at night and live mainly on mice and other small animals.

own (ohn)
adjective Used to show that something belongs to or is connected with someone.
verb **1.** To possess or have something. **2.** If you **own up** to something, you admit to having done something wrong.
idiom **on your own** Alone or by your own efforts.
▶ *verb* **owning, owned**

own·er (**oh**-nur) *noun* The person to whom something belongs.

O

own·er·ship (**oh**-nur-*ship*) *noun* The act of owning something.

ox (ahks) *noun* **1.** An adult male cow that is used as a work animal or for meat. **2.** An animal that is related to cattle, such as a buffalo, bison, or yak. ▶ *noun, plural* **oxen** (**ahk**-suhn)

ox·ford (**ahks**-furd) *noun* **1.** A low shoe that fastens with laces. **2.** A lightweight cotton cloth used to make clothing.

ox·i·dize (**ahk**-si-*dize*) *verb* To undergo a chemical change by combining with oxygen. ▶ *verb* **oxidizing, oxidized** ▶ *noun* **oxidizer** ▶ *noun* **oxidation** (ahk-si-**day**-shuhn)

ox·y·gen (**ahk**-si-juhn) *noun* A colorless gas found in the air and water. Humans and animals need oxygen to breathe, and fires need it to burn.

ox·y·mo·ron (*ahk*-si-**mor**-ahn) *noun* A short phrase that contains words or ideas that seem to be the opposite of each other, for example, "sweet sorrow."

oy·ster (**oi**-stur) *noun* A flat shellfish that has a hinged shell and lives in shallow waters. Some oysters can be eaten, and some produce pearls.

oz. (ouns) Short for **ounce** or the plural form **ounces.**

o·zone (**oh**-zone) *noun* **1.** A form of oxygen that has a pale blue color and a strong smell. **2. ozone layer** A layer in the earth's upper atmosphere that contains ozone and blocks out some of the sun's harmful rays.

P

pace (pase)
noun **1.** A step or a stride. **2.** The average length of a step when you are walking, about two feet for an adult. **3.** A rate of speed.
verb **1.** To measure distance in paces. **2.** To walk back and forth. ▶ *verb* **pacing, paced**

pace·mak·er (**pase**-*may*-kur) *noun* An electronic device put into someone's body to help the heart beat more regularly.

Pa·cif·ic O·cean (puh-**sif**-ik **oh**-shuhn) The world's largest ocean, covering about 30 percent of the earth's surface. The Pacific Ocean is bordered by the continents of Asia and Australia on one side and by the continents of North and South America on the other. It is divided at the equator into the North Pacific and the South Pacific.

pac·i·fist (**pas**-uh-fist) *noun* A person who believes very strongly that war and violence are wrong, and who refuses to fight or to enter the armed forces. ▶ *noun* **pacifism**

pac·i·fy (**pas**-uh-*fye*) *verb* **1.** To make a person feel calmer and more peaceful. **2.** To settle an agitated situation. ▶ *verb* **pacifies, pacifying, pacified**

pack (pak)
verb **1.** To put objects into a box, case, bag, or other container, especially in order to move or store them. **2.** To fill a space tightly.
noun **1.** A group of similar animals, people, or things. **2.** A bundle of things tied or wrapped together for carrying. **3.** A sturdy bag for carrying things on your back. **4.** A large quantity or amount. ▶ *verb* **packing, packed** ▶ *noun* **packing**

pack·age (**pak**-ij)
noun **1.** A parcel, or a bundle of something that is packed, wrapped, or put into a box. **2.** A carton, box, or case that can be packed with something.
verb To make into or put inside a package, often in order to be sold or mailed. ▶ *verb* **packaging, packaged**

pack·ag·ing (**pak**-uh-jing) *noun* The wrapping on something, especially something that you buy.

pack an·i·mal (**pak** *an*-uh-muhl) *noun* An animal, usually a horse or mule, that can carry heavy supplies.

pack·et (**pak**-it) *noun* A small container, package, or bundle.

pact (pakt) *noun* A formal agreement between two individuals, groups, or countries.

pad (pad)
verb 1. To walk softly and steadily. 2. To add words to a speech or piece of writing just to make it longer. 3. To fill or cover with something soft. 4. **pad a bill** To charge someone for more work than you really did.
noun 1. A wad or cushion of soft material, usually used to absorb liquid, give comfort, or provide protection. 2. Sheets of paper fastened together along one edge. 3. The soft part on the bottom of the feet of dogs and many other animals. 4. A platform from which a rocket is fired.
▶ *verb* **padding, padded**

pad·ding (**pad**-ing) *noun* Cotton, foam rubber, or any other material used to make or stuff a pad, or to protect items being packed into a container.

pad·dle (**pad**-uhl)
noun 1. A short, wide oar used to move and steer some kinds of small boats. 2. A small board with a short handle used to strike a ball in table tennis and other games. 3. A flat, wooden tool used for stirring, mixing, or beating.
verb 1. To walk or splash with your hands in shallow water. 2. To spank with a paddle or the hand. 3. To move a boat with a paddle.
▶ *verb* **paddling, paddled**

pad·dle wheel (**pad**-uhl *weel*) *noun* An engine-driven wheel placed at the back or side of a ship to propel it through the water.

pad·dock (**pad**-uhk) *noun* An enclosed field or area where horses can graze or exercise.

pad·dy (**pad**-ee) *noun* A flooded field where rice is grown. ▶ *noun, plural* **paddies**

pad·lock (**pad**-*lahk*)
noun A lock with a U-shaped metal bar that can be put through an opening or link and snapped shut.
verb To secure something with a padlock.
▶ *verb* **padlocking, padlocked**

pa·gan (**pay**-guhn)
noun A person who is not a member of the Christian, Jewish, or Muslim religion. A pagan may worship many gods or have no religion at all.
adjective Of or having to do with pagans or their beliefs.

page (payj)
noun 1. One side of a sheet of paper in a book, newspaper, or magazine. 2. In the past, a **page** was a boy servant. Today, a page can be a person of any age who assists someone, such as a senator. A page can also be a boy attendant at a wedding.
verb 1. To find someone by calling out or announcing the person's name or by using a pager. 2. To turn pages in a book or other printed material.
▶ *verb* **paging, paged**

pag·eant (**paj**-uhnt) *noun* A public entertainment where people walk in a procession, often in costume, or act out historical scenes.

pag·eant·ry (**paj**-uhn-tree) *noun* Elaborate display or ceremony.

pag·er (**pay**-jur) *noun* A small, electronic beeping device that doctors and other emergency personnel wear so that they can be contacted quickly.

pa·go·da (puh-**goh**-duh) *noun* A shrine or temple in eastern religions. A pagoda is shaped like a tower with many roofs that curve upward.

paid (payd)
verb The past tense and the past participle of **pay.**
adjective 1. Involving the exchange of money for something. 2. Some jobs include a **paid** vacation, which means that an employee continues to receive regular pay while away from work.

P

pail (payl) *noun* A bucket.

pain (payn)
noun **1.** Physical or emotional suffering caused by injury, illness, or great unhappiness. **2.** A nuisance, or an unpleasant experience.
verb To cause someone pain.
noun, plural **pains** Great care or effort.
Pain sounds like **pane**. ▶ *verb* **paining, pained**

pain·ful (**payn**-fuhl) *adjective* Causing physical or emotional distress. ▶ *adverb* **painfully**

pain·kill·er (**payn**-*kil*-ur) *noun* Medicine taken to stop pain.

pain·less (**payn**-lis) *adjective* Free from pain. ▶ *adverb* **painlessly**

pains·tak·ing (**paynz**-*tay*-king) *adjective* Very thorough and careful. ▶ *adverb* **painstakingly**

paint (paynt)
noun A liquid that you spread over a surface to color or decorate it, or to make a picture.
verb To cover something with paint, or to use paint to make a picture.
▶ *verb* **painting, painted** ▶ *noun* **painter** ▶ *noun* **painting**

paint·brush (**paynt**-*bruhsh*) *noun* A brush for applying paint. ▶ *noun, plural* **paintbrushes**

paint·er (**payn**-tur) *noun* **1.** Someone whose job is to paint. **2.** An artist.

paint·ing (**payn**-ting) *noun* **1.** A work of art that has been created with paint. **2.** The process of putting paint onto something. **3.** The occupation of a painter.

pair (pair)
noun **1.** A set of two things that are used together or make one unit. **2.** One thing that is made up of two parts. **3.** Two persons or animals that are alike or that work together.
verb **1.** To join or put together. **2. pair off** To form a pair or into pairs.
Pair sounds like **pare** and **pear**. ▶ *verb* **pairing, paired**

pa·ja·mas (puh-**jah**-muhz *or* puh-**jam**-uhz) *noun, plural* A set of clothes to sleep in, consisting of a loose shirt and pants or shorts.

Pak·i·stan (**pak**-i-*stan*) A country in South Asia. The majority of the country's population is Muslim. Pakistan was once the western part of India, a predominantly Hindu country. It became a separate nation after the British rule of India ended in 1947, and today it is an Islamic republic.

pal (pal) *noun* A good friend or a buddy.

pal·ace (**pal**-is) *noun* A large, grand residence for a king, queen, or other ruler.

pal·ate (**pal**-it) *noun* **1.** The roof of the mouth. **2.** A person's appreciation of taste.
Palate sounds like **palette**.

Pa·lau (puh-**lou**) An island nation in the Pacific Ocean consisting of the westernmost cluster of the Caroline Islands. One of the youngest and smallest countries in the world, it was a United Nations Trust Territory until 1994.

pale (payl)
adjective **1.** Having a light skin color, often because of an illness. **2.** Not bright in color.
verb To become pale.
Pale sounds like **pail**. ▶ *adjective* **paler, palest** ▶ *verb* **paling, paled** ▶ *noun* **paleness**

pa·le·on·tol·o·gy (*pay*-lee-uhn-**tah**-luh-jee) *noun* The science that deals with fossils and other ancient life forms. A person who studies paleontology is called a *paleontologist*.

Pa·le·o·zo·ic (*pay*-lee-uh-**zoh**-ik)
noun An era in the earth's history that began about 540 million years ago and ended about 250 million years ago. During this time, land plants, fish, amphibians, and reptiles began to appear.
adjective Of or having to do with the Paleozoic era.

pal·ette (**pal**-it) *noun* A flat board held in the hand, with a hole for the thumb. A palette is used for mixing paints.
Palette sounds like **palate**.

pal·in·drome (**pal**-in-*drohm*) *noun* A word, sentence, or number that reads the same backward as forward.

P

pal·i·sade (*pal*-i-**sayd**) *noun* A line of steep cliffs, often bordering a river.

pal·lid (**pal**-id) *adjective* Pale-looking, especially in the face or skin. ▶ *noun* **pallor** (**pal**-ur)

palm (pahm)
noun 1. The flat inside surface of your hand. 2. A tall, tropical tree with large leaves shaped like feathers or fans at the top.
verb To hide something in your palm. ▶ *verb* **palming, palmed**

pal·met·to (pal-**met**-oh) *noun* A kind of palm tree with leaves shaped like fans. Palmettos grow in the southern United States. ▶ *noun, plural* **palmettos** *or* **palmettoes**

palm·ist·ry (**pah**-mi-stree) *noun* The practice of telling people's fortunes by looking at the lines in the palms of their hands. ▶ *noun* **palmist**

pal·o·mi·no (*pal*-uh-**mee**-noh) *noun* A golden-tan or cream horse with a white mane and tail.

pam·pas (**pam**-puhz) *noun, plural* Large, treeless plains in South America. The pampas are mainly in central Argentina and Uruguay.

pam·per (**pam**-pur) *verb* To take very good care of yourself or someone else with food, kindness, or anything special. ▶ *verb* **pampering, pampered**

pam·phlet (**pam**-flit) *noun* A small, thin booklet that usually contains an essay or information on one particular topic.

pan (pan)
noun A wide, shallow metal container that is used for cooking.
verb 1. To wash gravel in a pan or sieve, looking for gold. 2. To move a movie or television camera over a wide area in order to display that area or to follow an action. 3. (informal) To criticize someone or something harshly. 4. **pan out** (informal) To turn out well; to succeed. ▶ *verb* **panning, panned**

Pan·a·ma (pan-uh-*mah*) The southernmost country in Central America. The Panama Canal, which cuts through the narrow piece of land that connects North and South America, was completed in 1914.

Pan·a·ma Ca·nal (**pan**-uh-*mah* kuh-**nal**) A ship canal located in Panama, stretching between the Atlantic Ocean and the Pacific Ocean. The Panama Canal was built by the United States between 1904 and 1914, and it is located on a narrow strip of land only 48 miles (77 kilometers) long. It remains an important passageway for international maritime shipping and trade.

pan·cake (**pan**-*kake*) *noun* A thin, flat cake made from batter and cooked in a pan or on a griddle.

pan·cre·as (**pan**-kree-uhs) *noun* A gland near your stomach that makes a fluid that helps you digest food. The pancreas also makes insulin, a hormone that helps your body use glucose.

pan·da (**pan**-duh) *noun* 1. An animal found in China that looks like a bear and has thick, black and white fur. It is also called a *giant panda*. 2. A small, reddish-brown animal that is found in Asia. It looks like a raccoon and has short legs, a long, bushy tail with rings, and a white face. It is also called a *lesser panda* or *red panda*.

pan·dem·ic (pan-**dem**-ik) *noun* An outbreak of a disease that affects a very large region or the whole world.

pan·de·mo·ni·um (*pan*-duh-**moh**-nee-uhm) *noun* Noisy chaos or confusion.

pane (payn) *noun* A sheet of glass or plastic in a window or door. **Pane** sounds like **pain**.

pan·el (**pan**-uhl)
noun 1. A flat piece of wood or other material made to form part of a surface such as a wall. 2. A board with instruments or controls on it. 3. A group of people chosen to do something such as judge a competition or discuss a topic.
verb To cover or decorate with panels. ▶ *verb* **paneling, paneled** ▶ *noun* **paneling** ▶ *noun* **panelist**

pang (pang) *noun* A sudden, brief pain or emotion.

pan·ic (**pan**-ik)
noun A sudden feeling of terror or fright, often affecting many people at once, and so severe that people cannot act normally or make good decisions.
verb To feel sudden, overwhelming fear or anxiety.
adjective **panic-stricken** Struck with sudden fear.
▶ *verb* **panicking, panicked** ▶ *adjective* **panicky**

pan·o·ram·a (*pan*-uh-**ram**-uh) *noun* A wide or complete view of an area. ▶ *adjective* **panoramic**

pan·sy (**pan**-zee) *noun* A small garden flower with five rounded petals that are often purple, yellow, or white. ▶ *noun, plural* **pansies**

pant (pant) *verb* To breathe quickly and loudly because you are exhausted. ▶ *verb* **panting, panted**

pan·ther (**pan**-thur) *noun* One of several wildcats found in Asia, Africa, and the Americas, called variously leopard, mountain lion, puma, cougar, and jaguar.

pan·to·mime (**pan**-tuh-*mime*)
noun 1. The telling of a story with gestures, body movements, and facial expressions rather than words. 2. A play or scene acted out with gestures instead of words.
verb To express with gestures and body movements.
▶ *verb* **pantomiming, pantomimed**

pan·try (**pan**-tree) *noun* A small room or a closet in or near a kitchen where food and kitchen supplies are kept. ▶ *noun, plural* **pantries**

pants (pants) *noun, plural* A piece of clothing with two legs that covers your body from the waist to the ankles.

pan·ty hose (**pan**-tee *hohz*) *noun, plural* An undergarment, similar to tights, that covers the hips, legs, and feet and is often made of nylon.

pa·pa·ya (puh-**pah**-yuh) *noun* The yellow or orange sweet fruit that grows on a tropical tree. It looks like a melon.

pa·per (**pay**-pur)
noun 1. A thin piece or sheet of material made from wood pulp or rags. Paper is used for writing, printing, drawing, wrapping, and covering walls. 2. A single sheet of paper. 3. A document, or a sheet of paper with something printed or written on it. 4. A written report or essay for school. 5. A newspaper.
verb To put wallpaper up, or to cover something with paper.
▶ *verb* **papering, papered**

pa·per·back (**pay**-pur-*bak*) *noun* A book with a paper cover.

pa·per clip (**pay**-pur *klip*) *noun* A bent piece of thin wire that is used to hold sheets of paper together.

pa·per·weight (**pay**-pur-*wayt*) *noun* A heavy, often decorative object used to hold down papers on a desk or other flat surface.

pa·per·work (**pay**-pur-*wurk*) *noun* The part of a job that involves writing down information and keeping records.

pa·pier-mâ·ché (*pay*-pur-muh-**shay**)
noun Paper that has been soaked in glue, which hardens when it dries. Before hardening, this material can be molded into dolls, toys, furniture, and other shapes.
adjective Made out of papier-mâché.

pap·ri·ka (pa-**pree**-kuh) *noun* A reddish-orange spice made from sweet red peppers.

Pa·pu·a New Guin·ea (**pah**-poo-uh noo **gin**-ee) A country consisting of the eastern half of the island of New Guinea and many offshore islands in the southwestern Pacific Ocean. Papua New Guinea remains largely unexplored. Researchers believe that many as yet undiscovered species of plants and animals live in the country's dense, mountainous rain forests.

pa·py·rus (puh-**pye**-ruhs) *noun* 1. A tall water plant that grows in northern Africa and southern Europe. 2. Paper made from the stems of this plant. The ancient Egyptians wrote on papyrus.
▶ *noun, plural* **papyri** (puh-**pye**-ree) *or* **papyruses**

P

par (pahr) *noun* **1.** An equal level. **2.** An accepted or normal level. **3.** In golf, the number of strokes it should take a player to get the ball into the hole or finish a particular course.

par·a·ble (**par**-uh-buhl) *noun* A story that illustrates a moral or religious lesson.

par·a·chute (**par**-uh-*shoot*)
noun A large piece of strong but lightweight fabric attached to thin ropes that spreads out in the air to slow the descent of whatever is attached to it. A parachute is used to drop people or loads safely from airplanes.
verb To drop or to descend by parachute.
▶ *verb* **parachuting, parachuted** ▶ *noun* **parachutist**

pa·rade (puh-**rade**)
noun **1.** A procession of people and vehicles as part of a ceremony or festivity. **2.** A series of people or things appearing one after the other.
verb **1.** To walk or march as if in a parade. **2.** To show something off.
▶ *verb* **parading, paraded**

par·a·dise (**par**-uh-*dise*) *noun* **1.** A place that is considered extremely beautiful and that makes people feel happy and contented. **2.** In some religions, **paradise** is another word for heaven.

par·a·dox (**par**-uh-*dahks*) *noun* **1.** A statement that seems to contradict itself but in fact may be true. **2.** A person or thing that seems to contradict itself.
▶ *noun, plural* **paradoxes** ▶ *adjective* **paradoxical**

par·af·fin (**par**-uh-fin) *noun* A white, waxy substance used in making candles and for sealing jars.

par·a·graph (**par**-uh-*graf*) *noun* A section in a piece of writing that begins on a new line and often is indented. A paragraph is made up of one or more sentences about a single subject or idea.

Par·a·guay (**par**-uh-*gwye* or **par**-uh-*gway*) A country in South America.

Because it is located in the middle of the continent, it is sometimes referred to as *el Corazón de América*, or "the Heart of America."

par·a·keet (**par**-uh-*keet*) *noun* A small parrot with brightly colored feathers and a long, pointed tail. Parakeets often are kept as pets.

par·a·le·gal (*par*-uh-**lee**-guhl)
noun A trained person who assists a lawyer.
adjective Of or having to do with a person who assists a lawyer.

par·al·lel (**par**-uh-*lel*)
adjective **1.** Staying the same distance from each other and never crossing or meeting. **2.** Very similar and often occurring at the same time.
noun **1.** A situation very similar to another one. **2.** Any of the imaginary lines that circle the earth parallel to the equator. On a map, parallels represent degrees of latitude.
verb To be very similar to something else, and often to occur at the same time.
▶ *verb* **paralleling, paralleled**

par·al·lel bars (**par**-uh-lel *bahrz*)
noun, plural A pair of horizontal wooden bars at the same or different heights used for doing exercises in gymnastics.

par·al·lel·o·gram (*par*-uh-**lel**-uh-*gram*) *noun* A four-sided figure with opposite sides that are parallel and equal in length.

pa·ral·y·sis (puh-**ral**-i-sis) *noun* **1.** A loss of the power to move or feel a part of the body. **2.** An inability to act or function.

par·a·lyze (**par**-uh-*lize*) *verb* **1.** To cause paralysis in. **2.** To make someone or something helpless or unable to function.
▶ *verb* **paralyzing, paralyzed**

par·a·me·ci·um (*par*-uh-**mee**-see-uhm) *noun* A microscopic organism with only one cell that lives in freshwater. It is shaped like a slipper. ▶ *noun, plural* **paramecia** (*par*-uh-**mee**-see-uh)

par·a·med·ic (*par*-uh-**med**-ik) *noun*
A person who is trained to give emergency medical treatment but who is not a doctor or a nurse.

par·a·mount (**par**-uh-*mount*) *adjective*
Above all others in rank, power, or importance.

par·a·pher·na·lia (*par*-uh-fur-**nayl**-yuh)
noun Numerous pieces of equipment, belongings, and other personal items, especially those needed for a particular activity.

par·a·phrase (**par**-uh-*fraze*)
verb To say or write something again in a different way.
noun A restatement in different words of something that has been said or written.
▶ *verb* **paraphrasing, paraphrased**

par·a·ple·gic (*par*-uh-**plee**-jik)
noun A person who has no feeling or movement in the lower part of his or her body, usually because of an injury or a disease of the spinal cord.
adjective Affected by paralysis in the lower half of the body.

par·a·site (**par**-uh-*site*) *noun* **1.** An animal or plant that lives on or inside of another animal or plant. **2.** A person who gets money, food, and shelter from another without doing anything in return.
▶ *adjective* **parasitic** (*par*-uh-**sit**-ik)

par·a·sol (**par**-uh-*sawl*) *noun* A small, light umbrella that shades you from the sun.

par·a·troops (**par**-uh-*troops*) *noun, plural* Soldiers who are trained to jump by parachute into battle. ▶ *noun* **paratrooper**

par·cel (**pahr**-suhl)
noun **1.** A package, or something that is packed, wrapped, or put into a box. **2.** A section or plot of land.
verb To divide into parts and give out.
▶ *verb* **parceling, parceled**

parch (pahrch) *verb* **1.** To make very dry. **2.** To make very thirsty.
▶ *verb* **parches, parching, parched** ▶ *adjective* **parched**

parch·ment (**pahrch**-muhnt) *noun*
Heavy sheets of paper-like material

made from the skin of sheep, goats, or other animals and used for writing on.

par·don (**pahr**-duhn)
verb To forgive or excuse someone, or to cancel a person's punishment or other consequences.
noun The act of forgiving someone for wrongdoing or a mistake.
interjection You say **I beg your pardon** as a polite way of asking someone to repeat what he or she has said or asking someone for forgiveness.
▶ *verb* **pardoning, pardoned**

pare (pair) *verb* **1.** To cut off the outer layer. **2.** To reduce or make less step by step, as if by cutting.
Pare sounds like **pair** and **pear.** ▶ *verb* **paring, pared**

par·ent (**pair**-uhnt)
noun **1.** A mother or a father. **2.** A plant or an animal that produces offspring.
verb To be or to act like a parent.
▶ *verb* **parenting, parented** ▶ *noun* **parenthood**

pa·ren·tal (puh-**ren**-tuhl) *adjective* Of or having to do with being a parent.

pa·ren·the·sis (puh-**ren**-thuh-sis)
noun One of the curved lines () used to enclose a word or phrase in a sentence or to enclose symbols or numbers in a mathematical expression. ▶ *noun, plural* **parentheses** (puh-**ren**-thuh-seez)

par·ish (**par**-ish) *noun* **1.** A particular church and the people who attend it. **2.** In Louisiana, a county.
▶ *noun, plural* **parishes**

pa·rish·ion·er (puh-**rish**-uh-nur) *noun*
A person who attends a particular church.

park (pahrk)
noun **1.** An area of land with trees, benches, and sometimes playgrounds, used by the public for recreation. **2.** An area of land set aside by the government so that it can be kept in its natural state.
verb To leave a car or other vehicle in a space in a garage or lot or at the curb of a street.
▶ *verb* **parking, parked**

P

par·ka (**pahr**-kuh) *noun* A large, heavy jacket suitable for winter weather. It has a hood and is usually made of fur or a windproof material filled with down.

park·ing me·ter (**pahr**-king *mee*-tur) *noun* A machine that you put money into in order to pay for parking. The meter allows you a certain amount of time for each coin you put into it.

park·way (**pahrk**-*way*) *noun* A wide highway or road that has grass, bushes, trees, and flowers planted down the middle or along the sides.

par·lia·ment (**pahr**-luh-muhnt) *noun* The group of people who have been elected to make the laws in some countries, such as Canada, the United Kingdom, and Israel. ▶ *adjective* **parliamentary**

par·lor (**pahr**-lur) *noun* 1. A formal living room, especially in an old house. 2. A room or rooms used for a business.

Par·me·san cheese (**pahr**-muh-zahn **cheez**) *noun* A very hard cheese with a sharp flavor, usually grated and used especially with pasta dishes. Parmesan cheese was originally made in Parma, Italy.

pa·ro·chi·al (puh-**roh**-kee-uhl) *adjective* 1. Of or having to do with a church parish. 2. Having a narrow, short-sighted point of view.

par·o·dy (**par**-uh-dee) *noun* An imitation of a serious piece of writing or a song that makes fun of the original work. *verb* To imitate someone or something, such as a serious piece of writing or a song, in order to make fun of the person or original work. ▶ *noun, plural* **parodies**

pa·role (puh-**role**) *noun* The early release of a prisoner, usually for good behavior, on the condition that he or she continue to obey the law. *verb* To release a prisoner on parole. ▶ *verb* **paroling, paroled**

par·ox·ysm (**par**-uhk-*siz*-uhm) *noun* A sudden outburst or fit.

par·rot (**par**-uht) *noun* 1. A brightly colored tropical bird with a curved beak and a rough voice. Some parrots can learn to repeat things that are said to them. 2. A person who repeats or imitates words without understanding what they mean. *verb* To repeat something in a mechanical way. ▶ *verb* **parroting, parroted**

parse (pahrs) *verb* To identify the parts of speech and the grammatical structures of a sentence. ▶ *verb* **parsing, parsed**

pars·ley (**pahr**-slee) *noun* A leafy, green herb with small leaves, used to season or to decorate food.

pars·nip (**pahr**-snip) *noun* A plant with a pale yellow root eaten as a vegetable. Parsnips resemble carrots.

par·son (**pahr**-suhn) *noun* A minister, especially a Protestant minister.

part (pahrt) *noun* 1. A portion or division of a whole. 2. A piece in a machine or device. 3. An expected share of responsibility or work. 4. A character or role in a play or film. 5. A line in your hair where the hair is combed in two directions. *verb* 1. To separate or to divide. 2. **part with something** To give something away or give it up. *adjective* Not completely or entirely. *idiom* **take part** To join with others in an activity. ▶ *verb* **parting, parted**

par·tial (**pahr**-shuhl) *adjective* 1. Incomplete. 2. Favoring one person or side over another. 3. **partial to** Especially fond of a particular thing. ▶ *noun* **partiality** (*pahr*-shee-**al**-i-tee) ▶ *adverb* **partially**

par·tial·ly (**pahr**-shuh-lee) *adverb* To a degree; not entirely.

par·tic·i·pant (pahr-**tis**-uh-puhnt) *noun* Someone who takes part in something.

par·tic·i·pate (pahr-**tis**-uh-*pate*) *verb* To join with others in an activity or event. ▶ *verb* **participating, participated** ▶ *noun* **participation**

P

par·ti·ci·ple (**pahr**-ti-*sip*-uhl) *noun* A form of a verb that is used with a helping verb or that can be used as an adjective. English has two kinds of participles: the present participle, ending in -*ing*, as in *walking* or *singing*, and the past participle, often but not always ending in -*ed* or -*en*, as in *finished* or *swollen*.

par·ti·cle (**pahr**-ti-kuhl) *noun* An extremely small piece or amount of something.

par·ti·cle phys·ics (**pahr**-ti-kuhl **fiz**-iks) *noun* The study of the behavior of the components of atoms.

par·tic·u·lar (pur-**tik**-yuh-lur)
adjective 1. Individual or special.
2. Very careful about details. 3. Special or unusual.
noun A detail.
phrase **in particular** Especially.

par·tic·u·lar·ly (pur-**tik**-yuh-lur-lee)
adverb Especially.

part·ing (**pahr**-ting)
noun A departure or a separation.
adjective Of or having to do with a departure or separation.

par·ti·tion (pahr-**tish**-uhn)
noun A movable wall or panel used to divide an area or a room.
verb 1. To section something off or to separate something. 2. To divide into sections or parts.
▶ *verb* **partitioning, partitioned**

part·ly (**pahrt**-lee) *adverb* In part or to some extent.

part·ner (**pahrt**-nur) *noun* A person who works or does some other activity with another person or persons.

part·ner·ship (**pahrt**-nur-*ship*) *noun*
1. The state of being a partner. 2. An association or business involving two or more people as partners.

part of speech (**pahrt** uhv **speech**)
noun A grammatical class into which a word can be placed according to the way it is used in a phrase or sentence, such as whether it is a noun, verb, or adjective. ▶ *noun, plural* **parts of speech**

par·tridge (**pahr**-trij) *noun* A plump game bird that has gray, brown, and white feathers.

part-time
adjective (**pahrt**-*time*) Done for only a few hours each day or a few days each week.
adverb **part time** (**pahrt**-*time*) For only part of the day or week.
▶ *noun* **part-timer**

par·ty (**pahr**-tee)
noun 1. An organized occasion when people enjoy themselves in a group, often to celebrate a special event.
2. A group of people working together on a particular task. 3. An organized group of people with similar political beliefs who sponsor candidates in elections. 4. A person or group that is involved in a particular activity, such as a legal case.
verb To enjoy yourself with other people at a party.
▶ *noun, plural* **parties** ▶ *verb* **parties, partying, partied**

pass (pas)
verb 1. To go by someone or something. 2. To give something to somebody who is farther away from it. 3. To kick, throw, or hit a ball to someone on your own team in a game or sport. 4. To succeed in a test or course. 5. To move on or to go by. 6. To approve or to make into law.
7. **pass away** To die. 8. **pass out** To faint. 9. **pass up** To give up the opportunity to have or do something.
noun 1. A narrow passage in a mountain range. 2. Written permission. 3. A free ticket.
▶ *noun, plural* **passes** ▶ *verb* **passes, passing, passed** ▶ *noun* **passer**

pas·sage (**pas**-ij) *noun* 1. A hall or a corridor. 2. A short section of a book or piece of music. 3. A journey by ship or airplane. 4. Approval of a bill into law by a legislature.

pas·sage·way (**pas**-ij-*way*) *noun* An alley, a hallway, a tunnel, or anything that allows you to pass from one place to another.

pas·sen·ger (**pas**-uhn-jur) *noun* Someone besides the driver who travels in a vehicle.

P

pass·er·by (**pas**-ur-*bye*) *noun* A person who happens to be passing. ▸ *noun, plural* **passersby**

pas·sion (**pash**-uhn) *noun* **1.** A very strong feeling, such as anger, love, or hatred. **2.** Great devotion or enthusiasm.

pas·sion·ate (**pash**-uh-nit) *adjective* Having or showing very strong feelings. ▸ *adverb* **passionately**

pas·sive (**pas**-iv) *adjective* **1.** Not inclined to fight back, react to, or resist things that happen. **2.** The subject of a **passive** verb has something done to it. It receives an action, while the subject of an active verb performs an action. *See* **active.** ▸ *adverb* **passively**

Pass·o·ver (**pas**-*oh*-vur) *noun* An important Jewish holiday celebrated in the spring. It commemorates the Jews' escape from slavery in Egypt.

pass·port (**pas**-*port*) *noun* An official document that verifies that you are a citizen of a certain country and allows you to cross international borders.

pass·word (**pas**-*wurd*) *noun* A secret word, code, or phrase that you need to know to get into a guarded area or a computer system.

past (past) *noun* **1.** The period of time before the present. **2.** **past tense** The form of a verb that shows that an action took place in the past. *adjective* **1.** Just finished or ended. **2.** Former. *adverb* So as to pass or go beyond. *preposition* To or on the far side of. *We went past the exit.*

pas·ta (**pah**-stuh) *noun* A food made from dough that is formed into shapes and dried. It is boiled in a liquid and usually served with a sauce.

paste (payst) *noun* **1.** A soft, sticky mixture used to hold things together. **2.** Any soft, creamy mixture. *verb* **1.** To fasten with paste. **2.** On a computer, to insert text or graphics copied or cut from another location. ▸ *verb* **pasting, pasted**

pas·tel (pa-**stel**) *noun* **1.** A chalky crayon that is used in drawing. **2.** A picture made with pastels. **3.** A light, soft shade of a color. *adjective* Pale and soft in color.

pas·teur·ize (**pas**-chuh-*rize*) *verb* To heat milk or another liquid to a temperature that is high enough to kill harmful bacteria. ▸ *noun* **pasteurization** (*pas*-chur-i-**zay**-shuhn) ▸ *adjective* **pasteurized**

pas·time (**pas**-*time*) *noun* A hobby, an activity, or an entertainment that makes the time pass in an enjoyable way.

pas·tor (**pas**-tur) *noun* A minister or priest in charge of a church or parish.

pas·tor·al (**pas**-tur-uhl) *adjective* **1.** Of or having to do with rural areas. **2.** Having to do with or coming from a pastor.

past par·ti·ci·ple (past pahr-ti-*sip*-uhl) *noun* A form of a verb that often, but not always, ends in *-ed* or *-en* and can be used with a helping verb to show that an action or a condition is completed. In the sentence "I have wrapped his gift," the word *wrapped* is a past participle. A past participle is also used to help form a passive verb, such as *kicked* in the sentence "The ball was kicked." Past participles may also be used as adjectives, such as *swollen* in "a swollen ankle."

pas·try (**pay**-stree) *noun* **1.** A dough that is used for pie crusts. **2.** Pies, tarts, and other sweet baked goods. ▸ *noun, plural* **pastries**

past tense (past tens) *noun* A form of a verb that shows that an action took place in the past, such as the verb *went* in the sentence "She went to school late this morning."

pas·ture (**pas**-chur) *noun* Grazing land for animals.

pas·ty (**pay**-stee) *adjective* Pale and sickly looking. ▸ *adjective* **pastier, pastiest**

P

pat (pat)
verb To touch something gently with your hand.
noun **1.** A small, flat piece. **2.** A gentle or light blow with the hand. **3. pat on the back** Praise for a person who has done something well.
▶ *verb* **patting, patted**

patch (pach)
verb **1.** To repair a small hole or tear by covering it with the same or similar material. **2. patch up** To settle or to smooth over.
noun **1.** A small part or area of something. **2.** A small piece of ground.
▶ *noun, plural* **patches** ▶ *verb* **patches, patching, patched**

patch·work (pach-*wurk*) *noun* A type of needlework consisting of a pattern made by sewing small patches of different material together. Some quilts are patchwork.

patch·y (pach-ee) *adjective* Uneven; made up of or similar to patches. ▶ *adjective* **patchier, patchiest**

pâ·té (pah-**tay** or pa-**tay**) *noun* A smooth spread made of meat, fish, or vegetables that is usually eaten on toast or crackers.

pat·ent
noun (**pat**-uhnt) **1.** A legal document giving the inventor of an item the sole rights to manufacture or sell it. **2. patent leather** Very shiny leather used for shoes, belts, handbags, and other accessories.
verb (**pat**-uhnt) To obtain a patent for.
adjective (**pay**-tuhnt or **pat**-uhnt) Obvious or open.
▶ *verb* **patenting, patented** ▶ *adverb* **patently**

pat·er·nal (puh-**tur**-nuhl) *adjective*
1. Having to do with or like a father. **2.** Related through your father.
▶ *adverb* **paternally**

path (path) *noun* **1.** A trail or track for walking. **2.** The line or route along which a person or thing moves.

pa·thet·ic (puh-**thet**-ik) *adjective*
1. Causing pity, sorrow, or sympathy. **2.** Completely inadequate.
▶ *adverb* **pathetically**

pa·tience (**pay**-shuhns) *noun* The ability to put up with problems and delays without getting angry or upset.

pa·tient (**pay**-shuhnt)
noun A person who is receiving treatment from a doctor or other health-care provider.
adjective Able to put up with problems and delays without getting angry or upset.
▶ *adverb* **patiently**

pat·i·o (**pat**-ee-*oh*) *noun* A paved area next to a house, used for relaxing or eating outdoors.

pa·tri·arch (**pay**-tree-*ahrk*) *noun* **1.** The male head of a family or tribe. **2.** An older man in a group, tribe, or village who is respected and who holds a place of honor. **3.** The head of any of several Orthodox churches.

pa·tri·ot (**pay**-tree-uht) *noun* A person who loves his or her country and is ready to defend it. ▶ *noun* **patriotism** (**pay**-tree-uh-*tiz*-uhm) ▶ *adjective* **patriotic** (*pay*-tree-ah-tik)

pa·tri·ot·ic (*pay*-tree-**ah**-tik) *adjective* A person who is **patriotic** has a strong loyalty to his or her own country. ▶ *adverb* **patriotically**

pa·trol (puh-**trohl**)
verb To walk or travel around an area to watch or protect it or the people within it.
noun **1.** A group of people who watch and protect an area. **2.** A group of soldiers, sometimes aboard ships or airplanes, sent out to find or learn about the enemy.
▶ *verb* **patrolling, patrolled**

pa·tron (**pay**-truhn) *noun* **1.** A customer. **2.** A person who gives money to or helps another person, an activity, or a cause.
▶ *noun* **patronage** (**pay**-truh-nij)

pa·tron·ize (**pay**-truh-*nize* or **pat**-ruh-*nize*) *verb* **1.** To act or talk to someone as though you are better or more knowledgeable than he or she is. **2.** To go to a store, restaurant, or other business regularly.
▶ *verb* **patronizing, patronized**

P

pa·tron saint (**pay**-truhn **saynt**) *noun*
A saint who is believed to look after an individual, a group of people, a particular activity, a city, or a country.

pat·ter (**pat**-ur)
verb To make light, quick sounds.
noun **1.** Continuous, fast talking, especially in order to distract someone. **2.** Repeated light, soft, tapping sounds.
▶ *verb* **pattering, pattered**

pat·tern (**pat**-urn)
noun **1.** A repeating arrangement of colors, shapes, and figures. **2.** A sample or model that you can follow as a guide. **3.** A repeated set of actions or characteristics.
verb To make a sample or model of something that you can follow as a guide.
▶ *verb* **patterning, patterned**
▶ *adjective* **patterned**

pat·ty (**pat**-ee) *noun* **1.** A round, flat piece of chopped or ground food. **2.** A round, flat piece of candy.
▶ *noun, plural* **patties**

pau·per (**paw**-pur) *noun* A very poor person.

pause (pawz)
verb To stop briefly.
noun A brief or temporary stop.
▶ *verb* **pausing, paused**

pave (payv) *verb* **1.** To cover a road or other surface with a hard material such as concrete or asphalt. **2. pave the way** To lead the way, or to make progress easier.
▶ *verb* **paving, paved**

pave·ment (**payv**-muhnt) *noun* **1.** A hard material, such as concrete or asphalt, that is used to cover roads or sidewalks. **2.** A paved road or a sidewalk.

pa·vil·ion (puh-**vil**-yuhn) *noun* **1.** An open building that is used for shelter or recreation or for a show or an exhibit. **2.** One of a group of buildings, especially a building that is part of a hospital.

paw (paw)
noun The foot of an animal that has four feet and claws.

verb **1.** To touch with a paw. **2.** To handle roughly or carelessly.
▶ *verb* **pawing, pawed**

pawn (pawn)
verb To leave a valuable item at a pawnbroker's in return for a loan. The item is returned to you if you repay the money, or it may be sold if you do not.
noun **1.** The smallest piece in the game of chess, having the lowest value.
2. A person or thing that is used by someone else to get something or to gain an advantage.
▶ *verb* **pawning, pawned**

pawn·brok·er (**pawn**-broh-kur) *noun* A person whose business is to make loans to people who leave valuable objects as security for the loans.

pay (pay)
verb **1.** To give money for something. **2.** To be worthwhile or advantageous. **3.** To give or offer. **4.** To suffer consequences for an action.
noun Money earned from working.
▶ *verb* **pays, paying, paid**

pay·a·ble (**pay**-uh-buhl) *adjective* Able to be paid or that must be paid.

pay·ment (**pay**-muhnt) *noun* Money given in return for something.

pay-per-view (**pay**-pur-**vyoo**) *noun* A service for cable television viewers in which customers order and view a single movie or televised event for a fee.

pay·roll (**pay**-rohl) *noun* **1.** A list of workers who are paid by a company, along with the amount each is to be paid. **2.** The total of all money paid to workers.

PC (**pee-see**)
noun Short for **personal computer.**
adjective (informal) A person who is **PC** makes a great effort to be sensitive to the needs and wishes of all groups, including minorities, women, and the disabled. PC is short for *politically correct.*

PDF (**pee**-dee-**ef**) *noun* A popular format for electronic documents, or a document formatted in this way. PDF is short for *portable document format.*

P

PE (pee-ee) *noun* A period in school during which you play sports or do any kind of physical exercise. PE is short for *physical education*.

pea (pee) *noun* A small, round, green vegetable that grows as a seed in a pod.

peace (pees) *noun* 1. A period without war or fighting. 2. Calmness of mind or environment. 3. Public security, or law and order.
Peace sounds like **piece**. ▶ *adverb* **peacefully** ▶ *noun* **peacetime**

peace·ful (pees-fuhl) *adjective* 1. Quiet and without any disturbance. 2. Tending to avoiding conflict.

peace·keep·ing (pees-*kee*-ping) *noun* A policy of keeping law and order; especially, an arrangement by which international troops who do not support either side in a conflict are sent to try to prevent war.

peach (peech)
noun 1. A soft, round, sweet fruit with a fuzzy, reddish-yellow skin and a pit at the center. 2. A pink-yellow color.
adjective Pinkish yellow.
▶ *noun, plural* **peaches**

pea·cock (pee-*kahk*) *noun* A large bird that is related to the pheasant. The male peacock has brilliant blue and green feathers that spread out in a fan shape when he raises his tail.

peak (peek)
noun 1. The pointed top of a high mountain. 2. A mountain with a pointed top. 3. The highest or best point.
verb To reach the highest or best point.
Peak sounds like **peek**. ▶ *verb* **peaking, peaked**

peal (peel)
verb To ring out loudly.
noun A loud sound or series of sounds.
Peal sounds like **peel**. ▶ *verb* **pealing, pealed**

pea·nut (pee-nuht) *noun* A nutlike seed that grows in underground pods. Peanuts are eaten roasted or made into peanut butter and cooking oil.

peanut butter (pee-nuht *buht*-ur) *noun* A thick, light brown spread made from ground, roasted peanuts.

pear (pair) *noun* A juicy and sweet yellow, green, red, or brown fruit with a smooth skin. **Pear** sounds like **pair** and **pare.**

pearl (purl) *noun* 1. A small, round object that grows inside oysters and is used to make valuable jewelry. 2. A valuable person, thing, or idea.

peas·ant (pez-uhnt) *noun* A person who owns a small farm or works on a farm, especially in Europe and some Asian nations.

peat (peet) *noun* Dark brown, partly decayed plant matter that is found in bogs and swamps. Peat can be used as fuel or compost.

peb·ble (peb-uhl) *noun* A small, round, smooth stone. ▶ *adjective* **pebbly**

pe·can (pee-kan *or* pi-**kahn**) *noun* A sweet nut with a thin, smooth shell. Pecans grow on large trees.

peck (pek)
verb 1. To strike or pick up something with the beak. 2. To eat in small bites or without enthusiasm.
noun 1. (informal) A quick, light kiss. 2. A unit of measure for dry things, such as produce or grain. A peck is equal to eight quarts, or one-fourth of a bushel.
▶ *verb* **pecking, pecked**

pe·cu·liar (pi-**kyool**-yur) *adjective* 1. Odd or unusual. 2. **peculiar to** Belonging to or having to do with a certain person, group, place, or thing.
▶ *noun* **peculiarity** (pi-*kyoo*-lee-**ar**-i-tee) ▶ *adverb* **peculiarly**

ped·al (ped-uhl)
noun A lever that you push with your foot, such as on a bicycle or a car.
verb To operate something by using a pedal or pedals.
Pedal sounds like **peddle**. ▶ *verb* **pedaling, pedaled**

ped·dle (ped-uhl) *verb* To sell things by going from house to house or place to place. **Peddle** sounds like **pedal**. ▶ *verb* **peddling, peddled** ▶ *noun* **peddler**

P

ped·es·tal (**ped**-i-stuhl) *noun* 1. The base of a statue. 2. Any base or support, as for a large vase. **3. put someone on a pedestal** To admire a person excessively.

pe·des·tri·an (puh-**des**-tree-uhn) *noun* A person who travels on foot. *adjective* Ordinary and dull.

pe·di·a·tric·ian (pee-dee-uh-**tri**-shuhn) *noun* A doctor who specializes in the care and treatment of babies and children.

pe·di·at·rics (pee-dee-**at**-riks) *noun* The branch of medicine that is concerned with babies and children. ▶ *adjective* **pediatric**

ped·i·gree (**ped**-i-gree) *noun* A line or list of ancestors, especially of an animal.

peek (peek)
verb 1. To look at something secretly or quickly. 2. To be barely visible.
noun A quick or secretive look.
Peek sounds like **peak**. ▶ *verb* **peeking, peeked**

peel (peel)
noun The outer skin of a fruit.
verb 1. To remove the skin of a vegetable or a fruit. 2. To remove or to pull off. 3. To come off in pieces or strips.
Peel sounds like **peal**. ▶ *verb* **peeling, peeled**

peep (peep)
verb To peek or look secretly at something.
noun The high, sharp sound that a young bird or chicken makes.
▶ *verb* **peeping, peeped**

peer (peer)
verb To look at something with difficulty.
noun 1. An equal, or a person of the same age, rank, or standing as another. 2. A member of the British nobility, such as a duke or an earl.
Peer sounds like **pier**. ▶ *verb* **peering, peered** ▶ *noun* **peerage**

peg (peg)
noun A short, cylindrical piece of wood, metal, or plastic, used to hold

things together, hang things on, or mark a position.
verb To fasten or mark with a peg.
▶ *verb* **pegging, pegged**

Pe·king·ese (pee-ki-**neez**) *noun* A breed of small dog originally from China. A Pekingese has a long, silky coat and a flat face. ▶ *noun, plural* **Pekingese**

pel·i·can (**pel**-i-kuhn) *noun* A large waterbird with a long bill and a pouch below the bill that can hold the fish it catches.

pel·let (**pel**-it) *noun* A small, hard ball of something, such as food or ice.

pell-mell (**pel**-**mel**) *adverb* In a confused or disorderly way.

pelt (pelt)
verb To strike or beat again and again.
noun An animal's skin with the hair or fur still on it.
▶ *verb* **pelting, pelted**

pen (pen)
noun 1. An instrument used for writing or drawing with ink. 2. A small, enclosed area for sheep, cattle, pigs, or other animals.
verb 1. To keep or shut up in a pen. 2. To write something.
▶ *verb* **penning, penned**

pe·nal·ize (**pee**-nuh-lize) *verb* To punish someone in some way, or to put someone at a disadvantage. ▶ *verb* **penalizing, penalized**

pen·al·ty (**pen**-uhl-tee) *noun* 1. A punishment. 2. In sports, a disadvantage or punishment that a team or player suffers for breaking the rules.

pen·cil (**pen**-suhl)
noun 1. An instrument used for drawing and writing, made of a stick of graphite in a wooden, metal, or plastic casing. 2. A similar instrument containing a cosmetic, medication, or other material.
verb To write or draw something with a pencil.
▶ *verb* **penciling, penciled**

pen·dant (**pen**-duhnt) *noun* A hanging ornament, especially one worn on a necklace.

P

pen·du·lum (**pen**-juh-luhm *or* **pen**-dyuh-luhm) *noun* A weight in a large clock that moves from side to side and keeps the clock's mechanism in regular motion.

pen·e·trate (**pen**-i-*trate*) *verb* 1. To go inside or through something. 2. To understand or to solve.
▶ *verb* **penetrating, penetrated** ▶ *noun* **penetration**

pen·guin (**pen**-gwin *or* **peng**-gwin) *noun* A waterbird of the Antarctic region that cannot fly. Instead, the penguin uses its wings as flippers for swimming underwater.

pen·i·cil·lin (*pen*-i-**sil**-uhn) *noun* A drug made from a mold called *penicillium* that kills bacteria and helps fight some diseases. Penicillin was the first antibiotic. It was discovered in 1928 by Sir Alexander Fleming, a British scientist.

pen·in·su·la (puh-**nin**-suh-luh) *noun* A piece of land that sticks out from a larger landmass and is almost completely surrounded by water. ▶ *adjective* **peninsular**

pe·nis (**pee**-nis) *noun* The male organ for urinating or reproduction. ▶ *noun, plural* **penises** *or* **penes** (**pee**-neez)

pen·i·tent (**pen**-i-tuhnt) *adjective* Extremely sorry for what you have done wrong. ▶ *noun* **penitence**

pen·i·ten·tia·ry (pen-i-**ten**-chur-ee) *noun* A state or federal prison for people found guilty of serious crimes. ▶ *noun, plural* **penitentiaries**

pen·knife (**pen**-*nife*) *noun* A small knife with different kinds of blades that fold into a case. ▶ *noun, plural* **penknives**

pen·man·ship (**pen**-muhn-*ship*) *noun* 1. The art of writing with a pen. 2. The style or quality of handwriting.

pen name (**pen** *name*) *noun* A made-up name used by an author instead of his or her real name.

pen·nant (**pen**-uhnt) *noun* 1. A long, triangular flag, often with the name of a school or team on it. 2. A championship, especially in professional baseball, symbolized by a flag.

pen·ni·less (**pen**-ee-lis) *adjective* Having no money at all.

Penn·syl·va·nia (*pen*-suhl-**vayn**-yuh) A state in the Mid-Atlantic region of the United States. One of the original 13 colonies, it was founded by William Penn, a Quaker pacifist who strongly believed that the English colonies in America should unite. Its largest city, Philadelphia, has many historical landmarks, including the Liberty Bell and Independence Hall, where the Declaration of Independence was signed.

pen·ny (**pen**-ee) *noun* The coin that is the smallest unit of money in the United States and Canada. A penny equals one cent. One hundred pennies equal one dollar. ▶ *noun, plural* **pennies**

pen pal (**pen** *pal*) *noun* Someone, often from another country, who exchanges letters with you.

pen·sion (**pen**-shuhn) *noun* A regular payment of money to a person who has retired from work, or who cannot work because of a disability. ▶ *noun* **pensioner**

pen·ta·gon (**pen**-tuh-*gahn*) *noun* 1. A shape with five sides. 2. **the Pentagon** A building with five sides in Arlington, Virginia, that is the headquarters of the U.S. Department of Defense.
▶ *adjective* **pentagonal** (pen-**tag**-uh-nuhl)

pent·house (**pent**-*hous*) *noun* An apartment located on the top floor of a tall building.

pe·o·ny (**pee**-uh-nee) *noun* A garden plant with large flowers that may be red, pink, or white. ▶ *noun, plural* **peonies**

peo·ple (**pee**-puhl) *noun* 1. Persons or human beings. 2. A collection of human beings who make up a nation, race, tribe, or group. 3. Family or relatives.

pep (pep)
noun Great energy and high spirits.
verb **pep up** To fill someone with energy.

P

adjective Designed to increase energy and high spirits.
▶ *verb* **pepping, pepped**

pep·per (**pep**-ur)
noun 1. A spicy powder made from the dried berries of a tropical climbing plant. 2. A hollow vegetable that is usually red, green, or yellow, with a taste ranging from slightly sharp to extremely hot.
verb 1. To season a food with pepper. 2. To hit repeatedly with small objects. 3. To overwhelm someone with suggestions or questions.
▶ *adjective* **peppery**

pep·per·mint (**pep**-ur-*mint*)
noun 1. A kind of mint plant. The oil from peppermint leaves is used as a flavoring, especially in candy and toothpaste. 2. A candy flavored with peppermint oil.
adjective Tasting of, smelling of, or flavored with peppermint.

pep·per·o·ni (*pep*-uh-**roh**-nee) *noun* A kind of hard Italian sausage made from beef or pork and seasoned with pepper.

per (pur) *preposition* In each or for each. *His job pays $7 per hour.* **Per** sounds like **purr.**

per cap·i·ta (pur **kap**-i-tuh) *adjective and adverb* For each person in a population.

per·ceive (pur-**seev**) *verb* 1. To become aware of through the senses, especially through sight or hearing. 2. To understand.
▶ *verb* **perceiving, perceived**

per·cent (pur-**sent**) *noun* A part that is one one-hundredth. A quarter is 25 percent of one dollar. Percent is also written using the symbol %.

per·cent·age (pur-**sen**-tij) *noun* A fraction or proportion of something, expressed as a number out of a hundred.

per·cep·ti·ble (pur-**sep**-tuh-buhl) *adjective* Noticeable and clear. ▶ *adverb* **perceptibly**

per·cep·tion (pur-**sep**-shuhn) *noun* 1. The act of noticing something with one of your senses or with your mind.

2. An idea based on what you have seen, heard, or experienced.

per·cep·tive (pur-**sep**-tiv) *adjective* Quick to notice or understand things.

perch (purch)
noun 1. A bar or branch on which a bird can rest. 2. Any raised place where a person can sit or stand. 3. An edible freshwater fish.
verb To sit or stand on the edge of something, often high up.
▶ *noun, plural* **perches** or **perch** ▶ *verb* **perches, perching, perched**

per·cus·sion in·stru·ment (pur-**kuhsh**-uhn *in*-struh-muhnt) *noun* A musical instrument, such as a drum, that is played by being hit or shaken. ▶ *noun* **percussionist** (pur-**kuhsh**-uh-nist)

per·en·ni·al (puh-**ren**-ee-uhl)
noun A plant that lives and flowers for more than two years.
adjective Lasting for a long time, or never ending.
▶ *adverb* **perennially**

per·fect
adjective (**pur**-fikt) Without any flaws or mistakes.
verb (pur-**fekt**) To make something as flawless as possible.
▶ *verb* **perfecting, perfected** ▶ *noun* **perfection** (pur-**fek**-shuhn)

per·fect·ly (**pur**-fikt-lee) *adverb* 1. In a way that couldn't be better or more perfect. 2. Completely.

per·fo·rate (**pur**-fuh-*rayt*) *verb* 1. To make a hole or holes in something. 2. To make a row of small holes through something, usually paper, so that a portion can be torn off easily.
▶ *verb* **perforating, perforated** ▶ *noun* **perforation** ▶ *adjective* **perforated**

per·form (pur-**form**) *verb* 1. To do or accomplish something. 2. To entertain an audience.
▶ *verb* **performing, performed**

per·form·ance (pur-**for**-muhns) *noun* 1. The public presentation of a play, movie, or piece of music. 2. The way something works, compared to a standard.

P

per·form·er (pur-**for**-mur) *noun* A person who entertains an audience in public.

per·fume (**pur**-fyoom) *noun* 1. A liquid you put on your skin to make yourself smell pleasant. 2. Any pleasing smell. *verb* To give a pleasant odor to something.
▶ *verb* **perfuming, perfumed**
▶ *adjective* **perfumed**

per·haps (pur-**haps**) *adverb* Maybe or possibly.

per·il (**per**-uhl) *noun* 1. Danger. 2. Something dangerous.
▶ *adjective* **perilous** ▶ *adverb* **perilously**

pe·rim·e·ter (puh-**rim**-i-tur) *noun* 1. The boundary of an area. 2. The distance around the edge of a shape or an area.

pe·ri·od (**peer**-ee-uhd) *noun* 1. A length of time. 2. A part of a school day. 3. The punctuation mark (.) used to show that a sentence has ended or that a word has been abbreviated.

pe·ri·od·ic (peer-ee-**ah**-dik) *adjective* Happening or repeating at regular intervals. ▶ *adverb* **periodically**

pe·ri·od·i·cal (peer-ee-**ah**-di-kuhl) *noun* A journal or magazine that is published at regular intervals, most often once a week or once a month.

pe·ri·od·ic ta·ble (**peer**-ee-*ah*-dik **tay**-buhl) *noun* A table that displays all of the chemical elements in a way that shows their relationships to each other.

pe·riph·er·al (puh-**rif**-ur-uhl) *adjective* Of or having to do with the outer part or edge of something. *noun* An external device, such as a printer or modem, that is connected to and controlled by a computer.
▶ *adverb* **peripherally**

pe·riph·er·y (puh-**rif**-ur-ee) *noun* The outside edge of something. ▶ *noun, plural* **peripheries**

per·i·scope (**per**-i-skope) *noun* A vertical tube containing a series of prisms or mirrors and lenses that allows you to see an object that is far above you or behind an obstacle. Periscopes are often used in submarines.

per·ish (**per**-ish) *verb* To die, or to be destroyed. ▶ *verb* **perishes, perishing, perished**

per·ish·a·ble (**per**-i-shuh-buhl) *adjective* Likely to spoil or decay quickly. *noun, plural* **perishables** Something, usually food, that is likely to decay or spoil.

per·ju·ry (**pur**-jur-ee) *noun* The act of lying in a court of law while under oath to tell the truth. Perjury is a crime. ▶ *noun, plural* **perjuries** ▶ *verb* **perjure**

perk (purk) *verb* **perk up** To become more cheerful. *noun* (informal) An extra advantage or benefit that comes with a particular job.
▶ *verb* **perking, perked** ▶ *adjective* **perky**

perm (purm) *noun* (informal) Short for **permanent** (the hair treatment).

per·ma·nent (**pur**-muh-nuhnt) *adjective* Lasting or meant to last for a long time. *noun* A method of setting hair in waves or curls and treating it with chemicals to make the style last for a few months. The original term for a permanent was *permanent wave*.
▶ *noun* **permanence**

per·ma·nent·ly (**pur**-muh-nuhnt-lee) *adverb* In a lasting or uninterrupted way.

per·me·ate (**pur**-mee-*ate*) *verb* To spread throughout something. ▶ *verb* **permeating, permeated**

per·mis·si·ble (pur-**mis**-uh-buhl) *adjective* Allowed or permitted.

per·mis·sion (pur-**mish**-uhn) *noun* Consent; an agreement to allow something to happen.

per·mis·sive (pur-**mis**-iv) *adjective* Not strict; allowing more freedom than others might allow in the same situation. ▶ *noun* **permissiveness**

per·mit
    verb (pur-**mit**) To allow or consent to something.
    noun (**pur**-mit) An official document giving someone permission to do something.
    ▸ *verb* **permitting, permitted**

per·mu·ta·tion (*pur*-myuh-**tay**-shuhn) *noun* One of several different ways in which a set of things can be ordered or arranged.

per·pen·dic·u·lar (*pur*-puhn-**dik**-yuh-lur) *noun* A line that is at right angles to another line or to a surface.
    adjective 1. Straight up and down or extremely steep. 2. At a 90-degree angle to another surface or to the ground.

per·pet·u·al (pur-**pech**-oo-uhl) *adjective* Without ending or changing. ▸ *adverb* **perpetually**

per·pet·u·ate (pur-**pech**-oo-ate) *verb* To make something last or continue for a very long time. ▸ *verb* **perpetuating, perpetuated** ▸ *noun* **perpetuation**

per·plex (pur-**pleks**) *verb* To make someone puzzled or unsure. ▸ *verb* **perplexes, perplexing, perplexed** ▸ *noun* **perplexity** (pur-**pleks**-i-tee) ▸ *adjective* **perplexed**

per·se·cute (**pur**-suh-*kyoot*) *verb* To continually treat someone cruelly and unfairly, especially because of that person's ideas or political beliefs. ▸ *verb* **persecuting, persecuted** ▸ *noun* **persecution** (*pur*-suh-**kyoo**-shuhn)

per·se·vere (*pur*-suh-**veer**) *verb* To continue to do or try to do something, even if you have difficulties or are unlikely to succeed. ▸ *verb* **persevering, persevered** ▸ *noun* **perseverance**

Per·sian (**pur**-zhuhn)
    noun The language that the people of Iran and some parts of Afghanistan speak. This language is also called **Farsi.**
    adjective Of or having to do with Iran or made in Iran.

Per·sian Gulf (**pur**-zhuhn **guhlf**) An inland sea of the Indian Ocean, bordered by Iran to the northeast and by the Arabian Peninsula along the west side. The Persian Gulf is surrounded by land except for its southeastern tip, which empties into the Indian Ocean.

per·sim·mon (pur-**sim**-uhn) *noun* An orange-red fruit that is shaped like a plum and is sweet and soft when ripe.

per·sist (pur-**sist**) *verb* 1. To last or to continue steadily. 2. To keep on doing something in spite of obstacles or warnings.
    ▸ *verb* **persisting, persisted** ▸ *noun* **persistence** ▸ *adverb* **persistently**

per·sist·ent (pur-**sis**-tuhnt) *adjective* 1. Continuing to do something in spite of difficulty or obstacles. 2. Lasting or continuing over a long period of time.

per·son (**pur**-suhn) *noun* 1. An individual human being. 2. In grammar, the *first person* means "I" or "we"; the *second person* means "you"; the *third person* means "he," "she," "it," or "they." 3. **in person** Physically present.

per·son·al (**pur**-suh-nuhl) *adjective* 1. Private, or having to do with one person only. 2. Done or made in person.

per·son·al com·put·er (**pur**-suh-nuhl kuhm-**pyoo**-tur) *noun* A desktop or portable computer that can be used at home, at school, or in an office.

per·son·al·i·ty (*pur*-suh-**nal**-i-tee) *noun* 1. All of the qualities or traits that make one person different from others. 2. A famous person, especially in entertainment or sports.
    ▸ *noun, plural* **personalities**

per·son·al·ly (**pur**-suh-nuh-lee) *adverb* 1. Without assistance; directly. 2. For oneself. 3. As an individual.

per·son·nel (*pur*-suh-**nel**)
    noun The group of people who work for a company or an organization.
    adjective Of or having to do with the people who work for a company or an organization.
    ▸ *noun, plural* **personnel**

P

per·spec·tive (pur-**spek**-tiv) *noun*
1. A particular attitude toward or way of looking at something. 2. The way things or events relate to each other in size or importance. 3. **in perspective** Drawn or painted so as to give the illusion of depth and distance, with distant objects smaller than closer ones.

per·spire (pur-**spire**) *verb* To sweat. ▶ *verb* **perspiring, perspired** ▶ *noun* **perspiration**

per·suade (pur-**swade**) *verb* To succeed in making someone do or believe something by giving the person good reasons. ▶ *verb* **persuading, persuaded** ▶ *noun* **persuasion** (pur-**sway**-zhuhn) ▶ *adjective* **persuasive**

per·tain (pur-**tayn**) *verb* To be connected or related. ▶ *verb* **pertaining, pertained**

per·ti·nent (**purt**-uh-nuhnt) *adjective* Having to do with what is being discussed or considered.

per·turb (pur-**turb**) *verb* To make someone uncomfortable or anxious. ▶ *verb* **perturbing, perturbed**

Pe·ru (puh-**roo**) A country in western South America. In the 15th century, Peru was the home of the Inca Empire, and tourists from all over the world go there to see the ruins of Machu Picchu, also known as "The Lost City of the Incas."

per·verse (pur-**vurs**) *adjective* Deliberately stubborn and unreasonable. ▶ *noun* **perversity**

pe·so (**pay**-soh) *noun* The main unit of money in Mexico, the Philippines, and several South and Central American countries.

pes·si·mis·tic (pes-uh-**mis**-tik) *adjective* Always seeing the worst side of a situation or believing that the worst will happen. ▶ *noun* **pessimism** (**pes**-uh-miz-uhm) ▶ *noun* **pessimist** ▶ *adverb* **pessimistically**

pest (pest) *noun* 1. An insect or other animal that destroys or damages crops, food, or livestock. 2. Any creature that interferes dangerously with human activity. 3. An annoying person or thing; a nuisance.

pes·ter (**pes**-tur) *verb* To annoy someone with frequent questions, interruptions, or reminders. ▶ *verb* **pestering, pestered**

pes·ti·cide (**pes**-ti-side) *noun* A chemical used to kill pests, such as insects.

pes·tle (**pes**-uhl *or* **pes**-tuhl) *noun* A short, heavy stick with a thick, rounded end, used to crush things such as herbs and medicine in a container called a mortar.

pet (pet)
noun 1. A tame animal kept for company or pleasure and treated with affection. 2. A person who is unfairly treated with special favor.
verb To stroke or pat an animal affectionately.
adjective Referring to something that a person is especially interested in.
▶ *verb* **petting, petted**

pet·al (**pet**-uhl) *noun* One of the colored outer parts of a flower.

pe·ti·tion (puh-**tish**-uhn)
noun A letter signed by many people asking those in power to change their policy or actions or telling them how the signers feel about a certain issue or situation.
verb To formally request; to ask for by petition.
▶ *verb* **petitioning, petitioned**

pet·ri·fied (**pet**-ruh-fide) *adjective* 1. So frightened that you are unable to move. 2. **petrified wood** Dead wood that has become hard like stone because minerals have seeped into its cells. ▶ *verb* **petrify**

pe·tro·le·um (puh-**troh**-lee-uhm) *noun* A thick, oily liquid found below the earth's surface. It is used to make gasoline, kerosene, heating oil, and many other products.

pet·ti·coat (**pet**-ee-kote) *noun* A light, loose undergarment that hangs from the shoulders or the waist and is worn underneath a dress or skirt.

pet·ty (**pet**-ee) *adjective* 1. Small and unimportant. 2. Mean or spiteful. ▶ *adjective* **pettier, pettiest**

P

pe·tu·nia (puh-**toon**-yuh) *noun* A garden plant with colorful flowers shaped like trumpets.

pew (pyoo) *noun* A long, wooden bench with a high back that people sit on in a church.

pew·ter (**pyoo**-tur)
noun 1. A metal made of tin mixed with lead or copper. Pewter is used to make plates, pitchers, and other utensils. 2. Utensils made of pewter.
adjective Made of pewter.

pH (**pee**-aych) *noun* A measure of how acidic or alkaline a substance is. The initials pH are short for *potential of hydrogen*. Acids have pH values less than 7, and alkalis have pH values greater than 7. If a substance has a pH value of 7, it is neutral.

phan·tom (**fan**-tuhm)
noun A ghost, or an imagined figure.
adjective Imaginary or nonexistent.

phar·aoh (**fair**-oh) *noun* The title given to kings in ancient Egypt.

phar·ma·ceu·ti·cal (*fahr*-muh-**soo**-ti-kuhl) *adjective* Of or having to do with medicines or drugs. A pharmaceutical company manufactures medicines and drugs.

phar·ma·cist (**fahr**-muh-sist) *noun* A person who is trained to prepare and dispense drugs and medicines.

phar·ma·cy (**fahr**-muh-see) *noun* A drugstore, or a special department of a larger store where medicines are sold. ▸ *noun, plural* **pharmacies**

phase (faze)
noun 1. A stage in something or someone's growth or development. 2. A stage of the moon's change in shape as it appears from Earth. 3. One part or side of something.
verb 1. **phase in** To start something gradually. 2. **phase out** To stop something gradually.
▸ *verb* **phasing, phased**

pheas·ant (**fez**-uhnt) *noun* A large, brightly colored bird with a long tail that is hunted for sport and for food. Peacocks, partridges, grouse, and quail are related to pheasants.

phe·nom·e·nal (fuh-**nah**-muh-nuhl) *adjective* Amazing, extraordinary. ▸ *adverb* **phenomenally**

phe·nom·e·non (fuh-**nah**-muh-*nahn*) *noun* 1. An event or a fact that can be seen or felt. 2. Something very unusual and remarkable.
▸ *noun, plural* **phenomena** (fuh-**nah**-muh-*nuh*) or **phenomenons**

phil·an·thro·pist (fuh-**lan**-thruh-pist) *noun* A person who helps others by giving time or money to causes and charities.

Phil·ip·pines (**fil**-uh-*peenz*) A country in Southeast Asia in the western Pacific Ocean. Consisting of more than 7,000 islands, the Philippines are on the western edge of an area known as the Pacific Ring of Fire. Made up of a ring of volcanoes surrounding the Pacific, this area is frequently struck by earthquakes and volcanic eruptions.

phil·o·den·dron (*fil*-uh-**den**-druhn) *noun* A tropical American climbing vine with leaves that are shaped like hearts. The philodendron is a popular indoor plant.

phi·los·o·pher (fuh-**lah**-suh-fur) *noun* Someone who thinks deeply and writes about the basic problems and questions of human existence.

phil·o·soph·i·cal (*fil*-uh-**sah**-fi-kuhl) *adjective* 1. Of or having to do with philosophy. 2. Accepting difficulties and problems calmly.
▸ *adverb* **philosophically**

phi·los·o·phy (fuh-**lah**-suh-fee) *noun* 1. The study of truth, wisdom, the nature of reality, and knowledge. 2. The systematic study of the basic ideas in any field. 3. A person's basic ideas and beliefs that guide his or her actions and decisions.

phish·ing (**fish**-ing) *noun* The activity of trying to steal someone's identity or credit information by lying about who you really are. Phishing usually involves sending emails that trick people into entering personal information at a fake website.

P

phlegm (flem) *noun* The thick substance, produced by the mucous membranes of the lungs, that you cough up when you have a cold.

pho·bi·a (**foh**-bee-uh) *noun* An extremely strong fear. ▶ *adjective* **phobic** (**foh**-bik)

Phoe·ni·cian (fuh-**nee**-shuhn) *adjective* Of or having to do with an ancient Mediterranean civilization that had a major influence on ancient Greece and Rome.
noun The language of this ancient civilization, which is no longer spoken. Modern Arabic and Hebrew are related to Phoenician.

phone (fone) *noun* Short for **telephone.**
verb To make a telephone call to someone.
▶ *verb* **phoning, phoned**

pho·net·i·cal·ly (fuh-**net**-ik-lee) *adverb* If something is spelled **phonetically**, it is spelled as it is pronounced, sometimes by using special symbols to represent sounds. The words in this dictionary are spelled phonetically in parentheses.

pho·net·ics (fuh-**net**-iks) *noun* The study of the sounds that are used in speaking.

pho·no·graph (**foh**-nuh-graf) *noun* A machine that picks up and reproduces the sounds that have been recorded in the grooves cut into a record.

pho·ny (**foh**-nee) *adjective* Intended to deceive; not the real thing.
noun A person or thing that is not honest or genuine; a fraud.
▶ *noun, plural* **phonies**

phos·pho·res·cence (*fahs*-fuh-**res**-uhns) *noun* 1. Light that is given off from a substance after the source of energy has been removed. 2. The light that is given off by a living thing, such as a fish or an insect.
▶ *adjective* **phosphorescent**

phos·pho·rus (**fahs**-fur-uhs) *noun* A chemical element that glows in the dark. It is used in making matches, fertilizers, glass, and steel.

pho·to (**foh**-toh) *noun* Short for **photograph.**

pho·to·cop·i·er (**foh**-toh-*kah*-pee-ur) *noun* A machine that copies documents using a special lens and ink called toner.

pho·to·cop·y (**foh**-toh-*kah*-pee) *noun* A copy of a document made by a photocopier.
verb To make a photocopy of something.
▶ *noun, plural* **photocopies** ▶ *verb* **photocopies, photocopying, photocopied**

pho·to fin·ish (**foh**-toh **fin**-ish) *noun* A very close end to a race, where the winner can be identified only by examining a photograph taken as the contestants crossed the finish line. ▶ *noun, plural* **photo finishes**

pho·to·gen·ic (*foh*-tuh-**jen**-ik) *adjective* Having a particularly good appearance in photographs.

pho·to·graph (**foh**-tuh-*graf*) *noun* 1. A picture taken by a camera on film and developed on paper. 2. A picture taken with a digital camera and printed on paper or shown on a computer screen.
verb To take a photograph of someone or something.
▶ *verb* **photographing, photographed**

pho·tog·ra·pher (fuh-**tah**-gruh-fur) *noun* Someone who takes a picture with a camera, especially as a job.

pho·tog·ra·phy (fuh-**tah**-gruh-fee) *noun* 1. The recording of visual images by exposing film inside a camera to light. 2. The recording of visual images using a digital camera to make an image that can be reproduced by a computer.
▶ *adjective* **photographic**

pho·to·jour·nal·ist (*foh*-toh-**jur**-nuh-list) *noun* A photographer who takes photographs of news events and tells the story of what has happened through the photos. ▶ *noun* **photojournalism**

pho·to·syn·the·sis (*foh*-toh-**sin**-thi-sis) *noun* A chemical process by

P

which green plants and some other organisms make their food. Plants use energy from the sun to turn water and carbon dioxide into food, and they produce oxygen as a by-product.

phrase (fraze)

noun 1. A group of words that have a meaning but do not form a sentence. *In the dark* is a phrase. 2. In music, a group of notes that are played as a unit and which can be performed on a single breath by a singer or wind instrumentalist.

verb To put into words in a particular way.

▶ *verb* **phrasing, phrased** ▶ *noun* **phrasing**

phy·lum (**fye**-luhm) *noun* A group of related plants or animals that is larger than a class but smaller than a kingdom. ▶ *noun, plural* **phyla** (**fye**-luh)

phys·i·cal (**fiz**-i-kuhl)

adjective 1. Of or having to do with the body. 2. Of or having to do with matter and energy. 3. Of or having to do with nature or natural objects.

noun A complete examination of a person's body, made by a doctor or nurse, to check the person's health.

▶ *adverb* **physically**

phys·i·cal fit·ness (**fiz**-i-kuhl **fit**-nis) *noun* The state of being in good health as a result of exercising and eating nutritious foods.

phys·i·cal ther·a·py (**fiz**-i-kuhl **ther**-uh-pee) *noun* The treatment of diseased or injured muscles and joints by physical and mechanical means, such as exercise, massage, and heat. ▶ *noun* **physical therapist**

phy·si·cian (fi-**zish**-uhn) *noun* Someone with a medical degree who has been trained and licensed to treat injured and sick people; a doctor. Physicians are also authorized to write prescriptions for medicine.

phys·ics (**fiz**-iks) *noun* The science that deals with matter and energy.

It includes the study of light, heat, sound, electricity, motion, and force. ▶ *noun* **physicist** (**fiz**-i-sist)

pi (pye) *noun* In math, a symbol (π) for the ratio of the circumference of a circle to its diameter. Pi equals about 3.1416. **Pi** sounds like **pie.**

pi·an·o

noun (pee-**an**-oh *or* **pyan**-oh) A large keyboard instrument that produces musical sounds when fingers strike the keys, causing padded hammers inside the piano to strike tuned metal strings.

adverb (**pyah**-noh) Softly. This word is used in music.

▶ *noun* **pianist** (**pyan**-ist *or* **pee**-uh-nist)

pic·co·lo (**pik**-uh-*loh*) *noun* An instrument that looks like a flute but is smaller and has a higher pitch.

pick (pik)

verb 1. To choose or select. 2. To collect or to gather, especially taking fruits or flowers from the plants on which they grow. 3. To cause on purpose. 4. **pick on** To tease someone or treat him or her in a mean way. 5. **pick at** To take bits off of something.

noun 1. A tool with pointed metal ends, used for breaking up soil or rocks. 2. A small piece of plastic or metal used to strum or pluck banjo or guitar strings. 3. The right to choose, or a turn to choose. 4. The best of a group.

▶ *verb* **picking, picked** ▶ *noun* **picker**

pick·ax *or* **pick·axe** (**pik**-aks) *noun* A tool with a long handle and a metal head. One end of the head is a sharp blade, and the other is a pick. A pickax can be used to cut through roots, loosen soil, and break up rocks. ▶ *noun, plural* **pickaxes**

pick·er·el (**pik**-ur-uhl) *noun* A freshwater fish found in the waters of North America. The pickerel has a long, pointed head and is used for food. ▶ *noun, plural* **pickerel** *or* **pickerels**

P

pick·et (**pik**-it)
verb To stand outside a place in protest. When a person or group pickets a location, they often carry signs and shout slogans to get attention and sometimes try to prevent others from entering.
noun A pointed stake that is driven into the ground to hold something in place or to build a fence.
▶ *verb* **picketing, picketed** ▶ *noun* **picketer**

pick·le (**pik**-uhl)
verb To preserve food in vinegar or saltwater.
noun 1. Any food, such as a cucumber, that has been pickled. 2. (informal) A difficult or awkward situation.
▶ *verb* **pickling, pickled**

pick·pock·et (**pik**-*pah*-kit) *noun* A person who steals from people's pockets or handbags.

pick·up (**pik**-*uhp*) *noun* 1. An increase in speed. 2. A small truck with a driver's cab and an open back.

pick·y (**pik**-ee) *adjective* (informal) Particular or choosy. ▶ *adjective* **pickier, pickiest**

pic·nic (**pik**-nik)
noun A party or trip that includes a meal eaten out of doors.
verb To have or take part in a picnic.
▶ *verb* **picnicking, picnicked** ▶ *noun* **picnicker**

pic·to·graph (**pik**-tuh-*graf*) *noun* 1. A picture used as a symbol in ancient writing systems. 2. Another name for **picture graph.**

pic·to·ri·al (pik-**tor**-ee-uhl) *adjective* Using pictures, or expressed in pictures. ▶ *adverb* **pictorially**

pic·ture (**pik**-chur)
noun 1. An image, such as a painting, photograph, or drawing. 2. An image on a television screen. 3. A movie.
verb 1. To imagine something. 2. To describe something vividly in words or images.
▶ *verb* **picturing, pictured**

pic·ture graph (**pik**-chur *graf*) *noun* A graph that shows information by means of picture symbols instead of lines or bars. Another name for picture graph is **pictograph** (**pik**-tuh-*graf*).

pic·tur·esque (*pik*-chuh-**resk**) *adjective* Pretty or charming to look at.

pie (pye) *noun* Pastry filled with fruit, custard, meat, or vegetables and baked in an oven. **Pie** sounds like **pi.**

piece (pees) *noun* 1. A part or section of something larger. 2. A part that has been broken, torn, or cut from a whole. 3. An artistic creation. 4. A coin. 5. A small object used in playing checkers, chess, and other board games. 6. An example of something, or one of a set. 7. **a piece of cake** Something that is easy to do.
Piece sounds like **peace.**

piece·work (**pees**-*wurk*) *noun* Work that is paid for by the amount completed, not by the time it takes to do it.

pie chart (**pye** *chahrt*) *noun* A chart in the shape of a circle that is divided into sections by lines coming from the center to show the size of different parts relative to the whole.

pier (peer) *noun* 1. A platform of metal, stone, concrete, or wood that extends over a body of water. A pier can be used as a landing place for ships and boats. 2. A pillar that supports a bridge.
Pier sounds like **peer.**

pierce (peers) *verb* 1. To make a hole in something. 2. To pass into or through, as if with a sharp instrument.
▶ *verb* **piercing, pierced**

pierc·ing (**peer**-sing) *adjective* Going through or seeming to go through something.

pi·e·ty (**pye**-i-tee) *noun* The quality of being religious or reverent; taking one's religion seriously.

pig (pig)
noun 1. A farm animal with a blunt snout that is raised for its meat, which is called pork. 2. (informal) A greedy, messy, or disgusting person.
verb **pig out** To eat a lot, usually in a greedy or messy way.

pi·geon (**pij**-uhn) *noun* A plump bird sometimes used for racing or for carrying messages. Pigeons are

P

often found in cities. They are related to doves.

pig·gy·back (**pig**-ee-*bak*) *adverb* Carried on the shoulders or back.

pig·gy bank (**pig**-ee *bangk*) *noun* A small bank, often in the shape of a pig, used mainly by children for saving coins.

pig·ment (**pig**-muhnt) *noun* A substance that gives color to something. Pigments can be natural, as in people's skin, or added to something, as in paint.

pig·pen (**pig**-*pen*) *noun* An enclosed area where pigs are kept. It is also called a **sty** or a **pigsty.**

pig·sty (**pig**-*stye*) *noun* **1.** A pigpen. **2.** (informal) A very messy and often dirty place.
  ▶ *noun, plural* **pigsties**

pig·tail (**pig**-*tayl*) *noun* A length of hair that has been divided into three sections and braided.

pike (pike) *noun* **1.** A large, thin freshwater fish with a flat snout and very sharp teeth. **2.** A type of dive in which the diver bends at the waist to touch the toes while in midair, then enters the water with the body fully extended. **3.** A gymnastics movement in which a person's body bends at the waist to touch the toes and then is fully extended again. **4.** A weapon used in the Middle Ages, consisting of a sharp metal head attached to a long pole.

pile (pile)
  noun **1.** A heap of something. **2.** A very great amount of something. **3.** A heavy wood or steel beam that is driven into the ground to support a bridge or pier. **4.** The raised loops or pieces of yarn that form the surface of a carpet.
  verb To make a pile by adding things.
  ▶ *verb* **piling, piled**

pil·fer (**pil**-fur) *verb* To steal small amounts of something or small things. ▶ *verb* **pilfering, pilfered** ▶ *noun* **pilferer** ▶ *noun* **pilferage**

pil·grim (**pil**-gruhm)
  noun A person who travels to a holy place to worship there.
  noun, plural **the Pilgrims** The group of people who left England because of religious persecution, came to America, and founded Plymouth Colony in 1620.
  ▶ *noun* **pilgrimage**

pill (pil) *noun* A small, solid tablet of medicine, such as aspirin.

pil·lage (**pil**-ij)
  verb To rob a place violently, especially during a war.
  noun The act of robbing a place violently in wartime.
  ▶ *verb* **pillaging, pillaged**

pil·lar (**pil**-ur) *noun* **1.** A column that supports part of a building or that stands alone as a monument. **2.** A person who is looked up to or relied upon in a particular way.

pil·low (**pil**-oh) *noun* A large, soft cushion for your head when you are sleeping. Some pillows are used to support the back or to sit on.

pil·low·case (**pil**-oh-*kase*) *noun* A cloth cover that you put over a pillow to keep it clean.

pi·lot (**pye**-luht)
  noun **1.** A person who flies an aircraft. **2.** A person who guides a ship in and out of port.
  verb To test or guide something.
  adjective Done as an experiment.
  ▶ *verb* **piloting, piloted**

pim·ple (**pim**-puhl) *noun* A small, raised spot on the skin that is sometimes painful and filled with pus. ▶ *adjective* **pimply**

pin (pin)
  noun **1.** A thin, pointed piece of metal, usually used to fasten fabric together. **2.** A piece of jewelry or a badge fastened to clothing with a pin or clasp. **3.** One of ten pieces of wood shaped like bottles that are knocked over in bowling. **4.** In golf, the flag that indicates where the hole is on the green.
  verb **1.** To fasten things together with a pin. **2.** To hold something or someone firmly in position.
  ▶ *verb* **pinning, pinned**

P

PIN (pin) *noun* A number used to identify a person who is using an automatic bank machine, a computer program, or other kinds of equipment. PIN is short for *personal identification number*.

pi·ña·ta (peen-**yah**-tuh) *noun* A decorated container filled with candies and gifts. It is hung from the ceiling at parties to be broken with sticks by blindfolded children. Piñatas are traditionally Latin American in origin and now are common at all kinds of parties and celebrations.

pin·ball (**pin**-*bawl*) *noun* A game in which you shoot small balls around a number of obstacles and targets on an enclosed, slanted table.

pin·cer (**pin**-sur) *noun* The pinching claw of a crustacean such as a crab.

pinch (pinch)
verb **1.** To squeeze someone's skin sharply between the thumb and index finger. **2.** To make thin or wrinkled. **3. pinch pennies** To spend money only when absolutely necessary.
noun **1.** A small amount of something. **2.** An emergency or time of need.
▶ *verb* **pinches, pinching, pinched** ▶ *noun, plural* **pinches**

pin·cush·ion (**pin**-*kush*-uhn) *noun* A small cushion used to stick pins in when they are not being used.

pine (pine)
noun A tall evergreen tree that produces cones and leaves that look like needles.
verb **pine for** To feel very sad because someone has gone away and you miss him or her.
▶ *verb* **pining, pined**

pine·ap·ple (**pine**-*ap*-uhl) *noun* A large, tropical fruit with yellow flesh and a tough, prickly skin. Pineapples grow on plants with long, stiff leaves.

Ping-Pong (**ping**-*pahng*) *noun* Another word for table tennis. Ping-Pong is a trademark. *See* **table tennis.**

pink (pingk)
noun A pale red color made by mixing red and white.

adjective Between red and white in color.
▶ *adjective* **pinkish**

pink·eye (**pingk**-*eye*) *noun* A highly contagious disease that causes the surface of the eyeball and the inside of the eyelid to become red, sore, and itchy.

pin·point (**pin**-*point*)
adjective Very exact or precise.
verb To locate something precisely.
▶ *verb* **pinpointing, pinpointed**

pins and nee·dles (pinz uhn **nee**-duhlz) *noun, plural* **1.** A prickly, tingling feeling that you get when some of the blood supply to part of your body has been temporarily cut off. **2. on pins and needles** Very nervous or excited about something that is going to happen soon.

pin·stripe (**pin**-*stripe*) *noun* A very narrow stripe woven into a fabric.

pint (pinte) *noun* A unit of measure equal to half a quart or 16 fluid ounces.

pin·to (**pin**-toh) *noun* **1.** A horse or pony that has spots or patches of two or more colors. **2.** A type of kidney bean that is spotted. It is grown mainly in the southwestern part of the United States and is used for food.

pin·wheel (**pin**-*weel*) *noun* A toy wheel that spins in the wind. It is made of colored paper or plastic that is pinned to a stick.

pi·o·neer (*pye*-uh-**neer**)
noun **1.** One of the first people to investigate or work in a new and unknown field of knowledge. **2.** A person who explores unknown territory and settles there.
adjective Referring to one of the first people or attempts to develop or study something.
verb To be the first to develop or use something.
▶ *verb* **pioneering, pioneered**

pi·ous (**pye**-uhs) *adjective* Practicing a religion faithfully and seriously. ▶ *adverb* **piously**

pipe (pipe)
noun **1.** A tube, usually used to carry

P

a liquid or gas. **2.** A narrow tube with a bowl on the end of it, for smoking tobacco. Pipes are usually made of wood or clay. **3.** A tube with holes along its length, played as a musical instrument or joined with other similar pipes to make a larger instrument. **4. piped music** Music that can be heard through speakers all over a building.
verb **1.** To send something along pipes, tubes, or wires. **2.** To play music on pipes. **3. pipe up** To speak suddenly, or more loudly than before. **4. pipe down** To speak more quietly, or to make less noise.
▶ *verb* **piping, piped**

pipe·line (**pipe**-*line*) *noun* **1.** A line of large pipes that carry water, gas, or oil over long distances. **2.** A direct route for sending information or supplies.

pip·ing (**pye**-ping)
noun **1.** A system of pipes. **2.** A shrill sound or call. **3.** A thin line of decoration on a cake, piece of clothing, or furniture.
adjective **piping hot** Very hot, usually describing food.

pi·ra·cy (**pye**-ruh-see) *noun* **1.** The crime of attacking and robbing ships at sea. **2.** Illegal copying or use of material such as computer software, a book, or music that has been created by someone else.
▶ *noun, plural* **piracies**

pi·rate (**pye**-rit)
noun A person who attacks and robs ships at sea.
verb To make unauthorized copies of music, film, a computer game, or other entertainment created by someone else and sell them illegally.
▶ *verb* **pirating, pirated** ▶ *adjective* **pirated**

pis·ta·chi·o (pi-**stash**-ee-*oh*) *noun* **1.** A small, green nut with a hard shell that is sometimes dyed red. **2.** A light green color.

pis·til (**pis**-tuhl) *noun* The female part of a flower, which is shaped like a stalk. It is the place where the seeds are produced. The pistil includes the ovule, the style, and the stigma of a flower. **Pistil** sounds like **pistol.**

pis·tol (**pis**-tuhl) *noun* A small gun designed to be held in the hand. **Pistol** sounds like **pistil.**

pis·ton (**pis**-tuhn) *noun* A disk or cylinder that moves back and forth in a larger cylinder. Automobile engines have pistons. Their back-and-forth movement is converted to rotational motion.

pit (pit)
noun **1.** A hole in the ground, often one from which something is being dug out. **2.** The large, hard seed in the middle of some fruits, such as peaches and plums. **3. the pit of one's stomach** An indefinite place in your abdomen where you seem to feel fear, excitement, or anxiety. **4. pit stop** A short break when a race car stops for fuel and repairs in a separate area called the pit.
verb **pitted against** Made to compete with someone or something else.
▶ *verb* **pitting, pitted**

pi·ta (**pee**-tuh) *noun* A thin, flat Middle Eastern bread that can be separated into two layers to form a pocket for meat, vegetables, or another filling.

pitch (pich)
verb **1.** To throw or toss something, such as a baseball or horseshoe. **2.** To fall or plunge forward. **3.** To put up a tent. **4. pitch in** To join in to help with a task.
noun **1.** A dark, sticky substance that is made from tar or petroleum. Pitch is used to waterproof roofs and pave streets. **2.** A high point or degree. **3.** The highness or lowness of a musical sound. **4.** (informal) A talk meant to persuade you to do or buy something. **5.** In baseball, a throw of the ball by the pitcher to the batter.
▶ *noun, plural* **pitches** ▶ *verb* **pitches, pitching, pitched**

pitch·er (**pich**-ur) *noun* **1.** A container with an open top for liquids. Pitchers usually have a handle and a lip or spout. **2.** A baseball player who throws the ball to the batter.

P

pitch·fork (**pich**-*fork*) *noun* A large fork with a long handle and two or three prongs, used for lifting and throwing hay.

pit·fall (**pit**-*fawl*) *noun* A hidden or unsuspected danger or difficulty.

pit·i·ful (**pit**-i-fuhl) *adjective* 1. Deserving or causing pity. 2. Inadequate.
▶ *adverb* **pitifully**

pit·i·less (**pit**-i-lis) *adjective* Showing no pity or sympathy for anyone. ▶ *adverb* **pitilessly**

pit·y (**pit**-ee)
verb To feel sorry for someone.
noun 1. A feeling of sorrow or sympathy for the suffering of someone else. 2. A sad or unfortunate situation.
▶ *verb* **pities, pitying, pitied** ▶ *noun, plural* **pities** ▶ *adverb* **pityingly**

piv·ot (**piv**-uht)
noun A central point on which something turns or balances.
verb To turn suddenly as if on a pivot.
▶ *verb* **pivoting, pivoted**

piv·ot·al (**piv**-uh-tuhl) *adjective* Very important in determining the outcome of something.

pix·el (**piks**-uhl) *noun* One of the tiny dots on a video screen or computer monitor that make up the visual image.

pix·ie *or* **pix·y** (**pik**-see) *noun* A small, mischievous elf or fairy in legends and fairy tales. ▶ *noun, plural* **pixies**

piz·za (**peet**-suh) *noun* A flat pie that is baked with toppings of tomato sauce, cheese, and various meats and vegetables.

piz·ze·ri·a (*peet*-suh-**ree**-uh) *noun* A place where pizza is made and sold.

plac·ard (**plak**-ahrd) *noun* A poster, sign, or notice that is put up in a public place.

pla·cate (**play**-kate) *verb* To make someone calm or less angry, often by giving the person something that he or she wants. ▶ *verb* **placating, placated**

place (plase)
noun 1. A particular location. 2. A particular position or rank. 3. A space

for a person or thing.
verb 1. To put something in a particular location. 2. To identify by putting in context.
phrase **in place** In its proper spot or location.
▶ *verb* **placing, placed**

pla·ce·bo (pluh-**see**-boh) *noun* A pill that contains no medicine but that is given to patients because the doctor thinks they will feel better if they believe they are taking medicine.

plac·id (**plas**-id) *adjective* Calm or peaceful. ▶ *adverb* **placidly**

pla·gia·rize (**play**-juh-*rize*) *verb* To steal the ideas or words of another and present them as your own. ▶ *verb* **plagiarizing, plagiarized** ▶ *noun* **plagiarism** ▶ *noun* **plagiarist**

plague (playg)
noun 1. A very serious disease that spreads quickly to many people and often causes death. 2. A large number of an annoying or destructive thing.
verb To trouble and annoy someone severely.
▶ *verb* **plaguing, plagued**

plaid (plad) *noun* A pattern of squares in cloth formed by weaving stripes of different widths and colors that cross each other.

plain (playn)
adjective 1. Easy to see or hear. 2. Easy to understand. 3. Not decorated or elaborate. 4. Simple and honest. 5. Not beautiful or handsome.
noun A large, flat area of land.
Plain sounds like **plane**. ▶ *adjective* **plainer, plainest**

plain·tive (**playn**-tiv) *adjective* Sounding sad and mournful. ▶ *adverb* **plaintively**

plan (plan)
verb 1. To figure out ahead of time what you will do or how you will do it. 2. To intend to do something.
noun 1. An idea about how you intend to do something. 2. A diagram or drawing that shows how the parts of something are arranged or put together.
▶ *verb* **planning, planned**

P

plane (playn)
noun **1.** A machine with wings that flies through the air. Plane is short for **airplane**. **2.** A hand tool with a sharp blade used for smoothing wood. **3.** A level of difficulty or achievement. **4.** A more or less flat surface, either real or imaginary. **5.** In geometry, a flat, two-dimensional surface.
verb To use a plane to smooth or finish something.
Plane sounds like **plain**. ▶ *verb* **planing, planed**

plan·et (**plan**-it) *noun* **1.** One of the eight large heavenly bodies circling the sun. **2.** A large heavenly body orbiting a star.
▶ *adjective* **planetary** (**plan**-i-*ter*-ee)

plan·e·tar·i·um (*plan*-i-**tair**-ee-uhm) *noun* A building with equipment for reproducing the positions and movements of the sun, moon, planets, and stars by projecting their images onto a curved ceiling.

plank (plangk) *noun* A long, flat piece of wood used, for example, for flooring in a house.

plank·ton (**plangk**-tuhn) *noun* Tiny animals and plants that drift or float in oceans and lakes.

plant (plant)
noun **1.** A living organism with a green pigment called chlorophyll that allows the organism to make food from the energy of the sun. Many land plants have stems, roots, leaves, and flowers. **2.** The buildings and equipment used to make a product or carry out a process; a factory.
verb **1.** To put a plant or seed in the ground so that it can grow. **2.** To put something firmly in place.
▶ *verb* **planting, planted**

plan·tain (**plan**-tin) *noun* A tropical fruit that looks like a banana but is eaten cooked.

plan·ta·tion (plan-**tay**-shuhn) *noun* A large farm found in warm climates where crops such as coffee, rubber, and cotton are grown.

plaque (plak) *noun* **1.** A metal plate with words inscribed on it, commemorating a person or an event, usually placed on a wall in a public place. **2.** A sticky deposit of food and bacteria that forms on your teeth and can cause tooth decay.

plas·ma (**plaz**-muh) *noun* **1.** The clear, yellow, liquid part of the blood that carries red and white blood cells. **2.** A gas or liquid that contains particles with positive and negative electrical charge, used in electronic displays.

plas·ter (**plas**-tur)
noun **1.** A soft mixture of lime, sand, and water that is spread on walls and ceilings and forms a smooth, hard surface when it dries. **2. plaster cast** A hard, white case that immobilizes broken bones so that they can heal properly.
verb To cover or coat something as if you were using plaster.
▶ *verb* **plastering, plastered** ▶ *noun* **plasterer**

plas·tic (**plas**-tik) *noun* A synthetic substance that is light and strong and can be molded into different shapes. Cellophane and vinyl are plastics.

plas·tic sur·ger·y (**plas**-tik **sur**-jur-ee) *noun* Operations done to improve someone's appearance or to repair visible damage caused by injury or disease.

plate (plate)
noun **1.** A flat dish from which food is served or eaten. **2.** A flat sheet of a hard substance. **3.** A color illustration in a book. **4.** Home base in baseball. **5.** One of the flat, rigid, rocky pieces that make up the earth's outer crust.
verb To cover something with a thin layer of metal, such as gold or silver.
▶ *verb* **plating, plated**

pla·teau (pla-**toh**) *noun* An area of level ground that is higher than the surrounding area.

plate·let (**plate**-lit) *noun* A disk-shaped body in the blood that helps the blood clot.

plate tec·ton·ics (**plate** tek-**tah**-niks) *noun* The theory that the earth's crust is made up of huge rigid sections, or "plates," that move very slowly.

P

plat·form (**plat**-form) *noun* **1.** A flat, raised structure where people or objects can stand. **2.** A statement of beliefs of a group. **3.** The hardware or software of a computer that determines what programs will run on it and what devices can be connected to it.

plat·ing (**play**-ting) *noun* A thin coating or layer of metal, often gold or silver.

plat·i·num (**plat**-uh-nuhm) *noun* A very valuable silvery-white metal that is often used in jewelry.

pla·toon (pluh-**toon**) *noun* A group of soldiers made up of two or more squads. A platoon is usually commanded by a lieutenant.

plat·ter (**plat**-ur) *noun* A large, shallow plate used to serve food.

plat·y·pus (**plat**-uh-pus) *noun* An Australian mammal with webbed feet, a broad bill, and dense fur. The platypus is one of the few mammals that lay eggs. ▶ *noun, plural* **platypuses**

plau·si·ble (**plaw**-zuh-buhl) *adjective* Believable or probable. ▶ *adverb* **plausibly**

play (play)
verb **1.** To take part in a game or other recreation. **2.** To make music on. **3.** To take part in a sport or game. **4.** To act a part in a play. **5.** To be available for an audience to enjoy. **6.** To act or to behave.
noun **1.** Fun or recreation. **2.** A story that is acted out on a stage. **3.** A move, a turn, or an action in a game. **4.** An amount of movement or slack in something.
▶ *verb* **playing, played**

play·er (**play**-ur) *noun* **1.** Someone who participates in a game or sport. **2.** Someone who plays a musical instrument. **3.** An active or influential participant in an activity.

play·ful (**play**-fuhl) *adjective* **1.** Frisky and willing to play. **2.** Humorous, or meant to amuse or tease.

play·ground (**play**-ground) *noun* An outdoor area, often with swings, slides, seesaws, and other equipment, where children can play.

play·ing card (**play**-ing kahrd) *noun* A card used in a game. The most common type of playing card set has 52 cards divided into four suits called spades, clubs, hearts, and diamonds.

play·mate (**play**-mate) *noun* A child who plays with another child or children.

play·off (**play**-awf) *noun* One of a series of games after the regular season that determine which teams will compete for the championship.

play·pen (**play**-pen) *noun* A usually square folding structure that is a safe place for a baby to play in.

play·room (**play**-room) *noun* A room intended for children to play in.

play·wright (**play**-rite) *noun* A person who writes plays.

pla·za (**plaz**-uh *or* **plah**-zuh) *noun* **1.** A public square. **2.** An open area near large city buildings that often has walkways, trees, shrubs, and benches.

plea (plee) *noun* **1.** An emotional request. **2.** A defendant's answer to a charge in a court of law.

plead (pleed) *verb* **1.** To beg someone to do something. **2.** To say whether you are guilty or not guilty in a court of law.
▶ *verb* **pleading, pleaded** *or* **pled** (pled)

pleas·ant (**plez**-uhnt) *adjective*
1. Enjoyable or giving pleasure.
2. Likeable or friendly.
▶ *adverb* **pleasantly**

please (pleez)
adverb A polite word used when you ask for something. It means "be so kind as to."
verb **1.** To satisfy or to give pleasure. **2.** To choose or to prefer.
▶ *verb* **pleasing, pleased** ▶ *adjective* **pleased** ▶ *adjective* **pleasing**

pleas·ure (**plezh**-ur) *noun* **1.** A feeling of satisfaction or enjoyment.
2. Something that gives you a feeling of satisfaction or enjoyment.
▶ *adjective* **pleasurable**

pleat (pleet) *noun* One or more parallel folds in a piece of clothing such as a skirt, held in place by stitching at one end. ▶ *adjective* **pleated**

P

pledge (plej)
verb 1. To make a sincere promise.
2. To promise to give an amount of money for a particular purpose.
noun A promise to do something.
▶ *verb* **pledging, pledged**

plen·ti·ful (**plen**-ti-fuhl) *adjective* Available in large amounts. ▶ *adverb* **plentifully**

plen·ty (**plen**-tee) *noun* A great number or amount that is more than enough.

pli·a·ble (**plye**-uh-buhl) *adjective* 1. Easily bent or shaped. 2. Easily influenced.

pli·ers (**plye**-urz) *noun, plural* A tool with two handles and jaws that can grip and bend objects or cut wire.

plight (plite) *noun* A dangerous, difficult, or unfortunate situation.

plod (plahd) *verb* 1. To walk in a slow and heavy way. 2. To work in a dull, slow way.
▶ *verb* **plodding, plodded** ▶ *noun* **plodder**

plot (plaht)
verb 1. To make a secret plan, usually to do something wrong or illegal.
2. To mark out something based on calculations, such as a graph or a route on a map.
noun 1. A small area of land. 2. The main story of a novel, movie, play, or any work of fiction. 3. A secret plan to do something.
▶ *verb* **plotting, plotted**

plo·ver (**pluhv**-ur *or* **ploh**-vur) *noun* A bird with long, pointed wings and a short bill. It runs along the beach to find food.

plow (plou)
noun 1. A piece of farm equipment pulled by an animal or a tractor and used to dig up soil and cut furrows before seeds are planted. 2. A device used to remove or push aside matter, such as snow, from roads and sidewalks.
verb 1. To break up soil using a plow.
2. **plow through** To work hard to complete a task.
▶ *verb* **plowing, plowed**

pluck (pluhk)
verb 1. To pull feathers out of a bird. 2. To play notes on a stringed instrument by pulling on the strings with your fingers or by using a pick.
3. To pull something briskly from its place.
noun Courage and determination.
▶ *verb* **plucking, plucked** ▶ *adjective* **plucked** ▶ *adjective* **plucky** ▶ *adverb* **pluckily**

plug (pluhg)
noun 1. An object that blocks a hole or a pipeline. 2. A device at the end of a wire that is put into an electrical outlet to make a connection with a source of electricity. Plugs have metal prongs.
verb 1. To close or repair something by blocking or filling it in. 2. (informal) To mention something in order to get publicity for it, often on radio or television. 3. To work in a steady way.
▶ *verb* **plugging, plugged**

plug and play (**pluhg** uhn **play**) *noun* A computer that has the essential software and programs already installed when you buy it. ▶ *adjective* **plug-and-play**

plug-in (**pluhg**-*in*) *noun* A small program that works with another program on a computer, usually to provide a specific function.

plum (pluhm) *noun* A fruit that is soft when ripe and has purple, red, or yellow skin and a pit in the center.

plum·age (**ploo**-mij) *noun* A bird's feathers, considered all together.

plumb·er (**pluhm**-ur) *noun* A person who installs and repairs water and sewage systems in buildings.

plumb·ing (**pluhm**-ing) *noun* The system of water and drainage pipes in a building.

plume (ploom)
noun 1. A long, fluffy feather often used as an ornament on clothing.
2. Something that has a feathery shape.
verb To emerge or spread out in a way that resembles a plume.
▶ *verb* **pluming, plumed**

P

plump (pluhmp)
adjective Somewhat fat or round in shape.
verb 1. To make a pillow or cushion fluffier by patting it. 2. To land, or to set something down, heavily.
▸ *adjective* **plumper, plumpest** ▸ *verb* **plumping, plumped**

plun·der (**pluhn**-dur)
verb To steal things by force, often during a battle.
noun Things that are stolen or taken by force.
▸ *verb* **plundering, plundered**

plunge (pluhnj) *verb* 1. To dive into water. 2. To put or push something in suddenly or with force. 3. To fall steeply or sharply. 4. To do something suddenly. 5. **take the plunge** To decide to do something you've never done before and feel nervous about.
▸ *verb* **plunging, plunged**

plu·ral (**ploor**-uhl)
noun The form of a word used for two or more of something. The plural of *foot* is *feet*. The plural of *desk* is *desks*.
adjective Referring to more than one.

plus (pluhs)
noun 1. In math, a sign (+) used in addition that is also known as a *plus sign*. 2. An advantage.
preposition 1. Added to. *Three plus three equals six.* 2. In addition to. *The dining room set consists of a table plus six chairs.*
adjective Slightly higher than.
▸ *noun, plural* **pluses**

Plu·to (**ploo**-toh) *noun* A dwarf planet in our solar system. Pluto is farther from the sun than the planet Neptune and can be seen only through a telescope. Until 2006 Pluto was classified as a planet, and its designation is still under debate.

plu·to·ni·um (ploo-**toh**-nee-uhm) *noun* A radioactive metallic element that is made artificially from uranium. Plutonium is used as a fuel in nuclear reactors and to make atomic bombs.

ply·wood (**plye**-wud) *noun* Board made from several thin sheets of wood that have been glued together. Plywood is used for building and carpentry.

p.m. (pee-em) *abbreviation* The initials of the Latin phrase *post meridiem*, which means "after midday." It is used to indicate the time between noon and 11:59 at night.

pneu·mat·ic (noo-**mat**-ik) *adjective* 1. Filled with air. 2. Operated by compressed air.

pneu·mo·nia (noo-**mohn**-yuh) *noun* A serious disease that causes the lungs to become inflamed and filled with a thick fluid that makes breathing difficult.

poach (pohch) *verb* 1. To hunt or fish illegally on someone else's property. 2. To cook food, such as eggs or fish, by heating it in gently boiling liquid.
▸ *verb* **poaches, poaching, poached**

poach·er (**poh**-chur) *noun* 1. A person who hunts or fishes illegally on someone else's land. 2. A pot designed to poach eggs or fish.

pock·et (**pah**-kit)
noun 1. A small cloth pouch that is sewn into clothing and used for carrying small items. 2. A compartment within a larger carrier. 3. A small area or an isolated group.
verb To take something secretly.
adjective Small enough to be carried in your pocket.
▸ *verb* **pocketing, pocketed**

pock·et·book (**pah**-kit-buk) *noun* A woman's purse or handbag that is used to carry personal items such as a wallet and keys.

pock·et·knife (**pah**-kit-nife) *noun* A small knife with a blade or blades that fold into the handle. ▸ *noun, plural* **pocketknives**

pock·et mon·ey (**pah**-kit *muhn*-ee) *noun* Money for minor expenses, such as bus fare or snacks.

pod (pahd) *noun* 1. A long, thin case that grows on certain plants and contains seeds. 2. A unit that is detachable from a larger vehicle and

P

has a special function. **3.** A group of certain kinds of sea animals.

pod·cast (pahd-kast**)**
verb To supply a program over the Internet for people to listen to or watch on a mobile device or on a computer.
noun A program for viewing or listening that is distributed in this way.
▸ *verb* **podcasting, podcast** *or* **podcasted**

po·di·um (poh-dee-uhm**)** *noun* **1.** A stand with a surface for holding things such as papers, for use by a person who is speaking to an audience. **2.** A small platform, such as the one that an orchestra conductor stands on.
▸ *noun, plural* **podiums** *or* **podia**

po·em (poh-uhm**)** *noun* A piece of writing arranged in lines, often with a regular rhythm and some words that rhyme. Many poems are written to help the reader or listener share an experience or feel a strong emotion. In a poem, words are often chosen for their sounds as well as their meanings.

po·et (poh-it**)** *noun* A person who writes poetry.

po·et·ry (poh-i-tree**)** *noun* **1.** Literary work in the form of poems.
2. Anything that has the effect of a poem.
▸ *adjective* **poetic**

poin·set·ti·a (poin-set-uh *or* poin-**set-**ee-uh**)** *noun* A decorative plant with large red, white, or pink leaves that look like flower petals.

point (point)
noun **1.** The sharp end of something. **2.** A dot in writing. **3.** A very small mark on a surface or in an area.
4. The main purpose or reason for saying or doing something. **5.** An idea presented in speech or writing. **6.** A specific place or location. **7.** A unit for scoring in a game. **8.** In geometry, a location in space with no dimensions. **9.** A particular time or moment. **10.** A quality or a trait.
verb **1.** To show where something is by

using your index finger or your arm.
2. To aim at someone or something.
3. point out To draw attention to something.
▸ *verb* **pointing, pointed** ▸ *adjective* **pointed**

point-blank (point-blangk) *adjective*
1. Very close. **2.** Plain and blunt.

point·less (point-lis**)** *adjective* Useless, or without purpose. ▸ *adverb* **pointlessly**

point of view (point uhv **vyoo)** *noun* An attitude, a viewpoint, or a way of looking at or thinking about something.

poise (poiz)
verb To balance.
noun A confident and graceful manner.
▸ *verb* **poising, poised**

poised (poizd) *adjective* Self-confident and graceful.

poi·son (poi-zuhn**)**
noun A substance that can kill or harm a person, animal, or plant if it is swallowed, inhaled, absorbed, or sometimes even touched.
verb To give a person, animal, or plant poison, or to put poison in something.
▸ *verb* **poisoning, poisoned**

poi·son ivy (poi-zuhn **eye-**vee**)** *noun* A shrub or climbing vine with clusters of three shiny, green leaves. Poison ivy causes an itchy rash on most people who touch it.

poi·son·ous (poi-zuh-nuhs**)** *adjective* Having a poison that can harm or kill. Some snakes, insects, and even plants are poisonous.

poi·son su·mac (poi-zuhn **soo-**mak**)** *noun* A variety of sumac that can cause a rash similar to that from poison ivy.

poke (pohk)
verb **1.** To jab sharply with a finger or pointed object. **2.** To stick out or thrust quickly. **3.** To move slowly.
noun A quick thrust or jab.
▸ *verb* **poking, poked** ▸ *adjective* **poky** *or* **pokey**

P

pok·er (**poh**-kur) *noun* 1. A long, metal tool used for stirring up a fire or arranging the burning wood. 2. A card game in which a player bets that the value of his or her cards is greater than that of the cards held by the other players.

Po·land (**poh**-luhnd) A country in Central Europe. It has almost 10,000 lakes, one of the highest number of lakes in the world. Formerly a Soviet satellite state, Poland is now a democracy and a member of the European Union.

po·lar (**poh**-lur) *adjective* Near or having to do with the icy regions around the North or South Pole.

po·lar bear (**poh**-lur *bair*) *noun* A large bear with thick, white fur that lives in Arctic regions.

pole (pole) *noun* 1. A long, smooth piece of wood, metal, or plastic. 2. One of the two geographical points, the North Pole or the South Pole, that are farthest away from the equator. 3. One of the two opposite ends of a magnet. 4. **poles apart** Very different or having very different ideas. **Pole** sounds like **poll**.

pole·cat (**pohl**-*kat*) *noun* 1. A European animal of the weasel family that has brown or black fur. A polecat gives off a strong, unpleasant odor when attacked or frightened. 2. (informal) A skunk.

pole vault (**pole** *vawlt*) *noun* An athletic event that involves jumping over a very high bar with the help of a long, flexible pole. *verb* **pole-vault** To jump over a high bar with the help of a long, flexible pole.
▶ *verb* **pole-vaulting, pole-vaulted**
▶ *noun* **pole-vaulter**

po·lice (puh-**lees**)
noun, plural The people whose job is to keep order, make sure that the law is obeyed, stop crimes that are being committed, and investigate crimes that have occurred.

verb To guard or patrol an area and keep order.
▶ *verb* **policing, policed**

po·lice·man (puh-**lees**-muhn) *noun* A man who is a member of a police force. ▶ *noun, plural* **policemen**

po·lice of·fic·er (puh-**lees** *aw*-fi-sur) *noun* A man or woman who is a member of a police department.

po·lice·wom·an (puh-**lees**-*wum*-uhn) *noun* A woman who is a member of a police force. ▶ *noun, plural* **policewomen**

pol·i·cy (**pah**-li-see) *noun* 1. A general plan or principle that people use to help them make decisions or take action. 2. An insurance contract.
▶ *noun, plural* **policies**

po·li·o (**poh**-lee-oh) *noun* An infectious viral disease that attacks the brain and spinal cord. Polio occurs mainly in children. In serious cases, it can cause paralysis. This disease is now easily prevented with a vaccine. Polio is short for *poliomyelitis*.

pol·ish (**pah**-lish)
verb 1. To rub something to make it shine, often using a special substance designed for that purpose. 2. To revise or prepare something to the best of your ability.
noun A substance used to clean things and make them shine.
▶ *verb* **polishes, polishing, polished** ▶ *noun, plural* **polishes**

pol·ished (**pah**-lisht) *adjective* 1. Smooth and shiny. 2. Well rehearsed and skillfully presented.

po·lite (puh-**lite**) *adjective* Having good manners; being well behaved and courteous to others. ▶ *adjective* **politer, politest** ▶ *noun* **politeness** ▶ *adverb* **politely**

po·lit·i·cal (puh-**lit**-i-kuhl) *adjective* 1. Of or having to do with governments and how they are run, or with politicians. 2. A **political party** is an organization that elects representatives to be candidates for government and creates or supports their policies.
▶ *adverb* **politically**

P

pol·i·ti·cian (*pah*-li-**tish**-uhn) *noun*
A person who runs for or holds a
government office, such as a senator.

pol·i·tics (**pah**-li-tiks)
noun The activity and discussions
involved in governing a country, state,
or city.
noun, plural **1.** The activities of
politicians and political parties. **2.** An
individual's beliefs about how the
government should be run.
▶ *adjective* **political** ▶ *adverb*
politically

pol·ka (**pohl**-kuh *or* **poh**-kuh) *noun* A
fast dance in which couples swirl
around the floor in a circular pattern.
The polka came from central Europe.

pol·ka dots (**poh**-kuh *dahts*) *noun,*
plural Round, colored dots that form
a regular pattern on fabric or other
materials. ▶ *adjective* **polka-dot**

poll (pohl)
noun A survey of people's opinions or
beliefs.
noun, plural **polls** The place where
votes are cast and recorded during an
election.
verb To record people's opinions or
votes.
Poll sounds like **pole.** ▶ *verb* **polling,**
polled

pol·len (**pah**-luhn) *noun* **1.** Tiny yellow
grains produced in the anthers of
flowers. Pollen grains are the male
cells of flowering plants. **2. pollen**
count A measurement of the amount
of pollen in the air, which indicates
how badly people with pollen allergies
will be affected.

pol·li·nate (**pah**-luh-*nate*) *verb* To carry
or transfer pollen from the stamen
to the pistil of the same flower or
another flower where female cells can
be fertilized to produce seed. ▶ *verb*
pollinating, pollinated ▶ *noun*
pollination

pol·lut·ant (puh-**loo**-tuhnt) *noun* A
substance that contaminates another
substance.

pol·lute (puh-**loot**) *verb* To
contaminate or make dirty or

impure, especially with industrial
waste or other products produced by
humans. ▶ *verb* **polluting, polluted**

pol·lu·tion (puh-**loo**-shuhn) *noun*
1. Harmful materials that damage or
contaminate the air, water, and soil,
such as chemicals, gasoline exhaust,
industrial waste, and excessive noise
and light. **2.** The act of polluting or the
state of being polluted.

po·lo (**poh**-loh) *noun* A game played
on horseback by two teams of four
players. The players try to hit a small
ball using long, wooden mallets.

pol·y·es·ter (*pah*-lee-**es**-tur) *noun* A
synthetic substance used to make
plastic products and fabric.

pol·y·gon (**pah**-li-*gahn*) *noun* A shape
with three or more straight sides.
Triangles, squares, pentagons, and
hexagons are all polygons.

pol·y·mer (**pah**-luh-mur) *noun* A natural
or synthetic compound made up
of small, simple molecules linked
together in long chains of repeating
units.

pol·yp (**pah**-luhp) *noun* **1.** A small sea
animal with a tubular body and a
round mouth surrounded by tentacles.
Coral is an example of a polyp. **2.** A
tumor or mass on the lining of the
nose, mouth, or other body passage
open to the outside.

pol·y·sty·rene (*pah*-lee-**stye**-reen) *noun*
A light, firm plastic often used to
make disposable cups, foams, and
packing materials. Styrofoam is one
form of polystyrene.

pol·y·un·sat·u·rates (*pah*-lee-uhn-
sach-ur-its) *noun, plural* Vegetable
fats and oils thought to be healthier
for you than other fats. ▶ *adjective*
polyunsaturated (*pah*-lee-uhn-**sach**-
uh-*ray*-tid)

pome·gran·ate (**pah**-muh-*gran*-it)
noun A round fruit that has a tough,
reddish-yellow skin and many
seeds covered with juicy red flesh.
Pomegranates have a tart flavor.

pomp (pahmp) *noun* Elaborate and
stately ceremony or display.

P

pomp·ous (pahm-puhs) *adjective* Self-important to a degree that irritates other people. ▶ *adverb* **pompously**

pon·cho (pahn-choh) *noun* 1. A cloak that looks like a blanket with a hole in the center for the head. Ponchos were originally worn in South America. 2. A similar waterproof garment with a hood.

pond (pahnd) *noun* An enclosed body of freshwater that is smaller than a lake.

pon·der (pahn-dur) *verb* To think about something carefully. ▶ *verb* **pondering, pondered**

pon·der·ous (pahn-dur-uhs) *adjective* 1. Heavy and slow or clumsy. 2. Hard to understand and dull.
▶ *adverb* **ponderously**

po·ny (poh-nee) *noun* 1. A breed of horse that stays small when fully grown. 2. Any horse, especially a small one.
▶ *noun, plural* **ponies**

Po·ny Ex·press (poh-nee ik-*spres*) *noun* A mail service in which a series of riders carried the mail on horseback from Missouri to California. Pony Express service started in April 1860 and ended in October 1861.

po·ny·tail (poh-nee-*tayl*) *noun* A hairstyle that looks like a pony's tail, in which the hair is pulled together and held with a band.

poo·dle (poo-duhl) *noun* A breed of dog with thick, curly hair that is usually cut in a fancy style. Poodles range in size from the fairly large standard poodle to the very small toy poodle.

pool (pool) *noun* 1. A small, shallow area of water or other liquid. 2. A swimming pool. 3. A game in which players use a stick called a cue to hit wooden balls into pockets around the edges of a table. 4. A group of people who share something.
verb To put things together to be shared, such as ideas or money.
▶ *verb* **pooling, pooled**

poor (poor) *adjective* 1. Having little or no money. 2. Worse than normal, or

worse than what people might desire. 3. Deserving sympathy or pity.
▶ *adjective* **poorer, poorest**

poor·ly (poor-lee) *adverb* Badly.

pop (pahp)
verb 1. To explode with a small bang or bursting sound. 2. To move or appear quickly or unexpectedly. 3. **pop out** In baseball, to hit a fly ball that is caught by a player on the other team.
noun 1. A sweet, carbonated soft drink. Also called **soda** or **soda pop.** 2. A sudden, explosive sound. 3. (informal) Father. 4. Short for **pop music.**
idiom **pop the question** To propose marriage.
▶ *verb* **popping, popped**

pop·corn (pahp-*korn*) *noun* Kernels of corn that are heated until they swell up and burst open into a fluffy mass with a popping sound. Popcorn is eaten as a snack.

pope *or* **Pope** (pohp) *noun* The head of the Roman Catholic Church.

pop·lar (pahp-lur) *noun* A tall tree with wide leaves. The aspen and the cottonwood are both poplar trees.

pop mu·sic (pahp myoo-zik) *noun* Modern popular music with a strong, and usually fast, beat.

pop·py (pah-pee) *noun* A plant with large, brightly colored flowers. Some species are grown on a large scale to produce drugs or seeds. Poppy seeds are used as toppings or fillings for baked goods. ▶ *noun, plural* **poppies**

pop·u·lar (pahp-yuh-lur) *adjective* 1. Liked or used by many people. 2. Having many friends, or liked by many people. 3. Of or for the people.
▶ *adverb* **popularly**

pop·u·lar·i·ty (pahp-yuh-lar-i-tee) *noun* The state of being liked or admired by many or by a particular group of people.

pop·u·lat·ed (pahp-yuh-lay-tid) *adjective* Having people living in it.

pop·u·la·tion (pahp-yuh-lay-shuhn) *noun* 1. The total number of people who live in a place. 2. All of the people living in a certain place.

P

pop-up (pahp-*uhp*)
adjective **1.** Appearing on a computer screen in front of another window. **2.** Having a section that opens outward.
noun Something that pops up on a computer screen, especially an ad.

por·ce·lain (por-suh-lin) *noun* Very fine china, often used to make ornaments or cups and saucers or to cover bathroom fixtures.

porch (porch) *noun* A structure with a roof that is attached to the outside of a house, usually near a door. ▶ *noun, plural* **porches**

por·cu·pine (por-kyuh-*pine*) *noun* A large rodent covered with long, sharp quills that are used for protection.

pore (por)
noun One of the tiny holes in your skin through which you sweat.
verb To read or study something carefully.
Pore sounds like **pour.** ▶ *verb* **poring, pored**

pork (pork) *noun* The meat from a pig.

po·rous (por-uhs) *adjective* Full of tiny holes that let liquid or gas pass through.

por·poise (por-puhs) *noun* An ocean mammal with a rounded head and a short, blunt snout. The porpoise is related to but is usually smaller than the dolphin and the whale.

por·ridge (por-ij) *noun* A kind of hot cereal made by boiling oats or other grains in milk or water until the mixture is thick.

port (port)
noun **1.** A harbor or place where boats and ships can dock or anchor safely. **2.** A town or city with a harbor where ships can dock and load and unload cargo. **3.** The left side of a ship or an aircraft as one faces forward. **4.** A place on a computer that is designed for a particular kind of plug. **5.** A strong, sweet red wine.
adjective Of or having to do with the left side of a ship or aircraft.

port·a·ble (por-tuh-buhl) *adjective* Able to be carried or moved easily.

por·tal (por-tuhl) *noun* **1.** An entrance, especially a large or important one. **2.** A website that provides links to many other websites.

port·cul·lis (*port*-**kuhl**-is) *noun* A strong, heavy grating that can be raised and lowered to defend the entrance to a castle. ▶ *noun, plural* **portcullises**

por·ter (por-tur) *noun* **1.** A person who carries luggage for people at a railroad station or hotel. **2.** A person who waits on train passengers. **3.** A person who carries equipment on an expedition.

port·hole (port-*hohl*) *noun* A small, round window in the side of a ship or boat.

por·ti·co (por-ti-*koh*) *noun* A porch or walkway with a roof that is supported by columns. ▶ *noun, plural* **porticos** or **porticoes**

por·tion (por-shuhn)
noun **1.** A part, section, or piece of something. **2.** An amount of food that is served to someone.
verb To divide something up into parts or shares.
▶ *verb* **portioning, portioned**

port·ly (port-lee) *adjective* Heavy or stout. ▶ *noun* **portliness**

por·trait (por-trit *or* **por**-trayt) *noun* **1.** A drawing, painting, photograph, or engraving of a person, especially one that shows only the face or the head and shoulders. **2.** A description.

por·tray (por-**tray**) *verb* **1.** To describe in words. **2.** To make a picture of something or someone. **3.** To act a part in a play or movie.
▶ *verb* **portraying, portrayed** ▶ *noun* **portrayal**

Por·tu·gal (por-chuh-guhl) A country in southwestern Europe on the Atlantic Ocean. It was a major maritime power during the 15th and 16th centuries, but it lost much of its influence after an earthquake devastated its capital, Lisbon, in 1755, and its largest colony, Brazil, became independent in 1822.

P

pose (pohz)
verb 1. To take a particular position and stay there so that you can be photographed, painted, or drawn.
2. To pretend to be someone else in order to deceive people. 3. **pose a question** To ask a question.
noun A bodily attitude or position.
▶ *verb* **posing, posed**

posh (pahsh) *adjective* (informal) Very stylish or expensive. ▶ *adjective* **posher, poshest**

po·si·tion (puh-**zish**-uhn)
noun 1. The place where someone or something is located. 2. A person's opinion or point of view on a particular issue or subject. 3. The way in which someone or something is standing, sitting, or lying. 4. The right place to be. 5. A particular job. 6. A set of circumstances. 7. A particular role on a team.
verb To put someone or something in a particular place, or to arrange people or things in a particular order.
▶ *verb* **positioning, positioned**

pos·i·tive (**pah**-zi-tiv) *adjective* 1. Certain, definite. 2. Helpful or constructive.
3. Showing approval or acceptance.
4. A **positive** number is more than zero. 5. Having one of two opposite kinds of electrical charge. 6. Showing that a particular disease, condition, or organism is present.

pos·i·tive·ly (**pah**-zi-tiv-lee) *adverb* 1. In a constructive or confident way. 2. Used to emphasize that something is the case or that someone means what they are saying.

pos·se (**pah**-see) *noun* A group of people gathered together by a sheriff to help capture a criminal.

pos·sess (puh-**zes**) *verb* 1. To have or to own. 2. If you are **possessed by** someone or something, you are in its power.
▶ *verb* **possessing, possessed**

pos·ses·sion (puh-**zesh**-uhn) *noun*
1. Something that belongs to you.
2. **in your possession** Owned or held by you.

pos·ses·sive (puh-**zes**-iv)
adjective Wanting to keep someone or something for yourself and not wanting to share it.
noun The form of a noun or pronoun that shows that something belongs to the one referred to. In "This coat is yours" and "Carolina's hair," "yours" and "Carolina's" are possessives.

pos·si·bil·i·ty (pah-suh-**bil**-i-tee) *noun*
1. An event that may happen. 2. One thing among several that may be chosen.
▶ *noun, plural* **possibilities**

pos·si·ble (**pah**-suh-buhl) *adjective* Able to be done.

pos·si·bly (**pah**-suh-blee) *adverb* Perhaps.

pos·sum (**pah**-suhm) *noun* 1. An opossum. 2. **play possum** To pretend to be asleep or dead.

post (pohst)
noun 1. A long, thick piece of wood, concrete, or metal that is fixed in the ground to support or mark something. 2. A place where someone is on duty. 3. A military base where soldiers are stationed or trained. 4. A particular job that someone has.
verb 1. To put up a notice or an announcement of information. 2. To assign someone to a post. 3. **keep posted** (informal) To give someone information or the latest news.
▶ *verb* **posting, posted**

post·age (**poh**-stij) *noun* The cost of sending a letter or package by mail.

post·age stamp (**poh**-stij *stamp*) *noun* A small printed piece of paper issued by a government and attached to mail to show that postage has been paid.

Post·al Serv·ice (**poh**-stuhl *sur*-vis) *noun* The agency that is in charge of selling stamps and delivering the mail. Although the Postal Service is run by the U.S. government, it is an independent agency.

post·card (**pohst**-kahrd) *noun* A card, sometimes with a picture on one side, that you send by mail. A postcard does not require an envelope to be mailed.

P

post·er (**poh**-stur) *noun* A large, printed sign that often has a picture. A poster can be put up as an advertisement, a notice, or a decoration.

post·hu·mous (**pahs**-chuh-muhs) *adjective* Coming or happening after death. ▶ *adverb* **posthumously**

post·man (**pohst**-muhn) *noun* A mail carrier, if the person is a man. ▶ *noun, plural* **postmen**

post·mark (**pohst**-*mahrk*) *noun* An official stamp on a piece of mail that marks, or cancels, the postage stamp and shows the place and date of mailing.

post·mast·er (**pohst**-*mas*-tur) *noun* The head of a post office, if the person is a man.

post·mis·tress (**pohst**-*mis*-tris) *noun* The head of a post office, if the person is a woman.

post of·fice (**pohst** *aw*-fis) *noun* The place where people go to buy stamps and to send letters and packages.

post·pone (**pohst**-**pone**) *verb* To put something off until later. ▶ *verb* **postponing, postponed** ▶ *noun* **postponement**

post·script (**pohst**-*skript*) *noun* A short message beginning "P.S." that is added to the end of a letter, after the writer's signature.

post·trau·mat·ic stress dis·or·der (**pohst**-traw-**mat**-ik **stres** dis-*or*-dur) *noun* A difficult condition experienced by people who have experienced war, physical attack, or great violence and are unable to behave normally as a result. Abbreviated as *PTSD*.

pos·ture (**pahs**-chur) *noun* The position of your body when you stand, sit, or walk.

post·war (**pohst**-**wawr**) *adjective* Happening or being after a war.

pot (paht)
noun 1. A deep, round container used for cooking or storing food. 2. A container made of clay or plastic that is used for growing plants.
verb To place something in a pot. ▶ *verb* **potting, potted**

po·tas·si·um (puh-**tas**-ee-uhm) *noun* A silvery-white, metallic chemical element that is necessary for good nutrition. It is found in foods such as bananas and potatoes and is also used in making fertilizers, explosives, and soap.

po·ta·to (puh-**tay**-toh) *noun* The thick underground tuber of a leafy plant, eaten as food. This vegetable was originally grown in South America. ▶ *noun, plural* **potatoes**

po·tent (**poh**-tuhnt) *adjective* Very strong. ▶ *noun* **potency** (**poh**-tuhn-see) ▶ *adverb* **potently**

po·ten·tial (puh-**ten**-shuhl) *noun* 1. What a person is capable of achieving in the future. 2. The possibility of being developed into something better.
adjective Possible but not yet actual or real.
▶ *adverb* **potentially**

pot·hole (**paht**-hohl) *noun* A large hole in the surface of a road.

po·tion (**poh**-shuhn) *noun* A liquid drunk as a medicine or poison or to bring about a magical or mysterious result.

pot·ter (**pah**-tur) *noun* A person who makes dishes, cups, and other objects out of clay.

pot·ter·y (**pah**-tur-ee) *noun* 1. Objects made of baked clay, such as bowls, plates, or vases. Pottery can be used for decorative or practical purposes. 2. A place where clay objects are made.
▶ *noun, plural* **potteries**

pouch (pouch) *noun* 1. A leather or fabric bag. 2. A pocket in the mother's body in which kangaroos and other marsupials carry their young.
▶ *noun, plural* **pouches**

poul·try (**pohl**-tree) *noun* Farm birds raised for their eggs and meat. Chickens, turkeys, ducks, and geese are poultry.

pounce (pouns) *verb* To jump forward and grab something suddenly. ▶ *verb* **pouncing, pounced**

P

pound (pound)
noun 1. A unit of weight equal to 16 ounces. A soccer ball weighs about one pound. Pound is abbreviated as *lb.* 2. A unit of money used in the United Kingdom and several other countries. 3. A place where stray dogs and other animals are kept.
verb To hit heavily and repeatedly.
▶ *verb* **pounding, pounded**

pour (por) *verb* 1. To make something flow in a steady stream. 2. To rain heavily. 3. To move in a steady stream and in large numbers.
Pour sounds like **pore.** ▶ *verb* **pouring, poured**

pout (pout)
verb To push out your lips to express annoyance or disappointment.
noun A sulky or disappointed facial expression.
▶ *verb* **pouting, pouted**

pov·er·ty (**pah**-vur-tee) *noun* The state of being poor.

pow·der (**pou**-dur)
noun 1. Tiny particles made by grinding, crushing, or pounding a solid substance. 2. A cosmetic or other preparation made from powder.
verb 1. To make or turn something into powder. 2. To cover something with powder.
▶ *verb* **powdering, powdered**
▶ *adjective* **powdery** ▶ *adjective* **powdered**

pow·er (**pou**-ur) *noun* 1. The strength or ability to do something. 2. The authority or right to command, control, or make decisions. 3. A person, group, or nation that has great strength, influence, or control over others. 4. Electricity or other forms of energy. 5. In mathematics, the number of times you use a number as a factor in multiplication. Three to the fifth power means three multiplied by three five times, or $3 \times 3 \times 3 \times 3 \times 3$, equaling 243.

pow·er·ful (**pou**-ur-fuhl) *adjective* Having great power, strength, or authority. ▶ *adverb* **powerfully**

pow·er·less (**pou**-ur-lis) *adjective* Having no power, strength, or authority.

prac·ti·cal (**prak**-ti-kuhl) *adjective* 1. Of or having to do with experience or practice rather than theory and ideas. 2. Useful. 3. Sensible, or showing good judgment.

prac·ti·cal joke (**prak**-ti-kuhl **johk**) *noun* A mischievous trick often done to make someone look or feel foolish.

prac·ti·cal·ly (**prak**-tik-lee) *adverb* 1. Almost or nearly. 2. In a sensible way.

prac·tice (**prak**-tis)
noun 1. The repetition of an action regularly in order to improve a skill. 2. A custom or a habit. 3. The business of a doctor, lawyer, or other professional.
verb 1. To do something repeatedly so that you get better at it. 2. To work as a doctor, lawyer, or other professional. 3. To follow the teachings of a religion and attend its services or ceremonies. 4. To put something into action.
phrase **in practice** In the way that actually happens, rather than what someone thinks will happen.
▶ *verb* **practicing, practiced**

prai·rie (**prair**-ee) *noun* A large area of flat or rolling grassland with few or no trees.

prai·rie dog (**prair**-ee *dawg*) *noun* A small burrowing mammal that is related to the squirrel. Prairie dogs live in large colonies mainly in the plains of west-central North America. Their call sounds like a dog's bark.

prai·rie schoon·er (**prair**-ee *skoo*-nur) *noun* A large covered wagon used by pioneers to journey westward over the flat, grassy prairies of central North America.

praise (praze)
noun Words of approval or admiration.
verb 1. To offer approval or admiration to someone or about something. 2. To worship and express thanks to.
▶ *verb* **praising, praised**

praise·wor·thy (**praze**-*wur*-THee) *adjective* Deserving praise.

prance (prans) *verb* **1.** To walk or move in a lively or proud way. **2.** To spring forward on hind legs.
▶ *verb* **prancing, pranced**

prank (prangk) *noun* A playful or mischievous trick.

pray (pray) *verb* **1.** To talk to God to give thanks or ask for help. **2.** To hope very much that something happens. **Pray** sounds like **prey.** ▶ *verb* **praying, prayed**

prayer (prair) *noun* **1.** The act of praying. **2.** An expression of appeal or thanks to God. **3.** A set of words used in praying. **4.** Something requested or prayed for.

pray·ing man·tis (**pray**-ing **man**-tis) *noun* An insect that is related to the grasshopper. When it rests, the praying mantis folds its front legs, which then look like hands folded in prayer.

preach (preech) *verb* **1.** To talk on a religious subject, especially during a worship service. **2.** To tell other people what you think they should do, often in an annoying way.
▶ *verb* **preaches, preaching, preached** ▶ *noun* **preacher**

pre·car·i·ous (pri-**kair**-ee-uhs) *adjective* Not in a secure position. ▶ *adverb* **precariously**

pre·cau·tion (pri-**kaw**-shuhn) *noun* Something you do in advance in order to prevent a dangerous or unpleasant occurrence. ▶ *adjective* **precautionary** (pri-**kaw**-shuh-*ner*-ee)

pre·cede (pree-**seed**) *verb* To come before something else. ▶ *verb* **preceding, preceded** ▶ *adjective* **preceding**

prec·e·dent (**pres**-i-duhnt) *noun* Something done, said, or written that becomes an example to be followed in the future.

pre·cinct (**pree**-singkt) *noun* **1.** An area or a district in a city or town. **2.** A police station in such a district.

pre·cious (**presh**-uhs) *adjective* **1.** Very valuable. **2.** Very special or dear.

prec·i·pice (**pres**-uh-pis) *noun* A tall, steep cliff.

pre·cip·i·tate (pri-**sip**-i-*tate*) *verb* **1.** To rain, sleet, hail, or snow. **2.** To make something happen suddenly or sooner than expected.
▶ *verb* **precipitating, precipitated**

pre·cip·i·ta·tion (pri-*sip*-i-**tay**-shuhn) *noun* The falling of water from the sky in the form of rain, sleet, hail, or snow.

pre·cise (pri-**sise**) *adjective* **1.** Very accurate or exact. **2.** Very neat and careful about details.

pre·cise·ly (pri-**sise**-lee) *adverb* In exact or precise terms.

pre·ci·sion (pri-**sizh**-uhn) *noun* Exactness. Something done with precision is done very carefully and accurately.

pre·co·cious (pri-**koh**-shuhs) *adjective* Advanced in development or abilities beyond what is normal for your age.

pred·a·tor (**pred**-uh-tur) *noun* An animal that lives by hunting other animals for food. Lions, sharks, and hawks are predators.

pred·a·to·ry (**pred**-uh-*tor*-ee) *adjective* **1.** Of or having to do with predators. **2.** A **predatory** person, organization, or action uses others unfairly.

pred·e·ces·sor (**pred**-uh-*ses*-ur) *noun* A person who held an office or a job before another person.

pre·dic·a·ment (pri-**dik**-uh-muhnt) *noun* A difficult or embarrassing situation.

pred·i·cate (**pred**-i-kit) *noun* The part of a sentence or clause that tells what the subject does or what is done to the subject. In the sentence "The kitten purred softly," the predicate is "purred softly."

pre·dict (pri-**dikt**) *verb* To say what will happen in the future. ▶ *verb* **predicting, predicted**

pre·dic·tion (pri-**dik**-shuhn) *noun* **1.** A statement about what will happen in the future. **2.** The action of predicting something.

pre·dom·i·nant (pri-**dah**-muh-nuhnt) *adjective* More important, dominant, or obvious than all others.

pre·dom·i·nant·ly (pri-**dah**-muh-nuhnt-lee) *adverb* For the most part; mainly.

P

pre·dom·i·nate (pri-**dah**-mi-*nate*)
verb To be larger, stronger, or more numerous than others. ▸ *verb* **predominating, predominated** ▸ *noun* **predominance** ▸ *adjective* **predominant**

preen (preen) *verb* **1.** To clean and arrange birds' feathers with their beaks. **2.** To fuss over your appearance and then admire yourself.
▸ *verb* **preening, preened**

pref·ace (**pref**-is)
noun An introduction to a book or speech.
verb To introduce by or to begin with introductory remarks.
▸ *verb* **prefacing, prefaced**

pre·fer (pri-**fur**) *verb* To like one person or thing better than another. ▸ *verb* **preferring, preferred**

pref·er·ence (**pref**-ruhns) *noun* **1.** Something that you prefer over another thing. **2.** An advantage that a particular group or person enjoys.

pre·fix (**pree**-fiks) *noun* A word part added to the beginning of a word or root to change the meaning. *Sub-*, *un-*, and *re-* are all prefixes. The prefix *un-*, which means "not," is used in the words *unhappy* and *unusual*. ▸ *noun, plural* **prefixes**

preg·nant (**preg**-nuhnt) *adjective* Having a baby (for a woman) or young (for animals) growing inside the uterus. ▸ *noun* **pregnancy**

pre·his·tor·ic (*pree*-hi-**stor**-ik) *adjective* Belonging to a time before history was recorded in written form. ▸ *noun* **prehistory**

prej·u·dice (**prej**-uh-dis)
noun **1.** An opinion or a judgment formed unfairly or without knowing all the facts. **2.** An immovable, unreasonable, or unfair opinion about someone based on the person's race, religion, or other characteristic. **3.** Hatred or unfair treatment that results from having fixed opinions about some group of people.
verb To cause or create prejudice or bias.

▸ *adjective* **prejudicial** (*prej*-uh-**dish**-uhl)

prej·u·diced (**prej**-uh-dist) *adjective* Disliking, mistreating, or mistrusting someone unfairly, because of prejudice.

pre·lim·i·nar·y (pri-**lim**-uh-*ner*-ee) *adjective* Preparing the way for something more important or more complete that comes later.
noun An early round in a sports competition.

pre·ma·ture (*pree*-muh-**choor** or *pree*-muh-**toor**) *adjective* Happening, appearing, or done too soon. ▸ *adverb* **prematurely**

pre·med·i·tat·ed (pree-**med**-i-*tay*-tid) *adjective* Planned in advance, usually a crime or other wrong action. ▸ *verb* **premeditate**

pre·mier (pri-**meer**)
adjective Leading or most important.
noun A prime minister.

pre·miere (pri-**meer** or prim-**yair**) *noun* The first public performance of a film, play, dance, or work of music.

prem·ise (**prem**-is)
noun A statement or principle that is accepted as true or taken for granted.
noun, plural **premises** Land and the buildings on it.

pre·mi·um (**pree**-mee-uhm)
noun **1.** Something that is free or less expensive than usual when you buy something else. **2.** An amount added to the normal cost. **3.** Money that is paid to take out and maintain an insurance policy. **4. at a premium** Scarce and in demand.
adjective Of better quality, and therefore sold at a higher price.

pre·mo·ni·tion (*pree*-muh-**nish**-uhn or *prem*-uh-**nish**-uhn) *noun* A feeling that something is going to happen, especially something bad or harmful.

pre·oc·cu·pied (pree-**ahk**-yuh-*pide*) *adjective* Thinking so much about something that you cannot pay attention to anything else. ▸ *noun* **preoccupation**

prep·a·ra·tion (*prep*-uh-**ray**-shuhn) *noun* **1.** The act or process of getting

P

ready. **2.** Something done in order to get ready for something else. **3.** A substance that is made up for a specific purpose, such as food or medicine.

pre·pare (pri-**pair**) *verb* **1.** To get ready. **2.** To put together various parts or ingredients. **3. be prepared to** To be willing to do something.
▶ *verb* **preparing, prepared**

prep·o·si·tion (*prep-uh-***zish**-uhn) *noun* A word such as *of, after, with,* or *on* that shows the relation of a noun or pronoun to some other word in a sentence, usually a verb, adjective, or another noun.

prep·o·si·tion·al phrase (**prep**-uh-zish-uh-nuhl **fraze**) *noun* A phrase that begins with a preposition. The phrase "in the secret garden" is a prepositional phrase, because it begins with the word "in," which is a preposition.

pre·pos·ter·ous (pri-**pah**-stur-uhs) *adjective* Completely absurd. ▶ *adverb* **preposterously**

prep school (**prep** *skool*) *noun* A private school that prepares students for college. Prep school is short for *preparatory school.*

pre·school (**pree**-*skool*)
adjective Of or having to do with children who are younger than elementary-school age.
noun A school for children who are too young for elementary school, such as a child care center or a nursery school.

pre·scribe (pri-**skribe**) *verb* **1.** To recommend strongly, or to order. **2.** To write an order for a specific kind of medicine for a patient.
▶ *verb* **prescribing, prescribed**

pre·scrip·tion (pri-**skrip**-shuhn) *noun* An order for drugs or medicine written by a doctor to a pharmacist. A prescription specifies what type and quantity of medicine to give.

pres·ence (**prez**-uhns) *noun* **1.** Being in a place at a certain time. **2.** The fact of being around a person or thing.

pre·sent
verb (pri-**zent**) **1.** To give someone a gift or a prize in a formal way. **2.** To introduce a person or thing.
noun (**prez**-uhnt) **1.** Something that you give to somebody. **2.** The time that is happening now. **3.** The **present tense.**
adjective (**prez**-uhnt) In a place.
▶ *verb* **presenting, presented** ▶ *noun* **presenter** (pri-**zen**-tur)

pres·en·ta·tion (*prez*-uhn-**tay**-shuhn) *noun* **1.** The act of giving a prize or present. **2.** A speech or other way of giving information. **3.** The way that something is produced and the way it looks.

pres·ent·ly (**prez**-uhnt-lee) *adverb* Now or at the present time.

pres·ent par·ti·ci·ple (**prez**-uhnt **pahr**-ti-*sip*-uhl) *noun* A form of a verb that ends in *-ing* and can be used with a helping verb to form certain tenses and to show that an action or condition is in progress. In the sentence "I am working," the word *working* is a present participle. Present participles may also be used as adjectives.

pres·ent tense (**prez**-uhnt **tens**) *noun* A form of the verb that is used to indicate present time.

pres·er·va·tion (*prez*-ur-**vay**-shuhn) *noun* Keeping something from being damaged or destroyed.

pre·serv·a·tive (pri-**zur**-vuh-tiv) *noun* Something used to preserve an item, especially a chemical used to keep food from spoiling.
adjective Preventing something from spoiling.

pre·serve (pri-**zurv**)
verb **1.** To protect something so that it stays in its original or current state. **2.** To treat food so that it does not become spoiled.
noun A place where plants and animals are protected in their natural environment.
noun, plural **preserves** Jam that contains chunks of fruit.
▶ *verb* **preserving, preserved**

P

pre·side (pri-**zide**) *verb* To be in authority over something. ▶ *verb* **presiding, presided**

pres·i·dent (**prez**-i-duhnt) *noun* **1.** The elected leader or chief executive of a republic. **2.** The head of a company, society, college, club, or organization. ▶ *noun* **presidency** ▶ *adjective* **presidential** (*prez*-i-**den**-shuhl)

pres·i·dent-e·lect (*prez*-i-duhnt-i-**lekt**) *noun* The person who has won the election for president but has not yet been sworn into office.

Pres·i·dents' Day (**prez**-i-duhnts *day*) *noun* A holiday observed in most of the United States on the third Monday in February, celebrating the birthdays of George Washington and Abraham Lincoln.

press (pres) *verb* **1.** To push firmly. **2.** To try hard to persuade someone to do something. **3.** To remove the wrinkles in clothes with an iron. *noun* **1.** A machine for printing. **2. the press** The journalists and the organizations that collect, publish, and broadcast the news. *idiom* **pressed for time** In a big hurry. ▶ *verb* **presses, pressing, pressed** ▶ *noun, plural* **presses** ▶ *noun* **presser**

press·ing (**pres**-ing) *adjective* Urgent and very important.

pres·sure (**presh**-ur) *noun* **1.** The force produced by pressing on something. **2.** Strong influence, force, or persuasion. **3.** A burden or a strain. *verb* To force or persuade someone to do something. ▶ *verb* **pressuring, pressured**

pres·sur·ize (**presh**-uh-*rize*) *verb* To seal off an aircraft cabin, a spacecraft, or a diving chamber so that the air pressure inside is the same as the pressure at the earth's surface. ▶ *verb* **pressurizing, pressurized** ▶ *adjective* **pressurized**

pres·tige (pre-**steezh**) *noun* The great respect and high status that come from being successful, powerful, rich,

or famous. ▶ *adjective* **prestigious** (pres-**tij**-uhs)

pres·to (**pres**-toh) *interjection* A word used to indicate that something happens suddenly, as if by magic.

pre·sum·a·bly (pri-**zoo**-muh-blee) *adverb* Probably.

pre·sume (pri-**zoom**) *verb* **1.** To think that something is true without being certain or having all the facts. **2.** To dare. ▶ *verb* **presuming, presumed**

pre·sump·tion (pri-**zuhmp**-shuhn) *noun* **1.** A belief that something is true without knowing for certain. **2.** Behavior that others think is arrogant or inappropriate.

pre·teen (pree-**teen**) *noun* A boy or girl who has not turned 13 yet. *adjective* Made for or happening in the two or three years before a child's thirteenth birthday.

pre·tend (pri-**tend**) *verb* **1.** To make believe. **2.** To claim falsely. **3.** To give a false show in order to trick or deceive. ▶ *verb* **pretending, pretended**

pre·tense (pree-tens *or* pri-tens) *noun* **1.** Dishonest behavior that is intended to make something false appear true. **2.** A false excuse or justification for something.

pre·text (**pree**-tekst) *noun* A false reason or excuse given to hide a real reason.

pret·ty (**prit**-ee) *adjective* Pleasant to look at. *adverb* Quite. ▶ *adjective* **prettier, prettiest** ▶ *noun* **prettiness** ▶ *adverb* **prettily**

pret·zel (**pret**-suhl) *noun* Dough that has been shaped into a stick or a knot and baked until it is crisp. Pretzels are usually salted on the outside.

pre·vail (pri-**vayl**) *verb* **1.** To succeed in spite of difficulties. **2.** To be common or usual in a particular area at a particular time. ▶ *verb* **prevailing, prevailed** ▶ *adjective* **prevalent** (**prev**-uh-luhnt)

pre·vent (pri-**vent**) *verb* **1.** To keep something from happening. **2.** To keep someone from doing something.

P

▶ *verb* **preventing, prevented** ▶ *noun*
prevention (pri-**ven**-shuhn)

pre·ven·tive (pri-**ven**-tiv)
adjective Meant to prevent or stop
something.
noun Something that prevents,
especially something that prevents a
disease.

pre·view (**pree**-*vyoo*)
noun A limited performance of a play,
a movie, or another kind of show
before it is released to the general
public.
verb To provide or have a preliminary
viewing of something.
▶ *verb* **previewing, previewed**

pre·vi·ous (**pree**-vee-uhs) *adjective*
Former, or happening before.

pre·vi·ous·ly (**pree**-vee-uhs-lee) *adverb*
Before now.

prey (pray)
noun 1. An animal that is hunted by
another animal for food. 2. The victim
of an attack or robbery.
verb 1. **prey on** To hunt and eat
another animal. 2. To rob, attack, or
take advantage of someone who is
helpless or unable to fight back.
Prey sounds like **pray.** ▶ *verb* **preying,
preyed**

price (prise)
noun 1. The amount that you pay
for something. 2. The cost at which
something is accomplished.
verb To assign a price to something.
▶ *verb* **pricing, priced**

price·less (**prise**-lis) *adjective* Too
precious for anyone to put a value
on it.

prick (prik)
verb 1. To make a small hole in
something with a sharp point. 2. To
raise up.
noun A small, sharp pain.
▶ *verb* **pricking, pricked**

prick·le (**prik**-uhl)
noun A small, sharp point, such as a
thorn.
verb To have or cause a tingling
feeling.
▶ *verb* **prickling, prickled** ▶ *adjective*
prickly

prick·ly pear (**prik**-lee **pair**) *noun* A
cactus with yellow flowers and fruit
shaped like a pear.

pride (pride)
noun 1. Self-respect, or a sense of your
own importance or worth. 2. A feeling
of satisfaction in something that you
or someone else has achieved. 3. An
exaggerated opinion of yourself or
your own importance.
verb **pride oneself on** To be proud of a
specific quality or accomplishment.

priest (preest) *noun* In certain Christian
and other religions, a member of
the clergy who can lead services and
perform rites.

prim (prim) *adjective* Stiffly formal
and proper. ▶ *adjective* **primmer,
primmest**

pri·ma don·na (**pree**-muh **dah**-nuh)
noun 1. A female opera or concert
star. 2. (informal) A person who is
demanding, selfish, or conceited.

pri·mar·i·ly (prye-**mair**-uh-lee) *adverb*
Mainly or chiefly.

pri·mar·y (**prye**-mer-ee *or* **prye**-mur-ee)
adjective 1. Biggest or most important.
2. Earliest or most basic.
noun An election to choose a party
candidate who will run in the general
election.

pri·mar·y col·ors (**prye**-mer-ee **kuhl**-urz)
noun, plural Red, yellow, and blue,
which can be mixed to make all the
other colors.

pri·mar·y school (**prye**-mer-ee *skool*)
noun A school that includes the first
three or four grades and sometimes
kindergarten.

pri·mate (**prye**-mate) *noun* Any member
of the group of mammals that
includes monkeys, apes, and humans.

prime (prime)
adjective 1. Most important. 2. Of the
best quality or kind.
verb 1. To prepare a surface to be
painted. 2. To pour water into a dry
pump in order to start it working
properly.
noun The best part.
▶ *verb* **priming, primed**

P

prime min·is·ter (prime min-i-stur)
noun The person in charge of a
government in many countries.
Great Britain and Canada have prime
ministers.

prime num·ber (prime nuhm-bur) *noun*
A number that can be evenly divided
only by itself or 1. The numbers 2, 3,
5, 7, 11, 13, and 19 are the first eight
prime numbers.

pri·me·val (prye-**mee**-vuhl) *adjective*
Belonging to the earliest stages in the
history of the world.

prim·i·tive (**prim**-i-tiv) *adjective* 1. Very
simple or crude. 2. Very basic and
unrefined. 3. Of or having to do with
an early stage of development.

prim·rose (**prim**-roze) *noun* A small
garden plant with clusters of brightly
colored flowers.

prince (prins) *noun* 1. The son of a king
or queen. 2. The husband of a queen.
3. A nobleman of high rank.

Prince Ed·ward Is·land (prins **ed**-wurd
eye-luhnd) A province of Canada
located north of Nova Scotia. It is
Canada's smallest province. Prince
Edward Island is known for its lush
green landscape and is the setting for
the novel *Anne of Green Gables*.

prin·cess (**prin**-sis *or* **prin**-ses)
noun 1. The daughter of a king or
queen. 2. The wife of a prince. 3. A
noblewoman of high rank.
▶ *noun, plural* **princesses**

prin·ci·pal (**prin**-suh-puhl)
adjective Main or most important.
noun The head of a school.
Principal sounds like **principle**.
▶ *adverb* **principally**

prin·ci·ple (**prin**-suh-puhl)
noun 1. A basic truth, law, or belief.
2. A basic rule that governs a person's
behavior.
phrase **in principle** With regard to the
general idea, but not the details or the
way in which the idea will be carried
out.
Principle sounds like **principal**.

print (print)
verb 1. To produce words or pictures
on a page with a machine that uses

ink or a special powder called toner.
2. To write using letters that are
separate. 3. To publish.
noun 1. A photograph or a printed
copy of a painting or drawing. 2. A
fingerprint.
▶ *verb* **printing, printed** ▶ *noun*
printer ▶ *adjective* **printed**

print·ing press (**prin**-ting pres) *noun* A
large machine that prints words and
designs by pressing sheets of paper
against a surface, such as a metal
plate, that has ink on it.

print·out (**print**-out) *noun* Information
or pictures printed from a computer.

pri·or (**prye**-ur) *adjective* Earlier, or
existing before.

pri·or·i·tize (prye-**or**-i-tize) *verb* 1. To put
things in order from most important
to least important. 2. To make
something more important or most
important.
▶ *verb* **prioritizes, prioritizing,
prioritized**

pri·or·i·ty (prye-**or**-i-tee) *noun* Something
that is more important or more urgent
than other things.

prism (**priz**-uhm) *noun* A clear, solid
glass or plastic shape that breaks up
light into the colors of the spectrum.
Prisms usually have a triangular base.

pris·on (**priz**-uhn) *noun* A building
where people are confined as
punishment for a crime.

pris·on·er (**priz**-uh-nur) *noun* 1. A person
who is in prison. 2. Any person who
has been captured or is held by force.

pri·va·cy (**prye**-vuh-see) *noun* A state
in which others do not disturb or
interfere with your personal matters.

pri·vate (**prye**-vit)
adjective 1. Belonging to or concerning
one person or group and no one else.
2. Not meant to be shared. 3. Not
holding a public office. 4. Owned
by one or more individuals or by a
company, not by the government.
5. Free from intrusion or observation.
6. Unwilling to share thoughts and
feelings with others.
noun A soldier of the lowest rank.
▶ *adverb* **privately**

P

pri·vate school (**prye**-vit **skool**) *noun*
A school where parents pay for their
children's education, as opposed to a
public school, which is supported by
tax dollars.

priv·i·lege (**priv**-uh-lij) *noun* A special
right or advantage given to a person
or a group of people. ▸ *adjective*
privileged

prize (prize)
noun A reward for winning a
competition.
adjective 1. Good enough to win a
prize, or likely to win a prize. 2. Highly
valued.
verb To value something very much.
▸ *verb* **prizing, prized**

pro (proh)
preposition In favor of something. *This
newspaper article is strongly pro-union.*
noun A person who is very skilled at
something. It is a shortened form of
the word *professional* and is often used
in sports.
phrase **pros and cons** (kahnz)
Advantages and disadvantages.

prob·a·bil·i·ty (*prah*-buh-**bil**-i-tee) *noun*
1. The likelihood that a particular thing
will happen. 2. The most probable
thing.

prob·a·ble (**prah**-buh-buhl) *adjective*
Likely to happen or be true.

prob·a·bly (**prah**-buh-blee) *adverb*
1. In all likelihood; with little doubt.
2. Approximately.

pro·ba·tion (proh-**bay**-shuhn) *noun* 1. A
period of time for testing a person's
behavior or job qualifications. 2. A
period of time during which a person
who has commited a crime is not
kept in prison but is allowed to go
free under the close supervision of a
probation officer.

probe (prohb)
noun 1. A thorough examination or
investigation. 2. A tool or device used
to explore or examine something.
verb To explore or examine something.
▸ *verb* **probing, probed**

prob·lem (**prah**-bluhm)
noun 1. A difficult situation that needs
to be solved. 2. A puzzle or question

that requires an answer.
adjective Being or creating a problem.

pro·ce·dure (pruh-**see**-jur) *noun* A way
of doing something, especially by a
series of steps.

pro·ceed
verb (pruh-**seed**) To move forward or
continue.
noun, plural (**proh**-seedz) **proceeds**
The sum of money that is raised by
an event.
▸ *verb* **proceeding, proceeded**

proc·ess (**prah**-ses *or* **proh**-ses)
noun A series of actions or steps that
produces a particular result.
verb To prepare or change by a series
of steps.
▸ *noun, plural* **processes** ▸ *verb*
processes, processing, processed
▸ *noun* **processing** ▸ *adjective*
processed

pro·ces·sion (pruh-**sesh**-uhn) *noun*
1. A number of people walking or
driving along a route in an orderly way
as part of a public festival, a religious
service, or a parade. 2. A number of
people, animals, or vehicles moving
along as if they were in a parade.

proc·es·sor (**prah**-ses-ur) *noun* 1. A
person, machine, or company that
processes something. 2. A computer's
CPU.

pro·claim (pruh-**klaym**) *verb* To
announce something publicly. ▸ *verb*
proclaiming, proclaimed ▸ *noun*
proclamation (*prah*-kluh-**may**-shuhn)

pro·cras·ti·nate (proh-**kras**-tuh-
nate) *verb* To put off or delay doing
something that you really need
to do. ▸ *verb* **procrastinating,
procrastinated** ▸ *noun* **procrastination**
▸ *noun* **procrastinator**

prod (prahd)
verb 1. To poke or jab something or
someone. 2. To push or urge someone
into action.
noun 1. A poke or a jab, either
physical or mental, to make or
remind someone to do something.
2. A stick or other sharp or electrified
instrument used to control animals.
▸ *verb* **prodding, prodded**

P

prod·i·gy (**prah**-di-jee) *noun* A person, especially a young one, who has exceptional ability in a particular area. ▶ *noun, plural* **prodigies**

pro·duce
verb (pruh-**doos**) 1. To make or manufacture something. 2. To bring something out for inspection or use. 3. To be in charge of putting on a play or making a movie or TV program.
noun (**prah**-doos or **proh**-doos) Things that are produced or grown for eating, especially fruits and vegetables.
▶ *verb* **producing, produced** ▶ *noun* **producer**

prod·uct (**prah**-duhkt) *noun*
1. Something that is manufactured or made by a natural process. 2. The result you get when you multiply two numbers.

pro·duc·tion (pruh-**duhk**-shuhn) *noun*
1. The process of creating, growing, or manufacturing something. 2. The total amount produced. 3. Any form of entertainment that is presented to others. 4. **production line** A system of manufacturing in which the steps needed to make the product are carried out one at a time, in a specific order, as the product moves along slowly on a belt or track.

pro·duc·tive (pruh-**duhk**-tiv)
adjective Making a lot of products, accomplishing a lot of work, or producing good results.

pro·duc·tiv·i·ty (*proh*-duhk-**tiv**-i-tee) *noun* The state of being productive, or the rate at which production happens.

pro·fess (pruh-**fes**) *verb* 1. To state openly or to make known. 2. To say something insincerely, or to pretend that something is true.
▶ *verb* **professes, professing, professed**

pro·fes·sion (pruh-**fesh**-uhn) *noun*
1. An occupation for which you need special training or study. 2. The whole group of people in an occupation that requires special training or study. 3. Something that you state openly.

pro·fes·sion·al (pruh-**fesh**-uh-nuhl)
noun 1. A member of a profession, such as a doctor, teacher, nurse, or lawyer. 2. A person who is very skilled or paid to engage in a particular activity.
adjective 1. Making money for doing something others do for fun. 2. Of or having to do with the standards of a particular profession or occupation.

pro·fes·sor (pruh-**fes**-ur) *noun* A teacher of the highest teaching rank at a college or university.

pro·fi·cient (pruh-**fish**-uhnt) *adjective* Able to do something properly and skillfully. ▶ *noun* **proficiency** ▶ *adverb* **proficiently**

pro·file (**proh**-file)
noun 1. A side view or drawing of someone's head. 2. A brief account of someone's life or work.
verb To describe someone in a written article.
▶ *verb* **profiling, profiled**

prof·it (**prah**-fit)
noun 1. The amount of money left after all the costs of running a business have been subtracted from the money earned. 2. A gain or a benefit.
verb To gain or benefit in some way.
Profit sounds like **prophet.** ▶ *verb* **profiting, profited**

prof·it·a·ble (**prah**-fi-tuh-buhl) *adjective* Producing a profit.

pro·found (pruh-**found**) *adjective* Very deep or intense. ▶ *adverb* **profoundly**

pro·fuse (pruh-**fyoos**) *adjective* Plentiful or more than enough. ▶ *noun* **profusion** (pruh-**fyoo**-zhuhn) ▶ *noun* **profuseness**

pro·gram (**proh**-gram)
noun 1. A television or radio show. 2. A booklet that gives you information about a performance or a sporting event. 3. A schedule or plan for doing something. 4. A series of instructions, written in a computer language, that controls the way a computer works.
verb To give a computer or other machine instructions to make it work in a certain way.
▶ *verb* **programming, programmed**

P

pro·gram·mer (**proh**-gram-ur) *noun* A person whose job is to program a computer.

pro·gram·ming (**proh**-gram-ing) *noun* 1. The entire set of broadcasts or performances of a television station, a radio station, or a theater. 2. The process of creating programs for computers.

prog·ress
verb (pruh-**gres**) To move forward or to improve.
noun (**prah**-gres) A forward movement or improvement.
phrase **in progress** (**prah**-gres) Happening.
▶ *verb* **progresses, progressing, progressed**

pro·gress·ive (pruh-**gres**-iv)
adjective 1. Moving forward or happening steadily. 2. In favor of improvement, progress, or reform, especially in political or social matters.
noun A person who favors improvement or reform, especially in political, social, or educational matters.

pro·hib·it (proh-**hib**-it) *verb* To forbid or ban something officially. ▶ *verb* **prohibiting, prohibited** ▶ *noun* **prohibition**

proj·ect
noun (**prah**-jekt) 1. A plan or a proposal. 2. A job or assignment worked on over a period of time. 3. A group of apartment buildings planned and built as a unit.
verb (pruh-**jekt**) 1. To stick out. 2. To display an image or a movie on a screen. 3. To predict or to forecast. 4. To make your voice carry very far.
▶ *verb* **projecting, projected**
▶ *adjective* **projecting**

pro·jec·tile (pruh-**jek**-tuhl *or* pruh-**jek**-tile) *noun* An object, such as a bullet or missile, that is thrown or shot through the air.

pro·jec·tion (pruh-**jek**-shuhn) *noun* 1. Something that sticks out. 2. An estimate or a prediction. 3. **map**

projection A way of representing the globe on a flat page.

pro·jec·tor (pruh-**jek**-tur) *noun* A machine that shows slides or movies on a screen.

pro·li·fic (pruh-**lif**-ik) *adjective* Producing a large quantity of something.

pro·logue (**proh**-lawg) *noun* The introductory section of a literary work or a musical composition.

pro·long (pruh-**lawng**) *verb* To make something last longer. ▶ *verb* **prolonging, prolonged**

prom (prahm) *noun* A formal dance for high-school students that is usually held near the end of the school year.

prom·e·nade (*prah*-muh-**nade** *or* *prah*-muh-**nahd**)
noun 1. A walk taken for pleasure. 2. A place for taking a leisurely walk.
verb To walk for pleasure.
▶ *verb* **promenading, promenaded**

prom·i·nent (**prah**-muh-nuhnt)
adjective 1. Very noticeable. 2. Famous or important.
▶ *noun* **prominence**

prom·ise (**prah**-mis)
verb To declare that you will definitely do a particular thing, or that a particular thing will happen.
noun 1. A pledge given by someone that he or she will do something. 2. The likelihood of doing well in the future.
▶ *verb* **promising, promised**
▶ *adjective* **promising**

prom·on·tor·y (**prah**-muhn-tor-ee) *noun* A high point of land or rock that sticks out into a body of water.

pro·mote (pruh-**mote**) *verb* 1. To move someone to a higher job or to a higher grade in school. 2. To help with the growth or development of something. 3. To make the public aware of something or someone.
▶ *verb* **promoting, promoted**

pro·mo·tion (pruh-**moh**-shuhn) *noun* 1. Advancement to a higher job or a higher grade in school. 2. Encouragement or publicity.

P

prompt (prahmpt)
adjective 1. Immediate, without delay.
2. On time.
noun A reminder or encouragement to do something.
verb 1. To move someone to action.
2. To remind actors of their lines when they have forgotten them during a play.
▶ *verb* **prompting, prompted**
▶ *adjective* **prompter, promptest**
▶ *noun* **prompter** ▶ *adverb* **promptly**

prone (prohn) *adjective* 1. Likely to act, feel, or be a certain way. 2. Lying with your face down.

prong (prahng) *noun* One of the sharp points of a fork or other tool.

prong·horn (**prahng**-horn) *noun* A wild animal with horns that lives in western North America. Pronghorns look a little like antelopes, but they are not closely related to any other animals.

pro·noun (**proh**-noun) *noun* A word that takes the place of a noun. The words *I*, *you*, *him*, and *it* are all pronouns.

pro·nounce (pruh-**nouns**) *verb* 1. To say words or sounds in a particular way.
2. To make a formal announcement.
▶ *verb* **pronouncing, pronounced**
▶ *noun* **pronouncement**

pro·nun·ci·a·tion (pruh-*nuhn*-see-**ay**-shuhn) *noun* The way a word is pronounced.

proof (proof) *noun* Facts or evidence that something is true.

proof·read (**proof**-reed) *verb* To read something carefully and correct any mistakes in spelling, punctuation, and grammar that you find. ▶ *verb* **proofreading, proofread** ▶ *noun* **proofreader**

prop (prahp)
verb To support something in order to keep it from falling down.
noun 1. Something used as a support.
2. Any item other than costumes or furniture that appears on a stage or a movie set. Prop is short for *property*.
▶ *verb* **propping, propped**

prop·a·gan·da (*prah*-puh-**gan**-duh) *noun* Information that is spread to influence the way people think, to gain supporters, or to damage an opposing group. Propaganda is often incomplete or biased information.

pro·pel (pruh-**pel**) *verb* To push something forward. ▶ *verb* **propelling, propelled**

pro·pel·lant (pruh-**pel**-uhnt) *noun*
1. A chemical or fuel that propels something when it is burned. 2. A compressed gas or a liquid that releases the contents of an aerosol can.

pro·pel·ler (pruh-**pel**-ur) *noun* A set of rotating blades that provide force to move an object through air or water.

prop·er (**prah**-pur) *adjective* 1. Right or suitable for a given purpose or occasion. 2. Stiffly formal or respectable.

prop·er·ly (**prah**-pur-lee) *adverb* 1. In a correct, appropriate, or suitable way.
2. In an exact or strict sense.

prop·er noun (**prah**-pur **noun**) *noun* The name of a particular person, place, or thing, such as *Jane*, *New York*, and *Washington Monument*. A proper noun begins with a capital letter.

prop·er·ty (**prah**-pur-tee) *noun*
1. Anything that is owned by an individual. 2. Buildings and land belonging to a person or a company.
3. A special quality or characteristic of something.
▶ *noun, plural* **properties**

proph·e·cy (**prah**-fuh-see) *noun* A prediction. ▶ *noun, plural* **prophecies** ▶ *verb* **prophesy** (**prah**-fuh-*sye*)

proph·et (**prah**-fit) *noun* 1. A person who speaks or claims to speak for God.
2. A person who predicts the future. **Prophet** sounds like **profit**.

pro·por·tion (pruh-**por**-shuhn) *noun* 1. A part of something. 2. The size, number, or amount of something in relation to another thing. 3. In mathematics, a statement that two ratios are equal. 4. **in proportion** The correct size in relation to something else.

P

noun, plural **proportions** The measurements or size of something. ▶ adjective **proportional** ▶ adverb **proportionally**

pro·pos·al (pruh-**poh**-zuhl) noun 1. A plan or suggestion for others to consider. 2. An offer of marriage.

pro·pose (pruh-**poze**) verb 1. To suggest an idea or a course of action. 2. To ask someone to marry you.
▶ verb **proposing, proposed** ▶ noun **proposal**

pro·po·si·tion (prah-puh-**zish**-uhn) noun 1. An offer or a suggestion. 2. Anything brought up for discussion.

pro·pul·sion (pruh-**puhl**-shuhn) noun 1. The force by which a vehicle or some other object is pushed along. 2. The act of moving forward by means of some kind of force.

prose (proze) noun Ordinary written or spoken language, as opposed to verse or poetry. Short stories and essays are examples of prose.

pros·e·cute (**prah**-si-kyoot) verb To begin and carry out a legal action in a court of law against a person accused of a crime.

pros·e·cu·tion (prah-si-**kyoo**-shuhn) noun The side in a lawsuit that represents the person bringing a complaint or accusing someone of a crime.

pros·e·cu·tor (**prah**-si-kyoo-tur) noun A lawyer who represents the government in criminal trials.

pros·pect (**prahs**-pekt)
noun 1. Something that is looked forward to or expected. 2. A wide view of a landscape. 3. A possible customer or a possible winner in a political or athletic contest.
verb To explore or search for something, especially gold or silver.
▶ verb **prospecting, prospected**
▶ noun **prospector**

pro·spec·tive (pruh-**spek**-tiv) adjective 1. Possible or likely. 2. Future or likely to become.

pro·spec·tus (pruh-**spek**-tuhs) noun A brochure giving information about a company or any organization. ▶ noun, plural **prospectuses**

pros·per (**prahs**-pur) verb To succeed or thrive. ▶ verb **prospering, prospered** ▶ noun **prosperity** (prah-**sper**-i-tee) ▶ adjective **prosperous**

pros·the·sis (prahs-**thee**-sis) noun An artificial device that replaces a missing part of a body. ▶ noun, plural **prostheses** (prahs-**thee**-seez)

pro·tect (pruh-**tekt**) verb To guard or keep something safe from harm, attack, or injury. ▶ verb **protecting, protected** ▶ noun **protector**

pro·tec·tion (pruh-**tek**-shuhn) noun 1. The act of protecting something. 2. The state of being protected.

pro·tec·tive (pruh-**tek**-tiv) adjective 1. Intended to protect someone or something from harm, damage, or destruction. 2. Having a strong wish to keep someone or something safe from harm or injury.

pro·tein (**proh**-teen) noun A type of chemical compound found in all living plant and animal cells. Foods such as meat, cheese, eggs, beans, and fish are sources of dietary protein.

pro·test
verb (pruh-**test**) To object strongly to something.
noun (**proh**-test) 1. A demonstration or statement against something. 2. An objection to something.
▶ verb **protesting, protested**

Prot·es·tant (**prah**-tuh-stuhnt)
noun A Christian who does not belong to either the Roman Catholic Church or the Eastern Orthodox Church.
adjective Of or having to do with any of the Protestant Churches.

pro·tist (**proh**-tist) noun Any organism from the kingdom Protista. Protists include amoebas, paramecia, and some algae.

pro·to·col (**proh**-tuh-kawl) noun 1. The correct and official rules for the way something should be done or arranged. 2. An international agreement about a particular subject. 3. A set of rules about how data is moved between computers or over a network so that no information is lost.

P

pro·ton (**proh**-tahn) *noun* One of the very small parts in the nucleus of an atom. A proton carries a positive electrical charge.

pro·to·plasm (**proh**-tuh-*plaz*-uhm) *noun* The colorless, jellylike material that makes up the living part of all cells.

pro·to·type (**proh**-tuh-*tipe*) *noun* The first version of an invention that tests an idea to see if it will work.

pro·to·zo·an (*proh*-tuh-**zoh**-uhn) *noun* A microscopic animal with one cell that reproduces by dividing. Paramecia and amoebas are protozoans.
▶ *noun, plural* **protozoans** or **protozoa** (*proh*-tuh-**zoh**-uh)

pro·trac·tor (proh-**trak**-tur) *noun* A semicircular instrument used for measuring and drawing angles. Protractors are marked off in degrees.

pro·trude (proh-**trood**) *verb* To extend beyond, above, or into something. ▶ *verb* **protruding, protruded** ▶ *noun* **protrusion** (proh-**troo**-zhuhn)

proud (proud) *adjective* **1.** Pleased and satisfied with what you or someone else has achieved. **2.** Having self-respect and a sense of your own worth. **3.** Having too high an opinion of your own value or abilities.
▶ *adjective* **prouder, proudest**

prove (proov) *verb* To demonstrate definitely that something is true. ▶ *verb* **proving, proved**

prov·erb (**prah**-vurb) *noun* A familiar saying that tells a common truth. "A stitch in time saves nine" is a proverb. ▶ *adjective* **proverbial**

pro·vide (pruh-**vide**)
verb **1.** To make something available for use. **2.** To set down as a rule or condition.
conjunction **provided** On condition that; as long as.
▶ *verb* **providing, provided** ▶ *noun* **provider**

prov·ince (**prah**-vins) *noun* A district or a region of some countries. Canada is made up of provinces.

pro·vin·cial (pruh-**vin**-shuhl) *adjective* **1.** Of or having to do with a province.

2. Narrow-minded or having a limited or prejudiced point of view.

pro·vi·sion (pruh-**vizh**-uhn)
noun **1.** The act of providing something. **2.** Something that is named as a condition in an agreement, a law, or a document.
noun, plural **provisions** A supply of groceries or food.

pro·vi·sion·al (pruh-**vizh**-uh-nuhl) *adjective* Temporary or not yet final. ▶ *adverb* **provisionally**

pro·voke (pruh-**voke**) *verb* **1.** To annoy someone and make the person angry. **2.** To bring on or to arouse.
▶ *verb* **provoking, provoked** ▶ *noun* **provocation** (*prah*-vuh-**kay**-shuhn)
▶ *adjective* **provocative** (pruh-**vah**-kuh-tiv)

prow (prou) *noun* The bow or front part of a boat or ship.

prow·ess (**prou**-is) *noun* Skill or bravery.

prowl (proul) *verb* To move around quietly and secretly, like an animal looking for prey. ▶ *verb* **prowling, prowled** ▶ *noun* **prowler**

prox·im·i·ty (prahk-**sim**-i-tee) *noun* Nearness in space, time, or relationship.

pru·dent (**proo**-duhnt) *adjective* Cautious, giving thought to the future or to the consequences of your actions. ▶ *noun* **prudence** (**proo**-duhns) ▶ *adverb* **prudently**

prune (proon)
noun A dried plum.
verb To cut off branches from a tree or bush in order to increase its growth.
▶ *verb* **pruning, pruned**

pry (prye) *verb* **1.** To inquire too closely into someone else's business. **2.** To remove, raise, or pull apart with force, as with a lever. **3.** To get with difficulty or much effort.
▶ *verb* **pries, prying, pried**

P.S. (pee-es) *noun* Short for **postscript** or **public school.**

psalm (sahm) *noun* A religious song or poem, especially one from the Book of Psalms in the Bible.

pseu·do·nym (**soo**-duh-nim) *noun* A false name, especially one used by an author instead of his or her real name.

P

psy·chi·a·trist (sye-**kye**-uh-trist) *noun* A medical doctor who is trained to treat emotional and mental illness. ▶ *noun* **psychiatry** ▶ *adjective* **psychiatric** (*sye-kee-***at**-rik)

psy·chic (**sye**-kik)
adjective Seeming or claiming to be able to tell what people are thinking or to predict the future.
noun Someone who is thought to have, or who claims to have, psychic powers.

psy·cho·log·i·cal (*sye*-kuh-**lah**-ji-kuhl) *adjective* **1.** Of or having to do with psychology. **2.** Having to do with or arising from the mind.

psy·chol·o·gist (sye-**kah**-luh-jist) *noun* A person who studies people's minds and emotions and the ways that people behave.

psy·chol·o·gy (sye-**kah**-luh-jee) *noun* The study of the mind, the emotions, and human behavior.

psy·cho·path (**sye**-kuh-*path*) *noun* A person who is mentally unbalanced, especially a person who is violent or dangerous. ▶ *adjective* **psychopathic**

pter·o·dac·tyl (*ter*-uh-**dak**-til) *noun* A prehistoric flying reptile with wide wings supported by very large fourth fingers.

pub (puhb) *noun* A bar where adults can go to drink alcohol.

pu·ber·ty (**pyoo**-bur-tee) *noun* The time when a person's body changes from a child's to an adult's.

pub·lic (**puhb**-lik)
adjective **1.** Of or having to do with the people or the community. **2.** Belonging or available to everybody. **3.** Working for the government of a town, city, or country.
adverb **in public** In front of or among other people.
noun **the public** People in general.
▶ *adverb* **publicly**

pub·li·ca·tion (*puhb*-li-**kay**-shuhn) *noun* **1.** A book, magazine, or newspaper. **2.** The production and distribution of a book, magazine, or newspaper.

pub·lic do·main (**puhb**-lik doh-**mayn**) *noun* The state of being unprotected by copyright and therefore available to everyone to use or copy.

pub·lic·i·ty (puh-**blis**-i-tee) *noun* Information about a person or an event that is given out to get the public's attention or approval.

pub·li·cize (**puhb**-li-size) *verb* To make something known to as many people as possible. ▶ *verb* **publicizing, publicized**

pub·lic o·pin·ion (**puhb**-lik uh-**pin**-yuhn) *noun* The views or beliefs of most of the people in a town, city, or country, usually found out through a public opinion poll.

pub·lic re·la·tions (**puhb**-lik ri-**lay**-shuhnz) *noun, plural* The methods or activities an organization or a business uses to promote goodwill or a good image with the public.

pub·lic school (**puhb**-lik *skool*) *noun* A school supported by tax money, offering free education to students who live within a certain area.

pub·lish (**puhb**-lish) *verb* To produce and distribute a book, magazine, newspaper, or any other material so that many people can read it. ▶ *verb* **publishes, publishing, published** ▶ *noun* **publisher** ▶ *noun* **publishing**

puck (puhk) *noun* A hard, round, flat piece of rubber used in ice hockey.

puck·er (**puhk**-ur)
verb To wrinkle, fold, or draw together.
noun A small fold or wrinkle.
▶ *verb* **puckering, puckered**

pud·ding (**pud**-ing) *noun* A sweet, soft dessert.

pud·dle (**puhd**-uhl) *noun* A small pool of water or other liquid.

pueb·lo (**pweb**-loh) *noun* **1.** A village consisting of stone and adobe buildings built next to and on top of each other. Pueblos were built by Native American tribes in the southwestern United States. **2. Pueblo** A member of a Native American tribe of New Mexico and Arizona.
▶ *noun, plural* **Pueblo** or **Pueblos**
▶ *noun, plural* **pueblos**

P

Puer·to Ri·co (**pwer**-toh **ree**-koh *or* **por**-tuh **ree**-koh) An unincorporated territory of the United States, located in the northeastern Caribbean Sea. It consists of a main island and several smaller ones, and it is a popular vacation destination for Americans.

puff (puhf)
noun **1.** A short, sudden burst of air, breath, or smoke. **2.** Anything that looks soft, light, and fluffy.
verb **1.** To blow or come out in puffs. **2. puff up** To swell.
▶ *verb* **puffing, puffed** ▶ *adjective* **puffy**

puf·fin (**puhf**-in) *noun* A seabird of northern regions that has black and white feathers, a short neck, and a colorful beak.

pug (puhg) *noun* A dog with short hair, a flat nose, a wrinkled face, and a curled tail.

pug·na·cious (puhg-**nay**-shuhs) *adjective* Eager to pick fights. ▶ *adverb* **pugnaciously**

pull (pul)
verb **1.** To move something forward or toward you. **2.** To tug or pluck something. **3.** To stretch or strain a part of the body. **4. pull off** To do something with great success. **5. pull out** To withdraw from an activity. **6. pull through** To get through a hard, painful, or dangerous time.
noun **1.** The act of pulling something, or the effort required to pull something. **2.** Attraction or influence.
▶ *verb* **pulling, pulled**

pul·ley (**pul**-ee) *noun* **1.** A wheel with a grooved rim around which a rope or chain can run. A pulley is used to lift heavy loads more easily. **2.** A lifting machine made from a rope or chain and a set of pulleys linked together.

pull·o·ver (**pul**-oh-vur) *noun* A shirt or sweater that you can pull over your head.

pulp (puhlp)
noun **1.** The soft, juicy, or fleshy part of fruits and vegetables. **2.** Any soft, wet mixture. **3.** The soft inner part of a tooth.

verb To crush or reduce something to a soft, wet mixture.
▶ *verb* **pulping, pulped**

pul·pit (**puhl**-pit) *noun* A raised, enclosed platform in a church where a minister stands to speak to a congregation.

pul·sate (**puhl**-sate) *verb* To beat, vibrate, or change in intensity regularly. ▶ *verb* **pulsating, pulsated**

pulse (puhls)
noun A steady beat or throb, especially the feeling of the heart moving blood through your body.
verb To beat or pulsate.
▶ *verb* **pulsing, pulsed**

pu·ma (**pyoo**-muh *or* **poo**-muh) *noun* Another name for **cougar, mountain lion,** and **panther.**

pum·ice (**puhm**-is) *noun* A light, grayish volcanic rock that is used for cleaning, smoothing, or polishing.

pum·mel (**puhm**-uhl) *verb* To punch someone or something repeatedly. ▶ *verb* **pummeling, pummeled**

pump (puhmp)
noun A machine that forces liquids or gases from one place to another.
verb **1.** To empty or fill using a pump. **2.** To keep asking someone questions.
noun, plural **pumps** Plain women's shoes with a medium to high heel.
▶ *verb* **pumping, pumped**

pump·kin (**puhmp**-kin) *noun* A big, round, orange squash with a thick rind and many seeds that grows on a vine along the ground. People often carve faces in pumpkins at Halloween.

pun (puhn)
noun A joke based on one word that has two meanings or two words that sound the same but have different meanings.
verb To make a pun.
▶ *verb* **punning, punned**

punch (puhnch)
verb **1.** To hit someone or something with your fist. **2.** To make a hole in something.
noun **1.** The action of hitting someone with force, or the impact of this.

P

2. A drink made by mixing several ingredients, usually fruit juices and soda. **3.** A metal tool for making holes. **4. punch line** The last line of a joke or story that makes it funny or surprising.
▶ *noun, plural* **punches** ▶ *verb* **punches, punching, punched** ▶ *noun* **puncher**

punc·tu·al (**puhngk**-choo-uhl) *adjective* Arriving or happening right on time. ▶ *noun* **punctuality** (puhnk-choo-**al**-i-tee) ▶ *adverb* **punctually**

punc·tu·a·tion (puhngk-choo-**ay**-shuhn) *noun* **1.** The use of periods, commas, and other marks to help make the meaning of written material clear. **2.** One or more punctuation marks.
▶ *verb* **punctuate**

punc·tu·a·tion mark (puhngk-choo-**ay**-shuhn *mahrk*) *noun* A written mark, such as a comma, period, colon, semicolon, question mark, or exclamation point, used in writing.

punc·ture (**puhngk**-chur) *noun* A hole made by a sharp object. *verb* To make a hole in something.
▶ *verb* **puncturing, punctured**

pun·gent (**puhn**-juhnt) *adjective* Having a strong or sharp smell or taste.

pun·ish (**puhn**-ish) *verb* To inflict a penalty for committing a crime or to make a person suffer for behaving badly. ▶ *verb* **punishes, punishing, punished**

pun·ish·ment (**puhn**-ish-muhnt) *noun* The act of punishing someone, or the penalty imposed on someone who is punished.

punk (puhngk) *noun* **1.** (slang) A young person who is always getting into trouble. **2.** A style of music and dress that became popular in the late 1970s. People who dressed in this style wore black clothes, used safety pins for decoration, and had brightly colored hair. **3. punk rock** Loud, hard rock music that became popular in the late 1970s.

punt (puhnt) *noun* A boat with a flat bottom that you push along with a long pole.

verb To kick a football or soccer ball dropped from the hands before it strikes the ground.
▶ *verb* **punting, punted** ▶ *noun* **punter**

pu·ny (**pyoo**-nee) *adjective* Small and weak, or unimportant. ▶ *adjective* **punier, puniest** ▶ *noun* **puniness** ▶ *adverb* **punily** (**pyoo**-nuh-lee)

pu·pa (**pyoo**-puh) *noun* An insect in an inactive stage of development between a larva and an adult. ▶ *noun, plural* **pupas** or **pupae** (**pyoo**-pee)

pu·pil (**pyoo**-puhl) *noun* **1.** A person who is being taught, especially in school. **2.** The round, black center of your eye that lets light enter.

pup·pet (**puhp**-it) *noun* A movable model in the shape of a person or an animal that you control by pulling strings that are attached to it or by moving your hand inside it.

pup·py (**puhp**-ee) *noun* A dog that is not fully grown. ▶ *noun, plural* **puppies**

pur·chase (**pur**-chuhs) *verb* To buy something. *noun* **1.** Something that has been bought. **2.** The act of purchasing.
▶ *verb* **purchasing, purchased** ▶ *noun* **purchaser**

pure (pyoor) *adjective* **1.** Not mixed with anything else. **2.** Not dirty or not polluted. **3.** Innocent or free from evil or guilt. **4.** Complete or nothing but.
▶ *adjective* **purer, purest** ▶ *noun* **purity** (**pyoor**-i-tee)

pure·bred (**pyoor**-bred) *adjective* Having ancestors of the same breed or kind of animal.

pu·ree *or* **pu·rée** (pyoo-**ray**) *noun* A thick paste made from food that has been put through a sieve or blender. *verb* To make a puree.
▶ *verb* **pureeing** *or* **puréeing, pureed** *or* **puréed**

purge (purj) *verb* To clean thoroughly by getting rid of unwanted items. *noun* The act or process of getting rid of unwanted people or things.
▶ *verb* **purging, purged**

P

pu·ri·fy (**pyoor**-uh-*fye*) *verb* To make something pure or clean. ▸ *verb* **purifies, purifying, purified** ▸ *noun* **purification** (*pyoor-uh-fi-kay-shuhn*)

Pur·i·tan (**pyoor**-i-tuhn) *noun* One of a group of Protestants in 16th- and 17th-century England who sought simple church services and a strict moral code. Many Puritans fled from England and settled in America.

pur·ple (**pur**-puhl)
noun The color that is made by mixing red and blue.
adjective Having the color purple.
▸ *adjective* **purpler, purplest**

pur·pose (**pur**-puhs) *noun* 1. A goal or an aim. 2. The reason why something is made or done, or an object's function. 3. **on purpose** Deliberately rather than by accident.
▸ *adjective* **purposeful**

pur·pose·ly (**pur**-puhs-lee) *adverb* With a particular effect in mind; on purpose.

purr (pur)
verb 1. To make a low, vibrating sound in the throat. 2. To make a low, vibrating sound like a cat.
noun A purring sound, like that made by a cat.
Purr sounds like **per**. ▸ *verb* **purring, purred**

purse (purs)
noun 1. A handbag or a pocketbook. 2. A small container for carrying money. 3. A sum of money given as a prize in an athletic contest.
verb **purse your lips** To press your lips together into wrinkles.
▸ *verb* **pursing, pursed**

pur·sue (pur-**soo**) *verb* 1. To follow or chase someone in order to catch him or her. 2. To continue something. 3. To try to accomplish a goal.
▸ *verb* **pursuing, pursued** ▸ *noun* **pursuer**

pur·suit (pur-**soot**) *noun* 1. A chase, in order to catch someone or something. 2. An activity, hobby, or interest.

pus (puhs) *noun* A thick, yellow liquid that comes out of an infected wound or sore.

push (push)
verb 1. To make something move by pressing on or against it. 2. To shove or press roughly. 3. To use your hands or arms to press past someone or something. 4. To try very hard to sell or do something. 5. To try to make someone do something.
noun 1. An act of pushing or shoving. 2. A great effort or drive.
▸ *verb* **pushes, pushing, pushed** ▸ *noun, plural* **pushes** ▸ *noun* **pusher**

push-up (**push**-uhp) *noun* An exercise in which you raise your body off the floor from a facedown position by pushing with your arms.

pus·sy wil·low (**pus**-ee **wil**-oh) *noun* A shrub with gray, furry flowers on long, thin branches.

put (put) *verb* 1. To place or lay something. 2. To state in words. 3. To cause someone to undergo or experience something. 4. **put away** To put something where it is stored when not in use. 5. **put down** To insult someone. 6. **put off** To delay doing something. 7. **put someone up** To let the person sleep overnight at your house. 8. **put up with** To tolerate something or allow it to continue.
▸ *verb* **putting, put**

putt (puht)
verb To hit a golf ball lightly into the hole on a green.
noun A gentle stroke with a golf club.
▸ *verb* **putting, putted** ▸ *noun* **putter**

put·ter (**puht**-ur) *verb* To work aimlessly without getting much done. ▸ *verb* **puttering, puttered**

put·ty (**puht**-ee) *noun* A kind of soft cement made of powdered chalk and linseed oil. It dries hard and is used to fasten windows into frames and to fill holes in wood.

put-upon (**put**-uh-pahn) *adjective* Treated unfairly or taken advantage of.

puz·zle (**puhz**-uhl)
noun 1. A game or an activity that involves solving a mystery, a problem, or a complex task. 2. Someone or something that is hard to understand.
verb To make someone confused

or unsure.
▶ *verb* **puzzling, puzzled** ▶ *adjective* **puzzled** ▶ *adjective* **puzzling**

py·lon (**pye**-lahn) *noun* A tall metal tower that supports electrical cables.

pyr·a·mid (**pir**-uh-mid) *noun* **1.** A solid shape with a polygon as a base and triangular sides that meet at a point on top. Most pyramids have a square base and four sides. **2.** An ancient Egyptian stone monument where pharaohs and their treasures were buried.

Pyr·e·nees (**pir**-uh-*neez*) A mountain range of southwestern Europe that forms a border between France and Spain. The Pyrenees extend for about 300 miles (482 kilometers), reaching the Mediterranean Sea at their southeastern end and the Atlantic at their northwestern tip.

py·thon (**pye**-thahn) *noun* A large, powerful snake that wraps itself around its prey and crushes it.

Qa·tar (**kah**-tahr *or* kuh-**tahr**) A country in the Middle East on the northeast coast of the Arabian Peninsula. Qatar is rich in oil and natural gas reserves, and its citizens have a high standard of living, with one of the highest per capita incomes in the world.

qt. (kwort) Short for **quart** or the plural form **quarts.**

quack (kwak)
verb To make the sound that is typical of a duck.
noun **1.** The sound made by a duck.
2. A dishonest person who pretends to be a doctor or have medical skills.
adjective Characteristic of a quack.
▶ *verb* **quacking, quacked**

quad (kwahd) *noun* A rectangular yard with buildings around it, especially at a college. Quad is short for **quadrangle.**

quad·ran·gle (**kwahd**-*rang*-guhl) *noun*
1. A closed shape with four sides and four angles; a quadrilateral. **2.** A quad, as at a college.

quad·rant (**kwahd**-ruhnt) *noun* A quarter of a circle, or a quarter of its circumference.

quad·ri·lat·er·al (*kwahd*-ruh-**lat**-ur-uhl) *noun* A closed shape with four straight sides and four angles. Squares and rectangles are quadrilaterals.
adjective Having four straight sides.

quad·ru·ped (**kwahd**-ruh-*ped*) *noun* An animal with four feet. Horses are quadrupeds.

qua·dru·ple (kwah-**droo**-puhl *or* **kwahd**-ruh-puhl)
verb To multiply something by four.
adjective Four times as many, or as big.
▶ *verb* **quadrupling, quadrupled**

qua·dru·plet (kwah-**droo**-plit) *noun* One of four babies born at the same time to one mother.

quag·mire (**kwag**-mire) *noun* **1.** A wet and muddy area of ground. **2.** A situation that is difficult to get out of.

qua·hog (**kwaw**-*hawg*) *noun* A round clam that you can eat. Quahogs have thick, heavy shells and are found on the eastern coast of North America. The word *quahog* is of Native American origin.

quail (kwayl) *noun* A small, fat bird with a short tail and gray or brown feathers. ▶ *noun, plural* **quail** *or* **quails**

quaint (kwaynt) *adjective* Old-fashioned, charming, and attractive. ▶ *adjective* **quainter, quaintest** ▶ *noun* **quaintness** ▶ *adverb* **quaintly**

quake (kwake)
verb **1.** To shake or tremble, especially with fear. **2.** To shake or to tremble.
noun **1.** An earthquake, or a trembling of the ground. **2.** Any trembling or shaking.
▶ *verb* **quaking, quaked**

Quak·er (**kway**-kur) *noun* A member of the Society of Friends, a Christian group founded in 1660 that prefers simple religious services and opposes war.

qual·i·fi·ca·tion (*kwahl*-uh-fi-**kay**-shuhn) *noun* A skill or an ability that makes you able to do a job or a task.

qual·i·fied (**kwah**-luh-fide) *adjective* Meeting the necessary standards or conditions.

qual·i·fy (**kwah**-luh-*fye*) *verb* 1. To reach a standard or level that allows you to do something. 2. To limit or restrict something you have just said in order to make it more specific or less severe. 3. To limit or modify the meaning of a word or phrase.
▸ *verb* **qualifies, qualifying, qualified**

qual·i·ty (**kwah**-li-tee) *noun* 1. The degree of excellence of something. 2. A special characteristic of something or someone.
▸ *noun, plural* **qualities**

qualm (kwahm *or* kwahlm) *noun* 1. A feeling of concern or doubt over whether what you are doing is right or wrong. 2. A brief, sudden feeling of sickness.

quan·da·ry (**kwahn**-dur-ee) *noun* If you are **in a quandary,** you are in a difficult situation and do not know what to do about it. ▸ *noun, plural* **quandaries**

quan·ti·ty (**kwahn**-ti-tee) *noun* 1. A number or amount. 2. A large number or amount.
▸ *noun, plural* **quantities**

quan·tum leap (**kwahn**-tuhm **leep**) *noun* A sudden, extremely large change or improvement.

quan·tum the·o·ry (**kwahn**-tuhm *thee*-ur-ee) *noun* A scientific method for describing matter and energy at a level smaller than atoms.

quar·an·tine (**kwor**-uhn-teen) *noun* A situation in which a person, animal, or plant is kept away from others for a period of time to stop a disease from spreading.
verb To isolate or keep separate.
▸ *verb* **quarantining, quarantined**

quark (kwork) *noun* In physics, any of several particles that are believed to

come in pairs. A quark is smaller than an atom.

quar·rel (**kwor**-uhl)
verb 1. To disagree or argue. 2. To find fault.
noun An argument, especially between people who know each other well.
▸ *verb* **quarreling, quarreled**

quar·rel·some (**kwor**-uhl-suhm) *adjective* If you are **quarrelsome,** you tend to argue a lot with other people.

quar·ry (**kwor**-ee)
noun 1. A place where stone, slate, or sand is dug from the ground. 2. A person or an animal that is being hunted or chased.
verb To take stone or some other material from a quarry.
▸ *noun, plural* **quarries** ▸ *verb* **quarries, quarrying, quarried**

quart (kwort) *noun* A unit of liquid measure equal to 32 ounces, or two pints.

quar·ter (**kwor**-tur)
noun 1. One of four equal parts of something. 2. A coin of the United States and Canada equal to 25 cents. 3. One of four equal periods that make up a game such as football or basketball. 4. An area of a town.
noun, plural **quarters** Rooms where people such as soldiers live, especially as part of their job.
verb 1. To divide into quarters. 2. To provide people, usually soldiers, with food and a place to sleep.
▸ *verb* **quartering, quartered**

quar·ter·back (**kwor**-tur-*bak*) *noun* In football, the player who leads the offense by throwing the ball or handing it to a runner.

quart·er·ly (**kwor**-tur-lee)
adjective Happening once every three months.
adverb Once every three months.

quar·tet (kwor-**tet**) *noun* 1. A piece of music that is written to be played or sung by four people. 2. Four people who play music or sing together.

quartz (kworts) *noun* A hard mineral that is used to make very accurate clocks, watches, and electronic equipment.

Q

qua·sar (**kway**-zahr) *noun* An object in space that is larger than a star but smaller than a galaxy. Quasars give off powerful radio waves and huge amounts of light and radioactivity.

quash (kwahsh) *verb* 1. To stop something from continuing, especially by force. 2. To officially decide that a legal decision is no longer valid.
▶ *verb* **quashes, quashing, quashed**

qua·ver (**kway**-vur)
verb If your voice **quavers,** it sounds unsteady.
noun A quivering sound or tremble in a voice.
▶ *verb* **quavering, quavered**

quay (kee) *noun* A place built on land near water where boats can stop to load or unload goods or passengers. **Quay** sounds like **key.**

quea·sy (**kwee**-zee) *adjective* 1. Sick to your stomach or nauseated. 2. Uneasy or troubled.
▶ *adjective* **queasier, queasiest** ▶ *noun* **queasiness**

Que·bec (kwuh-**bek** *or* kuh-**bek**) A province in east-central Canada. It is the only Canadian province whose sole official language is French.

queen (kween) *noun* 1. A female ruler of a country who comes from a royal family. 2. The wife of a king. 3. A playing card that has a picture of a queen on it. 4. The most powerful chess piece. It can move in any direction. 5. A female bee, wasp, or ant that can lay eggs.

queer (kweer) *adjective* Strange or odd. ▶ *adjective* **queerer, queerest** ▶ *adverb* **queerly**

quell (kwel) *verb* To stop something happening, especially by force. ▶ *verb* **quelling, quelled**

quench (kwench) *verb* 1. If you **quench** your thirst, you drink something until you are no longer thirsty. 2. If you **quench** a fire, you stop it from burning.
▶ *verb* **quenches, quenching, quenched**

que·ry (**kweer**-ee)
noun A question or request for information, especially because you have a doubt about something.
verb 1. To ask a question to. 2. To express doubt about something.
▶ *verb* **queries, querying, queried**
▶ *noun, plural* **queries**

que·sa·dil·la (*kay*-suh-**dee**-yuh) *noun* A folded, usually fried tortilla filled with a mixture of cheese and vegetables or meat.

quest (kwest)
noun 1. A long and difficult search. 2. A long journey made to do or to find something.
verb To search for something.
▶ *verb* **questing, quested**

ques·tion (**kwes**-chuhn)
noun 1. A sentence that asks for information. 2. A problem, or something that needs to be dealt with. 3. Doubt.
verb 1. To ask questions in order to get information. 2. To have suspicions or doubt about something.
▶ *verb* **questioning, questioned**

ques·tion mark (**kwes**-chuhn *mahrk*) *noun* The punctuation mark (?) used in writing at the end of a question.

ques·tion·naire (*kwes*-chuh-**nair**) *noun* A list of questions used to get information or to find out about people's opinions.

quet·zal (ket-**sahl**) *noun* A bird of Mexico and Central America with red and green feathers. The male has long tail feathers.

queue (kyoo)
noun 1. A line of people who are waiting for something. 2. A list of items or jobs on a computer that are dealt with in order.
verb 1. To add an item or job to a queue on a computer. 2. To form or wait in a line of people.
Queue sounds like **cue.** ▶ *verb* **queuing, queued**

quib·ble (**kwib**-uhl)
verb To argue about things that are not important.
noun A petty distinction or minor criticism.
▶ *verb* **quibbling, quibbled**

Q

quiche (keesh) *noun* A food like a pie made with a pastry crust and filled with eggs, milk, cheese, vegetables, and sometimes meat.

quick (kwik) *adjective* 1. Moving or doing something fast. 2. Done or happening in a short period of time. 3. Able to understand things fast.
▶ *adjective* **quicker, quickest** ▶ *verb* **quicken** ▶ *adverb* **quick**

quick·ly (**kwik**-lee) *adverb* Taking very little time.

quick·sand (**kwik**-sand) *noun* Loose, wet sand that is dangerous because you can sink into it.

qui·et (**kwye**-it)
adjective 1. Not loud. 2. Calm and peaceful.
noun The state of being quiet.
verb To make a person or group of people be quiet, or to become quiet.
▶ *adjective* **quieter, quietest** ▶ *verb* **quieting, quieted** ▶ *noun* **quietness** ▶ *adverb* **quietly**

quill (kwil) *noun* 1. The long, hollow central part of a feather. 2. One of the hollow, sharp spines on a porcupine. 3. **quill pen** A pen made from a bird's feather, with the end of its quill carved to form a point.

quilt (kwilt)
noun A warm, thick covering for a bed that usually has a decorative, stitched top layer of fabric.
verb To make or work on a quilt.
▶ *verb* **quilting, quilted**

quilt·ed (**kwil**-tid) *adjective* If material is **quilted,** it is padded with soft material and sewn in lines or patterns.

quin·tet (kwin-**tet**) *noun* 1. A piece of music that is written to be played or sung by five people. 2. Five people who play music or sing together.

quin·tup·let (kwin-**tuhp**-lit) *noun* One of five babies born at the same time to one mother.

quip (kwip)
noun A funny and clever remark.
verb To make a clever remark.
▶ *verb* **quipping, quipped**

quirk (kwurk) *noun* 1. An odd trait or a strange way of acting. 2. A sudden and strange thing that happens.
▶ *noun* **quirkiness** ▶ *adjective* **quirky**

quit (kwit) *verb* 1. To stop doing something. 2. To leave something, such as your job or school.
▶ *verb* **quitting, quit** or **quitted** ▶ *noun* **quitter**

quite (kwite) *adverb* 1. Entirely. 2. Actually or really. 3. Rather or very.

quiv·er (**kwiv**-ur)
verb To shake slightly.
noun 1. A container for arrows.
2. A shaking movement or sound.
▶ *verb* **quivering, quivered**

quix·ot·ic (kwik-**sah**-tik) *adjective* Showing imagination but not reasonable or practical.

quiz (kwiz)
noun A short test.
verb To ask someone a lot of questions about something.
▶ *noun, plural* **quizzes** ▶ *verb* **quizzes, quizzing, quizzed**

quo·ta (**kwoh**-tuh) *noun* A limit on an amount or share of something.

quo·ta·tion (kwoh-**tay**-shuhn) *noun* 1. A sentence or short passage from something such as a book, play, or speech that is repeated by someone else. 2. The act of repeating another person's words.

quo·ta·tion mark (kwoh-**tay**-shuhn mahrk) *noun* One of the punctuation marks (", ", ', or ') used in writing to show where speech begins and ends.

quote (kwote)
verb To repeat the exact words that someone else spoke or wrote.
noun A quotation.
▶ *verb* **quoting, quoted**

quo·tient (**kwoh**-shuhnt) *noun* The number that is the result when you divide one number by another.

QWERTY (**kwur**-tee) *adjective* Of or having to do with a standard English-language keyboard, in which the top row of letters from left to right begins *q,w,e,r,t,y.*

Q

R

rab·bi (**rab**-eye) *noun* A Jewish religious leader and teacher.

rab·bit (**rab**-it) *noun* A small, furry mammal with long ears that lives in a hole that it digs in the ground.

rab·ble (**rab**-uhl) *noun* A noisy crowd.

ra·bies (**ray**-beez) *noun* An often fatal disease that can affect humans, dogs, bats, and other warm-blooded animals. ▶ *adjective* **rabid** (**rab**-id)

rac·coon (ra-**koon**) *noun* A mammal with rings on its tail and black-and-white face markings that look like a mask.

race (rase)
noun **1.** A competition to see which person, animal, or vehicle is the fastest. **2.** One of the major groups into which human beings can be divided. People of the same race have similar physical characteristics, such as skin color, which are passed on from generation to generation.
verb **1.** To run, go, or move very fast. **2.** To have a race or to enter a car or an animal in a race.
▶ *verb* **racing, raced**

race car (**rase** *kahr*) *noun* A car designed to race at very high speeds.

race re·la·tions (**rase** ri-*lay*-shuhnz) *noun, plural* The way that people of different races get along with each other when they live in the same community.

race·track (**rase**-*trak*) *noun* A round or oval path that is used for racing.

ra·cial (**ray**-shuhl) *adjective* **1.** Of or having to do with a person's race. **2.** Between or among races.

rac·ist (**ray**-sist) *noun* A person who thinks that a particular race is better than others or treats people unfairly or cruelly because of their race. ▶ *noun* **racism** ▶ *adjective* **racist**

rack (rak)
noun **1.** A frame for holding or hanging things. **2.** An instrument of torture used in the past to stretch the body of a victim.
verb If you **rack your brain,** you try hard to remember something or figure something out.
▶ *verb* **racking, racked**

rack·et (**rak**-it) *noun* **1. racket** *or* **racquet** An oval stringed frame with a handle that you use in games such as tennis and badminton. **2.** A lot of noise; a din. **3.** A dishonest scheme or business activity.
▶ *noun, plural* **rackets** *or* **raquets**

rac·quet·ball (**rak**-it-*bawl*) *noun* A game played by two or four players who use short rackets to hit a small rubber ball against the walls, floor, and ceiling of an enclosed court.

ra·dar (**ray**-dahr) *noun* A way that ships and planes find solid objects by reflecting radio waves off them and by receiving the reflected waves. Radar is short for *radio detection and ranging*.

ra·di·al (**ray**-dee-uhl)
adjective **1.** Spreading out from the center or arranged like rays. **2.** Of or having to do with a kind of automobile or truck tire whose design makes it grip the road better than traditional tires.
noun A radial tire.

ra·di·ant (**ray**-dee-uhnt) *adjective* **1.** Shining brightly. **2.** If someone looks **radiant,** he or she looks very healthy and filled with happiness.
▶ *noun* **radiance**

ra·di·ate (**ray**-dee-*ate*) *verb* **1.** To give off rays of light or heat. **2.** To spread out from the center. **3.** To send out an emotion strongly.
▶ *verb* **radiating, radiated**

ra·di·a·tion (ray-dee-**ay**-shuhn) *noun* **1.** The giving off of energy in the form of light or heat. **2.** Atomic particles that are sent out from a radioactive substance.

ra·di·a·tor (**ray**-dee-*ay*-tur) *noun*
1. A series of pipes through which hot liquid, steam, or air circulates, sending heat into a room. 2. A metal device through which a liquid, usually water, circulates to cool a vehicle's engine.

rad·i·cal (**rad**-i-kuhl)
adjective 1. If a change is **radical,** it is thorough and has a wide range of important effects. 2. If a person is **radical,** he or she is in favor of extreme political change.
noun A person who is in favor of extreme political change.
▸ *adverb* **radically**

ra·di·o (**ray**-dee-oh)
noun 1. A way of communicating using electromagnetic waves broadcast from a central antenna. 2. A device that sends or receives these broadcasts and converts them into sound.
verb To send a message using radio signals.
▸ *verb* **radios, radioing, radioed**

ra·di·o·ac·tive (**ray**-dee-oh-**ak**-tiv)
adjective **Radioactive** materials are made up of atoms whose nuclei break down, giving off harmful radiation. ▸ *noun* **radioactivity**

ra·di·o but·ton (**ray**-dee-oh *buht*-uhn)
noun A small colored circle on a webpage that you can click to make something happen, such as choosing an option.

ra·di·og·ra·phy (**ray**-dee-**ah**-gruh-fee)
noun The science and techniques of taking X-ray photographs of people's bones or organs. ▸ *noun* **radiographer**

rad·ish (**rad**-ish) *noun* A crisp, small root vegetable, usually white inside with red skin, that you eat raw in salads. ▸ *noun, plural* **radishes**

ra·di·um (**ray**-dee-uhm) *noun* A highly radioactive chemical element sometimes used to treat cancer.

ra·di·us (**ray**-dee-uhs) *noun* 1. A straight line segment drawn from the exact center of a circle to its edge. 2. The outer bone in your lower arm. 3. The geographic area that makes a circle around a thing or a place.
▸ *noun, plural* **radii** (**ray**-dee-*eye*)

ra·don (**ray**-dahn) *noun* An odorless, colorless, radioactive gas that can seep up from the earth and rocks. Radon is a chemical element produced by radium.

raf·fle (**raf**-uhl)
noun A form of lottery to raise money by selling tickets and then giving small prizes to those holding winning tickets.
verb To offer something as a prize in a raffle.
▸ *verb* **raffling, raffled**

raft (raft)
noun 1. A floating platform made of wood and used to carry people or things. 2. An inflatable rubber boat that is propelled by oars.
verb To travel on a raft.
▸ *verb* **rafting, rafted** ▸ *noun* **rafting**

rag (rag)
noun An old, worn piece of material.
noun, plural **rags** Old, worn-out clothing, often ripped or torn.

rage (rayj)
noun Violent anger.
verb To happen with great force.
▸ *verb* **raging, raged**

rag·ged (**rag**-id) *adjective* Old, torn, and worn-out. ▸ *adjective* **raggedy** ▸ *adverb* **raggedly**

rag·time (**rag**-time) *noun* An early style of jazz having a strong, syncopated rhythm.

rag·weed (**rag**-weed) *noun* A weed whose pollen is a cause of hay fever in the fall.

raid (rayd)
noun 1. A sudden, surprise attack on a place. 2. A surprise visit by the police, especially to search for criminals or seize illegal drugs or stolen goods.
verb To carry out a raid on a place.
▸ *verb* **raiding, raided** ▸ *noun* **raider**

rail (rayl)
noun 1. A fixed bar supported by posts. 2. Railroad.
adjective Made of rails.

R

rail·ing (**ray**-ling) *noun* A wooden or metal bar that is a part of a fence or a staircase.

rail·road (**rayl**-rohd) *noun* 1. A track of double rails for a train. 2. A system of transport using trains.

rail·way (**rayl**-*way*) *noun* A railroad, or the tracks of a railroad.

rain (rayn)
noun 1. Water that falls in drops from clouds. 2. A falling of rain.
verb 1. To fall in rain. 2. To fall or pour like rain.
Rain sounds like **reign** and **rein.** ▸ *verb* **raining, rained** ▸ *adjective* **rainy**

rain·bow (**rayn**-boh) *noun* An arc of different colors caused by the bending of sunlight as it shines through water vapor.

rain·coat (**rayn**-koht) *noun* A waterproof coat that keeps you dry when it is raining.

rain·drop (**rayn**-*drahp*) *noun* A drop of rain.

rain·fall (**rayn**-*fawl*) *noun* The amount of rain that falls in a certain place during a period of time.

rain for·est (**rayn** *for*-ist) *noun* A dense, tropical forest where a lot of rain falls much of the year.

raise (rayz)
verb 1. To lift something to a higher position. 2. To assemble or collect something. 3. To take care of children or young animals until they are grown. 4. To ask or to bring up.
noun An increase in salary.
▸ *verb* **raising, raised**

rai·sin (**ray**-zin) *noun* A sweet grape that has been dried.

rake (rayk)
noun A garden tool with a row of teeth or prongs for working over soil or collecting leaves.
verb 1. To use a rake to level soil, collect leaves, cut grass, or the like. 2. (informal) If you **rake it in,** you make a lot of money, especially without working hard.
▸ *verb* **raking, raked**

ral·ly (**ral**-ee)
verb 1. To bring together again.

2. To join together to help or support a person or thing. 3. To regain strength, energy, or health.
noun 1. A large meeting for a purpose. 2. A long exchange of shots before a point is scored in a game such as tennis or badminton.
▸ *noun, plural* **rallies** ▸ *verb* **rallies, rallying, rallied**

ram (ram)
noun A male sheep.
verb 1. To crash into something with great force. 2. To force something into a space.
▸ *verb* **ramming, rammed**

RAM (ram) *noun* The part of a computer's memory that is lost when you turn the computer off. RAM is short for *random access memory.*

Ram·a·dan (*rah*-muh-**dahn**) *noun* The ninth month of the Muslim year, when Muslims fast each day from sunrise to sunset.

ram·ble (**ram**-buhl)
verb 1. To wander around without direction or purpose. 2. To go on a long walk for pleasure. 3. To speak for a long time or write a lot without sticking to the point.
noun A walk that is taken for pleasure.
▸ *verb* **rambling, rambled** ▸ *noun* **rambler**

ram·bling (**ram**-bling) *adjective* Going or growing in many directions.

ramp (ramp) *noun* A sloping passageway or roadway linking one level with another.

ram·page (**ram**-payj)
noun If someone goes **on a rampage,** the person rushes around in a violent and excited way.
verb To rush around in a violent and excited way.
▸ *verb* **rampaging, rampaged**

ram·pant (**ram**-puhnt) *adjective* Wild and without restraint.

ram·part (**ram**-pahrt) *noun* A wall or embankment surrounding a fort or castle, built to protect against attack.

ram·shack·le (**ram**-*shak*-uhl) *adjective* Rickety, poorly built, or likely to fall apart.

R

ran (ran) *verb* The past tense of **run.**

ranch (ranch)
noun A large farm for cattle, sheep, or horses.
verb To run or work on a ranch.
▶ *noun, plural* **ranches** ▶ *verb* **ranches, ranching, ranched** ▶ *noun* **rancher**

ran·cid (**ran**-sid) *adjective* Spoiled and not fit to eat.

ran·dom (**ran**-duhm) *adjective*
1. Without any order or purpose. 2. If you make a **random** selection from a group of items, each item in the group has the same chance of being chosen. 3. If you do something **at random,** you do it without any order or method.
▶ *adverb* **randomly**

range (raynj)
verb 1. To vary within certain limits. 2. To roam over a large area.
noun 1. An area of variation between limits. 2. The distance that a bullet or rocket can travel or a person can see. 3. A place for shooting at targets or testing rockets. 4. An area of open land used for grazing animals. 5. A chain of mountains. 6. A stove with several burners and at least one oven.
▶ *verb* **ranging, ranged**

rang·er (**rayn**-jur) *noun* A person in charge of a park or forest.

rank (rangk)
noun An official job level or position.
verb To assign a position to.
adjective 1. Having a strong and unpleasant odor or taste. 2. Complete or absolute.
▶ *verb* **ranking, ranked** ▶ *adjective* **ranker, rankest**

ran·sack (**ran**-sak) *verb* To search a place violently, usually looking for things to steal. ▶ *verb* **ransacking, ransacked**

ran·som (**ran**-suhm)
noun Money that is demanded before someone who is being held captive can be set free.
verb To obtain someone's freedom by paying a ransom.
▶ *verb* **ransoming, ransomed**

rant (rant) *verb* To talk loudly and angrily. ▶ *verb* **ranting, ranted**

rap (rap)
verb 1. To hit something with a quick, sharp blow. 2. (slang) To talk.
noun 1. A type of popular music in which the words are spoken rhythmically to a musical background. 2. A quick, sharp blow or knock. **Rap** sounds like **wrap.** ▶ *verb* **rapping, rapped** ▶ *noun* **rapper**

rap·id (**rap**-id) *adjective* Very fast or quick. ▶ *noun* **rapidity** (ra-**pid**-i-tee)

rap·id·ly (**rap**-id-lee) *adverb* Quickly or within a short period of time.

rap·ids (**rap**-idz) *noun, plural* A place in a river where the water flows very fast.

ra·pi·er (**ray**-pee-ur) *noun* A long sword with two edges, often used in duels in the 16th and 17th centuries.

rap·ture (**rap**-chur) *noun* Great happiness, joy, or delight.

rare (rair) *adjective* 1. Not often seen, found, or happening. 2. Not cooked very much. 3. Unusually good or excellent.
▶ *adjective* **rarer, rarest** ▶ *noun* **rarity**

rare·ly (**rair**-lee) *adverb* Not very often.

ras·cal (**ras**-kuhl) *noun* 1. Someone who is very mischievous. 2. A dishonest person.

rash (rash)
noun 1. An occurrence of small spots or blotchy red patches on the skin caused by an allergy or disease. 2. An occurrence of many events of the same type.
adjective Acting quickly, without thinking first.
▶ *noun, plural* **rashes** ▶ *adjective* **rasher, rashest** ▶ *adverb* **rashly**

rasp (rasp)
verb To speak in a harsh, grating voice.
noun 1. A harsh, grating sound. 2. A coarse file with cone-shaped teeth, used to smooth wood or metal.
▶ *verb* **rasping, rasped**

rasp·ber·ry (**raz**-ber-ee) *noun* 1. A small, sweet, black or red berry with very small seeds that grows on a prickly bush. 2. A dark purple-red color.
▶ *noun, plural* **raspberries**

R

rat (rat) *noun* 1. A rodent that looks like a large mouse and has a long tail. Rats sometimes spread disease.
2. (informal) A disloyal person.
3. **rat race** A very stressful routine or competition at work.

rate (rate)
noun 1. A degree of speed. 2. A fee or price. 3. A standard amount used to calculate a total.
verb 1. To judge the quality or worth of a person or thing. 2. To place in a particular position or rank.
▶ *verb* **rating, rated** ▶ *noun* **rating**

rath·er (**raTH**-ur) *adverb* 1. Fairly or quite; more than a little. 2. More willingly. 3. More correctly.

rat·i·fy (**rat**-uh-*fye*) *verb* To agree to or approve officially. ▶ *verb* **ratifies, ratifying, ratified** ▶ *noun* **ratification**

ra·ti·o (**ray**-shee-*oh* or **ray**-shoh) *noun* A comparison of two quantities or numbers using division. Ratios are usually expressed as fractions, or using the word *to*.

ra·tion (**rash**-uhn or **ray**-shuhn)
noun A limited amount or share, especially of food.
verb To give out in limited amounts.
▶ *verb* **rationing, rationed** ▶ *noun* **rationing**

ra·tion·al (**rash**-uh-nuhl) *adjective*
1. Logical and sensible and not emotional. 2. Reasonable and sane.
▶ *adverb* **rationally**

rat·tle (**rat**-uhl)
verb 1. To make a series of short, sharp noises. 2. **rattle off** To talk or say quickly. 3. To upset or embarrass.
noun 1. A rattling sound. 2. A baby's toy that makes a rattling sound. 3. The end part of a rattlesnake's tail that produces a rattling sound.
▶ *verb* **rattling, rattled**

rat·tle·snake (**rat**-uhl-*snayk*) *noun* A poisonous snake of North and South America with a tail that makes a rattling noise as it shakes.

rau·cous (**raw**-kuhs) *adjective* 1. Harsh or loud in a way that is unpleasant.
2. Loud and rowdy.
▶ *adverb* **raucously**

rave (rayv) *verb* 1. To talk wildly.
2. (informal) To praise something enthusiastically.
▶ *verb* **raving, raved**

ra·vel (**rav**-uhl) *verb* To fray or separate into single loose threads; to untangle. ▶ *verb* **raveling, raveled**

ra·ven (**ray**-vuhn)
noun A large bird with shiny black feathers, belonging to the crow family.
adjective Black and glossy.

rav·en·ous (**rav**-uh-nuhs) *adjective* Extremely hungry.

ra·vine (ruh-**veen**) *noun* A steep, extremely narrow valley.

raw (raw) *adjective* 1. Not cooked.
2. Not treated, processed, or refined.
3. Not trained or inexperienced.
4. Having the skin rubbed off.
5. Unpleasantly damp and chilly.
▶ *adjective* **rawer, rawest**

raw·hide (**raw**-*hide*) *noun* The skin of cattle or other animals before it has been soaked in a special solution and made into leather.

raw ma·te·ri·al (**raw** muh-**teer**-ee-uhl) *noun* A substance that is treated or processed and made into a useful finished product. Crude oil is the raw material from which we get gasoline.

ray (ray) *noun* 1. A narrow beam of light or other radiation. 2. A type of fish with a flat body, large winglike fins, and a thin, whiplike tail. 3. A tiny amount. 4. Part of a line that extends on and on in one direction from a single point.

ray·on (**ray**-ahn) *noun* A synthetic fabric made from cellulose that has the look and feel of silk.

ra·zor (**ray**-zur) *noun* A tool with a sharp blade used to shave hair from the skin.

re (ree) *preposition* Concerning. The word *re* is used to introduce the subject to be talked about. *His letter to the editor began, "I am writing to you re the traffic problems in my neighborhood."*

R

reach (reech)
verb 1. To stretch or hold out to
something with your hand. 2. To
go as far as. 3. To get to or arrive
somewhere. 4. To contact.
noun 1. The distance a person or thing
can reach. 2. An expanse. 3. The act of
reaching.
▸ *verb* **reaches, reaching,
reached** ▸ *noun, plural* **reaches**

re·act (ree-**akt**) *verb* 1. To behave in a
particular way as a response to words,
actions, or events. 2. If a substance
reacts with another, a chemical
change occurs in one or both of the
substances as they are mixed together.
▸ *verb* **reacting, reacted**

re·act·ion (ree-**ak**-shuhn) *noun* An
action in response to something; a
response.

re·ac·tion·ar·y (ree-**ak**-shuh-**ner**-ee)
adjective Against change and wanting
things to return to the way they were
in the past.
noun A person who has reactionary
views and opinions.
▸ *noun, plural* **reactionaries**

re·ac·tor (ree-**ak**-tur) *noun* A large
device in which nuclear energy is
produced by splitting atoms under
controlled conditions.

read (reed) *verb* 1. To look at and
understand written or printed words.
2. To say aloud something that
is written. 3. To learn by reading.
4. To understand some form of
communication, especially by
observing someone's behavior.
5. To show or to register.
▸ *verb* **reading, read** (red)

read·er (**ree**-dur) *noun* 1. A person who
reads. 2. A book with passages to
practice reading or to read about a
particular subject; an anthology.

read·i·ly (**red**-uh-lee) *adverb* 1. Easily.
2. Willingly and quickly.

read·ing (**ree**-ding) *noun* 1. The activity
of someone who reads. 2. The spoken
performance of a written work in front
of an audience.

read·y (**red**-ee)
adjective 1. Prepared. 2. Willing.

3. Likely or about to do something.
4. Quick.
verb To prepare something or
someone.
▸ *adjective* **readier, readiest**

re·al (**ree**-uhl *or* reel) *adjective* 1. True
and not made up. 2. Genuine and not
imitation or artificial.

re·al es·tate (**ree**-uhl e-*state*) *noun* Land
and the buildings that are on it.

re·al·is·tic (ree-uh-**lis**-tik) *adjective*
1. Very similar to the real thing.
2. Seeing things as they really are.
▸ *noun* **realism** ▸ *adverb* **realistically**

re·al·i·ty (ree-**al**-i-tee) *noun* 1. Truth, or
what actually happens, especially in
contrast to what you want or expect.
2. The actual facts that must be dealt
with.
▸ *noun, plural* **realities**

re·al·ize (**ree**-uh-*lize*) *verb* 1. To come to
understand something. 2. To make
real or to achieve.
▸ *verb* **realizing, realized** ▸ *noun*
realization

re·al·ly (**ree**-uh-lee *or* **ree**-lee) *adverb*
1. Actually, or in fact. 2. Very.

realm (relm) *noun* 1. An area or field of
knowledge or interest. 2. A kingdom.

reap (reep) *verb* 1. To cut grain or to
gather a crop by hand or machine.
2. To get as a reward.
▸ *verb* **reaping, reaped** ▸ *noun* **reaper**

re·ap·pear (ree-uh-**peer**) *verb* To come
into view again. ▸ *verb* **reappearing,
reappeared** ▸ *noun* **reappearance**

rear (reer)
verb 1. To give birth to and bring up
young animals. 2. To care for and
raise. 3. If a horse **rears**, it stands on
its hind legs. 4. To lift up.
noun The back part of something.
adjective Located in the back.
▸ *verb* **rearing, reared**

re·ar·range (ree-uh-**raynj**) *verb* To
arrange things in a new way. ▸ *verb*
rearranging, rearranged

rea·son (**ree**-zuhn)
noun 1. The basis or cause of a belief,
fact, or action. 2. An explanation or
an excuse.
verb 1. To think logically. 2. To try to

R

persuade someone that what you suggest is sensible.

noun The power to understand and to think in a logical, rational way.

▶ *verb* **reasoning, reasoned**

rea·son·a·ble (**ree**-zuh-nuh-buhl) *adjective* **1.** Fair or just. **2.** Sensible and not foolish. **3.** Costing a fair price.

▶ *adverb* **reasonably**

rea·son·ing (**ree**-zuh-ning) *noun* **1.** The process of thinking in an orderly fashion, drawing conclusions from facts. **2.** The reasons used in this process.

re·as·sure (*ree*-uh-**shoor**) *verb* To make someone feel calm and confident and give the person courage. ▶ *verb* **reassuring, reassured** ▶ *noun* **reassurance** ▶ *adjective* **reassuring**

re·bate (**ree**-bayt) *noun* Money that is given back to the purchaser of a product, as a sales promotion.

verb To give back part of the price paid for something.

▶ *verb* **rebating, rebated**

reb·el

noun (**reb**-uhl) Someone who fights against a government or against the people in charge of something.

verb (ri-**bel**) To oppose or fight against a government or against the people in charge of something.

▶ *verb* **rebelling, rebelled**

re·bel·lion (ri-**bel**-yuhn) *noun* **1.** Armed fight against a government. **2.** Any struggle against the people in charge of something.

re·bel·lious (ri-**bel**-yuhs) *adjective* Resistant to or disrespectful of authority.

re·boot (ree-**boot**) *verb* To start a computer again. ▶ *verb* **rebooting, rebooted**

re·bound

verb (ree-**bound**) **1.** To bounce or spring back after hitting something. **2.** To recover from a defeat or an upset, as if bouncing back. **3.** To get hold of a rebound in basketball.

noun (**ree**-bound) **1.** The action of bouncing back. **2.** Something that

bounces back, such as a basketball off the backboard. **3.** If you catch a ball that bounces off a wall, you can say that you caught it **on the rebound.**

▶ *verb* **rebounding, rebounded**

re·build (ree-**bild**) *verb* To build something again after it has been damaged or destroyed. ▶ *verb* **rebuilding, rebuilt**

re·buke (ri-**byook**)

verb To scold someone because he or she has done something wrong.

noun An expression of strong disapproval or criticism.

▶ *verb* **rebuking, rebuked**

re·call

verb (ri-**kawl**) **1.** To bring something to your mind; to remember. **2.** To call back a purchased product that has a defect. **3.** To summon someone to return.

noun (ri-**kawl** or **ree**-kawl) An official order to return someone or something.

▶ *verb* **recalling, recalled**

re·cap (**ree**-kap)

verb (informal) To repeat the main points of something that has already been said.

noun A repetition or summary.

▶ *verb* **recapping, recapped**

re·cede (ri-**seed**) *verb* **1.** To move back. **2.** To fade little by little.

▶ *verb* **receding, receded** ▶ *adjective* **receding**

re·ceipt (ri-**seet**) *noun* A piece of paper showing that money, goods, mail, or a service has been received.

re·ceive (ri-**seev**) *verb* **1.** To get or accept something that has been sent or given. **2.** To experience. **3.** To greet or to welcome.

▶ *verb* **receiving, received**

re·ceiv·er (ri-**see**-vur) *noun* **1.** The part of a wired telephone that you hold in your hand next to your ear and mouth. **2.** A piece of equipment that receives radio or television signals and changes them into sounds or pictures. **3.** A person who receives something. **4.** A member of the offensive team in football who is expected to catch the ball.

re·cent (**ree**-suhnt) *adjective* Done, made, or taking place a short time ago.

R

re·cent·ly (**ree**-suhnt-lee) *adverb* Not very long ago.

re·cep·ta·cle (ri-**sep**-tuh-kuhl) *noun* A container.

re·cep·tion (ri-**sep**-shuhn) *noun* 1. The way in which someone or something is received. 2. A large formal party.

re·cep·tion·ist (ri-**sep**-shuh-nist) *noun* A person whose job is to greet people in an office, clinic, or other place of business and sometimes to answer the telephone.

re·cess (**ree**-ses)
noun 1. A break from schoolwork during the morning or afternoon.
2. A part of a wall set back farther than the rest of the wall.
verb To halt activity for a set amount of time.
▶ *verb* **recessing, recessed** ▶ *adjective* **recessed**

re·ces·sion (ri-**sesh**-uhn) *noun* A time when business slows down and more workers than usual are unemployed.

rec·i·pe (**res**-uh-pee) *noun* Instructions for preparing food.

re·cip·i·ent (ri-**sip**-ee-uhnt) *noun* A person who receives something.

re·cit·al (ri-**sye**-tuhl) *noun* 1. A performance, usually given by a single performer or a small group. 2. A detailed account or report.

re·cite (ri-**site**) *verb* 1. To say aloud, in front of others, something that you memorized. 2. To tell about in detail.
▶ *verb* **reciting, recited** ▶ *noun* **recitation** (res-i-**tay**-shuhn)

reck·less (**rek**-lis) *adjective* Careless about your own or other people's safety. ▶ *adverb* **recklessly**

reck·on (**rek**-uhn) *verb* 1. To calculate or figure the value of. 2. To have an opinion; to think.
▶ *verb* **reckoning, reckoned** ▶ *noun* **reckoning**

re·claim (ri-**klaym**) *verb* 1. To get back something that belongs to you. 2. To make land suitable for building, farming, or grazing by clearing or draining it.
▶ *verb* **reclaiming, reclaimed** ▶ *noun* **reclamation** (rek-luh-**may**-shuhn)

re·cline (ri-**kline**) *verb* To lean back or lie down. ▶ *verb* **reclining, reclined**

rec·og·ni·tion (rek-uhg-**nish**-uhn) *noun* Appreciation or acknowledgment of someone or something.

rec·og·nize (**rek**-uhg-*nize*) *verb* 1. To see someone and know who the person is. 2. To understand a situation and accept it as true or right.
▶ *verb* **recognizing, recognized** ▶ *adjective* **recognizable** ▶ *adverb* **recognizably**

rec·ol·lect (rek-uh-**lekt**) *verb* To remember or to recall something. ▶ *verb* **recollecting, recollected** ▶ *noun* **recollection**

rec·om·mend (rek-uh-**mend**) *verb* 1. To suggest as being good or worthy. 2. To advise.
▶ *verb* **recommending, recommended** ▶ *noun* **recommendation**

rec·om·men·da·tion (rek-uh-men-**day**-shuhn) *noun* 1. A suggestion or proposal. 2. A favorable statement about someone's character or qualifications for something.

rec·on·cile (**rek**-uhn-*sile*) *verb* 1. To make up or become friendly again after a disagreement. 2. If you **reconcile yourself** to something, you decide to put up with it.
▶ *verb* **reconciling, reconciled** ▶ *noun* **reconciliation**

re·con·sid·er (ree-kuhn-**sid**-ur) *verb* To think again about a previous decision, especially with the idea of making a change. ▶ *verb* **reconsidering, reconsidered**

re·con·struct (ree-kuhn-**struhkt**) *verb* 1. To rebuild something that has been destroyed. 2. To carefully piece together past events.
▶ *verb* **reconstructed, reconstructing** ▶ *noun* **reconstruction**

re·cord
verb (ri-**kord**) 1. To write something down so that it can be kept. 2. To put music or other sounds onto a tape, compact disk, or record.
noun (**rek**-urd) 1. The facts about what a person or group has done. 2. A disk with grooves on which sound,

especially music, used to be recorded to be played by a phonograph. Also called *a phonograph record*. **3.** If you **set a record** in something such as a sport, you do it faster, better, higher, or the like, than anyone has ever done it before.
▸ *verb* **recording, recorded**

re·cord·er (ri-**kor**-dur) *noun* **1.** A device for recording sounds on magnetic tape. **2.** A woodwind musical instrument that you play by blowing into the mouthpiece and covering holes with your fingers to make different notes.

re·cord·ing (ri-**kor**-ding) *noun* **1.** A tape, compact disk, or record. **2.** The sounds on a tape, compact disk, or record.

re·count
verb **1.** (ri-**kount**) To narrate or tell about. **2.** (ree-**kount**) To count again. Also spelled as "re-count."
noun (**ree**-kount) An instance of recounting. Also spelled as "re-count."
▸ *verb* **recounting, recounted**

re·cov·er (ri-**kuhv**-ur) *verb* **1.** To get better after an illness, accident, or other difficulty. **2.** To get back something that has been lost, stolen, or taken away. **3.** To make up for.
▸ *verb* **recovering, recovered**

re·cov·er (ree-**kuhv**-ur) *verb* To cover again. ▸ *verb* **re-covering, re-covered**

re·cov·er·y (ri-**kuhv**-ur-ee) *noun* **1.** A return to health or to a normal state or condition. **2.** The process of regaining something that was lost or stolen.

rec·re·a·tion (rek-ree-**ay**-shuhn) *noun* The games, sports, and hobbies that you like to do in your spare time. ▸ *adjective* **recreational**

re·cruit (ri-**kroot**)
noun Someone who has recently joined the armed forces or any group or organization.
verb To get a person to join.
▸ *verb* **recruiting, recruited** ▸ *noun* **recruitment**

rec·tan·gle (**rek**-*tang*-guhl) *noun* A shape with four sides and four right angles. ▸ *adjective* **rectangular**

rec·ti·fy (**rek**-tuh-*fye*) *verb* To make right or correct. ▸ *verb* **rectifies, rectifying, rectified**

rec·tum (**rek**-tuhm) *noun* The lowest portion of the large intestine, ending at the anus. ▸ *adjective* **rectal** (**rek**-tuhl)

re·cu·per·ate (ri-**koo**-puh-*rate*) *verb* To recover from an illness or injury. ▸ *verb* **recuperating, recuperated** ▸ *noun* **recuperation**

re·cur (ri-**kur**) *verb* To appear or happen again. ▸ *verb* **recurring, recurred** ▸ *noun* **recurrence** ▸ *adjective* **recurrent**

re·cy·cle (ree-**sye**-kuhl) *verb* To process old items such as glass, plastic, newspapers, and aluminum and tin cans so that they can be used to make new products. ▸ *verb* **recycling, recycled** ▸ *adjective* **recyclable**

red (red)
noun One of the three primary colors, along with blue and yellow. Red is the color of beets and blood.
adjective **1.** Having the color of strawberries. **2.** Having a pink color in your face, for example because you are embarrassed, angry, or hot.
▸ *adjective* **redder, reddest** ▸ *adjective* **reddish**

red blood cell (**red bluhd** *sel*) *noun* A cell in your blood that carries oxygen from your lungs to all the tissues and cells of your body.

red·coat (**red**-koht) *noun* A British soldier during the time of the Revolutionary War and later wars. These soldiers' uniforms included bright red coats.

Red Cross (**red kraws**) *noun* An international organization that helps victims of disasters of all kinds, from floods and earthquakes to war and famine.

red·den (**red**-uhn) *verb* **1.** To make red or to become red. **2.** To blush.
▸ *verb* **reddening, reddened**

R

re·deem (ri-**deem**) *verb* 1. To exchange something for money or merchandise. 2. To save, or to make up for.
▶ *verb* **redeeming, redeemed** ▶ *noun* **redemption** (ri-**demp**-shuhn)

red-eye (**red**-*eye*) *noun* 1. A flight that leaves at night and reaches its destination in the morning, with tired passengers. 2. The appearance of redness in the eyes of people in a photograph because of the way that the camera captures light.

red-hand·ed (**han**-did) *adjective* If you catch someone **red-handed,** you catch the person in the act of doing something wrong.

red her·ring (**red her**-ing) *noun* Something that distracts a person's attention from the real issue.

Red Sea (**red see**) An inlet of the Indian Ocean that lies between Africa and Asia. The Red Sea is bounded by Egypt, Sudan, and Eritrea to the west, and by the Arabian Peninsula to the east. At its southern tip, it flows into the Gulf of Aden.

red tape (**red tape**) *noun* Excessive rules and regulations and detailed paperwork that make it hard to get things done.

re·duce (ri-**doos**) *verb* To decrease something in size, amount, or weight. ▶ *verb* **reducing, reduced**

re·duced (ri-**doost**) *adjective* Smaller or less in size, amount, or degree.

re·duc·tion (ri-**duhk**-shuhn) *noun* The act or process of making something smaller or less.

re·dun·dant (ri-**duhn**-duhnt) *adjective* Using repetitive words for what you mean to say or write. ▶ *noun* **redundancy**

red·wood (**red**-*wud*) *noun* A very large evergreen tree found along the western coast of the United States, especially in Northern California. The world's tallest redwood, found in Humboldt County, California, is 379 feet (115 meters) tall.

reed (reed) *noun* 1. A tall grass with long, thin, hollow stems that grows in or near water. 2. A piece of thin wood, metal, or plastic in the mouthpieces of some musical instruments, such as the clarinet, oboe, and saxophone. When you blow over the reed the right way, it vibrates and makes a sound.

reef (reef) *noun* A strip of rock, sand, or coral close to the surface of the ocean or another body of water.

reek (reek)
verb To give off an unpleasant smell.
noun A strong bad smell.
Reek sounds like **wreak.** ▶ *verb* **reeking, reeked**

reel (reel)
verb 1. To stagger. 2. If you **reel** something **off,** you say it quickly, especially from memory.
noun 1. A cylinder on which something, such as thread, fishing line, or film, is wound. 2. A type of folk dance that is lively and spirited.
▶ *verb* **reeling, reeled**

re·e·lect (ree-i-**lekt**) *verb* To elect for another term. ▶ *verb* **reelecting, reelected** ▶ *noun* **reelection**

re·en·try (ree-**en**-tree) *noun* The return of a spacecraft or missile to the earth's atmosphere. ▶ *noun, plural* **reentries** ▶ *verb* **reenter**

ref (ref) *noun* Short for **referee.**

re·fer (ri-**fur**) *verb* 1. To look at something for information. 2. To bring attention to something by mentioning it when you speak or write. 3. To send someone for additional or more detailed information or advice.
▶ *verb* **referring, referred** ▶ *noun* **referral**

ref·er·ee (ref-uh-**ree**)
noun An official who supervises a sports match or a game and makes sure that the players obey the rules.
verb To act as a referee.
▶ *verb* **refereeing, refereed**

ref·er·ence (**ref**-ur-uhns) *noun* 1. A mention of something or someone, or the act of mentioning something or someone. 2. A statement about someone's personal qualities and abilities. 3. A book, magazine, website, or the like from which you get

R

information that you use in an essay or other piece of work.

ref·er·ence book (**ref**-ur-uhns *buk*) *noun* A book that you use to find information quickly and easily. Encyclopedias, dictionaries, atlases, and almanacs are reference books.

ref·er·en·dum (*ref*-uh-**ren**-duhm) *noun* A vote by the people on a public measure. ▸ *noun, plural* **referendums** or **referenda** (*ref*-uh-**ren**-duh)

re·fill
verb (ree-**fil**) To fill a glass, cup, or container again.
noun (**ree**-*fil*) A second or later filling of something, such as a cup or glass. ▸ *verb* **refilling, refilled**

re·fi·nance (*ree*-fuh-**nans** or ree-**fye**-nans) *verb* To agree to new terms with a bank about how you will pay back a loan, usually for a house. ▸ *verb* **refinancing, refinanced**

re·fine (ri-**fine**) *verb* **1.** To purify, or to remove unwanted matter from a substance such as oil or sugar. **2.** To improve or perfect something, especially by making minor changes. ▸ *verb* **refining, refined**

re·fined (ri-**fined**) *adjective* **1.** A **refined** person is well educated and very polite, with good taste and elegant manners. **2.** Purified or processed.

re·fine·ment (ri-**fine**-muhnt) *noun* **1.** Good taste, elegance, and good manners. **2.** A slight change made to something in order to improve it.

re·fin·er·y (ri-**fye**-nur-ee) *noun* A factory where raw materials, such as crude oil or sugar, are purified and made into finished products. ▸ *noun, plural* **refineries**

re·fit (ree-**fit**) *verb* To prepare something for additional use by replacing parts and equipment. ▸ *verb* **refitting, refitted**

re·flect (ri-**flekt**) *verb* **1.** To show an image of something on a shiny surface, such as water or a mirror. **2.** To throw back heat, light, or sound from a surface. **3.** To think carefully or seriously about something. **4.** To bring about an impression of

someone or something, either good or bad. **5.** To show or to express. ▸ *verb* **reflecting, reflected**

re·flec·tion (ri-**flek**-shuhn) *noun* **1.** An image that you see in a mirror or on a shiny surface. **2.** One thing that indicates or gives you information about another thing. **3.** Thinking about something, or the result of thinking.

re·flec·tive (ri-**flek**-tiv) *adjective* **1.** Able to reflect light, images, or sound waves. **2.** Tending to think deeply and seriously about things. ▸ *adverb* **reflectively**

re·flec·tor (ri-**flek**-tur) *noun* A shiny surface or device that bounces back light or heat.

re·flex (**ree**-*fleks*)
noun An automatic action or movement that happens without a person's control or effort.
adjective Produced or performed as an automatic response. ▸ *noun, plural* **reflexes**

re·flex an·gle (**ree**-fleks *ang*-guhl) *noun* An angle between 180 degrees and 360 degrees.

re·for·est (ree-**for**-est) *verb* To replant trees where all the original trees were cut down or destroyed by fire or disaster. ▸ *verb* **reforesting, reforested** ▸ *noun* **reforestation**

re·form (ri-**form**)
verb **1.** To make changes in something so that it is corrected or improved. **2.** To change for the better, especially to abandon bad behavior.
noun An improvement, or the correcting of something unsatisfactory. ▸ *verb* **reforming, reformed**

re·for·ma·to·ry (ri-**for**-muh-*tor*-ee) *noun* A special school or institution for young people who have broken the law. ▸ *noun, plural* **reformatories**

re·fract (ri-**frakt**) *verb* When a ray of light is **refracted,** it bends because it has entered another medium, such as water or glass. ▸ *verb* **refracting, refracted** ▸ *noun* **refraction** (ri-**frak**-shuhn)

R

re·frain (ri-**frayn**)
verb To hold yourself back from doing or saying something you want to do. *noun* A regularly repeated part of a song or poem.
▶ *verb* **refraining, refrained**

re·fresh (ri-**fresh**) *verb* 1. To bring someone new energy and strength. 2. If a webpage **refreshes** or if you **refresh** it, you see the newest version of it. 3. If something **refreshes your memory**, it makes you remember something more clearly than you did before.
▶ *verb* **refreshes, refreshing, refreshed** ▶ *adjective* **refreshing**

re·fresh·ments (ri-**fresh**-muhnts) *noun, plural* Light snacks and drinks.

re·frig·er·a·tor (ri-**frij**-uh-ray-tur) *noun* A cabinet, a room, or an appliance with a very cold interior, used for storing food and drink. ▶ *noun* **refrigeration** ▶ *verb* **refrigerate**

re·fu·el (ree-**fyoo**-uhl) *verb* To supply or to take on more fuel. ▶ *verb* **refueling, refueled**

ref·uge (**ref**-yooj) *noun* 1. Protection or shelter from danger or trouble. 2. A place that provides protection or shelter.

ref·u·gee (ref-yoo-**jee**) *noun* A person who is forced to leave his or her home or country to escape war, religious persecution, or a natural disaster.

re·fund
verb (ri-**fuhnd**) To return or repay money. *noun* (**ree**-fuhnd) An amount of money that is returned or repaid to someone who has bought something, for example because a product does not work properly.
▶ *verb* **refunding, refunded**

re·fus·al (ri-**fyoo**-zuhl) *noun* An instance or expression of unwillingness to do something.

re·fuse
verb (ri-**fyooz**) To say you will not do, accept, or allow something. *noun* (**ref**-yoos) Trash.
▶ *verb* **refusing, refused**

re·gain (ree-**gayn**) *verb* To get something back, especially after you have lost control, possession, or use of it. ▶ *verb* **regaining, regained**

re·gal (**ree**-guhl) *adjective* Of or having to do with or suitable for a king or queen. ▶ *adverb* **regally**

re·gale (ri-**gale**) *verb* 1. To give great pleasure, delight, or entertainment. 2. To entertain lavishly with a lot of food and drink.
▶ *verb* **regaling, regaled**

re·gard (ri-**gahrd**)
verb 1. To think of someone or something in a particular way or from a particular point of view. 2. To look at closely. 3. To respect or show consideration for someone or something.
noun 1. A good opinion; esteem. 2. Respect or consideration.
noun, plural **regards** Good wishes.
▶ *verb* **regarding, regarded**

re·gard·ing (ri-**gahr**-ding) *preposition* About, in reference to, or concerning. *The teacher wrote a note regarding Maureen's lateness.*

re·gard·less (ri-**gahrd**-lis)
adjective Without considering anyone or anything else; heedless.
adverb In spite of everything.

re·gat·ta (ri-**gat**-uh *or* ri-**gah**-tuh) *noun* A boat race, or a series of boat races.

reg·gae (**reg**-ay) *noun* A type of popular music with a strong beat that comes from Jamaica in the West Indies.

re·gime (ri-**zheem** *or* ray-**zheem**) *noun* A government that rules a people during a specific period of time.

reg·i·ment (**rej**-uh-muhnt) *noun* A military unit made up of two or more battalions.

re·gion (**ree**-juhn) *noun* A general area, or a specific district or territory.
▶ *adjective* **regional** ▶ *adverb* **regionally**

reg·is·ter (**rej**-i-stur)
noun 1. A formal list of names or items, or a book in which official records are kept. 2. The range of notes that a human voice or a musical instrument can produce. 3. A machine that automatically records and counts. *verb* 1. To enter someone or something

R

on an official list. **2.** To express or to show an emotion. **3.** To show on a scale or other device.
▶ *verb* **registering, registered**

reg·is·tered nurse (**rej**-i-sturd **nurs**) *noun* A nurse who has completed certain training and is licensed by the state in which he or she practices.

reg·is·tra·tion (*rej*-i-**stray**-shuhn) *noun* **1.** The process of recording or registering someone or something. **2.** A certificate stating that someone or something has been registered.

reg·is·try (**rej**-i-stree) *noun* **1.** An official list of something, or a department that keeps such a list. **2.** A system file on a computer that keeps track of all the hardware and software on it.

re·gret (ri-**gret**)
verb To be sad, sorry, or disappointed about something.
noun A feeling of sadness or disappointment.
▶ *verb* **regretting, regretted** ▶ *adjective* **regretful**

re·gret·ta·ble (ri-**gret**-uh-buhl) *adjective* Causing or deserving regret. ▶ *adverb* **regrettably**

reg·u·lar (**reg**-yuh-lur) *adjective* **1.** Usual or customary. **2.** According to habit or usual behavior. **3.** Always happening at the same time. **4.** Occuring at normal or healthy intervals. **5.** A **regular** verb is one whose main parts are formed according to a regular pattern. *Love* is a regular verb because its past tense is *loved.*
▶ *noun* **regularity** (*reg*-yuh-**lar**-i-tee)

reg·u·lar·ly (**reg**-yuh-lur-lee) *adverb* At short and regular intervals.

reg·u·late (**reg**-yuh-*late*) *verb* **1.** To control or manage according to the rules. **2.** To adjust or to keep at some standard.
▶ *verb* **regulating, regulated**

reg·u·la·tion (*reg*-yuh-**lay**-shuhn) *noun* **1.** An official rule or order. **2.** The state of being controlled, or the act of controlling or adjusting something.

re·gur·gi·tate (ri-**gur**-ji-*tate*) *verb* To bring food that has been swallowed back up to your mouth. ▶ *verb* **regurgitating, regurgitated**

re·hears·al (ri-**hur**-suhl) *noun* A practice, especially for a performance.

re·hearse (ri-**hurs**) *verb* **1.** To practice in preparation for a public performance. **2.** To review or recount something in order.
▶ *verb* **rehearsing, rehearsed**

reign (rayn)
verb **1.** To rule a country as a king or queen. **2.** To be the most common thing everywhere.
noun The period during which a king or queen rules.
Reign sounds like **rain** and **rein.**
▶ *verb* **reigning, reigned**

re·im·burse (*ree*-im-**burs**) *verb* To pay back money spent on your behalf, or to be paid back for money that you have spent. ▶ *verb* **reimbursing, reimbursed** ▶ *noun* **reimbursement**

rein (rayn)
noun, plural **reins** Straps attached to a bridle to control or guide a horse.
noun A controlling or restraining force.
Rein sounds like **rain** and **reign.**

re·in·car·na·tion (*ree*-in-kahr-**nay**-shuhn) *noun* **1.** Being born on earth again in another body after dying. Reincarnation is part of the beliefs of some religions, such as Hinduism. **2.** Something that is very similar to something from the past.

rein·deer (**rayn**-*deer*) *noun* A deer that lives in the earth's far north regions. Both male and female reindeer have large, branching antlers. ▶ *noun, plural* **reindeer**

re·in·force (*ree*-in-**fors**) *verb* To make something stronger or more effective. ▶ *verb* **reinforcing, reinforced**

re·in·force·ment (*ree*-in-**fors**-muhnt)
noun The act of making something stronger or more effective.
noun, plural **reinforcements** Extra troops sent to strengthen an army or other fighting force.

re·ject
verb (ri-**jekt**) To refuse to accept, consider, or agree to something.
noun (**ree**-jekt) Something that has been discarded.
▶ *verb* **rejecting, rejected**

R

re·jec·tion (ri-**jek**-shuhn) *noun* An act of rejecting something.

re·joice (ri-**jois**) *verb* To feel great joy or happiness. ▶ *verb* **rejoicing, rejoiced**

re·lapse
noun (**ree**-laps *or* ri-**laps**) The act of falling back to a former condition, especially the return of an illness after you were feeling better.
verb (ri-**laps**) To fall back to a former condition, especially after a period of improvement.
▶ *verb* **relapsing, relapsed**

re·late (ri-**late**) *verb* 1. To tell the story or to give an account of something. 2. To have a relationship or connection. 3. To understand, to get along with, or to feel sympathy for someone or something.
▶ *verb* **relating, related**

re·lat·ed (ri-**lay**-tid) *adjective*
1. Belonging to the same family.
2. Having some connection.

re·la·tion (ri-**lay**-shuhn)
noun 1. A connection between two or more people or things. 2. A relative or member of your family.
noun, plural **relations** The way in which two or more persons, groups, or nations behave toward one other.

re·la·tion·ship (ri-**lay**-shuhn-*ship*) *noun*
1. The way in which people feel about and behave toward one another. 2. The way in which two or more things are connected.

rel·a·tive (**rel**-uh-tiv)
noun A family member or someone connected to you by marriage.
adjective Compared with others or to something else.

rel·a·tive·ly (**rel**-uh-tiv-lee) *adverb* In comparison with others or to something else; somewhat.

re·lax (ri-**laks**) *verb* 1. To take a rest from work or to do something enjoyable.
2. To become less tense, anxious, or strained. 3. To make something less strict or intense.
▶ *verb* **relaxes, relaxing, relaxed**

re·lax·a·tion (ree-lak-**say**-shuhn) *noun*
1. A state of rest, recreation, or freedom from tension or worry.

2. The action of making something looser, more relaxed, or less strict.

re·lay (**ree**-lay)
noun A team race, usually in running or swimming, in which each team member covers a portion of the total distance.
verb To pass along.
▶ *verb* **relaying, relayed**

re·lease (ri-**lees**)
verb 1. To set someone or something free. 2. If a CD, DVD, or movie is **released,** it is made available to the public for the first time.
noun A CD, DVD, or movie that has been made available to the public.
▶ *verb* **releasing, released**

rel·e·gate (**rel**-uh-*gate*) *verb* 1. To send to a place or position of less importance.
2. To turn over or assign a task to another person.
▶ *verb* **relegating, relegated**

re·lent (ri-**lent**) *verb* 1. To become less strict or more forgiving. 2. To become less intense.
▶ *verb* **relenting, relented**

re·lent·less (ri-**lent**-lis) *adjective* Unlikely to stop or grow weaker. ▶ *adverb* **relentlessly**

rel·e·vance (**rel**-uh-vuhns) *noun* The quality of being important or appropriate in relation to something else.

rel·e·vant (**rel**-uh-vuhnt) *adjective* Concerned with or connected to what is being dealt with or discussed.

re·li·a·ble (ri-**lye**-uh-buhl) *adjective* Able to be relied upon or trusted. ▶ *noun* **reliability** ▶ *adverb* **reliably**

rel·ic (**rel**-ik) *noun* 1. An object, belief, or custom that has survived from the past. 2. An object that belonged to or is associated with a saint or other holy person.

re·lief (ri-**leef**) *noun* 1. A feeling of release from pain, anxiety, or distress.
2. Assistance given to people in need. 3. Freedom from a job or duty, especially when one person takes over for another. 4. A type of sculpture in which figures or details stand out from the surface. 5. **relief map** A map

that uses shading or a model that uses relief to show hills and valleys.

re·lieve (ri-**leev**) *verb* **1.** To ease someone's pain, trouble, or difficulty. **2.** To take over someone's post, station, or duty.
▸ *verb* **relieving, relieved**

re·lig·ion (ri-**lij**-uhn) *noun* **1.** Belief in, devotion to, and worship of a God or gods. **2.** A specific system of belief, faith, and worship. Some world religions are Buddhism, Christianity, Hinduism, Islam, and Judaism. **3.** A principle, a cause, or a pursuit that is very important to someone.

re·li·gious (ri-**lij**-uhs) *adjective* **1.** Of or about religion. **2.** A **religious** person is one who believes in a religion and follows its teachings.
noun A member of a religious organization, such as a nun or a monk.

rel·ish (**rel**-ish) *verb* To take great pleasure in something.
noun **1.** A mixture of spices and chopped vegetables, such as olives or pickles, used to flavor food. **2.** Enjoyment.
▸ *verb* **relishes, relishing, relished** ▸ *noun, plural* **relishes**

re·luc·tant (ri-**luhk**-tuhnt) *adjective* Hesitant or unwilling to do something. ▸ *noun* **reluctance** ▸ *adverb* **reluctantly**

re·ly (ri-**lye**) *verb* To have trust in or to be dependent on someone or something. ▸ *verb* **relies, relying, relied** ▸ *noun* **reliance** (ri-**lye**-uhns) ▸ *adjective* **reliant** (ri-**lye**-uhnt)

re·main (ri-**mayn**) *verb* **1.** To stay in the same place. **2.** To be left after others have been used up, removed, or destroyed. **3.** To continue being.
▸ *verb* **remaining, remained**

re·main·der (ri-**mayn**-dur) *noun* **1.** The part or amount that is left over. **2.** The number found when one number is subtracted from another. **3.** The number left over when one number cannot be divided evenly by another.

re·mains (ri-**maynz**) *noun, plural* **1.** All that is left over. **2.** Parts of something that was once alive. **3.** A dead body.

re·mark (ri-**mahrk**) *verb* To mention or make a comment about something.
noun A comment or observation.
▸ *verb* **remarking, remarked**

re·mark·a·ble (ri-**mahr**-kuh-buhl) *adjective* Worth noticing; extraordinary. ▸ *adverb* **remarkably**

re·me·di·al (ri-**mee**-dee-uhl) *adjective* Intended to help or correct something.

rem·e·dy (**rem**-i-dee) *noun* Something that relieves pain, cures a disease, or corrects a disorder.
verb To relieve or to set something right.
▸ *noun, plural* **remedies** ▸ *verb* **remedies, remedying, remedied**

re·mem·ber (ri-**mem**-bur) *verb* **1.** To recall or to bring back to mind. **2.** To keep in mind carefully.
▸ *verb* **remembering, remembered**

re·mind (ri-**minde**) *verb* To cause someone to remember something. ▸ *verb* **reminding, reminded**

re·mind·er (ri-**mine**-dur) *noun* Something that helps a person remember.

rem·i·nisce (rem-uh-**nis**) *verb* To think or talk about past events or experiences. ▸ *verb* **reminiscing, reminisced** ▸ *noun* **reminiscence**

re·mis·sion (ri-**mish**-uhn) *noun* If the symptoms of a disease start to disappear or become less severe, the disease is in **remission.**

rem·nant (**rem**-nuhnt) *noun* A small piece or amount of something that is left over, especially a piece of cloth.

re·mod·el (ree-**mah**-duhl) *verb* To make a major change to the structure or design of something. ▸ *verb* **remodeling, remodeled**

re·morse (ri-**mors**) *noun* A strong feeling of guilt or distress over something wrong that you have done in the past. ▸ *adjective* **remorseful** ▸ *adverb* **remorsefully**

R

re·mote (ri-**moht**) *adjective* **1.** Far away in time or space; secluded or isolated. **2.** Extremely small or slight. ▸ *adjective* **remoter, remotest** ▸ *noun* **remoteness** ▸ *adverb* **remotely**

re·mote con·trol (ri-**moht** kuhn-**trohl**) *noun* A system or device for operating machines from a distance by means of radio signals or a beam of light. ▸ *adjective* **remote-controlled**

re·mov·a·ble (ri-**moo**-vuh-buhl) *adjective* Able to be easily removed.

re·mov·al (ri-**moo**-vuhl) *noun* The process or activity of taking something off or away.

re·move (ri-**moov**) *verb* **1.** To take something away from a place or position. **2.** To take off. ▸ *verb* **removing, removed**

Re·nais·sance (**ren**-uh-*sahns*) *noun* The revival of art and learning, inspired by the ancient Greeks and Romans, that took place in Europe between the 14th and 16th centuries. The Renaissance marked the transition from medieval to modern times.

ren·der (**ren**-dur) *verb* **1.** To make or cause to become. **2.** To give or to deliver. ▸ *verb* **rendering, rendered**

ren·dez·vous (**rahn**-duh-*voo* or **rahn**-day-*voo*) *noun* **1.** An appointment to meet at a certain time or place. **2.** The place chosen for a meeting. *verb* To meet at a time and place that have been agreed upon. ▸ *noun, plural* **rendezvous** ▸ *verb* **rendezvousing, rendezvoused**

re·new (ri-**noo**) *verb* **1.** To make something that is broken or worn look new again; to restore. **2.** To start something again after a break or interruption; to resume. **3.** To extend the period of a library loan, license, subscription, contract, or club membership. ▸ *verb* **renewing, renewed** ▸ *noun* **renewal** (ri-**noo**-uhl) ▸ *adjective* **renewable** ▸ *adjective* **renewed**

re·new·a·ble en·er·gy (ri-**noo**-uh-buhl **en**-ur-jee) *noun* Power from sources that can never be used up, such as wind, tides, sunlight, and geothermal heat.

ren·o·vate (**ren**-uh-*vate*) *verb* To modernize or restore something to good condition by cleaning, repairing, or remodeling. ▸ *verb* **renovating, renovated** ▸ *noun* **renovation**

re·nowned (ri-**nound**) *adjective* Famous and widely acclaimed. ▸ *noun* **renown**

rent (rent) *noun* Money paid by a tenant to the owner of a building or other property in return for living in it or using it. *verb* To get or give the right to use something in return for payment. ▸ *verb* **renting, rented**

rent·al (**ren**-tuhl) *noun* **1.** The amount paid to rent something. **2.** Something that is hired or rented, such as a car or property. *adjective* Having to do with or available for rent.

re·pair (ri-**pair**) *verb* To restore something that has been damaged or broken to good working condition; to fix. *noun* The act of fixing something that has been damaged or broken. ▸ *verb* **repairing, repaired**

re·pa·tri·a·tion (ree-*pay*-tree-*ay*-shuhn) *noun* The return of someone to the country where he or she was born or where he or she is a citizen. ▸ *verb* **repatriate**

re·pay (ree-**pay**) *verb* **1.** To pay someone back. **2.** To give or do something in return. ▸ *verb* **repaying, repaid** ▸ *noun* **repayment**

re·peal (ri-**peel**) *verb* To cancel or do away with something officially, such as a law. *noun* The official cancellation of something. ▸ *verb* **repealing, repealed**

re·peat *verb* (ri-**peet**) To say or do something again or more than once. *noun* (ri-**peet** or ree-**peet**) Something that happens or is done again. ▸ *verb* **repeating, repeated**

R

re·peat·ed·ly (ri-**pee**-tid-lee) *adverb* More than once or at frequent intervals.

re·pel (ri-**pel**) *verb* **1.** To drive back or keep away. **2.** To cause disgust or horror.
▶ *verb* **repelling, repelled**

re·pel·lent (ri-**pel**-uhnt)
noun A chemical that wards off insects and other pests.
adjective Repulsive or disgusting.

re·pent (ri-**pent**) *verb* To feel or to express regret for something that you have done. ▶ *verb* **repenting, repented** ▶ *noun* **repentance** ▶ *adjective* **repentant**

rep·er·toire (**rep**-ur-*twahr*) *noun* The songs, jokes, plays, stories, or musical compositions that an individual or a company is prepared to perform in public.

rep·e·ti·tion (rep-i-**tish**-uhn) *noun* The act of repeating something.
▶ *adjective* **repetitious** ▶ *adjective* **repetitive** (ri-**pet**-i-tiv)

re·place (ri-**plase**) *verb* **1.** To take the place of or to substitute for someone or something. **2.** To put something back in its former place or position. **3.** To put something new in the place of something that is worn or damaged.
▶ *verb* **replacing, replaced**

re·place·ment (ri-**plase**-muhnt) *noun* **1.** The activity or process of replacing someone or something. **2.** Someone or something that takes the place of another.

re·play
verb (ree-**play**) **1.** To play a recording again. **2.** To play a second contest or match between two teams or players because the first one ended in a tie.
noun (**ree**-play) The playing of a recording.
▶ *verb* **replaying, replayed**

rep·li·ca (**rep**-li-kuh) *noun* An exact copy of something, especially a copy made on a smaller scale than the original. ▶ *verb* **replicate** (**rep**-li-*kate*)

re·ply (ri-**plye**)
verb To answer or respond in speech or in writing.
noun An answer that is spoken or written.
▶ *verb* **replies, replying, replied** ▶ *noun, plural* **replies**

re·port (ri-**port**)
noun A detailed written or spoken account of an event.
verb **1.** To give a report or to make known. **2.** To make a formal charge or complaint about someone. **3.** To present yourself as ready to do something. **4.** If you **report to** someone, you work for him or her.
▶ *verb* **reporting, reported**

re·port card (ri-**port** *kahrd*) *noun* A listing of a student's grades that is compiled and sent home several times a year. A report card can also include comments from a teacher about a student's behavior.

re·port·er (ri-**por**-tur) *noun* Someone who gathers and reports the news for radio or television or for a newspaper, magazine, or website.

rep·re·sent (rep-ri-**zent**) *verb* **1.** To speak or act for someone else. **2.** To be a sign or symbol of something.
▶ *verb* **representing, represented**

rep·re·sen·ta·tion (rep-ri-zen-**tay**-shuhn) *noun* **1.** An image or model that stands for something. **2.** The act of representing or being represented.
▶ *adjective* **representational**

rep·re·sen·ta·tive (rep-ri-**zen**-tuh-tiv)
noun **1.** Someone who is chosen to speak or act for others. **2.** A person or thing that is typical of a class or group.
adjective Typical of a class or group.

re·press (ri-**pres**) *verb* **1.** If you **repress** an emotion, you try not to let it show. **2.** To use force to keep someone or something under very strict control.
▶ *verb* **represses, repressing, repressed** ▶ *noun* **repression** ▶ *adjective* **repressed** ▶ *adjective* **repressive**

re·prieve (ri-**preev**)
verb To cancel or delay a punishment.
noun Postponement or cancellation of a punishment.
▶ *verb* **reprieving, reprieved**

R

rep·ri·mand (**rep**-ruh-*mand*)
verb To criticize someone sharply or formally.
noun A sharp, formal, or official expression of disapproval.
▶ *verb* **reprimanding, reprimanded**

re·pri·sal (ri-**prye**-zuhl) *noun* An act of revenge or retaliation.

re·proach (ri-**prohch**)
verb To show that you disapprove of or are disappointed by what someone has done or said; to blame.
noun An expression of disapproval or disappointment; blame.
▶ *noun, plural* **reproaches** ▶ *verb* **reproaches, reproaching, reproached**

re·pro·duce (ree-pruh-**doos**) *verb* 1. To make an image or copy of something. 2. To produce offspring or individuals of the same kind.
▶ *verb* **reproducing, reproduced**

re·pro·duc·tion (ree-pruh-**duhk**-shuhn) *noun* 1. An image or copy of something, such as a work of art. 2. The act of producing offspring or individuals of the same kind.

rep·tile (**rep**-tile *or* **rep**-tuhl) *noun* A cold-blooded animal that crawls or creeps on short legs. Reptiles have backbones and most of them reproduce by laying eggs. ▶ *adjective* **reptilian** (rep-**til**-ee-uhn *or* rep-**til**-yuhn)

re·pub·lic (ri-**puhb**-lik) *noun* 1. A form of government in which the people have the power to elect representatives who manage the government. Republics often have presidents. 2. A country that has such a form of government. The United States is a republic.

re·pub·li·can (ri-**puhb**-li-kuhn) *adjective* Of or having to do with, typical of, or supporting a republic.

Re·pub·li·can Par·ty (ri-**puhb**-li-kuhn **pahr**-tee) *noun* One of the two main political parties in the United States. The other is the Democratic Party.

re·pug·nant (ri-**puhg**-nuhnt) *adjective* Disgusting or offensive.

re·pulse (ri-**puhls**) *verb* 1. To drive back by using force. 2. To refuse or reject something.
▶ *verb* **repulsing, repulsed**

re·pul·sive (ri-**puhl**-siv) *adjective* Very distasteful or disgusting. ▶ *noun* **repulsion** ▶ *adverb* **repulsively**

rep·u·ta·ble (**rep**-yuh-tuh-buhl) *adjective* Honorable and trustworthy; having a good reputation. ▶ *adverb* **reputably**

rep·u·ta·tion (rep-yuh-**tay**-shuhn) *noun* Your worth or character, as judged by other people.

re·pute (ri-**pyoot**) *noun* The state of being highly esteemed; fame.

re·put·ed (ri-**pyoo**-tid) *adjective* Generally supposed or believed to be. ▶ *adverb* **reputedly**

re·quest (ri-**kwest**)
verb To ask politely or formally for something.
noun Something that you ask for politely or formally.
▶ *verb* **requesting, requested**

re·qui·em (**rek**-wee-uhm) *noun* 1. A church service, especially in the Roman Catholic Church, for the souls of the dead or for someone who has died. 2. A piece of music composed in memory of someone who has died, often a musical setting of the Mass for the dead.

re·quire (ri-**kwire**) *verb* 1. To need something. 2. If you are **required** to do something, you are told or expected to do it.
▶ *verb* **requiring, required**

re·quired (ri-**kwired**) *adjective* Necessary.

re·quire·ment (ri-**kwire**-muhnt) *noun* Something that you need to do or are required to have.

re·read (ree-**reed**) *verb* To read a passage or piece of writing again.
▶ *verb* **rereading, reread** (ree-**red**)

re·run
verb (ree-**ruhn**) To run again.
noun (**ree**-ruhn) A television program that has been shown before.
▶ *verb* **rerunning, reran** (ree-**ran**)

res·cue (**res**-kyoo)
verb To save someone who is in danger or in a difficult situation.
noun An act of rescuing someone or something.
▶ *verb* **rescuing, rescued** ▶ *noun* **rescuer**

R

re·search (ri-**surch** or **ree**-*surch*)
verb To collect information about a subject through reading, investigating, or experimenting.
noun A study or investigation in a particular field, usually to learn new facts or to solve a problem.
▶ *verb* **researches, researching, researched** ▶ *noun, plural* **researches** ▶ *noun* **researcher**

re·sem·ble (ri-**zem**-buhl) *verb* To look like or be similar to something or someone. ▶ *verb* **resembling, resembled** ▶ *noun* **resemblance** (ri-**zem**-bluhns)

re·sent (ri-**zent**) *verb* To feel anger or annoyance toward someone or about something. ▶ *verb* **resenting, resented** ▶ *noun* **resentment** ▶ *adjective* **resentful**

res·er·va·tion (*rez*-ur-**vay**-shuhn) *noun*
1. An arrangement to save space or a seat for someone. **2.** An area of land set aside by the government for a special purpose. **3.** A doubt, fear, or reason to hesitate.

re·serve (ri-**zurv**)
verb **1.** To arrange for something to be kept for later or future use. **2.** To save for a special purpose or later use. **3.** To keep for oneself.
noun A protected place where hunting is not allowed and where animals can live and breed safely.
noun, plural **reserves** The part of the armed forces that is kept ready to serve in an emergency.
▶ *verb* **reserving, reserved**

re·served (ri-**zurvd**) *adjective* **1.** Kept for someone to use later. **2.** A **reserved** person is reluctant to reveal his or her feelings or opinions.

res·er·voir (**rez**-ur-*vwahr*) *noun* A natural or artificial lake in which water is collected and stored for use.

re·set
verb (**ree**-set) **1.** To make a machine, program, or device start again from the beginning. **2.** To change something from the setting it had before.
noun (**ree**-*set*) **reset button** A button

that you push to reset a device or machine.
▶ *verb* **resetting, reset**

re·side (ri-**zide**) *verb* To live in a place. ▶ *verb* **residing, resided**

res·i·dence (**rez**-i-duhns) *noun* The place where someone lives; a home.

res·i·dent (**rez**-i-duhnt) *noun* Someone who lives in a particular place on a long-term basis.

res·i·den·tial (rez-i-**den**-shuhl) *adjective* Of or having to do with a neighborhood or an area where people live.

res·i·due (**rez**-i-doo) *noun* **1.** What is left after something burns up or evaporates. **2.** Anything that remains after the main part has been taken away.
▶ *adjective* **residual** (ri-**zij**-oo-uhl)

re·sign (ri-**zine**) *verb* **1.** To give up a job, a position, or an office voluntarily.
2. If you **resign yourself** to something, you accept it because you realize it cannot be avoided.
▶ *verb* **resigning, resigned** ▶ *adjective* **resigned**

res·ig·na·tion (*rez*-ig-**nay**-shuhn) *noun* **1.** The act of giving up a job or position. **2.** A letter formally stating your intention to give up a job or position. **3.** The acceptance of something undesirable that can't be avoided.

res·in (**rez**-in) *noun* A yellow or brown, sticky substance that oozes from pine, balsam, and other trees and plants. Resin is used to make varnishes, lacquers, plastics, glue, and rubber.

re·sist (ri-**zist**) *verb* **1.** To refuse to accept; to oppose. **2.** To fight back or to struggle against someone or something. **3.** To stop yourself from having or doing something you want.
▶ *verb* **resisting, resisted**

re·sis·tance (ri-**zis**-tuhns) *noun*
1. The act of resisting or fighting back. **2.** The ability to fight off or overcome something. **3.** A force that opposes the motion of an object. **4.** The ability of a substance or a device to resist the passage of an electrical current.

R

res·o·lute (**rez**-uh-*loot*) *adjective* Strongly determined to do something. ▶ *adverb* **resolutely**

res·o·lu·tion (*rez*-uh-**loo**-shuhn) *noun*
1. A promise that you make to yourself, particularly at the start of a new year.
2. The state of being very determined.
3. A measure of the quality of an image, often measured in dots per inch.

re·solve (ri-**zahlv**)
verb 1. To make a firm decision about something. 2. To find a solution to a problem or to settle a difficulty.
noun Determination.
▶ *verb* **resolving, resolved**

res·o·nant (**rez**-uh-nuhnt) *adjective*
1. Having a full, deep sound. 2. Able to amplify sounds or make them last longer.
▶ *noun* **resonance** ▶ *verb* **resonate**

re·sort (ri-**zort**)
noun 1. A place where people go for rest and recreation. 2. If you do something as **a last resort,** you do it because everything else you have tried has failed.
verb If you **resort to** something, you do it because you have no other way of resolving a difficult situation.
▶ *verb* **resorting, resorted**

re·sound (ri-**zound**) *verb* 1. To be filled with sound. 2. To make a long, loud, echoing sound.
▶ *verb* **resounding, resounded**

re·source (**ree**-sors *or* **ree**-zors) *noun*
1. Something that is of value or use.
2. Something that you can go to for help or support.

re·source·ful (ri-**sors**-fuhl *or* ri-**zors**-fuhl) *adjective* If you are **resourceful,** you are good at knowing what to do or where to get help in any situation.

re·spect (ri-**spekt**)
verb To feel admiration and esteem for someone or something.
noun 1. A feeling of admiration or high regard for someone or something.
2. A particular feature or detail of something.
noun, plural **respects** Regards or greetings.
▶ *verb* **respecting, respected**

re·spect·a·ble (ri-**spek**-tuh-buhl) *adjective* 1. Behaving honestly and decently. 2. Acceptable or reasonably good.
▶ *adverb* **respectably**

re·spect·ful (ri-**spekt**-fuhl) *adjective* Showing proper respect, consideration, or courtesy. ▶ *adverb* **respectfully**

re·spec·tive (ri-**spek**-tiv) *adjective* Belonging to or having to do with each one. ▶ *adverb* **respectively**

res·pi·ra·tion (*res*-puh-**ray**-shuhn) *noun* The act or process of breathing in and breathing out. ▶ *adjective* **respiratory** (**res**-pur-uh-*tor*-ee)

re·spond (ri-**spahnd**) *verb* 1. To reply or to give an answer. 2. To react to someone or something.
▶ *verb* **responding, responded**

re·sponse (ri-**spahns**) *noun* A spoken or written reply; a reaction.

re·spon·si·bil·i·ty (ri-*spahn*-suh-**bil**-i-tee) *noun* 1. A duty or a job. 2. If you **take responsibility** for something that has happened, you agree that it is your burden or that you should take the blame for it.
▶ *noun, plural* **responsibilities**

re·spon·si·ble (ri-**spahn**-suh-buhl) *adjective* 1. If someone is **responsible** for something, it is their duty to do it. 2. If a person is **responsible,** he or she can be trusted. 3. Being the cause. 4. Having or involving important duties.
▶ *adverb* **responsibly**

rest (rest)
verb 1. To stop doing something in order to relax or sleep. 2. To lean against something. 3. To sit, lie, or be supported in a specific position. 4. To finish presenting evidence in a court of law.
noun 1. A stopping of work or some activity. 2. Sleep. 3. The others, or those that remain. 4. The state or fact of not moving. 5. A pause or period of silence in a piece of music.
Rest sounds like **wrest.** ▶ *verb* **resting, rested**

R

res·tau·rant (**res**-tuh-*rahnt* or **res**-tur-uhnt) *noun* A place where meals can be purchased and eaten.

rest·less (**rest**-lis) *adjective* Unable to relax or be still because of anxiety or boredom. ▶ *adverb* **restlessly**

res·to·ra·tion (res-tuh-**ray**-shuhn) *noun* 1. The return of something to its former condition, place, or owner. 2. The renovation or repair of a building or a work of art.

re·store (ri-**stor**) *verb* 1. To bring back or to establish again. 2. To bring back to an original condition. 3. To give something back or to put someone back in a former position.
▶ *verb* **restoring, restored** ▶ *noun* **restorer**

re·strain (ri-**strayn**) *verb* 1. To prevent someone from doing what he or she wants to do. 2. To hold back or keep under control.
▶ *verb* **restraining, restrained**

re·strained (ri-**straynd**) *adjective* Very reserved and unemotional.

re·straint (ri-**straynt**) *noun* 1. The act of limiting or controlling something. 2. A force, device, or influence that limits or controls.

re·strict (ri-**strikt**) *verb* To confine or keep within limits. ▶ *verb* **restricting, restricted** ▶ *adjective* **restricted**

re·stric·tion (ri-**strik**-shuhn) *noun* 1. The act of keeping or confining someone or something within limits. 2. A rule, measure, or condition that limits or controls.

rest·room (**rest**-room) *noun* A bathroom, especially in a public building.

re·sult (ri-**zuhlt**)
noun Something that is produced or caused by something else.
verb To be caused by or to happen because of something else.
▶ *verb* **resulting, resulted**

re·sume (ri-**zoom**) *verb* To start doing or to return to something after an interruption. ▶ *verb* **resuming, resumed**

ré·su·mé (**rez**-uh-*may*) *noun* A brief list or summary of a person's education, jobs, and achievements.

re·sus·ci·tate (ri-**suhs**-i-*tate*) *verb* To make conscious again, or to bring back from a near-death condition. ▶ *verb* **resuscitating, resuscitated** ▶ *noun* **resuscitation** (ri-*suhs*-i-**tay**-shuhn)

re·tail (**ree**-tayl)
adjective Of or having to do with the sale of goods directly to customers. *noun* 1. The sale of goods directly to customers. 2. The **retail price** of something is the price at which it is sold in stores.
verb To be sold for a specified price.
▶ *verb* **retailing, retailed**

re·tail·er (**ree**-tay-lur) *noun* Someone who sells goods to the public, usually in a store.

re·tain (ri-**tayn**) *verb* 1. To continue to have or to keep something. 2. To hold in or to contain. 3. If you **retain** a lawyer, you pay him or her a fee to represent you.
▶ *verb* **retaining, retained** ▶ *noun* **retention** (ri-**ten**-shuhn)

re·tal·i·ate (ri-**tal**-ee-*ate*) *verb* To get revenge or to respond to an injury or attack with similar behavior. ▶ *verb* **retaliating, retaliated** ▶ *noun* **retaliation** ▶ *adjective* **retaliatory**

re·tard (ri-**tahrd**) *verb* To slow down or to hold back. ▶ *verb* **retarding, retarded**

re·tard·ed (ri-**tahr**-did) *adjective* Slow or limited in mental or emotional development. Many people find this word offensive and use the words *challenged* or *disabled* instead. ▶ *noun* **retardation** (ree-tahr-**day**-shuhn)

retch (rech)
verb To try to vomit or to start vomiting.
noun An act of vomiting or trying to vomit.
▶ *verb* **retches, retching, retched**

ret·i·cent (**ret**-i-suhnt) *adjective* Reluctant to tell people what you know, think, or feel. ▶ *noun* **reticence**

ret·i·na (**ret**-uh-nuh) *noun* The lining at the back of the eyeball. The retina is sensitive to light and sends images of the things you see to your brain.

R

re·tire (ri-**tire**) *verb* **1.** To stop working, usually because you have reached a certain age. **2.** To go to bed. **3.** To go to a quieter or more private place. **4.** To put out in baseball.
▶ *verb* **retiring, retired** ▶ *adjective* **retired**

re·tire·ment (ri-**tire**-muhnt) *noun* The period in your life after you've stopped working.

re·tir·ing (re-**tire**-ing) *adjective* Shy and reserved; preferring to spend time alone rather than with other people.

re·tort
verb (ri-**tort**) To respond in a quick, sharp, or witty manner.
noun (ri-**tort** or **ree**-tort) **1.** A quick, witty response. **2.** A long-necked glass container used in laboratories.
▶ *verb* **retorting, retorted**

re·trace (ri-**trays**) *verb* To go back over the same route or path that you have just taken. ▶ *verb* **retracing, retraced**

re·treat (ri-**treet**)
verb To withdraw from an attack or move away from a difficult situation.
noun **1.** A quiet place where you can go to relax, to think, or to be alone; a refuge. **2.** The process of going backward or withdrawing from something.
▶ *verb* **retreating, retreated**

re·trieve (ri-**treev**) *verb* **1.** To get or bring something back; to regain. **2.** To locate information in storage, especially by using a computer.
▶ *verb* **retrieving, retrieved** ▶ *noun* **retrieval**

re·triev·er (ri-**tree**-vur) *noun* Any of several popular breeds of large dogs. Retrievers can be trained to find and bring back game shot by hunters.

re·tro·rock·et (**ret**-roh-*rah*-kit) *noun* A small rocket that slows down or turns a spacecraft.

ret·ro·vi·rus (**ret**-roh-*vye*-ruhs) *noun* Any of a group of viruses that contain RNA instead of the usual DNA. HIV, the virus that causes AIDS, is an example of a retrovirus. It works by inserting

a copy of itself into human DNA so that it will be reproduced by its host. ▶ *noun, plural* **retroviruses**

re·turn (ri-**turn**)
verb **1.** To come back or to go back. **2.** To take, put, or send something back. **3.** To appear or happen again. **4.** To give back in the same way.
noun **1.** The act of returning. **2.** Money made as a profit. **3.** An official form. **4.** A large key on a keyboard that you hit to end a line or to move to another place on your screen. It has that name because in some programs, hitting this key causes you to return to the left margin and start a new line. Also called **enter**. **5. return ticket** A ticket that covers travel to and from a place.
phrase **in return** In exchange for or as a payment for something else.
▶ *verb* **returning, returned**

re·un·ion (ree-**yoon**-yuhn) *noun* A meeting or gathering of two or more people who have not seen each other for a long time.

re·us·a·ble (ree-**yoo**-zuh-buhl) *adjective* Capable of being used again rather than thrown away.

rev (rev) *verb* (informal) To increase the speed of an engine by pressing on the accelerator. ▶ *verb* **revving, revved**

re·veal (ri-**veel**) *verb* **1.** To make known. **2.** To show or bring into view.
▶ *verb* **revealing, revealed** ▶ *adjective* **revealing**

rev·el (**rev**-uhl) *verb* If you **revel in** something, you find great pleasure or enjoyment in it. ▶ *verb* **reveling, reveled**

rev·e·la·tion (*rev*-uh-**lay**-shuhn) *noun* A very surprising and previously unknown fact that is made known.

re·venge (ri-**venj**)
noun Something you do to get back at someone for the injury or harm that the person has done to you or to someone you care about.
verb To do something to get back at someone for something that person has done to you or someone you care about.

re·venge·ful (ri-**venj**-fuhl) *adjective*
Seeking or motivated by revenge.

rev·e·nue (**rev**-uh-noo) *noun* **1.** The
money that a government gets from
taxes and other sources. **2.** The money
that is made from property or other
investments.

re·ver·ber·ate (ri-**vur**-buh-rate) *verb*
To echo or resound as if in a series
of echoes. ▶ *verb* **reverberating,
reverberated** ▶ *noun* **reverberation**

rev·er·ence (**rev**-ur-uhns) *noun*
Honor and respect that is felt or
shown. ▶ *verb* **revere** (ri-**veer**)
▶ *adjective* **reverent** (**rev**-ur-uhnt)
▶ *adverb* **reverently**

re·verse (ri-**vurs**)
verb **1.** To turn something around,
upside down, or inside out. **2.** To
transfer telephone fees to someone
receiving the call. **3.** To cancel or
change to the opposite position.
noun **1.** The opposite of something.
2. The back or rear side of something.
3. A position of gears that allows a
motor vehicle to move backward.
adjective Opposite in position, order,
or direction.
▶ *verb* **reversing, reversed** ▶ *adjective*
reversible ▶ *noun* **reversal** (ri-**vur**-
suhl)

re·vert (ri-**vurt**) *verb* To go back to a
previous state or condition. ▶ *verb*
reverting, reverted ▶ *noun* **reversion**
(ri-**vur**-zhuhn)

re·view (ri-**vyoo**)
noun **1.** A piece of writing that gives
an opinion about a movie, a written
work, or a performance. **2.** A careful
or formal inspection of something.
verb **1.** To study something carefully
and to make changes if necessary.
2. To study or go over again. **3.** To
write a review of a book, movie, or
some other work. **4.** To make a formal
inspection of.
▶ *verb* **reviewing, reviewed** ▶ *noun*
reviewer

re·vise (ri-**vize**) *verb* **1.** To examine and
change something, often to make it

more up-to-date. **2.** To reconsider and
change something in the light of new
information.
▶ *verb* **revising, revised**

re·vi·sion (ri-**vizh**-uhn) *noun* **1.** The
preparation of a new version of
something. **2.** A new version or form
of something, especially a piece of
writing.

re·viv·al (ri-**vye**-vuhl) *noun* **1.** The act
of making something popular,
known, or useful again. **2.** A return
to good health or consciousness.
3. A reawakening of religious faith or
a meeting intended to achieve this.

re·vive (ri-**vive**) *verb* **1.** To bring
someone back to life or
consciousness. **2.** To restore interest
in something or to bring it back
into use. **3.** To give new strength or
freshness to.
▶ *verb* **reviving, revived** ▶ *noun*
revival (ri-**vye**-vuhl)

re·voke (ri-**voke**) *verb* To take away
or to cancel. ▶ *verb* **revoking,
revoked** ▶ *noun* **revocation**
(*rev*-uh-**kay**-shuhn)

re·volt (ri-**vohlt**)
verb **1.** To try to overthrow a ruler
or a government. **2.** If something
revolts you, it fills you with disgust.
noun A rebellion against a
government or an authority.
▶ *verb* **revolting, revolted**

re·volt·ing (ri-**vohl**-ting) *adjective* Very
unpleasant or disgusting.

rev·o·lu·tion (*rev*-uh-**loo**-shuhn) *noun*
1. A violent overthrow of a country's
government or ruler by the people
who live there. **2.** A sudden, radical,
or far-reaching change. **3.** A complete
movement of one object around
another, such as of the earth around
the sun.

rev·o·lu·tion·ar·y (*rev*-uh-**loo**-shuh-*ner*-
ee) *adjective* **1.** Involving or bringing
about a dramatic change. **2.** Of or
having to do with a political or social
revolution.

R

Rev·o·lu·tion·ar·y War (*rev*-uh-**loo**-shuh-*ner*-ee **wor**) *noun* The war in which the 13 American colonies won their independence from Great Britain. The war lasted from 1775 to 1783 and is also known as the *American Revolution.*

rev·o·lu·tion·ize (*rev*-uh-**loo**-shuh-nize) *verb* To bring about a complete change in something. ▶ *verb* **revolutionizing, revolutionized**

re·volve (ri-**vahlv**) *verb* **1.** To keep turning in a circle or orbit around a central point or object. **2.** To spin around or to rotate. **3. revolve around** To center or focus on. ▶ *verb* **revolving, revolved**

re·volv·er (ri-**vahl**-vur) *noun* A small pistol with a revolving cylinder that enables it to be fired several times before it needs to be reloaded.

re·ward (ri-**word**)
noun Something that you receive in recognition of your efforts or achievements.
verb To give someone a reward for their service or achievements.
▶ *verb* **rewarding, rewarded**

re·ward·ing (ri-**wor**-ding) *adjective* If something is **rewarding,** it offers or brings you satisfaction.

re·word (ree-**wurd**) *verb* To say or write something using different words. ▶ *verb* **rewording, reworded**

Reye's syn·drome (**rize** *sin*-drohm or **rayz** *sin*-drohm) *noun* A rare children's disease whose symptoms include vomiting and swelling of the liver and brain.

rheu·mat·ic fever (roo-**mat**-ik **fee**-vur) *noun* A serious disease, especially in children, that causes fever, joint pain, and possible heart damage.

rheu·ma·tism (**roo**-muh-*tiz*-uhm) *noun* A disease that causes pain, swelling, and stiffness in the joints and muscles. ▶ *adjective* **rheumatic** (roo-**mat**-ik)

rhi·noc·er·os (rye-**nah**-sur-uhs) *noun* A large mammal from Africa and Asia that has thick, folded skin and

one or two upright horns on its nose. ▶ *noun, plural* **rhinoceroses** or **rhinoceros**

Rhode Isl·and (*rohd* **eye**-luhnd) A New England state in the northeastern United States. It is the smallest state in the U.S. and was the first of the 13 original colonies to declare independence from British rule. One of its main attractions is the city of Newport, famous for its mansions built in the 19th century, when it was a summer resort for the country's wealthiest families.

rho·do·den·dron (roh-duh-**den**-druhn) *noun* A large evergreen shrub with showy clusters of bell-shaped flowers.

rhom·bus (**rahm**-buhs) *noun* A parallelogram with four straight sides of equal length but often no right angles. ▶ *noun, plural* **rhombuses** or **rhombi** (**rahm**-*bye*)

rhu·barb (**roo**-bahrb) *noun* A tall plant with reddish or greenish stems that can be cooked and eaten. Its leaves are poisonous.

rhyme (rime)
verb If words **rhyme,** they have the same ending sounds. The word *love* rhymes with *dove* and *above.*
noun **1.** A short poem that rhymes. **2.** A word that ends with the same sound as another.
▶ *verb* **rhyming, rhymed**

rhythm (**riTH**-uhm) *noun* A repeated pattern of sound or movement in music, poetry, or dance.

rhyth·mic (**riTH**-mik) *adjective* Of, relating to, or having a rhythm. ▶ *adjective* **rhythmical** ▶ *adverb* **rhythmically**

rib (rib) *noun* **1.** One of the curved bones that enclose your chest and protect your heart and lungs. **2.** Something that looks or functions like a rib.

rib·bon (**rib**-uhn) *noun* **1.** A long, thin band of material, such as satin or velvet, that is used for tying something or for decoration.

R

2. A long, thin band of material used for something other than decoration.

rice (rise) *noun* The seeds of a grasslike cereal plant that is grown for food in flooded fields.

rich (rich)
adjective **1.** Having a great deal of money or many possessions.
2. Existing in large quantities or having an abundant supply of something. **3.** Very expensive and impressive. **4.** Containing a lot of fat or sugar. **5.** Fertile.
noun, plural **riches** Material wealth or abundant natural resources.
noun People who have a great deal of money or possessions.
▸ *adjective* **richer, richest** ▸ *adverb* **richly**

rick·et·y (**rik**-i-tee) *adjective* Poorly made and likely to break or collapse.

rick·shaw *or* **rick·sha** (**rik**-*shaw*) *noun* A small carriage with two wheels and a cover that usually is pulled by one person. Rickshaws originally were used in Asia.

ric·o·chet (**rik**-uh-*shay*) *verb* To rebound off a hard surface. ▸ *verb* **ricocheting, ricocheted**

rid (rid)
verb To remove an unwanted or annoying person or thing.
phrase If you **get rid of** something, you free yourself of it by throwing it away or removing it.
▸ *verb* **ridding, rid**

rid·dle (**rid**-uhl) *noun* A statement or question that makes you think hard and that usually has a clever answer.

ride (ride)
verb **1.** To travel on an animal or in a vehicle. **2.** To be supported or carried along.
noun **1.** A journey on an animal or in a vehicle. **2.** A device or machine such as a merry-go-round that people ride for fun.
▸ *verb* **riding, rode, ridden**

rid·er (**rye**-dur) *noun* **1.** Someone who rides a horse. **2.** Some who rides a two-wheeled vehicle, or who is a passenger in a motor vehicle.
3. An addition to a document that modifies or adds to information in the main part.

ridge (rij) *noun* **1.** A narrow, raised strip on the surface of something.
2. A long, narrow chain of mountains or hills.
▸ *adjective* **ridged**

rid·i·cule (**rid**-i-kyool)
verb To make fun of someone or something in a mocking or unkind way.
noun The act of making fun or someone or something in a mocking or unkind way.
▸ *verb* **ridiculing, ridiculed**

ri·dic·u·lous (ri-**dik**-yuh-luhs) *adjective* Absurd, silly, or foolish. ▸ *adverb* **ridiculously**

ri·fle (**rye**-fuhl)
noun A gun with a long barrel that is fired from the shoulder.
verb To search through and rob.
▸ *verb* **rifling, rifled**

rift (rift) *noun* **1.** A split or crack in a rock or other hard substance.
2. A serious disagreement between people who used to have a close relationship.

rig (rig)
verb **1.** To provide or to equip.
2. To equip a ship with the necessary masts, sails, ropes, and other gear.
3. To manage, arrange, or control something in a dishonest way.
4. If you **rig up** something, you put it together in a casual or makeshift way, using whatever you can find.
noun **1.** The arrangement of a boat's or ship's masts and sails.
2. A structure specially designed to drill for oil or gas. **3.** A carriage led by a horse or horses that is used for moving people or goods. **4.** A truck that has a small cab for the driver and a larger trailer in back, used for hauling commercial goods.
5. Equipment or gear used for a special purpose.
▸ *verb* **rigging, rigged**

R

rig·ging (**rig**-ing) *noun* The system of ropes, chains, and wires that support and control the sails on a boat or ship.

right (rite)
adjective 1. On the side opposite the left. 2. Conforming to fact, reason, or truth; correct. 3. Morally good, fair, or acceptable. 4. Suitable.
adverb 1. Toward the right-hand side or direction. 2. Correctly. 3. Exactly in a particular position or location. 4. Immediately. 5. In a straight line; directly.
noun 1. The side that is not the left. 2. If you have **the right** to do something, then you are legally or morally entitled to do it. 3. In politics, **the right** refers to people, parties, or groups that have conservative views.
Right sounds like **write**. ▸ *adverb* **rightly**

right an·gle (**rite ang**-guhl) *noun* An angle of 90 degrees, such as one of the corners of a square.

right-click (**rite-klik**) *verb* To click the button on the right side of a computer mouse that has more than one button. ▸ *verb* **right-clicking, right-clicked**

right·eous (**rye**-chuhs) *adjective* 1. Without guilt or sin; morally good. 2. Morally justified.
▸ *noun* **righteousness** ▸ *adverb* **righteously**

right-hand·ed (**rite-han**-did) *adjective* Using your right hand more easily than your left hand. ▸ *noun* **right-hander**

right tri·an·gle (**rite trye**-ang-guhl) *noun* A triangle that includes one right angle.

rig·id (**rij**-id) *adjective* 1. Stiff and difficult to bend or move. 2. Strict and not easily changed.
▸ *noun* **rigidity** (ri-**jid**-i-tee) ▸ *adverb* **rigidly**

rile (rile) *verb* To annoy or to irritate. ▸ *verb* **riling, riled**

rim (rim) *noun* The border or outside edge of something round.

rind (rinde) *noun* The tough outer skin of some fruits, or the hard outer edge of some cheeses and bacon.

ring (ring)
noun 1. A small, circular band of metal or some other material, worn on your finger as a piece of jewelry. 2. A circular form or arrangement. 3. (informal) A telephone call. 4. A resounding tone, like that of a bell. 5. The enclosed space in which a boxing or wrestling match is held. 6. A group of people working together for some unlawful purpose.
verb 1. To make or form a circle around. 2. To make or cause to make a clear, musical sound.
Ring sounds like **wring**. ▸ *verb* **ringing, rang** (rang), **rung** (ruhng)

ring·lead·er (**ring**-lee-dur) *noun* A person who leads others, especially those who commit crimes or cause trouble.

ring·let (**ring**-lit) *noun* A long, spiral curl of hair.

rink (ringk) *noun* An enclosed area with a smooth surface that is used for ice-skating, roller-skating, or hockey.

rinse (rins)
verb 1. To get rid of soap or dirt by washing something in clean water. 2. To wash lightly.
noun 1. A special liquid that you can use to color or condition your hair. 2. The process of washing something in clean water.
▸ *verb* **rinsing, rinsed**

ri·ot (**rye**-uht)
verb To take part in a noisy or violent public disturbance involving a lot of people.
noun 1. (informal) A person or thing that is extremely funny. 2. A violent public disturbance.
▸ *verb* **rioting, rioted** ▸ *noun* **rioter** ▸ *noun* **rioting** ▸ *adjective* **riotous** (**rye**-uh-tuhs)

rip (rip)
verb 1. To tear or pull something forcefully apart or away. 2. To copy music or sound files from one place to another, especially from a CD to your hard drive. 3. (slang) If someone **rips** you **off,** the person cheats, steals

R

from, or takes advantage of you.
noun A long tear or cut in
something.

▸ *verb* **ripping, ripped**

ripe (ripe) *adjective* Fully developed
or mature; ready to be harvested,
picked, or eaten. ▸ *adjective* **riper,
ripest** ▸ *noun* **ripeness** ▸ *verb* **ripen**

rip-off (**rip**-awf) *noun* Something that
is a lot more expensive than it is
worth.

rip·ple (**rip**-uhl)
noun **1.** A very small wave or series
of waves on the surface of a body of
water. **2.** Anything that looks like a
ripple. **3.** A small wave of sound, or
a feeling that moves through a place
or a group of people.
verb To form or show little waves on
the surface.

▸ *verb* **rippling, rippled**

rise (rize)
verb **1.** To move from a lower to a
higher position. **2.** To stand up from
a sitting, kneeling, or lying position.
3. To get out of bed. **4.** To increase in
value, number, amount, or intensity.
5. To move up in position, rank, or
importance. **6.** To rebel.
noun **1.** An upward slope. **2.** An
increase in price, power, importance,
influence, or the like.

▸ *verb* **rising, rose** (rohz) **risen**
(**riz**-uhn)

risk (risk)
noun The possibility of loss or harm;
danger.
verb **1.** To expose to risk. **2.** To take
the risk or chance of.

▸ *verb* **risking, risked** ▸ *adjective*
risky

rit·u·al (**rich**-oo-uhl)
noun **1.** An act or series of acts that
are always performed in the same
way, usually as part of a religious or
social ceremony. **2.** An action or set
of actions that you repeat often.
adjective Done or performed as a
ritual.

▸ *adverb* **ritually**

ri·val (**rye**-vuhl)
noun One of two or more people

who are competing against one
another.
verb To be equal to or almost as good
as something or someone else.
adjective Striving for competitive
advantage.

▸ *verb* **rivaling, rivaled** ▸ *noun* **rivalry**

riv·er (**riv**-ur) *noun* A large, natural
stream of fresh water that flows into
a lake, an ocean, or another river.

riv·et (**riv**-it)
noun A short metal pin or bolt that
is used to fasten pieces of metal
together. Once the rivet is in place,
the plain end is hammered down to
form a second head.
verb **1.** To fasten or join with a rivet
or rivets. **2.** If you are **riveted** by
something, it holds your attention
completely.

▸ *verb* **riveting, riveted** ▸ *noun*
riveter ▸ *adjective* **riveting**

RNA (**ahr**-en-**ay**) *noun* The complex
molecule produced by living cells
and viruses that is responsible for
manufacturing the protein in a cell.
RNA is short for *ribonucleic acid.*

road (rohd) *noun* **1.** A wide path with
a smooth, hard surface on which
vehicles and people travel. **2.** The
route or path a person takes to
achieve a goal. **Road** sounds like
rode.

road map (**rohd** map) *noun* A map for
motorists that shows the streets and
highways of a particular area.

road rage (**rohd** rayj) *noun* Dangerous
and uncontrollable anger experienced
by the driver of a car when another
driver does something irritating or
upsetting.

road·run·ner (**rohd**-*ruhn*-ur) *noun* A
small bird with brown-black feathers
and a long tail found mainly in the
southwestern United States. It gets
around by running very fast instead
of flying.

road·side (**rohd**-*side*)
noun The area beside a road.
adjective Located near or beside
a road.

R

R

roam (rohm) *verb* To wander around without a purpose or plan. ▶ *verb* **roaming, roamed**

roar (ror)
verb 1. To make a loud, deep, prolonged sound. 2. To laugh very loudly.
noun A loud, deep, prolonged sound.
▶ *verb* **roaring, roared**

roast (rohst)
verb 1. To cook meat or vegetables with dry heat, in a hot oven or over a fire. 2. To make or to be very hot.
noun A piece of meat that has been roasted or that is suitable for roasting.
adjective Roasted.
▶ *verb* **roasting, roasted** ▶ *adjective* **roasting** ▶ *adjective* **roasted**

rob (rahb) *verb* To steal something from a person or place. ▶ *verb* **robbing, robbed** ▶ *noun* **robber**

rob·ber·y (**rah**-bur-ee) *noun* The act or crime of stealing from a person or place. ▶ *noun, plural* **robberies**

robe (rohb) *noun* 1. A long, loose outer garment. 2. A bathrobe.

rob·in (**rah**-bin) *noun* A songbird that has a reddish-orange chest.

ro·bot (**roh**-baht) *noun* A machine that is programmed to perform complex human tasks and that sometimes resembles a human being. ▶ *adjective* **robotic** (roh-**bah**-tik)

ro·bot·ic arm (roh-**bah**-tik ahrm) *noun* A mechanical arm that works like a human arm to control tools or operate machines.

ro·bot·ics (roh-**bah**-tiks) *noun* The science of designing, making, and using robots.

ro·bust (roh-**buhst**) *adjective* 1. Strong and healthy. 2. Powerfully built. 3. Rich; strong in flavor.
▶ *adverb* **robustly**

rock (rahk)
noun 1. A stone of any size, especially one small enough to be picked up and thrown. 2. The hard mineral matter that forms an important part of the earth's crust. 3. Popular music, usually played on electric guitars and other amplified instruments, with a strong beat and a simple, repetitive tune; rock 'n' roll. Also called *rock music*.
verb 1. To move backward and forward or from side to side, as if in a cradle. 2. To shake or move violently.
▶ *verb* **rocking, rocked**

rock climb·ing (rahk *klye*-ming) *noun* The sport of climbing steep rock faces, usually with the help of ropes, harnesses, and other special equipment.

rock·er (**rah**-kur) *noun* 1. One of the curved pieces of wood or metal on which a rocking chair, cradle, or other item rocks. 2. A rocking chair. 3. A person who plays or likes rock 'n' roll music.

rock·et (**rah**-kit)
noun A tube-shaped vehicle, propelled by a very powerful engine, that is designed for traveling through space or carrying missiles.
verb To increase very quickly and suddenly.
▶ *verb* **rocketing, rocketed**

Rock·ies (**rah**-keez) A large mountain range covering over 3,000 miles (4,827 kilometers) in North America. The Rockies originate in western Canada and extend south to New Mexico in the United States. The Rockies are also called the Rocky Mountains.

rock·ing chair (**rah**-king *chair*) *noun* A chair mounted on curved runners that allow the sitter to rock back and forth.

rock·ing horse (**rah**-king *hors*) *noun* A toy horse mounted on curved runners so that it can rock back and forth.

rock 'n' roll (rahk uhn rohl)
noun A kind of popular music with a strong beat, a simple melody, and lyrics that often repeat.
adjective Of or having to do with rock 'n' roll music.

rod (rahd) *noun* 1. A long, thin pole or stick. 2. A unit of length equal to 5.5 yards, or 16.5 feet.

rode (rohd) *verb* The past tense of **ride**. **Rode** sounds like **road**.

ro·dent (**roh**-duhnt) *noun* A mammal with large, sharp front teeth that are constantly growing and used for gnawing things. Rats, beavers, and squirrels are all rodents.

ro·de·o (**roh**-dee-*oh* or roh-**day**-oh) *noun* A contest in which cowboys and cowgirls compete at riding wild horses and bulls and catching cattle with lassos.

roe (roh) *noun* The eggs of a fish, often eaten as food.

rogue (rohg) *noun* **1.** A worthless or dishonest person. **2.** A person whose behavior you disapprove of but whom you still like. **3.** A vicious and dangerous animal, especially an elephant, that lives apart from the herd.

role (rohl) *noun* **1.** An actor's part in a play or movie. **2.** The job or purpose of someone or something in a particular situation.
Role sounds like **roll.**

role mod·el (rohl *mah*-duhl) *noun* A person whose behavior in a particular area is imitated by others.

roll (rohl)
verb **1.** To move by turning over and over. **2.** To form the shape of a ball or cylinder. **3.** To flatten something by pushing a roller or cylindrical object over it. **4.** To move in a side-to-side or up-and-down way. **5.** To make a deep, loud sound.
noun **1.** Something that is in the shape of a cylinder or tube. **2.** A small, round piece of baked bread dough. **3.** A list of names.
Roll sounds like **role.** ▶ *verb* **rolling, rolled**

roll·er (**roh**-lur) *noun* **1.** A cylinder or rod that has something rolled around it, such as a window shade. **2.** A cylinder that is used to spread, squeeze, smooth, or crush something.

Rollerblade (**roh**-lur-*blade*) *noun* A trademark for an in-line skate.

roll·er coast·er (**roh**-lur *koh*-stur) *noun* An amusement park ride consisting of a train of open cars in which people ride at high speeds over a track with steep slopes and tight turns.

roll·er-skat·ing (**roh**-lur-*skay*-ting) *noun* The sport of gliding across a smooth surface wearing shoes or boots with wheels attached. ▶ *noun* **roller skate** ▶ *verb* **roller-skate**

roll·ing pin (**roh**-ling *pin*) *noun* A cylinder, often made of wood, that is used to flatten out dough.

Rom (rohm) *noun* A member of a group of people who originated in India and who now live mainly in Europe and North America. *See* **Gypsy.** ▶ *noun, plural* **Roma** (**roh**-muh) ▶ *adjective* **Romany** or **Romani** (**rah**-muh-nee *or* **roh**-muh-nee)

ROM (rahm) *noun* Memory in a computer with data that can be used but not changed. ROM is short for *read-only memory.*

Ro·man (**roh**-muhn)
noun **1.** A person who lived in ancient Rome. **2.** A person who was born or is living in modern Rome, Italy. **3. roman** A style of type with upright letters. This sentence is in roman.
adjective Of or having to do with the people or culture of ancient or modern Rome.

Ro·man Cath·o·lic (**roh**-muhn **kath**-lik) *noun* A member of the Roman Catholic Church.
adjective Of or having to do with the Roman Catholic Church and its beliefs.

Ro·man Cath·o·lic Church (**roh**-muhn **kath**-lik **church**) *noun* A Christian church that has the pope as its leader.

ro·mance (roh-**mans**) *noun* **1.** An affectionate relationship between people who are in love. **2.** A poem or story about the loves and adventures of heroes and heroines. **3.** A quality of mystery, excitement, and adventure.

Ro·mance lan·guage (roh-**mans** *lang*-gwij) *noun* One of a group of languages that developed from Latin. The Romance languages include Spanish, Italian, French, Portuguese, and Romanian.

Ro·ma·ni·a (roh-**may**-nee-uh) A country in Central and Southeastern Europe whose eastern boundary lies on the Black Sea. Once under Soviet rule, it is now a democracy. Transylvania, a mountain region in the center of Romania, has become famous as the setting for the vampire novel *Dracula*.

Ro·man nu·mer·als (**roh**-muhn **noo**-mur-uhlz) *noun, plural* Letters that represent numbers in the ancient Roman numbering system. The number 16, for example, is written XVI.

ro·man·tic (roh-**man**-tik) *adjective* **1.** Of or having to do with love or romance. **2.** Imaginative but not practical.

romp (rahmp)
verb To run or play in a noisy, carefree, and energetic way.
noun A period of noisy, energetic play.
▶ *verb* **romping, romped**

roof (roof *or* ruf) *noun* **1.** The covering on the top of a house, building, or vehicle. **2.** The top inner surface of something.

rook (ruk)
noun **1.** A chess piece, shaped like a battlement and also known as a castle, that can move across the board in straight lines but not diagonally. **2.** A type of crow with black feathers and a bare face.
verb (informal) To cheat someone.
▶ *verb* **rooking, rooked**

rook·ie (**ruk**-ee) *noun* **1.** Someone who has just joined a group and lacks experience and training, especially an inexperienced police officer. **2.** An athlete who is in his or her first season with a professional sports team.

room (room *or* rum)
noun **1.** One of the separate parts of a house or building that is enclosed by walls, a floor, and a ceiling. **2.** Empty space that can be occupied or used for something. **3.** An opportunity or chance.
verb To share a room or living space with one or more people.
▶ *verb* **rooming, roomed**

room·mate (**room**-mate) *noun* Someone who shares a room or living space with one or more people.

room·y (**roo**-mee) *adjective* Large, or having a lot of space. ▶ *adjective* **roomier, roomiest**

roost (roost)
noun A place where birds or other winged animals, such as chickens, gather to rest at night.
verb When birds **roost,** they settle somewhere to rest or sleep.
▶ *verb* **roosting, roosted**

roost·er (**roo**-stur) *noun* An adult male chicken.

root (root *or* rut)
noun **1.** The part of a plant or tree that grows under the ground, where it collects water and nutrients. **2.** A part that functions like a root or resembles one. **3.** The source, origin, or cause of something. **4.** A word to which a prefix or suffix is added to make another word. *Hungry* is the root of *hungriest*.
verb **1.** To grow roots. **2.** To cheer.
noun, plural If you have **roots** in a particular place, that place is where your family comes from or where you grew up. Many Americans have their roots in Europe, Africa, or Asia.
▶ *verb* **rooting, rooted**

root ca·nal (**root** kuh-**nal**) *noun* **1.** A groove in a tooth's root through which the nerve passes. **2.** A dental procedure to replace the pulp in a tooth's root with another substance in order to save the tooth.

rope (rohp)
noun A strong, thick cord made from twisted or braided strands of hemp, nylon, or some other material.
verb **1.** To fasten with a cord. **2.** To catch with a lasso or rope. **3.** To separate an area or object with ropes.
▶ *verb* **roping, roped**

rose (roze)
noun **1.** A garden flower that grows on a prickly bush and usually has a sweet smell. Roses may be red, pink, yellow, or white. **2.** A light red or warm pink color.
adjective Having a light red or warm pink color.

rose·bud (**roze**-buhd) *noun* The bud from which the rose flower blooms.

R

rose·mar·y (**rohz**-*mair*-ee) *noun* An evergreen plant of the mint family that has needle-like leaves used for adding flavor in cooking.

Rosh Ha·sha·na (**rohsh** huh-**shah**-nuh) *noun* The Jewish New Year, occurring in September or October.

ros·ter (**rah**-stur) *noun* A list of people, especially a list that shows duties or assignments.

ros·y (**roh**-zee) *adjective* 1. Having a pinkish color. 2. Promising or hopeful.
▶ *adjective* **rosier, rosiest**

rot (raht)
verb To make or become rotten; to decay.
noun A disease that causes tissues to decay, especially in plants.
▶ *verb* **rotting, rotted**

ro·ta·ry (**roh**-tur-ee) *adjective* Having a part or parts that turn around and around or rotate.

ro·tate (**roh**-tate) *verb* 1. To move in a circle around a central point, like a wheel. 2. To take turns doing things in a regular, repeated order. 3. To grow different crops, one after the other, on the same piece of land.
▶ *verb* **rotating, rotated** ▶ *noun* **rotation** ▶ *adjective* **rotational**

ro·ta·tor cuff (**roh**-tay-tur *kuhf*) *noun* The muscles and tendons that attach the upper arm to the shoulder and allow the arm to rotate in its socket.

ro·tor (**roh**-tur) *noun* 1. The part of an engine or other machine that turns or rotates. 2. The blades of a helicopter that turn and lift the helicopter into the air.

rot·ten (**rah**-tuhn) *adjective* 1. Used to describe food that has gone bad or has started to decay from the action of bacteria or fungi. 2. Used to describe wood that is weak and likely to crack, break, or give way. 3. (informal) Very bad or extremely unpleasant.

Rott·wei·ler (**raht**-*wye*-lur) *noun* One of a breed of powerful black and brown dogs with short hair and a short tail, often used as guard dogs.

rouge (roozh) *noun* Red or pink makeup put on the cheeks to make them look less pale.

rough (ruhf)
adjective 1. Not smooth or level; having an irregular surface with many bumps or dents. 2. Not calm or gentle. 3. Not sensitive or polite and often loud or violent. 4. (informal) Difficult and unpleasant. 5. Not completely worked out or not exact. 6. Preliminary, hastily done, or unfinished.
verb (informal) If you **rough it,** you manage with only the basic necessities or comforts.
Rough sounds like **ruff.** ▶ *adjective* **rougher, roughest** ▶ *verb* **roughing, roughed**

rough·age (**ruhf**-ij) *noun* The fiber found in fruit, cereals, vegetables, and other foods, which cannot be digested but helps food move through the intestines.

rough·ly (**ruhf**-lee) *adverb* 1. In a rough, harsh, or violent way. 2. Approximately.

round (round)
adjective 1. Shaped like a circle, a sphere, or a cylinder. 2. Having a curved surface or outline.
noun 1. Something round in shape. 2. A long burst. 3. A series of repeated actions or events. 4. A period of play in a sport or contest. 5. A complete game. 6. A simple song for three or more voices in which people sing the same melody but start at different times, one after the other. 7. One shot fired by a weapon or by each person in a military unit.
noun, plural **rounds** A regular route or course of action followed by someone such as a mail carrier, doctor, or guard.
verb 1. To make or become round. 2. To go around. 3. **round off** To make into a round number. 4. **round up** To gather together.
preposition Around. *The hikers gathered round the campfire.*
adverb Around.
▶ *adjective* **rounder, roundest** ▶ *verb* **rounding, rounded** ▶ *adjective* **rounded**

R

round·a·bout (**roun**-duh-*bout*) *adjective* Indirect in travel, thought, or conversation.

round·house (**round**-*hous*) *noun* A circular building with a large turntable in the center, used for storing, repairing, and switching locomotive engines.

round num·ber (**round nuhm**-bur) *noun* A number rounded off to the nearest whole number or to the nearest ten, hundred, thousand, and so on. Rounding off 158 to the nearest ten gives you a round number of 160. Rounding off 158 to the nearest hundred gives you a round number of 200.

round-trip (**round**-trip) *noun* A trip to a place and back again.

round·up (**round**-uhp) *noun* 1. The gathering together of cattle for branding or shipping to market. 2. A gathering together of people, things, or facts.

rouse (rouz) *verb* 1. To wake up or to awaken someone. 2. To make someone feel angry, interested, or excited; to stir up.
▶ *verb* **rousing, roused** ▶ *adjective* **rousing**

rout (rout)
noun A complete or overwhelming defeat.
verb 1. To defeat or beat totally. 2. To drive or force out.
▶ *verb* **routing, routed**

route (root *or* rout)
noun 1. The road, path, or course that you follow to get from one place to another. 2. A series of places or customers visited regularly by a person who delivers or sells something.
verb To send or direct someone or something along a particular course.

rout·er (**rou**-tur) *noun* 1. A device that handles signals between computers or computer networks. 2. An electric tool used in woodworking that digs out holes or spaces in wood.

rou·tine (roo-**teen**)
noun A regular sequence of actions or way of doing things.
adjective Commonplace; done as part of a regular procedure.

row
noun 1. (roh) People or things arranged in a straight line. 2. (roh) A trip made by rowboat. 3. (rou) A noisy fight or quarrel.
verb (roh) To move a boat through water by using oars.
▶ *verb* **rowing, rowed** ▶ *noun* **rower**

row·boat (**roh**-boht) *noun* A small boat that is moved through the water by using oars.

row·dy (**rou**-dee) *adjective* Noisy and wild or disorderly. ▶ *adjective* **rowdier, rowdiest** ▶ *noun* **rowdiness** ▶ *adverb* **rowdily**

roy·al (**roi**-uhl) *adjective* 1. Relating to or belonging to a king or queen or a member of his or her family. 2. Magnificent or fit for a king or queen.
▶ *noun* **royalty**

RSS feed (**ahr**-es-es feed) *noun* An electronic news service that sends new information to your computer whenever it is available. RSS is short for *really simple syndication*.

RSVP (**ahr**-es-**vee**-pee) The initials of the French phrase *Répondez s'il vous plaît*, meaning "please reply," that is often written at the end of an invitation.

rub (ruhb)
verb 1. To move one thing against the surface of another with firm pressure. 2. To put on or spread something by using pressure. 3. To clean, polish, or make smooth by pressing something against a surface and moving it back and forth. 4. (informal) If you **rub it in,** you keep reminding someone about something unpleasant.
noun The act of rubbing.
▶ *verb* **rubbing, rubbed**

rub·ber (**ruhb**-ur)
noun A waterproof, elastic substance made from the milky sap of a tropical plant or produced artificially.
noun, plural **rubbers** Low boots that protect shoes from water.

R

rub·ber band (ruhb-ur **band)** *noun*
A loop of thin rubber that can be
stretched and used to hold things
together.

rub·ber stamp (ruhb-ur **stamp)**
noun A stamp with a rubber end.
Raised letters or a design in the
rubber can be covered with ink and
used to print something.
verb **rubber-stamp** (informal) To
approve or vote for without question.

rub·bish (ruhb-ish) *noun* **1.** Things that
you throw away; waste or worthless
items. **2.** Nonsense or foolish talk.

rub·ble (ruhb-uhl) *noun* Broken
fragments of stone, brick, and
concrete that are left after a building is
destroyed or falls down.

ru·ble (roo-buhl) *noun* The main unit of
money in Russia.

ru·by (roo-bee)
noun **1.** A precious stone of a deep red
color. **2.** A deep red color.
adjective Deep red in color.
▶ *noun, plural* **rubies**

rud·der (ruhd-ur) *noun* A hinged piece
of wood or metal attached to the back
of a boat, ship, or airplane and used
for steering.

rude (rood) *adjective* **1.** Bad-mannered
or offensive. **2.** Roughly or crudely
made.
▶ *adjective* **ruder, rudest** ▶ *adverb*
rudely

rude·ness (rood-nis) *noun* Rude
behavior or speech.

ruff (ruhf) *noun* **1.** A starched, ruffled
collar worn by men and women in
western Europe from the mid-16th
to the mid-17th century. **2.** A collar of
feathers or hair on certain birds or
animals.
Ruff sounds like **rough.**

ruf·fi·an (ruhf-ee-uhn) *noun* A rough
or violent person, especially one who
breaks the law.

ruf·fle (ruhf-uhl)
verb **1.** To disturb the surface of
something, or to make it uneven or
messy. **2.** To annoy, irritate, or upset
someone.
noun A strip of gathered material used

as a decoration or trimming; a frill.
▶ *verb* **ruffling, ruffled**

rug (ruhg) *noun* A thick mat made from
wool or other fibers and used as a
floor covering.

rug·by (ruhg-bee) *noun* A form of
football played by two teams that kick,
pass, or carry an oval ball.

rug·ged (ruhg-id) *adjective* **1.** Rough
and uneven, or having a jagged
outline. **2.** Tough, strong, and able
to withstand rough handling or
conditions. **3.** Harsh or difficult;
requiring determination and
toughness.

ru·in (roo-in)
verb **1.** To spoil or destroy something
completely. **2.** To make someone lose
all of his or her money.
noun **1.** The destruction of something.
2. Loss of wealth or social position.
noun, plural **ruins** The remains of
something that has collapsed or been
destroyed.
▶ *verb* **ruining, ruined**

rule (rool)
noun **1.** An official instruction or
principle that governs behavior or
actions. **2.** Control, or government.
3. The normal or usual state of things;
what is usually done.
verb **1.** To govern or to have power
and authority over something, usually
a country. **2.** To make an official
decision or to state with authority
that something is the case. **3.** If you
rule something **out,** you exclude or
eliminate it as a possibility.
phrase If you do something **as a rule,**
you do it most of the time, but not
always.
▶ *verb* **ruling, ruled**

rul·er (roo-lur) *noun* **1.** A flat, smooth-
edged strip of wood, plastic, or metal
used to measure something or to
draw straight lines. **2.** Someone who
rules a country or a group of people.

rul·ing (roo-ling) *noun* A decision or
a statement made by someone in
authority.

rum (ruhm) *noun* An alcoholic drink
made from sugarcane.

R

rum·ble (ruhm-buhl)
verb To make or move with a low, deep, continuous noise like the sound of thunder.
noun A low, continuous sound like thunder.
▶ *verb* **rumbling, rumbled**

rum·mage (ruhm-ij) *verb* To search for something in a haphazard or careless way. ▶ *verb* **rummaging, rummaged**

ru·mor (roo-mur)
noun A story or report that is spread by word of mouth but that may not be true.
verb To be spread or reported as a rumor.
▶ *verb* **rumoring, rumored** ▶ *adjective* **rumored**

rump (ruhmp) *noun* The hindquarters or buttocks of a mammal, or the lower back part of a bird.

rum·ple (ruhm-puhl) *verb* To wrinkle or crease. ▶ *verb* **rumpling, rumpled** ▶ *adjective* **rumpled**

run (ruhn)
verb **1.** To move at a speed faster than a walk, using your legs. **2.** To function or to make something function. **3.** To manage or be in charge of people or an organization. **4.** To travel a regular route. **5.** To be a candidate in an election. **6.** To continue. **7.** To flow in a steady stream. **8.** To organize, carry out, or proceed with something. **9.** To operate a computer program. **10.** If you **run away,** you escape from a person, place, or situation. **11.** If you have **run out of** something, you have used it all up. **12.** If you **run into** or **run across** someone or something, you meet the person or find the thing by chance.
noun **1.** The act of running. **2.** A running pace. **3.** A small enclosure for pets or other animals. **4.** Freedom to move about or use something. **5.** A series of actions that continue to happen. **6.** A length of torn stitches. **7.** In baseball, a score made by touching home plate after touching the other three bases.
▶ *verb* **running, ran** (ran), **run**

run·a·way (ruhn-uh-*way*)
noun A person, usually a young person, who has run away from home or an institution.
adjective Happening quickly, easily, or uncontrollably.

run-down (ruhn-doun) *adjective* **1.** Old and in need of repair. **2.** Tired or weak.

rung (ruhng) *noun* One of the horizontal bars on a ladder where you put your foot. **Rung** sounds like **wrung.**

run·ner (ruhn-ur) *noun* **1.** Someone who runs in a race or in a particular way. **2.** The long, narrow part of an object that enables it to move or slide, as the blade on an ice skate or a sled. **3.** A long, narrow carpet, often used on stairs.

run·ner-up (ruhn-ur-*uhp*) *noun* The person or team that takes second place in a race or competition.
▶ *noun, plural* **runners-up**

run·ning mate (ruhn-ing *mate*) *noun* A person who runs for public office with another candidate in a less important position.

run·ny (ruhn-ee) *adjective* **1.** More like liquid than you expected, or tending to flow like a liquid. **2.** If you have a **runny** nose, it tends to drip mucus.
▶ *adjective* **runnier, runniest**

run·way (ruhn-*way*) *noun* **1.** A strip of hard, level ground that aircraft use for taking off and landing. **2.** A raised aisle that extends from a stage into the audience, used in fashion shows.

rup·ture (ruhp-chur)
verb To break open or to burst.
noun A sudden bursting or breaking open.
▶ *verb* **rupturing, ruptured**

ru·ral (roor-uhl) *adjective* Of or having to do with the countryside, country life, or farming.

ruse (rooz *or* **roos)** *noun* A clever trick meant to confuse or mislead someone.

rush (ruhsh)
verb To move or act quickly.
noun **1.** The act of rushing. **2.** A sudden burst of speed or flurry of activity.

R

adjective Requiring or done with speed or urgency.

noun, plural **rushes** Tall, marshy plants with hollow stems, used for making baskets and chair seats.

▶ *verb* **rushes, rushing, rushed**

Rus·sia (**ruhsh**-uh) A country in northern Eurasia. It is the largest country in the world and has the world's largest energy and mineral reserves. Russia was once the leading republic of the Soviet Union, which dissolved in 1991.

rust (ruhst)

noun **1.** The flaky, reddish-brown coating that can form on iron and steel when they are exposed to moist air. **2.** A reddish-brown color. **3.** Red or brown disease spots on plants, caused by a fungus.

verb To form rust.

▶ *verb* **rusting, rusted** ▶ *adjective* **rusty**

rus·tic (**ruhs**-tik) *adjective* Of or having to do with life in the country; simple and unsophisticated.

rus·tle (**ruhs**-uhl)

verb **1.** To make a soft, fluttering sound like dry leaves or pieces of paper. **2.** To steal horses, cattle, or sheep.

noun A soft, fluttering sound like dry leaves or pieces of paper.

▶ *verb* **rustling, rustled** ▶ *noun* **rustler** ▶ *noun* **rustling**

rust·y (**ruhs**-tee) *adjective* **1.** Covered with rust or having rust spots on it. **2.** Not as good as before, especially because of a lack of practice or use.

rut (ruht) *noun* **1.** A deep, narrow track in the ground made by the repeated passage of wheels or vehicles. **2.** If someone is **in a rut,** he or she keeps doing things in the same dull, boring way.

ruth·less (**rooth**-lis) *adjective* Someone who is **ruthless** has no pity or sympathy for other people. ▶ *noun* **ruthlessness** ▶ *adverb* **ruthlessly**

Rwan·da (ruh-**wahn**-duh) A country in eastern Central Africa. Mountain gorillas live in Rwanda's Volcanoes National Park and are the country's main tourist attraction. In 1994, Rwanda was the site of a massive genocide, the result of a conflict between the nation's Hutu and Tutsi tribes.

rye (rye) *noun* **1.** A cereal grass that looks like wheat and is used to make flour and whiskey. **2.** A chewy, dark brown bread made from rye flour, usually with caraway seeds added.

S

Sab·bath (**sab**-uhth) *noun* A day of the week that is supposed to be used for rest and religious activities.

sa·ber (**say**-bur) *noun* A heavy sword with a curved blade and one cutting edge.

sa·ber-toothed ti·ger (**say**-bur-*tootht* **tye**-gur) *noun* A prehistoric animal related to the lion and tiger that had long, curved teeth in its upper jaw.

sa·ble (**say**-buhl) *noun* **1.** A small European animal with soft, dark brown fur that looks like a weasel. **2.** The color of a sable, either black or dark brown.

▶ *noun, plural* **sable** *or* **sables**
▶ *adjective* **sable**

sab·o·tage (**sab**-uh-*tahzh*)

noun The deliberate damage or destruction of property, especially to prevent or stop something.

verb To try to make something fail, using violence or destruction.

▶ *verb* **sabotaging, sabotaged**

sab·o·teur (*sab*-uh-**toor**) *noun* A person who deliberately damages or destroys property in order to stop something.

sac (sak) *noun* A bag or pouchlike structure in a plant or animal that often contains a liquid. **Sac** sounds like **sack.**

sac·cha·rin (**sak**-ur-in) *noun* A sweet artificial compound with no calories that is used as a sugar substitute.

sac·cha·rine (**sak**-ur-in) *adjective*
1. Sickeningly sweet or sentimental.
2. Of or having to do with sugar.

sack (sak)
noun A large bag made of strong material that is used for storing and carrying things.
verb 1. To fire a person from a job.
2. To steal things from a place that has been captured in a war or battle; loot. **Sack** sounds like **sac.** ▶ *verb* **sacking, sacked**

sa·cred (**say**-krid) *adjective* 1. Holy, or having to do with religion. 2. Very important and deserving great respect.

sac·ri·fice (**sak**-ruh-*fise*)
verb To give up something you value or enjoy for the sake of something that is more important.
noun 1. The offering of something to God or a god. 2. Something that you do without, even though it is difficult.
3. In baseball, a **sacrifice hit** is a bunt that advances a base runner but results in the batter being put out.
4. In baseball, a **sacrifice fly** is a fly ball to the outfield that is caught but still allows a base runner to advance.
▶ *verb* **sacrificing, sacrificed**
▶ *adjective* **sacrificial**

sac·ri·lege (**sak**-ruh-lij) *noun* Treating something that is holy or very important with disrespect. ▶ *adjective* **sacrilegious** (*sak*-ruh-**lij**-uhs) ▶ *adverb* **sacrilegiously**

sad (sad) *adjective* 1. Unhappy or sorrowful. 2. Causing you to feel sorrowful or gloomy.
▶ *adjective* **sadder, saddest** ▶ *noun* **sadness** ▶ *adverb* **sadly**

sad·den (**sad**-uhn) *verb* To cause someone to feel sad. ▶ *verb* **saddening, saddened**

sad·dle (**sad**-uhl)
noun 1. A leather seat for a rider that is strapped to a horse's back. 2. A seat on a bicycle or motorcycle.
verb 1. To cause difficulty or hardship.
2. To put a saddle on.
▶ *verb* **saddling, saddled**

sa·fa·ri (suh-**fahr**-ee) *noun* A trip taken, especially in Africa, to see or hunt large wild animals.

safe (sayf)
adjective 1. Protected from danger, injury, theft, or risk. 2. Unable or unlikely to cause trouble or harm; not dangerous. 3. Careful. 4. In baseball, a hitter is **safe** if he or she reaches a base without being tagged by an opposing player or called out by the umpire.
noun A fireproof box or container with a lock for storing money or valuables.
▶ *adjective* **safer, safest** ▶ *adverb* **safely**

safe·guard (**sayf**-gahrd)
verb To guard or protect someone or something.
noun Something that protects.
▶ *verb* **safeguarding, safeguarded**

safe·ty (**sayf**-tee) *noun* The condition of being protected from or unlikely to cause harm or danger.

safe·ty belt (**sayf**-tee *belt*) *noun*
1. A belt or harness that fastens a person who works at great heights to a fixed object. Safety belts prevent falls. 2. Another word for **seat belt.**

safe·ty pin (**sayf**-tee *pin*) *noun* A fastening pin with a guard at one end that covers and holds the point.

sag (sag) *verb* 1. To sink, droop, bend, or settle as a result of weight or pressure. 2. To lose strength.
▶ *verb* **sagging, sagged**

sage (sayj)
noun 1. An herb with grayish-green leaves that are often used in cooking.
2. A person, especially an elderly man, who is widely respected for his judgment and wisdom.
adjective Very wise.

sage·brush (**sayj**-*bruhsh*) *noun* A common shrub on the dry plains of the western United States.

Sa·har·a (suh-**har**-uh) The largest hot desert in the world, covering an area nearly the size of the United States or Europe. The Sahara is located

S

in the northern region of Africa, and stretches horizontally from the Red Sea to the Atlantic Ocean. It includes areas of sand dunes, rocky outcroppings, and regions with more dense vegetation.

said (sed) *verb* The past tense and past participle of **say.**

sail (sayl)
noun **1.** A large piece of canvas or other strong material that is attached to the mast of a boat or ship and moves it forward by catching the wind. **2.** Something that resembles or works like a sail, such as the arm of a windmill.
verb **1.** To travel by water. **2.** When a boat or ship **sails**, it begins a voyage. **3.** To glide or move smoothly.
Sail sounds like **sale.** ▶ *verb* **sailing, sailed** ▶ *noun* **sailing**

sail·board (**sayl**-*bord*) *noun* A flat board that resembles a surfboard with a mast and sail, used for windsurfing.

sail·boat (**sayl**-*boht*) *noun* A boat that is moved through the water by the wind blowing against its sail or sails.

sail·or (**say**-lur) *noun* **1.** A person who works as a member of the crew on a ship or boat. **2.** A member of a country's navy.

saint (saynt) *noun* **1.** In the Christian church, a person who has been officially recognized for having lived a very holy life. The short form of *Saint* is *St*. **2.** A very kind and patient person.
▶ *adjective* **saintly** ▶ *adjective* **sainted**

Saint Ber·nard (**saynt** bur-**nahrd**) *noun* A very large, powerful dog with a big head and fur that is white and reddish brown. The Saint Bernard was originally used to locate lost travelers in the snowy mountains of Switzerland.

sake (sayk) *noun* **1.** A benefit or an advantage. **2.** A reason or a purpose.

sal·ad (**sal**-uhd) *noun* **1.** A combination of raw vegetables, usually served with a dressing. **2.** A cold dish of chopped fruit, meat, eggs, fish, or some other food, mixed in with a dressing.

sal·a·man·der (**sal**-uh-*man*-dur) *noun* An animal that looks like a small, brightly colored lizard.

sal·a·ried (**sal**-ur-eed) *adjective* Paid a certain agreed-upon amount of money for working at a job, instead of being paid by the hour.

sal·a·ry (**sal**-ur-ee) *noun* The fixed amount of money someone is paid for his or her work. ▶ *noun, plural* **salaries**

sale (sayl)
noun **1.** The act of exchanging property or services for money. **2.** A period of time when items are sold at lower than usual prices. **3.** **for sale** Available for purchase. **4.** **on sale** For sale at reduced prices.
noun, plural **sales** The number or amount of things sold.
Sale sounds like **sail.**

sales·man (**saylz**-muhn) *noun* A man who sells goods or services. ▶ *noun, plural* **salesmen**

sales·per·son (**saylz**-*pur*-suhn) *noun* A man or woman who sells goods or services. ▶ *noun, plural* **salespeople**

sales·wom·an (**saylz**-*wum*-uhn) *noun* A woman who sells goods or services. ▶ *noun, plural* **saleswomen**

sa·lin·i·ty (suh-**lin**-i-tee) *noun* Saltiness, or the amount of salt in something. ▶ *adjective* **saline** (**say**-leen *or* **say**-line)

sa·li·va (suh-**lye**-vuh) *noun* The watery fluid in your mouth that keeps it moist and helps you soften and swallow food.

salm·on (**sam**-uhn) *noun* **1.** A large fish with silvery skin and edible pink flesh. Most salmon live in saltwater but swim to freshwater to lay their eggs. **2.** A yellowish-pink or light orange color.
▶ *noun, plural* **salmon**

sal·mo·nel·la (*sal*-muh-**nel**-uh) *noun* Any of a group of bacteria that are shaped like rods and that can cause disease in humans and other warm-blooded animals. ▶ *noun, plural* **salmonellas** *or* **salmonellae** (*sal*-muh-**nel**-ee)

sa·loon (suh-**loon**) *noun* A place where people can buy and drink alcoholic beverages; a bar or tavern.

sal·sa (**sahl**-suh) *noun* **1.** A hot, spicy tomato sauce that can be flavored with onions and hot peppers and eaten with tortilla chips. **2.** A popular style of music that originated in the Caribbean. It has been influenced by jazz and rock.

salt (sawlt)
noun **1.** A white substance in the form of crystals, found in seawater and under the ground. Salt is used to season and preserve food. **2.** In chemistry, a compound formed from an acid and a base. **3.** If you take something with **a grain of salt,** you are aware that it might be exaggerated or not absolutely true.
verb To put salt on.
▶ *verb* **salting, salted** ▶ *noun* **saltiness**

salt·wa·ter (**sawlt**-*waw*-tur)
noun Water that is very salty, such as that found in the oceans.
adjective Of or having to do with saltwater.

salt·y (**sawl**-tee) *adjective* **1.** Containing salt, especially too much salt. **2.** A **salty** story or **salty** language is impolite or about sex.

sa·lute (suh-**loot**) *verb* **1.** To show your respect by raising your hand to your forehead. **2.** To express admiration or respect for something someone has done.
▶ *verb* **saluting, saluted**

sal·vage (**sal**-vij)
verb To rescue property from a shipwreck, fire, flood, or other disaster.
noun Property from a shipwreck, fire, flood, or other disaster.
▶ *verb* **salvaging, salvaged** ▶ *noun* **salvager**

sal·va·tion (sal-**vay**-shuhn) *noun* **1.** The state of being saved or protected from sin, evil, harm, or destruction. **2.** Someone or something that saves or protects.

salve (sav) *noun* An ointment or a cream that relieves pain and helps heal wounds, burns, or sores.

same (saym)
adjective **1.** Exactly alike. **2.** Being the very one and not another. **3.** Not changed or different.
pronoun The identical person or thing.
phrase **the same** In an identical manner.

Sa·mo·a (suh-**moh**-uh) An island nation in the western part of the Samoan Islands, located in the South Pacific Ocean. Formerly administered by New Zealand, in 1962 it became the first Polynesian country to establish its independence in the 20th century.

sam·ple (**sam**-puhl)
noun A small part or quantity of something that shows what the whole of it is like.
verb To take a small amount of something to test its quality or to see if you like it.
▶ *verb* **sampling, sampled**

sam·u·rai (**sam**-u-*rye*) *noun* A Japanese warrior who lived in medieval times. ▶ *noun, plural* **samurai**

sanc·tion (**sangk**-shuhn)
verb To permit or to give approval.
noun Permission or approval.
noun, plural **sanctions** A punishment, such as a blockade of shipping, that a nation or group of nations enforces against another.
▶ *verb* **sanctioning, sanctioned**

sanc·tu·ar·y (**sangk**-choo-*er*-ee) *noun* **1.** Safety or protection. **2.** A natural area where birds or animals are protected from hunters. **3.** A holy or sacred place, such as a church, temple, or mosque.
▶ *noun, plural* **sanctuaries**

sand (sand)
noun The small, loose particles made of rock and shell that cover beaches and deserts.
verb **1.** To sprinkle or cover with sand. **2.** To smooth a surface with sandpaper or other abrasive substance.
▶ *verb* **sanding, sanded** ▶ *adjective* **sandy**

S

san·dal (**san**-duhl) *noun* A shoe that is partly open on top or has straps that attach the sole to the foot.

sand·bag (**sand**-*bag*) *noun* A sturdy bag filled with sand and used to build a protective wall against floods, bullets, or explosives.

sand·bar (**sand**-*bahr*) *noun* A ridge of sand in a river or bay or along an ocean's shore.

sand·box (**sand**-*bahks*) *noun* A large wooden box with low sides that is filled with sand for children to play in. ▶ *noun, plural* **sandboxes**

sand·pa·per (**sand**-*pay*-pur) *noun* Heavy paper coated with grains of sand and used for smoothing rough surfaces.

sand·pip·er (**sand**-*pye*-pur) *noun* A small shorebird with a long bill, brown or gray feathers, and long, slender legs.

sand·stone (**sand**-*stohn*) *noun* A kind of rock made up mostly of sandlike grains of quartz cemented together by lime or other materials.

sand·wich (**sand**-wich) *noun* Two or more slices of bread with cheese, meat, or some other filling between them. ▶ *noun, plural* **sandwiches**

sane (sayn) *adjective* **1.** Mentally healthy. **2.** Sensible, or showing good judgment.
▶ *adjective* **saner, sanest** ▶ *adverb* **sanely**

sang (sang) *verb* The past tense of **sing.**

san·i·tar·y (**san**-i-*ter*-ee) *adjective* Clean, healthful, and free of germs.

san·i·ta·tion (*san*-i-**tay**-shuhn) *noun* Systems for cleaning the water supply and disposing of sewage and garbage in a town or city.

san·i·ty (**san**-i-tee) *noun* Good mental health.

sank (sangk) *verb* The past tense of **sink.**

San Ma·ri·no (*san* muh-**ree**-noh) A country on the eastern side of the Apennine Mountains, completely surrounded by Italy. It is believed to be the world's oldest republic, founded by a Christian stonemason in the year 301.

São To·mé and Prín·ci·pe (**sou** tu-**may** and **prin**-suh-puh) An island nation in the Gulf of Guinea off the western coast of Africa. It consists of two islands that are part of an extinct volcanic mountain range, and it is the smallest Portuguese-speaking country in the world.

sap (sap)
noun The liquid that flows through a plant, carrying water and food from one part of the plant to another.
verb To gradually weaken or to drain someone's strength or power.
▶ *verb* **sapping, sapped**

sap·ling (**sap**-ling) *noun* A young, slender tree.

sap·phire (**saf**-ire) *noun* A transparent blue gemstone.

sar·cas·tic (sahr-**kas**-tik) *adjective* Using bitter or mocking words that are meant to hurt or make fun of someone or something. ▶ *noun* **sarcasm** (**sahr**-*kaz*-uhm) ▶ *adverb* **sarcastically**

sar·dine (sahr-**deen**) *noun* A small saltwater fish, often packed tightly in cans and sold for eating.

sa·ri (**sahr**-ee) *noun* A long piece of light material worn wrapped around the body and over one shoulder. Saris are worn mainly by Indian and Pakistani women and girls.

sa·rong (suh-**rahng**) *noun* A long piece of brightly colored cloth wrapped around the body and tucked in at the waist or under the armpits. Sarongs are worn by men and women in Malaysia, Indonesia, and the Pacific Islands.

sash (sash) *noun* **1.** A wide strip of material worn around the waist or over one shoulder as an ornament or as part of a uniform. **2.** A frame that holds the glass in a window or door.
▶ *noun, plural* **sashes**

sa·shi·mi (sah-**shee**-mee) *noun* A Japanese dish made up of thinly sliced raw fish served with a sauce for dipping.

S

Sas·katch·e·wan (sas-**kach**-uh-*wahn*) A landlocked, prairie province of Canada, just north of Montana and North Dakota. It is the only Canadian province whose borders are determined by lines of longitude and latitude rather than by geographical features such as rivers and mountains.

sat (sat) *verb* The past tense and past participle of **sit**.

Sa·tan (**say**-tuhn) *noun* The devil in the Old Testament. Satan is described as an evil spirit that was sent away from the presence of God and confined to hell.

satch·el (**sach**-uhl) *noun* A bag or small suitcase sometimes carried over the shoulder.

sat·el·lite (**sat**-uh-*lite*) *noun* 1. A spacecraft that is sent into orbit around the earth, the moon, or another heavenly body. 2. A moon or other heavenly body that travels in an orbit around a larger heavenly body.

sat·el·lite dish (**sat**-uh-lite *dish*) *noun* A receiver for radio or television signals sent by satellite. Satellite dishes are shaped like a dish and are usually attached to the outside wall of a house or building. ▶ *noun, plural* **satellite dishes**

sat·in (**sat**-in) *noun* A very smooth fabric that is shiny on one side and dull on the other.

sat·ire (**sat**-ire) *noun* A type of mocking humor intended to show how foolish or misguided someone or something is. ▶ *noun* **satirist** ▶ *adjective* **satirical** (suh-**tir**-i-kuhl)

sat·is·fac·tion (*sat*-is-**fak**-shuhn) *noun* A feeling of being pleased or content because you have achieved something or met certain needs.

sat·is·fac·to·ry (*sat*-is-**fak**-tur-ee) *adjective* Good enough but not outstanding. ▶ *adverb* **satisfactorily**

sat·is·fied (**sat**-is-*fide*) *adjective* Happy because a need or want has been met.

sat·is·fy (**sat**-is-*fye*) *verb* 1. To please someone by meeting his or her needs or desires. 2. To convince or to free from doubt. ▶ *verb* **satisfies, satisfying, satisfied**

sat·u·rate (**sach**-uh-*rate*) *verb* To soak thoroughly. ▶ *verb* **saturating, saturated** ▶ *noun* **saturation** ▶ *adjective* **saturated**

sat·u·ra·tion point (**sach**-uh-**ray**-shuhn *point*) *noun* The limit beyond which no more of something can be absorbed.

Sat·ur·day (**sat**-ur-day *or* **sat**-ur-dee) *noun* The seventh day of the week, after Friday and before Sunday.

Sat·urn (**sat**-urn) *noun* The sixth planet in distance from the sun and the second-largest planet in our solar system. Saturn has at least 62 known moons and is surrounded by rings that are thought to be made of ice, rock, and frozen gases.

sauce (saws) *noun* 1. A thick liquid served with food to add flavor and make it more appealing. 2. Stewed fruit eaten as dessert or as a side dish.

sauce·pan (**saws**-pan) *noun* A deep metal or glass cooking pot with a long handle and a lid.

sau·cer (**saw**-sur) *noun* A small, shallow plate designed to go under a cup and catch spills.

Sau·di A·ra·bi·a (**sou**-dee uh-**ray**-bee-uh *or* **saw**-dee uh-**ray**-bee-uh) The largest Arab country in the Middle East. It is home to 20 percent of the world's oil reserves as well as to Islam's two holiest shrines, Mecca and Medina.

sau·na (**saw**-nuh) *noun* 1. A bath using dry heat, or a steam bath in which the steam is made by throwing water on hot stones. 2. A room for such a bath.

saun·ter (**sawn**-tur) *verb* To walk in a slow, leisurely, or casual way. ▶ *verb* **sauntering, sauntered**

sau·sage (**saw**-sij) *noun* Chopped and seasoned meat that is sometimes stuffed into a thin case shaped like a tube.

sav·age (**sav**-ij) *adjective* 1. Not tamed, or not under human control. 2. Fierce, dangerous, or violent. 3. Not civilized. *noun* 1. A person who lives in a way that is not civilized. 2. A fierce or violent person.

▶ *adverb* **savagely**

sa·van·na *or* **sa·van·nah** (suh-**van**-uh) *noun* A flat, grassy plain with few or no trees. Savannas are found in tropical and subtropical areas.

save (sayv)

verb **1.** To rescue someone or something from danger or harm. **2.** To make the best use of something and not waste it. **3.** To store or keep something, especially money, for future use. **4.** To stop a ball or puck from going into a goal in soccer or hockey. **5.** To copy a file from a computer's RAM (random access memory) onto a disk or other storage device.

preposition Except. *All the kids were dressed and ready to go, save one.*

▶ *verb* **saving, saved** ▶ *noun* **saver**

sav·ings (**say**-vingz) *noun, plural* Money that has been saved or not spent.

sav·ior (**sayv**-yur) *noun* A person or thing that saves someone from danger, difficulty, or death.

sa·vor·y (**say**-vur-ee) *adjective* Pleasing to the taste or smell.

saw (saw)

noun A hand- or power-driven tool with sharp teeth on its blade, used for cutting wood.

verb **1.** To use a saw for cutting something. **2.** The past tense of **see.**

▶ *verb* **sawing, sawed, sawn** (sawn)

saw·dust (**saw**-duhst) *noun* Tiny particles of wood that fall off when you saw wood.

saw·mill (**saw**-mil) *noun* A place where people use machines to saw logs into lumber.

sax·o·phone (**sak**-suh-fone) *noun* A wind instrument made of brass, with a mouthpiece that holds a reed, keys for the fingers, and a body that is usually curved. ▶ *noun* **saxophonist**

say (say)

verb **1.** To speak. **2.** To state, or to express in words. **3.** To repeat or to recite.

noun The chance to speak.

▶ *verb* **says** (sez), **saying, said** (sed)

say·ing (**say**-ing) *noun* A well-known phrase or proverb that gives advice or expresses a truth. "Don't cry over spilled milk" is a saying.

scab (skab) *noun* The hard crust that forms over a sore or wound when it is healing.

scab·bard (**skab**-urd) *noun* A case that holds a sword, dagger, or bayonet when it is not in use.

scaf·fold (**skaf**-uhld) *noun* A temporary structure made of planks and poles attached to the outside of a building that workers stand on.

scald (skawld) *verb* To burn with very hot liquid or steam. ▶ *verb* **scalding, scalded** ▶ *adjective* **scalding**

scale (skale)

noun **1.** One of the thin, flat, overlapping pieces of hard skin that cover the body of a fish, snake, or other reptile. **2.** Musical notes arranged in a series of rising or falling pitches. **3.** A series of numbers, units, or values used to measure something. **4.** The ratio between the measurements on a map, model, drawing, or plan and the actual measurements. **5.** A device for weighing things. **6.** A series of stages or steps.

verb **1.** To remove all the scales from something. **2.** To climb or go up something.

▶ *verb* **scaling, scaled** ▶ *adjective* **scaly**

sca·lene tri·an·gle (skay-**leen** trye-**ang**-guhl) *noun* In geometry, a triangle with three sides of different lengths.

scal·lion (**skal**-yuhn) *noun* An onion with long, grasslike leaves and a small bulb.

scal·lop (**skah**-luhp *or* **skal**-uhp) *noun* **1.** A shellfish with two fan-shaped, hinged shells that swims by snapping its shells together and shooting out a jet of water. **2.** One of a series of small curves in a decorative border that looks like the edge of a scallop shell.

▶ *adjective* **scalloped**

scalp (skalp) *noun* The skin covering the top and back of your head, usually covered with hair.

scal·pel (**skal**-puhl) *noun* A small, straight knife with a very sharp blade, used in surgery.

scam·per (**skam**-pur) *verb* To run lightly and quickly. ▸ *verb* **scampering, scampered**

scan (skan) *verb* 1. To read quickly, without looking for details. 2. To examine in a searching way. 3. To move a beam of light over something to obtain or transmit an image.
▸ *verb* **scanning, scanned**

scan·dal (**skan**-duhl) *noun* 1. A dishonest or immoral act that shocks people and disgraces those involved. 2. Harmful gossip.
▸ *adjective* **scandalous**

Scan·di·na·vi·an (*skan*-duh-**nay**-vee-uhn)
noun Someone who was born in or is a citizen of Norway, Denmark, or Sweden. Iceland and Finland also are sometimes considered Scandinavian countries.
adjective Of or having to do with the countries, people, or languages of of Norway, Denmark, or Sweden.

Scan·di·na·vi·an Pe·nin·su·la (*skan*-duh-**nay**-vee-uhn puh-**nin**-suh-luh) A region of northern Europe, connected to the mainland but predominantly surrounded by the Norwegian, North, and Baltic Seas. The Scandinavian Peninsula is the largest peninsula in Europe, and includes Norway and Sweden, and part of Finland.

scan·ner (**skan**-ur) *noun* A machine that uses a beam of light to copy an image or read information.

scant (skant) *adjective* 1. Barely enough, or not enough. 2. Not quite the full amount.

scant·y (**skan**-tee) *adjective* Too little in size or amount. ▸ *adjective* **scantier, scantiest**

scape·goat (**skape**-goht) *noun* A person who is made to take the blame for the mistakes or wrongdoings of others.

scar (skahr)
noun A mark left on your skin by an injury or wound that has healed.
verb To leave a permanent mark

on your skin.
▸ *verb* **scarring, scarred**

scarce (skairs) *adjective* Hard to get or find, or available in quantities too small to meet the demand. ▸ *noun* **scarcity** (**skair**-si-tee)

scarce·ly (**skairs**-lee) *adverb* 1. Hardly; almost not. 2. Probably not or certainly not.

scare (skair)
verb To frighten or be frightened by someone or something.
noun Widespread fear or panic.
▸ *verb* **scaring, scared** ▸ *adjective* **scared**

scare·crow (**skair**-kroh) *noun* A figure made of straw that is shaped and dressed to look like a person and put in a field to frighten birds away from crops.

scarf (skahrf) *noun* A square or strip of material worn around the neck or head for decoration or warmth. ▸ *noun, plural* **scarfs** or **scarves** (skahrvz)

scar·let (**skahr**-lit)
noun A bright red color.
adjective Having a bright red color.

scar·y (**skair**-ee) *adjective* Causing feelings of fear. ▸ *adjective* **scarier, scariest**

scat·ter (**skat**-ur) *verb* 1. To throw things here and there. 2. To move off in different directions.
▸ *verb* **scattering, scattered**

scav·enge (**skav**-uhnj) *verb* To search through garbage for something useful or edible. ▸ *verb* **scavenging, scavenged** ▸ *noun* **scavenger**

sce·nar·i·o (suh-**nair**-ee-oh) *noun* 1. An outline of a movie, a play, or an opera that summarizes the story. 2. An outline of a series of events that might happen in a particular situation.

scene (seen) *noun* 1. A view of people or places. 2. A part of a story, play, or movie that shows what is happening in one particular place and time. 3. The place where something happens. 4. **make a scene** To show your anger or other emotion in a very public way.

S

scen·er·y (**see**-nur-ee) noun 1. The natural features of a landscape, such as trees, lakes, and mountains. 2. The painted screens and backdrops that are used on stage to represent the location of a scene in a play, an opera, or a ballet.
▶ noun, plural **sceneries**

sce·nic (**see**-nik) adjective Having beautiful natural surroundings.

scent (sent)
noun 1. A distinctive smell, especially a pleasant one. 2. A pleasant-smelling liquid that you put on your skin; a perfume. 3. The odor or trail of a hunted animal or person.
verb To feel that something exists or is about to happen.
Scent sounds like **cent** and **sent**.
▶ verb **scenting, scented** ▶ adjective **scented**

scep·ter (**sep**-tur) noun A rod or staff carried by a king or queen as a symbol of authority.

sched·ule (**skej**-ool or **skej**-ul)
noun A plan, a list of events, or a timetable.
verb To plan an event for a certain date or time.
▶ verb **scheduling, scheduled**

scheme (skeem)
noun A plan or plot for doing something.
verb To make plans for something in a secret or underhanded way.
▶ verb **scheming, schemed** ▶ noun **schemer** ▶ adjective **scheming**

schol·ar (**skah**-lur) noun 1. A person who has a great deal of knowledge in a particular field. 2. A serious student.
▶ adjective **scholarly**

schol·ar·ship (**skah**-lur-ship) noun
1. Money given to pay for you to go to college or to follow a course of study. 2. Knowledge achieved by studying hard.

scho·las·tic (skuh-**las**-tik) adjective Of or having to do with school and learning.

school (skool)
noun 1. A place where people go to be taught and to learn. 2. Learning that takes place in school. 3. All the people in a school. 4. A part of a university. 5. A group of fish or sea creatures swimming or feeding together.
verb To teach or train someone.
▶ verb **schooling, schooled** ▶ noun **schooling**

school·child (**skool**-childe) noun A **schoolchild** is a boy or girl who goes to school. ▶ noun, plural **schoolchildren**

schoon·er (**skoo**-nur) noun A fast ship with two masts, a narrow hull, and sails that run lengthwise.

schwa (shwah) noun The sound of a short, unstressed vowel in English, such as the sound of the letter a in the word ago, or the sound of the o in gallop. Dictionaries represent the schwa by the symbol ə.

sci·ence (**sye**-uhns) noun 1. The study of nature and the physical world through observation and experiment. 2. Any of the branches or fields of scientific study, such as biology, physics, or geology.

sci·ence fic·tion (**sye**-uhns **fik**-shuhn) noun Fantasy stories that are set in the future and usually involve science and technology, space travel, or life on other planets.

sci·en·tif·ic (sye-uhn-**tif**-ik) adjective 1. Of or having to do with science. 2. To use the **scientific method** when you do an experiment, you first collect and organize information about the problem you are trying to solve, and then you test your ideas about it very carefully.
▶ adverb **scientifically**

sci·en·tist (**sye**-uhn-tist) noun A person who is trained and works in science. Many scientists work in laboratories, doing experiments.

scis·sors (**siz**-urz) noun, plural A sharp tool for cutting cloth and paper, with looped handles and two blades that press against each other.

scoff (skahf or skawf) verb To mock or to treat someone or something in a scornful way. ▶ verb **scoffing, scoffed**

scold (skohld) *verb* To tell someone in an angry way that he or she has done something wrong or done a bad job. ▸ *verb* **scolding, scolded**

sco·li·o·sis (*skoh*-lee-**oh**-sis) *noun* An abnormal curving of the spine to the side.

scoop (skoop)
verb To pick up or gather up something in a quick, smooth movement.
noun **1.** A utensil shaped like a spoon with a short handle and a deep hollow. **2.** A story reported in a newspaper before other papers have a chance to report it.
▸ *verb* **scooping, scooped**

scoot·er (**skoo**-tur) *noun* **1.** A child's vehicle with a handle, two wheels, and a board that you stand on with one foot while pushing against the ground with the other. **2.** A small, light motorcycle.

scope (skohp) *noun* **1.** The opportunity or possibility. **2.** The area or range of operation.

scorch (skorch)
verb **1.** To burn something on the surface, as with an iron. **2.** To wither or dry up with intense heat.
adjective If the weather is **scorching**, it is almost too hot to bear.
▸ *verb* **scorches, scorching, scorched** ▸ *noun* **scorch**

score (skor)
verb **1.** To make a point or points in a game, contest, or test. **2.** To arrange a piece of music so that it can be played by different instruments. **3.** To mark the surface of something with cuts, scratches, notches, or lines.
noun **1.** The number of points made by each person or team in a game, contest, or test. **2.** A written piece of music, showing all the parts for voices or instruments. **3.** Twenty.
noun, plural **scores** A large number.
idiom **know the score** (informal) To be well informed about the situation.
▸ *verb* **scoring, scored** ▸ *noun* **scorer**

scorn (skorn)
noun A feeling of contempt for someone or something you think of as worthless or bad.
verb **1.** To treat with contempt. **2.** To refuse something because you think it is not worth your while.
▸ *verb* **scorning, scorned** ▸ *adjective* **scornful**

scor·pi·on (**skor**-pee-uhn) *noun* An animal related to the spider with a long, jointed tail that ends in a poisonous stinger.

scoun·drel (**skoun**-druhl) *noun* Someone who deceives or takes advantage of others.

scour (skour) *verb* **1.** To clean or polish something by rubbing it hard with soap and water or something rough. **2.** To search a place thoroughly.
▸ *verb* **scouring, scoured** ▸ *noun* **scourer**

scourge (skurj) *noun* Someone or something that causes serious trouble and suffering.

scout (skout)
noun Someone sent to find out and bring back information.
verb To search in the hope of discovering something.
▸ *verb* **scouting, scouted**

scowl (skoul)
verb To make an angry frown.
noun An angry frown.
▸ *verb* **scowling, scowled**

scram·ble (**skram**-buhl)
verb **1.** To crawl or climb in a hurried way, using hands and feet. **2.** To rush or struggle to get somewhere or something. **3.** To mix up or throw together. **4.** To alter an electronic signal so that it requires a special receiver to decode the message.
5. scrambled eggs Egg yolks and whites mixed together and cooked in a frying pan.
noun The act of rushing or struggling to get somewhere or do something.
▸ *verb* **scrambling, scrambled**
▸ *adjective* **scrambled** ▸ *noun* **scrambler**

scrap (skrap)
noun **1.** A small piece or bit of something. **2.** Metal that is saved from old cars or machines for reuse.

S

verb **1.** To abandon or get rid of something. **2.** (informal) To quarrel or to fight.

▸ *verb* **scrapping, scrapped** ▸ *noun* **scrapper**

scrap·book (**skrap**-buk) *noun* A book with blank pages on which you mount pictures, newspaper clippings, and other items you wish to keep.

scrape (skrape)
verb **1.** To clean, smooth, or scratch something with a rough or sharp object. **2. scrape together** To gather or collect with great difficulty. **3. scrape by** To manage or make your way with difficulty.
noun **1.** An injury caused by something sharp or hard scraping your skin. **2.** (informal) An awkward or embarrassing situation.

▸ *verb* **scraping, scraped** ▸ *noun* **scraper**

scratch (skrach)
verb **1.** To scrape lightly with your fingernails a part of you that itches. **2.** To mark or cut the surface of something. **3.** To tear or dig at with the fingernails or claws. **4.** (informal) To erase or cancel something.
noun A mark left on something as a result of scratching.
idioms **1. from scratch** (informal) Starting from fresh ingredients or from the very beginning. **2. up to scratch** (informal) Acceptable, ready, or up to standard.

▸ *verb* **scratches, scratching, scratched** ▸ *noun, plural* **scratches**

scratch·y (**skrach**-ee) *adjective* **1.** Causing an itch. **2.** Rough and irritating.

▸ *adjective* **scratchier, scratchiest**

scrawl (skrawl)
verb To write in a hurried, careless way.
noun Sloppy handwriting that is difficult to read.

▸ *verb* **scrawling, scrawled**

scream (skreem)
verb To make a loud, shrill, piercing cry or sound.
noun **1.** A loud, shrill, piercing cry or sound. **2.** (informal) Someone or something that is considered very funny.

▸ *verb* **screaming, screamed**

screech (skreech)
verb To make a loud, high-pitched sound.
noun A loud, high-pitched sound.

▸ *verb* **screeches, screeching, screeched** ▸ *noun, plural* **screeches**

screen (skreen)
noun **1.** Wire or plastic netting in a frame. **2.** A light, movable partition used to hide or divide a room. **3.** The flat front surface of a television or computer monitor. **4.** The white surface on which movies or slides are projected.
verb **1.** To show on a screen. **2.** To test someone to find out whether or not they have a disease. **3.** To examine carefully in order to make a selection, or to separate into groups.

▸ *verb* **screening, screened**

screen·play (**skreen**-play) *noun* A play written to be made into a movie, with all the actors' lines and their directions.

screen·sav·er (**skreen**-say-vur) *noun* A computer program that replaces the still image on a computer monitor with one that changes or that uses less light.

screen·shot (**skreen**-shaht) *noun* An image of what appears on a computer monitor. Screenshots are often used to show people how different programs work.

screw (skroo)
noun A device for fastening things together that looks like a nail with a spiral thread and a slotted head.
verb **1.** To fasten something with screws. **2.** To turn or twist something until it is tightly fastened. **3.** To twist into an unnatural shape or position. **4. screw up** (informal) To make a really bad mistake.

▸ *verb* **screwing, screwed**

screw·driv·er (**skroo**-drye-vur) *noun* A tool with a tip that fits into the slot in the head of a screw so that you can turn it.

S

scrib·ble (skrib-uhl)
verb **1.** To write or draw something carelessly or in a rush. **2.** To make or cover with meaningless marks.
noun Handwriting or drawing that is not very clear or easy to make out.
▸ *verb* **scribbling, scribbled**

scribe (skribe) *noun* A person who copied documents by hand before printing was invented.

script (skript) *noun* **1.** The written text of a play, a movie, or a television or radio show. **2.** Writing in which the letters are joined together.

scrip·ture (skrip-chur) *noun* The sacred writings of a religion.

scroll (skrohl)
noun A piece of paper or parchment with writing on it that is rolled up into the shape of a tube.
verb To move text or graphics up or down on a computer screen.
▸ *verb* **scrolling, scrolled**

scroll bar (skrohl *bahr***)** *noun* A horizontal or vertical bar on a computer monitor that you can move with your mouse to see different parts of a document.

scroll wheel (skrohl *weel***)** *noun* A small disk on a mouse that you turn in order to scroll through a document or zoom into or out of an image on your computer monitor.

scrounge (skrounj) *verb* **1.** To get things from people without paying. **2.** To get or collect things with difficulty.
▸ *verb* **scrounging, scrounged**
▸ *noun* **scrounger**

scrub (skruhb)
verb To clean something by rubbing or brushing it hard.
noun Low bushes or short trees that grow thickly together and cover an area of land.
▸ *verb* **scrubbing, scrubbed**

scruff·y (skruhf-ee) *adjective* Shabby and messy or dirty. ▸ *adjective* **scruffier, scruffiest** ▸ *adverb* **scruffily**

scru·ple (skroo-puhl) *noun* A strong feeling about what is right that keeps you from doing something wrong.

scru·pu·lous (skroo-pyuh-luhs) *adjective* **1.** Having strict beliefs about what is right and proper. **2.** Very careful and exact.
▸ *adverb* **scrupulously**

scru·ti·nize (skroo-tuh-*nize*) *verb* To examine, observe, or inspect something closely. ▸ *verb* **scrutinizing, scrutinized**

scru·ti·ny (skroo-tuh-nee) *noun* Close and critical observation or inspection of someone or something.

scu·ba div·ing (skoo-buh *dye*-ving) *noun* Underwater swimming with a tank of compressed air on your back that you can breathe through a hose. Scuba is short for *self-contained underwater breathing apparatus.* ▸ *noun* **scuba diver**

scuff (skuhf) *verb* To scratch or scrape something and leave a mark. ▸ *verb* **scuffing, scuffed**

scuf·fle (skuhf-uhl)
noun A confused and disorderly struggle or fight.
verb To engage in or cause a scuffle.
▸ *verb* **scuffling, scuffled**

scull (skuhl) *noun* **1.** One of a pair of lightweight oars used to propel a boat through water. **2.** A small, light boat that is propelled by oars, often used for racing.
Scull sounds like **skull.**

sculp·ture (skuhlp-chur) *noun* **1.** Something carved or shaped out of stone, wood, marble, or clay or cast in bronze or another metal. **2.** The art or practice of making sculpture.
▸ *noun* **sculptor (skuhlp-tuhr)** ▸ *verb* **sculpt (skulpt)**

scum (skuhm) *noun* A filmy layer that forms on the surface of a liquid or body of water, especially stagnant water.

scur·ry (skur-ee) *verb* To hurry, or to move with light, quick steps. ▸ *verb* **scurries, scurrying, scurried**

scur·vy (skur-vee) *noun* A disease characterized by bleeding gums and extreme weakness. Scurvy is caused by a lack of vitamin C, which is found in citrus fruits and vegetables.

S

scuz·zy (**skuhz**-ee) *adjective* (slang) Dirty, grimy, or disgusting in some way. ▶ *adjective* **scuzzier, scuzziest**

scythe (siTHe) *noun* A tool with a long handle and a large, curved blade used for cutting grass or crops by hand.

sea (see) *noun* **1.** The body of saltwater that covers nearly three-fourths of the earth's surface; the ocean. **2.** A body of saltwater that may be partly enclosed or mostly or fully enclosed by land, such as the Caribbean or Mediterranean seas. **3.** An overwhelming amount or number. **Sea** sounds like **see.**

sea anemone (see uh-*nem*-uh-nee) *noun* A sea animal with a body shaped like a tube and a mouth opening that is surrounded by brightly colored tentacles.

sea·board (**see**-bord) *noun* The land along or near the ocean shore.

sea·coast (**see**-*kohst*) *noun* The area of land along the edge of a sea or an ocean.

sea·far·er (**see**-*fair*-ur) *noun* Someone who travels by sea, especially a sailor.

sea·far·ing (**see**-*fair*-ing) *adjective* **1.** Earning your living by working at sea. **2.** Of or having to do with sailors or the sea.

sea·food (**see**-*food*) *noun* Edible fish and shellfish.

sea·gull (**see**-*guhl*) *noun* A gray and white bird that is commonly found near the seacoast.

sea horse (see *hors*) *noun* A small ocean fish with a head shaped like that of a horse that swims through the water in an upright position.

seal (seel) *noun* **1.** A sea mammal that lives in coastal waters and has thick fur and flippers. **2.** Something that securely closes up a container. **3.** A design pressed into wax and made into a stamp. A seal is used to secure the contents of an envelope or to make a document official. *verb* To shut, fasten, or close something up. ▶ *verb* **sealing, sealed** ▶ *noun* **sealant** (**see**-luhnt)

sea lev·el (**see** *lev*-uhl) *noun* The average level of the ocean's surface, used as a starting point from which to measure the height or depth of a place.

sea lion (**see** *lye*-uhn) *noun* A large marine mammal similar to a seal but with ear flaps and longer front flippers.

seam (seem) *noun* **1.** A line of sewing that joins two pieces of material. **2.** A band of mineral or metal in the earth. **Seam** sounds like **seem.**

seam·stress (**seem**-stris) *noun* A woman who sews for a living. ▶ *noun, plural* **seamstresses**

sea·plane (**see**-*plane*) *noun* An airplane that can take off from and land on water. A seaplane has floats attached to its underside.

sea·port (**see**-*port*) *noun* **1.** A port or harbor for seafaring ships. **2.** A city or town with such a port or harbor.

search (surch) *verb* **1.** To explore or examine something carefully and thoroughly in order to find someone or something. **2.** To look for something on the Internet, using a search engine. *noun* **1.** The activity of looking or searching for something or someone. **2. search warrant** An order from a court that allows the police to enter and search a place. **3. search engine** A computer program that will search the World Wide Web for the words or data you request. ▶ *verb* **searches, searching, searched** ▶ *noun, plural* **searches** ▶ *noun* **searcher**

search·ing (**sur**-ching) *adjective* Examining thoroughly; probing.

search·light (**surch**-*lite*) *noun* A large lamp with a powerful beam of light that can be focused in any direction.

sea·shell (**see**-*shel*) *noun* The shell of a sea animal such as an oyster or a clam.

sea·shore (**see**-*shor*) *noun* The land along the seacoast.

sea·sick (**see**-*sik*) *adjective* Feeling nauseous and dizzy because of the rolling or tossing movement of a boat or ship.

sea·son (**see**-zuhn) *noun* 1. One of the four natural parts of the year. The four seasons are spring, summer, autumn or fall, and winter. 2. A part of the year when a certain activity or event takes place. 3. **season ticket** A ticket for a series of events in a season, such as to all the home games of a sports team or performances of a ballet or an opera company.
verb To add flavor to food by adding herbs, salt, or spices.
phrase If a food is **in season,** it is available fresh for eating.
▸ *verb* **seasoning, seasoned**
▸ *adjective* **seasonal** ▸ *adverb* **seasonally**

sea·son·ing (**see**-zuh-ning) *noun* Anything that is added to food to give it more flavor, such as salt, herbs, or spices.

seat (seet)
noun 1. Something such as a chair or bench that you can sit on. 2. Anyplace where you can sit. 3. The part of the body you sit on, or the fabric that covers it. 4. The central location of something.
verb 1. To cause to sit. 2. To have enough seats for a certain number of people.
▸ *verb* **seating, seated**

seat belt (**seet** *belt*) *noun* A strap or harness that holds a person securely in the seat of a car, a truck, or an airplane for protection in case of an accident.

sea tur·tle (**see** *tur*-tuhl) *noun* A large turtle with paddle-like feet that lives in the sea, has a very long life span, and migrates across huge distances.

sea ur·chin (**see** *ur*-chin) *noun* A sea creature with a hard, spiny shell. The spines are used for protection and also help the sea urchin move around.

sea·weed (**see**-*weed*) *noun* Any of various types of algae that grow in the sea and need sunlight to make their own food. ▸ *noun, plural* **seaweed**

se·cede (si-**seed**) *verb* To formally withdraw from a group or an organization, often to form another organization. ▸ *verb* **seceding, seceded** ▸ *noun* **secession** (si-**sesh**-uhn)

se·clud·ed (si-**kloo**-did) *adjective* Quiet and private; not seen or visited by many people. ▸ *noun* **seclusion** (si-**kloo**-zhuhn)

sec·ond (**sek**-uhnd)
adjective Next after the first of something, written numerically as 2nd.
noun 1. A unit of time equal to one-sixtieth of a minute. 2. Any very short period of time.
noun, plural **seconds** Another, or a second, helping of food.
verb To support or approve a suggestion or idea.
▸ *verb* **seconding, seconded** ▸ *adverb* **secondly**

sec·on·dar·y (**sek**-uhn-*der*-ee) *adjective* 1. Coming after or less important than. 2. Based on something that is not original. 3. Of or having to do with the second stage of something.
▸ *adverb* **secondarily** (**sek**-uhn-*der*-uh-lee)

sec·on·dar·y school (**sek**-uhn-*der*-ee *skool*) *noun* A school between elementary school and college; a high school.

sec·ond-guess (**sek**-uhnd-**ges**) *verb* To think that your own opinion about a person or a decision is better or more accurate than someone else's.

sec·ond·hand (**sek**-uhnd-*hand*) *adjective* 1. Owned, worn, or used by someone else before you. 2. Selling used goods.

sec·ond·hand smoke (**sek**-uhnd-*hand* *smohk*) *noun* Smoke that a person inhales from cigarettes, cigars, or pipes that other people are smoking.

sec·ond-rate (**sek**-uhnd-**rate**) *adjective* Of poor quality.

S

se·cre·cy (**see**-kruh-see) *noun* 1. The practice or habit of keeping things secret. 2. The condition of being secret.

se·cret (**see**-krit)
noun Something that is kept hidden or that only a few people know.
adjective Not known or seen by many people.
phrase **in secret** Without anyone else knowing.
▶ *adverb* **secretly**

secret agent *noun* A spy or a person who obtains secret information, usually from another government.

sec·re·tar·y (**sek**-ri-ter-ee) *noun* 1. A person who handles letters, telephone calls, appointments, and other office tasks for an employer. 2. A person in charge of a cabinet department in a government.
▶ *noun, plural* **secretaries** ▶ *adjective* **secretarial**

se·crete (si-**kreet**) *verb* 1. To produce and release a liquid. 2. To put in a secret place; to hide.
▶ *verb* **secreting, secreted** ▶ *noun* **secretion**

se·cre·tive (**see**-kri-tiv) *adjective* Tending to be silent about your thoughts, feelings, and activities.

sect (sekt) *noun* A group whose members share the same beliefs and practices or follow the same leader. A sect is often a small group that has broken away from a larger religious group.

sec·tion (**sek**-shuhn) *noun* 1. One of the parts into which something is divided. 2. A part of a town, city, or country. 3. A **cross section.**

sec·tor (**sek**-tur) *noun* 1. A part of a circle between two straight lines drawn from the center to the circumference. 2. A part or division of a city or group of people.

sec·u·lar (**sek**-yuh-lur) *adjective* Belonging to the physical world; not religious or sacred.

se·cure (si-**kyoor**)
adjective 1. Safe, confident, and not worried or anxious. 2. Safely kept or

firmly fastened so that it can't become loose or be lost. 3. Firm and steady, or strong. 4. Certain or guaranteed.
verb 1. To make something safe, especially by fastening, tying, or closing it tightly. 2. To get.
▶ *verb* **securing, secured** ▶ *adverb* **securely**

se·cu·ri·ty (si-**kyoor**-i-tee) *noun* 1. The state of being free from danger; safety. 2. Protection from danger or disruption. 3. A private service providing protection for a specific business, school, or area.

se·dan (si-**dan**) *noun* An enclosed car for four or more people with either two or four doors and a full-sized rear seat.

se·date (si-**date**)
adjective 1. Calm, unhurried, and relaxed. 2. Serious or dignified.
verb To give someone a drug to make him or her calm down or fall asleep.
▶ *verb* **sedating, sedated** ▶ *noun* **sedation** ▶ *adverb* **sedately**

sed·a·tive (**sed**-uh-tiv) *noun* A drug that makes you calm or sleepy.

sed·i·ment (**sed**-uh-muhnt) *noun* 1. Material that settles at the bottom of a liquid. 2. Rock, sand, or dirt that has been carried to a place by water, wind, or a glacier.
▶ *noun* **sedimentation** (sed-uh-muhn-**tay**-shuhn)

sed·i·men·tar·y (sed-uh-**men**-tur-ee) *adjective* **Sedimentary** rock is formed by layers of sediment that have been pressed together.

see (see) *verb* 1. To become aware of something or someone with your eyes. 2. To understand or to get a clear mental impression of something. 3. To find out or to discover. 4. To visit and spend some time with someone. 5. To date someone regularly. 6. **see about** To investigate or look into something. 7. **see through** To be able to recognize the true nature of someone or something. 8. To **see** a job **through** is to finish a job.
See sounds like **sea.** ▶ *verb* **seeing, saw, seen** (seen)

S

seed (seed)
noun 1. The part of a flowering plant from which a new plant can grow, especially a grain, nut, or kernel. 2. The source or beginning of something.
verb 1. To plant land with seeds.
2. To remove seeds from.
▶ *verb* **seeding, seeded**

seed·ling (**seed**-ling) *noun* A young plant that has been grown from a seed rather than a cutting.

seek (seek) *verb* 1. To try to find something. 2. To try. 3. To ask for.
▶ *verb* **seeking, sought** (sawt) ▶ *noun* **seeker**

seem (seem) *verb* 1. To appear to be, or to give the impression of being.
2. To appear to oneself.
Seem sounds like **seam**. ▶ *verb* **seeming, seemed**

seem·ing·ly (**see**-ming-lee) *adverb* In a way that appears to be real or true; apparently.

seep (seep) *verb* To flow or leak slowly. ▶ *verb* **seeping, seeped** ▶ *noun* **seepage**

see·saw (**see**-*saw*)
noun A long board balanced on a support in the middle. When people sit on opposite sides, one end goes up as the other goes down.
verb 1. To ride on a seesaw. 2. To move up and down or back and forth.
▶ *verb* **seesawing, seesawed**

seethe (seeTH) *verb* 1. To be very angry without expressing that anger. 2. To bubble or foam as if a liquid were boiling.
▶ *verb* **seething, seethed** ▶ *adjective* **seething**

see-through (**see**-*throo*) *adjective* Able to be seen through; transparent.

seg·ment (**seg**-muhnt) *noun* 1. A part or section of something. 2. In geometry, the portion of a line between two points on the line.
▶ *adjective* **segmental** (seg-**men**-tuhl)

seg·re·gate (**seg**-ri-*gate*) *verb* To separate or keep people or things apart from the main group. ▶ *verb* **segregating, segregated** ▶ *adjective* **segregated**

seg·re·ga·tion (*seg*-ri-**gay**-shuhn) *noun* The act or practice of keeping people or groups apart.

seis·mo·graph (**size**-muh-*graf*) *noun* An instrument that detects earthquakes and measures their power. ▶ *noun* **seismography** (size-**mah**-gruh-fee)

seize (seez) *verb* 1. To grab or take hold of something suddenly. 2. To arrest or capture someone or something.
▶ *verb* **seizing, seized**

sei·zure (**see**-zhur) *noun* 1. A sudden attack of illness, especially of a disease such as epilepsy. 2. The act of seizing something or someone.

sel·dom (**sel**-duhm) *adverb* Rarely; not often.

se·lect (suh-**lekt**)
verb 1. To choose someone or something carefully. 2. To mark text or an image on a computer screen in order to do something with it.
adjective Carefully chosen as the best.
▶ *verb* **selecting, selected** ▶ *noun* **selector**

se·lec·tion (suh-**lek**-shuhn) *noun* 1. The act of picking or choosing something. 2. A person or thing that has been chosen. 3. A section of data on a computer screen that you have selected. 4. A range of things from which you can choose.

se·lec·tive (suh-**lek**-tiv) *adjective* Choosing carefully.

self (self) *noun* One's individual nature or personality. ▶ *noun, plural* **selves**

self-as·sur·ance (**self**-uh-**shoor**-uhns) *noun* Confidence in yourself and your abilities.

self-cen·tered (**self-sen**-turd) *adjective* Thinking only about your own feelings or needs; selfish.

self-con·fi·dent (**self-kahn**-fi-duhnt) *adjective* Sure of one's own abilities or worth. ▶ *noun* **self-confidence** ▶ *adverb* **self-confidently**

self-con·scious (**self-kahn**-shuhs) *adjective* Constantly worried about how you look to other people and what they are thinking. ▶ *adverb* **self-consciously**

S

self-con·trol (**self**-kuhn-**trohl**) *noun* Control of your feelings and behavior. ▸ *adjective* **self-controlled**

self-de·fense (**self**-di-**fens**) *noun* The act of protecting yourself against attacks or threats.

self-de·struct (**self**-di-**struhkt**) *verb* To destroy itself or oneself. ▸ *verb* **self-destructing, self-destructed** ▸ *noun* **self-destruction** ▸ *adjective* **self-destructive**

self-em·ployed (**self**-em-**ploid**) *adjective* Working as your own boss or running your own business.

self-es·teem (**self**-e-**steem**) *noun* A feeling of personal pride and of respect for yourself.

self-ex·plan·a·to·ry (**self**-ik-**splan**-uh-*tor*-ee) *adjective* Easily understood and requiring no further explanation.

self·ish (**sel**-fish) *adjective* Concerned only with one's own needs and wishes. ▸ *noun* **selfishness** ▸ *adverb* **selfishly**

self-re·spect (**self**-ri-**spekt**) *noun* Pride and confidence in yourself and your abilities. ▸ *adjective* **self-respecting**

self-right·eous (**self**-rye-chuhs) *adjective* Too confident that you are right and that others are wrong.

self-ris·ing flour (**self**-*rye*-zing **flour**) *noun* Flour that contains baking powder, which makes cakes or breads rise when baked in an oven.

self-serv·ice (**self**-**sur**-vis) *adjective* If a store or gas station is **self-service,** you help yourself to what you want and then pay a cashier.

self-start·er (**self**-**stahr**-tur) *noun* A person who has the ability or willingness to take a first step in doing or learning something.

self-suf·fi·cient (**self**-suh-**fish**-uhnt) *adjective* Able to take care of one's own needs without help from others. ▸ *noun* **self-sufficiency**

sell (sel) *verb* 1. To exchange something for money. 2. To offer for sale. 3. To be sold or to be on sale. 4. To help the sale of something. 5. (informal) To persuade someone that he or she wants something.

Sell sounds like **cell.** ▸ *verb* **selling, sold** (sohld)

sell·er (**sel**-ur) *noun* Someone who sells something or who has something for sale.

selves (selvz) *noun, plural* The plural of **self.**

se·mes·ter (suh-**mes**-tur) *noun* One of two terms that make up a school year.

sem·i·cir·cle (**sem**-i-*sur*-kuhl) *noun* A half of a circle. ▸ *adjective* **semicircular**

sem·i·co·lon (**sem**-i-*koh*-luhn) *noun* The punctuation mark (;) used to separate parts of a sentence. A semicolon shows a greater separation of thoughts or ideas than a comma does.

sem·i·con·duc·tor (*sem*-ee-kuhn-**duhk**-tur) *noun* A substance, such as silicon, that doesn't conduct electricity well at low temperatures but whose conductivity improves at higher temperatures.

sem·i·fi·nal (**sem**-ee-*fye*-nuhl) *noun* A match or game to decide who will play in the final match or game of a series or tournament. ▸ *noun* **semifinalist**

sem·i·nar (**sem**-uh-*nahr*) *noun* 1. A conference or meeting for the purpose of training or discussion. 2. A college class with a small number of students who meet with a professor to discuss a particular topic.

sem·i·nar·y (**sem**-uh-*ner*-ee) *noun* A school that trains students to become priests, ministers, or rabbis. ▸ *noun, plural* **seminaries**

Sem·i·nole (**sem**-uh-*nole*) *noun* A member of a group of Native Americans who originally lived in Florida. Today, the Seminoles mainly live in Oklahoma, but some still live in Florida. ▸ *noun, plural* **Seminoles** or **Seminole**

sen·ate (**sen**-it) *noun* 1. A body of officials elected to make laws.
2. **Senate** One of the two houses of the U.S. Congress that make laws. Each state has two senators.
▸ *noun* **senator** (**sen**-uh-tur)

S

send (send) *verb* **1.** To make someone or something go or be taken somewhere. **2.** To cause something to move quickly over an area. **3. send for** To ask a person to come to you, or to ask for something to be brought to you.
▶ *verb* **sending, sent** (sent) ▶ *noun* **sender**

send-off (send-*awf*) *noun* (informal) A gathering to say good-bye to someone and to wish him or her good luck.

Sen·e·gal (sen-i-**gawl** *or* sen-i-**gahl**) A country in West Africa on the Atlantic Ocean. Senegal is the westernmost nation on the African mainland. A colony of France until 1960, it has one of the steadiest democracies in Africa.

se·nile (**see**-nile) *adjective* Showing a loss of mental ability as a result of old age. ▶ *noun* **senility** (si-**nil**-i-tee)

sen·ior (**see**-nyur)
adjective **1.** When a father and son have identical names, **senior** is placed after the surname to indicate the father. **2.** Older than someone else, or higher in rank or status.
noun A student in the fourth year of high school or college.
▶ *noun* **seniority**

sen·ior cit·i·zen (**seen**-yur **sit**-i-zuhn) *noun* An elderly person, especially someone who is older than 65 and has retired.

sen·sa·tion (sen-**say**-shuhn) *noun* **1.** The ability to feel or be aware of something through one of the senses. **2.** A feeling or an awareness. **3.** Someone or something that causes widespread excitement or interest.

sen·sa·tion·al (sen-**say**-shuh-nuhl) *adjective* **1.** Very good, and so attracting a lot of positive attention. **2.** Attracting a lot of attention because people are shocked or disapprove.
▶ *adverb* **sensationally**

sense (sens)
noun **1.** One of the powers a living being uses to learn about its surroundings. Sight, hearing, touch, taste, and smell are the five senses. **2.** A feeling. **3.** An understanding or an appreciation. **4.** Good judgment.

5. Meaning, especially when there are several meanings available.
verb To be or become aware of something.
phrase **make sense** To be understandable or logical.
▶ *verb* **sensing, sensed**

sense·less (**sens**-lis) *adjective* **1.** Without purpose or meaning; pointless. **2.** Unconscious.
▶ *adverb* **senselessly**

sense or·gan (**sens** or-guhn) *noun* An organ in the body that receives information, or stimuli, from its surroundings. The human sense organs include the eyes, ears, nose, taste buds, and skin.

sen·si·ble (**sen**-suh-buhl) *adjective* Showing common sense and sound judgment. ▶ *adverb* **sensibly**

sen·si·tive (**sen**-si-tiv) *adjective* **1.** Easily offended or upset. **2.** Painful. **3.** Aware of other people's attitudes, feelings, or circumstances. **4.** Affected by even slight changes.
▶ *adverb* **sensitively**

sen·si·tiv·i·ty (sen-si-**tiv**-i-tee) *noun* An awareness or appreciation of the feelings of others.

sen·sor (**sen**-sur) *noun* An instrument that can detect and measure changes and transmit the information to a controlling device.

sent (sent) *verb* The past tense and past participle of **send. Sent** sounds like **cent** and **scent.**

sen·tence (**sen**-tuhns)
noun **1.** A group of words that has a subject and a verb and expresses a complete thought. **2.** A punishment given to someone who has been found guilty in court.
verb To punish someone found guilty in a court in a particular way.
▶ *verb* **sentencing, sentenced**

sen·ti·ment (**sen**-tuh-muhnt) *noun* **1.** An opinion about a specific matter. **2.** A thought or an attitude that is based on feeling or emotion instead of reason. **3.** Tender or sensitive feeling.

sen·ti·ment·al (sen-tuh-**men**-tuhl) *adjective* **1.** Of or having to do

with emotion rather than reason.
2. Too emotional, or emotional in a superficial way. ▸ *noun* **sentimentality** (*sen*-tuh-**men**-tal-i-tee) ▸ *adverb* **sentimentally**

sen·try (**sen**-tree) *noun* A person who stands guard and warns others of danger. ▸ *noun, plural* **sentries**

se·pal (**see**-puhl) *noun* The green outer covering of a flower bud. The sepal opens to allow the flower to bloom and remains to protect the petals.

sep·a·rate
verb (**sep**-uh-*rate*) **1.** To set, put, or keep apart. **2.** To stop living together as husband and wife.
adjective (**sep**-ur-it) Different, individual, or not joined together.
noun, plural (**sep**-ur-its) **separates** Pieces of clothing, such as a skirt or jacket, that you can buy separately and wear in combination with other clothes.
▸ *verb* **separating, separated**

sep·a·rate·ly (**sep**-ur-it-lee) *adverb* Apart from others or from each other.

sep·a·ra·tion (*sep*-uh-**ray**-shuhn) *noun* **1.** The act or process of being moved or coming apart. **2.** A situation in which a husband and wife remain married but live apart.

Sep·tem·ber (sep-**tem**-bur) *noun* The ninth month on the calendar, after August and before October. September has 30 days.

se·quel (**see**-kwuhl) *noun* A book or movie that continues the story of an earlier work.

se·quence (**see**-kwuhns) *noun* **1.** The following of one thing after another in a regular or fixed order. **2.** A series or collection of things that follow each other in a particular order.
▸ *adjective* **sequential** (si-**kwen**-shuhl)

se·quin (**see**-kwin) *noun* A small, shiny disk, often in a bright color, that can be sewn onto clothing for decoration.

se·quoi·a (si-**kwoi**-uh) *noun* A giant evergreen tree that can reach a height of over 300 feet (90 meters). Redwoods are a type of sequoia.

Ser·bi·a (**sur**-bee-uh) A country located where Central and Southeastern Europe meet. Serbia was the site of ethnic warfare following the breakup of the former Yugoslavia in the early 1990s. The territory of Kosovo, to the south of Serbia, is still a disputed region. Kosovo declared its independence in 2008, but Serbia has not recognized it as a separate country.

ser·en·dip·i·ty (*ser*-uhn-**dip**-i-tee) *noun* An accidental occurrence that brings good luck or a happy outcome. ▸ *adjective* **serendipitous** (*ser*-uhn-**dip**-i-tuhs)

se·rene (suh-**reen**) *adjective* Calm, peaceful, or untroubled. ▸ *noun* **serenity** (suh-**ren**-i-tee) ▸ *adverb* **serenely**

serf (surf) *noun* In medieval times, a farm worker who was owned by a lord and treated as a slave. **Serf** sounds like **surf**. ▸ *noun* **serfdom** (**surf**-duhm)

ser·geant (**sahr**-juhnt) *noun* A military officer who ranks above a corporal and is in charge of troops.

se·ri·al (**seer**-ee-uhl)
noun A story or play that is published or broadcast in several parts, which are presented one at a time on television or radio or in a magazine.
adjective Repeatedly committing the same criminal act or following the same behavior pattern.
Serial sounds like **cereal**. ▸ *noun* **serialization** ▸ *verb* **serialize**

se·ri·al num·ber (**seer**-ee-uhl *nuhm*-bur) *noun* A number that identifies a member of the armed forces or a vehicle, an appliance, or another product.

se·ries (**seer**-eez) *noun* **1.** A group of related things that come one after another. **2.** A number of books or television or radio programs that deal with the same characters or are linked in some way. **3.** Electrical parts that are connected **in series** are arranged so that the current passes though each one of them in turn.
▸ *noun, plural* **series**

se·ri·ous (**seer**-ee-uhs) *adjective*
1. Solemn or caused by deep thought.
2. Meaning what you say or do; sincere. 3. Dangerous, or giving cause for concern. 4. Important and requiring a lot of thought.
▶ *noun* **seriousness** ▶ *adverb* **seriously**

ser·mon (**sur**-muhn) *noun* 1. A speech given during a religious service.
2. Any serious talk, especially one that deals with morals or correct behavior.
▶ *verb* **sermonize**

ser·pent (**sur**-puhnt) *noun* A snake.

ser·rat·ed (**ser**-ay-tid) *adjective* Having a blade like that of a saw.

se·rum (**seer**-uhm) *noun* 1. The clear, thin, liquid part of the blood. It separates from blood when a clot forms. 2. A liquid used to prevent or cure a disease. Serum is taken from the blood of an animal that has had the disease and is already immune to it.
▶ *noun, plural* **serums** or **sera** (**seer**-uh)

serv·ant (**sur**-vuhnt) *noun* Someone who is employed to do housework, cooking, or other domestic chores in someone else's house.

serve (surv)
verb 1. To work for someone as a servant. 2. To give someone food or drink, or to help a customer in a store. 3. To do your duty in some form of service. 4. To supply. 5. To spend. 6. In games such as tennis and volleyball, to begin play by hitting the ball.
noun The act of hitting a ball over a net to begin play in games such as tennis and volleyball.
▶ *verb* **serving, served**

serv·er (**sur**-vur) *noun* 1. Someone who serves others, such as a waiter or waitress. 2. The player who serves the ball in tennis, volleyball, or other games. 3. A computer shared by two or more users in a network. This kind of computer is also known as a *file server.*

serv·ice (**sur**-vis)
noun 1. The way in which the staff in a store or restaurant helps and takes care of you. 2. Work that helps others. 3. Employment as a servant. 4. A system or way of providing something useful or necessary. 5. A branch of the armed forces. 6. A ceremony of religious worship. 7. A branch of the government. 8. The repairing of a car or an appliance. 9. A complete set of matched dishes. 10. A serve in tennis, volleyball, or any game in which a ball is hit over a net.
verb To repair or work on something such as a car, a machine, or a piece of equipment.
▶ *verb* **servicing, serviced**

serv·ice sta·tion (**sur**-vis stay-shuhn) *noun* Another term for **gas station.**

ser·vile (**sur**-vile) *adjective* Too eager to serve or please someone.

serv·ing (**sur**-ving) *noun* An amount of food for one person at a meal; a helping.

ses·a·me (**ses**-uh-mee) *noun* A small oval seed, or the tropical plant from which this seed comes. Sesame seeds and their oil are used in cooking and baking.

ses·sion (**sesh**-uhn) *noun* 1. A formal meeting. 2. A series of meetings of a court or legislature. 3. A period of time devoted to a certain activity.

set (set)
noun 1. A group of people or things that go together. 2. The stage or scenery for a play or movie. 3. A device for sending out or receiving electronic signals. 4. In math, a collection of items that are grouped together or have something in common.
adjective 1. Ready to do or begin something. 2. Fixed or established ahead of time.
verb 1. To put or to place. 2. To lay out, arrange, or put in order. 3. To begin or to start. 4. To decide on. 5. To establish or provide something as a model for other people to follow. 6. To become firm or hardened. 7. To go toward or below the horizon. 8. **set aside** To save

S

something for another time. **9. set out** To begin a trip. **10. set up** To arrange something, especially for a particular use.

idiom **be set on something** To want something very much and to be determined to get or achieve it.

▶ *verb* **setting, set**

set·back (**set**-bak) *noun* A problem that delays you or keeps you from making progress.

set·ting (**set**-ing) *noun* **1.** Background or surroundings. **2.** A set for a play or movie, or a background for a story. **3.** The way in which a machine or appliance is set or adjusted. **4.** The frame in which something, such as a jewel, sits.

set·tle (**set**-uhl) *verb* **1.** To decide or agree on something. **2.** To sit or place comfortably. **3.** To make a home or to live in a new place. **4.** To sink. **5.** To calm. **6. settle in** To get used to a new situation. **7. settle up** To pay a bill or a debt.

▶ *verb* **settling, settled** ▶ *noun* **settler**

set·tle·ment (**set**-uhl-muhnt) *noun* **1.** An agreement or a decision about something that was in doubt. **2.** A small village or group of houses where people live. **3.** A colony or community of people who have left one place to make a home in another.

set·up (**set**-uhp) *noun* The way that something is arranged.

sev·en (**sev**-uhn)
noun The number that comes after six and before eight, written numerically as 7.
adjective Referring to the number that comes after six and before eight.

sev·enth (**sev**-uhnth)
adjective Next after sixth and before eighth, written numerically as 7th.
noun One part of something that has been divided into seven equal parts, written numerically as 1/7.

sev·en·ti·eth (**sev**-uhn-tee-ith) *adjective* Next after 69th and before 71st, written numerically as 70th.

sev·en·ty (**sev**-uhn-tee) *noun* The number that is equal to 7 times 10, written numerically as 70.

sev·er (**sev**-ur) *verb* **1.** To cut off or apart. **2.** To end or to break off.

▶ *verb* **severing, severed**

sev·er·al (**sev**-ur-uhl)
adjective More than two, but not many.
noun More than two, or a few, people or things.

se·vere (suh-**veer**) *adjective* **1.** Strict or harsh. **2.** Extreme, intense, or dangerous. **3.** Violent, or causing great discomfort or difficulty.

▶ *adjective* **severer, severest** ▶ *noun* **severity** (suh-**ver**-i-tee) ▶ *adverb* **severely**

sew (soh) *verb* To make, repair, or fasten something with stitches made by a needle and thread. **Sew** sounds like **so.** ▶ *verb* **sewing, sewed, sewn** (sohn) ▶ *noun* **sewing**

sew·age (**soo**-ij) *noun* Liquid and solid waste that is carried off by sewers and drains.

sewage plant (**soo**-ij *plant*) *noun* A place where sewage is treated to make it safe and not toxic.

sew·er (**soo**-ur) *noun* An underground pipe that carries off drainage water and liquid and solid waste.

sewing machine (**soh**-ing muh-*sheen*) *noun* A machine for sewing very fast or making special stitches.

sex (seks) *noun* **1.** One of the two classes, male or female, into which people and most other living things are divided. **2.** The fact or condition of being male or female. **3.** The activity that people or animals engage in in order to reproduce or for pleasure.

▶ *noun, plural* **sexes** ▶ *adjective* **sexual**

sex·ist (**sek**-sist) *adjective* Discriminating on the basis of a person's sex. ▶ *noun* **sexism**

Sey·chelles (say-**shel** *or* say-**shelz**) An island nation in the Indian Ocean, located nearly 1,000 miles (1,600 kilometers) off the eastern coast of Africa. It consists of 115 islands northeast of the island of Madagascar, and has fewer people than any other country in Africa.

S

shab·by (**shab**-ee) *adjective* 1. Showing signs of wear and tear; worn out. 2. Mean or unfair.
▶ *adjective* **shabbier, shabbiest**
▶ *adverb* **shabbily** ▶ *noun* **shabbiness**

shack (shak) *noun* A small, roughly built hut or cabin.

shack·les (**shak**-uhlz) *noun, plural* A pair of metal rings locked around the wrists or ankles of a prisoner or a slave.

shade (shayd)
verb 1. To protect or screen someone or something from the light. 2. To make part of a drawing or picture darker by reproducing the effects of shade.
noun 1. A device that provides shelter or protection from light. 2. A place that is protected from the heat and light of the sun. 3. The degree of darkness of a color. 4. A small amount or difference.
noun, plural **shades** (slang) Sunglasses.
▶ *verb* **shading, shaded** ▶ *noun* **shading**

shad·ow (**shad**-oh)
noun 1. An area of shade on a surface made by something blocking out the light. 2. A faint trace or suggestion.
verb To follow or stay close to someone, usually secretly.
▶ *verb* **shadowing, shadowed**
▶ *adjective* **shadowy** (**shad**-oh-ee)

shad·y (**shay**-dee) *adjective* 1. Out of the light or out of the sun. 2. Dishonest or underhanded.

shaft (shaft) *noun* 1. The long, narrow handle of a spear, an arrow, a paddle, or a tool. 2. A rotating rod that transmits power in a machine or engine. 3. A ray or beam. 4. A long, narrow passage that goes straight down.

shag·gy (**shag**-ee) *adjective* Having or covered with long, rough hair or wool. ▶ *adjective* **shaggier, shaggiest**

shake (shayk)
verb 1. To move quickly up and down or back and forth. 2. To remove or scatter something by making short, quick movements. 3. To tremble, or to cause to tremble. 4. To upset. 5. To clasp someone's hand as a way of greeting or agreeing with the person.
noun A short quick movement from side to side or up and down.
▶ *verb* **shaking, shook** (shuk), **shaken** (**shay**-kuhn)

shak·y (**shay**-kee) *adjective* 1. Not sturdy or reliable. 2. Trembling or quivering. 3. Questionable or unpromising.
▶ *adjective* **shakier, shakiest**

shale (shayl) *noun* A rock that is formed from hardened clay or mud. It has many thin layers that separate easily.

shall (shal) *verb* A helping verb that is used in the following ways: 1. To show an action that will take place in the future. 2. To show that an action is required. 3. To ask a question, or to offer a suggestion.

shal·low (**shal**-oh) *adjective* 1. Not deep. 2. Lacking depth of thought, feeling, or knowledge.
▶ *adjective* **shallower, shallowest**

sham (sham) *noun* 1. Something that is meant to deceive or is not what it seems to be. 2. A decorative cover.

sha·man (**shay**-muhn) *noun* A healer in some traditional societies who deals with beings in the spirit world.

sham·bles (**sham**-buhlz) *noun* A total mess or a state of chaos.

shame (shame)
noun 1. A feeling of embarrassment and upset that you get when you know you have done something wrong or foolish. 2. Something that is unfortunate or a pity. 3. Dishonor or disgrace.
verb To make someone feel guilty or embarrassed about something.
▶ *verb* **shaming, shamed**

shame·ful (**shaym**-ful) *adjective* A **shameful** act is one that should cause the person who did it to feel ashamed. ▶ *adverb* **shamefully**

sham·poo (sham-**poo**)
noun A liquid soap used for washing hair, carpets, or upholstery.

verb To wash hair, carpets, or upholstery.
▶ *verb* **shampooing, shampooed**

sham·rock (**sham**-*rahk*) *noun* A small, cloverlike plant with three leaves. The shamrock is the national emblem of Ireland.

shan·ty (**shan**-tee) *noun* 1. A roughly built shack or cabin. 2. A **sea shanty** is a song sung by sailors in rhythm with their work.
▶ *noun, plural* **shanties**

shape (shayp)
noun 1. The form or outline of an object or a figure. 2. Good or fit condition.
verb 1. To mold or to determine how someone or something will develop. 2. **shape up** (informal) To develop.
▶ *verb* **shaping, shaped**

shape·less (**shape**-lis) *adjective* Having no clearly defined shape, or having an unattractive shape.

share (shair)
verb 1. To divide something between two or more people. 2. To use together. 3. To take part.
noun 1. The portion of something that someone receives or that belongs to someone. 2. One of many equal parts into which the ownership of a business is divided.
▶ *verb* **sharing, shared**

share·ware (**shair**-*wair*) *noun* Computer software that has a copyright but is provided free on a trial basis. If a person decides to continue using the software, he or she is expected to pay a fee to the author. ▶ *noun, plural* **shareware**

shark (shahrk) *noun* 1. A large and often fierce fish with a fin on its back, a torpedo-like body, and very sharp teeth. 2. Someone who is very skilled at a certain activity and uses that skill to cheat people.

sharp (shahrp)
adjective 1. Having an edge or a point that cuts or pierces easily. 2. Pointed. 3. Able to think or notice things quickly. 4. Abrupt or sudden. 5. Strong, biting, or harsh. 6. Distinct or clearly outlined. 7. In music, a **sharp** note is one that is higher in pitch than the usual note. 8. (slang) Very attractive or stylish.
adverb Exactly.
▶ *adjective* **sharper, sharpest**

sharp·en (**shahr**-puhn) *verb* To make sharp. ▶ *verb* **sharpening, sharpened**

shat·ter (**shat**-ur) *verb* 1. To break suddenly into many small pieces. 2. To destroy completely or to ruin.
▶ *verb* **shattering, shattered**

shave (shayv)
verb 1. To remove hair from the face or body with a razor or an electric shaver. 2. To cut off or slice in thin layers.
noun 1. An instance of removing hair from the body or face with a razor. 2. **close shave** An occasion when you come very close to or barely manage to escape something.
▶ *verb* **shaving, shaved**

shawl (shawl) *noun* A piece of soft material that is worn over the shoulders or around the head.

Shaw·nee (shaw-**nee**) *noun* A member of a group of Native Americans who once lived in the central Ohio Valley. The Shawnee now live mainly in Oklahoma. ▶ *noun, plural* **Shawnee** or **Shawnees**

she (shee) *pronoun* The female person or animal mentioned before.

sheaf (sheef) *noun* A bundle or collection of things gathered together. ▶ *noun, plural* **sheaves** (sheevz)

shear (sheer) *verb* 1. To clip or cut with scissors or shears. 2. To cut the hair or wool off a sheep or other animal. **Shear** sounds like **sheer.** ▶ *verb* **shearing, sheared** or **shorn** (shorn)

shears (sheerz) *noun, plural* A large cutting tool that resembles a pair of scissors. Shears are used in gardening and for cutting metal.

sheath (sheeth) *noun* A case for a knife, sword, or dagger.

she'd (sheed) *contraction* A short form of *she had* or *she would.*

S

shed (shed)
noun A small building, often attached to a larger one, used for storing things.
verb 1. To lose, to get rid of, or to let something fall. 2. To give off or to supply.
▶ *verb* **shedding, shed**

sheen (sheen) *noun* A soft shine or luster.

sheep (sheep) *noun* A grass-eating farm animal raised for its wool and meat. ▶ *noun, plural* **sheep**

sheep·dog (**sheep**-dawg) *noun* A dog that has been trained to guard and round up sheep.

sheep·ish (**shee**-pish) *adjective* Embarrassed because of having done something foolish. ▶ *adverb* **sheepishly**

sheer (sheer) *adjective* 1. So thin as to be almost transparent. 2. Total; nothing but. 3. Vertical or close to vertical.
Sheer sounds like **shear.** ▶ *adjective* **sheerer, sheerest**

sheet (sheet) *noun* 1. A large, rectangular piece of cotton or other fabric used to cover a bed or to lie under. 2. A broad, thin piece of paper, glass, metal, or other material.

sheik (sheek *or* shayk) *noun* The head or chief of an Arab family, tribe, or village.

shelf (shelf) *noun* 1. A length of wood or other rigid material, inside a cupboard or fastened to a wall, used for holding or storing things. 2. Something flat that looks like a shelf, such as a ledge of rock.
▶ *noun, plural* **shelves** (shelvz)

shell (shel)
noun 1. A hard outer covering or case. Nuts, tortoises, and eggs all have shells. 2. A type of small bomb that is fired from a cannon. 3. A metal or paper case that holds a bullet and its explosive and is fired from a gun.
verb 1. To remove something from its shell. 2. To bombard or to attack with shells.
▶ *verb* **shelling, shelled**

she'll (sheel) *contraction* A short form of *she will* or *she shall.*

shel·lac (shuh-**lak**) *noun* A hard varnish used on wooden floors and furniture to protect them and give them a shiny finish.

shell·fish (**shel**-*fish*) *noun* A creature with a shell that lives in water, such as a crab, oyster, or mussel. ▶ *noun, plural* **shellfish** *or* **shellfishes**

shel·ter (**shel**-tur)
noun 1. A place that offers protection from bad weather or danger. 2. Protection from something unpleasant or dangerous. 3. A place where a homeless person, a victim of a disaster, or an animal that is not wanted can stay.
verb To provide protection for someone or something, especially from the weather.
▶ *verb* **sheltering, sheltered**

shelve (shelv) *verb* 1. To cancel or decide not to continue with something. 2. To place something on a shelf or shelves.
▶ *verb* **shelving, shelved**

shep·herd (**shep**-urd)
noun Someone whose job is to herd, guard, and take care of sheep.
verb To watch over or to guide.
▶ *verb* **shepherding, shepherded**

sher·bet (**shur**-bit) *noun* A frozen dessert made of fruit juices, water, sugar, and milk, egg white, or gelatin.

sher·iff (**sher**-if) *noun* The person in charge of enforcing the law in a county or town.

sher·ry (**sher**-ee) *noun* A strong, sweet wine made from grapes grown near the town of Jerez, Spain. ▶ *noun, plural* **sherries**

she's (sheez) *contraction* A short form of *she is* or *she has.*

Shet·land po·ny (**shet**-luhnd **poh**-nee) *noun* A small horse with a long mane and tail and a rough coat, originally bred in Scotland's Shetland Islands.

S

shield (sheeld)
noun **1.** A piece of armor carried in front of the body to protect it from attack. **2.** Someone or something that provides protection. **3.** A police officer's badge.
verb To protect someone or something from something that is risky, harmful, or unpleasant.
▶ *verb* **shielding, shielded**

shift (shift)
verb **1.** To change or move something. **2.** To change the gears in a motor vehicle that does not have an automatic transmission.
noun **1.** A movement or a change. **2.** A period of several hours' continuous work, or the group of people who work those hours.
▶ *verb* **shifting, shifted**

shii·ta·ke (shee-*tah*-kee) *noun* A dark brown, edible Asian mushroom.

shil·ling (**shil**-ing) *noun* **1.** A coin that was used in Great Britain until 1971. Twenty shillings equaled one pound. **2.** A coin that is used in several African countries, including Kenya, Somalia, Tanzania, and Uganda. One shilling equals 100 cents.

shim·mer (**shim**-ur) *verb* To shine with a faint, unsteady light. ▶ *verb* **shimmering, shimmered**

shin (shin)
noun The front part of your leg, below your knee and above your ankle.
verb To climb by using your hands and legs to hold on and pull your weight.
▶ *verb* **shinning, shinned**

shine (shine)
verb **1.** To give off or reflect light. **2.** To aim light in a particular direction. **3.** To be bright; to make bright or polish. **4.** To do something very well.
noun The brightness that occurs when light reflects off something.
▶ *verb* **shining, shone** (shohn) *or* **shined**

shin·gle (**shing**-guhl) *noun* A thin, flat piece of wood or other material used to cover roofs or outside walls. Shingles are put on in overlapping rows so that water runs off them.

Shin·to (**shin**-toh) *noun* The main religion of Japan, which involves the worship of nature and of ancestors and ancient heroes.

shin·y (**shye**-nee) *adjective* Reflecting a lot of light. ▶ *adjective* **shinier, shiniest**

ship (ship)
noun **1.** A large boat that can travel across deep water. **2.** An airplane, an airship, or a spacecraft.
verb **1.** To send on a ship, a truck, a train, or an airplane. **2.** To go on a ship, usually to work.
▶ *verb* **shipping, shipped**

ship·ment (**ship**-muhnt) *noun* **1.** A package or a group of packages that is sent from one place to another. **2.** The act of shipping.

ship·shape (**ship**-shayp) *adjective* Neat, clean, and in good order.

ship·wreck (**ship**-rek) *noun* **1.** The sinking or destruction of a ship at sea. **2.** The remains of a ship that has sunk or been destroyed at sea.
▶ *adjective* **shipwrecked**

ship·yard (**ship**-yahrd) *noun* A place where ships are built or repaired.

shirk (shurk) *verb* To avoid doing something that should be done. ▶ *verb* **shirking, shirked** ▶ *noun* **shirker**

shirt (shurt) *noun* A piece of clothing that covers the upper half of your body.

shish ka·bob *or* **shish ke·bob** (**shish** kuh-*bahb*) *noun* Small pieces of meat and vegetables cooked on a skewer.

shiv·er (**shiv**-ur)
verb To shake with or as if with cold.
noun An act or instance of shivering.
▶ *verb* **shivering, shivered** ▶ *adjective* **shivery**

shoal (shole) *noun* **1.** An area of shallow water or a submerged sandbar that can be seen at low tide. **2.** A large number of fish swimming together.

S

shock (shahk)
noun 1. A sudden, violent event, such as an accident or a death, that upsets or disturbs you greatly. 2. The mental or emotional upset caused by such an event. 3. A medical condition caused by a serious drop in blood pressure, sometimes causing loss of consciousness. Shock may be caused by severe injury or great emotional upset. 4. A sudden, violent impact. 5. Injury to the body caused by an electric current passing through it. 6. A thick, heavy mass of something, especially hair.
verb 1. To surprise, horrify, or disgust someone. 2. To cause electric current to go through someone.
▶ *verb* **shocking, shocked** ▶ *adjective* **shocking**

shod·dy (**shah**-dee) *adjective* Poorly made or made from cheap materials. ▶ *adjective* **shoddier, shoddiest** ▶ *noun* **shoddiness**

shoe (shoo)
noun 1. An outer covering for the foot with a thick sole and a heel. Shoes are usually made of leather or vinyl. 2. A horseshoe. 3. The part of a brake that presses against a wheel to slow or stop it.
verb To fit a shoe or shoes on a horse.
▶ *verb* **shoeing, shod** (shahd) *or* **shoed**

shoe·lace (**shoo**-lace) *noun* A cord or string used for fastening a shoe.

shoe·string (**shoo**-string)
noun 1. Another word for **shoelace**. 2. If a person starts a business **on a shoestring,** that means that he or she has very little money to work with.
adjective Shaped like a shoestring.

shone (shone) *verb* The past tense and past participle of **shine. Shone** sounds like **shown.**

shook (shuk) *verb* The past tense of **shake.**

shoot (shoot)
verb 1. To wound or kill a person or an animal with a bullet or an arrow. 2. To fire a gun. 3. To film a movie or video or to photograph someone or something. 4. To move with great speed and sudden force. 5. To aim and kick, hit, or throw a ball or puck toward a goal or net. 6. To strive for.
noun A new sprout or twig growing from the main trunk or stem of a plant or tree.
Shoot sounds like **chute.** ▶ *verb* **shooting, shot**

shoot·ing star (**shoo**-ting **stahr**) *noun* A meteor that burns up as it enters the earth's atmosphere.

shop (shahp)
noun 1. A place where goods are offered for sale. 2. A place where a particular kind of work is done.
verb To visit a store so that you can look at or buy goods.
▶ *verb* **shopping, shopped** ▶ *noun* **shopper** ▶ *noun* **shopping**

shop·a·hol·ic (shah-puh-**haw**-lik) *noun* (informal) Someone who really enjoys shopping, or who cannot control the urge to shop.

shop·keep·er (**shahp**-kee-pur) *noun* Someone who owns or runs a small shop or store.

shop·lift·er (**shahp**-lif-tur) *noun* Someone who takes something from a store without paying for it. ▶ *noun* **shoplifting** ▶ *verb* **shoplift**

shopping center (**shah**-ping **sen**-tur) *noun* A group of stores with one central parking lot.

shore (shor) *noun* The land along the edge of an ocean, a river, or a lake.

shore·bird (**shor**-burd) *noun* A bird that lives or feeds mainly on the shores of lakes, rivers, or seas.

short (short)
adjective 1. Less than the average or expected length, height, distance, time, or scope. 2. **short of** *or* **short on** Lacking the full amount that you need. 3. Abrupt in a rude or unfriendly way; curt. 4. **short for** Shortened from something longer. For example, the word *dorm* is short for *dormitory.*
adverb Suddenly.
noun A **short circuit.**
▶ *adjective* **shorter, shortest** ▶ *adverb* **shorter, shortest** ▶ *noun* **shortness**

S

short·age (**shor**-tij) *noun* A situation where there is not enough of something that is needed or expected.

short·bread (**short**-*bred*) *noun* A rich cookie made with flour, sugar, and butter.

short cir·cuit (**short sur**-kit) *noun* An electric circuit that bypasses a device that was designed to be included in the circuit. Sometimes a short circuit can cause a fire or blow a fuse.
verb **short-circuit** To bypass.

short·com·ing (**short**-*kuhm*-ing) *noun* A weakness or fault in something or someone.

short·cut (**short**-*kuht*) *noun* 1. A shorter route for getting somewhere, or a quicker way of doing something. 2. Short for **keyboard shortcut.**

short·en (**shor**-tuhn) *verb* To make short or shorter. ▶ *verb* **shortening, shortened**

short·en·ing (**shor**-tuh-ning) *noun* Butter, lard, or other fat used in baking, especially to make pastry crisp or flaky.

short·hand (**short**-*hand*) *noun* Any system for writing quickly that uses symbols or abbreviations instead of words.

short·hand·ed (**short**-**han**-did) *adjective* Not having enough or the usual number of people to do a job.

short·ly (**short**-lee) *adverb* In a short time; very soon.

short·ness (**short**-nis) *noun* 1. The state of being short. 2. An insufficient amount.

short-range (**short**-*raynj*) *adjective* Not reaching far in time or distance.

shorts (shorts) *noun, plural* 1. Pants that reach to or above the knees. 2. A man's or boy's underpants.

short·sight·ed (**short**-**sye**-tid) *adjective* 1. Not thinking carefully about future consequences. 2. Nearsighted.
 ▶ *noun* **shortsightedness**

short·stop (**short**-*stahp*) *noun* In baseball or softball, the player whose position is between second and third base.

short-tem·pered (**short**-**tem**-purd) *adjective* Tending to lose your temper easily.

shot (shaht)
verb The past tense and past participle of **shoot.**
noun 1. The firing of a gun or cannon. 2. A person who shoots. 3. A single bullet fired from a gun. 4. A single metal ball or pellet fired from a gun or cannon. 5. A throw or thrust of a ball or puck toward a net or other goal in various sports. 6. The distance or range over which something such as a missile or bullet can travel. 7. A photograph. 8. An injection. 9. A heavy metal ball thrown at a track-and-field event. 10. (informal) An attempt or a chance.
 ▶ *noun, plural* **shots** *or* **shot**

shot·gun (**shaht**-*guhn*) *noun* A gun with a long barrel that fires cartridges filled with pellets, often used in hunting small game.

shot put (**shaht** put) *noun* A track-and-field event in which a heavy metal ball is thrown as far as possible. ▶ *noun* **shot-putter** ▶ *noun* **shot-putting**

should (shud) *verb* A helping verb that is used in the following ways: 1. To show a duty or an obligation. 2. To show that something is likely or expected. 3. To make a suggestion or invite others' opinions. 4. To show that something might happen.

shoul·der (**shohl**-dur)
noun 1. The joint or part of the body between your neck and your upper arm. 2. A similar part on an animal's body. 3. The sloping side or edge of a road or highway.
verb 1. To push with your shoulder or shoulders. 2. To take on a burden.
 ▶ *verb* **shouldering, shouldered**

shoul·der blade (**shohl**-dur *blade*) *noun* One of two large, flat bones in the upper back, just below the shoulder.

should·n't (**shud**-uhnt) *contraction* A short form of *should not.*

shout (shout)
verb To speak or call out loudly.
noun A loud cry or yell.
 ▶ *verb* **shouting, shouted**

S

shove (shuhv)
verb To push hard or roughly.
noun A hard or rough push.
▶ *verb* **shoving, shoved**

shov·el (**shuhv**-uhl)
noun A tool with a long handle and a flattened scoop, used for moving earth, snow, and other materials.
verb **1.** To dig, clear, or make something with a shovel. **2.** To move something with a shovel. **3.** To move, put, or throw something in large quantities, as if with a shovel.
▶ *verb* **shoveling, shoveled**

show (shoh)
verb **1.** To let see or be seen. **2.** To explain something to someone by doing it yourself. **3.** To make known or clear. **4.** To guide or lead. **5.** To be or to make visible. **6. show up** To arrive or make an appearance somewhere.
noun A public display, performance, or exhibition.
▶ *verb* **showing, showed, shown**

show busi·ness (shoh **biz**-nis) *noun* Popular entertainment such as music, television, and movies, and the industry that provides it.

show·case (**shoh**-kase)
noun **1.** A case or cabinet for displaying items, especially in a store. **2.** A place for displaying something to advantage.
verb To display something or someone boldly and elaborately.
▶ *verb* **showcasing, showcased**

show·er (**shou**-er)
noun **1.** A mounted device that sprays water over a person's body for washing. **2.** A washing of the body by means of this. **3.** A brief rainfall. **4.** A party at which a woman who is about to marry or give birth is honored and receives presents.
verb **1.** To wash yourself under a shower. **2.** To pour down on, to scatter over, or to cover. **3.** To give someone lots of things.
▶ *verb* **showering, showered**
▶ *adjective* **showery**

shown (shohn) *verb* The past participle of **show. Shown** sounds like **shone.**

show-off *noun* (**shoh**-*awf*) Someone who behaves in a bragging way about his or her possessions or abilities. ▶ *verb* **show off** (shoh-**awf**)

show·room (**shoh**-room) *noun* A room used to display cars, furniture, or other items that are for sale.

show·y (**shoh**-ee) *adjective* **1.** Striking, or attracting attention because of color or size. **2.** Flashy, or too bright and colorful.
▶ *adjective* **showier, showiest**

shrank (shrank) *verb* The past tense of **shrink.**

shrap·nel (**shrap**-nuhl) *noun* Small pieces of metal thrown out by an exploding shell or bomb.

shred (shred)
noun **1.** A long, thin strip of something made by tearing or cutting. **2.** A small amount; a bit.
verb To tear or cut into long, thin strips.
▶ *verb* **shredding, shredded**

shred·der (**shred**-ur) *noun* A machine for cutting documents into thin strips or small pieces so that no one can read them.

shrew (shroo) *noun* **1.** A small, insect-eating mammal that resembles a mouse, with a pointed nose and tiny eyes. **2.** A nagging, scolding woman.

shrewd (shrood) *adjective* Showing cleverness or sharp powers of judgment in practical situations. ▶ *adjective* **shrewder, shrewdest** ▶ *adverb* **shrewdly**

shriek (shreek)
verb To make a shrill, piercing cry.
noun A shrill, piercing cry.
▶ *verb* **shrieking, shrieked**

shrill (shril) *adjective* Having a high, sharp sound. ▶ *adjective* **shriller, shrillest**

shrimp (shrimp) *noun* A small shellfish with a long tail that is highly valued as food. ▶ *noun, plural* **shrimp** or **shrimps**

shrine (shrine) *noun* **1.** A building or small structure that contains objects associated with a holy person. **2.** A place that is honored for its history or

S

because it is connected to something important.

shrink (shringk)
verb 1. To make or to become smaller, often as a result of heat, cold, or moisture. 2. To draw back or turn away because you are frightened or disgusted.
noun (slang) A psychiatrist or a psychologist.
▶ *verb* **shrinking, shrank** (shrangk) or **shrunk** (shruhngk), **shrunk** or **shrunken**

shriv·el (**shriv**-uhl) *verb* To shrink and become wrinkled, often after exposure to heat or sunlight. ▶ *verb* **shriveling, shriveled** ▶ *adjective* **shriveled**

shroud (shroud)
noun 1. A cloth used to wrap a dead body for burial. 2. Something that covers or hides.
verb To cover or hide with a thin veil or haze.
▶ *verb* **shrouding, shrouded**

shrub (shruhb) *noun* A plant or bush with woody stems that branch out at or near the ground.

shrub·ber·y (**shruhb**-ur-ee) *noun* A number of shrubs planted together.

shrug (shruhg) *verb* To raise your shoulders briefly to show that you don't know or don't care about someone or something. ▶ *verb* **shrugging, shrugged** ▶ *noun* **shrug**

shrunk (shruhngk) *verb* The past participle of **shrink**.

shrunk·en (**shruhng**-kuhn)
verb A past participle of **shrink**.
adjective Made smaller.

shud·der (**shuhd**-ur)
verb To shake or tremble violently from cold, fear, or disgust.
noun A shaking or trembling caused by cold, fear, or disgust.
▶ *verb* **shuddering, shuddered**

shuf·fle (**shuhf**-uhl) *verb* 1. To walk slowly, without lifting your feet completely off the floor or ground. 2. To mix playing cards so that they are in a random order. 3. To move something from one place to another. ▶ *verb* **shuffling, shuffled**

shun (shuhn) *verb* To avoid or ignore someone or something on purpose. ▶ *verb* **shunning, shunned**

shunt (shuhnt)
verb To move something off to one side.
noun A new path, created by surgery, for the flow of blood.
▶ *verb* **shunting, shunted**

shut (shuht) *verb* 1. To close an opening or passage, or to fasten something securely. 2. To confine or to enclose. 3. **shut down** To stop operating or to close. 4. **shut out** To stop the opposing team from scoring any points. 5. **shut up** To stop talking or to make someone stop talking.
▶ *verb* **shutting, shut**

shut·ter (**shuht**-ur) *noun* 1. One of a pair of hinged panels attached to a window that can be closed to keep out weather or the light. 2. The part of a camera that opens and closes to expose the film to light when a picture is taken.

shut·tle (**shuht**-uhl) *noun* 1. The part of a loom that carries the thread from side to side as a piece of cloth is being woven. 2. A bus, train, or aircraft that travels frequently between two places. *See also* **space shuttle.**

shut·tle·cock (**shuht**-uhl-*kahk*) *noun* A small object, usually made of plastic, that is hit back and forth over the net in the game of badminton.

shy (shye)
adjective 1. Bashful and uncomfortable around people or with strangers. 2. Easily frightened or startled; timid. 3. Lacking, or short.
verb If a horse **shies**, it moves suddenly backward or sideways because it has been frightened or startled.
▶ *adjective* **shyer, shier, shyest, shiest** ▶ *verb* **shying, shied** ▶ *noun* **shyness** ▶ *adverb* **shyly**

Si·a·mese cat (**sye**-uh-*meez* kat) *noun* A slender breed of cat that has blue eyes, short hair, and a pale brown or gray coat. Its ears, paws, and tail are often dark.

S

sib·ling (**sib**-ling) *noun* A brother or a sister.

sick (sik) *adjective* 1. Suffering from a disease; ill. 2. Nauseated, or feeling as though you are going to vomit. 3. Tired, annoyed, bored by, or disgusted with someone or something. 4. Upset or very unhappy.
▸ *adjective* **sicker, sickest**

sick·en (**sik**-uhn) *verb* To make someone feel nauseated or disgusted. ▸ *verb* **sickening, sickened** ▸ *adjective* **sickening** ▸ *adverb* **sickeningly**

sick·le (**sik**-uhl) *noun* A tool with a short handle and a curved blade that is used for cutting grain, grass, or weeds.

sick·le-cell dis·ease (**sik**-uhl-*sel* di-*zeez*) *noun* A form of anemia in which many normal red blood cells take on a sickle shape and cannot carry oxygen. Sickle-cell disease is inherited and occurs mainly in people of African ancestry.

sick·ly (**sik**-lee) *adjective* 1. In poor health and often ill. 2. Caused by or showing sickness.
▸ *adjective* **sicklier, sickliest**

sick·ness (**sik**-nuhs) *noun* Illness or disease. ▸ *noun, plural* **sicknesses**

side (side)
noun 1. One of the lines or surfaces that form the boundaries or limits of a shape or object. 2. An outer part of something that is not the top, bottom, front, or back. 3. The right or left part of the body. 4. One of two opposing individuals, groups, teams, or positions. 5. The area next to someone. 6. A line of ancestors.
verb **side with** To agree with or support someone.
adjective At or near one side.
▸ *verb* **siding, sided**

side·burns (**side**-burnz) *noun, plural* The hair that grows down the sides of a man's face, just in front of his ears.

side ef·fect (**side** i-*fekt*) *noun* A usually unpleasant or undesired effect of taking a medicine.

side·line (**side**-*line*) *noun* 1. A line that marks the side boundary of the playing area in sports such as football, basketball, and soccer. 2. An activity or work done in addition to a regular job.

side·show (**side**-*shoh*) *noun* A small show in addition to the main attraction at a fair or circus.

side·step (**side**-*step*) *verb* 1. To step to one side. 2. To avoid a problem or decision.
▸ *verb* **sidestepping, sidestepped**

side·track (**side**-*trak*) *verb* To distract or to be distracted from the main issue or something important. ▸ *verb* **sidetracking, sidetracked**

side·walk (**side**-*wawk*) *noun* A paved path beside a street.

side·ways (**side**-*wayz*)
adjective 1. To or from one side. 2. Moving or directed toward one side. *adverb* With one side forward.

sid·ing (**sye**-ding) *noun* 1. A short section of railroad track next to the main track, used for storing or shunting cars. 2. Material that covers the outside of a house.

siege (seej) *noun* The surrounding of a place such as a castle or city to cut off supplies and then wait for those inside to surrender.

si·er·ra (see-**er**-uh) *noun* A chain of hills or mountains with peaks that look like sharp, jagged teeth.

Si·er·ra Le·one (see-*er*-uh lee-**ohn**) A small country in West Africa on the Atlantic Ocean. Its name means "lion mountains." It has mountains, plains, rain forests, savannas, and beaches. The former British colony is now rebuilding its economy after a civil war that ended in 2002. Sierra Leone has an abundant supply of many kinds of minerals, among them diamonds and gold.

si·es·ta (see-**es**-tuh) *noun* An afternoon nap or rest, usually taken after a midday meal.

sieve (siv) *noun* A container consisting of a wire or plastic mesh in a frame, used for separating large pieces from small pieces or liquids from solids.

S

sift (sift) *verb* 1. To pass a substance through a mesh to get rid of lumps or large chunks. 2. To examine something carefully to determine what is most important or useful.
▶ *verb* **sifting, sifted**

sigh (sye)
verb To let out a long, deep breath, often to express sadness, weariness, or relief.
noun A long, deep breath that can express sadness, weariness, or relief.
▶ *verb* **sighing, sighed**

sight (site)
noun 1. The ability to see; vision. 2. The act of seeing. 3. The range or distance a person can see. 4. Something that is seen; a view. 5. A small metal device on a rifle that helps you aim. 6. Something funny or odd to look at.
verb To see or to spot.
Sight sounds like **cite** and **site**. ▶ *verb* **sighting, sighted**

sight·se·er (*site-see*-ur) *noun* A person who visits places of interest. ▶ *noun* **sightseeing** ▶ *verb* **sightsee**

sign (sine)
noun 1. A symbol that has a specific meaning. 2. A publicly displayed notice that gives information about or advertises something. 3. A trace, or evidence left by someone. 4. Something that points out what is to come.
verb 1. To write your name as a signature on something. 2. To communicate using sign language.
▶ *verb* **signing, signed**

sig·nal (**sig**-nuhl)
noun 1. A sign or device that sends a message or warning. 2. The electrical pulses transmitted for radio, television, or telephone communications.
verb To send a message or warning with a sign or device.
▶ *verb* **signaling, signaled**

sig·na·ture (**sig**-nuh-chur) *noun* A person's name, written in his or her own individual way, usually in script.

sig·nif·i·cance (sig-**nif**-i-kuhns) *noun* Importance or meaning.

sig·nif·i·cant (sig-**nif**-i-kuhnt) *adjective* Important, meaningful, or likely to have a major effect. ▶ *adverb* **significantly**

sign lan·guage (**sine** *lang*-gwij) *noun* A language in which hand gestures, in combination with facial expressions and larger body movements, are used instead of speech.

sign·post (**sine**-*pohst*) *noun* A post with signs on it to direct travelers.

Sikh (seek) *noun* A member of a religious sect, founded in India in the 16th century, that believes in a single god.

si·lence (**sye**-luhns) *noun* Absence of sound; stillness and quiet.

si·lenc·er (**sye**-luhn-sur) *noun* A device that reduces noise, especially from a gun.

si·lent (**sye**-luhnt) *adjective* Making no sound; absolutely quiet. ▶ *adverb* **silently**

sil·hou·ette (*sil*-oo-et) *noun* 1. A drawing made by filling in the outline of a figure with a solid color, usually black. 2. A dark outline of someone or something, visible against a light background.

sil·i·con (**sil**-i-kuhn or **sil**-i-*kahn*) *noun* A chemical element found in sand and rocks and used to make glass, microchips, and transistors.

sil·i·cone (**sil**-i-*kohn*) *noun* A stable chemical compound containing silicon, used for making plastics, lubricants, and artificial body parts.

silk (silk) *noun* A soft, shiny fiber produced by silkworms, or the thread or fabric made from this fiber.

silk·worm (**silk**-*wurm*) *noun* A caterpillar that spins a cocoon made of silk fibers.

silk·y (**sil**-kee) *adjective* Made of silk or like silk in texture; smooth.

sill (sil) *noun* A piece of wood or stone that runs across the bottom of a door or window.

sil·ly (**sil**-ee) *adjective* 1. Foolish or showing a lack of common sense. 2. Ridiculous or laughable.
▶ *adjective* **sillier, silliest** ▶ *noun* **silliness**

S

si·lo (**sye**-loh) *noun* **1.** A tall, round tower used to store food for farm animals. **2.** An underground structure for storing and launching a guided missile.

silt (silt) *noun* The fine particles of soil that are carried along by flowing water and that eventually settle to the bottom of a river or lake.

sil·ver (**sil**-vur)
noun **1.** A soft, shiny, white metal that is used to make jewelry, coins, bowls, and utensils. **2.** Coins made from silver or a metal that looks like silver. **3.** Forks, spoons, and other items made of or coated with silver; silverware. **4.** A grayish-white color.
adjective Made of silver.
▶ *adjective* **silvery**

sil·ver·smith (**sil**-vur-*smith*) *noun* A person who makes or repairs silver objects.

sil·ver·ware (**sil**-vur-*wair*) *noun* Objects made of or coated with silver, especially forks, spoons, and knives.

sim·i·lar (**sim**-uh-lur) *adjective* Nearly but not exactly alike.

sim·i·lar·i·ty (*sim*-uh-**lar**-i-tee) *noun* The quality of being similar or alike. ▶ *noun, plural* **similarities**

sim·i·lar·ly (**sim**-uh-lur-lee) *adverb* In a way that resembles but is not identical to someone or something else.

sim·i·le (**sim**-uh-lee) *noun* A way of describing something by comparing it to something quite different. A simile uses the word *like* or *as*. For example: *His smile is as warm as the sun.*

sim·mer (**sim**-ur)
verb **1.** To stay at or just below the boiling point. **2. simmer down** (informal) To become calmer.
noun The state of a liquid just below the boiling point.
▶ *verb* **simmering, simmered**

sim·ple (**sim**-puhl) *adjective* **1.** Easily done or understood. **2.** With nothing added. **3.** Plain, or not fancy.
▶ *adjective* **simpler, simplest** ▶ *noun* **simplicity** (sim-**plis**-i-tee)

sim·ple sen·tence (**sim**-puhl **sen**-tuhns) *noun* A sentence that consists of only

one independent clause. "The lion roared" is a simple sentence.

sim·pli·fy (**sim**-pluh-*fye*) *verb* To make something less complicated or easier to understand. ▶ *verb* **simplifies, simplifying, simplified** ▶ *noun* **simplification** (*sim*-pluh-fi-**kay**-shuhn)

sim·ply (**sim**-plee) *adverb* **1.** In a simple way, or plainly. **2.** Merely, or just. **3.** Very.

sim·u·la·tion (*sim*-yuh-**lay**-shuhn) *noun* **1.** A trial run to act out a real event. **2.** A copy or an imitation.
▶ *verb* **simulate** (**sim**-yuh-*layt*)

sim·u·la·tor (**sim**-yuh-*lay*-tur) *noun* A machine that allows you to experience or perform a complex task, such as flying a plane, by imitating the conditions and controls.

si·mul·ta·ne·ous (*sye*-muhl-**tay**-nee-uhs) *adjective* Happening or done at the same time.

si·mul·ta·ne·ous·ly (*sye*-muhl-**tay**-nee-uhs-lee) *adverb* At the same time.

sin (sin)
noun An act that goes against moral or religious laws, especially when it is done on purpose.
verb To commit an act that goes against moral or religious laws.
▶ *verb* **sinning, sinned** ▶ *noun* **sinner** ▶ *adjective* **sinful** ▶ *adverb* **sinfully**

Si·nai Pe·nin·su·la (**sye**-nye puh-**nin**-suh-luh) A triangular peninsula of Egypt that lies at the north end of the Red Sea. On its northeastern side, the peninsula shares a border with Israel.

since (sins)
conjunction **1.** During the period following the time when. **2.** As, or because.
adverb **1.** Ago; before now. **2.** From then until now.
preposition From or during the time after. *I've been here since July.*

sin·cere (sin-**seer**) *adjective* Straightforward and honest.
▶ *adjective* **sincerer, sincerest** ▶ *noun* **sincerity** (sin-**ser**-i-tee)

sin·cere·ly (sin-**seer**-lee) *adverb* In a way that expresses your true feelings.

S

sin·ew (**sin**-yoo) *noun* A band of tissue that connects a muscle to a bone; a tendon or ligament.

sing (sing) *verb* 1. To produce musical sounds and words with your voice. 2. To perform by singing. 3. To produce musical sounds.
▶ *verb* **singing, sang** (sang), **sung** (suhng)

Sing·a·pore (**sing**-uh-*por*) An island nation off the southern tip of the Malay Peninsula in Southeast Asia. Originally a British trading colony, Singapore is now an important center for international trade and one of the wealthiest countries in the world.

singe (sinj) *verb* To burn something slightly. ▶ *verb* **singeing, singed**

sing·er (**sing**-ur) *noun* Someone who sings, especially who sings well or who sings professionally.

sin·gle (**sing**-guhl)
adjective 1. One and no more than one. 2. Intended for one person or family. 3. Not married.
verb **single out** To choose out of a group.
noun 1. A recording that features one main song. 2. A hit in baseball that allows the runner to get to first base.
▶ *verb* **singling, singled**

sin·gle-hand·ed (**sing**-guhl-**han**-did) *adjective* Done alone or without help from others. ▶ *adverb* **single-handedly**

sin·gle-mind·ed (**sing**-guhl-**mine**-did) *adjective* Focused on one main purpose or goal.

sin·gu·lar (**sing**-gyuh-lur)
adjective Of or having to do with the form of a word that refers to just one person or thing. *Chair* and *singer* are singular nouns.
noun The form of a word that refers to just one person or thing. *Chair* and *singer* are singulars.

sin·is·ter (**sin**-i-stur) *adjective* Suggesting or threatening harm, evil, or misfortune.

sink (singk)
noun A basin used for washing, with faucets for hot and cold water and a drain.

verb 1. To go down slowly or gradually. 2. To go or to make someone or something go beneath the surface. 3. To fall or drop into a certain state. 4. To become lower in amount. 5. To fall in pitch or volume. 6. To penetrate or go through or into deeply.
▶ *verb* **sinking, sank, sunk** ▶ *noun* **sinking**

si·nus (**sye**-nuhs) *noun* One of the hollow spaces in the skull, above the eyes and on either side of the nose that lead to the nose. ▶ *noun, plural* **sinuses**

Sioux (soo) *noun* A member of a group of Native Americans who live in Minnesota and North and South Dakota. ▶ *noun, plural* **Sioux**

sip (sip)
verb To drink slowly, a little at a time.
noun A small amount of a drink.
▶ *verb* **sipping, sipped**

si·phon (**sye**-fuhn)
noun A bent tube through which liquid can drain upward and then down to a lower level, using the difference in pressure at the two ends to keep the liquid flowing.
verb To drain liquid through a siphon.
▶ *verb* **siphoning, siphoned**

sir (sur) *noun* 1. A polite way to address a man, used in speaking and writing. 2. **Sir** The title of someone who has been made a knight.

si·ren (**sye**-ruhn) *noun* A device that makes a loud, shrill sound. A siren is often used as a signal or warning.

sis·ter (**sis**-tur) *noun* 1. A girl or woman who has the same parents as another person. 2. A nun. 3. A woman who shares an interest or cause with another.
▶ *adjective* **sisterly**

sis·ter·hood (**sis**-tur-hud) *noun* 1. The warm, close feeling between sisters or among women. 2. A group of women who share a common interest, aim, or cause.

sis·ter-in-law (**sis**-tur-in-*law*) *noun* The sister of a person's spouse or the wife of a person's brother. ▶ *noun, plural* **sisters-in-law**

sit (sit) *verb* 1. To rest your weight on your buttocks. 2. To be in a place or on a surface. 3. To pose. 4. To take a place as an official member of a club or legislature. 5. To hold a session or meeting. 6. To babysit. 7. **sit in** To take someone's place temporarily. ▶ *verb* **sitting, sat** (sat)

sit·com (**sit**-kahm) *noun* (informal) A humorous television program that features the same group of characters each week. Sitcom is short for *situation comedy*.

site (site) *noun* 1. The place where something is located or taking place. 2. **On site** means at the same place where something is happening. 3. Short for **website**. 4. **site map** A page that serves as an index for a website, showing you all the pages on the site and how they are connected with each other.
Site sounds like **cite** and **sight**.

sit·ting room (**sit**-ing *room*) *noun* A room in a home or hotel in which people can sit and relax or talk with others.

sit·u·ate (**sich**-oo-ate) *verb* To place something in a particular spot or location. ▶ *verb* **situating, situated**

sit·u·a·tion (*sich*-oo-**ay**-shuhn) *noun* The circumstances that exist at a particular time and place.

sit-up (**sit**-uhp) *noun* An exercise for stomach muscles that is done by lying down and then raising the body to a sitting position without lifting the feet or legs.

six (siks)
noun The number that comes after five and before seven, written numerically as 6.
adjective Referring to the number that comes after five and before seven.
▶ *noun, plural* **sixes**

sixth (siksth)
adjective Next after fifth and before seventh, written numerically as 6th.
noun One part of something that has been divided into six equal parts, written numerically as 1/6.

six·ti·eth (**siks**-tee-ith) *adjective* Next after 59th and before 61st, written numerically as 60th.

six·ty (**siks**-tee) *noun* The number that is equal to 6 times 10, written numerically as 60.

siz·a·ble *or* **size·a·ble** (**sye**-zuh-buhl) *adjective* Fairly large.

size (size) *noun* 1. The measurements or extent of something. 2. One in a series of standard measurements for items of clothing or other articles.

siz·zle (**siz**-uhl) *verb* To make a hissing, crackling noise, especially when frying food. ▶ *verb* **sizzling, sizzled**

skate (skate)
noun 1. A boot with a blade fastened to the sole. Skates are used for gliding over ice. 2. A roller skate. 3. A large, flat, saltwater fish with a long, narrow tail and a diamond-shaped body. Skates are related to sharks and rays.
verb To glide or move along on skates.
▶ *verb* **skating, skated**

skate·board (**skate**-bord)
noun A small board with four roller skate wheels on the bottom that you ride in a standing or crouching position.
verb To ride or travel on a skateboard.
▶ *verb* **skateboarding, skateboarded**
▶ *noun* **skateboarding**

ske·dad·dle (ski-**dad**-uhl) *verb* (informal) To move along quickly or to run away from something that scares you. ▶ *verb* **skedaddling, skedaddled**

skel·e·ton (**skel**-uh-tuhn) *noun* The framework of bones that supports and protects the body of an animal with a backbone.

skep·tic (**skep**-tik) *noun* Someone who does not accept views or opinions readily from others. ▶ *noun* **skepticism** (**skep**-ti-siz-uhm)

skep·ti·cal (**skep**-ti-kuhl) *adjective* Doubting that something is really true. ▶ *adverb* **skeptically**

sketch (skech)
noun 1. A rough or unfinished drawing, done quickly and without much detail. 2. A short essay or written description of someone or something. 3. A short

S

play, skit, or story that is usually humorous.
verb To draw quickly.
▶ *noun, plural* **sketches** ▶ *verb* **sketches, sketching, sketched**

sketch·y (**skech**-ee) *adjective* **1.** Roughly drawn or done without detail. **2.** Incomplete and not very clear.
▶ *adjective* **sketchier, sketchiest**

skew·er (**skyoo**-ur) *noun* A long metal or wooden pin for holding pieces of meat or vegetables together while they are being cooked.

ski (skee)
noun One of a pair of long, narrow runners that curve up in the front and are fastened to special boots, used for gliding over snow.
verb To move over snow with skis on.
▶ *verb* **skiing, skied** ▶ *noun* **skiing**

skid (skid)
verb To slide out of control on a slippery surface.
noun **1.** A runner on the bottom of a helicopter or other aircraft, used in place of wheels for landing. **2.** An instance of sliding out of control on a slick surface.
▶ *verb* **skidding, skidded**

skiff (skif) *noun* A boat small enough to be sailed or rowed by one person.

skill (skil) *noun* The ability to do something well, usually as a result of training or practice.

skilled (skild) *adjective* Having, showing, or requiring mastery or expertise.

skil·let (**skil**-it) *noun* A frying pan.

skim (skim) *verb* **1.** To remove something that is floating on the top of a liquid. **2.** To read through something quickly, just to get the main ideas. **3.** To glide across or pass quickly and lightly over something.
▶ *verb* **skimming, skimmed**
▶ *adjective* **skimmed**

skim milk (**skim** milk) *noun* Milk from which the cream has been removed. It is also known as *skimmed milk*.

skin (skin)
noun **1.** The thin layer of tissue that forms the outer covering of human and animal bodies. **2.** The peel or outer layer of a fruit or vegetable.
verb **1.** To scrape your skin. **2.** To remove the skin from a killed animal.
▶ *verb* **skinning, skinned**

skin diving *noun* Underwater swimming with a face mask, flippers, and a snorkel. ▶ *verb* **skin dive** ▶ *noun* **skin diver**

skin·ny (**skin**-ee) *adjective* **1.** Very thin. **2.** Fitting very tightly.
▶ *adjective* **skinnier, skinniest**

skip (skip) *verb* **1.** To move along by hopping on one foot and then the other. **2.** To jump over. **3.** To leave something out or to pass over it. **4.** (informal) To leave a place quickly or secretly.
▶ *verb* **skipping, skipped**

skirt (skurt)
noun A piece of clothing worn by women and girls that hangs from the waist and covers all or part of the legs.
verb **1.** To pass around a place or to lie around its border or edge. **2.** To avoid a question, a discussion, or an issue because it is difficult or because you are afraid that others might disagree with you.
▶ *verb* **skirting, skirted**

skit (skit) *noun* A short, usually funny play.

skit·tish (**skit**-ish) *adjective* Excitable or easily frightened and therefore hard to control.

skull (skuhl) *noun* The bony framework of the head that protects the brain.
Skull sounds like **scull**.

skunk (skuhngk) *noun* **1.** A black and white mammal with a stripe down its back and a bushy tail. Skunks spray a foul-smelling liquid when they are frightened or in danger. **2.** (informal) An obnoxious or offensive person.

sky (skye) *noun* The upper atmosphere, or the area of space that seems to arch over the earth. ▶ *noun, plural* **skies**

sky·box (**skye**-bahks) *noun* An elevated, enclosed room at a sports stadium where spectators can watch the action in privacy and luxury. ▶ *noun, plural* **skyboxes**

S

sky·div·ing (skye-*dye*-ving) *noun* The sport of jumping from an airplane and falling as far as safely possible before opening a parachute. Skydiving often involves stunts. ▶ *noun* **skydiver** ▶ *verb* **skydive**

sky·lark (skye-*lahrk*) *noun* A brown and white European bird that sings while flying.

sky·light (skye-*lite*) *noun* A window in a roof or ceiling.

sky·line (skye-*line*) *noun* 1. The outline of buildings, mountains, or other objects seen against the sky from a distance. 2. The horizon, or the line at which the earth and sky seem to meet.

sky mar·shal (skye *mahr*-shuhl) *noun* See **air marshal.**

Skype (skipe)
noun A trademark for a service that allows you to use your Internet connection as a telephone.
verb To call someone or take part in a conversation using Skype.
▶ *verb* **Skyping, Skyped** or **skyping, skyped**

sky·rock·et (skye-*rah*-kit)
noun A type of firework that shoots into the air and explodes in a shower of many-colored sparks.
verb To rise suddenly and quickly.
▶ *verb* **skyrocketing, skyrocketed**

sky·scrap·er (skye-*skray*-pur) *noun* A very tall building.

slab (slab) *noun* A broad, flat, thick piece of something.

slack (slak) *adjective* 1. Not tight or firm; loose. 2. Not busy or active. 3. Careless or lazy in your work.
▶ *adjective* **slacker, slackest** ▶ *verb* **slacken**

slacks (slaks) *noun, plural* Pants for casual wear.

sla·lom (slah-luhm) *noun* An athletic event in which athletes ski down a hill, zigzagging between gates.

slam (slam)
verb 1. To close something loudly and forcefully. 2. To strike something with great force.
noun The act of slamming something,

or the sound this makes.
▶ *verb* **slamming, slammed**

slan·der (**slan**-dur)
noun An untrue statement about someone that damages that person's reputation.
verb To make an untrue statement about someone publicly.
▶ *adjective* **slanderous**

slang (slang) *noun* Colorful or lively words and phrases used in ordinary conversation but not in formal speech or writing. Slang often gives new and different meanings to old words.

slant (slant)
verb To slope, lean, or be at an angle.
noun An attitude, opinion, or point of view.
▶ *verb* **slanting, slanted**

slap (slap)
verb 1. To hit someone or something with a flat object or the palm of your hand. 2. To throw down or put on with great force.
noun The act of slapping someone or something, or the sound this makes.
▶ *verb* **slapping, slapped**

slap·dash (**slap**-dash) *adjective* Done carelessly and in a rush.

slap·stick (**slap**-stik) *noun* Comedy that stresses loud, rough action or horseplay and visual jokes.

slash (slash)
verb 1. To cut or wound with a forceful, sweeping motion. 2. To reduce something drastically.
noun A symbol (/) that is used to separate choices, to indicate where lines of text should be broken, and in many computer commands.
▶ *verb* **slashes, slashing, slashed** ▶ *noun, plural* **slashes**

slat (slat) *noun* A long, narrow strip of wood or metal.

slate (slayt) *noun* 1. A grayish-green or bluish-gray rock that can be split into thin, smooth layers. 2. A tile for roofs or floors made from slate. 3. A piece of slate or other material used for writing on. 4. A dark blue-gray color. 5. A complete list of candidates who are running for office.

S

slaugh·ter (**slaw**-tur)
verb To kill animals for food.
noun **1.** The killing of an animal for food. **2.** The killing of a large number of people in a brutal, violent way.
▶ *verb* **slaughtering, slaughtered**

slave (slayv)
noun **1.** A person who is owned by another person and thought of as property. **2.** A person who is completely dominated by a habit or influence. **3.** A person who works as hard as a slave.
verb To work very hard or like a slave.
▶ *verb* **slaving, slaved**

slav·er·y (**slay**-vur-ee) *noun* **1.** The condition of being a slave, or a system in which some people own slaves. **2.** The period in American history, ending in 1863, in which people could legally own slaves.

slay (slay) *verb* To kill violently. **Slay** sounds like **sleigh.** ▶ *verb* **slaying, slayed, slew** (sloo), **slain** (slayn)

sled (sled) *noun* A vehicle with wooden or metal runners that can be pushed, pulled, or allowed to slide over snow and ice.

sledge·ham·mer (**slej**-ham-ur) *noun* A heavy hammer with a long handle. A sledgehammer is usually held with both hands.

sleek (sleek) *adjective* Smooth and glossy, as if polished. ▶ *adjective* **sleeker, sleekest**

sleep (sleep)
verb To rest with the eyes closed, the muscles relaxed, and no conscious thought or movement.
noun The state of rest with the eyes closed, the muscles relaxed, and no conscious thought or movement.
▶ *verb* **sleeping, slept** (slept)

sleep·ing bag (**slee**-ping *bag*) *noun* A warm, zippered, padded bag in which you can sleep outdoors, especially while camping.

sleep·walk·er (**sleep**-waw-kur) *noun* A person who gets out of bed and walks around while asleep. ▶ *verb* **sleepwalk**

sleep·y (**slee**-pee) *adjective* Drowsy, or ready for sleep. ▶ *adjective* **sleepier, sleepiest** ▶ *noun* **sleepiness**

sleet (sleet)
noun Frozen or partly frozen rain; a mixture of rain and snow.
verb When sleet is falling from the sky, people say that it is **sleeting.**

sleeve (sleev) *noun* **1.** The part of a shirt, coat, or other garment that covers the upper or the entire arm. **2. up your sleeve** Hidden or secret but ready to be used when needed.

sleigh (slay) *noun* A vehicle on runners with one or more seats, used in snow and usually pulled by horses or other animals. **Sleigh** sounds like **slay.**

slen·der (**slen**-dur) *adjective* **1.** Slim or thin in an attractive way. **2.** Limited in amount, size, or extent; barely enough.
▶ *adjective* **slenderer, slenderest**

slept (slept) *verb* The past tense and past participle of **sleep.**

sleuth (slooth) *noun* A detective, or anyone good at finding out facts.

slice (slise)
noun A thin, flat piece cut from something larger.
verb To cut something into slices.
▶ *verb* **slicing, sliced**

slick (slik)
adjective **1.** Very smooth, wet, and slippery. **2.** Very clever, efficient, or professional.
noun A layer of oil on the surface of water or on a road.
▶ *adjective* **slicker, slickest**

slide (slide)
verb **1.** To move smoothly over a surface while never losing contact with it. **2.** To move or fall suddenly.
noun **1.** A smooth, slanted surface or chute down which people can slide. **2.** A photographic transparency inside a frame that you view by projecting the image onto a screen. **3.** One of a series of pictures or text that make up a computer presentation. **4.** A small piece of glass on which you put specimens that you want to examine under a microscope. **5.** A large mass of snow, earth, or rock that falls down a slope from a great height.
▶ *verb* **sliding, slid**

S

slide·show (**slide**-*shoh*) *noun* **1.** A series of photographic slides that tell a story, usually of an interesting place that someone visited. **2.** A series of images or text arranged to be viewed as a single presentation, either on a computer or projected onto a screen.

slight (slite)
adjective **1.** Not very significant. **2.** Slender, small, or short.
verb **1.** To treat something as unimportant or to do something carelessly. **2.** To insult someone or to treat a person coldly.
noun An action that makes someone feel that they have been treated badly.
▶ *verb* **slighting, slighted** ▶ *adjective* **slighter, slightest**

slight·ly (**slite**-lee) *adverb* **1.** To a small degree or extent. **2.** In a slender or delicate way.

slim (slim)
adjective **1.** Slender and graceful. **2.** Small in quantity or amount; meager.
verb To try to reduce your weight.
▶ *verb* **slimming, slimmed** ▶ *adjective* **slimmer, slimmest**

slime (slime) *noun* A moist, soft, and slippery substance. ▶ *adjective* **slimy**

sling (sling)
noun **1.** A loop of cloth, suspended from the neck and used to support an injured arm. **2.** A strap or loop of leather used for throwing stones. **3.** A strong loop of cable, chain, or rope used to raise heavy objects.
verb To hang or throw something loosely or in a rough way.
▶ *verb* **slinging, slung** (sluhng)

sling·shot (**sling**-*shaht*) *noun* A piece of metal or wood shaped like a Y with an elastic band attached. Slingshots are used for shooting small stones.

slip (slip)
verb **1.** To lose your footing on a slippery surface. **2.** To move quickly and quietly, without attracting attention. **3.** To put on or take off quickly and easily. **4.** To escape. **5.** To move or slide from a place.
noun **1.** A small mistake. **2.** A light undergarment worn by girls and women under a skirt or dress. **3.** A small piece. **4.** A small shoot or twig cut from a plant for grafting or planting. **5.** A place where a boat or ship is docked.
verb To make a mistake in speech or writing.
▶ *verb* **slipping, slipped**

slip·per (**slip**-ur) *noun* A soft, lightweight shoe that you slip on and wear indoors.

slip·per·y (**slip**-ur-ee) *adjective* Smooth, oily, or wet and very hard to hold on to or stand on.

slip·shod (**slip**-*shahd*) *adjective* Careless or sloppy in appearance or workmanship.

slit (slit)
verb To make a long, straight, narrow cut or opening in something.
noun A long, straight, narrow cut or opening.
▶ *verb* **slitting, slit**

slith·er (**sliTH**-ur) *verb* To move along by sliding, like a snake. ▶ *verb* **slithering, slithered**

sliv·er (**sliv**-ur) *noun* A very thin and sometimes pointed piece of something.

slo·gan (**sloh**-guhn) *noun* A phrase or motto used by a business, a group, or an individual to express a goal or belief.

sloop (sloop) *noun* A sailboat with one mast and sails that are set from front to back.

slop (slahp) *verb* To splash or spill a liquid over the edge of a container. ▶ *verb* **slopping, slopped**

slope (slohp)
verb To slant or be at an angle.
noun A surface such as a hillside that is slanted.
▶ *verb* **sloping, sloped** ▶ *adjective* **sloping**

slop·py (**slah**-pee) *adjective* **1.** Messy and disorganized. **2.** Carelessly done. **3.** Muddy or slushy.
▶ *adjective* **sloppier, sloppiest** ▶ *noun* **sloppiness** ▶ *adverb* **sloppily**

slot (slaht) *noun* A small, narrow opening or groove.

sloth (slawth *or* slahth) *noun* **1.** A tropical mammal with long arms and legs, curved claws, and a shaggy coat. Sloths move very slowly and hang upside down in trees. **2.** A tendency to avoid exerting yourself or making much of an effort; laziness.
▶ *adjective* **slothful**

slouch (slouch)
verb To sit, stand, or walk with your head and shoulders drooping or bent forward.
noun An awkward, lazy, or incompetent person.
▶ *verb* **slouches, slouching, slouched** ▶ *noun, plural* **slouches**

Slo·va·ki·a (sloh-**vah**-kee-uh) A country in Central Europe that was formerly part of Czechoslovakia. The Slovaks formed their own country after peacefully separating from the Czechs in 1993.

Slo·ve·ni·a (sloh-**vee**-nee-uh) A mountainous country in Central Europe bordered by the Alps and the Mediterranean Sea. Forests cover more than half of it, and over a million new trees are planted in the country each year, making it the third most forested nation in Europe, after Finland and Sweden. Part of the former Yugoslavia, Slovenia became independent in 1991 following a ten-day war.

slov·en·ly (**sluhv**-uhn-lee) *adjective* Careless, dirty, and untidy in dress, habits, or appearance. ▶ *noun* **slovenliness**

slow (sloh)
adjective **1.** Moving at a low speed or taking a long time. **2.** Behind the correct time. **3.** Not busy. **4.** Not able to learn or understand quickly.
verb To cut down your speed.
adverb In a slow way or at a slow speed.
▶ *adjective* **slower, slowest** ▶ *adverb* **slower, slowest** ▶ *verb* **slowing, slowed** ▶ *noun* **slowness** ▶ *adverb* **slowly**

sludge (sluhj) *noun* Mud, ooze, or any heavy, slimy industrial waste.

slug (sluhg)
noun **1.** A slimy creature that looks like a snail without a shell. **2.** A bullet. **3.** A metal disk that is used in place of a coin, often illegally.
verb To hit with force.
▶ *verb* **slugging, slugged**

slug·gish (**sluhg**-ish) *adjective* Moving slowly and without energy or alertness. ▶ *noun* **sluggishness**

slum (sluhm) *noun* An overcrowded area in a town or city where poor people live in run-down buildings.

slum·ber (**sluhm**-bur)
verb To sleep.
noun Sleep.
▶ *verb* **slumbering, slumbered**

slump (sluhmp)
verb **1.** To sink down heavily and suddenly. **2.** To decrease in amount or activity.
noun A sudden drop or decline.
▶ *verb* **slumping, slumped**

slur (slur)
verb To speak in an unclear way by running words together.
noun An insult or accusation that hurts a person's reputation.
▶ *verb* **slurring, slurred**

slurp (slurp) *verb* To drink or eat something noisily. ▶ *verb* **slurping, slurped**

slush (sluhsh) *noun* Partly melted snow or ice. ▶ *adjective* **slushy**

sly (slye) *adjective* Crafty and cunning, or suggesting that you know something that could be embarrassing or damaging. ▶ *adjective* **slier, sliest** ▶ *adverb* **slyly** (**slye**-lee)

smack (smak)
verb **1.** To strike or hit someone or something with the palm of your hand or a flat object. **2.** To strike or hit something noisily and with force. **3.** To close and open the lips quickly, making a sharp sound.
noun **1.** A loud kiss. **2.** An act of hitting someone or something, or the sound this makes.
▶ *verb* **smacking, smacked**

S

small (smawl)
adjective **1.** Less than average in size, number, or amount; little. **2.** Not important. **3.** Low, soft, or weak.
noun **small talk** Casual conversation about unimportant things.
▶ *adjective* **smaller, smallest**

small in·tes·tine (smawl in-**tes**-tin)
noun The long, coiled part of the digestive system between the stomach and the large intestine, where most nutrients are removed from food and passed into the bloodstream.

small·pox (**smawl**-*pahks*) *noun* A very contagious and often lethal disease that causes a rash, high fever, and blisters that can leave permanent scars.

smart (smahrt)
adjective **1.** Clever and quick-witted; bright. **2.** Nicely dressed, tidy, and clean. **3.** Fashionable or stylish.
verb To cause or to feel a sharp, stinging pain.
▶ *adjective* **smarter, smartest** ▶ *verb* **smarting, smarted** ▶ *noun* **smartness** ▶ *adverb* **smartly**

smart·phone (**smahrt**-fone) *noun* A cell phone that can run programs and applications similar to the ones that you use on a computer, such as email and Internet access.

smash (smash)
verb **1.** To break something into many pieces suddenly and noisily. **2.** To collide violently with something. **3.** To destroy or defeat completely.
noun **smash hit** (informal) A recording, movie, or show that is a huge popular success.
▶ *verb* **smashes, smashing, smashed**

smear (smeer)
verb **1.** To spread a sticky or greasy substance over a surface. **2.** To become messy or blurred. **3.** To try to damage someone's reputation by accusing the person of things that aren't true.
noun A mark or streak of a dirty or greasy substance.
▶ *verb* **smearing, smeared**

smell (smel)
verb **1.** To sense an odor with your nose. **2.** To give off a particular odor or scent. **3.** To give off a strong or unpleasant odor. **4.** To sniff.
noun **1.** An odor or a scent. **2.** The ability to sense odors with the nose.
▶ *verb* **smelling, smelled** *or* **smelt**

smell·y (**smel**-ee) *adjective* Having a strong and usually unpleasant smell. ▶ *adjective* **smellier, smelliest**

smelt (smelt)
verb To melt ore so that the metal can be removed.
noun A thin, silvery food fish that lives in cold ocean waters and swims up rivers to lay its eggs.
▶ *verb* **smelting, smelted**

smile (smile)
verb To turn up the corners of your mouth and make a facial expression that shows you are pleased, happy, or amused.
noun An expression on your face that shows you are happy, with the corners of your mouth turned up.
▶ *verb* **smiling, smiled**

smil·ey (**smye**-lee) *noun* A simple image of a smiling face that people sometimes add to written messages to show that they are happy or laughing.

smirk (smurk)
verb To smile in a smug, knowing, or annoying way.
noun A smug or annoying smile.
▶ *verb* **smirking, smirked**

smock (smahk) *noun* A garment that looks like a long, loose shirt. Smocks are worn over other clothes to keep them from getting dirty.

smog (smahg) *noun* Fog that has become mixed with smoke or other pollution and hangs in the air over a city or industrial area.

smoke (smohk)
noun The vapor that is produced when something burns.
verb **1.** To give off smoke. **2.** To draw the smoke from a cigarette, pipe, or cigar into your mouth and lungs and blow it out again. **3.** To preserve meat

S

or fish by hanging it in smoke.
▶ *verb* **smoking, smoked** ▶ *adjective* **smoky** ▶ *noun* **smoker** ▶ *noun* **smoking** ▶ *adjective* **smoked**

smoke a·larm (**smohk** uh-*lahrm*) *noun* Another name for a **smoke detector.**

smoke de·tec·tor (**smohk** di-*tek*-tur) *noun* A device that warns people of smoke or fire by letting out a loud, piercing sound.

smoke·stack (**smoke**-*stak*) *noun* A chimney that allows smoke or gases to escape from a factory, a ship, or a locomotive.

smol·der (**smohl**-dur) *verb* 1. To burn slowly, with smoke but no flames. 2. To show hidden anger, hate, or jealousy. 3. To exist or continue in a hidden state.
▶ *verb* **smoldering, smoldered**

smooth (smooTH)
adjective 1. Having a regular or even surface, without roughness or bumps. 2. Happening without interruptions, problems, or difficulties. 3. Able or skillful.
verb To make things more level, even, or flat.
▶ *adjective* **smoother, smoothest**
▶ *verb* **smoothing, smoothed** ▶ *adverb* **smoothly** ▶ *noun* **smoothness**

smor·gas·bord (**smor**-guhs-*bord*) *noun* 1. A meal consisting of many different dishes displayed on a long table so that people can choose what they want. 2. A wide variety of something.

smoth·er (**smuTH**-ur) *verb* 1. To keep someone from breathing by covering his or her nose and mouth. 2. To cover someone or something thickly or entirely. 3. To hide or to hold back.
▶ *verb* **smothering, smothered**

smudge (smuhj)
verb To blur or smear by rubbing something.
noun A blur or smear.
▶ *verb* **smudging, smudged**
▶ *adjective* **smudged**

smug (smuhg) *adjective* So pleased with yourself that you annoy other people. ▶ *adjective* **smugger, smuggest** ▶ *noun*

smugness ▶ *adverb* **smugly**

smug·gle (**smuhg**-uhl) *verb* 1. To move goods into or out of a country illegally. 2. To bring someone or something into or out of a place secretly.
▶ *verb* **smuggling, smuggled** ▶ *noun* **smuggler**

snack (snak)
noun A light meal or small quantity of food.
verb To eat a snack.
▶ *verb* **snacking, snacked**

snag (snag)
noun An unexpected problem or drawback.
verb To catch on something.
noun An obstacle or tangle.
▶ *verb* **snagging, snagged**

snail (snayl) *noun* 1. A small animal with a soft, slimy body and a spiral shell on its back. Snails live on land or in water, and some are used as food. 2. A person who moves slowly.

snake (snake) *noun* A long, slender reptile without limbs that slithers along the ground. In the United States, only rattlesnakes, copperheads, water moccasins, and coral snakes have poisonous bites.

snap (snap)
verb 1. To break with a sudden, sharp, cracking sound. 2. To bite suddenly or bring the jaws together as if to bite. 3. To speak to someone quickly and sharply. 4. To open or close with a click or snapping sound.
noun 1. A sudden cracking sound. 2. **cold snap** A brief period of cold weather. 3. (informal) A snapshot. 4. The moment in a football game when the ball is put in play by the center, a lineman on the offense.
▶ *verb* **snapping, snapped**

snap·drag·on (**snap**-*drag*-uhn) *noun* A garden plant with brightly colored flowers that grow on spikes. Each flower has two petals that look like lips.

snap·py (**snap**-ee) *adjective* 1. Short and clever. 2. Neat, stylish, and elegant. 3. Irritable and sharp. 4. **make it snappy** To do something immediately.

snap·shot (**snap**-*shaht*) *noun* An informal photograph, especially one taken with a simple, handheld camera.

snare (snair)
noun A trap for catching birds or small animals, consisting of a loop of wire that pulls tight when a trigger is released.
verb To catch a bird or an animal in a trap or snare.
▸ *verb* **snaring, snared**

snare drum (**snair** *druhm*) *noun* A double-headed drum with strings or wires stretched across the bottom head that produce a rattling sound.

snarl (snahrl)
verb 1. To growl with bared teeth. 2. To say something angrily or theateningly. 3. If something such as traffic is **snarled,** it has stopped or is moving very slowly.
noun 1. A tangle or knot. 2. A sound like growling, or the act of making this sound.
▸ *verb* **snarling, snarled**

snatch (snach)
verb To take or grab something quickly or eagerly.
noun A fragment of something.
▸ *verb* **snatches, snatching, snatched** ▸ *noun, plural* **snatches**

sneak (sneek)
verb 1. To move in a quiet, secretive way. 2. To put, carry, or take someone or something secretly into or out of a place.
adjective Done secretly or with no warning.
noun Someone who is tricky and dishonest.
▸ *verb* **sneaking, sneaked** or **snuck** (snuhk) ▸ *adjective* **sneaky** ▸ *adverb* **sneakily**

sneak·ers (**snee**-kurz) *noun, plural* Athletic shoes with rubber soles.

sneer (sneer)
verb To smile in a hateful or scornful way.
noun A hateful or scornful smile.
▸ *verb* **sneering, sneered**

sneeze (sneez)
verb To push air out through your nose and mouth suddenly and explosively.
noun The act of suddenly forcing air out through your nose and mouth.
▸ *verb* **sneezing, sneezed**

snick·er (**snik**-ur)
noun A mean or disrespectful little laugh.
verb To laugh in such a way.
▸ *verb* **snickering, snickered**

sniff (snif)
verb 1. To breathe in through your nose with enough force to be heard. 2. To smell something.
noun The act of breathing forcefully through your nose or the sound this makes.
▸ *verb* **sniffing, sniffed**

snif·fle (**snif**-uhl)
verb To take short breaths noisily and repeatedly, usually because you are crying or have a cold.
noun The act of sniffling, or the sound it makes.
▸ *verb* **sniffling, sniffled**

snip (snip) *verb* To cut, clip, or separate something using shears or scissors in short, quick strokes. ▸ *verb* **snipping, snipped**

snipe (snipe)
verb To shoot at a person or persons from a hidden place.
noun A marsh bird with a long bill and brown feathers spotted with black and white.
▸ *verb* **sniping, sniped** ▸ *noun* **sniper**

sniv·el (**sniv**-uhl) *verb* To whine or complain tearfully. ▸ *verb* **sniveling, sniveled**

snob (snahb) *noun* 1. Someone who looks down on people who are not rich, successful, or intelligent. 2. A person who thinks that he or she is better than or superior to others.
▸ *noun* **snobbery**

snoop (snoop)
verb (informal) To pry or look around in a sly or sneaky way.
noun A nosy person who pries into other people's business.
▸ *verb* **snooping, snooped** ▸ *adjective* **snoopy**

snooze (snooz)
verb (informal) To sleep lightly and briefly, usually during the day; to doze.
noun A short, light nap.
▶ *verb* **snoozing, snoozed**

snore (snor) *verb* To breathe with harsh, snorting noises while you are asleep. ▶ *verb* **snoring, snored**

snor·kel (**snor**-kuhl) *noun* A long tube that you hold in your mouth and use to breathe when you're swimming underwater. ▶ *noun* **snorkeling**

snort (snort)
verb 1. To breathe out forcefully through your nose with a harsh sound. 2. To show scorn, anger, or disbelief by snorting.
noun The act of breathing out loudly and forcefully through your nose.
▶ *verb* **snorting, snorted**

snout (snout) *noun* The long front part of an animal's head. It includes the nose, mouth, and jaws.

snow (snoh)
noun White crystals of ice that form when water vapor freezes in the air.
verb To fall from the sky as snow.
▶ *verb* **snowing, snowed** ▶ *adjective* **snowy**

snow·ball (**snoh**-bawl)
noun Snow that has been packed together into a ball.
verb To grow quickly in size or importance.
▶ *verb* **snowballing, snowballed**

snow·board (**snoh**-bord)
noun A board like a wide ski for riding downhill on snow.
verb To ride on a snowboard.
▶ *verb* **snowboarding, snowboarded** ▶ *noun* **snowboarding**

snow·fall (**snoh**-fawl) *noun* The amount of snow that falls in one place in a given period of time.

snow·flake (**snoh**-flake) *noun* A single flake or crystal of snow.

snow·man (**snoh**-man) *noun* A figure made out of large, stacked balls of snow, that resembles a person. ▶ *noun, plural* **snowmen**

snow·mo·bile (**snoh**-muh-beel) *noun* A vehicle with an engine and skis or runners, used to travel over snow.

snow·plow (**snoh**-plou)
noun A device or vehicle used to push snow off a road, sidewalk, or other surface.
verb In skiing, to spread your skis apart and turn the tips inward so that you can slow down or turn.
▶ *verb* **snowplowing, snowplowed**

snow·shoe (**snoh**-shoo) *noun* A webbed frame that is shaped like a racket and attached to a boot to keep the foot from sinking into the snow.

snow·storm (**snoh**-storm) *noun* A storm with strong winds and heavy snow.

snub (snuhb)
verb To treat someone coldly or with disrespect; to ignore a person.
noun An instance of disrespecting someone by ignoring them or not treating them properly.
▶ *verb* **snubbing, snubbed**

snuck (snuhk) *verb* (informal) A past tense and past participle of **sneak.**

snuff (snuhf)
noun Powdered tobacco that is sniffed up the nose, chewed, or rubbed into the gums.
verb **snuff out** To extinguish.
▶ *verb* **snuffing, snuffed**

snug (snuhg) *adjective* 1. Cozy and comfortable. 2. Fitting closely or tightly.
▶ *adjective* **snugger, snuggest** ▶ *adverb* **snugly**

snug·gle (**snuhg**-uhl) *verb* To lie close to someone, or to hold something close for warmth or protection or to show affection. ▶ *verb* **snuggling, snuggled** ▶ *adjective* **snuggly**

so (soh)
adverb 1. In this or that way. 2. To that extent. 3. Very. 4. Very much. 5. Too or also.
conjunction 1. Therefore. 2. In order that.
adjective True.
pronoun 1. More or less. 2. That way, or the same.
interjection A word that shows surprise, shock, or annoyance.
So sounds like **sew.**

S

soak (sohk) *verb* 1. To make something completely wet. 2. To put something in water for a long period of time. 3. **soak up** To take in a liquid by absorbing it.
▶ *verb* **soaking, soaked**

soak·ing (**soh**-king) *adjective* Thoroughly wet.

soap (sohp)
noun A substance used for washing and cleaning. Soap is usually made from fat and lye.
verb To apply soap to someone or something.
▶ *adjective* **soapy**

soap opera (**sohp** ah-pur-uh) *noun* A television series about the difficult lives of a group of people. Soap operas stress suspense and exaggerated emotions.

soar (sor) *verb* 1. To fly or to rise high in the air. 2. To rise or increase quickly above the usual or normal level.
Soar sounds like **sore**. ▶ *verb* **soaring, soared**

sob (sahb)
verb To take short, gasping breaths because you have been crying.
noun The act of sobbing, or the sound it makes.
▶ *verb* **sobbing, sobbed**

so·ber (**soh**-bur)
adjective 1. Not drunk. 2. Solemn, serious, and sensible. 3. Dark in color, not bright or flashy.
verb To make someone more serious, solemn, or sober.
▶ *adjective* **soberer, soberest** ▶ *verb* **sobering, sobered** ▶ *adverb* **soberly**

soc·cer (**sah**-kur) *noun* A game played by two teams of 11 players who try to score by kicking a ball into goals at each end of a field.

so·cia·ble (**soh**-shuh-buhl)
adjective Friendly, enjoying the company of other people. ▶ *noun* **sociability** ▶ *adverb* **sociably**

so·cial (**soh**-shuhl)
adjective 1. Of or having to do with the way that people live together as a society. 2. Of or having to do with people getting together in a friendly way or for companionship. 3. Friendly or sociable. 4. Living in colonies or communities rather than on their own.
noun A party or a gathering of people.
▶ *adverb* **socially**

so·cial·ism (**soh**-shuh-liz-uhm) *noun* An economic system in which the government, rather than private individuals, owns and operates the factories, businesses, and farms. ▶ *noun* **socialist** ▶ *adjective* **socialist**

so·cial net·work·ing (**soh**-shuhl **net**-wur-king) *noun* 1. The activity of using computer networks to communicate and form friendly relationships with other people. 2. **social networking site** A website that helps people to connect with each other in a friendly way.

So·cial Se·cu·ri·ty (**soh**-shuhl si-**kyoor**-i-tee) *noun* A U.S. government program that pays money to people who are elderly, retired, unemployed, or disabled. Sometimes also spelled "social security."

so·cial stud·ies (**soh**-shuhl **stuhd**-eez) *noun* A subject in school that includes geography, history, and government.

so·ci·e·ty (suh-**sye**-i-tee) *noun* 1. All people, or people as a group. 2. All the people who live in the same country or region and share the same culture, customs, laws, and organizations. 3. An organization or club for people who share the same interests or activities. 4. The social group that often sets or follows current fashions and style.
▶ *noun, plural* **societies**

so·ci·ol·o·gy (soh-see-**ah**-luh-jee) *noun* The study of human social behavior and the development of human society. ▶ *noun* **sociologist** ▶ *adjective* **sociological** (soh-see-uh-**lah**-ji-kuhl)

sock (sahk)
noun A knitted item of clothing that covers your foot and the lower part of your leg.
verb (informal) To hit someone hard, especially with your fist.
▶ *verb* **socking, socked**

sock·et (**sah**-kit) *noun* A hole or hollow place where something fits in.

sock pup·pet (**sahk** *puhp*-it) *noun* 1. A simple puppet made from a sock. 2. An online identity that someone uses to say flattering things about himself or herself.

sod (sahd)
noun 1. The top layer of soil and the grass that grows in it. 2. A piece of sod that is held together by matted roots and cut in a square or strip.
verb To cover with pieces of sod.
▶ *verb* **sodding, sodded**

so·da (**soh**-duh) *noun* 1. A soft drink made with soda water. 2. A drink made with soda water, flavoring, and ice cream. 3. Soda water. 4. Baking soda.

so·da wa·ter (**soh**-duh *waw*-tur) *noun* A drink with bubbles, made by mixing water with carbon dioxide gas.

sod·den (**sah**-duhn) *adjective* Soaking wet.

so·di·um (**soh**-dee-uhm) *noun* A silver-white metallic element found in salt.

so·di·um bi·car·bon·ate (**soh**-dee-uhm bye-**kahr**-buh-nit) *noun* A white substance used in baking powder, fire extinguishers, and medicines. Also called **baking soda.**

so·fa (**soh**-fuh) *noun* A long, padded seat with a fixed back, arms, and room for two or more people; a couch.

soft (sawft) *adjective* 1. Easy to press, bend, or mold into a different shape, as in *a soft pillow.* 2. Smooth or fine to the touch; not rough. 3. Pleasantly mild or gentle. 4. Kind.
▶ *adjective* **softer, softest** ▶ *noun* **softness** ▶ *adverb* **softly**

soft·ball (**sawft**-bawl) *noun* A sport, similar to baseball, that is played on a smaller field with a larger, softer ball that is pitched underhand.

soft drink (**sawft dringk**) *noun* A beverage, made with soda water, that contains no alcohol.

soft·en (**saw**-fuhn) *verb* 1. To become soft or make something soft. 2. To make someone or something weaker, less intense, or more agreeable, or to become this way.
▶ *verb* **softening, softened**

soft·heart·ed (**sawft**-*hahr*-tid) *adjective* Very kind, caring, and sympathetic.

soft·ware (**sawft**-*wair*) *noun* Computer programs that control the workings of the equipment, or hardware, and direct it to do specific tasks.

sog·gy (**sah**-gee) *adjective* Very wet, heavy, and soft. ▶ *adjective* **soggier, soggiest**

soil (soil)
noun 1. The top layer of earth in which plants grow. 2. A land or a country.
verb To make something dirty or bring disgrace upon it.
▶ *verb* **soiling, soiled**

so·lace (**sah**-lis)
noun 1. Comfort, or relief from sorrow or grief. 2. Something that gives such comfort.
verb To comfort or console someone who is sad or grieving.
▶ *verb* **solacing, solaced**

so·lar (**soh**-lur) *adjective* 1. Of or having to do with the sun. 2. Powered by energy from the sun.

so·lar en·er·gy (**soh**-lur **en**-ur-jee) *noun* Energy from the sun that can be used for heating and generating electricity.

so·lar heat·ing (**soh**-lur **hee**-ting) *noun* Heating powered by energy from the sun.

so·lar sys·tem (**soh**-lur *sis*-tuhm) *noun* The sun together with the eight planets, many moons, and asteroids and comets that move in orbit around it.

sold (sohld) *verb* The past tense and past participle of **sell.**

sol·der (**sah**-dur)
verb To join pieces of metal by putting a small amount of heated, melted alloy between them. As the alloy cools, it hardens.
noun The soft metal that you use when you solder something.
▶ *verb* **soldering, soldered**

S

531

sol·dier (**sohl**-jur) *noun* A person serving in an army.

sole (sole)
noun **1.** The bottom part of the foot. **2.** The bottom part of a shoe, boot, or sock. **3.** A kind of edible ocean flatfish.
adjective One and only.
Sole sounds like **soul.** ▸ *adverb* **solely**

sol·emn (**sah**-luhm) *adjective* Grave or very serious. ▸ *noun* **solemnness** ▸ *noun* **solemnity** (suh-**lem**-ni-tee) ▸ *adverb* **solemnly**

sol·id (**sah**-lid)
adjective **1.** Hard and firm; not a liquid or a gas. **2.** Not mixed with anything else. **3.** Having no spaces or gaps; not hollow. **4.** Dependable. **5.** Not interrupted; continuous.
noun A three-dimensional object or geometric figure.
▸ *adverb* **solidly** ▸ *noun* **solidity**

sol·i·dar·i·ty (*sah*-li-**dar**-i-tee) *noun* Unity and mutual support among a group of people who share the same opinions, interests, or goals.

so·lid·i·fy (suh-**lid**-uh-*fye*) *verb* To become solid, hard, and firm. ▸ *verb* **solidifies, solidifying, solidified**

sol·i·tar·y (**sah**-li-*ter*-ee) *adjective* **1.** Not requiring or without the companionship of others. **2.** Single or only. **3.** Isolated and remote.

sol·i·tar·y con·fine·ment (**sah**-li-*ter*-ee kuhn-**fine**-muhnt) *noun* A punishment in which a prisoner is kept in a separate cell and not allowed to see or talk to the other prisoners.

so·lo (**soh**-loh)
noun A song, dance, or piece of music that is performed by one person, with or without accompaniment.
adjective Done by one person.
verb To fly a plane alone, especially for the first time.
adverb Alone; without anyone else.
▸ *verb* **soloing, soloed** ▸ *noun* **soloist**

Sol·o·mon Is·lands (**sah**-luh-muhn **eye**-luhndz) A nation consisting of almost 1,000 islands, located east of Papua New Guinea. Guadalcanal, one of the southern Solomon Islands, was the site of some of the fiercest fighting that occurred between the U.S. and Japan during World War II.

sol·stice (**sahl**-stis *or* **sohl**-stis) *noun* The moment of time during the year when the overhead sun reaches its farthest point north or south of the equator. In the Northern Hemisphere, the summer solstice occurs about June 21 and the winter solstice about December 21.

sol·u·ble (**sahl**-yuh-buhl) *adjective* Easily dissolved in liquid, especially water.

so·lu·tion (suh-**loo**-shuhn) *noun* **1.** The answer to or the means of solving a problem. **2.** A mixture made up of a substance that has been dissolved in a liquid.

solve (sahlv) *verb* To find an answer to or a way of dealing with a problem. ▸ *verb* **solving, solved** ▸ *noun* **solver**

sol·vent (**sahl**-vuhnt)
noun A substance, usually a liquid, that can make another substance dissolve.
adjective Having enough money to pay one's debts.

So·ma·li·a (suh-**mah**-lee-uh) A country in the Horn of Africa along the Gulf of Aden and the Indian Ocean. Somalia has been the site of civil unrest in recent years. It has the longest coastline on the African continent, and acts of piracy by Somalis are affecting international shipping. The country has metals, ores, gas, and other natural resources that have yet to be developed, and may have large oil reserves.

som·ber (**sahm**-bur) *adjective* **1.** Dark, gloomy, and dull. **2.** Very serious and lacking any humor.

som·bre·ro (sahm-**brair**-oh) *noun* A tall hat with a wide brim that is worn in Mexico and the southwestern United States.

some (suhm)
adjective **1.** An unknown number or amount of something. **2.** (informal) Remarkable.
pronoun A certain small number of people or amount of something.
Some sounds like **sum.**

S

some·bod·y (**suhm**-*buhd*-ee or **suhm**-bah-dee)
pronoun A person who is not specified or known.
noun An important or famous person.

some·day (**suhm**-*day*) *adverb* At some future time.

some·how (**suhm**-*hou*) *adverb* In a way that is not known or understood.

some·one (**suhm**-*wuhn*) *pronoun* Somebody; some person.

som·er·sault (**suhm**-ur-*sawlt*)
noun A gymnastic move in which you tuck your chin into your chest and roll in a complete circle forward or backward.
verb To perform a somersault.
▶ *verb* **somersaulting, somersaulted**

some·thing (**suhm**-*thing*)
pronoun A thing that is not specified or known.
adverb A little bit.

some·time (**suhm**-*time*) *adverb* At a time that is not specified or known.

some·times (**suhm**-*timez*) *adverb* Now and then; occasionally.

some·what (**suhm**-*waht*)
adverb Rather.
pronoun Something.

some·where (**suhm**-*wair*)
adverb **1.** To, in, or at a place that is not specified or known. **2.** At some time, or in some amount.
noun A place.

son (suhn) *noun* Someone's male child; a boy or man in relation to his parents. **Son** sounds like **sun.**

so·nar (**soh**-nahr) *noun* An instrument used on ships and submarines that sends out underwater sound waves to determine the location of objects and the distance to the bottom. Sonar is short for *sound navigation and ranging.*

so·na·ta (suh-**nah**-tuh) *noun* A piece of classical music written for a solo instrument, often with a piano, and consisting of several movements or sections.

song (sawng)
noun **1.** A piece of music that has words and is meant to be sung.
2. The musical sounds made by a whale, a bird, or an insect.
idiom **for a song** At a very cheap price.

song·bird (**sawng**-*burd*) *noun* A bird that has a musical call or song. Larks, finches, and cardinals are songbirds.

son·ic (**sah**-nik) *adjective* **1.** Of or having to do with sound waves. **2.** Of or having to do with the speed of sound in air, or about 760 miles per hour at sea level.

son·ic boom (**sah**-nik **boom**) *noun* The loud noise produced by a vehicle when it travels faster than the speed of sound and breaks through the sound barrier.

son-in-law (**suhn**-in-*law*) *noun* The husband of a person's daughter. ▶ *noun, plural* **sons-in-law**

son·net (**sah**-nit) *noun* A poem with 14 lines that uses any of a number of fixed patterns of rhyme.

soon (soon)
adverb **1.** In or after a short time; shortly. **2.** Before the usual time; early. **3.** Quickly; without delay.
phrase If someone **would sooner** do something, they would rather do it than something else.
▶ *adverb* **sooner, soonest**

soot (sut) *noun* Black powder that is produced when a fuel such as coal, wood, or oil is burned. ▶ *adjective* **sooty**

soothe (sooTH) *verb* **1.** To gently calm someone who is angry or upset. **2.** To relieve something that is painful or uncomfortable.
▶ *verb* **soothing, soothed** ▶ *adjective* **soothing**

so·phis·ti·ca·ted (suh-**fis**-tuh-*kay*-tid) *adjective* **1.** Having a lot of knowledge about the world, especially when it comes to culture and fashion. **2.** Very complicated or advanced; highly developed.
▶ *noun* **sophistication**

soph·o·more (**sahf**-*mor* or **sah**-fuh-*mor*) *noun* A student in the second year of high school or college.

sop·ping (**sah**-ping) *adjective* Wet all the way through.

S

so·pran·o (suh-**pran**-oh)
noun 1. The highest singing voice. 2. A person who sings in a soprano voice.
adjective Of or having to do with the highest singing voice.

sor·bet (sor-**bay** or **sor**-bit) *noun* A frozen dessert made from fruit juice.

sor·cer·er (**sor**-sur-er) *noun* A person who practices magic by controlling evil spirits; a wizard. ▶ *noun* **sorcery**

sor·did (**sor**-did) *adjective* 1. Dirty or filthy. 2. Evil and disgusting.
▶ *noun* **sordidness** ▶ *adverb* **sordidly**

sore (sor)
adjective 1. Aching or painful. 2. Angry or upset.
noun An area of raw or painful skin, especially one that has become infected.
Sore sounds like **soar.** ▶ *adjective* **sorer, sorest** ▶ *noun* **soreness**

sor·rel (**sor**-uhl or **sahr**-uhl) *noun* 1. A reddish-brown color. 2. A horse of this color with a mane and tail of a lighter color. 3. A plant with long clusters of small flowers and edible leaves that are shaped like hearts.

sor·row (**sahr**-oh)
noun Great sadness, grief, or regret.
verb To feel great sadness, grief, or regret.
▶ *adjective* **sorrowful** ▶ *adverb* **sorrowfully**

sor·ry (**sahr**-ee)
adjective 1. Feeling sadness, sympathy, or regret because you have done something wrong or because someone is suffering. 2. Worthless, inferior, or poor.
phrase If someone or something is **in a sorry state,** it is in very bad condition.
▶ *adjective* **sorrier, sorriest**

sort (sort)
noun A group of people or things that have something in common; a type or a kind.
verb To arrange or separate things.
▶ *verb* **sorting, sorted**

SOS (**es**-oh-*es*) *noun* An international signal of distress, sent out by ships or planes in need of urgent help.

sought (sawt) *verb* The past tense and past participle of **seek.**

soul (sole)
noun 1. The spiritual part of a person that is often thought to control the ability to think, feel, and act. 2. A person.
adjective Of or having to do with African Americans or black culture.
Soul sounds like **sole.**

sound (sound)
noun 1. Something that you sense with your ears. 2. One of the noises that make up human speech. *Write* begins with an *r* sound. 3. A long, narrow arm of water between two bodies of water or between the mainland and an island.
verb 1. To make a noise. 2. To appear to be or to give an impression. 3. To be said or pronounced.
adjective 1. Healthy or strong. 2. Sensible or reliable. 3. Deep and undisturbed.
▶ *verb* **sounding, sounded**

sound bar·ri·er (**sound** bar-ee-ur) *noun* When an object breaks the **sound barrier,** it is going faster than the sound waves it produces. As a result, all of the sound waves get bunched together, resulting in a single loud boom.

sound bite (**sound** bite) *noun* A small portion of a political speech or interview that is recorded and played on a newscast or other program.

sound ef·fects (**sound** i-*fekts*) *noun, plural* Sounds, other than speech or music, that are used to make a play, a movie, or a radio or television program seem more realistic.

sound·proof (**sound**-*proof*)
adjective Not allowing any sound to enter or escape.
verb To make something soundproof.

sound track (**sound** *trak*) *noun* 1. A recording of music from a movie or play. 2. The narrow strip on a motion-picture film or videotape that carries the sound recording.

sound wave (**sound** *wave*) *noun* A wave or series of vibrations in the air, in a solid, or in a liquid that can be heard.

S

soup (soop)
noun A liquid food made by cooking vegetables, meat, or fish in broth, milk, or water.
verb **soup up** (slang) To increase the power of an engine or motor vehicle.
▶ *verb* **souping, souped** ▶ *adjective* **soupy**

sour (sour)
adjective **1.** Having a sharp, acid taste. **2.** Disagreeable.
verb To make or become acid through spoiling.
▶ *adjective* **sourer, sourest** ▶ *verb* **souring, soured** ▶ *noun* **sourness**

source (sors) *noun* **1.** The place, person, or thing from which something comes or develops. **2.** The starting point of a stream or river. **3.** A person, book, or document that provides information.

sour·dough (*sour*-doh) *noun* A fermented dough used in making breads and rolls.

south (south)
noun **1.** One of the four main points of the compass. South is to your left when you face the direction where the sun sets. **2. South** Any area or region that is lying in this direction. **3. the South** In the United States, the states lying south of Pennsylvania and the Ohio River and east of the Mississippi River.
adjective To do with or existing in the south.
adverb Toward the south.

South Af·ri·ca (*south* **af**-ri-kuh) A country on the southern tip of Africa. Its long-standing policy of apartheid, which discriminated against the nonwhite majority of its citizens, was repealed in 1991. South Africa has three capital cities: Pretoria, the administrative capital; Cape Town, the legislative capital; and Bloemfontein, the judicial capital.

South A·mer·i·ca (*south* uh-**mer**-i-kuh) A continent of the Western Hemisphere, located to the south of North America. South America is the fourth-largest continent, and the fifth most populated. It is surrounded by the Pacific Ocean to the west, the Atlantic Ocean to the east, and the Caribbean Sea to the northeast.

South Car·o·li·na (*south* **kar**-uh-**lye**-nuh) A state in the southern part of the United States. South Carolina was the first state to secede from the Union before the outbreak of the Civil War, and was the site for the start of the war. It began on April 12, 1861, when the Confederates fired on the Union troops who held Fort Sumter, a military fortification in the harbor of the city of Charleston.

South Chi·na Sea (*south* **chye**-nuh see) A large sea of the Pacific Ocean, located to the south of China and Taiwan. It contains a large number of small islands.

South Da·ko·ta (*south* duh-**koh**-tuh) A state in the Midwest region of the United States. Its popular attractions include the Badlands National Park, Mount Rushmore, and the site of the Wounded Knee massacre. Mount Rushmore is in the Black Hills, an area with low, pine-forested mountains that are sacred to the Sioux, also known as the Lakota.

South·east (*south*-**eest**) *noun* **the Southeast** The area of the United States to the south and east that stretches from Virginia to Florida and Louisiana.

south·ern (**suhTH**-urn) *adjective* **1.** In or toward the south. **2.** Coming from the south.

South·ern Hem·i·sphere (**suhTH**-urn **hem**-i-*sfeer*) *noun* The half of the earth that is south of the equator.

South Pole (**south pole**) *noun* The most southern part of the earth, located at the bottom tip of the earth's axis.

south·ward (**south**-wurd) *adverb, adjective* To or toward the south.

South·west (*south*-**west**) *noun* **the Southwest** The area of the United States that includes the states west of the Mississippi River and south of Missouri and Kansas.

S

sou·ve·nir (soo-vuh-**neer**) noun An object that you keep to remind you of a place, a person, or something that happened.

sov·er·eign (**sahv**-rin)
noun A king or queen.
adjective 1. Having the highest power. 2. Independent.

sov·er·eign·ty (**sahv**-rin-tee) noun Supreme authority or the power to rule.

So·vi·et Un·ion (**soh**-vee-et **yoon**-yuhn) noun A former country of 15 republics that included Russia, Ukraine, and other nations of eastern Europe and northern Asia. It is also known as the Union of Soviet Socialist Republics, abbreviated as U.S.S.R.

sow
verb (soh) To scatter seeds over the ground so that they will grow; to plant.
noun (sou) An adult female pig.
▶ verb **sowing, sowed, sown** (sohn) or **sowed**

soy·bean (**soi**-been) noun A seed that grows in pods on bushy plants. Soybeans are a good source of protein and oil.

soy sauce (soi) noun A dark liquid that is made from soaked and fermented soybeans. It is used as a sauce to flavor food.

space (spase)
verb To leave an empty area between things.
noun 1. The physical universe beyond the earth's atmosphere. Also called **outer space**. 2. An area that is unoccupied or available. 3. A period of time, usually of a specified length. 4. The open area in which all objects are located. Space has height, width, and depth.
▶ verb **spacing, spaced**

space bar (spase bahr) noun A bar at the bottom of a computer or typewriter keyboard that adds a space to the right of a character when pressed.

space·craft (**spays**-kraft) noun A vehicle that travels or is used in space. ▶ noun, plural **spacecraft**

space·ship (**spays**-ship) noun A spacecraft designed and built to break free of the earth's atmosphere and travel into space.

space shut·tle (spase shuht-uhl) noun A spacecraft designed to make repeated journeys into space, carrying astronauts and equipment back and forth between the earth and a space station.

space sta·tion (spase stay-shuhn) noun A spacecraft that stays in orbit and is large enough to house a crew for long periods of time.

space·suit (**spays**-soot) noun The sealed and pressurized suit that an astronaut wears in space.

space·walk (**spays**-wawk)
noun A period of time during which an astronaut leaves his or her spacecraft and moves around in space.
verb To move outside a spacecraft while being attached to it.
▶ verb **spacewalking, spacewalked**
▶ noun **spacewalker**

spa·cious (**spay**-shuhs) adjective Having plenty of space.

spade (spayd)
noun A tool used for digging, with a long, sturdy handle and a flat blade that you can push into the earth with your foot.
noun, plural **spades** One of the four suits in a deck of playing cards. Spades have a black symbol that looks like an upside-down heart with a stalk.
verb To dig or move earth with a spade.
▶ verb **spading, spaded**

spa·ghet·ti (spuh-**get**-ee) noun Long, thin strands of pasta that are cooked by boiling and usually served with a sauce.

Spain (spayn) A country in southwestern Europe. A world empire in the 16th and 17th centuries, Spain sent out explorers to the Americas to claim colonies for Spain. As a result, Spanish is the official language of most of Central and South America.

S

spam (spam)
noun Messages or advertisements sent by email to people who did not ask for them.
verb To send email messages to people who have not asked for them.
▶ *verb* **spamming, spammed**

span (span)
noun 1. The distance between two points. The span of a bridge is its length from one end to the other. 2. The full reach or length of something. 3. The length of time that something lasts.
verb To reach over or stretch across something.
▶ *verb* **spanning, spanned**

spank (spangk) *verb* To hit someone with an open hand or a flat object, especially on the buttocks, as a punishment. ▶ *verb* **spanking, spanked**

spare (spair)
adjective 1. Kept for use when needed; extra. 2. Not taken up by work; free. 3. With no excess fat; lean.
verb 1. To give something that you have enough of or to make something available. 2. To show mercy, or to not hurt someone. 3. To free from the need to do something.
noun 1. An item like another one that you have, for use in case the first one is lost or broken. 2. The knocking down of all ten pins in bowling with two rolls of the ball.
▶ *verb* **sparing, spared**

spark (spahrk)
noun 1. A small bit of burning material thrown off by a fire. 2. A quick flash of light. 3. A small bit or trace.
verb 1. To make something happen or to stir something up. 2. To throw off sparks.
▶ *verb* **sparking, sparked**

spar·kle (spahr-kuhl)
verb 1. To shine with or to reflect flashes of light; to glitter. 2. To fizz or bubble. 3. To accomplish something in a brilliant or lively way.
noun A bright flash of light.
▶ *verb* **sparkling, sparkled**

spark plug (spahrk pluhg) *noun* A device in a gasoline engine that ignites the fuel-and-air mixture in a cylinder by producing an electrical spark.

spar·row (spar-oh) *noun* A small, common songbird with brown, white, and gray feathers and a short bill.

sparse (spahrs) *adjective* Thinly spread; not crowded or dense. ▶ *adverb* **sparsely**

spasm (spaz-uhm) *noun* 1. A sudden tightening of a muscle that cannot be controlled. 2. A short, sudden burst of energy, activity, or emotion.

spat (spat) *noun* A short, unimportant argument or quarrel.

spat·ter (spat-ur) *verb* To scatter or splash in drops or small bits. ▶ *verb* **spattering, spattered**

spat·u·la (spach-uh-luh) *noun* A tool with a broad, flat blade that bends easily. It is used to mix, spread, or lift food or to mix plaster or paint.

spawn (spawn)
noun The large number of eggs produced by fish, mollusks, and amphibians.
verb To produce a large number of eggs.
▶ *verb* **spawning, spawned**

speak (speek) *verb* 1. To talk, or to say words in an ordinary voice. 2. To tell or make known your ideas, opinions, or feelings. 3. To deliver a speech. 4. To talk in a certain language. 5. **speak out** *or* **speak up** To speak loudly, or to speak openly and honestly about what you really believe.
▶ *verb* **speaking, spoke** (spohk), **spoken** (spoh-kin)

speak·er (spee-kur) *noun* 1. The one who is speaking. 2. Somebody who makes a speech. 3. A loudspeaker, especially one attached to a sound system.

spear (speer)
noun 1. A weapon with a long handle and a pointed head. 2. A long blade, shoot, or stalk of a plant.
verb To pick up with something sharp.
▶ *verb* **spearing, speared**

S

spear·mint (**speer**-*mint*) *noun* A fragrant mint plant with spear-shaped leaves that is used to flavor candy and food.

spe·cial (**spesh**-uhl)
adjective 1. Different or unusual. 2. For a particular purpose or occasion. *noun* A television program intended as a single show rather than as one in a series.
▶ *adverb* **specially**

spe·cial·ist (**spesh**-uh-list) *noun* An expert in a particular field of knowledge or kind of work.

spe·cial·ize (**spesh**-uh-*lize*) *verb* To focus on one area of work, or to learn a lot about one subject. ▶ *verb* **specializing, specialized** ▶ *noun* **specialization** (*spesh*-uh-li-*zay*-shuhn)

spe·cial·ty (**spesh**-uhl-tee) *noun* 1. The skill or area of study that you are particularly good at. 2. A particular product or service.
▶ *noun, plural* **specialties**

spe·cies (**spee**-sheez *or* **spee**-seez) *noun* One of the groups into which animals and plants of the same genus are divided. Members of the same species can mate and have offspring. ▶ *noun, plural* **species**

spe·cif·ic (spuh-**sif**-ik) *adjective* Precise, definite, or of a particular kind. ▶ *adverb* **specifically**

spec·i·fi·ca·tions (*spes*-uh-fi-**kay**-shuhnz) *noun, plural* A detailed statement about the design, materials, and workmanship required for something that is to be built or made.

spec·i·fy (**spes**-uh-*fye*) *verb* To mention, describe, or define something in an exact or detailed way. ▶ *verb* **specifies, specifying, specified**

spec·i·men (**spes**-uh-muhn) *noun* A sample, or an example used to stand for a whole group.

speck (spek) *noun* 1. A small spot or mark. 2. A tiny particle or bit.

speck·led (**spek**-uhld) *adjective* Covered with small, irregular spots or patches of color.

spec·ta·cle (**spek**-tuh-kuhl) *noun* A remarkable or impressive sight.

spec·ta·cles (**spek**-tuh-kuhlz) *noun, plural* Eyeglasses.

spec·tac·u·lar (spek-**tak**-yuh-lur) *adjective* Remarkable or very impressive. ▶ *adverb* **spectacularly**

spec·ta·tor (**spek**-*tay*-tur) *noun* 1. Someone who watches an event but does not participate in it. 2. A **spectator sport** is one that large groups of people enjoy watching.

spec·ter (**spek**-tur) *noun* A ghost or phantom. ▶ *adjective* **spectral** (**spek**-truhl)

spec·trum (**spek**-truhm) *noun* 1. The bands of color that are revealed when light shines through a prism or through drops of water, as in a rainbow. 2. A wide range of activities, qualities, or ideas.
▶ *noun, plural* **spectrums** *or* **spectra** (**spek**-truh)

spec·u·late (**spek**-yuh-*late*) *verb* 1. To make a guess or form an opinion about something without knowing all the facts. 2. To invest in something that is risky, such as a business or a stock.
▶ *verb* **speculating, speculated** ▶ *noun* **speculator**

spec·u·la·tion (*spek*-yuh-**lay**-shuhn) *noun* Reasoning based on evidence that is insufficient or not firm.

sped (sped) *verb* The past tense and past participle of **speed.**

speech (speech) *noun* 1. The ability to speak or the act of speaking. 2. A talk given to an audience. 3. The way in which someone speaks.
▶ *noun, plural* **speeches**

speech·less (**speech**-lis) *adjective* Temporarily unable to speak, especially as a result of shock or emotion.

speed (speed)
noun 1. The rate at which someone or something moves. 2. The rate of any action. 3. Swiftness of movement. *verb* To move or travel at a rate faster than what is safe or allowed.
▶ *verb* **speeding, sped** (sped) *or* **speeded**

S

speed bump (**speed** buhmp) *noun* A ridge of asphalt or hard rubber that has been laid across a road or parking lot to make drivers slow down.

speed·om·e·ter (spi-**dah**-mi-tur) *noun* An instrument on a vehicle, such as a bike or a car, that tells you how fast you are traveling.

speed trap (**speed** trap) *noun* A stretch of road where drivers typically speed and police catch them using radar.

speed·y (**spee**-dee) *adjective* Done, happening, or moving quickly. ▸ *adverb* **speedily**

spell (spel)
verb 1. To name or write the letters that make up a word in their correct order. 2. To mean. 3. To take someone's place for a time. 4. **spell out** To explain something clearly and in detail.
noun 1. A brief period of time. 2. A brief period during which something is abnormal. 3. Words or a formula believed to have magical powers. 4. An irresistible charm or fascination.
▸ *verb* **spelling, spelled**

spell·bound (**spel**-bound) *adjective* Held in a state of deep fascination or amazement, as if by a spell.

spell check·er (**spel** chek-ur) *noun* A computer program that searches for misspelled words in a document.

spell·ing (**spel**-ing) *noun* 1. The letters used to write a word. 2. Writing or saying the correct letters to form a word or words.

spe·lunk·ing (spi-**luhng**-king) *noun* Exploring caves, especially as a hobby. ▸ *noun* **spelunker**

spend (spend) *verb* 1. To use money to buy goods or services. 2. To pass time. 3. To use up or to devote time, energy, or resources.
▸ *verb* **spending, spent** (spent)

sperm (spurm) *noun* A male reproductive cell that is capable of fertilizing eggs in a female.

sphere (sfeer) *noun* 1. A solid form like that of a basketball or globe, with all points on the surface the same distance from the center. 2. An area of activity, interest, or knowledge.
▸ *adjective* **spherical** (**sfer**-i-kuhl *or* **sfeer**-i-kuhl)

sphinx (sfingks) *noun* 1. In Egyptian mythology, a creature with the body of a lion and the head of a man, ram, or hawk. 2. **the Sphinx** A large statue of this creature in Giza, Egypt.
▸ *noun, plural* **sphinxes**

spice (spise)
noun 1. A plant substance with a distinctive smell or taste, such as cinnamon or paprika, that is used to flavor food. 2. Anything that adds excitement or interest.
verb To add spice to a dish.
▸ *verb* **spicing, spiced**

spi·cy (**spye**-see) *adjective* Containing lots of spices; having a pungent taste. ▸ *adjective* **spicier, spiciest**

spi·der (**spye**-dur) *noun* An insectlike creature with eight legs, a body divided into two parts, and no wings. Spiders spin webs to trap insects for food.

spig·ot (**spig**-uht) *noun* A device used to control the flow of liquid in a pipe; a faucet.

spike (spike)
noun 1. A large, heavy nail often used to fasten rails to railroad ties. 2. One of several pointed pieces of metal attached to the sole of a shoe to help athletes avoid slipping. 3. **spike heel** A very high, narrow heel on a woman's shoe. 4. An ear of wheat or grain, such as corn. 5. A long cluster of flowers on one stem.
verb 1. To form something into sharp points. 2. To hit a volleyball down and over the net with force so that it is difficult to return.
▸ *verb* **spiking, spiked** ▸ *adjective* **spiked**

spill (spil)
verb 1. To let the contents of a container flow or fall out, often accidentally. 2. To shed.
noun A serious fall.
▸ *verb* **spilling, spilled** *or* **spilt** (spilt)

S

spin (spin)
verb **1.** To make thread by twisting fine fibers together. **2.** To make a web or cocoon by giving off a liquid that hardens into thread. **3.** To rotate or to whirl around. **4.** To tell or to relate. **5.** To feel dizzy, or as if your head is whirling around.
noun **1.** A short ride. **2.** A special interpretation or point of view.
▶ *verb* **spinning, spun**

spin·ach (**spin**-ich) *noun* A vegetable with edible dark green leaves.

spi·nal col·umn (**spye**-nuhl *kah*-luhm) *noun* A series of connected bones in your back that support and protect the spinal cord; the backbone.

spi·nal cord (**spye**-nuhl *kord*) *noun* A thick cord of nerve tissue that starts at the brain and runs through the center of the spinal column. The spinal cord links the brain to the nerves in the rest of the body.

spin·dle (**spin**-duhl) *noun* The round stick or rod on a spinning wheel that holds and winds thread.

spin·dly (**spind**-lee) *adjective* Slender and rather weak. ▶ *adjective* **spindlier, spindliest**

spine (spine) *noun* **1.** The backbone. **2.** A hard, sharp, pointed growth, such as a thorn or quill, on some plants and animals. **3.** The central, vertical piece of a book's cover.
▶ *adjective* **spinal** ▶ *adjective* **spiny**

spin·ning wheel (**spin**-ing *weel*) *noun* A device worked by hand consisting of a large wheel and a spindle. A spinning wheel is used to spin fibers into thread or yarn.

spin-off *noun* (**spin**-*awf*) **1.** An unrelated benefit or product that comes from something used or developed earlier. **2.** A television show starring a character who had a popular but less important role on an earlier program.
▶ *verb* **spin off** (spin *awf*)

spin·ster (**spin**-stur) *noun* A woman who has stayed single beyond the age at which most women marry.

spi·ral (**spye**-ruhl)
adjective Winding in a continuous curve around a fixed point or central axis.
noun A spiral shape or something that has this shape.
verb To move following the shape of a spiral.
▶ *verb* **spiraling, spiraled**

spire (spire) *noun* A structure that comes to a point at the top. Spires are often built on top of church towers.

spir·it (**spir**-it)
noun **1.** The invisible part of a person that is believed to control thoughts and feelings; the soul. **2.** The essential character, quality, or mood of a person or group of people. **3.** Courage, enthusiasm, and determination. **4.** A ghost or supernatural being. **5.** The real meaning or intent.
noun, plural **spirits** A person's mood or state of mind.
verb **spirit away** To carry off mysteriously or secretly.
▶ *verb* **spiriting, spirited** ▶ *adjective* **spirited**

spir·i·tu·al (**spir**-i-*choo*-uhl)
adjective **1.** Of or having to do with the soul and not with material or physical things. **2.** Of or having to do with religion.
noun A type of religious folk song that was originated by African Americans in the South.
▶ *adverb* **spiritually**

spit (spit)
verb **1.** To force food, liquid, or saliva out of your mouth. **2.** To make an angry, hissing sound.
noun **1.** Saliva. **2.** A long, pointed rod that holds meat over a fire for cooking. **3.** A narrow point of land that sticks out into the water.
▶ *verb* **spitting, spat** (spat) *or* **spit**

spite (spite)
noun A deliberate wish to hurt, annoy, humiliate, or offend someone.
verb To be mean or nasty to someone.
phrase **in spite of** Without being hindered by; regardless, or even though.
▶ *verb* **spiting, spited** ▶ *adjective* **spiteful** ▶ *adverb* **spitefully**

splash (splash)
verb **1.** To throw or scatter a liquid so

S

that it falls in drops. **2.** To make wet by splashing.
noun The sound or movement of liquid being thrown or scattered.
▶ *verb* **splashes, splashing, splashed** ▶ *noun, plural* **splashes**

splash·down (**splash**-doun) *noun* The landing of a spacecraft in the ocean.

splen·did (**splen**-did) *adjective* **1.** Very beautiful or impressive; brilliant.
2. Very good; excellent.
▶ *adverb* **splendidly**

splen·dor (**splen**-dur) *noun* Great or magnificent beauty.

splint (splint) *noun* A strip of something rigid, used to support a broken or injured limb.

splin·ter (**splin**-tur)
noun A thin, sharp piece of wood, glass, bone, or metal that has broken off from a larger piece.
verb To break into thin, sharp pieces.
▶ *verb* **splintering, splintered**

split (split)
verb **1.** To break along the grain. **2.** To divide. **3.** To burst or break apart by force. **4.** (slang) To leave a place.
noun A crack or a break.
noun, plural **the splits** An acrobatic or dance move in which you slide to the floor with your legs spread in opposite directions.
▶ *verb* **splitting, split**

spoil (spoil) *verb* **1.** To ruin or take the joy out of something. **2.** To become rotten or unfit for eating. **3.** To give someone, especially a child, everything that they want, so that eventually they expect to have their way all the time.
▶ *verb* **spoiling, spoiled** ▶ *verb* **spoiling, spoiled** *or* **spoilt** (spoilt)

spoke (spoke)
verb The past tense of **speak.**
noun One of the thin rods that connect the rim of a wheel to the hub.

spo·ken (**spoh**-kuhn)
verb The past participle of **speak.**
adjective Said out loud rather than written.

sponge (spuhnj)
noun **1.** A sea animal that has a

rubbery skeleton with many holes. The dried skeletons of sponges absorb water easily and are often used for washing and cleaning. **2.** A cleaning pad made of a sponge skeleton or artificial material that absorbs water.
verb To wash or wipe something with a sponge.
▶ *verb* **spongeing, sponged** ▶ *adjective* **spongy**

spon·sor (**spahn**-sur)
verb **1.** To give money and support to a worthwhile program or activity. **2.** To pay the costs of a radio or television broadcast in return for having your products advertised.
noun A person who is responsible for someone or something.
▶ *verb* **sponsoring, sponsored** ▶ *noun* **sponsorship**

spon·ta·ne·ous (spahn-**tay**-nee-uhs) *adjective* **1.** Done on impulse, without previous thought or planning.
2. Happening by itself, without any apparent outside cause.
▶ *noun* **spontaneity** (spahn-tuh-**nee**-i-tee) ▶ *adverb* **spontaneously**

spool (spool) *noun* A cylinder or roller on which film, wire, thread, or string is wound.

spoon (spoon)
noun A utensil with a handle on one end and a surface shaped like a shallow bowl on the other.
verb To pick up food or some other substance with a spoon.
▶ *verb* **spooning, spooned**

spore (spor) *noun* A plant cell that develops into a new plant. Spores are produced by plants that do not flower, such as mosses and ferns.

sport (sport) *noun* **1.** A game involving physical effort and skill. **2.** A person who plays fair and accepts losing with good grace.

sports jack·et (**sports** jak-it) *noun* An informal jacket, similar to a suit jacket, that a man wears with slacks.

sports·man·ship (**sports**-muhn-*ship*) *noun* Fair and reasonable behavior, especially in playing a sport.

spot (spaht)
noun 1. A small mark or stain.
2. An area on the skin or fur that is different from the area around it.
3. A particular place or position.
verb To notice something or someone.
idioms 1. **hit the spot** To be satisfying and exactly the right thing to have at that moment. 2. **in a tight spot** In a lot of trouble and unable to get out of it easily.
▶ *verb* **spotting, spotted** ▶ *adjective* **spotted**

spot·less (**spaht**-lis) *adjective*
1. Perfectly clean. 2. Without a flaw or fault.
▶ *adverb* **spotlessly**

spot·light (**spaht**-*lite*)
noun 1. A powerful beam of light aimed at a particular person, thing, or area. 2. A lamp that sends a strong beam of light, used especially on a theater stage or in an exhibit to highlight items on display.
verb To draw attention to something, with or as if with a spotlight.
idiom **in the spotlight** In the news, or the focus of a lot of public attention.
▶ *verb* **spotlighting, spotlighted**

spouse (spous) *noun* A husband or a wife.

spout (spout)
noun A pipe, a tube, or an opening through which liquid flows or is poured.
verb To shoot or pour out with force.
▶ *verb* **spouting, spouted**

sprain (sprayn)
verb To injure a joint by twisting or tearing its muscles or ligaments.
noun An injury that results from twisting a joint or muscles.
▶ *verb* **spraining, sprained**

sprang (sprang) *verb* The past tense of **spring.**

sprawl (sprawl)
verb 1. To sit, lie, or fall with your arms and legs spread out in a relaxed or awkward way. 2. To spread out unevenly over a large area.
noun 1. The spread of buildings on the outskirts of a city, often growing in an unplanned and uncontrolled way that most people think is excessive or unattractive. 2. An awkward posture.
▶ *verb* **sprawling, sprawled**

spray (spray)
verb To scatter liquid in fine droplets or a mist.
noun Liquid in the form of mist or droplets.
▶ *verb* **spraying, sprayed**

spread (spred)
verb 1. To open or stretch out. 2. To cover a surface with something, or to apply an even layer of something.
3. To reach out or extend over an area.
4. To distribute or to make something more widely known.
noun 1. The process of something moving or increasing over an area.
2. (informal) An elaborate meal put on a table.
▶ *verb* **spreading, spread**

spread·sheet (**spred**-*sheet*) *noun*
1. A wide sheet of paper that is divided into rows and columns. Spreadsheets are used for organizing numerical data. 2. A computer program that allows you to keep track of and use information in a table format.

spree (spree) *noun* A period of excessive or unrestrained activity.

spring (spring)
noun 1. The season after winter and before summer, when the weather becomes warmer and plants and flowers begin to grow. 2. A spiral coil of metal that returns to its original shape or position after being stretched or pressed down. 3. A place where water rises to the surface from an underground source.
verb 1. To move suddenly forward or upward from the ground; to leap.
2. To appear suddenly. 3. To make known suddenly.
▶ *verb* **springing, sprang** (sprang), **sprung** (spruhng)

spring·board (**spring**-*bord*) *noun*
A flexible board used in diving or gymnastics to help a person jump high in the air.

S

542

spring clean·ing (**spring klee**-ning)
noun A thorough cleaning of a house or room, usually done once a year.

spring fe·ver (**spring fee**-vur) *noun* A lazy or restless feeling that often is associated with the coming of spring.

sprin·kle (**spring**-kuhl)
verb **1.** To scatter something in small drops or bits. **2.** To rain in small amounts.
noun A small amount of something.
▸ *verb* **sprinkling, sprinkled**

sprin·kler (**spring**-klur) *noun* A device that attaches to a hose and sprays water over a lawn or garden.

sprint (sprint)
verb To run fast for a short distance.
noun A short race, run at the fastest possible speed.
▸ *verb* **sprinting, sprinted** ▸ *noun* **sprinter**

sprock·et (**sprah**-kit) *noun* A wheel with a rim made of toothlike points that fit into the holes of a chain. The chain then drives the wheel.

sprout (sprout)
verb **1.** To begin to grow and produce shoots or buds. **2.** To grow, appear, or develop suddenly or quickly.
noun A new or young plant growth, such as a bud or shoot.
noun, plural **sprouts** The young edible shoots of various plants that are often eaten raw.
▸ *verb* **sprouting, sprouted**

spruce (sproos) *noun* An evergreen tree with short leaves shaped like needles, drooping cones, and wood that is often used in making pulp for paper.

sprung (spruhng) *verb* The past participle of **spring.**

spun (spuhn) *verb* The past tense and past participle of **spin.**

spur (spur)
noun **1.** A pointed device, often a spiked wheel, on the heel of a rider's boot. Spurs are used to make a horse go faster or obey commands. **2.** Something that encourages someone to do something.
verb **spur on** To encourage someone to make more of an effort.
▸ *verb* **spurring, spurred**

spurt (spurt)
verb To come out suddenly in a stream or gush.
noun A sudden, brief burst of energy, growth, or activity.
▸ *verb* **spurting, spurted**

sput·ter (**spuht**-ur) *verb* **1.** To make popping, spitting, or coughing noises. **2.** To speak quickly and in a confused way. **3.** To spit out small bits of food or saliva, especially when you are talking in an excited way.
▸ *verb* **sputtering, sputtered**

spy (spye)
verb **1.** To watch someone or something closely and secretly. **2.** To sight.
noun Someone who secretly collects information about an enemy or a competitor.
▸ *noun, plural* **spies** ▸ *verb* **spies, spying, spied**

spy·ing (**spye**-ing) *noun* The activity of observing someone or something secretly in order to get information.

spy·ware (**spye**-wair) *noun* Software that is secretly installed on your computer in order to gather information about you and how you use your computer.

squab·ble (**skwah**-buhl)
noun A noisy argument or quarrel, usually over something unimportant.
verb To argue over something unimportant.
▸ *verb* **squabbling, squabbled**

squad (skwahd) *noun* A small group of people who work together or are involved in the same activity, such as soldiers, football players, or police officers.

squad·ron (**skwah**-druhn) *noun* A group of ships, cavalry troops, or other military units.

squal·id (**skwah**-lid) *adjective* Dirty and miserable, usually because of neglect or poverty.

squall (skwawl) *noun* A sudden, violent wind that usually brings rain, snow, or sleet with it.

squa·lor (**skwah**-lur) *noun* The condition of being dirty, miserable, and very poor.

S

squan·der (**skwahn**-dur) *verb* To spend money, time, or opportunity wastefully or foolishly. ▶ *verb* **squandering, squandered**

square (skwair)
noun **1.** A shape with four straight, equal sides and four right angles. **2.** A number is a **square** if it can be expressed as the product of the same two numbers. Four is the square of 2 because 2 × 2 = 4. **3.** An open area in a town or city with streets on all four sides. **4.** A person who is considered boring or too conservative.
verb To multiply a number by itself.
adjective **1.** In the shape of a square. **2.** Honest or fair, especially in business affairs. **3.** Nutritious and filling. **4.** (slang) Not cool or not hip; old-fashioned.
▶ *verb* **squaring, squared** ▶ *adjective* **squarer, squarest**

square dance (**skwair** dans) *noun* A dance in which four couples form the sides of a square and move to spoken commands.

square root (**skwair** root) *noun* A number that, when multiplied by itself, produces a given number. The square root of 25 is 5, because 5 × 5 = 25. The symbol for a square root is √.

squash (skwahsh)
verb To crush or to squeeze someone or something into a soft, flat mass.
noun **1.** A game in which two players with rackets hit a small rubber ball against the walls of an enclosed court. **2.** A fleshy fruit that grows on a vine in many shapes, sizes, and colors. Squash are related to pumpkins and gourds.
▶ *verb* **squashes, squashing, squashed** ▶ *noun, plural* **squash** or **squashes**

squat (skwaht)
verb **1.** To crouch, or to sit on your heels with your knees bent. **2.** To settle on an area of land or to live in an empty house that does not belong to you.
adjective Short and wide.

noun A posture in which you are on your feet with your rear end low to the ground.
▶ *adjective* **squatter, squattest** ▶ *verb* **squatting, squatted** ▶ *noun* **squatter**

squawk (skwawk)
noun **1.** A loud, harsh screech like the sound made by a parrot or a chicken. **2.** (informal) Any loud complaint or protest.
verb **1.** To make this sound. **2.** (informal) To complain loudly.
▶ *verb* **squawking, squawked** ▶ *noun* **squawker**

squeak (skweek)
verb To make a short, sharp, high-pitched sound.
noun A short, sharp, high-pitched sound.
▶ *verb* **squeaking, squeaked** ▶ *adjective* **squeaky**

squeal (skweel)
verb **1.** To make a shrill, high sound or cry. **2.** (informal) To betray a friend or secret; to inform on someone.
noun A short, loud, high-pitched cry.
▶ *verb* **squealing, squealed**

squea·mish (**skwee**-mish) *adjective* Easily shocked, disgusted, or nauseated. ▶ *adverb* **squeamishly**

squeeze (skweez)
verb **1.** To exert pressure on someone or something from two or more sides. **2.** To barely get into or through a space. **3.** To hug someone.
noun The act of exerting pressure on someone or something from two or more sides.
▶ *verb* **squeezing, squeezed** ▶ *noun* **squeezer**

squid (skwid) *noun* A sea creature with a long, soft body and ten arms or tentacles that swims by squirting out water with great force. ▶ *noun, plural* **squid** or **squids**

squint (skwint)
verb To look at something through partly closed eyes, especially when there is too much light.
noun An act or instance of squinting.
▶ *verb* **squinting, squinted**

S

squire (skwire) *noun* 1. In medieval times, a young nobleman who served as an attendant to a knight. 2. An English country gentleman who owns land.

squirm (skwurm) *verb* 1. To wriggle or twist about, especially because you are nervous or uncomfortable. 2. To show or feel discomfort because you are embarrassed or ashamed.
▶ *verb* **squirming, squirmed**

squir·rel (skwurl) *noun* A rodent that climbs trees and has a long, bushy tail.

squirt (skwurt)
verb To force out a stream or jet of liquid.
noun A jet or stream of liquid, or a small amount squirted out.
▶ *verb* **squirting, squirted**

squish·y (skwish-ee) *adjective* (informal) Soft and spongy. ▶ *adjective* **squishier, squishiest**

Sri Lan·ka (*sree* lahng-kuh *or shree* lahng-kuh) An island nation in South Asia off the southern coast of India. Formerly called Ceylon, it is known for its tropical forests and beaches. In 1960, Sri Lanka elected the world's first female prime minister.

stab (stab)
verb 1. To thrust a knife or other sharp instrument into someone. 2. To stick or drive a pointed object into something.
noun 1. A sharp, brief feeling or pang. 2. A wound caused by stabbing.
idiom **take a stab at** *or* **make a stab at** (informal) To attempt something.
▶ *verb* **stabbing, stabbed**

sta·bil·i·ty (stuh-bil-i-tee) *noun* The quality of being firm and steady.

sta·ble (stay-buhl)
noun A building or a part of a building where horses or cattle are fed and housed.
adjective 1. Firmly fixed; not likely to fail or give way. 2. Mentally and emotionally steady or secure.
verb To accommodate in a stable.
▶ *verb* **stabling, stabled** ▶ *adjective*

stabler, stablest ▶ *verb* **stabilize** (stay-buh-*lize*)

stac·ca·to (stuh-kah-toh) *adverb, adjective* In music, when you play notes **staccato,** you play them abruptly and separately, so that each sound is distinct.

stack (stak)
verb To arrange things in a pile.
noun 1. A large, neat pile of hay, straw, or grain. 2. A neat pile of something arranged in layers. 3. A chimney or a smokestack.
▶ *verb* **stacking, stacked**

sta·di·um (stay-dee-uhm) *noun* A large structure in which sports events and concerts are held. It usually has an open field surrounded by rows of rising seats. ▶ *noun, plural* **stadiums** or **stadia** (stay-dee-uh)

staff (staf)
noun 1. A group of people who work for a company, an institution, or a person. 2. A stick or pole used as a support in walking or as a weapon. 3. A flagpole. 4. The set of lines and spaces on which music is written.
verb To provide an organization with employees.
▶ *verb* **staffing, staffed**

stag (stag) *noun* A fully grown male deer.

stage (stayj)
noun 1. A raised platform on which actors and other entertainers perform. 2. The profession of acting. 3. A step, level, or point in a process. 4. A period of development.
verb To present a public performance of a play or similar event.
▶ *verb* **staging, staged**

stage·coach (stayj-kohch) *noun* A four-wheeled, horse-drawn coach, used in the past to carry mail and passengers on scheduled trips over regular routes. ▶ *noun, plural* **stagecoaches**

stag·ger (stag-ur) *verb* 1. To walk or move unsteadily, as if you're about to collapse. 2. To arrange events so that they don't all occur at the same time. 3. To shock someone deeply.
▶ *verb* **staggering, staggered**
▶ *adjective* **staggered**

S

stag·ger·ing (**stag**-ur-ing) *adjective* Causing great amazement or upset.

stag·nant (**stag**-nuhnt) *adjective* **1.** Not moving or not flowing; still. **2.** Foul or polluted as a result of not moving. **3.** Not active or not growing.

stag·nate (**stag**-nate) *verb* **1.** When water **stagnates,** it becomes dirty or polluted, changes color, and often gives off a foul odor. **2.** If situations or persons **stagnate,** they stop developing or progressing and remain the same.
▸ *verb* **stagnating, stagnated** ▸ *noun* **stagnation**

staid (stayd) *adjective* Proper, serious, and not very adventurous. ▸ *adjective* **staider, staidest** ▸ *noun* **staidness** ▸ *adverb* **staidly**

stain (stayn)
noun **1.** A mark or spot that is hard to remove. **2.** A dye used to color wood.
verb To mark or discolor something.
▸ *verb* **staining, stained**

stained glass (staynd glas) *noun* Colored pieces of glass, held in place by lead strips, that form a picture, pattern, or design. ▸ *adjective* **stained-glass**

stain·less steel (**stayn**-lis **steel**) *noun* A type of steel that contains chromium and therefore does not rust or tarnish.

stair (stair)
noun One of a group of fixed steps that allow you to walk from the ground to the entrance of a building or from one level to another.
noun, plural **stairs** Another word for **stairway.**
Stair sounds like **stare.**

stair·way (**stair**-way) *noun* A flight of steps with a railing and a structure that supports it.

stake (stayk)
noun **1.** A post with a point at one end that can be driven into the ground to support something, such as a tree or a fence. **2.** Something, especially money, that is bet or risked.

verb **1.** To secure something using a stake. **2.** To risk or to gamble.
idioms and phrases **1. have a stake in** To have a personal interest or involvement in something. **2. at stake** At risk of being lost, ruined, injured, or damaged. **3. pull up stakes** To leave a place.
Stake sounds like **steak.** ▸ *verb* **staking, staked**

sta·lac·tite (stuh-**lak**-*tite*) *noun* An icicle-shaped mineral deposit that hangs from the roof of a cave. Stalactites form as dripping water, full of minerals, slowly evaporates.

sta·lag·mite (stuh-**lag**-*mite*) *noun* A tapering column that sticks up from the floor of a cave. Stalagmites are formed when water containing minerals drips from the ceiling to the floor of the cave and slowly solidifies.

stale (stale) *adjective* **1.** No longer fresh. **2.** No longer new or interesting.
▸ *adjective* **staler, stalest**

stale·mate (**stale**-*mate*) *noun* **1.** A situation in a game of chess in which a player cannot make a move without placing his or her king in check. **2.** Any position or situation that results in a deadlock, with no progress possible.

stalk (stawk)
noun The main stem of a plant from which the leaves and flowers grow.
verb **1.** To hunt or track a person or an animal in a quiet, secret way. **2.** To walk in a proud, stiff, or angry way.
▸ *verb* **stalking, stalked** ▸ *noun* **stalker**

stall (stawl)
verb **1.** When a vehicle **stalls,** its engine stops running and it loses power. **2.** To deliberately put off doing something.
noun **1.** A counter or booth where things are displayed for sale at a market. **2.** An enclosed space for one animal in a stable or barn. **3.** An act or instance of stalling.
▸ *verb* **stalling, stalled**

S

stal·lion (**stal**-yuhn) *noun* An adult male horse.

sta·men (**stay**-muhn) *noun* The part of a flower that produces pollen. It consists of a thin stalk, called the filament, and a tip, called the anther, that has pollen on it.

stam·i·na (**stam**-uh-nuh) *noun* The energy and strength to keep doing something, or to resist fatigue and illness.

stam·mer (**stam**-ur)
verb To speak in an unsure way, stopping often and repeating certain sounds.
noun The act of stammering.
▶ *verb* **stammering, stammered**

stamp (stamp)
noun **1.** A small piece of gummed paper that you stick on a letter or package that is going to be mailed; a postage stamp. **2.** An object used to transfer a mark, signature, or design to paper by pressing it against a pad of ink first. **3.** An instance of bringing down your foot or another object hard.
verb To bring your foot down hard.
▶ *verb* **stamping, stamped**

stam·pede (stam-**peed**) *verb* To make a sudden, wild rush in one direction, usually out of fear. ▶ *verb* **stampeding, stampeded** ▶ *noun* **stampede**

stance (stans) *noun* **1.** The way someone stands; posture. **2.** Attitude or point of view.

stand (stand)
verb **1.** To be on your feet or to rise to an upright position. **2.** To put something in an upright position. **3.** To be located. **4.** To be in a certain rank or order. **5.** To have an opinion or to take a position. **6.** To continue without change or to remain valid. **7.** To tolerate or put up with something. **8. stand by** To support and remain loyal to someone. **9. stand for** To represent. **10. stand out** To show up clearly or to be easily seen.
noun **1.** An object or piece of furniture for holding or displaying things. **2.** A small booth, counter, or stall where goods are sold. **3.** A position or opinion on some matter.
noun, plural **stands** A covered area for spectators at a ballpark or stadium.
phrase **take a stand** To state your opinion on an issue in a clear and forceful way.
▶ *verb* **standing, stood**

stand·a·lone (**stand**-uh-lohn) *adjective* Available or able to operate by itself; not depending on another thing.

stan·dard (**stan**-durd)
noun **1.** A rule or model that is used to judge or measure how good something is. **2.** The flag or banner of a nation or military group.
adjective **1.** Normal or average. **2.** Used or accepted as a standard, rule, or model. **3.** Widely used or accepted as correct.

stand·by (**stand**-bye) *noun* **1.** Someone or something that is kept in reserve, to be used if needed. **2.** The state of being available if needed. **3.** A setting for an electrical device that takes less power, for times when it is not being used. **4.** Someone who doesn't hold a ticket for a flight but will get a seat if there is one available. **5.** Your favorite or most frequent choice.

stand·in (**stand**-*in*) *noun* A person who takes the place of another person. ▶ *verb* **stand in**

stand·ing (**stan**-ding)
noun Position, rank, or reputation.
noun, plural **standings** The positions or rankings of all the teams within a sport during a regular season of play.
phrase **in good standing** Respected and accepted within a group.

stand·still (**stand**-*stil*) *noun* A complete halt.

stand·up (**stand**-*uhp*) *adjective* A **stand-up** comic or comedian performs while standing alone on a stage or in front of a camera.

stank (stangk) *verb* The past tense of **stink.**

stan·za (**stan**-zuh) *noun* One of the units, consisting of two or more lines, into which a poem or song is divided; a verse.

S

sta·ple (**stay**-puhl)

noun **1.** A thin piece of wire that is shaped like a U and punched through sheets of paper to fasten them together. **2.** Any food or product that is used regularly and kept in large amounts. **3.** A main product that is grown or produced in a country or region.

verb To attach paper or other thin objects using a staple.

▶ *verb* **stapling, stapled** ▶ *noun* **stapler**

star (stahr)

noun **1.** A mass of burning gas, seen in the sky at night as a glowing point of light. **2.** A shape with five or more points. **3.** A person who plays a leading role in a movie, television program, or play. **4.** A person who is outstanding in some field.

verb To take the leading role in a movie, television program, or play.

▶ *verb* **starring, starred** ▶ *adjective* **starry**

star·board (**stahr**-burd *or* **stahr**-bord)

noun The right-hand side of a ship or an aircraft when you are facing forward.

adjective Of or on the starboard.

starch (stahrch)

noun **1.** A tasteless, odorless white substance found in potatoes, rice, corn, wheat, and other plant foods that is considered an important part of the human diet. **2.** A substance used in laundering for making fabric stiff.

verb To apply starch to clothes.

▶ *noun, plural* **starches** ▶ *verb* **starches, starching, starched**

stare (stair)

verb To look at someone or something steadily with your eyes wide open.

noun An instance of staring.

Stare sounds like **stair.** ▶ *verb* **staring, stared**

star·fish (**stahr**-*fish*) *noun* A sea animal with a flattened, star-shaped body and five or more arms. ▶ *noun, plural* **starfish** *or* **starfishes**

stark (stahrk) *adjective* **1.** Bare and grim; having little or no plant life. **2.** Complete or extreme.

▶ *adjective* **starker, starkest**

star·ling (**stahr**-ling) *noun* A songbird with a pointed yellow bill and dark, shiny feathers. Starlings are found in most parts of the world.

Stars and Stripes (**stahrz** uhn **stripes**)

noun The flag of the United States. The red and white stripes represent the 13 original colonies. The white stars represent the 50 states.

start (stahrt)

verb **1.** To begin to move, act, or happen. **2.** To make something move, act, or happen. **3.** To jump or move suddenly.

noun **1.** A place where or time when something begins. **2.** An advantage at the beginning of a race or contest. **3.** A moment when something surprises or scares you a little.

▶ *verb* **starting, started**

star·tle (**stahr**-tuhl) *verb* To surprise, frighten, or alarm someone, often causing a quick, involuntary movement. ▶ *verb* **startling, startled** ▶ *adjective* **startled** ▶ *adjective* **startling**

start-up *or* **start·up** (**stahrt**-*uhp*) *noun* A new company, formed by the people who are going to run it.

starve (stahrv) *verb* **1.** To suffer or die from lack of food. **2.** To need or want something very much.

▶ *verb* **starving, starved** ▶ *noun* **starvation**

starv·ing (**stahr**-ving) *adjective* **1.** Suffering or dying from lack of food. **2.** (informal) Very hungry.

state (state)

verb To say something in words; to tell or explain.

noun **1.** A group of people united under one government; a nation. **2.** Any of the political and geographical units that make up a country such as the United States. **3.** The condition that someone or something is in.

▶ *verb* **stating, stated** ▶ *noun* **statehood** (**state**-*hud*)

S

state·ly (**state**-lee) *adjective* Grand, dignified, or majestic.

state·ment (**state**-muhnt) *noun*
1. Something that is said in words.
2. A monthly report from a bank listing all the amounts paid into and out of an account.

state-of-the-art (**state**-uhv-THee-**ahrt**) *adjective* At the highest level of development; very up-to-date.

states·man (**stayts**-muhn) *noun* A person respected for great experience and leadership in government. ▶ *noun, plural* **statesmen**

states·wom·an (**stayts**-*wum*-uhn) *noun* A woman respected for great experience and leadership in government. ▶ *noun, plural* **stateswomen**

stat·ic (**stat**-ik)
adjective Not moving, changing, or growing.
noun Electrical discharges in the air that interfere with radio or television signals and cause a hissing, crackling sound.

stat·ic e·lec·tric·i·ty (**stat**-ik i-lek-**tris**-i-tee) *noun* Electricity that builds up in an object as a result of friction and is released in the form of sparks or a mild electric shock.

sta·tion (**stay**-shuhn) *noun* 1. A place where tickets for trains, buses, or other vehicles are sold and where passengers are let on and off. 2. A building where a service is provided. 3. A place with equipment to send out television or radio signals. 4. A place where a person or thing stands or is supposed to stand while carrying out a duty.

sta·tion·ar·y (**stay**-shuh-*ner*-ee) *adjective* 1. Not moving or not able to be moved. 2. Not changing.
Stationary sounds like **stationery.**

sta·tion·er·y (**stay**-shuh-*ner*-ee) *noun* 1. Materials used for writing, such as paper, pens, and notebooks; office supplies. 2. Paper and envelopes used to write letters.
Stationery sounds like **stationary.**

station wagon (**stay**-shuhn *wag*-uhn) *noun* A motor vehicle with a large, enclosed cargo area behind the rear seats, where the trunk would ordinarily be. The rear seats can be folded down for extra storage space.

sta·tis·tic (stuh-**tis**-tik) *noun* A fact or piece of information taken from a study that covers a much larger quantity of information. ▶ *adjective* **statistical** ▶ *adverb* **statistically**

stat·ue (**stach**-oo) *noun* A model of a person or an animal, especially one that is life-size or larger, made from metal, ston

stat·ure (**stach**-ur) *noun* 1. Height. 2. Good reputation.

sta·tus (**stay**-tuhs *or* **stat**-uhs) *noun* 1. A person's rank or position in a group, an organization, or a society. 2. The condition of a person, situation, project, or event.

sta·tus bar (**stay**-tuhs *bahr or* **stat**-uhs *bahr*) *noun* An area at the bottom of the screen in many computer programs and browsers that shows information about what is currently happening in the main display area.

stat·ute (**stach**-oot) *noun* A written rule or law.

stat·u·to·ry (**stach**-uh-*tor*-ee) *adjective* Required, permitted, or regulated by a statute or law.

stave (stayv)
noun 1. One of the long, thin strips of wood that form the sides of a barrel. 2. The set of lines and spaces on which musical notes are written; a staff.
verb 1. **stave in** To break by forcing inward or to smash a hole in something. 2. **stave off** To manage to prevent or delay something.
▶ *verb* **staving, staved** *or* **stove** (stohv)

stay (stay)
verb 1. To remain in one place or condition. 2. To live or spend time somewhere.
noun A period of time spent somewhere as a guest or visitor.
▶ *verb* **staying, stayed**

S

stead·fast (**sted**-fast) *adjective* Firm and steady or not changing.

stead·y (**sted**-ee)
adjective 1. Uniform and continuous.
2. Firm or stable; not shaky.
3. Sensible, reliable, or dependable.
4. Regular.
verb To stop something from shaking, trembling, or tottering.
▶ *adjective* **steadier, steadiest** ▶ *verb* **steadies, steadying, steadied** ▶ *adverb* **steadily**

steak (stayk) *noun* A thick slice of beef or some other meat or fish. **Steak** sounds like **stake.**

steal (steel)
verb 1. To take something that does not belong to you, without permission and with no thought of returning it. 2. To do something in a secret or tricky way. 3. To get to the next base in baseball without a hit or an error.
noun 1. Something bought at a very low price; a bargain. 2. An instance of stealing a base in baseball.
Steal sounds like **steel.** ▶ *verb* **stealing, stole** (stohl), **stolen** (stohl-in)

stealth·y (**stel**-thee) *adjective* Acting with or characterized by silence, secrecy, and caution. ▶ *adjective* **stealthier, stealthiest** ▶ *noun* **stealth** ▶ *adverb* **stealthily**

steam (steem)
noun 1. The vapor that water turns into when it boils. 2. The mist formed when water vapor condenses.
verb 1. To cook using steam.
2. **steam up** To become covered with condensed water vapor.
idioms 1. **let off steam** or **blow off steam** (informal) To release the energy or angry feelings that you have stored up. 2. **run out of steam** (informal) To lose your energy or enthusiasm.
▶ *verb* **steaming, steamed**

steam·boat (**steem**-boht) *noun* A boat powered by a steam engine.

steam en·gine (**steem** en-jin) *noun* An engine that uses pressurized steam to drive pistons up and down in closed cylinders, which in turn creates the mechanical energy to move a ship,

car, locomotive, or other vehicle forward.

steam·er (**stee**-mur) *noun* 1. A boat powered by steam. 2. A pot or appliance used to cook foods with steam.

steam locomotive (**steem** loh-kuh-**moh**-tiv) *noun* A steam-powered engine used for pulling a train. Steam locomotives were used on most trains in the United States until about 1940.

steam·roll·er (**steem**-roh-lur) *noun* A heavy vehicle with a roller that is used to flatten road surfaces.

steam·ship (**steem**-ship) *noun* A ship powered by a steam engine.

steed (steed) *noun* A horse, especially one that is spirited.

steel (steel)
noun A hard, strong metal made chiefly from iron and carbon, used in heavy construction.
verb To prepare oneself by becoming determined and hard, like steel.
Steel sounds like **steal.** ▶ *verb* **steeling, steeled**

steel band (**steel band**) *noun* A group that plays music on percussion instruments made from oil drums. The depth of each drum determines its pitch.

steel wool (**steel wul**) *noun* A mass of very fine threads of steel. Steel wool is used for cleaning, smoothing, and polishing things.

steep (steep)
adjective 1. Having a sharp rise or slope. 2. Very large or at a rapid rate.
3. Very high.
verb 1. To soak in a liquid for the purpose of cleaning, softening, or drawing the essence out of something. 2. To be full of something.
▶ *adjective* **steeper, steepest** ▶ *verb* **steeping, steeped** ▶ *adverb* **steeply**

stee·ple (**stee**-puhl) *noun* A high tower on a church or other building, often with a spire on top.

stee·ple·chase (**stee**-puhl-chase) *noun* A long horse race that requires jumping over hedges, fences, and ditches.

S

steer (steer)
verb **1.** To make a vehicle go in a particular direction by using a wheel, rudder, or paddle. **2.** To be guided. **3.** To guide or to direct.
noun A young male of the domestic cattle family, raised especially for its beef. ▶ *verb* **steering, steered**

steer·ing wheel (**steer**-ing *weel*) *noun* A wheel in a vehicle that is turned by hand to control its direction.

steg·o·sau·rus (*steg*-uh-**sor**-uhs) *noun* A dinosaur that fed on plants and had bony plates along its back, a small head, and a long tail with spikes. ▶ *noun, plural* **stegosauruses** or **stegosaurus**

stem (stem)
noun The main, upward-growing part of a plant from which the leaves and flowers grow; the stalk.
verb **1. stem from** To originate or come from. **2.** To stop or check the flow or progress of something.
▶ *verb* **stemming, stemmed**

stem cell (**stem** *sel*) *noun* A cell in the body or in an embryo that can develop into different kinds of cells with special purposes.

stench (stench) *noun* An offensive odor. ▶ *noun, plural* **stenches**

sten·cil (**sten**-suhl)
noun A piece of paper, plastic, or metal with letters or a pattern cut out of it. Applying paint or ink over the holes transfers the design to a surface below.
verb To create a design or sign using stencils.
▶ *verb* **stenciling, stenciled**

step (step)
noun **1.** One of the flat surfaces on a stairway where you put your foot. **2.** The distance covered by a step. **3.** The sound of a footstep. **4.** A defined move using your feet in a dance. **5.** A level in a hierarchy. **6.** One of a series of actions taken to make or achieve something. **7.** The difference in pitch between notes in a musical scale. A half step is the difference between two adjacent keys on a piano, such as F and F sharp; a whole step is the difference between most of the notes in a major scale, such as between F and G.
noun, plural **steps** A set of stairs.
verb To move your foot forward and put it down in walking, climbing, or dancing.
idioms **1. step by step** In a gradual and steady way. **2. watch your step** Walk or act carefully.
Step sounds like **steppe.** ▶ *verb* **stepping, stepped**

step·broth·er (**step**-*bruhTH*-ur) *noun* A person's **stepbrother** is that person's stepparent's son from a former marriage.

step·child (**step**-*childe*) *noun* A child that a person's husband or wife had by a former marriage.

step·daugh·ter (**step**-*daw*-tuhr) *noun* A female stepchild.

step·fam·i·ly (**step**-*fam*-uh-lee) *noun* The family of your stepfather or stepmother.

step·fa·ther (**step**-*fah*-THur) *noun* The man who married a person's mother after the death or divorce of the person's father.

step·moth·er (**step**-*muhTH*-ur) *noun* The woman who married a person's father after the death or divorce of the person's mother.

step·par·ent (**step**-*pair*-uhnt) *noun* A stepfather or a stepmother.

steppe (step) *noun* Any of the wide, treeless plains found in southeastern Europe and Asia. **Steppe** sounds like **step.**

step·sis·ter (**step**-*sis*-tur) *noun* A person's **stepsister** is that person's stepparent's daughter from a former marriage.

step·son (**step**-*suhn*) *noun* A male stepchild.

ste·re·o (**ster**-ee-*oh*)
noun A phonograph, radio, or other sound system that uses two or more channels of sound so that the listener hears sounds in a more natural way.
adjective Designed for, reproducing in, or having to do with stereo.

ste·re·o·type (ster-ee-oh-*tipe*)
noun A widely held but overly simple idea, opinion, or image of a person, group, or thing.
verb To have a widely held but overly simple idea, opinion, or image of a person, group, or thing.
▶ *verb* **stereotyping, stereotyped** ▶ *adjective* **stereotypical** (*ster*-ee-oh-**tip**-i-kuhl)

ster·ile (**ster**-uhl) *adjective* Free from germs and dirt.

ster·i·lize (**ster**-uh-*lize*) *verb* To rid something of germs and dirt by exposing it to heat or chemicals.
▶ *verb* **sterilizing, sterilized** ▶ *noun* **sterilization** (*ster*-uh-li-**zay**-shuhn)

ster·ling (**stur**-ling) *noun* The currency of the United Kingdom.

stern (sturn)
adjective Strict or harsh.
noun The rear end of a ship or boat.
▶ *adjective* **sterner, sternest**

ste·roid (**ster**-oid) *noun* A chemical substance found naturally in plants and animals, including humans. The use of steroids by athletes to improve their strength and performance is banned in most sports competitions.

steth·o·scope (**steth**-uh-*skope*) *noun* A medical instrument used by doctors and nurses to listen to the sounds from a patient's heart, lungs, and other parts of the body.

stew (stoo)
noun A dish made of meat or fish and vegetables, boiled or simmered slowly over a long period of time.
verb 1. To cook something for a long time over low heat. 2. To worry about something.
idiom **stew in your own juices** To suffer as a result of your own actions.
▶ *verb* **stewing, stewed** ▶ *adjective* **stewed**

stew·ard (**stoo**-urd) *noun* 1. A man who serves passengers on an airplane or a ship. 2. A person who serves food and drink at a hotel, club, or restaurant.

stew·ard·ess (**stoo**-ur-dis) *noun* A woman who serves passengers, especially on an airplane.

stick (stik)
noun 1. A long, thin piece of wood, especially one that has fallen off a tree. 2. Something shaped like a stick.
verb 1. To fasten or attach one thing to another with something sticky, such as glue or tape. 2. To push a pointed object into or through something else. 3. To remain attached, as if glued. 4. To remain attached or become fixed in a particular position. 5. **stick out** To be prominent, often because the object is higher or longer than other things nearby. 6. **stick up for** (informal) To support or defend a person. 7. **stick to** To continue doing or using something.
▶ *verb* **sticking, stuck** (stuhk)

stick·er (**stik**-ur) *noun* A paper or plastic label with glue on the back.

stick·y (**stik**-ee) *adjective* 1. Tending to stick to things when touched. 2. Uncomfortably humid. 3. Likely to cause upset or hurt feelings, and so difficult to deal with.
▶ *adjective* **stickier, stickiest**

stiff (stif) *adjective* 1. Difficult to bend, stretch, turn, or operate. 2. Difficult to move easily or without pain. 3. Not flowing easily; thick. 4. Severe or difficult to deal with. 5. Not natural or easy in manner; formal. 6. Strong and steady; powerful.
▶ *adjective* **stiffer, stiffest** ▶ *verb* **stiffen** ▶ *adverb* **stiffly**

sti·fle (**stye**-fuhl) *verb* 1. To hold back or to stop. 2. To feel smothered because of a lack of fresh or cool air.
▶ *verb* **stifling, stifled** ▶ *adjective* **stifling**

stig·ma (**stig**-ma) *noun* 1. A mark or sign of disgrace or embarrassment. 2. The tip of the pistil of a flower, where pollen is received.
▶ *noun, plural* **stigmata** (stig-**mat**-uh) *or* **stigmas**

still (stil)
adjective 1. Without sound; silent. 2. Without motion; quiet and calm.
noun A state of quietness.
verb To calm or quiet.
adverb 1. Without moving. 2. Even now, or at a particular time. 3. All the same; nevertheless. 4. Even; yet.

▶ *adjective* **stiller, stillest** ▶ *noun* **stillness**

stilt (stilt) *noun* **1.** One of two poles, each with a rest or strap for the foot, used to raise the wearer above the ground in walking. **2.** One of the posts that holds a building, pier, or other structure above the ground or water level.

stim·u·lant (**stim**-yuh-luhnt) *noun* A substance that stimulates activity in a part of the body. *adjective* Causing increased levels of activity or awareness.

stim·u·late (**stim**-yuh-*late*) *verb* **1.** To encourage something to grow, develop, or become more active. **2.** To make someone interested, excited, or enthusiastic. ▶ *verb* **stimulating, stimulated** ▶ *noun* **stimulation** ▶ *adjective* **stimulating**

stim·u·lus (**stim**-yuh-luhs) *noun* **1.** Anything that excites or causes an action. **2.** Something that causes or speeds up a reaction in a person, an animal, or a plant. Your eyes, ears, and nose receive stimuli from your surroundings. ▶ *noun, plural* **stimuli** (**stim**-yuh-*lye*)

sting (sting) *verb* **1.** To pierce or wound with a small, sharp point. **2.** To hurt with or as if with a sharp, pricking pain. *noun* **1.** A stinger. **2.** An injury caused by an insect or animal's stinging you. **3.** A sensation of heat, tingling, and pain. ▶ *verb* **stinging, stung**

sting·er (**sting**-ur) *noun* A sharp, pointed part of an insect or animal that can be used to sting.

sting·ray (**sting**-ray) *noun* A fish with a flat body; large, winglike fins; and a whiplike tail with poisonous spines that can cause a painful wound.

stin·gy (**stin**-jee) *adjective* Not willing to give or spend money; not generous. ▶ *adjective* **stingier, stingiest** ▶ *adverb* **stingily** (**stin**-juh-lee)

stink (stingk) *verb* **1.** To give off a strong, unpleasant smell. **2.** (slang) To be very bad or worthless. *noun* A bad smell. ▶ *verb* **stinking, stank** (stangk), **stunk** (stuhngk) ▶ *adjective* **stinky**

stir (stur) *verb* **1.** To mix a liquid or soft substance thoroughly by moving a spoon or stick around and around in it. **2.** To move slightly or to become active. **3.** To excite or cause strong feelings in someone. *noun* A state of excitement or disturbance. ▶ *verb* **stirring, stirred**

stir-fry (**stur**-*frye*) *verb* To fry food quickly over high heat in a lightly oiled pan or wok while stirring continuously. ▶ *verb* **stir-fries, stir-frying, stir-fried**

stir·rup (**stur**-uhp *or* **stir**-uhp) *noun* **1.** A ring or loop that hangs down from a saddle and holds a rider's foot. **2.** One of the three small bones in the middle ear. It looks somewhat like a stirrup.

stitch (stich) *noun* **1.** A complete movement of a needle with thread on it, used in sewing and embroidery and to close wounds. **2.** A loop of yarn produced in knitting or crocheting. **3.** A sudden, sharp pain in your side, usually caused by running. *verb* **1.** To make stitches in sewing or knitting. **2.** To close up a wound with stitches. ▶ *noun, plural* **stitches** ▶ *verb* **stitches, stitching, stitched**

St. Kitts and Ne·vis (*saynt* **kits** and **nee**-vis) A two-island nation in the Leeward Islands of the West Indies. St. Kitts is where the first British and French colonies in the Caribbean were established.

St. Lu·cia (*saynt* **loo**-shuh *or saynt* **loo**-see-uh) An island country, part of the Lesser Antilles in the eastern Caribbean Sea. Two Nobel Prize winners—poet Derek Walcott, born in 1930, and economist Arthur Lewis (1915–1991)—were natives of St. Lucia.

S

stock (stahk)
verb 1. To keep a supply of a product to sell. **2. stock up** To gather or store a large supply of something for sale or future use.
noun 1. The supply of merchandise or materials that a factory, warehouse, or store has to sell. 2. Cattle, sheep, pigs, and other animals raised on a ranch or farm; livestock. 3. Water in which meat, fish, or vegetables have been cooked slowly. 4. If you own **stock** in a company, you have invested money in it and own a part of the company. 5. Ancestors.
▶ *verb* **stocking, stocked**

stock·ade (stah-**kade**) *noun* 1. A fence or enclosure made of strong posts set firmly in the ground to protect against attacks. 2. A jail for people in the military.

stock·bro·ker (stahk-*broh*-kur) *noun* A person who buys and sells stocks and shares in companies on behalf of other people.

stock car (stahk khar) *noun* A car for racing, made from a regular model sold to the public.

stock·hold·er (stahk-*hohl*-dur) *noun* A person who owns shares, or stock, in a company.

stock·ing (stah-king) *noun* A tight, knitted covering for the foot and leg.

stock mar·ket (stahk *mahr*-kit) *or* **stock ex·change** (stahk iks-*chaynj*) *noun* A place where stocks and shares in companies are bought and sold.

stock·pile (stahk-*pile*)
verb To gather a large supply of food or weapons in case you run out or face an emergency in the future.
noun A supply of something gathered for present or future use.
▶ *verb* **stockpiling, stockpiled**

stocks (stahks) *noun, plural* A heavy, wooden frame with holes for confining people by their ankles and sometimes wrists, used in the past to punish people publicly for minor offenses.

stock·y (stah-kee) *adjective* Having a short, sturdy build. ▶ *adjective* **stockier, stockiest**

stock·yard (stahk-*yahrd*) *noun* An enclosed area where livestock are kept before being shipped or slaughtered.

stodg·y (stah-jee) *adjective* 1. Very dull or boring. 2. Very old-fashioned and stuffy.
▶ *adjective* **stodgier, stodgiest**

sto·ic (stoh-ik)
noun A person who is not moved or affected by pain or pleasure.
adjective Not showing any emotion or weakness, especially in a difficult situation. You can also use the form *stoical* for this meaning.
▶ *adverb* **stoically**

stoke (stohk) *verb* To add fuel to a fire or furnace. ▶ *verb* **stoking, stoked**

stole (stole) *verb* The past tense of **steal.**

sto·len (stoh-luhn)
verb The past participle of **steal.**
adjective Taken away illegally from the owner.

stom·ach (stuhm-uhk)
noun 1. The muscular, pouchlike organ of your body where chewed food begins to be digested. 2. The front part of your body, between your chest and thighs, containing this organ; the belly or abdomen.
verb To accept or put up with something.
▶ *verb* **stomaching, stomached**

stomp (stahmp)
verb 1. To walk heavily or loudly across a floor. 2. To bang your foot down, especially in anger.
noun The action of stomping, or the sound made by stomping.
▶ *verb* **stomping, stomped**

stone (stone)
noun 1. Naturally hardened mineral matter that is found in the earth; rock. 2. A small piece of this material. 3. A valuable jewel or gem. 4. The hard covering that encloses the seed in the middle of certain fruits.
verb To hit with stones.
▶ *verb* **stoning, stoned** ▶ *adjective* **stony**

Stone Age (stone *ayj*) *noun* A period in history when stone was

S

commonly used to make tools and weapons. Different parts of the world experienced a Stone Age at different times.

stone·wall (**stone**-*wawl*) *verb* To ignore a question, or to stand in the way of an investigation by refusing to give information. ▶ *verb* **stonewalling, stonewalled**

stone·washed (**stone**-*wahsht*) *adjective* Washed with stones that soften and fade the fabric.

stood (stud) *verb* The past tense and past participle of **stand.**

stool (stool) *noun* A seat without a back or arms.

stoop (stoop)
verb 1. To bend forward and down, often with the knees bent. 2. To carry your head and shoulders, or the upper part of your body, bent forward all the time. 3. To lower yourself to do something; to condescend or degrade yourself.
noun 1. A small porch with steps outside a doorway. 2. A standing posture that is slightly bent forward. ▶ *verb* **stooping, stooped**

stop (stahp)
verb 1. To come or bring something to an end. 2. To prevent something from moving, continuing, or operating. 3. To be no longer moving or operating. 4. To close up or block an opening.
noun 1. The act of stopping. 2. One of the regular places on a route where someone or something pauses, such as the place where a bus or train picks up and drops off passengers. 3. A brief stay or visit. ▶ *verb* **stopping, stopped**

stop·light (**stahp**-*lite*) *noun* 1. Another word for **traffic light.** 2. A light on the rear part of a motor vehicle that comes on when the driver steps on the brakes.

stop·per (**stah**-*pur*) *noun* Something that fits into the top of a container to keep the contents from escaping.

stop·watch (**stahp**-*wahch*) *noun* A watch that you can start and stop with

buttons to see how long something takes.

stor·age (**stor**-ij)
noun 1. Space where you can keep something that you are not using. 2. **storage device** A disk, tape, or drive that can be used to store computer files.
phrase **in storage** Put away until it is needed.

store (stor)
noun 1. A place where things are sold. 2. A supply or stock of something kept for future use.
verb 1. To put things away for future use. 2. To copy data into the memory of a computer or onto a floppy disk or other storage device. ▶ *verb* **storing, stored**

store·keep·er (**stor**-*kee*-pur) *noun* A person who owns or runs a store.

stork (stork) *noun* A large wading bird with long, thin legs; a long neck; and a long, straight bill.

storm (storm)
noun 1. Heavy rain, snow, sleet, or hail accompanied by strong winds. Some storms also can have thunder and lightning. 2. A sudden, strong outburst.
verb 1. To attack suddenly or violently. 2. If the weather is very violent with wind, rain, snow, or lightning, you can say **it storms.** 3. **storm out** To leave a place angrily or violently. ▶ *verb* **storming, stormed**

storm·y (**stor**-mee) *adjective* **Stormy** weather is weather in which there is wind and frequent rain or snow, sometimes with thunder and lightning. ▶ *adjective* **stormier, stormiest**

sto·ry (**stor**-ee) *noun* 1. A spoken or written account of something that happened. 2. A tale made up to entertain people. 3. A lie. 4. A floor or level of a building. ▶ *noun, plural* **stories**

stout (stout) *adjective* 1. Quite fat; large and heavily built. 2. Strong and sturdy. 3. Brave or determined. ▶ *adjective* **stouter, stoutest**

S

stove (stohv) *noun* A piece of equipment used for cooking or heating, fueled by gas, electricity, wood, or oil.

stow (stoh) *verb* To put away or to store. ▶ *verb* **stowing, stowed** ▶ *noun* **stowage** (stoh-ij)

stow·a·way (stoh-uh-*way*) *noun* A person who secretly boards a plane, ship, or other vehicle to avoid paying a fare or to escape unnoticed. ▶ *verb* **stow away**

strag·gle (strag-uhl) *verb* To trail slowly behind a group of people; to wander or stray. ▶ *verb* **straggling, straggled** ▶ *noun* **straggler**

straight (strayt)
adjective **1.** Without a curve or bend. **2.** Not curly or not wavy. **3.** Not crooked or not stooping. **4.** Level or even. **5.** Honest, sincere, or correct.
adverb Immediately or directly.
Straight sounds like **strait.** ▶ *adjective* **straighter, straightest**

straight·a·way (strayt-uh-*way*)
adverb Immediately; at once.
noun A section of a road or racetrack that doesn't curve.

straight·en (stray-tuhn) *verb* **1.** If you **straighten** something **out** or **up,** you put it in the proper order. **2.** To make something straight or to become straight.
▶ *verb* **straightening, straightened**

straight·for·ward (strayt-**for**-wurd) *adjective* **1.** Honest and open. **2.** Easy to understand.

strain (strayn)
verb **1.** To draw or pull tight; to stretch. **2.** To pour a mostly liquid substance through a sieve or colander to separate out the solid pieces. **3.** To injure a muscle by making it work too hard. **4.** To make as much of an effort as you possibly can to do something.
noun A state of tension or exhaustion.
▶ *verb* **straining, strained** ▶ *noun* **strainer** ▶ *adjective* **strained**

strait (strayt)
noun A narrow strip of water that connects two larger bodies of water.
idiom **dire straits** A very difficult

situation.
Strait sounds like **straight.**

strand (strand)
noun **1.** One of the lengths of thread or wire that are twisted together to form a rope, string, or cable. **2.** Something that looks like a thread. **3.** Something made up of objects strung or twisted together. **4.** An area of seafront.
verb **1.** To force onto the shore; to drive onto a beach, reef, or sandbar. **2.** To leave in a strange or unpleasant place, especially without any money or way to depart.
▶ *verb* **stranding, stranded**

strange (straynj) *adjective* **1.** Different from the usual; odd or peculiar. **2.** Not known, heard, or seen before; not familiar. **3.** Ill at ease; not comfortable.
▶ *adjective* **stranger, strangest** ▶ *noun* **strangeness** ▶ *adverb* **strangely**

strang·er (strayn-jur) *noun* **1.** Someone you do not recognize and have never met. **2.** A newcomer or an outsider.

stran·gle (strang-guhl) *verb* **1.** To kill someone by squeezing the person's throat and cutting off his or her air supply. **2.** To be unable to breathe; to choke.
▶ *verb* **strangling, strangled** ▶ *noun* **strangler** ▶ *noun* **strangulation** (*strang*-gyuh-**lay**-shuhn)

strap (strap)
noun A strip of leather or some other flexible material used to fasten, carry, or hold on to someone or something.
verb To use a strap to fasten or to hold things in place.
▶ *verb* **strapping, strapped**

strat·e·gy (strat-i-jee) *noun* A clever plan for winning a military battle or achieving a goal. ▶ *noun, plural* **strategies** ▶ *noun* **strategist**
▶ *adjective* **strategic** (struh-**tee**-jik)
▶ *adverb* **strategically**

strat·o·sphere (strat-uh-*sfeer*) *noun* The layer of the earth's atmosphere that begins about 8 miles (13 kilometers) above the earth and ends about 31 miles (50 kilometers) above the earth.

straw (straw) *noun* **1.** The dried stalks of wheat, barley, oats, or other cereal

S

plants that are left after the grain has been removed. **2.** A thin, hollow plastic or paper tube used to suck liquid from a container.

straw·ber·ry (**straw**-ber-ee) *noun* The red, juicy fruit of a small, low plant of the rose family. ▶ *noun, plural* **strawberries**

stray (stray)
verb To wander off without a destination; to become lost.
noun A cat or dog that has wandered away from its home or that has no home.
adjective Without a home; wandering about.
▶ *verb* **straying, strayed**

streak (streek)
noun **1.** A long, thin mark or stripe. **2.** A character trait. **3.** A small series of events.
verb To move very fast.
▶ *verb* **streaking, streaked** ▶ *adjective* **streaky**

stream (streem)
noun **1.** A body of flowing water, especially a brook or a small river. **2.** A steady flow of anything.
verb **1.** To move or flow steadily. **2.** To float or to wave in the wind. **3.** To watch or listen to video or music at the same time that it is being downloaded to your computer.
▶ *verb* **streaming, streamed**

stream·er (**stree**-mur) *noun* A long, thin strip of cloth, ribbon, or colored paper used as a decoration.

stream·lined (**streem**-lined) *adjective* **1.** Designed or shaped to minimize resistance to air or water. **2.** Made simpler or more efficient.

street (street) *noun* **1.** A road in a city or town, often with sidewalks, houses, or other buildings along it. **2.** Everyone who lives or works on a street.

street·car (**street**-kahr) *noun* An electricity-powered vehicle that holds many passengers and runs on rails through city streets; a trolley.

street·light (**street**-lite) *noun* A light mounted on a pole by the side of a street to help drivers and pedestrians see at night.

street·wise (**street**-wize) *adjective* Having the skills and experience needed to survive in a difficult or dangerous, usually urban, environment.

strength (strengkth *or* strength) *noun* **1.** The quality of being strong; force; power. **2.** The power to resist or hold up under strain or stress; toughness. **3.** A good quality or something at which you excel.

strength·en (**streng**-thuhn) *verb* To make stronger. ▶ *verb* **strengthening, strengthened**

stren·u·ous (**stren**-yoo-uhs) *adjective* **1.** Requiring great energy or effort. **2.** Very active or energetic.
▶ *adverb* **strenuously**

stress (stres)
noun **1.** Mental or emotional strain or pressure. **2.** Emphasis in pronunciation.
verb **1.** To emphasize one or more syllables within a word. **2.** To emphasize something because you think it's important.
▶ *noun, plural* **stresses** ▶ *verb* **stresses, stressing, stressed** ▶ *adjective* **stressful**

stretch (strech)
verb **1.** To spread out your arms, legs, or body to full length. **2.** To extend or spread out over an area. **3.** To make something reach or extend farther. **4. stretch out** To lie fully extended.
noun **1.** An unbroken period of time. **2.** An unbroken length or distance. **3.** An act of stretching a part of your body.
▶ *verb* **stretches, stretching, stretched** ▶ *noun, plural* **stretches**

stretch·er (**strech**-ur) *noun* A piece of canvas attached to two poles, used for carrying an injured or sick person.

strew (stroo) *verb* **1.** To scatter, sprinkle, or throw here and there. **2.** To cover a surface with things that have been scattered or sprinkled.
▶ *verb* **strewing, strewed, strewn** (stroon)

S

strict (strikt) *adjective* **1.** Demanding that the rules be followed exactly. **2.** Enforced all the time. **3.** Complete or absolute.
▶ *adjective* **stricter, strictest** ▶ *noun* **strictness** ▶ *adverb* **strictly**

stride (stride)
verb To take long, energetic steps.
noun The way a person runs or walks.
▶ *verb* **striding, strode** (strode), **stridden** (strid-uhn)

strife (strife) *noun* A bitter conflict between enemies; a fight or a struggle.

strike (strike)
verb **1.** To hit or attack suddenly and forcefully. **2.** To announce the time with a chime or other sound. **3.** To make an impression on someone or to seem to be something. **4.** To find or discover suddenly. **5.** To light a match by rubbing it quickly and forcefully against something rough. **6.** To refuse to go to work until an employer meets certain demands.
noun **1.** A situation in which workers refuse to work until their demands are met. **2.** In baseball, a ball pitched over the plate between the batter's chest and knees, or any pitch that is swung at and missed. **3.** In bowling, the act of knocking down all ten pins with the first ball.
▶ *verb* **striking, struck** (struhk) ▶ *noun* **striker**

strik·ing (strye-king) *adjective* Attracting attention or notice. ▶ *adverb* **strikingly**

string (string)
noun **1.** A thin cord or rope made of twisted fiber. **2.** A thin cord of wire, gut, or nylon on a musical instrument such as a guitar or violin. **3.** A number of things of the same or similar kind all in a row.
verb **1.** To run a cord, thread, or piece of wire through a row of objects. **2.** To put the strings on an instrument.
adjective **strung out** Very tense or nervous about something.
▶ *verb* **stringing, strung** (struhng) ▶ *adjective* **stringed**

string bean (**string** *been*) *noun* A long, thin, green pod that is eaten as a vegetable.

strings (stringz) *noun, plural* Stringed instruments that are played with a bow or plucked.

strip (strip)
verb **1.** To take off clothing; to undress. **2.** To pull, tear, or take something off.
noun A long, narrow piece of something.
▶ *verb* **stripping, stripped**

stripe (stripe)
noun A narrow band of color.
verb To decorate with stripes.
▶ *verb* **striping, striped** ▶ *adjective* **striped**

strive (strive) *verb* To try very hard to achieve or prevent something. ▶ *verb* **striving, strove** (strohv), **striven** (striv-in)

strobe (strohb) *noun* A device that produces very brief, high-intensity flashes of light.

stroke (strohk)
verb To draw your hand gently over the surface of something.
noun **1.** An unexpected action or event that has a powerful effect. **2.** A hit or a blow. **3.** A mark made by a pen, pencil, or brush. **4.** A sudden lack of oxygen in part of the brain caused by the blocking or breaking of a blood vessel. **5.** A movement of the hand over something. **6.** One of a series of repeated movements in swimming or rowing, or a method of hitting the ball in tennis.
▶ *verb* **stroking, stroked**

stroll (strohl)
noun A slow, relaxed walk.
verb To walk in a slow or casual way.
▶ *verb* **strolling, strolled**

strol·ler (stroh-lur) *noun* A small, folding carriage for a baby or small child to sit in and be pushed around.

strong (strawng) *adjective* **1.** Physically powerful or exerting great force. **2.** Tough, firm, long-lasting, or hard to break. **3.** Having a sharp or bitter taste or odor.
▶ *adjective* **stronger, strongest**
▶ *adverb* **strongly**

S

strong·hold (**strawng**-hohld) *noun* A place that is well protected against attack or danger.

struc·ture (**struhk**-chur)
noun 1. Something that has been built, such as a house, an office building, a bridge, or a dam. 2. How something is arranged, organized, or put together.
verb To arrange, organize, or put something together in a particular way.
▶ *adjective* **structural**

strug·gle (**struhg**-uhl)
verb 1. To try very hard or make a great effort to do something. 2. To fight or compete with someone. 3. To fight against a problem or difficulty.
noun A situation in which someone encounters difficulties and obstacles.
▶ *verb* **struggling, struggled**

strum (struhm) *verb* To play a musical instrument such as a guitar or harp by sweeping your thumb or fingers over the strings. ▶ *verb* **strumming, strummed**

strut (struht)
verb To walk with a swagger or in a proud way.
noun A wooden or metal bar designed to brace or stabilize a structure.
▶ *verb* **strutting, strutted**

stub (stuhb)
noun A short part of something that remains after the rest has been used or torn off.
verb To accidentally hit something with your toe or foot.
▶ *verb* **stubbing, stubbed** ▶ *adjective* **stubby**

stub·ble (**stuhb**-uhl) *noun* 1. Short, spiky stalks of corn or grain that are left in the ground after harvesting. 2. The short, stiff hairs that grow on a man's face when he has not shaved for a while.
▶ *adjective* **stubbly**

stub·born (**stuhb**-urn) *adjective* 1. Not willing to give in or change; set on having your own way. 2. Hard to treat or deal with.

▶ *noun* **stubbornness** ▶ *adverb* **stubbornly**

stuck (stuhk)
verb The past tense and past participle of **stick**.
adjective Firmly fixed in a position and not able to move or be moved.
phrases 1. If you are **stuck in** a place, you are not able to leave it. 2. If you are **stuck with** something or someone, you are not able to get rid of it or of him or her.

stu·dent (**stoo**-duhnt) *noun* 1. A person who studies at a school. 2. A person who studies or observes something on his or her own.

stu·di·o (**stoo**-dee-oh) *noun* 1. A room or building in which an artist, dancer, or photographer works or practices. 2. A place where movies, television and radio shows, or recordings are made. 3. A place that transmits radio or television programs. 4. A one-room apartment.

stu·di·ous (**stoo**-dee-uhs) *adjective* Liking or tending to study very hard. ▶ *noun* **studiousness** ▶ *adverb* **studiously**

stud·y (**stuhd**-ee)
verb 1. To spend time learning a subject or skill by reading about it or by practicing it. 2. To look at something closely.
noun 1. A room used for studying or reading. 2. A detailed experiment aimed at getting information, or a report written as a result of this.
▶ *verb* **studies, studying, studied** ▶ *noun, plural* **studies**

stuff (stuhf)
noun 1. The substance, material, or ingredients out of which something is made. 2. Personal belongings. 3. Useless or worthless things; junk.
verb 1. To cram something into a container; to fill a space tightly. 2. To fill the inside of something. 3. To fill yourself with too much food.
adjective **stuffed up** Having a blocked nose because of a cold or an allergy.
▶ *verb* **stuffing, stuffed**

S

stuff·ing (**stuhf**-ing) *noun* **1.** Soft material used to fill pillows, cushions, and other articles made of or covered with cloth. **2.** A mixture of chopped food that is cooked inside poultry or meat or a hollowed-out vegetable.

stuf·fy (**stuhf**-ee) *adjective* **1.** Hard to breathe in because it lacks fresh air. **2.** Dull, old-fashioned, and narrow-minded. ▶ *adjective* **stuffier, stuffiest** ▶ *adverb* **stuffily** ▶ *noun* **stuffiness**

stum·ble (**stuhm**-buhl) *verb* **1.** To trip and lose your balance briefly; to walk unsteadily. **2.** To speak or act in a blundering or confused way. **3. stumble on** *or* **stumble upon** To come upon or discover something unexpectedly. ▶ *verb* **stumbling, stumbled**

stump (stuhmp) *noun* **1.** The part of a tree trunk that is left in the ground after a tree has been cut down. **2.** A piece of something that remains after the rest of it has broken off or worn away. *verb* (informal) To puzzle or to confuse. ▶ *verb* **stumping, stumped**

stump·y (**stuhm**-pee) *adjective* Short and thick, like a stump. ▶ *adjective* **stumpier, stumpiest**

stun (stuhn) *verb* To shock, overwhelm, or knock unconscious. ▶ *verb* **stunning, stunned**

stung (stuhng) *verb* The past tense and past participle of **sting.**

stunk (stuhngk) *verb* The past participle of **stink.**

stun·ning (**stuhn**-ing) *adjective* **1.** (informal) Extremely beautiful or attractive. **2.** Amazing or remarkable. **3.** Hard enough to knock you out. ▶ *adverb* **stunningly**

stunt (stuhnt) *noun* **1.** An act that shows great skill or daring. **2.** Something that is done to show off or attract attention. **3. stunt person** A person who takes the place of an actress or actor in an action scene or when a special skill or great risk is involved. Also known as a *stunt man, stunt woman,* or *stunt double.* *verb* To stop the growth or development of something. ▶ *verb* **stunting, stunted** ▶ *adjective* **stunted**

stu·pen·dous (stoo-**pen**-duhs) *adjective* Amazing or awesome. ▶ *adverb* **stupendously**

stu·pid (**stoo**-pid) *adjective* **1.** Slow to learn or understand; not intelligent. **2.** Lacking common sense; foolish or silly. ▶ *adjective* **stupider, stupidest** ▶ *noun* **stupidity** (stoo-**pid**-i-tee) ▶ *adverb* **stupidly**

stur·dy (**stur**-dee) *adjective* Strong and solidly made or built. ▶ *adjective* **sturdier, sturdiest**

stur·geon (**stur**-juhn) *noun* A large food fish covered with rows of bony, pointed scales. Its eggs, called caviar, are also eaten.

stut·ter (**stuht**-ur) *verb* To involuntarily repeat the first sound or syllable of a word before saying the whole word. *noun* A way of speaking in which sounds or syllables are repeated uncontrollably. ▶ *verb* **stuttering, stuttered** ▶ *noun* **stutterer**

St. Vin·cent and the Gren·a·dines (saynt **vin**-suhnt and THuh gren-uh-**deenz**) An island nation in the Lesser Antilles, where the Caribbean Sea meets the Atlantic Ocean. It consists of the main island, St. Vincent, and the northern two-thirds of the chain of islands known as the Grenadines, which extend from St. Vincent south to the island nation of Grenada.

sty (stye) *noun* **1.** A pen or enclosed area where pigs live. **2.** A small, inflamed swelling on the rim of an eyelid. ▶ *noun, plural* **sties** *or* **styes**

style (stile) *noun* **1.** The way in which something is written, spoken, made, or done. **2.** The way in which people act and dress in a particular time period, especially

S

the most recent one; fashion. **3.** A particular way that someone's hair is arranged. **4.** An elegant manner. **5.** The slender structure that joins the ovary of a flower to the stigma.
verb To arrange or design something in a particular way.
▶ *verb* **styling, styled** ▶ *noun* **stylist**

sty·lish (**stye**-lish) *adjective* Displaying the latest style; fashionable. ▶ *adverb* **stylishly**

sty·lus (**stye**-luhs) *noun* A small stick that you use like a pen to input data to some devices.

Sty·ro·foam (**stye**-ruh-*fohm*) *noun* The trademark for a very lightweight, rigid plastic that is used in many items, from building insulation to drinking cups.

suave (swahv) *adjective* Pleasant, charming, and attractive, but perhaps not to be trusted. ▶ *adjective* **suaver, suavest**

sub·con·scious (suhb-**kahn**-shuhs) *noun* The part of the mind where hidden thoughts are, as well as feelings of which you are not aware.
adjective Present but not immediately available to your awareness.
▶ *adverb* **subconsciously**

sub·con·ti·nent (suhb-**kahn**-tuh-nuhnt) *noun* A large area of land that is part of a continent but is considered a separate geographical or political unit.

sub·di·vide (*suhb*-duh-**vide**) *verb* **1.** To divide something that has already been divided into even smaller parts. **2.** To divide an area of land into lots for building homes.
▶ *verb* **subdividing, subdivided**
▶ *noun* **subdivision** (*suhb*-duh-*vizh*-uhn)

sub·due (suhb-**doo**) *verb* **1.** To defeat in battle; to conquer. **2.** To control.
▶ *verb* **subduing, subdued**

sub·dued (suhb-**dood**) *adjective* **1.** Unusually quiet and thoughtful. **2.** Not harsh; muted.

sub·ject
noun (**suhb**-jikt) **1.** The person or thing that is discussed, studied, dealt with,

or written about. **2.** An area of study in a school or college. **3.** A word or group of words in a sentence that tells who or what performs the action expressed by the verb. In the sentence "John likes milk," *John* is the subject. **4.** A person or thing that is studied or examined. **5.** A person who lives in a kingdom or under the authority of a king or queen.
adjective (**suhb**-jikt) **subject to** Having a tendency to be affected by something, especially if it is something unpleasant.
verb (suhb-**jekt**) To force someone to go through an unpleasant experience.
▶ *verb* **subjecting, subjected**

sub·jec·tive (suhb-**jek**-tiv) *adjective* Of or having to do with your feelings, tastes, or opinions rather than with facts. ▶ *adverb* **subjectively**

sub·ma·rine (**suhb**-muh-*reen* or *suhb*-muh-**reen**) *noun* A ship that can travel both on the surface and under the water.

sub·merge (suhb-**murj**) *verb* **1.** To sink or plunge beneath the surface of a liquid, especially water. **2.** To cover with water or another liquid.
▶ *verb* **submerging, submerged**

sub·mis·sion (suhb-**mish**-uhn) *noun* **1.** Acceptance of or giving in to the will or authority of someone or something. **2.** A proposal, application, or some other document that is submitted for consideration or judgment.

sub·mit (suhb-**mit**) *verb* **1.** To propose, offer, hand in, or present something. **2.** To give in to or to agree to obey someone or something.
▶ *verb* **submitting, submitted**

sub·or·di·nate
adjective (suh-**bor**-duh-nit) Less important; lower in rank.
noun (suh-**bor**-duh-nit) A person who is under the authority or control of someone else and can therefore be told what to do.
verb (suh-**bor**-duh-*nate*) To make one thing less important than another.
▶ *verb* **subordinating, subordinated**

S

sub·scribe (suhb-**skribe**) *verb* **1.** To pay money regularly for a product or service such as a newspaper, magazine, or cable television. **2.** To agree with or go along with a belief or an idea.
▶ *verb* **subscribing, subscribed** ▶ *noun* **subscriber** ▶ *noun* **subscription**

sub·se·quent (**suhb**-si-kwuhnt) *adjective* Coming after something in time, place, or order. ▶ *adverb* **subsequently**

sub·set (**suhb**-*set*) *noun* A set of items that are all contained within a larger set. For example, the numbers 1 through 10 are a subset of the numbers 1 through 1,000.

sub·side (suhb-**side**) *verb* **1.** To sink to a lower or more normal level. **2.** To become less intense or active.
▶ *verb* **subsiding, subsided**

sub·sid·i·ar·y (suhb-**sid**-ee-*er*-ee) *adjective* Related but not as important; secondary.
noun A company that is owned or controlled by a larger company.

sub·si·dy (**suhb**-si-dee) *noun* Money that a government or person contributes to help a worthy enterprise or to keep the price of a product or service low. ▶ *noun, plural* **subsidies** ▶ *verb* **subsidize** (**suhb**-si-*dize*)

sub·stance (**suhb**-stuhns) *noun* **1.** Something that has weight and takes up space; matter. **2.** The physical matter of which someone or something is made. **3.** The most important or essential part of something; the gist.

sub·stan·tial (suhb-**stan**-shuhl) *adjective* **1.** Of great size, value, or importance. **2.** Solidly built; strong or firm. **3.** Not imaginary; real.

sub·stan·tial·ly (suhb-**stan**-shuh-lee) *adverb* **1.** To a significant extent. **2.** For the most part.

sub·sti·tute (**suhb**-sti-*toot*) *noun* Something or someone acting or used in place of another, such as a teacher who takes over when another teacher is ill.
verb To put, use, or be one thing or

person in place of another.
▶ *verb* **substituting, substituted** ▶ *noun* **substitution** (suhb-sti-**too**-shuhn)

sub·ti·tle (**suhb**-*tye*-tuhl) *noun* A second title that explains the main title of a book, movie, play, essay, or song.
noun, plural **subtitles** The translated words that appear at the bottom of the screen when a foreign-language movie or television program is shown.

sub·tle (**suht**-uhl) *adjective* **1.** Not strong; faint or delicate. **2.** Clever and not overly obvious.
▶ *adjective* **subtler, subtlest** ▶ *noun* **subtlety** (**suht**-uhl-tee) ▶ *noun* **subtleness** ▶ *adverb* **subtly** (**sut**-uh-lee)

sub·tract (suhb-**trakt**) *verb* To take one number or amount away from another. ▶ *verb* **subtracting, subtracted**

sub·trac·tion (suhb-**trak**-shuhn) *noun* The operation in arithmetic of taking away one quantity from another.

sub·tra·hend (**suhb**-truh-*hend*) *noun* A number that is subtracted from another number. In the equation $7 - 4 = 3$, 4 is the subtrahend.

sub·urb (**suhb**-urb) *noun* An area or a district on or close to the outer edge of a city. A suburb is made up mostly of homes, with few businesses. ▶ *noun* **suburbia** (suh-**bur**-bee-uh) ▶ *noun* **suburbanite** (suh-**bur**-buh-*nite*) ▶ *adjective* **suburban**

sub·way (**suhb**-*way*) *noun* An electric train or a system of trains that runs underground in a city.

suc·ceed (suhk-**seed**) *verb* **1.** To achieve or accomplish something. **2.** To have or to enjoy success. **3.** To come after and take the place left by someone else.
▶ *verb* **succeeding, succeeded**

suc·cess (suhk-**ses**) *noun* **1.** A good or favorable outcome; desired results. **2.** A person or thing that has achieved success.
▶ *noun, plural* **successes**

S

suc·cess·ful (suhk-**ses**-fuhl) *adjective*
1. Producing a favorable and intended result. 2. Able to do something well and make money at it.
▸ *adverb* **successfully**

suc·ces·sion (suhk-**sesh**-uhn) *noun*
1. A number of persons or things that follow one after another in order; a series. 2. The coming of one person or thing after another. 3. The order in which one person after another takes over a title, a throne, or a political office.

suc·cess·ive (suhk-**ses**-iv) *adjective* Following in order or sequence. ▸ *adverb* **successively**

suc·ces·sor (suhk-**ses**-ur) *noun* One who follows another in a position or sequence.

suc·cu·lent (**suhk**-yuh-luhnt) *adjective* Full of juice.
noun A plant, such as a cactus, that has thick, fleshy leaves for storing moisture.
▸ *noun* **succulence**

such (suhch)
adjective 1. Of the same or that kind. 2. Like, or similar. 3. So much, or so great.
pronoun Others of that kind.

suck (suhk) *verb* 1. To draw air or a liquid into your mouth by using your lungs, tongue, or lips. 2. To pull strongly or draw in. 3. To hold something in your mouth as if you were sucking.
▸ *verb* **sucking, sucked**

suck·er (**suhk**-ur) *noun* 1. A body part of certain animals that is used to stick to surfaces. 2. (slang) A person who is easily cheated or fooled. 3. A piece of candy, such as a lollipop, that is held in the mouth until it dissolves.

suc·tion (**suhk**-shuhn) *noun* The act of drawing air out of a space to create a vacuum. This causes the surrounding air or liquid to be sucked into the empty space.

Su·dan (soo-**dan**) A country in northeast Africa. It is the largest country in Africa, and it is also the largest Arab country. Lord Kitchener,

a governor-general of Sudan when it was a British colony, laid out the streets of its capital, Khartoum, in the shape of the British flag. Since gaining independence in 1956, Sudan has endured famines and two civil wars.

sud·den (**suhd**-uhn) *adjective* 1. Happening without warning; unexpected. 2. Quick, hasty, or abrupt.
▸ *noun* **suddenness** ▸ *adverb* **suddenly**

sud·den in·fant death syn·drome (**suhd**-uhn **in**-fuhnt **deth** sin-drohm) *noun* The death, usually during sleep, of a seemingly healthy infant for no known cause. Also known as *SIDS*.

suds (suhdz) *noun, plural* The bubbles that form on top of a substance, such as water, that contains soap.

sue (soo) *verb* To start a suit or case against someone in a court of law. ▸ *verb* **suing, sued**

suede (swayd) *noun* Soft leather with a velvety finish on one side.

su·et (**soo**-it) *noun* A hard fat from cattle and sheep that is used in cooking.

suf·fer (**suhf**-ur) *verb* 1. To have pain, discomfort, or sorrow. 2. To experience or undergo something unpleasant. 3. To be damaged, or to become worse.
▸ *verb* **suffering, suffered** ▸ *noun* **suffering**

suf·fer·er (**suhf**-ur-ur) *noun* Someone who must endure a condition, illness, or something unpleasant.

suf·fi·cient (suh-**fish**-uhnt) *adjective* As much as is needed; adequate. ▸ *adverb* **sufficiently**

suf·fix (**suhf**-iks) *noun* A syllable or syllables added at the end of a word or root that changes its meaning. For example, in *sadness* the suffix is *-ness*. ▸ *noun, plural* **suffixes**

suf·fo·cate (**suhf**-uh-*kate*) *verb* 1. To kill by cutting off the supply of air or oxygen. 2. To die from lack of oxygen. 3. To have difficulty breathing.
▸ *verb* **suffocating, suffocated** ▸ *noun* **suffocation** (*suhf*-uh-**kay**-shuhn)

S

suf·frage (**suhf**-rij) *noun* The right to vote.

sug·ar (**shug**-ur) *noun* A sweet substance that comes from sugar beets and sugarcane and is used in foods and drinks. ▶ *adjective* **sugary** (**shug**-ur-ee)

sug·ar beet (**shug**-ur *beet*) *noun* A vegetable with fleshy white roots from which sugar is produced.

sugar·cane (**shug**-ur-kane) *noun* A tropical grass whose tall, woody stems are used to make sugar.

sug·gest (suhg-**jest** *or* suh-**jest**) *verb* 1. To mention something as an idea, a plan, or a possibility. 2. To bring or call to mind. 3. To hint or show indirectly. ▶ *verb* **suggesting, suggested**

sug·ges·tion (suhg-**jes**-chuhn *or* suh-**jes**-chuhn) *noun* 1. Something that you suggest, such as an idea, a piece of advice, or a plan. 2. A small but noticeable amount.

su·i·cide (**soo**-i-side) *noun* The act of killing oneself on purpose. ▶ *adjective* **suicidal** (soo-i-**sye**-duhl) ▶ *adverb* **suicidally**

suit (soot)
noun 1. A set of matching clothes, usually a man's jacket and pants or a woman's jacket and skirt. 2. One of the sets into which playing cards are divided. The four suits are clubs, diamonds, hearts, and spades. 3. A case that is brought before a court of law; a lawsuit.
verb 1. To be acceptable or convenient; to be right or appropriate for someone or something. 2. To look good on someone. ▶ *verb* **suiting, suited**

suit·a·ble (**soo**-tuh-buhl) *adjective* Right for a particular purpose, occasion or condition. ▶ *noun* **suitability** (soo-tuh-**bil**-i-tee) ▶ *adverb* **suitably**

suit·case (**soot**-kase) *noun* A flat case with a handle and a hinged lid, used for carrying clothes and belongings when you travel.

suite (sweet) *noun* 1. A group of rooms that are connected. 2. A set of matching furniture or other items. 3. A piece of music made up of several parts.

suit·or (**soo**-tur) *noun* A man who courts a woman.

sul·fur (**suhl**-fur) *noun* A yellow chemical element used in gunpowder, matches, and fertilizer.

sul·fur di·ox·ide (**suhl**-fur dye-**ahk**-side) *noun* A poisonous gas found in some industrial waste. Sulfur dioxide causes air pollution.

sulk (suhlk)
verb To be angry, resentful, or disappointed but also very quiet and withdrawn.
noun A bad mood in which someone doesn't speak very much. ▶ *verb* **sulking, sulked** ▶ *adjective* **sulky**

sul·len (**suhl**-uhn) *adjective* Gloomy and silent because you feel angry, bitter, or hurt. ▶ *adverb* **sullenly**

sul·tan (**suhl**-tuhn) *noun* An emperor or ruler of some Muslim countries.

sul·try (**suhl**-tree) *adjective* Very hot and humid. ▶ *adjective* **sultrier, sultriest** ▶ *noun* **sultriness**

sum (suhm)
noun 1. A particular amount of money. 2. A number that you get from adding two or more numbers together. 3. **sum** *or* **sum total** The whole or final amount.
verb **sum up** To briefly summarize the main points.
Sum sounds like **some.** ▶ *verb* **summing, summed**

su·mac (**soo**-mak) *noun* A bush or tree with pointed leaves and clusters of flowers or red berries.

sum·ma·ry (**suhm**-ur-ee) *noun* A brief statement that gives the main points or ideas of something that has been said or written. ▶ *noun, plural* **summaries** ▶ *verb* **summarize**

sum·mer (**suhm**-ur) *noun* The season after spring and before autumn, when the days are long and the weather is warm. ▶ *adjective* **summery**

S

sum·mit (**suhm**-it) *noun* 1. The highest point; the top. 2. A meeting of the heads of government or highest officials from different countries.

sum·mon (**suhm**-uhn) *verb* 1. To request or to order that someone come or appear. 2. To make an effort to show a certain quality or response.
▸ *verb* **summoning, summoned**

sum·mons (**suhm**-uhnz) *noun* An order to appear in a court of law. ▸ *noun, plural* **summonses** ▸ *verb* **summons**

su·mo wres·tling (**soo**-moh **res**-ling) *noun* A Japanese form of wrestling. ▸ *noun* **sumo wrestler**

sun (suhn)
noun 1. The star that the earth and other planets revolve around and that gives us light and warmth. Sometimes capitalized as *Sun.* 2. Any star that is the center of a system of planets. 3. The light or warmth that comes from the sun.
verb To sit or lie in the sun.
Sun sounds like **son.** ▸ *verb* **sunning, sunned**

sun·bathe (**suhn**-bayTH) *verb* To sit or lie in the sun so you can get a suntan. ▸ *verb* **sunbathing, sunbathed** ▸ *noun* **sunbath** (**suhn**-bath)

sun·burn (**suhn**-burn) *noun* Redness or blistering of the skin caused by spending too much time in the sun. ▸ *adjective* **sunburned** or **sunburnt**

sun·dae (**suhn**-day or **suhn**-dee) *noun* Ice cream served with one or more toppings, such as syrup, whipped cream, nuts, or fruit.

Sun·day (**suhn**-day or **suhn**-dee) *noun* The first day of the week, after Saturday and before Monday.

sun·di·al (**suhn**-dye-uhl) *noun* An instrument that shows the time with a pointer that casts a shadow on a flat dial similar to the face of a clock.

sun·down (**suhn**-doun) *noun* Sunset, the time of day just before nightfall, when the sun dips below the horizon.

sun·flow·er (**suhn**-flou-ur) *noun* A large flower with yellow petals and a dark center, grown for its edible seeds and their oil.

sung (suhng) *verb* The past participle of **sing.**

sun·glass·es (**suhn**-glas-iz) *noun, plural* Eyeglasses with a dark tint that protects your eyes from the glare of sunlight.

sunk (sungk) *verb* The past participle of **sink.**

sunk·en (**suhng**-kuhn) *adjective* 1. Below the surface. 2. Below the other areas nearby.

sun·light (**suhn**-lite) *noun* The light of the sun.

sun·rise (**suhn**-rize) *noun* The event or the time of day when the sun first appears above the eastern horizon.

sun·screen (**suhn**-skreen) *noun* A substance containing a chemical that protects the skin from the harmful rays of the sun.

sun·set (**suhn**-set) *noun* The event or the time in the evening when the sun sinks below the western horizon.

sun·shine (**suhn**-shine) *noun* The light from the sun or the sun's direct rays.

sun·stroke (**suhn**-strohk) *noun* An illness caused by too much exposure to the sun. Symptoms of sunstroke include fever, dizziness, and headaches.

sun·tan (**suhn**-tan) *noun* A darkening of the skin as a result of being out in the sun. ▸ *adjective* **suntanned**

su·per (**soo**-pur)
adjective Very good; excellent.
noun (informal) Short for **superintendent.**

su·perb (soo-**purb**) *adjective* Excellent or outstanding. ▸ *adverb* **superbly** (soo-**purb**-lee)

su·per·fi·cial (soo-pur-**fish**-uhl) *adjective* 1. Existing or happening on the surface. 2. Concerned only with what is obvious and easy to understand; not deep or thorough.
▸ *adverb* **superficially**

su·per·flu·ous (su-**pur**-floo-uhs) *adjective* More than is needed or wanted; not necessary.

S

su·per·her·o (*soo*-pur-*heer*-oh) *noun* A fictional character with superhuman powers such as extraordinary strength or the ability to fly. ▶ *noun, plural* **superheroes**

su·per·hu·man (*soo*-pur-**hyoo**-muhn) *adjective* Having or requiring characteristics or abilities beyond those of an ordinary human.

su·per·in·ten·dent (*soo*-pur-in-**ten**-duhnt) *noun* **1.** An official who directs or manages an organization. **2.** A person in charge of a building; a janitor or custodian.

su·pe·ri·or (su-**peer**-ee-ur) *adjective* **1.** Higher in rank or position. **2.** Above average in quality or ability; excellent. **3.** Believing that or behaving as if you are better than other people. *noun* A person who has a higher rank or position than others.
▶ *noun* **superiority** (su-*peer*-ee-**or**-i-tee)

su·per·la·tive (su-**pur**-luh-tiv) *adjective* **1. Superlative** adjectives and adverbs are used to describe the highest degree of a certain quality. *Largest* is the superlative form of *large*, and *most difficult* is the superlative form of *difficult*. **2.** The very best. *noun* A superlative adverb or adjective.
▶ *adverb* **superlatively**

su·per·mar·ket (*soo*-pur-*mahr*-kit) *noun* A large self-service store that sells food and household goods.

su·per·nat·u·ral (*soo*-pur-**nach**-ur-uhl) *noun* Things that exist outside normal human experience or knowledge. *adjective* Existing outside normal human experience or knowledge.
▶ *adverb* **supernaturally**

su·per·no·va (*soo*-pur-**noh**-vuh) *noun* An extremely bright exploding star that can give off millions of times more light than the sun. ▶ *noun, plural* **supernovas** or **supernovae** (*soo*-pur-**noh**-vee)

su·per·son·ic (*soo*-pur-**sah**-nik) *adjective* At or having to do with a speed faster than that of sound.

su·per·sti·tion (*soo*-pur-**stish**-uhn) *noun* A belief that explains the cause of something in a magical way that cannot be tested or proven.

su·per·sti·tious (*soo*-pur-**stish**-uhs) *adjective* **1.** More influenced by superstition than by reason or facts. **2.** Based on or resulting from superstition.

su·per·tank·er (*soo*-pur-*tang*-kur) *noun* A very large oil tanker used to transport large amounts of crude oil to refineries.

su·per·vise (*soo*-pur-*vize*) *verb* To watch over or direct a group of people; to be in charge of someone or something. ▶ *verb* **supervising, supervised**

su·per·vi·sion (*soo*-pur-**vizh**-uhn) *noun* Direct oversight or management of someone or something, especially a person's work.

su·per·vi·sor (*soo*-pur-**vye**-zur) *noun* Someone who watches over and directs the work of other people.

sup·per (**suhp**-ur) *noun* A light evening meal or a dinner.

sup·ple (**suhp**-uhl) *adjective* Able to move or bend easily; limber or flexible. ▶ *adjective* **suppler, supplest** ▶ *noun* **suppleness**

sup·ple·ment (**suhp**-luh-muhnt) *noun* Something added to complete another thing or to make up for what is missing. *verb* To add to something.
▶ *verb* **supplementing, supplemented**
▶ *adjective* **supplementary** (*suhp*-luh-**men**-tur-ee)

sup·pli·er (suh-**plye**-ur) *noun* Someone who provides something that is needed or who makes something available.

sup·ply (suh-**plye**) *verb* To provide something that is needed or wanted. *noun* An amount of something that is available for use. *noun, plural* **supplies** Materials needed to do something.
▶ *verb* **supplies, supplying, supplied** ▶ *noun, plural* **supplies**

sup·port (suh-**port**) *verb* **1.** To bear the weight of someone or something. **2.** To earn a living for; to provide for. **3.** To give help, comfort,

S

or encouragement to someone or something. **4.** To believe in someone or to be in favor of something. **5.** To show to be true.
noun **1.** The act of helping, comforting, or encouraging someone or something. **2.** Something, especially money, given to support someone or something. **3.** Something that bears the weight of someone or something.
▶ *verb* **supporting, supported**
▶ *adjective* **supportive**

sup·port·er (suh-**por**-tur) *noun* Someone who promotes or encourages someone or something, such as a sports team or a political party.

sup·pose (suh-**poze**) *verb* **1.** To imagine or assume that something is true or possible. **2.** To believe or to guess. **3.** To expect.
▶ *verb* **supposing, supposed**
▶ *adjective* **supposed** ▶ *adverb* **supposedly**

sup·press (suh-**pres**) *verb* **1.** To put a stop to something, especially by using authority or force. **2.** To hold back or to control the expression of something.
▶ *verb* **suppresses, suppressing, suppressed** ▶ *noun* **suppression** (suh-**presh**-uhn)

su·preme (su-**preem**) *adjective* **1.** The highest in power, authority, or importance. **2.** The greatest or most excellent.
▶ *noun* **supremacy** (su-**prem**-uh-see)
▶ *adverb* **supremely**

Su·preme Court (su-**preem** kort) *noun* **1.** The highest and most powerful court in the United States. It has the power to overturn decisions made in lower courts and also to declare laws unconstitutional. **2.** The highest court in a state.

sure (shoor)
adjective **1.** Having no doubt; certain; confident. **2.** Certain to happen; impossible to avoid. **3.** Firm or steady.
adverb Without a doubt; certainly.
▶ *adjective* **surer, surest**

sure·ly (**shoor**-lee) *adverb* With certainty; absolutely; without a doubt.

surf (surf)
noun Waves as they break on the shore.
verb **1.** To balance on a surfboard and ride the crest of a breaking wave toward shore. **2.** To look through pages or sites on the World Wide Web.
Surf sounds like **serf.** ▶ *verb* **surfing, surfed** ▶ *noun* **surfer** ▶ *noun* **surfing**

sur·face (**sur**-fis)
noun **1.** The outside or outermost layer of something. **2.** One of the sides of something that has several sides.
verb **1.** To rise to the surface. **2.** To appear, especially from a hidden location.
phrase **on the surface** In its outward appearance.
▶ *verb* **surfacing, surfaced**

surf·board (**surf**-bord) *noun* A long, narrow board with rounded ends on which surfers stand as they ride breaking waves.

surge (surj)
verb **1.** To rush or sweep forward with force, like a wave. **2.** To increase sharply and suddenly.
noun **1.** A sudden, strong rush. **2.** A sudden increase.
▶ *verb* **surging, surged**

sur·geon (**sur**-juhn) *noun* A doctor who specializes in performing operations.

surge pro·tec·tor (**surj** pruh-*tek*-tur) *noun* A device that protects devices plugged into it from being damaged by a sudden increase in voltage.

sur·ger·y (**sur**-jur-ee) *noun* **1.** Medical treatment that involves repairing, removing, or replacing injured or diseased parts of the body, usually by cutting. **2.** The branch of medicine that deals with injury and disease in this way. **3.** An operation performed by a surgeon.
▶ *adjective* **surgical** (**sur**-ji-kuhl)

Su·ri·na·me (**soor**-uh-nah-muh) A country on the coast of northern South America. A Dutch colony for almost 300 years, it was formerly known as Dutch Guiana. It became independent in 1975.

S

sur·ly (**sur**-lee) *adjective* Mean, rude, and unfriendly. ▶ *adjective* **surlier, surliest**

sur·name (**sur**-*name*) *noun* A person's last name or family name.

sur·pass (sur-**pas**) *verb* 1. To be better, greater, or stronger than another person or thing. 2. To go beyond the limits or powers of something. ▶ *verb* **surpasses, surpassing, surpassed**

sur·plus (**sur**-pluhs)
noun An amount greater than what is used or needed; excess.
adjective more than what is needed; excess.

sur·prise (sur-**prize**)
verb 1. To amaze or astonish someone by doing or saying something unexpected. 2. To come upon suddenly and without warning.
noun An event or fact that you become aware of suddenly and don't expect.
▶ *verb* **surprising, surprised**
▶ *adjective* **surprising**

sur·ren·der (suh-**ren**-dur)
verb 1. To give up or to stop resisting someone or something. 2. To give something up or to hand something over.
noun The act of surrendering.
▶ *verb* **surrendering, surrendered**

sur·round (suh-**round**) *verb* To be on all sides of someone or something; to encircle. ▶ *verb* **surrounding, surrounded**

sur·round·ings (suh-**roun**-dingz) *noun, plural* The conditions or objects around a person or thing; the environment.

sur·vey
noun (**sur**-vay) 1. A study of the opinions or experiences of a group of people, based on their responses to questions. 2. A report based on measurement and inspection of a piece of land or a building.
verb 1. (sur-**vay**) To examine someone or something carefully and thoroughly. 2. (sur-**vay**) To measure the lines and angles of a piece of land in order to

make a map or plan. 3. (**sur**-vay) To ask a group of people their opinion on a matter in order to gather statistical information.
▶ *verb* **surveying, surveyed** ▶ *noun* **surveyor** (sur-**vay**-ur)

sur·vive (sur-**vive**) *verb* 1. To continue to live after or in spite of an accident or dangerous event. 2. To continue to live or exist. 3. To live longer than someone or something.
▶ *verb* **surviving, survived** ▶ *noun* **survival** (sur-**vye**-vuhl)

sur·vi·vor (sur-**vye**-vur) *noun* Someone who lives through a disaster or other horrible event.

su·shi (**soo**-shee) *noun* A Japanese dish made of small cakes of cooked rice with raw fish or vegetables, wrapped in seaweed.

sus·pect
verb (suh-**spekt**) 1. To think that something may be true; to guess or suppose. 2. To think that someone is guilty with little or no proof. 3. To have doubts about; to distrust.
noun (**suhs**-pekt) Someone who is thought to have committed a crime.
adjective (**suhs**-pekt) Causing you to be suspicious.
▶ *verb* **suspecting, suspected**

sus·pend (suh-**spend**) *verb* 1. To attach something to a support so that it hangs downward. 2. To keep from falling as if attached from above. 3. To stop something for a brief period of time. 4. To punish someone by not allowing him or her to participate.
▶ *verb* **suspending, suspended**

sus·pend·ers (suh-**spen**-durz) *noun, plural* A pair of elastic straps worn over the shoulders and attached to pants or a skirt to hold up the garment.

sus·pense (suh-**spens**) *noun* An anxious and uncertain feeling caused by not knowing what might happen next.

sus·pen·sion (suh-**spen**-shuhn) *noun* 1. A period during which an activity is not allowed or does not take place.

S

2. The dismissal of someone from a place or position by an authority for a period of time. **3.** The state of being suspended from something.

sus·pen·sion bridge (suhs-**pen**-shuhn brij) *noun* A bridge hung from cables or chains strung from towers.

sus·pi·cion (suh-**spish**-uhn) *noun* A thought, based more on feeling than on fact, that something is wrong or bad.
phrase **under suspicion** Believed to have done something wrong.

sus·pi·cious (suh-**spish**-uhs) *adjective* **1.** Thinking that something is wrong or bad, but having little or no proof to back up your feelings. **2.** Giving an impression of being wrong, untrustworthy, or dangerous.

sus·tain (suh-**stayn**) *verb* **1.** To keep something going; to maintain. **2.** To encourage someone, or to give someone the energy and strength to keep going. **3.** To suffer or experience something unpleasant.
▶ *verb* **sustaining, sustained**

sus·tain·a·ble (suh-**stay**-nuh-buhl) *adjective* Done in a way that can be continued and that doesn't use up natural resources. ▶ *noun* **sustainability** (suh-*stay*-nuh-**bil**-i-tee)

sus·te·nance (**suhs**-tuh-nuhns) *noun* The food and drink that someone requires to live; nourishment.

SUV (**es**-*yoo*-**vee**) *noun* A large car that is built like a truck and that can be driven where there are no roads. SUV is short for *sport utility vehicle.*

swag·ger (**swag**-ur) *verb* To walk or act in a bold, confident way.
noun A bold, confident way of walking.
▶ *verb* **swaggering, swaggered**

swal·low (**swah**-loh) *verb* **1.** To make food or drink go from your mouth down to your stomach. **2.** To cause to disappear as if by swallowing. **3.** To suppress or hold back. **4.** (informal) To accept or believe without question.

noun **1.** An act of instance of swallowing. **2.** A migrating, insect-eating bird with long, pointed wings and a forked tail.
▶ *verb* **swallowing, swallowed**

swam (swam) *verb* The past tense of **swim.**

swamp (swahmp) *noun* An area of wet, spongy ground; a marsh.
verb **1.** To fill with or sink in water. **2.** To overwhelm.
▶ *verb* **swamping, swamped**
▶ *adjective* **swampy**

swan (swahn) *noun* A large, usually white waterbird with webbed feet and a long, graceful neck.

swap (swahp) *verb* To trade or exchange someone or something for another.
noun An act of items being exchanged, or an event where people do this.
▶ *verb* **swapping, swapped**

swarm (sworm) *noun* A group of people or insects that gather or move in large numbers.
verb **1.** To fly closely together, forming a dense mass. **2. swarm with** To be filled with.
▶ *verb* **swarming, swarmed**

swar·thy (**swor**-THee) *adjective* Dark-skinned. ▶ *adjective* **swarthier, swarthiest**

swas·ti·ka (**swah**-sti-kuh) *noun* An ancient symbol consisting of a cross with the arms bent at right angles. During the 20th century, the swastika was adopted as the emblem of the Nazi party in Germany.

swat (swaht) *verb* To hit with a quick, sharp blow.
noun A quick, sharp blow.
▶ *verb* **swatting, swatted**

sway (sway) *verb* **1.** To move or swing slowly backward and forward or from side to side. **2.** To change or influence the way someone thinks or acts.
noun **1.** A rhythmical movement from side to side. **2.** Influence or control.
▶ *verb* **swaying, swayed**

S

Swa·zi·land (*swah*-zee-*land*) A small, landlocked kingdom in southern Africa, surrounded by South Africa and Mozambique. It is mainly mountainous and hilly but has some plains, as well as a rain forest. Swaziland has two capitals: Mbabane, the administrative capital, and Lobamba, the royal and legislative capital.

swear (swair) *verb* 1. To make a solemn promise; to vow. 2. To use rude or bad language; to curse.
▶ *verb* **swearing, swore** (swor), **sworn** (sworn)

sweat (swet)
verb To have salty drops of moisture come out through the pores in your skin; to perspire.
noun The salty drops of moisture that come out through the pores in your skin when you are hot.
▶ *verb* **sweating, sweat** *or* **sweated**

sweat·er (swet-ur) *noun* A knitted or crocheted piece of clothing that you wear on your upper body.

sweat·shirt (swet-*shurt*) *noun* A casual, collarless, long-sleeved top made of cotton jersey with a fleece backing.

Swe·den (swee-duhn) A country in northern Europe on the Scandinavian Peninsula. It has not participated in any war for almost 200 years and remained neutral during World War I and II. Sweden is known for awarding the Nobel Prizes. Alfred Nobel (1833–1896), a Swedish industrialist who invented dynamite, bequeathed his fortune to fund the prizes, given for literature, medicine, and other achievements.

sweep (sweep)
verb 1. To clean or clear away with a brush or broom. 2. To move or carry rapidly and forcefully. 3. To touch or brush lightly. 4. To move or pass over a wide area quickly and steadily.
noun 1. The complete range or extent of something. 2. The act of cleaning or clearing away with a brush or broom.
▶ *verb* **sweeping, swept** (swept)

sweep·ing (swee-ping) *adjective* Affecting many people or things; wide-ranging.

sweet (sweet)
adjective 1. Tasting like sugar or honey. 2. Pleasant in taste, smell, or sound. 3. Gentle and kind; good-natured.
noun, plural **sweets** Candy, cookies, or other sweet-tasting foods.
▶ *adjective* **sweeter, sweetest** ▶ *adverb* **sweetly**

sweet·en (swee-tuhn) *verb* To make something sweet or sweeter, usually by adding sugar. ▶ *verb* **sweetening, sweetened**

sweet·heart (sweet-*hahrt*) *noun* 1. Either person of a loving couple. 2. A lovable person.

sweet po·ta·to (sweet puh-*tay*-toh) *noun* The thick, sweet, orange root of a vine, eaten as a vegetable. ▶ *noun, plural* **sweet potatoes**

swell (swel)
verb To grow larger, greater, or stronger.
noun A long, rolling wave or waves.
adjective (slang) Wonderful.
▶ *verb* **swelling, swelled, swollen** ▶ *noun* **swelling**

swel·ter·ing (swel-tur-ing) *adjective* Uncomfortably hot. ▶ *verb* **swelter**

swept (swept) *verb* The past tense and past participle of **sweep.**

swerve (swurv)
verb To turn aside suddenly while moving forward, usually to avoid hitting something.
noun An act or instance of turning sharply.
▶ *verb* **swerving, swerved**

swift (swift)
adjective 1. Moving or able to move very fast. 2. Happening or done quickly.
noun A migrating bird, similar to a swallow, with long, narrow wings.
▶ *adjective* **swifter, swiftest** ▶ *noun* **swiftness** ▶ *adverb* **swiftly**

swig (swig)
verb To drink a liquid in large gulps, usually from a bottle or

S

other container.

noun A big swallow.

▶ *verb* **swigging, swigged**

swim (swim)

verb **1.** To move through the water using the arms and legs or the fins, flippers, or tail. **2.** To float on or be covered by liquid.

noun A period of time that you spend swimming.

▶ *verb* **swimming, swam** (swam), **swum** (swuhm) ▶ *noun* **swimmer**

swim·suit (**swim**-soot) *noun* A piece of clothing worn for swimming.

swin·dle (**swin**-duhl)

verb To cheat someone out of money, property, or possessions.

noun An instance of cheating someone out of something.

▶ *verb* **swindling, swindled** ▶ *noun* **swindler** (**swind**-luhr)

swine (swine) *noun* **1.** A pig or a hog. **2.** A hateful, vicious, or greedy person.

swine flu (**swine** *floo*) *noun* A form of flu that was first found in pigs and that spread to humans.

swing (swing)

verb **1.** To move back and forth or from side to side while hanging from above. **2.** To move on a hinge or pivot. **3.** To move or turn with a curved, sweeping motion.

noun **1.** A piece of playground equipment, consisting of a seat hanging from ropes or chains on which you sit and move back and forth. **2.** The act of moving on a hinge or pivot, especially the movement of a batter's arm in baseball. **3.** A style of lively jazz music originally played by large dance bands in the 1930s.

▶ *verb* **swinging, swung** (swuhng)

swipe (swipe)

verb **1.** (informal) To hit someone or something with a hard, sweeping blow or stroke. **2.** (slang) To steal something. **3.** To run a card with a magnetic strip through a machine in order to do something, such as make a payment.

noun An instance of swiping something.

▶ *verb* **swiping, swiped**

swirl (swurl)

verb To move with a twisting, spiraling, or whirling motion.

noun A pattern in which there are twisting or curving lines.

▶ *verb* **swirling, swirled**

swish (swish)

verb To move with a soft, rustling sound.

noun A soft, rustling sound.

▶ *verb* **swishes, swishing, swished** ▶ *noun, plural* **swishes**

switch (swich)

verb **1.** To trade one thing for something similar. **2.** To shift, transfer, or change from one thing to another. **3.** To turn a piece of electrical equipment on or off.

noun **1.** A change or a trade. **2.** A device that interrupts the flow of electricity in a circuit. **3.** A long, thin stick or rod used for whipping. **4.** A quick, jerking motion. **5.** A section of railroad track used to move a train from one track to another.

▶ *verb* **switches, switching, switched** ▶ *noun, plural* **switches**

switch·board (**swich**-bord) *noun* The control center or panel for connecting the lines of a telephone system.

Switz·er·land (**swit**-sur-luhnd) A country in western Europe. Switzerland is one of the most prosperous countries in the world. It has a long history of being neutral: It did not take sides in World War I or II and has not participated in a war since 1815. The country is known for its alpine resorts, precision-made watches, Swiss chocolates, and Swiss cheese.

swiv·el (**swiv**-uhl)

verb To turn or rotate around a central point.

noun A mechanism that allows one part to rotate around another.

▶ *verb* **swiveling, swiveled**

S

swol·len (swoh-luhn)
verb The past participle of **swell.**
adjective Made large by swelling.

swoon (swoon) *verb* To faint, often from excitement. ▶ *verb* **swooning, swooned**

swoop (swoop)
verb To rush down or pounce upon suddenly.
noun A quick movement downwards, especially to get something.
▶ *verb* **swooping, swooped**

sword (sord) *noun* A weapon with a handle and a long, pointed blade with a sharp edge on one or both sides.

sword·fish (sord-*fish*) *noun* A large saltwater food fish with a swordlike bone sticking out from its upper jaw. ▶ *noun, plural* **swordfish**

swore (swor) *verb* The past tense of **swear.**

sworn (sworn) *verb* The past participle of **swear.**

swum (swuhm) *verb* The past participle of **swim.**

syc·a·more (sik-uh-*mor*) *noun* A North American and European tree with smooth, brown bark that peels off in layers.

syl·la·ble (sil-uh-buhl) *noun* A unit of sound in a word. A syllable contains a vowel and possibly one or more consonants. For example, the word *long* has one syllable, and the word *table* has two syllables. The word *syllable* has three syllables.

syl·la·bus (sil-uh-buhs) *noun* An outline or a summary of work that must be covered for a particular course of study. ▶ *noun, plural* **syllabuses** or **syllabi** (**sil**-uh-*bye*)

sym·bol (sim-buhl) *noun* A design or an object that stands for, suggests, or represents something else. **Symbol** sounds like **cymbal.**

sym·bol·ic (sim-**bah**-lik) *adjective* Standing for something else.

sym·bol·ize (sim-buh-*lize*) *verb* To stand for or represent something else. ▶ *verb* **symbolizing, symbolized**

sym·met·ri·cal (si-**met**-ri-kuhl) *adjective* Having matching points, parts, or shapes on both sides of a dividing line. The capital letters "M" and "X" are symmetrical because you can draw a line dividing them into two matching halves. ▶ *adverb* **symmetrically**

sym·me·try (sim-i-tree) *noun* A balanced arrangement of parts on either side of a line or around a central point.

sym·pa·thet·ic (*sim*-puh-**thet**-ik) *adjective* Feeling or showing sympathy toward someone or something. ▶ *adverb* **sympathetically**

sym·pa·thize (sim-puh-*thize*) *verb* **1.** To understand or appreciate other people's troubles. **2.** To be in agreement.
▶ *verb* **sympathizing, sympathized**

sym·pa·thy (sim-puh-thee)
noun The ability to identify with and to share other people's feelings.
phrase If you are **in sympathy with** someone or something, you agree with them.
▶ *adjective* **sympathetic** (sim-puh-**thet**-ik) ▶ *adverb* **sympathetically**

sym·pho·ny (sim-fuh-nee) *noun*
1. A long piece of music written for a full orchestra, usually consisting of several parts called movements.
2. A large orchestra that usually plays classical music.
▶ *noun, plural* **symphonies** ▶ *adjective* **symphonic** (sim-**fah**-nik)

symp·tom (simp-tuhm) *noun* **1.** A sign of an illness. **2.** An indication of something.

syn·a·gogue (sin-uh-*gahg*) *noun* A building for Jewish worship and religious study.

sync (singk)
verb Short for **synchronize.**
noun If two things are **in sync,** they work well together. If two things are **out of sync,** there is a problem with the way they work together.

S

syn·chro·nize (**sing**-kruh-*nize*) *verb* **1.** To arrange events so that they happen at the same time or in a certain order. **2.** To set to the same time.
▶ *verb* **synchronizing, synchronized** ▶ *noun* **synchronization** (*sin*-kruh-ni-**zay**-shuhn)

syn·chro·nized swim·ming (**sing**-kruh-*nized* **swim**-ing) *noun* Swimming that is synchronized to a musical accompaniment and that uses movements to form dancelike patterns.

syn·co·pate (**sing**-kuh-*pate*) *verb* To change the rhythm of a piece of music by stressing beats that are normally unstressed. ▶ *verb* **syncopating, syncopated** ▶ *noun* **syncopation** (*sing*-kuh-**pay**-shuhn) ▶ *adjective* **syncopated**

syn·drome (**sin**-drohm) *noun* A group of signs and symptoms that occur together and are characteristic of a particular disease or disorder.

syn·o·nym (**sin**-uh-nim) *noun* A word that has the same or nearly the same meaning as another word in the same language. For example, the word *shut* is a synonym for the word *close*.

syn·on·y·mous (si-**nah**-nuh-muhs) *adjective* **1.** Having the same or almost the same meaning. For example, the words *gigantic* and *huge* are synonymous. **2.** Closely associated with or suggesting something.

syn·op·sis (si-**nahp**-sis) *noun* A brief summary or outline. ▶ *noun, plural* **synopses** (si-**nahp**-seez)

syn·tax (**sin**-taks) *noun* **1.** The arrangement of words and phrases in a sentence. **2.** The rules that govern a programming or command language and determine the way that letters, numbers, and symbols must be entered.
▶ *adjective* **syntactic** (sin-**tak**-tik)

syn·the·siz·er (**sin**-thuh-*sye*-zur) *noun* An electronic keyboard instrument that can imitate the sound of various musical instruments or produce sounds that ordinary instruments cannot.

syn·thet·ic (sin-**thet**-ik) *adjective* Manufactured or artificial rather than found in nature.
noun Something that is manufactured rather than naturally occurring, especially a fabric.
▶ *adverb* **synthetically**

Syr·i·a (**seer**-ee-uh) A country in western Asia on the Mediterranean Sea. Its capital, Damascus, was founded around 2500 B.C. and is thought to be one of the oldest continuously inhabited cities in the world. The Golan Heights, a border region between Syria and Israel, has been a source of conflict in the area since the 1940s. Israel captured it from Syria during the 1967 Arab-Israeli War.

sy·ringe (suh-**rinj**) *noun* A tube with a plunger and a hollow needle, used for giving injections and drawing out blood or bodily fluids.

syr·up (**sir**-uhp) *noun* **1.** A sweet, thick liquid made by boiling sugar and water, usually with some flavoring. **2.** A sweet, thick liquid made by boiling down the sap of a tree or plant.
▶ *adjective* **syrupy** (**sir**-uh-pee)

sys·tem (**sis**-tuhm) *noun* **1.** A group of things or parts, related or connected so that they work together in an organized way. **2.** An organized and coordinated way of getting something done. **3.** A method or procedure.
▶ *adjective* **systematic** (*sis*-tuh-**mat**-ik)
▶ *adverb* **systematically**

S

T

tab (tab) *noun* **1.** A small flap or loop that is attached to something, such as a file folder or soda can. Tabs are used for labeling, pulling, or opening. **2.** A key on a computer keyboard that you use to move around in tables. **3.** The character that your keyboard sends to the computer when you hit the tab key. **4.** One of a group of displays that you have open in a web browser, allowing you to have views of several webpages at once. **5.** (informal) If you **keep tabs on** someone, you watch the person closely to see what he or she is doing. **6.** (informal) If you **pick up the tab,** you pay for something for a group of people, such as the bill in a restaurant.

tab·by (**tab**-ee) *noun* **1.** A cat with a striped coat. **2.** Any domestic cat, especially a female. ▶ *noun, plural* **tabbies**

tab·er·na·cle (**tab**-ur-*nak*-uhl) *noun* **1.** A building used for worship by some Christian groups. **2.** A case or box for holy objects.

ta·ble (**tay**-buhl) *noun* **1.** A piece of furniture that has a flat top resting on legs. **2.** A chart that lists facts and figures, usually in columns. **3.** Food put on a table. **4.** If you **turn the tables** on someone, you reverse the situation so that things are in your favor. **5.** If something is done **under the table,** it is done in secret or illegally.

ta·ble·cloth (**tay**-buhl-*klawth*) *noun* A piece of material put over a table to protect or decorate it.

ta·ble man·ners (**tay**-buhl *man*-urz) *noun, plural* Your behavior when you are eating a meal, especially with other people.

ta·ble·spoon (**tay**-buhl-*spoon*) *noun* A large spoon that you use to serve food or as a measure in cooking. A tablespoon is equal to three teaspoons. ▶ *noun* **tablespoonful**

tab·let (**tab**-lit) *noun* **1.** A pad of writing paper glued together at one end. **2.** A small, hard piece of medicine that you swallow. **3.** A piece of stone with writing carved into it.

ta·ble ten·nis (**tay**-buhl *ten*-is) *noun* A game for two or four players who use wooden paddles to hit a small, light ball over a low net on a table. Also called **Ping-Pong.**

tab·loid (**tab**-loid) *noun* A newspaper that contains brief articles and many pictures. The pictures and articles are often intended to stir up interest or excitement.

ta·boo (tuh-**boo** or ta-**boo**) *adjective* If a subject is **taboo,** it may offend or upset people if you talk about it. *noun* Something that is taboo.

tab·u·lar (**tab**-yuh-lur) *adjective* Arranged in the form of a table or chart.

tab·u·late (**tab**-yuh-*late*) *verb* To arrange information into a table or chart. ▶ *noun* **tabulation**

tac·it (**tas**-it) *adjective* Agreed to or understood without being stated. ▶ *adverb* **tacitly**

tac·i·turn (**tas**-i-turn) *adjective* Quiet and shy and not saying much.

tack (tak) *noun* **1.** A small nail with a sharp point and a large, flat head. **2.** A way of doing something. **3.** Equipment that you need for riding a horse, such as a bridle and saddle. *verb* **1.** To add or attach something extra or different. **2.** To sew material loosely before doing it neatly. **3.** To turn a boat so that the wind blows into the sails from the opposite side. ▶ *verb* **tacking, tacked**

tack·le (**tak**-uhl)
verb 1. In football, to knock or throw a player to the ground in order to stop the person from moving forward.
2. To try to take the ball from another player in a sport such as soccer.
3. To attempt to deal with a difficult problem.
noun 1. An instance of tackling in sports. 2. The equipment that you need for a particular activity. 3. A system of ropes and pulleys used to raise, lower, or move heavy loads.
▶ *verb* **tackling, tackled** ▶ *noun* **tackler**

ta·co (**tah**-koh) *noun* A Mexican food consisting of a fried or soft tortilla that is folded around one or more fillings such as beef, chicken, or cheese.

tact (takt) *noun* The ability to deal with a difficult situation or person without causing anyone to be upset or embarrassed. ▶ *adjective* **tactful** ▶ *adverb* **tactfully**

tac·tic (**tak**-tik) *noun* An action or plan undertaken to achieve a specific goal. ▶ *adjective* **tactical** ▶ *adverb* **tactically**

tad·pole (**tad**-pole) *noun* A young frog or toad that lives in water, breathes through gills, and has a long tail but no legs.

taf·fy (**taf**-ee) *noun* A thick, chewy candy that is made of brown sugar or molasses and butter. The ingredients are boiled together, then stretched and folded over and over until the mixture holds its shape. ▶ *noun, plural* **taffies**

tag (tag)
noun 1. A label that identifies or gives information. 2. A children's game in which the player called "It" has to chase the other players and touch one of them. 3. A code that tells a computer how it should deal with text or data.
verb 1. In baseball, to put a runner out by touching him or her with the ball.
2. To put a label on something that identifies or gives information about it. 3. If you **tag along** with someone, you follow the person.
▶ *verb* **tagging, tagged**

tail (tayl)
noun 1. A part that sticks out at the back end of an animal's body and is often long and thin. 2. Something that is shaped like a tail. 3. The rear part or end of something. 4. **tails** The side of a coin that doesn't have a head or face; the back of the coin.
verb (informal) If you **tail** someone, you follow him or her closely.
Tail sounds like **tale**. ▶ *verb* **tailing, tailed**

tail·gate (**tale**-gayt)
noun A board or gate at the rear of a vehicle that can be folded down or removed for loading and unloading.
verb 1. To drive very closely behind another vehicle in a way that is considered dangerous. 2. To set up a picnic or barbecue on the tailgate of a vehicle, especially in the parking lot of a sports stadium.
▶ *verb* **tailgating, tailgated** ▶ *noun* **tailgater**

tai·lor (**tay**-lur)
noun Someone who makes or alters clothes.
verb 1. To design or change something for a particular purpose. 2. To make or alter clothes.
▶ *verb* **tailoring, tailored**

Tai·wan (*tye*-**wahn**) An island in East Asia off the southeastern coast of China. Its political status has been a subject of controversy for many years, since most of the international community now regards Taiwan as part of the People's Republic of China rather than as an independent state.

Ta·ji·ki·stan (tuh-**jee**-ki-*stan*) A country in Central Asia. Ninety percent of its land is mountainous. Most of its people belong to the Persian-speaking Tajik ethnic group. The word *Tajik* was an old Turkish term for someone who spoke Persian, and *Tajikistan* means "land of the Tajiks."

T

take (tayk) *verb* **1.** To get, seize, or capture something with the hands. **2.** To move, carry, or remove something. **3.** To accept something. **4.** To use something. **5.** To receive or to accept something, especially something bad. **6.** To do or perform an action. **7.** To tolerate, or to permit something. **8.** To win something. **9.** To lead. **10.** To understand or believe something. **11.** To require or need something, such as an amount of time or work. **12.** If you **take after** someone in your family, you look or act like the person. **13.** (informal) If you are **taken in** by someone, you believe the lies that the person tells you. **14.** If you **take off** something, you remove it. **15.** If you **take up** something, you begin it. **16.** If you **take to** something or someone, you like the thing or person.
▶ *verb* **taking, took** (tuk), **taken** (**tay**-kin)

take·off (**tayk**-*awf*) *noun* The process of an aircraft leaving the ground. ▶ *verb* **take off**

take·out (**tayk**-*out*)
noun **1.** A restaurant selling meals that you take and eat somewhere else. **2.** Food that you buy from this kind of restaurant.
adjective **take-out** Of or having to do with a takeout.

take·o·ver (**tayk**-*oh*-vur) *noun* **1.** The action of one company taking control of another company by buying lots of its stock. **2.** If there is a **takeover** of a country, a new group or individual seizes possession or control.
▶ *verb* **take over**

talc (talk) *noun* A soft mineral that is ground up to make talcum powder, face powder, paint, and plastics.

tal·cum pow·der (**tal**-kuhm *pou*-dur) *noun* A fine, white powder made from talc. You can use talcum powder to dry your body or to make it smell good.

tale (tale) *noun* **1.** A story about exciting and imaginary events. **2.** An interesting story about someone's experiences that may not be completely true.
Tale sounds like **tail.**

tal·ent (**tal**-uhnt) *noun* **1.** A natural ability or skill. **2.** A person with talent.

tal·ent·ed (**tal**-uhn-tid) *adjective* Good at a particular skill or talent, especially without much training.

talk (tawk)
verb **1.** To say words; to speak. **2.** To discuss something, especially something important. **3.** If you **talk** a person or group **into** doing something, you persuade that person or group to do something.
noun **1.** A conversation. **2.** A speech or a lecture.
▶ *verb* **talking, talked** ▶ *noun* **talker**

talk·a·tive (**taw**-kuh-tiv) *adjective* Someone who is **talkative** talks a lot.

talk show (**tawk** *shoh*) *noun* A television or radio program in which a host interviews or has discussions with guests, audience members, and callers.

tall (tawl) *adjective* **1.** Higher than usual; not short or low. **2.** Having a certain height.
▶ *adjective* **taller, tallest**

tal·low (**tal**-oh) *noun* Fat from cattle and sheep that is used mainly to make candles and soap.

tall tale (**tawl** tale) *noun* A story that is difficult to believe.

tal·ly (**tal**-ee)
noun An account, a record, or a score.
verb **1.** To add up an account, record, or score. **2.** To match, or to agree.
▶ *verb* **tallies, tallying, tallied**

Tal·mud (**tal**-mud) *noun* The collection of Jewish civil and religious laws.

tal·on (**tal**-uhn) *noun* A sharp claw of a bird such as an eagle, hawk, or falcon.

ta·ma·le (tuh-**mah**-lee) *noun* A Mexican dish made up of seasoned chopped meat rolled in cornmeal, then wrapped in husks of corn and steamed.

tam·a·rind (**tam**-ur-ind) *noun* A tropical tree, or the soft, sticky fruit that grows on this tree.

tam·bou·rine (*tam*-buh-**reen**) *noun* A small, round musical instrument that

T

is similar to a drum. It has small, metal disks around the rim and is played by shaking or striking it with the hand.

tame (taym)
adjective **1.** Taken from a wild or natural state and trained to live with or be useful to people. **2.** Gentle and not afraid around people. **3.** Not exciting or interesting enough.
verb To take an animal from a wild or natural state and train it to live with or be useful to people.
▶ *adjective* **tamer, tamest** ▶ *adverb* **tamely** ▶ *noun* **tamer**

tam·per (**tam**-pur) *verb* To interfere with something so that it becomes harmed or damaged. ▶ *verb* **tampering, tampered**

tan (tan)
noun **1.** A light yellow-brown color. **2.** If you have a **tan,** your skin has become darker because you have spent time in the sun.
adjective Being of a light yellow-brown color.
verb **1.** To become darker or brown from the sun. **2.** To make animal skin into leather by soaking it in a chemical solution.
▶ *adjective* **tanner, tannest** ▶ *verb* **tanning, tanned** ▶ *noun* **tannery**

tan·dem (**tan**-duhm)
noun A bicycle for two people, with one seat behind the other.
phrases **1. in tandem** Together with or at the same time as someone or something else. **2. in tandem** One in front of another.

tan·door·i (tan-**door**-ee) *noun* An Indian method of cooking meat, bread, or any food by baking it in a clay pot.

tan·gent (**tan**-juhnt) *noun* **1.** In geometry, a straight line that touches a curve in one place. **2.** If you **go off on a tangent,** you suddenly start talking about something that is not related to the main topic of discussion.

tan·ger·ine (tan-juh-**reen**) *noun* A sweet, orange citrus fruit that is smaller than an orange and easier to peel.

tan·gle (**tang**-guhl)
verb To twist together in a messy way and become difficult to separate.
noun Something twisted together in a messy way.
▶ *verb* **tangling, tangled**

tang·y (**tang**-ee) *adjective* Having a strong, sharp flavor or odor. ▶ *adjective* **tangier, tangiest** ▶ *noun* **tang**

tank (tangk)
noun **1.** A large container for gas or liquid. **2.** A military vehicle covered in heavy armor with a large gun at the front. Tanks have two metal belts with wheels inside them that allow them to move over rough ground.
verb (informal) To decrease sharply or fail suddenly.

tank·er (**tang**-kur) *noun* A ship, a truck, or an airplane that contains large tanks for carrying liquids or gas.

tan·trum (**tan**-truhm) *noun* A sudden outburst of uncontrolled anger or bad temper, considered to be typical of a child.

Tan·za·ni·a (tan-zuh-**nee**-uh) A country in central East Africa. Once known as Tanganyika, it includes the islands of Zanzibar, which are in the Indian Ocean off the country's eastern coast. Tanzania was established in 1964 when Tanganyika united with Zanzibar.

tap (tap)
verb **1.** To hit something gently or lightly. **2.** To make or do by tapping again and again. **3.** To make a hole in order to draw off a liquid. **4.** To secretly listen in on a telephone conversation using a special device.
noun **1.** A gentle or light hit. **2.** A small metal plate attached to the sole of a shoe for tap dancing. **3.** A device used to control the flow of a liquid in a pipe; a faucet.
▶ *verb* **tapping, tapped**

tap danc·ing (tap *dan*-sing) *noun* Dancing in which shoes with taps are worn in order to make a clicking sound with the feet. ▶ *noun* **tap dance** ▶ *noun* **tap dancer** ▶ *verb* **tap-dance**

T

tape (tape)
noun 1. A thin strip of material, paper, or plastic. 2. A long piece of plastic covered with a magnetic substance and used to record sound or pictures. The tape is usually contained in a plastic case called a cassette.
verb 1. To fasten together, wrap, or bind with tape. 2. To record sound or pictures on tape.
▸ verb **taping, taped**

tape mea·sure (tape *mezh*-ur) noun A long, thin piece of ribbon or steel marked in inches or centimeters so that you can measure things easily.

ta·per (**tay**-pur)
verb 1. To make or become narrower at one end. 2. **taper off** To gradually become smaller or less.
noun A slender candle.
Taper sounds like **tapir**. ▸ verb **tapering, tapered**

tape re·cord·er (tape re-*kor*-dur) noun A machine that you use to play back or record music and sound on magnetic tape. ▸ noun **tape recording** ▸ verb **tape-record**

tap·es·try (**tap**-i-stree) noun A heavy piece of cloth with threads woven into it to make pictures or patterns. ▸ noun, plural **tapestries**

ta·pir (**tay**-pur) noun A large animal that has hoofs and a long, flexible snout. It is distantly related to the horse and rhinoceros. **Tapir** sounds like **taper.**

taps (taps) noun A song played on a bugle at the end of the day in military camps as a signal that all lights must be put out. Taps is also played at military funerals.

tar (tahr)
noun A thick, black, sticky substance used for making roads and patching roofs. Tar is made from coal or wood.
verb To apply tar to something.
▸ verb **tarring, tarred**

ta·ran·tu·la (tuh-**ran**-chuh-luh) noun A large, hairy spider found mainly in warm regions. Its bite is painful but not seriously poisonous to people.

tar·dy (**tahr**-dee) adjective Not on time; late. ▸ adjective **tardier, tardiest** ▸ noun **tardiness**

tar·get (**tahr**-git)
noun 1. A mark, a circle, or an object at which you aim and shoot. 2. Someone or something that is criticized or made fun of. 3. A goal or an aim.
verb If you **target** something, you direct attention to it.
▸ verb **targeting, targeted**

tar·iff (**tar**-if) noun A tax charged on goods that are imported or exported.

tar·nish (**tahr**-nish) verb If something **tarnishes,** it becomes less bright. ▸ verb **tarnishes, tarnishing, tarnished**

tar·pau·lin (**tahr**-puh-lin) noun A heavy, waterproof covering, usually made of canvas, that is used to protect playing fields, boats, or any outdoor item from wet weather. A tarpaulin is also known as a *tarp*.

tart (tahrt)
noun A small pie or pastry that usually contains fruit.
adjective 1. Sour-tasting. 2. A **tart** remark is mean, sharp, or bitter in tone.
▸ adjective **tarter, tartest** ▸ adverb **tartly** ▸ noun **tartness**

tar·tan (**tahr**-tuhn) noun A type of plaid, or a woolen cloth with a plaid pattern. Tartan is used especially for Scottish kilts.

tar·tar (**tahr**-tur) noun A yellow substance that forms on the teeth. Tartar consists of food particles, saliva, and calcium. If not removed, it becomes hard.

tar·tar sauce (**tahr**-tur *saws*) noun A sauce made with mayonnaise and chopped pickles, often served with fish.

Ta·ser (**tay**-zur) noun A trademark for a weapon used especially by police that sends a very powerful and painful electric shock through a person's body.

task (task) noun A piece of work to be done, especially work assigned by another person.

T

task·bar (**task**-*bahr*) *noun* A horizontal bar at the bottom of your computer screen that shows which programs you have open.

task force (**task** *fors*) *noun* A group formed for a limited period of time to deal with a specific problem.

tas·sel (**tas**-uhl) *noun* **1.** A bunch of threads tied at one end and used as a decoration on shoes, clothing, graduation caps, furniture, or rugs. **2.** Something that is like a tassel, such as the tassel of silk on an ear of corn. ▸ *adjective* **tasseled**

taste (tayst)
noun **1.** Your sense of **taste** allows you to identify a food by its flavor. **2.** The **taste** of a food is its flavor, for example, sweet, sour, salty, or bitter. **3.** If you have good **taste,** you choose clothes, furniture, and other things carefully and well.
verb **1.** To have a certain flavor. **2.** To try a bit of food or drink to see if you like it.
▸ *verb* **tasting, tasted** ▸ *adjective* **tasty** ▸ *adjective* **tasteful**

taste bud (**tayst** *buhd*) *noun* One of the groups of cells in the tongue that sense whether something is sweet, sour, salty, or bitter.

taste·less (**tayst**-lis) *adjective* **1.** Having little or no flavor; bland. **2.** Showing little sense of what is appropriate; rude.

tat·tered (**tat**-urd) *adjective* Old and torn.

tat·tle (**tat**-uhl) *verb* To tell someone in authority that someone else is doing something wrong. This word is used especially by and about children. ▸ *verb* **tattling, tattled** ▸ *noun* **tattler**

tat·tle·tale (**tat**-uhl-*tale*) *noun* Someone who tells other people's secrets. This word is used especially by and about children.

tat·too (ta-**too**) *noun* A picture or words that have been printed on somebody's skin with needles and ink.

taught (tawt) *verb* The past tense and past participle of **teach.**

taunt (tawnt)
verb To try to make someone angry or upset by saying unkind things about him or her.
noun Something said to make someone angry or upset.
▸ *verb* **taunting, taunted**

taut (tawt) *adjective* Stretched tight. ▸ *adjective* **tauter, tautest**

tav·ern (**tav**-urn) *noun* A place where people can sit and drink alcoholic beverages; a bar.

taw·ny (**taw**-nee) *adjective* Having a light, sandy-brown color. ▸ *adjective* **tawnier, tawniest**

tax (taks)
noun Money that people and businesses must pay in order to support a government.
verb To make heavy demands on; to strain.
▸ *noun, plural* **taxes** ▸ *verb* **taxes, taxing, taxed** ▸ *adjective* **taxing**

tax·a·ble (**tak**-suh-buhl) *adjective* If something is **taxable,** you have to pay tax on it.

tax·a·tion (tak-**say**-shuhn) *noun* **1.** The system a government uses to collect money from people and businesses. **2.** The money a government collects from people and businesses.

tax·i (**tak**-see)
noun A car with a driver whom you pay to take you somewhere.
verb When planes **taxi,** they move along the ground before taking off or after landing.
▸ *verb* **taxies, taxiing, taxied**

tax·on·o·my (tak-**sah**-nuh-mee) *noun* The system that scientists use for classifying and naming plants, animals, and microbes. ▸ *adjective* **taxonomic** (*tak*-suh-**nah**-mik)

TB (**tee**-bee) *noun* **1.** Short for **tuberculosis. 2.** Short for **terabyte.**

T cell (**tee** *sel*) *noun* Any of a group of cells found in the lymph glands that help protect the body against disease.

T

tea (tee) *noun* **1.** A drink made from the leaves of a plant that is grown in China, Japan, and India. **2.** This plant or its dried leaves. **3.** A similar drink made from the leaves of other plants. **4.** A late-afternoon social gathering at which tea and other refreshments are served.

teach (teech) *verb* To tell or show someone how to do something. ▸ *verb* **teaches, teaching, taught** (tawt)

teach·er (**tee**-chur) *noun* Someone who teachers or instructs, especially as a job.

tea·ket·tle (**tee**-*ket*-uhl) *noun* A kettle with a handle and a spout.

teal (teel) *noun* **1.** A dark color between green and blue. **2.** Any of several small ducks with short necks. Teal live in rivers and marshes. The males often have brightly colored feathers. ▸ *noun, plural* **teal** or **teals** ▸ *adjective* **teal**

team (teem) *noun* **1.** A group of people who work together or play a sport together against another group. **2.** Two or more animals that are fastened together to do work.
verb **team up** To join together to achieve something.
Team sounds like **teem.** ▸ *verb* **teaming, teamed**

team·mate (**teem**-*mate*) *noun* Someone who is a member of your team.

tear *noun* **1.** (teer) A drop of clear, salty liquid that comes from your eye. **2.** (tair) A rip in a piece of paper or other substance.
verb (tair) **1.** To pull or be pulled apart by force. **2.** To make a hole in something by pulling; to rip. **3.** To move very quickly. ▸ *verb* **tearing, tore** (tor), **torn** (torn) ▸ *adjective* **tearful** (**teer**-fuhl) ▸ *adjective* **teary** (**teer**-ee)

tease (teez) *verb* To say unkind things to someone in a way that is meant to be playful. ▸ *verb* **teasing, teased** ▸ *noun* **teaser**

tea·spoon (**tee**-*spoon*) *noun* A small spoon that you use as a measure in cooking or for stirring liquids. Three teaspoons equal one tablespoon. ▸ *noun* **teaspoonful**

tech·ni·cal (**tek**-ni-kuhl) *adjective* **1.** Of or having to do with science, engineering, or the mechanical or industrial arts. **2.** Using words that only experts in a particular field or subject understand.
▸ *adverb* **technically**

tech·ni·cian (tek-**nish**-uhn) *noun* Someone who works with specialized equipment or does practical laboratory work.

tech·nique (tek-**neek**) *noun* A method or way of doing something that requires skill, as in the arts, sports, or the sciences.

tech·nol·o·gy (tek-**nah**-luh-jee) *noun* The use of science and engineering to do practical things, such as make businesses and factories more efficient. ▸ *noun, plural* **technologies** ▸ *adjective* **technological** (*tek*-nuh-**lah**-ji-kuhl)

ted·dy bear (**ted**-ee *bair*) *noun* A soft, stuffed toy bear.

te·di·ous (**tee**-dee-uhs *or* **tee**-juhs) *adjective* Tiring and boring. ▸ *adverb* **tediously**

teem (teem) *verb* If a place is **teeming with** people or animals, there are many of them moving around. **Teem** sounds like **team.**

teen·ag·er (**teen**-*ay*-jur) *noun* A person who is between the ages of 13 and 19. ▸ *adjective* **teenage** or **teenaged**

teens (teenz) *noun, plural* The years of a person's life between 13 and 19.

tee·ny (**tee**-nee) *adjective* (informal) Tiny. ▸ *adjective* **teenier, teeniest**

tee·pee (**tee**-*pee*) *noun* Another spelling of **tepee.**

teeth (teeth) *noun, plural* The plural of **tooth.**

teethe (teeTH) *verb* If a baby is **teething,** teeth are coming through his or her gums for the first time. ▸ *verb* **teething, teethed**

T

Tef·lon (**tef**-lahn) *noun* The trademark for a type of plastic used especially on the insides of pans to prevent sticking.

tel·e·cast (**tel**-i-kast)
noun A program broadcast by television.
verb To broadcast a program by television.
▶ *verb* **telecasting, telecasted**

tel·e·com·mu·ni·ca·tion (*tel*-i-kuh-*myoo*-nih-**kay**-shuhn) *noun* 1. The science that deals with the sending of messages over long distances by telephone, satellite, radio, and other electronic means. Also known as *telecommunications.* 2. Any message sent this way.

tel·e·com·mute (*tel*-i-kuh-**myoot**) *verb* To do your work by staying at home and communicating with your office using a computer and other devices. ▶ *verb* **telecommuting, telecommuted** ▶ *noun* **telecommuter**

tel·e·gram (**tel**-i-*gram*) *noun* A message that is sent by telegraph.

tel·e·graph (**tel**-i-*graf*) *noun* An old system for sending messages over long distances using a code of electrical signals.

tel·e·mar·ket·ing (*tel*-uh-**mahr**-ki-ting) *noun* The selling of goods and services by telephone. ▶ *noun* **telemarketer**

te·lem·e·try (tuh-**lem**-i-tree) *noun* The use of radio waves to transmit and record information from a measuring instrument.

tel·e·phone (**tel**-uh-*fone*)
noun 1. A device for sending and receiving sounds, especially speech, by changing them into electrical signals. 2. A system for sending sounds over distances in this way.
verb To call on a telephone.
▶ *verb* **telephoning, telephoned**

tel·e·pho·to lens (**tel**-uh-*foh*-toh **lenz**) *noun* A camera lens that makes distant objects seem larger and closer.

tel·e·scope (**tel**-uh-*skope*) *noun* An instrument that makes distant objects seem larger and closer.

Telescopes are used especially for studying the stars and other heavenly bodies. ▶ *adjective* **telescopic** (*tel*-uh-**skah**-pik)

tel·e·vise (**tel**-uh-*vize*) *verb* To broadcast by television. ▶ *verb* **televising, televised**

tel·e·vi·sion (**tel**-uh-*vizh*-uhn) *noun* 1. A piece of electrical equipment with a screen that receives and shows moving pictures with sound; also known as a *television set* or a *TV set.* 2. The system of sending sounds and moving pictures along radio waves to be picked up by a television set. 3. The programs that are broadcast on television.

tell (tel) *verb* 1. To put into words by speaking or writing. 2. To report information to someone. 3. To show or indicate something. 4. To order or to command. 5. To recognize or to identify. 6. If you **tell** someone **off,** you speak to the person in an angry way because he or she has done something wrong. 7. If you **tell on** someone, you report to someone else what that person has done.
▶ *verb* **telling, told** (tohld)

tel·ler (**tel**-ur) *noun* 1. Someone who tells or relates stories. 2. A bank employee who gives out and receives money.

tem·per (**tem**-pur)
noun 1. A tendency to suddenly get angry. 2. A person's usual attitude or mood. 3. A calm state of mind.
verb 1. To make something less severe. 2. To make something hard or strong.
▶ *verb* **tempering, tempered**

tem·per·a·ment (**tem**-pur-uh-muhnt) *noun* Your nature or personality; the way you usually think, act, or respond to other people or to situations.

tem·per·a·men·tal (*tem*-pur-uh-**men**-tuhl) *adjective* Moody, unpredictable, or too sensitive. ▶ *adverb* **temperamentally**

tem·per·ate (**tem**-pur-it) *adjective* If an area has a **temperate** climate, the temperature is rarely very high or very low.

tem·per·a·ture (**tem**-pur-uh-chur) *noun* **1.** The degree of heat or cold in something, usually measured by a thermometer. **2.** If you have a **temperature,** your body is hotter than normal. Normal human body temperature is around 98.6 degrees Fahrenheit, or 37 degrees Celsius.

tem·pest (**tem**-pist) *noun* **1.** A violent storm with strong winds. **2.** A violent or noisy commotion.

tem·plate (**tem**-plit) *noun* **1.** A shape or pattern that you draw or cut around to make the same shape in another material, such as paper or metal. **2.** In computers, a document or pattern that is used to create similar documents.

tem·ple (**tem**-puhl) *noun* **1.** The flat area on either side of the forehead, above the cheek and in front of the ear. **2.** A building used for worshiping a god or gods.

tem·po (**tem**-poh) *noun* The speed or rhythm of a piece of music. ▶ *noun, plural* **tempos** or **tempi** (**tem**-pee)

tem·po·rar·y (**tem**-puh-*rer*-ee) *adjective* Lasting for only a short time. ▶ *adverb* **temporarily** (*tem*-puh-**rer**-uh-lee)

tempt (tempt) *verb* **1.** To try to get someone to do or want something that is wrong or foolish. **2.** To appeal strongly to someone.
▶ *verb* **tempting, tempted** ▶ *noun* **tempter** ▶ *adjective* **tempting**

temp·ta·tion (temp-**tay**-shuhn) *noun* **1.** Something that you want to have or do, although you know you should not. **2.** The act of being tempted.

ten (ten) *noun* The number that comes after 9 and before 11, written numerically as 10.
adjective Referring to the number that comes after 9 and before 11.

ten·ant (**ten**-uhnt) *noun* Someone who rents a house or other property that belongs to someone else.

tend (tend) *verb* **1.** If something **tends** to happen, it usually or often happens. **2.** To take care of a person, an animal, or a plant.
▶ *verb* **tending, tended**

ten·den·cy (**ten**-duhn-see) *noun* If you have a **tendency** to do something, you usually or often do it. ▶ *noun, plural* **tendencies**

ten·der (**ten**-dur) *adjective* **1.** Sore or painful. **2.** Soft or easy to chew. **3.** Kind and gentle.
▶ *adverb* **tenderly** ▶ *noun* **tenderness**

ten·don (**ten**-duhn) *noun* A strong, thick cord or band of tissue that joins a muscle to a bone or other body part.

ten·dril (**ten**-druhl) *noun* A threadlike, curly stem. Some climbing plants climb by means of tendrils that curl around supports.

ten·e·ment (**ten**-uh-muhnt) *noun* A large building divided into apartments, especially one that is crowded and in a poor part of a city.

Ten·nes·see (*ten*-uh-**see**) A state in the southeastern region of the United States. Tennessee has played a large role in American music. Its largest city, Memphis, is considered the birthplace of the blues and was important in the development of rock 'n' roll. Nashville, its capital, is the center of the country music industry and is the home of the Grand Ole Opry.

ten·nis (**ten**-is) *noun* A game in which two or four players use rackets to hit a ball over a net on a court.

ten·or (**ten**-ur) *noun* **1.** An adult male singing voice in the highest range. **2.** A person with a tenor voice.
adjective Of or having to do with the highest male singing voice.

tense (tens) *adjective* **1.** Nervous or worried. **2.** Stretched stiff and tight.
noun A form of a verb that indicates whether an action happened in the past, is happening in the present, or will happen in the future. *I was, I am,* and *I will be* are examples of the past, present, and future tenses of the verb *to be.*
verb To become stiff and tight, or to make your muscles do this.
▶ *adjective* **tenser, tensest** ▶ *adverb* **tensely** ▶ *noun* **tenseness**

T

ten·sion (**ten**-shuhn) *noun* 1. A feeling of nervousness, stress, or suspense that makes it difficult to relax. 2. The stiffness or tightness of something such as a rope or wire. 3. If there is **tension** between two people, there is difficulty in their relationship and they may suddenly start arguing.

tent (tent) *noun* A portable shelter made of nylon or canvas supported by poles and ropes.

ten·ta·cle (**ten**-tuh-kuhl) *noun* One of the long, flexible limbs of some animals, such as the octopus and squid. Tentacles are used for moving, feeling, and grasping.

ten·ta·tive (**ten**-tuh-tiv) *adjective* 1. Unsure or not confident. 2. Not certain or definite, and may be changed.
▶ *adverb* **tentatively**

ten·ter·hooks (**ten**-tur-*huks*) *noun, plural* If you are on **tenterhooks,** you are nervously waiting for something to happen.

tenth (tenth)
noun 1. One part of something that has been divided into ten equal parts, written numerically as 1/10. 2. In decimal notation, the **tenths place** is the position of the number to the right of the decimal point. In the number 4.0129, the digit 0 is in the tenths place.
adjective Next after 9th and before 11th, written numerically as 10th.

ten·u·ous (**ten**-yoo-uhs) *adjective* Not very strong or certain. ▶ *adverb* **tenuously**

te·pee (**tee**-*pee*) *noun* A tent shaped like a cone and made from animal skins by Native Americans in North America.

tep·id (**tep**-id) *adjective* Slightly warm.

ter·a·byte (**ter**-uh-*bite*) *noun* A unit used to measure large amounts of data. A terabyte is one thousand gigabytes.

ter·i·ya·ki (*ter*-ee-**yah**-kee) *noun* A Japanese dish of chicken, meat, or fish that has been soaked in soy sauce and broiled or grilled.

term (turm)
noun 1. A word with a specific meaning in some particular field. 2. A definite or limited period of time. 3. A part of the school year.
noun, plural 1. **terms** The conditions of an agreement, a contract, a will, or a sale. 2. **terms** A relationship between people.

ter·mi·nal (**tur**-muh-nuhl)
noun 1. A station at either end of a transportation line. 2. A computer keyboard and screen that are connected to a network. 3. **terminal velocity** The maximum speed an object can reach falling through the air.
adjective A **terminal** illness cannot be cured and causes death, often slowly.
▶ *adverb* **terminally**

ter·mi·nate (**tur**-muh-*nate*) *verb* 1. To stop or to end. 2. To remove someone from a job.
▶ *verb* **terminating, terminated**

ter·mi·nol·o·gy (*tur*-muh-**nah**-luh-jee) *noun* The special vocabulary of a particular field of knowledge. Each of the sciences has its own terminology.

ter·mite (**tur**-mite) *noun* An insect like an ant that eats wood. Termites live together in large colonies and can severely damage wooden buildings.

ter·race (**ter**-is) *noun* 1. A paved, open area next to a building where you can sit. 2. A balcony of an apartment building. 3. A raised, flat platform of land with sloping sides.
▶ *adjective* **terraced**

ter·ra·cot·ta (**ter**-uh-**kah**-tuh) *noun* A hard, waterproof clay used in making pottery and roofs.

ter·rain (tuh-**rayn**) *noun* An area of land.

ter·ra·pin (**ter**-uh-pin) *noun* A North American turtle that lives in or near freshwater or along seashores.

ter·rar·i·um (tuh-**rair**-ee-uhm) *noun* A glass or plastic container for growing small plants or raising small land animals. ▶ *noun, plural* **terrariums** or **terraria** (tuh-**rair**-ee-uh)

ter·res·tri·al (tuh-**res**-tree-uhl) *adjective* Of or having to do with the earth, or living on the earth.

T

ter·ri·ble (**ter**-uh-buhl) *adjective* **1.** Very great; extreme or severe. **2.** Very bad or unpleasant. **3.** Causing great fear or terror.

ter·ri·bly (**ter**-uh-blee) *adverb* **1.** Extremely. **2.** Very badly.

ter·ri·er (**ter**-ee-ur) *noun* Any of several breeds of small, lively dogs that were originally used for hunting small animals.

ter·ri·fic (tuh-**rif**-ik) *adjective* **1.** Extremely good; excellent. **2.** Very large or great, in a way that is surprising. **3.** Causing great fear or terror.
▸ *adverb* **terrifically**

ter·ri·fy (**ter**-uh-*fye*) *verb* To frighten someone greatly. ▸ *verb* **terrifies, terrifying, terrified** ▸ *adjective* **terrifying** ▸ *adverb* **terrifyingly**

ter·ri·to·ry (**ter**-i-tor-ee) *noun* **1.** Any large area of land. **2.** The land and waters under the control of a state, nation, or ruler. **3.** An area connected with or owned by a country that is outside the country's main borders.
▸ *noun, plural* **territories** ▸ *adjective* **territorial** (*ter*-i-**tor**-ee-uhl)

ter·ror (**ter**-ur) *noun* **1.** Very great fear. **2.** A person or thing that causes very great fear.

ter·ror·ist (**ter**-ur-ist) *noun* Someone who uses violence and threats in order to frighten people, obtain power, or force a government to do something. ▸ *noun* **terrorism** (**ter**-uh-**riz**-uhm)

ter·ror·ize (**ter**-uh-*rize*) *verb* To frighten someone a great deal. ▸ *verb* **terrorizing, terrorized**

terse (turs) *adjective* Brief and direct in a way that may be considered rude. ▸ *adjective* **terser, tersest**

tes·sel·late (**tes**-uh-*late*) *verb* When shapes **tessellate,** they fit together exactly on a flat surface, without leaving gaps. ▸ *verb* **tessellating, tessellated** ▸ *noun* **tessellation** ▸ *adjective* **tessellated**

test (test)
noun **1.** A set of questions, problems, or tasks used to measure your knowledge or skill. **2.** A way of studying something to find out what something is like, what it contains, or how good it is. **3.** An examination of a small amount of something to check if it works correctly or is finished, or to learn more information about it.
verb To try something out.
▸ *verb* **testing, tested**

tes·ta·ment (**tes**-tuh-muhnt) *noun* **1.** Proof that something exists or is true. **2. Testament** Either of the two main divisions of the Christian Bible, the New Testament or the Old Testament.

tes·ti·fy (**tes**-tuh-*fye*) *verb* To state what you have witnessed or what you know in a court of law. ▸ *verb* **testifies, testifying, testified**

tes·ti·mo·ny (**tes**-tuh-*moh*-nee) *noun* A formal statement given by a witness or an expert in a court of law. ▸ *noun, plural* **testimonies**

test pi·lot (**test** *pye*-luht) *noun* A pilot who flies new airplanes in order to test them for safety and strength.

test tube (**test** *toob*) *noun* A narrow glass tube that is closed at one end. Test tubes are used in laboratory tests and experiments.

tet·a·nus (**tet**-uh-nuhs) *noun* A serious, sometimes fatal disease caused by bacteria getting into a cut or wound. Tetanus makes your muscles, especially those in your jaw, become very stiff. It is also called *lockjaw.*

teth·er (**teTH**-ur)
noun **1.** A rope or chain that is used to tie up an animal so that it cannot move far. **2.** If you are **at the end of your tether,** you have run out of patience or energy and can no longer deal with a difficult situation.
verb To tie with a rope or chain.
▸ *verb* **tethering, tethered**

Tex·as (**tek**-suhs) A state in the South Central region of the United States. It is the second-largest state in the country, after Alaska. Before becoming a state, Texas belonged to Mexico, then was an independent republic. Texas was identified with cowboys and the cattle industry, but after the discovery of oil in the state in the early 1900s, it also became associated with oil exploration.

Tex-Mex (**teks**-meks) *adjective* Of or having to do with a style of cooking or music that originated in southern Texas and combines Mexican and American culture.

text (tekst)
noun **1.** The main section of writing in a book, not including the pictures, notes, or index. **2.** The original or exact words of a speaker or writer. **3.** The topic or theme of a piece of writing or a speech. **4.** A textbook. **5.** In a computer word-processing program, words and sentences as opposed to things such as art or graphs. **6.** A written message sent by using the keys of a cell phone to spell words that will appear on the display screen of the phone receiving it.
verb To send a text message by cellular telephone.
▶ *verb* **texting, texted**

text·book (**tekst**-buk) *noun* A book used to teach and study a subject.

text ed·i·tor (**tekst** ed-i-tur) *noun* A computer program that you can use to create and edit documents that contain text.

tex·tile (**tek**-stuhl *or* **tek**-stile) *noun* A woven or knitted fabric or cloth.

tex·ture (**teks**-chur) *noun* The way something feels, especially how rough or smooth it is.

Thai·land (**tye**-land) A country in Southeast Asia. Formerly known as Siam, Thailand is the only country in Southeast Asia never to have been ruled by a European power.

than (THan *or* THuhn) *conjunction* **1.** In comparison with. **2.** Except; besides.

thank (thangk)
verb **1.** To tell someone that you are grateful for something. **2.** To hold someone or something responsible for something, especially something bad or unpleasant.
interjection **thanks** An expression showing that you are grateful.
noun, plural **thanks** Gratitude.
▶ *verb* **thanking, thanked**

thank·ful (**thangk**-fuhl) *adjective* Showing thanks; grateful. ▶ *adverb* **thankfully**

thank·less (**thangk**-lis) *adjective* **1.** Not appreciated. **2.** A **thankless** person is not likely to give thanks or show gratitude.

Thanks·giv·ing Day (*thangks*-**giv**-ing day) *noun* **1.** A holiday observed in the United States on the fourth Thursday in November in order to remember the first Pilgrims' harvest feast, which was held in 1621. **2.** A similar holiday observed in Canada on the second Monday in October.

that (THat)
pronoun **1.** A person or thing mentioned or indicated. **2.** A thing farther away than or contrasted with another thing. **3.** Used to introduce a clause defining which person or thing you are referring to. In the sentence *I took a bite of the cake that he baked,* "that he baked" defines which cake is meant.
adjective **1.** Used to indicate a person, place, or thing present or already mentioned. **2.** Used to indicate a person or thing farther away than or contrasted with another thing.
conjunction **1.** Used to show reason or cause. **2.** Used to introduce a clause in a sentence. **3.** Used to indicate a result.
adverb To the extent that is stated; so.
▶ *pronoun, plural* **those** ▶ *adjective, plural* **those**

thatch (thach) *noun* Dried plants, such as straw or reeds, used to make a roof, or a roof made from these materials. ▶ *noun, plural* **thatches** ▶ *adjective* **thatched**

that's (THats) *contraction* A short form of *that is* or *that has.*

thaw (thaw)
verb **1.** To melt. **2.** To become room temperature after being frozen.
noun A time of year when snow and ice melt because the weather has become warmer.
▶ *verb* **thawing, thawed**

the (THuh *or* THee)
definite article **1.** Used before a noun or noun phrase that stands for a particular or previously mentioned person or thing. *The chair in the hall is an antique.* **2.** Used to show that a thing is the only one of it there is. **3.** Used to show that a person or thing is thought of as the best, most important, or greatest, and therefore one of a kind. *It was the movie to see last year.* **4.** Used to make a singular noun general. *The hippopotamus lives in central and southern Africa.*
adverb To that degree; that much; by that much.

the·a·ter *or* **the·a·tre** (**thee**-uh-tur) *noun* **1.** A building where plays or movies are shown. **2.** The work of writing, producing, or acting in plays.

the·at·ri·cal (thee-**at**-ri-kuhl) *adjective* **1.** Of or having to do with the theater. **2.** Done in a way that is intended to create a dramatic effect.

thee (THee) *pronoun* An old word for **you.**

theft (theft) *noun* The act of stealing.

their (THair) *adjective* Belonging to or having to do with them. **Their** sounds like **there** and **they're.**

theirs (THairz) *pronoun* The one or ones belonging to or having to do with them.

them (THem) *pronoun* The form of the word *they* that is used as the object of a verb or preposition. It refers to the things or people just mentioned.

theme (theem) *noun* **1.** The main subject or idea of a piece of writing or a talk. **2.** A short essay or piece of writing on one subject. **3.** The main melody in a piece of music. **4. theme park** A park with rides and attractions based on a particular subject, such as space travel.

them·selves (THem-**selvz** *or* THuhm-**selvz**) *pronoun* Them and no one else; their own selves.

then (THen)
adverb **1.** At that time. **2.** After that; next. **3.** In that case; therefore.
noun That time.

the·ol·o·gy (thee-**ah**-luh-jee) *noun* The study of religion and religious beliefs. ▶ *adjective* **theological** (thee-uh-**lah**-ji-kuhl)

the·o·rem (**thee**-ur-uhm *or* **theer**-uhm) *noun* A statement, especially in mathematics, that can be proved to be true.

the·o·ret·i·cal (thee-uh-**ret**-i-kuhl) *adjective* **1.** Existing only as a theory; not practically possible. **2.** Of or having to do with a theory.
▶ *adverb* **theoretically**

the·o·ry (**thee**-ur-ee *or* **theer**-ee) *noun* **1.** An idea or a statement that explains how or why something happens. **2.** An idea or opinion based on some facts or evidence but not proved. **3.** The rules and principles of an art or a science, rather than its practice. **4.** If something is true or should happen **in theory,** it should be true or happen but it may not.

ther·a·pist (**ther**-uh-pist) *noun* A person whose work is providing therapy for illnesses, injuries, or psychological problems.

ther·a·py (**ther**-uh-pee) *noun* A treatment for an illness, injury, disability, or psychological problem. ▶ *noun, plural* **therapies** ▶ *noun* **therapist** (**ther**-uh-pist)

there (THair)
adverb At, to, or in a particular place.
pronoun A word used to introduce a sentence in which the verb comes before the subject.
noun That place.
There sounds like **their** and **they're.**

there·a·bouts (**thair**-uh-*bouts*) *adverb* Near the place or near the time that is being talked about.

there·af·ter (THair-**af**-tur) *adverb* Afterward; from that time on.

there·by (THair-**bye** *or* **THair-bye**) *adverb* In that way; by that means.

there·fore (**THair**-for) *adverb* As a result; for that reason.

therm (thurm) *noun* A unit for measuring heat.

ther·mal (**thur**-muhl)
adjective Of or having to do with heat

T

or holding in heat.

noun A rising current of warm air.

ther·mom·e·ter (thur-**mah**-mi-tur) *noun* An instrument that is used to measure temperature.

ther·mos (**thur**-muhs) *noun* A container that keeps liquids hot or cold for many hours. Also known as a *thermos bottle.* ▸ *noun, plural* **thermoses**

ther·mo·stat (**thur**-muh-stat) *noun* A device that automatically controls the temperature of furnaces, refrigerators, air conditioners, and other heating and cooling systems.

the·sau·rus (thi-**sor**-uhs) *noun* A book that groups together words that have similar and opposite meanings. ▸ *noun, plural* **thesauri** (thi-**sor**-eye) *or* **thesauruses**

these (THeez) *adjective and pronoun, plural* The plural of **this.**

the·sis (**thee**-sis) *noun* An idea or argument that is to be debated or proved. ▸ *noun, plural* **theses** (**thee**-seez)

they (THay) *pronoun* **1.** The people, animals, or things mentioned before. **2.** People in general.

they'd (THayd) *contraction* A short form of *they had* or *they would.*

they'll (THayl) *contraction* A short form of *they will* or *they shall.*

they're (THair) *contraction* A short form of *they are.* **They're** sounds like **their** and **there.**

they've (THayv) *contraction* A short form of *they have.*

thick (thik)

adjective **1.** Great in width or depth; not thin. **2.** As measured from one side or surface to the other. **3.** Growing, being, or having parts that are close together; dense. **4.** Not flowing or pouring easily.

adverb In a way that will make something thick.

▸ *adjective* **thicker, thickest** ▸ *noun* **thickness** ▸ *verb* **thicken** ▸ *adverb* **thickly**

thick·en (**thik**-uhn) *verb* To make thick or to become thick. ▸ *verb* **thickening, thickened** ▸ *noun* **thickener**

thick·et (**thik**-it) *noun* An area of plants, bushes, or small trees growing very close together.

thief (theef) *noun* Someone who steals things from a person or place. ▸ *noun, plural* **thieves** (theevz) ▸ *verb* **thieve** (theev) ▸ *adjective* **thieving**

thigh (thye) *noun* The top part of your leg, between your knee and your hip.

thim·ble (**thim**-buhl) *noun* A small cap worn on the finger to protect it while you are sewing.

thin (thin)

adjective **1.** Small in width or depth; not thick. **2.** Not fat; slender. **3.** Not close together; not dense. **4.** Containing mostly water and so flowing or pouring easily. **5.** Not deep or firm; weak. **6.** Not very effective.

verb To make something become less thick, crowded, or dense.

▸ *adjective* **thinner, thinnest** ▸ *noun* **thinness** ▸ *adverb* **thinly**

thing (thing)

noun **1.** An object that is not alive. **2.** An object whose name you do not know or do not state. **3.** An idea, action, or event.

noun, plural **1. things** Items that belong to someone. **2. things** Life in general at a particular time.

think (thingk) *verb* **1.** To use your mind in order to form an idea, solve a problem, or make a decision. **2.** To have an opinion or believe that something is true. **3.** To have as a thought; to imagine. **4.** To remember something. **5.** To consider someone and that person's particular situation or needs.

▸ *verb* **thinking, thought** ▸ *noun* **thinker**

third (thurd)

adjective Next after second and before fourth, written numerically as 3rd.

noun One part of something that has been divided into three equal parts, written numerically as 1/3.

▸ *adverb* **thirdly**

Third World (**thurd wurld**) *noun* The poorer, developing countries of the world.

T

thirst (thurst) *noun* **1.** A dry feeling in the mouth, caused by a need to drink liquids. **2.** A need or desire for liquid. **3.** The feeling of wanting something very much.

thirst·y (**thur**-stee) *adjective* Needing or wanting to drink something. ▶ *adjective* **thirstier, thirstiest** ▶ *adverb* **thirstily** (**thur**-stuh-lee)

this (THis) *pronoun* **1.** A person or thing present, nearby, or just mentioned. **2.** Something that is nearer than or is being compared to something else. **3.** Something about to be said. *adjective* **1.** Used to indicate a person or thing present, nearby, or just mentioned. **2.** Used to indicate a person or thing nearer than or contrasted with another thing. *adverb* To this extent.
▶ *pronoun and adjective, plural* **these**

this·tle (**this**-uhl) *noun* A wild plant that has leaves with sharp points and purple, pink, white, blue, or yellow flowers.

thong (thawng) *noun* **1.** A narrow strip of leather used to fasten things together. **2.** A sandal held to the foot with a piece of leather or plastic that goes between the first two toes.

tho·rax (**thor**-aks) *noun* **1.** The part of your body between your neck and your abdomen. **2.** The part of an insect's body between its head and its abdomen.
▶ *noun, plural* **thoraxes** or **thoraces** (**thor**-uh-seez)

thorn (thorn) *noun* A sharp point that sticks out from a branch or stem of a plant such as a rose.

thorn·y (**thor**-nee) *adjective* **1.** Covered with thorns. **2.** Causing difficulty.
▶ *adjective* **thornier, thorniest**

thor·ough (**thur**-oh) *adjective* Done in a careful and complete way. ▶ *noun* **thoroughness**

thor·ough·bred (**thur**-uh-bred) *noun* **1.** **Thoroughbred** A breed of English horses developed especially for racing. **2.** An animal whose parents are of the same breed.

thor·ough·fare (**thur**-uh-*fair*) *noun* A main road.

thor·ough·ly (**thur**-uh-lee) *adverb* In a complete, detailed, or very careful manner.

those (THoze) *pronoun, plural* The plural of **that**. *adjective, plural* The plural of **that**.

thou (THou) *pronoun* An old word for **you.**

though (THoh) *conjunction* **1.** In spite of the fact that; although. **2.** Yet; but; however. *adverb* However; nevertheless.

thought (thawt) *verb* The past tense and past participle of **think.** *noun* **1.** If you are **deep in thought** or **lost in thought,** you are thinking so hard that you do not notice what is going on around you. **2.** An idea or an opinion. **3.** Close attention to something.

thought·ful (**thawt**-fuhl) *adjective* **1.** Involving a lot of thought. **2.** Kind and considering other people's feelings and needs.
▶ *adverb* **thoughtfully**

thought·less (**thawt**-lis) *adjective* **1.** Not concerned about other people's feelings and needs. **2.** Careless.
▶ *adverb* **thoughtlessly**

thou·sand (**thou**-zuhnd) *noun* The number that is equal to 10 times 100, written numerically as 1,000. *adjective* Of or having to do with the number 1,000.

thou·sandth (**thou**-zuhndth) *adjective* Of or having to do with the last in a sequence of a thousand items, written numerically as 1,000th. *noun* **1.** One part of something that has been divided into 1,000 equal parts, written numerically as 1/1000. **2.** In decimal notation, the **thousandth place** is the position of the third number to the right of the decimal point. In the number 4.0129, the digit 2 is in the thousandths place.

thrash (thrash) *verb* **1.** To beat or defeat someone severely. **2.** To move wildly or violently. **3.** To beat someone thoroughly in a game. **4.** If you **thrash out** an idea or a problem, you talk about it until you make a decision.
▶ *verb* **thrashes, thrashing, thrashed** ▶ *noun* **thrashing**

thread (thred)
noun **1.** A strand of material such as cotton or silk that is used for sewing. **2.** The theme or main idea that connects different ideas or events. **3.** The raised line that winds continuously around a screw or nut.
verb **1.** To pass something such as a thread or piece of string through a hole. **2.** To move through a place by going between and around things or people that are in your way.
▶ *verb* **threading, threaded**

thread·bare (thred-bair) *adjective* If your clothes are **threadbare,** they are old and in bad condition.

threat (thret) *noun* **1.** A warning that punishment or harm will follow if a certain thing is done or not done. **2.** A sign or possibility that something harmful or dangerous might happen. **3.** A person or thing regarded as a danger.

threat·en (thret-uhn) *verb* To say that you will hurt or cause trouble for someone if you do not get what you want. ▶ *verb* **threatening, threatened**

three (three)
noun The number that comes after two and before four, written numerically as 3.
adjective Referring to the number that comes after two and before four.

three·di·men·sion·al (three-duh-men-shuh-nuhl) *or* **3-D** (three-dee) *adjective* **1.** Having or seeming to have the three dimensions of length, width, and height. **2.** Having or seeming to have depth.

thresh (thresh) *verb* To separate the grain or seed from a cereal plant such as wheat by beating. ▶ *verb* **threshes, threshing, threshed**

thresh·old (thresh-hohld) *noun* **1.** The bottom of a door frame, usually made of wood, metal, or stone. **2.** The level at which something starts to happen or change. **3.** The start of something new, especially something important.

threw (throo) *verb* The past tense of **throw.**

thrift (thrift) *noun* Careful management of money or other resources.

thrift·y (thrif-tee) *adjective* Careful not to waste money. ▶ *adjective* **thriftier, thriftiest**

thrill (thril) *noun* A strong feeling of excitement and pleasure. ▶ *adjective* **thrilling**

thril·ler (thril-ur) *noun* An exciting story that is filled with action, mystery, or suspense.

thrive (thrive) *verb* To become successful or healthy and strong. ▶ *verb* **thriving, thrived** ▶ *adjective* **thriving**

throat (throht) *noun* **1.** The front of your neck. **2.** The tube inside the neck that runs from the mouth into the stomach or lungs.

throb (thrahb) *verb* **1.** If a part of your body **throbs,** you feel a pain there that stops and starts in a regular pattern. **2.** If music or a sound **throbs,** it beats repeatedly with a strong regular rhythm.
▶ *verb* **throbbing, throbbed**

throne (throhn) *noun* **1.** A special chair for a king or queen to sit on during a ceremony. **2.** The power or authority of a king or queen.

throng (thrawng)
noun A large group of people.
verb To gather in a large group.
▶ *verb* **thronging, thronged**

throt·tle (thrah-tuhl)
verb To injure or kill someone by squeezing the person's throat so that he or she cannot breathe.
noun A piece of equipment that controls the amount of fuel that flows in a vehicle's engine.
▶ *verb* **throttling, throttled**

T

through (throo)
preposition 1. In one side and out the other. *I walked through the hall and into the kitchen.* 2. To many places in; around. *We traveled through Europe.* 3. By way of; because of. *Peter got the job through a friend.* 4. As a result of. *We lost the game through inexperience.* 5. From the beginning to the end of. *School goes through June.* 6. In the midst of; among or between. *A hiking path winds through the trees.* 7. Finished with. *We are through the worst part of the storm now.*
adverb 1. From one side or end to the other. 2. Completely. 3. From beginning to end.
adjective 1. Allowing passage from one end or side to the other. 2. Finished.

through·out (*throo*-**out**)
preposition 1. All the way through; in every part. *The company has stores throughout the West Coast.* 2. During the whole of a particular period of time. *The person sitting behind me coughed throughout the entire movie.*
adverb In every part; everywhere.

through·way (throo-*way*) *noun* Another spelling of **thruway.**

throw (throh)
verb 1. To use your hand to send something through the air. 2. To make someone or something fall to the ground. 3. To put on or take off quickly or carelessly. 4. To put in a certain condition or place. 5. (informal) To make someone feel confused or surprised. 6. **throw away** To get rid of something that you do not want. 7. **throw up** (informal) To vomit.
noun The act of throwing something, such as a ball.
▶ *verb* **throwing, threw** (throo), **thrown** (throhn)

thrush (thruhsh) *noun* A small songbird. Robins and bluebirds are types of thrushes. ▶ *noun, plural* **thrushes**

thrust (thruhst)
verb To push something suddenly and roughly.
noun 1. The forward force produced by the engine of a jet or rocket. 2. The main point of an argument.
▶ *verb* **thrusting, thrust**

thru·way (throo-*way*) *noun* A wide highway used especially for traveling at high speeds over long distances.

thud (thuhd) *noun* The dull thump made when a heavy object falls to the ground or hits something else.

thug (thuhg) *noun* A rough, violent person.

thumb (thuhm)
noun The short, thick finger that you have on the end of each hand.
verb **thumb through** To turn over the pages of a book.
idiom If someone is **all thumbs,** the person is very clumsy.
▶ *verb* **thumbing, thumbed**

thumb drive (thuhm *drive*) *noun* Another name for a **flash drive.**

thumb·tack (**thuhm**-*tak*) *noun* A small pin with a flat, round head, used for attaching paper to bulletin boards, walls, and other surfaces.

thump (thuhmp)
noun 1. An act of hitting someone or something hard. 2. A deep, heavy sound made when something heavy hits a surface.
verb To beat heavily with a steady rhythm.
▶ *verb* **thumping, thumped**

thun·der (**thuhn**-dur)
noun The loud sound that comes during a storm after a flash of lightning.
verb To make a very loud noise like thunder.
▶ *verb* **thundering, thundered**

thun·der·cloud (**thuhn**-dur-*kloud*) *noun* A large, dark cloud that produces lightning and thunder during a storm.

thun·der·storm (**thuhn**-dur-*storm*) *noun* A storm with heavy rain, thunder, and lightning.

Thurs·day (**thurz**-*day* or **thurz**-dee) *noun* The fifth day of the week, after Wednesday and before Friday.

thus (THuhs) *adverb* 1. In this way. 2. As a result.

T

thwart (thwort) *verb* To prevent a plan from happening or succeeding. ▸ *verb* **thwarting, thwarted**

thy (THye) *pronoun* An old word for **your.**

thyme (time) *noun* An herb used in cooking that grows as a low shrub. **Thyme** sounds like **time.**

thy·roid (**thye**-roid) *noun* A gland in the throat that produces a hormone that regulates the body's growth and metabolism.

ti·ar·a (tee-**ar**-uh *or* tee-**ahr**-uh) *noun* A piece of jewelry like a small crown, typically worn by women.

tick (tik)
noun **1.** The light clicking sound that a clock or watch makes. **2.** A mark that someone makes to show that an answer is correct or that something has been done. **3.** A very small insect that looks like a spider. Ticks suck blood from under the skin of animals and people.
verb **1.** To make such a sound. **2.** To mark time passing by ticking. **3.** To put a mark next to something on a list. **4.** If you **tick** someone **off,** you make the person extremely angry.
▸ *verb* **ticking, ticked**

tick·et (**tik**-it)
noun **1.** A printed piece of paper or card that proves you have paid to do something, such as ride on a train or sit in a movie theater. **2.** A written order to pay a fine or appear in court for breaking a traffic law. **3.** A price tag or a label. **4.** The list of candidates belonging to a particular political party to be voted on in an election.
verb **1.** To attach a price tag or label to something. **2.** To give a traffic ticket to someone.
▸ *verb* **ticketing, ticketed**

tick·le (**tik**-uhl)
verb **1.** To keep touching or poking someone gently in order to try to make the person laugh. **2.** To have a slightly uncomfortable feeling in a part of your body. **3.** To please or amuse someone.
noun A slightly uncomfortable feeling

in a part of your body.
▸ *verb* **tickling, tickled**

tick·lish (**tik**-lish) *adjective* **1.** Easily tickled. **2.** Requiring sensitivity or delicate treatment.

tic-tac-toe *or* **tick-tack-toe** (tik-tak-**toh**) *noun* A game played on a grid of nine squares. Two players take turns putting an X or an O in an empty square. The winner is the first person to get three Xs or Os in a row.

ti·dal wave (**tye**-duhl *wave*) *noun* An extremely large and powerful ocean wave, often caused by an underwater earthquake.

tid·bit (**tid**-bit) *noun* **1.** A small piece of food. **2.** A small piece of interesting news or information.

tide (tide) *noun* **1.** The constant change in sea level that is caused by the pull of the sun and the moon on the earth. **2.** Something that changes like the tides of the sea.

tid·ings (**tye**-dingz) *noun, plural* News or information.

ti·dy (**tye**-dee) *adjective* Neat, clean, and organized. ▸ *adjective* **tidier, tidiest** ▸ *noun* **tidiness**

tie (tye)
verb To join two pieces of something such as string or rope together with a knot or bow.
noun **1.** A long narrow piece of fabric that is worn knotted around the collar of a shirt; a necktie.
2. Something that holds or bonds people together. **3.** A situation in which two people or teams have exactly the same score in a competition.
▸ *verb* **ties, tying, tied**

tie-break·er (**tye**-bray-kur) *noun* A special or extra game played to decide the winner of a tie game.

tier (teer) *noun* One of several rows or layers placed one above the other, such as a row of seats in a stadium or layers on a wedding cake.

ti·ger (**tye**-gur) *noun* A large, striped, wild cat that lives in Asia. The tiger is the largest member of the cat family.

ti·ger lil·y (**tye**-gur *lil*-ee) *noun* A large flower that is shaped like a trumpet and has red or orange flowers and black spots.

tight (tite) *adjective* 1. Fitting closely. 2. Fastened or held firmly; secure. 3. Fully stretched; not loose. 4. Not letting water or air pass through. 5. (informal) Not generous with money; stingy. 6. Having little time to spare. 7. Difficult. 8. Even or almost even in score; close.
▶ *adjective* **tighter, tightest** ▶ *adverb* **tightly**

tight·en (**tye**-tuhn) *verb* To make something tight or to become tight. ▶ *verb* **tightening, tightened**

tight·rope (**tite**-rope) *noun* A rope or wire stretched high above the ground on which circus performers walk.

tights (tites) *noun, plural* A piece of clothing that fits closely and covers the hips, legs, and feet.

Ti·gris (**tye**-gris) A major river of the Middle East, flowing through parts of Turkey, Syria, and Iraq. The Tigris originates in the mountains of Turkey. It meets the Euphrates in Iraq and ultimately flows into the Persian Gulf.

til·de (**til**-duh) *noun* An accent that is used over the letter *n* in Spanish, and over other letters in other languages. For example, the English word *canyon* is spelled "cañon" in Spanish, but has a similar pronunciation.

tile (tile) *noun* A square made of stone, plastic, or baked clay, often used to make roofs or to cover floors or walls.

till (til)
preposition and conjunction Another word for **until**.
noun A drawer or box in a store, used to hold money; part of a cash register.
verb To prepare land for growing crops.
▶ *verb* **tilling, tilled**

till·er (**til**-ur) *noun* A handle attached to the rudder of a small boat. The tiller is used to steer the boat.

tilt (tilt) *verb* To lean or tip to one side. ▶ *verb* **tilting, tilted**

tim·ber (**tim**-bur) *noun* 1. Cut wood used for building; lumber. 2. A long, heavy piece of wood; a beam. 3. Trees; forest.

tim·ber·line (**tim**-bur-line) *noun* The highest point at which trees can grow on a mountain, or the farthest northern point in the arctic regions where trees can grow.

time (time)
noun 1. The past, present, and future measured in seconds, minutes, hours, and so on. 2. A particular moment shown on a clock or watch in hours and minutes. 3. An amount of time. 4. A specific period in someone's life. 5. A specific period in history. 6. One in a series of repeated actions. 7. The beat in a piece of music.
verb 1. To measure how long it takes to do something. 2. To arrange for something to happen at a particular time.
Time sounds like **thyme**. ▶ *verb* **timing, timed** ▶ *noun* **timer** ▶ *adjective* **timely**

time·less (**time**-lis) *adjective* 1. Not affected, changed, or weakened by time. 2. Not referring to a particular time or date.
▶ *adverb* **timelessly**

time·line (**time**-line) *noun* A chart or graph of a period of time with important events noted at points where they happened or are supposed to happen.

times (timez)
noun, plural A particular period of time.
preposition Multiplied by. *Seven times six is 42.*

time·ta·ble (**time**-tay-buhl) *noun* A list of the times when buses, trains, planes, or boats arrive and depart; a schedule.

time zone (**time** zone) *noun* A region in which all the clocks are set to the same time. The earth is divided into 24 time zones.

tim·id (**tim**-id) *adjective* Shy and without courage. ▶ *noun* **timidity** (ti-**mid**-i-tee) ▶ *adverb* **timidly**

T

Ti·mor-Leste (**tee**-mor-**lest**) An island nation in Southeast Asia. The main part of the country is the eastern half of the island of Timor, whose western half belongs to Indonesia. Also known as East Timor, Timor-Leste declared its independence from Indonesia in 1975 and suffered many years of violence and instability in its struggle to become a separate country. Timor-Leste also includes a small area on the northwestern side of Timor and two islands off Timor's coast.

tin (tin) *noun* 1. A soft, silvery metal that does not rust easily. Tin is used to coat steel cans. 2. A container that is made of or coated with tin.

tin·foil (**tin**-*foil*) *noun* A paper-thin, flexible sheet of tin or aluminum used for wrapping food.

tinge (tinj) *noun* A very small amount of a color, quality, or emotion.

tin·gle (**ting**-guhl)
verb To sting or tickle slightly.
noun A slight sting or tickle.
▶ *verb* **tingling, tingled**

tin·ker (**ting**-kur)
verb To make small adjustments to something in a casual way, especially in order to repair it.
noun A person in the past who traveled from place to place fixing metal objects such as pots and pans.
▶ *verb* **tinkering, tinkered**

tin·kle (**ting**-kuhl)
verb To make a light, ringing sound such as that made by a small bell.
noun A light, ringing sound.
▶ *verb* **tinkling, tinkled**

tint (tint)
noun 1. A variety of a color, often one with white added. 2. A pale, delicate color.
verb To give a slight color to.
▶ *verb* **tinting, tinted** ▶ *adjective* **tinted**

ti·ny (**tye**-nee) *adjective* Very small. ▶ *adjective* **tinier, tiniest**

tip (tip)
verb 1. To cause something to move into a slanted position or fall over. 2. To move into a slanted position or fall over. 3. To raise or touch your hat

as a greeting to someone. 4. **tip off** To give information or a warning to someone.
noun 1. The end part or point of something. 2. A helpful piece of advice. 3. An amount of extra money that you give to someone such as a taxi driver or waitress as thanks for good service.
▶ *verb* **tipping, tipped**

tip·toe (**tip**-*toh*) *verb* To walk very quietly on or as if you were on your toes. ▶ *verb* **tiptoeing, tiptoed**

tire (tire)
noun A band of rubber that fits around the outside of a wheel and usually is filled with air.
verb 1. To become weak or unable to continue because you need rest, or to make someone do this. 2. To become bored.
▶ *verb* **tiring, tired**

tired (tired *or* **tye**-urd) *adjective* 1. Ready for sleep, because you have been awake a long time or you have worked hard. 2. When people talk about a **tired** excuse, cliché, formula, or other idea expressed in language, they mean that it has been said or used too often and is not effective or convincing. 3. If you are **tired of** something, you have had enough of it and don't want any more.
▶ *noun* **tiredness**

tire·some (**tire**-suhm) *adjective* Making you feel annoyed or bored.

tis·sue (**tish**-oo) *noun* 1. Soft, thin paper used as a handkerchief, or for cleaning or wrapping things. 2. A mass of similar cells that form a particular part or organ of an animal or a plant.

ti·tle (**tye**-tuhl) *noun* 1. The name of a book, movie, song, painting, or other work. 2. A word used to show a person's status, rank, or occupation. *Ms., Dr., Lord,* and *Senator* are titles. 3. Legal ownership, or a document that shows legal ownership. 4. A championship.
▶ *verb* **title**

T

ti·tle bar (**tye**-tuhl *bahr*) *noun* The horizontal bar that appears at the top of a computer program that you are using, with the name of the program in it.

Tlin·git (**tling**-git) *noun* A member of a group of Native Americans who live on the islands and coast of southern Alaska. ▶ *noun, plural* **Tlingit** or **Tlingits**

to (too *or* tuh) *preposition* **1.** Toward; in the direction of. *The kitten ran to me.* **2.** As far as. *The astronauts went to the moon.* **3.** On, against, or in contact with. *Nail the wreath to the door.* **4.** In or for each. *There are four quarts to a gallon.* **5.** Until. *Our booth is open from nine to eight.* **6.** Compared with. *The score was nine to eight.* **7.** For the attention, benefit, or purpose of. *Mom came to my rescue.* **8.** Concerning or regarding. *What do you say to that?* **9.** Before. *It's ten minutes to two.* **10.** Used before a verb to form an infinitive. *I'd like to go now.* **11.** Used to show the receiver of an action. *We gave the trophy to her.* **12.** In agreement with. *Dinner was not cooked to my liking.*
To sounds like **too** and **two.**

toad (tohd) *noun* An amphibian that looks like a frog but has rougher, drier skin. Toads live mainly on land.

toad·stool (**tohd**-*stool*) *noun* A mushroom, especially one that is poisonous.

toast (tohst)
noun Bread browned by heat.
verb **1.** To warm thoroughly. **2.** To hold up your glass and drink something such as a glass of wine in honor of someone.
▶ *verb* **toasting, toasted**

toast·er (**toh**-stur) *noun* An electrical appliance that toasts bread.

to·bac·co (tuh-**bak**-oh) *noun* The chopped, dried leaves of the tobacco plant. Tobacco is used for smoking, as in cigarettes, or chewing.

to·bog·gan (tuh-**bah**-guhn)
noun A long, flat sled with a front edge that turns up.

verb To travel downhill on a toboggan.
▶ *verb* **tobogganing, tobogganed**

to·day (tuh-**day**)
noun This present day or time.
adverb **1.** On or during this day. **2.** At the present time; nowadays.

tod·dler (**tahd**-lur) *noun* A very young child who has just learned to walk.

toe (toh) *noun* **1.** One of the five slender parts at the end of your foot. **2.** The part of a shoe, boot, sock, or stocking that covers the toes.
Toe sounds like **tow.**

tof·fee (**taw**-fee) *noun* A hard, chewy candy made by boiling sugar and butter together.

to·fu (**toh**-foo) *noun* A soft food with a texture like cheese that is made from soybeans.

to·ga (**toh**-guh) *noun* A piece of clothing worn by people in ancient Rome. It was wrapped around the body and draped over the left shoulder.

to·geth·er (tuh-**geTH**-ur) *adverb* **1.** With one another. **2.** Into one group, mass, or place. **3.** At the same time. **4.** In agreement or cooperation.

To·go (**toh**-goh) A country in West Africa on the Gulf of Guinea. After gaining its independence from France in 1960, it was under military rule for many years but is now holding democratic elections. A sub-Saharan nation, it has savannas and a tropical climate.

toil (toil)
verb **1.** To work very hard for a long time. **2.** To move slowly with pain or effort.
noun Hard, exhausting work.
▶ *verb* **toiling, toiled** ▶ *noun* **toiler**

toi·let (**toi**-lit) *noun* **1.** A device connected to plumbing in which people get rid of waste from their bodies. **2.** A room containing a toilet; a bathroom.

to·ken (**toh**-kuhn) *noun* **1.** Something that stands for something else; a sign or symbol. **2.** A piece of stamped metal that can be used in place of money.

told (tohld) *verb* The past tense and past participle of **tell.**

tol·er·ance (**tah**-lur-uhns) *noun* 1. The willingness to respect or accept the customs, beliefs, or opinions of others. 2. The ability to put up with or endure something such as pain or hardship.

tol·er·ant (**tah**-lur-uhnt) *adjective* Willing to put up with something or someone, such as a challenging situation or a person who is very different from you. ▶ *adverb* **tolerantly**

tol·er·ate (**tah**-luh-rate) *verb* To put up with or endure something or someone. ▶ *verb* **tolerating, tolerated** ▶ *noun* **toleration**

toll (tohl)
verb To ring a bell slowly and regularly.
noun 1. A charge or tax paid for using a highway, bridge, or tunnel. 2. The number of deaths or injuries as a result of something such as an accident, war, or illness. 3. A charge for a service such as a long-distance telephone call. 4. The sound made by a bell ringing.
idiom If something **takes its toll** on someone or something, it causes serious damage or suffering.
▶ *verb* **tolling, tolled**

tom·a·hawk (**tah**-muh-*hawk*) *noun* A small ax once used by some Native Americans as a tool or weapon.

to·ma·to (tuh-**may**-toh or tuh-**mah**-toh) *noun* A red, juicy fruit eaten as a vegetable either raw or cooked. ▶ *noun, plural* **tomatoes**

tomb (toom) *noun* A grave, room, or building for holding a dead body.

tom·boy (**tahm**-*boi*) *noun* A girl who enjoys activities that were once associated with boys, such as climbing trees or playing sports.

tomb·stone (**toom**-*stone*) *noun* A carved block of stone that marks the place where someone is buried.

tom·cat (**tahm**-*kat*) *noun* A male cat.

to·mor·row (tuh-**mor**-oh)
noun 1. The day after today. 2. The future.
adverb On the day after today.

tom-tom (**tahm**-*tahm*) *noun* 1. A small drum that is usually beaten with the hands. 2. A small to medium-size drum in a drum set that makes a low, hollow sound.

ton (tuhn) *noun* A unit of weight equal to 2,000 pounds in the United States and Canada and 2,240 pounds in Great Britain.

tone (tohn) *noun* 1. A single sound, especially one that is musical, thought of in terms of its pitch, length, quality, or loudness. 2. A way of speaking or writing that shows a certain feeling or attitude. 3. The general quality, feeling, or style of something. 4. In music, a **tone** is the difference in pitch between certain musical notes. 5. A tint or shade of a color. 6. The normal, healthy firmness of the muscles.

Ton·ga (**tahng**-guh) A kingdom consisting of a group of islands in the South Pacific Ocean. It is the only island nation in the area that did not become a European colony, and is the only one that is still ruled by a native king.

tongs (tawngz) *noun, plural* A tool with two connected arms used for picking up or holding things.

tongue (tuhng) *noun* 1. The movable muscle in your mouth that is used for tasting, swallowing, and talking. 2. The tongue of an animal such as a cow, cooked and used as food. 3. A language. 4. The ability to speak. 5. The flap of material under the laces of a shoe. 6. **hold your tongue** To stop yourself from saying something.

tongue twist·er (**tuhng** *twis*-tur) *noun* A sentence or verse that is very hard to say or repeat quickly, such as "red leather, yellow leather."

ton·ic (**tah**-nik) *noun* Something that makes you feel stronger or refreshed.

to·night (tuh-**nite**)
noun This evening or night.
adverb On this evening or night.

ton·sil·li·tis (*tahn*-suh-**lye**-tis) *noun* An illness that makes your tonsils infected and painful.

ton·sils (**tahn**-suhlz) *noun, plural* Two flaps of soft tissue that lie one on each side of the throat.

T

too (too) *adverb* **1.** As well; also; in addition. **2.** More than enough. **3.** Very; extremely. *Too* is used in this way especially with negatives.

Too sounds like **to** and **two.**

took (tuk) *verb* The past tense of **take.**

tool (tool) *noun* **1.** A piece of equipment that you use to do a particular job, for example, to repair or make things. **2.** Anything that helps you accomplish something.

tool·bar (**tool**-*bahr*) *noun* A horizontal bar near the top of the screen in some computer programs that you click on to use various commands and features.

tool·box (**tool**-*bahks*) *noun* A box designed for storing or carrying hand tools. ▶ *noun, plural* **toolboxes**

toon (toon) *noun* (informal) A cartoon.

toot (toot) *verb* To sound a horn or whistle in short blasts. ▶ *verb* **tooting, tooted**

tooth (tooth) *noun* **1.** One of the white, bony parts of your mouth that you use for biting and chewing food. **2.** One of a row of parts that stick out on a saw, comb, or gear. ▶ *noun, plural* **teeth**

tooth·ache (**tooth**-*ake*) *noun* A pain in or near a tooth.

tooth·brush (**tooth**-*bruhsh*) *noun* A small brush that is used to clean the teeth. ▶ *noun, plural* **toothbrushes**

tooth·paste (**tooth**-*payst*) *noun* A paste that is put on a toothbrush and used to clean the teeth.

tooth·pick (**tooth**-*pik*) *noun* A small, thin piece of wood or plastic that is used to remove food from between the teeth.

top (tahp)
noun **1.** The highest point or part of something. **2.** A cover or a lid. **3.** The highest rank or position. **4.** A piece of clothing worn on the upper part of your body. **5.** The highest or greatest degree or pitch. **6.** A toy that is shaped like a cone and spins on a pointed end.
verb **1.** To do better than someone or something. **2.** To put at the top of

something.
adjective Highest in rank or position.
▶ *verb* **topping, topped**

to·paz (**toh**-paz) *noun* A clear mineral that is used as a gem. It is usually a color ranging from yellow to brown.

top·ic (**tah**-pik) *noun* The subject of a discussion, study, lesson, speech, or piece of writing.

top·i·cal (**tah**-pi-kuhl) *adjective* **1.** Of interest now; in the news at present. **2.** A **topical** medicine is applied directly to the skin.

to·pog·ra·phy (tuh-**pah**-gruh-fee) *noun* The detailed description of the physical features of an area, including hills, valleys, mountains, plains, and rivers. ▶ *noun* **topographer**

top·o·nym (**tah**-puh-nim) *noun* The name of a place.

top·ple (**tah**-puhl) *verb* **1.** To become unsteady and fall over, usually from a height. **2.** To make something fall. **3.** To remove a leader or government from power, especially by force; overthrow. ▶ *verb* **toppling, toppled**

top·soil (**tahp**-*soil*) *noun* The top layer of soil that contains the nutrients that plants need to grow.

top·sy-tur·vy (**tahp**-see-**tur**-vee) *adjective, adverb* Upside down, mixed-up, or confused.

To·rah (**tor**-uh *or* **toh**-ruh) *noun* The first five books of the Jewish Bible which make up the traditional principles of Judaism.

torch (torch)
noun **1.** A flaming light that can be carried in the hand. **2.** A tool that gives off a very hot flame used to weld or cut metals; a blowtorch.
verb To set fire to something.
▶ *verb* **torches, torching, torched** ▶ *noun, plural* **torches**

tore (tor) *verb* The past tense of **tear.**

to·re·a·dor (**tor**-ee-uh-*dor*) *noun* A bullfighter.

tor·ment
verb (tor-**ment**) To annoy or upset someone deliberately.
noun (**tor**-ment) Great pain or suffering.

T

▸ *verb* **tormenting, tormented** ▸ *noun* **tormentor** (tor-**men**-tur)

torn (torn) *verb* The past participle of **tear.**

tor·na·do (tor-**nay**-doh) *noun* A violent and very destructive windstorm that appears as a dark cloud shaped like a funnel. ▸ *noun, plural* **tornadoes** or **tornados**

Tor·na·do Al·ley (tor-**nay**-doh **al**-ee) *noun* The central part of the United States where tornadoes are frequent, including some or all of Kansas, Nebraska, Oklahoma, the Dakotas, Missouri, and Iowa.

tor·pe·do (tor-**pee**-doh) *noun* An underwater bomb shaped like a tube that explodes when it hits a target, such as a ship. ▸ *noun, plural* **torpedoes**

tor·rent (**tor**-uhnt) *noun* A violent, quickly moving stream of water or other liquid. ▸ *adjective* **torrential** (tuh-**ren**-chuhl)

tor·rid (**tor**-id) *adjective* Extremely hot. ▸ *noun* **torridness** ▸ *adverb* **torridly**

tor·so (**tor**-soh) *noun* The part of your body between your neck and your waist, not including your arms; the trunk.

tor·til·la (tor-**tee**-yuh) *noun* A round, flat bread made from cornmeal or flour. Tortillas are often served with a topping or filling.

tor·toise (**tor**-tuhs) *noun* A turtle, especially one that lives on land.

tor·ture (**tor**-chur) *verb* To deliberately cause someone extreme pain or mental suffering as punishment or as a way to force the person to do or say something. *noun* 1. The act of causing extreme pain as a punishment or as a way of forcing someone to do or say something. 2. Extreme pain or mental suffering. ▸ *verb* **torturing, tortured**

toss (taws) *verb* 1. To throw something with little force. 2. To move, fling, or rock something back and forth. 3. To mix a salad lightly. 4. To throw a coin into the air to decide something according to which side lands face up.

▸ *verb* **tosses, tossing, tossed** ▸ *adjective* **tossed**

tot (taht) *noun* (informal) A small child.

to·tal (**toh**-tuhl) *adjective* 1. Making up the whole amount; entire. 2. Complete. *noun* A number gotten by adding; a sum. *verb* 1. To add up numbers. 2. (informal) To damage a vehicle so badly that it cannot be repaired or is not worth repairing. ▸ *verb* **totaling, totaled**

to·tal·ly (**toh**-tuh-lee) *adverb* Completely, entirely, or absolutely.

tote (toht) *verb* (informal) To carry something. ▸ *verb* **toting, toted**

to·tem pole (**toh**-tuhm *pole*) *noun* A pole carved and painted with animals, plants, and other natural objects that represent a family or clan. Certain North American Native Americans placed totem poles in front of their homes.

tot·ter (**tah**-tur) *verb* 1. To walk in an unsteady way. 2. To tremble or rock as if about to fall; to sway. ▸ *verb* **tottering, tottered**

tou·can (**too**-kan) *noun* A brightly colored tropical American bird that has a very large beak.

touch (tuhch) *verb* 1. To make contact with your hand or finger, or another area of your body. 2. To make light contact with another object. 3. To affect emotionally. *noun* 1. The act of touching. 2. The sense that you use to feel things with your fingers or other parts of your body. 3. A very small amount. *idiom* **keep in touch** To contact someone regularly, for example, by telephone or email. ▸ *verb* **touches, touching, touched** ▸ *noun, plural* **touches**

touch·down (**tuhch**-doun) *noun* 1. In football, a play in which the ball is carried over the opponent's goal line, scoring six points. 2. The moment when an aircraft or a spacecraft lands after a flight.

touch·ing (**tuhch**-ing) *adjective*
Making you feel an emotion such as compassion or sympathy. ▶ *adverb* **touchingly**

touch·y (**tuhch**-ee) *adjective* Sensitive and easily annoyed. ▶ *adjective* **touchier, touchiest** ▶ *noun* **touchiness**

tough (tuhf)
adjective 1. Difficult to do. 2. Able to deal with pain or difficult situations; rugged. 3. Strong and difficult to damage. 4. Hard to cut or chew. 5. Difficult to deal with. 6. Rough or violent. 7. Unhappy or unlucky.
noun A rough and violent person.
▶ *adjective* **tougher, toughest**

tou·pee (too-**pay**) *noun* A wig used to cover a man's baldness.

tour (toor)
noun 1. A trip around an area or place in order to see different parts of it and learn about it. 2. When a band, team, or theater group goes **on tour**, it travels to different places to play or perform.
verb To go on a tour.
▶ *verb* **touring, toured**

tour·ist (**toor**-ist) *noun* Someone who is traveling and visiting a place for pleasure. ▶ *noun* **tourism**

tour·na·ment (**toor**-nuh-muhnt) *noun* 1. A series of contests in which a number of people or teams try to win the championship. 2. In the Middle Ages, **tournaments** were events in which knights jousted against each other.

tour·ni·quet (**tur**-nuh-kit) *noun* A bandage or band twisted tightly around a limb to prevent a wound or cut from bleeding too much.

tout (tout) *verb* To praise or publicize someone or something in order to convince other people that the person or thing is important or good. ▶ *verb* **touting, touted**

tow (toh) *verb* To pull a vehicle by attaching it behind another vehicle, usually with a rope or chain. **Tow** sounds like **toe.** ▶ *verb* **towing, towed**

to·ward (tord *or* tword) *or* **to·wards** (tordz *or* twordz) *preposition* 1. In the direction of. *The crowd started moving toward the exit.* 2. With regard to; concerning. *The children showed great respect toward their grandparents.* 3. Just before; near. *It started to snow toward morning.* 4. In order to buy; for. *My parents are saving money toward a new car.*

tow·el (**tou**-uhl) *noun* A piece of thick, soft cloth or paper that is used for drying or wiping wet things.

tow·er (**tou**-ur)
noun 1. A tall and narrow structure that stands by itself or is part of a building, such as a castle or church. 2. The case of a desktop computer that contains the CPU and the hard drive, often shaped like a tall box.
verb To be much taller than the people or things around someone or something.
▶ *verb* **towering, towered** ▶ *adjective* **towering**

town (toun) *noun* A place where people live and work that has things such as houses, stores, offices, and schools. A town is larger than a village but smaller than a city.

town·ship (**toun**-ship) *noun* A division of a county in some states.

tox·ic (**tahk**-sik) *adjective* Poisonous. ▶ *noun* **toxin** (**tahk**-sin) *noun* **toxicity** (tahk-**sis**-i-tee)

toy (toi)
noun An object that children can play with.
verb If you **toy** with an idea or plan, you consider it but not in a serious way.
▶ *verb* **toying, toyed**

trace (trase)
verb 1. To find someone or something that has disappeared after looking carefully. 2. To copy a picture or shape by following lines visible through a piece of thin paper. 3. To follow, study, or describe the history or development of something.

T

noun A small, visible sign that something has happened or that someone has been somewhere.
▶ *verb* **tracing, traced** ▶ *noun* **tracing**

track (trak)
noun 1. The marks left behind by a moving animal, person, or vehicle. 2. A path or a trail. 3. A prepared path or course for runners or racing animals. 4. A rail or set of rails for vehicles to run on.
verb To look for someone or something by following marks left behind on the ground.
▶ *verb* **tracking, tracked** ▶ *noun* **tracking** ▶ *noun* **tracker**

track and field (trak uhn **feeld**) *noun* A group of sports events that includes running, jumping, and throwing contests, such as the hurdles, pole vault, and shot put. ▶ *adjective* **track-and-field**

tract (trakt) *noun* 1. A large area of land. 2. A group of parts or organs in the body that perform a specific function. 3. A booklet or pamphlet, especially one on a religious or political subject.

trac·tion (trak-shuhn) *noun* The force that keeps a moving body from slipping on a surface.

trac·tor (trak-tur) *noun* 1. A powerful vehicle used on farms to, for example, plow fields or pull heavy loads. 2. A truck that has a cab and no body. It is used for pulling a trailer.

trade (trade)
noun 1. The business of buying and selling goods; commerce. 2. A particular job or craft, especially one that requires working with the hands or with machines. 3. The exchange of something for something else.
verb 1. To exchange something you have for something someone else has; swap. 2. To buy and sell goods.
▶ *verb* **trading, traded**

trade·mark (trade-mahrk) *noun* A word, picture, or design that shows that a product is made by a particular company.

trad·er (tray-dur) *noun* 1. A person whose business is buying and selling or bartering goods. 2. A person who buys and sells stocks in hopes of making short-term profits.

trad·ing post (tray-ding *pohst*) *noun* A store in a wilderness area where people can exchange local products such as furs or hides for food and supplies.

tra·di·tion (truh-**dish**-uhn) *noun* 1. The handing down of customs, ideas, and beliefs from one generation to the next. 2. A custom, an idea, or a belief that is handed down in this way.

tra·di·tion·al (truh-**dish**-uh-nuhl) *adjective* Of or having to do with customs, beliefs, or activities that are handed down from one generation to the next; long-established.

traf·fic (traf-ik)
noun All the moving vehicles on a particular road at a particular time.
verb To buy and sell illegal goods.
▶ *verb* **trafficking, trafficked** ▶ *noun* **trafficking**

traf·fic cir·cle (traf-ik sur-kuhl) *noun* An intersection formed by a circle around which the traffic moves in only one direction. Each vehicle enters the circle from a street and continues around the circle until it arrives at the street where the vehicle's driver wishes to turn.

traf·fic light (traf-ik *lite*) *noun* A set of lights that controls traffic. Traffic lights are usually placed where streets intersect.

trag·e·dy (traj-i-dee) *noun* 1. A very sad and shocking event, especially one that involves death. 2. A serious play, movie, or book with a sad ending, such as the death of the main character, or plays of this type in general.
▶ *noun, plural* **tragedies**

trag·ic (traj-ik) *adjective* 1. Of or having to do with or in the style of a tragedy or sad story. 2. Causing great sadness, especially because someone has died or suffered in a shocking way.
▶ *adverb* **tragically**

T

trail (trayl)
noun 1. A track or path for people to follow, especially in the woods. 2. A mark, scent, or path left behind by an animal or a person. 3. Something that follows along behind.
verb 1. To follow a scent or tracks in order to catch an animal or a person. 2. To walk or move slowly behind others.
▶ *verb* **trailing, trailed**

trail bike (**trayl** *bike*) *noun* A light, strong motorcycle built for cross-country racing and riding.

trail·er (**tray**-lur) *noun* 1. A vehicle that is pulled by another vehicle, especially a car or truck, and used to carry things. 2. Another name for **mobile home.** 3. A group of scenes that are used to advertise a movie.

train (trayn)
noun 1. A group of railroad cars that are connected to each other and pulled along a railway by an engine. 2. A group of people, animals, or vehicles traveling in a line. 3. The long piece of fabric at the back of a bride's dress.
verb 1. To prepare yourself to be something or do something by practicing or learning. 2. To teach a person or an animal how to do something. 3. To bring up children a certain way. 4. To make a plant grow in a certain direction or shape.
▶ *verb* **training, trained**

train·ee (tray-**nee**) *noun* Someone who is being trained, especially for a job.

train·er (**tray**-nur) *noun* 1. A person who trains circus animals, show animals, or pets. 2. Someone who helps people, especially athletes, get in the best possible physical condition.

train·ing (**tray**-ning) *noun* 1. The activity of teaching a person or animal how to do something or how to behave in a certain way. 2. The process of becoming physically fit for an activity through diet and exercise.

traipse (trayps) *verb* To walk or travel around without a plan or purpose. ▶ *verb* **traipsing, traipsed**

trait (trayt) *noun* A quality or characteristic that makes one person or thing different from another.

trai·tor (**tray**-tur) *noun* 1. Someone who helps the enemy of his or her country. 2. Someone who is unfaithful to a friend, cause, or trust.

tramp (tramp)
verb 1. To walk with heavy steps. 2. To go for a long walk or hike.
noun 1. Someone who wanders from place to place and does not have a permanent home. 2. The sound made by heavy steps.
▶ *verb* **tramping, tramped**

tram·ple (**tram**-puhl) *verb* To damage or crush something by walking heavily all over it. ▶ *verb* **trampling, trampled**

tram·po·line (tram-puh-**leen**) *noun* A piece of equipment used for jumping up and down on, either as a sport or for pleasure. A trampoline consists of a sheet of canvas attached to a frame by elastic ropes or springs.

trance (trans) *noun* A mental state in which you are conscious but not really aware of what is happening around you.

tran·quil (**trang**-kwuhl) *adjective* Peaceful and calm. ▶ *noun* **tranquility** *or* **tranquillity** (trang-**kwil**-i-tee)

trans·ac·tion (tran-**sak**-shuhn *or* tran-**zak**-shuhn) *noun* An exchange of goods, services, or money. ▶ *verb* **transact**

trans·at·lan·tic (*trans*-uht-**lan**-tik) *adjective* 1. Crossing the Atlantic Ocean. 2. Involving countries or people on both sides of the Atlantic Ocean. 3. On or coming from the other side of the Atlantic Ocean.

trans·con·ti·nen·tal (*trans*-kahn-tuh-**nen**-tuhl) *adjective* Crossing a continent.

trans·fer
verb (**trans**-fur *or* trans-**fur**) 1. To move someone or something from one person or place to another. 2. To change from one vehicle or method of transportation to another.
noun (**trans**-fur) 1. The moving of someone or something from one place or person to another. 2. A printed ticket that permits you to change from one

T

vehicle or route to another without paying more money.
▶ verb **transferring, transferred**

trans·form (trans-**form**) verb To completely change something. ▶ verb **transforming, transformed**

trans·for·ma·tion (trans-for-**may**-shuhn) noun A complete or dramatic change in form, appearance, or character.

trans·form·er (trans-**for**-mur) noun A piece of equipment that reduces or increases the voltage of an electric current.

trans·fu·sion (trans-**fyoo**-zhuhn) noun The injection of blood from one person into the body of someone else who is injured or sick.

tran·sient (**tran**-shuhnt or **tran**-zee-uhnt)
adjective Lasting for only a short time.
noun A person without a permanent home who moves from place to place.

tran·sis·tor (tran-**zis**-tur) noun A small electronic device that controls the flow of electric current in items such as radios, television sets, and computers.

tran·sit (**tran**-sit or **tran**-zit) noun **1.** A system for carrying people or goods from one place to another on trains, buses, and other vehicles. **2. in transit** In the process of going from one place to another.

tran·si·tion (tran-**zish**-uhn) noun A change from one form, condition, or place to another.

tran·si·tive (**tran**-si-tiv) adjective If a verb is **transitive,** it needs an object in order to complete its meaning. For example, in the sentence "We called our friends and then visited them," the verbs called and visited depend on their objects (our friends and them) to be clear and meaningful. See also **intransitive.**

trans·late (trans-**late**) verb To change spoken or written words from one language into another. ▶ verb **translating, translated** ▶ noun **translator**

trans·la·tion (trans-**lay**-shuhn) noun **1.** The activity of translating words or a text from one language into another. **2.** A text in a language other than the original, after it has been translated.

trans·lu·cent (trans-**loo**-suhnt) adjective A **translucent** substance is not completely clear like glass but will let some light through. ▶ noun **translucence**

trans·mis·sion (trans-**mish**-uhn) noun **1.** The act of transmitting or sending something from one person or place to another. **2.** Something that is transmitted, such as a telegram. **3.** In a car, a series of gears that send power from the engine to the wheels.

trans·mit (tranz-**mit** or trans-**mit**) verb **1.** To send or pass something from one place or person to another. **2.** To send out radio or television signals. **3.** To cause or allow something such as light, heat, or sound to pass through a material or substance.
▶ verb **transmitting, transmitted**
▶ noun **transmitter**

tran·som (**tran**-suhm) noun A small window over a door or another window.

trans·par·en·cy (trans-**pair**-uhn-see or trans-**par**-uhn-see) noun A sheet of thin, clear plastic with writing or pictures on it that you can shine light through in order to view the writing or pictures on a screen. ▶ noun, plural **transparencies**

trans·par·ent (trans-**pair**-uhnt or trans-**par**-uhnt) adjective **1.** A **transparent** substance is clear like glass and lets light through so that objects on the other side can be seen clearly. **2.** Obvious.

tran·spi·ra·tion (tran-spuh-**ray**-shuhn) noun The process by which plants give off moisture. ▶ verb **transpire** (tran-**spire**)

trans·plant
noun (**trans**-plant) A medical operation in which a damaged organ, such as a kidney, is replaced by a healthy one.
verb (trans-**plant**) To dig up a plant and plant it somewhere else.
▶ verb **transplanting, transplanted**

trans·port

verb (trans-**port**) 1. To move people or freight from one place to another. 2. To feel very strong emotions, such as happiness.

noun (**trans**-port) A vehicle that carries people or freight, such as a ship or plane.

▶ *verb* **transporting, transported**

trans·por·ta·tion (*trans*-pur-**tay**-shuhn) *noun* A means or system for moving people and freight from one place to another.

trap (trap)

noun 1. A device for capturing an animal. 2. Anything used to trick or catch someone.

verb To capture a person or an animal in a trap.

▶ *verb* **trapping, trapped** ▶ *noun* **trapper**

trap·door (**trap**-dor) *noun* A door in a floor, ceiling, or roof.

tra·peze (tra-**peez**) *noun* A horizontal bar hanging from two ropes used especially by circus performers and gymnasts.

tra·pe·zi·um (truh-**pee**-zee-uhm) *noun* A shape with four sides, none of which is parallel to another. ▶ *noun, plural* **trapeziums** *or* **trapezia** (truh-**pee**-zee-uh)

trap·e·zoid (**trap**-uh-*zoid*) *noun* A shape with four sides of which only two are parallel.

trap·per (**trap**-ur) *noun* Someone who makes a living by trapping wild animals, usually for their fur.

trash (trash)

noun 1. Things that you have thrown away because they are worthless; garbage. 2. Nonsense. 3. A place on some computers where you can move files that you don't need anymore.

verb 1. (informal) To damage or destroy something, making a big mess. 2. (informal) To criticize something or someone in a very harsh way.

trau·ma (**trou**-muh *or* **traw**-muh) *noun* 1. A severe and painful emotional

shock. 2. A severe physical wound or injury.

trau·mat·ic (traw-**mat**-ik) *adjective* Shocking and very upsetting.

trav·el (**trav**-uhl)

verb 1. To go from one place to another, especially a place that is far away. 2. To move a particular distance, in a particular direction, or at a particular speed. 3. To pass or to move; to be transmitted. 4. In basketball, to move illegally by failing to bounce the ball while walking or running.

noun The act of going from one place to another, especially to places that are far away.

▶ *verb* **traveling, traveled** ▶ *adjective* **traveling**

trav·el a·gent (**trav**-uhl *ay*-juhnt) *noun* A person or company that arranges travel and vacations for its customers. ▶ *noun* **travel agency**

trav·el·er (**trav**-uh-lur) *noun* Someone who travels.

trawl·er (**traw**-lur) *noun* A boat that drags a large net through the water to catch fish. ▶ *verb* **trawl**

tray (tray) *noun* A flat container made of metal, plastic, or wood with a low rim around the edges that is used for carrying things.

treach·er·ous (**trech**-ur-uhs) *adjective* 1. Disloyal and not to be trusted. 2. Dangerous.

▶ *adverb* **treacherously** ▶ *noun* **treachery**

tread (tred)

verb 1. To walk on, over, or along. 2. To press or crush with the feet.

noun 1. The flat, horizontal part of a step. 2. The ridges on a car tire or the sole of a shoe that help prevent you from slipping.

idiom **tread water** To swim in one place with your body in a vertical position.

▶ *verb* **treading, trod** (trahd), **trodden** (**trah**-duhn)

tread·mill (**tred**-*mil*) *noun* 1. An exercise machine with a large moving belt that you can walk or run on while staying in the same place. 2. A situation that is

T

boring or tiring because you always do the same things without making any progress.

trea·son (**tree**-zuhn) *noun* The crime of being disloyal to your country by spying for another country or by helping an enemy during a war.

treas·ure (**trezh**-ur)
noun 1. Gold, jewels, money, or other valuable things that have been collected or hidden. 2. Something considered to be very valuable.
verb To consider something to be very valuable.
▶ *verb* **treasuring, treasured**
▶ *adjective* **treasured**

treas·ur·er (**trezh**-ur-ur) *noun* The person in charge of the money of a government, company, or club.

treas·ur·y (**trezh**-ur-ee) *noun* 1. The funds of a government, company, or club. 2. **Treasury** A government department that is in charge of collecting taxes and managing the public's money. 3. A place where money or treasure is stored.
▶ *noun, plural* **treasuries**

treat (treet)
verb 1. To deal with or act toward people or things in a certain way. 2. To try to cure or heal a sickness or injury; to give medical attention to someone. 3. To use a chemical substance to clean, change, or protect something. 4. To pay for something for someone, especially when you do not usually do this.
noun An experience or gift that comes as a pleasant surprise.
▶ *verb* **treating, treated**

treat·ment (**treet**-muhnt) *noun* 1. The way that you treat someone or something. 2. The actions of a medical professional to cure or treat patients.

trea·ty (**tree**-tee) *noun* A formal written agreement between two or more countries. ▶ *noun, plural* **treaties**

treb·le (**treb**-uhl)
adjective 1. Three times as big or three times as many; triple. 2. High in pitch or tone.
verb To increase to three times the

original amount; to triple.
noun The highest musical part, voice, or instrument.
▶ *verb* **trebling, trebled**

tree (tree)
noun 1. A large plant with a long trunk, roots, branches, and leaves. 2. Something that looks like a tree, such as the diagram used to show family relationships or a pole for hanging up clothes.
verb To pursue and chase up a tree.
▶ *verb* **treeing, treed**

tree house (**tree** *hous*) *noun* A platform built in a tree, sometimes with walls, for children to play in.

trek (trek)
verb To make a slow, difficult journey.
noun A slow, difficult walk or journey.
▶ *verb* **trekking, trekked**

trel·lis (**trel**-is) *noun* A framework made up of thin strips of wood that cross each other. Trellises are used to support growing plants. ▶ *noun, plural* **trellises**

trem·ble (**trem**-buhl) *verb* 1. To shake in a way that you are unable to control, especially from cold, fear, or excitement. 2. To vibrate.
▶ *verb* **trembling, trembled**

tre·men·dous (truh-**men**-duhs) *adjective* 1. Very large. 2. Excellent or very good.
▶ *adverb* **tremendously**

trem·or (**trem**-ur) *noun* A shaking movement.

trench (trench) *noun* A long, narrow ditch, especially one used to protect soldiers in battle. ▶ *noun, plural* **trenches**

trend (trend) *noun* 1. The general direction in which things are developing. 2. The newest fashion.

tres·pass (**tres**-puhs *or* **tres**-*pas*)
verb To go on someone's private property without permission.
noun A sin.
▶ *verb* **trespasses, trespassing, trespassed** ▶ *noun, plural* **trespasses** ▶ *noun* **trespasser**

tress·es (**tres**-iz) *noun, plural* A woman's or girl's hair, especially when it is worn long and loose.

T

tres·tle (**tres**-uhl) *noun* A frame shaped like the letter *A* that supports a bridge or railroad track.

tri·al (**trye**-uhl) *noun* 1. The examination of evidence in a court of law to decide if a charge or claim is true. 2. The act of trying or testing something; a test. 3. A frustrating or difficult experience that reveals how strong or patient you are.

tri·an·gle (**trye**-*ang*-guhl) *noun* 1. A shape with three straight sides and three angles. 2. A steel percussion instrument in the shape of a triangle. You play it by striking it with a small metal rod. ▶ *adjective* **triangular** (trye-**ang**-gyuh-lur)

tri·ath·lon (trye-**ath**-lahn) *noun* A long-distance race made up of three parts—usually swimming, bicycling, and running. ▶ *noun* **triathlete** (trye-**ath**-leet)

tribe (tribe) *noun* A large group of related people who share the same language, customs, and laws, and who usually live in the same area.

trib·u·la·tion (trib-yuh-**lay**-shuhn) *noun* 1. Unhappiness or suffering. 2. A difficult experience.

tri·bu·nal (trye-**byoo**-nuhl) *noun* A court of law.

trib·u·tar·y (**trib**-yuh-*ter*-ee) *noun* A stream that flows into a larger stream, river, or lake. ▶ *noun, plural* **tributaries**

trib·ute (**trib**-yoot) *noun* Something done, given, or said to show thanks or respect.

tri·cer·a·tops (trye-**ser**-uh-*tahps*) *noun* A large dinosaur that ate plants and had three horns and a bony collar in the shape of a fan at the back of its head. ▶ *noun, plural* **triceratops** or **triceratopses**

trich·i·no·sis (trik-uh-**noh**-sis) *noun* A disease caused by tiny worms often found in pork that has not been fully cooked.

trick (trik) *verb* To make someone believe something that is not true. *noun* 1. A clever or skillful action that you do to entertain someone. 2. A prank or a practical joke. ▶ *verb* **tricking, tricked** ▶ *noun* **trickery**

trick·le (**trik**-uhl) *verb* To flow very slowly in a thin stream, or to fall in drops. *noun* A slow flow of liquid. ▶ *verb* **trickling, trickled**

trick or treat (**trik** ur **treet**) *noun* The words that children say to ask for candy when they go from house to house on Halloween. ▶ *verb* **trick-or-treat**

trick·y (**trik**-ee) *adjective* 1. Someone who is **tricky** is clever and likely to try to deceive you. 2. Difficult in an unexpected way; requiring careful thought or handling. ▶ *adjective* **trickier, trickiest**

tri·cy·cle (**trye**-sik-uhl) *noun* A children's vehicle that has three wheels.

tri·fle (**trye**-fuhl) *noun* 1. Something that is not very valuable or important. 2. A small amount; a bit. *verb* To play with or not take seriously. ▶ *verb* **trifling, trifled** ▶ *adjective* **trifling**

trig·ger (**trig**-ur) *noun* The lever on a gun that you pull to fire the gun. *verb* To cause something to happen immediately. ▶ *verb* **triggering, triggered**

tril·o·gy (**tril**-uh-jee) *noun* A group of three related works, such as plays, novels, or programs, that together make a series. ▶ *noun, plural* **trilogies**

trim (trim) *verb* 1. To cut small pieces off something in order to improve its shape or to get rid of what is not needed or wanted. 2. To add ornaments or decorations to something. *adjective* Neat, tidy, or in good condition. ▶ *verb* **trimming, trimmed** ▶ *adjective* **trimmer, trimmest**

trim·mings (**trim**-ingz) *noun, plural* The things that are added to something or that go with it.

T

Trin·i·dad and To·ba·go (**trin**-i-*dad* and tuh-**bay**-goh) An island nation in the southern Caribbean Sea, northeast of Venezuela. It includes the islands of Trinidad and Tobago, as well as smaller islands. Unlike most other Caribbean islands, which depend on tourism, its economy is based largely on oil and gas production. The country is the birthplace of calypso music.

trin·ket (**tring**-kit) *noun* A small, cheap souvenir, decoration, or piece of jewelry.

tri·o (**tree**-oh) *noun* **1.** Three things or people together as a group. **2.** A piece of music for three musicians.

trip (trip)
verb **1.** To hit your foot on something by accident and fall or almost fall. **2.** To catch someone's foot and cause the person to fall or almost fall. **3. trip up** To make a mistake or to cause another person to make a mistake.
noun A journey to a place.
▶ *verb* **tripping, tripped**

tripe (tripe) *noun* **1.** The lining of the stomach of an ox or a cow. Tripe is eaten as food. **2.** (informal) Anything that is useless or worthless.

trip·le (**trip**-uhl)
adjective **1.** Three times as big, or three times as many. **2.** Made up of three parts.
noun In baseball, a hit that allows you to reach third base.
verb **1.** To multiply or cause to multiply by three. **2.** To hit a triple.
▶ *verb* **triples, tripling, tripled**

trip·let (**trip**-lit) *noun* One of three children born to the same mother at the same birth.

tri·pod (**trye**-*pahd*) *noun* A stand with three legs that is used to steady a camera or other piece of equipment.

trite (trite) *adjective* Not interesting or important because of being too simple or being used too much.

tri·umph (**trye**-uhmf) *noun* A great victory, success, or achievement. ▶ *verb* **triumph** ▶ *adjective* **triumphant** (trye-**uhm**-fuhnt)

triv·i·al (**triv**-ee-uhl) *adjective* Not very important. ▶ *noun, plural* **trivia** (**triv**-ee-uh)

Tro·jan horse (**troh**-juhn **hors**) *noun* **1.** A person, action, or thing that seems harmless but that people believe will later prove to be harmful. **2.** A kind of software that is advertised as something useful but that in fact damages your computer after you install it.

troll (trohl)
verb To fish by pulling a line with bait from behind a slowly moving boat.
noun In fairy tales, an ugly creature that is very large or very small and lives in a cave, in the hills, or under a bridge.
▶ *verb* **trolling, trolled** ▶ *noun* **troller**

trol·ley (**trah**-lee) *noun* An electric streetcar that runs on tracks and gets its power from an overhead wire.

trom·bone (trahm-**bone**) *noun* A brass musical instrument with a long, bent tube that the player slides back and forth to change the tones.

troop (troop)
noun An organized group of people, such as soldiers or scouts.
verb To walk somewhere in a group.
▶ *verb* **trooping, trooped**

troop·er (**troo**-pur) *noun* A state police officer.

tro·phy (**troh**-fee) *noun* A prize such as a large silver cup given to the winner of a competition, or to someone who has done something outstanding. ▶ *noun, plural* **trophies**

trop·i·cal (**trah**-pi-kuhl) *adjective* Of or having to do with the hot, rainy area of the tropics.

trop·i·cal fish (**trah**-pi-kuhl **fish**) *noun* Any of various small or brightly colored fish that originally come from the tropics. Tropical fish are often kept as pets in aquariums. ▶ *noun, plural* **tropical fish** or **tropical fishes**

trop·ics (**trah**-piks) *noun, plural* The extremely hot area of the earth near the equator.

T

trot (traht)
verb 1. When a horse **trots,** it moves at a pace that is faster than a walk but not as fast as a run. 2. When a person **trots,** he or she runs slowly or jogs. *noun* A slow pace.
▶ *verb* **trotting, trotted** ▶ *noun* **trotter**

trou·ble (**truhb**-uhl)
noun 1. A difficult, dangerous, or upsetting situation. 2. A cause of difficulty, worry, or annoyance.
verb 1. To disturb or worry someone. 2. To ask someone for help, or to make an extra effort.
phrase If you **take the trouble** to do something, you make a special effort to do it.
▶ *verb* **troubling, troubled**
▶ *adjective* **troublesome** (**truhb**-uhl-suhm) ▶ *adjective* **troubling** ▶ *adjective* **troubled**

trough (trawf) *noun* 1. A long, narrow container from which animals can eat or drink. 2. The lowest part of something.

trounce (trouns) *verb* To beat soundly in a competition or game. ▶ *verb* **trouncing, trounced**

trou·sers (**trou**-zurz) *noun, plural* Another word for **pants.** ▶ *adjective* **trouser**

trout (trout) *noun* A freshwater fish, related to the salmon, that you can eat.

trow·el (**trou**-uhl) *noun* 1. A hand tool with a flat blade shaped like a diamond. Trowels are used for doing things such as laying cement or filling holes in plaster. 2. A hand tool with a small, curved blade, used for planting and other light garden work.

tru·ant (**troo**-uhnt) *noun* A student who stays away from school without permission. ▶ *noun* **truancy**

truce (troos) *noun* An agreement between enemies to stop fighting for a short time.

truck (truhk) *noun* A large motor vehicle with space in the back to carry loads.

trudge (truhj) *verb* To walk slowly and with effort; to plod. ▶ *verb* **trudging, trudged**

true (troo) *adjective* 1. Correct or agreeing with the facts. 2. Loyal or faithful. 3. Real or genuine.
▶ *adjective* **truer, truest**

tru·ly (**troo**-lee) *adverb* 1. Really or actually. 2. Used to emphasize that you really mean what you are saying.

trum·pet (**truhm**-pit) *noun* 1. A brass musical instrument that consists of a long tube with a wide funnel shape at one end. You play it by blowing into it and pressing a combination of three valves on top to change the tones. 2. A loud sound like that of a trumpet, such as the cry of an elephant.

trunk (truhngk)
noun 1. The thick, main part of a tree. 2. A large case used for storing things or carrying things such as clothes on a long journey. 3. The upper part of your body, not including your arms and head. 4. The long nose of an elephant. 5. An enclosed compartment in a car, usually at the back, where things such as bags and a spare tire can be stored.
noun, plural **trunks** Shorts worn by men or boys for swimming or boxing.

trust (truhst)
verb To believe that someone is honest and reliable.
noun The belief that someone is honest and reliable.
▶ *verb* **trusting, trusted** ▶ *adjective* **trusting**

trust·ee (truh-**stee**) *noun* 1. A person who has the legal authority to manage property for the benefit of another person or people. 2. A person who directs the funds and policies of an organization or institution.

trust·wor·thy (**truhst**-wur-THee) *adjective* Able to be trusted and relied on to do what is right.

trust·y (**truhs**-tee) *adjective* Something that is **trusty** can be relied on, especially because you have had it for a long time.

truth (trooth) *noun* 1. The real facts about something, rather than what is false or not known. 2. The quality of being true, real, honest, or accurate.

T

try (trye)
verb **1.** To attempt to do something. **2.** To examine in a court of law someone accused of a crime. **3.** To test the quality, strength, or effect of something. **4.** If someone or something **tries your patience,** that person or thing causes you to feel impatient.
noun An attempt to do something. ▶ *noun, plural* **tries** ▶ *verb* **tries, trying, tried**

try·ing (**trye**-ing) *adjective* Annoying or difficult to deal with.

try·out (**trye**-out) *noun* A trial or test to see if a person is qualified to do something, such as perform a role in a play or play on a team; an audition. ▶ *verb* **try out**

T-shirt *or* **tee shirt** (**tee**-shurt) *noun* A light cotton shirt or undershirt with no collar and usually short sleeves.

tsu·na·mi (tsu-**nah**-mee) *noun* A very large, destructive wave caused by an underwater earthquake or volcano.

tub (tuhb) *noun* **1.** A bathtub. **2.** A round, open container used for packing or storing foods. **3.** A large, wide container used for washing clothes or bathing.

tu·ba (**too**-buh) *noun* A large, brass wind instrument with several valves. Tubas play very low notes.

tube (toob) *noun* **1.** A long, hollow cylinder, especially one used to carry or hold liquids. **2.** A long container made of soft metal or plastic with a cap that screws on. **3.** The hollow rubber ring that is put inside some bicycle tires and filled with air. **4. the tube** (informal) Television.

tu·ber (**too**-bur) *noun* The thick underground stem of a plant such as a potato.

tu·ber·cu·lo·sis (tu-**bur**-kyuh-**loh**-sis) *noun* A highly contagious disease caused by bacteria, that usually affects the lungs. Abbreviated as *TB*.

tu·bu·lar (**too**-byuh-lur) *adjective* In the shape of a tube.

tuck (tuhk)
verb **1.** To fold or push the ends of something into place. **2. tuck in** To make someone warm and comfortable in bed by pulling up the blankets around him or her. **3. tuck away** To hide something in a safe place.
noun A small fold sewn into clothing as a decoration or to make the clothes fit better.
▶ *verb* **tucking, tucked**

Tues·day (**tooz**-day *or* **tooz**-dee) *noun* The third day of the week, after Monday and before Wednesday.

tuft (tuhft) *noun* A bunch of individual pieces of something such as hair, grass, or feathers that are attached together at the bottom. ▶ *adjective* **tufted**

tug (tuhg)
verb To pull something hard with a short, quick movement.
noun **1.** A brief, forceful pull. **2.** See **tugboat**.
▶ *verb* **tugging, tugged**

tug·boat (**tuhg**-boht) *noun* A small, powerful boat that pulls or pushes large ships.

tug-of-war (**tuhg**-uhv-**wor**) *noun* A contest between two teams, each holding on to opposite ends of a rope, who try to pull each other over a center line.

tu·i·tion (too-**ish**-uhn) *noun* Money paid to a college or private school in order for a student to study there.

tu·lip (**too**-lip) *noun* A plant with a tall stem and a colorful flower on top that is shaped like a cup.

tum·ble (**tuhm**-buhl) *verb* **1.** To fall down suddenly and hit the ground several times. **2.** To do somersaults, handsprings, or other acrobatic movements. **3.** To roll or toss around. **4.** To move in a quick and uncontrolled way.
▶ *verb* **tumbling, tumbled**

tum·bler (**tuhm**-blur) *noun* **1.** A tall drinking glass with straight sides. **2.** Someone who does acrobatic movements, such as somersaults or handsprings.

T

tum·ble·weed (**tum**-buhl-*weed*) *noun*
A bushy plant found in the deserts of
the western United States that breaks
off from its roots and blows around in
the wind.

tum·my (**tuhm**-ee) *noun* (informal) The
stomach. ▶ *noun, plural* **tummies**

tu·mor (**too**-mur) *noun* An abnormal
lump or mass of cells in the body.

tu·mult (**too**-muhlt) *noun* A state
of noisy confusion. ▶ *adjective*
tumultuous (tuh-**muhl**-choo-
uhs) ▶ *adverb* **tumultuously**

tu·na (**too**-nuh) *noun* A large, edible fish
that is found in warm seas throughout
the world. ▶ *noun, plural* **tuna** or
tunas

tun·dra (**tuhn**-druh) *noun* A very cold
area of northern Europe, Asia, and
Canada where there are no trees
and the soil under the surface of the
ground is always frozen.

tune (toon)
noun 1. A series of musical notes
arranged in a pattern; a simple
melody that is easy to remember.
2. The condition of having the correct
musical pitch. 3. Agreement or
understanding.
verb 1. To adjust the pitch of a musical
instrument. 2. If you **tune in** a radio
or television program or station, you
adjust the dial to receive it. 3. If you
tune a car engine **up,** you put it in
good working order by adjusting the
parts.
▶ *verb* **tuning, tuned** ▶ *adjective*
tuneful ▶ *noun* **tuner**

tung·sten (**tung**-stuhn) *noun* A hard,
gray metallic element that has a very
high melting point and is used to
make steel and the thin wire inside
lightbulbs.

tu·nic (**too**-nik) *noun* A loose shirt
without sleeves.

tun·ing fork (**too**-ning *fork*) *noun* A
piece of metal with two long thin parts
joined together at one end, used for
tuning musical instruments. When
you hit it, it vibrates to produce a
particular musical note.

Tu·ni·sia (too-**nee**-zhuh) The
northernmost country in Africa, on
the Mediterranean Sea. Its coastline
extends for about 800 miles, and
the area around its capital and main
port, Tunis, was once the site of
the Phoenician city of Carthage, an
important maritime power in ancient
times.

tun·nel (**tuhn**-uhl) *noun* 1. A passage
built beneath the ground or water or
through a mountain for cars, trains, or
other vehicles to use. 2. An animal's
underground passage.

tun·nel vi·sion (**tuhn**-uhl *vizh*-uhn)
noun 1. A tendency to only think about
one part of a problem or situation
and ignore other parts. 2. A condition
in which the eye can only see things
that are straight ahead, as if through
a tunnel.

tur·ban (**tur**-buhn) *noun* A long scarf
wound around the head or around
a cap. Turbans are worn especially by
men in Arab countries and India.

tur·bine (**tur**-buhn or **tur**-bine) *noun* An
engine powered by water, steam, wind,
or gas passing through the blades of
a wheel and making it spin.

tur·bo (**tur**-boh) *adjective* A **turbo** or
turbo-charged engine has high-
pressure air forced into it to create
extra power.

tur·bo·fan (**tur**-boh-*fan*) *noun* A type
of aircraft engine in which a large
fan, powered by a turbine, pushes air
into the hot exhaust at the rear of the
engine, giving extra power.

tur·bu·lent (**tur**-byuh-luhnt) *adjective*
Wild, confused, or violent. ▶ *noun*
turbulence

turf (turf) *noun* The top layer of grass
and earth on a lawn or playing field.

tur·key (**tur**-kee) *noun* 1. A large North
American bird with red-brown feathers
and a tail that spreads out like a fan.
2. (slang) A silly or foolish person.

Tur·key (**tur**-kee) A country that extends
from Southeast Europe to West Asia. It
was the center of the former Ottoman
Empire, whose capital, Constantinople,
is now called Istanbul.

T

Turk·me·ni·stan (turk-**men**-i-*stan*) A country in Central Asia. Turkmenistan has vast reserves of natural gas, the fourth largest in the world. Most of the country is covered by a desert called the Karakum, which means "black sand," where it rains only about once every ten years.

tur·moil (**tur**-moil) *noun* Great confusion.

turn (turn)
verb 1. To go in a new direction. 2. To rotate, or to make something rotate. 3. To change appearance or state, or to make something do this. 4. To become. 5. If something **turns** your stomach, it makes you feel sick. 6. If you **turn** something or someone **down,** you refuse an opportunity or invitation. 7. **turn down** To move a switch on a piece of equipment so that you lower the amount of heat, sound, or light being produced. 8. **turn in** To go to bed. 9. If you **turn** something **off,** you make it stop working by, for example, moving a switch. 10. If you **turn** something **on,** you make it start to work by, for example, moving a switch. 11. **turn up** To appear, especially when you are not expected. 12. **turn up** To move a switch on a piece of equipment so that you increase the amount of heat, sound, or light being produced. 13. (slang) If something **turns** you **on,** it makes you interested or excited.
noun 1. A change in direction or position, or the point where such a change takes place. 2. The act of turning; a rotation. 3. A change in events or time. 4. A chance or duty to do something. 5. A **good turn** is an action that helps someone.
▸ *verb* **turning, turned**

tur·nip (**tur**-nip) *noun* A white or yellow root vegetable with a round shape.

turn·out (**turn**-*out*) *noun* The number of people at a gathering or an event.

turn·pike (**turn**-*pike*) *noun* A highway that you have to pay to drive on.

turn·stile (**turn**-*stile*) *noun* A metal bar inside an entrance or exit gate that moves forward in a circle when pushed so that only one person at a time can pass through.

turn·ta·ble (**turn**-*tay*-buhl) *noun* A flat round surface that turns around and around in a circle. A turntable is used for playing phonograph records.

tur·pen·tine (**tur**-puhn-*tine*) *noun* A clear liquid made from the sap of certain pine trees. Turpentine is often used to thin paints.

tur·quoise (**tur**-koiz *or* **tur**-kwoiz) *noun* 1. A valuable, blue-green stone used in making jewelry. 2. A blue-green color.
adjective Being blue-green in color.

tur·ret (**tur**-it) *noun* 1. A round or square tower on a building, usually on a corner. Many castles have turrets. 2. A structure on a tank, warship, or fighter plane that holds one or more guns. It usually rotates so that the gun can be fired in different directions.

tur·tle (**tur**-tuhl) *noun* A reptile that can pull its head, legs, and tail into its hard shell for protection. Turtles live on land and in water.

tur·tle·neck (**tur**-tuhl-*nek*) *noun* 1. A high collar that turns down and fits tightly around the neck. 2. A sweater or shirt with such a collar.

tusk (tuhsk) *noun* One of the pair of long, curved, pointed teeth that stick out of the mouth of an animal such as an elephant, walrus, or wild boar.

tus·sle (**tuhs**-uhl)
noun A short fight, argument, or struggle.
verb To engage in a tussle.
▸ *verb* **tussling, tussled**

tu·tor (**too**-tur) *noun* A teacher who gives private lessons to only one student or a few students at a time.

tu·tor·i·al (too-**tor**-ee-uhl) *noun* A short course in which you learn to do, or learn about, a particular thing. Many tutorials are designed so that people can do them alone on a computer.

tu·tu (**too**-too) *noun* A short skirt made of several layers of stiff net, worn by a ballet dancer.

T

Tu·va·lu (**too**-vuh-*loo* or too-**vah**-loo)
An island nation in the Pacific Ocean,
about halfway between Hawaii and
Australia. Formerly known as the
Ellice Islands, it consists of four reef
islands and five atolls. It was once a
British colony, and like many former
colonies, it has retained the design
of the British flag inside its own flag,
shown at the top left of the flag. The
nine stars represent Tuvalu's islands
and atolls.

tux·e·do (tuhk-**see**-doh) *noun* **1.** A
man's jacket, usually black, worn with
a bow tie for formal occasions. **2.** A
man's suit that includes this jacket.

TV (**tee-vee**) *noun* Short for **television.**

tweed (tweed) *noun* A rough wool
cloth woven with yarns of two or
more colors.

tween (tween) *noun* (informal) A child
between 10 and 14; a pre-teenager or
young teenager.

tweet (tweet)
noun **1.** A short, high sound; a chirp.
2. A short message that you send
using the Internet service Twitter.
verb **1.** If a bird **tweets,** it makes a
short, high-pitched sound. **2.** To
send a message or messages using
Twitter.

twee·zers (**twee**-zurz) *noun, plural* A
small metal tool with two long pieces
joined at one end, used for pulling
out hairs or for picking up very small
objects.

twelfth (twelfth)
adjective Next after 11th and before
13th, written numerically as 12th.
noun One part of something that
has been divided into 12 equal parts,
written numerically as 1/12.

twelve (twelv)
noun The number that comes after
11 and before 13, written numerically
as 12.
adjective Referring to the number that
comes after 11 and before 13.

twen·ty (**twen**-tee) *noun* The number
that is equal to 2 times 10, written
numerically as 20.

twice (twise) *adverb* Two times.

twig (twig) *noun* A small, thin branch of
a tree or other woody plant.

twi·light (**twye**-*lite*) *noun* The time when
the day is ending and the night is
beginning, when the sun has just set
and it is beginning to get dark.

twin (twin)
noun One of two children born at the
same birth to the same mother.
adjective Belonging to a pair that are
exactly the same.

twine (twine)
noun A very strong string made of two
or more strands twisted together.
verb To wind or grow in a coil.
▶ *verb* **twining, twined**

twinge (twinj) *noun* A sudden slight
pain or unpleasant feeling.

twin·kle (**twing**-kuhl)
verb To shine with quick flashes of
light; to sparkle.
noun A flash of light.
▶ *verb* **twinkling, twinkled**

twirl (twurl) *verb* To turn or spin around
quickly. ▶ *verb* **twirling, twirled**

twist (twist) *verb* **1.** To turn, wind, or
bend, or to do this to something. **2.** To
wind two pieces of something like
thread or wire together. **3.** To turn a
part of your body, such as your knee
or wrist, suddenly in a way that is
painful but does not cause a serious
injury. **4.** When you **twist someone's
words,** you purposely change the
meaning of what he or she said.
▶ *verb* **twisting, twisted**

twis·ter (**twis**-tur) *noun* (informal)
A tornado.

twitch (twich) *verb* To make small,
sudden movements. ▶ *verb* **twitches,
twitching, twitched** ▶ *adjective*
twitchy

twit·ter (**twit**-ur) *noun* **1.** The short, high,
chirping sounds that a bird makes.
2. A state of nervous excitement.
3. Twitter A trademark for an online
service that lets you post short
messages for anyone to read.
▶ *verb* **twitter**

T

two (too)
noun The number that comes after one and before three, written numerically as 2.
adjective Referring to the number that comes after one and before three.
Two sounds like **to** and **too.**

ty·coon (tye-**koon**) *noun* A very wealthy, powerful businessperson.

type (tipe)
noun **1.** A sort or a kind. **2.** Small pieces of metal with raised letters, numbers, punctuation marks, or other symbols on their surfaces. These pieces of type were formerly used in printing. Today, printing is mainly done with computers. **3.** Printed numbers and letters.
verb To write something with a typewriter or computer.
▶ *verb* **typing, typed**

type·face (**tipe**-*fase*) *noun* A particular style of type used in printing and desktop publishing.

type·set (**tipe**-*set*) *verb* To put a piece of writing into a typed form that can be used in printing. ▶ *verb* **typesetting, typeset** ▶ *noun* **typesetter**

type·writ·er (**tipe**-*rye*-tur) *noun* A machine that prints letters, numbers, and punctuation marks when you press keys with your fingers.

ty·phoid (**tye**-foid) *noun* A serious infectious disease caused by germs in food or water. Typhoid's symptoms include high fever and diarrhea, and it sometimes leads to death.

ty·phoon (tye-**foon**) *noun* A violent tropical storm that occurs in the western Pacific Ocean.

typ·i·cal (**tip**-i-kuhl) *adjective* **1.** Having traits or qualities that are normal for a particular type or class. **2.** If someone does something that is **typical,** the person behaves in a way that is expected or not surprising.

typ·i·cal·ly (**tip**-ik-lee) *adverb* In an expected or usual manner; normally.

typ·ist (**tye**-pist) *noun* Someone who uses a computer or typewriter to write things, especially as a job.

ty·ran·no·saur (ti-**ran**-uh-*sor*) *noun* A huge dinosaur that ate meat and walked upright.

tyr·an·ny (**tir**-uh-nee) *noun* Government in which unfair laws are enforced with power and punishment and a cruel leader has all the power.

ty·rant (**tye**-ruhnt) *noun* Someone who rules other people in a cruel or unjust way. ▶ *adjective* **tyrannical** (ti-**ran**-i-kuhl)

U

ud·der (**uhd**-ur) *noun* The baglike part of a female cow, sheep, or other similar mammal that hangs down near its back legs. The udder contains the glands that produce milk.

UFO (**yoo**-*ef*-**oh**) *noun* An object that is seen or is thought to be seen flying in the sky, and that some people believe to be a spaceship from another planet. UFO is short for *unidentified flying object.*

U·gan·da (yoo-**gan**-duh *or* oo-**gahn**-duh) A country in East Africa on Lake Victoria. Named for Queen Victoria of Great Britain, the freshwater lake is the largest in Africa. The White Nile, the only river that flows out of the lake, is one of the two main tributaries of the Nile. The other is the Blue Nile, which originates in Ethiopia.

ug·ly (**uhg**-lee) *adjective* **1.** Not attractive or pleasant to look at. **2.** Disgusting or unpleasant. **3.** Nasty or mean.
▶ *adjective* **uglier, ugliest**

U·kraine (yoo-**krayn**) A country in eastern Europe. Formerly part of the Soviet Union, Ukraine became independent after the collapse of the Soviet Union in 1991. It is the largest of the European countries whose borders are entirely within the continent of Europe, and it includes the republic of Crimea, a peninsula on the Black Sea.

u·ku·le·le (yoo-kuh-**lay**-lee) noun A small, four-stringed guitar originally made popular in Hawaii.

ul·cer (**uhl**-sur) noun An open, painful sore on the skin or on the lining of the stomach.

ul·ti·mate (**uhl**-tuh-mit) adjective 1. Final, or happening at the end of a process. 2. Basic, original, or fundamental. 3. Greatest or best.

ul·ti·mate·ly (**uhl**-tuh-mit-lee) adverb In the end; eventually.

ul·ti·ma·tum (uhl-tuh-**may**-tuhm) noun A final offer or demand, especially one that carries with it the threat of punishment or the use of force if rejected. ▶ noun, plural **ultimatums** or **ultimata** (uhl-tuh-**may**-tuh)

ul·tra·light (**uhl**-truh-lite) noun A very light aircraft, usually for one person, which is powered by a small engine.

ul·tra·sound (**uhl**-truh-sound) noun Sound whose frequency is too high for the human ear to hear. Ultrasound waves are used in medical scans.

ul·tra·vi·o·let light (**uhl**-truh-vye-uh-lit lite) noun A type of light that cannot be seen by the human eye. It is given off by the sun and causes the skin to get darker.

um·bil·i·cal cord (uhm-**bil**-i-kuhl kord) noun The flexible tube containing blood vessels that connects an unborn baby to its mother's body. The baby receives food and oxygen through this cord, and it also lets the baby's body eliminate wastes.

um·brel·la (uhm-**brel**-uh) noun A folding frame with a circular cloth stretched over it that you hold over your head to protect you from the rain.

um·pire (**uhm**-pire) noun An official who rules on plays in baseball, tennis, and certain other sports.

un·a·ble (uhn-**ay**-buhl) adjective Lacking the ability to do something.

un·ac·cept·a·ble (uhn-uhk-**sep**-tuh-buhl) adjective Not good enough, or not allowable. ▶ adverb **unacceptably**

un·ac·cus·tomed (uhn-uh-**kuhs**-tuhmd) adjective Not used to something.

un·adul·ter·at·ed (uhn-uh-**duhl**-tuh-ray-tid) adjective Pure, with nothing extra or artificial added to it.

un·aid·ed (uhn-**ay**-did) adjective Without any help.

u·nan·i·mous (yoo-**nan**-uh-muhs) adjective Agreed on by everyone. ▶ adverb **unanimously**

un·ap·proach·a·ble (uhn-uh-**proh**-chuh-buhl) adjective 1. Not easy to talk to or to get to know; unfriendly. 2. Difficult or impossible to get to.

un·armed (uhn-**ahrmd**) adjective Not carrying any weapons.

un·au·tho·rized (uhn-**aw**-thuh-rized) adjective Done without official permission.

un·a·void·a·ble (uhn-uh-**voi**-duh-buhl) adjective Impossible to avoid or prevent. ▶ adverb **unavoidably**

un·a·ware (uhn-uh-**wair**) adjective Not knowing that something exists or is happening.

un·bear·a·ble (uhn-**bair**-uh-buhl) adjective Too bad or unpleasant to tolerate. ▶ adverb **unbearably**

un·be·com·ing (uhn-bi-**kuhm**-ing) adjective 1. Not attractive or not flattering. 2. Not in good taste; not proper.

un·be·liev·a·ble (uhn-bi-**lee**-vuh-buhl) adjective Impossible to believe, or unlikely to be true.

un·bend·ing (uhn-**ben**-ding) adjective Unwilling to change your mind.

un·break·a·ble (uhn-**bray**-kuh-buhl) adjective Not able to be broken, or not likely to be broken.

un·bro·ken (uhn-**broh**-kuhn) adjective 1. Not broken; whole. 2. Not interrupted; without a stop or break; continuous. 3. Not tamed or trained

U

for use with a harness. **4.** Not bettered or topped.

un·bur·den (uhn-**bur**-duhn) *verb* To relieve yourself of something that is causing worry or distress. ▶ *verb* **unburdening, unburdened**

un·can·ny (uhn-**kan**-ee) *adjective* **1.** Very strange and difficult to explain or understand; mysterious; eerie. **2.** Remarkable or extraordinary. ▶ *adverb* **uncannily**

un·cer·tain (uhn-**sur**-tuhn) *adjective* **1.** Not sure. **2.** Likely to change.

un·cer·tain·ty (uhn-**sur**-tuhn-tee) *noun* Unsureness or lack of confidence about something.

un·civ·i·lized (uhn-**siv**-uh-*lized*) *adjective* **1.** Considered to be less advanced socially or culturally. **2.** Impolite or unruly.

un·cle (**uhng**-kuhl) *noun* The brother of your mother or father, or the husband of your aunt.

un·com·fort·a·ble (uhn-**kuhm**-fur-tuh-buhl) *adjective* **1.** Not relaxed or at ease in your body or your mind. **2.** Causing worry or pain. ▶ *adverb* **uncomfortably**

un·com·mon (uhn-**kah**-muhn) *adjective* Rare or unusual; out of the ordinary. ▶ *adverb* **uncommonly**

un·com·pli·men·ta·ry (*uhn*-kahm-pluh-**ment**-ree) *adjective* Insulting, rude, or negative.

un·com·pro·mis·ing (uhn-**kahm**-pruh-*mye*-zing) *adjective* Refusing to give in, change your ideas, or accept something as it is. ▶ *adverb* **uncompromisingly**

un·con·cerned (*uhn*-kuhn-**surnd**) *adjective* **1.** Not interested; indifferent. **2.** Not worried, anxious, or upset.

un·con·di·tion·al (*uhn*-kuhn-**dish**-uh-nuhl) *adjective* Not limited by any conditions; without limitations. ▶ *adverb* **unconditionally**

un·con·firmed (*uhn*-kuhn-**furmd**) *adjective* Not yet known to be definitely true.

un·con·scious (uhn-**kahn**-shuhs) *adjective* **1.** Not awake; not able to see,

feel, or think. **2.** Unaware. **3.** Done without realizing it.

un·con·sti·tu·tion·al (*uhn*-kahn-sti-**too**-shuh-nuhl) *adjective* Not in keeping with the basic principles or laws set forth in the constitution of a state or country, especially the Constitution of the United States.

un·con·trol·la·ble (*uhn*-kuhn-**troh**-luh-buhl) *adjective* Not able to be stopped, held in, or restrained. ▶ *adverb* **uncontrollably**

un·co·op·er·a·tive (*uhn*-koh-**ah**-pur-uh-tiv) *adjective* Unwilling to help or work with others.

un·couth (uhn-**kooth**) *adjective* Lacking good manners or refinement.

un·cov·er (uhn-**kuhv**-ur) *verb* **1.** To remove a cover from something. **2.** To discover or reveal something; to make something known. ▶ *verb* **uncovering, uncovered**

un·daunt·ed (uhn-**dawn**-tid) *adjective* Not discouraged or frightened by dangers or difficulties.

un·de·cid·ed (*uhn*-di-**sye**-did) *adjective* **1.** Not having made up your mind. **2.** Not yet settled.

un·de·ni·a·ble (*uhn*-di-**nye**-uh-buhl) *adjective* So clearly true that it cannot be denied. ▶ *adverb* **undeniably**

un·der (**uhn**-dur) *preposition* **1.** Below or beneath. *The suitcases are in a closet under the stairs.* **2.** Less than a particular number or amount. *Use the express checkout if you have under 12 items in your cart.* **3.** According to. *Under the rules, she can't reenter the game.* **4.** Controlled or bound by, as in *under oath*. **5.** Subordinate to or responsible for. *Jeff has 20 people working under him.* **6.** Hidden by something. *Under his rough appearance, Blake is a polite and considerate person.* *adverb* Below or beneath something.

un·der·arm (**uhn**-dur-*ahrm*) *adverb, adjective* Underhand; with your arm below shoulder level. *noun* The armpit, or the part of the body that is under the arm.

un·der·brush (**uhn**-dur-*bruhsh*) *noun*
Bushes, shrubs, and other plants that grow beneath the large trees in the forest or woods.

un·der·clothes (**uhn**-dur-*kloze*) *noun, plural* Underwear.

un·der·cov·er (*uhn*-dur-**kuhv**-ur) *adjective* Working or done in secret, especially police work or espionage. *adverb* Secretly.

un·der·de·vel·oped (*uhn*-dur-di-**vel**-uhpt) *adjective* 1. Not completely or normally developed. 2. Having an economy that is not very advanced compared to others.

un·der·dog (**uhn**-dur-*dawg*) *noun* A person, team, or group that is expected to lose a game, a race, an election, or other contest.

un·der·es·ti·mate (*uhn*-dur-**es**-tuh-mate) *verb* 1. To think that something is smaller, weaker, or less important than it really is. 2. To make a guess that is too low.
  ▶ *verb* **underestimating, underestimated** ▶ *noun* **underestimation**

un·der·foot (*uhn*-der-**fut**) *adverb*
1. Under your feet; on the ground.
2. In the way.

un·der·gar·ment (**uhn**-dur-*gahr*-muhnt) *noun* A piece of clothing that you wear next to your skin, under other clothes, such as a T-shirt.

un·der·go (*uhn*-dur-**goh**) *verb* To experience or have to go through something. ▶ *verb* **undergoes, undergoing, underwent** (*uhn*-dur-**went**), **undergone** (*uhn*-dur-**gawn**)

un·der·grad·u·ate (*uhn*-dur-**graj**-oo-it) *noun* A college or university student who has not yet completed studies for a first-level degree, called a bachelor's degree.
adjective Of or having to do with study for a bachelor's degree.

un·der·ground (**uhn**-dur-*ground*) *adjective, adverb* 1. Below the ground.
2. Secret or hidden.

Un·der·ground Rail·road (**un**-dur-*ground* **rayl**-*rohd*) *noun* A network of people who secretly helped slaves

from the South escape to free states in the North or to Canada before the American Civil War.

un·der·growth (**uhn**-dur-*grohth*) *noun* Saplings, seedlings, shrubs, and other plants, especially those that grow beneath the tall, mature trees in a forest.

un·der·hand (**uhn**-dur-*hand*) *adjective, adverb* Thrown or pitched with the hand below the shoulder or elbow level.

un·der·hand·ed (**uhn**-dur-*han*-did) *adjective* Sneaky or dishonest; done in secret; unfair.

un·der·line (**uhn**-dur-*line*) *verb*
1. To draw a line under something.
2. To emphasize the importance of something.
  ▶ *verb* **underlining, underlined**

un·der·mine (**uhn**-dur-*mine*) *verb* To weaken or destroy something slowly and often secretly. ▶ *verb* **undermining, undermined**

un·der·neath (*uhn*-dur-*neeth*) *preposition, adverb* Under or below.

un·der·nour·ished (*uhn*-dur-**nur**-isht) *adjective* Weak and unhealthy from lack of nutritious food.

un·der·pants (**uhn**-dur-*pants*) *noun, plural* Short pants worn as underwear.

un·der·pass (**uhn**-dur-*pas*) *noun* A road or passage that goes underneath another road or a bridge.

un·der·priv·i·leged (*uhn*-dur-**priv**-uh-lijd) *adjective* Lacking the advantages or opportunities that other people have, usually because of poverty.

un·der·sea (*uhn*-dur-**see**) *adjective* Located, done, or used below the surface of the ocean.

un·der·shirt (**uhn**-dur-*shurt*) *noun* A shirt with short sleeves or no sleeves worn as underwear.

un·der·side (**uhn**-dur-*side*) *noun* The bottom side or surface of something.

un·der·stand (*uhn*-dur-**stand**) *verb* 1. To grasp the meaning of something or the way something works. 2. To know very well. 3. To have sympathy for someone. 4. To believe that something is true; to gather from indirect

U

information.

▶ *verb* **understanding, understood** (*uhn*-dur-**stud**) ▶ *adjective* **understanding**

un·der·stand·a·ble (*uhn*-dur-**stan**-duh-buhl) *adjective* 1. Easy to understand. 2. Natural, to be expected.

▶ *adverb* **understandably**

un·der·stand·ing (*uhn*-dur-**stan**-ding) *noun* 1. The ability to understand something. 2. Someone's perception of a fact or a situation. 3. Sympathy or tolerance. 4. An informal agreement.

un·der·take (*uhn*-dur-**take**) *verb* 1. To agree to do a job or task; to accept a responsibility. 2. To set about; to try or attempt.

▶ *verb* **undertaking, undertook, undertaken**

un·der·tak·er (**uhn**-dur-*tay*-kur) *noun* A person whose job is to prepare dead bodies for burial or cremation and to arrange funerals.

un·der·tak·ing (**uhn**-dur-*tay*-king) *noun* A task, project, or assignment that someone takes on.

un·der·tow (**uhn**-dur-*toh*) *noun* A strong current below the surface of a body of water that can pull swimmers away from the shore.

un·der·wa·ter (**uhn**-dur-**waw**-tur) *adjective, adverb* Located, used, or done under the surface of the water.

un·der·wear (**uhn**-dur-*wair*) *noun* Clothes that you wear next to your skin, under your outer clothes; underclothes.

un·der·weight (**uhn**-dur-**wayt**) *adjective* Having less than the normal or required weight; weighing too little.

un·der·world (**uhn**-dur-*wurld*) *noun* 1. The part of society that is involved in organized crime. 2. In Greek and Roman mythology, the place under the ground where the spirits of dead people go.

un·de·sir·a·ble (*uhn*-di-**zye**-ruh-buhl) *adjective* Not wanted or not pleasant.

un·dis·turbed (*uhn*-dis-**turbd**) *adjective* Not bothered, or not interrupted; peaceful and calm.

un·do (uhn-**doo**)

verb 1. To untie, unfasten, or open something. 2. To remove or reverse the effects of something.

noun A function in some computer programs that allows you to undo commands or actions and return to an earlier version or state.

▶ *verb* **undoes, undoing, undid, undone**

un·done (uhn-**duhn**) *adjective* Not finished or not completed.

un·doubt·ed·ly (uhn-**dou**-tid-lee) *adverb* In a way that is beyond question or doubt.

un·dress (uhn-**dres**) *verb* To take clothes off. ▶ *verb* **undresses, undressing, undressed** ▶ *adjective* **undressed**

un·dy·ing (uhn-**dye**-ing) *adjective* Lasting forever.

un·earth (uhn-**urth**) *verb* 1. To dig up something. 2. To find, discover, or uncover something after searching for it.

▶ *verb* **unearthing, unearthed**

un·eas·y (uhn-**ee**-zee) *adjective* 1. Worried, nervous, or anxious. 2. Awkward, uncomfortable, or embarrassed.

▶ *noun* **uneasiness** ▶ *adverb* **uneasily**

un·em·ployed (*uhn*-em-**ploid**) *adjective* Without a job or paid work of any kind. ▶ *noun* **unemployment**

un·e·qual (uhn-**ee**-kwuhl) *adjective* 1. Not the same in amount, size, or value. 2. Not well matched or not well balanced.

▶ *adverb* **unequally**

un·e·ven (uhn-**ee**-vuhn) *adjective* 1. Not flat, smooth, or straight. 2. Not regular, or not consistent. 3. **uneven number** A whole number that does not have two as a factor.

▶ *adverb* **unevenly**

un·e·vent·ful (*uhn*-i-**vent**-fuhl) *adjective* With nothing interesting or exciting happening. ▶ *adverb* **uneventfully**

un·ex·pect·ed (*uhn*-ik-**spek**-tid) *adjective* Surprising because you did not think it would happen. ▶ *adverb* **unexpectedly**

U

un·fair (uhn-**fair**) *adjective* Not fair, right, or just. ▶ *adjective* **unfairer, unfairest** ▶ *noun* **unfairness** ▶ *adverb* **unfairly**

un·faith·ful (uhn-**fayth**-fuhl) *adjective* Not trustworthy; disloyal. ▶ *adverb* **unfaithfully**

un·fa·mil·iar (*uhn*-fuh-**mil**-yur) *adjective* **1.** Not well known or not easily recognized; strange. **2.** Not knowing about something, or having no experience using it.

un·fas·ten (uhn-**fas**-uhn) *verb* **1.** To release or to detach. **2.** To open something that has been fastened. ▶ *verb* **unfastening, unfastened**

un·feel·ing (uhn-**fee**-ling) *adjective* Without kindness or sympathy; cruel.

un·fit (uhn-**fit**) *adjective* **1.** Not suitable or good enough for a particular purpose. **2.** Unhealthy or in poor physical condition.

un·fold (uhn-**fohld**) *verb* **1.** To open and spread out something that was folded. **2.** To become known gradually. ▶ *verb* **unfolding, unfolded**

un·fore·seen (*uhn*-for-**seen**) *adjective* Not expected or not planned.

un·for·get·ta·ble (*uhn*-fur-**get**-uh-buhl) *adjective* So special, in some way, that you cannot forget it. ▶ *adverb* **unforgettably**

un·for·giv·a·ble (*uhn*-fur-**giv**-uh-buhl) *adjective* So bad that it cannot be forgiven. ▶ *adverb* **unforgivably**

un·for·tu·nate (uhn-**for**-chuh-nit) *adjective* **1.** Unlucky. **2.** Not wise, proper, or suitable. ▶ *adverb* **unfortunately**

un·friend (*uhn*-**frend**) *verb* (informal) To remove someone from your list of friends on a social networking site.

un·friend·ly (uhn-**frend**-lee) *adjective* **1.** Not friendly; feeling or showing dislike. **2.** Not pleasant or not favorable. ▶ *adjective* **unfriendlier, unfriendliest** ▶ *noun* **unfriendliness**

un·grate·ful (uhn-**grate**-fuhl) *adjective* Not thankful or appreciative for something. ▶ *adverb* **ungratefully**

un·hap·py (uhn-**hap**-ee) *adjective* **1.** Without joy; sad. **2.** Not lucky or fortunate. **3.** Not suitable. ▶ *adjective* **unhappier, unhappiest** ▶ *noun* **unhappiness** ▶ *adverb* **unhappily**

un·health·y (uhn-**hel**-thee) *adjective* **1.** Not healthy; in poor health; not well. **2.** Resulting from poor health. **3.** Harmful to one's health.

un·heard-of (uhn-**hurd**-uhv) *adjective* Not known or done before.

u·ni·corn (**yoo**-ni-korn) *noun* An imaginary animal that looks like a horse with a single straight horn growing from its forehead.

un·i·den·ti·fied (*uhn*-eye-**den**-tuh-*fide*) *adjective* Not identified; not known or recognized. ▶ *adjective* **unidentifiable**

u·ni·form (**yoo**-nuh-*form*) *noun* A special set of clothes worn by all the members of a particular group or organization. Nurses, soldiers, police officers, and mail carriers wear uniforms. *adjective* **1.** Always the same; never changing. **2.** All alike; not different in any way. ▶ *adjective* **uniformed** ▶ *noun* **uniformity** (yoo-nuh-**for**-mi-tee) ▶ *adverb* **uniformly**

u·ni·fy (**yoo**-nuh-*fye*) *verb* To bring or join together into a whole or a unit; to unite. ▶ *verb* **unifies, unifying, unified** ▶ *noun* **unification** (*yoo*-nuh-fi-**kay**-shuhn)

un·im·por·tant (*uhn*-im-**por**-tuhnt) *adjective* Not important; of no special value or interest; minor.

un·in·hab·it·ed (*uhn*-in-**hab**-i-tid) *adjective* Having no one living there.

un·in·tel·li·gi·ble (*uhn*-in-**tel**-i-juh-buhl) *adjective* Not able to be understood. ▶ *adverb* **unintelligibly**

un·in·ten·tion·al (*uhn*-in-**ten**-shuh-nuhl) *adjective* Done by accident, not on purpose. ▶ *adverb* **unintentionally**

un·in·ter·est·ed (uhn-**in**-tri-stid) *adjective* Having no interest in something, or not wanting to know anything about it.

U

un·ion (**yoon**-yuhn) *noun* 1. An organized group of workers set up to help improve such things as working conditions, wages, and health benefits. 2. The joining together of two or more things or people to form a larger group. 3. **the Union** The United States of America. 4. **the Union** The Northern states that remained loyal to the federal government during the Civil War.

u·nique (yoo-**neek**) *adjective* Being the only one of its kind; unlike anything else. ▶ *adverb* **uniquely**

u·ni·sex (**yoo**-ni-*seks*) *adjective* Able to be worn or used by both men and women.

u·ni·son (**yoo**-ni-suhn) *noun* Saying, singing, or doing something together.

u·nit (**yoo**-nit) *noun* 1. An individual thing or person, considered complete in itself. 2. A single person, thing, or group that is part of a larger group or whole. 3. An amount used as a standard of measurement. 4. A machine or piece of equipment that has a special purpose. 5. The number one.

u·nite (yoo-**nite**) *verb* 1. To join together or work together to achieve something. 2. To put or join together in order to make a whole. ▶ *verb* **uniting, united**

u·nit·ed (yoo-**nye**-tid) *adjective* Joined together for a common purpose.

U·nit·ed Ar·ab Em·ir·ates (yoo-**nye**-tid **ar**-uhb **em**-ur-its) A federation of seven states in the southeastern part of the Arabian Peninsula on the Persian Gulf. It has one of the largest oil reserves in the world and is a global finance center. The two most populous states are Abu Dhabi and Dubai.

U·nit·ed King·dom (yoo-**nye**-tid **king**-duhm) An island country off the northwestern coast of Europe, surrounded by the Atlantic Ocean, the North Sea, the Irish Sea, and the English Channel. The United Kingdom consists of four countries: England, Northern Ireland, Scotland, and Wales. Also known as Great Britain, it was the world's leading power in the 19th and early 20th centuries.

U·nit·ed States (yoo-**nye**-tid **states**) A country in North America consisting of 50 states and lying between the Atlantic and Pacific oceans. It is one of the largest and most ethnically diverse nations in the world, and it has the world's largest economy.

u·ni·ver·sal (*yoo*-nuh-**vur**-suhl) *adjective* 1. True of everyone or everything, or applying to everyone or everything. 2. Found everywhere. ▶ *adverb* **universally**

u·ni·verse (**yoo**-nuh-*vurs*) *noun* All existing matter and space.

u·ni·ver·si·ty (*yoo*-nuh-**vur**-si-tee) *noun* A school for higher learning after high school where people can study for degrees, do research, or learn a profession such as law or medicine. ▶ *noun, plural* **universities**

un·just (uhn-**juhst**) *adjective* Not just, fair, or right. ▶ *adverb* **unjustly**

un·kempt (uhn-**kempt**) *adjective* 1. Not combed. 2. Not tidy or neat in appearance.

un·kind (uhn-**kinde**) *adjective* Not kind; harsh or cruel. ▶ *adjective* **unkinder, unkindest** ▶ *adverb* **unkindly**

un·known (uhn-**nohn**) *adjective* Not familiar or not known about. *noun* An unknown person or thing.

un·less (uhn-**les**) *conjunction* Except on the condition that.

un·like (uhn-**like**) *adjective* 1. Not alike; different. 2. In a pair of magnets, **unlike** poles attract each other while like poles repel each other. *preposition* 1. Different from; not like. *Unlike Tina, I love music.* 2. Not typical of. *It's unlike Doug to be late.*

un·like·ly (uhn-**like**-lee) *adjective* 1. Not probable. 2. Not likely to be true or to succeed.

un·lim·it·ed (uhn-**lim**-i-tid) *adjective* Having no limits, bounds, or restrictions.

U

un·load (uhn-**lohd**) *verb* **1.** To remove things from a container, ship, or vehicle. **2.** To remove ammunition from a gun.
▶ *verb* **unloading, unloaded**

un·lock (uhn-**lahk**) *verb* **1.** To open something with a key. **2.** To solve, or to provide a key to.
▶ *verb* **unlocking, unlocked**

un·luck·y (uhn-**luhk**-ee) *adjective* **1.** Unfortunate, having bad luck. **2.** Happening by chance and unfortunate. **3.** Bringing or believed to bring bad luck.
▶ *adjective* **unluckier, unluckiest** ▶ *adverb* **unluckily**

un·mis·tak·a·ble (*uhn*-mi-**stay**-kuh-buhl) *adjective* Very obvious and impossible to confuse with anything else. ▶ *adverb* **unmistakably**

un·nat·u·ral (uhn-**nach**-ur-uhl) *adjective* **1.** Not usual or not normal; not happening in nature. **2.** False or insincere.
▶ *adverb* **unnaturally**

un·nec·es·sar·y (uhn-**nes**-uh-*ser*-ee) *adjective* Not necessary or required. ▶ *adverb* **unnecessarily**

un·no·ticed (uhn-**noh**-tist) *adjective* Ignored or not noticed.

un·ob·served (*uhn*-uhb-**zurvd**) *adjective* Not seen or not noticed.

un·oc·cu·pied (uhn-**ahk**-yuh-pide) *adjective* **1.** Having no occupants; vacant. **2.** Not held by enemy forces. **3.** Not busy or in use.

un·of·fi·cial (*uhn*-uh-**fish**-uhl) *adjective* **1.** Not issued or approved by someone in authority. **2.** Informal.
▶ *adverb* **unofficially**

un·pack (uhn-**pak**) *verb* To take objects out of a box, suitcase, trunk, vehicle, or container of any kind. ▶ *verb* **unpacking, unpacked**

un·pleas·ant (uhn-**plez**-uhnt) *adjective* Not pleasing; offensive; disagreeable. ▶ *adverb* **unpleasantly**

un·plug (uhn-**pluhg**) *verb* **1.** To disconnect an electrical device by removing its plug from an electric socket. **2.** To remove a stopper or something that blocks an opening.
▶ *verb* **unplugging, unplugged**

un·pop·u·lar (uhn-**pahp**-yuh-lur) *adjective* Not liked or approved of by many people.

un·prec·e·dent·ed (un-**pres**-i-*den*-tid) *adjective* Not known or done before; without a previous example.

un·pre·dict·a·ble (*uhn*-pri-**dik**-tuh-buhl) *adjective* **1.** Not able to be predicted. **2.** Behaving in a way that cannot be predicted.
▶ *adverb* **unpredictably**

un·pre·pared (*uhn*-pri-**paird**) *adjective* **1.** Not ready. **2.** Unwilling.

un·pro·voked (*uhn*-pruh-**vohkt**) *adjective* Not caused by anyone or anything.

un·rav·el (uhn-**rav**-uhl) *verb* **1.** To unwind a tangled mass of string, yarn, or strands of any kind. **2.** To undo or pull apart a woven or knitted fabric. **3.** To search for and discover the truth about a complex situation.
▶ *verb* **unraveling, unraveled**

un·rea·son·a·ble (uhn-**ree**-zuh-nuh-buhl) *adjective* **1.** Not showing reason or good sense. **2.** Unfair or unacceptable. **3.** Too great, excessive.
▶ *adverb* **unreasonably**

un·rec·og·niz·a·ble (uhn-**rek**-uhg-*nye*-zuh-buhl) *adjective* Unable to be recognized.

un·re·li·a·ble (*uhn*-ri-**lye**-uh-buhl) *adjective* Not dependable; not to be trusted.

un·re·solved (*uhn*-ri-**zahlvd**) *adjective* Not resolved or solved; still outstanding.

un·rest (uhn-**rest**) *noun* Disturbance and trouble; a lack of calm; dissatisfaction.

un·re·strict·ed (*uhn*-ri-**strik**-tid) *adjective* Without limitations or restrictions.

un·ripe (uhn-**ripe**) *adjective* Not mature enough to be harvested or eaten.

un·ri·valed (uhn-**rye**-vuhld) *adjective* Better than anyone or anything of the same type; having no equal.

un·roll (uhn-**role**) *verb* To open or spread out something that is rolled up. ▶ *verb* **unrolling, unrolled**

U

un·ruf·fled (uhn-**ruhf**-uhld) *adjective*
Completely calm, especially after a
disturbing incident.

un·rul·y (uhn-**roo**-lee) *adjective* Hard
to control or discipline. ▶ *adjective*
unrulier, unruliest

un·sat·is·fac·to·ry (*uhn*-sat-is-**fak**-tur-ee)
adjective Not good enough to meet a
certain need or standard. ▶ *adverb*
unsatisfactorily

un·scathed (uhn-**skay**THd) *adjective*
Not hurt or damaged.

un·scru·pu·lous (uhn-**skroo**-pyuh-luhs)
adjective Not guided by principles;
not concerned about whether your
actions are right or wrong. ▶ *adverb*
unscrupulously

un·seen (uhn-**seen**) *adjective* Not seen
or noticed.

un·set·tle (uhn-**set**-uhl) *verb* To upset
or to disturb. ▶ *verb* **unsettling,
unsettled**

un·set·tled (uhn-**set**-uhld) *adjective*
1. Not calm or not orderly; disturbed.
2. Not decided or not determined.
3. Not inhabited. **4.** Likely to change;
uncertain. **5.** Not paid.

un·sight·ly (uhn-**site**-lee) *adjective*
Unattractive, not pleasant to look at.

un·skilled (uhn-**skild**) *adjective* Having
no particular skill, training, or
experience.

un·sound (uhn-**sound**) *adjective* **1.** Not
strong or not solid; weak; unsafe.
2. Not based on good judgment or
clear thinking; not sensible. **3.** Not
healthy.

un·sta·ble (uhn-**stay**-buhl) *adjective*
1. Not firm; unsteady or shaky. **2.** Likely
to change. **3.** Showing rapid changes
of behavior and mood.

un·stead·y (uhn-**sted**-ee) *adjective*
Shaky or wobbly; not firm. ▶ *adverb*
unsteadily

un·suc·cess·ful (*uhn*-suhk-**ses**-fuhl)
adjective Unable to do something well
or to get what you want. ▶ *adverb*
unsuccessfully

un·suit·a·ble (uhn-**soo**-tuh-buhl)
adjective Not right for a particular
purpose or occasion. ▶ *noun*
unsuitability ▶ *adverb* **unsuitably**

un·sure (uhn-**shoor**) *adjective* **1.** Not
definite or not certain. **2.** Lacking
confidence and certainty.

un·tan·gle (uhn-**tang**-guhl) *verb* **1.** To
remove knots or tangles. **2.** To clear up
or explain.
▶ *verb* **untangling, untangled**

un·think·a·ble (uhn-**thing**-kuh-buhl)
adjective So unlikely or undesirable that
it cannot be considered or imagined.

un·ti·dy (uhn-**tye**-dee) *adjective* Not neat;
messy. ▶ *noun* **untidiness** ▶ *adverb*
untidily

un·tie (uhn-**tye**) *verb* **1.** To loosen or
undo something that has been tied.
2. To free from something that ties,
fastens, or restrains.
▶ *verb* **untying, untied**

un·til (uhn-**til**)
preposition **1.** Up to the time of. *Wait
until tomorrow before you decide.*
2. Before. *I won't be ready until Monday.*
conjunction **1.** Up to the time that.
2. Before. **3.** To the point, degree, or
place that.

un·to (**uhn**-too) *preposition* An old word
for **to.**

un·told (uhn-**tohld**) *adjective* **1.** Too great
to be counted or measured. **2.** Not told
or not revealed.

un·touched (uhn-**tuhcht**) *adjective*
1. Not handled or touched by anyone.
2. Ignored or undisturbed. **3.** Not
moved or not affected.

un·true (uhn-**troo**) *adjective* **1.** False or
incorrect. **2.** Not faithful or not loyal.

un·used *adjective* **1.** (uhn-**yoozd**) Never
used. **2.** (uhn-**yoost**) Not accustomed.

un·u·su·al (uhn-**yoo**-zhoo-uhl) *adjective*
Not usual, common, or ordinary;
rare. ▶ *adverb* **unusually**

un·wel·come (uhn-**wel**-kuhm) *adjective*
Not needed, wanted, or willingly
received.

un·well (uhn-**wel**) *adjective* Sick or ill.

un·wield·y (uhn-**weel**-dee) *adjective*
Difficult to hold or manage because of
shape, size, weight, or complexity.

un·will·ing (uhn-**wil**-ing) *adjective* Not
eager to do something. ▶ *adverb*
unwillingly

U

un·wind (uhn-**winde**) *verb* **1.** To undo something that has been rolled or wound up. **2.** To relax after being tense or worried.
> ▸ *verb* **unwinding, unwound**

un·wor·thy (uhn-**wur**-THee) *adjective* **1.** Not deserving. **2.** Not fitting, proper, or appropriate.
> ▸ *adverb* **unworthily**

un·wrap (uhn-**rap**) *verb* To remove the packaging or outer layer from something. ▸ *verb* **unwrapping, unwrapped**

un·zip (uhn-**zip**) *verb* **1.** To unfasten a zipper or garment. **2.** To expand a computer file or set of files that has been compressed in zipped form.
> ▸ *verb* **unzipping, unzipped**

up (uhp)
adverb **1.** From a lower to a higher place. **2.** In, at, or to a higher place or position. **3.** To a higher point or degree. **4.** On one's feet; in an upright position. **5.** Entirely. **6.** To a higher volume. **7.** Out of bed.
adjective **1.** Moving upward. **2.** Above the horizon.
preposition **1.** From a lower to a higher position or place in or on. *We hiked up the mountain.* **2.** At or to a farther point in or on. *They walked up the street.* **3.** Toward the source or inner part of. *We sailed up the river.*
phrases **1. up against** Faced with. **2. up for** Ready or eager to do something. **3. up to** Capable of performing or dealing with something. **4. up to** Depending on a particular person, or being his or her responsibility. **5. up to** Doing or occupied with something.

up·beat (**uhp**-beet) *adjective* (informal) Cheerful and optimistic.

up·bring·ing (**uhp**-bring-ing) *noun* The care and training a person receives while growing up.

up·date
verb (**uhp**-date or uhp-**date**) **1.** To provide someone with the latest information. **2.** To make something more modern or up to date.
noun (**uhp**-date) **1.** The latest information about something. **2.** A modern or up-to-date version of something.
> ▸ *verb* **updating, updated**

up front (uhp **fruhnt**)
adverb Before anything else; at the very beginning.
adjective **1. up-front** Being or coming in first or at the front. **2. up-front** Open and willing to share information.

up·grade
verb (**uhp**-grade) **1.** To promote someone to a better or more important job or status. **2.** To improve something. **3.** To replace a computer part or a piece of software with a better, more powerful, or more recently released version.
noun (**uhp**-grade) **1.** The upward slope of a hill or road. **2.** A newer version of something, especially software.
> ▸ *verb* **upgrading, upgraded**

up·heav·al (uhp-**hee**-vuhl) *noun* **1.** A sudden and violent upset or disturbance. **2.** A forceful lifting up of part of the earth's crust, especially during an earthquake.

up·hill (uhp-**hil**)
adjective, adverb Sloping upward.
noun **uphill battle** Something that is very tiring or difficult to accomplish.

up·hold (**uhp**-hohld) *verb* **1.** To support something. **2.** To confirm a claim or a decision.
> ▸ *verb* **upholding, upheld**

up·hol·ster (uhp-**hohl**-stur)
verb To put new upholstery on a piece of furniture. ▸ *verb* **upholstering, upholstered** ▸ *noun* **upholsterer** ▸ *adjective* **upholstered**

up·hol·ster·y (uhp-**hohl**-stur-ee) *noun* The stuffing, springs, cushions, and covering that are put on furniture. ▸ *noun, plural* **upholsteries**

up·keep (**uhp**-keep) *noun* The work or cost of keeping something in good condition.

up·load (**uhp**-lohd) *verb* To send information to another computer over a network. ▸ *verb* **uploading, uploaded**

up·on (uh-**pahn**) *preposition* On.

up·per (**uhp**-ur) *adjective* Higher in position or rank.

up·per·case (**uhp**-ur-kase) *adjective* **Uppercase** letters are capital letters.

up·per hand (**uhp**-ur hand) *noun* A position of advantage or control.

up·per·most (**uhp**-ur-*mohst*) *adjective* Highest in place, rank, or importance.
adverb In the highest or most important place or rank.

up·right (**uhp**-*rite*) *adjective, adverb* 1. Standing straight up; vertical. 2. Honorable and moral. *noun* Also **upright piano.** A piano whose strings are arranged vertically, or up and down.

up·ris·ing (**uhp**-*rye*-zing) *noun* A revolt or a rebellion.

up·roar (**uhp**-ror) *noun* A confused, noisy disturbance.

up·roar·i·ous (uhp-**ror**-ee-uhs) *adjective* 1. Noisy or confused; full of uproar. 2. Extremely funny.

up·root (**uhp**-root) *verb* 1. To tear or pull out by the roots. 2. To force someone to leave.
▶ *verb* **uprooting, uprooted**

up·set
verb (**uhp**-set) 1. To make someone nervous or worried. 2. To tip, turn, or knock something over. 3. To make someone feel ill. 4. To interfere with. 5. To defeat unexpectedly.
adjective (**uhp**-set) Nervous, worried, or disturbed about something.
noun (**uhp**-set) 1. An unexpected victory. 2. A period of time when you feel nervous or worried because of something that has happened.
▶ *verb* **upsetting, upset**

up·side down (**uhp**-*side* doun) *adverb* 1. With the top at the bottom. 2. In a confused or messy condition.
▶ *adjective* **upside-down**

up·stairs
adverb (**uhp**-stairz) 1. Up the stairs. 2. To or on a higher floor.
adjective (**uhp**-stairz) On an upper floor.
noun (**uhp**-stairz) The upper floor or floors of a building.

up·stream (**uhp**-streem) *adverb, adjective* Toward the source of a stream or river; against the current.

up·tight (**uhp**-tite) *adjective* (slang) Tense, nervous, or anxious.

up-to-date (**uhp**-tuh-date) *adjective* Containing the most recent information or in the latest style.

up·ward (**uhp**-wurd) *or* **up·wards** (**uhp**-wurdz)
adverb Toward a higher place or position.
adjective Moving or rising toward a higher place or position.

ur·a·ni·um (yu-**ray**-nee-uhm) *noun* A silver-white radioactive metal that is the main source of nuclear energy. Uranium is a chemical element.

Ur·a·nus (**yur**-uh-nuhs *or* yu-**ray**-nuhs) *noun* The seventh planet in distance from the sun. Uranus is the third-largest planet in our solar system. It has 27 known moons as well as 13 rings circling its equator.

ur·ban (**ur**-buhn) *adjective* Having to do with or living in a city.

ur·chin (**ur**-chin) *noun* A homeless child who begs in the street.

urge (urj)
verb To try very hard to persuade someone to do something.
noun A strong desire to do something.
▶ *verb* **urging, urged**

ur·gent (**ur**-juhnt) *adjective* Requiring immediate action or attention. ▶ *noun* **urgency** (**ur**-juhn-see) ▶ *adverb* **urgently**

u·rin·ar·y system (**yoor**-uh-*ner*-ee sis-tuhm) *noun* The organs and body parts that produce, store, and release urine. In humans and other mammals, it includes the kidneys, bladder, and tubes that carry urine.

u·ri·nate (**yoor**-uh-nate) *verb* To pass urine from the body. ▶ *verb* **urinating, urinated** ▶ *noun* **urination**

u·rine (**yoor**-uhn) *noun* The yellowish liquid that people and animals pass out of their bodies. Urine consists of water and wastes taken out of the blood by the kidneys. It is stored in the bladder.

U

URL (yoo-*ahr*-**el**) *noun* The address of a file on the Internet or the World Wide Web. URL is short for *Uniform Resource Locator* or *Universal Resource Locator*.

urn (urn) *noun* **1.** A vase with a base or pedestal. An urn is used as an ornament or a container. **2.** A large metal container with a faucet used for making and serving coffee or tea. **Urn** sounds like **earn.**

U·ru·guay (*yoor*-uh-*gwye* or *yoor*-uh-*gway*) A country in the southeastern part of South America. Its economy is mainly based on agriculture. Uruguay is one of the most economically advanced countries in South America and is socially progressive. In 2009, the Uruguayan government completed its project of giving every child in the country's elementary schools a free laptop and a free wireless Internet account.

us (uhs) *pronoun* The form of the pronoun *we* that is used after a verb or preposition.

U.S. *or* **US** (yoo-*es*) An abbreviation for United States.

us·age (*yoo*-sij or *yoo*-zij) *noun* **1.** The way that something is used. **2.** The way that words and phrases are used in a language.

USB (yoo-*es*-**bee**) *noun* A common type of computer connection used for many different devices. Computers usually have a number of USB ports where these devices can be plugged in. USB is short for *Universal Serial Bus.*

use
verb (yooz) **1.** To do a job with something. **2.** To spend or consume by using. **3.** To take advantage of a person in order to get something that you want.
noun (yoos) **1.** The action of using something. **2.** The right or ability to use something. **3.** A purpose for which something can be used. **4.** Advantage or benefit.
▶ *verb* **using, used** ▶ *noun* **user** (*yoo*-zur)

used
adjective **1.** (yoozd) Already made use of; secondhand. **2.** (yoost) Accustomed to something.
verb (yoost) Did something in the past.

use·ful (*yoos*-fuhl) *adjective* Helpful, or able to be used in a practical way. ▶ *noun* **usefulness**

use·less (*yoos*-lis) *adjective* **1.** Not helpful, or having no value. **2.** Hopeless; not capable of producing any result. **3.** (informal) Not very good or not very skilled.

us·er-friend·ly (*yoo*-zur-**frend**-lee) *adjective* Easy for people without experience to learn and operate.

us·er·name (*yoo*-zur-*naym*) *noun* A name that you use to identify yourself to a computer, network, or website.

ush·er (**uhsh**-ur) *noun* A person who shows people to their seats in a church, theater, or stadium.

u·su·al (*yoo*-zhoo-uhl) *adjective* Normal, common, or expected.

u·su·al·ly (*yoo*-zhoo-uh-lee) *adverb* Almost always.

U.S. Vir·gin Is·lands (yoo-*es* **vur**-jin **eye**-luhndz) A group of islands in the Caribbean Sea that is an unincorporated territory of the United States. The main islands are Saint Croix, Saint John, and Saint Thomas. To the northeast lie the British Virgin Islands, an overseas territory of the United Kingdom.

U·tah (*yoo*-taw or *yoo*-tah) A state in the western United States. More than half of its inhabitants are members of The Church of Jesus Christ of Latter-day Saints, also known as the Mormon Church. Its headquarters is in Salt Lake City, the state's capital. The Salt Lake Tabernacle, built by Mormon pioneers, is the home of the famous Mormon Tabernacle Choir.

u·ten·sil (yoo-**ten**-suhl) *noun* A tool or container, often used in the kitchen, that has a special purpose.

U

u·ter·us (yoo-tur-uhs) *noun* The hollow organ in women and other female mammals that holds and nourishes a fetus; the womb. ▶ *noun, plural* **uteri (yoo-**tuh-*rye*) *or* **uteruses**

u·til·i·ty (yoo-til-i-tee) *noun* **1.** A basic service supplied to a community, such as telephone, water, gas, or electricity. **2.** A company that supplies a basic utility. **3.** Usefulness. **4. utility program** A computer program that performs a specific task that allows the computer to run more efficiently.
▶ *noun, plural* **utilities**

ut·most (uht-*mohst*) *noun* The greatest or most extreme extent or amount.

u·to·pi·a (yoo-toh-pee-uh) *noun* An imaginary place where life is always good and free from social problems. ▶ *adjective* **utopian (yoo-toh-**pee-uhn)

ut·ter (uht-ur) *verb* To speak or to make a sound with your voice. *adjective* Complete or total.
▶ *verb* **uttering, uttered**

ut·ter·ance (uh-tur-uhns) *noun* Something that is said aloud, such as a spoken word or statement or a vocal sound.

ut·ter·ly (uht-ur-lee) *adverb* Absolutely; totally.

U-turn (yoo-*turn*) *noun* **1.** A turn made by a vehicle in the shape of a U, in order to go in the opposite direction. **2.** A complete reversal of plan, policy, or attitude.

Uz·bek·i·stan (uz-bek-i-*stan*) A country in Central Asia. Part of the former Soviet Union, Uzbekistan has been independent since 1991. Its second-largest city, Samarkand, was centrally located on the Silk Road, the ancient trade route between China and the West, and it is one of the world's oldest cities.

V

va·can·cy (vay-kuhn-see) *noun* **1.** A place, such as an apartment or a hotel room, that is available. **2.** A job or position that is unfilled.
▶ *noun, plural* **vacancies**

va·cant (vay-kuhnt) *adjective* **1.** Unoccupied or empty. **2.** Not filled.

va·cate (vay-kate) *verb* To leave, or to leave something empty. ▶ *verb* **vacating, vacated**

va·ca·tion (vay-kay-shuhn) *noun* A time of rest from school, work, and other regular duties; especially a pleasure trip away from home.

vac·ci·nate (vak-suh-*nate*) *verb* To protect someone against a disease by giving the person an injection or a dose of vaccine. ▶ *verb* **vaccinating, vaccinated** ▶ *noun* **vaccination**

vac·cine (vak-seen) *noun* A substance containing dead, weakened, or living organisms that can be injected or taken orally. A vaccine causes a person to produce antibodies that protect him or her from the disease caused by the organisms.

vac·u·um (vak-yoom) *noun* **1.** A sealed space or container from which all air or gas has been removed. **2.** A vacuum cleaner. *verb* To operate a vacuum cleaner.
▶ *verb* **vacuuming, vacuumed**

vac·u·um clean·er (vak-yoom *clee-nur) noun* A machine that picks up dirt from carpets, furniture, and other surfaces. To work, a vacuum cleaner reduces the air pressure inside itself. Then dirt is carried into it by outside air rushing to fill the partial vacuum.

va·gi·na (vuh-jye-nuh) *noun* The passage in women and other female mammals that leads from the uterus, through which babies are born.

vague (vayg) *adjective* Indefinite or unclear. ▶ *adjective* **vaguer, vaguest**

vain (vayn) *adjective* 1. Having too high an opinion of your appearance, your abilities, or your worth. 2. Unsuccessful or useless. **Vain** sounds like **vane** and **vein**. ▶ *adjective* **vainer, vainest**

val·en·tine (**val**-uhn-*tine*) *noun* 1. A gift or greeting card sent to a friend, relative, or loved one on Valentine's Day. 2. A sweetheart or loved one chosen on Valentine's Day.

Val·en·tine's Day (**val**-uhn-tinez *day*) *noun* February 14, a day named in honor of Saint Valentine, a Christian martyr of the third century A.D. It is celebrated by sending valentines.

val·iant (**val**-yuhnt) *adjective* Showing courage or determination. ▶ *adverb* **valiantly**

val·id (**val**-id) *adjective* 1. Acceptable in support of a claim. 2. Legal or officially acceptable.
▶ *noun* **validity** (vuh-**lid**-i-tee)

val·i·date (**val**-i-*date*) *verb* 1. To affirm or support the truth or value of something. 2. To make valid or legal.

val·ley (**val**-ee) *noun* 1. A low area of land between two hills or mountains, often containing a river or stream. 2. An area of land drained by a river system.

val·or (**val**-ur) *noun* Great bravery or courage, especially in battle.

val·u·a·ble (**val**-yoo-uh-buhl *or* **val**-yuh-buhl)
adjective Worth a lot of money, or very important or useful in some other way.
noun, plural **valuables** Possessions that are very important or worth a lot of money.

val·ue (**val**-yoo)
noun 1. The amount of money that something is worth. 2. In mathematics, an assigned or calculated number or quantity.
noun, plural **values** A person's principles of behavior and beliefs about what is most important in life.
verb 1. To think that something is precious or important. 2. To estimate how much something is worth.
▶ *verb* **valuing, valued**

valve (valv) *noun* A movable part that controls the flow of a liquid or gas through a pipe or other channel.

vam·pire (**vam**-pire) *noun* A dead person who rises from the grave at night to feed on the blood of humans, according to folktales and horror stories.

vam·pire bat (**vam**-pire *bat*) *noun* Any of the bats of Central America and South America that feed on the blood of birds and mammals.

van (van) *noun* 1. A large, enclosed truck used for moving animals or household goods from place to place. 2. A smaller motor vehicle that is shaped like a box and used for carrying passengers or cargo. A van has rear or side doors and side panels that often have windows.

van·dal (**van**-duhl) *noun* A person who deliberately damages or destroys other people's property. ▶ *noun* **vandalism**

van·dal·ize (**van**-duh-*lize*) *verb* To deliberately damage or destroy property for no reason. ▶ *verb* **vandalizing, vandalized**

vane (vayn) *noun* 1. See **weather vane**. 2. The flat part on the shaft of a bird's feather.
Vane sounds like **vain** and **vein**.

va·nil·la (vuh-**nil**-uh) *noun* A flavoring made from the seed pods of a tropical orchid. It is used in ice cream, candies, cookies, and other foods.

van·ish (**van**-ish) *verb* 1. To disappear suddenly and completely. 2. To cease to exist.
▶ *verb* **vanishes, vanishing, vanished**

van·i·ty (**van**-i-tee) *noun* Excessive pride in your own appearance or achievements. ▶ *noun, plural* **vanities**

van·i·ty plate (**van**-i-tee *plate*) *noun* A motor vehicle license plate with letters or numbers selected by the owner.

van·quish (**vang**-kwish) *verb* 1. To defeat or conquer an enemy in battle. 2. To defeat an opponent in a contest or competition. 3. To overcome an emotion or a fear.
▶ *verb* **vanquishes, vanquishing, vanquished**

V

Va·nu·a·tu (*vah*-noo-**ah**-too) An island nation in the South Pacific Ocean, east of northern Australia. The chain of islands was known as the New Hebrides when it was a colony, jointly ruled by the French and the British. Its name was changed to Vanuatu after the islands became independent in 1980.

va·por (**vay**-pur) *noun* 1. Fine particles of mist, steam, or smoke that can be seen hanging in the air. 2. A gas formed from something that is usually a liquid or solid at normal temperatures.

var·i·a·ble (**vair**-ee-uh-buhl) *adjective* Likely to change.
noun 1. A factor or quantity that can be changed in an experiment in order to measure its effect on some other element or process. 2. In mathematics, a symbol, such as x, y, or z, that stands for a number.

var·i·a·tion (*vair*-ee-**ay**-shuhn) *noun* 1. A change from the usual. 2. Something that is slightly different from another thing of the same type.

va·ri·e·ty (vuh-**rye**-i-tee) *noun* 1. Difference, or change. 2. A selection of different things in a particular category. 3. A different type of the same thing.
▸ *noun, plural* **varieties**

var·i·ous (**vair**-ee-uhs) *adjective* 1. Of different kinds. 2. An indefinite number; several.

var·mint (**vahr**-muhnt) *noun* 1. (informal) An undesirable animal, such as one that kills a rancher's livestock. 2. (informal) A person who is undesirable, obnoxious, or troublesome.

var·nish (**vahr**-nish)
noun A clear coating that you put on wood or other materials to protect it and make it shiny.
verb To coat something with varnish.
▸ *noun, plural* **varnishes** ▸ *verb* **varnishes, varnishing, varnished**

var·y (**vair**-ee) *verb* 1. To change or to be different in some way from other similar things. 2. To make changes to something.
▸ *verb* **varies, varying, varied** ▸ *noun* **variant**

vase (vays *or* vayz *or* vahz) *noun* A decorative container, usually made of glass, clay, or china, and often used for displaying flowers.

vas·sal (**vas**-uhl) *noun* In the Middle Ages, a person who was given land and protection by a lord in return for loyalty and military service.

vast (vast) *adjective* Very large in extent or amount. ▸ *adjective* **vaster, vastest** ▸ *noun* **vastness** ▸ *adverb* **vastly**

vat (vat) *noun* A large tank or container used for storing liquids.

Vat·i·can Cit·y (**vat**-i-kuhn **sit**-ee) A city-state entirely surrounded by the city of Rome, Italy. It is the home of the pope, who is the leader of the Roman Catholic Church. The Vatican is the only country in the world whose sole purpose is to administer a religion.

vault (vawlt)
verb To jump over something using your hands or a pole for support.
noun 1. A room or compartment for keeping money and other valuables safe. 2. An underground burial chamber. 3. A jump over something using your hands or a pole for support.
adjective **vaulted** In the form of an arch.
▸ *verb* **vaulting, vaulted**

V-chip (**vee**-*chip*) *noun* A device that can be installed in a TV set to allow parents to block certain programs so that children cannot watch them.

VCR (**vee**-*see*-**ahr**) *noun* An electronic machine that is connected to a television set. It uses magnetic tape to record or play back movies or television programs. VCR is short for *videocassette recorder*.

V

veal (veel) *noun* The meat from a calf.

vee·jay (**vee**-*jay*) *noun* An announcer on a television program that features music videos. Veejay is short for *video jockey* and is abbreviated as *VJ*.

veer (veer) *verb* To change direction or turn suddenly. ▶ *verb* **veering, veered**

veg·an (**vee**-guhn) *noun* A person who does not eat or use any animal or dairy products. ▶ *noun* **veganism**

veg·e·ta·ble (**vej**-tuh-buhl *or* vej-i-tuh-buhl) *noun* A plant or part of a plant used as food. Vegetables are usually eaten as side dishes or in salads.

veg·e·tar·i·an (*vej*-i-**tair**-ee-uhn) *noun* A person who eats only plants and plant products and sometimes eggs or dairy products. *adjective* Containing no meat. ▶ *noun* **vegetarianism**

veg·e·ta·tion (*vej*-i-**tay**-shuhn) *noun* Plant life or the plants that cover an area.

ve·he·ment (**vee**-uh-muhnt) *adjective* Showing strong feeling about something. ▶ *noun* **vehemence** (**vee**-uh-muhns) ▶ *adverb* **vehemently**

ve·hi·cle (**vee**-i-kuhl) *noun* A thing, such as a car or cart, that is used to transport people or things.

veil (vayl)
noun 1. A piece of material worn by women as a covering for the head or face. 2. Something that hides like a veil or curtain.
verb To hide something using a veil or something like a veil.
▶ *verb* **veiling, veiled**

vein (vayn) *noun* 1. One of the vessels through which blood is sent back to the heart from other parts of the body. 2. One of the stiff, narrow tubes that form the framework of a leaf or an insect's wing. 3. A narrow band of mineral in rock.
Vein sounds like **vain** and **vane**.

Vel·cro (**vel**-*kroh*) *noun* The trademark for a fastener that consists of two pieces of fabric. One piece is covered with tiny hooks that stick to the tiny loops on the second piece.

vel·lum (**vel**-uhm) *noun* 1. Fine parchment paper made from the skin of a calf, lamb, or baby goat. 2. Very high quality writing paper.

ve·loc·i·ty (vuh-**lah**-si-tee) *noun* Speed, especially in scientific work. ▶ *noun, plural* **velocities**

vel·vet (**vel**-vit)
noun 1. A thick, soft fabric made from cotton, silk, or other materials, slightly fuzzy on one side. 2. The soft skin that covers a deer's antlers while they are growing.
adjective 1. Made of velvet, or covered in velvet. 2. Smooth and soft like velvet.

ven·det·ta (ven-**det**-uh) *noun* A long-lasting feud between two families, gangs, or other groups.

vend·ing ma·chine (**ven**-ding muh-sheen) *noun* A machine into which you insert money to buy food items, beverages, or other products.

ven·dor (**ven**-dur) *noun* A person who sells something.

ve·ne·tian blind (vuh-**nee**-shuhn **blinde**) *noun* An indoor window covering made from thin strips of metal or plastic that can be raised or tilted to vary the amount of light that comes in.

Ven·e·zue·la (*ven*-uh-**zway**-luh) A country on the northern coast of South America. Venezuela is one of the most urbanized countries in Latin America. It has a range of habitats, from the Andes Mountains to rain forests, plains, coastal regions, and Caribbean islands, and is known for its diverse wildlife.

ven·geance (**ven**-juhns) *noun* Action that you take to pay someone back for harm that he or she has done to you or someone you care about.

ven·i·son (**ven**-i-suhn) *noun* The meat of a deer.

ven·om (**ven**-uhm) *noun* 1. Poison produced by some snakes and spiders. Venom is usually passed into a victim's body through a bite or sting. 2. Ill will; spite or malice.

vent (vent)
noun 1. An opening through which smoke or fumes can escape. 2. The

V

opening in a volcano through which smoke and lava escape.
verb To express an emotion.
▶ *verb* **venting, vented**

ven·ti·late (**ven**-tuh-*late*) *verb* To allow fresh air into a place and let stale air out. ▶ *verb* **ventilating, ventilated** ▶ *noun* **ventilation** (*ven*-tuh-**lay**-shuhn) ▶ *noun* **ventilator** (**ven**-tuh-*lay*-tur)

ven·tri·cle (**ven**-tri-kuhl) *noun* Either one of the two lower chambers of the heart. The ventricles receive blood from the atria and pump it to the arteries.

ven·tril·o·quism (ven-**tril**-uh-*kwiz*-uhm) *noun* The art of throwing your voice so that your words don't seem to be coming from you but from another source, such as a puppet. ▶ *noun* **ventriloquist** (ven-**tril**-uh-*kwist*)

ven·ture (**ven**-chur)
noun A risky or daring journey or project.
verb To go somewhere or do something daring, dangerous, or unpleasant.
▶ *verb* **venturing, ventured**

ven·ue (**ven**-yoo) *noun* The place where an event is held.

Ve·nus (**vee**-nuhs) *noun* The second planet in distance from the sun. Venus is the sixth-largest planet in our solar system and is brighter in our sky than any other heavenly body except the sun and moon.

ve·ran·da *or* **ve·ran·dah** (vuh-**ran**-duh) *noun* An open porch around the outside of a house, often with a roof.

verb (vurb) *noun* A word that expresses an action or a state of being. *Do, run, be, have,* and *think* are verbs.

ver·bal (**vur**-buhl) *adjective* **1.** Of or having to do with words. **2.** Spoken.

ver·dict (**vur**-dikt) *noun* **1.** The decision of a jury on whether an accused person is guilty or not guilty. **2.** An opinion or judgment.

verge (vurj)
noun The edge, rim, or margin of something.
verb To be very near to something.

phrase **on the verge** About to do something very soon.
▶ *verb* **verging, verged**

ver·i·fy (**ver**-uh-*fye*) *verb* **1.** To prove that something is true. **2.** To test or check the accuracy of something.
▶ *verb* **verifies, verifying, verified**
▶ *noun* **verification** (*ver*-uh-fi-**kay**-shuhn) ▶ *adjective* **verifiable**

ver·min (**vur**-min) *noun* **1.** Any of various small, common insects or animals that are harmful pests. Fleas, rats, and lice are vermin. **2.** An offensive person, or a person who is regarded as bad or troublesome.
▶ *noun, plural* **vermin**

Ver·mont (vur-**mahnt**) A New England state in the northeastern United States. It is known for its Green Mountains, rural landscapes, and maple syrup production. Its capital, Montpelier, is the smallest state capital in the U.S., with fewer than 8,000 residents.

ver·sa·tile (**vur**-suh-tuhl) *adjective* Able to function or to be used in many different ways. ▶ *noun* **versatility** (*vur*-suh-**til**-i-tee)

verse (vurs) *noun* **1.** One section of a poem or song. A verse is made up of several lines. **2.** Poetry, or a poem.

ver·sion (**vur**-zhuhn) *noun* **1.** One description or account given from a particular point of view. **2.** A different or changed form of something such as a book or car.

ver·sus (**vur**-suhs) *preposition* Against: *Today's game is the Baltimore Orioles versus the New York Yankees.* In general, versus is abbreviated *vs.* When referring to court cases, however, it is abbreviated *v.*

ver·te·bra (**vur**-tuh-bruh) *noun* One of the small bones that make up the backbone. ▶ *noun, plural* **vertebrae** (**vur**-tuh-*bree* or **vur**-tuh-*bray*)

ver·te·brate (**vur**-tuh-brit or **vur**-tuh-*brate*) *noun* Any animal that has a backbone. Fish, amphibians, reptiles, birds, and mammals are all vertebrates.

V

ver·tex (**vur**-teks) *noun* **1.** The top or highest point of something. **2.** The meeting point of two lines that form an angle.
▸ *noun, plural* **vertices** (**vur**-tuh-*seez*) *or* **vertexes**

ver·ti·cal (**vur**-ti-kuhl) *adjective* Upright, or straight up and down. ▸ *adverb* **vertically**

ver·y (**ver**-ee)
adverb To a great degree.
adjective Exact.

ves·sel (**ves**-uhl) *noun* **1.** A ship or a large boat. **2.** A tube in the body that fluids pass through. Arteries and veins are blood vessels. **3.** A hollow container for holding liquids, such as a bowl, vase, or jar.

vest (vest)
noun A short, sleeveless piece of clothing that is worn over a blouse or shirt.
verb To give power or authority to some person or group.
▸ *verb* **vesting, vested**

ves·tige (**ves**-tij) *noun* A trace or sign of something that is hard to perceive or that no longer exists.

vet (vet) *noun* **1.** (informal) A veterinarian. **2.** (informal) A veteran of the armed forces.

vet·er·an (**vet**-ur-uhn) *noun* **1.** Someone with a lot of experience in a profession, a position, or an activity. **2.** A person who has served in the armed forces, especially during a war.

Vet·er·ans Day (**vet**-ur-uhnz *day*) *noun* November 11, a day honoring men and women who served in the armed services and fought in wars for the United States. Formerly known as *Armistice Day*, this national holiday was first observed to celebrate the armistice, or truce, that ended World War I on November 11, 1918.

vet·er·i·nar·i·an (*vet*-ur-uh-**nair**-ee-uhn) *noun* A doctor who is trained to diagnose and treat sick or injured animals.

vet·er·i·nar·y (**vet**-ur-uh-*ner*-ee) *adjective* Of or having to do with the treatment of animals.

ve·to (**vee**-toh)
noun The right or power of a president, a governor, or an official group to reject a bill that has been passed by a legislature and to keep it from becoming a law.
verb **1.** To stop a bill from becoming a law. **2.** To forbid, or to refuse to approve.
▸ *noun, plural* **vetoes** ▸ *verb* **vetoes, vetoing, vetoed**

vex (veks) *verb* To annoy or worry somebody. ▸ *verb* **vexes, vexing, vexed** ▸ *noun* **vexation** (vek-**say**-shuhn) ▸ *adjective* **vexatious** (vek-**say**-shuhs) ▸ *adjective* **vexed**

vi·a (**vye**-uh *or* **vee**-uh) *preposition* By way of. *This train goes to Los Angeles via Denver.*

vi·a·ble (**vye**-uh-buhl) *adjective* Capable of succeeding. ▸ *noun* **viability** (*vye*-uh-**bil**-i-tee)

vi·a·duct (**vye**-uh-*duhkt*) *noun* A large bridge that carries a railroad track, road, or pipeline across a valley or over a city street.

vi·brant (**vye**-bruhnt) *adjective* **1.** Full of energy or enthusiasm. **2.** Bright or lively.
▸ *noun* **vibrancy** (**vye**-bruhn-see)
▸ *adverb* **vibrantly**

vi·bra·phone (**vye**-bruh-*fone*) *noun* An electronic xylophone with two rows of metal keys.

vi·brate (**vye**-brate) *verb* To move back and forth rapidly. ▸ *verb* **vibrating, vibrated**

vi·bra·tion (vye-**bray**-shuhn) *noun* An instance of something vibrating, or the sensation that this produces.

vice (vise) *noun* Immoral or harmful behavior. **Vice** sounds like **vise**.

vice pres·i·dent (**vise prez**-i-duhnt) *noun* An officer who ranks second to a president and acts for the president when necessary.

vice ver·sa (**vye**-suh **vur**-suh *or* **vise vur**-suh) *adverb* A Latin phrase meaning "the other way around."

vi·cin·i·ty (vi-**sin**-i-tee) *noun* The area surrounding a particular place. ▸ *noun, plural* **vicinities**

vi·cious (**vish**-uhs) *adjective* 1. Cruel and mean. 2. Evil or wicked. 3. Fierce or dangerous.
▶ *noun* **viciousness** ▶ *adverb* **viciously**

vic·tim (**vik**-tuhm) *noun* 1. A person who is hurt, killed, or made to suffer. 2. A person who is cheated or tricked.

vic·tim·ize (**vik**-tuh-*mize*) *verb* To single someone out for cruel or unfair treatment. ▶ *verb* **victimizing, victimized** ▶ *noun* **victimization** (*vik*-tuh-mi-**zay**-shuhn)

vic·tor (**vik**-tur) *noun* The winner in a battle, war, game, or contest.

vic·to·ry (**vik**-tur-ee) *noun* A win in a battle, war, game, or contest. ▶ *noun, plural* **victories** ▶ *adjective* **victorious** (vik-**tor**-ee-uhs) ▶ *adverb* **victoriously**

vid·e·o (**vid**-ee-oh) *adjective* Of or having to do with the visual part of a television program or with a computer display. *noun* 1. The visual part of television. 2. A recording of a movie or television show that can be played on a VCR. 3. A videotaped performance of a song.

vid·e·o·cas·sette (*vid*-ee-oh-kuh-**set**) *noun* A plastic case that contains videotape. It can be inserted into a VCR and used to record or play back movies and television programs.

vid·e·o dis·play ter·mi·nal (**vid**-ee-oh dis-*play* tur-muh-nuhl) *noun* The monitor or display screen of a computer. A video display terminal is also known as a *VDT*.

vid·e·o game (**vid**-ee-oh *game*) *noun* An electronic or computerized game played by using buttons or levers to move images around on a television or computer screen.

vid·e·o·tape (**vid**-ee-oh-*tape*) *noun* 1. Magnetic tape for recording and playing sound and pictures. 2. A recording on this kind of tape. *verb* To record something on videotape.
▶ *verb* **videotaping, videotaped**

vie (vye) *verb* To compete. ▶ *verb* **vying, vied**

Vi·et·nam (vee-*et*-**nahm**) A country in Southeast Asia on the South China Sea. During the Vietnam War, American forces supported the anti-communist government in the southern part of the country as it tried to resist the communist north, but the U.S. withdrew in 1973, and the north eventually won. Vietnam has reestablished diplomatic relations with the United States, and its economy is one of the fastest-growing in the world.

view (vyoo) *noun* 1. What you can see from a certain place. 2. The range or field of sight. 3. What you think about something, or your opinion. *verb* 1. To look at something. 2. To consider something in a particular way.
▶ *verb* **viewing, viewed**

view·er (**vyoo**-ur) *noun* 1. Someone who looks at something; a spectator or onlooker. 2. A device for looking at something, such as slides or photographic images.

view·point (**vyoo**-*point*) *noun* 1. The place or position from which a person views a situation or an event. 2. An attitude or a way of thinking.

vig·i·lant (**vij**-uh-luhnt) *adjective* Keeping a careful watch. ▶ *noun* **vigilance** ▶ *adverb* **vigilantly**

vig·or (**vig**-ur) *noun* 1. Great force or energy. 2. Physical energy or strength.

vig·or·ous (**vig**-ur-uhs) *adjective* Involving physical effort, strength, or energy. ▶ *adverb* **vigorously**

Vi·king (**vye**-king) *noun* A member of one of the Scandinavian peoples who invaded the coasts of Europe and explored the North American coast between the 8th and 11th centuries.

vile (vile) *adjective* 1. Evil or immoral. 2. Disgusting or repulsive.
▶ *adjective* **viler, vilest** ▶ *noun* **vileness**

vil·la (**vil**-uh) *noun* A large, luxurious house, especially one in the country.

vil·lage (**vil**-ij) *noun* A small group of houses that make up a community. A village is usually smaller than a town. ▶ *noun* **villager**

V

vil·lain (**vil**-uhn) *noun* An evil person, often a character in a play. ▸ *adjective* **villainous**

vin·dic·tive (vin-**dik**-tiv) *adjective* Unforgiving and seeking revenge. ▸ *noun* **vindictiveness** ▸ *adverb* **vindictively**

vine (vine) *noun* A plant with a long, twining stem that grows along the ground or climbs on trees, fences, or other supports. Melons, cucumbers, grapes, and pumpkins grow on vines.

vin·e·gar (**vin**-i-gur) *noun* A sour liquid made from fermented wine, cider, or other liquids, and used to flavor and preserve food.

vine·yard (**vin**-yurd) *noun* An area of land where grapes are grown.

vin·tage (**vin**-tij)
noun The wine or grapes of a particular season.
adjective **1.** Among the best of a person's work. **2.** Old but in good condition and valued for style and still valuable.

vi·nyl (**vye**-nuhl) *noun* A flexible, waterproof, shiny plastic that is used to make floor coverings, raincoats, and other products.

vi·o·la (vee-**oh**-luh) *noun* A stringed musical instrument that looks like a violin but is slightly larger and has a deeper tone.

vi·o·late (**vye**-uh-*late*) *verb* **1.** To break or ignore a promise, a rule, or a law. **2.** To treat a sacred place with disrespect. **3.** To disturb rudely or without any right.
▸ *verb* **violating, violated** ▸ *noun* **violation** (vye-uh-**lay**-shuhn) ▸ *noun* **violator** (**vye**-uh-*lay*-tur)

vi·o·lence (**vye**-uh-luhns) *noun* **1.** The use of physical force to cause harm. **2.** Great force or strength.

vi·o·lent (**vye**-uh-luhnt) *adjective* **1.** Showing or caused by great physical force. **2.** Showing or caused by strong feeling or emotion.

vi·o·let (**vye**-uh-lit)
noun **1.** A plant that grows close to the ground, with small purple, yellow, or white flowers. **2.** A blue-purple color.
adjective Being of a blue-purple color.

vi·o·lin (*vye*-uh-**lin**) *noun* A musical instrument with four strings, held under the chin and played with a bow. ▸ *noun* **violinist**

VIP (**vee**-*eye*-**pee**) *noun* Someone who is famous or important and so gets special treatment or consideration. Short for *very important person.*

vi·per (**vye**-pur) *noun* Any poisonous snake.

vir·gin (**vur**-jin) *adjective* In its natural state; untouched.

Vir·gin·ia (vur-**jin**-yuh) A state on the Atlantic coast of the southern United States. It was the site of the first permanent English colony in the New World, when Jamestown was established in 1607. It is the birthplace of eight U.S. presidents, including George Washington, Thomas Jefferson, James Madison, and Woodrow Wilson.

vir·tu·al (**vur**-choo-uhl) *adjective* **1.** Almost, but not complete or exact. **2.** Made to seem like the real thing, but consisting mainly of sound and images.

vir·tu·al·ly (**vur**-choo-uh-lee) *adverb* Almost, nearly.

vi·tu·al re·al·i·ty (**vur**-choo-uhl ree-**al**-i-tee) *noun* An environment that looks three-dimensional, created through a computer. Virtual reality seems real to the person who experiences it.

vir·tue (**vur**-choo) *noun* **1.** Moral goodness. **2.** An example of moral goodness. **3.** Any good quality or trait.
▸ *adjective* **virtuous** (**vur**-choo-uhs) ▸ *adverb* **virtuously**

vir·tu·o·so (*vur*-choo-**oh**-soh) *noun* A particularly skillful performer, especially a musician. ▸ *noun, plural* **virtuosos** or **virtuosi** (*vur*-choo-**oh**-see)

vir·u·lent (**vir**-uh-luhnt) *adjective* **1.** Very severe, aggressive, or harmful. **2.** Bitter, spiteful, or full of hate.
▸ *noun* **virulence** (**vir**-uh-luhns) ▸ *adverb* **virulently**

V

vi·rus (**vye**-ruhs) *noun* **1.** A very tiny organism that can reproduce and grow only when inside living cells. Viruses are smaller than bacteria. They cause diseases such as polio, measles, the common cold, and AIDS. **2.** The illness caused by a virus. **3.** A computer program, often hidden within another, seemingly innocent program, that produces many copies of itself and is designed to destroy a computer system or damage data.
▶ *noun, plural* **viruses**

vi·sa (**vee**-zuh) *noun* A document, usually stamped in a passport, giving permission for someone to enter a foreign country or stay there for a certain period of time.

vise (vise) *noun* A device with two jaws that open and close with a screw or lever. A vise is used to hold an object firmly in place while it is being worked on. **Vise** sounds like **vice.**

vis·i·ble (**viz**-uh-buhl) *adjective* Able to be seen. ▶ *noun* **visibility** (viz-uh-**bil**-i-tee) ▶ *adverb* **visibly** (**viz**-uh-blee)

vi·sion (**vizh**-uhn) *noun* **1.** The sense of sight. **2.** A lovely or beautiful sight. **3.** The ability to think ahead and plan. **4.** Something that you imagine or dream about.
▶ *adjective* **visionary** (**vizh**-uh-**ner**-ee)

vis·it (**viz**-it)
verb To go to see people or places and spend a certain amount of time there.
noun An occasion when a person goes to see people or places.
▶ *verb* **visiting, visited**

vis·i·tor (**viz**-i-tur) *noun* Someone who visits a place or person.

vi·sor (**vye**-zur) *noun* **1.** A brim that sticks out of the front of a cap to shade the eyes from the sun. **2.** A movable shade inside a car, above the windshield, that protects the eyes from glare. **3.** The movable, see-through shield on the front of a helmet that protects the face.

vis·u·al (**vizh**-oo-uhl) *adjective* **1.** Of or having to do with seeing. **2.** Designed or able to be seen.
▶ *adverb* **visually**

vi·su·al·ize (**vizh**-oo-uh-*lize*) *verb* To imagine something; to see something in your mind. ▶ *verb* **visualizing, visualized** ▶ *noun* **visualization** (*vizh*-oo-uh-li-**zay**-shuhn)

vi·tal (**vye**-tuhl) *adjective* **1.** Very important or essential. **2.** Of or having to do with life. **3.** Necessary for life. **4.** Full of life or energetic.
▶ *adverb* **vitally**

vi·tal·i·ty (vye-**tal**-i-tee) *noun* A state of being strong and lively.

vi·ta·min (**vye**-tuh-min) *noun* One of the substances in food that is essential for good health and nutrition.

vi·va·cious (vi-**vay**-shuhs) *adjective* Having a lively and animated personality. ▶ *noun* **vivacity** (vi-**vas**-i-tee) ▶ *adverb* **vivaciously**

viv·id (**viv**-id) *adjective* **1.** Bright and strong. **2.** Lively or active. **3.** Sharp and clear.
▶ *noun* **vividness** ▶ *adverb* **vividly**

viv·i·sec·tion (*viv*-i-**sek**-shuhn) *noun* The practice of operating on live animals for scientific and medical research.

vo·cab·u·lar·y (voh-**kab**-yuh-*ler*-ee) *noun* All the words that a person can use and understand. ▶ *noun, plural* **vocabularies**

vo·cal (**voh**-kuhl)
adjective **1.** Of or having to do with the voice. **2.** Outspoken and unafraid to express opinions.
noun, plural In music, the **vocals** are the parts that are sung.
▶ *adverb* **vocally**

vo·cal cords (**voh**-kuhl kordz) *noun, plural* Either of two pairs of bands or folds of membranes in the larynx. When air from the lungs passes through the lower pair, it causes them to vibrate and produce sound.

vo·cal·ist (**voh**-kuh-list) *noun* A singer.

vo·ca·tion (voh-**kay**-shuhn) *noun* **1.** A job, profession, or occupation. **2.** A strong feeling for a particular job, especially a religious career.
▶ *adjective* **vocational** (voh-**kay**-shuh-nuhl)

V

vo·cif·er·ous (voh-**sif**-ur-uhs) *adjective*
Noisy and vehement. ▶ *adverb*
vociferously

vod·ka (**vahd**-kuh) *noun* A strong
alcoholic drink that is clear in color
and is made from grain or potatoes.

vogue (vohg) *noun* The fashion or style
at a particular time.

voice (vois)
noun 1. The sound produced by air
passing through the larynx and out
of the mouth. 2. The power to speak
and sing. 3. The right to express your
opinion.
verb To express in words.
▶ *verb* **voicing, voiced**

voice mail (**vois** mayl) *noun* A system
that allows you to leave and play back
spoken messages by telephone.

voice·print (**vois**-print) *noun* A graph
that shows the special patterns
and characteristics of an individual
speaker's voice.

void (void)
noun A completely empty space.
adjective Not valid or legal.
verb To declare that something is not
valid or legal.
▶ *verb* **voiding, voided**

vol·a·tile (**vah**-luh-tuhl) *adjective*
1. Evaporating easily, or unstable in
some other way. 2. Showing rapid
changes of mood.
▶ *noun* **volatility** (*vah*-luh-**til**-i-tee)

vol·ca·no (vahl-**kay**-noh) *noun* A
mountain with openings through
which molten lava, ash, and hot
gases erupt. Volcanoes are found
along the boundaries of the earth's
plates. ▶ *noun, plural* **volcanoes** or
volcanos

vol·ley (**vah**-lee)
noun 1. In games such as tennis or
soccer, a shot in which the ball is
hit or kicked before it can bounce.
2. The firing of a number of bullets or
missiles at the same time. 3. A burst
or outburst of many things at the
same time.
verb To kick a soccer ball before it
bounces to the ground.
▶ *verb* **volleying, volleyed**

vol·ley·ball (**vah**-lee-bawl) *noun* 1. A
team game in which the players use
their hands and forearms to hit a
large ball over a net and try to make
the ball land on the ground on their
opponent's side. Volleyball can be
played on a court or on a beach. 2. The
ball used in this game.

volt (vohlt) *noun* A unit for measuring
the force of an electrical current or the
stored power of a battery. Volts are
used to measure voltage.

volt·age (**vohl**-tij) *noun* The force of an
electrical current, expressed in volts.

vol·ume (**vahl**-yoom or **vahl**-yuhm)
noun 1. A book. 2. One book of a
set. 3. The amount of space taken
up by a three-dimensional object,
such as a box, or by a substance
within a container. 4. The amount of
something, especially a large amount.
5. Loudness.

vol·un·tar·y (**vah**-luhn-ter-ee) *adjective*
1. Willing; not forced. 2. Controlled by
the will. 3. Done on purpose and not
by accident.

vol·un·teer (*vah*-luhn-teer)
verb To offer to do a job without pay.
noun A person who works without pay
because they wish to.
adjective Formed or made up of
volunteers, or done as a volunteer.
▶ *verb* **volunteering, volunteered**

vom·it (**vah**-mit) *verb* To bring up food
and other substances from your
stomach and expel them from your
mouth. ▶ *verb* **vomiting, vomited**

vote (voht)
verb To make a choice in an election.
noun 1. A choice or opinion expressed
in an election. 2. All of the ballots in
an election, considered as a whole.
▶ *verb* **voting, voted** ▶ *noun* **voter**

vouch (vouch) *verb* To say that
someone or something is true,
honest, or reliable. ▶ *verb* **vouching,
vouched**

vow (vou)
verb To make a solemn and important
promise.
noun An important promise.
▶ *verb* **vowing, vowed**

vow·el (**vou**-uhl) *noun* A speech sound made with a free flow of air through the mouth. Vowels are represented by the letters *a, e, i, o, u,* and sometimes *y,* or combinations of these letters.

voy·age (**voi**-ij) *noun* A long journey by sea or in space. ▸ *noun* **voyager**

vul·gar (**vuhl**-gur) *adjective* Rude or in bad taste. ▸ *noun* **vulgarity** (vuhl-**gar**-i-tee)

vul·ner·a·ble (**vuhl**-nur-uh-buhl) *adjective* In a position or condition where a person or thing could easily be damaged. ▸ *noun* **vulnerability** (vuhl-nur-uh-**bil**-i-tee) ▸ *adverb* **vulnerably**

vul·ture (**vuhl**-chur) *noun* A large bird of prey that has dark feathers and a bald head and neck. Vultures feed mainly on the meat of dead animals.

wack·y (**wak**-ee) *adjective* (slang) Odd or crazy in a silly or amusing way. ▸ *adjective* **wackier, wackiest** ▸ *noun* **wackiness** ▸ *adverb* **wackily**

wad (wahd)
noun **1.** A small, tightly packed ball or piece of something soft. **2.** A tight, thick roll.
verb To press or roll something into a wad.
▸ *verb* **wadding, wadded**

wad·dle (**wah**-duhl) *verb* To walk awkwardly, taking short steps and moving slightly from side to side. ▸ *verb* **waddling, waddled**

wade (wayd) *verb* **1.** To walk through water or mud. **2.** To move through something slowly and with difficulty.
▸ *verb* **wading, waded**

wad·er (**way**-dur)
noun A bird such as the crane or heron that wades in shallow water looking for food.
noun, plural **waders** High, waterproof boots used for fishing in deep water.

wa·fer (**way**-fur) *noun* **1.** A thin, light, crisp cookie or cracker. **2.** A thin, flat piece of candy.

waf·fle (**wah**-fuhl)
noun A type of cake baked in an appliance that presses a crisscross pattern into it.
verb (informal) To avoid giving a direct answer to a question; to keep changing your mind or position.
▸ *verb* **waffling, waffled** ▸ *noun* **waffler**

waft (wahft) *verb* To float or be carried through the air, as if by a breeze. ▸ *verb* **wafting, wafted**

wag (wag)
verb To move something quickly from side to side or up and down.
noun An instance of wagging something, usually a body part.
▸ *verb* **wagging, wagged**

wage (waje)
noun **wage** or **wages** The money someone is paid for the work he or she does.
verb If you **wage** a war or a campaign, you start it and continue it.
▸ *verb* **waging, waged**

wa·ger (**way**-jur)
noun A bet.
verb To make a bet.
▸ *verb* **wagering, wagered**

wag·on (**wag**-uhn) *noun* **1.** A vehicle with four wheels that is used to carry heavy loads and is pulled by a horse or horses. **2.** A child's toy vehicle or cart with four wheels and a long handle that is used for pulling and carrying things.

wag·on train (**wag**-uhn *trayn*) *noun* In frontier times, a line or group of covered wagons that traveled west together for safety.

waif (wayf) *noun* **1.** Someone, especially a young child, who is small, pale, and thin and looks like he or she has no home. **2.** A stray animal.

W

wail (wayl)
verb To make a long cry of pain or sadness.
noun A long cry of pain or sadness.
▶ *verb* **wailing, wailed**

waist (wayst) *noun* **1.** The middle part of your body between your ribs and your hips. **2.** The part of a piece of clothing that covers the body around the waist area.
Waist sounds like **waste.**

wait (wayt)
verb **1.** To stay in a place or do nothing for a period of time until someone comes or something happens. **2.** To look forward to something. **3.** To be delayed or put off. **4.** If you **wait on** someone, you serve as the person's waiter, waitress, salesperson, or servant.
noun A period of time spent waiting.
Wait sounds like **weight.** ▶ *verb* **waiting, waited**

wait·er (**way**-tur) *noun* A man who serves people food and drinks in a restaurant.

wait·ing room (**way**-ting *room*) *noun* A room or an area where people sit and wait for something such as a train or a doctor's appointment.

wait·ress (**way**-tris) *noun* A woman who serves people food and drinks in a restaurant. ▶ *noun, plural* **waitresses**

waive (wayv) *verb* **1.** To give up something by choice. **2.** To postpone or to set aside.
Waive sounds like **wave.** ▶ *verb* **waiving, waived**

waiv·er (**way**-vur) *noun* **1.** A document that you can sign to say that you are choosing to give up your legal right to do or have something. **2.** The act of choosing to give up your legal right to do or have something.
Waiver sounds like **waver.**

wake (wake)
verb **1.** To stop sleeping and become fully conscious. **2.** To cause someone to stop sleeping.
noun **1.** An occasion before or after a funeral in which people meet to remember the dead person. **2.** The trail in the water left by a boat as it moves away. **3.** What is left behind by something or someone.
▶ *verb* **waking, woke** (wohk) *or* **waked, waked** *or* **woken** (**woh**-kuhn)

walk (wawk)
verb **1.** To move along by placing one foot on the ground before lifting the other. **2.** To go with someone to a place. **3.** To make or help walk.
noun **1.** A way or style of walking. **2.** A trip that you make by walking. **3.** A path or other area that is set apart or designed for walking. **4.** In baseball, the right of the batter to go to first base after the pitcher has thrown four pitches that are not swung at and are not called strikes by the umpire.
idiom (informal) If you **walk all over** somebody, you treat the person badly and take advantage of him or her.
▶ *verb* **walking, walked** ▶ *noun* **walker**

walk·ie-talk·ie (**waw**-kee-**taw**-kee) *noun* A radio that is held in the hand, powered by batteries, and is used to communicate over short distances.

walk·o·ver (**wawk**-oh-vur) *noun* (informal) A very easy victory.

walk·way (**wawk**-*way*) *noun* A path or passage for walking.

wall (wawl) *noun* **1.** A vertical, solid structure, usually made of brick or stone, that surrounds an area or separates one area from another. **2.** The vertical side of a room or building that supports a roof. **3.** Anything that divides one thing from another, shuts something in, or stops anything from getting past; a barrier. **4.** A situation in which no one will talk to you, help you, or give you information.

wal·la·by (**wah**-luh-*bee*) *noun* A small marsupial that is related to the kangaroo. Wallabies are found in Australia, New Zealand, and New Guinea. ▶ *noun, plural* **wallabies**

wal·let (**wah**-lit) *noun* A small, flat case, usually made of leather, for holding money, photographs, and/or cards.

W

wal·lop (**wah**-luhp)
verb 1. (informal) To hit someone or something very hard. 2. (informal) To defeat severely.
noun A hard hit or punch.
▶ *verb* **walloping, walloped**

wal·low (**wah**-loh) *verb* 1. To roll around in mud or water. 2. To enjoy something greatly, or to get completely involved in something.
▶ *verb* **wallowing, wallowed**

wall·pa·per (**wawl**-*pay*-pur)
noun 1. Paper that is pasted in sections to a wall in order to decorate a room. 2. A pattern or image that serves as the background of a computer desktop.
verb To apply wallpaper to a wall.
▶ *verb* **wallpapering, wallpapered**

wal·nut (**wawl**-nuht) *noun* A sweet nut that grows on a tall tree and has a hard, wrinkled shell. The wood of the walnut tree is often used to make furniture. ▶ *noun, plural* **walnuts**

wal·rus (**wawl**-ruhs) *noun* A large sea animal that lives in the Arctic. Walruses have tusks, flippers, tough skin, and a thick layer of blubber. ▶ *noun, plural* **walruses** or **walrus**

waltz (wawlts)
noun 1. A ballroom dance in which a couple turns continuously in a regular series of three steps. 2. A piece of music that is used with a waltz.
verb To dance the waltz.
▶ *noun, plural* **waltzes** ▶ *verb* **waltzes, waltzing, waltzed** ▶ *noun* **waltzer**

wam·pum (**wahm**-puhm) *noun* Beads made from polished shells strung together or woven to make belts, collars, and necklaces. Wampum was used by some Native American tribes as money.

wand (wahnd) *noun* A thin rod or stick, especially one used by magicians.

wan·der (**wahn**-dur) *verb* 1. To move around without a particular purpose or place to go; to roam. 2. To walk away from where you ought to be; to stray. 3. If your mind or thoughts **wander,** you become distracted from

something and start thinking about something else.
▶ *verb* **wandering, wandered** ▶ *noun* **wanderer**

wane (wane) *verb* 1. To become less or smaller in size, importance, or strength. 2. When the moon **wanes,** it seems to get smaller.
▶ *verb* **waning, waned**

wan·gle (**wang**-guhl) *verb* (informal) To gain something by clever or dishonest methods. ▶ *verb* **wangling, wangled**

want (wahnt)
verb 1. To feel that you would like to have, do, or get something; to wish for; to desire. 2. To need or require something.
noun 1. A lack of something.
2. Something that you need or desire.
3. The condition of being very poor or needy; poverty.
▶ *verb* **wanting, wanted**

war (wor) *noun* 1. A long period of fighting between two or more opposing countries or groups. 2. A struggle over a long period of time to stop or control something harmful. **War** sounds like **wore.**

war·bler (**wor**-blur) *noun* Any of several small songbirds, many of which have brightly colored feathers.

ward (word)
noun 1. A large room or section in a hospital where many patients are taken care of. 2. A person who is officially cared for by a guardian or the court. 3. For voting purposes, a district of a town or city.
verb **ward off** To do something to protect yourself from something attacking or hurting you.
▶ *verb* **warding, warded**

war·den (**wor**-duhn) *noun* 1. Someone in charge of a prison. 2. An official who is responsible for making sure certain laws are obeyed.

ward·robe (**wor**-drobe) *noun* 1. A collection of clothes, especially all the clothes belonging to one person. 2. A tall piece of furniture or a closet used for storing clothes.

W

ware·house (**wair**-*hous*) *noun* A large building used for storing goods or merchandise.

wares (wairz) *noun, plural* Things that are for sale; goods.

war·fare (**wor**-*fair*) *noun* The fighting of wars, especially using a particular method.

war·like (**wor**-*like*) *adjective* 1. Aggressive and liking to fight. 2. Ready and likely to start a war.

warm (worm)
adjective 1. Slightly hot. 2. Holding in body heat. 3. Very friendly.
verb 1. To raise the temperature of something. 2. If you **warm up** before a sports match or athletic activity, you stretch or exercise lightly in preparation. 3. If you **warm up** an engine, you turn it on and let it run until it is ready to be used.
▶ *adjective* **warmer, warmest** ▶ *verb* **warming, warmed** ▶ *adverb* **warmly** ▶ *noun* **warm-up**

warm-blood·ed (**worm-bluhd**-id) *adjective* **Warm-blooded** animals have a warm body temperature that does not change, even if the temperature around them is very hot or very cold.

warmth (wormth) *noun* 1. The feeling or condition of being warm. 2. Friendliness, kindness, or enthusiasm.

warn (worn) *verb* 1. To tell someone to do or not do something in order to avoid danger or something bad. 2. To give someone advice about something bad that might happen.
Warn sounds like **worn**. ▶ *verb* **warning, warned** ▶ *noun* **warning**

warp (worp) *verb* If an object **warps,** it gets twisted, curved, or bent out of shape, especially because of dampness or heat. ▶ *verb* **warping, warped**

war·rant (**wor**-uhnt)
noun An official piece of paper that gives someone the right to do something.
verb 1. To guarantee. 2. To deserve.
▶ *verb* **warranting, warranted**

war·ran·ty (**wor**-uhn-tee) *noun* A written agreement in which a company agrees that it is responsible for repairing or replacing a product it has sold if it breaks within a specific period of time.

war·ren (**wor**-uhn) *noun* A system of underground holes and tunnels where rabbits live.

war·ri·or (**wor**-ee-ur) *noun* A soldier, or someone who fights with courage and determination.

war·ship (**wor**-ship) *noun* A ship with heavy guns that is used in war.

wart (wort) *noun* 1. A small, hard lump on the skin that is caused by a virus. 2. A small lump or bump that grows on a plant.
▶ *adjective* **warty**

war·y (**wair**-ee) *adjective* Nervous and cautious. ▶ *adjective* **warier, wariest** ▶ *noun* **wariness** ▶ *adverb* **warily**

was (wuhz *or* wahz) *verb* The form of **be** used with *I, he, she,* or *it* or with singular nouns in the past tense.

wash (wahsh)
verb 1. To clean with water or soap and water. 2. To be carried by the movement of water. 3. **wash up** To clean your hands and face using soap and water. 4. If waves or the sea **washes** something **up,** it brings it to the shore.
noun 1. Clothing that needs to be or has been washed. 2. A liquid containing soap that is used for cleaning.
▶ *verb* **washes, washing, washed** ▶ *noun, plural* **washes** ▶ *noun* **washing**

wash·a·ble (**wah**-shuh-buhl) *adjective* If a material is **washable,** you can wash it without causing any damage to it.

wash·er (**wah**-shur) *noun* 1. A washing machine. 2. A ring that fits between a nut and a bolt to give a tighter fit or prevent a leak.

wash·ing ma·chine (**wah**-shing muh-sheen) *noun* A machine for washing clothes.

Wash·ing·ton (**wah**-shing-tuhn) A state in the Pacific Northwest region of the

W

United States, bordering Canada. It has several active volcanoes, including Mount St. Helens, which erupted in 1980. Another active volcano, Mount Rainier, is the highest mountain in the state. The volcanoes are part of the Cascades, a mountain range that divides the state. The eastern half is arid, while the western half is wetter and cooler, and has some rain forests near the Pacific Ocean, among the few temperate rain forests in the U.S.

Wash·ing·ton (**wah**-shing-tuhn) The capital of the United States. It is the home of the federal government, which includes the White House, Congress, and the Supreme Court. It is also referred to as the District of Columbia, its legal name, or as D.C., or as Washington, D.C. The city was created from land that originally belonged to the states of Maryland and Virginia.

Wash·ing·ton's Birth·day (**wah**-shing-tuhnz **burth**-day) *noun* A holiday that honors the birthday of George Washington, the first president of the United States. Originally celebrated on February 22, Washington's actual birthday, this holiday is now observed on the third Monday in February as part of **Presidents' Day.**

was·n't (**wuhz**-uhnt) *contraction* A short form of *was not.*

wasp (wahsp) *noun* A thin, flying insect with black and yellow stripes. Female wasps can sting.

waste (wayst)
verb **1.** To use or spend something foolishly or carelessly. **2.** If someone **wastes away,** the person gets thinner and weaker, especially because of sickness.
noun **1.** Garbage, or something left over and not needed. **2.** What the body does not use or need after food has been digested. **3.** A large area of land with few people, plants, or animals.
adjective Referring to things that are not wanted or not useful.
Waste sounds like **waist.** ▶ *verb* **wasting, wasted**

waste·bas·ket (**wayst**-*bas*-kit) *noun* A small basket or open container used for scraps of paper or other small items of trash.

waste·ful (**wayst**-fuhl) *adjective* If you are **wasteful,** you use things up carelessly and do not think about saving them. ▶ *noun* **wastefulness** ▶ *adverb* **wastefully**

waste·land (**wayst**-*land*) *noun* An area of land that is barren or empty, and where few plants or animals can live.

watch (wahch)
noun **1.** A small clock that you can wear on your wrist. **2.** A person or group that guards someone or something, or the activity of doing this. **3.** The time that a guard is on duty.
verb **1.** To look at something or someone for a period of time. **2.** To be alert or careful about something. **3.** To keep guard over someone or something.
▶ *noun, plural* **watches** ▶ *verb* **watches, watching, watched**

watch·dog (**wahch**-*dawg*) *noun*
1. A dog trained to guard a house, property, or people. **2.** A person or group of people who make sure companies or the government do not do anything illegal.

watch·ful (**wahch**-fuhl) *adjective* Observing carefully; alert. ▶ *noun* **watchfulness** ▶ *adverb* **watchfully**

wa·ter (**waw**-tur)
noun The colorless liquid that falls as rain and fills oceans, rivers, and lakes.
noun, plural **waters** The water in an ocean, a river, or a lake.
verb **1.** To pour water on something. **2.** If your mouth **waters,** it produces saliva because you are hungry. **3.** If your eyes **water,** they become full of tears. **4. water down** To add water or another liquid to make something weaker. **5. water down** To make something less effective, less difficult, or less offensive.
▶ *verb* **watering, watered**

W

wa·ter·bird (**waw**-tur-*burd*) *noun* A bird that lives near the water and can swim or wade.

wa·ter buf·fa·lo (**waw**-tur *buhf*-uh-loh) *noun* A buffalo with long horns that curve upward and outward. Found in Asia, it is often used to pull or carry heavy loads. ▶ *noun, plural* **water buffaloes** *or* **water buffalos** *or* **water buffalo**

wa·ter·col·or (**waw**-tur-*kuhl*-ur) *noun* **1.** Paint that is mixed with water instead of oil. **2.** A picture painted with watercolors.

wa·ter·cress (**waw**-tur-*kres*) *noun* A plant that grows in wet soil or running water with sharp-tasting, edible leaves.

wa·ter cy·cle (**waw**-tur *sye*-kuhl) *noun* The constant movement of the earth's water. Plants give off moisture, and water from lakes, rivers, and oceans evaporates, making water vapor. This vapor rises, forms clouds, and eventually falls as rain, hail, or snow.

wa·ter·fall (**waw**-tur-*fawl*) *noun* Water from a stream or river that falls from a high place to a lower place.

wa·ter·front (**waw**-tur-*fruhnt*) *noun* An area of a city or town that is located beside a body of water.

wa·ter·ing can (**waw**-tur-ing *kan*) *noun* A container with a handle and a long spout that is used for watering plants.

wa·ter lil·y (**waw**-tur *lil*-ee) *noun* A plant with wide, flat leaves and colorful flowers that grows in freshwater ponds and lakes. ▶ *noun, plural* **water lilies**

wa·ter·logged (**waw**-tur-*lawgd*) *adjective* If something is **waterlogged,** it is so filled or soaked with water that it becomes heavy or hard to manage.

wa·ter main (**waw**-tur *mayn*) *noun* A large, main pipe in a system of pipes that carry water.

wa·ter·mark (**waw**-tur-*mahrk*) *noun* **1.** A mark or design in paper that you can see when you hold the paper up to the light. **2.** A mark on a wall or other surface left by water in a river, a lake, or an ocean.

wa·ter·mel·on (**waw**-tur-*mel*-uhn) *noun* A large, sweet, juicy fruit that grows on vines. It usually has a thick, green skin, many black seeds, and pink or red flesh.

wa·ter moc·ca·sin (**waw**-tur *mah*-kuh-sin) *noun* A poisonous snake that lives near water and in swamps in the southeastern part of the United States. It is also called a **cottonmouth.**

wa·ter·proof (**waw**-tur-*proof*) *adjective* If something is **waterproof,** it does not allow water to enter.

wa·ter·shed (**waw**-tur-*shed*) *noun* **1.** A ridge or area of high land that separates two river basins. **2.** The region or land area that drains into a river or lake. **3.** An important factor; a turning point.

wa·ter·ski (**waw**-tur-*skee*) *verb* To travel on skis over water while being pulled by a boat. ▶ *verb* **water-skiing, water-skied** ▶ *noun* **water-skier** ▶ *noun* **waterskiing**

wa·ter·tight (**waw**-tur-*tite*) *adjective* **1.** Completely sealed so that water cannot enter or leave. **2.** If an argument is **watertight,** it has no mistakes or flaws.

wa·ter va·por (**waw**-tur *vay*-pur) *noun* Water in the form of gas or very tiny drops.

wa·ter·way (**waw**-tur-*way*) *noun* A river, canal, or other body of water on which ships and boats can travel.

wa·ter·wheel (**waw**-tur-*weel*) *noun* A large wheel that is turned by water flowing over or under it.

wa·ter·works (**waw**-tur-*wurks*) *noun, plural* The system that provides water to a community or town, including reservoirs, pipes, machinery, and buildings. *Waterworks* can be used with a singular or a plural verb.

watt (waht) *noun* A unit for measuring electrical power. ▶ *noun* **wattage** (**wah**-tij)

W

wave (wave)

verb **1.** To move your hand back and forth to get someone's attention or to say hello or good-bye. **2.** To move or sway back and forth or up and down, or to make something do this. *noun* **1.** A line of water that rises up and moves across the surface of an ocean or sea. **2.** A slight curl in your hair. **3.** An amount of energy that travels through air or water in the shape of a wave. **4.** A period of time in which there is a sudden change or increase in something.

Wave sounds like **waive.** ▶ *verb* **waving, waved** ▶ *adjective* **wavy**

wave·length (**wayv**-*lengkth*) *noun* **1.** The distance between one point on a wave of light or sound and the next. **2.** (informal) The state of having similar thoughts or opinions as another person.

wa·ver (**way**-vur) *verb* **1.** To be uncertain about what you think or believe about someone or something. **2.** To become weak or unsteady.

Waver sounds like **waiver.** ▶ *verb* **wavering, wavered**

wax (waks)

noun **1.** A hard substance made from oils or fats and used to make candles, crayons, and polish. Wax becomes soft when heated. **2.** A substance like this produced by bees; beeswax. *verb* **1.** To put wax or polish on something such as a car or furniture. **2.** When the moon **waxes,** it appears to get bigger. **3.** To grow, or to become.

▶ *verb* **waxes, waxing, waxed**
▶ *adjective* **waxy**

way (way)

noun **1.** A direction. **2.** A road or a route to get to a place. **3.** A method or style that you use to do something. **4.** A particular manner or a style. **5.** Distance. **6.** The opportunity to do or get what you wish. **7.** A point or a detail. **8.** Space or a path.

noun, plural **ways** A group of people's typical habits or customs.

Way sounds like **weigh.**

we (wee) *pronoun, plural* The people who are speaking or writing. **We** sounds like **wee.**

weak (week) *adjective* **1.** Having little strength, force, or power. **2.** Likely to break, fall, or collapse. **3.** Lacking flavor. **4.** Lacking in skill or knowledge. **5.** Your **weak** points are the things that you are not very good at.

Weak sounds like **week.** ▶ *adjective* **weaker, weakest** ▶ *adverb* **weakly**

weak·en (**wee**-kuhn) *verb* **1.** To make something less strong, concentrated, or potent, or to become this way. **2.** To make something less effective or convincing. **3.** To lose physical strength or vigor, or to cause this.

▶ *verb* **weakening, weakened**

weak·ling (**week**-ling) *noun* A person without physical or moral strength.

weak·ness (**week**-nis) *noun* **1.** The condition of being weak or at a disadvantage. **2.** A personal fault or defect. **3.** A special fondness or desire for something.

wealth (welth) *noun* **1.** A great amount of money, property, or valuable possessions. **2.** A great amount of anything.

wealth·y (**wel**-thee) *adjective* Someone who is **wealthy** has a lot of money, property, or possessions. ▶ *adjective* **wealthier, wealthiest**

wean (ween) *verb* **1.** When you **wean** babies, you start giving them food other than their mothers' milk or formula. **2.** If you **wean** someone **from** something, you help him or her stop doing it or give it up gradually.

▶ *verb* **weaning, weaned**

weap·on (**wep**-uhn) *noun* **1.** Something that can be used in a fight to attack or defend, such as a sword, gun, knife, or bomb. **2.** Anything that can be used to win a fight, struggle, or contest.

▶ *noun* **weaponry**

W

wear (wair)
verb 1. To be dressed in something, or to have something on your body. 2. To have your hair in a particular style. 3. To show a particular expression on your face. 4. To last a long time. 5. **wear away** To destroy something slowly and gradually. 6. **wear off** To gradually decrease or stop. 7. If an activity **wears** you **out**, it makes you extremely tired. 8. If you **wear out** your clothes, you use them so much that they are damaged and no longer useful.
noun 1. Clothes worn by a particular group of people, or for a particular occasion. 2. The gradual damage done to something that has been used a lot over a period of time.
▶ *verb* **wearing, wore** (wor), **worn** ▶ *noun* **wearer**

wea·ry (**weer**-ee) *adjective* 1. Extremely tired. 2. Having little patience or interest; bored.
▶ *adjective* **wearier, weariest** ▶ *noun* **weariness** ▶ *adverb* **wearily**

wea·sel (**wee**-zuhl)
noun 1. A small animal with a long, thin body, short legs, and soft, thick, reddish-brown fur. It eats other small animals. 2. (informal) A person who uses tricks and lies to get what he or she wants.
verb **weasel out** (informal) To use tricks and lies in order to avoid doing something.

weath·er (**weTH**-ur)
noun The condition of the outside air or atmosphere at a particular time and place. Weather can be described, for example, as hot or cold, wet or dry, calm or windy, clear or cloudy.
verb 1. If wood, stone, or another material **weathers,** it changes after being outside for a long time. 2. If you **weather** a difficult situation, such as a storm or crisis, you manage to get through it safely.
idiom If you are **under the weather,** you are sick.
▶ *verb* **weathering, weathered**

weath·er·beat·en (**weTH**-ur-*bee*-tuhn) *adjective* Damaged or worn by the weather.

weath·er vane (**weTH**-ur *vayn*) *noun* A pointer that swings around on a pole to show which way the wind is blowing.

weave (weev)
verb 1. To make cloth, baskets, or other objects by passing threads or strips over and under each other. 2. To spin a web or cocoon. 3. To move from side to side or in and out in order to get through something.
noun A method or pattern of weaving.
Weave sounds like **we've.** ▶ *verb* **weaving, wove** (wohv) *or* **weaved, woven** (**woh**-vuhn) *or* **weaved** ▶ *noun* **weaver**

web (web) *noun* 1. A very thin net of sticky threads made by a spider to catch flies and other insects. 2. Short for the **World Wide Web.** 3. A pattern of related things put together in a careful or complicated way. 4. The fold of skin or tissue that connects the toes of a duck, frog, or other animal that swims.

web brows·er (**web** *brou*-zur) *noun* The full form of **browser** (sense 1).

web·cam (**web**-*kam*) *noun* A video camera that broadcasts directly to a website so that people online can watch it.

web·foot·ed (**web**-*fut*-id) *adjective* Having toes that are connected by a web or fold of skin.

web·host·ing (**web**-*hoh*-sting) *noun* The business of providing Internet addresses and server storage space for people or companies who have websites.

web·log (**web**-*lawg*) *noun* A blog.

web·mas·ter (**web**-*mas*-tur) *noun* Someone whose job or responsibility is to take care of a website and make sure that all its links and other functions are working properly.

web·page (**web**-*payj*) *noun* A single page on a website.

W

web·site (**web**-site) *noun* A group of linked computer files on the World Wide Web.

we'd (weed) *contraction* A short form of *we had* or *we would*. **We'd** sounds like **weed.**

wed (wed) *verb* **1.** To get married to someone. **2.** To perform a marriage ceremony.
▶ *verb* **wedding, wedded** *or* **wed**

wed·ding (**wed**-ing) *noun* A marriage ceremony.

wedge (wej)
noun A piece of food, wood, metal, or plastic that is thin and pointed at one end and thick at the other.
verb **1.** To split, force apart, or hold in place with a wedge. **2.** To squeeze or crowd into a limited space.
▶ *verb* **wedging, wedged**

Wed·nes·day (**wenz**-day *or* **wenz**-dee)
noun The fourth day of the week, after Tuesday and before Thursday.

wee (wee) *adjective* Very small; tiny.
Wee sounds like **we.**

weed (weed)
noun A plant that is seen as useless or harmful and grows where it is not wanted.
verb **1.** If you **weed** your garden, you pull unwanted plants out. **2.** If you **weed** people or things **out,** you remove them from a group because they are useless, harmful, or not wanted.
Weed sounds like **we'd.** ▶ *verb* **weeding, weeded**

week (week) *noun* **1.** A period of seven days, usually measured from Sunday to Saturday. **2.** The hours or days that a person works or spends in school each week.
Week sounds like **weak.**

week·day (**week**-day) *noun* Any day of the week except Saturday or Sunday.

week·end (**week**-end) *noun* The period of time from Friday night through Sunday night.

week·ly (**week**-lee)
adjective, adverb Done, happening, or appearing once a week or every week.

adverb Once a week, or every week.
noun A newspaper or magazine that is published once a week.
▶ *noun, plural* **weeklies**

weep (weep) *verb* To cry because you feel great sadness or emotion. ▶ *verb* **weeping, wept** (wept) ▶ *adjective* **weepy**

wee·vil (**wee**-vuhl) *noun* A small beetle that is a pest to farmers because it eats and damages crops.

weigh (way) *verb* **1.** To measure how heavy or light someone or something is by using a scale. **2.** To have a particular weight. **3.** To consider something carefully before deciding. **4.** If you are **weighed down,** you have too much to carry, do, or think about.
Weigh sounds like **way.** ▶ *verb* **weighing, weighed**

weight (wate)
noun **1.** A measurement that shows how heavy someone or something is. **2.** The heaviness of someone or something. **3.** A unit, such as the ounce, pound, or ton, that is used for measuring weight. **4.** A heavy object used to hold things down. **5.** Something that causes you a lot of worry because you are responsible for it. **6.** Something that has the power to influence people.
noun, plural **weights** Heavy objects that people lift as an exercise to make their muscles stronger.
Weight sounds like **wait.**

weight·less (**wate**-lis) *adjective* **1.** Having little or no weight. **2.** Free of the pull of gravity.
▶ *noun* **weightlessness** ▶ *adverb* **weightlessly**

weight·lift·er (**wate**-lif-tur)
noun A person who lifts weights in competitions or for pleasure. ▶ *noun* **weightlifting**

weird (weerd) *adjective* Unusual or mysterious. ▶ *adjective* **weirder, weirdest** ▶ *noun* **weirdness** ▶ *adverb* **weirdly**

W

wel·come (wel-kuhm)
verb 1. If you **welcome** someone, you greet the person in a warm and friendly way. 2. If you **welcome** something, you are glad to have it.
adjective 1. If something is **welcome,** you are glad to have it because you need it. 2. "You're **welcome**" is the polite response when someone says, "Thank you."
noun 1. The way in which someone is greeted. 2. The state of being welcome in a place.
▶ *verb* **welcoming, welcomed**
▶ *adjective* **welcoming**

weld (weld) *verb* To join two pieces of metal or plastic by heating them until they are soft enough to be joined together. ▶ *verb* **welding, welded** ▶ *noun* **welder**

wel·fare (wel-fair) *noun* 1. Someone's **welfare** is the person's health, happiness, and comfort. 2. Money or other help given by a government to people who are in need.

we'll (weel) *contraction* A short form of *we will* or *we shall.*

well (wel)
adverb 1. If you do something **well,** you do it in a good, skillful, or satisfactory way. 2. Completely and thoroughly. 3. Much; to a great extent. 4. In a close or familiar way.
adjective Healthy.
noun A deep hole in the ground from which you can remove water, oil, or natural gas.
interjection You say **well** to show surprise or doubt.

well-bal·anced (wel-bal-uhnst) *adjective* 1. Nicely or evenly balanced. 2. A **well-balanced** person is sensible and not easily upset.

well-be·haved (wel-bi-**hayvd**) *adjective* Acting properly and with good manners.

well-be·ing (wel-bee-ing) *noun* A feeling of being healthy and happy.

well-known (wel-nohn) *adjective* Known by many people; famous.

well-off (wel-awf) *adjective* If someone is **well-off,** he or she has a lot of money.

well-round·ed (wel-roun-did) *adjective* A **well-rounded** person has experience or interests in many different areas.

went (went) *verb* A verb form that is used as the past tense of **go.** *Went* is actually the past tense of *wend,* an old-fashioned verb that is not used very much today.

wept (wept) *verb* The past tense and past participle of **weep.**

we're (weer) *contraction* A short form of *we are.*

were (wur) *verb* The form of **be** used with *we, you,* or *they* or with plural nouns in the past tense.

weren't (wurnt *or* **wur**-uhnt) *contraction* A short form of *were not.*

west (west)
noun 1. One of the four main points of the compass. West is the direction in which the sun sets. 2. **West** Any area or region lying in this direction. 3. **the West** In the United States, the region that is west of the Great Plains.
adjective, adverb Of or having to do with or existing in the west.
▶ *adverb* **westerly (wes**-tur-lee)

west·ern (wes-turn)
adjective 1. In, of, toward, or from the west. 2. Of or having to do with a western region. 3. **Western** Of or having to do with the West.
noun **Western** *or* **western** A cowboy movie or television show set in the western part of the United States, especially during the last half of the 19th century.

West·ern Hem·i·sphere (wes-turn **hem**-i-*sfeer*) *noun* The half of the world west of the Atlantic Ocean. It includes North, Central, and South America and surrounding waters.

West In·dies (west in-deez) A group of islands in the Western Hemisphere that separates the Caribbean Sea from the Atlantic Ocean. The West Indies are subdivided into island clusters called the Antilles, the Lesser Antilles, and the Bahamas. The region is generally considered a subregion of North America.

W

West Vir·gin·ia (**west** vur-**jin**-yuh) A state in the Mid-Atlantic region of the United States. West Virginia became a state during the Civil War, when it joined the Union after separating from Virginia, a Confederate state. It is in the Appalachian range and is mountainous and heavily forested. Coal mining is the state's main industry. Tourism is also important to its economy. Its wildlife areas are popular with tourists who come to the state for outdoor sports, including river rafting, fishing, hiking, and mountain biking.

west·ward (**west**-wurd) *adverb, adjective* To or toward the west.

wet (wet)
adjective **1.** Covered with or full of liquid, especially water. **2.** Not yet dry; still moist. **3.** Rainy.
verb To make something wet.
▶ *adjective* **wetter, wettest** ▶ *verb* **wetting, wet** *or* **wetted**

wet·land (**wet**-land) *or* **wet·lands** (**wet**-landz) *noun* Land where there is a lot of moisture in the soil.

we've (weev) *contraction* A short form of *we have*. **We've** sounds like **weave**.

whack (wak)
noun **1.** (informal) A hard, sharp hit or slap. **2.** (slang) An attempt.
verb To hit or slap something sharply.
▶ *verb* **whacking, whacked**

whale (wale)
noun A large sea animal that looks like a fish but is actually a mammal that breathes air. Dolphins and porpoises are members of the whale family.
verb To hunt for whales.
▶ *verb* **whaling, whaled**

whal·er (**way**-lur) *noun* **1.** Someone who hunts whales. **2.** A boat used for hunting whales.
▶ *noun* **whaling**

wharf (worf) *noun* A long platform, built along a shore, where boats and ships can load and unload. ▶ *noun, plural* **wharves** (worvz) *or* **wharfs**

what (waht *or* wuht)
pronoun **1.** The word **what** is used in questions to get information about something or someone. **2.** The thing or things that.
adjective The word **what** is used to emphasize a particular quality, such as how great, small, or strange something or someone is.
adverb In which way; how.
interjection The word **what** is used to show surprise or anger.

what·ev·er (waht-**ev**-ur *or* wuht-**ev**-ur)
pronoun **1.** Anything that. **2.** No matter what. **3.** Which thing or things; what.
adjective **1.** Any that. **2.** Of any kind or type; at all.

what's (wahts *or* wuhts) *contraction* A short form of *what is* or *what has*.

wheat (weet) *noun* A plant that produces grain that is used for making flour, pasta, and breakfast foods.

wheat·grass (**weet**-gras) *noun* **1.** A kind of grass that is grown in the western United States for feeding animals. **2.** Blades of grass from wheat, which are ground up very fine with water to make a healthy drink.

wheel (weel)
noun **1.** A round frame or object that turns on an axle. Wheels are used to move a vehicle or work machinery. **2.** Anything that uses or is shaped like a wheel.
noun, plural **wheels** (slang) An automobile.
verb **1.** To push something that has wheels. **2.** To turn.
▶ *verb* **wheeling, wheeled**

wheel·bar·row (**weel**-bar-oh) *noun* A small cart with one or two wheels at the front, often used to carry things around in yards or gardens.

wheel·chair (**weel**-chair) *noun* A chair on wheels for people who are not able to walk because they are sick, injured, or disabled.

wheel·ie (**wee**-lee) *noun* (informal) If you do a **wheelie** on a bicycle or motorcycle, you ride for a short time with the front wheel off the ground.

W

wheeze (weez) *verb* To breathe with difficulty, making a whistling noise. People sometimes wheeze when they have asthma or a bad cold. ▸ *verb* **wheezing, wheezed** ▸ *noun* **wheeziness** ▸ *adjective* **wheezy**

whelk (welk) *noun* A large snail that lives in saltwater and has a spiral shell.

when (wen)
adverb The word **when** is used to ask about the time of an event.
conjunction 1. At the time that. 2. At any time; whenever. 3. Although; but. 4. Considering the fact that.

when·ev·er (wen-**ev**-ur) *conjunction* At any time.

where (wair)
adverb The word **where** is used to ask about the position or place of someone or something.
conjunction 1. In, at, or to the place that or in which. 2. In or at which place.
pronoun What place.

where·a·bouts (wair-uh-*bouts*)
adverb Approximately where.
noun The place where a person or thing is. *Whereabouts* can be used with a singular or plural verb.

where·as (wair-**az**) *conjunction* On the other hand.

where·up·on (wair-uh-**pahn**)
conjunction After which; at which time; and then.

wher·ev·er (wair-**ev**-ur) *conjunction, adverb* In, at, or to any place or situation.

wheth·er (**weTH**-ur) *conjunction* 1. If. 2. The word **whether** is used to indicate a choice between two things or possibilities.

whew (hwyoo) *interjection* A word used to show relief, discomfort, or surprise.

whey (way) *noun* The watery part of milk that separates when milk sours or when you make cheese.

which (wich)
adjective The word **which** is used to ask about a choice among a limited number of people or things.
pronoun 1. What one or ones. 2. The

one or ones that.
conjunction The one or ones mentioned; that.

which·ev·er (wich-**ev**-ur) *pronoun, adjective* 1. Any one or ones. 2. No matter which.

whiff (wif) *noun* 1. A light puff of air or smoke. 2. A faint smell in the air.

while (wile)
noun A period of time.
conjunction 1. During the time that. 2. Although. 3. Used to contrast two different people, things, or situations.
verb To pass or spend time in a pleasant or relaxed way.
▸ *verb* **whiling, whiled**

whim (wim) *noun* A sudden wish to do or have something, especially when it seems unnecessary or silly.

whim·per (**wim**-pur)
verb To make quiet, crying noises.
noun A quiet, crying noise.
▸ *verb* **whimpering, whimpered**

whine (wine) *verb* 1. To complain about something in an annoying way. 2. To make a long, high sound that is sad or unpleasant.
▸ *verb* **whining, whined** ▸ *noun* **whiner**

whin·ny (**win**-ee)
verb If a horse **whinnies,** it makes a gentle, high-pitched sound.
noun A gentle, high-pitched neigh.
▸ *verb* **whinnies, whinnying, whinnied** ▸ *noun, plural* **whinnies**

whip (wip)
noun A long piece of rope or leather on a handle, used especially for hitting horses and cattle.
verb 1. To hit or beat with a whip. 2. To beat something, such as eggs or cream, until it is stiff. 3. To move, pull, or take something suddenly. 4. (informal) To defeat an opponent badly.
▸ *verb* **whipping, whipped**

whip·poor·will (**wip**-uhr-*wil*) *noun* A brown North American bird with brown, gray, and black spots. Its call sounds very much like its name.

whir (wur)
verb To move, fly, or operate with

W

a buzzing or humming sound.

noun A buzzing or humming sound.

▶ *verb* **whirring, whirred**

whirl (wurl)

verb 1. To move around quickly in a circle, or to make someone or something do this. 2. To turn around quickly.

noun Fast or confused activity and movement.

idiom (informal) If you **give** something **a whirl,** you try it out to see if you like it or if you can do it.

▶ *verb* **whirling, whirled**

whirl·pool (**wurl**-*pool*) *noun* 1. A powerful current of water that moves quickly in a circle and pulls floating objects toward its center. 2. A special bathtub in which strong currents of hot water move in circles around all or part of the body. Also known as a *whirlpool bath.*

whirl·wind (**wurl**-*wind*)

noun A wind that rotates in a tall column, smaller and less violent than a tornado.

adjective Happening very quickly.

whisk (wisk)

noun A kitchen tool consisting of loops of wire attached to a handle.

verb 1. To move something or someone quickly or suddenly. 2. To brush or remove something with a quick, sweeping motion. 3. To mix or beat with a whisk.

▶ *verb* **whisking, whisked**

whisk·er (**wis**-kur)

noun One of the long, stiff hairs near the mouth of some animals, such as cats and rabbits.

noun, plural **whiskers** The hairs that grow on a man's face.

whis·key (**wis**-kee) *noun* A strong, alcoholic drink made from barley, corn, or rye.

whis·per (**wis**-pur)

verb To talk very quietly or softly.

noun 1. Soft, quiet speech. 2. A soft, rustling sound.

▶ *verb* **whispering, whispered**

whis·tle (**wis**-uhl)

noun 1. An instrument that makes a loud, shrill sound when you blow into it. 2. A whistling sound made by the lips or by a whistle.

verb 1. To make a high, loud sound by blowing air through your lips. 2. To make a whistling sound. 3. To move very fast while making a whistling sound.

▶ *verb* **whistling, whistled**

white (wite)

noun 1. The lightest color; the color of snow or milk. 2. The **white** of an egg is the clear part around the yolk.

adjective 1. Light in color. 2. Belonging to or related to the race of people with light-colored skin. 3. Looking pale, especially because you are sick or frightened. 4. Pale gray or silver.

▶ *adjective* **whiter, whitest**

white blood cell (wite blud *sel*) *noun* A colorless blood cell that helps to protect the body against infection.

white·board (**wite**-*bord*) *noun* A white surface, similar to a blackboard, that can be written on with special markers and wiped clean afterwards.

White House (wite *hous*) *noun* 1. The official home of the president of the United States, located at 1600 Pennsylvania Avenue in Washington, D.C. 2. The office or power of the president of the United States.

whit·en (**wye**-tuhn) *verb* To make white or become white. ▶ *verb* **whitening, whitened**

white noise (wite noiz) *noun* 1. A mixture of sound waves that creates a noise used to cover annoying or distracting sounds. 2. Background noise from appliances, such as air conditioners and fans.

white·wash (**wite**-*wahsh*)

noun 1. A mixture of white powder and water used for painting walls and wooden fences white. 2. Something that hides a crime or wrong action.

verb 1. To paint with whitewash. 2. To hide a crime or wrong action.

▶ *noun, plural* **whitewashes** ▶ *verb* **whitewashes, whitewashing, whitewashed**

W

whit·tle (**wit**-uhl) *verb* **1.** To cut or shave small pieces from wood or soap with a knife. **2.** To make or carve something by doing this. **3. whittle away** To reduce little by little.
▶ *verb* **whittling, whittled** ▶ *noun* **whittling**

whiz *or* **whizz** (wiz)
verb To move very quickly, often with a buzzing sound.
noun (slang) A person who has great skill or ability in a particular field or activity.
▶ *verb* **whizzes, whizzing, whizzed**
▶ *noun, plural* **whizzes**

who (hoo) *pronoun* **1.** The word **who** is used to ask questions about people, for example, to find out a person's name. **2.** The word **who** is used to show which person or people you are talking about or to give more information about a person or persons.

who'd (hood) *contraction* A short form of *who would* or *who had.*

who·ev·er (*hoo*-**ev**-ur) *pronoun* **1.** Any person at all, or no matter which person. **2.** Who.

whole (hole)
adjective **1.** Entire or total; all of. **2.** Complete, with nothing missing.
noun The entire thing, including all of its parts.
phrases **1. on the whole** In general. **2. as a whole** Considering all the parts of something together.
Whole sounds like **hole.**

whole num·ber (**hole** *nuhm*-bur) *noun* Any of the set of numbers beginning with 0 and continuing with each number being one more than the number before it. The whole numbers are 0, 1, 2, 3, 4, ... They go on and on without end.

whole·sale (**hole**-*sale*)
adverb, adjective When storekeepers buy things **wholesale,** they buy them cheaply in large quantities in order to sell them at a profit.
adjective Affecting a large number of things or people.
▶ *noun* **wholesaler**

whole·some (**hole**-suhm) *adjective* **1.** Good for your health. **2.** Considered to have a good moral influence.

whole wheat (**hole weet**) *adjective* Made from the entire grain of wheat.

who'll (hool) *contraction* A short form of *who will* or *who shall.*

whol·ly (**hoh**-lee) *adverb* Completely. **Wholly** sounds like **holy.**

whom (hoom) *pronoun* What or which person or people. **Whom** is the form of **who** when it is the object of a verb or preposition. It is often used in formal speech and writing.

whom·ev·er (*hoom*-**ev**-ur) *pronoun* The form of **whoever** used as the object of a verb or preposition.

whoop (hoop *or* hup *or* wup) *noun* A loud cry or shout.

whoop·ing cough (**hoo**-ping *kawf*) *noun* An infectious disease, especially affecting children, that makes them cough violently and have trouble breathing.

whoop·ing crane (**hoo**-ping *krane*) *noun* A large, white waterbird with a red face and black tips on its wings. Whooping cranes live in Canada and the United States. There are very few of them left.

who's (hooz) *contraction* A short form of *who is* or *who has.* **Who's** sounds like **whose.**

whose (hooz) *pronoun* **1.** The word **whose** is used to ask which person or people something belongs to. **2.** The word **whose** is used to indicate which person or thing you are talking about. **Whose** sounds like **who's.**

why (wye)
adverb The word **why** is used to ask for the reason for something.
conjunction The reason for which.
interjection The word **why** is used to show mild surprise or to show that a person is pausing to think.

wick (wik) *noun* The twisted cord in a candle, an oil lamp, or a lighter, that soaks up the fuel and burns when lit.

wick·ed (**wik**-id) *adjective* Evil or cruel. ▶ *noun* **wickedness** ▶ *adverb* **wickedly**

W

wick·er (wik-ur)
noun Thin twigs or branches, usually from a willow tree, that are bent and woven to make baskets and furniture.
adjective Made of wicker.

wick·et (wik-it) *noun* One of several small wire arches through which balls are hit in croquet.

wide (wide)
adjective 1. Large from side to side; broad. 2. Having a certain distance from one side to the other or from edge to edge. 3. Involving or including a large number of people or things. 4. Completely open.
adverb 1. Not close to. 2. Over a large area. 3. To the full extent.
▶ *adjective* **wider, widest** ▶ *adverb* **widely**

wid·en (wye-duhn) *verb* To increase the width or scope of something. ▶ *verb* **widening, widened**

wide·spread (wide-spred) *adjective* 1. Happening or existing in many places or among many people. 2. Fully open.

wid·ow (wid-oh) *noun* A woman whose husband has died and who has not married again. ▶ *adjective* **widowed**

wid·ow·er (wid-oh-ur) *noun* A man whose wife has died and who has not married again. ▶ *adjective* **widowed**

width (width) *noun* The distance from one side of something to the other; breadth.

wie·ner (wee-nur) *noun* A long, thin, pink sausage; the kind of sausage used to make a hot dog.

wife (wife) *noun* The female partner in a marriage, or any married woman. ▶ *noun, plural* **wives (wivez)**

Wi-Fi (wye-fye) *noun* A trademark for the standard kind of wireless signal that allows computers and other devices to connect to the Internet where there is a signal available.

wig (wig) *noun* A covering of real or artificial hair made to be worn on someone's head.

wig·gle (wig-uhl)
verb To make short, quick movements from side to side or up and down, or to move something in this way.
noun An act or instance of wiggling.
▶ *verb* **wiggling, wiggled** ▶ *noun* **wiggler** ▶ *adjective* **wiggly**

wig·wam (wig-wahm) *noun* A hut made of poles and covered with bark or animal skins. Some Native American tribes once lived in wigwams.

wi·ki (wik-ee) *noun* A website that grows by allowing users to change or add knowledge, information, and images.

wild (wilde)
adjective 1. Living in natural conditions and not controlled or cared for by humans. 2. Not controlled, or not disciplined. 3. Overcome with an emotion such as grief, anger, or happiness. 4. Crazy, fantastic, or reckless.
noun **the wild** An area that has been left in its natural state; wilderness.
▶ *adjective* **wilder, wildest** ▶ *noun* **wildness** ▶ *adverb* **wildly**

wild·cat (wilde-kat) *noun* Any of several wild members of the cat family that are small or medium in size, including the bobcat, ocelot, and lynx.

wil·der·ness (wil-dur-nis) *noun* An area of wild land where no people live, such as a forest or desert. ▶ *noun, plural* **wildernesses**

wild·flow·er (wilde-flou-ur) *noun* Any flower of a plant that grows in a field, woods, or any wild area without the help of human beings.

wild·life (wilde-life) *noun* Wild animals living in their natural environment.

will (wil) *verb* A helping verb that is used in the following ways: 1. To show that something is going to take place or exist in the future. 2. To show a possible action that depends on something that could happen in the future. 3. To ask someone to do something. 4. To give an order or say what must happen or not happen. 5. To say what is true or likely to happen in a particular situation.

W

will (wil)
> *noun* 1. A legal document that contains instructions stating what should happen to someone's property and money when the person dies. 2. The power to choose or control what you will and will not do. 3. Strong purpose; determination.
> *verb* 1. To leave money, property, or possessions to someone still living after you die. 2. To make something happen by a very strong determination.
> ▶ *verb* **willing, willed**

will·ful (**wil**-fuhl) *adjective* 1. Deliberate. 2. Someone who is **willful** is determined to have his or her own way.
> ▶ *noun* **willfulness** ▶ *adjective* **willfully**

will·ing (**wil**-ing) *adjective* Ready and eager to offer help or do what is asked. ▶ *noun* **willingness** ▶ *adverb* **willingly**

wil·low (**wil**-oh) *noun* A tree with narrow leaves and thin branches that bend easily. Willows are often found near water.

wilt (wilt) *verb* 1. If a plant **wilts,** it begins to bend over because it is dying or needs water. 2. To become tired because you are hot, have no energy, or need food.
> ▶ *verb* **wilting, wilted**

wimp (wimp) *noun* (informal) A weak or cowardly person.

win (win)
> *verb* 1. To be the best or most successful in a competition, such as a game or an election. 2. To get something as a prize. 3. To gain something good that you want or deserve.
> *noun* A victory.
> ▶ *verb* **winning, won** ▶ *noun* **winner**

wince (wins) *verb* To make a sudden expression on your face because you are in pain, embarrassed, or disgusted. ▶ *verb* **wincing, winced**

winch (winch) *noun* A machine that lifts or pulls heavy objects. A winch is made up of cable wound around a rotating drum. ▶ *noun, plural* **winches**

wind
> *noun* (wind) 1. Moving air. 2. Breath, or the ability to breathe.
> *verb* (winde) 1. To wrap or twist something around something else. 2. To have a series of turns and curves. 3. To turn a knob or handle around several times in order to make a machine start working. 4. **wind up** (slang) If you **wind** something **up,** you finish it. 5. **wind up** To become, finally.
> ▶ *verb* **winding, wound** (wound)

wind·break·er (**wind**-*bray*-kur) *noun* A light jacket that protects you from the wind.

wind-chill fac·tor (**wind**-chil *fak*-tur) *noun* A measurement given in degrees that reports the combined effect of low temperature and wind speed on the human body. Also known as the *chill factor* or the *wind-chill index.*

wind·ed (**win**-did) *adjective* If you are **winded,** you have difficulty breathing because of exercise or a sudden blow to the stomach.

wind·fall (**wind**-*fawl*) *noun* 1. A sudden piece of good news or good luck that you get unexpectedly, especially an amount of money. 2. Fruit that has fallen off a tree.

wind farm (**wind** *fahrm*) *noun* A windy place with a lot of wind turbines or windmills for generating electricity.

wind in·stru·ment (**wind** in-struh-muhnt) *noun* A musical instrument, such as a flute, trumpet, or harmonica, played by blowing.

wind·mill (**wind**-mil) *noun* A structure with long blades that turn in the wind. This produces power that is used to grind grain into flour, pump water, or generate electricity.

win·dow (**win**-doh) *noun* 1. An opening, especially in the wall of a building or vehicle, that lets in air and light. Windows are usually covered with a sheet of glass. 2. A single sheet of glass in a window. 3. The viewing space on a computer screen in which you can see information and work with a program.

W

win·dow·pane (**win**-doh-*pane*) *noun*
A single sheet or section of glass in
a window.

win·dow-shop (**win**-doh *shahp*) *verb*
To look at items in store windows but
not buy anything. ▶ *verb* **window-
shopping, window-shopped**

wind·pipe (**wind**-*pipe*) *noun* The tube
that connects the lungs with the
throat and carries air for breathing.

wind·shear (**wind**-*sheer*) *noun* A
sudden change in wind speed
and direction that is caused
by a downward flow of cool
air. Windshears occur during
thunderstorms. They can cause
aircraft to lose altitude quickly.

wind·shield (**wind**-*sheeld*) *noun* The
large window in the front of a motor
vehicle that protects the driver and
passengers from the wind.

wind·surf·ing (**wind**-*sur*-fing) *noun*
The sport of sailing across water by
standing on a surfboard and holding
and moving a large sail attached to
the board. ▶ *noun* **windsurfer**

wind·swept (**wind**-*swept*) *adjective*
Exposed to strong winds or blown
by the wind.

wind tur·bine (**wind** *tur*-buhn) *noun* An
engine that is powered by long blades
that turn in the wind. This produces
energy that makes electricity.

wind·y (**win**-dee) *adjective*
Exposed to or being hit by strong
winds. ▶ *adjective* **windier, windiest**

wine (wine) *noun* An alcoholic drink
made from the juice of grapes that
has been allowed to ferment.

wing (wing)
noun **1.** One of the parts of a bird's,
insect's, or bat's body that it uses in
order to fly. **2.** A structure that sticks
out of the side of an aircraft that
makes it able to fly. **3.** An outer part
or extension of a building. **4.** The far
left or right side of a sports field, or
a person who plays in that area in
sports such as soccer or hockey.
noun, plural **wings** The sides of a
theater stage that cannot be seen by
the audience.

wing·span (**wing**-*span*) *noun* The
distance between one end of a wing
of a bird or an aircraft and the other.

wink (wingk)
verb To close one eye quickly as a
signal or a friendly gesture.
noun **1.** The act of closing and
opening your eye as a signal to
someone. **2.** A very short time; an
instant.
idiom If you **do not sleep a wink,** you
do not sleep at all.
▶ *verb* **winking, winked**

win·ner (**win**-ur) *noun* **1.** A person, a
team, an animal, or a thing that wins
a contest. **2.** (informal) A person, an
idea, or a plan that seems likely to
succeed.

win·ning (**win**-ing)
adjective **1.** Successful or victorious.
2. Pleasing, attractive, or charming.
noun, plural **winnings** Something that
is won in a game or competition,
especially money.

win·ter (**win**-tur) *noun* The season
between fall and spring, when the
weather is coldest. ▶ *adjective* **wintry**

win·ter·green (**win**-tur-*green*)
noun A low evergreen plant with
white flowers and red berries. Its
leaves produce a minty oil used in
medicines and flavorings.
adjective Flavored with wintergreen.

wipe (wipe) *verb* **1.** To clean or dry
something by rubbing. **2.** To clear
or remove something by rubbing.
3. wipe out To destroy something
completely.
▶ *verb* **wiping, wiped**

wire (wire *or* **wye**-ur)
noun **1.** A long, thin, flexible thread
of metal. Wire can be used to pull
or support things or to conduct an
electrical current. **2.** A telegram.
verb **1.** To fasten things together with
a piece of wire. **2.** To install or put in
wires for electricity or data transfer.
3. To send by telegraph.
▶ *verb* **wiring, wired** ▶ *noun* **wiring**

wire·less (**wire**-lis) *adjective* Not
requiring wires to send or receive
data or to work properly.

W

wir·y (**wye**-ree) *adjective* **1.** Strong and stiff. **2.** A **wiry** person is thin but strong. ▶ *adjective* **wirier, wiriest**

Wis·con·sin (wis-**kahn**-suhn) A state in the Midwest region of the United States. Wisconsin is bordered by Michigan, Iowa, Illinois, and Minnesota, and by two Great Lakes that separate it from Canada: Lake Superior and Lake Michigan. It is known for its production of cheese, milk, and butter, and its citizens, especially the fans of its football and baseball teams, are often referred to as cheeseheads.

wis·dom (**wiz**-duhm) *noun* Knowledge, experience, and good judgment.

wis·dom tooth (**wiz**-duhm *tooth*) *noun* Any of the four teeth at the back of your mouth that come in last, usually when you are a young adult. ▶ *noun, plural* **wisdom teeth**

wise (wize) *adjective* Having or showing good judgment and intelligence. ▶ *adjective* **wiser, wisest** ▶ *adverb* **wisely**

wish (wish)
verb **1.** To want something very much. **2.** To hope for something for another person.
noun **1.** A strong desire for something. **2.** Something that you want or that you want to have happen. **3.** The act of wanting something and hoping you will get it or that it will happen. ▶ *verb* **wishes, wishing, wished** ▶ *noun, plural* **wishes**

wish·bone (**wish**-bohn) *noun* A bone shaped like a Y in front of the breastbone of most birds. According to superstition, when two people pull a wishbone apart, the one who gets the longer piece will have a wish granted.

wisp (wisp) *noun* A long, thin piece or streak of something. ▶ *adjective* **wispy**

wis·te·ri·a (wi-**steer**-ee-uh) *noun* A climbing vine plant with bunches of blue, white, pink, or purple flowers that hang down.

wist·ful (**wist**-fuhl) *adjective* Feeling sad because you are thinking of something you would like to have but cannot, especially something you had in the past. ▶ *adverb* **wistfully**

wit (wit)
noun **1.** The ability to say things that are clever and funny. **2.** Someone who has the ability to say clever and funny things.
noun, plural **wits** The ability to think quickly and make good decisions.

witch (wich) *noun* A person, especially a woman, believed by some people to have magic powers. ▶ *noun, plural* **witches**

with (wiTH *or* with) *preposition* **1.** In the company or care of. *Come with me. You can leave the package with me.* **2.** Having. *I'm looking for someone with a good sense of humor.* **3.** In a way that shows. *She dressed with care.* **4.** In addition to. *We had chicken with rice.* **5.** In the opinion of. *It's OK with me.* **6.** By using. *You cut meat with a knife.* **7.** In regard to. *Are you happy with your grades?* **8.** Against. *The brothers fought with each other constantly.* **9.** In support of. *Are you with me on this issue?*

with·draw (wiTH-**draw** *or* with-**draw**) *verb* **1.** To take away or remove something. **2.** To go away or drop out of an event. ▶ *verb* **withdrawing, withdrew** (wiTH-**droo** *or* with-**droo**), **withdrawn** (wiTH-**drawn** *or* with-**drawn**)

with·draw·al (wiTH-**draw**-uhl *or* with-**draw**-uhl) *noun* **1.** The act of taking back something that has been granted. **2.** A retreat or removal from a place or position. **3.** The removal of money from a bank account.

with·drawn (wiTH-**drawn** *or* with-**drawn**) *adjective* Very shy and quiet.

with·er (**wiTH**-ur) *verb* To dry up or become smaller and weaker. ▶ *verb* **withering, withered**

with·hold (with-**hohld** *or* wiTH-**hohld**) *verb* To keep something back, or to refuse to give something to someone. ▶ *verb* **withholding, withheld**

W

with·in (wiTH-**in** *or* with-**in**)
preposition **1.** Inside. *I could hear a dog barking from within the house.* **2.** Not beyond the limits of. *I want you back within the next ten minutes.*
adverb Inside a place.

with·out (wiTH-**out** *or* with-**out**)
preposition **1.** Not having something. *I completed the project without help.* **2.** Not being with someone or something. *My parents went on vacation without me.* **3.** In a way that avoids something. *We ate dinner without speaking.*

with·stand (with-**stand** *or* wiTH-**stand**) *verb* To stand strongly against something. ▶ *verb* **withstanding, withstood**

wit·ness (**wit**-nis)
noun **1.** A person who has seen or heard something. **2.** A person who gives evidence in a court of law. **3.** A person who signs an official paper to prove that he or she watched a contract, will, or other legal document being signed.
verb **1.** To see something that is happening or has happened. **2.** To sign an official paper to prove that you saw someone else sign it.
▶ *noun, plural* **witnesses** ▶ *verb* **witnesses, witnessing, witnessed**

wit·ty (**wit**-ee) *adjective* Funny and clever. ▶ *adjective* **wittier, wittiest** ▶ *adverb* **wittily** (**wit**-uh-lee)

wives (wivez) *noun, plural* The plural of **wife.**

wiz·ard (**wiz**-urd) *noun* **1.** A person, especially a man, believed to have magical powers. **2.** Someone who is extremely good at doing something. **3.** A small computer program that takes you through a task step by step to make it easier.

wob·ble (**wah**-buhl) *verb* To move from side to side in an unsteady way, or to make something do this. ▶ *verb* **wobbling, wobbled** ▶ *adjective* **wobbly**

woe (woh) *noun* Great sadness and suffering. ▶ *adjective* **woeful** ▶ *adverb* **woefully**

wok (wahk) *noun* A large pan shaped like a bowl that is used especially for cooking Asian food.

woke (woke) *verb* The past tense of **wake.**

wok·en (**wo**-kuhn) *verb* The past participle of **wake.**

wolf (wulf)
noun A wild mammal that is related to the dog and hunts in a group for food.
verb If you **wolf** something **down,** you eat it quickly.
▶ *noun, plural* **wolves** ▶ *verb* **wolfing, wolfed**

wol·ver·ine (**wul**-vuh-reen) *noun* A powerfully built mammal, related to the weasel, with dark brown fur and a long, bushy tail.

wom·an (**wum**-uhn) *noun* An adult female human being. ▶ *noun, plural* **women** (**wim**-in) ▶ *adverb* **womanly**

wom·an·hood (**wum**-uhn-hud) *noun* **1.** The time or state of being a female adult. **2.** Women as a group.

womb (woom) *noun* The organ in female mammals where babies grow before they are born; the uterus.

wom·bat (**wahm**-bat) *noun* An Australian animal that looks like a small bear.

won (wuhn) *verb* The past tense and past participle of **win. Won** sounds like **one.**

won·der (**wuhn**-dur)
verb **1.** To want to know or learn more about something. **2.** To be surprised or impressed by something.
noun **1.** Something so remarkable or impressive that it causes surprise or amazement. **2.** The feeling caused by something remarkable or impressive.
▶ *verb* **wondering, wondered**

won·der·ful (**wuhn**-dur-fuhl) *adjective* **1.** Very good; excellent. **2.** Remarkable and making you feel admiration.
▶ *adverb* **wonderfully**

won't (wohnt) *contraction* A short form of *will not.*

W

wood (wud)
> *noun* The hard substance that the trunk and branches of trees are made of.
> *noun, plural* **woods** An area of land with many trees growing close together; a forest.
> **Wood** sounds like **would.**

wood·chuck (**wud**-*chuhk*) *noun* A name used in some areas for a **groundhog.**

wood·en (**wud**-uhn) *adjective* 1. Made out of wood. 2. Stiff and awkward.

wood·land (**wud**-*land*) *noun* Land covered mainly by trees; a forest.

wood·peck·er (**wud**-*pek*-ur) *noun* Any of a number of birds that live in forests throughout the world. Woodpeckers have strong, pointed bills, which they use to drill holes in trees to get insects.

wood·wind (**wud**-*wind*)
> *adjective* The **woodwind** section of an orchestra is made up of wind instruments that were originally made of wood, such as the flute, clarinet, and oboe.
> *noun* A wind instrument.

wood·work (**wud**-*wurk*) *noun* Things made out of wood, especially wooden parts inside a house, such as window frames, doors, and moldings. ▶ *noun* **woodworker**

wool (wul) *noun* 1. The soft, thick, curly hair of sheep and certain other animals, such as the llama and alpaca. Wool is spun into yarn, which is used to make fabric. 2. Yarn or fabric made of wool.
> ▶ *adjective* **woolly**

wool·en (**wul**-uhn) *adjective* Made from wool.

word (wurd)
> *noun* 1. A unit of one or more spoken sounds or written letters that has a meaning in a particular language. 2. A brief remark or comment. 3. A short conversation. 4. A message or a piece of information.
> *verb* To put into words.
> *phrase* If you **give your word,** you promise you will do something.
> ▶ *verb* **wording, worded**

word·ing (**wur**-ding) *noun* The way in which words are chosen and arranged in something that is said or written.

word proc·es·sing (wurd *prah*-ses-ing) *noun* The use of a computer or similar machine to type and print documents. Words can be seen on the screen and are easily changed, moved, copied, and stored. ▶ *noun* **word processor**

word·y (**wur**-dee) *adjective* Having or using too many words. ▶ *adjective* **wordier, wordiest**

wore (wor) *verb* The past tense of **wear.**
> **Wore** sounds like **war.**

work (wurk)
> *noun* 1. Effort or labor to get something done. 2. A person's job; what someone does to make money. 3. A task. 4. Something produced by an artist, such as a piece of music, a painting, or a sculpture.
> *noun, plural* **works** The moving parts of a watch or machine.
> *verb* 1. To have a job. 2. To get something done by using your energy or ability. 3. If a machine or device **works,** it operates in the proper way. 4. To bring about or to cause. 5. **work out** To solve a problem by thinking hard. 6. **work out** To do physical exercise, especially in a gym.
> ▶ *verb* **working, worked**

work·a·ble (**wur**-kuh-buhl) *adjective* Practical and likely to be successful.

work·a·hol·ic (*wur*-kuh-**haw**-lik) *noun* Someone who chooses to work a lot and has little interest in anything else.

work·bench (**wurk**-*bench*) *noun* A strong table used by someone who works with tools, such as a carpenter or a mechanic. ▶ *noun, plural* **workbenches**

work·book (**wurk**-*buk*) *noun* A book with problems and exercises to be done by students.

work·er (**wur**-kur) *noun* 1. Someone who does a particular type of job in order to make money. 2. A female bee, ant, termite, or other insect that does all the work for the colony but does not reproduce.

work·man (**wurk**-muhn) *noun* A man who does manual work or who

W

works with machines. ▶ *noun, plural* **workmen**

work·man·ship (wurk-muhn-*ship*) *noun* The skill and care with which something is made, usually by hand.

work·out (**wurk**-out) *noun* A period of exercise or physical work.

work·shop (**wurk**-*shahp*) *noun* 1. A room or building where things are made or fixed. 2. A meeting where a group of people discuss, learn about, or practice a particular skill.

work·sta·tion (**wurk**-*stay*-shuhn) *noun* 1. An area, usually for one person, with the equipment needed to do a specific job. 2. A computer that runs programs and allows people to gain access to a computer network.

world (wurld) *noun* 1. The earth. 2. A particular part of the earth. 3. Everyone who lives on earth. 4. An area of activity or interest and the people connected with it. 5. A large amount. 6. Living things, considered as a group.

world-class (**wurld-klas**) *adjective* Of the highest rank or level in the world.

world·ly (**wurld**-lee) *adjective* 1. Concerned with ordinary life and activities, rather than with spiritual or religious ideas. 2. Having a lot of practical knowledge and life experience.

World War I (**wurld** *wor* **wuhn**) *noun* A war fought from 1914 to 1918, mainly in Europe. The United States, Great Britain, France, Russia, Italy, Japan, and other allied nations defeated Germany, Austria-Hungary, Turkey, and Bulgaria.

World War II (**wurld** *wor* **too**) *noun* A war fought from 1939 to 1945 in which the United States, France, Great Britain, the Soviet Union, and other allied nations defeated Germany, Italy, and Japan.

world·wide (**wurld-wide**) *adjective* Existing or known about throughout the world.

World Wide Web (**wurld** *wide* **web**) *noun* The system of websites connected on the Internet. Also called the **web.** Abbreviated as *WWW.*

worm (wurm) *noun* 1. A small animal that lives in the soil. Worms have long, thin, soft bodies and no backbones or legs. 2. A small, harmful computer program that makes copies of itself and then travels on the Internet, causing damage to different computers. *verb* If you **worm into** or **through** something, you move slowly like a worm by twisting and turning from side to side.

▶ *verb* **worming, wormed**

worn (worn) *verb* Past participle of **wear.** *adjective* Damaged by wear or use. **Worn** sounds like **warn.**

worn-out (**worn-out**) *adjective* 1. No longer useful or in good condition. 2. Very tired.

wor·ry (**wur**-ee) *verb* To think about your problems or about bad things that could happen. *noun* 1. Something that makes you anxious or concerned. 2. The feeling of being anxious or nervous.

▶ *verb* **worries, worrying, worried**
▶ *noun, plural* **worries** ▶ *noun* **worrier** ▶ *adjective* **worrying** ▶ *adverb* **worriedly**

worse (wurs) *adjective* 1. More inferior; less good. 2. More evil or bad. 3. More unpleasant, severe, or harmful. 4. More sick or in poorer health than before. *adverb* Less well. *noun* Something that is worse.

wor·ship (**wur**-ship) *verb* 1. To show love and devotion to God or a god, especially by praying or going to a church service. 2. To admire and love someone or something very much. *noun* 1. The act of showing love and devotion to God or a god, especially by praying or singing in a religious building with others. 2. Admiration or love for someone or something.

▶ *verb* **worshiping** or **worshipping, worshiped** or **worshipped**

W

worst (wurst)
adjective The most inferior, harmful, or unpleasant; worse than any other one.
adverb In the worst way.
noun Someone or something that is the worst.

worth (wurth)
adjective, preposition 1. Having a certain value in money. *He has a rare coin that's worth a fortune. How much do you think my old car is worth?* 2. Deserving, or good enough for doing something. *It's worth going to the movie just to see the special effects.*
noun The quality that makes someone or something valuable or important.

worth·less (**wurth**-lis) *adjective* Useless or having no value. ▶ *noun* **worthlessness**

worth·while (**wurth**-wile) *adjective* Useful and important.

wor·thy (**wur**-THee) *adjective* 1. Having value; good or worthwhile. 2. Good enough for something; deserving.
▶ *adjective* **worthier, worthiest**

would (wud) *verb* A helping verb that is used in the following ways:
1. As the past tense of the helping verb **will.** 2. To express a possibility based on something that is not true right now. 3. To express action that happened often or regularly in the past. 4. To make a request.
Would sounds like **wood.**

would·n't (**wud**-uhnt) *contraction* A short form of *would not.*

wound
noun (woond) An injury in which the skin is cut, usually because of an accident or violence.
verb 1. (woond) To injure someone. 2. (woond) To hurt someone's feelings. 3. (wound) Past tense and past participle of **wind.**
▶ *verb* **wounding, wounded**

wove (wove) *verb* The past tense of **weave.**

wov·en (**wo**-vuhn) *verb* The past participle of **weave.**

wran·gle (**rang**-guhl)
verb 1. To argue for a long time in a noisy or angry way. 2. To herd and take care of horses and cattle on a ranch.
noun A loud or angry argument.
▶ *verb* **wrangling, wrangled** ▶ *noun* **wrangler**

wrap (rap)
verb 1. To cover something completely by winding paper or another material around it. 2. To wind something around someone or something else. 3. To hide by covering.
noun 1. A piece of clothing worn around your upper body, such as a coat or shawl. 2. A sandwich consisting of a soft tortilla that has been rolled up with a filling inside.
phrase If you are **wrapped up** in something, you are totally involved in it.
Wrap sounds like **rap.** ▶ *verb* **wrapping, wrapped**

wrap·per (**rap**-ur) *noun* The thin material that wraps and protects something.

wrath (rath) *noun* Great anger that is openly expressed.

wreak (reek) *verb* To cause great problems or damage. **Wreak** sounds like **reek.** ▶ *verb* **wreaking, wreaked**

wreath (reeth) *noun* A group of flowers, leaves, or branches that are twisted together in the shape of a circle.

wreck (rek)
verb To destroy or ruin something.
noun The remains of a vehicle that has been destroyed or damaged.
▶ *verb* **wrecking, wrecked**

wreck·age (**rek**-ij) *noun* The broken parts or pieces lying around at the site of a crash or an explosion.

wren (ren) *noun* A small songbird with a long, thin bill, brown feathers, and a small tail that sticks up.

wrench (rench)
noun A tool used for tightening and loosening bolts and nuts.
verb 1. To pull something suddenly and with a lot of force. 2. To injure yourself by twisting a part of your body.
▶ *noun, plural* **wrenches** ▶ *verb* **wrenches, wrenching, wrenched**

W

wrest (rest) *verb* **1.** To twist, pull, or tear something away. **2.** To take something by force or violence. **Wrest** sounds like **rest.**

wres·tle (**res**-uhl) *verb* **1.** To fight by gripping or holding your opponent and trying to push the person to the ground. **2.** If you **wrestle** with a problem, you try to find a solution by thinking very hard. ▶ *verb* **wrestling, wrestled**

wres·tling (**res**-ling) *noun* A sport in which two opponents hold each other and try to force each other to the ground. ▶ *noun* **wrestler**

wretch·ed (**rech**-id) *adjective* **1.** Miserable or unfortunate. **2.** Very low in quality of ability. ▶ *noun* **wretch**

wrig·gle (**rig**-uhl) *verb* To twist and turn your body. ▶ *verb* **wriggling, wriggled**

wring (ring) *verb* **1.** To remove most of the liquid out of wet material by twisting it with your hands. **2.** To get something from someone by using force or threats. **Wring** sounds like **ring.** ▶ *verb* **wringing, wrung** (ruhng) ▶ *noun* **wringer**

wrin·kle (**ring**-kuhl) *noun* One of a number of lines that appear in skin, cloth, or paper as a result of aging, folding, crumpling, or some other process. *verb* To form lines as a result of aging, folding, or crumpling, or movement. ▶ *verb* **wrinkling, wrinkled**

wrist (rist) *noun* The joint that connects the hand and the arm.

wrist·watch (**rist**-*wahch*) *noun* A watch worn on a strap or band that fits around the wrist. ▶ *noun, plural* **wristwatches**

write (rite) *verb* **1.** To produce letters, words, or numbers on a surface, such as paper, especially using a pen or pencil. **2.** To create stories, poems, articles, or music. **3.** To use words to create a letter or email and send it to someone. **Write** sounds like **right.** ▶ *verb* **writing, wrote** (rote), **written** (**rit**-in)

writ·er (**rye**-tur) *noun* A person who writes something, especially if this is their job.

writhe (riTHe) *verb* To twist and turn around, as in pain. ▶ *verb* **writhing, writhed**

writ·ing (**rye**-ting) *noun* **1.** The act of putting letters on paper. **2.** A written work such as a story, book, or poem. **3.** Written form. **4.** Handwriting.

wrong (rawng) *adjective* **1.** Not correct or not true. **2.** Bad or immoral. **3.** Not appropriate for a particular situation. **4.** If something is **wrong** with a machine or vehicle, it is not working properly. *adverb* In a way that is not correct or does not produce the result you want. *verb* To treat someone badly or in an unfair way. *noun* **1.** An act that is illegal or unfair. **2.** Behavior that is bad or immoral. ▶ *verb* **wronging, wronged** ▶ *adverb* **wrongly**

wrong·do·ing (**rawng**-doo-ing) *noun* Behavior that is wrong, evil, or illegal.

Wy·o·ming (wye-**oh**-ming) A state in the western United States. It is the least populous state in the U.S. and is known for its Rocky Mountain ranges and for Yellowstone National Park. The state motto is "Equal Rights." The women in Wyoming were the first in the country to vote. They were also the first to serve on juries and hold public office.

W

Xe·rox (**zeer**-ahks)
noun Trademark name for a kind of photocopier.
verb To copy on a photocopier.
▶ *verb* **Xeroxes, Xeroxing, Xeroxed**

X·mas (**kris**-muhs *or* **eks**-muhs)
noun An informal abbreviation for **Christmas.**

XML (**eks**-*em*-**el**) *noun* The set of computer codes that is often used to make complicated webpages. XML is short for *extensible markup language.*

X-ray (**eks**-*ray*)
noun 1. An invisible and powerful beam of light that can pass through solid objects. X-rays are used to take pictures of teeth, bones, and organs inside the body. 2. A picture of the inside of a person's body, taken using X-rays.
verb To photograph something using X-rays.
▶ *verb* **X-raying, X-rayed**

xy·lo·phone (**zye**-luh-*fone*) *noun* A musical instrument with wooden bars of different lengths that you hit with two small sticks to produce different notes.

yacht (yaht) *noun* A large boat or small ship with sails, used for pleasure or for racing.

yak (yak) *noun* An ox of Tibet and central Asia that has long, shaggy hair. Yaks are used as work animals, and are raised for their milk and meat.

yam (yam) *noun* 1. The thick root of a tropical plant that is ground into flour or eaten as a vegetable. 2. A large sweet potato that has orange flesh.

yank (yangk)
verb To suddenly pull something with force.
noun A sudden and hard pull.
▶ *verb* **yanking, yanked**

Yan·kee (**yang**-kee) *noun* 1. A person born or living in one of the northern states, especially a state in New England. 2. A person who fought for the Union during the Civil War. 3. Any person born or living in the United States.

yap (yap) *verb* 1. If a small dog **yaps,** it barks repeatedly with short, high sounds. 2. (slang) To talk in a noisy,

irritating way.
▶ *verb* **yapping, yapped**

yard (yahrd) *noun* 1. A unit of length equal to 3 feet or 36 inches. 2. An area of ground around or next to a house, school, or other building. 3. An enclosed area used for a certain type of work or business. 4. An area next to a railroad station where trains are switched, repaired, or stored.

yard·stick (**yahrd**-*stik*) *noun* 1. A measuring stick that is one yard long. 2. A standard used to judge or compare things or people.

yar·mul·ke (**yah**-muh-kuh *or* **yahr**-muhl-kuh) *noun* A small, round cap that Jewish men and boys wear on their heads, especially during religious services.

yarn (yahrn)
noun Fibers such as wool or cotton that are twisted or spun into long strands for knitting or weaving.
idiom (informal) If someone **spins a yarn,** he or she tells a long story that may not be completely true.

yawn (yawn)
verb 1. To open your mouth wide and breathe in deeply, especially because you are tired or bored. 2. To open wide.
noun An act or instance of yawning.
▶ *verb* **yawning, yawned**

year (yeer) *noun* 1. The period of time in which the earth makes one trip around the sun, about 365 days and 6 hours. 2. On the calendar that we commonly use today, a **year** is a period of 365 days, or 366 in a leap year, divided into 52 weeks or 12 months. The year begins January 1 and ends December 31. 3. Any period of 12 months. 4. A part of a year spent in a particular activity.

year·ly (yeer-lee) *adjective, adverb* Happening or done each year.

yearn (yurn) *verb* To wish for something very strongly, especially something that is difficult to get or achieve. ▶ *verb* **yearning, yearned** ▶ *noun* **yearning**

year-round (yeer-round) *adjective, adverb* Happening or operating through the entire year.

yeast (yeest) *noun* A yellow fungus used to make bread dough rise and to make alcoholic drinks.

yell (yel)
verb To shout, cry out, or scream loudly.
noun A loud shout or scream.
▶ *verb* **yelling, yelled**

yel·low (yel-oh)
noun 1. One of the three primary colors, along with red and blue. Yellow is the color of lemons. 2. The yolk of an egg.
verb To become or make yellow.
adjective 1. Having the color of lemons. 2. Easily scared; cowardly.
▶ *verb* **yellowing, yellowed** ▶ *adjective* **yellower, yellowest**

yel·low jack·et (yel-oh jak-it) *noun* A wasp that has black and bright yellow stripes. It usually builds its nest in or near the ground and has a painful sting.

yelp (yelp)
verb To make a sharp, high, crying sound, usually of pain.
noun A sharp, high, crying sound.
▶ *verb* **yelping, yelped**

Yem·en (yem-uhn) A desert country on the Arabian Peninsula in Southwest Asia. Yemen used to be divided into a northern and a southern state, but the two were unified in 1990 as the Republic of Yemen.

yen (yen) *noun* 1. The unit of money in Japan. 2. (informal) A strong desire.

yes (yes)
adverb, interjection A word used to show that you agree or that something is true.
noun 1. An answer that shows agreement, approval, or acceptance. 2. A vote or voter in favor of something.
▶ *noun, plural* **yeses** or **yesses**

yes·ter·day (yes-tur-*day* or yes-tur-dee)
noun 1. The day before today. 2. The recent past.
adverb On the day before today.

yet (yet)
adverb 1. Up to now; so far. 2. At the present time; now. 3. In addition; even. 4. At some future time; eventually.
conjunction But.

yew (yoo) *noun* An evergreen tree or shrub with poisonous, dark green needles and red berries. **Yew** sounds like **ewe** and **you.**

yield (yeeld)
verb 1. To produce or provide something. 2. To allow an opponent to have something or to win a fight or an argument.
noun The amount that something produces.
▶ *verb* **yielding, yielded**

yo (yoh) *interjection* (slang) A word used to get someone's attention, say hello, or acknowledge being called.

yo·del (yoh-duhl) *verb* To sing loudly in a voice that changes quickly between high and low sounds. Yodeling is traditionally done in the mountains of Switzerland. ▶ *verb* **yodeling, yodeled** ▶ *noun* **yodeler**

Y

yo·ga (**yoh**-guh) *noun* A system of exercises and meditation that helps people control their minds and bodies and become physically fit. Yoga came originally from Hindu teachings.

yo·gurt (**yoh**-gurt) *noun* A slightly sour food prepared by adding bacteria to milk. Yogurt is often prepared with fruit or flavors such as vanilla.

yoke (yoke) *noun* 1. A wooden frame attached to the necks of work animals, such as oxen, to connect them so they can plow or pull a heavy load. 2. The part of a shirt, blouse, or dress that fits around the shoulders and neck. **Yoke** sounds like **yolk**.

yolk (yoke) *noun* The yellow part of an egg. **Yolk** sounds like **yoke**.

Yom Kip·pur (*yahm* **kip**-ur *or* **yohm** ki-**poor**) *noun* A Jewish religious holiday that falls ten days after Rosh Hashanah during September or October. On Yom Kippur, Jewish people do not eat or drink and ask God to forgive the things they have done wrong.

yon·der (**yahn**-dur) *adverb* Over there.

you (yoo) *pronoun* 1. The person or people that someone is speaking or writing to. 2. People in general. **You** sounds like **ewe** and **yew**.

you'd (yood) *contraction* A short form of *you had* or *you would*.

you'll (yool) *contraction* A short form of *you shall* or *you will*. **You'll** sounds like **Yule**.

young (yuhng)
adjective 1. Having lived or existed for only a short time. 2. Youthful.
noun, plural The young animals that belong to a particular mother, considered as a group.
▶ *adjective* **younger, youngest**

young·ster (**yuhng**-stur) *noun* A young person, especially a child.

your (yoor *or* yor) *adjective* Belonging to or having to do with you.

you're (yoor *or* yur) *contraction* A short form of *you are*.

yours (yoorz *or* yorz) *pronoun* The one or ones belonging to or having to do with you.

your·self (yoor-**self**) *pronoun* Your own self. ▶ *pronoun, plural* **yourselves**

youth (yooth) *noun* 1. The time of life when a person is no longer a child but is not yet an adult. 2. The quality or state of being young. 3. A young person, especially a young male between 13 and 18 years of age. 4. Young people in general.

you've (yoov) *contraction* A short form of *you have*.

yowl (youl)
noun A long, loud cry of pain or unhappiness.
verb To cry loudly with pain or unhappiness.
▶ *verb* **yowling, yowled**

yo-yo (**yoh**-yoh) *noun* A toy that consists of a piece of string wound around a circular plastic or wooden object. You wrap the string around your finger and make the yo-yo go up and down by raising and lowering your hand.

Yu·kon (**yoo**-kahn) A territory in northern Canada. It is the westernmost and smallest of Canada's three federal territories, which include Nunavut and the Northwest Territories. Sparsely populated, it borders the U.S. state of Alaska on the west, the Canadian province of British Columbia to the south, and the Northwest Territories to the east. Mount Logan, in southwestern Yukon near the Alaskan border, is the highest mountain in Canada.

Yule (yool) *noun* Another word for **Christmas. Yule** sounds like **you'll**.

Yule·tide (**yool**-tide) *noun* The Christmas season.

yup·pie (**yuhp**-ee) *noun* A young adult with an expensive lifestyle and a job that pays a lot of money. Yuppie comes from the phrase *young urban professional*.

Y

Z

Zam·bi·a (zam-bee-uh) A country in southern Africa. Formerly known as Northern Rhodesia, its name was changed to Zambia when it became independent from the United Kingdom in 1964. Victoria Falls, on the Zambezi River between Zambia and Zimbabwe, is among the largest waterfalls in the world.

za·ny (zay-nee) *adjective* Unusual or crazy in a way that is funny. ▶ *adjective* **zanier, zaniest** ▶ *adverb* **zanily**

zap (zap) *verb* **1.** (slang) To shoot or destroy with force, as in an electronic game. **2.** (slang) To cook something in a microwave oven. **3.** (slang) To change channels on a television set with a remote control.
▶ *verb* **zapping, zapped**

zeal (zeel) *noun* A lot of energy and enthusiasm. ▶ *adjective* **zealous (zel-**uhs)

zeal·ot (zel-uht) *noun* Someone who has very strong beliefs about something, such as politics or religion, and tries to convince other people to share the same beliefs, especially if this is done in a way that is considered excessive.

ze·bra (zee-bruh) *noun* A wild animal of southern and eastern Africa. A zebra is similar to a horse except that it is smaller and has black and white stripes on its body.

ze·nith (zee-nith) *noun* **1.** The period of time when something or someone is most effective or successful. **2.** The highest point in the sky reached by the sun or moon, directly overhead.

zep·pe·lin (zep-uh-lin) *noun* An airship with a rigid frame. A zeppelin is shaped like a cigar.

ze·ro (zeer-oh)
noun **1.** The number that indicates that there is no quantity of something, written numerically as 0. **2.** A point on a thermometer or other scale at which numbering or measurement begins. **3.** Nothing.
adjective Not any.
verb If you **zero in on** something or someone, you focus all of your attention on that thing or person.
▶ *noun, plural* **zeros** *or* **zeroes** ▶ *verb* **zeroes, zeroing, zeroed**

zest (zest) *noun* Enthusiasm and enjoyment.

zig·zag (zig-zag)
noun A line or course that moves in short, sharp turns or angles from one side to the other.
adjective Having short, sharp turns or angles from one side to the other.
verb To move in the shape of a zigzag.
▶ *verb* **zigzagging, zigzagged**

zilch (zilch) *noun* (slang) Absolutely nothing; zero.

Zim·bab·we (zim-bahb-way *or* zim-**bahb-**wee) A country in southern Africa. Formerly known as Southern Rhodesia, it had been a British colony and became independent in 1980. Mining is an important industry in Zimbabwe, which has diamond fields and some of the biggest platinum reserves in the world, as well as gold, copper, and other minerals.

zinc (zingk) *noun* A blue-white metal that is mixed with copper to make brass and used to coat other metals so that they will not rust. Zinc is a chemical element.

zin·ni·a (zin-ee-uh) *noun* A garden plant with round, brightly colored flowers.

zip (zip)
verb **1. zip up** To fasten clothes with a zipper. **2.** To make a computer file or set of files smaller so that they will be easier to store or send to someone. **3.** (informal) To move fast or to make something do this.
noun A short, hissing sound.
▶ *verb* **zipping, zipped**

ZIP code or **zip code** (**zip** *kode*) *noun* A number given by the Postal Service to each delivery area in the United States in order to speed the sorting and delivery of mail.

zip file (**zip** *file*) *noun* A computer file that contains one or more compressed files and that can only be opened with a special program that returns the files to their normal size.

zip line (**zip** *line*) *noun* A pulley attached to a cable that is hung between two high places. People ride on a zip line by sitting in a sling that is attached to the pulley.

zip·per (**zip**-ur) *noun* A fastener for clothes or other objects. A zipper consists of two strips of metal or plastic teeth that link up when the strips are pulled together.

zith·er (**ziTH**-ur or **zith**-ur) *noun* A musical instrument made up of a flat box with strings stretched across it. Instruments in the zither family can have up to 40 strings, which are plucked with a pick or with the fingers.

zo·di·ac (**zoh**-dee-*ak*) *noun* An imaginary area in the sky in the shape of a circle that the sun, the moon, and the planets travel through. The zodiac is divided into 12 equal parts, each named for a different constellation.

zone (zone)
noun **1.** An area that is separate from other areas and used for a special purpose. **2.** Any of the five areas of the earth divided according to climate. There are two frigid zones, two temperate zones, and one torrid zone.
verb To divide an area of land into smaller sections so that each can be used for a special purpose.

zoo (zoo) *noun* A place where many different animals are kept so that people can see or study them.

zo·ol·o·gy (zoh-**ah**-luh-jee) *noun* The science that deals with the study of animal life. ▶ *noun* **zoologist** (zoh-**ah**-luh-jist) ▶ *adjective* **zoological** (*zoh*-uh-**lah**-ji-kuhl)

zoom (zoom) *verb* **1.** To move quickly with a loud, humming sound. **2.** To increase or rise rapidly and suddenly. **3. zoom in** To adjust a camera's lens so that the person or thing you are taking a picture of appears to be closer. **4. zoom out** To adjust a camera's lens so that the person or thing you are taking a picture of appears to be farther away.
▶ *verb* **zooming, zoomed**

zuc·chi·ni (zoo-**kee**-nee) *noun* A long squash that has green skin. ▶ *noun, plural* **zucchini** or **zucchinis**

Zu·ni (**zoo**-nee) or **Zu·ñi** (**zoon**-yee) *noun* A member of a group of Native Americans who now live in western New Mexico. ▶ *noun, plural* **Zuni** or **Zunis,** or **Zuñi** or **Zuñis**

Z

The Parts of Speech

All the words in English can be divided into eight groups called the parts of speech.

Nouns

Persons	Places	Things	Ideas
grandmother	farm	pencil	freedom
Margaret	continent	window	happiness
teacher	city	banana	bravery
kitten	house	telephone	childhood

Uses of Nouns

Subject: who or what performs the action of the verb	The **dog** bit the man.
Direct Object: who or what receives the action of the verb	The dog bit the **man**.
Indirect Object: shows to or for whom	She baked the **girl** a cake and gave the **boy** a cookie.
Object of a Preposition: comes after a preposition	They went to a **restaurant** after the **movies**.
Possession: shows ownership	The **kid's** sneakers were new.
Noun of Direct Address: the person spoken to	**David**, please help me fix my computer.
Predicate Noun: comes after the verb of being, means the same thing as the subject	My mother is the **mayor** of this town.
Appositive: follows a noun, gives information about it	Jen, my **neighbor**, has two cats.

Verbs

A verb shows action (doing) or being.

Tense: tells time. Verbs have six tenses.

Present	Karen **writes** a poem.
Past	Karen **wrote** a poem.
Future	Karen **will write** a poem.
Present Perfect	Karen **has written** a poem.
Past Perfect	Karen **had written** a poem.
Future Perfect	Karen **will have written** a poem.

The verb **to be** (of being) is
am, are, is, was, were, be, being, been.

Adjectives

An adjective describes a noun or pronoun and answers these questions:

What kind of?	It was a **beautiful** day.
How many? How much?	I'd like **three** apples and **some** grapes, please.
Which one? Which ones?	**That** tie is mine; **those** socks are yours.

Adverbs

An adverb describes a verb, adjective, or other adverb and answers four questions:

How?	The cat howled **loudly**.
When?	The cat howled **today**.
Where?	The cat howled **there**.
To what extent (by how much)?	The cat howled **extremely** loudly.

Prepositions

A preposition shows the relationship of one noun to another.

The mouse is **in** the house.
The cow is **near** the plow.
The fish is **on** the dish.
The bug is **under** the rug.
The bee is **between** the tree and the sea.

Pronouns

A pronoun takes the place of a noun.

Subject pronouns	I, you, he, she, it, we, they
Object pronouns	me, you, him, her, it, us, them
Possessive pronouns	my, mine, your, yours, his, her, hers, its, our, ours, their, theirs

Mary told **Christopher** to wash **Christopher's** hands.
She told **him** to wash **his** hands.

Conjunctions

A conjunction joins words or parts of sentences together. Some common conjunctions are:

and	either/or	when
so	but	therefore
if	after	yet
while	though	because
nor	however	where
or	for	nevertheless
since	although	unless

*The boy **and** the girl are related, **but** they don't look alike, **so** they must be in disguise, **or** my glasses are foggy.*

Interjections

An interjection is a word that expresses strong feelings or emotions.

***Wow**, it's great!*	***Hurray**, it's raining!*
***Eek**, a snake!*	***Ouch**, that hurts.*
***Hey**, don't do that!*	***Well**, that's all, folks.*
***Gosh**, that's nice.*	***Whoa**, slow down!*
***Yippee**, we won!*	***Ugh**, how disgusting!*

Four Kinds of Sentences

Declarative: states a **fact**
The baseball game is tomorrow.

Interrogative: asks a **question**
How many feet are in a mile?

Imperative: gives an **order**
Please line up in single file.

Exclamatory: expresses **strong feelings**
The animals have escaped from their cages!

Glossary of Grammar Terms

Articles: *a, an, the*

Clause: a group of words with a subject and a verb

Paragraph: a group of sentences written together about the same thing

Phrase: a group of words

Sentence: a group of words with a subject and a verb that makes complete sense

Apostrophes '

Use an apostrophe in contractions to take the place of missing letters.
it is = it's   you are = you're   they will = they'll

Use an apostrophe in all possessive nouns.
the boy's jackets, the babies' toys

Colons :

Use a colon to introduce a list.
Take the following items: a blanket, food, and a first aid kit.

Put a colon after headings in a memo.
To: Mrs. Youngman
From: Ms. Stevens

Use a colon after the greeting of a business letter.
Dear Customer Service Department:

Commas ,

Use commas to separate three or more items in a series.
David, Jennifer, and Tim went to the movies.

Use a comma to separate the name of the person spoken to.
After you move, Lorraine, you'll be closer to work.

Use commas to set off a direct quotation.
I said, "Your dog needs a haircut," and Roslyn laughed.

Use a comma between clauses in a sentence
Audrey baked the cake, and Irwin ate it.

Use a comma between adjectives describing the same noun.
Karen took beautiful, colorful, spectacular nature photos.

Dashes —

Use dashes when you interrupt a thought.
Abraham Lincoln—we celebrate his birthday in February—was our 16th president.

Ellipses . . .

Put ellipses where you leave words out.
She had many pets . . . when she lived in Chelsea.

Exclamation Points !

Put an exclamation point at the end of an exclamatory sentence.
A 95-pound chicken just escaped from the coop!

Hyphens -

Use a hyphen to connect parts of some compound words.
custom-made   well-known   mother-in-law

Use a hyphen to separate syllables in a word when a word can't fit at the end of a line.
In the 1990s, my grandparents lived in a building in the heart of New York City.

Use hyphens in word numbers from twenty-one to ninety-nine.
sixty-seven   thirty-five   forty-two

Parentheses ( )

Put parentheses around extra words that give more facts.
Post Imaging (that's my brother's company) is on Madison Avenue.

Periods .

Put a period at the end of a sentence.
She was born on July 19, 2003.

Use periods after initials.
Franklin D. Roosevelt was president during World War II.

Use periods after abbreviations.
Shawmut St.   N.Y.   3:00 a.m.   Dr. Sen

Question Marks ?

Put a question mark at the end of a question.
Are you a student at Columbia Prep School?

Quotation Marks " "

Put quotation marks around words you are quoting directly.
"My goose just laid a golden egg!" shouted the farmer.

Semicolons ;

Use a semicolon to join two main clauses in a sentence.
She retouches photographs; he sings in a heavy metal band.

Use a semicolon before some conjunctions or phrases.
It had rained all morning; therefore, the picnic was called off.

Slashes /

Put a slash between words used in pairs.
either/or   neither/nor

Put slashes between parts of an Internet address.
http://www.scholastic.com/kids

The following section shows you how to capitalize words. Abbreviations often include periods.

Capitalize the first word of a sentence.
My teacher's pet frog fell into a bucket of paint.

Capitalize the first word of a direct quote.
Abby said, "Mommy, I like alligators."

Capitalize the first word of each line of poetry.
A cow flew by
While chewing gum;
She ate a pie;
Do you want some?

Capitalize the pronoun *I*.
I couldn't stop laughing after I heard that joke.

Capitalize people's names.
Richard Soghoian, Sue Kilmer, Lorrie Gerson

Capitalize the names of buildings and monuments.
Chrysler Building, Sears Tower, Lincoln Memorial

Capitalize the names of organizations.
Internet Society, American Medical Association

Capitalize the names of colleges and museums.
Tufts University, San Francisco Museum of Modern Art

Capitalize the names of sports teams.
Chicago Bears, Denver Nuggets

Capitalize proper adjectives (made from proper nouns).
French cooking, Italian opera, Japanese cars

Capitalize initials in a person's name.
John F. Kennedy, J. K. Rowling

Capitalize official titles used with people's names.
General Jones, President Freedman, Queen Rozzie

Capitalize the names of the days of the week.
Monday, Tuesday, Wednesday, etc.

Capitalize the names of the months of the year.
January, February, March, etc.

Capitalize the first word in the greeting and closing of a letter.
Dear Mr. Greenblatt,   Sincerely yours,

Capitalize the main words in the titles of books, movies, plays, and songs.
Island of the Blue Dolphins, The Sound of Music

Capitalize the names of college or school courses.
Introduction to Cartography, Advanced Physics

Capitalize geographic locations.
He lived in the East but moved to the Southwest.

Capitalize the names of religions, nationalities, and races.
Muslims, Christians, Canadians

Capitalize the names of holidays, festivals, and special events.
Thanksgiving, Rosh Hashana, Christmas, Fall Fair

Capitalize the names of languages.
Greek, Hebrew, Swahili, English

Capitalize the names of historical periods, documents, and events.
the Civil War, the Constitution, the Middle Ages

Capitalize the names of gods and deities.
Buddha, Allah, God, Jehovah

Capitalize the names of religious books and books of the Bible.
the Koran, the Torah, Genesis, Bible

Capitalize the names of the planets.
Mars, Venus, Saturn, Jupiter

Capitalize the abbreviations of titles after someone's name.
Herbert Wigglesworth, Jr.
Anthony Smart, M.D.

Capitalize the postal abbreviations for states.
MA, TX, NY, FL, CA

Capitalize the names of products and companies.
Tylenol, Ford Motor Company, Adidas, Wikipedia

Capitalize A.D. and B.C.
*I saw ancient statues from **A.D.** 230 and 51 **B.C.***

An idiom is an expression that has a special meaning that is different from what the individual words usually mean. For instance, "Keep a stiff upper lip" means "be brave." Here are some other well-known idioms and their meanings:

ants in your pants: extreme restlessness

apple of your eye: something or someone greatly loved

at the drop of a hat: immediately

baker's dozen: 13 for the price of 12

beat around the bush: avoid answering a question

between a rock and a hard place: in a difficult situation

bite the bullet: prepare for an unpleasant experience

blow your own horn: praise yourself

bolt from the blue: something unexpected and surprising

break a leg: good luck in a show

burn the candle at both ends: work late into the night

bury the hatchet: settle an argument

butter someone up: flatter someone

butterflies in your stomach: a feeling of nervousness

calm before the storm: a period of quiet before a crisis

climbing the walls: be restless and frustrated

cold feet: a fear of doing something

cool as a cucumber: very calm

cost an arm and a leg: very expensive

cry wolf: give a false alarm

dime a dozen: very common and cheap

drop in the bucket: a very small amount of something

eat your words: take back what you've said

elbow grease: hard work

eleventh hour: the last minute

face the music: accept the punishment you deserve

feather in your cap: a great achievement or honor

fight tooth and nail: fight fiercely

fish out of water: a person out of his or her usual place

fly off the handle: lose your temper; become angry

forty winks: a short nap

from soup to nuts: everything from beginning to end

get a kick out of something: really enjoy something

get under someone's skin: to bother or annoy someone

gift of gab: skill in talking

give me five: slap a person's hand as a greeting

go bananas: act in a crazy manner

green thumb: good at growing flowers and plants

head in the clouds: absent-minded; lost in thought

hit the books: do your homework or study harder

hit the jackpot: win a lot of money; be very lucky

in hot water: in big trouble

jump the gun: start too soon

keep your shirt on: remain calm; don't get angry

lend an ear: listen carefully; pay attention

like two peas in a pod: exactly alike in looks or behavior

make waves: cause trouble

needle in a haystack: something very hard to find

no dice: absolutely not!

on cloud nine: very happy

on top of the world: feeling joyously happy

open a can of worms: cause trouble

out like a light: fast asleep

pass the hat: ask for money

piece of cake: very easy to do

play with fire: do something dangerous

pull yourself together: get control of yourself

raining cats and dogs: raining very heavily

red-letter day: a very significant and happy day

ring a bell: sound familiar

scratch the surface: just begin to deal with a problem

shake a leg: speed up; go faster

skate on thin ice: take a big chance

spill the beans: give away a secret

throw in the towel: give up

tickled pink: very pleased or amused

tighten your belt: spend less money

two-faced: dishonest; false

under the weather: sick

walking on air: very happy, excited, joyful

wet blanket: a dull or sour person who spoils the fun

white elephant: something useless and unwanted

An initial is a letter, usually followed by a period, that takes the place of a whole word.
An acronym is a group of initials that forms another word or phrase.
An abbreviation is a shortened form of a word, followed by a period.

AA = Alcoholics
Anonymous
ACLU = American Civil
Liberties Union
aka = also known as
AM = amplitude
modulation
anon = anonymous
ASAP = as soon as
possible
ASPCA = American Society
for the Prevention of
Cruelty to Animals
Aug. = August
AWOL = absent without
leave
C = Celsius or centigrade
CEO = chief executive
officer
CIA = Central Intelligence
Agency
cm = centimeter
co. = company
COD = cash on delivery
corp. = corporation
dB = decibel
D.C. = District of
Columbia
DDS = Doctor of Dental
Science
Dec. = December
dept. = department
DOB = date of birth
e.g. = for example
EMT = emergency medical
technician
EPA = Environmental
Protection Agency
ERA = Equal Rights
Amendment
ESL = English as a second
language
F = Fahrenheit
FBI = Federal Bureau of
Investigation
Feb. = February
FM = frequency
modulation
Fri. = Friday
ft. = foot
FYI = for your information
g = gram
GCF = greatest common
factor

GOP = Grand Old Party
(Republican Party)
govt. = government
HDTV = high-definition
television
HQ = headquarters
hr. = hour
ICU = intensive care unit
ID = identification
i.e. = that is
in. = inch
inc. = incorporated
IRS = Internal Revenue
Service
Jan. = January
Jr. = junior
kg = kilogram
km = kilometer
l = liter
lb. = pound
LCD = lowest (or least)
common denominator
LCM = lowest (or least)
common multiple
m = meter
MADD = Mothers Against
Drunk Driving
MC = master of
ceremonies
MD = *medicinae doctor*
(Latin for
"doctor of medicine")
mi. = mile
min. = minute
misc. = miscellaneous
mm = millimeter
mo. = month
Mon. = Monday
NAACP = National
Association for the
Advancement of Colored
People
NASA = National
Aeronautics and Space
Administration
NASCAR = National
Association for Stock
Car Auto Racing
NBA = National Basketball
Association
NFL = National Football
League
NHL = National Hockey
League

no. = number
Nov. = November
NOW = National
Organization for
Women
Oct. = October
OPEC = Organization of
Petroleum Exporting
Countries
oz. = ounce
PA = public address
PIN = personal
identification number
P.O. = post office
POW = prisoner of war
PTA = Parent-Teacher
Association
PTO = Parent-Teacher
Organization
RN = registered nurse
RV = recreational vehicle
SADD = Students Against
Drunk Driving
SASE = self-addressed
stamped envelope
Sat. = Saturday
sec. = second
Sept. = September
SIDS = sudden infant
death syndrome
sq. = square
Sr. = senior
Sun. = Sunday
t. = ton
T or tbsp. = tablespoon
tsp. = teaspoon
TBA = to be announced
Thurs. = Thursday
TM = trademark
Tues. = Tuesday
UN = United Nations
UNICEF = United Nations
Children's Fund
UPC = Universal Product
Code
U.S. = United States
U.S.A. = United States of
America
VP = vice president
Wed. = Wednesday
w/o = without
WWW = World Wide Web
yd. = yard
yr. = year